Y0-DLF-943

CANADIAN PERSONNEL/ HUMAN RESOURCE MANAGEMENT:

A Diagnostic Approach

CANADIAN PERSONNEL/ HUMAN RESOURCE MANAGEMENT:

A Diagnostic Approach

George T. Milkovich
Cornell University

William F. Glueck
Late of The University of Georgia

Richard T. Barth
Faculty of Business Administration
Memorial University of Newfoundland

Steven L. McShane
Faculty of Business Administration
Simon Fraser University

1988

BUSINESS PUBLICATIONS, INC.
Plano, Texas 75075

© BUSINESS PUBLICATIONS, INC., 1988

All rights reserved. No part of this publication may be reproduced, stored in a retrieval system, or transmitted, in any form or by any means, electronic, mechanical, photocopying, recording, or otherwise, without the prior written permission of the publisher.

Acquisitions editor: Rod Banister
Project editors: Ann Cassady and Jean Roberts
Production manager: Stephen K. Emry
Compositor: The Clarinda Company
Typeface: 10/13 Caledonia
Printer: R. R. Donnelley & Sons Company

ISBN 0-256-05997-7
Library of Congress Catalog Card No. 87-73025

Printed in the United States of America

1 2 3 4 5 6 7 8 9 0 DO 5 4 3 2 1 0 9 8

To Anneli, Reija, and Richard

To Donna, my wife and best friend

PREFACE

Personnel/human resource management (P/HRM) has become one of the most complex and challenging areas of Canadian business. Significant changes are occurring in employment legislation, work force composition, and product market competition. Consequently, Canadian organizations need managers who understand the technical dimensions of P/HRM problems and opportunities and are able to make effective human resource management decisions.

Canadian Personnel/Human Resource Management: A Diagnostic Approach shows readers how to make effective human resource management decisions by diagnosing organizational conditions such as business strategies and cultures, and external conditions such as increased foreign competition, government regulations, and union pressures. The latest relevant theories and practices are introduced so that readers know "how to" address human resource problems and opportunities. The balanced integration of managerial and technical material makes this book an important source of information as well as a valuable learning tool.

KEY FEATURES

Canadian Personnel/Human Resource Management: A Diagnostic Approach includes several valuable features that enhance its contribution to this field. Here are the major distinguishing characteristics.

- *A strategic and managerial emphasis.* P/HRM managers see themselves as boundary spanners who play an important role in managing the relationship between the organization and its internal and external environments. This book introduces each chapter with a diagnostic assessment of the organization's environment and its relationship to the subject of that chapter. Through this diagnostic perspective, readers learn how P/HRM decisions affect and are affected by the organization's environment. They develop a broader understanding of P/HRM beyond the technical issues.
- *Comprehensive integration of Canadian P/HRM practices.* A good Canadian P/HRM text must integrate the conceptual material with examples of actual practices and programs in Canada. The authors believe that, compared with other available texts, *Canadian Personnel/Human*

Resource Management: A Diagnostic Approach provides the best coverage and integration of actual P/HRM practices and experiences across Canada. For example, readers will learn about assessment centres at General Motors Canada, labour-management relations at Budd Canada, suggestion systems at Sears Canada, "flexible firm" practices in several Canadian industries, performance evaluations at Imperial Oil and First City Trust, flexible benefits at Cominco, wrongful dismissal at General Motors of Canada, management succession planning at Ontario's Ministry of Transportation and Communications, and a host of other practices and experiences right here in Canada. This helps readers to identify with the conceptual material and increases the book's interest.

- *A balance of theory and practice.* This text maintains a good balance between the theories/models of relevance to P/HRM managers and the "how to" issues of implementation. The latest concepts are introduced in a way that university and community college students can understand. Extensive and up-to-date references are included throughout the text to support the pertinent theory and research. These concepts are integrated with real life P/HRM practices. For example, the text describes how to implement employee assistance programs, calculate employment demand forecasts, conduct employee orientation programs, implement employment equity programs, and reduce employee benefit costs.

- *Original and adapted Canadian cases on a variety of P/HRM topics.* In keeping with the managerial perspective of this book, new cases within the Canadian context have been added together with the best of those previously published by Professor Glueck. The cases vary in length and difficulty and are based in several settings. Some address technical issues, while others concentrate on managerial decision making. All cases have been classroom tested. They are separated from the chapters (in alphabetical order at the end of the text) so the instructor has the option of either letting students discover the relevant issues or telling them which chapters apply.

Canadian Personnel/Human Resource Management: A Diagnostic Approach has been written with the purpose of informing and exciting its readers about the challenges and importance of P/HRM in Canada. We are confident it will achieve this purpose.

ACKNOWLEDGEMENTS

A book is always the product of many people, this book perhaps more than others. Our first debt goes to the late Bill Glueck who, during his lifetime, set new standards of excellence in P/HRM textbook writing and teaching. We hope this edition remains true to those laudable standards.

Several colleagues shared their ideas with us as reviewers of the Canadian edition. The detailed comments and suggestions of the following are especially appreciated:

>   David E. Dimick, York University
>   John R. Goodwin, Concordia University
>   Terry Hercus, University of Manitoba
>   Edison L. Roach, Algonquin College
>   Michael Rock, Seneca College

We also extend a special thanks to Brian Bemmels at the University of Alberta for his excellent contribution to this book by writing the labour relations chapter.

Numerous P/HRM managers, consultants, and government officials helped shape this book by providing examples, material, and wisdom on a variety of subjects. They stand out as the role models for future generations of Canadian managers and specialists. It is not possible to list them all, but several deserve special mention:

>   Trudy Baal, Continuing Care Employee Relations Association
>   Debbie Cleveland, First City Trust
>   Randy Daurve, Eatons
>   John B. Egan, HAY Management Consultants
>   R. Emery, Canada Employment and Immigration Commission
>   G. K. Griffin, Sears Canada
>   Doug Lawson, Lawson and Associates
>   Kim Miller, Trimac
>   Gordon Pickle, Royal Trust
>   R. B. Shearer, British Columbia Telephone Company
>   Stan Summerville, Canada Employment and Immigration Commission
>   Hayne Wai, Canadian Human Rights Commission
>   Walt Walmesley, Chevron Canada

Our deans, James G. Barnes (Memorial) and Stan Shapiro (Simon Fraser) provided supportive work climates, for which we thank them. We are also appreciative of the research assistance support made available through a grant from the Associates Program of Memorial's Faculty of Business Administration.

Rod Banister and Jim Evans at Irwin-Dorsey of Canada deserve much of the credit for ensuring that this book was completed on time and at a high standard of quality. We are proud to be associated with both of them and with Irwin-Dorsey of Canada. The professional work of Ann Cassady and Jean Roberts, our project editors at Irwin-Dorsey of Canada, is also appreciated.

Finally, our students deserve special mention. They continue to motivate and challenge us in the classroom and educate us by sharing their thoughts and experiences. We thank them all.

Richard T. Barth
Steven L. McShane

CONTENTS

PART ONE   INTRODUCTION AND EXTERNAL CONDITIONS   3

CHAPTER 1   THE DIAGNOSTIC APPROACH   5
P/HRM—INTRODUCTION, 6   A DIAGNOSTIC APPROACH TO HUMAN RESOURCE MANAGEMENT, 8   *Tailoring Decisions to the Circumstances. A Diagnostic Approach.*   THE DIAGNOSTIC MODEL, 11   *External Conditions. Organization Conditions. Human Resource Activities. Objectives. The Book Plan.*   WHO MANAGES HUMAN RESOURCES?, 19   *The Role of the Canadian Human Resource Manager. P/HRM—A Field in Transition. The Interaction of Operating and Human Resource Managers-Partners.*   SUMMARY   25
APPENDIX A / *Certification and Professionalization*   26
APPENDIX B / *Publications and Other Sources*   27
APPENDIX C / *A Brief History of Canadian P/HRM*   30

CHAPTER 2   EXTERNAL CONDITIONS   38
EXTERNAL CONDITIONS AND THE DIAGNOSTIC MODEL, 40   *Diagnosing External Conditions. Environmental Scanning.*   ECONOMIC CONDITIONS, 43   *The Population and the Labour Force. Labour Markets. Product/Service Market Conditions. Canada–U.S. Free(r) Trade. Privatization. Takeovers and Mergers.*   TECHNOLOGY, 67   GOVERNMENT REGULATIONS, 78   *Terms and Conditions—Employment. The Regulatory Process. Deregulation.*   UNION EXPECTATIONS AND CONCERNS, 81   INTERNATIONAL DIMENSIONS, 83   SUMMARY   84

PART TWO   ORGANIZATION CONDITIONS   95

CHAPTER 3   NATURE OF THE ORGANIZATION   97
ORGANIZATION INFLUENCES AND THE DIAGNOSTIC APPROACH, 99   *Strategies and Operational Objectives. Financial Condition and Flexibility. Technologies Employed. Culture and*

Philosophy. The State of Knowledge. HUMAN RESOURCE PLANNING: THE LINK, 110 *Human Resource Planning: An Important Distinction. Establishing Human Resource Objectives. Assessing Current Human Resource Conditions. Designing and Evaluating Human Resource Activities. Monitoring and Evaluating Results. Human Resource Planning: Who Is Doing It?* HUMAN RESOURCE INFORMATION SYSTEMS, 122 *Design Process. Information Requirements. Basic Components of HRIS. Common Mistakes.* STRATEGY, STRUCTURE, AND STAFF, 129 *Centralized-Decentralized. Congruency. Staffing.*
SUMMARY 132
APPENDIX / *System Description: Merck and Company, Inc.* 133

CHAPTER 4 NATURE OF THE WORK 141
THE NATURE OF WORK AND THE DIAGNOSTIC MODEL, 142 DEFINING WORK, 143 *Qualifications Required. Rewards and Returns.* JOB DESIGN, 144 *Overview. Scientific Management. Human Relations. Current Approaches. Job Characteristics Model. Employee Focus of Attention. Tailoring Jobs to Organization and Environmental Conditions. Hours of Work and Work Schedules.* JOB ANALYSIS, 154 *Why Analyze Jobs? What Data to Collect. Manager/Employee Acceptance. How to Collect Data. Conventional Job Analysis. Quantitative Job Analysis. Usefulness of Methods. Sources of Error in Job Analysis. Job Descriptions and Specifications.* CANADIAN JOB-OCCUPATIONAL INFORMATION, 168
SUMMARY 170
APPENDIX A / *Procedures for Gathering Job Information* 171
APPENDIX B / *Sample Job Descriptions* 173

CHAPTER 5 NATURE OF THE EMPLOYEES 189
INDIVIDUAL DIFFERENCES AND THE DIAGNOSTIC MODEL, 190 DETERMINANTS OF INDIVIDUAL PERFORMANCE, 190 *Ability. Motivation. Role Perceptions and Situational Contingencies.* THEORIES OF MOTIVATION, 194 *Content Theories. Process Theories.* CAREERS, 202 *Career Orientation. Career Stages. Careers and Organizational Effectiveness.* THE SUPERVISOR, 206 *Leadership Styles.* THE WORK GROUP, 208 *Organization Advantages. Designing Work Groups. P/HRM and Work Groups.*
SUMMARY 210

PART THREE HUMAN RESOURCE ACTIVITIES: STAFFING   217

CHAPTER 6   EMPLOYMENT PLANNING   219
A DIAGNOSTIC APPROACH TO EMPLOYMENT PLANNING, 220 EMPLOYMENT PLANNING, 227 *Reasons for Employment Planning. Three Phases of Analysis. Who Performs Employment Planning?* FORECASTING DEMAND FOR EMPLOYEES, 230 *Estimated Organization Performance Goals. Productivity. An Illustration. Tailoring Tools to the Situation. Prediction Accuracy versus Objectives Achieved. Keep Employment Forecasts in Perspective.* FORECASTING HUMAN RESOURCE SUPPLY, 240 *Turnover Rates as an Objective. Human Resource Supply Estimates. Skills Inventories. Replacement and Succession Charts. Transitional Matrixes.* DESIGNING PROGRAMS, 255
SUMMARY 260

CHAPTER 7   EMPLOYMENT EQUITY   269
A DIAGNOSTIC APPROACH TO EMPLOYMENT EQUITY, 270 WHAT IS EMPLOYMENT EQUITY?, 271 *The Need for Employment Equity in Canada.* LEGAL FOUNDATIONS OF EMPLOYMENT EQUITY, 278 *Canadian Charter of Rights and Freedom. Human Rights Legislation.* EMERGING CONCEPTS IN EMPLOYMENT EQUITY, 283 *From Intent to Effect. Bona Fide Occupational Qualification. Reasonable Accommodation. Sexual and Other Harassment. Mandatory Retirement.* EMPLOYMENT EQUITY PROGRAMS IN CANADA, 293 *Mandatory Employment Equity Programs.* IMPLEMENTING EMPLOYMENT EQUITY PROGRAMS, 295 *Step One: EEP Planning. Step Two: Utilization Analysis. Step Three: Employment Systems Review. Step Four: Plan Design and Implementation.*
SUMMARY 309
APPENDIX / *Prohibited Grounds for Screening and Selection in Employment* 309

CHAPTER 8   RECRUITING AND JOB SEARCH   320
INTRODUCTION, 321 *Recruitment Process—Components. Dual Responsibility for Recruiting. The Recruiter.* A DIAGNOSTIC APPROACH TO RECRUITING, 325 *Recruitment Planning. External Influences. Organization Influences. Individual Candidate's Preferences. Employer–Applicant Matching.* SOURCES AND METHODS, 331 *Internal Recruiting. External Recruiting. Locating Other External Candidates.* EVALUATING RECRUITING

PROGRAMS, 340 *Recruiting Costs and Benefits.* REALISM OR FLYPAPER?, 345 *Realistic Job Previews.* THE POTENTIAL EMPLOYEE'S VIEW OF RECRUITING, 347 *Occupational Choice. Organizational Choice.*
SUMMARY 352
APPENDIX / *How to Get a Job* 353

CHAPTER 9 SELECTION 369
A DIAGNOSTIC APPROACH TO SELECTION, 372 EMPLOYMENT TESTING, 375 RELIABILITY, 376 *Reliability Methods.* VALIDATION, 378 *Empirical (Criterion-Related) Validation Methods. Rational Methods.* USEFULNESS OF A SELECTION PROCEDURE, 383 VALIDITY GENERALIZATION, 391 SELECTION PROCESS, 392 SELECTION PROCEDURES, 393 *Application Blanks/Biographical Data. Employment Interview. Employment Tests. Medical Testing/Screening. Formal Education. Experience. Reference Checks and Recommendation Letters. Comparison of Job Performance Predictors.* INTERNATIONAL DIMENSIONS, 415
SUMMARY 416
APPENDIX A / *Technical Note—Selection Study* 417
APPENDIX B / *Valid Selection Means Higher Work Force Productivity* 417

PART FOUR HUMAN RESOURCE ACTIVITIES: DEVELOPMENT 431

CHAPTER 10 ORIENTATION, SOCIALIZATION, AND TRAINING 433
THE ORIENTATION PROCESS, 434 THE SOCIALIZATION PROCESS, 442 THE TRAINING PROCESS, 443 *Introduction.* A DIAGNOSTIC APPROACH TO TRAINING, 444 *External Influences. Internal Influences. Who Is Involved in Training? Major Decisions.* DETERMINING TRAINING NEEDS AND OBJECTIVES, 451 *Organizational Analysis. Operational Analysis. Individual Performance Analysis. Training Needs as a Function of Organizational Level. Stating Objectives.*
TRANSLATING NEEDS INTO PROGRAMS, 457 *Learning Principles. Individual Differences. Instructional Techniques,* 461 *On-the-Job Training. Off-the-Job Training. Combinations.*
EVALUATING RESULTS, 471 *Four Evaluation Questions. Criteria for Evaluation. Experimental Designs. Costs and Benefits. Cost, Benefits, and Productivity.*
SUMMARY 481
APPENDIX / *Orientation—International Assignments* 482

CHAPTER 11 PERFORMANCE EVALUATION **489**
A DIAGNOSTIC APPROACH TO PERFORMANCE EVALUATION, 491 *Environmental Conditions. Organizational Conditions.* PERFORMANCE EVALUATION EFFECTIVENESS, 494 *Purpose of Performance Evaluation. Reliability and Validity. Sensitivity. Acceptability. Practicality.* EVALUATION CRITERIA AND STANDARDS, 498 *Multiple, Global, or Composite Criteria. Measuring Performance Criteria. Standard of Evaluation.* PERFORMANCE EVALUATION METHODS, 504 *Subjective Criteria, Absolute Standard. Objective Criteria, Absolute Standard. Relative Evaluation Methods. Assessment Centres. Using Multiple Techniques.* THE EVALUATION PROCESS, 519 *Who Should Evaluate? Processing Performance Information. Performance Evaluation Training. Observing Performance.* THE EVALUATION INTERVIEW, 526
SUMMARY, 529
APPENDIX A / *Performance Evaluation at First City Trust* 530
APPENDIX B / *Performance Evaluation at Chevron Canada Limited* 534

PART FIVE HUMAN RESOURCE ACTIVITIES: EMPLOYMENT RELATIONS **551**

CHAPTER 12 EMPLOYEE RELATIONS AND RIGHTS **553**
A DIAGNOSTIC APPROACH TO EMPLOYEE RELATIONS AND RIGHTS, 555 *External Factors. Internal Factors.* QUALITY OF WORK LIFE, 557 *QWL Approaches. QWL Outcomes.* EMPLOYEE COUNSELLING AND CONFLICT RESOLUTION, 563 *Career Development. Employee Assistance. Conflict Resolution.* OCCUPATIONAL HEALTH AND SAFETY, 576 *Costs and Causes of Occupational Injuries and Diseases. Occupational Health and Safety Legislation.* TERMINATION OF EMPLOYMENT, 584 *Statutory Rights. Common Law Wrongful Dismissal.*
SUMMARY, 590

CHAPTER 13 LABOUR RELATIONS
A DIAGNOSTIC APPROACH TO LABOUR RELATIONS, 601 *External Conditions. Organizational Conditions.* CANADIAN UNIONISM: A HISTORICAL PERSPECTIVE, 605 WHY EMPLOYEES JOIN UNIONS, 610 THE ORGANIZING CAMPAIGN, 611 UNION STRUCTURE, 613 NEGOTIATING A

CONTRACT, 615 *Preparation for Contract Negotiations. Negotiation Issues. Formalizing the Contract.* IMPASSES IN COLLECTIVE BARGAINING, 618 *Mediation and Conciliation. Interest Arbitration. Strikes and Lockouts. Labour Disputes in Canada.* COLLECTIVE AGREEMENT ADMINISTRATION, 625 *Grievance Process. Grievance Arbitration.* THE PUBLIC SECTOR, 627 LABOR UNION EFFECTS, 628 *Union Impact on Wages. Union Impact on Productivity. Union Impact on Employee "Voice."*
SUMMARY 631

PART SIX HUMAN RESOURCE ACTIVITIES: COMPENSATION 639

CHAPTER 14 PAY LEVEL AND STRUCTURE 641
INTRODUCTION, 642 A DIAGNOSTIC APPROACH TO PAY ADMINISTRATION, 645 *External Influences on Pay. Organizational Influences on Pay.* A PAY MODEL, 651 *Compensation Objectives. Equity: The Conceptual Foundation.* PAY DECISIONS AND TECHNIQUES, 655 *External Equity. Internal Equity. Job Evaluation and the Pay Model.*
SUMMARY 673
APPENDIX / *The Hay Guide Chart–Profile Method* 674

CHAPTER 15 INDIVIDUAL PAY AND ADMINISTRATION 683
INDIVIDUAL PAY POLICIES, 684 INDIVIDUAL PAY TECHNIQUES, 685 *Pay Ranges. Pay Increase Guidelines. External, Internal, and Employee Equity.* PAY-FOR-PERFORMANCE, 692 *Is Money Important? Should Pay Increases Be Based on Performance? Is Pay Based on Performance? Negative Evidence.* PAY AND SATISFACTION, 695 INCENTIVES, 697 *Individual Incentives. Group Incentives.* PAY ADMINISTRATION, 704 *Cost Controls. Communication. Participation. Special Groups.* EXECUTIVE PAY, 707 *Compensation Decisions. Is Executive Pay Effective?* PAY EQUITY, 714 *Equal Pay versus Pay Equity: An Example. Features of Pay Equity Legislation. The Continuing Controversy.*
SUMMARY, 720

CHAPTER 16 BENEFITS   **727**
A DIAGNOSTIC APPROACH TO BENEFITS, 729 *External Influences. Internal Influences.* TYPES OF EMPLOYEE BENEFITS, 732 *Compensation for Time Not Worked. Insurance-Based Benefits. Employee Services.* CANADA'S RETIREMENT INCOME SYSTEM, 739 *Government Income Security Programs. Canada/Quebec Pension Plan. Employer-Sponsored Pensions and Individual Savings.* MANAGING BENEFITS, 749 *Benefit Objectives. Benefits Communication. Containing Benefit Costs. Flexible Benefits.*
SUMMARY 762

PART SEVEN HUMAN RESOURCE ACTIVITIES: EVALUATION   **769**

CHAPTER 17 EVALUATION   **771**
A DIAGNOSTIC APPROACH TO EVALUATION, 773 *P/HRM as a Collection of Activities: Maintenance and Control. P/HRM as an Integrated System: Achieving Effectiveness.* APPROACHES TO EVALUATION, 774 *Process-Oriented Audits. Reputational Approach. Quantitative Approaches.*
SUMMARY, 791

CASES:
BLOCK DRUG COMPANY 794
CANADA EAST INSURANCE COMPANY LTD. 795
CANADIAN GLOVE COMPANY LTD. 804
CONSOLIDATED DEFENSE MANUFACTURING 806
EASTERN SCHOOL DISTRICT 807
EGLOFF PLASTICS 808
FLINT MEMORIAL HOSPITAL 809
GIBSON PETROLEUM, LTD. 813
GIGANTIC AIRCRAFT COMPANY 814
HALIFAX MANUFACTURING, LTD. 816
HICKLING ASSOCIATES LTD. 818
MINISTRY OF TRADE AND COMMERCE 829
PACIFIC FINANCIAL SERVICES LTD. 833
PEMBERTON MINING SYSTEMS LTD. 835
STRATEGIC HUMAN RESOURCE PLANNING 839
SUDBURY SHOES 841

TIMBER CRAFT LIMITED 844
TYLER MANUFACTURING COMPANY 852

NAME INDEX   **855**

SUBJECT INDEX   **857**

PART ONE
INTRODUCTION AND EXTERNAL CONDITIONS

Personnel/human resource management is concerned with the effective management of people at work. It examines what is, what can be, and what should be done to make people both more productive and more satisfied with their working lives.

This book is for students who will become employers, supervisors, or managers. Its goal is to help them develop into effective *managers of human resources*.

Chapter One introduces the diagnostic approach. To diagnose means to analyse, to seek the underlying causes. Our diagnostic approach considers underlying factors and relationships that can affect, and are affected by, human resources. Chapter Two examines the external conditions: economic influences, governmental pressures, technological changes, and union expectations.

CHAPTER ONE
THE DIAGNOSTIC APPROACH

CHAPTER OUTLINE

I. P/HRM—Introduction
II. A Diagnostic Approach to Human Resource Management
    A. Tailoring Decisions to the Circumstances
    B. A Diagnostic Approach
III. The Diagnostic Model
    A. External Conditions
    B. Organization Conditions
    C. Human Resource Activities
    D. Objectives
    E. The Book Plan
IV. Who Manages Human Resources?
    A. The Role of the Canadian Human Resource Manager
    B. P/HRM—A Field in Transition
    C. The Interaction of Operating and Human Resource Managers-Partners
V. Summary
    Appendix A / Certification and Professionalization
    Appendix B / Publications and Other Sources
    Appendix C / A Brief History of Canadian P/HRM

A lot of personnel types and even P/HRM managers have no idea what the real business of their company is.[1]

If I had known when I started in P/HRM what I know now, I'd get some exposure to the major functional areas. Too often we come in with the idea of keeping P/HRM separate from the rest of the organization.[2]

A well-informed, well-balanced, commonsense, pragmatic human resource manager, who understands how the company's business operates, is a treasure, a tremendous asset to the company, probably a greater asset than even s/he realizes.[3]

The truly effective P/HRM manager is one who can achieve a well-balanced, pragmatic view of concerns *both* for people *and* profit.[4]

I believe the successful human resources executive of the 1980s and 90s must not only know the functional specialties in some depth, but must have the ability to anticipate and integrate new developments across all business disciplines.[5]

The preceding comments provide glimpses of how the exciting field of personnel/human resource management (P/HRM) is viewed by executives and managers, and human resource specialists with whom they must assume joint responsibility for the acquisition, development, and retention of human resource talent. These and other examples, inserted at various points, introduce the reader to the importance of personnel/human resource management and its expanding role in today's modern organization.

P/HRM—INTRODUCTION

> **Definition**
> *Personnel/human resource management (P/HRM)* consists of the decisions and activities involving human resources that are intended to influence the effectiveness of the employees *and* the organization. This means achieving an optimal fit among the nature of the employees, the nature of the job, and the nature of the organization and external conditions.

Although money and materials are resources of organizations, employees—the human resources—are particularly important. First and foremost, human resources influence productivity and profitability. People design and produce the goods and services, control quality and market the products, allocate financial resources, and set overall strategies and objectives for the organization. Without effective people, an organization cannot achieve its objectives.

Because an employer's human resources comprise an important determinant of organizational effectiveness, managing human resources is a central concern of every organization. It is part of every manager's job. A plant manager whose job includes coordinating electronic components, production designs, and financial budgets may be trying to manufacture personal computers capable of quality performance at a cost that can withstand worldwide pricing pressures. Achieving this depends on effective human resource management. This plant manager probably has a human resource specialist to help make human resource decisions; but an informed plant manager increases the quality of those decisions and thereby boosts productivity and profitability. At Bertha's Kitty Boutique, where Bertha makes all the decisions, human resources still must be managed. The same is true in public sector organizations. City managers must deliver police and fire protection, sanitation, and social services to a public that often believes the quality of service is too low and the taxes too high. Effective human resource management is required here, too. So whether in the public or private sector, or in local, national, or international markets, effective management of human resources is critical for all organizations.

Recently, a number of trends have made human resource management even more important, and more complex. One of the most important reasons is the changing nature of work. Work has become more varied and dynamic. Consequently, employers are seeking employees who are more flexible, better trained, and capable of learning new skills as job requirements change.[6] Such workers seem to have higher expectations about the work they are willing to perform, as well as a desire for involvement in managing their own jobs and sharing in the financial gains achieved by the organization.[7] Another reason is changing demographics of the population and labour force.[8] Women's increased attachment to the work force, dual-career families, single-parent families, the influx of immigrants and undocumented workers, and the aging of the labour force are all demographic changes that affect the work force.[9] As a result, employers cannot afford to view workers as interchangeable economic units. Pegging employees into narrowly defined jobs that offer little discretion, with little regard for the needs of the employee, deserves to become obsolete practice.

Not only are workers changing but organizations are changing too. Government regulation of the employment relationship, economic competition on a global scale, attention to justice and equity in the workplace, and a host of other factors forced this change. Rigidly bureaucratized organizations that require layer upon layer of approval for decisions are restructuring. New organization forms, more decentralized profit centres, and employee work teams with greater autonomy and control over the work performed are evolving. For example, both General Motors and Ford agreed with their employees to form new work teams and change production methods to improve product quality and reduce costs. In the process, a layer of middle management was cut from assembly plants.[10]

The dynamic nature of work, workers, and organizations requires rethinking traditional approaches to human resource management. This book is about meeting the challenges and opportunities presented by these changes.

A DIAGNOSTIC APPROACH TO HUMAN RESOURCE MANAGEMENT

In today's world, specialization might have gone too far. Often we are taught how to do things without understanding *why* we do them. Thus, we fail to discern the overall framework in which our own jobs fit. The stereotype of the paper-shuffling bureaucrat who provides indifferent service is an example. If that employee better understood the agency's objectives, service might improve. Similarly, the arc welder on a General Motors assembly line who receives information about the relationship of the number and quality of welds to the costs and quality of the car may improve the quality, as well as the competitiveness, of the product.

Human resource professionals also can suffer from narrow perspectives. They may have the technical knowledge to decide how many and whom to hire, whom to promote to which job, and how much to pay. But *if they do not link* this technical knowledge with an understanding of the financial and marketing strategies of the organization, the people involved, the work to be performed, and the environment in which decisions are being made, the decisions are less likely to be effective.

Tailoring Decisions to the Circumstances

So what is the point? First, human resource managers are more likely to be effective if, in addition to the technical expertise related to particular human resource decisions, they can tailor the decision to the proper organizational and environmental context. A second point is that the manager does not act in a fixed context. Economic conditions change, organizations change, people change. The context varies and influences the decisions made and techniques used.

A quick example illustrates this second point: Suppose two firms have a vacancy for a marketing research manager. One organization goes outside the company to fill the position; the other promotes a current employee. Both decisions may have merit. Promotion from within is a common policy in firms that choose to develop or "grow" their own talent. IBM Canada is a classic illustration. But hiring from outside suits firms seeking "new blood" with new ideas and approaches. Also, relatively young organizations, such as Micronav in Nova Scotia, MacDonald Dettwiler in British Columbia, or other high-tech firms, may need immediate marketing expertise and may not have time to develop the necessary skills in a current employee. So different decisions may be correct in differing environmental and organizational contexts. While technical knowledge is critical for making decisions, application of that knowledge must be tailored to variations in the contextual circumstances.

A Diagnostic Approach

To help you understand all the factors affecting human resource decisions, we developed an approach to human resource management. It is called a *diagnostic approach*, based on the analogue of the physician. Think of a particularly effective physician you have visited. The physician's general objective is to maintain or improve your health. With this objective in mind, as much data as feasible will be gathered—data on your medical history and the symptoms or conditions that precipitated your visit. After combining these data with the physician's technical knowledge and skills, a treatment program is prescribed. If that treatment fails to yield the desired results, adjustments may be made, and the next most likely treatment is prescribed.

Human resource managers can follow a similar model,[11] outlined in Exhibit 1-1. First, the P/HRM manager *identifies* certain *symptoms*. Operating managers, because of their close contact with employees, are frequently a good source of information. The next step, *diagnosis*, involves data collection and analysis to identify potential causes of the problem. This may include information on the organization's conditions, such as its financial objectives or marketing strategies. Current behaviour and problems of employees and the quality of work are analysed. The external environment is scanned to assess its influence and to note any directional changes. With this information, managers formulate a *plan* designed to alleviate the problem. This third step involves setting human resource objectives and designing the most likely treatment—or human resource activities—to achieve these objectives. In designing the activity, the manager, like the physician, must make a judgement based on personal expertise and the information gathered. Next, *implementation* of the plan activates the treatment, often with the complementary efforts of operating managers. The fifth step, often overlooked, is *follow-up*, which reexamines the initial symptoms of the problem(s) to detect improvements. Like the physician, a manager does not give up if the first treatment does not achieve the desired results. Rather, he or she proceeds to analyse, diagnose, and adjust the treatment until the desired results are achieved.

EXHIBIT 1–1
Steps of the Diagnostic Approach

```
                                    Follow-up
                                   ↗
                        Implementation
                       ↗
                  Plan
                 ↗
          Diagnosis
         ↗
Identification of symptoms
```

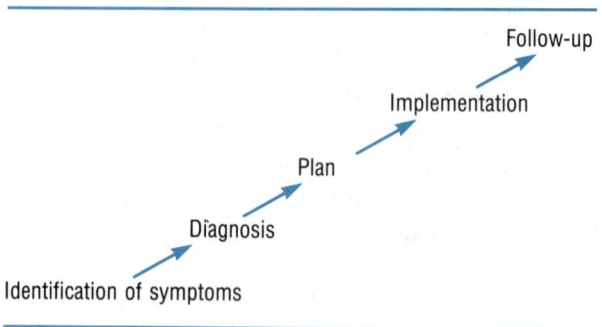

Sometimes there is sufficient time to gather more data, consult experts, and conduct research before prescribing actions. Other times, the manager, like the physician, must simply react to an emergency and "stop the bleeding"; no amount of planning or anticipation can foresee all possibilities.

Let us examine some situations that illustrate this approach. Consider a manager whose unit's productivity has declined (symptom). A number of potential causes exist. Perhaps raw materials have been delayed, are of poor quality, or equipment is not working. Such problems can be identified fairly easily. But perhaps the problem is with the employees. Maybe experienced hands have left, leaving replacements who lack the necessary experience to do the work effectively. If the manager diagnoses worker inexperience as the major factor in the present production decline, possible prescriptions for boosting experience will be examined. Common remedies include more and better training, higher pay to attract skilled and experienced workers, redesigning jobs to reduce the skill required to perform them, and improving communication between supervisors and employees. The manager has diagnosed the situation, set objectives (improve performance and quality), considered the external environment (the pay offered by other employers) and the organization environment (inexperienced employees compared to job requirements), and decided on a course of action. In this case, the manager may decide that increasing training seems the best option. To select the best option, the relative costs, feasibility, and chances of success must be weighed. More often than not, rather than doing a complex cost–benefit analysis, the choice of treatment, like the physician's, is based on the manager's knowledge of research results *and* on personal experience.

But in addition to simply reacting to a problem after it occurs, managers must also anticipate and prevent issues from arising.[12] They must be proactive. Suppose top management of a business machine manufacturer concludes that declining sales of electric typewriters will result in the need for fewer engineers than the number currently employed. The plant's human resource manager could diagnose the situation and decide to let naturally occurring turnover combine with a hiring freeze to solve the engineer surplus. However, life is seldom that simple. Suppose top management also decides to enter the electronic typewriter and word processor business. This strategic marketing decision has a cascading effect on human resource decisions. Perhaps considerable engineering talent and new ideas will be required to design these new products. Senior engineers whose talents lie in the electric typewriter business may be obsolete. They can be retrained for other jobs, encouraged to take advantage of an early retirement program, or offered help in seeking employment with other firms. At the same time, some engineers with expertise required for the new products will be hired. Once again, the manager has diagnosed the organization's objectives and strategies, examined human resource conditions, scanned the external environment, and developed a set of human resource actions to anticipate the future. This is not a hypothetical textbook example. It is part of Smith Corona's human resource management plan. If, as is often the case, the company's objectives shift or conditions change, then the manager will need to adjust the human resource actions accordingly.

THE DIAGNOSTIC MODEL

We have developed a diagnostic model based on this approach. As Exhibit 1–2 shows, our diagnostic model has four basic components.

External conditions.
Organization conditions.
Human resource activities.
Objectives.

Human resource professionals must be extremely well-versed in all social, economic, political, and international issues. (See reference 3.)

External Conditions

The external environment influences and restricts the organization's strategies and activities and, ultimately, its effectiveness. The external environment is an amalgam of societal, cultural, political, technological, and economic factors that influence the organization and its employees. These include:

EXHIBIT 1–2
The Diagnostic Model

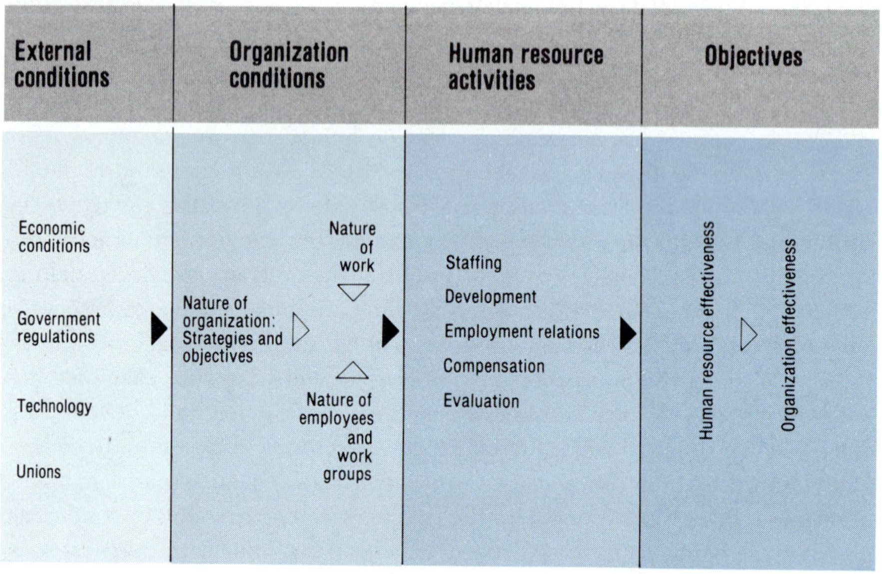

External conditions	Organization conditions	Human resource activities	Objectives
Economic conditions Government regulations Technology Unions	Nature of work Nature of organization: Strategies and objectives Nature of employees and work groups	Staffing Development Employment relations Compensation Evaluation	Human resource effectiveness Organization effectiveness

Economic Conditions. Changing economic conditions directly influence all operations of any organization, including its human resource activities. A manager's decision to hire additional people, to lay off current employees, or to grant a cost-of-living wage increase are all influenced by economic conditions. Economic conditions also influence employees. For example, high unemployment rates may make employees reluctant to leave their present jobs, and thus may restrict turnover. Or a worker squeezed by inflation may request overtime hours, in order to increase a pay cheque.

Technology. Technological change constitutes a powerful economic and competitive force. The identification of technological trends and the assessment of their likely impact on the nature and extent of an organization's need for human resources, capital, raw materials, and processing equipment are of major importance.

The effects of externally produced technological change on various P/HRM activities depend on the type, or "depth," of innovation it represents. Direct consequences include new skill demands, a higher degree of interdependent activities, and smaller margins for error. Second-order effects occur in terms of revised P/HRM practices such as: selection/training (higher selection requirements, more emphasis on the ability to learn, the capacity to be trained, and the possession of multiple skills), job design (broader jobs, which imply fewer job classifications), work team structures (more emphasis on team processes and shared responsibility), compensation/appraisal (pay-for-knowledge systems, emphasis on team performance), and organization (pushing more operating decisions downward, more consultative decision making). Successful application of these practices requires supporting policies based on employee involvement, employment continuity, and union/management cooperation.[13]

Government Influences. Laws reflect a society's response to social, political, or economic problems. Human rights and employment equity laws, regulations of federal, provincial and municipal governments, as well as the courts' interpretation of these laws, have become increasingly important to employers. Employment equity and pay equity (equal pay for work of equal value) have been especially significant. These and related concepts require a reexamination of every P/HRM policy and program to ensure their fairness.

Union Expectations. Unions form for several reasons; too often the reason is poor management of human resources.[14] In many cases, unions have forced employers into sound human resource programs. However, the presence of a union affects an organization's flexibility in designing human resource programs. Therefore, many organizations wish to maintain or achieve union-free status. Labour/management relationships range from hostile to highly cooperative. Unions have an impact beyond their membership. Many nonunionized employers set their wage levels according to union rates in the area. This is called the spillover effect. Additionally, unions become involved in the political process, seeking to influence the way the government responds to problems. So directly or indirectly, unions affect all employers.

Organization Conditions

The second component of our diagnostic model is labelled organizational conditions. The organization's internal environment is made up of many factors. Three of the key ones are included here, but the list is not exhaustive.

Nature of the Organization. Several factors make up the nature of the organization; its strategies and objectives, technology, structure, and culture are examples. When viewed as an internal factor, technology is broadly defined as the techniques and processes an employer uses to convert inputs (capital, materials, knowledge) into outputs (products, services). Strategy refers to the fundamental direction of the organization. One company's decision to leave, and IBM's decision to enter, the personal computer market reflect different strategic directions for those companies. So does a steel firm's decision to concentrate on three types of steel products where it had unique competitive advantages: sheet steel for automakers, seamless pipe for energy exploration, and plates and beams for construction. This decision may mean that plants producing other steel products have to be closed or retooled. It also has profound implications for human resources. Some employees, both steelworkers and managers, may have to be permanently laid off, others retrained to operate new equipment and facilities. Perhaps pay plans based on profit sharing, cost reduction, or improved quality need to be designed. Organization strategies shape human resource actions. Organization resources—financial, material, and human resources—must be deployed in a manner consistent with these strategic directions, and human resource activities must be designed and administered to be consistent with these strategies. Other factors in the nature of the organization are examined in Chapter Three.

Nature of the Work. How do you structure and design organizations? What tasks and responsibilities are considered when examining the nature of the work? The types of jobs to be performed influence the skill and training required, the kinds of compensation and rewards that can be offered, how the jobs can be designed, and other human resource activities. For example, the work at Peoples' Jewellers differs from the work at General Motors' highly automated plant in Oshawa. While each organization requires human resources, the differences in the work require differing P/HRM systems.

Nature of the Employees and Work Groups. Each employee possesses unique abilities, needs, and motivation. The characteristics of an organization's employees in part determine if work teams or individualized jobs are appropriate, if decisions are centralized at corporate headquarters or delegated to units and work teams. Successful human resource activities must be designed and managed with the uniqueness of individuals and work groups in mind. Human resource planning ensures that human resource activities are consistent with the nature of the organization and ensures the match between the nature of the individuals and the nature of the work. Strategic human resource planning makes certain that all human resource decisions are linked with the manufacturing, marketing, financial, and other organization decisions. It also ensures that human resource activities are integrated and do not work at cross-purposes.

The failure of so many P/HRM professionals to thoroughly tune in to business matters might account for their lack of participation in the tough process of pounding out a new strategy. The "house humanist" must possess a practical business orientation backed up by knowledge of finance, markets, economic factors, and technology. (See reference 3.)

Human Resource Activities

The third major component in the diagnostic model is human resource activities. We identified five of them in terms of *programs* designed and administered to achieve human resource and organization objectives. These parallel the five parts of the book that follow the chapters on external and organization conditions.

Staffing
Staffing activities determine the composition of an organization's human resources. Issues addressed include: How many people to employ? What types of knowledge, skills, abilities, other characteristics (KSAOs), and experience are required? Where and how should people be recruited? How do we select, fairly, the correct individuals from among applicants? Pertinent P/HRM activities are employment planning, employment equity, recruitment, and selection.

Development
Most people prefer to work in organizations that provide the opportunity to learn new skills and to advance to higher-level jobs that utilize those skills.[15] Organizations choose to spend substantial sums on training programs, either to teach employees new skills or to sharpen their performance on present jobs.[16] Performance evaluation and training activities are developmental activities designed to enhance employee skills for the benefit of the organization and the employee.

Employment Relations and Rights
These activities promote harmonious relationships among managers and employees. In some organizations, this means reducing employer and employee hostilities, or at least keeping employee dissatisfaction to a tolerable murmur. In others, it means fair and equitable treatment of all employees. Quality of work life, guaranteed employment, grievance procedures, or assistance programs such as drug counselling are part of employee relations. It also includes occupational health and safety activities to reduce work-related accidents, health hazards, and deaths. Labour relations, in which conditions of employment are collectively negotiated with unionized employees, is the most visible activity in employment relations.

Compensation
The design and administration of compensation systems address issues related to rewards and returns for employees' expertise and services. How much to pay an employee, how to ensure fair and equitable pay differences among employees, how large a pay increase each person should receive, and what forms compensation should take (cash, incentives, bonuses, health and medical care, pensions, and so on) all need to be addressed. Some managers include challenging work assignments, the sense of personal accomplishment, and other intrinsic aspects of work as a reward or compensation, too. The

three activities of compensation are determining pay level and structure, individual pay levels and administration of pay systems, and benefits.

Evaluation

Evaluation, including cost analysis, of each program and the entire human resource system is the final human resource activity in the diagnostic approach. Evaluation involves analysis and research to improve the design and administration of the human resource system. It includes the use of integrated information systems and the economic analysis of human resource programs. What are the costs and potential benefits of each alternative? Under what organizational conditions are some programs more likely to be effective than others? How do we evaluate the costs as well as the contributions of P/HRM programs to the organization goals? Evaluative activities enhance the professional judgement of human resource managers.

The biggest mistake a human resource professional can make is to approach senior management with a proposal and not be able to demonstrate how it would affect the company and tie into the strategic plan. (See reference 1.)

These sets of human resource activities (staffing, development, employment relations, compensation, and evaluation) are designed to influence the match between elements of organization and external conditions and, hence, engender human resource effectiveness. They include support and functional activities. P/HRM *support* activities have an indirect influence and serve in a supportive role for, or as an input to, functional activities.[17] The three major support activities are analysing the nature of work (job design, job analysis) and of individuals (ability, motivation), human resource planning, and assessing outcomes. *Functional* P/HRM activities have a more direct effect. The major functional activities are staffing and development, employment relations (employee relations, labour relations), and compensation.

Although discussed separately, human resource activities are highly interrelated. Suppose, for example, a recently conducted job analysis contains errors. As Chapter Four will show, such errors may feed into selection standards, job evaluation, and a number of other activities. Errors in selection may lead to additional orientation and training costs, to less promotability, and so on. In short, a wrong decision made as part of one activity frequently affects other activities.

The design and administration of human resource activities depend on the previous two components of the model: conditions internal and external to the organization. All these activities are designed to accomplish objectives, the last component of the model.

Objectives

Human resource activities are designed to achieve two sets of objectives: organization effectiveness and human resource effectiveness.

Objectives serve several purposes. First, objectives shape the human resource activities—they must be tailored to help managers achieve the organization and human resource objectives. For example, objectives of improving productivity or achieving employment equity affect each of the major human resource activities shown in the diagnostic model. Recruiting, training, compensation, and promotion decisions must be made with regard to their impact on these objectives.

Organization objectives also serve another purpose. Objectives become the standards against which the success of the managers' decisions and performance is evaluated. If the objective is to retain market share, or to reach a specific return on investment or level of profit, then these indexes become a measure of the organization's success. Of course, many factors outside the human resource system can affect the organization's success. However, the objectives do provide a standard for judging overall organization performance and human resource management.

Organizational Effectiveness

There probably are as many different definitions of organizational effectiveness as there are organizations. Typical examples include return on investments, sales, profits, market share, and the like. Highly diversified organizations may even have different definitions of effectiveness for different business units. For example, some units may be operating in booming markets, while others are in declining markets. At TRW Canada, some divisions make products for the auto industry, which in the early 1980s experienced a calamitous decline. Other TRW divisions make space and defence systems, a booming business. The objective for one division may be to maintain the present position in a declining market, while another division's objective may be to capture a greater market share.

Human Resource Effectiveness

Effective employees are the key to all human resource management. Consequently, human resource effectiveness is a key objective of the diagnostic approach shown in the model. Specifics vary among organizations. However, some common definitions of human resource effectiveness include:

High performance is attained.

Quality products are produced.

The right number of employees with the required skills and experience are employed.

Labour costs, turnover, and absenteeism are controlled.

Competitive pay rates are established.

Work environment provides the opportunity for employees to attain job satisfaction and self-esteem.

There is compliance with laws and regulations providing employment equity, a safe work environment, and protection of individual employee rights.

Training is timely, relevant, and anticipatory in nature.

It has also been suggested that P/HRM effectiveness is ultimately determined by its reputation with the various "client" groups it serves.[18] These include managers, other employees, union leaders, and even government officials.

Reality Is More Complex

The diagnostic model uses arrows depicting relationships that flow from left to right. Environmental conditions affect organizations, which in turn shape human resource activities, which influence effectiveness. But that does not mean all influence is in only one direction. The reality of human resource management is more complex. Exhibit 1–3 illustrates this. *Interaction* occurs

EXHIBIT 1–3
Human Resource Activities May Also Affect the Organization and the External Environment

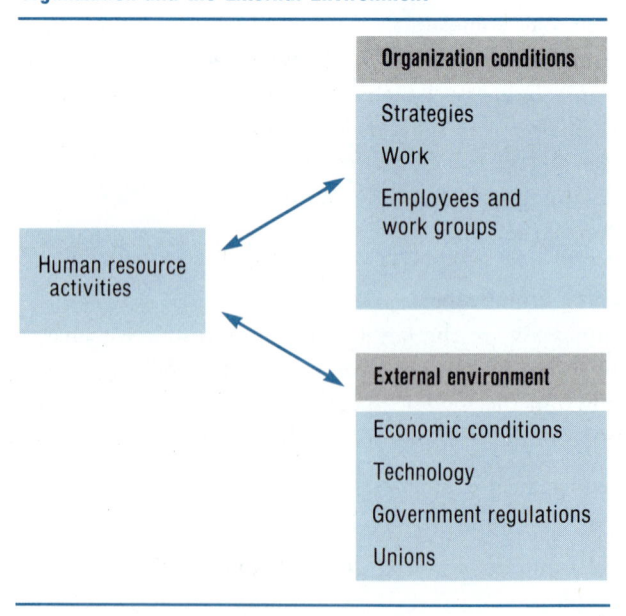

Human resource activities ↔ Organization conditions
- Strategies
- Work
- Employees and work groups

Human resource activities ↔ External environment
- Economic conditions
- Technology
- Government regulations
- Unions

among and within the four model components. For example, achieving human resource effectiveness affects the nature of the employees. Some research has found that productive employees (effective human resources) who achieve work goals are more satisfied than those who are less productive. Employees and organizations lobby to affect the political/social policies instituted by governments. Safety and employment equity regulations are shaped in response to employer and employee pressures. Even organization strategies may be adjusted to capitalize on the interests and abilities of employees; organizations have bought out smaller companies to obtain certain management talent. And an effective and efficient organization can influence product/labour market conditions. The interrelationships among components in the model are complex and multidirectional, but the diagnostic model captures the critical ones.

At first the model seems simple. But as you progress through the book, you will discover the interactions among the factors making up human resource management are very complex. The diagnostic model serves as a framework for understanding and analysing them.

The Book Plan

This book is divided into seven major parts. The organization of the parts parallels the diagnostic model (Exhibit 1–2), so it is useful to keep this model in mind.

Part One introduces the diagnostic model and, in Chapter Two, examines the factors that comprise one of the four basic components: *external conditions*. The next major component—*organization conditions*—is the focus of Part Two. Here we address the nature of work, nature of employees, and nature of organization (in terms of strategies and objectives).

Parts Three through Seven deal with specifics of the third major component—*human resource activities*—and cover the following: staffing, development, employment relations, compensation, and evaluation.

WHO MANAGES HUMAN RESOURCES?

As we pointed out earlier, every organization, no matter its size, needs to manage its human resources. Very small organizations do not hire a person who specializes in human resource management. The owners or operating managers do it. But as organizations increase in size and complexity, the operating manager's work is divided up and some of it becomes specialized. Human resource management is one such function, as is accounting or marketing.

P/HRM is not separate from the management function; it must be seen as an integral part of the enabling process to meet organizational goals. (See reference 1.)

Several studies have examined human resource staffing ratios, that is, the number of human resource specialists hired for every 100 employees.[19] On average, the ratio is 0.5 P/HRM professional per 100 employees.[20] (The median ratio for U.S. employers is 0.6 specialist for every 100 employees. This figure has not changed much since 1960.) In contrast, public sector P/HRM ratios have been found to be as high as 2.0, or four times the all-industry average.

Human resource staff ratios vary by environmental and organizational factors as well as by types of employees and work. Ratios vary by industry, with a high of 0.7 per 100 in finance, insurance, and real estate, to lows of 0.2 in forestry and 0.1 in construction.[21] Smaller firms usually require higher ratios, as they are unable to benefit fully from economies of scale in P/HRM activities. Generally, human resource ratios are higher in firms with greater percentages of professional, engineering, and managerial workers than nonprofessional, production workers.

Why do some industries and firms devote more resources to human resource management than others? Why do professional/engineering/managerial employees seem to have more resources devoted to them than production/blue-collar workers? One answer may be that certain types of employees require greater resources to recruit, train, and pay than others. Some employers believe that more resources devoted to human resource activities will improve overall organization effectiveness. Exhibits 1–4 and 1–5 show IBM's human resource philosophy and some of its human resource programs. But little systematic research has been directed at understanding the effects of human resource staffing ratios and resource deployment on the effectiveness of organizations.

EXHIBIT 1–4
IBM Human Resource Philosophy

"IBM people are our greatest asset—increased efficiency cannot be paid for by debiting our traditional respect for the individual—There can and need be no compromise on that. The management of people remains paramount."

JOHN OPEL

EXHIBIT 1–5
IBM's Human Resource Policies Focus on the Employee, and Programs Are Designed to Increase Each Employee's Involvement

Comments on a number of the specific policies IBM is using:

Compensation: ". . . everyone employed by IBM is salaried. All employees were placed on salary in 1958, and at the same time, all time clocks in the company were removed. . . . Today, employees fill out weekly time sheets that are verified by their managers."

Benefits: "All of IBM's benefit programs are noncontributory. . . . The benefit programs provide wide coverage and we try to be as innovative as possible."

The Line Manager: "We try to maintain a very close employee and manager relationship. We give the manager full human resource responsibility, including merit evaluation and salary."

Training for Managers: "To enable managers to function well in this environment, we provide them with a broad base of management training. In addition, we require all managers, at all levels, to have 40 hours of specific management training each year."

Opinion Surveys: "Opinion surveys, routinely conducted about once a year in most units, are an anonymous process that allows employees to express their opinions on anything about the business, including top management."

Performance Appraisal: "There is a long tradition of individual treatment in IBM. I mentioned the merit system earlier. . . . The appraisal and counselling program is an integral part of that. This program requires that managers and employees sit down and develop objectives, and that employees be evaluated against these objectives at least annually."

Flexible Hours: "We announced in 1981 that individualized work schedules—popularly known as flextime—would be extended to the entire IBM Corporation. Employees are enthusiastic, and management and employees both have seen this program as a current and tangible manifestation of our commitment to respect for the individual."

Quality Circles: "At present, we have in operation over 1,000 excel circles—commonly known as quality circles. Their numbers are increasing, consistent with the company's continuing emphasis on quality. This approach is an excellent way for employees to participate in job-related decisions that affect them."

Manager's Expense Fund: "Our managers are expected to be concerned with their people. To support their human relations efforts, managers are provided with funds for personalized gestures or recognition—or concern—such as a gift for a hospitalized employee."

The Role of the Canadian Human Resource Manager

In 1981, more than 58,000 people were employed as P/HRM professionals. This represents a doubling of the P/HRM profession between 1971 and 1981.[22] In 1986, Canada Employment and Immigration predicted that new professional employment (new positions *and* replacements) in human resource administration would require 6,900 additional P/HRM managers and directors and 9,400 P/HRM officers by 1992.[23] This means that, on average, some 2,300 new positions will be available each year. While this demand was not reflected in the recession-wracked marketplace of the early 1980s, a pent-up demand for P/HRM professionals exists. Thus, as the economy recovers and gathers momentum, that demand will break loose.

Not only are P/HRM professionals in demand, but they are also relatively well paid. Their average pay increased more rapidly than for other categories of managerial occupations.[24]

Overall, each increase of 100,000 jobs created about 500 jobs in the P/HRM field.[25] This may not be the ratio in the future, if various levels of government play a less dominant role in economic activity. The private sector may provide a more important source of P/HRM jobs than it has in the past.[26]

P/HRM has been moving toward greater education and professionalism. Although Kumar noted in 1975 that only about one fourth of Canadian personnel and industrial relations employees were university trained, about two thirds of his 1980 respondents indicated that a university degree is essential; they also felt that five or more years of work experience is necessary for effective performance in P/HRM jobs.[27] Today's employers recognize that the P/HRM function requires a university education, and more individuals employed in the field have a degree in, or directly related to, P/HRM.[28] College and university training include comprehensive courses such as this one, covering topics such as human resource planning, employment equity, compensation administration, training, recruiting, labour relations, and collective bargaining.

Also, a number of professional associations, such as the Personnel Association of Ontario, offer a variety of membership categories based on experience and education, and nurture professional standards through seminars and certificate programs with cooperating colleges and universities (see Appendix A). There is also a wealth of professional and academic journals, and a variety of government reports and updating and retrieval services. (See Appendix B.)

P/HRM—A Field in Transition

The chapter introduction and the highlighted items suggest that the road to professional maturity has not always been smooth for Canadian P/HRM practitioners. To appreciate the field's growth, it is useful to take a brief overview of how it has developed and changed. A more detailed look is given in Appendix C.

The foundation of modern P/HRM emerged from nine interrelated sources.[29] These range from the increased specialization of labour associated with the Industrial Revolution to early industrial psychology, the emergence of personnel specialists, the behavioural science approach to managing people, to the social and employment-related legislation of the last two decades.

According to Cascio, P/HRM developed in three stages—file maintenance, government accountability, and organizational accountability.[30]

The *file maintenance* stage typified P/HRM through the mid-1960s. "Personnel" responsibilities included applicant screening, orientation, collection and storage of personal data of employees (birth date, education, and so on), and circulating memos. Some companies also included planning the company picnic in Personnel's duties.

The other two stages developed in response to changes in external conditions. The growth stage of *government accountability* began with the more intensive passage of legislation pertaining to employment equity laws, pension laws, health and safety laws, employment standards, the introduction of provincial and federal regulatory agencies and their interpretive guidelines, and court rulings affecting virtually every aspect of employment. All of these accelerated the rise in importance of P/HRM.[31] Although this stage of the field began earlier in the United States (where intensive legislation in these areas started in the 1960s), Canadian managers and executives outside the P/HRM function have realized that ineptitude in complying with employment-related legislation cannot be tolerated. Staying "clean" has become a priority in many organizations, and P/HRM professionals are paying attention to signals pointing out the need for special expertise in each aspect of the activities comprising the third component of the diagnostic model.

Somewhat in conjunction with this stage, Canadian P/HRM also entered a phase of *organizational accountability*. This stage evolved due to a combination of economic and political forces (high interest rates, worldwide recession), which led top management to insist on greater accountability (in dollar terms) from functional and staff areas. In contrast to prior years, P/HRM was asked to justify its activities and programs in terms of costs and benefits. In addition, "the responsibility for effective management of people, along with the effective management of physical and financial resources, was placed squarely on the shoulders of line managers—those directly responsible for the operations of the business."[32] This contemporary view, which is reflected in the definition of P/HRM, suggests that all managers, "no matter what their line of responsibility, are accountable to their organizations in terms of the financial impact of P/HRM operations."[33]

Recent research suggests that another element of the third and future stages is the need for a more macro-level perspective. Data from a sample of chief executive officers reveal that a more generalist orientation by *senior* P/HRM managers increases the function's influence on organizational decision making and helps nurture P/HRM's importance and status as an equal partner.[34] However, internal boundary spanning and influence building must still have a core of specialized expertise to draw on. They also require some "political" savvy and, as succinctly put by Kanter, the capacity to develop lines of supply, information, and support.[35]

Given the changing roles of P/HRM and operating managers, we suggest the most fruitful approach may result from close interaction between the two. This is not always easy to achieve.

The Interaction of Operating and Human Resource Managers—Partners

With two managers—operating managers and human resource managers—making decisions, there may be conflict if authority for specific decisions is blurred. Additionally, operating and human resource managers may have different orientations or even different objectives. For example, an operating manager may wish to minimize costs by paying only the minimum wage necessary to attract sufficient workers to do the job at minimum levels of competence. On paper, the operating manager looks good. But over time, inferior goods or services may drive away formerly loyal customers, and resentful workers may take out their frustration on product quality and equipment. Eventually, profits may plummet, but by then the short-sighted operating manager may have moved to a new location. In contrast, some human resources managers have the long-term needs of the employees and the organization in mind and try to ensure consistent, fair treatment.

The potential conflict between human resource professionals and operating managers is most manifest where the decisions must be joint efforts, as on such issues as discipline, physical working conditions, termination, transfer, promotion, and employment planning. Operating managers are *the* managers of human resources. They are responsible for the effective utilization of all the organization's resources. Yet the human resource professional, like the financial or marketing or engineering professional, must advise and counsel to make certain the human resource decisions are correct under the circumstances. Ideally, human resource professionals and operations managers will complement each other rather than compete.

Good sources for P/HRM opportunities are found in conversations with operating managers about the business—where it's going, where it's hurting.

The key to plugging P/HRM more into the company is to plug operating managers into P/HRM.

Nothing you or your department could do will have the impact of several operating managers who have "bought" into what you're doing.

P/HRM should involve operating managers not only in the implementation, but also the design of programs. (See reference 1.)

To encourage a productive partnership between human resource professionals and operating managers, chapters dealing with specific activities include a delineation of each manager's contribution to effective P/HRM. These show that operating managers and supervisors play an important role in performing most of the P/HRM activities discussed in this book. They also reemphasize that P/HRM must be viewed as a joint responsibility.

Consequently, and in light of the definition of human resource management, this book is directed at two groups: P/HRM students and professionals as well as operating managers and supervisors. We hope to reach both halves of the partnership so, together, they can make informed choices when designing, implementing, and managing activities that are intended to influence the effectiveness of the employees and the organization.

SUMMARY

Human resource management is an important topic, not only because labour is expensive but also because people make the decisions and do the work in organizations. Human resources *are* the organization. The job of managing human resources is changing because organizations are changing and employees are becoming more insistent that their needs be met. In response, managers are required to tailor their decisions to the particular circumstances of the organization and the environment, as well as to the needs of the employees. That is what the diagnostic model of human resource management is all about.

In our model, conditions outside the organization—government, economic, technological, and union influences—and conditions inside the organization—organization strategies, nature of the work, nature of employees and work groups—all affect what human resource programs are designed, and how effective they will be in achieving objectives.

The next component of the model is human resource activities. These are the programs designed to achieve the objectives. Objectives in the model include organization effectiveness and human resource effectiveness. Human resource activities are tailored to meet whatever objectives an organization adopts; these objectives then become the standards for evaluating the activities and the human resource manager.

Two points about the model need to be emphasized. First, there is considerable *interaction* among all components. While economic conditions affect human resource programs, the opposite also holds true. Sound human resource programs can increase the attractiveness of an organization to a potential employee, and hence change conditions in the labour market. The second point is that *conditions change*. Society's expectations change, technology and jobs change—in fact, change is a constant, and as conditions change, human resource activities must change too. As the rate of change has accelerated in the past two decades, human resource management has grown in complexity, importance, and professional maturity. The challenge of diagnosing conditions and designing activities to fit changing conditions is what makes human resource management so exciting.

APPENDIX A / Certification and Professionalization

Canadian practitioners who are seconded to U.S. locations should consider accreditation courses of the American Society of Personnel Administrators (ASPA). The ASPA Accreditation Institute offers executives the opportunity to be accredited as specialists (in functional areas such as employment, placement and planning, or training and development) or as generalists (multiple specialties). This institute is a nonprofit organization formed for the purpose of accrediting human resource professionals.

ASPA accreditation is based on mastery of a body of knowledge, as demonstrated by passing a comprehensive written examination, and on varying amounts of full-time professional experience in the field, as practitioners, consultants, educators, or researchers. Individuals must currently be serving in the role appropriate to the type of accreditation they seek.

In Canada, the Council of Canadian Personnel Associations (CCPA) has in the past been seen as a national voice for practitioners and has been promoted as the overall body to institutionalize and oversee certification programs.[36] More recent efforts at certification, however, have been executed on a provincial level.

In general, there is considerable similarity among the certification programs offered.[37] This is illustrated in Exhibit A–1, which compares two sets of courses: one based on a survey conducted by Queen's University's Industrial Relations Centre, and the Certificate in Personnel Management (CPM) course established by the Personnel Association of Ontario (PAO) as the basic standards of knowledge for the P/HRM field. Successful completion of the CPM is part of the requirement to become an accredited full member of the PAO.

The recent formation (in 1987) of HR Canada (properly The Federation of Human Resource Development Associations of Canada) provides an umbrella organization that helps tie together the various provincial training and development societies. Another organization, the International Association for Personnel Women (IAPW), was founded in 1950. Its purpose is to expand and improve the professionalism of women in P/HRM. The approximately 2,000 members are generalists and specialists working in various industries.[38]

EXHIBIT A–1
Subject Areas in Accreditation/Certification Courses: Queen's University's Survey and PAO

Industrial Relations Centre Survey, Queen's University (in order of importance)

1. Human Resource Management
2. Sociology/Psychology
3. Management Skills
4. Industrial Relations
5. Economics/Labour Economics
6. Labour Law
7. Communication Skills
8. Labour Relations
9. Collective Bargaining
10. Statistics/Computers
11. Organizational Theory/Behaviour
12. Labour History

PAO

Tier I — Foundations of Human Resources
1. Finance and Accounting
2. Labour Economics
3. Organizational Behaviour
4. Human Resources Administration

Tier II — Areas of Specialization
5. Compensation
6. Health and Safety
7. Human Resource Planning
8. Labour Relations
9. Training and Development
10. Human Resource Research and Information Systems

Source: D. A. Ondrack, "P/IR Professional Certification in Ontario: The PAO Model," paper presented at a symposium on professional education in P/IR, Canadian Industrial Relations Association (CIRA), Dalhousie University, Halifax, N.S., May 26, 1981. The PAO courses are listed from PAO's 1987 "Curriculum Summary—Certificate in Personnel Management."

APPENDIX B / Publications and Other Sources

Canadian P/HRM students, managers, and practitioners can develop and advance their knowledge of the field by reading a cross section of professional journals and gaining access to a number of information sources. The following list, while not exhaustive, is divided into several categories:

1. Journals for the general human resource manager:
    Administrative Management
    Canadian HR Reporter
    Human Resource Management
    The Human Resource
    The Personnel Administrator
    Personnel
    Personnel Journal
    Supervisory Management
2. Scholarly journals: The following publications are written for both scholars and executives. Reading these requires more technical training than the journals listed above.

Academy of Management Journal
Academy of Management Review
Canadian Journal of Administrative Sciences
Canadian Journal of Behavioural Science
Canadian Psychology
Relations Industrielles
Journal of Applied Psychology
Journal of Human Resources
Journal of Management
Journal of Vocational Behavior
Organizational Behavior and Human Decision Processes (formerly *Organizational Behavior and Human Performance*)
Personnel Psychology

3. Specialized journals: These are available to the P/HRM specialist in several distinct fields. They include:
Benefits Canada
Canadian Human Rights Reporter
Canadian Social Trends
Human Resource Planning
International Reviews of Ergonomics
Journal of Occupational Behaviour
Managerial Planning
Managing Automation
Occupational Health & Safety Canada
Robotics
Training
Training and Development Journal
Work and Stress

4. General management and business journals: The coverage of these sources is more business/management–oriented, but certain issues include articles on P/HRM topics and developments.
Academy of Management Executive
Business Quarterly
Business Horizons
Business Journal/Outlook
Canadian Public Administration
The Canadian Business MAGAZINE
The Canadian Business REVIEW
Harvard Business Review
Organizational Dynamics
Report on Business Magazine (The Globe and Mail)
Sloan Management Review

5. Information and current awareness services: Several companies and organizations offer management information services. The best established are CCH Canadian Limited, and The Conference Board of Canada. "Human Resource Management in Canada" comprises a third source.

   CCH Canadian Limited provides a service covering the following:

   Canadian Labour Law Reports: Reproduces and explains federal and provincial laws on employer-employee relations, fair wages, vacations, statutory holidays, hours of work, industrial standards, fair employment practices, and so on. Outline of Unemployment Insurance and of Workers' Compensation Law. Court, Labour Relations Board, and Human Rights labour decisions. "Labour Notes" newsletter summary is included. Bimonthly reporting; three volumes.

   Canadian Industrial Relations and Personnel Developments: Reports significant developments in industrial relations and personnel fields. Monthly digests present Canadian economic indicators on the labour market. Regular reports on key subjects and periodic special research studies. Weekly newsletter; one volume.

   Canadian Employment Benefits and Pension Guide: Covers Canada and Québec Pension Plans and provincial legislation regulating private pension plans. Fringe benefit plans, group insurance, medicare and executive compensation also covered. Consolidated text of relevant laws reproduced. Report letter summary included. Monthly reporting; two volumes.

   Canadian Employment Safety and Health Guide: Reports on federal and provincial legislation on employment safety and health. Relevant case law, statute law, plus editorial commentary. Report letter summary. Monthly reporting; two volumes.

   Canadian Payroll Management Guide: Practical reference provides a single, complete source of information on all federal and provincial legislation and regulations, and step-by-step instructions on preparing the payroll. Monthly reporting; one volume.

   Focus on Canadian Employment and Equality Rights: Prepared by the Labour Department of the law firm Fraser & Beatty, this newsletter is intended to keep employers and service providers up-to-date on all equality requirements. Monthly reporting; one volume.

   The Conference Board of Canada offers many of its products and services through computers, bringing subscribers timely, current, useful information when and where they need it. Subscribers have access to the board's quarterly survey of forecasters, Statistics Canada CANSIM, bilingual Conference Board releases, and advance executive summaries. New on-line services in 1986 included a microcomputer model of the Canadian economy and extended provincial forecasts.

Other related current awareness services are available (consult your library). These include: ABI/INFORM, which indexes approximately 550 journals covering all aspects of management and business, including personnel and labour relations; AP NEWS, with the full text of national, international, and business news from the AP Data Stream service; CANADIAN BUSINESS AND CURRENT AFFAIRS, an index of 170 Canadian business periodicals and 10 newspapers; INDUSTRY DATA SOURCES, which provides access to industry-intensive data on 65 major industries and includes Canada as well as the United States and other foreign countries; and MANAGEMENT CONTENTS, with current information on a variety of business and management-related topics from approximately 700 U.S. and international journals.

6. Government sources: These include publications and reports (sometimes in terms of "special studies") by Canada Employment and Immigration, the Economic Council of Canada, the Canadian Centre for Occupational Health and Safety, Labour Canada, and Statistics Canada. Provincial agencies also issue reports dealing with issues pertaining to various aspects of P/HRM.

7. International sources: Two important sources are the International Labour Organization (ILO) and the Organization for Economic Cooperation and Development (OECD). For example, recent ILO publications include an encyclopedia on occupational health and safety and reports dealing with the impact of microtechnology on employment. OECD, of which Canada is a member country, publishes analyses and comparisons of employment and output levels and various other studies.

APPENDIX C / A Brief History of Canadian P/HRM[39]

By the 1880s, industrialization was in its first flowering in Canada. The government, middle-class reformers, and the fledgling trade union movement were concerned that the worst excesses of the British Industrial Revolution (e.g., the use of child labour) should not be repeated here. A Royal Commission on the Relations of Labour and Capital, established in 1886, issued a report in 1889 that documented a number of abuses (e.g., children as young as 10 were working in factories; awareness of safety issues was minimal). Also by 1889, provincial governments in both Ontario and Quebec had passed their first factory acts, regulating safety conditions, child labour, and hours of work. Employers were increasingly required to accept responsibility for the general welfare of their workers.

Many employers took to this notion, which became known as the industrial betterment or industrial welfare movement. That movement reached its peak in the early 1900s, with factories providing facilities such as baths, lunchrooms, and mutual benefit societies. Bell Telephone, for example, established a health program for employees as early as the 1880s. A number of other companies, such as Canadian Pacific Railway, introduced formal pension plans. Some employers may have adopted betterment policies to prevent formation of unions.

Influenced by similar programs in the United States and Great Britain, companies appointed the first "industrial welfare" workers in the 1890s.

In 1906, the Toronto branch executive of the Canadian Manufacturers' Association observed, "The intelligent manufacturer . . . knows that human beings, like machines, give best service and require less time and expense for repair when carefully treated, and that good ventilation, wholesome food, and wise recreation are as necessary for the efficiency of the individuals in his employ as are oil and brush for the machinery."[40]

Over time, a number of industrial welfare workers got involved in the selection, education, and training of workers, and in the study of wage payments, becoming precursors of the modern P/HRM practitioner. As enterprises grew, it became necessary to maintain extensive employment records. This led to another precursor of the modern personnel practitioner: record keeping became the job of employment clerks. The Bank of Nova Scotia, for example, employed its first "staff clerk" in 1912.

Many Canadian companies began to centralize their hiring procedures after World War I. Centralization of employment activities and a more orderly approach to hiring reflected the advances in selection procedures made by the military during the war. Still, it took a number of years before the involvement of personnel specialists in hiring was universally accepted.

The end of World War I also saw the emergence of the industrial relations function, in its modern sense, in Canada. Although the Canadian union movement started to pick up speed after 1900, its real growth was still ahead. Development of trade unionism generally paralleled the growth of the personnel function.

As unions grew in influence, employers turned increasingly to personnel practitioners, either attempting to keep unions out or to deal more effectively with an established union. The union movement proved to be an accidental benefactor to the personnel profession. For example, unionization was a major factor in stimulating the improvement of job descriptions (which had to be defined much more exactly in contract negotiations). Demands for higher wages and new services and benefits (pensions, group life insurance) created the need for specialists in wages and benefits negotiation and administration.

Fall of 1934 saw the formation of the Montreal Personnel Association, the first such association in Canada, with an initial membership of nine people. The new group immediately mounted a 10-week night course, titled "Personnel Administration in Industry," using materials prepared by personnel staff at CNR, CPR, Bell Telephone, C-I-L, Sun Life, and faculty at McGill University. In June 1935, a group of counterparts in Toronto started to meet weekly for informal discussions on personnel subjects.

By the mid-1930s, the majority of Canadian companies, including some of the largest, had no real personnel function beyond the most rudimentary recordkeeping. This would remain the case for several years. However, the modern personnel and industrial relations function had begun to take shape, at least in a handful of the more progressive companies. Practitioners still tended to be largely self-educated; there were no Canadian university degree-credit personnel courses to attend. Those so inclined had to travel to Dartmouth College in New Hampshire, which offered its first course in employment management in 1915. Not until 1936 did Queen's University, under prodding from the personnel associations of Montreal and Toronto, set up Canada's first industrial relations section. The few magazines to carry articles on the personnel function (e.g., *Supervision, Personnel Journal*) came from across the border, as did the first textbooks in the field.

World War II led to an increase in the importance of the personnel function. Factories doubled in size almost overnight, and then doubled again. Workers had to be recruited and trained as rapidly as possible for jobs that, in many cases, had not even existed before. In addition, the federal government added new layers of regulation and bureaucracy to the workplace to facilitate war production. Suddenly, personnel and industrial relations skills were important. The federal government even sponsored special extension courses in personnel administration at universities including Dalhousie, Queen's, the University of Manitoba, and the University of British Columbia. One of the key elements in these courses was job description and evaluation.

The shortage of trained personnel staff pulled many new and untrained individuals into the field from other areas. J. Rae Perigoe, who in 1954 became the founder and longtime editor of the *Canadian Personnel and Industrial Relations Journal*, attended meetings with the Personnel Association of Toronto (PAT) and helped organize a number of personnel associations in locations such as Windsor and Chatham.

Another impact of the war was the steady advance of industrial psychology. The military placed increasing reliance on psychological testing to improve methods of selection and placement. Overall, the personnel profession emerged from the war years stronger than ever. Personnel people, personnel associations, courses, and centres of industrial relations grew and kept growing.

In the early 1950s, a fundamental split began to develop in the personnel function. On one hand was the traditional approach, characteristic of individuals in labour relations and to some degree in employment and remuneration.

Choosing a "very pragmatic approach, often involving hostility between management and workers—an advocacy system of power-based relationships and conflicts," they "had typically come up through minor functions in their companies, without any special educational qualifications but with extensive experience in these functions."[41] The dominance of this group was challenged by "better-educated people who had a base in theory and not nearly as extensive in experience,"[42] who were applying the new concepts of human relations and techniques such as human resource planning and management development. In the United States, this new wave of practitioners had already moved to the forefront in several companies. In Canada, they gained an initial foothold at Ontario Hydro. From the mid-1950s onward, as younger and better-educated individuals joined personnel associations, interest in this new approach was in the ascendancy.

Canada's postwar economic boom, combined with the low birth rates during the Depression, created major skills shortages in the 1950s and 1960s. These extended all the way up to the management level. Human resource planning and management development had become an absolute necessity. Increasingly, new skills and new expertise were needed to supplement the traditional labour relations approach to personnel. Peter Drucker deplored the fact that the personnel function had so far confined itself largely to rank-and-file employees. Innovative companies were moving ahead with management development programs, including communications skills training, performance appraisal systems, and management by objectives. Herzberg's theory of motivation had become influential, as had the need hierarchy ideas of Maslow. Studies in group dynamics and group behaviour, which had helped trigger the human relations movement, were leading increasingly to a focus on the organization itself and the factors that made it effective. Interest in the old-style labour relations had slackened to a degree in favour of organizational behaviour and development. Union Carbide was one of the first Canadian corporations to establish an organization development group.

The emergence of a younger breed of chief executive officers (CEOs) also helped generate respect for the personnel function. They were more willing to expose their employees to personnel research and more receptive to adoption of new techniques. This was partly in response to changing social trends: the postwar baby boom had come to maturity and entered the work force. Their views of the work ethic were different from their parents'. Companies responded by incorporating ideas drawn from the behavioural sciences on job design/enrichment, employee participation, and conflict resolution. Alliance with the behavioural sciences brought not only new techniques, but also a new source of prestige within organizations. However, enthusiasm for new ideas was sometimes carried through to the point of faddishness. The struggle for professional recognition was a key theme throughout this period.

By the mid-1970s, more practitioners were winning acceptance at the senior level. As a result, some felt less pressure to play the behavioural science guru. The less affluent economic conditions also depressed the enthusiasm for some of the new ideas. However, some continued to grow in popularity, including MBO, the emphasis on human resource planning as a part of corporate strategic planning, and assessment centres.

The 1970s also saw an upsurge of Canadian nationalism. According to Murray, one spinoff "was a move on the part of many foreign-owned multinational companies to decentralize control of the human resource function,"[43] so their Canadian subsidiaries would develop policies more closely reflecting the Canadian situation.

Another emerging trend was the growing participation of women in the work force. In the years ahead, this would mean adjustments to new human rights and equal opportunity initiatives, as well as to a growing influx of ambitious and intelligent women into the personnel/human resource management field.

As organizations grappled with the increasing rate of inflation into the early 1980s and unions pushed hard for cost-of-living increases, many companies began to drastically cut managerial and professional staff. New specialties emerged rapidly on the personnel scene, with labels such as "out-placement" consultant and relocation counselling.

At the same time, interest was growing in Japanese management techniques (particularly quality circles) and in organization effectiveness and productivity improvement efforts, which often involved elements of employee participation and introduction of new technology. The timely appearance of the popular *In Search of Excellence* and *The Renewal Factor,* and companies' determination to remain lean and productive, help an understanding and appreciation of P/HRM to permeate the entire managerial culture.[44] In progressive organizations, the senior P/HRM manager has become an integral part of the senior management team, on a par with such traditional functions as manufacturing and marketing.

DISCUSSION AND REVIEW QUESTIONS

1. Define human resource management and tell why it is important in an organization.
2. What are some of the outside forces of change that influence human resource management?
3. What is the major purpose of human resource activities?
4. How do top management's strategic decisions interact with human resource management?

5. Describe the importance of interactions of operating and human resource managers in making decisions.
6. What are some of the reasons for the increasing importance of human resource management in the organization?
7. What are some reasons for using the diagnostic model of human resource management?
8. How are human resource activities related to organization conditions?
9. What basic results do human resource activities seek to affect? What data measure these results?

NOTES AND REFERENCES

1. Several of the items used for special emphasis in this chapter were adapted in order to provide the desired P/HRM specificity. Jack Gordon, "What They Don't Teach You about Being a Training Manager," *Training*, June 1986, pp. 22–27, 29–32, 34.
2. Ibid.
3. These items were extracted from Fred K. Foulkes, ed., *Strategic Human Resources Management: A Guide for Effective Practice* (Englewood Cliffs, N.J.: Prentice-Hall, 1986), p. 385.
4. Ibid., p. 374.
5. Ibid., p. 148.
6. Some writers make the case that work will be more complex. Yet others argue it will be greatly simplified, except for a small proportion of jobs. Eli Ginzberg, D. Mills, J. D. Owen, H. Sheppard, and M. L. Wachter, eds., *Work Decision in the 1980s* (Boston: Auburn House Publishing, 1981); Sar A. Levitan and Clifford M. Johnson, *Second Thoughts on Work* (Kalamazoo, Mich.: W. E. Upjohn Institute for Employment Research, 1982); "Work in the 21st Century," *Personnel Administrator*, December 1983.
7. D. Quinn Mills, "Human Resources in the 1980s," *Harvard Business Review*, 1979, pp. 154–62; John J. Leach, "Merging the Two Faces of Personnel: A Challenge for the 1980s," *Personnel*, January–February 1980, pp. 52–58; Jack W. English, "The Road Ahead for the Human Resources Function," *Personnel*, March–April 1980, pp. 35–40; George S. Odiorne, "Personnel Management for the 1980s," in *ASPA Handbook of Personnel and Industrial Relations*, ed. D. Yoder and H. Heneman, Jr. (Washington, D.C.: Bureau of National Affairs, 1979), chap. 1.8; David E. Dimick, "Who Makes Personnel Decisions?" *Canadian Personnel & Industrial Relations Journal*, January 1978, pp. 23–29; Daniel R. Hoyt and J. D. Lewis, "Planning for a Career in Human Resource Management," *Personnel Administrator*, October 1980, pp. 53–54, 67–68; Robert H. Meehan, "The Future Personnel Executive," *Personnel Administrator*, January 1981, pp. 25–28; Stella M. Nkomo, "Stage Three in Personnel Administration: Strategic Human Resources Management," *Personnel*, July–August 1980, pp. 69–77; Neil A. Palomba, "Accreditation of Personnel Administrator: Theory and Reality," *Personnel Administrator*, January 1981, pp. 37–40; and Mary Zippo, "Human Resources Professionals: The New Corporate Heroes," *Personnel*, January–February 1981, pp. 43–44.

8. Statistics Canada, "The Labour Force Survey," *Work for Tomorrow*, report by the Parliamentary Task Force on Employment Opportunities for the 1980s (Ottawa: Published under the authority of the Speaker of the House of Commons, Cat. No. XC2-321/4-01E); Economic Council of Canada, *Changing Times*, Twenty-Third Annual Review 1986 (Ottawa: Minister of Supply and Services Canada, 1986, Cat. No. EC21-1/1986E).
9. See Chapter Two, External Conditions.
10. C. G. Burck, "Will Success Spoil General Motors?" *Fortune*, August 22, 1983, pp. 94–106.
11. This five-step model is also useful for establishing a consultant-client relationship between P/HRM and operating managers.
12. This is similar to physicians' practicing preventive medicine.
13. See the detailed discussion of technology and P/HRM interaction presented in Chapter Two. The specific points summarized here were drawn from Richard E. Walton and Gerald A. Susman, "People Policies for the New Machines," *Harvard Business Review*, March–April 1987, pp. 98–106; see also Joseph N. Fry and J. Peter Killing, *Strategic Analysis and Action* (Scarborough: Prentice-Hall Canada, 1986); Cindy Moser, "Hi-Tech Tools," *Occupational Health and Safety Canada*, March–April 1986, pp. 28–30, 34; Keith Newton and Gordon Betcherman, "Innovating on Two Fronts: People and Technology in the 1990s," *Canadian Business REVIEW*, Autumn 1987, pp. 18–26.
14. Union-management relations are discussed in Chapter Thirteen; also see John A. Willes, *Contemporary Canadian Labour Relations* (Toronto: McGraw-Hill Ryerson Limited, 1984).
15. Phil Ebersole, "A New Pattern: Women as Engineers," *Democrat & Chronicle* (Rochester, N.Y.), March 25, 1984, p. 3F; Rosabeth Moss Kanter and Barry A. Stein, *Life in Organizations* (New York: Basic Books, 1979).
16. Andrew Campbell, "Training Helps Keep Employees on Toes," *The Globe and Mail*, March 10, 1986, p. B2; "$16 Million in Job Fund Goes to Youth," *The Vancouver Sun*, May 31, 1986, p. A6; Thomas F. Gilbert, "Training: The $100 Billion Opportunity," *Training and Development Journal*, November 1976, pp. 3–8.
17. Herbert G. Heneman III, Donald P. Schwab, John A. Fossum, and Lee D. Dyer, *Personnel/Human Resource Management*, 3rd. ed. (Homewood, Ill.: Richard D. Irwin, 1986).
18. A. S. Tsui, "Personnel Department Effectiveness: A Tripartite Approach," *Industrial Relations* 23 (1984), pp. 184–97.
19. Jean-Michel Cousineau, "Labour Market Trends and Their Implications for P/HRM Training in Canada," Document No. 86–06 (Montréal: Ecole de relations industrielles, Université de Montreal, March 1986); Oscar A. Onantic and Edward J. Giblin, "The Personnel Department: Its Staffing and Budgeting," cited in *Personnel*, November–December 1982, p. 6.
20. Cousineau, "Labour Market Trends."
21. Ibid.
22. Ibid.
23. Derived from data in *Job Futures: An Occupational Outlook to 1992* (Ottawa: Minister of Supply and Services Canada, 1986; Cat. No. MP43-181/1986E).
24. Cousineau, "Labour Market Trends."
25. Ibid.

26. Ibid.
27. Pradeep Kumar, *Personnel Management in Canada: A Manpower Profile* (Kingston, Ont.: Industrial Relations Centre, Queen's University, 1975); Pradeep Kumar, "Professionalism in Canadian Personnel and Industrial Relations," *The Canadian Personnel and Industrial Relations Journal*, January 1981, pp. 27–31.
28. James W. Thacker and R. Julian Cattaneo, "The Canadian Personnel Function: Status and Practices," *ASAC Proceedings* (Personnel and Human Resources: Special Interest Group, June 1–3, 1987, Toronto, Ontario), pp. 56–66.
29. Wendell L. French, *The Personnel Management Process*, 5th ed. (Boston: Houghton-Mifflin, 1982).
30. Wayne F. Cascio, *Managing Human Resources* (New York: McGraw–Hill, 1986).
31. Ibid; and *PAT: The First 50 Years (Building the Human Resource Function)*, (Toronto: Personnel Association of Toronto, 1986).
32. Ibid., p. 44.
33. Ibid., p. 44.
34. R. William Blake, "The Role of the Senior Human Resource Executive in Managing Corporate Excellence: Orientation and Influence," Ph.D. dissertation, University of Western Ontario, London, Ontario, 1987.
35. Rosabeth Moss Kanter, "Power Failure in Management Circuits," *Harvard Business Review*, July–August 1979, pp. 65–75; for the new kind of human resource manager needed, see also Jeffrey Gandz and James C. Rush, "Change Will Be the Norm," *Financial Times* of Canada, March 28, 1983, p. 11.
36. C. W. Nemeth and J. I. A. Rowney, "Professionalize or Perish," *The Canadian Personnel and Industrial Relations Journal*, January 1981, pp. 27–31.
37. D. A. Ondrack, "P/IR Professional Certification in Ontario: The PAO Model," paper presented at a symposium on professional education in P/IR, Canadian Industrial Relations Association (CIRA), Dalhousie University, Halifax, N.S., May 26, 1981.
38. Denise S. Akey, ed., *Encyclopedia of Associations*, 16th ed. (Detroit: Gale Research, 1982).
39. This section is compiled from the history of the Personnel Association of Toronto, *PAT: The First 50 Years (Building the Human Resource Function)*. The authors are grateful to PAT for granting permission to adapt this material.
40. Ibid.
41. Ibid.
42. Ibid.
43. Ibid.
44. Robert H. Waterman, Jr., *The Renewal Factor: How the Best Get and Keep the Competitive Edge* (New York: Bantam Books, 1987).

CHAPTER TWO
EXTERNAL CONDITIONS

CHAPTER OUTLINE

I. External Conditions and the Diagnostic Model
    A. Diagnosing External Conditions
    B. Environmental Scanning
II. Economic Conditions
    A. The Population and the Labour Force
    B. Labour Markets
    C. Product/Service Market Conditions
    D. Canada–U.S. Free(r) Trade
    E. Privatization
    F. Takeovers and Mergers
III. Technology
IV. Government Regulations
    A. Terms and Conditions—Employment
    B. The Regulatory Process
    C. Deregulation
V. Union Expectations and Concerns
VI. International Dimensions
VII. Summary

Demand for labour was so keen that an employee could quit a job in the morning and have employment in another organization at noon. The term "five day worker" or "floater" came into use to describe the undependable work force. Labour turnover was enormous. One organization's average yearly employment was 14,300, but 50,448 employees left in that year.[1]

It was evident that such turnover was an expensive indulgence. Some sort of program that would insure a stable, experienced work force was badly wanted. After a series of studies, human resource programs were designed to increase work force stability. These included profit sharing, training programs to insure employees could use the modern technology, a department store, legal aid (with six full-time lawyers to give employees legal advice), medical and dental facilities (with a staff of 12), and employee athletic and musical programs. While demand for labour continued unabated, the turnover and absenteeism dropped dramatically following the onset of these programs.[2]

Is this the success story of a human resource manager in a high-tech organization, competing for computer and software design engineers in the 1980s? No, it is the Ford Motor Company's experience from 1913 to 1920.

Ford found that conditions in the *external* environment in 1913 affected employees' work behaviours as well as management's ability to achieve organization objectives. High demand for labour and the unmet needs and expectations of new workers led Ford to instigate programs to be run by a department of sociology, a forerunner to the modern human resource management function. The department's activities ranged from forecasting future availability of labour to visiting workers' homes to discuss their needs and behaviours. Improved work force stability has been attributed to these programs.[3]

Ford's experience needs to be rediscovered. Conditions external to the organization have a significant influence on human resource and organization effectiveness. Improved human resource management is often a direct response to external pressures. Jacoby argues that personnel programs arose as the result of widespread labour unrest and union pressures.[4] He states, "According to various surveys, the proportion of large firms with personnel departments rose markedly during 1919 to 1935"[5]; the proportion of the industrial work force covered by personnel departments increased substantially.

Analysis of more recent data on personnel budgets reveals that increased government regulation of human rights, employment equity, and occupational safety and health has affected the magnitude of organization resources allocated to related human resources programs.[6] To more fully understand human resource management requires an understanding of these and other external influences. This chapter addresses those issues.

EXTERNAL CONDITIONS AND THE DIAGNOSTIC MODEL

The diagnostic model shows four key sources of external pressures on human resource management:

Economic pressures.

Governmental regulations.

Expectations or threat of a union.

Technological change.

Diagnosing External Conditions

Exhibit 2–1 lists some of the devices used to diagnose the nature of relevant external pressures.

Most of the analysis, conducted for specific P/HRM activities, involves the human resources manager in an important boundary-spanning role. For example, staffing and recruiting activities require searches to assess the quantity and quality of various skills and abilities available in the external labour market. Wage and benefit surveys are conducted to determine competitive pay rates.

One procedure shown in the exhibit, environmental scanning, is used to assess economic, governmental, and union trends. Because of its flexibility, it illustrates how organizations may diagnose external conditions.

Environmental Scanning

External environmental scanning (EES) for general business purposes is reasonably well developed, but little has been written on human resource management applications, and there is virtually no research.[7] However, most formal (and probably most informal) EES applications follow some variant of the process shown in Exhibit 2–2, which includes monitoring, screening, conducting issues research, and communicating.

Monitoring the Environment

Like an early warning system, monitoring involves gathering intelligence about the organization's environment with emphasis on patterns and discontinuities.[8] Most organizations scan all regions in which they have facilities. In practice, domestic and overseas areas tend to be treated separately, and the domestic emphasis is national rather than regional or local. Time frames tend to extend as far as the planning horizon. The subject matter considered appears to be fairly consistent from company to company. Honeywell, a typical

EXHIBIT 2–1
Devices Used to Diagnose External Conditions for the Key Human Resource Programs

Device	External Conditions Analysed	Human Resource Programs
External environmental scanning	Economic conditions Governmental regulations Societal values Union expectations and power Technological changes	Human resource planning
Salary and benefit surveys	Economic conditions: Wages and benefits paid by competitors in labour and product markets	Compensation and benefits
Recruiting and availability analysis	Economic conditions: Availability of required skills and experience Availability of designated groups (women, aboriginal peoples, visible minorities, and persons with disabilities)	Recruiting Employment equity/human rights action and planning
Labour settlement surveys	Union expectation and power: Recent contract settlement provisions	Labour relations

EXHIBIT 2-2
The External Environmental Scanning Process

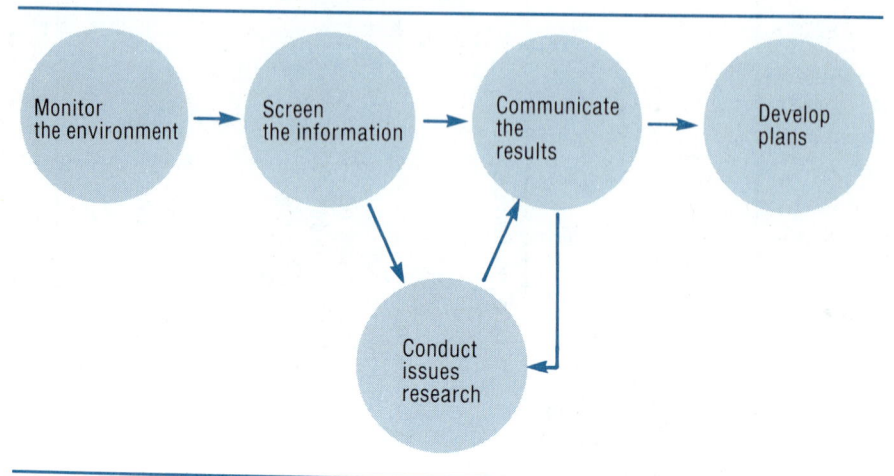

Monitor the environment → Screen the information → Communicate the results → Develop plans

Conduct issues research

Source: G. Milkovich, L. Dyer, T. Mahoney, "HRM Planning," in *Human Resources Management in the 1980's*, ed. Stephen J. Carroll and Randall S. Schuler (Washington, D.C.: Bureau of National Affairs, 1983), pp. 2–18. Copyright © 1983 by The Bureau of National Affairs, Inc. Reprinted by permission.

example, concentrates on several major topic areas, such as work force demographics, economic conditions, technological developments, work force social trends (including attitudes, values, expectations), legal and regulatory matters, and regional/metropolitan characteristics.[9] Each of these has subtopics. Work force dynamics, for example, includes the changing composition of the work force, supply of engineers, supply of nonengineering technical labour, work force mobility, and offshore labour markets.

Screening the Information

Monitoring tends to turn up more information than is useful. Also, the information tends to come in bits and pieces, whereas planners and decision makers need to be aware of patterns (i.e., trends and discontinuities in the environment). Screening separates the wheat from the chaff and begins to bundle the wheat into meaningful entities, or issues. Screening can be done by one or a few members of a scanning staff group or by a committee.

Issues Research

Issues research further investigates topics identified during the monitoring process. Its purpose is to assess probable implications for human resource management in the context of known business plans.

Communication

Even the most sophisticated monitoring and analysis are to no avail unless the results are transmitted to planners and managers on a timely basis and in an understandable and usable form.

A variety of communications approaches are used, ranging from annual written reports to abstracts and seminars. The effectiveness of these various approaches can only be guessed. A common complaint about written reports is that they are less specific than required in drawing out the human resources implications of environmental conditions.

While a variety of procedures are used to diagnose external conditions, EES is one that monitors the overall trends across the entire external environment. Next we will discuss some of the significant trends in the external conditions enumerated in the diagnostic model. Our discussion of these is more comprehensive than usually found in books on P/HRM. Today's P/HRM professional needs to be aware of—and understand—the interplay of relevant external conditions and how they affect both P/HRM and the more traditional functional areas. A certain degree of macroperspective is necessary for furthering the professional role of P/HRM.

ECONOMIC CONDITIONS

Many economic factors affect human resource decisions, including the makeup of the population and the labour force, and labour market and product/service market conditions. Also important are technology and, especially in the Canadian context, free trade negotiations, the emerging privatization of federal firms, and corporate takeovers-mergers.

The Population and the Labour Force

According to Statistics Canada, the population of Canada is estimated to be 26.55 million in 1990 and 27.3 million in 1996.[10] Only a part of the population is eligible to work. The *labour force* is the number of people in the civilian noninstitutional working age population (15 years of age and older) who are classified as employed or unemployed (but seeking or available for work) during the reference period covered by Statistics Canada's *Labour Force Survey* (*LFS*).[11] The *LFS* samples about 98 percent of the population 15 years and older.

The labour force changed from 12.64 million in 1985 to 13.03 million in 1987, and it is estimated to reach about 14 million by 1990.[12] Changes in the labour force derive from two components. Part of the change is due to shifts in the size and age distribution of the working age population (also known as *source population*). The other component springs from variations in the overall labour force *participation rate*, which expresses the labour force statistic as a percentage reflecting the proportion of working age population that actually participates in the labour force.

The overall participation rate is expressed as a percentage of the working age population. The participation rate of a particular subgroup (by gender, age, marital status, education) is the percentage of that group's working age population accounted for by that group's labour force. For example, a given participation rate for women designates the percentage of working age women in the labour force; it is *not* the percentage depicting their share of the total labour force.

As summarized in Exhibit 2–3, the overall participation rate has increased moderately from its 54.1 percent in 1961 to 66.6 percent in 1988, and is expected to reach 67.6 percent by 1991, followed by a small increase into the mid-1990s. The participation rate of men has declined marginally. The change in women's participation rate was relatively dramatic—from only 28.7 percent in 1961 to 51.7 percent in 1981, and is still increasing.[13] In the 1970s, about one third of the increase in the labour force was attributable to increases in participation rates, primarily as a result of the very large increase in female participation.[14]

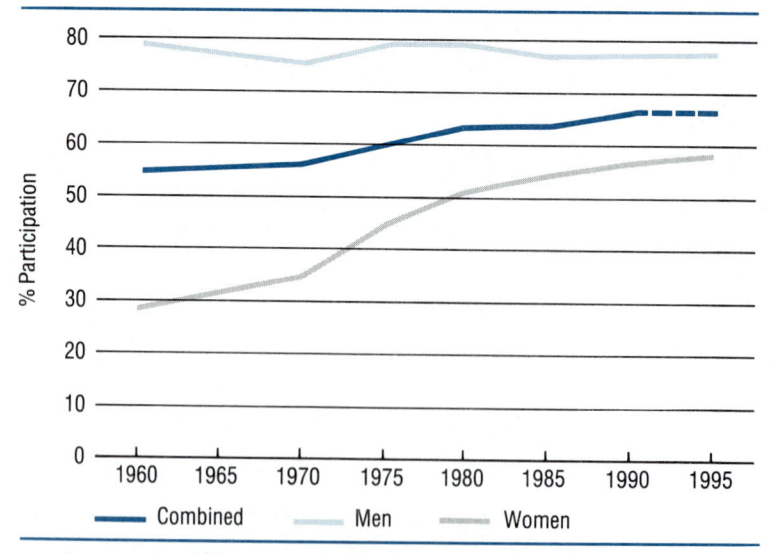

EXHIBIT 2–3
Labour Force Participation Rates

Source: Woods Gordon and Clarkson Gordon, *Tomorrow's Customers*, 20th ed. (Toronto: Woods Gordon and Clarkson Gordon, 1986). Used with permission.

EXHIBIT 2–4
Labour Force Participation Rate

Participation rate by percentage as a function of age

Age	1961	1971	1981	1985	1986
15–19	36.2%	35.1%	55.6%	52.9%	54.3%
20–24	68.9	71.8	79.7	79.5	80.4
25–44	63.0	68.7	80.3	82.4	83.5
45–64	60.7	62.9	64.6	64.3	63.7
65 and older	17.3	11.9	8.7	7.7	7.1

Participation rate by percentage as a function of level of schooling

Education	1961	1971	1981	1985	1986
Primary	50.4%	46.4%	46.2%	40.7%	39.2%
Secondary	54.1	56.8	62.6	66.4	67.0
Postsecondary	66.0	72.9	73.2	79.2	79.3

Source: Adapted from Pradeep Kumar with Mary Lou Coates and David Arrowsmith, *The Current Industrial Relations Scene in Canada: 1986* (Kingston, Ont.: Queen's University, Industrial Relations Centre, 1986), pp. 131–32; 1986 data from Kumar et al.'s 1987 report, pp. 172–73. Used with permission.

Exhibit 2–4 views participation rate as a function of age and level of education. The largest segment of the labour force is consistently comprised of 20- to 44-year-olds, followed by the next older group. There has been a steady decline in the participation of the 65 and older group. For any given year, a higher level of education produced higher participation rates.

Age and education are only two of a host of demographic, economic, and social factors that reflect population characteristics, influence the makeup of the labour force, and determine individual participation rates.

Understanding the makeup, and changes in it, of the labour force is important in the diagnostic approach to human resource management. The makeup provides the basis for the supply of human resources available to employers and has other implications for P/HRM. For example, the qualifications, opinions, attitudes, beliefs, values, career interests, lifestyle preferences, and motivations of people in the labour force influence human resource activities and ultimately the effectiveness of the organization. The percentage of minorities and women influence employment equity decisions; qualifications and skills influence training decisions and the design of jobs; the relative numbers of various skills available, along with the demand for these skills by employers, influence wage decisions.

Canada's population growth has been slowing for the past decade. Average annual percentage increases have slowed from 1.7 percent for 1961–71 to 1.0 percent for 1981–85; they are expected to fall to only 0.8 percent per year between 1986 and 1991 and as low as 0.5 percent between 1991 and 1996. As already noted, this is expected to result in a population increase to 27.3

million by 1996.[15] Exhibit 2–5 shows the population profiles by age for 1976 to 1996. These and other source data offer a departure point for discussing several shifts in the population and labour force.

Shift 1—Shortage of Young Employees. Because of the low birth rates of the 1960s and 70s, the percentage of young people is expected to decline. By 1996, there will be 370,000 fewer children under 9 years of age, about 50,000 fewer teens, and nearly 600,000 fewer adults age 20 to 34.[16] This suggests not only a potential shortage of teen-age workers throughout the 1980s and into the 90s, but also a smaller supply of middle-management talent near the end of the next decade.

Shift 2—The Middle Age Bulge of the Baby Boom Generation. The decade ahead will see the demographic bunching of the labour force in the 35 to 49 age bracket. The entry of the baby boomers into middle age means there will be nearly 1.6 million more adults age 35 to 49, an increase of 32.4 percent from 1986.[17] These are individuals who are typically competing for promotion,

EXHIBIT 2–5
Canada's Aging Population: 1976 to 1996 (percent of total population)

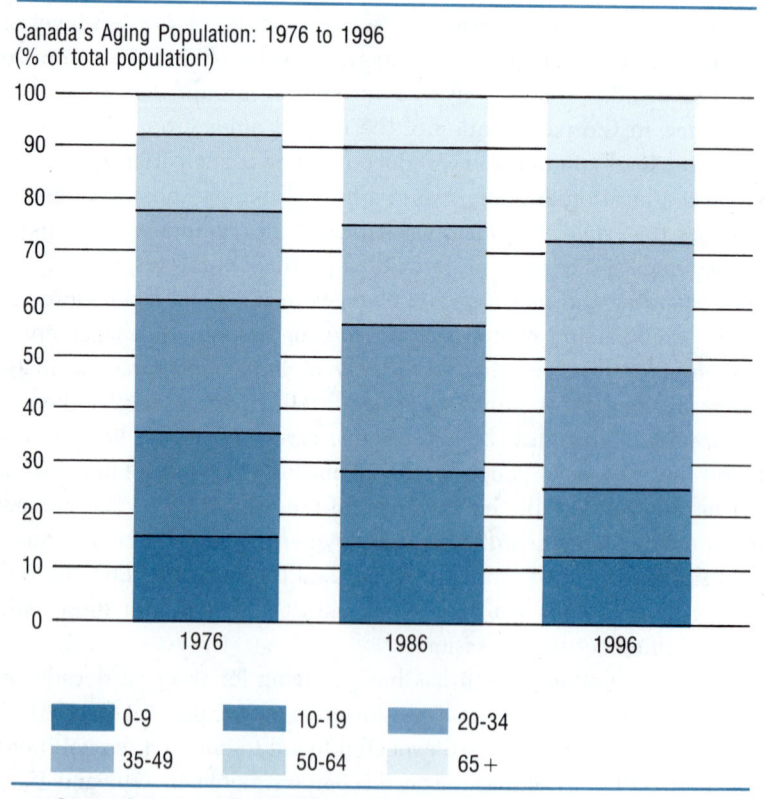

Canada's Aging Population: 1976 to 1996
(% of total population)

Legend: 0-9 | 10-19 | 20-34 | 35-49 | 50-64 | 65+

Source: Census and Statistics Canada Population Forecast.

professional recognition, and more supervisory responsibilities. Their bulge in the population is working its way through the age distribution and the labour force. This bulge has tremendous implications for human resource management. We can predict increased competition for promotions, severe disappointments, and pressure on training and pay programs. This age group experienced the same problem when they were competing for college and university admission. Now they are competing for opportunities in the organization. These pressures may increase interest in protection of workers' rights and perhaps unions.

Shift 3—The Increasing Role of Women. A great number of women entered the labour force during the 1974–84 decade. The number of women in the labour force increased by 50.4 percent, even though the female population 15 years and older grew only 21 percent.[18]

We've already pointed out the dramatic rise in women's overall participation rate since 1961 (see Exhibit 2–3). As shown in Exhibit 2–6, it is projected that 57 percent of women of working age will be participating in the labour force by 1995. Historically, female participation rates are at their highest for the two groups encompassing the 15-to-44-year age range. Relative to many other industrialized nations, the participation rate of Canadian women in the labour force is high.[19]

The female participation rate is expected to continue to increase, although its rate of growth will decelerate. One projection estimates that 85 percent of women aged 25 to 54 will be working or looking for work by the year 2005; it also expects that women will provide most of Canada's new workers in the future.[20]

The rise in female participation rates has been due in large part to the dramatic change in the attitudes and aspirations of women and the increasing need for both wife and husband to enter the work force to cover the rising cost of living. The fast growth in the service sector, many segments of which are dominated by female employees, is also responsible for some of the increase. Be it due to need or desire, there has been an increase in dual-career

EXHIBIT 2–6
Labour Force Participation Rate for Women (by age groups)

Age	1961	1975	1985	1995
15–24	39.5%	56.8%	64.7%	72.0%
25–44	29.2	52.3	70.3	76.2
45–64	28.5	39.4	46.9	50.1
65 +	5.9	4.9	4.8	7.2
Average	28.7	44.4	54.2	57.0

Source: Woods Gordon forecast; 1961 data from P. Kumar et al., *The Current Industrial Relations Scene in Canada: 1987* (Kingston, Ont.: Queen's University, Industrial Relations Centre, 1987), p. 173. Used with permission.

families, and more women are continuing to work after having children. Women's attachment to the work force has become more permanent.

The female labour force has also seen a shift from the nonprofessional cluster (e.g., clerical, service occupations) to the professional grouping of managerial and administrative occupations. The number of bachelor's and postgraduate degrees granted to women has risen dramatically. Higher education levels lead to higher participation rates in the labour force. Women also are shifting from traditional female-dominated courses of study (e.g., fine and applied arts, humanities) to management programs, law, medicine, and engineering.[21]

Some companies have seen the light and are accommodating employees with working spouses. For example, when promotions involve relocation, employing both spouses at the new location or assisting the employee's spouse in finding suitable alternate employment in the new location is often considered. In addition, employer-sponsored day-care assistance is becoming more common.

Another challenge facing employers is whether they are willing to make certain short-term concessions for women during their childbearing years. Some have made the choice already. Clarkson Gordon, one of Canada's largest accounting/consulting firms, says, "We can't afford to lose our (managerial) recruits who are balancing a job and family. . . . We have to give a lot more thought to accommodating people juggling the ongoing building of their career in the company with a young family."[22]

Shift 4—Employment of Older Workers. Another shift that will become increasingly apparent is the "grey revolution." By 1996, about 28 percent of the population (see Exhibit 2–5)—almost 7.6 million Canadians—will be more than 50 years old. Nearly 3.6 million of these (or 13.1 percent) will be older than 65 (8.7 percent in 1976). By the year 2000, the 65-plus age group may climb to 13.49 percent of that year's population of 28.39 million.[23]

It still is not clear whether changes in mandatory retirement legislation will impel more employees to remain in the labour force beyond the traditional retirement age of 65. If so, that would run counter to recent trends toward earlier retirement. As was shown in Exhibit 2–4, participation rates for this age group have shown a steady decline (from 17.3 percent in 1961 to 7.7 percent in 1985). Viewed according to gender, males' participation rate decreased from 29.3 percent to 12.3 percent; women's, from 5.9 to 4.2 percent.[24] Projections to 1990 indicate a continuing decline for males (to 11.7 percent), but an increase in female participation rate (to 6.0 percent)[25] that is expected to reach 7.2 percent by 1995 (see Exhibit 2–6).

Many factors affect the retirement decision, including the adequacy of pensions, health status, physical demands of the job, and absence of being conditioned to expect retirement at age 65. Many Canadian workers have chosen to retire earlier, and certain pension reforms may encourage that.[26] However, keeping workers on the job longer makes for a more stable and mature work force, possibly yielding greater productivity than when relying on inexperienced workers.

Asking workers to remain employed beyond age 65 will necessitate a loosening of Canada Pension restrictions, more flexible working arrangements, phased retirements, job redesign to accommodate the physical and psychological needs to capitalize on these workers' experience, and a general set of management policies that are responsive to the older labour force.

Shift 5—Part-Time Workers.[27] The fastest-growing segment of the Canadian work force consists of part-time workers. The growth rate of this segment in the 1980s is 10 times that of full-time employees,[28] which means that about one in every six Canadian workers is a part-timer. Total part-time employment is estimated to be 1.8 million.[29] Most part-time work is concentrated in the service industries, especially banks, transport, education, health care, personal services, business services, and recreation. Generally, "part-time workers tend to be younger, less well educated, are more likely to be female (especially married females), are less likely to be unionized,"[30] are paid less, and are often denied access to pensions and benefits as well as bargaining rights.[31]

Job sharing, a special type of part-time work, means one job is divided between two workers. Because it requires schedule compatibility between the two people sharing the job, as well as roughly equivalent or complementary skills, most job sharing is initiated by employees. More organizations seem willing to consider this alternative as they become familiar with its advantages.

Shift 6—Literacy. Although we pride ourselves on our educational system, about 4 million Canadians are functionally illiterate (i.e., have an eighth grade education or less).[32] More disturbing is that about 40 percent of the illiterates are younger than 45, and almost 30 percent of all teen-agers drop out of secondary school. That can add up to serious problems for business and society, in terms of both direct and hidden costs.

Workers' illiteracy is a major contributor to safety violations and accidents.[33] Other workplace problems caused by illiteracy concern the inability to understand written material pertaining to instructions about work procedures and methods, and requiring remedial preparation in order to benefit from training courses. A number of Canadian firms have begun to pay attention to this issue and have established in-house courses in cooperation with the Canadian Business Task Force on Literacy.

Shift 7—Influx of Immigrants, Refugees, and Illegals. Canada is a stable, prosperous, and open society. These features and our tolerance for cultural diversity serve as a magnet to draw successive waves of legal immigrants to our shores from various countries. While Canada's history of immigration and immigration policies have been called incoherent and controversial,[34] Canadians generally believed that the emerging ethnic mosaic was desirable, and that there was control over who gets in, how many, when, with what skills and other resources, and their potential contribution to Canadian society.

In the past few years, debate has been intense about our lack of a long-term immigration policy and our perceived (if not actual) loss of control over who enters the country. Lax enforcement of control regulations for visitors who "overstayed" to seek employment led to an amnesty in 1973. Illegals who have entered since hope for another one. Use of fraudulent documents, what some refer to as "refugee roulette," and other stratagems to gain back-door entry has also increased. This was seen as unfair to legitimate immigration and refugee applicants willing to follow established procedures. When the situation of illegals reached epidemic proportions in late 1986, the Employment and Immigration Minister imposed tighter requirements for visitors and refugee applicants from certain countries.[35] Estimates of the number of illegals in Canada range from 50,000 to 200,000.[36]

Immigrants are vital to Canada's population growth, and they represent an important factor in the supply of labour. Government projections of source population and labour force usually include assumptions incorporating different immigration levels. Given Canada's current low birth rate, our population will start declining by the year 2021 if immigration levels are not increased. Estimates by Statistics Canada suggest that our static birth rates should justify

EXHIBIT 2–7
Average Annual Immigration between 1861 and 1990 (as percent of population)

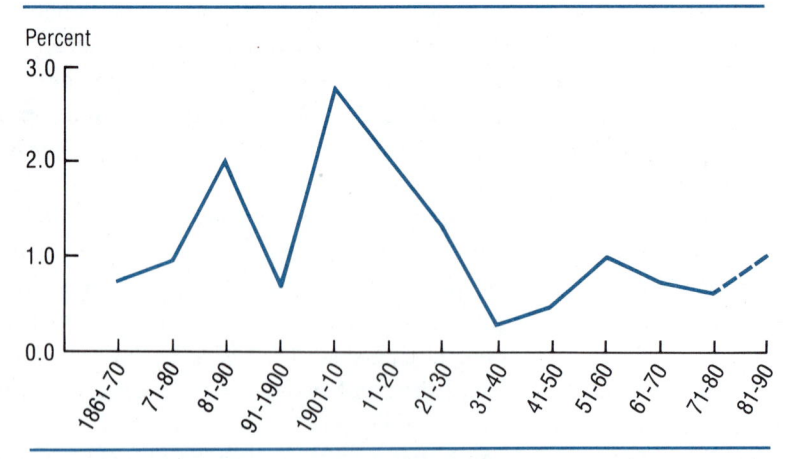

Source: Adapted from *The Financial Post*, September 6, 1986, p. 12; the dashed segment represents estimates. Used with permission.

about 275,000 immigrants a year (about three times the current level) to "keep the national population growing by just 1 percent."[37] Immigration ceilings are expected to meet an eventual annual target of 200,000.[38] This is still less than 1 percent of our population (see Exhibit 2–7 for the uneven path of average annual immigration as a percentage of population).

Labour markets and the state of the economy affect the need for labour. That's why (except for cases involving humanitarian reasons) immigration was reduced as unemployment rates increased (see Exhibit 2–8). Between 40 and 50 percent of immigrants are destined for the labour force.[39] Our desire to import primarily skilled labour has been so successful that we have neglected training and apprenticeship programs. For example, the Parliamentary Task Force on Employment Opportunities in the 80s concluded that Canadian employers have relied too heavily and too long on immigration to meet their *skilled* labour requirements.

Two relatively recent government measures expand immigration categories to include "business immigrants." They can enter under the investor class category (which requires a net worth of at least $500,000) or as entrepreneurs. The latter must set up and manage a new business. In one year, the more than 2,000 entrepreneurs (from about 85 countries, but primarily from Hong Kong, West Germany, and the United States) who entered Canada brought $1.2 billion in capital and created almost 10,000 jobs.[40]

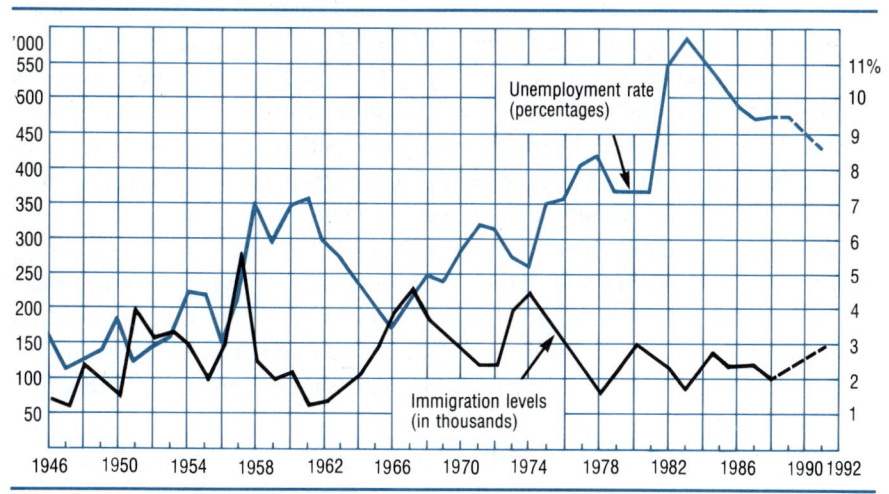

EXHIBIT 2–8
Unemployment Rate and Immigration Levels

Source: Ken MacQueen, "Opening the Doors," *Maclean's*, October 13, 1986, p. 14. Projection to 1991 based on *Changing Times*, Twenty-Third Annual Review of the Economic Council of Canada (Ottawa: Minister of Supply and Services Canada, 1986; Cat. No. EC21-1/1986E). Used with permission.

The major population and labour force shifts predicted for the remainder of the 1980s and 90s are already having significant effects on traditional P/HRM practices and are a major factor explaining why human resource management is such a complex, challenging, and significant field.

Labour Markets

Labour markets comprise another aspect of economic conditions in the diagnostic model and need to be considered at more than one level.

A labour market may be defined as a *bounded entity wherein labour supply* (individuals looking for work) *and demand for labour* (employers looking for workers) *interact*.[41] Its boundaries can vary according to geography, occupation, and so on. Our definition implies that an exchange between employers and job seekers is an essential part of a labour market. The exchange involves sharing and evaluating information about job opportunities and inducements offered by the employer and the skills and contributions offered by the job seeker. If the inducements and contributions offered are acceptable to both parties, a contract is executed, either in formal or implied terms. The result is allocation of job seekers to job opportunities at various pay rates.

Labour markets are usually analysed at various levels of aggregation—national, regional, and local. The practical relevance of one or more of these to a given employer depends on a number of factors, which are explained below.

The primary federal government department responsible for performing analyses of, and projections for, the national labour market is the Canada Employment and Immigration Commission (CEIC). The macrolevel analysis forms an integral part of Canada's efforts to engage in effective human resource planning at the national level. The effort centres on assessing the current state of the national labour market, anticipating future imbalances, and designing and implementing policies and programs directed at providing a balance between supply and demand. This requires forecasting tools (discussed in Chapter Six), certain supply and demand initiatives (e.g., the Canadian Jobs Strategy programs discussed in Chapter Ten), and a labour market intelligence function. The latter provides the fundamental underpinning for both supply- and demand-side activities to accommodate information requirements of governments, workers, and employers (see Exhibit 2–9).

An illustrative projection of the demand for several broad occupational categories is shown in Exhibit 2–10 (as a percentage of total labour demand) for different economic growth rate scenarios. With relatively fast economic growth (Scenario A) for 1986–90, the forecast projects the aggregate demand

EXHIBIT 2-9
Labour Market Intelligence Function

Supply Side Activities
- Placement and information services
- Career counselling
- Mobility assistance
- Industrial training assistance
- Short-term training
- Apprenticeship programs
- Post-secondary education
- Immigration

Demand Side Activities
- Regional development
- Direct employment
- Assistance to industry for employment creation

Labour Market Intelligence

Employers
- Current hiring
- Manpower planning
- Strategic planning
- Corporate training
- Apprenticeship training
- Capital investment

Workers
- Career choice
- Decisions to undertake training courses
- Mobility decisions

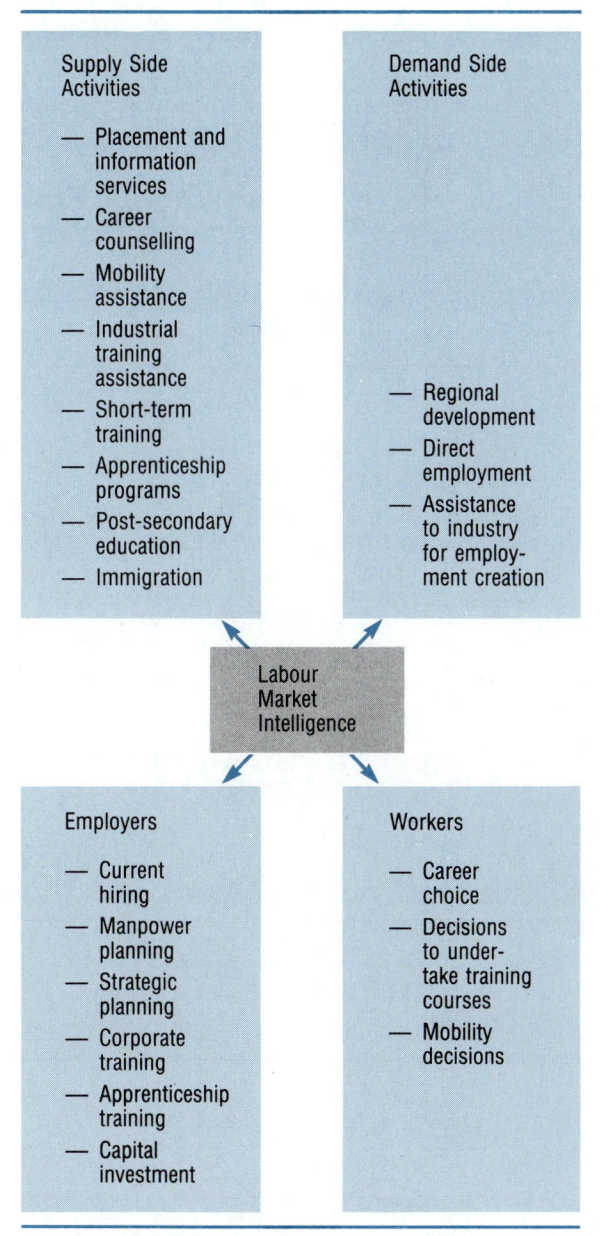

Source: *Labour Market Development in the 1980s* (Ottawa: Minister of Supply and Services Canada, 1981; Cat. No. MP15-3/1-1981E). Reproduced with permission of the Minister of Supply and Services Canada.

EXHIBIT 2–10
Forecast Occupational Demand under Various Assumptions for the National Labour Market (percent contribution to overall employment growth)

	1972–1979	1980–1985 A	1980–1985 B	1980–1985 C	COFOR-85	1986–1990 A	1986–1990 B
Highly qualified occupations	19.1%	13.2%	13.0%	14.4%	11.6%	13.9%	14.0%
Highly skilled occupations	27.0	24.4	24.5	27.7	28.9	27.6	27.3
Medium-skilled occupations	23.8	29.6	29.6	28.0	26.0	30.0	30.3
Low-skilled occupations	30.2	32.7	32.9	30.0	33.4	28.5	28.4
Total employment	100.0	100.0	100.0	100.0	100.0	100.0	100.0

Note: Columns may not total due to rounding.
Source: *Labour Market Developments in the 1980s* (Ottawa: Minister of Supply and Services Canada, 1981; Cat. No. MP15-3/1-1981E), p. 53. Reproduced with permission of the Minister of Supply and Services Canada.

for "highly qualified occupations" as 13.9 percent of the total national demand for labour. Within this occupational group, greater demand is forecast for managerial and related occupations than for the other four subgroups.

A more finely tuned analysis is performed for regional differences in labour market conditions across Canada. These differences are due to regional variations in economic activity, which can lead to substantial regional labour market imbalances. To highlight this, one need only contrast Calgary's "Bitter Spring" of 1986 with the resurgence of Canada's heartland the same year.[42] Things were lean and slow in the oil patch, leading to a steady stream of layoff notices. In the Golden Horseshoe (the stretch of land that hugs the western tip of Lake Ontario from Oshawa to Niagara Falls), manufacturers had rebounded from the 1982 recession, and both the manufacturing and service sectors were humming along. The local construction industry experienced such an extreme shortage of skilled tradespeople that advertising campaigns were launched to tap labour markets in other regions (British Columbia, the Maritimes) and preliminary plans were considered for requesting special work permits to bring in foreign workers.[43] A similar case can be characterized by "they came from across Canada—and from as far away as California."[44] Lured by the prospects of securing 1 of 3,000 new jobs at two American Motors Canada plants northwest of Toronto, the crush of applicants—mainly from British Columbia, Alberta, Nova Scotia, and Quebec—reached 60,000. Thus, the buoyant economic growth of one region acts as a strong magnet for job seekers from other parts of Canada. In 1985, approximately 36,000 Canadians migrated to Ontario; the same was expected to occur in 1986 through 1988. These examples demonstrate the fluidity of labour market boundaries and illustrate that regional labour market imbalances are usually alleviated through interprovincial migration.

The Economic Services section of the CEIC publishes regional labour market bulletins on a regular basis. Also, CEIC's Occupational Analysis and Classification Division of its Occupational and Career Analysis Branch is developing the JOBSCAN Project.[45] This system is intended to accommodate the unique needs of different levels and sectors of the labour market, each of which requires different approaches. For example, the greatest transferability of workers between types of jobs occurs at the lowest level of the labour market (the so-called labouring level); the least occurs at the highly technical or professional level. A wide middle range exists with varying degrees of skill transferability and interoccupational mobility.

Relevant Labour Market

The relevant labour market—national, regional, or local—varies with the situation. Labour markets may be flexible or rigid, fixed or in a state of change, and excess supply and demand for labour can exist simultaneously in different labour markets in a country or region.

Of practical concern to the P/HRM professional are the factors usually used to define the boundaries of the relevant labour market. They are:[46]

- Geography (distances people are willing to move/relocate or, on a local scale, commute daily).
- Occupation (education, qualifications, and skills required).
- Other employers that compete with similar products and services (the industry factor).
- Union membership.
- Licencing and certification requirements.

Human resource professionals need to conceive of labour markets in terms of all these factors. The skills and qualifications required in an occupation are important because they tend to limit mobility among occupations or are in shortage or oversupply (e.g., the oversupply of professional engineers in British Columbia for several years as of 1985; the shortage of registered nurses in parts of Atlantic Canada in 1986–87).

Qualifications interact with geography to further define the scope of the relevant labour markets. Those skills possessed by degreed professionals are recruited nationally; others (technicians, craftworkers, and operatives) are recruited regionally, although extremes can occur and necessitate interregional recruiting; still others (e.g., office workers) are recruited locally. Exhibit 2–11 summarizes how qualifications interact with geography. Basically, as the importance and complexity of qualifications increase, the geographic limits also increase.

However, the geographic scope of a market is not fixed. It changes in response to workers' willingness to relocate or commute certain distances. This "propensity to be mobile" may be affected by personal and economic circumstances as well as the pay level established by an employer. As already indicated, it is also influenced by an economic boom in certain regions. Configurations of local labour markets can even be shaped by convenient public transportation, such as a monorail, bus lines to suburbs, and so on. Also, the geographic limits may not be the same for all in a broad skill group. Not all MBAs (they are *not* a homogeneous group) operate in a national market; some firms recruit them locally, others nationally, or from only a few preferred programs.

In addition to occupation and geography, the industry in which the organization competes for labour and sells its products/services is also important.[47] Industry affects the employer's ability to pay and the skills required. The importance of qualifications and experience tailored to particular industries is often overlooked in theoretical analysis of labour markets.

EXHIBIT 2–11
Relevant Labour Markets, by Geographic and Employee Groups

	Employee Groups/Occupations					
Relevant Labour Market	Production	Office and Clerical	Technicians	Scientists and Engineers	Managerial Professional	Executive
Local: Within relatively small areas such as cities	Most likely	Most likely	Most likely			
Regional: Within a particular area of the province, or several provinces	Only if in short supply or critical	Only if in short supply or critical	Most likely			
National: Across the country				Most likely	Most likely	
International: Across several countries				Only for critical skills or those in very short supply	Only for critical skills or those in very short supply	Most likely

Source: Adapted and modified from George T. Milkovich and Jerry Newman, *Compensation* (Plano, Tex.: Business Publications, 1984).

EXHIBIT 2–12
Selected Labour Market Indicators (base case projection, 1986–1996)*

	1986	1987	1988	1989	1990	1991	Averages 1986–1991	Averages 1992–1996
Change in:								
Labour force	2.3%	1.5%	1.6%	1.6%	1.2%	1.2%	1.6%	1.4%
Employment	3.1	2.0	1.4	1.6	1.8	1.6	1.9	1.9
Productivity (output per person-hour)	0.5	2.4	2.4	0.6	1.7	2.7	1.7	2.4
Real wage rate	1.8	2.7	2.5	1.7	2.6	2.9	2.4	2.8
Nominal wage rage	5.0	5.2	5.4	5.6	6.5	6.6	5.7	7.0
Unemployment rate:								
Base case	9.8	9.4	9.5	9.5	9.0	8.6	9.3	7.1
Low-growth scenario	10.1	10.1	9.0	9.3	9.5	9.5	9.6	—
High-growth scenario	9.8	9.4	9.5	9.2	8.4	7.6	9.0	—
Participation rate†	65.7	66.2	66.6	67.1	67.5	67.6	66.8	68.4

*Including low-growth and high-growth scenarios for unemployment rate.
†Participation rate in terms of labour force as a proportion of the population aged 15 and older.
Source: Economic Council of Canada, CANDIDE Model 3.0, August 1986 (Adapted from Tables 2–3 and 2–4 of *Changing Times*, Twenty-third Annual Review, Economic Council of Canada, Cat. No. EC21-1/1986E). Reproduced with permission of the Minister of Supply and Services Canada.

Labour Market Prospects into the 1990s

Projections of the future state of labour markets are usually portrayed in terms of unemployment rates, supply and demand for labour, participation rates, productivity, employment, and estimates of the total labour force. These are derived from major economic indicators such as gross national product, consumer price index, and so on. Two scenarios in addition to what is termed the "base case" are often considered: a "high-growth" (of the economy) scenario and a "low-growth" scenario. The base case is considered the conditional forecast, based on historical relationships, and is the Economic Council of Canada's best judgement about the factors shaping our economy in the medium term.[48]

Exhibit 2–12 shows a forecast extending into the 1990s. The base case projection reveals only a small improvement in unemployment rates in the near term. From 1986 to 1991 the unemployment rate is expected to decline from 9.8 percent to 8.6 percent, averaging 9.3 percent for the five-year period. This is because the growth in the labour force is estimated to continue to keep pace with the rise in employment. The forecast for 1992–96 suggests that employment growth is projected to consistently outstrip growth in the labour force, causing a gradual decline in the unemployment rate to about 7 percent by 1996. A continuing rise in participation rate is also indicated. This may be primarily due to the wider participation of women in the work force. Exhibit 2–13 portrays the distribution of the 2.2 million new jobs expected to be created between 1985 and 1995.

Exhibits 2–10 and 2–14 illustrate projections with more specific focuses. The former shows demand projections for categories according to skill levels. Exhibit 2–14 provides an occupational outlook to 1992 for several occupational groups in CEIC's *Canadian Classification and Dictionary of Occupations* (CCDO). This forecast is based on the recently developed Canadian Occupational Projection System (COPS), which can project demand and supply simultaneously. The COPS forecast is that the country's required level of persons in the Personnel and IR management occupations (Group 1136) will be 29,200 by 1992, an increase of 3,600 over 1985. Combined with the estimated attrition of 3,300 (due to death and retirement, but excluding movement to other occupational groups), this means a total requirement for new talent of 6,900 between 1985 and 1992. The total requirement for nonmanagement P/HRM positions (Group 1174) is 9,400.

Exhibits 2–15 and 2–16 show the occupational fields with the largest and smallest expected job growth.[49] The lists in these exhibits may hold some initial surprises; many of us would expect that any job concerned with computer-related technologies would rank near the top. Instead, we find a reflection of the economic shift to the service sector (health services and education, plus the broad range of personal services). For example, a number of tradi-

EXHIBIT 2–13
2.2 Million New Jobs between 1985 and 1995

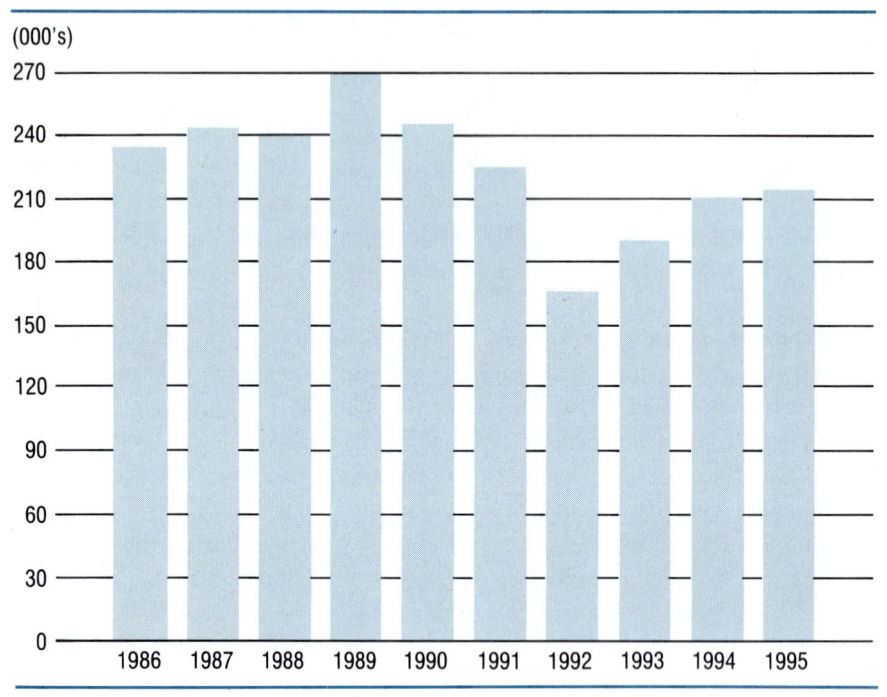

(000's)

[Bar chart showing approximate values: 1986: 235, 1987: 242, 1988: 240, 1989: 268, 1990: 244, 1991: 225, 1992: 168, 1993: 192, 1994: 210, 1995: 215]

Source: Statistics Canada and Woods Gordon Forecast. (Used with permission.)

tional jobs will experience growth. More workers will be needed to drive trucks, to deliver goods, to provide janitorial/custodial services, to perform health and personal services, and to maintain and repair the increased number of cars, appliances, and other equipment. According to the projections, the wider use of word-processing equipment, compact discs, and other features of the electronic office does not negate the need for more bookkeepers, secretaries, receptionists, and typists. Financial services call for significant growth in the number of accountants and auditors. The combined demand for supervisory/managerial talent is also considerable (64,500 new openings).

Before you rush off and make any career decisions based on the source data for the exhibits, realize that the projections are imprecise. How well we respond on the supply side will have a great impact on our ability to protect Canadian jobs in light of increasing competitiveness from overseas. On a per capita basis, Canada is way behind Japan in engineers. But, as an acquaintance pointed out recently, we are way ahead with lawyers.

EXHIBIT 2–14
Occupational Outlooks to 1992 (in thousands)

Occupational Group	Employment Trends 1985	Employment Trends 1992	Change	Attrition*	Total Requirements†
(1136)‡ Personnel and IR management occupations (e.g., employment manager, manager of personnel department, labour relations director)	25.6	29.2	3.6	3.3	6.9
(1143) Production management occupations (e.g., plant superintendent, operation manager)	45.8	50.9	5.1	6.2	11.3
(1174) Personnel and related officers (e.g., staff training officer, labour relations representative, job and wage analyst)	31.5	36.0	4.5	4.9	9.4
(2117) Physical sciences, technologists (e.g., biochemistry technician, X-ray technician)	19.2	21.5	2.3	1.9	4.2
(2183) Systems analysts, computer programmers, and related occupations (e.g., simulation systems analyst, software systems programmer)	59.7	67.3	7.6	4.2	11.8
(3131) Nurses (registered), graduate, and nurses-in-training (e.g., graduate nurse, occupational health nurse)	193.6	225.8	32.2	32.7	64.9
(4141) Electronic data processing equipment operators (e.g., word processing machine operator, data processor, computer operator)	75.0	84.4	9.4	9.7	19.1

*This estimate is the number of projected withdrawals from the labour force because of death and retirement; it does not include movement from one occupational group to another.

†Demand requirements in order to staff projected additional jobs and the projected number of jobs vacated through attrition.

‡The code numbers (1136, 1143, etc.) and occupational titles come from Employment and Immigration's *Canadian Classification and Dictionary of Occupations* (CCDO), fifth edition.

Source: Adapted from *Job Futures: An Occupational Outlook to 1992* (Ottawa: Minister of Supply and Services, Canada, 1986, Cat. No. MP 43-181/1986E, Employment and Immigration Canada). Used with permission of the Minister of Supply and Services Canada.

EXHIBIT 2–15
Twenty-Five Fastest-Growing Occupations, 1985–1992 (in thousands)

CCDO Code*	Job Classification	New Requirements to 1992
4131	Bookkeepers and accounting clerks	126.1
4111	Secretaries and stenographers	117.9
6191	Janitors, charworkers, and cleaners	94.8
6125	Food and beverage serving	90.5
5135	Salesclerks and salespersons	69.7
9175	Truck drivers	69.3
3131	Nurses (registered, graduate, and nurses-in-training)	64.9
4133	Cashiers and tellers	64.6
6121	Chefs and cooks	62.2
4197	General office clerks	46.1
1171	Accountants, auditors, etc.	42.3
1137	Sales and advertising	40.1
6115	Guards, related security	39.1
5130	Supervisors: sales, commodities	36.3
4171	Receptionists and information clerks	31.8
4113	Typists and clerk-typists	31.6
2731	Elementary and kindergarten teachers	30.2
6143	Barbers, hairdressers, related	28.3
1130	General managers/senior officials	28.2
8581	Motor vehicle mechanics and repair	27.0
6198	Occupations in labouring and other elemental work: other services	24.0
5133	Commercial travellers	23.8
5172	Real estate sales	23.1
4155	Stock clerks, related	23.1
6120	Supervisors: food and beverage preparation	22.1

*Canadian Classification and Dictionary of Occupations.
Source: Rankings compiled from data in *Job Futures: An Occupational Outlook to 1992* (Ottawa: Minister of Supply and Services, 1986, Cat. No. MP 43-181/1986E, Employment and Immigration Canada).

Product/Service Market Conditions

Change in the product/service markets in which an organization operates is the third aspect of economic conditions considered in the diagnostic approach. Pressures from inflation and technology also affect product/service markets, and hence human resource decisions.

Product/Service Demands

Conditions in a firm's markets affect both its ability to pay and the quantity and quality of people employed. Product market pressures, for example, lead management to attempt to maximize output and employment in times of growth and to economize on use of human resources in times of market decline or excess capacity. All organizations must, over time, receive enough revenues to cover expenses, including those for P/HRM programs. Thus, an

EXHIBIT 2–16
Twenty-Five Slowest-Growing Occupations, 1985–1992 (in thousands)

CCDO Code*	Job Classification	New Requirements to 1992
2791	Community college vocational teachers	0.0
2151	Metallurgical/materials engineering	0.2
2113	Physicists	0.3
2189	Mathematicians, statisticians and actuaries, systems analysts, computer programmers, related	0.3
2313	Sociologists, anthropologists, related	0.3
2153	Mining engineering	0.4
7311	Captains and other officers, fishing	0.4
7516	Log inspecting, grading, scaling, related	0.4
7715	Blasting	0.4
2157	Community engineers	0.5
8316	Inspecting, testing, grading, and sampling: metal machinery	0.5
8336	Inspecting, testing, grading, and sampling: metal shaping and forming excluding machining	0.5
2139	Life sciences	0.5
2142	Chemical engineers	0.6
8795	Glaziers	0.6
9153	Engineering officers, ship	0.6
9555	Sound and video recording and reproduction equipment operators	0.6
9512	Printing press	0.6
3115	Veterinarians	0.7
8786	Insulating	0.8
2353	Technicians in library, museum, and archival	0.9
3154	Dispensing opticians	0.9
8337	Boilermakers, platers, and structural metal workers	0.9
8783	Concrete finishing, related	0.9
9111	Air pilots, navigators, flight engineers	0.9
9551	Radio and television broadcasting equipment operators	0.9

*Canadian Classification and Dictionary of Occupations.
Source: Rankings compiled from data in *Job Futures: An Occupational Outlook to 1992* (Ottawa: Minister of Supply and Services, 1986, Cat. No. MP 43-181/1986E, Employment and Immigration Canada).

employer's ability to pay employees is constrained by its ability to compete in the product market and generate sales revenues.

In effect, the product market puts a lid on the maximum pay level an employer can set.[50] If the employer pays more, it has two options. It can try to pass on the higher pay level through price increases or fix prices and allocate a greater share of total revenues to cover labour costs.

Consider the auto firms' recent experiences.[51] For many years, automakers were able to cover increased pay levels through increased car prices for the consumer. While competition existed among domestic producers, they all passed on the pay increases. But then the product market changed. Competition from Europe and Japan, and their import penetration of the North American market, increased. Due to the depressed economy, the total demand for cars actually declined. Canadian vehicle manufacturers and the larger parts producers undertook aggressive capital spending programs for more efficient equipment to increase competitiveness. This left the industry in a weakened financial position between 1980 and 1982. These forces combined to constrain the firms' ability to pay workers and their ability to change the pay level. In response, some autoworkers took pay cuts, accepted smaller wage increases, and agreed to work rule changes intended to improve productivity.

So an employer's ability to finance higher pay levels through price increases depends on the product market conditions. Employers in highly competitive markets are less able to raise prices without loss of revenues.

Demand for a firm's products (along with productivity, plant capacity, and inventory levels) directly affects staffing decisions—the quantity and quality of human resources to employ. This occurs in public organizations as well as profit-making companies. Consider a city government, a symphony, or a college or university. Changes in demand for their services (e.g., increased enrollments) eventually affect the people employed (professors, teaching assistants). Consequently, employment forecasting uses product demand data to answer questions such as how many employees with what skills and experience will be required.

Inflationary Pressures

Inflation is the rate of change in prices paid for goods and services. The most obvious impact of inflation on human resources is on cost-of-living adjustments (COLAs) to wages and pension plans. But inflation influences human resources in less obvious ways. For example, a study done for Exxon Chemicals reports that relocating a transferred employee costs more than $25,000, in the form of low-interest "bridge loans" and low-interest mortgages, lump sum payments for new home expenses, and relocation expenses.[52] Inflation also affects the costs of interviewing, recruiting, and training employees. One estimate of the net total investment per professional employee (degreed managerial/technical) after two years is more than $100,000 and may be $1 million over a 20-year career.[53]

Canada-U.S. Free(r) Trade[54]

On September 26, 1985, the Prime Minister announced in the House of Commons the government's interest in pursuing a new trade agreement with the

United States. The chief negotiators, Simon Reisman for Canada and Peter Murphy for the United States, were appointed in 1986. Their discussions have been referred to as "free trade talks," although "enhanced" or "freer" trade may be closer to the intent of the negotiations. Shortly before midnight on October 3, 1987, the two countries agreed in principle on the elements to be included in the Canada–United States Agreement. The Agreement's reduction of trade barriers requires transitional measures and an adjustment period of about 10 years (to start January 1, 1989).[55]

Nonnegotiable items are those that define the distinctive nature and cultural integrity of Canada and our control over them. For example, the discussions exclude Canadian medicare, our unemployment insurance system, bilingualism, the Canada Council, and the CBC.

Freer trade relates to P/HRM because the struggle to make Canadian industry more competitive will be fruitless if our firms are shut out of the U.S. market. Canada is the U.S.' biggest trading partner: three quarters of our exports of manufactured goods, which account for 80 percent of Canada's total exports, go to the United States.[56] Without a bilateral free trade agreement, we're not assured of continuous access to U.S. markets. As free-traders point out, in 1986 Canada was the only industrial country of its size without assured access to markets (in the United States, Japan, and the European Community) of more than 100 million people. The U.S. market, with a population 10 times greater than Canada's, is some 15 times larger than ours in terms of consumption. It constitutes one of the most important factors affecting the health of our economy. Even before the initiation of free trade talks, the U.S. market accounted for a quarter of our gross national product and upwards of 2 million jobs. A mere 10 percent reduction of our exports to the United States could cause some 250,000 Canadians to lose their jobs.[57] The Economic Council suggests that freer trade would generally be beneficial to the Canadian economy.[58] Its projection to 1995 reveals that freer trade could yield an unemployment rate one percentage point below the base case. That translates into a lot more jobs for Canadians.

A free trade agreement with our principal trading partner will save Canadian jobs, heretofore threatened by protectionist measures, and create better jobs for the future. According to Mr. Reisman, more and more Canadian industries and business leaders are "expressing confidence in their ability to survive and flourish in a North American free trade environment."[59] By allowing goods to flow freely, Canadian producers will have the benefits of a "domestic" North American market of more than a quarter of a billion people.[60]

Privatization

In 1986, the Minister of State for Privatization inherited a mandate calling for difficult judgement about how the public policy functions of Crown corporations should be translated into the private sector. Hundreds of federal firms had been examined for their private-sector potential.[61] The government wants to dispose of "a stable of lack-lustre corporate nags only a government could love" and subsidize.[62] Creation of a separate ministry sent the message that privatization had become a higher priority.

The sale of Crown-owned Canadair Ltd. to Montreal's Bombardier Inc. was one of the first to be reviewed. Also considered were Teleglobe Canada and Eldorado Nuclear Ltd. Fishery Products International was privatized in 1987. Along with Canadian private firms, foreign bidders are also eligible. This is rationalized on the grounds that we are a capital-short country. Crown-corporation assets amount to more than $50 billion, spread over a wide array of companies.[63] In the long run, the privatization issue may be less political than economic. With this in mind, the government's program does not simply establish annual privatization targets, as is done in Britain, France, and West Germany, but rather makes decisions on a case-by-case basis. According to the Minister, considerable weight is given to such factors as "timeliness, market conditions, and *long-term employment opportunities.*"[64]

Takeovers and Mergers

Just as takeover fever gripped the United States a few years ago, Canada is rife with takeover bids and "corporate marriages." Imasco, the restaurant, tobacco, and drugstore company, made a successful bid for Genstar, whose varied Canadian and American interests range from financial services to waste management; Canada Trust acquired The Permanent; Pacific Western Airlines gobbled up CPAir; and so on. The number of takeovers valued at more than $100 million increased sevenfold between 1982 and 1985.[65] A subsequent wave of takeover seminars appeared, with a focus on refining the tactics of corporate siege, (such as defensive measures, strategies for launching a takeover bid, new legislation in the anticombines area, anticipated regulatory response, and government enforcement tools).

A merger leads to a collision of different corporate cultures, even if the merging organizations are from the same industry sector, and requires integration of the organizations' systems, particularly information systems, and personnel. Employees of the target company often find that the acquirer's imprimatur extends beyond a change in the company logo.

There is evidence that human resources problems are at the heart of many merger/acquisition failures. For example, the following have been documented as P/HRM problems that can prevent mergers from achieving their stated goals:

- Reduced productivity because of the psychological effects of uncertainty about job security and the future.
- Staff reductions, transfers, and other "cost consolidation efforts."
- Employees not feeling "attached" to the new organization.
- Unwanted turnovers, especially among the most competent (who are the most mobile).
- Unexpected employee benefits costs (e.g., underfunded pension plans).
- Dysfunctional leadership struggles.
- Wrong mix of human resource skills (because of superficial analysis of new requirements in the merged organization).[66]

Such problems are not surprising when P/HRM planning and development are excluded from merger plans. Too often, human resources managers are still seen as *softball* players and the merger as a *hardball* game played primarily (to their disadvantage, we might add) by CEOs, strategic planners, and financial executives.[67] As firms try to strengthen their competitive edge through mergers, acquisitions, and divestitures, P/HRM managers should become more involved in their strategic role.

TECHNOLOGY

Another important external factor is comprised of technological changes and developments.[68] The infusion of some forms of technology is accelerating at an exponential rate, and technological changes of the last 80 years will be surpassed by the changes anticipated for the remainder of this century.[69] The pace is such that new terms are introduced quite frequently; those relevant to our discussion are outlined in Exhibit 2-17.[70] Knowledge of these will enhance your credibility when dealing with top management, operating managers, and unions on questions pertaining to technological change and P/HRM issues.

Examples of new technology are all around us: the CANADARM, the Concorde, piggyback rail containerization, microprocessors (i.e., chip technology, with its miniaturized circuitry), robots on the production line, the application of lasers to surgical procedures and various industrial uses (e.g., metal cutting), revolutions in information processing, and telecommunications satellites. Informatics—the marriage of information processing and telecommunications technology—provides the basis for office automation and the anticipated "office of the future." "Good ears" voice activation/recognition computing exists, and laser printers already are being challenged by ion printers.

EXHIBIT 2-17
Glossary of Technical Terms

Artificial intelligence (AI): The capability of a computer to perform functions that are normally attributed to human intelligence, such as learning, adapting, recognizing, classifying, reasoning, self-correction, and improvement.

Automated system (cell): A small group of machines able to do a variety of manufacturing tasks on several different parts. The system cell will sometimes include robots, but not necessarily.

Automation: The theory, art, or technique of making a process automatic, self-moving, or self-controlling; the process of a system by mechanical or electronic devices that take the place of human observation, effort, and decision.

Biochip: Experimental electronic device that functions as integrated circuit; uses biological molecules as framework for semiconducting molecules.

Biotechnology: Use of biological processes to provide goods and services.

CAD (computer-aided design): A system that allows drawings to be constructed on a video display unit (VDU) screen and subsequently stored, manipulated, and updated electronically. Geometric transformations (including rotation of the design about any axis) can be carried out at high speed.

CAD/CAM: The integration of computers into the entire design-to-fabrication cycle of a product or plant (a common database is used and the output of CAD is available to CAM).

CAE (computer-aided engineering): Computerized creation and analysis of designs for error-checking, manufacturability, performance, and economy of production.

CAL (computer-aided learning or instruction): The application of computers to present instructional material, monitor students' learning, and adjust the presentation of material based on students' responses.

CAM (computer-aided manufacturing): The use of computer technology to generate manufacturing-oriented data. CAM techniques can be used to produce process plans for fabricating a complete assembly, to program robots, and to coordinate plant operation.

CAT (Computer-aided testing): Enables the output of CAD to be submitted to a series of assessments.

CHIP: A small piece of silicon that is a complete semiconductor device; commonly used name for integrated circuit (IC). The silicon is impregnated with impurities in a pattern to form transistors; electrical paths are formed on it by depositing thin layers of aluminum or gold.

CIM (computer-integrated manufacturing): Refers to the totally automated factory in which *all* manufacturing processes are integrated and controlled by a CAD/CAM system. CIM enables production planners and schedulers, shop floor supervisors, and accountants to use the same database as product designers and engineers.

CRT (cathode ray tube): Is used to display computer programs on TV-like screen, or monitor.

Electronic office: Office environment that uses electronic means for text and data handling, information storage and retrieval, communications, etc.

EXHIBIT 2–17 *(continued)*

Ergonomics: Derived from the Greek words *ergon* (work) and *nomos* (natural laws of). The word has become synonymous with the study of the problems of people in adjusting to their environment, especially the science that seeks to adapt work or working conditions to suit the worker.

Fifth generation: Term used to describe the most advanced generation of computers.

FMS (flexible manufacturing system): Machines interconnected by a transport system and controlled by central computer; allows a variety of parts to be processed simultaneously. Often, it involves robotic functions.

IC (integrated circuit): Semiconductor circuit in which electronic components are formed on small wafer of materials, usually silicon; also known as a *chip*.

Informatics: Derived from French *informatique*; concerned with information and its handling, especially integration of computer and communications technologies.

Island of automation: Stand-alone automation products (robots, CAD/CAM systems, NC machines) without the integration required for a cohesive system.

Laser: Light amplification by stimulated emission of radiation; a highly concentrated beam of light. Used in a variety of ways by some computers; also has applications in the cutting of metal and fabric, surgery, etc.

Just-in-time (JIT): Delivery of parts to assembly line just before needed.

Microchip: (Same as *chip*).

Microelectronics: Branch of electronics dealing with extremely small electronic components.

NC (numerical control): Operating machine tools (or similar equipment) in response to numerically coded commands. These commands may be generated by a CAD/CAM system on punched tapes.

Robomation: A contraction of the words *robot* and *automation*, meaning the use of robots to control and operate equipment or machines automatically.

Robot: A reprogrammable, multifunctional manipulator designed to move material, parts, tools, or specialized devices through variable programmed motions for the performance of a variety of tasks. (*Note:* This Robot Institute of America definition was accepted worldwide at the recent 11th International Symposium on Industrial Robots in Tokyo). A *material handling* robot is designed to grasp, move, transport, or otherwise handle parts of materials in a manufacturing operation; a *material processing* robot is designed and programmed so it can machine, cut, form, or in some way change the shape, function, or properties of the materials it handles; a *playback* robot is initially operated by a human operator who inputs instructions relevant to a desired operation (sequence, conditions, positions) into a "memory." The information can be "played back," and the operations are repetitively executed automatically from memory.

Robotic cell: One or two robots working together.

Robotics: The use of computer-controlled manipulators or arms to automate a variety of manufacturing processes such as welding, material handling, painting, and assembly.

EXHIBIT 2–17 *(concluded)*

Semiconductor: Material whose electrical conductivity is less than that of a conductor (e.g., metals like copper) and greater than that of an insulator (e.g., glass).

SPC (Statistical process control): Use of basic statistical concepts to monitor how consistently products fit engineering specifications.

VDT (video display terminal): Device equipped with a cathode ray tube that displays information visually; generally connected to a keyboard for entering and editing information; often used as a synonym for VDU (visual display unit).

Vision system (machine vision): Sensory capability to scan and/or look at a given piece or part, and determine where said part is in relation to where it should be; after digesting that information, the system's logic tells a robot what to do.

Wafer: A slice of silicon on which, typically, a large number of integrated circuit chips are simultaneously produced.

Work cell: A manufacturing unit consisting of one or more workstations.

Work envelope: Robot operations envelope; the set of points representing the maximum extent or reach of the robot "hand" or working tool in all directions.

Compiled from various sources. See Note 70.

Robots are an essential component of computer-aided design/manufacturing (CAD/CAM) systems, the cornerstone of the "factory of the future." New technology[71] also allows ocean farming, instant communication worldwide, the cloning of plants and animals, bacterial engineering (the use of bacteria in the extraction of gold, copper, and nickel, for example), and the use of solar energy and nuclear fusion as alternative sources of energy.

Rarely before have technological advancements been so pervasive. Their results, especially those due to the high-tech (r)evolution, have already had numerous—and portend more—impacts on our society and the workplace. However, while hindsight allows us to view past effects in perspective, the effects of new technology cannot be predicted as accurately as the changes themselves.[72] There are essentially four points of view about the effects of new technology.[73] Optimists see the current wave of technological developments as just the latest in a long series, leading to higher output, employment, and living standards. Pessimists see the potential for massive displacements of workers and express little faith in the ability of the output effect to stave off job loss. A third group is generally neutral about the overall net employment effects. A fourth point of view contends that rather than asking how many jobs will be lost if the new technologies are adopted, the more relevant question should inquire about the number of jobs lost *if we don't*. This fourth view is rooted in the belief that Canada stands to lose international markets, along with the industries and jobs that supply them, if other countries forge ahead technologically and we do not.[74] Yet others may fear that new technologies may spawn "a techno-nobility with the information and skills to control the new production processes, and techno-peasants whose lives are shaped and paid by them."[75] This would lead to some polarization of certain skill and occupation structures.

What we do know is that technology has become a "competitive weapon"[76] for many firms; a series of "techno-battles" is in the offing, not only between firms of different countries, but also among domestic competitors. We can also anticipate that the impact of technologies will not be uniform: different segments of the labour force, the various industry sectors, regions of economic activity across Canada, organizational structures, and input-output processes employed have different absorptive and reactive capabilities.

The following sections examine the growth of demand for industrial robots, some applications, the factory of the future, and some effects of technology and their implications for P/HRM and Canada's workplaces.

Industrial Robots (Silico Sapiens?).[77] It's been estimated that the world population of robots increased from about 1,000 in 1970 to more than 22,000 in 1981, an annual growth rate of 32 percent.[78] Although estimates vary, a forecast growth rate of 30 to 35 percent annually from 1980 to 1990 implies a world stock of industrial robots of between 230,000 and 333,000 by 1990.[79] Canada's robot stock was estimated at about 250 in 1981. Later data suggest the Canadian growth will probably accelerate to somewhat over 3,000 in 1988, and about 7,000 units by 1990.[80] General Motors alone plans to have 1,200 robots in service in Canada by 1990 and about 14,000 worldwide.[81]

As important as the absolute numbers is the distribution of robots across industries. The automobile industry accounts for 30 percent of the robot stock in Japan and 60 percent in Canada. This suggests that, in general, the rest of Canada's manufacturing sector has been slow to invest in robots.

Until a few years ago, robots were used primarily in work situations that were hazardous, involved health risks, or were monotonous and repetitive (spray painting, spot welding). However, the scope of applications widened as improvements in software and sensor technology allowed development of robots with greater capabilities. The new generation of robots will have tactile (feel) and vision capabilities. (A prototype was on display in the General Motors exhibit at EXPO 86.) By 1995, 60 percent of all robots are expected to incorporate robotic vision and other sensory devices.[82]

The more sophisticated robots become, the more they provide an essential component of CAD/CAM systems. Robots come into play in CAM. CAM has lagged behind CAD, for which systems have been in existence since the use of computer graphics. The lag was caused by the slow development of machines that can directly accept computerized design specifications (for both product and process) and perform the physical work required in manufacturing. Without computerized robots, there would be no CAM.[83]

The Factory of the Future. The "factories on autopilot" material in Exhibit 2–18 is the best introduction to the factory of the future. This section examines some efforts in that direction and presents a scheme that represents much of the current thinking.

Canadian General Electric built a new automated plant in Bromont, Quebec. The plant, designed to produce blades and vanes for high-tech jet engines, is "fully automated, with 40 robots, laser-making systems, and computers for measuring the contours of blades and vanes. CAD and CAM are used throughout the plant and tied to a central computer."[84] General Motors of Canada spent $2 billion on its GM Autoplex in Oshawa.[85] The new highly automated, low-inventory production system abandons the traditional assembly line; cars are built in sections at successive workstations, each with teams of up to 15 workers.[86]

The ultimate factory technology is computer-integrated manufacturing (CIM). By totally automating and linking all the factory and corporate headquarters functions, "a manufacturer would be able to turn out essentially perfect, one-of-a-kind products—at the lowest possible cost and almost overnight."[87] Thus, a company could conceive new products on its CAD system, pass the CAD data to the computer-aided engineering (CAE) system (to verify

EXHIBIT 2–18
Factories on Autopilot

The scene: Midnight at a deserted showcase "factory of the future." Inside, the sound of machines in motion, producing parts for tools and robots. Finished trays of parts are *automatically* stacked and removed for packaging and distribution. Countless details of production, from *microprocessors* throughout the factory, are relayed to a *central computer*. The factory operates untended by humans during the nightshift. The lights stay off all night.

Suddenly computer sensors detect a malfunction in one of the automated tools. Within milliseconds, production at this work area or "cell" is halted. A central computer calls the homes of the technicians on duty to request repairs. Suppliers and head office are *automatically advised* of any changes to the production schedule resulting from the breakdown.

This is the fully automated factory—still largely the stuff of management dreams and labour nightmares. Today, *only a few hundred fully automated factories are operating* around the world. And, for the time being, most experts expect the factory of the future to remain just that. Introduction costs are high, and paybacks are still uncertain.

But computers, data links, industrial robots, and automated machinery are winning an increasingly central place in industrial production. In the process, they are inspiring a new vision of what manufacturing is all about.

Source: "A Guide to New Technology," *Au Courant* 7, no. 2 (1986), p. 10. Based on *Workable Futures: Notes on Emerging Technologies*, Economic Council of Canada, Cat. No. EC22-132/1986E. Used with permission of the Minister of Supply and Services Canada.

that the design will do the job intended, and economically so), extract information required for manufacturing the product from the CAE data, and send this information to the CAM system, which would send electronics instructions for making the product to computer-controlled machine tools, robotic assembly stations, and other automated equipment on the shop floor. All this would be coordinated with computerized management systems (e.g., manufacturing-resource and manufacturing-process planning), and the factory's mainframe computer would continuously update corporate data banks used by marketing, finance, purchasing, and other headquarters functions.[88]

High-Tech Profile—Canada. A crucial concern of the "microchip" age and its effects on P/HRM is the degree of penetration of computer-based technology in Canada. To what extent has high technology spread across the country? What factors inhibit or enhance its adoption? What is the impact on personnel? Answers to these and other questions can be drawn from a new Economic Council survey of more than 1,000 Canadian firms in all provinces and industries, except agriculture, fishing, construction, and public administration. A summary of the findings follows (complemented by the data in Exhibit 2–19).[89]

- Much of the new technology introduced in the first half of the 1980s involved personal computers, word processors, and office applications. There was a fair amount of process automation (CAD/CAM), which is expected to account for a much higher proportion of new technology up to 1990. The application of robots is estimated to more than double.
- The introduction of new technology was most prevalent in the West, with the percentage of firms in British Columbia (80 percent) and the Prairies (81 percent) exceeding Ontario's 76 percent, which was also the average for Canada. As one proceeded eastward, new technology tapered off, but even in the Atlantic provinces more than two thirds of firms had introduced new technology. This regional difference reflects the distribution of industries, but also suggests that geography is part of Canada's high-tech story.
- Fewer Canadian-owned firms (72 percent) adopted new technology than U.S.-owned (94 percent) and other foreign-owned companies (88 percent) operating in Canada.
- The rate of introduction of technology is a function of industry sector.

Exhibit 2–19 reveals that the median number of employees for innovators and noninnovators grew at about the same rate (12 percent versus 13 percent). Wages were consistently higher in innovating establishments, as were wage gains, increasing 40 percent on average for innovators. Technology primarily affects personnel in terms of internal transfers, reduced hours, permanent layoffs, and early retirement. The two sets of factors identified as

EXHIBIT 2-19
High-Tech Profile Summary—Canada

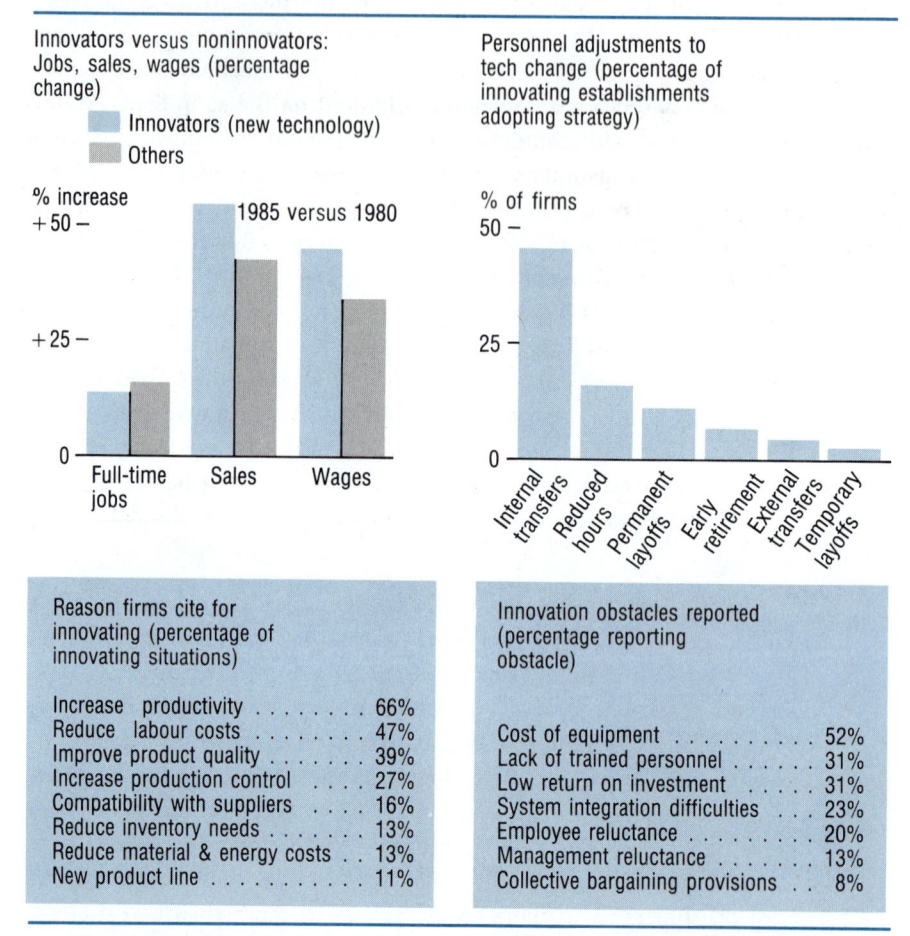

Innovators versus noninnovators: Jobs, sales, wages (percentage change)

- Innovators (new technology)
- Others

% increase 1985 versus 1980
+50 —
+25 —
0 —
Full-time jobs | Sales | Wages

Personnel adjustments to tech change (percentage of innovating establishments adopting strategy)

% of firms
50 —
25 —
0 —
Internal transfers, Reduced hours, Permanent layoffs, Early retirement, External transfers, Temporary layoffs

Reason firms cite for innovating (percentage of innovating situations)	
Increase productivity	66%
Reduce labour costs	47%
Improve product quality	39%
Increase production control	27%
Compatibility with suppliers	16%
Reduce inventory needs	13%
Reduce material & energy costs	13%
New product line	11%

Innovation obstacles reported (percentage reporting obstacle)	
Cost of equipment	52%
Lack of trained personnel	31%
Low return on investment	31%
System integration difficulties	23%
Employee reluctance	20%
Management reluctance	13%
Collective bargaining provisions	8%

Source: Adapted from Gordon Betcherman and Kathryn McMullen, *Working with Technology: A Survey of Automation in Canada* (Ottawa: Minister of Supply and Services Canada, 1986; Cat. No. EC22-133/1986E, Economic Council of Canada). Used with permission of the Minister of Supply and Services Canada.

enhancing adoption or obstacles are similar to ones identified in other studies.[90] Both point out again the importance of P/HRM issues: productivity, labour costs, product quality, lack of trained personnel, employee as well as management reluctance, and collective bargaining provisions.

Implications

Some of the major implications of technology for Canada's workplace were examined by Labour Canada's Task Force on Microelectronics and Employment.[91] Among the areas covered were occupational health and safety, job content, electronic monitoring of performance, organization of work time, training and education (including integrated and cross-training), job security, changing expectations of the work force, legislative treatment of technological change, and anticipated disproportionate impact on women workers in positions that are prime targets for efficiency and productivity improvements via the introduction of this technology. Several other Canadian studies also provide useful data. For example, one suggests that employees—and the general public—may be neutral or guardedly optimistic about new technology, and that socioeconomic status, education, gender, positive experience with new technology, and degree of optimism are significantly related.[92] Indications are that women workers worry significantly more than men about losing their jobs because of new technology in the workplace. Other findings show that implementation problems are not only technical: about 50 percent of the problems encountered by clients of Ontario's CAD/CAM Centre are of a "human and organizational" nature.[93] It is clear that technology has an influence on many facets of the workplace. The extent and intensity of many of the effects are summarized in Exhibit 2–20. Even a cursory look suggests they are relevant to the P/HRM topics covered in this book.

EXHIBIT 2–20
Some Effects of Technology on P/HRM and P/HRM-Related Systems

Robots can raise the quality of life.

A recent study (by a West German bank) on the effect of robotics on employment estimated a loss of 5 to 10 jobs for each second-generation robot installed.

There doesn't seem to be much dispute that robots are "eliminating" human work, without offering an equal amount of alternative employment in return.

There are still unions that look on technology as the villain in unemployment.

The perception that overall employment problems necessarily result from technological change is wrong.

General Motors is developing a robotic safety system to stop a robot's motion when an "intruder" enters the robot's work envelope.

Robots can have differential effects on both the psychological and physical aspects of the quality of work life.

The maintenance of robots is a more complex job than the traditional maintenance job; the future is for the "electro-mechanical" technician.

Power may shift from "supervisor of workers" to "supervisor of machines."

A study of the impacts of robotics by 1990 concluded that there will be a gradual "skill twist" (50 percent of the jobs created will require a significant technical background).

Robotic technology would eventually allow setting up profitable plants with a relatively small number of workers.

Facilitating employee acceptance of the introduction of robots into the workplace is a major task facing P/HRM managers.

EXHIBIT 2–20 *(continued)*

Perhaps the most important economic data for the P/HRM is the cost-per-hour comparison of robots and the human worker.

P/HRM managers should strive to recognize specific areas (processes, jobs, and people) of immediate impact of robotics technology.

Viable cross-training, if developed with pending robot usage, may help keep personnel obsolescence to a minimum.

The P/HRM manager should actively recruit those who make the most successful "robotists"—technical generalists with a broad technical experience base that allows them to contribute to a wider variety of possible applications.

The P/HRM director should be aware of top management's commitment to CAD/CAM.

The P/HRM manager should evaluate what happened in other countries that have gone through the infusion of robotics.

In a number of "hostile" (to health and safety) work environments, there may be an extra incentive for robotization.

Worker reaction to technology tends to be most negative when employees perceive the danger of job loss, when management imposes the technology with little consultation, and when little employee participation in decisions about their jobs is allowed.

The incorporation of robots must be done as part of an overall system change, not as "patchwork" replacements of outdated equipment.

A major challenge for P/HRM is anticipating what lies beyond immediate robotics infusion.

There is a need to rethink job designs.

The future human resources impacts of robotics (and the parent microprocessor technology) will extend beyond manufacturing personnel.

Technology is now a competitive weapon.

Technology provides the freedom to move administrative and decision processes anywhere in the country.

New technologies may be creating a techno-nobility and a techno-peasant class.

Technological change will require substantial internal training for its implementation.

*R*eeducation and *r*etraining will be featured prominently.

In implementing new technologies, human and organizational dimensions are at least as important as the technical ones.

A Canadian strategy in high-technology development cannot be developed by our governments alone, for they are only one group of players in the game.

Some clusters of high-tech industries have begun to blossom in Canadian cities.

The "chip," smaller than a fingernail, contains hundreds of thousands of electronic components and complex circuits.

Microelectronics drives an entire cluster of technologies (e.g., robotics, CAD, CAM, digital signal processing).

Ontario, Manitoba, British Columbia, and Quebec have been actively engaged in making high technology an integral part of their economic development efforts.

EXHIBIT 2-20 *(continued)*

- It is vital to create an independent body, a Canadian Centre of Technology, Work, and Human Priorities.
- We are the first generation to face the end of the Industrial Revolution and to define the values and structures of the new economy.
- Microelectronics will create new industries and render others obsolete.
- Microelectronics will change not only the content, but also the organization of work.
- A greater adaptive flexibility needs to be built into training and educational institutions as well as our places of work.
- The balance of responsibilities for training among governments, postsecondary training institutions, vocational schools, unions, and employers may need a fresh look.
- In Canada, we need more research to develop and adopt ergonomic standards for office automation equipment and workplaces.
- Questions and concerns about occupational health and safety implications of microelectronic technology were expressed repeatedly (in submissions to the Labour Canada Task Force on Micro-electronics and Employment).
- Extremely pessimistic forecasts of technological unemployment would appear most likely to be misleading.
- The likelihood of becoming technologically redundant by the year 2000 is universally related to the level of education.
- There is a lack of consensus regarding the impact of new technology on job content.
- Technological change directly affects the structure of the production process and changes the role of the labour market in the allocation of human resources.
- Until a few years ago, robots were utilized mostly in work positions that were hazardous or monotonous, or posed long-term health risks.
- The impact of industrial robots will not be the same across all industrial sectors.
- One reason for the relatively rapid adoption of CAM is that our manufacturing concepts are de-emphasizing standardization/assembly line techniques in favour of more production variability. This facilitates fast alignment with engineering changes and quick adjustment to changes in consumer demand.
- In Canada particularly, the shortage of engineers and technicians with experience in CAM and robot applications is inhibiting the pace of robotics infusion.
- Projections of the interplay between technological change, industry, and occupational employment are more highly developed in the United States than in Canada.
- The pace of technological change and diffusion, although affecting jobs and the workplace, probably should not cause undue worry.
- Over the years, we've gone from the vertical to the divisional, and then to the matrix organizational structure. The next innovation may be the "network corporation"—small central organizations relying on other companies to perform on a contract basis. This allows them to better tap outside technology.

EXHIBIT 2–20 *(concluded)*

We are at the turning point in the next era of the Industrial Revolution, with all the implications it had for demand for labour, job content, job security, and so on.

The primary cost reduction target is labour.

Among the benefits associated with advanced manufacturing technology are: reductions in turnover, training costs, and supervisory costs; reduction of throughput times; progressive company image for customers and suppliers; and increased employee morale (by eliminating dirty, dull, or dangerous jobs).

Source: Compiled from various sources. (See Note 117.)

Given the external factors discussed so far, Canada fares well in terms of general competitive capability. A recent comparison of 22 countries showed Canada emerging as number 6, up from 7th place in 1985 and 11th place in 1983.[94] Within the overall rankings, Canada placed fourth on the human resources factor, comprised of education levels, motivation of the work force, and structure of the labour force. These are welcome signals, especially for jobs in the vitally important manufacturing sector.[95] More good news comes in a report by the Institute for Research on Public Policy: many Canadian plants have reduced costs significantly through increased specialization and longer production runs.[96] If this country puts even more emphasis on dedicating businesses and workers to a lifelong process of skills training, for example, and realizes that computer-based technologies represent Canada's best chance to maintain and expand employment in the long run, we can become a techno-winner.[97]

Diagnosing relevant external factors is important to effective P/HRM management. The trick is to determine which factors and conditions are relevant, when, and what their effects will be on the proactive organization.

GOVERNMENT REGULATIONS

Government intervention in the workplace is not new. Much of Canada's economic growth stems from government actions favouring the formation of capital. Additionally, the federal government's spending as a percentage of the gross national product has expanded. The services and products purchased by the government affect the types of jobs and workers employed. So the government, through its actions as a consumer, affects P/HRM decisions. The government also affects P/HRM by regulating terms and conditions of employment. This type of regulation has changed qualitatively in the past two decades and has increased the importance of the P/HRM manager. The upcoming chapters include an examination of the impact of governmental regulations on each P/HRM activity.

Terms and Conditions—Employment

Today's manager needs to be aware of several main trends of government forays into P/HRM matters: employment equity (EE), occupational health and safety (OHS), labour standards, and collective bargaining. The unique Canadian mix of division of powers between the federal and provincial-territorial levels of government makes this task difficult. Both levels can enact legislation in these areas, although the type of organizations covered by each government body is clearly defined. This still leaves 13 jurisdictions and does not necessarily make for uniform legislation by the 10 provinces and 2 territories for businesses not under federal jurisdiction.

Federal Jurisdiction. Federal legislation pertaining to EE, OHS, and labour standards applies to employees and employers in works, undertakings, or businesses under the legislative authority of the Parliament of Canada. The activities within federal jurisdiction include: (1) interprovincial and international services such as highway transport, railways, telephone, telegraph, and cable systems, ferries, tunnels and bridges, pipelines, canals, and shipping and shipping services; (2) radio and television broadcasting; (3) air transport, aircraft operations, and aerodromes; (4) banks; (5) primary fishing where the fishermen work for wages; (6) grain elevators, flour and feed mills, feed warehouses, grain seed cleaning plants, and uranium mining and processing; and (7) most federal Crown corporations, such as Canada Post and the Canada Mortgage and Housing Corporation.

Federal labour standards and occupational health and safety regulations are delineated in Parts III and IV, respectively, of the Canada Labour Code. Collective bargaining is covered by Part V. Federal human rights legislation is embodied in the Canadian Human Rights Act (passed by Parliament in 1977) and the Canadian Charter of Rights and Freedoms. The Charter's Section 15 (which came into force in 1985) protects every individual's right to equality. Legislation in these areas is amended occasionally, either to clarify, cover new areas, or extend coverage to additional units of the work force. For example, amendments to Part IV of the Labour Code became effective on March 31, 1986, making its OHS provisions also apply to some 3 million employees of the Public Service of Canada. In the area of human rights, new legislation proclaimed in August 1986 expanded the federal government's role in employment equity: the new Employment Equity Act, in effect since October 1, 1986, requires certain federally regulated employers to implement employment equity and report annually to Ottawa. The first reports are due in 1988.

Provincial-Territorial Jurisdiction. The provinces and territories also have legislation pertaining to employment standards, health and safety, and human rights. This legislation is usually embodied in various acts, orders, and codes.

Federal and provincial legislative requirements appear in appropriate chapters of this book. The issue of employment equity pervades many management decisions and is treated in Chapter Seven. Occupational health and safety are addressed in Chapter Twelve. Collective bargaining is included in Chapter Thirteen.

The Regulatory Process

P/HRM programs must be in compliance with laws and regulations. By understanding the regulatory process, managers can better comply with the intent of legislative action. Generally, problems in society instigate pressure for legislative action. If enough support develops, often as a result of compromises and trade-offs, laws are passed. Once passed, agencies must enforce the laws through rulings, regulations, inspections, and investigations. Management responds to enforcement by auditing and/or altering P/HRM practices, defending lawsuits, and lobbying for policy change. Managers can perceive regulations as a constraint on organizations or as an objective—something that can be influenced and then achieved.

If seen as a desired objective, employers lobby to influence regulation through their governmental relations units or a consortium of employers such as the Canadian Manufacturers' Association, the Canadian Federation of Independent Businesses, the Canadian Chamber of Commerce, or the Canadian Advanced Technology Association. To influence legislation, the human resource professional must establish links with the firm's law and public relations departments as well as with professional societies and associations.

Some professional lobbyists have lately been viewed as "silent persuaders." As their influence has grown, so has concern that they may have become too powerful and too "invisible." As a result, the federal government has begun hearings on a proposal to monitor their activities, perhaps even forcing them to register and list their clients.[98]

Employers also attempt to influence interpretation of legislation by defending their practices in the courts, although this is a costly action that few employers actively seek. Yet all organizations benefit from greater emphasis on proactive activities that shape the regulations and force courts to examine management practices.

Deregulation

Like regulation, deregulation affects human resources. Deregulation is something many people wish would happen to someone else. While a move to deregulate certain industries may yield an overall gain for the economy in terms of increased productivity and lowered prices, wrenching dislocations may be an undesirable by-product, and some employers may try to dampen the effects of increased competition by demanding wage concessions and/or productivity increases from unions. For example, the 1986 strike against Pacific Western Airlines centred around the company's request for productivity increases in order to remain competitive in the recently deregulated Canadian airline industry. Other air carriers may reduce the level or frequency of services.

In order to adjust to new price competition resulting from deregulation, companies slash labour costs by cutting wage rates, dismissing employees, and/or negotiating more flexible work rules. (Work rules are the regulations that labour and management have set up to govern the workplace. They tend to be restrictive—limiting transfer of workers from one job to another, prescribing crew sizes, and the like.) Similarly, government regulations have inhibited managers' willingness to compete. Some organizations may have become comfortably inefficient and now face uncomfortable choices.

UNION EXPECTATIONS AND CONCERNS

Unions exist because employees sometimes believe it is necessary to put a third party between themselves and management. Employees, who perceive a lack of individual bargaining power, believe that by banding together as a trade union they can "collectively negotiate the conditions of their employment on a more equal footing with their employer."[99]

Unions in Canada represent about 37.6 percent of all nonagricultural paid workers, down from a high of 40 percent in 1983[100] and up from 33.6 percent in 1970.[101] Unions also appear to have lost some ground in the United States and parts of Europe. Although Canadian labour organizing attempts are booming, new members are barely compensating for losses caused by smaller crew sizes, plant shutdowns, layoffs, technological change, and public-sector cutbacks.[102] The economic recession of 1980–83 had a negative impact on our trade union movement, particularly in the primary industry and manufacturing sectors.[103] However, a recent study suggests a bright future for unions and predicts that, by the year 2000, unions will represent about 45 percent of the employed work force.[104] Much of the next decade's growth in union strength is expected to occur in the service sector (e.g., banks, the retail trade), which is currently less than 10 percent unionized.[105]

Although the rate of growth of union membership has slowed, unions remain powerful and strategic groups. For example, the Canadian Union of Public Employees, the largest, has about 330,000 members; the National Union of Provincial Government Employees has 278,000, followed by the Public Service Alliance of Canada with about 180,000. The largest private-sector unions are the United Steelworkers of America with 160,000 members, the United Food and Commercial Workers with 160,000, and the Canadian Autoworkers with 143,000. It is obvious that unions, with an estimated total Canadian membership of more than 3.78 million, comprise an external factor to be reckoned with (even if your work force is currently not unionized).[106]

What can P/HRM managers and employers expect from unions in the future? This depends on unions' expectations and concerns with certain issues. The following are likely to have an impact on the labour relations scene and P/HRM activities and provide some clues as to the track to be taken as unions confront the "corporate blueprint."[107]

One of the continuing principal concerns of unions will be preservation of jobs. This is due to the uneven and uncertain pace of economic growth, the threat of computer-based automation, anticipated shrinkage of resource-based and what are commonly referred to as "heavy smokestack" industries, and unions' perception of a strong "stay lean" philosophy on the part of private-sector management. There is also concern with restraint policies of the federal and provincial governments, trade negotiations, deregulation, and privatization.

The spectre of accelerating technological change, and unions' recognition of the need for Canada's firms to become true competitive peers of overseas and U.S. firms in international markets, will heighten the emphasis on job security through developing new skills, training programs, and job sharing. We expect that "robots on the bargaining table" will become a motto, along with measures intended to produce timely, genuine, and participative consultations on how to plan for and implement robotization and other computer-based technologies.

Another concern of unions that will affect P/HRM is their renewed interest in creating a different image. This will include measures designed to attract more white-collar workers and women. A doubling in the proportion of unionized women is causing unions to pay more attention to women's issues. For example, the Public Service Alliance of Canada has announced that future lists of bargaining priorities will include maternity leave, day care, employment equity, and protection from sexual harassment.[108]

Although we usually think only of employers in connection with human rights, a union must show that, as an organization, *it* does not discriminate.

In Ontario, the labour relations board requires that a union not discriminate against any person or persons because of their race, creed, colour, nationality, ancestry, place of origin, sex, or age.[109] Other provinces have similar provisions in their statutes or take a slightly different approach.[110] Women and visible minorities may discover that unions can offer a complementary beneficial route to wage parity and closer observation of employment equity guidelines by employers.

Labour leaders' emphasis on a strong commitment to equity and fairness in the workplace may mean there will be more pressure, both at the bargaining table and through lobbying, to achieve pay equity legislation (such as in Ontario and Manitoba) in both the public and private sectors. Trade liberalization with the United States (seen by some union members as leading to inadequate wages, poor working conditions, and cuts in unemployment insurance), extensive essential services legislation (narrowing the right to strike), and competition from nonunionized firms are also important concerns.[111]

The labour movement is also concerned with the potential impact of the Charter of Rights and Freedoms. Some argue that the charter could be used to "destroy the trade union movement as it exists."[112] The best-known charter case in this regard successfully challenged a union's use of compulsory union dues for social and political causes. It appears that Canadian unions prefer to enlarge their role to include broad matters of social and public policy.[113] In this vein, trade union strategies can be expected to include forging links with other groups (the unemployed, churches, peace activists, social agencies, the women's movement)[114] that stand to benefit from trade union initiatives.

Other union concerns with implications for P/HRM activities include the increasing proportion of part-time workers; occupational health and safety problems and measures due to new technology (such as posed by the use of video display terminals, lasers, and robots); more emphasis on an ergonomics approach to workplace design; and labour legislation that may widen or narrow the factors (e.g., common working conditions, similarity of work or common skills)[115] considered by labour relations boards in the determination of what the appropriate bargaining unit can be (the who, where, when and why of unionizing). Most aspects of human resource management—recruiting, selection, employment equity, performance appraisal, promotion, and others examined in this book—will continue to be directly affected by the presence of a union and its expectations.

INTERNATIONAL DIMENSIONS

Recent years have seen more Canadian employers increase their awareness of the globalization and interdependence of the world's economies. While the four types of factors significant in the international environment are essentially captured by the sources of external pressures shown in the diagnostic model, firms may find that a move into the arena of international/multinational business is not just domestic management on a grander scale. The complications of different economic systems, languages, customs, beliefs and values, social structures, topography and natural resources, and the level of government stability add markedly to the complexity of the decision to go international and the choice of appropriate P/HRM systems. For example, multinational corporations (MNCs) may face a bewildering web of government regulations and labour laws specific to each host country. Special cross-cultural orientation and training/development programs may be necessary. In some cultures (e.g., Latin American, Indian) family connections and social class considerations may take precedence over technical qualifications in hiring employees. Although it is not our intent to detail these factors, Chapters Nine and Ten pay some attention to several.[116]

SUMMARY

External conditions set the stage for the organization. They influence what actions an organization can take; actions of organizations in turn can influence these conditions to some degree. While the nature of the external conditions can be discussed in general terms, it is sometimes difficult to discuss specifics. This is so for several reasons.

First, the external conditions are interrelated and constantly changing. For example, we have classified relevant conditions as economic, technological, governmental, and union expectations in our diagnostic model. Yet economic and technological changes not only affect organizations but also affect unions, government, and all of society. So as one factor changes, the others inevitably change too. Their effects on P/HRM activities may vary, depending on the type of industry sector, the firm size, the diversity of its employee base, and the stage of sophistication in dealing with P/HRM issues.

Second, organizations differ, and they are constantly changing. So while an aging work force affects all organizations, repercussions will be different for various organizations. A technologically mature industry may experience a burdensome labour bill and little opportunity for career advancement among younger employees. Such an organization may decide it is advantageous to sweeten retirement packages in order to create more turnover at the top. A rapid-growth organization may hire those retired workers in order to cut the lead time required to obtain experienced employees. So the same external condition will have very different implications among organizations.

The next chapter discusses some of the characteristics that determine an organization's response to external conditions in managing its human resources.

DISCUSSION AND REVIEW QUESTIONS

1. Why is it important for P/HRM managers to keep track of external forces?
2. What devices do organizations use to scan the external environment, and what P/HRM programs are they related to?
3. What major economic forces influence human resource management decisions?
4. What is the difference between the population and the labour force?
5. Define labour force and labour force participation rate.
6. How does the diffusion of computer-related technologies affect labour markets? P/HRM activities?
7. Why are the effects of technology not uniformly distributed?
8. Discuss how government legislation has affected the sphere and importance of P/HRM.
9. Why is the concept of "relevant" labour markets important to P/HRM?
10. Invite a P/HRM manager from a local firm for a guest lecture on "How External Factors Affect My Company's P/HRM Activities."

NOTES AND REFERENCES

1. *Essays on American Industrialism: Selected Papers of Samuel Levin*, ed. Mark L. Kahn (Detroit, Mich.: Wayne State University, 1973), pp. 39–40.
2. Ibid., pp. 40–41.
3. Ibid., pp. 33–65.
4. Sanford M. Jacoby, "Industrial Labor Mobility in Historical Perspective," *Industrial Relations*, Spring 1983, pp. 261–82.
5. Ibid., p. 262.
6. *Bulletin to Management*, ASPA/BNA Survey No. 43, "Status of Human Resources Programs. Mid-Year 1983" (Washington, D.C.: Bureau of National Affairs, August 1983); Steven Langer, "Budgets and Staffing: A Survey, Part II," *Personnel Journal*, June 1982, pp. 464–68.
7. See, for example, H. L. Ansoff, "Managing Strategic Surprise by Response to Weak Signals," *California Management Review*, Winter 1975, pp. 21–33; J. F. Preble, "Corporate Use of Environmental Scanning," *Michigan Business Review*, September 1978, pp. 12–17; J. S. Mendall, "The Practice of Intuition," in *Handbook of Futures Research*, ed. J. Fowler (Westport, Conn.: Greenwood Press, 1978), pp. 149–61; P. T. Terry, "Mechanisms for Environmental Scanning," *Long-Range Planning*, June 1977, pp. 2–9; R. B. Frantzreb, ed., "Environmental Scanning," *Manpower Planning* 3, no. 11 (1980); J. A. Sheridan, "The Relatedness of Change: A Comprehensive Approach to Human Resource Planning in the

Eighties," *Human Resource Planning* 4, no. 2 (1982), pp. 11–17; J. A. Sheridan and J. O. Monaghan, "Environmental Issues Scanning: Starting a Self-Sustaining Research Program," *Human Resource Planning* 5, no. 2 (1982), pp. 57–69; J. K. Brown, *This Business of Issues: Coping with the Company's Environments* (New York: The Conference Board, 1979); David A. Aaker, "Organizing a Strategic Information Scanning System," *California Management Review* 25, no. 2 (1983), pp. 76–83.
8. Ibid., pp. 2–28.
9. Frantzreb, "Environmental Scanning," p. 3.
10. Statistics Canada estimates (from seminar notes, Executive Development Programmes, Faculty of Commerce, University of British Columbia, Vancouver, B.C., 1986); and Woods Gordon and Clarkson Gordon, *Tomorrow's Customers*, 20th ed. (Toronto: 1986), p. 1.
11. *Labour Force Survey* (Ottawa: Statistics Canada), p. 143; Pradeep Kumar with Mary Lou Coates and David Arrowsmith, *The Current Industrial Relations Scene in Canada: 1986* (Kingston, Ont.: Industrial Relations Centre, Queen's University, 1986), p. 95; "Now That We've Burned Our Boats . . ." The Report of the People's Commission on Unemployment—Newfoundland and Labrador (Ottawa: Mutual Press Ltd., 1978).
12. The 1985 and 1987 data are from "Stronger Growth Coming," *The Financial Post*, December 15, 1986, p. 32; the 1990 projection is from Table 2.2 (p. 39) of *Work for Tomorrow*, report by the Parliamentary Task Force on Employment Opportunities for the '80s (Ottawa: Published under authority of the Speaker of the House of Commons, Cat. No. XC2-321/4-01E).
13. The 1961, 1971, 1981, and 1985 data are from Kumar et al., *The Current Industrial Relations Scene in Canada*, p. 31; the five-year interval data for 1975–95 was adapted from Gordon and Gordon, *Tomorrow's Customers*, p. 8.
14. *Changing Times*, Twenty-Third Annual Review of the Economic Council of Canada (Ottawa: Minister of Supply and Services Canada, 1986; Cat. No. EC21-1/1986E).
15. Gordon and Gordon, *Tomorrow's Customers*, p. 1.
16. Ibid., p. 2.
17. Ibid.
18. *Women in the Labour Force: 1985–1986 Edition* (Ottawa: Minister of Supply and Services, 1986; Labour Canada Cat. No. L24-1468/86B).
19. Gordon and Gordon, *Tomorrow's Customers*, p. 8.
20. "In the Long Run, Good Reasons for Hope," *Financial Times*, March 26, 1984, pp. 21, 25.
21. *Women in the Labour Force;* "Innovation and Jobs in Canada," a research report prepared for the Economic Council of Canada (Ottawa: Minister of Supply and Services Canada, 1987; Cat. No. EC22-141/1987E), Chap. 9.
22. Dorothy Lipovenko, "Moms Choosing Nursery over Career," *The Globe and Mail*, February 26, 1987, pp. B1–B2.
23. Exhibit 2–5 data is from Gordon and Gordon, *Tomorrow's Customers*, p. 2; the year 2000 data is based on Statistics Canada estimates (see reference 10) and *The Globe and Mail*, January 24, 1987, p. B1.
24. Kumar et al., *The Current Industrial Regulations Scene in Canada: 1986*, p. 131.
25. *Work for Tomorrow*, Parliamentary Task Force on Employment Opportunities for the '80s, Table 2.1, p. 38.

26. "In the Long Run, Good Reasons for Hope," p. 21.
27. This issue also affects changes in work schedules, such as compressed workweeks and flextime (see Chapter Four).
28. "Employers Split over Benefits for Part-Timers," *The Globe and Mail*, July 25, 1986, pp. A1–A2.
29. "Part-Time Workers Fastest-Growing Element of the Canadian Workforce," *The Evening Telegram*, December 1, 1986, p. 25.
30. "Part-Time Wage Gap Studied," *Vancouver Sun*, January 3, 1987, p. C4 (quoting Prof. Wayne Simpson, University of Manitoba).
31. "Part-Time Workers Fastest-Growing Element of the Canadian Work Force." For details on the distribution of part-time employment, and benefit coverage of full-time versus part-time employees, see "Innovation and Jobs in Canada," Tables 7-1 and 7-2.
32. Morton Ritts, "What if Johnny Still Can't Read," *Canadian Business*, May 1986, pp. 54–57, 124; the definition of functional illiteracy is according to the United Nations Educational, Scientific and Cultural Organization.
33. Ibid.
34. For example, a study by the federal government concluded that a search of Canadian immigration history for public consensus or consistency in policy would be in vain (see Ken MacQueen, "Opening the Doors," *Macleans*, October 13, 1986, p. 13).
35. "Minister Ponders Change to Make Refugees Wait," *The Globe and Mail*, January 16, 1987, p. A5; "Minister Toughens Rules for Refugee Immigrants," *The Evening Telegram*, January 9, 1987, p. 19.
36. "Immigration: Scrap Unfair Law and Open Door Wide," *The Financial Post*, September 6, 1986, p. 12.
37. MacQueen, "Opening the Doors."
38. Ibid., p. 13.
39. Kumar et al., *The Current Industrial Relations Scene in Canada: 1986*, p. 125.
40. Michael Rose, "Assets of Any Creed or Color," *Maclean's*, October 13, 1986, p. 19; Renate Lerch, "More Entrepreneurs Wanted," *The Financial Post*, November 17, 1986, p. 2.
41. Larry F. Moore and Larry Charach, ed., *Manpower Planning for Canadians*, 2nd ed. (Vancouver: The University of British Columbia, Institute of Industrial Relations, 1979).
42. Michael Salter with Christopher Donville, "Calgary's Bitter Spring," *Maclean's*, March 31, 1986, pp. 38–39; Patricia Best with Sherri Aikenhead and Theresa Tedesco, "The Heartland's Resurgence," *Maclean's*, June 2, 1986, pp. 38–39.
43. "Ontario Launches Drive to Lure Skilled Workers," *The Sun*, February 25, 1986, p. B3.
44. T. Tedesco, "Help Wanted in Ontario," *Maclean's*, October 13, 1986, p. 46.
45. JOBSCAN CONCEPT (from Section D of a CEIC document), Economic and Labour Market Analysis, Regional Economic Services Branch, Vancouver, April 29, 1986.
46. Robert J. Flanagan, Robert S. Smith, and Ronald G. Ehrenberg, *Labour Economics and Labour Relations* (Glenview, Ill.: Scott, Foresman, 1984); M. J. Wallace and C. H. Fay, *Compensation Theory and Practice* (Boston: Kent, 1983).
47. George T. Milkovich and Jerry M. Newman, *Compensation*, 2nd ed. (Plano, Tex.: Business Publications, 1987).

48. *Changing Times*, Twenty-Third Annual Review of the Economic Council of Canada (Ottawa: Canadian Government Publishing Centre, 1986, Cat. No. EC 21-1/1986E).
49. Based on data shown in Kumar et al., *The Current Industrial Relations Scene in Canada: 1986*, pp. 154–58; another projection is in N. Leckie, "Projecting Canada's Occupational Requirements: Descriptive Analysis and Results," Strategic Policy Planning Section, CEIC, May 1984.
50. Walter A. Fogel, "Job Rate Ranges: A Theoretical and Empirical Analysis," *Industrial and Labor Relations Review*, July 1964, pp. 584–97.
51. "Automobile Industry's Comeback," *Business Week*, June 13, 1983, pp. 28–35.
52. Employee Relations Project on Relocation Expenses (Houston, Tex.: Exxon Chemicals Employee Relations Department, 1983).
53. Henry L. Dahl, "Measuring the Human ROI," *Management Review*, January 1979, pp. 44–50.
54. This section draws on the following sources: Peter Cook, "A Message of Hope from the Home of the Unfree Trader," *Report on Business Magazine*, September 1986, pp. 15–16; Simon Reisman, "Canada—United States Trade at the Crossroads: Options for Growth," *The Canadian Business Review*, Autumn 1985, pp. 17–23; R. J. Wonnacott and Paul Wonnacott, "Toward Free Trade between Canada and the United States," *The Canadian Business Review*, Autumn 1985, pp. 12–16; "Reluctant Pioneers," *The Economist*, February 15, 1986 (part of a special section titled *Canada Survey*), pp. 5–20; Alan Gotlieb, "The Trade Initiative in Context," *Canadian Banker*, June 1986, pp. 14–19; *Canadian Trade Negotiations: Introduction, Selected Documents, Further Reading*, (prepared under the authority of the Secretary of State for External Affairs and the Minister for International Trade (Ottawa: Minister of Supply and Services Canada, 1986; Cat. No. E 74-8/1986E); Alexander Ross, "Free Trade's Mr. Tough Guy," *Canadian Business*, March 1986, pp. 22, 24–29, 101–2.
55. *Changing Times*, Twenty-Third Annual Review of the Economic Council of Canada (Ottawa: Canadian Government Publishing Centre, 1986, Cat. No. EC 21-1/1986E); *Canada–U.S. Free Trade Agreement: Overview* (Ottawa: External Affairs Canada, 1987).
56. "Reluctant Pioneers," *The Economist*.
57. *Canadian Trade Negotiations*.
58. *Changing Times*, Economic Council of Canada.
59. Reisman, "Canada-United States Trade at the Crossroads," p. 20.
60. Wonnacott and Wonnacott, "Toward Free Trade between Canada and the United States."
61. James Bagnall, "Privatization Proceeds—But Cautiously," *The Financial Post*, August 16, 1986, p. 6; see also D. Hatter, "Privatization Gamble," *The Financial Post*, November 24, 1986, pp. 1–2.
62. Deborah McGregor, "McDougall Refines the Art of Privatization," *Financial Times*, August 11, 1986, pp. 1–2.
63. Ibid.
64. Bagnall, "Privatization Proceeds," p. 6 (quoting the Minister of State for Privatization, Barbara McDougall).
65. Douglas Martin, "A Takeover Wave in Canada," *New York Times*, April 10, 1986, pp. 31, 34; see also "Mergers, Acquisitions, Takeovers Spark Clashes between Corporate Cultures," *The Globe and Mail*, March 18, 1987, p. B8; "Counting the

Cost of the Decade's Mergers," *The Financial Post 500*, Summer 1987, pp. 61–62, 64.
66. John D. Gridley, "Mergers and Acquisitions, 1: Premerger Human Resources Planning," *Personnel*, September 1986, pp. 28–36; see also Robert M. Fullmer, "Mergers and Acquisitions, 2: Role of Management Development," *Personnel*, September 1986, pp. 37–49; and Michael A. Conway, "Mergers and Acquisitions, 3: Ten Pitfalls of Joint Ventures," *Personnel*, September 1986, pp. 50–51.
67. David W. Merrell, "Playing Hardball on a Mergers and Acquisitions Team," *Personnel*, October 1985, pp. 22–27; see also Diane Francis, *Controlling Interest: Who Owns Canada?* (Toronto: Macmillan of Canada, 1986); and J. M. Ivancevich, D. M. Schweiger, and F. R. Power, "Managing Human Resources during Mergers and Acquisitions," *Human Resource Planning* (forthcoming).
68. Here technology is viewed as an external force impinging on the organization. This may lead to a change in the procedures, methods, and techniques (i.e., "organization technology") employed by the organization to convert inputs from the environment into outputs (see Chapter Three).
69. A. Templer, "The Behavioural Implications of Introducing Robots and Other Forms of New Technology into Canadian Industry," proceedings of the Annual Conference of the Administrative Sciences Association of Canada (Organizational Behaviour Division), 1984, pp. 171–79; Douglas Austrom and Steve Graffi, "An Empirical Study of Attitudes towards Technological Change," proceedings of the Annual Conference of the Administrative Sciences Association of Canada (Organizational Behaviour Division), 1986, pp. 1–10; A. Ehrber, "Unemployment," *Fortune*, May 1983, pp. 107–12.
70. Words Associated and Keith Newton, "Workable Futures: Notes on Emerging Technologies," report prepared for the Economic Council of Canada (Ottawa: Supply and Services Canada, 1986; Cat. No. EC22-132/1986E); K. J. Blois, "Manufacturing Technology as a Competitive Weapon," *Long-Range Planning*, August 1986, pp. 63–70; *In the Chips: Opportunities, People, Partnerships*, report of the Labour Canada Task Force on Micro-Electronics and Employment (Ottawa: Minister of Supply and Services Canada, 1982; Cat. No. L35-1982/1E); "The Automation News Factory Management Glossary," *Automation News* (New York: Grant Publications, 1983).
71. Harold A. Gram, *An Introduction to Management: The Canadian Manager* (Toronto: Holt, Rinehart & Winston of Canada, 1986).
72. George Wise, "The Accuracy of Technological Forecasts, 1890–1940," *Futures*, October 1976, pp. 411–19.
73. Keith Newton, "Impact of New Technology on Employment," *Canadian Business Review*, Winter 1985, pp. 27–30.
74. Ibid.
75. Ibid., p. 30.
76. Michael E. Cornelissen, "Management Trends: People and Technology Are Key," *Business Quarterly*, Spring 1985, pp. 84–88.
77. This term is borrowed from Joseph Deken, *Silico Sapiens: The Fundamentals and Future of Robots* (Bantam, 1986).
78. *The Impact of Industrial Robots on the Manufacturing Industries of Member Countries*, (Paris: Organization for Economic Cooperation and Development, October 1982).
79. Ibid.; G. W. Nobbs, "Impact of Robots in Manufacturing," *Regional Economic*

Services, Canada Employment and Immigration, B.C./Yukon Region, June 1983; also see S. D. Saleh and Siva Pal, "Robotic Technology and Its Impact on Work Design and the Quality of Working Life," *Industrial Management*, May–June 1985, pp. 1–5.
80. Based on Evans Research Corporation, "The Canadian CAD/CAM Market," ERC Paper No. 65, Toronto, August 1985; Ronald Anderson, "Robots Can Raise the Quality of Life," *The Globe and Mail*, July 17, 1986, p. B2. (The estimates in this article are based on a report by the Japan Industrial Robot Association); see also *Innovation and Jobs in Canada*, a research report prepared for the Economic Council of Canada (Ottawa: Minister of Supply and Services Canada, 1987; Cat. No. EC22-141/1987E).
81. Words Associated and Keith Newton, "Workable Futures," 1986.
82. Ibid.
83. Edward M. Knod, Jr., Jerry L. Wall, John P. Daniels, Hugh M. Shane, and Theodore A. Wernimont, "Robotics: Challenges for the Human Resources Manager," *Business Horizons*, March–April 1984, pp. 38–46.
84. Gram, *An Introduction to Management*, p. 563.
85. "GM's New Era in Canada," *Maclean's*, March 31, 1986, p. 40.
86. Gram, *An Introduction to Management*.
87. Quoting from Richard Brandt and Otis Port, "How Automation Could Save the Day," *Business Week*, March 3, 1986, pp. 72–74; see also "Factory of the Future," *The Economist*, May 30, 1987.
88. Brandt and Port, "How Automation Could Save the Day."
89. Gordon Betcherman and Kathryn McMullen, *Working with Technology: A Survey of Automation in Canada*, report prepared for the Economic Council of Canada (Ottawa: Minister of Supply and Services Canada, 1986; Cat. No. EC22-133/1986E).
90. Hugh Munro and Hamid Noori, "Reflecting Corporate Strategy in the Decision to Automate," *Business Quarterly* (Special Supplement: Generating Profit from New Technology), Winter 1985–1986, pp. 43–48; Extracts from the 1986 *Thompson Lightstone Research Report* (Rexdale, Ont.: Ontario Centre for Advanced Manufacturing, 1986; 1986-09-18RP).
91. *In the Chips: Opportunities, People, Partnerships*, report of the Labour Canada Task Force on Microelectronics and Employment (Ottawa: Minister of Supply and Services Canada, 1982; Cat. No. L35-1982/1E).
92. Austrom and Graffi, "An Empirical Study of Attitudes towards Technological Change."
93. Carol A. Beatty, *Promoting Productivity with CAD*, (Kingston, Ont.: School of Business, Queen's University, September 1986), Working Paper Series, No. MC 86-05.
94. Dalton Robertson, "We're Moving up the Ladder," *The Financial Post*, August 23, 1986, p. 5; Joseph R. D'Cruz and James D. Fleck, "The 1986 Score Card on Canada's Competitiveness: Mixed but Encouraging," *Business Quarterly*, Summer 1986, pp. 78–87.
95. "Meeting the New Trade Challenge," *The Financial Post*, August 23, 1986, p. 8.
96. Ibid. (summarizing Don Daly and Don McCharles, *Canadian Manufactured Exports: Constraints and Opportunities*, Institute for Research on Public Policy).
97. Robert Ferchat, "Science Is Key to Future Well-Being," *The Financial Post*, August 23, 1986, p. 8.

98. Ken MacQueen, "The Power Brokers," *Maclean's*, February 24, 1986, pp. 13–16.
99. John A. Willes, *Contemporary Canadian Labour Relations* (Toronto: McGraw-Hill Ryerson Limited, 1984), p. 3.
100. Pradeep Kumar with Mary Lou Coates and David Arrowsmith, *The Current Industrial Relations Scene in Canada: 1987* (Kingston, Ont.: Queen's University, Industrial Relations Centre, 1987), pp. 39, 378.
101. "Labour-Intensive Drives Net Unions New Recruits," *The Globe and Mail*, September 1, 1986, p. 2.
102. Ibid., p. 1.
103. Willes, *Contemporary Canadian Labour Relations*.
104. See Kumar et al., *The Current Industrial Relations Scene in Canada: 1986*, p. 8 (the forecast is based on the report, "Will You Have a Union in 1995?" by Vector Union Report, a Canadian labour research and consulting organization); "Future Bright for Unions, Report Says," *The Globe and Mail*, January 23, 1986, p. A5.
105. "Future Bright for Unions."
106. Kumar et al. *The Current Industrial Relations Scene in Canada: 1987*, pp. 39–40.
107. The following discussion draws on a number of sources: Prem Benimadhu, "Industrial Relations 1986: Coping with Change," *Canadian Business Review*, Summer 1986, pp. 26–31; "Labour Intensive Drives Net Unions New Recruits," *The Globe and Mail*, September 1, 1986, pp. A1–A2; "Organized Labour on Increase," *The Metro*, August 31, 1986, p. B15; "Technological Change Presents Dilemma to Labour Movement," *The Globe and Mail*, April 14, 1986, p. B10; "Computers Blamed for Making Jobs Dead Ends," *The Globe and Mail*, November 17, 1986, p. C11; "Future Bright for Unions, Report Says," *The Globe and Mail*, January 23, 1986, p. A5; Duncan Cameron, "Labour's New Blueprint: Forge Links to Other Groups," Department of Political Science, University of Ottawa, 1986; "Part-Time Workers Fastest-Growing Element of Canadian Work Force," *The Evening Telegram*, December 1, 1986, p. 25; "Will Canadian Workers Accept Japanese Ways?" *The Globe and Mail*, September 6, 1986, p. D1; Karl H. Ebel, "The Impact of Industrial Robotics on the World of Work," *International Labour Review*, no. 1 (1986); Dan O'Hagan, "Our Canada or Theirs?" *Canadian Labour*, September 1986, pp. 15–18.
108. Benimadhu, "Industrial Relations 1986: Coping with Change."
109. *Labour Relations Act*, revised Statutes of Ontario, 1980, chap. 228, sec. 13.
110. Willes, *Contemporary Canadian Labour Relations*, p. 115.
111. Benimadhu, "Industrial Relations 1986: Coping with Change."
112. Ibid.
113. Ibid.
114. Cameron, "Labour's New Blueprint."
115. Willes, *Contemporary Canadian Labour Relations* (see his discussion on pp. 129–38).
116. For a thorough discussion of relevant factors, see Janice M. Miller and John A. Kilpatrick, *Issues for Managers: An International Perspective* (Homewood, Ill.: Richard D. Irwin, 1987); Ricky W. Griffin, *Management*, 2nd ed. (Boston: Houghton Mifflin, 1987), chap. 23; Wayne F. Cascio, *Managing Human Resources* (New York: McGraw-Hill, 1986), chap. 17; Rosalie L. Tung, *Managing Human Resources in the International Context* (Cambridge, Mass.: Ballinger Publishers, in

press); Nancy J. Adler, *International Dimensions of Organizational Behavior* (Boston: Kent Publishing, 1986); H. W. Lane and J. J. DiStefano, *International Management Behavior* (Toronto: Methuen, 1987).

117. Sources for Exhibit 2–20: Anderson, "Robots Can Raise the Quality of Life"; George Tombs, "Robots May Liberate Us, but They're Also a Threat," *The Financial Post*, March 1, 1986; Wilfred List, "Technological Change Presents Dilemma to Labor Movement," *The Globe and Mail*, April 14, 1986; Saleh and Pal, "Robotic Technology and Its Impact on Work Design and the Quality of Working Life"; Knod et al., "Robotics: Challenges for the Human Resources Manager"; Cornelissen, "Management Trends: People and Technology Are Key"; Newton, "Impact of New Technology on Employment"; Beatty, "Promoting Productivity with CAD"; Wilbrod Leclerc, *Canadian Strategy in Technology* (Faculty of Administration, University of Ottawa), Working Paper series 86-01; *In the Chips: Opportunities, People, Partnerships*; Austrom and Graffi, "An Empirical Study of Attitudes towards Technological Change"; *Steering the Course—Twenty-First Annual Review* (Economic Council of Canada, 1984); Brandt and Port, "How Automation Could Save the Day"; Christopher J. Piper and Russell W. Radford, "Process Automation and Just-In-Time: Critical Complements," *Business Quarterly*, Winter 1985–1986, pp. 37–42 (Special Supplement on Generating Profit from Technology); Neil Hill and Tony Dimnik, "Cost Justifying New Technologies," *Business Quarterly*, Winter 1985–1986, pp. 19–24 (Special Supplement on Generating Profit from Technology).

Exhibit II
THE DIAGNOSTIC MODEL

External conditions	Organization conditions	Human resource activities	Objectives
Economic conditions Government regulations Technology Unions	Nature of organization: Strategies and objectives Nature of work Nature of employees and work groups	Staffing Development Employment relations Compensation Evaluation	Human resource effectiveness Organization effectiveness

PART TWO
ORGANIZATION CONDITIONS

Part Two begins the discussion of the factors within the organization that influence P/HRM activities. These factors include the directions and objectives of the organization; its financial condition and technologies; its size and structure; the type of work that must be performed to accomplish the objectives; the abilities, motivation, and behaviour of individuals currently employed; the organization's philosophy and culture; and on and on. While the list may seem endless, the diagnostic model, shown in Exhibit II, groups these influences into three basic categories.

- Nature of the organization.
- Nature of the work.
- Nature of the employees.

This grouping provides a framework for Part Two. In Chapter Three, we discuss the organization's conditions and how they may be linked to P/HRM activities through planning. Human resource planning not only links these activities to the organization's conditions, but it also integrates all the activities to make sure they are directed toward employee and organization effectiveness. Chapter Four examines the nature of the work itself: how jobs are designed and analyzed to achieve employee and organizational effectiveness. Chapter Five discusses behaviour of personnel, including that of employees, supervisors, and work groups that employees may form.

CHAPTER THREE
NATURE OF THE ORGANIZATION

CHAPTER OUTLINE

I. Organization Influences and the Diagnostic Approach
    A. Strategies and Operational Objectives
    B. Financial Condition and Flexibility
    C. Technologies Employed
    D. Culture and Philosophy
    E. The State of Knowledge

II. Human Resource Planning: The Link
    A. Human Resource Planning: An Important Distinction
    B. Establishing Human Resource Objectives
    C. Assessing Current Human Resource Conditions
    D. Designing and Evaluating Human Resource Activities
    E. Monitoring and Evaluating Results
    F. Human Resource Planning: Who Is Doing It?

III. Human Resource Information Systems
    A. Design Process
    B. Information Requirements
    C. Basic Components of HRIS
    D. Common Mistakes

IV. Strategy, Structure, and Staff
    A. Centralized–Decentralized
    B. Congruency
    C. Staffing

V. Summary

    Appendix / System Description: Merck and Company, Inc.

TRW Corporation manufactures products ranging from microelectronic guidance systems to auto brakes (for General Motors) to zippers (for Levi's jeans).[1] To compete effectively in such diverse markets, TRW is organized into three sectors: Electronics and Space, Automotive, and Industrial Products. Each of these sectors is further subdivided into divisions and plants located in North America and overseas. The organization's conditions in the three sectors differ; so do many of the human resource programs. For example, the Electronics and Space sector must recruit and retain engineers and computer software specialists. These professionals are currently in very high demand and enjoy escalating salaries. Thus, Electronics and Space is operating under highly competitive conditions. At the same time, the Automotive and Industrial sectors have experienced less dependable markets and stiff foreign competition. Layoffs, retrenchment, changes in work rules, relocation and modernizing of plants and equipment, and controlled wage increases (even wage concessions) have been typical personnel actions in these sectors. So in one organization, business units face various conditions. Some units are going after an increased share of expanding markets; other units are regrouping and learning to operate leaner; still others are trying new ventures with new ideas and products.

Contrast TRW to Dunbar's Auto Repair. Dunbar's pumps gas, services cars, and does minor repair work. Dunbar's has a two-bay station, but as cars become more complex, it is getting harder and harder to keep up on the equipment and expertise needed to repair them. The regional marketing representative for the oil company suggested that Dunbar drop the repair-service part of the business and convert his garage into a convenience store. But Dunbar has no experience in marketing, purchasing, and inventorying convenience items. He is better at mechanics than mathematics. What business should Dunbar be in—auto service and repair or gasoline and other convenience items?

Dunbar's and TRW have something in common. No matter the size or complexity, differences in organizations influence human resource decisions, and in turn, human resources influence the nature of the organization. The demand for TRW's varied products translates into the need to employ diverse skills in the TRW work force. TRW's ability to successfully compete in its many markets depends, at least in part, on the ability of its employees to design, produce, and sell products. Similar relationships between product demand, human resources, and ability to compete are present in small organizations like Dunbar's. Dunbar sees a portion of his business threatened, but he lacks the expertise required to change business directions.

ORGANIZATION INFLUENCES AND THE DIAGNOSTIC APPROACH

What in the nature of the organization influences human resource decisions? This chapter discusses four key factors: strategic and operational directions, financial conditions, technology employed, and culture and philosophy. Not only do these four factors influence human resource activities, but human resource activities also influence these four factors.

Strategies and Operational Objectives

Business strategies and operational objectives are major influences on the design and management of P/HRM activities. The importance of linking P/HRM with strategic issues is becoming more widely accepted.[2] Business strategies and operational objectives are major influences on, but also affected by, the design and management of P/HRM.

Managers find it useful to distinguish between operational objectives and strategies. Strategic planning is the process of setting long-term goals, developing a broad formula for how the organization is going to compete, and deciding which policies will be needed to achieve the goals.[3] Different organizations may use somewhat different terms, such as *mission* or *objectives* instead of *goals*, and *tactics* instead of *operating* or *functional policies*.[4] Strategy making can be thought of as including three highly interdependent phases: formulation, implementation, and evaluation. Formulation is the phase in which human resource issues arise.[5] As outlined in Exhibit 3–1, strategy formulation is initiated through several assessments of anticipated conditions in the external environment, along with an analysis of the resources likely to be available and the organization's strengths and weaknesses. Strengths and weaknesses refer to assets and skills relative to competitors, including financial resources, technological posture, product identification, and so on. This information is translated into apparently feasible strategies. Desirable strategies reflect the values, preferences, and power of key implementors and stakeholders. Feasible and desirable alternatives are merged into what is hoped will be a workable strategy.[6] The appropriateness of a strategy is usually assessed by applying several criteria, which test the proposed goals and policies in terms of environmental fit, resource fit, communication and implementation (e.g., are goals well understood by key implementors; is managerial capability sufficient to allow for effective implementation), and internal consistency (e.g., are goals mutually achievable; do key operating policies reinforce each other).[7]

A strategy indicates an organization's direction, its long-term goals, its major deployment of resources. An example is a steel company's decision, in

EXHIBIT 3–1
The Strategy Formulation Process

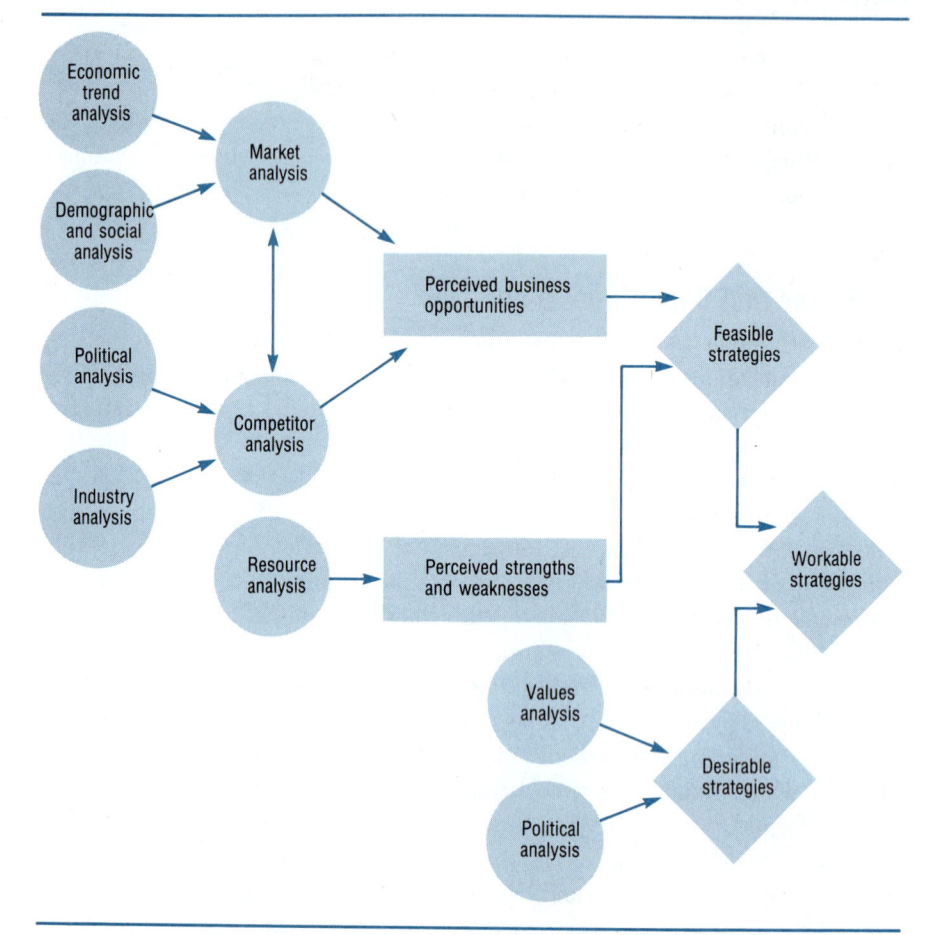

```
Economic
trend
analysis ──┐
           ├──→ Market
Demographic│    analysis
and social ┤      ↕
analysis   │      │ ──→ Perceived business
           │      │     opportunities ──┐
Political  │      ↕                     │──→ ⬥ Feasible
analysis ──┤    Competitor              │    strategies
           │    analysis ───────────────┘           │
Industry   │      │                                 │
analysis ──┘      │                                 ↓
                  ↓                             ⬥ Workable
                Resource ──→ Perceived strengths   strategies
                analysis     and weaknesses ──┐    ↑
                                              │    │
                              Values          │    │
                              analysis ──┐    │    │
                                         ├──→ ⬥ Desirable
                              Political ─┘    strategies
                              analysis
```

Source: Charles W. Hofer, "A Conceptual Scheme for Formulating a Total Business Strategy" (Dover, Mass.: Land Publishing, #BP0040, 1976, p. 6). Copyright © 1976 by Charles W. Hofer. Reproduced by permission. See also Lee Dyer, "Bringing Human Resources into the Strategy Formulation Process." Reprinted in *Perspectives on Personnel/Human Resource Management*, 3rd ed., ed. Herbert H. Heneman III and Donald P. Schwab (Homewood, Ill.: Richard D. Irwin, 1986).

the face of stiff foreign competition, to focus on specialized steel production and to phase out products that foreign steel industries can produce at lower cost. A different strategy may involve "forward" and/or "backward" integration. Primary steel companies in Canada have integrated forward into manufacturing and distribution of steel products and backward through ownership of mines that produce iron ore, coal, and limestone.

Other examples of strategic decisions include diversification, either through acquiring related products and services or creating a portfolio of relatively unrelated businesses. Montreal-based Molson diversified around its beer business into Beaver Lumber Co. (building supplies), Diversey Corporation (cleaning chemicals), and the Montreal Canadians (sports team).[8] Its competitor Labatt's, which dominates in beer sales, now produces more milk by volume in North America than beer and ale because of its strategic thrust into the dairy products industry. As part of its planned diversification, this company also added U.S.-based Johanna Farms to its agri-products group.[9] Holding true to its strategy of growth by acquisition, St. Catherine, Ontario-based Fleet Aerospace Corp., a manufacturer of components and subsystems for the aerospace and marine industries, targetted for takeover a North Carolina manufacturer of parts for the aerospace industry, Aeronca, Inc.[10]

Strategic business decisions influence human resource management decisions. Major changes in business direction, such as the steel company's repositioning in specialty steels, divestment, or diversification and integration strategies, involve a major redeployment of human resources. Plant closings and employee layoffs and additions may be involved, and management must learn to compete in new markets. Directional shifts usually involve adjustments in the nature of employees required and/or work performed. New jobs appear, and old ones disappear; new skills and training are required. All this takes time. For TRW, the importance of the Electronics and Space sector increased gradually and the Automotive sector declined gradually over a four-year period. The latter's previous major contribution to profits and sales was replaced by Electronics and Space. This change required many adjustments, including reallocation of employees from Automotive to various Space and Defence units.[11]

P/HRM decisions frequently affect a firm's strategies. The capacity of an organization to reach its strategic goals is influenced by human resources in several ways. Three fundamental areas of impact (as shown in Exhibit 3–2) are the capacity to undertake new enterprises and change operations, the capacity to operate effectively, and cost economics.[12] For example, the work rules and wage increases negotiated in labour contracts affect costs and, in turn, the price of goods and services.[13] As it becomes more difficult to control the costs of capital, equipment and materials, the focal point of management shifts to control over staffing levels, compensation and benefits, and staffing mix. While often taken for granted, the talents and efforts of employees do have tangible effects on management competencies, productivity, adaptivity to changes, and other factors supportive of an organization's strategic goals.[14] A good example is the selection of the chief executive and top management. Since these people supply the company's "vision" and are heavily involved in the organization's strategic decisions, changes in their ranks will affect the flavour of desirable strategies and subsequent strategic decisions. According

EXHIBIT 3-2
The Strategic Impact of Human Resources Factors

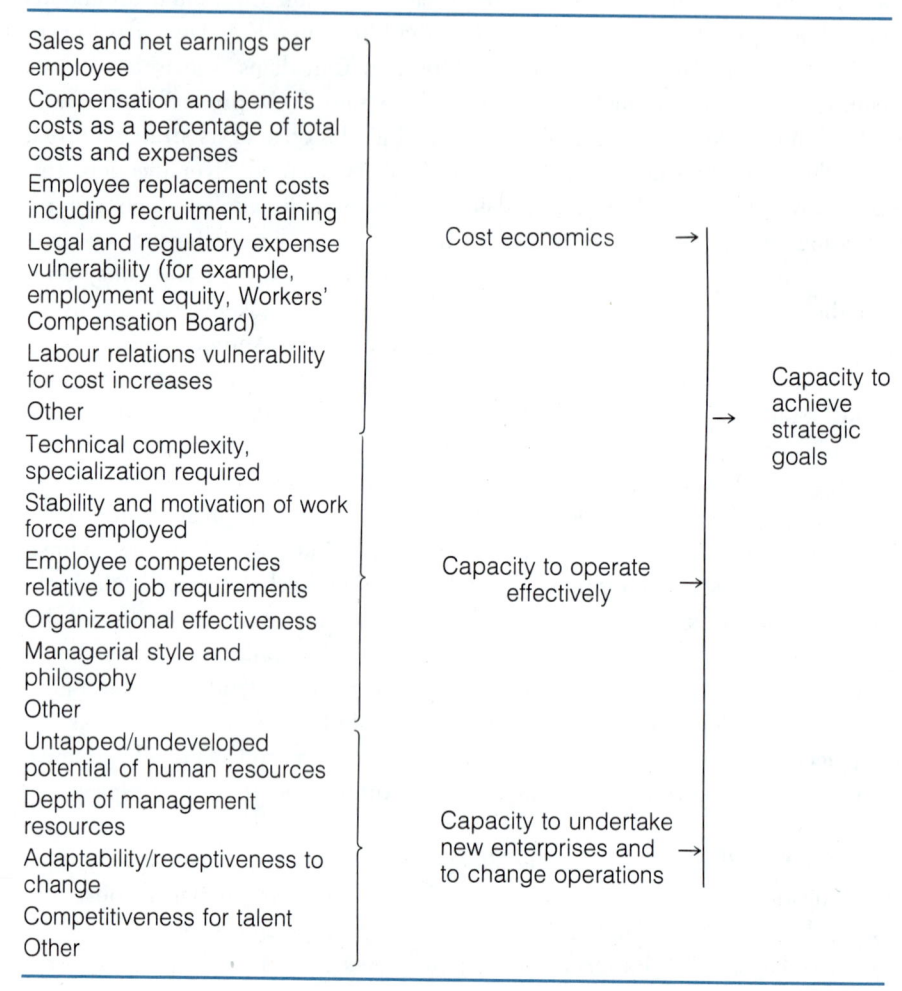

Factors	Grouping	Outcome
Sales and net earnings per employee Compensation and benefits costs as a percentage of total costs and expenses Employee replacement costs including recruitment, training Legal and regulatory expense vulnerability (for example, employment equity, Workers' Compensation Board) Labour relations vulnerability for cost increases Other	Cost economics →	
Technical complexity, specialization required Stability and motivation of work force employed Employee competencies relative to job requirements Organizational effectiveness Managerial style and philosophy Other	Capacity to operate effectively →	Capacity to achieve strategic goals
Untapped/undeveloped potential of human resources Depth of management resources Adaptability/receptiveness to change Competitiveness for talent Other	Capacity to undertake new enterprises and to change operations →	

Source: Modified from *Human Resource Planning* by James W. Walker. Copyright © 1980 by McGraw-Hill, Inc. Used with permission of the publisher.

to Porter, P/HRM can affect competitive advantage in any firm through, among other things, its "role in determining the skills and motivation of employees and the cost of hiring and training. In some industries, it holds the key to competitive advantage."[15]

While strategic planning and objectives involve major thrusts or shifts in the organization, operational planning and objectives are generally shorter term and involve very specific goals for current operations. They are more immediate (quarterly, annual, biannual), have more specific targets (rate of return, market share, production volumes), and typically concentrate on improving the way we are currently doing business, rather than changing the business.

Operational decisions have more immediate effects on P/HRM activities. Here, timing is critical. Production schedules must be met, quality standards achieved, and sales targets accomplished. Examples of personnel decisions resulting from operational decisions include hiring temporary salesclerks during a holiday rush, using overtime, second shifts, subcontracting, and so on.

Strategic Levels

Researchers of strategy and human resource management usually think of three levels of strategic decisions: the total organization, the unit, and the function.[16] The total organization refers to corporatewide decisions. Unit-level decisions focus on parts of the organization, often called profit centres, lines of business, or strategic business units (TRW's three sectors are examples). Functional decisions involve particular components of the organization, such as marketing, finance, and P/HRM.

Use of a three-level hierarchy of strategy helps resolve problems of scale and complexity for both strategic and human resource planning. Consider CP Ltd., for example. One of Canada's largest corporations, its subsidiaries are involved in businesses ranging from railway, shipping, and telecommunications operations to oil and gas, iron and steel, forest products, real estate, and hotel businesses. To understand and develop policy in such a context, it is necessary to shift from the encompassing notion of strategy at the corporate level to tangible and specific statements for separate business units and functions within the corporation.[17]

The strategic issues addressed by managers at each level differ.[18] As Exhibit 3–3 shows, at the total organization (corporate) level, managers must decide "what business should we be in?" At the business unit level, managers must decide "how do we compete in those businesses?" Finally, human resource managers, operating at the function level, must decide "how can we contribute to the unit and corporate objectives?"

EXHIBIT 3–3
Issues at Three Strategic Levels

Strategic Level	Issue
Corporatewide	What business(es) should we be in?
Business units	How do we compete?
Functions	How do we contribute to business unit and corporate objectives?

All organizations, even small ones like Dunbar's Auto Repair, must decide whether they want to fix cars or sell groceries, what specific products and services to offer, and whether to hire new employees with required skills or train present employees to do new jobs. So the issues addressed at each level vary, and managers of human resources must keep the strategic level in mind when they analyze the nature of the organization.

Strategic Types

Researchers have also discovered that organizations differ in the way they are designed or structured and in their approaches to human resource management. For example, Miles and Snow classify organizations into three basic strategic types, shown in Exhibit 3–4.[19] These three types are defined primarily in terms of their approaches to product/service markets. Briefly they are:

Defenders: Organizations operating in a few stable product markets. Managers are highly expert in their limited areas of operation but tend not to search for new product opportunities. Primary attention is on improving the efficiency of existing operations.

Prospectors: Organizations that continually search for new product and market opportunities and regularly take risks. Managers of these organizations tend to be creators of change and uncertainty, to which their market competitors must respond. The emphasis is on research and development, and on being first on the market with unique products, rather than on efficiency. An example in the computer industry is a company that tries to introduce new and innovative personal computers before its competitors do, or one that concentrates on technically unique products.

Analyzers: Organizations that operate in many types of product markets, some relatively stable, others changing. Managers in the stable areas operate routinely and efficiently through use of formalized structures and activities. In the more dynamic areas, managers watch competitors for new ideas, then rapidly adopt those that appear most promising. Examples include IBM and 3M.

Snow and Miles state that this typology is most useful when applied to business unit and functional levels of organizations (how should we compete and what can we contribute?) rather than to corporate-level decisions (which businesses should we be in?).[20]

Contingent Human Resource Activities

A major point in the diagnostic approach is that managers tend to design P/HRM activities to fit the nature of the organization. Each of Miles and Snow's three organizational types has a different approach to the human resource

EXHIBIT 3–4
Organization Types and Human Resource Management Activities

Organizational Characteristics	Type A (Defender)	Type B (Prospector)	Type C (Analyzer)
Product-market strategy	Limited, stable product line; predictable markets	Broad, changing product line; changing markets	Stable and changing product line; predictable and changing markets
Research and development	Limited mostly to product improvement	Extensive; emphasis on "first-to-market"	Focused; emphasis on "second-to-market"
Production	High volume/low cost; emphasis on efficiency and process engineering	Customized; prototypical emphasis on effectiveness and product design	High volume/low cost; emphasis on process engineering
Marketing	Limited mostly to sales	Focused heavily on market research	Extensive marketing campaigns
Human Resource Management Activities			
Basic role	Maintenance	Entrepreneurial	Coordination
Human resource planning	Formal; extensive	Informal; limited	Formal; extensive
Recruitment, selection, and placement	Make	Buy	Make and buy
Training and development	Skill building	Skill identification and application	Skill building and application
Compensation	Internal pay relationships; internal equity	External pay relationships; external competitiveness	Internal consistency and external competitiveness, a blend
Performance appraisal	Process-oriented; focus on training needs, individual/group performance	Results-oriented; focus on staffing needs, division/corporate performance	Mostly process-oriented; training and staffing needs, individual/group/division performance

Source: Adapted from R. E. Miles and C. C. Snow, *Organizational Strategy, Structure, and Processes* (New York: McGraw-Hill, 1978); reproduced with permission.

activities listed in our diagnostic model.[21] For example, a "defender" organization tends to design formal planning activities, hire new employees into lower entry-level jobs, promote from within for higher-level jobs, and focus on internal pay relationships among employees. "Prospectors," on the other hand, seek more entrepreneurial managers who may hire experienced employees at all job levels in the organization, tolerate only limited formal planning procedures, emphasize specific and technical training, and ensure that pay rates are competitive with those paid by competing employers.

A note of caution is required here. Research relating human resource programs to these various organization types is not well developed. Nevertheless, research suggests that differences in the nature of organizations, particularly in product-market strategies, do influence the design of P/HRM activities. We can even *describe* which programs appear to fit with different types of organizations. The field is not advanced enough to *prescribe*. Research does not yet permit us to stipulate which activity is most effective for different organization conditions.[22]

Financial Condition and Flexibility

In addition to affecting its direction, an organization's financial state has a critical influence on human resource activities. Here management is concerned with the extent to which a potential financial resource gap could hamper the organization's ability to marshal the human resources necessary to support its existing, or planned changes in, strategy. Another look at Exhibit 3-2 helps illustrate the link between financial and human resources. For example, a change to production technology involving more technical complexity incurs reskilling costs in order to maintain employee competencies relative to new job requirements. These costs are in addition to acquisition of equipment, but need to be considered as part of the cost package in the decision to modernize the plant. The level of financial assets also influences the organization's ability to be competitive, to absorb replacement costs, to maintain a competitive stance in compensation and benefits areas, and so on. Overall, the costs of acquiring, retaining, developing, and motivating needed talent must be compatible with estimates of allowable costs.[23]

Related to an organization's financial condition is its flexibility in pricing its products or services—in order to improve the financial condition. Some firms are able to pass increased costs on to consumers in the form of higher prices. Others in more competitive markets face loss of revenues if they raise prices. One recourse is to reduce costs by reducing the work force and/or controlling wages. Thus, flexibility in pricing products affects an organization's human resource decisions.

The organization's financial condition cannot be ignored in models of human resource management. An employer's ability to pay wages, fund training programs, and conduct other personnel activities are all affected by its financial condition and flexibility. And in turn, commitments to employees in the form of wages and benefits affect the organization's financial condition.

Technologies Employed

Variations in the technology employed are also important in the functioning of organizations and influence P/HRM activities. Technology can be defined as the techniques and processes used to generate goods and services.[24] A chemical distillation process used by Imperial Oil, a job shop in a small foundry, Ford's continuous assembly lines, even the computer, calculator, paper and pencil of a public accounting firm are examples of technological variety.

Technology influences the nature of work to be performed, how it is performed, and the skills and abilities required of employees.

Culture and Philosophy

How important are corporate culture and philosophy in achieving employee and organization effectiveness?[25] Culture refers to the set of important assumptions, values, beliefs, and traditions shared by members of the organization,[26] and has several layers.[27] According to Schein, the underlying assumptions include values viewed as so important that they are taken for granted, nondebatable, and accepted as automatically true.[28]

Culture is usually examined at three levels. The most superficial level includes audible and visible behavioural patterns, artifacts, and so on. Examples, while easy to see, are hard to interpret without an understanding of the deeper levels. The second level of culture pertains to how employees make sense of the first level—how they explain, rationalize, and justify the what and why of their behaviours and activities. The third level goes deeper still, to the learned underlying assumptions that steer and govern the other two levels. At this core level, we begin to understand how the assumptions interlock and combine to form patterns.[29]

Much of the literature on corporate culture and organizational performance can be interpreted as suggesting that culture has significant positive economic value for a firm.[30] One survey reported that a high percentage of the organizations questioned agreed that corporate culture was important to their business success.[31] Another indication of the importance of culture is the recent development of methods to conduct a culture "checkup."[32] Many organizations also believe that culture is important to their capacity to formulate and implement strategy and is related to human resource management. How becomes clear by considering the roles of culture content and strength (see Exhibit 3–5). Culture content influences the *direction* of behaviour; culture strength determines the *intensity* of behaviour.[33] An example is actions reflecting the eight principles espoused by Peters and Waterman (shown in Exhibit 3–6)[34] and Waterman's more recent lessons of "corporate renewal" (e.g., teamwork, empowerment of subordinates, commitment, delayering, declared management attention backed by changes in behaviour, productivity gains from employees' ideas, not only from improvements in technology).[35] Cultures supportive of the renewal lessons lead to new views on strategy formulation and implementation.

Exhibits 3–7 and 3–8 reveal IBM's and TRW's corporate philosophies toward human resources. Their P/HRM programs are designed to be consistent with and supportive of these philosophies. Hence, IBM emphasizes individual merit pay, internal grievance programs for airing dissatisfactions, a generous benefits program, a minimum of 40 hours of human resource training for all new managers, and other programs to instill the IBM philosophy in all employees.

According to Sathe, companies typically have one or more subcultures within the corporate culture. These may be of the enhancing or "countercul-

EXHIBIT 3–5
Corporate Culture Strength and Content: Factors Influencing and Effect on Behaviour

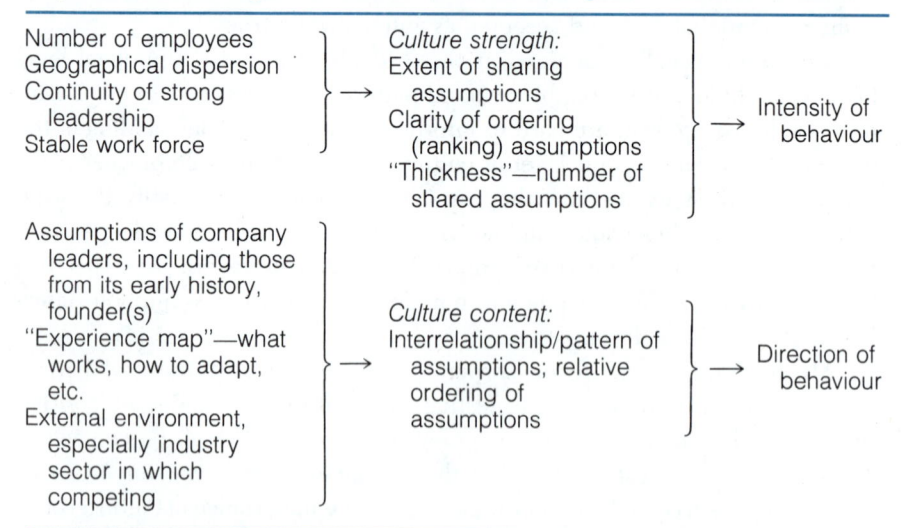

Factors		Culture Element		Effect
Number of employees Geographical dispersion Continuity of strong leadership Stable work force	→	*Culture strength:* Extent of sharing assumptions Clarity of ordering (ranking) assumptions "Thickness"—number of shared assumptions	→	Intensity of behaviour
Assumptions of company leaders, including those from its early history, founder(s) "Experience map"—what works, how to adapt, etc. External environment, especially industry sector in which competing	→	*Culture content:* Interrelationship/pattern of assumptions; relative ordering of assumptions	→	Direction of behaviour

Source: Compiled from several sources, especially Vijay Sathe, *Culture and Related Corporate Realities* (Homewood, Ill.: Richard D. Irwin, Inc., 1985).

EXHIBIT 3–6
Eight Attributes of Excellent Companies

1.	Bias for action	"Getting on with it." "Not paralyzed by analysis."
2.	Close to customer	"Learn from customers." "Get product ideas from customers; provide highest quality service."
3.	Autonomy and entrepreneurship	"Foster many leaders and innovators through the organization."
4.	Productivity through people	"Treat employees as the root source of quality and productivity gain." "Respect for the individual."
5.	Hands-on value driven	"Basic philosophy of an organization has more to do with its achievements than do technological or economic resources, organization structure, or innovation."
6.	Stick to the knitting	"Never acquire a business you cannot run."
7.	Simple form, lean staff	"The underlying structural forms and systems in excellent companies are elegantly simple."
8.	Simultaneously tight-loose properties	"Excellent companies are both centralized and decentralized." "Autonomy down to the shop floor best centralized about a few guiding core values."

Source: Adapted from Thomas J. Peters and Robert H. Waterman, Jr., *In Search of Excellence* (New York: Harper & Row, 1983).

ture" type. A counterculture has culture content that opposes the company culture; an enhancing subculture has the same content but is stronger than the company culture. In the case of a functionally organized company, for example, different functional cultures may coexist with the company culture and may be stronger than it. Or different cultures may prevail in different units.[36] Esso Resources, the exploration and production arm of Imperial Oil Ltd., has a corporate culture markedly different from Imperial's.[37] Given the three levels of strategic decisions, differences in subcultures do influence strategy formulation.

EXHIBIT 3–7
IBM Principles

> Respect for the individual
> Customer service
> Excellence
> Effective management leadership
> Obligation to stockholders
> Fair deal for suppliers
> Corporate citizenship

EXHIBIT 3–8
Organizational Values

TRW and the 80s . . . Fundamental Objectives
Objective one:
TRW seeks to adhere to the highest standards of conduct in all that it does.
Objective two:
TRW seeks to achieve superior performance as an economic unit, with special emphasis on high-quality products and services.
Objective three:
TRW seeks to achieve high quality in its internal operations with special focus on its many relationships with employees.
Objective four:
TRW seeks to augment its principal social contributions—those resulting from its economic performance and internal operations—by participation in a wide range of community activities and communication programs.

The State of Knowledge

It is easy to assert that models of human resource management must consider the nature of the organization, and it is even comparatively easy to list and discuss some factors that have an influence.[38] It is much more difficult to state definitively how these factors influence P/HRM management and in turn are influenced by its activities. Precise statements about the relationship between the particulars of organizational characteristics such as objectives and strategies, financial conditions, technology, and culture and human resource management are not well researched. Some research such as Snow and Mile's work has been discussed, but much more work is required.

HUMAN RESOURCE PLANNING: THE LINK

Human resource planning is the first P/HRM activity listed in the diagnostic model. It is discussed here because it provides the link between the organization conditions discussed above and the management of other personnel activities. It is through planning that managers diagnose changes in the firm's strategic directions, financial conditions, culture and technology, and integrate them into human resource decisions.[39]

So planning for the management of human resources can play a vital role. *It not only links the organizational and external environments, but it also integrates P/HRM decisions and focusses them toward employee and organization effectiveness.*

A widely used definition of human resource planning is:[40]

> **Definition**
>
> *Human resource planning* is the process by which management determines how the organization should move from its current (human resource) position to its desired (human resource) position.

This definition is deceptively simple. It assumes that we can answer four basic questions. These questions, along with a four-stage planning process, are shown in Exhibit 3–9.

1. *Where do we want to be and how do we contribute?* The answer to this question requires establishing human resource objectives that are consistent with the strategies and objectives of the business unit and function (see Exhibit 3–3). Human resource planning helps to make certain that human resource decisions are tailored to the unit's objectives.

EXHIBIT 3–9
Human Resources Planning—A Four-Stage Process

Issue	Diagnostic Process
1. Where do we want to be? How do we contribute to the organization?	*Scan the external environment* Economic conditions, government/legal regulations, union interests/expectations, societal expectations. *Analyze the internal organization environment* Strategic objectives, financial conditions, technologies employed. *Establish human resource objectives* Productivity, costs, compliance, employee work behaviours.
2. Where are we now?	*Assess current human resource conditions* Evaluate current personnel functions, activities and accomplishments. Analyze current employees and current jobs. Assess match between employees and jobs.
3. How do we get to goals?	*Generate and evaluate human resource programs and actions* Productivity, performance programming. Staff and allocation programming. Compliance programming. Problem area programming.
4. How did we do?	*Monitor and evaluate human resource results*

2. *Where are we now?* Answering this question involves *(a)* an analysis of the current personnel functions activities and responsibilities, *(b)* an analysis of the nature of the employees and the nature of the work, *(c)* an assessment of how effectively the organization is currently utilizing its human resources. Notice the focus is on how effectively the organization manages its human resources and how the personnel department currently contributes to improving human resource management.
3. *How do we get from where we are to where we want to be?* Answering this question is the heart of human resource decision making and programming. Managers generate alternatives to achieve human resource goals. Alternative activities may be designed to increase unit productivity and employee job performance, to ensure compliance with legislation and societal expectations, to control labour costs, and/or to resolve any current or anticipated problems the employees may face.
4. *How effective were our actions?* Answers here evaluate the results of the personnel activities, to assess if the actions taken did accomplish the human resource objectives set earlier, and to monitor any new problems that may have surfaced.

Human Resource Planning: An Important Distinction

Human resource planning is often confused with planning for each individual personnel activity.[41] For example, employment planning's goal is to get the right number of people in the right job at the right time. Compensation planning determines the salary increase budget. By contrast, human resource planning encompasses the *entire* personnel/human resource system—it is planning for the management of human resources for the entire unit and function. The goal of human resource planning is to develop an integrated set of human resource policies and programs designed to achieve the human resource and organizational objectives.

Let's now discuss each of the four major phases in the human resource planning process.

Establishing Human Resource Objectives

A basic step in any human resource planning effort is specifying objectives. To specify objectives requires consideration of various sources of objectives, the timing or planning period, and the techniques to use.

Human resource objectives come in many forms. They include improving productivity, controlling labour costs, ensuring compliance with regulations, and influencing a wide range of employee work behaviours such as job performance, absenteeism, and turnover. The ultimate objectives are employee and organization effectiveness. Examples of companies' human resource objectives are shown in Exhibits 3–10 and 3–11 for Ontario Hydro and Merck, the parent company of Merck Frosst Canada, Inc. Magna International, which has more than 75 plants in both Canada and the United States and is headquartered in Markham, Ontario, enshrines company philosophy and its belief in employees through its Magna Corporate Constitution.[42]

Human resource objectives are derived from several sources. The diagnostic model suggests four: the external environment, the strategic and operational objectives of the organization, current employee work behaviours, and the nature of work in the organization. Whatever the source, objectives serve two basic functions: they direct P/HRM activities toward goals and serve as standards against which to evaluate results.

The techniques used to establish objectives vary widely. They may require pulling together teams of people from different functions (finance, engineering, plant operations, P/HRM) to share information. Setting human resources objectives is an art rather than a science. Dyer says, "Research has so far failed to develop adequate means of determining whether organizations are currently at their desired human resource position, let alone techniques

EXHIBIT 3–10
Ontario Hydro's Corporate Policy—Human Resources Planning

1. The corporation shall forecast its human resources requirements as a necessary part of other forecasts.
2. Managers at all levels shall engage in human resources planning as an integrated and supporting part of work program planning.
3. The corporation shall consider future as well as present requirements when filing positions.
4. Managers at level X-1 shall recommend succession plans for level X and shall provide assistance to prepare candidates to meet position requirements.
5. Human resources planning for senior management positions at levels 2 and 3 shall be conducted and monitored by a policy and administration committee appointed by the president.
6. The policy and administration committee shall establish policy and procedures for forecasting of needs; identification of target jobs, nomination, assessment, succession planning, development and selection of candidates for positions at levels 2 and 3 as part of the senior management resources plan.
7. Employees shall have the primary responsibility for their own career development.
8. The corporation shall provide assistance to employees in individual career planning to the extent permitted by work priorities.
9. The corporation shall include consideration of the identified career aspirations, interests, and personal constraints on career mobility of potential candidates for positions in planning for its human resources requirements.

Source: James Rush and L. Bourne, "Human Resource Planning at Ontario Hydro: A Field Study" (London, Ont.: University of Western Ontario, 1983).

EXHIBIT 3–11
Merck's Corporate Human Resource Objectives

Detailed Action Plans (1982–1986) in Support of Strategic Priorities
Summary of Priorities:
1. Satisfy the long-term *Management Requirements* of the Company at all levels.
2. Continued concentration on improved and effective *Employee Relations* at all levels of the Company.
3. Continue to focus on *Affirmative Action*, with emphasis on developing a total environment conducive to equal employment opportunity.
4. Expanded use of various media for continued development and implementation of *Employee Communications*.
5. Continued emphasis on the importance of the *Supervisor* at all levels of the organization by providing training and communications support of our strategy of cooperation and understanding.
6. Develop new and more effective ways to accommodate *Employee Participation* in joint problem-solving areas and in appropriate policy/practice development.
7. Continue development and implementation of programs and policies which will strengthen *Employee Identification and Commitment* to the Company and its business goals and objectives.
8. Review and expand employee *Compensation and Reward Systems* to assure that they are truly motivating high performance. Merchandise the programs to assure their acceptance at all levels of the organization.
9. Continue development and expansion of the broad-based *Employee Health and Safety Program*, focused on health and well-being both on and off the job.
10. Develop innovative approaches to *Organization Design* and to *Job Design & Scheduling* to improve productivity.

Key Action Plans in Support of Strategic Priorities:

Priority #1. Satisfy the long-term *Management Requirements* of the Company at all levels

The long-term survival of the Company will depend in large measure on the availability of outstanding management talent at all levels of the organization. During the last few years, Human Resource planning and training and development efforts have been markedly expanded to meet growing present and future needs. Emphasis has been placed on management and supervisory programs to assure adequate numbers of personnel for leadership positions requiring strong skills in planning, communicating, problem resolution, coaching, and training others. We will need to continue to emphasize and expand the wide variety of activities required to develop effective leaders for the future:

- Recruitment, selection, and placement.
- Succession planning.
- Individual career planning and development.
- Identification of high potential management talent at all levels.
- Inter-divisional exchange of high potential employees.

EXHIBIT 3–11 *(concluded)*

Supporting Action Plans:

a. Continue strong emphasis on Human Resource planning and development activities which include recruitment of people with strong management potential, succession planning, individual career planning, and identification of high potential management talent throughout the Company.
  Timetable: 1981 & continuing   Cost: To be determined

b. Develop programs to require *minimum skills training* for all *new* supervisory and managerial personnel.
  Timetable: 1982–1983   Cost: To be determined

c. Expand our college recruiting program as a high-priority source of new talent.
  Timetable: 1981 & continuing   Cost: Budgeted

d. Implement a Senior Management Briefing Program to provide orientation on key issues, information on new management techniques, and reviews of materials and approaches being used in the supervisory and management development programs throughout the Company. Program will include leading outside authorities in the management and organization planning/development field.
  Timetable: 1981–1982   Cost: $20,000

e. In anticipation of loss of Human Resources people to other companies, possibly to other functions and to general turnover, continue the program of regular recruitment of high potential individuals.
  Timetable: 1981 & continuing   Cost: Budgeted

Source: Merck & Co., Inc.

to establish appropriate objectives for new business or emerging technologies."[43] Doeringer argues that the process of setting goals by itself has value since it requires managers to try to consider the human resource implications of organization decisions.[44]

An Illustration: Productivity Improvement

Excerpts from a major firm's human resource plan are presented as Exhibit 3–12. This employer's human resource objectives seek to improve employee performance and unit productivity through human resource programs designed to:

- Upgrade the current work force's ability to perform jobs.
- Motivate the top performers.
- Terminate so-called marginal performers.
- Upgrade managerial skills.

EXHIBIT 3–12
Strategic Focus to Achieve 5 Percent Annual Employee Performance and Unit Productivity

Actions Planned	Programs
Upgrade current work force's ability to perform job	Job skills training programs.
	Slow rates of job transfers and upgrading to ensure incumbent remains in job through two cycles.
	Identify marginal performers.
	Increase percent of budget allocation to job skills training.
Motivate top performers	Identify top performers.
	Investigate feasibility of cash (bonus) incentive programs.
	Increase percent of merit budget allocated to top performers.
	Career opportunities information dissemination.
	Allocate upgrading opportunities to top performers.
	Study feasibility of determining top performers' desired reward and job opportunities.
Terminate marginal performers	Implement "marginals" program.
	Monitor each unit's progress on "marginal" goals.
	Decrease percent of budget allocated (10 percent).
Upgrade managerial capabilities	Establish coordinate program for managers: search/succession planning.
	Complete project to ensure job relatedness of current management development programs.
	Implement the "management level retirement preparation program"; ensure that guidelines for age discrimination are understood and adhered to.
	Continue percent of budget allocation.

Source: Adapted from J. Walker, *Human Resource Planning* (New York: McGraw-Hill, 1980); reproduced with permission.

Managers may differ on which is the best way to bring about improved performance. This example represents what this firm's managers decided, and it illustrates an actual human resource plan.

Assessing Current Human Resource Conditions

The second phase of the human resource planning process analyzes where the organization currently is—its actual human resources situation. In the diagnostic approach, the current situation has three basic aspects:

- *Current P/HRM activities and responsibilities.* Here such devices as audits of its activities, and/or surveys of various users ("clients") of P/HRM, are conducted. Clients surveyed might include employees and managers.[45]
- *Nature of the work and employees to perform the work.* Work is defined in terms of the qualifications necessary to perform the work and the rewards of the work. Employee skills, experience, needs, and interests are the individual characteristics analyzed.
- *Match between the individual employee and the work to be performed.* The degree of correspondence between the individual employee's characteristics and the requirements of the job is also considered. Mismatches of employees and jobs may lead to reduced performance and low job satisfaction. Improving the match between employee skills and job requirements should lead to improved performance. Similarly, increased correspondence between employee interest and motivation and the rewards offered in a job should lead to improved performance.

The state of our knowledge related to each of these three aspects—the effectiveness of P/HRM activities, the individual and the work, and the match between them—is examined in the following chapters. Analysis of human resource activities and their roles in achieving the match between individuals and the work is an important aspect of human resource planning. Through ensuring this match, human resource planning is helping link P/HRM activities to the organization directions. It yields a wide range of information on possible problems such as marginal performance, low job satisfaction, absenteeism, and turnover. It also yields data on the skills available in the existing work force, and on the work itself. Human resource planning helps establish the contribution of personnel activities to the organization's objectives.

Designing and Evaluating Human Resource Activities

Human resource activities are designed to achieve human resource objectives. These activities were enumerated and shown in the diagnostic model and are covered individually in the upcoming chapters.

EXHIBIT 3–13
Programming Designed to Influence Employee Motivation and Performance

Alternative Human Resources Programs

Evaluation Criteria	Pay Incentive	Job Enrichment	Opportunity to Rotate and Qualify for Higher Pay	Convenient Work Schedule	Increased Job Security
Technical feasibility	Moderate	Moderate	High	Low	High
Likely payoff	High	High	Moderate	Low	Low
Relative costs	High	High	Moderate	Low	Low
Other consequences	Other pay systems	Work scheduling and flow	Lower experience levels	Staffing problems	?

Source: Adapted from a chemical firm's human resources plan.

Designing these activities is a most critical phase of human resource planning.

> **Definition**
> *Human resource programming* is the process of translating objectives into human resource activities.

One approach to generating and evaluating P/HRM activities is to focus on the following three elements.[46]

1. Generate alternative actions based on models of human resource management. These models may be derived from the human resource-related theories and research and from the practical experiences of managers and employees.[47]
2. Evaluate the various alternatives generated on four criteria: *(a)* the likely payoff, *(b)* the anticipated costs, *(c)* the technical feasibility of the action, and *(d)* the possible consequences (both positive and negative) for other P/HRM actions and other parts of the organization.
3. Undertake an integrated set of activities judged to most effectively achieve the human resources objectives.

Exhibit 3-13 illustrates the evaluation of alternative programs to influence employee motivation and performance. In this case, the programs are based on the judgement of a task force of managers. Ideally, their practical judgement would have the benefit of research results too. The managers evaluated the options on each of the four criteria mentioned earlier. Dimick and Murray suggest that the best we can hope to achieve in evaluating alternative P/HRM programs is to "satisfice"—to determine those actions that will meet the goal, rather than optimize.[48]

Human resource programming—the generation and evaluation of alternative actions to achieve objectives—is the weakest link in human resource planning. One fruitful approach is to draw upon the theories and research in fields related to human resource management—organization theory and behaviour, labour economics, sociology, and industrial psychology.[49] The modern P/HRM manager may draw upon theories and research in all of these fields.

Monitoring and Evaluating Results

Monitoring and evaluating results is the fourth phase of the human resource planning process shown in Exhibit 3-9. This phase involves both qualitative and quantitative features. Planners should assess:

1. The extent to which they are tuned into the organization's human resource problems and opportunities and the extent to which their priorities are sound.
2. The quality of their working relationships with others in the organization—financial specialists and line managers—who supply their data and make use of the results of human resource planning.
3. The quality of the communications that flow between the parties involved.
4. The extent to which forecasts, plans, and recommended actions are being heeded by organizational decision makers.
5. The perceived value of human resource planning and other P/HRM activities among various constituents.[50]

To effectively conduct human resource programming today, a sound information system is essential, as discussed below. Indeed, data deficiencies are often cited as a serious limitation to effective human resource planning.[51]

Human Resource Planning: Who Is Doing It?

Recent surveys of employers show that human resource planning is commonly practiced. Janger found 86 percent of the responding firms were involved in human resource planning and more than 50 percent regarded it as a major activity.[52] The Human Resources Planning Society, a professional society for human resource planners, was established in 1977.[53]

The responsibility for human resource planning seems to evolve as a firm gains experience with it. A recent study of the evolution of human resource planning at Merck is illustrative.[54] As Exhibit 3–14 shows, elements of human resource planning began in Merck more than 25 years ago. The first efforts were fragmented and focused on forecasting demand for labour replacement needs (employment planning). Gradually, the focus shifted to integrate (1) the various P/HRM activities (staffing, compensation, etc.) with each other, and (2) the human resource planning with the business planning process. At first, human resource planning was the sole responsibility of human resource managers. The operating managers played a secondary and advisory role. Gradually, responsibility shifted. Human resource planning at Merck is now primarily a tool of operating managers, and human resource professionals have taken on the consultant or advisory role. At Merck, human resource planning has become an integral part of its business planning process.[55]

EXHIBIT 3-14
Evolution of HRP at Merck

	Before 1965	1965–1969	1970–1974	1975 and Beyond
Special projects	First formal HRP (five-year rolling plan)	Continued use of HRP (five-year rolling plan)	Converted HRP (five-year plan to HR strategic plan)
Replacement plan	Subfunctional focus, organization development, compensation, and labour relations	Personnel area wide focus	HR strategic plan focus; external and internal HR factors relevant to business plans
Demand forecasts	Driving force: general shortage of managerial talent	Driving force: shortage of managerial talent and employment equity concerns	Biannual HRP
	Experimentation with various planning processes and statistical techniques	Formalization of HRPP (succession plan) and PPS (information system)	HRP focus; succession plan for managerial talent
		Emerging links with business planning through formal executive reviews of HRPP	Driving force: shifted to business strategic and operating missions
			Formal reviews of HRP and SHRP at all managerial levels
			Special projects emphasizing office productivity, aging, composition of managerial talent pool
			Use of statistical methods tailored to project needs

HUMAN RESOURCE INFORMATION SYSTEMS

A key building block in the foundation of all human resource management activities, including human resource planning, lies in effective human resource information systems (HRIS). All employers maintain information on their human resources; whether that information proves useful to the organization depends on how accessible it is. Computers have greatly enhanced the practicality of information analysis and have much to contribute to evaluating the effectiveness of the P/HRM function.

> **Definition**
>
> An *HRIS* is a systematic procedure for collecting, storing, maintaining, retrieving, and validating certain data needed by an organization about its human resources, P/HRM activities, and organization unit characteristics.[56]

A human resource information system (HRIS) is used to support a wide variety of P/HRM-related activities. Staffing makes use of data on applicants, new hires, employment equity, promotions, turnover; development uses data on skills training received and performance appraisals; compensation, on pay increases and salary forecasts; labour relations, on grievance and discipline experience; the list goes on and on. Computerized HRIS may also simplify administrative chores such as preparing mailing labels to employees or retired employees and generating certain routine reports. In addition, HRIS should enable the P/HRM professional to quickly respond to special requests. Such requests may come from an operating manager who may be concerned about what appears to be excess turnover, or a government agency that asks questions about the proportion of members of designated groups in the marketing function.

Properly designed and administered, HRIS becomes a key P/HRM tool. Some of the major issues to consider are: the design process, information requirements, major functional components, and common mistakes.

Design Process

If the data necessary to support the various human resource activities are available, then any activity can be aided by a computer-based HRIS. But it is necessary that the HRIS be well designed.

No best approach to the design process has emerged. The process used by TRW is fairly common and is shown in Exhibit 3–15.[57] The first and most

EXHIBIT 3–15
An Illustration of an HRIS Design Process

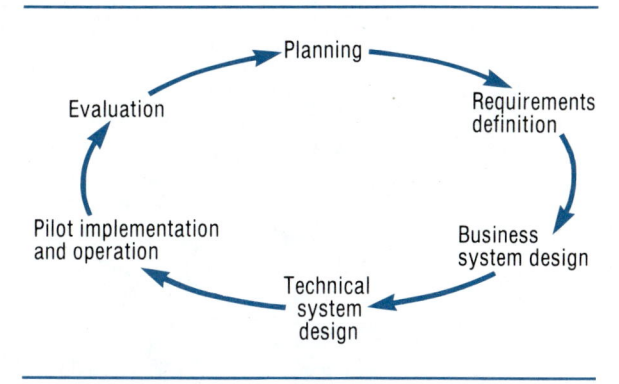

```
          Planning
Evaluation         Requirements
                   definition
Pilot implementation   Business
and operation          system design
          Technical
          system
          design
```

Source: TRW Task Force Report on Employee Information System 1983.

important step involves specifying the system requirements. These specifications are the heart of the system and include such decisions as the type of data to collect, the amount of data to collect, how to collect it, and when to collect it. This is such a critical step that it is discussed in greater detail in the references.[58] A nontechnical description of Merck's HRIS is included as an appendix to this chapter.

The next step in the design process is the business system design. It involves answering questions about who will use the system, how will they access it, how will it be updated, and so on. Technical design includes software system development and programming. Then the system is piloted at certain locations and evaluated.

Information Requirements

Most attempts to develop an HRIS start and stop at trying to determine the data requirements. Typically, a survey of all possible users is conducted to identify their data needs. An enormous wish list results, containing so many items that the project often is crushed by its own weight.

Rather than trying to tackle all P/HRM activities' needs at once, some organizations focus on a flexible, expandable modular system. A modular approach is illustrated in Exhibit 3–16. Each of the basic human resource activities then develops a module that draws upon a core data set. Exhibits 3–17 and 3–18 illustrate labour relations and compensation modules drawn from the core data.

EXHIBIT 3–16
Building the Employee Information Database

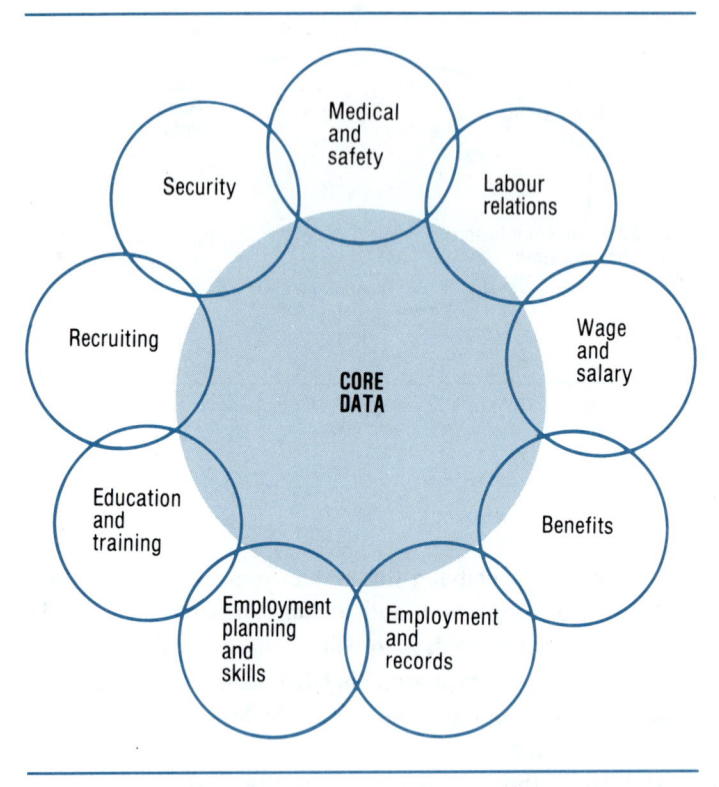

Core Data surrounded by: Medical and safety, Labour relations, Wage and salary, Benefits, Employment and records, Employment planning and skills, Education and training, Recruiting, Security.

Basic Components of HRIS

It is convenient to consider three major functional components in any HRIS; they are illustrated below:[59]

INPUT → DATA MAINTENANCE → OUTPUT

Each of these functions is briefly examined and illustrated.

Input Function

The input function provides the capabilities needed to enter P/HRM information into the HRIS. This includes the procedures required to collect the data; such details as who collects it, when, and how it is processed need to be specified. A typical HRIS input function, developed by Simon, is illustrated in Exhibit 3–19.[60] Note the first activity is to ensure all data are present and valid (no "garbage in").

Data Maintenance Function

After the data are processed by the input function, it enters the data maintenance function. This function updates and adds the new data to the existing database. Exhibit 3–20 illustrates a typical maintenance function.

Output Function

The most visible function of an HRIS is the output generated. It can take many forms, ranging from a standard version to special reports. The output reports are the crucial link to the user. The decision maker must be able to use the output if the HRIS is to be an effective tool. Interested readers should consult references to this chapter for more detailed discussions.

**EXHIBIT 3–17
An HRIS Compensation Module**

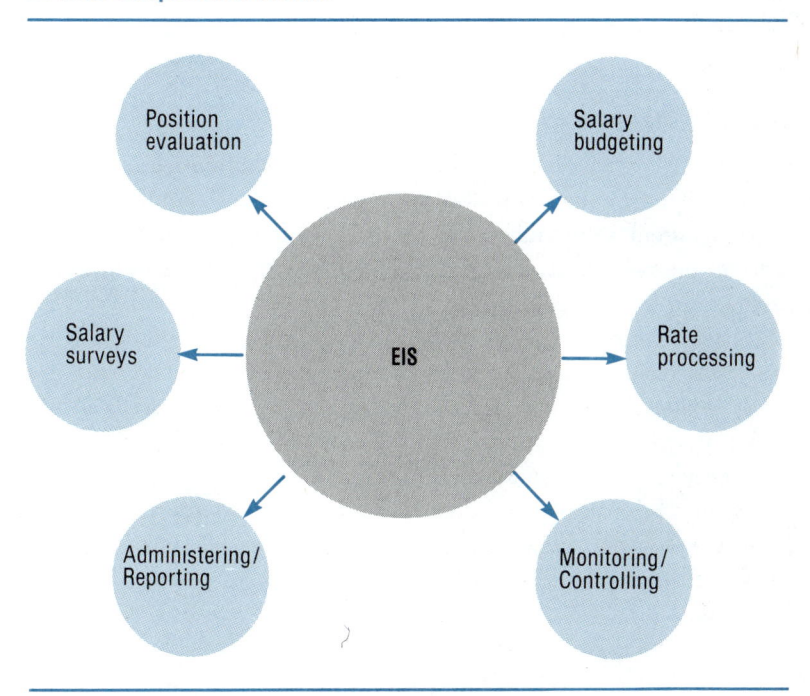

EXHIBIT 3-18
An HRIS Labour Relations Module

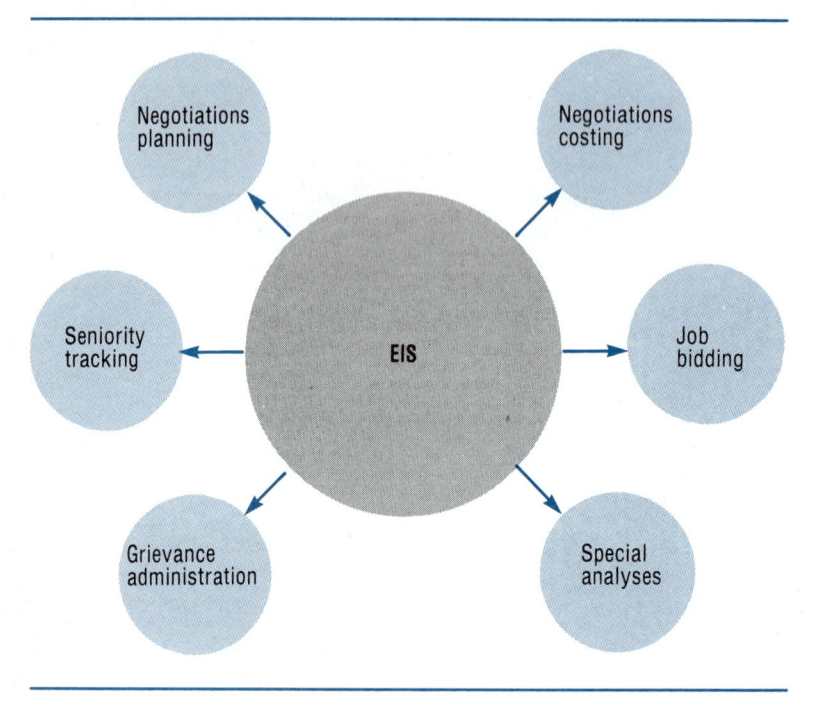

Central node: EIS

Connected nodes:
- Negotiations planning
- Negotiations costing
- Seniority tracking
- Job bidding
- Grievance administration
- Special analyses

Common Mistakes

Walker, after 15 years of building and installing computer-based HRIS, reported the "10 most common mistakes."[61] These mistakes are listed in Exhibit 3–21. Many seem self-evident but deserve comment. The first—being all things to all people, all at once—is a common error. Automated procedures can produce an almost infinite variety of complex reports and graphics and can be made to interface with financial, marketing, and other information systems.[62] Yet ensuring that the reports actually aid the user to manage more effectively is often overlooked. Walker's view is to keep the HRIS simple in design and output, and user-friendly.[63] He estimates it takes a minimum of two or three years to put an HRIS into operation from conception to installation. This may be a conservative estimate for more complex systems, since the TRW Employee Information System Project was begun in 1980 and by 1984 was just being piloted at a few sites.

**EXHIBIT 3–19
HRIS Input**

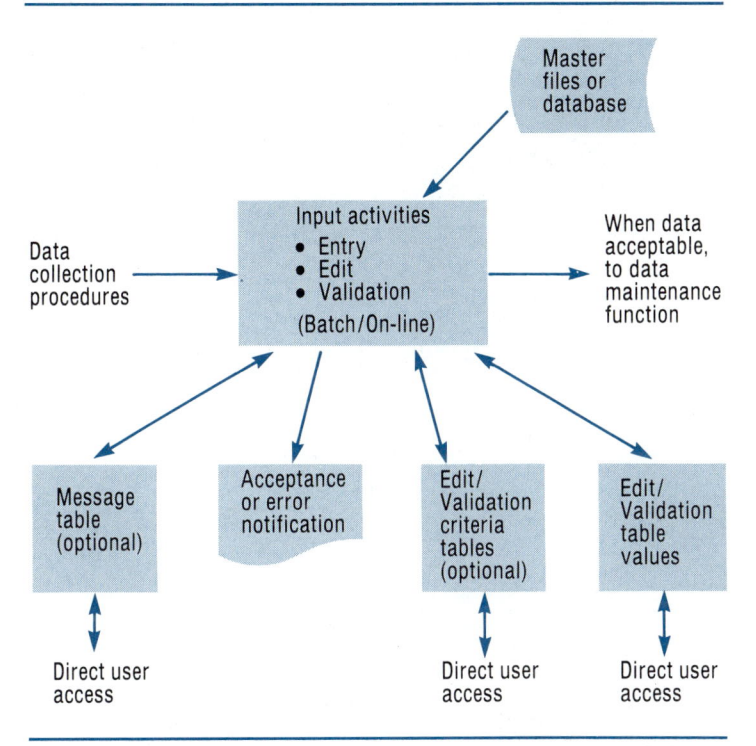

Source: Sidney H. Simon, "The HRIS: What Capabilities Must It Have?" *Personnel*, September–October 1983, pp. 36–49. Reprinted, by permission of the publisher, from "The HRIS: What Capabilities Must It Have?" by Sidney H. Simon, *Personnel*, September–October 1983, pp. 36–49 © 1983. Periodicals Division, American Management Associations, New York. All rights reserved.

The discussion to this point has assumed that an HRIS is a major undertaking. It is. However, microcomputers with software for P/HRM application are commercially available.[64] Software for specialized applications such as recruiting, employment equity analysis, job analysis, salary budgeting and planning, and succession planning are available.[65] So are generalized packages such as spread sheets and statistical programs. Even HRIS for microcomputers are available. They are designed for small- and moderate-size employers or plants.

**EXHIBIT 3-20
HRIS Data Maintenance**

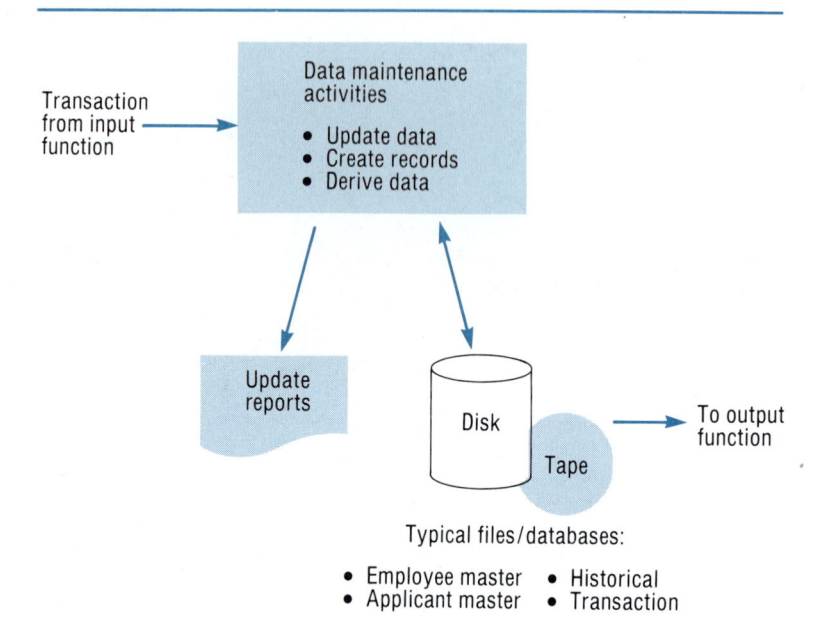

Transaction from input function → Data maintenance activities
- Update data
- Create records
- Derive data

→ Update reports

↕ Disk / Tape

→ To output function

Typical files/databases:
- Employee master
- Applicant master
- Historical
- Transaction

Source: Sidney H. Simon, "The HRIS: What Capabilities Must It Have?" *Personnel*, September–October 1983, pp. 36–49. Reprinted, by permission of the publisher, from "The HRIS: What Capabilities Must It Have?" by Sidney H. Simon, *Personnel*, September–October 1983, pp. 36–49 © 1983. Periodicals Division, American Management Associations, New York. All rights reserved.

**EXHIBIT 3-21
Ten Most Common Mistakes in Developing Computer-Based HRIS**

1. Being all things to all people, all at once.
2. No P/HRM expertise on the project team.
3. Separate systems for each P/HRM activity.
4. Too much complexity.
5. Insufficient operating management support.
6. No participation in design.
7. Technical marvels, but not "user-oriented."
8. Loose design project control.
9. Promising savings that don't occur.
10. Building, when you can buy.

Source: A. J. Walker, "The 10 Most Common Mistakes in Developing Computer-Based Personnel Systems," *Personnel Administrator*, July 1980, pp. 39–42.

STRATEGY, STRUCTURE, AND STAFF

Managers seem to be constantly reevaluating where to locate responsibility for the design and administration of P/HRM activities. The organizational arrangements chosen vary widely.

Centralized–Decentralized

An important issue related to structuring the function revolves around centralized–decentralized strategies. Decentralized refers to a management strategy of giving separate organization units the responsibility to design and administer their own P/HRM systems.[66] This contrasts with a centralized strategy that locates the design and administration responsibility in a single corporate unit. Some firms, such as IBM and Merck, have relatively large corporate staffs whose responsibility is to formulate human resource strategies and design the activities. Exhibit 3–22 shows a centralized human resource structure. Administration of human resource activities falls to those working in various units, often P/HRM generalists. Generalists handle all personnel activities, rather than specializing in any single one, such as compensation or recruiting.

Highly decentralized organizations, such as TRW, employ small corporate human resource staffs (professionals) whose primary responsibility is managing P/HRM systems for executive and corporate staff. These professionals operate in a purely advisory capacity to other organization units. The units in turn may employ their own human resource specialists (for example, compensation and staffing specialists) and generalists. A decentralized human resource structure is shown in Exhibit 3–23. Notice that each sector, Automotive World Wide (AWW), Electronics and Defence (E&D), and Industrial and Energy (I&E), has its own human resources staff plus generalists located in the subunits. The relationship of these sector staffs to corporate is advisory only (dotted line). The primary reporting (solid line) is to the sector line managers.

Another structural variation is to treat the corporate human resource function as internal consultants. As such, the human resource professionals must market and "sell" their products and services to the operating units. Certain activities, such as benefit plans and corporatewide profit sharing, remain under control of the corporate group. But the responsibility for other activities, such as recruiting, hiring, pay, and training are delegated to the units. The unit managers may decide to adopt corporate's services, design their own, or even use outside consultants.

Decentralizing certain aspects of human resource administration has considerable appeal. Pushing these responsibilities (and expenses) closer to the

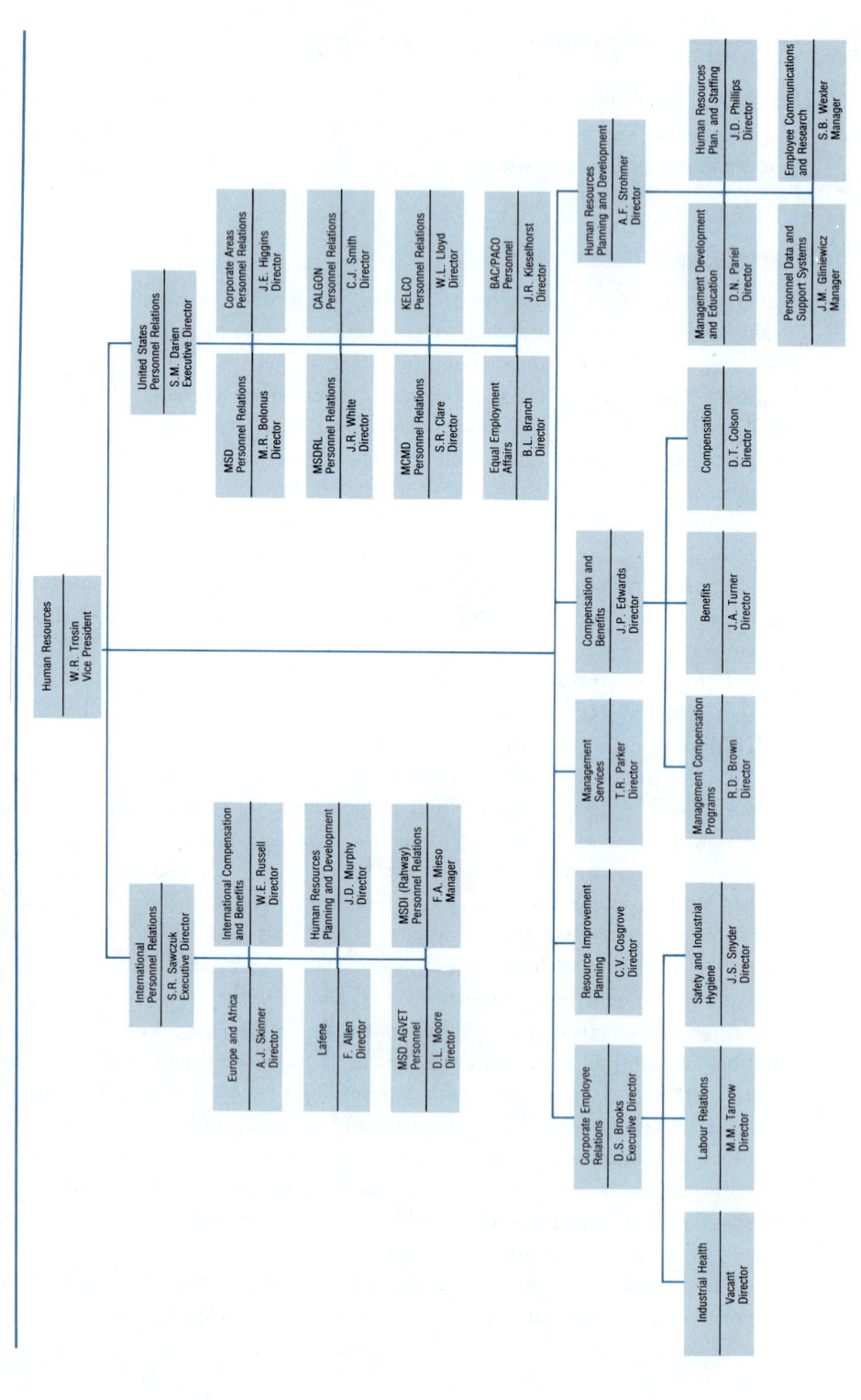

EXHIBIT 3–22 Merck's Centralized Human Resource Structure

- **Human Resources** — W. R. Trosin, Vice President
  - **International Personnel Relations** — S. R. Sawczuk, Executive Director
    - Europe and Africa — A. J. Skinner, Director
    - International Compensation and Benefits — W. E. Russell, Director
    - Lafene — F. Allen, Director
    - Human Resources Planning and Development — J. D. Murphy, Director
    - MSDI (Rahway) Personnel Relations — F. A. Mieso, Manager
    - MSD AGVET Personnel — D. L. Moore, Director
  - **United States Personnel Relations** — S. M. Darien, Executive Director
    - MSD Personnel Relations — M. R. Bolonus, Director
    - MSDRL Personnel Relations — J. R. White, Director
    - MCMD Personnel Relations — S. R. Clare, Director
    - Equal Employment Affairs — B. L. Branch, Director
    - Corporate Areas Personnel Relations — J. E. Higgins, Director
    - CALGON Personnel Relations — C. J. Smith, Director
    - KELCO Personnel Relations — W. L. Lloyd, Director
    - BAC/PACO Personnel — J. R. Kieselhorst
  - **Corporate Employee Relations** — D. S. Brooks, Executive Director
    - Resource Improvement Planning — C. V. Cosgrove, Director
    - Management Services — T. R. Parker, Director
    - Compensation and Benefits — J. P. Edwards, Director
      - Management Compensation Programs — R. D. Brown, Director
      - Benefits — J. A. Turner, Director
      - Compensation — D. T. Colson, Director
    - Labour Relations — M. M. Tarnow, Director
    - Safety and Industrial Hygiene — J. S. Snyder, Director
    - Industrial Health — Vacant, Director
  - **Human Resources Planning and Development** — A. F. Strohmer, Director
    - Management Development and Education — D. N. Pariel, Director
    - Personnel Data and Support Systems — J. M. Gliniewicz, Manager
    - Human Resources Plan. and Staffing — J. D. Phillips, Director
    - Employee Communications and Research — S. B. Wexler, Manager

EXHIBIT 3–23
TRW's Decentralized Human Resource Structure

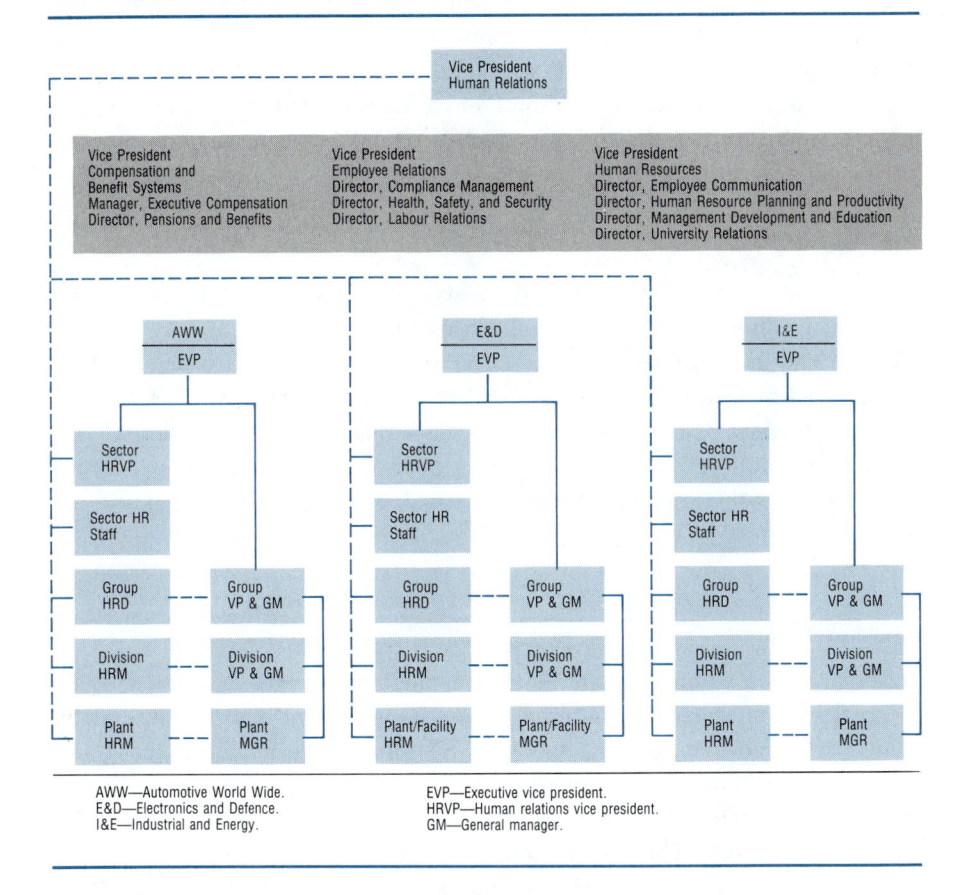

```
                              Vice President
                              Human Relations

Vice President              Vice President              Vice President
Compensation and            Employee Relations          Human Resources
Benefit Systems             Director, Compliance Management   Director, Employee Communication
Manager, Executive Compensation   Director, Health, Safety, and Security   Director, Human Resource Planning and Productivity
Director, Pensions and Benefits   Director, Labour Relations   Director, Management Development and Education
                                                         Director, University Relations
```

AWW	E&D	I&E
EVP	EVP	EVP

Under each:
- Sector HRVP
- Sector HR Staff
- Group HRD — Group VP & GM
- Division HRM — Division VP & GM
- Plant HRM — Plant MGR

(For E&D: Plant/Facility HRM — Plant/Facility MGR)

AWW—Automotive World Wide.
E&D—Electronics and Defence.
I&E—Industrial and Energy.
EVP—Executive vice president.
HRVP—Human relations vice president.
GM—General manager.

siderable appeal. Pushing these responsibilities (and expenses) closer to the units and managers affected by them may help ensure that decisions are related to organizational objectives. However, decentralization is not without dilemmas. Achieving consistent employee treatment across units can be difficult. As can designing human resource activities that support a unit's objectives but run counter to the overall corporate objectives.

The answer to these and related problems of decentralization can be found in developing corporatewide principles or guidelines that all must meet. For example, a decentralized employer would permit different P/HRM activities to be adopted by the units as long as the plans could be shown to be (1) job-related, (2) business-related, (3) acceptable to managers and employees, (4) cost-effective, and (5) able to withstand legal challenge.

Congruency

The human resource system is one of many management systems used in the organization. Consequently, P/HRM must be congruent with these other systems.[67] For example, it may be appealing, on paper at least, to decentralize some of the P/HRM functions. However, if financial data and other management systems are not also decentralized, the P/HRM system will not fit, and may even work at cross-purposes to other systems.

Staffing

A final issue related to structuring the responsibility for human resource management involves the skills and abilities required in human resource professionals. The grandest strategy and structure may seem well designed, well thought out in the abstract, but it could be a disaster if the staff lacks people qualified to carry it out. Experience suggests these skills include knowledge of the operation of the business, ability to use various techniques and approaches, plus the interpersonal skills to work with top management and operating managers (see Chapter One).

SUMMARY

An organization's human resource management is strongly influenced by its internal environment. The internal environment, in turn, is influenced by human resource management decisions. The diagnostic model groups these internal factors into three categories: the nature of the organization, the nature of the current work force employed, and the nature of the work to be performed. Chapter Three examined what it is about the nature of the organization that influences human resource activities. Strategic and operational directions, financial condition, technology, culture, and organization structure are identified as key features of organizations that influence human resource management.

These key features of the organization are integrated into human resource management through human resource planning. Planning provides the link between the organizational environment, the external environment, and human resource activities.

Human resource planning involves four questions: What are our human resource goals? What is our current human resource position? What is the best strategy to reach our desired goals? and Did we accomplish our objectives? Approaches to answering these four questions are addressed.

Also discussed are the design, information requirements, and major functional components of human resource information systems; common mistakes in these are pointed out.

The last section of the chapter considered alternatives for locating responsibility for human resource management inside the organization. Whatever arrangement is most logical for an organization, it must be guided by corporatewide principles, and it must fit with other management systems in the organization.

APPENDIX / System Description: Merck and Company, Inc.

The Personnel Management Information System (PMIS) is a computerized information system containing selected data extracted from the record jackets of the company's domestic employees. The system is under the direct control of the Human Resources Area with the data being processed by Merck computers. A special unit, Personnel Data Services, manages the entire process, and extensive security precautions are used to ensure complete confidentiality of all data.

What Is PMIS Used For?

PMIS is used for a wide variety of personnel-related activities. Common examples include salary planning, employee placement, and appraisal scheduling. PMIS simplifies certain administrative tasks, such as preparing mailing lists and repetitive reports that require only routine maintenance each month. And PMIS enables the company to quickly supply reports required by the government about the Merck work force without resorting to extra clerical support. In fact, PMIS is an essential management tool in a company with more than 30,000 employees.

What Types of Information Are Maintained by PMIS?

PMIS contains an "electronic record" on almost all domestic employees at Merck. Each record includes five major categories of data:

- *Personal data*—Personal facts such as name, address, social insurance number, and birth date are stored in this section.
- *Merck data*—Facts concerning an employee as they pertain to his or her employment at Merck are stored. These include date of hire, retirement date, organization, benefit plan data, and so forth.
- *Employment history data*—An employee's work history is stored in the computer, showing every action affecting pay, grade, location, and the like.
- *Educational data*—Facts concerning an employee's educational accomplishments are stored, to include the highest education level achieved and college/university degrees earned.

- *Evaluation data*—This information is maintained only on salaried employees and includes ratings taken from the employee's latest performance evaluation.

How Is Information Entered into PMIS?

Generally, data enter the system through the use of forms. As shown in the illustration, a supervisor starts the system by sending personnel forms to the Human Resources Area that services his or her department. These forms are reviewed, approved, and sent to Personnel Data Services and Payroll, if necessary. The data contained on the forms are then entered into PMIS at the Merck Computer Operations Centre. New forms containing the current status of employees are then returned to the supervisors through Personnel Data Services and the Human Resources Area.

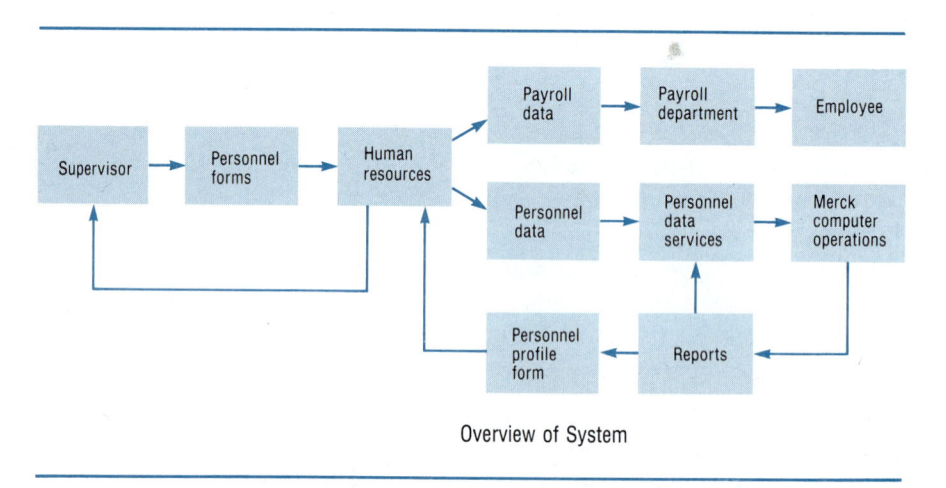

Overview of System

The same procedure is used to request a report from PMIS. The request is made to Personnel Data Services through the Human Resources Area and a PMIS report is printed. The report is returned to the requestor through the Human Resources Area. This procedure is one of the many ways that we ensure information is given only to authorized employees.

While Human Resources uses many forms to enter information into PMIS, the principal working documents of PMIS are the Personnel Profile and the Employment Requisition.

The computer-printed Personnel Profile form shows information about a particular employee. Managers use this form to report to Human Resources that changes to an employee's status have been initiated or to report corrections to an employee's record. When the information is entered into PMIS, the computer prints a Personnel Profile form that shows the new or changed data. This form is returned to the originating manager and serves as confirmation that the data has been entered properly.

The Employment Requisition is submitted to Human Resources whenever a manager seeks assistance in filling a position vacancy. Where appropriate and where requested, the computer is used to match position requirements on the Employment Requisition form with the data on employee's records. A report listing all employees with matched qualifications is forwarded to the employment manager to assist in filling the vacancy.

DISCUSSION AND REVIEW QUESTIONS

1. Define human resource planning.
2. Why is human resource planning considered a pivotal function in the diagnostic approach to human resource management?
3. Discuss the differences between operational and strategic objectives.
4. How does an organization's financial state influence P/HRM activities?
5. What are the four major phases in the human resource planning process?
6. What factors should be considered in setting human resource objectives?
7. What is the most critical phase of human resource planning? Discuss the state of the art of this function.
8. What is the present state of human resource planning in industry?
9. Discuss the skills, abilities, and experiences that you believe are required for a P/HRM professional. Does it make any difference if the firm is centralized or decentralized or if the job is specialized or for a generalist?
10. Based on Walker's 10 most common mistakes in developing an HRIS, how would you begin to design an HRIS?
11. How might environmental and organizational conditions affect the type of HRIS you would design?

NOTES AND REFERENCES

1. TRW Human Relations Strategic Corporate Plan (Cleveland: TRW Corporate Human Resources Department, 1983).
2. See, for example, Lee Dyer, "Bringing Human Resources into the Strategy Formulation Process." Reprinted in *Perspectives on Personnel/Human Resource Management*, 3rd ed., ed. Herbert H. Heneman III and Donald P. Schwab (Homewood, Ill.: Richard D. Irwin, 1986); Thomas A. Mahoney, "Emerging Strategic Issues of Human Resource Management," *ASAC Proceedings* (Personnel and Human Resources: Special Interest Group, Toronto, Ontario, June 1–3, 1987), pp. 67–75; Alain Gosselin, "Strategic HRM and Top Managers' Capabilities for Strategic Planning: A Review and a Suggested Framework," *ASAC Proceedings* (Per-

sonnel and Human Resources: Special Interest Group, Toronto, Ontario, June 1–3, 1987), pp. 20–36; Sylvie St.-Onge, "La strategie organisationelle et l'importance accordee à la gestion des ressources humaines," *ASAC Proceedings* (Personnel and Human Resources; Special Interest Group, Toronto, Ontario, June 1–3, 1987), pp. 98–108.
3. Michael E. Porter, *Competitive Strategy: Techniques for Analyzing Industries and Competitors* (New York: Free Press, 1980); Joseph N. Fry and J. Peter Killing, *Strategic Analysis and Action* (Scarborough, Ont.: Prentice-Hall Canada, 1986).
4. Porter, *Competitive Strategy*.
5. Lee Dyer, "Bringing Human Resources into the Strategy Formulation Process."
6. Ibid. The strategy formulation process and categories of environmental factors shown in Exhibit 3–1 serve the purpose of this chapter. Other models are basically similar in approach, using somewhat different terminology and detail. Useful sources are: Fry and Killing, *Strategic Analysis and Action* (especially their Diamond-E framework, p. 27); Michael E. Porter, *Competitive Strategy*; Michael E. Porter, *Competitive Advantage: Creating and Sustaining Superior Performance* (New York: Free Press, 1985); John A. Pearce II and Richard B. Robinson, Jr., *Formulation and Implementation of Competitive Strategy*, 2nd ed. (Homewood, Ill.: Richard D. Irwin, 1985); a variety of forecasting methods are presented in S. C. Wheelwright and S. Makridakis, *Forecasting Methods in Management*, 4th ed. (New York: John Wiley & Sons, 1985); for an extensive list of environmental components and classification of environments, see Robert Duncan, "What Is the Right Organization Structure?" Reprinted in *The Dynamics of Organization Theory*, 2nd ed., ed. John F. Veiga and John N. Yanouzas (New York: West Publishing Co., 1984).
7. Porter, *Competitive Strategy*.
8. Harold A. Gram, *The Canadian Manager: An Introduction to Management* (Toronto: Holt, Rinehart & Winston of Canada, 1986).
9. David Climie, "Breweries Gain Favor," *Financial Times*, May 26, 1986, p. 23.
10. Brian Brinks, "Fleet Aerospace Chases the U.S. Market," *Financial Times*, May 26, 1986, p. 14.
11. TRW Human Resources Strategic Plan (Cleveland: TRW Corporate Human Relations, 1983).
12. James W. Walker, *Human Resource Planning* (New York: McGraw-Hill, 1980).
13. Thomas A. Kochan, Robert B. McKersie, and Peter Cappelli, "Strategic Choice and Industrial Relations Theory," *Industrial Relations* 23, no. 1 (1984), pp. 16–40.
14. Walker, *Human Resource Planning*.
15. Porter, *Competitive Advantage*.
16. Fry and Killing, *Strategic Analysis and Action*; Rudi K. Bresser and Ronald C. Bishop, "Dysfunctional Effects of Formal Planning: Two Theoretical Explanations," *Academy of Management Review* 8, no. 4 (1983), pp. 588–99; R. L. Ackoff, *A Concept of Corporate Planning* (New York: John Wiley & Sons, 1970); Carl R. Anderson and Carl P. Zeithaml, "Stage of the Product Life Cycle, Business Strategy, and Business Performance," *Academy of Management Journal* 27, no. 1 (1984), pp. 5–25; Dyer, "Bringing Human Resources into the Strategy Formulation Process."
17. Fry and Killing, *Strategic Analysis and Action*.

18. Robert A. Burgelman, "Corporate Entrepreneurship and Strategic Management: Insights from a Process Study," *Management Science*, December 1983, pp. 1349–59; P. F. Drucker, *Management: Tasks, Responsibilities, Practices* (New York: Harper & Row, 1973).
19. Raymond E. Miles and Charles C. Snow, *Organizational Strategy, Structure and Processes* (New York: McGraw-Hill, 1978).
20. Charles C. Snow and Raymond E. Miles, "Organizational Strategy, Design and Human Resources Management" (working paper presented at Academy of Management meetings, Dallas, Texas, 1983).
21. Ibid., p. 4.
22. George Milkovich, "Human Resource Strategy and Evaluation: Introduction" *Industrial Relations* 23, no. 2 (1984), pp. 151–55; Lee Dyer, "Studying Human Resource Strategy: An Approach and an Agenda," *Industrial Relations* 23, no. 2 (1984), pp. 156–69; John W. Boudreau, "Decision Theory Contributions to HRM Research and Practice," *Industrial Relations* 23, no. 2 (1984), pp. 198–217.
23. Dyer, "Bringing Human Resources into the Strategy Formulation Process."
24. John H. Jackson, Cyril P. Morgan, and Joseph G. P. Paolillo, *Organization Theory: A Macro Perspective for Management*, 3rd ed. (Englewood Cliffs, N.J.: Prentice Hall, 1986), chap. 8; although there is some disagreement and conceptual confusion on the definition of technology, the overall conclusion of their recent review proposes limiting the definition to the transformation process of converting inputs into outputs (even though some have suggested including the input and output phases).
25. Vijay Sathe, *Culture and Related Corporate Realities* (Homewood, Ill.: Richard D. Irwin, 1985); Peter J. Frost, Larry F. Moore, Meryl Reis Louis, Craig C. Lundberg, and Joanne Martin, eds., *Organizational Culture* (Beverly Hills, Calif.: Sage Publications, 1985); J. Fierman, "The Corporate Culture Vultures," *Fortune*, October 17, 1983, pp. 66–73; Stanley M. Davis, "Corporate Culture and Human Resource Management: Two Keys to Implement Strategy," *Human Resource Planning* 6, no. 3 (1983), pp. 159–69; Ralph H. Kilman, Mary J. Saxton, Roy Serpa, and Associates, *Gaining Control of the Corporate Culture* (San Francisco: Jossey-Bass, 1986); Christian Scholz, "Corporate Culture and Strategy—The Problem of Strategic Fit," *Long Range Planning* 20, no. 4 (1987), pp. 78–87.
26. This definition draws on the following: Andrew M. Pettigrew, "On Studying Organizational Cultures," *Administrative Science Quarterly*, December 1979; Edgar H. Schein, "Corporate Culture: What It Is and How to Change It," excerpts from an invited address delivered to the 1983 Convocation of the Society of Sloan Fellows, MIT, October 14, 1983; Sathe, *Culture and Related Corporate Realities*, in which he points out the difference between his and Schein's use of assumptions, values and beliefs (pp. 539–40).
27. Schein, "Corporate Culture"; Sathe, *Culture and Related Corporate Realities*.
28. Schein, "Corporate Culture."
29. Ibid.
30. Jay B. Barney, "Organization Culture: Can It Be a Source of Sustained Competitive Advantage?" *Academy of Management Review* 11, no. 3 (1986), pp. 656–65.
31. Howard Schwartz and Stanley M. Davis, "Matching Corporate Culture and Business Strategy," *Organizational Dynamics*, Summer 1981, pp. 36–48.
32. See, for example, Human Performance Systems Inc., "The Corporate Culture Fitness System," as displayed at the 1986 Annual Conference of the Administra-

tive Sciences Association of Canada, Whistler, B.C., June 1–3, 1986; Richard Pascale, "The Paradox of 'Corporate Culture'; Reconciling Ourselves to Socialization," *California Management Review*, Winter 1985, pp. 26–41; Frost et al., *Organizational Culture*.
33. Sathe, *Culture and Related Corporate Realities*.
34. Thomas J. Peters and Robert H. Waterman, Jr., *In Search of Excellence* (New York: Harper & Row, 1983).
35. Robert H. Waterman, Jr., *The Renewal Factor: How the Best Get and Keep the Competitive Edge* (New York: Bantam Books, 1987).
36. Sathe, *Culture and Related Corporate Realities*.
37. Eva Innes, Robert L. Perry, and Jim Lyon, *The Financial Post Selects the 100 Best Companies to Work for in Canada* (Don Mills, Ont.: Collins, 1986).
38. James Sweet, "How Manpower Development Can Support Your Strategic Plan," *Journal of Business Strategy*, Summer 1981, pp. 77–87; Richard B. Higgins, "How Well Are We Rewarding Our Managers for Strategic Planning?" *Journal of Business Strategy*, Winter 1981, pp. 77–83; Eddie C. Smith, "Strategic Business Planning and Human Resources: Parts I and II," *Personnel Journal*, August–September 1982, pp. 680–91.
39. "Personnel Planning at IBM: The Integration of Resource and Business Planning" (Armonk, N.Y.: Corporate Personnel Department, 1983); J. Rush and L. Borne, *Human Resource Planning at Ontario Hydro: A Field Study* (London, Ont.: University of Western Ontario, 1983); D. Parker, J. Fossum, J. Blakslee, and A. Rucci, "Human Resource Planning at American Hospital Supply: A Field Study" (working paper, Ann Arbor, Mich., 1983); C. Fombrun, "Conversation with Reginald Jones and Frank Doyle," *Organizational Dynamics*, Winter 1982, pp. 42–63; David B. Jamison, "The Imperative of an Integrative Approach to Strategic Management Research," *Academy of Management Review* 6, no. 4 (1981), pp. 601–9; Carrie Dulan, "Apple's New Macintosh Computer Is Seen as Critical to Firm's Future," *The Wall Street Journal*, December 8, 1983, p. 33; Lee Dyer and Nelson O. Heyer, "Human Resources Planning at IBM: A Field Study" (working paper, ILR School, Ithaca, N.Y.: Cornell University, 1984); George Milkovich and Douglas Phillips, "Human Resources Planning at Merck: A Field Study" (working paper, ILR School, Ithaca, N.Y.: Cornell University, 1984); Lloyd Baird, Ilain Meshoulan, and Ghislaine Degiue, "Meshing Human Resource Planning with Strategic Business Planning: A Model Approach," *Personnel*, September–October 1983, pp. 14–24; Julia Reid Galosy, "Meshing Human Resource Planning with Strategic Business Planning: One Company's Experience," *Personnel*, September–October 1983, pp. 26–34.
40. Eric Vetter, *Manpower Planning for High Talent Personnel* (Ann Arbor: University of Michigan Press, 1967), p. 15; Lee Dyer, "Human Resource Planning," in *The Management of Personnel/Human Resources: New Perspectives*, ed. K. Rowland and G. Ferris (Boston: Allyn & Bacon, 1982); James A. Craft, "A Critical Perspective on Human Resource Planning," *Human Resource Planning* 3, no. 2 (1980), pp. 39–52; George T. Milkovich and Thomas A. Mahoney, "Human Resource Planning and PAIR Policy," in *ASPA Handbook of Personnel and Industrial Relations*, ed. D. Yoder and H. G. Heneman, Jr. (Washington, D.C.: Bureau of National Affairs, 1979); Milkovich and Mahoney, "Human Resource Planning Models: A Perspective," *Human Resource Planning*, Spring 1978; E. H. Burack and N. J. Mathys, *Human Resource Planning: A Pragmatic Approach to*

Manpower Staffing and Development (Lake Forest, Ill.: Brace-Park, 1979); James Walker, *Human Resource Planning* (New York: McGraw-Hill, 1980); Towers, Perrin, Forster, and Crosby, "Corporate Manpower Planning: A Study of Manpower Planning Practices in 220 Major U.S. Business Organizations," in *Policy Issues in Contemporary Personnel and Industrial Relations*, ed. M. G. Miner and J. B. Miner (New York: Macmillan, 1977).

41. George Milkovich, Lee Dyer, and Thomas Mahoney, "HR Planning," in *Human Resources Management in the 1980's*, ed. S. J. Carroll and R. S. Schuler (Washington, D.C.: Bureau of National Affairs, 1983), pp. 2–28.
42. Innes, Perry, and Lyon, *The 100 Best Companies to Work for in Canada*.
43. Lee Dyer, "Bringing Human Resources into the Strategy Formulation Process," *Human Resource Management*, Fall 1984, pp. 10–21.
44. Peter Doeringer, M. J. Piorie, and J. G. Scoville, *Corporate Manpower Planning* (New York: The Conference Board, August 1968), pp. 3, 8.
45. Center for Research in Career Development, "Client Questionnaire: Study of Employee Relations at Exxon Research and Engineering Co." (New York: working paper, Columbia Graduate School of Management, 1982).
46. J. P. Campbell and R. D. Pritchard, "Motivation Theory in Industrial and Organization Psychology" in *Handbook of Industrial and Organizational Psychology*, ed. M. D. Dunnette (Chicago: Rand McNally, 1976).
47. L. Cheeks, "Cost Effectiveness Comes to the Personnel Function," *Harvard Business Review* 51, no. 3, (1973), pp. 96–105; Wayne F. Cascio, *Costing Human Resources: The Financial Impact of Behavior in Organizations* (Boston: Kent Publishing, 1982).
48. David E. Dimick and Victor V. Murray, "Correlates of Substantive Policy Decisions on Organizations: The Case of Human Resource Management," *Academy of Management Journal*, December 1978, pp. 661–73.
49. M. D. Dunnette, ed., *Handbook of Industrial and Organizational Psychology* (Chicago: Rand McNally, 1976); *Annual Review of Sociology* (Palo Alto: Annual Reviews Inc., 1980 on); F. R. Marshall, V. M. Briggs, Jr., and A. G. King, *Labor Economics* (Homewood, Ill.: Richard D. Irwin, 1984).
50. Anne Tsui, "A Tripartite Approach to Research on Personnel/Human Resource Department Effectiveness," *Industrial Relations*, Spring 1984, pp. 184–97.
51. A. J. Walker, *HRIS Development* (New York: Van Nostrand Reinhold, 1982); Albert C. Hyde and Jay M. Shafritz, "HRIS: Introduction to Tomorrow's System for Managing Human Resources," *Public Personnel Management*, March 1977, pp. 70–77; G. A. Bassett, "PAIR Records and Information Systems," in *Planning and Auditing PAIR*, ed. D. Yoder and H. G. Heneman, Jr. (Washington, D.C.: Bureau of National Affairs, 1976); R. Frantzreb, "Confessions of a Manpower Modeler," in *Manpower Planning for Canadians*, 2nd ed., ed. L. F. Moore and L. Charach (Vancouver: Institute of Industrial Relations, University of British Columbia, 1979); Dyer, *Human Resource Planning*.
52. A. R. Janger, *Personnel Administration: Changing Scope and Organization*, Conference Board Report No. 203 (New York: The Conference Board, 1966); A. R. Janger, *The Personnel Function: Changing Objectives and Organization*, Conference Board Report No. 712 (New York: The Conference Board, 1977); Elmer H. Burack and Thomas G. Gutteridge, "Institutional Manpower Planning: Rhetoric versus Reality," *California Management Review*, Spring 1978, pp. 13–21; Harvey Kahalas, Harold Pazer, J. S. Hoegh, and Amy Levitt, "Human Resource Planning

Activities in U.S. Firms," *Human Resource Planning* 3, no. 2 (1980); TPF & C, *Corporate Manpower Planning*; Charles R. Greer and Daniel Armstrong, "Human Resource Forecasting and Planning: A State-of-the-Art Investigation," *Human Resource Planning* 3, no. 2 (1980), pp. 67–78; Kendrith M. Rowland and Scott L. Summers, "Human Resources Planning: A Second Look," *Personnel Administrator*, December 1981, pp. 73–81.
53. Human Resources Planning Society, P.O. Box 2553, Grand Central Station, New York, NY 10017.
54. Milkovich and Phillips, "HRP at Merck," 1984.
55. Ibid., p. 10.
56. This definition is adapted from A. J. Walker, *HRIS Development* (New York: Van Nostrand Reinhold, 1982).
57. TRW Employee Information System Task Force Report 1983; see also Stephen C. Ward, "How to Computerize Your Personnel Planning," *Long Range Planning* 20, no. 4 (1987), pp. 88–101.
58. Walker, *HRIS Development*; also see Lyman Seamans, Jr., "Establishing the Human Resource System Data Base," *Personnel Administrator*, November 1977, pp. 44–49; V. Ceriello, "A Guide for Building a Human Resource Data System," *Personnel Journal*, September 1978, pp. 496–503; Mary Jo Lavin, "HRDIS: A Computerized Human Resource Development Information System," *Human Resource Planning* 14, no. 1 (1981), pp. 25–35; William B. Miller, "Building an Effective Information Systems Function," *MIS Quarterly*, June 1980, pp. 21–30.
59. Sidney H. Simon, "The HRIS: What Capabilities Must It Have?" *Personnel*, September–October 1983, pp. 36–49.
60. Ibid.
61. A. J. Walker, "The 10 Most Common Mistakes in Developing Computer-Based Personnel Systems," *Personnel Administrator*, July 1980, pp. 39–42.
62. Ibid.
63. Ibid.
64. Corporate Education Resources, Inc., *Executrak: Microcomputer Succession Planning System* (Fairfield, Iowa, 1984); Integral Systems, Inc., *Human Resource System* (Walnut Creek, Calif.); *Decision Support Services and Tools for Human Resource Management* (Los Altos, Calif., SCOPOS 1983); *IBM System/370 Interactive Personnel System: General Information Manual* (White Plains, N.Y.: IBM Corporation, Data Processing Division).
65. Ibid.
66. Jay R. Galbraith, *Designing Complex Organizations* (Reading, Mass: Addison-Wesley Publishing, 1973).
67. John H. Grant and William R. King, "Strategic Formulation: Analytical and Normative Model," in *Strategic Management*, ed. Dan E. Schendel and Charles W. Hofer (Boston: Little, Brown, 1979), pp. 104–22.

CHAPTER FOUR
NATURE OF THE WORK

CHAPTER OUTLINE

I. The Nature of Work and the Diagnostic Model
II. Defining Work
    A. Qualifications Required
    B. Rewards and Returns
III. Job Design
    A. Overview
    B. Scientific Management
    C. Human Relations
    D. Current Approaches
    E. Job Characteristics Model
    F. Employee Focus of Attention
    G. Tailoring Jobs to Organization and Environmental Conditions
    H. Hours of Work and Work Schedules
IV. Job Analysis
    A. Why Analyze Jobs?
    B. What Data to Collect
    C. Manager/Employee Acceptance
    D. How to Collect Data
    E. Conventional Job Analysis
    F. Quantitative Job Analysis
    G. Usefulness of Methods
    H. Sources of Error in Job Analysis
    I. Job Descriptions and Specifications

V. Canadian Job-Occupational Identification
VI. Summary
   Appendix A / Procedures for Gathering Job Information
   Appendix B / Sample Job Descriptions

> I put on my hard hat, change into my safety shoes, put on my safety glasses, go to the bonderizer. They rake the metal, they wash it, they dip it in a paint solution, and we take it off. My arms get tired about the first half hour. After that, they don't get tired any more until maybe the last half hour at the end of the day.
>
> Interview with steelworker, *Working*, by Studs Terkel[1]

> Everything that happens in the market I see instantaneously. I have a machine in front of me that records and memorizes every transaction that takes place in the entire day. I watch the shares pass the tape. I look at every symbol, every transaction. I would go out of my mind, but my eye has been conditioned to screen maybe 200 stocks and ignore the others. I really put in an enormously exhausting day.
>
> Interview with stockbroker, *Working*, by Studs Terkel[2]

Work is a coat of many colours. It comes in different shapes and sizes, with different tasks to be performed, different qualifications required to perform it, and different pay offered to those who perform it. This variety is what makes work so difficult to define. A common definition is "purposeful effort." But some wag responds, "If work is purposeful effort, what is golf?"[3]

This chapter examines the nature of work and diagnoses its role in the management of human resources. Work is both designed and analyzed by P/HRM professionals. This chapter discusses alternative approaches to job design and job analysis.

THE NATURE OF WORK AND THE DIAGNOSTIC MODEL

Work is a critical concept in the diagnostic model. The skills and experience required to perform work influence the kind of education and training people seek. Work influences the pay employees receive, and thus their economic well-being. Many people find status and personal fulfillment in their work. So work is important to individuals, to society, and to organizations.

The work to be performed is based on the technology employed and the goods and services to be produced by organizations. Stelco, for example, sells specialty steel. To produce it requires raw steel made from iron ore. Stelco has many options. It can buy partially finished steel and finish it to customers' specifications, or it can buy iron ore to smelt in its own blast furnace. Many factors go into Stelco's decision on what business strategy to pursue. The decision it makes determines the nature of the work done at its facilities. All organizations face similar issues. The strategies and objectives managers decide on affect the work to be performed.

The nature of work affects human resource management activities. For example, pay is largely based on the job a person performs. Staffing and training activities help ensure that employees' skills and abilities match the job requirements. Human resource activities also affect the nature of work. Work is designed into jobs, and jobs can be redesigned to match the skills employees possess. A proper match helps achieve both organization and employee effectiveness.[4] So P/HRM activities both affect and are affected by the nature of the work.

DEFINING WORK

Definition
The nature of work includes (1) the content—duties, tasks, behaviours, functions, responsibilities; (2) the qualifications required to perform it—skills, abilities, experiences; and (3) returns and rewards for performing it—pay, promotions, intrinsic satisfaction.

Qualifications Required

Information about the skills and abilities, the personality makeup, and the experience and knowledge required to perform the work is important for human resource decision makers. Data about these qualifications are necessary to perform recruiting, selection, compensation, and training activities. Data on work-related qualifications also help ensure proper consideration of employment equity.

The steelworker and the stockbroker quoted at the beginning of this chapter had to develop different skills and qualifications for their work. Details of the precise qualifications required for different jobs are necessary to match individuals and the work.

Rewards and Returns

The rewards and returns from work are often categorized as extrinsic or intrinsic.[5] Extrinsic rewards are those that are external to the individual and are relatively concrete. Examples include pay, benefits, promotions, praise, pleasant working conditions, and so on. Intrinsic rewards are more conceptual—less observable to others—and to some extent less controlled by others.[6] Examples include feelings of accomplishment, freedom, or autonomy in the work. The rewards and returns designed into jobs are important. Since employee and organization effectiveness are influenced by the match between an individual's needs and goals and the rewards available in the job to satisfy those needs, jobs must be designed to include intrinsic reward systems.

Caution must be exercised in designing reward systems, however, because people do not agree on what is intrinsically and extrinsically rewarding. O'Reilly comments, "One's frame of reference, as represented by factors such as past experiences, present roles, expectations, may result in different perceptions and definitions of the same work."[7] For example, workers who have been on the job awhile may change the job; they may adopt short cuts and new routines. People with different educations, backgrounds, aspirations, or reference groups may also see the content, qualifications, and rewards of work differently.[8] Clearly, designing work and matching individuals' motivation and ability with it is complex.

JOB DESIGN

> **Definition**
> *Job design* integrates work content (tasks, functions, relationships), the rewards (extrinsic and intrinsic), and the qualifications required (skills, knowledge, abilities) for each job.

Both theory and research indicate job design affects employee and organization effectiveness.[9] Based on an extensive and still-growing theoretical base, job design has had considerable research attention in recent years and is being widely applied to the actual practice of management.

Overview

Job design activities have a long history. The technological advances of the 18th and 19th centuries gave rise to the factory system of work production. This in turn caused reconsideration of the nature of work and how jobs were designed. Formal concerns with job design started with the scientific management movement at the turn of the century. This approach evolved into what is today generally called "job engineering." The human relations movement emerged in the 1920s and flowered for a number of years. Starting in the 1950s, some practicing managers, such as Thomas Watson, founder of IBM, became concerned about the impact of job engineering approaches and began implementing job enlargement and job rotation programs. In the late 1960s, concern about employee dissatisfaction and declining productivity increased. A new look at job design seemed necessary.

The reported successes of job enlargement efforts, plus the increasingly popular motivation theories of Maslow and Herzberg, led to the job enrichment movement in job design. Today, with quality of work life (QWL) becoming a major societal issue in this country, job design takes a broader perspective. Job enrichment seems to have shifted its focus to job characteristics; goal setting has begun to be linked to the design of jobs; and QWL often utilizes the sociotechnical approach. The latter deals with more than just job design; it aims to incorporate job design into the entire operating system of the organization (see Chapter Twelve).

Scientific Management

First outlined by Frederick W. Taylor in 1911, "scientific management" emphasized the production process of work. His writings have been the basis for many jobs and organizations since.[10] Other pioneers of that era were Frank Gilbreth, Henry L. Gantt, and Harrington Emerson.

Taylor's earliest experiences at the Midvale Iron Company in Pennsylvania influenced his understanding of the work process and the goals of job design. He studied the technical aspects of the production process, the individual, and the groups employees form. He then calculated standards and specific methods based on the systematic organization of this information.

The goal was to develop universal principles to guide management and the control of work. Taylor's method for designing jobs emphasized:

- Narrow range of tasks in a job.
- Very specific job descriptions.
- Systematic routing and scheduling of work.
- Close supervision.

The core of the approach was the reduction of each job to its most essential elements (job simplification) to be performed under close supervision. However, Taylor was more farsighted and humane than imitators who applied his ideas by rote. For example, he believed in retraining rather than firing workers his reforms made redundant, and felt managers needed improvement just as much as workers.[11]

The Taylor (and Gilbreth) tradition reached Canada through Charles Bedaux, a French-born American efficiency expert.[12] In 1927, Ralph Presgrave, then a young foreman at York Knitting Mills in Toronto, heard about Bedaux's success in increasing productivity through time study and wage incentives.

Bedaux's experts were engaged by York Knitting to organize a wage incentive system. After two years, Presgrave knew the system as well as the consultants did, and the Bedaux people were sent home. The method was known in Canada as "the York Plan," and Presgrave and two colleagues decided to enter the consulting business themselves. J. Douglas Woods, president of York Knitting, liked the idea and wanted a part of it. They incorporated J.D. Woods & Co., were successful, and began expanding into other aspects of the companies they were visiting (e.g., inventory control, merchandising, sales). This appeared to be the period when time study began turning into management consulting. The partners joined their expertise with that of an accounting firm (Clarkson, Gordon, Dilworth & Nash) to form J.D. Woods Co. Ltd., which eventually became Toronto-based Woods Gordon. In terms of staff, Woods Gordon is Canada's biggest management consulting firm.

Taylor's scientific management principles were an early systematic effort at job design. But for some workers, simplified jobs led to dissatisfaction, alienation, and frustration.[13] The human relations movement highlighted these problems and called for job enrichment as a solution.

Human Relations

The human relations movement was in large part a reaction against the dehumanizing aspects of scientific management. Rather than emphasizing the production needs of the organization, the human relations movement looked at jobs from the perspective of the individual worker.[14]

The movement grew out of studies by Mayo in the early 1920s, now referred to as the Hawthorne Studies.[15] The Hawthorne Studies mark a critical turning point, away from an excessive emphasis on the technical aspects of job design by scientific management and toward a recognition of the social needs of workers and how these needs affect performance. The original goal of studies at the Western Electric Company's Hawthorne plant in 1924 was to test the effects of variations in working conditions on productivity. The striking conclusions were that variations in the work environment (lighting, ventilation, temperature) were less important than the social interaction with co-workers.[16]

The researchers discovered that workers spontaneously formed groups, organized the work environment, established norms, and enforced sanctions among themselves. In other words, economic incentives, the key motivation factor in scientific management theories, were now viewed as secondary to the need for social solidarity provided in work groups. Social and emotional needs of workers, if cultivated and controlled, seemed to lead to higher productivity. The human relations movement advocated job design as a way to direct these needs toward stable, predictable forms. Supportive work groups and nonauthoritarian supervisors were seen as keys to increasing worker motivation. There was less emphasis on the technology of the work. Quality circles and other worker participation programs, discussed in Chapter Twelve, may be viewed as recent applications of these ideas.[17]

Current Approaches

Several approaches to job design affect the degree of specialization, job characteristics, and psychological dimensions of work.

Job engineering is concerned with product, process, and tool design; plant layout; standard operating procedures; work measurement and standards; worker methods; and human-machine interactions. This approach went hand in hand with automation in the 1950s and 1960s.[18]

In *job rotation*, the employees take turns performing several different work-simplified jobs. Job rotation provides more flexible work assignments, makes it easier to staff unpleasant jobs (or heavier jobs), and reduces the boredom and monotony of doing only one work-simplified job.[19]

Job enlargement is the opposite of work simplification. If the work-simplified job consists of three operations, the job enlargement approach expands this until a meaningful component or part is completed by one person. The theory is that whole jobs reduce boredom through more variety and give more meaning to work.[20] Note that variety is achieved through enlargement in a horizontal direction.

Job enrichment represents an extension of the job rotation and job enlargement techniques of job design. It is a direct outgrowth of Herzberg's two-factor theory of motivation and involves increasing responsibility of the workers to provide them with more meaningfulness, challenge, autonomy, and control.[21]

There are at least two approaches to job enrichment. One is to increase the horizontal scope of a job. In the following diagram, Job 1 has five operations. To enlarge its scope, four operations would be added: two from the job

| Two operations | Basic tasks JOB 1 Five operations | Two operations |

←——————— Increased ———————→

that precedes it and two from the job that follows. Horizontal enlargement increases variety, lengthens the cycle time, provides the task with more wholeness and identity, and increases the knowledge necessary to perform it.

The second approach to enrichment is to increase the vertical scope of a job, as shown for Job 2 in the following diagram. Increased vertical scope gives the employees more responsibility for the tasks on which they work. For instance, an employee might be expected not only to perform certain

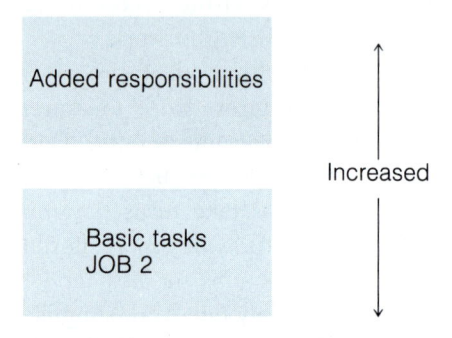

```
    ┌─────────────────────────┐           ↑
    │                         │           │
    │  Added responsibilities │           │
    │                         │           │
    └─────────────────────────┘           │
                                       Increased
    ┌─────────────────────────┐           
    │                         │           │
    │      Basic tasks        │           │
    │        JOB 2            │           │
    │                         │           │
    └─────────────────────────┘           ↓
```

operations on the product but also to order the materials necessary for these operations and inspect them for quality. This type of enrichment takes some of the authority from supervisors (or other departments) and adds it to the job. Thus, it can increase an employee's authority, responsibility, and autonomy. The advantages for job enrichment include greater intrinsic rewards available to employees, which in turn reduces absenteeism and turnover.[22]

These approaches to job design are part of various combinations of management innovations introduced with resounding success by companies such as the Copper Cliff, Ontario division of Inco Ltd., the Firestone Canada Inc. plant in Hamilton, and the McDonnell Douglas Canada Ltd. plant in Toronto. At Inco, for example, the work crew in the mines used to consist of 26 workers, each doing a specialized job. The company introduced a program to consolidate the crews' tasks; the new, smaller work team consists of only six workers, each doing several jobs.[23] The new emphasis on multiple skills allows more extensive job rotation (both horizontally and vertically), such as reported by Shell's Sarnia chemical plant in Ontario and Eldorado Nuclear in Port Hope, Ontario.[24] Says Rene Decelles of Canadian General Electric's plant in Bromont, Quebec: "It keeps you alert. I find it challenging. It's a little like operating your own business because you have responsibility in your area of work."[25] At Air Canada, a work improvement program which included redesigning the work process of the refund section around employee teams, each responsible for a geographical region, was proposed.[26] Following a successful test, teams of five to six employees were formed to handle *all* aspects of refunds pertaining to their section. What were the effects? One employee summarized her feelings this way: "Our jobs have more variety, challenge, and responsibility. Any time you have more responsibility and variety in your work you feel more satisfied with your job. We feel we can voice our opinions about ways to improve work and solve work-related problems."[27]

Job Characteristics Model

The Hackman-Oldham model of job enrichment (see Exhibit 4–1) is a more recent approach to job design.[28] The model is based on the view that five core job characteristics lead the worker to experience three key psychological states; these, in turn, affect motivation and satisfaction on the job. The more the three states are experienced, the more the worker will feel internal work motivation.

The five core job characteristics are:

1. Skill variety: The degree to which the job requires a variety of different activities in carrying out the work, which allows the use of a number of an individual's skills and talents;
2. Task identity: The degree to which the job requires completion of a "whole" and identifiable piece of work—that is, doing a job from the beginning to end with a visible outcome;
3. Task significance: The degree to which the job has a substantial impact on the lives or work of other people, whether in the immediate organization or in the external environment;

which contribute to the sense of meaningfulness (of the work) experienced by the employee;

4. Autonomy: The degree to which the job provides substantial freedom, independence, and discretion to the individual in scheduling the work and in determining the procedures to be used in carrying it out. This influences whether an individual feels personally responsible for the outcomes of the work performed;
5. Feedback: The degree to which carrying out the work activities required by the job results in the individual's obtaining direct and clear information about the effectiveness of his or her performance,[29] which provides the individual with knowledge of the actual results of the work.

The "moderators" at the bottom of the model account for individual differences among workers in the way they respond to jobs. Moderators explain why individuals react differently to jobs that theoretically should be motivating.[30] For example, if a worker is low on "growth need strength," job enrich-

EXHIBIT 4–1
Job Characteristics Model

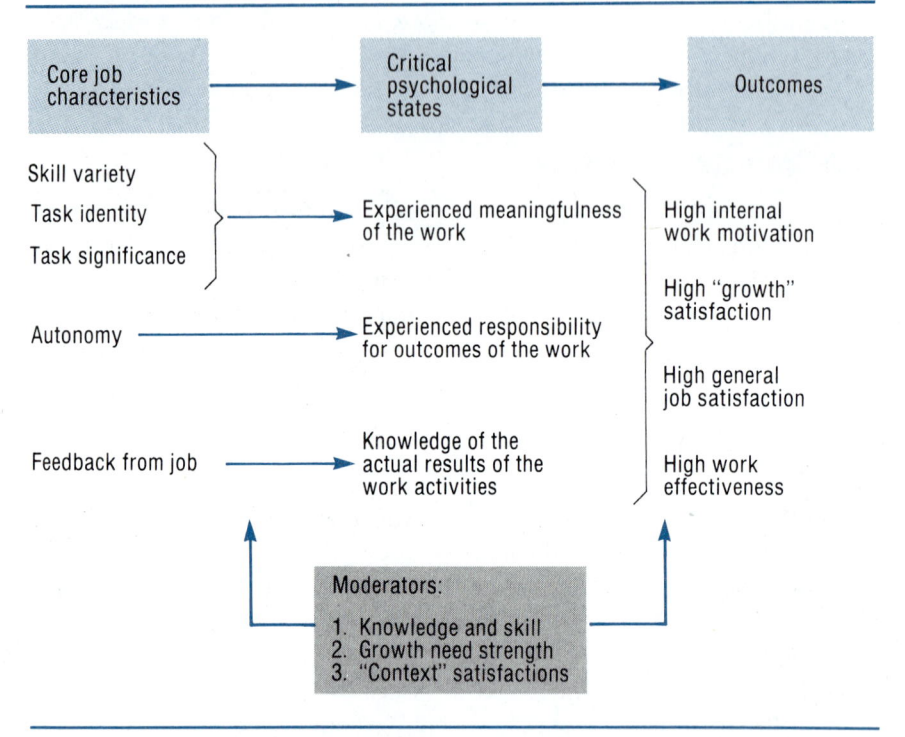

Core job characteristics	Critical psychological states	Outcomes

Skill variety
Task identity } → Experienced meaningfulness of the work
Task significance

Autonomy → Experienced responsibility for outcomes of the work

Feedback from job → Knowledge of the actual results of the work activities

High internal work motivation

High "growth" satisfaction

High general job satisfaction

High work effectiveness

Moderators:
1. Knowledge and skill
2. Growth need strength
3. "Context" satisfactions

Source: J. R. Hackman and G. R. Oldham, *Work Redesign* (Reading, Mass.: Addison-Wesley Publishing, 1980), p. 90. Used by permission.

ment in any or all of the core job characteristics will probably have little impact. The model focusses on the interaction between the individual and the job.

Continuing research on the job characteristics model is concerned with further clarifying whether the a priori five-factor structure varies across different study populations. So far the evidence is mixed.[31]

Employee Focus of Attention

An emerging area of research with practical implications for job design employs the construct of employee focus of attention,[32] which is assumed to influence employee reactions to systematic change efforts. Focus of attention refers to the employee's cognitive orientation toward each of multiple "targets." Focus represents what the employee thinks about, concentrates on, and mentally attends to while at work. Although there are a number of possible targets and daily fluctuations may occur, it is assumed that employees do characteristically (i.e., consistently) focus on identifiable classes of targets, such as job factors (in the traditional job design sense), work unit factors (including work unit size and independence from other units), and off-the-job factors.

A recent longitudinal study suggests that focus of attention moderates the effects of job change interventions for both "soft" (e.g., satisfaction) and "hard" (e.g., performance) variables.[33] The primary nature of the interventions used was techno-structural[34] (e.g., job enlargement/enrichment). The study also determined that high job focus employees (defined as those who characteristically focus a great deal on the work environment) reacted more favourably to the interventions in terms of better performance and less absenteeism and tardiness.[35]

Tailoring Jobs to Organization and Environmental Conditions

The best approach to job design has not yet emerged. One applicable to all circumstances probably does not exist. The current approaches face some unresolved issues. First, the models are very complex conceptually and difficult for managers to apply. Second, the approaches waver between focussing on an organization or a job or an individual. Rarely are all three integrated. The search for the perfect organization design is similar to the search for the Holy Grail.

The diagnostic model implies that any approach to job design is more likely to be effective if it considers the organization condition in which the job is performed as well as the nature of the work and the nature of the employees involved. Thus far, no approach does this.[36]

Other aspects of job design include hours of work and work schedules.

Hours of Work and Work Schedules

From the employee's perspective, an important aspect of a job is the number of hours of work required, the arrangement of the hours, and freedom in determining work schedules. The work schedule affects the nonwork part of a person's life, the time with family, in leisure, and in self-development.

Recent evidence indicates a sizable portion of job dissatisfaction is related to lack of control over hours of work, forced overtime, and lack of freedom to adjust hours to match personal needs.[37] However, workers are also concerned about the likely impact of work schedules on organization effectiveness. Employers have devoted considerable effort to rearranging employees' work schedules. Scales are now available to allow P/HRM managers to assess workers' attitudes toward various work schedules and to predict work schedule preferences.[38]

Work hours and schedules come in a variety of arrangements. Some of the most common methods are examined next.

Compressed Workweek

The compressed workweek is a modification of the traditional five-day, 37-hour week by scheduling the normal hours of weekly work in less than five days. The typical compressed workweek follows a four-day, 37-hour schedule (4/37). Others, such as fire departments or the nursing staff at some hospitals, use a three-day, 36-hour schedule (3/36). Another variation is the "weekend 2/24." Under a recently signed contract with the union, specially hired workers at 3M Canada's plant in London, Ontario, will work 12-hour shifts on Saturdays and Sundays but will be paid for 40 hours instead of only for the actual 24 hours worked.

Research results on the effects of compressed workweeks are uneven.[39] Some studies reported positive effects on productivity, absenteeism, and other behaviours; others reached different conclusions. Among the latter, it was noted that positive effects observed soon after introduction of the compressed workweek declined rapidly. Individual and job differences may explain many of the contradictions in the research findings.[40] In general, older employees seem to find a compressed workweek undesirable, especially where the work is physically or mentally taxing. Younger employees suggest it interferes with their social life. Another factor is the nature of the task involved. In general, if the task is physically or mentally taxing, it probably is not suitable for a compressed workweek schedule.

Flexible Hours (Flexitime)

Under flexitime, all employees are present at the workplace for a specified period (core time), but the rest of the required hours may be completed at the employees' discretion within a specified period.[41]

Going from the least to the most flexible, the different types of flexitime are:[42]

Flexitour: Employees are required to select specific starting and quitting times and to work this schedule for a specified period, such as a week or month. Each work day is of normal duration.

Gliding time: Variation in starting and quitting time is permitted, but workday total is usually eight hours.

Variable day: Credit and debit of work hours is permitted (such as working 10 hours one day and 6 hours another) as long as the total hours worked are even at the end of the week or month.

Maniflex: Credit and debit hours are permitted, and a core time is not required on all days. The core may be from 10 A.M. until 2 P.M. Monday and Friday only.

Flexiplace: Employees can change the location of work as well as the hours, such as working at home, at satellite locations, and so on.

Advocates of flexitime say it allows employees the freedom to manage their own time.[43] The major disadvantages of flexitime include:

- Not all employees are present when others want them.
- Keeping records of hours worked for pay purposes is difficult. This can increase costs.
- Middle management may perceive a loss of control, and unions may desire fewer hours for their members, not rearranged hours.
- Potential conflicts exist between flexitime and the present wage and hours laws, especially about overtime pay and lunch breaks.
- Flexitime may be hard to implement in *inter*dependent jobs. Manufacturing to inventory may be costly, and in service industries, coordination may be difficult.[44]

Flexitime can have a positive effect on employment equity. Since working parents frequently experience time conflicts resulting from family requirements, the discretion that flexitime allows may help an employer attract and retain more women employees.[45]

Another work arrangement beginning to attract more attention is working at home.

Home Work—Electronic Cottage?

With the widespread use of computer terminals and advanced telephone technology, some companies are beginning to contract out routine forms processing. For example, some insurance companies pay a flat rate per claim form processed to clerks who do the processing on computer terminals in their homes.

Other work that can be done this way includes processing catalogue sales, tape-recorded dictation, keypunching computer programs, or even writing software. People who have such work arrangements appreciate the convenience provided by this "electronic cottage" lifestyle. However, unions are unhappy and argue that such arrangements weaken their organizations, may erode wage standards, and open the way for worker exploitation. We may see proposals that would ban high-tech home work. For the immediate future, however, the practice is expected to spread.

Job design affects the nature of work as well as the work schedule and hours. Next we examine job analysis, the process of collecting information about the nature of work.

JOB ANALYSIS

> **Definition**
> *Job analysis* is a systematic process of collecting data and making certain judgements about all of the important information related to the nature of a specific job.

Job analysis usually collects information about specific tasks or what a person does.[46] A group of tasks performed by one person makes up a position. Identical positions make a job, and broadly similar jobs combine into an occupation.[47] Exhibit 4–2 summarizes these terms.

Why Analyze Jobs?

Job analysis is a basic tool in human resource management because information about the work performed serves so many purposes. Exhibit 4–3 lists some of the P/HRM uses (in addition to job design) of data gathered through job analysis. These include:

1. Training programs: Job analysis permits training programs to be tailored to actual qualifications required to perform the jobs, rather than some hypothetical ones dreamed up by managers.[48]

EXHIBIT 4–2
Job Analysis Terminology

Task	Smallest unit of analysis, a specific statement of what a person does: for example, operates an Apple II terminal, answers the telephone.
Position	Next level of analysis, *a group of tasks* performed by *one* person: for example, all tasks done by a computer operator or secretary.
Job	Many positions, all with the same basic tasks and with several people performing them.
Occupation	Grouping of jobs with broadly similar content, for example, managerial, technical, crafts.
Job descriptions	Systematic summary of the information collected in the job analysis.
Job specifications	The minimum skills, knowledge, and abilities required to perform the job.

Source: E. J. McCormick, "Job and Task Analysis" in *Handbook of Industrial and Organizational Psychology*, ed. M. D. Dunnette, © 1976, John Wiley & Sons, Inc. Reprinted by permission.

EXHIBIT 4–3
Uses of Job Analysis Information

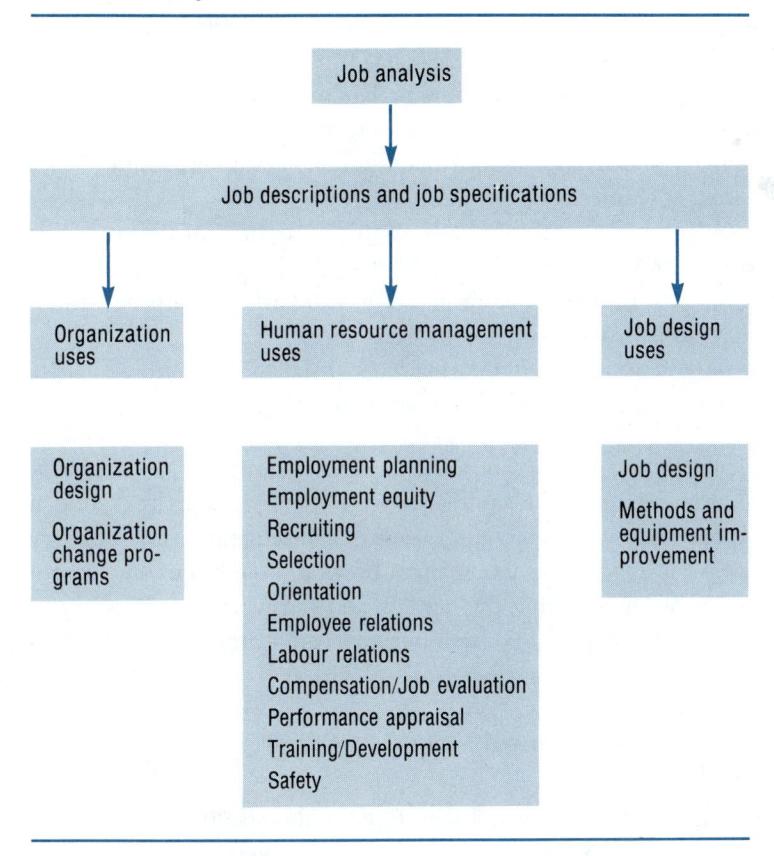

```
                        Job analysis
                             │
                             ▼
         Job descriptions and job specifications
         │              │              │
         ▼              ▼              ▼
   Organization   Human resource    Job design
   uses           management uses   uses

   Organization   Employment planning    Job design
   design         Employment equity
                  Recruiting             Methods and
   Organization   Selection              equipment im-
   change pro-    Orientation            provement
   grams          Employee relations
                  Labour relations
                  Compensation/Job evaluation
                  Performance appraisal
                  Training/Development
                  Safety
```

2. Job-related interviews and recruitment: Job analysis can tell interviewers which requirements are necessary for success on the job.[49] This can pay off in two ways: it allows the interviewer to better assess the fit between the candidate and the job, and it allows candidates to decide if they are really interested.
3. Test development, selection, and validation: Tests chosen or developed on the basis of measuring work-related information objectively and validly are useful in hiring decisions as well as in complying with employment equity concerns.[50]
4. Performance evaluation: Basing performance evaluation measures on job analysis information helps ensure they are job-related.[51]
5. Compensation: Job analysis is often a first step in evaluating the worth of a job for pay purposes.[52]

6. Employment equity: Job analysis data can be helpful in establishing that P/HRM decisions are work-related.[53] A well-done job analysis is an important step in both complying with and defending against actions brought under human rights legislation.
7. Career planning and development: The movement of individuals into and out of positions, jobs, and occupations is a common procedure in organizations. Job analysis provides clear and detailed information to those considering such career movement.
8. Safety: Safety on a job depends on proper layout, standards, equipment, and other physical conditions. What a job entails and the type of people needed also contribute information to establish safe procedures. This information is provided by job analysis.
9. Job design: Job analysis information is used to structure and modify the elements, duties, and tasks of specific jobs.

Despite the importance of job analysis, a survey by Jones and DeCotiis found that approximately 60 percent of 899 surveyed employers did not use it.[54] Reasons cited were time and expense. Consequently, it is important that the reasons for conducting job analysis be well thought out and properly understood. Those authorizing the activity and those carrying it out need to be aware of the time and cost commitment, as well as the nature of any changes that may result.

What Data to Collect

List upon list exist of suggested data to be gathered during job analysis. Exhibit 4–4 is typical. Some job analysis methods focus on work characteristics and on tasks and behaviours required, taking a task-oriented approach; others are designed to uncover primarily required worker characteristics in terms of *k*nowledge, *s*kills, *a*bility, and *o*ther characteristics (KSAOs), a worker-oriented approach. Note that the latter can usually be inferred from a description of tasks and required behaviours.

Deciding what information to collect depends on the following factors: existing data, purpose of the analysis,[55] cost of the procedure, and concerns of practicality (e.g., time to completion, amount of expertise required, sample size).[56] The more purposes to be served by a job analysis, the greater will be the variety of data that must be collected. For example, those interested in job design will focus on how differences in the work structure and content affect motivation and performance, while the specific behaviours and abilities required to perform a job are of interest to those making recruiting and selection decisions.

EXHIBIT 4–4
Typical Job Data Collected

Job Content/Context Factors
  Duties
  Functions
  Tasks
  Activities
  Performance criteria
  Critical incidents
  Organizational level
  Reporting relationships
  Communications network
  Output (e.g., reports, analyses)
  Working conditions
  Time allocation
  Resource responsibility
  Roles (e.g., negotiator, monitor, leader)

Worker Characteristics
  Professional/technical knowledge
  Prior experience
  Manual skills
  Verbal skills
  Written skills
  Quantitative skills
  Mechanical skills
  Conceptual skills
  Managerial skills
  Bargaining skills
  Leadership skills
  Consulting skills
  Human relations skills
  Aptitudes
  Values
  Style

Work Characteristics
  Risk or exposure
  Constraints
  Choices
  Conflicting demands
  Origin of activities
  Expected/unexpected
  Dependence/independence
  Pattern or cycle
  Time pressure
  Fragmentation
  Sustained attention
  Time orientation (short or long)

Interpersonal Relationships
  Internal
  Boss
  Other superiors
  Peers
  Subordinates
  Other juniors
  External
  Suppliers
  Customers
  Regulatory
  Consultants
  Professional/industry
  Community
  Union/employee group

Source: Howard Risher, "Job Analysis: A Management Perspective," *Employee Relations Law Journal*, Spring 1979, pp. 535–51.

Pay decisions are based on information about similarities and differences in the skill, effort, responsibility, and working conditions among jobs. It is not known whether a single job analysis procedure can collect data to accommodate so many diverse uses.[57] With the aid of computers, it has become feasible to collect and analyze vast amounts of job-related data. But the key issue remains: to make certain the data collected serve the purposes of managers and help employees better understand their jobs.

Manager/Employee Acceptance

Employee and manager acceptance of data collected is important and easily overlooked.[58] For example, a job analyst may believe the descriptions adequately describe a job, while jobholders, their supervisors, or the union may believe the data omit significant aspects of the work. No matter how well the rest of the P/HRM system is administered, if employees and managers are dissatisfied with the initial data collected, they are not likely to believe decisions based on that data can be fair. An appeal system to resolve such disagreements may be necessary. In a unionized setting, specifics of the appeal procedure can be part of the collective agreement.

How to Collect Data

Exhibit 4–5 categorizes the most common methods of job analysis data collection. Appendix A describes some procedures for collecting data.

The data collection methods (or combination thereof) used by the job analyst are a function of the job analysis method decided on. The choice is not an easy one: there are seven job analysis methods available:[59] Functional Job Analysis; Position Analysis Questionnaire; Job Elements Method; Task Inventory/CODAP (a computerized technique); Threshold Traits Analysis; Critical Incident Technique; and Ability Requirements Scales. Significant advances in collecting and analyzing job information have occurred in the past few years. Basically these include techniques to quantify the data and computerize the analysis. Such developments help minimize errors in data collection and,

EXHIBIT 4–5
Methods of Data Collection

Method	Descriptions	Characteristics
Questionnaire	Using standardized form, jobholders and/or supervisors describe the work. Data can be gathered either through mailed survey or through individual interview.	Variations include combining questionnaire with individual or group interview. As with all questionnaires, responses may be incomplete or difficult to interpret, a limitation minimized by combining with interviews. Standard format eases mathematical analysis. Interviews, however, may be time consuming and become more difficult with workers at multiple locations.

EXHIBIT 4–5 *(concluded)*

Method	Descriptions	Characteristics
Checklist	Jobholders and/or supervisors check items on a task inventory that apply to their particular job. Checklist can be tailor-made or purchased.	Depends on recognition rather than recall. Cheap, easy to administer and analyze. However, care must be taken that all significant aspects of work are included in the list.
Diary	Jobholders record activities as they are performed.	Has the advantage of collecting data as events occur, but it is often difficult to obtain continuous and consistent entries. Obtained data are not in a standardized format.
Observation	Analyst records perceptions formed while watching the work being done by one or more jobholders.	The absence of preconceived structures or artificial constraints can lead to richer data. Each job can be studied in any depth desired. However, validity and reliability of data can be a problem, and the relative emphasis of certain work aspects is dependent on the acuteness of the analyst's perceptions. Also, the observation of employee behaviour by an analyst influences the behaviour.
Activity sampling	Observations are made at random intervals.	
Activity matrix	Respondents identify time spent in relation to tasks and products or services.	Data collected is amenable to quantitative analysis, and is highly adaptable to other human resource management needs; however, another job analysis procedure must be used initially to develop the matrix.
Critical incidents	Behaviourally oriented incidents describe key job behaviours. Analyst determines degree of each type of behaviour present or absent in each job.	Analysis clearly based on concrete behaviour. Scales require some expertise to develop.

Source: George T. Milkovich and Jerry M. Newman, *Compensation*, 2nd ed. (Plano, Texas: Business Publications, 1987), p. 67.

insofar as possible, increase chances the jobs are analyzed on work-related factors.[60] To review the state of the art in job analysis, we grouped approaches to job analysis into two types—conventional and quantitative.

Conventional Job Analysis

Conventional procedures vary in specific details, but generally the job analysis is conducted by an analyst using a questionnaire in conjunction with interviews of job incumbents and supervisors.[61] The data collected are used to develop a summary job description. Often both job incumbents and supervisors have an opportunity to modify and approve the description.

Functional Job Analysis

Probably the most detailed conventional procedure is functional job analysis (FJA). This approach assumes that all jobs involve relationships to data, people, and things and that these relationships can be arranged (by the analyst) according to their complexity (see Exhibit 4–6). For example, the simplest relationship to people requires taking instructions or serving. The most complex people relationship is serving as a mentor (a role model or counsellor). J.A. Fine and other advocates of FJA see it as the cornerstone for all human resource systems.[62] But critics complain the typical essay descriptions of job

EXHIBIT 4–6
Worker Function Scales of Functional Job Analysis

	Data	People	Things
Higher level	Synthesizing	Mentoring	Precision working, setting up
	Coordinating		
	Innovating	Negotiating	Manipulating, operating-controlling, driving-controlling
	Analyzing	Supervising	
	Computing	Consulting, instructing, treating	
	Compiling		
		Coaching, persuading, diverting	Handling, feeding-offbearing, tending
	Copying	Exchanging information	
Lower level	Comparing	Taking instructions-helping, serving	

Source: Adapted from S. A. Fine and Wretha A. Wiley, *An Introduction to Functional Job Analysis: A Scaling of Selected Tasks from the Social Welfare Field* (Kalamazoo, Mich.: W. E. Upjohn Institute for Employment Research, 1971).

activities are not adequately descriptive of the jobs in question.[63] The method places considerable reliance on the analyst's ability to understand the work performed and to translate it into description sheets. Certain safeguards, such as multiple approvals by supervisors and incumbents, can help minimize that difficulty but cannot eliminate it.[64]

Quantitative Job Analysis

Quantitative job analysis (QJA) is intended to reduce reliance on the limitations of the analyst. The approach involves the detailed assessment—the quantification—of the tasks and worker traits involved in a job. QJA is more systematic, relies on computers for analysis, and is less subject to error than conventional job analysis. However, it is also more costly to develop.[65]

Inventories are the core of QJA. An inventory is essentially a structured questionnaire in which the work and worker attributes relevant for the group of jobs to be analyzed are listed. Exhibit 4–7 illustrates part of a QJA inventory. The item scales show that a task is measured in terms of time spent, importance, and learning time. The knowledge, skills, and abilities required to perform the work are measured in terms of degree of importance and prior

EXHIBIT 4–7
Example of Task or Activity-Oriented Job Inventory: Retail Clerical Work*

	Time spent	Importance	Learning time
	(1) This is a part of my job / (2) Much less time than other activities / (3) Less time than other activities / (4) About the same amount of time as other activities / (5) More time than other activities / (6) Much more time than other activities	(1) Unimportant / (2) Minor importance / (3) Important / (4) Very important / (5) Crucial	(1) 1 day or less / (2) 2 or 3 days / (3) 4 or 5 days / (4) Up to a month / (5) 1–3 months / (6) More than 3 months
153. Plan special sales promotions and see that they are carried out according to plan.			
154. Keep track of and follow up on the activities of subordinates.			
155. Transcribe from dictating machine records or tapes.			
156. Schedule dates or times for appointments, meetings, etc. or delivery, pick-up, and repair of merchandise by checking with those involved for time and place.			
157. Perform routine preventive mechanical maintenance on machines or equipment.			
158. Look up, search for, or locate information in readily available sources such as files, parts lists, records, manuals, tables, catalogs, etc.			
159. Set objectives for a department or unit of the company.			

*Used for describing nonexempt-level clerical, maintenance, warehousing, selling, and foreman jobs in a retail organization.
Source: L. M. Hough, *Job Activities Questionnaire for Retail Employees* (Minneapolis: Personnel Decisions Research Institute, 1977).

experience required.[66] The person presently holding a job is the one most likely to fill out one of these inventories.

Position Analysis Questionnaire

The most publicly available example of QJA is the Position Analysis Questionnaire (PAQ).[67] Exhibit 4–8 shows sample items from the work output section of PAQ. Additional sections include information input, mental processes, re-

---

EXHIBIT 4–8
Position Analysis Questionnaire (sample items of work output)

3.2 Manual Activities

This section describes manual activities in which tools may or may not be used.

78	1	Setting up/adjusting (adjusting, calibrating, aligning and/or setting up of machines or equipment, for example, setting up a lathe or drill press, adjusting an engine carburetor, adjusting, calibrating, and aligning electric circuitry, etc.)
79	1	Manually modifying (using hands *directly* to form or otherwise modify materials or products, for example, kneading dough by hand, folding letters, massaging, etc.)
80	1	Material controlling (manually controlling or guiding materials being processed, for example, in operating sewing machine, jig saws, etc.)
81	1	Assembling/disassembling (either manually or with the use of hand tools putting parts or components together to form more complete items, or taking apart or disassembling items into their component parts)
82	1	Arranging/positioning (manually placing objects, materials, persons, animals, etc., in a specific position or arrangement, for example, arranging library books, window displays, stocking shelves, positioning patients for certain medical and dental procedures, etc.; do *not* include here arranging/positioning which is a part of the operations listed in items 78–81)
83	1	Feeding/off-bearing (manually inserting throwing, dumping, or placing materials into or removing them from *machines* or *processing equipment*; this category is *not* to be used in describing operations in which the worker manually *guides* or *controls* the materials or parts during processing, as in item 80)
84	1	Physical handling (physically handling objects, materials, animals, human beings, etc., either manually or with nominal use of aiding devices, for example, in certain warehousing activities, loading/unloading conveyor belts or trucks, packaging, farming activities, hospital procedures, etc.; typically there is little requirement for carefully positioning or arrangement of objects; include here relatively uninvolved handling operations *not* provided for in items 78–83)

Source: PAQ Services, Inc., Logan, Utah. Copyright 1969 by Purdue Research Foundation, West Lafayette, Indiana 47906.

lationship with other persons, job context, and other job characteristics. Some users caution that the PAQ focusses only on similarities among jobs, whereas some uses of job analysis data, such as compensation, need to identify differences as well as similarities. Additionally, PAQ has been criticized for having a high reading comprehension level and complex instructions, which make it difficult for employees to complete the questionnaire without assistance.[68]

Position Description Questionnaire

Another popular QJA is Control Data Corporation's Position Description Questionnaire (PDQ).[69] An excerpt from an analysis for a personnel position is shown in Exhibit 4–9.

A major limitation of all QJA is cost. One study reports that before QJA systems can begin to pay, approximately one year is required to develop and administer the inventory plus about $10,000 to $20,000 for computer and consulting assistance.[70]

Advantages of Quantitative Job Analysis

Despite cost limitations, the practice of job analysis has been upgraded with the development of quantitative job analysis methods, and at least four factors are increasing its use. First, as more employers use it, the technology is becoming better understood and simpler to apply.[71] Second, sound information about the nature of work and the requirements to perform it is the basic foundation of effective human resource decision making.[72] Third, challenges from employees, unions, and human rights councils to verify the work-relatedness of P/HRM decisions require sound job analysis. And fourth, QJA lends itself to user-friendly computer applications.

Usefulness of Methods

Job analysis procedures, whether conventional or quantitative, are subjective and involve a high degree of judgement.[73] It is therefore important to consider the comparative usefulness of job analysis methods, particularly in terms of their reliability, validity, practicality, and organizational purposes.

Reliability. Reliability is the consistency of the results obtained. Are the results (whether the work is similar or dissimilar) the same regardless of who is involved (supervisors, incumbents, analysts, consultants) or the methods used?

Several studies comparing employee-supervisor descriptions of work content present a mixed picture of the reliability of job analysis.[74] The results indicate employees and supervisors often differ in how they view the employees' work, distribution of time among tasks, skills required to perform the work, and difficulties of the tasks performed. Developers of QJA inventories generally report more favourable reliability results.[75]

EXHIBIT 4–9 Control Data Corporation Personnel Task Questionnaire

SECTION II: TASK QUESTIONNAIRE (Cont.)

1. Review all tasks.
2. Mark "Do Perform" for all tasks you perform in your current job and "Do Not Perform" for all tasks you do not perform in your current job.
3. At the end of the OAQ, in the space provided, write in any unlisted tasks that you perform.

STEP I — Do perform / Do not perform

STEP II — TIME SPENT
Compared to all other tasks performed on your present job.

Scale: 1 = Extremely small compared to other tasks, 2 = Very small compared to other tasks, 3 = Small compared to other tasks, 4 = Slightly smaller than other tasks, 5 = About average, 6 = Slightly larger than other tasks, 7 = Larger than other tasks, 8 = Very large compared to other tasks, 9 = Extremely large compared to other tasks

1 ASSESS ORGANIZATIONAL AND HUMAN RESOURCE NEEDS

Identify and assess organizational needs

1. Identify and assess corporate or company-wide needs by consulting/conferring with requestor/client.
2. Evaluate effectiveness of corporate or company-wide implemented programs/practices.
3. Identify and assess division needs by consulting/conferring with requestor/client.
4. Evaluate effectiveness of division implemented programs/practices.
5. Analyze previous plan/program results (e.g. incentive payouts, training results, merit increases, affirmative action progress, enrollments, etc.).
6. Assist management in determining sales emphasis/incentives based on company strategy and direction.
7. Determine goals and objectives as a result of needs assessment.

Assess human resource requirements

8. Assess jobs and human resource skills necessary to meet business objectives.
9. Advise management of jobs and human resource skills necessary to meet business objectives.
10. Assess external market to determine human resource availability, deficiencies, needs.
11. Assess internal workforce to determine human resource availability, deficiencies, needs.

Establish human resource requirements

12. Establish corporate or company-wide headcount goals (e.g., growth, workforce balancing, etc.).
13. Establish division headcount goals (e.g., growth, workforce balancing, etc.).
14. Consult with management in establishing headcount goals (e.g., growth, workforce balancing, etc.).
15. Advise management in structuring/restructuring department and/or organization.

Monitor organizational environment issues

16. Determine organizational environment issues (e.g., morale, reactions, rumor mill, etc.).
17. Consult with management on organizational environment issues (e.g., morale, reactions, rumor mill, etc.).
18. Assess and develop alternative solutions to organizational environment issues (e.g., morale, reactions, rumor mill, etc.).

Traditional job analysis does not usually lend itself to formal reliability analysis because of the narrative and unstructured output. This imprecision and obscure structure make reliability a serious issue for traditional methods. Whatever method is adopted, it should be used independently by several people (analysts, supervisors, subordinates) and any differences should be investigated and resolved.

Validity. Validity refers to the accuracy of the results obtained. The validity of job analysis results is largely unknown. Reliable job information does not mean it is accurate, comprehensive, and uncontaminated (free from bias). Research on how to estimate the validity of job analysis is difficult since there is almost no way of showing the extent to which the results are accurate portraits of the work. The most promising approach may be to examine the convergence of results among multiple sources of job data (analysts, incumbents, supervisors) and multiple methods.[76] A common approach to increase accuracy of job analysis is to require the jobholder and the supervisor to mutually sign off on the results.

Practicality. The practicality of a job analysis method refers to concerns such as user acceptability of the results, cost of the method, its degree of standardization and off-the-shelf possibilities, and the degree of expertise required.

Acceptability of the results by the employees and managers remains the critical test. Traditional job analysis is not always well accepted by the parties involved, and the acceptability of QJA approaches is mixed. A project at Control Data Corporation describes experiences in which managers and employees refused to accept the results.[77] The inventory, developed over a four-year study, ran into several problems, which led most managers to refuse to use it. Among the problems faced were:

1. Employee/manager understanding. The statistical methods used were difficult to understand, and managers were unable to communicate the results to employees.
2. Behaviourally oriented versus "scope" data. Analysis that focused on work behaviours and omitted "scope" data (e.g., size of budgets, total payroll contribution to organization objectives) caused managers to question the accuracy (validity) of the analysis.
3. Abstract and ambiguous factors. The nature of the data collected (e.g., analyzing subordinates' weaknesses and strengths) was perceived to be too subjective and therefore open to personal interpretation.[78]

In another study, Levine et al. solicited expert judgements from 93 experienced job analysts about seven job analysis methods.[79] The analysts agreed that the PAQ was the most practical method in terms of being available for use off-the-shelf. It was also rated as the most standardized approach (although not significantly more so than the FJA), the most reliable, and the least costly, and seen as taking less time to complete. FJA was identified as producing the highest user acceptability, rated higher than the PAQ on quality of outcome, but was evaluated as more costly.

Organizational Purposes. The study by Levine et al. also produced effectiveness ratings of job analysis methods for a variety of organizational purposes (such as the ones listed in Exhibit 4–3). Focussing here only on the PAQ and FJA methods, the latter was rated more effective in producing information for job descriptions and specifications, job classification, job design, performance appraisal, efficiency/safety, and satisfying employment equity requirements. The PAQ was rated higher for job evaluation purposes.[80]

Even though the results of quantitative job analysis can be statistically manipulated, we must bear in mind that *people* make the decisions about what items go into a job analysis, and *people* respond to those items. As Dunnette states,

> I wish to emphasize the central role played in all these procedures by human judgement. I know of no methodology, statistical technique, or objective measurement that can negate the importance of, nor supplement, rational judgement as an important element in the process of deriving behaviour and task information about jobs and of using that information to develop or justify human resource programs.[81]

Quantitative and more systematic approaches to job analysis do not remove the judgement; they only permit us to become more systematic in the way we do it. This suggests that we guard against possible sources of error.

Sources of Error in Job Analysis

Major sources of error in job analysis include poor sampling of tasks, response sets by observers or the incumbent, changes in the job and environment, and changes in employee behaviour.[82] Such errors can occur in both the quantitative and qualitative approaches considered in this chapter.

Sampling Errors. Two types of sampling errors can be identified. The first, inadequate sampling, occurs because the analyst did not identify or elicit the entire domain of tasks involved, thus producing a deficient analysis. This can happen even when a comprehensive system such as the PAQ is used. Another problem that contributes to this error is jobholders' carelessness (sometimes intentional) in reporting what they do and how their time is distributed across job activities. The other type of sampling error occurs when the analyst includes (job) elements that are not really part of the job; the resulting analysis is said to be contaminated.[83]

Response Sets. Response sets can occur in several ways. For example, if jobholders are asked how much time they spend on a given activity and are offered possible answers ranging from "A great deal" to "None," different interpretations of "A great deal" result. The interpretations of qualitative labels is also influenced by the person's belief about what the job analyst plans to do with the information. Job analysts have also been found to have response sets, leading them to underestimate abilities necessary for job performance.[84]

Job Environment Changes. These stem from time- and situation-determined changes. They occur usually through the introduction of new processes and equipment. In the printing trade, for example, the advent of computerized typesetting equipment means that previously developed job descriptions and specifications are no longer applicable.[85]

Employee Behaviour Changes. Incumbents sometimes "redefine" their jobs and modify their behaviour, especially if procedural requirements are not entirely rigid. As Cascio states, "Strictly speaking, the job itself may not change, but . . . is frequently what the incumbent makes of it."[86] This points out the importance of including only employees who have been fully trained; otherwise the job analysis reflects behaviours that are still developing.

Job Descriptions and Specifications

The *job description* is one of the outputs of a systematic job analysis. Although there is no standard format for job descriptions, they typically contain three sections, which identify, define, and describe the job.[87]

1. *Job identification.* The job may be identified by its title, number of incumbents, where it is located (department, work site), and job number.
2. *Job definition.* This summary section reflects the purpose of the job, why the job exists, what constitutes satisfactory job performance, and how it fits in with other jobs and with overall organization objectives.
3. *Description of the job.* What are the major duties of this jobholder? What specific work is performed? How closely supervised is this job: how much discretion does the jobholder enjoy; what controls limit the actions of the jobholder? Besides job activities, this section describes working conditions and the physical environment, as well as the required interpersonal interactions.

The writing of a job description can range from the results-oriented to the duty-oriented approach. The former is preferred because it gives the employee a sense of purpose and participation by clarifying why the specified job duties are performed.[88] This is achieved by capturing the essence of the job through expressing job duties in relation to the results desired. The typical job-result statement involves three elements: (1) what the action is intended to produce (the result or "why" of the job); (2) an action verb; and (3) the "how" (job duty). A useful guideline applied to the writing format is to link the result(s) to be accomplished with *by* to the description of how it is to be done. The following are some examples (arbitrarily selected from different jobs for illustrative purposes): records accounting transactions (result or purpose) *by* posting to journals and ledgers, making closing entries, applying or verifying account transfers, and summarizing totals and balances (duty); provides diagnostic data to physicians *by* conducting appropriate laboratory tests; supplies power for building and equipment *by* maintaining electrical equipment and systems.[89]

Information for the *job specifications* evolves from the job description and addresses the question, "What KSAOs, education, previous work experience, and training, are needed to perform the job effectively?" The job specification, which is sometimes appended to the job description, offers guidelines for recruitment and selection by both identifying requirements and specifying the qualifying level for each. The employer should be able to demonstrate that the job specification items are truly job-related and that the minimum qualifications are realistic.

Appendix B at the end of this chapter contains sample job descriptions.

We now turn to a classification scheme for identifying jobs in terms of work content and abilities required to perform the work.

CANADIAN JOB-OCCUPATIONAL INFORMATION

The best-known source of standardized Canadian occupational information is the Canadian Classification and Dictionary of Occupations (CCDO), issued by Emloyment and Immigration Canada.[90] The CCDO is a systematic and comprehensive arrangement of occupational descriptions reflecting the work performed by Canadians. These descriptions represent a summary of the significant activities of a number of similar jobs that may be found in different establishments or industries.

The CCDO's classification structure consists of four levels of occupational categorization, each providing successively finer detail: the Major Group (there are 23), the Minor Group (81), the Unit Group (499), and the individual unique occupations (some 7,500 are included). An individual occupation is identified by a seven-digit code number and a title, such as 2797-120 *TRAINING SPECIALIST-COMPUTERS* (educ.). The last three digits (-120), called the terminal digits, provide the unique code number within the classification structure for each occupation.

An illustrative CCDO occupational description appears in Exhibit 4–10. Each of the 14 components has been numbered and labelled. The lead

Nature of the Work 169

EXHIBIT 4–10
CCDO Occupational Description

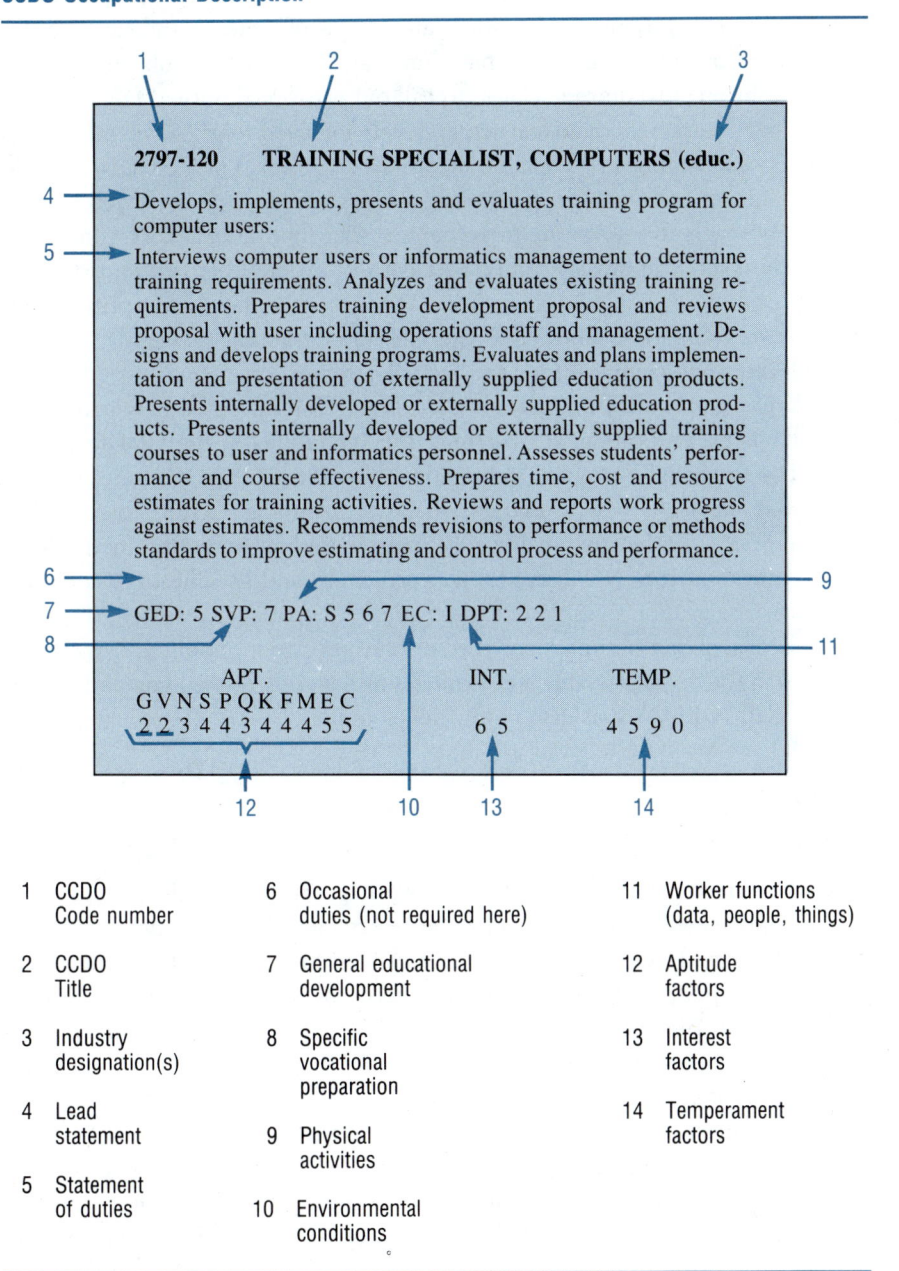

2797-120   TRAINING SPECIALIST, COMPUTERS (educ.)

Develops, implements, presents and evaluates training program for computer users:

Interviews computer users or informatics management to determine training requirements. Analyzes and evaluates existing training requirements. Prepares training development proposal and reviews proposal with user including operations staff and management. Designs and develops training programs. Evaluates and plans implementation and presentation of externally supplied education products. Presents internally developed or externally supplied education products. Presents internally developed or externally supplied training courses to user and informatics personnel. Assesses students' performance and course effectiveness. Prepares time, cost and resource estimates for training activities. Reviews and reports work progress against estimates. Recommends revisions to performance or methods standards to improve estimating and control process and performance.

GED: 5 SVP: 7 PA: S 5 6 7 EC: I DPT: 2 2 1

APT.	INT.	TEMP.
G V N S P Q K F M E C		
2 2 3 4 4 3 4 4 4 5 5	6 5	4 5 9 0

1 CCDO Code number	6 Occasional duties (not required here)	11 Worker functions (data, people, things)
2 CCDO Title	7 General educational development	12 Aptitude factors
3 Industry designation(s)	8 Specific vocational preparation	13 Interest factors
4 Lead statement	9 Physical activities	14 Temperament factors
5 Statement of duties	10 Environmental conditions	

Source: *CCDO Guide,* 4th ed. Employment and Immigration Canada, Ottawa, 1982, pp. 77–78. Adapted with permission of the Minister of Supply and Services Canada.

statement describes the principal duties of the worker and gives a general indication of how the occupation differs from others. The statement of duties is a broad description of the nature and scope of work; it indicates, either directly or by inference, the what, how, and why of the job and may be followed by an "if required" clause to call out occasional duties. Details of the remaining components and particular levels for each (e.g., GED:5 for 13 to 16 years of schooling) are available in various appendixes of the CCDO Guide. The component of "worker functions" is based on the functional job analysis (FJA) approach discussed in this chapter. The aptitude factors component draws on a set of aptitudes from a test battery (briefly referred to as GATB), which is discussed in Chapter Nine. When certain levels of aptitudes are underscored (as are G and V for the computer training specialist), they are considered to be significant for satisfactory job performance.

Employment and Immigration Canada (EIC) proposed a new concept in occupational classification to overcome the limitations of the CCDO's structure. The proposed National Occupational Classification (NOC) is designed to meet the needs of labour market analysis (including COPS, discussed in Chapter Six).[91] Rather than using a structure based on predetermined criteria for classification, the NOC will let the principles and specifications for occupational classification emerge from empirical occupational research. The new basis for classifying occupations will be interoccupation mobility, typical patterns of upward progression, and similar skill level. A related compatible system, called JOBSCAN, is also under development.[92]

SUMMARY

This chapter concentrates on how the work performed inside organizations affects employees as well as organizations. Attributes of work that are important to human resource management, and how to design and analyze them, are central topics. Work content (duties, tasks, behaviours, functions, responsibilities); the qualifications required to perform it (skills, abilities, experience); and returns and rewards for performing it (pay, promotions, challenging work) constitute the nature of work.

Job design is concerned with alternative arrangements of job content, rewards, and qualifications. The alternative approaches of job engineering, rotation, enlargement, and enrichment, and some of their advantages and disadvantages, are discussed. The job characteristics model, a more recent approach, is also introduced.

Job analysis is the tool used to assess work as it is performed in the organization. It provides input for a variety of P/HRM activities.

The nature of work plays a critical role in the management of human resources. Job analysis and job design are important tools in matching the nature of the individual with the nature of the work. It is through this matching process that employee and organization effectiveness is achieved.

APPENDIX A / Procedures for Gathering Job Information

Overview
A combination of on-site observations, interviews, and preinterview preparation and study is used to develop the necessary job information.

Data Sources
Sources of information for developing the job description include:
- Existing documents, such as job briefs; previously developed task lists; and training manuals.
- On-site observations of work operations.
- Interviews with first-level supervisors, job incumbents, and perhaps sources from whom or to whom the incumbent receives or passes on job inputs or outputs.

General Procedures
The general procedures are enumerated below, with detailed recommendations and reminders.

1. Develop preliminary job information.
   a. Review existing documents in order to develop an initial "big-picture" familiarity with the job: its main mission, its major duties or functions, its work flow patterns.
   b. Prepare a preliminary list of duties that will serve as a framework for conducting the interviews.
   c. Make a note of major items that are unclear, ambiguous, or need to be clarified during data gathering.

2. Conduct initial tour of work site.
   a. The initial tour is designed to familiarize the job analyst with the work layout, the tools and equipment used, the general conditions of the workplace and the mechanics associated with the end-to-end performance of major duties.

b. The initial tour is particularly helpful in those jobs where a firsthand view of a complicated or unfamiliar piece of equipment saves the interviewee the thousand words required to describe the unfamiliar or technical.
   c. For continuity, it is recommended that the first-level supervisor-interviewee be designated the guide for the job site observations.

3. Conduct interviews.
   a. It is recommended that the first interview be conducted with the first-level supervisor, who is considered to be in a better position than the jobholders to provide an overview of the job and how the major duties fit together.
   b. For scheduling purposes, it is recommended that no more than two interviews be conducted per day, each interview lasting no more than three hours.
   c. In selecting interviewees, the interviewees are considered subject matter experts by virtue of the fact that they perform the job (in the case of first-level supervisors). The job incumbent to be interviewed should represent the typical employee who is knowledgeable about the job (not the trainee who is just learning the ropes nor the most outstanding member of the work unit).

4. Conduct second tour of work site.
   a. The second tour of the work site is designed to clarify, confirm, and otherwise refine information developed in the interviews.
   b. As in the initial tour, it is recommended that the same first-level supervisor-interviewee conduct the second walk-through.

5. Consolidate job information.
   a. The consolidation phase of the job study involves piecing together into one coherent and comprehensive job description the data obtained from several sources: supervisor, jobholders, on-site tours, and written materials about the job.
   b. Past experience indicates that one minute of consolidation is required for every minute of interviewing. For planning purposes, at least five hours should be set aside for consolidation.
   c. A subject matter expert should be accessible as a resource person to the job analyst during the consolidation phase. The supervisor-interviewee fills this role.
   d. Check your initial preliminary list of duties and questions—all must be answered or confirmed.

6. Verify job description.
   a. The verification phase involves bringing all the interviewees together to determine if the consolidated job description is accurate and complete.
   b. The verification process is conducted in a group setting. Typed or legibly written copies of the job description (narrative description of the work setting and list of task statements) are distributed to the first-level supervisor and the job incumbent interviewees.
   c. Line by line, the job analyst goes through the entire job description and makes notes of any omissions, ambiguities, or needed clarifications.
   d. Collect all materials at the end of the verification meeting.

APPENDIX B / Sample Job Descriptions

EXHIBIT B-1

TITLE: Clerk Typist—Senior

SUMMARY
Works independently and performs a variety of relatively routine clerical duties, the majority of which require competence in the use of a typewriter.

TYPICAL DUTIES
1. Types letters, reports, tables, bills, and the like from rough or clear drafts.
2. Performs the most difficult typing assignments, such as statistical tables and graphs.
3. May combine data from several sources in order to type tables/reports and to post records.
4. Performs a variety of other relatively complex clerical duties which require a working knowledge of the organization.
5. Maintains administrative/technical records and furnishes information as necessary.
6. Instructs, trains, and assigns work to lower-classified employees as necessary.
7. Performs other related duties as required.

JOB SPECIFICATIONS
Education and Training Required: Grade 12 graduation or equivalent. Must be able to type.
Experience Required: One year of office clerical experience.

EXHIBIT B-2
3M Management Position Description

NAME: P.D.	**DATE COMPLETED:** 1/31/87
EMPLOYEE NUMBER: 000XXX	**SUPERVISOR:** R. S.
POSITION: PLANT MANAGER	**SUPERVISOR'S TITLE:** SITE MANAGER
FUNCTIONAL AREA: MANUFACTURING	**% OF JOB TAPPED:** 90%

I. ACCOUNTABILITY

A. HUMAN RESOURCES

—The jobholder has management responsibility for **379** employees.

    285.0 (75%) of these are Blue-Collar Workers.
    35.0 (9%) of these are Foremen.
    20.0 (5%) of these are in Job Groups 6–10.
    19.0 (5%) of these are in the T structure.
    13.0 (3%) of these are in Job Groups 1–5.
    7.0 (1%) of these are in Job Groups 11–15.

—**8.0** subordinate(s) report(s) directly to the jobholder and **2 worker(s) report(s)** to him/her on a dotted line basis.
—The highest direct subordinate reporting to this person is a(n) **QUALITY CONTROL MGR**, Grade **11**.
—The jobholder works approximately **80** days a year in locations other than his/her home location.

B. FINANCIAL RESPONSIBILITIES

—For the current fiscal year, the jobholder has responsibility for an annual operating budget of **19000.0** million lire.
—He/she has direct management responsibility for annual sales totaling **1** million lire.

II. PRIMARY RESPONSIBILITIES AND ACTIVITIES

A. SUPERVISING & CONTROLLING

—**75%** of the jobholder's time is spent Supervising subordinates and it is considered **an extremely important** part of the position.
—**15%** of his/her time is spent on Controlling activities and these are considered to be **an extremely important** aspect of the position.

—The most significant activities concerning Supervising & Controlling are:

Significance *Activity*
Crucial Defines areas of responsibility for managerial personnel.
Crucial Develops subordinates for improved job performance and future responsibility.
Crucial Maintains a smooth working relationship among various individuals who need to work cooperatively.
Crucial Analyzes at least monthly the effectiveness of operations.
Crucial Initiates requests for capital expenditures.
Crucial Develops evaluation criteria that serve to measure progress and effectiveness of the operation.
Crucial Reviews future product plans for adequacy and consistency with corporate objectives.
Substantial Interacts face-to-face with subordinates on an almost daily basis.
Substantial Develops executive-level management talent.
Substantial Motivates subordinates to change or improve performance.
Substantial Conducts regular performance reviews with subordinates.
Substantial Monitors subordinates' progress toward objectives of unit and adjusts activities as necessary to reach them.
Substantial Delegates work, assigns responsibility to subordinates, and establishes appropriate controls.
Substantial Forecasts manpower requirements.
Substantial Reviews and if necessary revises budget allocations.
Substantial Reviews project proposals for adequacy.

B. MONITORING BUSINESS INDICATORS

—**5%** of the jobholder's time is spent Monitoring Business Indicators and it is considered **an important** function of this position.

—The most significant activities for this aspect of the position are Monitoring:

Significance *Activity*
Crucial Long-range trends in management thinking.
Crucial Optimum return on investments.
Substantial The total sales volume of the division/subsidiary.
Substantial Price trends in the industry.
Substantial Commodity operating profit.
Substantial The financial health of the organization.
Substantial Latest technological developments affecting your function.

EXHIBIT B–2 *(continued)*

C. CONSULTING & INNOVATING

—**5%** of the jobholder's time is spent Consulting and it is considered **an important** part of this position.

—The most significant activities relating to Consulting & Innovating for this position are:

Significance	Activity
Substantial	Anticipate new or changed demands for products, services, or technologies.
Substantial	Is called on to consult on subsidiarywide problems.
Substantial	Applies advanced principles, theories, and concepts in more than one recognized field.
Substantial	Counsels organizational heads on organizational problems.
Substantial	Brainstorms to address unique problems.

D. ADMINISTRATION

—**5%** of the jobholder's time is spent Administering and it is considered **an important** function of this position.

—The most significant Administration activities for this position are:

Significance	Activity
Crucial	Evaluates and documents the effectiveness of plans, projects, etc., upon their completion.
Substantial	Works in pressure situations, such as increased workload periods, to meet tight deadlines.
Substantial	Frequently is required to react to unexpected events.
Substantial	Prepares speeches, briefings, or presentations.
Substantial	Switches strategies rapidly to achieve an objective.
Substantial	Schedules the work of two or more functions to ensure meeting the organization's commitments.
Substantial	Analyzes operating performance reports.
Substantial	Tracks project activities closely and ensures, where appropriate, that follow-up is made.
Substantial	Documents and files important details for future reference.

E. COORDINATING

—**15%** of this jobholder's time is spent Coordinating and it is considered **a very important** part of this position.

—The most significant Coordinating activities for this position are:

Significance	Activity
Crucial	Coordinates interdependent activities of different groups within the organization.
Crucial	Is aware of conflict between executive-level management personnel.
Crucial	Coordinates major activities in different departments/divisions of the organization.
Crucial	Makes formal presentations to higher management.
Crucial	Coordinates with other departments to meet previously established plans.
Substantial	Sounds out many different people before making major decisions.
Substantial	Integrates the plans of other departments/divisions.
Substantial	Works to increase cooperation among different departments/divisions.
Substantial	Works with other individuals/groups not under his/her direct supervision to solve problems.

F. REPRESENTING

—**0–2%** of the jobholder's time is spent Representing 3M and it is considered **an important** function of the position.

—The position's most significant activities relating to Representing are:

Significance	Activity
	There are no activities within this section that are of at least substantial significance.

G. PLANNING & ORGANIZING

—**0–2%** of the jobholder's time is spent on Long-Range Planning and it is considered **an unimportant** aspect of this position.
—**30%** of the jobholder's time is spent on Planning and Organizing, and it is considered **an extremely important** part of this position.

—Significant Planning and Organizing activities, broken down by the nature of the decision-making role, are:

APPROVAL:	Authority to approve without review by superiors
Crucial	Determining plans and performance objectives for an organization of 379 employees.
Crucial	Planning and coordinating the introduction of new products or services.
Crucial	Determining plans to phase out unprofitable products/services.
Crucial	Revising planning schedules to ensure project completion.
Substantial	Determining reductions in employee headcount, should this become necessary.
Substantial	Scheduling work of subordinates so that it flows evenly and steadily.

EXHIBIT B-2 (continued)

SHARED APPROVAL; Share authority for decisions with others, but without review by superiors.

Substantial Hiring an individual for an approved position.
Substantial Evaluating an organization of 200–400 employees to determine the best allocation and utilization of resources.
Substantial Allocating and scheduling resources to ensure that they will be available when needed.

PRIMARY RECOMMENDATION: Provide superiors with their sole or primary input for decisions.

Crucial Determining plans and performance objectives for an organization with annual sales of 0.0 million lire.
Substantial Developing implementation strategy for long-range plans.
Substantial Setting selling prices.

III. INTERNAL & EXTERNAL CONTACTS

A. INTERNAL CONTACTS

PURPOSE OF CONTACT

INTERNAL CONTACTS	SHARE INFORMATION regarding activities or decisions.	INFLUENCE OTHERS to act in a manner consistent with my objectives.	DIRECT and/or integrate the plans, activities or decisions of others.
Other Manager	SUBSTANTIAL	SUBSTANTIAL	SUBSTANTIAL
Supervisor	SUBSTANTIAL	SUBSTANTIAL	SUBSTANTIAL
Professional/Admin. Employees	SUBSTANTIAL	MODERATE	SUBSTANTIAL

B. EXTERNAL CONTACTS

PURPOSE OF CONTACT

EXTERNAL CONTACTS	PROVIDE INFORMATION or promote the organization or its products/services	SELL products/services	NEGOTIATE contracts, settlements, etc.
Senior Representatives of major suppliers	SUBSTANTIAL		SUBSTANTIAL

IV. KNOW-HOW

A. LEVEL OF KNOWLEDGE

—To perform the position requirements, the jobholder regularly uses Know-How from the following content areas, at the level of knowledge shown:

LEVEL 1: Sufficient familiarity to COMMUNICATE with individuals in this content area	LEVEL 2: Sufficient knowledge to SOLVE BASIC PROBLEMS by applying 3M policies/procedures related to this area	LEVEL 3: Thorough knowledge of basic principles to SOLVE COMPLEX PROBLEMS when policies/procedures are not clear	LEVEL 4: Thorough KNOWLEDGE OF ADVANCED PRINCIPLES to solve complex problems	LEVEL 5: Thorough knowledge of advanced principles + DEVELOP NEW ADVANCEMENTS in area to solve unique, complex problems
Safety Environmental Finance/Accounting Data Processing Law/Contracts Distribution Purchasing Transportation Personnel Marketing		Production Quality Control Production Planning	Process & Indus. Eng.	

EXHIBIT B–2 (concluded)

B. EDUCATION AND EXPERIENCE

—For each knowledge content area, the jobholder has the following amounts of on-the-job experience and formal education that contribute to proficient accomplishment of the position's responsibilities:

KNOW-HOW AREA	YEARS OF EXPERIENCE	AMOUNT OF FORMAL EDUCATION
Production	5	Pre-university qualifications equivalent to at least 13 years of education
Process & Indus. Eng.	5	
Quality Control	3	
Production Planning	3	

EXHIBIT B–3

Can-Corp.   Professional/Managerial Job Description

Job Title: DIRECTOR, EMPLOYEE BENEFITS

Job Number:

Reports To (Job Title): V. P., EMPLOYEE RELATIONS

Division/Staff Responsibility: EMPLOYEE RELATIONS

Location: TORONTO GHQ

I. Organization—Attach Chart
Number of People Supervised and Functionally Directed

Salaried Direct: Exempt ___1___ Nonexempt ___1___

Salaried Work Force: Exempt _____ Nonexempt ___4___

Hourly: Direct _____ Work Force _____

Functionally Directed _____

II. Position Summary
A. Position Objective

Direct the design, implementation and administration of all corporate salaried, hourly and retiree benefit programs, both domestic and foreign.

B. Position Functions
1. Direct the development and implementation of policies, improvements and modifications to all Corporate Employee Benefit Programs for salaried, hourly and retirees.
2. Provide procedures and policy interpretation necessary for the uniform administration of all benefit programs.
3. Direct personnel at GHQ, Plants, Mines and Regional Offices in uniform application and administration of employee benefit programs.
4. Establish and direct employee and management informative benefits communication programs.
5. Recommend and establish benefit plans unique to foreign nationals employed by wholly or partially owned overseas subsidiaries.
6. Advise and recommend modifications to benefit plans based on surveys and federal, provincial, and foreign legislation.

Description Prepared by   Date

Line Approver   Date

(If additional space is needed, please use back of form.)

DISCUSSION AND REVIEW QUESTIONS

1. What did the Hawthorne experiments reveal about group influences on individual productivity?
2. How does job enrichment differ from job enlargement?
3. Contrast the perspectives of scientific management and human relations.
4. What assumptions do these two perspectives make about what motivates employees?
5. How do hours of work limit/facilitate various job design strategies?
6. Applying the diagnostic model, what factors should an organization consider in designing jobs?
7. What is the critical advantage of quantitative job analysis over conventional approaches? Why is this important?
8. If human judgement is central to job analysis, why bother doing it?
9. Refer back to Miles and Snow's strategic organization types, (Defender, Analyzer, Prospector) discussed in Chapter Three. Would the organization strategy make any difference in the role job analysis might play?
10. Would strategic organization type make any difference in job design?
11. Discuss the effects and cost implications of errors in job analysis on the P/HRM uses shown in Exhibit 4–4.
12. Invite a job analyst from a local company to give a guest lecture on job analysis.

NOTES AND REFERENCES

1. Adapted from Studs Terkel, *Working: People Talk about What They Do All Day and How They Feel about What They Do* (New York: Pantheon Books, a Division of Random House, 1974), Copyright 1972, 1974 by Studs Terkel.
2. Ibid.
3. H. G. Heneman, Jr., "Work and Nonwork: Historical Perspectives," in *Work and Non-Work in the Year 2001*, ed. M. Dunnette (Monterey, Calif.: Brooks/Cole Publishing, 1973).
4. Richard T. Mowday, Lyman W. Porter, and Richard M. Steers, *Employee-Organization Linkages* (New York: Academic Press, 1982).
5. F. Herzberg, B. Mausner, and B. Snyderman, *The Motivation to Work*, 2nd ed. (New York: John Wiley & Sons, 1959); F. Herzberg, *Work and the Nature of Man* (Cleveland: World Publishing, 1966).
6. Herzberg et al., *Motivation*.
7. Charles O'Reilly, G. N. Parlette, and J. Blum, "Perceptual Measures of Task Characteristics: The Biasing Effects of Differing Frames of References and Job Attitudes," *Academy of Management Journal* 123, no. 1 (1980), pp. 118–31.
8. George H. Dreher, "Individual Needs or Correlates of Satisfaction and Involvement with a Modified Scanlon Plan Company," *Journal of Vocational Behavior*, August 1980, pp. 89–94; Joseph E. Champoux, "The World of Nonwork: Some Implications for Job Redesign Efforts," *Personnel Psychology*, Spring 1979, pp. 61–75; D. Robey, "Task Design, Work Values, and Worker Response: An Experimental Test," *Organizational Behavior and Human Performance*, October 1974, pp. 264–73.

9. Randall B. Dunham, "Reactions to Job Characteristics: Moderating Effects of the Organization," *Academy of Management Journal*, March 1977, pp. 42–65.
10. Edwin A. Locke, "The Ideas of Frederick W. Taylor: An Evaluation," *Academy of Management Review* 7, no. 1 (1982), pp. 14–25; F. W. Taylor, *Scientific Management* (New York: Harper & Row, 1964.)
11. Robert Fulford, "Firm Management," *Saturday Night*, September 1983, pp. 42–48, 52.
12. This summary of the trail that leads to Woods Gordon's 30th-floor head office in the Toronto-Dominion Centre in Toronto is abstracted from Fulford, "Firm Management."
13. J. Richard Hackman, Jone L. Pearce, and Jane Caminis Wolfe, "Effects of Changes in Job Characteristics on Work Attitudes and Behaviors: A Naturally Occurring Quasi-Experiment," *Organizational Behavior and Human Performance* 21, no. 2 (1978), pp. 289–304; D. Clawson, *Bureaucracy and the Labor Process: The Transformation of U.S. Industry, 1860–1920* (New York: Monthly Review Press, 1980); Peter Drucker, *The Practice of Management* (New York: Harper & Row, 1954); M. Nadworny, *Scientific Management and the Unions, 1900–1932* (Cambridge, Mass.: Harvard University Press, 1955); D. Noble, *America by Design: Science, Technology and the Rise of Corporate Capitalism* (Oxford, Eng.: Oxford University Press, 1977).
14. Gary J. Blau and Ralph Katerberg, "Toward Enhancing Research with the Social Information Processing Approach to Job Design," *Academy of Management Review* 7, no. 4 (1982), pp. 543–51; A. Carey, "The Hawthorne Studies: A Radical Criticism," *American Sociological Review* 32, no. 2 (1976), pp. 295–308; J. R. Hackman and G. R. Oldham, *Work Redesign*, (Reading, Mass.: Addison-Wesley Publishing, 1979).
15. E. Mayo, *The Human Problems of an Industrial Civilization* (New York: Macmillan, 1933); N. Mouzelis, *Organization and Bureaucracy* (London: Routledge & Kegan Paul, 1967).
16. Gary L. Cooper, "Humanizing the Work Place in Europe: An Overview of Six Countries," *Personnel Journal*, June 1980, pp. 488–91.
17. Stephen H. Fuller and Berth Jonsson, "Corporate Approaches to the Quality of Work Life," *Personnel Journal*, August 1980, pp. 645–48.
18. L. E. Davis, R. R. Canter, and J. Hoffman, "Current Job Design Criteria," *Journal of Industrial Engineering* 6 (1955), pp. 5–11.
19. M. J. Gannon, B. A. Poole, and R. E. Prangley, "Involuntary Job Rotation and Work Behavior," *Personnel Journal*, June 1972, pp. 446–48.
20. Denise M. Rousseau, "Technological Differences in Job Characteristics, Employee Satisfaction, and Motivation: A Synthesis of Job Design Research and Sociotechnical Systems Theory," *Organizational Behavior and Human Performance*, June 1977, pp. 18–42.
21. David J. Cherrington and J. Lynn England, "The Desire for an Enriched Job as a Moderator of the Enrichment-Satisfaction Relationship," *Organizational Behavior and Human Performance*, February 1980, pp. 139–59.
22. Kae H. Chung and Monica F. Ross, "Differences in Motivational Properties between Job Enlargement and Job Enrichment," *Academy of Management Review*, January 1977, pp. 113–21.
23. A. Campbell, "Management Styles Are Changing to Include Employee Participation," *The Globe and Mail*, October 7, 1985.

24. W. List, "When Workers and Managers Act as a Team," *Report on Business Magazine*, October 1985, pp. 60–67.
25. "A Study in Workplace Innovation," *Report on Business Magazine*, October 1985, p. 64.
26. Susan Wright and Serge Lareau, "An Analysis of a Work Improvement Program in Air Canada," in *Quality of Working Life: Contemporary Cases*, ed. J. B. Cunningham and T. H. White (Ottawa: Labour Canada, 1984).
27. Ibid., p. 153.
28. Hackman and Oldham, *Work Redesign*.
29. Ibid.
30. Ibid.
31. Robert J. Harvey, Robert S. Billings, and Kevin J. Nilan, "Confirmatory Factor Analysis of the Job Diagnostic Survey: Good News and Bad News," *Journal of Applied Psychology* 70, no. 3 (1985), pp. 461–68; Eileen A. Hogan and Daniel A. Martell, "A Confirmatory Structural Equations Analysis of the Job Characteristics Model," *Organizational Behavior and Human Decision Processes* 39, no. 2 (1987), pp. 242–63; Jacqueline R. Idaszak and Fritz Dragow, "A Revision of the Job Diagnostic Survey: Elimination of a Measurement Artifact," *Journal of Applied Psychology* 72, no. 1 (1987), pp. 69–74.
32. Donald G. Gardner, Randall B. Dunham, Larry L. Cummings, and Jon L. Pierce, "Focus of Attention at Work and Reactions to Organizational Change," *Journal of Applied Behavioral Science* 23, no. 3 (1987), pp. 351–70.
33. Ibid.
34. John M. Nicholas and Marsha Katz, "Research Methods and Reporting Practices in Organization Development: A Review and Some Guidelines," *Academy of Management Review* 10, no. 4 (1985), pp. 737–49.
35. Gardner et al., "Focus of Attention."
36. Sam Bacharach and Stephen Mitchell, *Job Reference Manual* (Ithaca, N.Y.: Organization Analysis and Practice, 1983).
37. William F. Glueck, "Changing Hours of Work: A Review and Analysis of the Research," *Personnel Administrator*, March 1979, pp. 44–62; Donald J. Petersen, "Flexitime in the United States: The Lessons of Experience," *Personnel*, January–February 1980, pp. 21–31.
38. Randall B. Dunham and Jon L. Pierce, "Attitudes Toward Work Schedules: Construct Definition, Instrument Development, and Validation," *Academy of Management Journal* 29, no. 1 (1986), pp. 170–82.
39. John W. Newstrom and Jon L. Pierce, "Alternative Work Schedules: The State of the Art," *Personnel Administrator*, October 1979, pp. 19–23.
40. John M. Ivancevich and Herbert L. Lyon, "The Shortened Workweek: A Field Experience," *Journal of Applied Psychology*, February 1977, pp. 34–37.
41. R. T. Golembiewski and C. W. Proehl, "A Survey of the Empirical Literature on Flexible Workhours: Character and Consequence of a Major Innovation," *Academy of Management Review* 3, no. 4 (1978), pp. 837–53; R. T. Golembiewski and C. W. Proehl, "Public Sector Applications of Flexible Workhours: A Review of Available Experience," *Public Administration Review* 40, no. 1 (1980), pp. 72–85; W. Hicks and R. J. Klimoski, "The Impact of Flexitime on Employee Attitudes," *Academy of Management Journal* 24, no. 2 (1981), pp. 333–41.
42. John M. Ivancevich and William F. Glueck, *Foundations of Personnel/Human Resource Management*, 3rd ed. (Plano, Tex.: Business Publications, 1986); see also

S. Nollen and V. H. Martin, *Alternative Work Schedules* (New York: AMACOM, 1978); and S. Nollen, *New Work Schedules in Practice: Managing Time in a Changing Society* (New York: Van Nostrand Reinhold, 1981).
43. John R. Turney and Stanley L. Cohen, "Alternative Work Schedules Increase Employee Satisfaction," *Personnel Journal*, March 1983, pp. 202–7; Cary B. Barad, "Flexitime under Scrutiny: Research on Work Adjustment and Organizational Performance," *Personnel Administrator*, May 1980, pp. 69–74.
44. Virginia E. Schein, Elizabeth H. Maurer, and Jan F. Jovak, "Impact of Flexible Working Hours on Productivity," *Journal of Applied Psychology*, August 1977, pp. 463–65.
45. B. Rosen, S. Rynes, and T. Mahoney, "Compensation, Jobs and Gender," *Harvard Business Review* 61, no. 4 (1983), pp. 170–72, 174, 176, 178, 184, 186, 190; Michael Frease and Robert A. Zawacki, "Job Sharing: An Answer to Productivity Problems," *Personnel Administrator*, October 1979, pp. 35–38; J. McCroskey, "Work and Families: What Is the Employer's Responsibility?" *Personnel Journal*, January 1982, pp. 30–33; R. E. Kopelman, J. H. Greenhaus, and T. E. Connolly, "A Model of Work, Family, and Interrole Conflict: A Construct Validation Study," *Organizational Behavior and Human Performance* 32, no. 1 (1983), pp. 198–215.
46. E. J. McCormick, *Job Analysis: Methods and Applications* (New York: AMACOM, 1979); George T. Milkovich and Jerry Newman, *Compensation* (Plano, Tex.: Business Publications, 1984); Stephen E. Bemis, Ann Holt Belenky, and Dee Ann Soder, *Job Analysis* (Washington, D.C.: Bureau of National Affairs, 1983).
47. E. J. McCormick, "Job and Task Analysis," in *Handbook of Industrial and Organizational Psychology*, ed. M. Dunnette (Chicago: Rand McNally, 1976).
48. Kenneth N. Wexley and Gary P. Latham, *Developing and Training Human Resources in Organizations* (Glenview, Ill.: Scott, Foresman, 1981).
49. See Chapter Eight.
50. K. Pearlman, "Job Families: A Review and Discussion of the Implications for Personnel Selection," *Psychological Bulletin* 82, no. 1 (1980), pp. 1–28.
51. Richard Henderson, *Performance Appraisal: Theory to Practice* (Reston, Va.: Reston Publishing, 1980); H. John Bernardin and Richard Beatty, *Performance Appraisal* (Boston: Kent Publishing, 1984).
52. Milkovich and Newman, *Compensation*; Ronald C. Page, "The Use of Job Content Information for Compensation and Reward Systems" (paper presented at Academy of Management Conference, August 1982, New York); Walter W. Tornow, "An Integrated Personnel Approach to Job Analysis and Job Evaluation" (paper presented at Conference on Job Analysis, Institute of Industrial Relations, University of California, Berkeley, February 1979).
53. M. D. Dunnette, L. M. Hough, and R. L. Rosse, "Task and Job Taxonomies as a Basis for Identifying Labor Supply Sources and Evaluating Employment Qualifications," *Human Resources Planning* 2, no. 1 (1979).
54. J. J. Jones and Thomas DeCotiis, "Job Analysis: National Survey Findings," *Personnel Journal*, October 1969, pp. 805–9.
55. Milkovich and Newman, *Compensation*.
56. Edward L. Levine, Ronald A. Ash, and Frank Sistrunk, "Evaluation of Job Analysis Methods by Experienced Job Analysts," *Academy of Management Journal* 26, no. 2 (1983), pp. 339–48.
57. George T. Milkovich and Charles Cogill, "Work Measurement," in *Handbook of*

Wage and Salary Administration, ed. Milton L. Rock (New York: McGraw-Hill, 1984); for a suggested approach to evaluating job analysis methods, see Ronald A. Ash and Edward L. Levine, "A Framework for Evaluating Job Analysis Methods," *Personnel*, November–December 1980, pp. 53–59.

58. Luis R. Gomez-Mejia, Ronald C. Page, and Walter W. Tornow, "A Comparison of the Practical Utility of Traditional, Statistical, and Hybrid Job Evaluation Approaches," *Academy of Management Journal* 25, no. 4 (1982), pp. 790–809.

59. See, for example, Fine and Wiley, *Functional Job Analysis*; E. J. McCormick, P. R. Jeanneret, and R. Mecham, "A Study of Job Characteristics and Job Dimensions Based on the Position Analysis Questionnaire," *Journal of Applied Psychology* 56 (1972), pp. 347–68; E. S. Primoff, *How to Prepare and Conduct Job Element Examinations* (Washington, D.C.: U.S. Government Printing Office, 1975); R. E. Christal, "The United States Air Force Occupational Research Project," *JSAS Catalog of Selected Documents in Psychology* 4 (1974), (Ms. no. 651), for a description of task inventory—CODAP; F. M. Lopez, G. A. Kesselman, and F. E. Lopez, "An Empirical Test of a Trait-Oriented Job Analysis Technique," *Personnel Psychology* 34 (1981), pp. 479–502; J. C. Flanagan, "The Critical Incident Technique," *Psychological Bulletin* 51 (1954), pp. 327–58; E. A. Fleishman, "Toward a Taxonomy of Human Performance," *American Psychologist* 30 (1975), pp. 1127–49, for ability requirements scales.

60. M. J. Wallace, "Methodology, Research Practice, and Progress in Personnel and Industrial Relations," *Academy of Management Review* 8, no. 1 (1983), pp. 6–13.

61. U.S. Department of Labor, Manpower Administration, *Handbook for Analyzing Jobs* (Washington, D.C.: U.S. Government Printing Office, 1972); S. A. Fine and W. W. Wiley, *An Introduction to Functional Job Analysis*, monograph no. 4 (Kalamazoo, Mich.: W. E. Upjohn Institute for Employment Research, 1971).

62. Fine and Wiley, *Functional Job Analysis*.

63. Ibid.

64. R. I. Henderson, *Compensation Management* (Reston, Va.: Reston Publishing, 1979); Alfred R. Brandt, "Describing Hourly Jobs," in *Handbook of Wage and Salary Administration*, ed. Milton L. Rock (New York: McGraw-Hill, 1972).

65. Frank Krzystofiak, Jerry M. Newman, and Gary Anderson, "A Qualified Approach to Measurement of Job Content: Procedures and Payoffs," *Personnel Psychology*, Summer 1979, pp. 341–57.

66. For some of the best research on scaling of quantitative job analysis inventories, see J. E. Morsh, "Job Analysis in the United States Air Force," *Personnel Psychology* 17, no. 17 (1964), pp. 7–17; J. E. Morsh, M. Joyce Giorgia, and J. M. Madden, "A Job Analysis of a Complex Utilization Field—The R&D Management Officer" (Personnel Research Laboratory, Aerospace Medical Division, Air Force Systems Command, 1965); J. N. Mosel, "The Domain of Worker Functions as a Partially Ordered Set" (paper presented at American Psychological Association Meetings, Philadelphia, 1963); A. I. Siegel and D. G. Schultz, "Post-Training Performance Criterion Development and Application: A Comparative Multidimensional Scaling Analysis of the Tasks Performed by Naval Aviation Electronics Technicians at Two Job Levels" (Wayne, Pa.: Applied Psychological Services, 1964).

67. McCormick, "Job Analysis"; Robert C. Mecham, "Quantitative Job Evaluation Using the Position Analysis Questionnaire," *Personnel Administrator*, June 1983, pp. 82–88, 124. Information on the PAQ is available from PAQ Services, P.O.

Box 3337, Logan, Utah 84321, telephone (801) 752-5698. For information on the Air Force Inventory, see J. E. Morsh and W. B. Archer, "Procedural Guide for Conducting Occupational Surveys in the United States Air Force," (Personnel Research Laboratory Aerospace Medical Division, Lackland Air Force Base, Texas: PRI-TR-67-11, September 1967); Morsh, "Job Analysis in the USAF."
68. Ronald A. Ash and S. L. Edgell, "A Note on the Readability of the Position Analysis Questionnaire (PAQ)," *Journal of Applied Psychology* 60, no. 4 (1975), pp. 765–66.
69. The PDQ is available from Control Data Corporation, 8200 34th Avenue South, Minneapolis, Minn.
70. Krzystofiak et al., "A Quantified Approach."
71. Milkovich and Newman, *Compensation*.
72. Howard Risher, "Job Analysis: A Management Perspective," *Employee Relations Law Journal*, Spring 1979, pp. 535–51.
73. Dunnette et al., "Task and Job Taxonomies."
74. Paul Sparks, "Job Analysis," in *Personnel Management*, ed. K. Rowland and G. Ferris (Boston: Allyn & Bacon, 1982).
75. Ernest J. McCormick: "Job Information: Its Development and Applications," in *Handbook of Personnel and Industrial Relations*, ed. D. Yoder and H. G. Heneman III (Washington, D.C.: Bureau of National Affairs, 1979); *Job Analysis* (New York: AMACOM, 1979); "Job and Task Analysis," in *Handbook of Industrial and Organizational Psychology*, ed. M. Dunnette (Chicago: Rand McNally, 1976); E. J. McCormick, R. H. Finn, and C. D. Scheips, "Patterns of Job Requirements," *Journal of Applied Psychology* 41 (1957), pp. 358–65. E. J. McCormick, P. R. Jeanneret, and R. C. Mecham: *The Development and Background of the Position Analysis Questionnaire (PAQ)* (West Lafayette, Ind.: Occupational Research Center, Purdue University, 1969); and *A Study of Job Characteristics and Job Dimensions as Based on the Position Analysis Questionnaire* (West Lafayette, Ind.: Occupational Research Center, Purdue University, 1969). P. R. Jeanneret and R. C. Mecham, "A Study of Job Characteristics and Job Dimensions as Based on the Position Analysis Questionnaire (PAQ)," *Journal of Applied Psychology* 56, no. 2 (1972), pp. 347–68. R. C. Mecham and E. J. McCormick, *The Rated Attribute Requirements of Job Elements in the Position Analysis Questionnaire* (West Lafayette, Ind.: Occupational Research Center, Purdue University, 1969); and *The Use of Data Based on the Position Analysis Questionnaire* (West Lafayette, Ind.: Occupational Research Center, Purdue University, 1969). R. C. Mecham, E. J. McCormick, and P. R. Jeanneret, *Technical Manual for the Position Analysis Questionnaire (PAQ) (System II)* (Logan, Utah: PAQ Services, 1977).
76. Paul Sparks, "Job Analysis," in *Personnel Management*, ed. K. Rowland and G. Ferris (Boston: Allyn & Bacon, 1982).
77. Gomez et al., "Comparison."
78. Ibid.
79. Levine et al., "Evaluation of Job Analysis Methods by Experienced Job Analysts."
80. Ibid.
81. Dunnette et al., "Task and Job Taxonomies."
82. Marvin D. Dunnette, *Personnel Selection and Placement* (Belmont, Calif.: Wadsworth, 1966).
83. Ibid., p. 89.
84. N. H. Trattner, S. A. Fine, and J. F. Kubis, "A Comparison of Worker Require-

ment Ratings by Reading Job Descriptions and by Direct Observation," *Personnel Psychology* 8 (1955), pp. 183–94; Herbert G. Heneman III, Donald P. Schwab, John A. Fossum, and Lee D. Dyer, *Personnel/Human Resource Management*, rev. ed. (Homewood, Ill.: Richard D. Irwin, 1983).

85. Wayne F. Cascio, *Applied Psychology in Personnel Management*, 2nd ed. (Reston, Va.: Reston Publishing, 1982).
86. Ibid., p. 50; also see Dunnette, *Personnel Selection*, chap. 5.
87. E. T. Cornelius III, T. J. Carron, and M. M. Collins, "Job Analysis Models and Job Classification," *Personnel Psychology* 32, no. 4 (1979), pp. 693–708; also see R. W. Lissitz, J. L. Mendoza, C. J. Huberty, and V. H. Markos, "Some Ideas on a Methodology for Determining Job Similarities/Differences," *Personnel Psychology* 32 (1979), pp. 517–28; and JoAnn Lee and Jorge L. Mendoza, "A Comparison of Techniques which Test for Job Differences," *Personnel Psychology* 34, no. 4 (1981), pp. 731–48.
88. Roger J. Plachy, "Writing Job Descriptions that Get Results," *Personnel*, October 1987, pp. 56–63.
89. Ibid., pp. 57, 59.
90. *CCDO Guide*, 6th ed. (Ottawa: Employment and Immigration Canada, 1986; Cat. No. MP53-8/1986E).
91. Interview with R. Emery, EIC Regional Economic Services Branch, BC/YT Region, April 25, 1986, and sections of written material supplied April 29, 1986.
92. Ibid.

CHAPTER FIVE
NATURE OF THE EMPLOYEES

CHAPTER OUTLINE

I. Individual Differences and the Diagnostic Model
II. Determinants of Individual Performance
    A. Ability
    B. Motivation
    C. Role Perceptions and Situational Contingencies
III. Theories of Motivation
    A. Content Theories
    B. Process Theories
IV. Careers
    A. Career Orientation
    B. Career Stages
    C. Careers and Organizational Effectiveness
V. The Supervisor
    A. Leadership Styles
VI. The Work Group
    A. Organization Advantages
    B. Designing Work Groups
    C. P/HRM and Work Groups
VII. Summary

As a world leader in aircraft and power plant simulators, CAE Electronics Ltd. of Montreal is one of Canada's shining stars in the field of advanced technology. The company credits a large share of this success to the quality and loyalty of its employees.[1] It does not pay the highest salaries, yet CAE Electronics is able to attract the best talent through a carefully nurtured supportive work environment. Responsibility is decentralized through project team management, job security and retraining are emphasized (unlike many engineering firms in Canada), and status differences within the organization are minimized. This corporate culture is a magnet to bright individuals who feel stifled in more impersonal organizations.

Like CAE Electronics, every organization reflects the nature of the employees it hires and develops. Through their everyday work relationships, people establish the social foundation of the firm, so understanding individuals and their work relationships is an important part of P/HRM.

In Part Two of this book we have been examining the organizational environment of P/HRM. The nature of organizations, particularly their objectives and strategic directions, was covered in Chapter Three; the nature of the work, its analysis and design, was discussed in Chapter Four. The nature of employees, supervisors, and work groups is discussed in this chapter.

INDIVIDUAL DIFFERENCES AND THE DIAGNOSTIC MODEL

In all organizations, the behaviour of employees is a significant influence on P/HRM.[2] Individuals vary in ability, motivation, and role perceptions.[3] Some of these differences have a genetic component. For example, new research supports the idea that many personality characteristics are determined by heredity rather than life experiences.[4] We also inherit certain physical characteristics that influence our ability to play hockey, do heavy physical labour, and perform other tasks. But no hockey player would question the value of years of practice honing the abilities required for that sport. While genetics may limit the behaviours at which we can become proficient, most differences in ability derive from learning experiences and practice. No P/HRM activity can become successful if it does not recognize these individual differences. Individual differences influence whom we hire, promote, train, and develop.[5]

DETERMINANTS OF INDIVIDUAL PERFORMANCE

A major function of P/HRM is to maximize organizational effectiveness. This includes implementing programs and practices that enhance the performance of individual employees. But what causes one employee to do a better job than another?

EXHIBIT 5–1
Determinants of Individual Performance

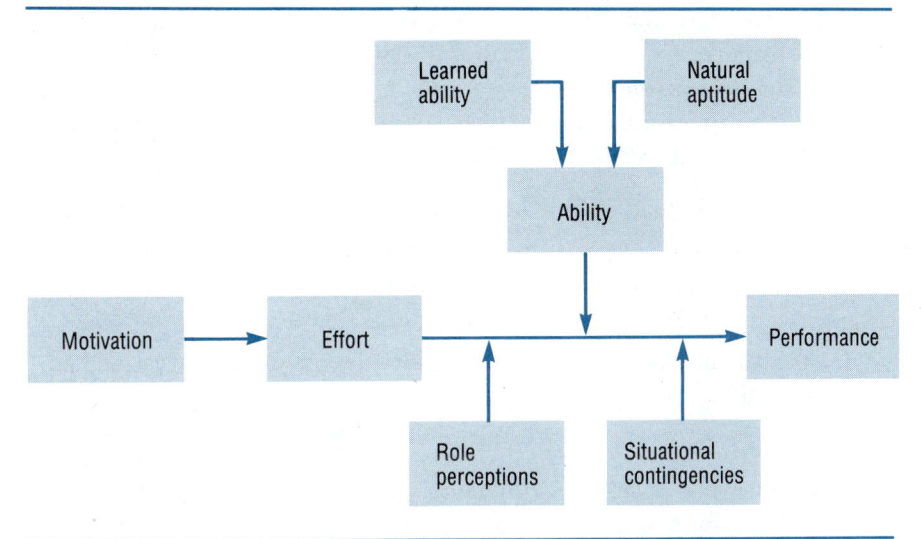

```
                    Learned              Natural
                    ability              aptitude
                         \              /
                          v            v
                           Ability
                              |
                              v
   Motivation --> Effort --------------> Performance
                     ^                ^
                     |                |
                   Role          Situational
               perceptions      contingencies
```

Source: Adapted from Dennis W. Organ and Thomas Bateman, *Organizational Behavior: An Applied Psychological Approach*, 3rd ed. (Plano, Tex.: Business Publications, 1986).

As Exhibit 5–1 illustrates, four factors directly influence individual performance. These variables include: (1) *ability*, the natural aptitude and learned capability to perform those specific tasks; (2) *motivation*, the human forces that determine the form, direction, intensity, and duration of the individual's effort; (3) *role perceptions*, the beliefs about job requirements and, more specifically, what the task actually involves; and (4) *situational contingencies*, the environmental constraints and facilitators to job performance that are beyond the employee's control.

Ability

> **Definition**
> *Ability* is the learned capability (i.e., developed from experience or practice) to engage in a task plus the person's innate aptitude for the task. *Aptitude* refers to a natural talent or facility in mastering a task.[6]

As this definition states, ability has two dimensions: natural ability (called *aptitude*) and learned ability. Natural aptitudes are genetically based talents or attributes that enable us to learn certain tasks faster and/or better than others. For example, some people learn to be artists more easily than others because they have innate aptitudes such as creativity, perceptual accuracy, and the appropriate motor skills. Some abilities are also learned from experience and practice. Examples abound of people with physical and mental disabilities who have accomplished remarkable feats.

Just as we differ from one another in appearance, we have diverse abilities and aptitudes. Psychologists categorize various kinds of abilities as:[7]

Mechanical ability—ability to visualize how parts fit together into a whole; comprehension of mechanical relationships.

Motor coordination ability—the ability to move the body effectively to perform physical acts.

Intellectual abilities—general intelligence or reasoning; verbal and numerical ability.

Creative abilities—innovative and artistic abilities; aesthetic judgement.

Whether a particular ability influences individual performance depends on the tasks performed. Finger dexterity—the ability to handle small objects with the fingers—is more important for employees working with tiny precision parts at Litton Systems Canada Ltd. than for warehouse workers in the same firm. In other words, specific individual abilities contribute to performance only when they are matched with corresponding job requirements.

The influence of individual ability on job performance is well documented.[8] However, the strength of this relationship is not as high as you might think, because the form of the relationship between ability and performance can be complex. General intelligence may be related to performance on assembly-line jobs, but this does not mean applicants with the highest intelligence are best suited to these tasks.[9] The lack of challenge may result in subpar performance by these high-ability individuals.

With this complex relationship between individual ability and job performance in mind, several P/HRM policies and practices have been developed.

P/HRM Influences on Ability

Job-related ability can be influenced by careful selection among job applicants, by training, and by designing jobs to increase the match between abilities possessed and those abilities required on the job.

Selection and Placement. Organizations have long realized the role of pay in the selection process. If an applicant pool is too small to ensure selection of enough qualified employees, one standard strategy is to raise the relative wage to attract more applicants.[10]

Paying above the market rate triggers several phenomena. First, the higher relative wage makes the job more attractive, which makes recruitment easier. Second, the larger pool of applicants means more opportunity to select individuals whose abilities better match job requirements. The better a match between individual abilities and job requirements, the higher the expected job performance, other things being equal (see Chapters Nine and Fourteen).

Training and Development. Performance can also be improved through training and development programs (see Chapter Ten). The P/HRM process is highly subject to errors. For example, some job applicants do not end up performing as well on the job as expected. To identify these errors, most organizations conduct formal performance evaluations. One outcome of this performance evaluation process is the identification of training and development needs intended to strengthen abilities necessary for improved job performance.

Motivation

Definition
Motivation is a person's inner forces of energy that initiate, shape, sustain, and direct behaviour to satisfy unmet needs.

Why are some people more willing than others to come to work? Why do some work harder than others to achieve organizational objectives? Motivation is a difficult concept to understand and apply. It fluctuates within each individual in response to so many factors that it is impossible to identify, much less control them all. We cannot see motivation. As an abstract construct, it can only be inferred from observable behaviour. Motivation also interacts with ability in complex ways to affect performance.[11]

Many psychologists interested in motivation agree that the key issue is the goal-directed nature of behaviour.[12] If managers could discover why behaviour occurs and why it is directed toward one of countless possible goals, considerable progress could be made in improving employee performance. Consider two junior accountants who work side by side on the same project. One accountant concentrates on the logical structure of the accounts while persevering to complete the job accurately and quickly. The other's energies are directed toward planning this weekend's ski trip while the task at hand receives cursory attention. Both of these employees are working on the same job in similar work environments; each receives the same pay and works the same hours. Yet their behaviours are directed to different goals.

Role Perceptions and Situational Contingencies

> **Definition**
> *Role perception* refers to the way in which employees define the job requirements. It includes the types of behaviour believed to be appropriate for the job in general as well as for specific tasks.

> **Definition**
> *Situational contingencies* are the environmental conditions surrounding the job that may facilitate or constrain performance. At least in the short term, they are beyond the employee's control.

Employees may have both the ability and motivation to perform the job well, but fail in their tasks because they misunderstand the job requirements. In this respect, job performance is also a function of role perceptions. Role perceptions steer employee efforts toward a particular set of goals. If those goals are inappropriate—that is, the employee lacks role clarity—performance suffers.[13] For an extreme example, one embarrassed warehouse employee mistakenly shipped a large piece of equipment at great expense to a customer's offices in London, England, rather than to the intended destination of London, Ontario. The employee was both motivated and able to ship the parcel; unfortunately, the task requirements were confused.

Finally, individual performance is influenced by situational contingencies. A job cannot be done well if there is not enough time, people, budget, or facilities.[14] Situational constraints are interventions between the individual's effort and the performance goal. Inhibiting conditions limit the potential performance of employees in a particular situation. Facilitating conditions, on the other hand, potentially increase performance without any changes in motivation, ability, or role clarity.

THEORIES OF MOTIVATION

As noted above, motivation is a complex concept. To shed some light on the countless motivational problems in the world of business, we present a few of the more prominent theories. We will discuss these theories as they bear on job performance, even though they may also have relevance for other work behaviours such as absenteeism and turnover.

Content Theories

Content theories can be distinguished by their emphasis on *what* motivates people rather than *how* people are motivated. The key variable in most of these theories is different types of needs. It has been speculated that psychologists have enumerated several hundred needs.[15]

The two most well-known content theories include the work by Maslow,[16] and by Herzberg, Mausner, and Snyderman.[17]

Maslow. Maslow's theory is based on a hierarchy of five needs (Exhibit 5–2), each assumed to motivate behaviour in varying degrees.[18] Maslow argues that lower-level needs in the hierarchy are prepotent: behaviour is directed toward satisfying these needs until they are sufficiently fulfilled to make the next higher order need dominant. For example, people living below the poverty line may direct their behaviour toward obtaining the necessary food to satisfy their physiological needs. If they obtain jobs that help to consistently satisfy these needs, the need for security becomes dominant, and behaviour is then directed toward obtaining physical and emotional security. Higher-order needs become progressively more important as lower-order needs are satisfied.

One of the major problems with this approach is that it is extremely difficult to identify which needs are prepotent at any given time. Without this information, it is virtually impossible to determine how a work environment should be structured to improve performance. For example, research indicates that needs vary by age, geographic location (urban/rural), socioeconomic

EXHIBIT 5–2
Maslow's Hierarchy of Needs

1.	Physiological needs	The need for food, water, and air.
2.	Safety needs	The need for security, stability, and the absence from pain, threat, or illness.
3.	Social needs	Need for affection, belongingness, love.
4.	Esteem needs	Need for personal feelings of achievement or self-esteem and also a need for recognition or respect from others.
5.	Self-actualization needs	Need to become all one is capable of becoming, to realize one's own potential, or achieve self-fulfillment.

Source: George T. Milkovich and Jerry M. Newman, *Compensation*, 2nd ed. (Plano, Tex.: Business Publications, 1987).

EXHIBIT 5–3
Herzberg's Two Factors

Hygiene Factors (context)	Motivating Factors (content)
Company policies	Feelings of accomplishment
Pay	
Benefits	
Supervision	Feelings of achievement
Working conditions	Recognition
Job security	Personal growth

status, and gender, to name a few. There is even speculation that the needs of the general population have been shifting toward a greater concern for such higher-level needs as autonomy and self-actualization.[19]

Herzberg. Herzberg's theory appears very similar to Maslow's.[20] He argues that two types of factors are present across organizations: hygienes and motivators (see Exhibit 5–3). Hygiene factors include such things as company policy, administration, supervision, salary, interpersonal relations, and working conditions. Motivators are represented by opportunities for advancement, achievement, responsibility, and recognition. In essence, it might be argued that Maslow's theory has gravitated in the same direction as Herzberg's. If in fact most lower-order needs are generally satisfied in our affluent society, then individual needs that are prepotent in Maslow's framework include esteem and self-actualization.[21] As conceived by Maslow, these needs are very similar to Herzberg's conception of advancement, achievement, and recognition. Since these factors are prepotent, they assume responsibility for a great deal of the goal direction of individuals. In Herzberg's terms, they become the motivators, the factors that can lead to job satisfaction if met by the organization.

Differences between Maslow and Herzberg. The one major difference that can be inferred from these two theories is the function assumed by pay. Numerous studies have shown that pay can satisfy, to some extent, Maslow's needs. In contrast, Herzberg's work is often interpreted as if he argued that pay is solely a hygiene factor, necessary to thwart job dissatisfaction, but not appropriate for motivating behaviour. While Herzberg's theory can be attacked on a number of grounds, it is inappropriate to assume Herzberg relegated pay only to the status of a hygiene factor.[22] The original work by Herzberg demonstrates that pay takes on significance as a source of satisfaction when it is perceived as a form of recognition or reward. In this context, pay provides feedback to an employee in the form of recognition for achievement.

Process Theories

Process theories of motivation focus on *how* people are motivated. They recognize the role of content theories in examining the types of needs and reinforcers that are part of the motivational process, but they also attempt to explain how this process operates.

Drive Theory. Perhaps the first major process theory of motivation to receive considerable attention was Hull's drive theory.[23] The model sought to explain how motivation occurred (i.e., choice to expend effort, level, and degree of persistence) and the direction of the behaviour that resulted. A distilled version of this model indicates that behaviour engaged in by an individual is a multiplicative function of three factors: (1) habit strength, which represents the effects of learning and gives behaviour its direction; (2) drive, which varies as a function of level of biological need (e.g., hunger, thirst); and (3) the incentive value of the expected reward.[24]

What relevance does this model have for improving employee performance? Much of the answer comes from an article by Opsahl and Dunnette,[25] which seeks to explain why a seemingly neutral object (money) with no direct ability to satisfy needs, becomes valuable to people and is capable of motivating behaviour. According to Opsahl and Dunnette, money can assume properties as a secondary reinforcer. Secondary reinforcers are objects which when frequently associated with other objects that reduce biological needs, eventually also become reinforcers. In Hull's framework, then, money can be associated with food and drink (which satisfy biological needs), for example, and subsequently become secondary reinforcers. Over time, as performance continues to be rewarded with pay increases, the pay-performance link may become stronger in terms of habit strength.

Expectancy Theory

The theory that has captured the most attention of motivation researchers over the past two decades is expectancy theory. Although slight variations of the theory exist,[26] expectancy theory basically postulates that people will direct their effort toward those actions perceived to lead to desired outcomes. This assumes a rational model of decision making whereby individuals assess the costs and benefits of alternate courses of action and select the course with the highest payoff.[27]

One of the more popular versions of expectancy theory is presented in Exhibit 5-4. The key variable to be explained in this model is effort level. According to Exhibit 5-4, effort level is dependent on three factors: (1) effort→performance expectancy, (2) performance→outcome expectancy, and (3) valence.

Effort→Performance Expectancy. The effort→performance expectancy (E→P) is the individual's subjective probability that a specific level of effort

EXHIBIT 5–4
Expectancy Theory of Motivation

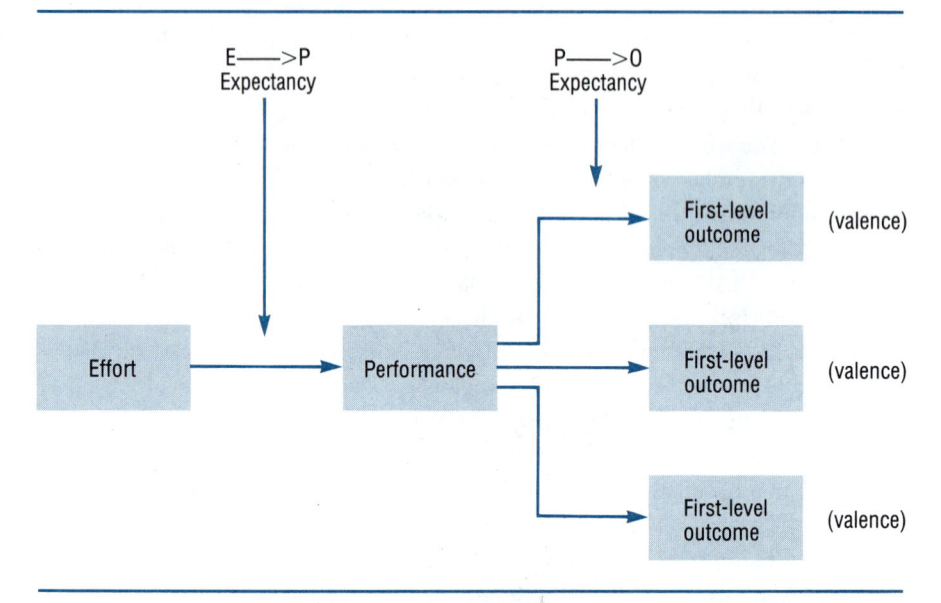

Source: James L. Gibson, John M. Ivancevich, and James H. Donnelly, Jr., *Organizations: Behavior, Structure, Processes*, 5th ed. (Plano, Tex.: Business Publications, 1985).

will lead to a specific level of performance. In general, employees are more motivated to achieve a particular performance goal as their E→P expectancy for that performance level rises. This perception is influenced by the individual's previous experience and perceptions of the situation. Expectancy is calculated as a value between 0.00 and 1.00.

In a simplified example, suppose you are a recruitment specialist and your boss asks you to prepare a report in five days diagnosing the quality of the firm's postsecondary recruiting practices. What is your E→P expectancy of completing this task satisfactorily within the time constraints? What is the chance the report could be submitted in four days rather than five? If the job is impossible to do in less than three weeks, you may argue for an extension or implicitly lower the quality of your performance goal. In other situations (where your job is not at stake), performance goals with low E→P expectancies might be abandoned.

The E→P expectancy has implications for training, coaching, and job design. Some employees might not put much effort toward a particular task because their skills are poorly matched with that task. As they experience repeated failure, E→P expectancy declines. Proper training, placement, or job design increases the probability of success and usually enhances the individual's perception that the task can be accomplished. In other cases, even employees equipped with the required skills may lack confidence. Thus, supervisory coaching may also increase effort by raising the relevant E→P expectancy.[28]

Performance→Outcome Expectancy. The performance→outcome expectancy (P→O) is the individual's subjective probability that a specific level of performance will lead to a specific level of each outcome. Some outcomes are basic needs. For example, what is the probability that completing the above-mentioned report satisfactorily and on time will fulfill your need for self-esteem for the day? Other outcomes, such as praise and money, are associated with basic needs. To continue our example, what is the probability that completing a good report on time will result in an "above-average" performance review this year? The performance review is not valued in itself. Rather, it is associated with certain basic needs. The number of potential outcomes is infinite. However, we tend to consider P→O expectancies only for those outcomes of interest to us at the time.

The P→O expectancy is important for organizational effectiveness. Inaccurate performance evaluations may hurt individual performance by weakening the P→O expectancy between good performance and valued rewards. Employees eventually learn there is little to gain by working hard if the performance evaluation does not recognize superior contributions. Instead, effort will be redirected toward actions that are rewarded.

Valence. Valence refers to the value or anticipated satisfaction/dissatisfaction an individual places on each outcome. This variable ranges from negative to positive (for example −10 to +10). Valences originate with the prepotence of basic needs. The higher the association with a prepotent need, the higher the valence of the outcome. Employees with a high need for social esteem would probably place a higher valence on public recognition for their accomplishments than those who do not have a strong need for social esteem.

The concept of valence also has implications for P/HRM, particularly organizational rewards. Notice that the valences attached to organizational rewards vary with each employee. Most people value a pay increase, but the strength of this outcome's valence depends on the individual's needs.[29] Consequently, to maximize the effectiveness of the reward system, we would ideally adapt the type of rewards offered to the needs of each individual. For outstanding performance, some employees prefer a large bonus. Others are more satisfied if some of that bonus is traded for more paid time off.

The Combined Expectancy Model. Researchers believe that valences and expectancies act on effort in a multiplicative manner. Using our earlier example of the report on postsecondary recruiting, Exhibit 5–5 illustrates this presumed relationship among the parts of the expectancy model. Only three performance levels are shown in this simplified example: completing

EXHIBIT 5–5
Application of Expectancy Theory

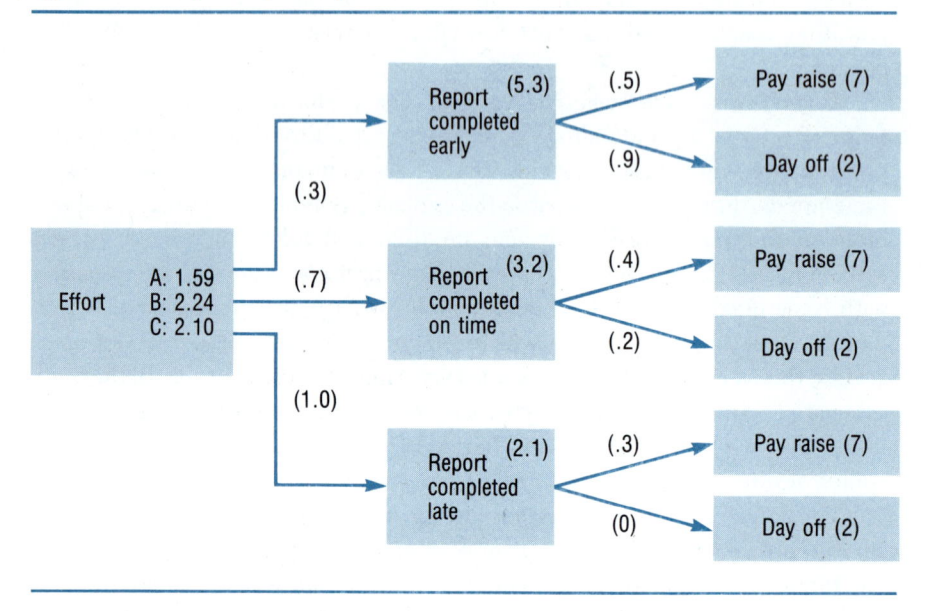

a satisfactory report one day early, on time, or one day late. The employee has considered (consciously or subconsciously) only two outcomes: an above-average pay raise and a day off with pay. Other outcomes could have negative values (getting fired) or could be a direct basic need. Notice that each performance level also has a valence derived from the outcome valences and P→O expectancies. For example, completing the report early has a value of 5.3 [i.e., $(7 \times .5) + (2 \times .9) = 5.3$]. Based on the employee's expectancies and valences in this situation, effort would be directed toward completing the report on time rather than the other two performance goals. Although completing the report early has the highest valence, the probability of achieving this performance goal is too slim.

Equity Theory

There has been some question about whether equity theory is really a distinct theory or whether it can be subsumed under expectancy theory. While there are a number of models dealing with the equity concept, two generated sufficient research or intriguing potential to warrant discussion. Adams argues that individuals compare their inputs and outcomes to those of some relevant other person in determining whether they are equitably (fairly) treated.[30]

Stated another way, the comparison process can be expressed as a comparison of ratios:

$$\frac{\text{Person's outcomes}}{\text{Person's inputs}} \quad \text{compared to} \quad \frac{\text{Other's outcomes}}{\text{Other's inputs}} \rightarrow \text{Employee behaviour}$$

Varying Perceptions. This model suggests that people compare the rewards they receive, relative to the inputs they have to make to receive those rewards, to the same ratio for some relevant other. If the two ratios are not equal, the employee will be motivated to reduce the "perceived" inequity. A key in this explanation is the word *perceived*. The inequity could result because some individuals evaluate and classify as inputs and outcomes factors that other individuals might consider irrelevant. For example, a physically attractive salesperson might consider attractiveness a relative input and expect to be compensated higher than a less attractive individual, other things being equal. Yet the organization may consider this an irrelevant input, pay the two individuals equally, and never realize the person views it as an inequitable exchange. Also, a person might evaluate an outcome as relevant that the organization is not even aware exists. As an example, consider a supervisor who keeps a particular employee abreast of information about company activities affecting the employee's job. Potentially, the supervisor could view this as a reward, treating the subordinate as a member of the "in" group, privy to information not disseminated to other subordinates.[31] If this is not perceived as a reward by the subordinate, yet the supervisor views it as a reward for above-average performance, feelings of inequity may result.

Perceptions and Performance. The possible impact this perceived inequity may have on motivation and subsequent performance is pointed out by Adams.[32] Granted, inequity is viewed in this theory as a source of motivation. However, the consequences do not necessarily bode well for improved performance. As Adams notes, people can (1) cognitively distort their or others' inputs and/or outcomes, (2) attempt to change their or others' inputs and/or outcomes, (3) change the comparison person, or (4) reduce their involvement in the exchange relationship. Several of these consequences have negative implications for performance. For example, accusing other work group members of being rate-busters and using social sanctions to get them to reduce outcomes could be viewed as an effort to get others to reduce inputs. Another example includes certain unionization efforts. Consider a company that has a union representing all blue-collar workers. If nonunionized clerical workers do not receive raises commensurate with those obtained by unionized workers, one possible outcome could be efforts by clerical workers to form their own union. This is particularly true if clerical workers use the unionized blue-collar workers as relevant others and perceive that rewards for the two groups are out of balance, given inputs. In this case, disgruntled clerical workers could view unionization as a way to improve outcomes and reestablish equity.

Viewing situations from the employee's perspective can help supervisors understand behaviour and direct it toward organizational objectives. A useful way to gain insight on motivational patterns in individuals is through the literature on organization careers.

CAREERS

The notion of careers offers an additional way to understand employee work behaviour.[33] However, it is a very speculative area, that is, still more descriptive than experimental.

> **Definition**
> An individual's *career* is a sequence of work-related experiences in which a person participates during the span of a work life.

This sequence of experiences is influenced both by the organization, which hires, trains, and promotes individuals into jobs, and the individual, who brings unique abilities and motivation to the job.

Career Orientation

In addition to finding differences in abilities and motivation, researchers have found that employees differ in their orientation to work; that is, what role work plays in their lives, and what it is that people seek in their work lives.[34]

Based on a longitudinal study of 44 management graduates, Schein developed the concept of "career anchor."[35] A career anchor is a self-concept based on differing work motives and abilities that guide, stabilize, and integrate a person's work experiences. Schein identifies five different anchors.[36]

1. *Technical/functional competence.* The primary orientation of these individuals is the actual work they do, and they wish to continue utilizing their skills in the kind of work they were trained to do. They avoid positions that remove them from these areas of competence or push them into general management. These people define growth as increasing skill, rather than rise in organization level. An example may be an engineer who wishes to pursue circuit design and has no wish to supervise others or manage a project.

2. *Managerial competence.* The primary work goal for this group is to develop the managerial abilities of *(a)* interpersonal competence, *(b)* analytical competence, and *(c)* emotional competence. Emotional competence enables an individual to make the difficult decisions that are required at the highest levels of management.

These first two types of career orientation were most common in Schein's sample, but even in this relatively homogenous group of management school graduates, other types of career anchors existed. They include:

3. *Security.* These managers see themselves primarily in terms of working in a particular organization or tied to a specific geographic area.
4. *Creativity.* A strong need to create something that is entirely their own—whether it is a product, a company, or a personal fortune—characterizes these people.
5. *Autonomy/independence.* These persons do not adapt well to working under the constraints of organization life; many leave it to become consultants or to start their own businesses.

Career anchors, according to Schein, reflect the underlying motives that a person brings into adulthood, as well as abilities.[37] A career anchor grows out of early work experiences and provides guidance as a career progresses through various stages. It aids our understanding of employee work behaviour.

Another facet of work behaviour is that it changes as a person matures. The classic work *The Seasons of a Man's Life* by Levinson and others has spurred a new area of research called career stages.[38] Career stage research examines how behaviour changes as people pass through organizations and accumulate work experience. Theoretically, ability should increase with experience. However, changes in motivation patterns may cause performance decreases as age increases. An understanding of career stages may help organizations prevent performance declines.

Career Stages

The work life experiences of individuals evolve through growth phases, similar to a biological model of growth and decay.[39] The issues to be resolved differ at each career phase or stage, and thus the effectiveness of P/HRM programs varies according to the stage a person is in. For example, a person in an early career stage may be less concerned with pensions and vesting rights than a person in a later career stage. Training needs differ among individuals at different stages and so may the willingness to work overtime. For these reasons, a P/HRM manager familiar with the literature on career stages

**EXHIBIT 5–6
Career Stages**

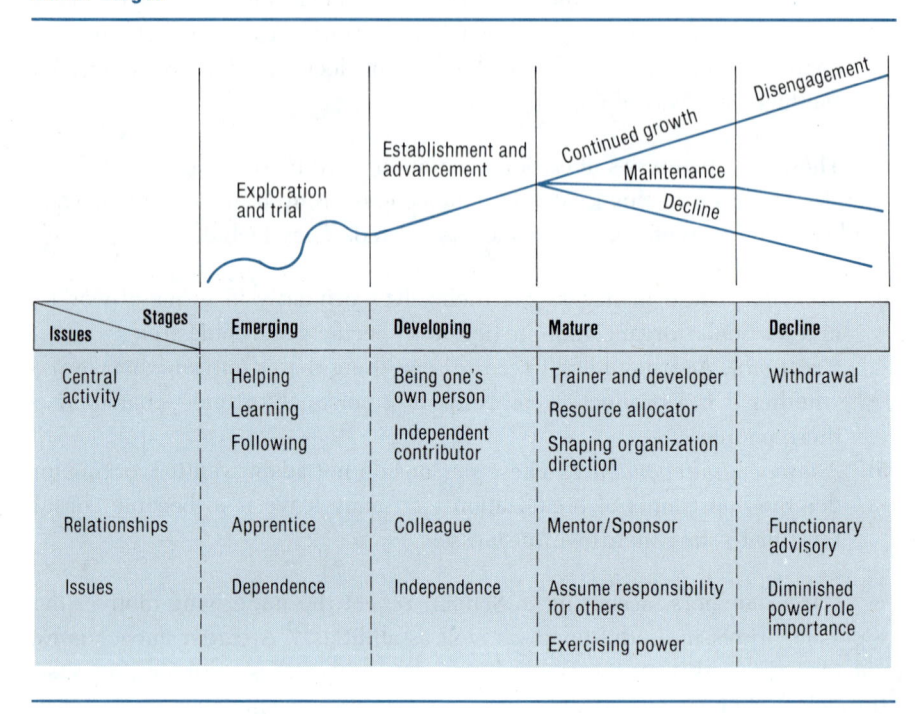

[Diagram showing career trajectory curves: Exploration and trial → Establishment and advancement → branching into Continued growth / Maintenance / Decline → Disengagement]

Issues \ Stages	Emerging	Developing	Mature	Decline
Central activity	Helping Learning Following	Being one's own person Independent contributor	Trainer and developer Resource allocator Shaping organization direction	Withdrawal
Relationships	Apprentice	Colleague	Mentor/Sponsor	Functionary advisory
Issues	Dependence	Independence	Assume responsibility for others Exercising power	Diminished power/role importance

may better understand the needs of the employees. Career stage literature views early adulthood as the starting point.[40] Exhibit 5–6 shows the four career stages.

Exploration

The young adult in the exploration stage is trying to fit into the world of work. Exploration activities include trying to clarify and identify one's interests and skills, building those skills through education or training programs, dealing with constraints such as finances and parental pressure, and making initial decisions on jobs and organizations of interest. Exploration is influenced by school, family, and friends. Jobs (and roles) may be tried and rejected, false starts may occur; but throughout all these "searching" activities, the young adult is gaining knowledge and developing a self-image in terms of possible career goals and directions. Then the young adult seeks permanent employment that utilizes skills and meets personal needs. This leads to the second stage, establishment.

Establishment

The establishment stage includes successful negotiation through the recruiting process, acceptance of a job, and orientation into the chosen organization. During this early socialization into an organization, an individual develops a sense of the likely future within that organization.

Socialization is followed by a process of "mutual acceptance." The individual, co-workers, and supervisors must all learn the capabilities and constraints of the others. Open exchanges of information and feedback on performance are necessary for this acceptance to occur. Opportunities to demonstrate capabilities on both sides must be provided. In addition to fostering mutual acceptance, a balance must be reached by the individual in the establishment stage between responding to directives and initiating activities.

Maintenance

Here the individual has become an important member of the organization; work assignments are of a more vital nature. The organization draws on the individual's accumulated wisdom and perspective. This person is expected to serve as role model and mentor for younger employees.

The maintenance stage may also be a time of midcareer crisis, which can be stimulated by events outside the work life and may include:

1. Family changes—children leaving home, divorce, illness, or death of parents.
2. Changed financial obligations, with resulting ability to consider options (for example, self-employment) that were previously unrealistic because of their financial risk.
3. A recognition of limits, including mortality, that may spur a reassessment of one's accomplishments and a change in goals.

Many people in mid career, with varying degrees of apprehension and success, cycle back to the exploration stage and make major changes in their lives at this time.

Decline

The latter years of a career are characterized as a time of decline. Preparation for retirement may involve a psychological withdrawal from the organization long before physical separation occurs. A reduced role with less responsibility may be assigned; personal and work relationships may be adjusted according to their value to the individual and the amount of effort the individual is willing to expend on maintaining them.

Sociologists and psychologists may make narrower distinctions and add more stages, or integrate life and career stages. Some emphasize the critical nature of the transition from one stage to the next.[41] Others postulate a "career clock," which affects the speed of movement among stages.[42]

Careers and Organizational Effectiveness

Understanding career processes is increasingly important for P/HRM. By managing these processes, the organization ensures that employee needs and abilities are congruent with organizational needs throughout the individual's career.[43] Career management recognizes that the needs and abilities of employees change throughout their working lives. Career management is the responsibility of each employee as well as the company. In Chapter Twelve, we describe some of these career management practices.

To make optimal use of its human resources, organizations must work within the dynamic processes of career orientation and stages. Otherwise, employee needs will be unmet, which could lead to higher turnover, absenteeism, and stress. In other situations, poor career planning could lead to mismatched abilities with job requirements, leading to lower performance levels.

Oliver postulates a concept of "career unrest," which explains the effects of careers on employee satisfaction and productivity.[44] Career unrest may stem from life unrest, career self unrest (dissatisfaction with one's personal effectiveness in one's chosen career), career content unrest (dissatisfaction with the work content of the chosen career), or job unrest (dissatisfaction with the work environment). Oliver claims career unrest diminishes an individual's ability to make a creative contribution and so affects productivity.

Finally, career management should be integrated with strategic management.[45] The organization's needs are changing at the same time as employee needs and abilities. Emerging organizational strategies, such as entering a new market or selling a subsidiary, may open new career paths and close others. In other words, P/HRM professionals must work with two sets of moving targets: the career stages of employees and the life cycles of the organization.

THE SUPERVISOR

The supervisor or manager is directly involved in many of the significant P/HRM activities. The supervisor and the work group constitute the social environment within which the individual learns the norms and expectations for work. A favourable and constructive social environment is conducive to positive individual motivation and productivity.[46] A negative social environment inhibits motivation, which hurts performance. The success of the entire

P/HRM system depends on how thoughtfully and fairly the supervisor manages it.[47] So a key ingredient in effective P/HRM is the quality of supervisory leadership.

Leadership Styles

Leadership is a mutual process. Not only do leaders affect workers, but workers also affect leaders. Additionally, other organization factors such as the organization objectives, finances, technology and culture, and the nature of the work—all factors in our diagnostic model—affect leadership.[48]

Considerable effort was spent trying to identify which personality characteristics determined a successful leader.[49] Such information would be helpful in selecting supervisors. One group classified leaders by their decision-making style:

Authoritarian—The leader makes decisions alone and tells subordinates what they are to do.

Democratic—The leader actively involves subordinates in the decision-making process, sharing problems, soliciting input, and sharing authority.

Laissez-faire—The leader avoids making decisions whenever possible and leaves it up to subordinates to make individual decisions with little guidance either from the leader or from the rest of the group.

Research on the effectiveness of alternative leadership styles has produced interesting results. For example, individuals under democratic leadership were found to be more satisfied, had higher morale, were more creative, and had better relationships with their superiors.[50] However, the quantity of output produced by workers was highest under the autocratic leadership style, slightly lower under democratic leadership, and lowest under laissez-faire leadership.

Most researchers now agree that no single leadership style is universally associated with effectiveness.[51] Rather, a *contingency approach* is advocated. A contingency approach recognizes that effective leadership depends on the circumstances. The nature of the organization, work, and employees all affect what is required of leaders. Effective leadership requires a match between the circumstances and the supervisor.

Effective supervisors are able to adapt their style of relating to employees to the employee's abilities and motivation. They encourage employee participation in key decisions in the work unit. And they help develop effective work groups. Development of an effective work group is significant to the success of an organization's P/HRM program and to the achievement of organizational and employee effectiveness.

THE WORK GROUP

> **Definition**
> A *work group* is a set of two or more people who see themselves as interdependent with one another for the accomplishment of a purpose, and who communicate and interact with one another on a more or less continuous basis. In many cases (but not always), they work closely together physically.

Effective work groups do a lot for employees. Work groups can offer support to the employee against "arbitrary" demands by outsiders (other work groups, managers, clients), thus giving employees more control over their work lives and a greater sense of power and dignity.[52]

Effective work groups also offer friendship and acceptance—a feeling of belonging. It is difficult to get such a feeling in most large organizations. The Canadian government and Canadian Pacific Ltd. employ tens of thousands. A feeling of belonging within organizations like these is enhanced by membership in small work groups.

Organization Advantages

What do groups do for organizations? First of all, along with the supervisor, they help orient the new employee to the job, teach the job, and socialize the new employee.[53] Unfortunately, work groups can also have negative effects whey they apply pressure on members to restrict production at artificially low levels.[54] This effect was first documented in the Hawthorne studies mentioned in the previous chapter. The work group decided on production quotas and ridiculed any group member who tried to exceed the quota. The group was able to enforce its norms despite a pay system based on output. Thus, the influence of the group can be powerful.[55] And it is in the organization's interest to have group goals compatible with those of the organization.

Designing Work Groups

How can an organization ensure that the work group will function for the good of the organization? There appear to be three key features in designing work groups that have an impact on group effectiveness (see Exhibit 5–7). These are task design, group composition, and group norms.

EXHIBIT 5–7
The Impact of Key Design Features on Various Facets of Work Group Effectiveness

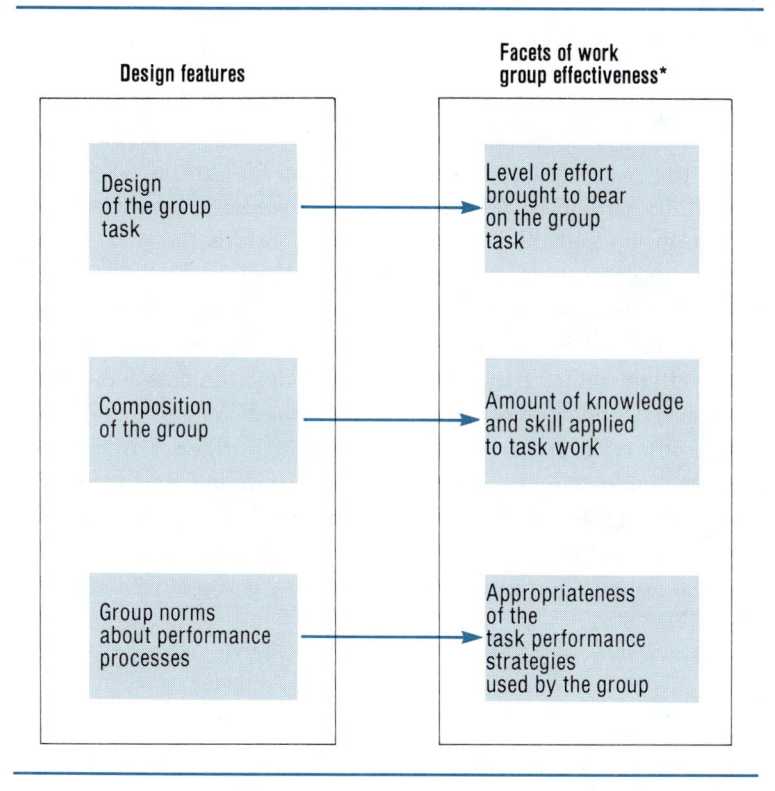

Design features	Facets of work group effectiveness*
Design of the group task	→ Level of effort brought to bear on the group task
Composition of the group	→ Amount of knowledge and skill applied to task work
Group norms about performance processes	→ Appropriateness of the task performance strategies used by the group

*Hackman and Oldham refer to these as "intermediate criteria of effectiveness."
Source: Adapted from J. R. Hackman and G. R. Oldham, *Work Redesign* (Reading, Mass.: Addison-Wesley Publishing, 1980). Used by permission.

Task Design

The tasks assigned the group influence the level of effort group members will exert. Well-designed tasks motivate members to work hard. The criteria for task design are those discussed in the previous chapter on job design: skill variety, task identity, task significance, autonomy, and feedback. (See Chapter Four for elaboration of these terms.)

Group Composition

The job-related ability available to be applied to the group's task is determined by who is in the group. Thus, the group must possess the skills to do the job, as well as the interpersonal skills to organize itself.

Group Norms

Just as organization strategies affect how the organization utilizes its resources, so, too, the group's strategies affect how it utilizes the motivation and abilities of its members.

P/HRM and Work Groups

In an effective work group, members function and act as a team, with all members fully participating in decisions and working toward achieving the goals of the group and the organization. So what difference do work groups make for human resource management? Hackman and Oldham emphasize that for work groups to be effective in generating high performance of members, several conditions must be met. First, performance standards must be set for the group, rather than for individuals. Commitment and cohesiveness will be fostered only if the organization's reward systems (pay, promotion) reinforce group effort rather than undermine it. Further, the group must be given a clear understanding of its tasks and constraints and it must be provided any training or other resources it may require to carry out its tasks. Thus, if the organization wishes to utilize and control its work teams, the P/HRM system must be tuned to foster effective group behaviour.[56]

SUMMARY

The basic premise of this chapter is that differences in employees, supervisors, and the groups they form play a key role in managing human resources. Understanding and utilizing these differences in P/HRM decisions help achieve employee and organization effectiveness.

The concept of individual differences is incorporated into the design and administration of many P/HRM activities. Selecting employees with required skills, granting larger pay increases to superior performers, promoting only those employees with the greatest potential, tailoring training programs to individual needs, and offering health insurance options with the flexibility to meet each employee's needs are all examples.

We have now examined the three basic components of organization conditions listed in the diagnostic model: nature of the organization, the work, and the employees. The design of P/HRM activities and their management are contingent on all three components. And these components are not simply constraints to be considered only once. Rather, they change over time and P/HRM professionals must adapt their decisions and activities to these changing circumstances.

DISCUSSION AND REVIEW QUESTIONS

1. Differentiate abilities from aptitudes. If you were trying to fill an assembly line job, what abilities would you look for in a prospective employee? How would these abilities differ from those you would seek in a person to fill the plant manager's position?
2. Suppose you are a human resource specialist. Why would it be important for you to understand employee motivation? Explain motivation to work in terms of the expectancy theory. Give some practical applications of the theory you could use to motivate employees.
3. Explain how work groups can help achieve employee and organization effectiveness.
4. What is the supervisor's role in affecting employee performance?
5. How may speculating about career anchors help a manager?
6. Do career anchor and career stage notions have any relevance for job design?
7. How do the tasks that people face at different stages of their careers influence their motivation?

NOTES AND REFERENCES

1. Ian Allaby, "From the Ground Up," *Canadian Business*, January 1986, pp. 29, 94–96; Robert MacKay, "Skinny Management Key to CAE Success," *Financial Times*, July 14, 1980; Carolyn Purden, "Reekie Looks Back on Long Career," *CAE News*, October 1985; Eva Innes, Robert L. Perry, and Jim Lyon, *The 100 Best Companies to Work for in Canada* (Don Mills, Ont.: Collins, 1986).
2. Marvin D. Dunnette, "Critical Concepts in the Assessment of Human Capabilities," in *Human Performance & Productivity*, ed. M. D. Dunnette and Edwin A. Fleishman, vol. 1 (Hillsdale, N.J.: Lawrence Erlbaum Associates, 1982); Lyle F. Schoenfeldt, "Intra-Individual Variations & Human Performance," in *Human Performance & Productivity*, ed. M. D. Dunnette and Edwin Fleishman, vol. 1 (Hillsdale, N.J.: Lawrence Erlbaum Associates, 1982).
3. Kurt Lewin, *Dynamic Theory of Personality* (New York: McGraw-Hill, 1935); James McConnell, *Understanding Human Behavior* (New York: Holt, Rinehart & Winston, 1984); Anne Anastasi, *Differential Psychology* (New York: Macmillan, 1970); Leona E. Tyler, *Individuality* (San Francisco: Jossey-Bass, 1978); Lyman Porter et al., *Behavior in Organizations* (New York: McGraw-Hill, 1975), p. 61; Norman Maier, *Psychology in Industrial Organizations* (Boston: Houghton Mifflin, 1973), pp. 159–60.
4. Daniel Goleman, "Genes Outweigh Upbringing, Twins Personality Study Says," *The Globe and Mail*, December 4, 1986, p. A11.
5. See, for example, Anastasi, *Differential Psychology*.
6. Adapted from Dennis W. Organ and Thomas Bateman, *Organizational Behavior: An Applied Psychological Approach*, 3rd ed. (Plano, Tex.: Business Publications, 1986); Craig C. Pinder, *Work Motivation* (Glenview, Ill.: Scott, Foresman, 1984).
7. C. N. Cofer and M. H. Appley, *Motivation: Theory and Research* (New York: John Wiley & Sons, 1964).

8. Bernard Bass, "Individual Capability, Team Performance & Team Productivity," in *Human Performance & Productivity*, ed. M. D. Dunnette and E. A. Fleishman (Hillsdale, N.J.: Lawrence Erlbaum Associates, 1982).
9. Ibid.
10. George Milkovich and Jerry Newman, *Compensation*, 2nd ed. (Plano, Tex.: Business Publications, 1987).
11. Abraham Korman, *The Psychology of Motivation* (Englewood Cliffs, N.J.: Prentice-Hall, 1974); David McClelland, *The Personality* (Hinsdale, Ill.: Dryden Press, 1951); Victor Vroom, *Work and Motivation* (New York: John Wiley & Sons, 1964); Clayton Alderfer, *Existence, Relatedness, and Growth* (New York: Free Press, 1972); J. W. Atkinson, *An Introduction to Motivation* (New York: American Book, 1964); John Campbell and Robert Pritchard, "Motivation Theory in Industrial and Organizational Psychology," in *Handbook of Industrial and Organizational Psychology*, ed. M. D. Dunnette (Chicago: Rand-McNally, 1976); *Motivation & Society: A Volume in Honor of David C. McClelland*, ed. Abigail J. Stewart (San Francisco: Jossey-Bass, 1982); Michael E. Cavanaugh, "In Search of Motivation," *Personnel Journal*, March 1984, pp. 76–80.
12. Edwin Locke, "The Motivational Effect of Knowledge of Results: Knowledge or Goal Setting?" *Journal of Applied Psychology* 51, no. 2 (1967), pp. 324–29.
13. Lyman W. Porter and Edward E. Lawler III, *Managerial Attitudes and Performance* (Homewood, Ill.: Richard D. Irwin, 1968).
14. Lawrence H. Peters, Edward J. O'Connor, and Joe R. Eulberg, "Situational Constraints: Sources, Consequences, and Future Considerations," in *Research in Personnel and Human Resources Management*, Vol. 3, ed. K. M. Rowland and G. R. Ferris (Greenwich, Conn.: JAI Press, 1985), pp. 79–115; Lawrence H. Peters and Edward J. O'Connor, "Situational Constraints and Work: The Influence of a Frequently Overlooked Construct," *Academy of Management Review* 5, no. 2 (1980), pp. 391–97.
15. Edward Lawler III, *Pay & Organization Effectiveness: A Psychological View* (New York: McGraw-Hill, 1971).
16. Abraham Maslow, *Motivation & Personality* (New York: Harper & Row, 1954).
17. Frederick Herzberg, Bernard Mausner, and Barbara Snyderman, *The Motivation to Work* (New York: John Wiley & Sons, 1959).
18. Maslow, *Motivation & Personality*.
19. Theodore Roszak, *The Making of a Counter-Culture: Reflections on the Technocratic Society and Its Youthful Opposition* (Garden City, N.Y.: Doubleday, 1969).
20. F. Herzberg et al., *The Motivation to Work*.
21. A. Maslow, *Motivation & Personality*.
22. F. Herzberg et al., *The Motivation to Work*.
23. Clark Hull, *A Behavior System* (New Haven, Conn.: Yale University Press, 1952).
24. Campbell and Pritchard, "Motivation Theory."
25. R. L. Opsahl and M. D. Dunnette, "The Role of Financial Compensation in Industrial Motivation," *Psychological Bulletin* 66 (1966), pp. 94–118.
26. D. A. Nadler and E. E. Lawler III, "Motivation: A Diagnostic Approach," in *Perspectives on Behavior in Organizations*, 2nd ed., ed. J. R. Hackman, E. E. Lawler III, and L. W. Porter (New York: McGraw-Hill, 1983); Vroom, *Work and Motivation*; Campbell and Pritchard, "Motivation Theory"; B. M. Staw, "Motivation in Organizations: Toward Synthesis and Redirection," in *New Directions in*

Organizational Behavior, ed. B. M. Staw and G. R. Salancik (Chicago: St. Clair Press, 1977).
27. Vroom, *Motivation and Work*, pp. 14–19.
28. Nadler and Lawler, "Motivation."
29. Kenneth R. Brousseau and J. Bruce Prince, "Job-Person Dynamics: An Extension of Longitudinal Research," *Journal of Applied Psychology* 66 (1981), pp. 59–62.
30. Opsahl and Dunnette, "Role of Financial Compensation."
31. J. Stacey Adams, "Inequity in Social Exchange," in *Advances in Experimental Social Psychology*, ed. Leonard Berkowitz (New York: Academic Press, 1965); J. Stacey Adams, "Toward an Understanding of Inequity," *Journal of Abnormal and Social Psychology* 67, no. 3 (1963), pp. 442–636.
32. Ibid.
33. E. Erickson, *Childhood and Society* (New York: W. W. Norton, 1950); Douglas Hall, *Careers in Organizations* (Santa Monica, Calif.: Goodyear Publishing, 1976); D. J. Levinson, C. Darrow, E. Klein, M. Levinson, and B. McKee, *The Seasons of a Man's Life* (New York: Alfred A. Knopf, 1978); J. Rush and A. Peacock, "A Review and Integration of Theories of Life/Career Stages" (working paper, University of Western Ontario, London, Ontario, 1980); J. Rush, A. Peacock, and G. Milkovich, "Career Stages: A Partial Test of Levinson's Model of Life/Career Stages," *Journal of Vocational Behavior* 16 (1980), pp. 347–59; E. G. Schein, *Career Dynamics: Matching Individual and Organizational Needs* (Reading, Mass.: Addison-Wesley Publishing, 1978); John Van Maanen and Edgar Schein, "Career Development," in *Improving Life at Work*, ed. J. Richard Hackman and J. Loyd Suttle (Santa Monica, Calif.: Goodyear Publishing, 1977).
34. D. Super and D. T. Hall, "Career Development: Exploration and Planning," in *Annual Review of Psychology*, ed. M. R. Rosenzweig and L. W. Porter (Palo Alto, Calif.: Annual Reviews, 1978); Hall, *Careers in Organizations*; George T. Milkovich and John C. Anderson, "Careers and Career Systems," in *Personnel Management: New Perspectives*, ed. K. Rowland and G. Ferris (Boston: Allyn & Bacon, 1982); and J. C. Anderson, G. T. Milkovich, and A. Tsui, "Intra-Organizational Mobility: A Model and Review," *Academy of Management Review*, October 1981, pp. 529–38; T. Gutteridge, "Commentary: A Comparison of Perspectives," in *Careers in Organizations*, ed. L. Dyer (Ithaca, N.Y.: Cornell University Press, 1976).
35. Schein, *Career Dynamics: Matching Individuals*.
36. Ibid.
37. Ibid.
38. Levinson et al., *The Seasons of a Man's Life*.
39. Hall, *Careers in Organizations*.
40. Ibid.; also see Rush and Peacock, "A Review and Integration of Theories of Life/Career Stages"; G. W. Dalton, P. H. Thompson, and R. L. Price, "The Four Stages of Professional Careers: A New Look at Performance by Professionals," *Organizational Dynamics*, Summer 1977, pp. 19–42.
41. Manuel London and Stephen A. Stumpf, *Managing Careers* (Reading, Mass.: Addison-Wesley Publishing, 1981).
42. J. Rush, A. Peacock, and G. Milkovich, "Career Stages: A Partial Test of Levinson's Model of Life/Career Stages."
43. Hall, *Careers in Organizations*.

44. Robert Oliver, *Career Unrest: A Source of Creativity* (New York: Center for Research in Career Development, Columbia University, 1981).
45. John Burdett, "Career Management: Where Do We Go from Here?" *The Human Resource*, October–November 1986, pp. 8–11; Stephen Stumpf and Nancy Hanrahan, "Designing Organizational Career Management Practices to Fit Strategic Management Objectives," in *Readings in Personnel and Human Resource Management*, 2nd ed., ed. Randall Schuler and Stuart Youngblood (St. Paul, Minn.: West Publishing, 1984), pp. 316–25.
46. H. Peter Dachler and Bernhard Wilpert, "Conceptual Dimensions and Boundaries of Participation in Organizations: A Critical Evaluation," *Administrative Science Quarterly*, March 1978, pp. 1–39; Ben Graham, Jr., and Parvin Titus, *The Amazing Oversight* (New York: AMACOM, 1979); "Eric Trist on the Quality of Working Life," *Labour Gazette*, August 1977, pp. 365–71; Joseph W. McGuire, "The 'New' Egalitarianism and Management Practice," *California Management Review*, Spring 1977, pp. 21–29.
47. Daniel C. Feldman and Hugh J. Arnold, *Managing Individual and Group Behavior in Organizations* (New York: McGraw-Hill, 1983).
48. S. R. Rhodes and Mildred Doering, "An Integrated Model of Career Motivation," *Academy of Management Review* 8, no. 4 (1983), pp. 631–40; Manuel London, "Toward a Theory of Career Motivation," *Academy of Management Review* 8, no. 4 (1983), pp. 620–31; Oliver, *Career Unrest: A Source of Creativity*; see, for example, R. M. Stogdill, *Handbook of Leadership: A Survey of Theory and Research* (New York: Free Press, 1984); R. Tannenbaum, R. Weschler, and F. Massarik, *Leadership & Organization* (New York: McGraw-Hill, 1961); G. Yukl, *Leadership in Organizations* (Englewood Cliffs, N.J.: Prentice-Hall, 1981); F. E. Fiedler, *A Theory of Leadership Effectiveness* (New York: McGraw-Hill, 1967); also see V. H. Vroom and P. W. Yetton, *Leadership & Decision Making* (Pittsburgh, Pa.: University of Pittsburgh Press, 1973).
49. K. Lewin, R. Lippitt, and R. K. White, "Patterns of Aggressive Behavior in Experimentally Created Social Climates," *Journal of Social Psychology* 10 (1939), pp. 271–99.
50. Yukl, *Leadership*.
51. See especially Fiedler, *Leadership Effectiveness*.
52. Feldman and Arnold, *Managing Individual & Group Behavior*.
53. Ibid.
54. Ibid.
55. Samuel B. Bacharach and Edward J. Lawler, *Power & Politics in Organizations* (San Francisco: Jossey-Bass, 1980).
56. J. H. Davis, *Group Performance* (Reading, Mass.: Addison-Wesley Publishing, 1969); J. R. Hackman, "Group Influences on Individuals in Organizations," in *Handbook of Industrial and Organizational Psychology*, ed. M. D. Dunnette (Chicago: Rand McNally, 1976); M. E. Shaw, *Group Dynamics*, 3rd ed. (New York: McGraw-Hill, 1981); M. Sherif, B. J. White, and O. J. Harvey, "Status in Experimentally Produced Groups," *American Journal of Sociology* 60, no. 2 (1955), pp. 370–79; P. E. Slater, "Contrasting Correlates of Group Size," *Sociometry* 21, no. 1 (1958), pp. 129–39; I. D. Steiner, "Models for Inferring Relationships between Group Size and Potential Group Productivity," *Behavioral Science* 11, no. 2 (1966), pp. 273–83.

Exhibit III
THE DIAGNOSTIC MODEL

External conditions	Organization conditions	Human resource activities	Objectives
Economic conditions Government regulations Technology Unions	Nature of organization: Strategies and objectives → Nature of work / Nature of employees and work groups	Staffing Development Employment relations Compensation Evaluation	Human resource effectiveness

PART THREE
HUMAN RESOURCE ACTIVITIES:
STAFFING

Part Three focusses on the P/HRM activities that make up the staffing process. The object of the process is to employ effective people in the right job at the right time. As the diagnostic model shows (Exhibit III), the staffing process is affected by external factors, most notably, employment equity legislation and product/labour market conditions. Within the organization, the culture, strategies, and objectives affect the employer's overall approach to recruiting. The nature of the job vacancies and the skills needed, (e.g., accountants or assemblers) affect many of the decisions in designing the staffing process.

The process begins with employment planning (Chapter Six), which involves analyzing and forecasting the employer's human resource requirements and supplies. Employment equity is in part a specialized application of the work force utilization analysis discussed in Chapter Six. But because employment equity encompasses all human resource processes, a separate chapter is devoted to analysis of and compliance with employment equity legislation (Chapter Seven).

The next part of the staffing process—recruiting (Chapter Eight)—starts with the data provided through employment planning and seeks to attract qualified applicants to fill job vacancies.

Selection (Chapter 9) occurs at several points in the staffing process. First, some rough screening of people who aspire to the jobs occurs during recruiting. Once job aspirants hear more about the work to be performed, the qualifications required, and so on, they may decide not to apply (self-selection), or recruiters may suggest further training or experience is necessary to qualify

PART THREE continued

for the job. Selection occurs again when the number of people who apply exceeds the number of jobs available. Care must be taken that the selection decisions do not discriminate against women and other designated groups.

It is useful to think of all these topics, employment planning, employment equity, recruitment, and selection as forming one major component of a human resource system—the staffing process—rather than separate and unrelated activities. In practice, the design and management of these activities must be integrated. Keep this in mind as you study each aspect, Chapters Six through Nine, of the staffing process.

CHAPTER SIX
EMPLOYMENT PLANNING

CHAPTER OUTLINE

I. A Diagnostic Approach to Employment Planning
II. Employment Planning
    A. Reasons for Employment Planning
    B. Three Phases of Analysis
    C. Who Performs Employment Planning?
III. Forecasting Demand for Employees
    A. Estimated Organization Performance Goals
    B. Productivity
    C. An Illustration
    D. Tailoring Tools to the Situation
    E. Prediction Accuracy versus Objectives Achieved
    F. Keep Employment Forecasts in Perspective
IV. Forecasting Human Resource Supply
    A. Turnover Rates as an Objective
    B. Human Resource Supply Estimates
    C. Skills Inventories
    D. Replacement and Succession Charts
    E. Transitional Matrixes
V. Designing Programs
VI. Summary

General Motors of Canada is one of the "corporate kings." For the third year in a row, GM, with sales of nearly $19 billion, topped The Financial Post 500 list of Canada's biggest companies.[1] Another of the "kings," General Electric, is in a dizzying array of businesses. Its products include turbines, televisions, light bulbs, robots, and CAT scanners.[2] At the other end of the spectrum, Tannereye Ltd., with only 125 employees, produces luxury eyeglass frames in a small manufacturing facility in Charlottetown, Prince Edward Island. The firm is branching out, and its workers are optimistic that expansion will create more supervisory openings.[3] Despite the difference in size, these organizations have something in common. As part of operating their businesses, managers in these companies must decide the number of people to employ, the types of skills needed, and at what point these employees are required. *All* managers face these questions. Finding the answers is the role of employment planning.

A DIAGNOSTIC APPROACH TO EMPLOYMENT PLANNING

The employment needs of an organization flow from the strategic, operational, and human resource decisions made by top management. Exhibit 6-1 illustrates the relationship of strategic management decisions to employment planning. Top management examines factors in the external and internal environments, analyzes the strategic advantages of the organization, and sets its objectives for the planning period. Strategic human resource planning translates the business decisions of top management into human resource implications.[4] Employment planning is one important part of the overall human resource plan. It focuses on the numbers of employees and the qualifications required to achieve the organization's objectives. Other parts of the total overall human resource plan (see Chapter Three) include compensation, training, employee relations, and so on.

Strategies and Objectives

Planning is an attempt by managers to cope with uncertainties and risks.[5] We expect employment planning to be most important during periods of great change and turbulence, such as rapid expansion, diversification, or any strategic changes. If a manager is faced with stable, highly predictable future conditions, then the need for and the potential contribution of employment planning seems less. Herein lies a contradiction and a dilemma for P/HRM professionals. We will discover in this chapter that some of the techniques for employment planning are based on sound historical data and accurate estimates of the future.[6] Often it seems that employment planning is easiest to apply in those stable and certain situations where its payoffs are likely to be the least.

EXHIBIT 6–1
Interaction between Strategic Organization Decisions, Strategic Human Resource Decisions, and Employment Planning

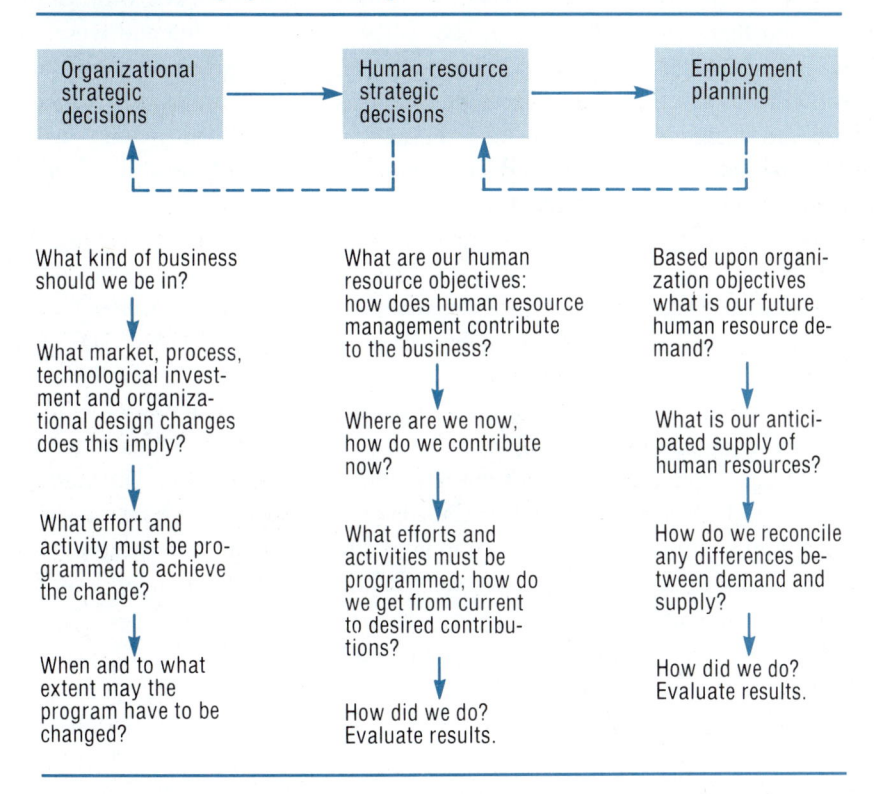

```
┌──────────────┐     ┌──────────────┐     ┌──────────────┐
│Organizational│────▶│Human resource│────▶│ Employment   │
│ strategic    │     │ strategic    │     │ planning     │
│ decisions    │     │ decisions    │     │              │
└──────┬───────┘     └──────┬───────┘     └──────┬───────┘
       ▲                    ▲                    │
       └────────────────────┴────────────────────┘
```

What kind of business should we be in?	What are our human resource objectives: how does human resource management contribute to the business?	Based upon organization objectives what is our future human resource demand?
What market, process, technological investment and organizational design changes does this imply?	Where are we now, how do we contribute now?	What is our anticipated supply of human resources?
What effort and activity must be programmed to achieve the change?	What efforts and activities must be programmed; how do we get from current to desired contributions?	How do we reconcile any differences between demand and supply?
When and to what extent may the program have to be changed?	How did we do? Evaluate results.	How did we do? Evaluate results.

While the nature of employment planning is strongly contingent on the nature of the organization's strategies and objectives, the diagnostic model points to a number of other influences that provide the context for micro-level planning. Chief among these in the macro environment are government activities and programs, the external labour market, technology, and the influence of unions. Also important is the nature of the work and the employees. The form and interplay of these factors can enhance or restrict the success of employment planning.

Government Activities and Programs

The primary federal government department responsible for human resource and employment planning at the national (macro) level is the Canada Employment and Immigration Commission (CEIC). CEIC's activities reflect Canada's interest in the judicious utilization and development of the national work force. Thus, it seeks to address imbalances between labour supply and demand for labour by analyzing and influencing labour markets at the national and regional levels.

Much of the government's recent effort in this area is in response to the realization that prior systems to project labour supply and demand were not good enough. Many of the systems formerly used were conducted in isolation, and there was no coordinated use of the information they produced.[7] Current efforts are designed to provide more integration for the main players in the labour market—government, industry, labour unions, and those involved in education, training, and employment planning.

Although a detailed technical discussion of each program is beyond the scope of this text, an outline of those most germane to this chapter follows.

Canadian Disaggregated Interdepartmental Econometric Model (CANDIDE).[8] Developed by the Economic Council of Canada, CANDIDE is a medium-term forecasting model that can be characterized as a simultaneous, nonlinear, econometric model of the Canadian economy. The model involves some 1,600 equations and employs regression analyses to forecast, among other things, unemployment and the real domestic product (i.e., the value of all goods and services produced in Canada, minus any increase due to inflation). CANDIDE allows for incorporation of different assumptions rather than simple extension of past trends. As mentioned below, other models use certain parts of its output.

Canadian Occupational Forecasting Program (COFOR).[9] Until recently, COFOR was the major tool used by the federal government to forecast future labour market demands. CEIC developed COFOR to provide employment forecasts—nationally and for each province—for the more than 500 occupational groups in the Canadian Classification and Dictionary of Occupations (see the discussion of CCDO in Chapter Four).

Because the broad macroeconomic environment is an important determinant of labour market conditions, COFOR uses a three-stage process based on the real domestic output data of CANDIDE. The first estimation concerns what the total employment of the industry in question would be. The second stage consists of distributing the estimate of national employment by industry to the provincial level. Finally, the model determines the level of employment by occupation, by industry, and by province.[10] To obtain this distribution, COFOR utilizes the occupational distribution of the experienced labour force from recent census data.

Canadian Occupational Projection System (COPS).[11] Work on this model began in 1982, and refinements are continuing. According to CEIC, COPS seeks to project both domestic occupational requirements and supply in Canada and the provinces for up to 10 years. Such expanded forecasting capability allows identification of occupations in which domestic skill imbalances could exist. This information can then be used in assessments of

EXHIBIT 6–2
Outline of Canadian Occupational Projection System—COPS

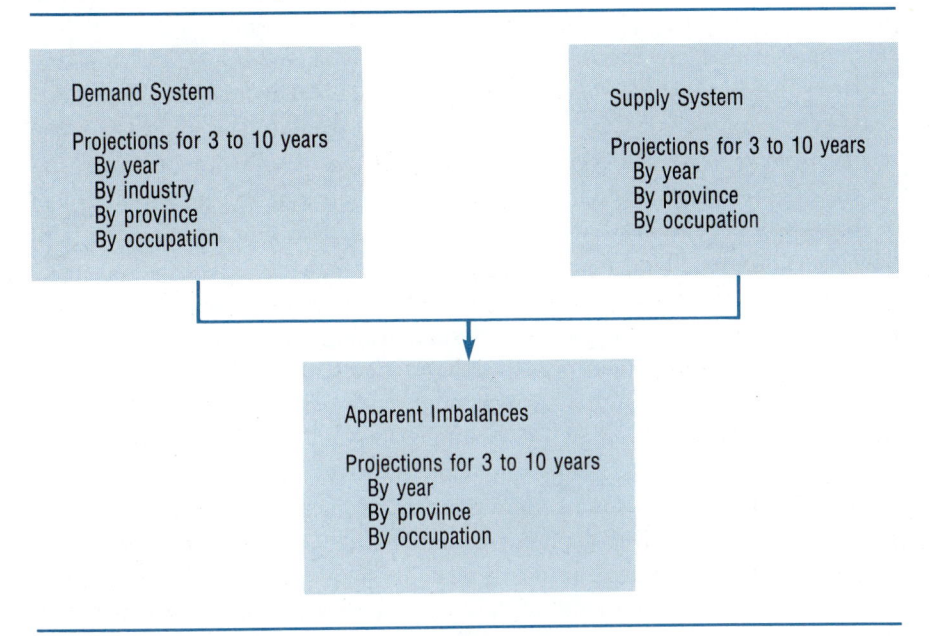

```
┌─────────────────────────────┐         ┌─────────────────────────────┐
│ Demand System               │         │ Supply System               │
│                             │         │                             │
│ Projections for 3 to 10 years│        │ Projections for 3 to 10 years│
│   By year                   │         │   By year                   │
│   By industry               │         │   By province               │
│   By province               │         │   By occupation             │
│   By occupation             │         │                             │
└──────────────┬──────────────┘         └──────────────┬──────────────┘
               │                                       │
               └───────────────────┬───────────────────┘
                                   ▼
                    ┌─────────────────────────────┐
                    │ Apparent Imbalances         │
                    │                             │
                    │ Projections for 3 to 10 years│
                    │   By year                   │
                    │   By province               │
                    │   By occupation             │
                    └─────────────────────────────┘
```

Source: "Notions and Numbers—The Canadian Occupational Projection System," Employment and Immigration Canada, WH-3-418 (no date), p. 2. Reproduced with permission of the Minister of Supply and Services Canada.

whether the imbalances might be self-correcting or require specific intervention by the private sector or governments.

Exhibit 6–2 outlines the main features of COPS. On the supply side, the model attempts to estimate how many workers and potential workers are expected to be available in certain occupations. Projections include the estimated number of workers coming from the education and training system, apprenticeships, net interprovincial migration, Canadian households, interoccupational mobility, and net immigration. The demand side of the system is driven by projected economic activity for the country and builds on methodology and data sources developed for COFOR. Alternative economic outlooks are considered through a set of economic scenarios (e.g., high growth) to provide a picture of the economy in terms of growth rate, rates of inflation, and employment growth, among others. Anticipated levels of industry output derived from these scenarios are then translated into employment projections for 69 industries. From these, provincial and national occupational requirements are produced for 496 occupational groups. CEIC also supplements these estimates with results from comprehensive studies of sectors undergoing rapid change.

Continuing improvements to the COPS system may lead to a finer disaggregation than the current 69-industry breakdown[12] and entail use of the proposed national occupational classification (NOC) system for classifying occupational groups (see the discussion of NOC in Chapter Four).

MicroElectronics SIMulation Model (MESIM).[13] This instrument was developed to supplement COPS, which fails to incorporate the impact of technological change on the occupational composition of industry employment. MESIM is an occupational employment protection tool able to take account of changes in occupational distribution associated with new technology—particularly computer-based technologies.

Additional government involvement comes through a combination of efforts at several levels. The federal government may insist on, and encourage, employment planning when private industry deals with national government agencies. This is considered a fair economic trade-off for industries hoping to win federal money or support. For example, the Department of Regional Expansion (now part of the Department of Industry, Trade, and Commerce) includes employment planning requirements when industries are supported through the Regional Development Incentives Act.[14] The most powerful inducement possible—human resource planning legislation—was implemented in bills relating to northern and offshore energy developments. The Northern Pipeline Act and the Canada Oil and Gas Act contain clauses requiring companies to develop comprehensive human resource plans.[15]

At the sectoral level, we find that several Canadian industries (involving some 3,000 firms and employing more than 430,000 people) are covered by national human resource planning agreements. These pacts with national industrial and professional associations provide a bridge between the CEIC and private-sector decision makers who share concerns about labour shortages and unemployment. Canada appears to be the first Western industrialized country to take this innovative step in national industrial human resource planning.[16]

The CEIC also offers a range of programs and services to management and workers to support the development and implementation of employment planning at the company level. Its Manpower Consultative Service (MCS) includes joint consultative employment planning committees whose costs are shared by the company and government. Some 350 MCS agreements are entered into each year by companies and their worker representatives.[17] Exhibit 6-3 summarizes some results of the government's efforts to encourage good employment planning.

The government also influences employment planning through employment equity guidelines that call for detailed analysis of the sharing of job opportunities with women, the disabled and visible minorities.

EXHIBIT 6–3
Examples of Industry-Government Cooperation in Human Resource/Employment Planning

The Alaska Highway Gas Pipeline is an example of company human resource planning on a "mega" scale. The Foothills Group of Companies will require some 17,000 person-years to build the 2,100 miles of pipeline in Canada. Unions, corporate management and the government cooperated on a range of approaches to ensure an adequate supply of workers and opportunities for Natives and women.

A special MCS agreement brought Quebec's major aerospace companies and unions together to develop provincial human resource planning strategies. CAMAQ—the Committee for Aerospace Manpower Assessment in Quebec—has taken the lead in encouraging improved training programs and greater public awareness of human resource planning issues.

Sperry Univac Defence Systems organized a special hiring and training plan when it opened an electronic instruments plant. The company arranged an aptitude testing and recruitment program with the Winnipeg West Canada Employment Centre, and workers were hired without problem. Human resource planning remains important to the firm and is an element in deciding new contracts.

Associations representing the mining, coal, plastics, graphic arts, aircraft and aerospace manufacturing, shipbuilding and repair, electrical and electronics and foundries industries have signed human resource planning agreements with the Minister of Employment and Immigration. The Canadian Council of Professional Engineers—representing more than 100,000 engineers—has also signed an agreement, the first of its kind between the government and a professional association. Other industrial groups and professional organizations are expected to join this national initiative.

Source: Adapted from *Human Resource Planning: A Challenge for the 1980s* (Ottawa: Minister of Supply and Services, 1983, Canada Employment and Immigration Commission, Cat. MP 43-125/83). Reproduced with the permission of the Minister of Supply and Services Canada.

Labour Markets

As was noted in Chapter Two, a labour market is a bounded entity in which labour supply and demand for labour interact. Labour markets exist at several levels (national, regional, local), and the preceding discussion of government activities suggests these markets can be viewed as targets of macro-level planning. In turn, their composition affects employment planning at the micro level.[18] For example, shortages of critical skills result in longer lead times to hire or train the needed personnel and, hence, make planning more important. Surpluses in the market shorten the time required to hire personnel. Planning does not need to be done as far ahead since people with the required skills are readily available. However, labour market surpluses driven by a downturn in the economy may combine with a need for downsizing. This presents a dilemma for organizations that care about their employees. Normal voluntary termination and retirement rates may be insufficient to balance the employer's reduced staffing level, and some employees may have to be terminated or placed on early retirement.

It is also well known that in a large country like Canada, economic activity varies regionally. An increase in economic activity in the industrial manufacturing belt of Ontario leads to an increase in employment opportunities in that area. If employment planners find that the local labour market is insufficient to supply the requisite quality and quantity of labour, the regional labour market may have to be tapped, and so on. This points out the importance of understanding the relevant external factors (see Chapter Two), especially the link between economic activity and labour markets. As was pointed out, environmental scanning is a useful activity to assess relative trends. A relatively comprehensive data source for assessing labour market trends is available through regional labour market bulletins published by CEIC.[19]

Technology

Technological change affects the design of employment planning through its effects on the nature of work and attendant changes in requisite KSAOs. For example, the number of employees required for unskilled work need not be specified three to five years ahead, since unskilled labour is usually easily obtainable. But requirements for critical technical and managerial positions may need to be forecast years ahead because it takes longer to develop, retrain, and/or recruit these skills.[20] For employers in the high-technology segment, potential supply problems can be viewed in terms of a hierarchy of shortages based on the length of postsecondary school training required to become fully proficient.[21]

- Unskilled workers: three to six months.
- Junior paraprofessionals (e.g., technicians, draftspeople, programmers): two to three years.
- Senior paraprofessionals: two to three years of training plus five years of industrial experience.
- Professionals (primarily professional engineers and managers): 5 years of training plus 10 to 25 years of on-the-job experience.

Unions

Unions may also exert an important influence on employment planning. Union-management agreements may regulate hiring, promotion, transfer, and layoff actions. Seniority provisions and "bumping rights" in collective agreements need to be tied into employment plans. Unions are also an important part of several joint initiatives with government and industry.[22]

The nature of employment planning at the organizational level is contingent on many factors. The following sections examine the major issues in the employment planning process and link this process to other human resource activities.

EMPLOYMENT PLANNING

> **Definition**
> *Employment planning* identifies the future needs for employees, both in terms of quality and quantity; compares the needs with the present work force; and determines the numbers and types of employees to be recruited or phased out, based on the organization's strategies and objectives.[23]

Simply stated, employment planning is planning how to staff the organization with effective human resources.

Reasons for Employment Planning

Many organizations do more talking about than actual planning for employment.[24] Yet more and more seem to be moving to formal planning systems as they discover that unsystematic approaches are inefficient in meeting employment needs. Some common reasons for formal employment planning are to achieve:[25]

More effective and efficient use of human resources.

More satisfied and more developed employees.

More effective employment equity planning.

Let's look at each of these reasons.

More Effective and Efficient Use of People at Work. Employment planning precedes other personnel activities. How could you schedule recruiting if you did not know how many people you needed? How could you select effectively if you did not know the kinds of people needed for job openings? How large an orientation program should you schedule? When? How large a training program should you schedule? Careful analysis of many human resource activities shows that their effectiveness and efficiency depend on answers to questions about how many people with what talents are required.

More Effective Employee Development and Greater Employee Satisfaction. Employment planning helps the company identify its future P/HRM needs, thereby increasing the opportunity for employees to plan for and participate in their career development. This may increase employee satisfaction and reduce absenteeism and turnover.[26] Employment planning may also help P/HRM specialists estimate future organizational demography. *Organizational demography* refers to the age, seniority, sex, or other demographic distribution of the company's work force at a specific time. This distribution is affected by the flow of people into, through, and out of the organization and has a significant effect on organizational effectiveness.[27]

If a company has a long-term hiring freeze or lays off recently hired employees, the average seniority level of those still employed increases substantially. For example, as a result of massive layoffs during the early 1980s, the *newest* production employee in some Canadian forest products firms has more than 10 years' seniority. Firms with a large percentage of long-term employees tend to be less flexible and innovative. Another problem occurs when these companies suddenly hire a large number of new people. The large gap between the age and seniority of new and current employees may lead to substantial organizational conflict. Some of these long-term problems may be avoided through well-planned employment practices.

More Effective Employment Equity Planning. Carefully designed human resource planning programs enhance an employer's ability to draw on, and develop further, a broader array of talent. Employment planning itself focusses managers' attention on the fair treatment of members of target groups. Data collected routinely during sound employment planning, especially on the supply side, may identify pockets of potential human resource inputs or contributions that have not been fully explored. Further, employment planning data may be required of certain employers to ensure compliance with employment equity and/or federal contract compliance legislation.

Three Phases of Analysis

Employment planning is designed to get the right number and types of employees in the right jobs at the right time. As Exhibit 6–4 indicates, employment planning does its part to ensure the success of the overall strategic human resource plan. It does this in three basic phases of analysis:

1. Forecasting human resource demand.
2. Analyzing human resources available.
3. Designing and evaluating alternative programs to reconcile demand and supply.

EXHIBIT 6–4
Employment Planning Process

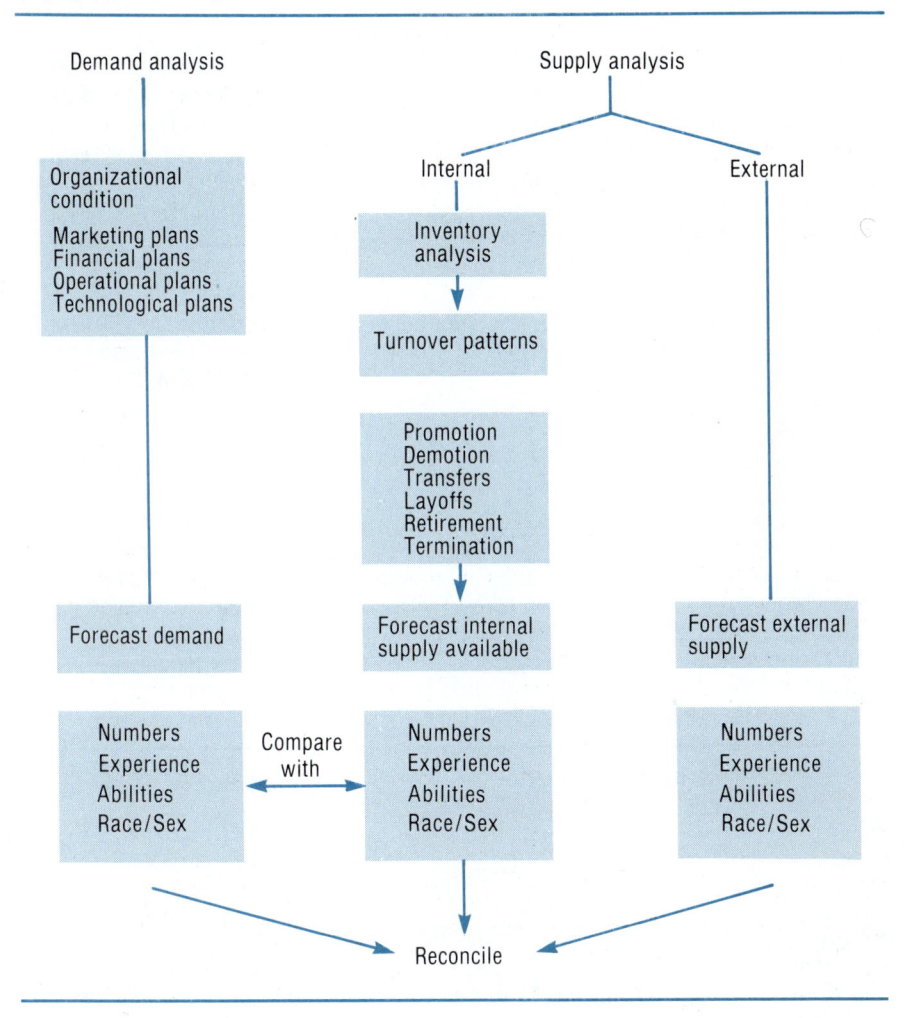

```
Demand analysis                          Supply analysis
     |                                  /              \
     |                            Internal           External
     |                               |
[Organizational                 [Inventory
 condition                       analysis]
                                    |
 Marketing plans                    v
 Financial plans              [Turnover patterns]
 Operational plans                  |
 Technological plans]               v
     |                         [Promotion
     |                          Demotion
     |                          Transfers
     |                          Layoffs
     |                          Retirement
     |                          Termination]
     |                               |
     v                               v                    v
[Forecast demand]            [Forecast internal      [Forecast external
                              supply available]       supply]
     |                               |                    |
     v         Compare               v                    v
[Numbers        with          [Numbers              [Numbers
 Experience  <------>          Experience            Experience
 Abilities                     Abilities             Abilities
 Race/Sex]                     Race/Sex]             Race/Sex]
     \                             |                    /
      \                            v                   /
       ---------------->      [Reconcile]     <--------
```

Who Performs Employment Planning?

The respective roles of operating and P/HRM managers in employment planning are outlined in Exhibit 6–5. The first two items, while not part of employment planning, are included as a reminder of the flow of decisions that lead to employment planning (see Exhibit 6–1). The state of knowledge and practice in each of the formal employment planning phases are discussed below; first, we turn to forecasting the demand for human resources.

EXHIBIT 6–5
Employment Planning Activities Performed by P/HRM and Operating Managers

Planning Activities	Operating Manager (OM)	P/HRM Manager
Strategic organizational decisions	Performed by OM with inputs from P/HRM	Provides information inputs for OM
Strategic human resource decisions	Provides information inputs for P/HRM	Performed by P/HRM with inputs from OM
Forecasting demand for human resources		Performed by P/HRM based on strategic management decisions
Forecasting supply of human resources	Provides information inputs for P/HRM	Performed by P/HRM with information inputs from OM
Work scheduling decisions	Joint responsibility	Joint responsibility
Action decision: Analyzing the composition of the work force		Performed by P/HRM
Action decision: Shortage of employees	Provides information inputs for P/HRM	Performed by P/HRM with information inputs from OM
Action decision: Surplus of employees	Policy decisions by OM with inputs from P/HRM	Implementation decisions by P/HRM

Source: Adapted from John M. Ivancevich and William F. Glueck, *Foundations of Personnel/Human Resource Management*, 3rd ed. (Plano, Tex.: Business Publications, 1986).

FORECASTING DEMAND FOR EMPLOYEES

There are several approaches to demand forecasting. The headquarters can forecast the total demand for the entire organization (*top-down* approach), or the individual units can forecast their own requirements, which are then added up to get total demand (*bottom-up* approach), or there can be a combination of these two approaches.[28]

Demand forecasting, like any process of predicting the future, is more art than science,[29] and it is less amenable to modelling than supply forecasts. Employment planners must use their judgements as well as models and formulas. The most perplexing problem in demand forecasting is identifying the relevant business factor(s) and using the appropriate forecasting technique to estimate the relationship between the demand for human resources and the output—goods and services—produced by the organization.

**EXHIBIT 6–6
Employment Planning Process**

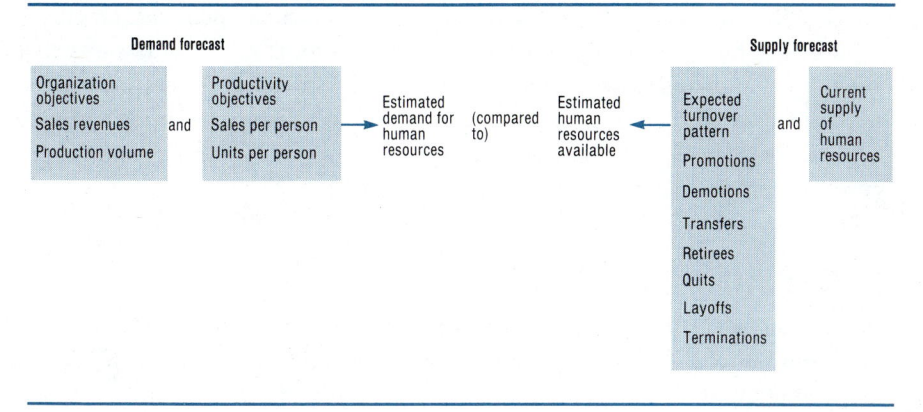

```
      Demand forecast                                                                              Supply forecast
┌──────────────┐   ┌──────────────┐                                    ┌──────────────┐   ┌──────────────┐
│ Organization │   │ Productivity │                                    │ Expected     │   │ Current      │
│ objectives   │   │ objectives   │   Estimated                Estimated│ turnover     │   │ supply       │
│ Sales revenues│ and│ Sales per person│→ demand for (compared  human   │ pattern      │and│ of           │
│ Production   │   │ Units per person│  human       to)       resources │ Promotions   │   │ human        │
│ volume       │   │              │   resources              available  │ Demotions    │   │ resources    │
└──────────────┘   └──────────────┘                                    │ Transfers    │   └──────────────┘
                                                                       │ Retirees     │
                                                                       │ Quits        │
                                                                       │ Layoffs      │
                                                                       │ Terminations │
                                                                       └──────────────┘
```

Selecting the appropriate business factor to which human resource demand can be related is a critical step.[30] To be useful in predicting demand, the business factor should satisfy at least two requirements. First, it should relate directly to the essential nature of the business[31] and be expressed in terms of units (e.g., dollar volume, sales per person) consistent with business planning. The second requirement stipulates that change in the factor selected be proportional to required human resources.[32] In a steel company, for example, tons of steel produced can be used if the number of required workers is proportional to the output of steel.

Choosing the proper business factor can be difficult for several reasons. Required staffing levels are not always proportional to product volume. Further, planners in a multiproduct organization may find the various products require different levels of labour input. This requires separate projections for different products or segments of the work force.[33]

Exhibit 6–6 shows the basic model for estimating demand for employees. The future need for employees is derived from the demand for products, the financial performance objectives of the organization, and a productivity factor. In practice, as indicated above, the difficulty lies in getting good measures of each.

Estimated Organization Performance Goals

Several measures are used in employment planning to determine an organization's financial performance and demand for its products. The 3M Company, for example, uses gross sales revenues.[34] An insurance firm such as London Life might use policies-in-force. Some firms use return on investment;

others utilize estimated production volumes or value added (the difference between the cost of raw materials and the price of the final product).[35]

The best measures to select in starting employment planning are those used in the financial, manufacturing, and marketing plans. This ensures that the employment plan will be better integrated with the business plans. The required data are usually readily available. The estimated revenues and production forecasts are typically generated in the overall business planning process and serve as inputs to employment forecasts.

Productivity

Productivity may be measured at various levels: organization, unit, product line, or whatever level seems logical. But in general it is the output produced per unit of input.[36] Output is measured in the terms discussed above. Human resource inputs can be measured as numbers of employees, person hours, or wage dollars.

What difference does the measurement of productivity make? Exhibit 6–7 contrasts several different measures of productivity.

The factors chosen to measure productivity focus our effort. In sales revenue per number of employees, productivity is dollar sales related to each employee. Contrast that with dollar sales generated for each dollar in compensation paid or with units produced per hours worked. The measures used shift our attention. The one to use depends on which factors (wages, hours, number of employees) we are trying to affect and control.

EXHIBIT 6–7
Productivity Measures for Human Resource Demand Forecasts

Measure	Definition	Focus
Sales revenues per number of employees	Dollar sales associated with each employee	Sales and number of employees; treats each employee identically
Sales revenues per wage bill	Dollar sales associated with each dollar paid in wages	Sales and costs of labour; recognizes different experience and skills receive different pay
Sales revenues per person-hour	Dollar sales associated with each hour worked	Sales and hours worked; used in manufacturing units
Production units per person-hour	Units produced per hour worked	Production and hours; used in manufacturing

Research literature tells little about which measures are most commonly used. Nor is much known about the effects of using various alternatives. Yet our experience suggests that firms that focus on controlling the numbers of employees use sales per person. Those that focus on return on investments and costs use sales per salaries.[37]

Next we illustrate an actual employee forecast. It usually involves the number of employees and the mix of qualifications required.

An Illustration

Employee Forecasts: Numbers Required

The numbers of employees required for a future plan period is a function of the estimated sales revenue (or production estimate) for that period and the productivity goal. In the example in Exhibit 6–8, the current year's revenues were $120 million; productivity was determined by dividing $120 million by the current work force, 857 employees, to get revenue of $140,000 per person. During the plan year, two forecasts were generated. The first used the current year's productivity figure, the second included a productivity improvement goal of 7 percent ($140,000 × 107 percent = $149,800 revenue per employee). With the improved productivity, 1,001 employees ($150 million ÷ 149,800 = 1,001) are required, which is 70 less than without the productivity improvement goal. If the average wage bill (pay plus benefits) is $20,000 per employee, then the savings generated by the productivity improvement equals $1.40 million ($20,000 × 70). Taking account of an anticipated change in productivity reflects the planners' view of how efficiently human and technical resources can be combined and utilized.

EXHIBIT 6–8
Human Resource Demand Forecast

	Current Year	Plan Year Estimate: No Change in Productivity	Plan Year Estimate: 7 Percent Productivity Improvement
Revenue	$120 million	$150 million	$150 million
Present employees	857		
Productivity (revenue per employee)	$140,000	$140,000	$149,800
Employees required		1,071	1,001

Other approaches to demand forecasting are more complex, but the basic concepts remain—demand for employees is derived from revenue or production targets and productivity objectives.[38]

Employee Forecasts: Skills Mix

The mix or combination of skills and experience required is more difficult to forecast. Many employers simply use the same distribution of skills that they have during the current period. Exhibit 6–9 shows the proportion of employees in each skill or job category during the current period. The forecast total number of employees derived above is simply allocated according to the current proportions. Then managers are asked to use their best judgements for any redeployment of employees.

The question of skill mix can be addressed in other ways, too. Some employers estimate support staff needs (accountants, human resource professionals) as a function of the number of a critical skill required.[39] For example, in firms in which engineering talent is critical, such as at Hewlett-Packard (Canada), SNC, and H. A. Simons, the number of engineers required may be used as the determinant of the level of clerical, accounting, and other support personnel. The ratio may be one support employee for every 20 engineers, for example.

Regardless of the approach used, the results of the demand forecasts serve as inputs to managers. They may be adjusted by managers with more intimate knowledge to fit the needs of a particular organization unit.[40]

Productivity Goals

As we have noted, productivity is one of the key objectives of P/HRM. Exhibit 6–10 shows there are five basic strategies for improving productivity.[41]

EXHIBIT 6–9
Employment Forecast: Skills Mix

	Current Year		Plan Year Forecast	
Work Force Category	Number	Percent	Number	Percent
Total employees	857	100%	1,000	100%
Executive	8	1	10	1
Manager—supervisor	128	15	150	15
Professional and staff specialist	171	20	200	20
Scientist—engineer	214	25	250	25
Office	86	10	100	10
Production—maintenance	250	29	290	29

EXHIBIT 6-10
Five Basic Strategies to Improve Productivity

$$\text{Productivity} = \frac{\text{Outputs}}{\text{Inputs}}$$

Strategy	Description	HRM Example
1. ↑/↑ (larger top)	Increase output faster than inputs	Increase sales or production faster than adding employees or person-hours
2. ↑/—	Increase output while holding inputs stable	Increase sales or production while keeping the work force numbers constant; no net additions to staff; replace exits
3. ↓/↓ (larger bottom)	Decrease inputs faster than output	In a declining situation, reduce the work force faster than the decline in production or sales revenues
4. —/↓	Maintain output with reduced inputs	Maintain sales or production with fewer employees
5. ↑/↓	Increase output with reduced inputs	Improve sales and production with a reduced work force

We can design programs that will either raise the numerator (output) more quickly than the denominator (input) or lower the denominator more quickly than the numerator.

In sum, improving productivity is a key objective of P/HRM. This is so for several reasons. First, the productivity goal plays a key role when determining the number of employees required. Next, productivity is directly linked to achieving the organization's goals. Finally, the desire to improve productivity focuses the human resource professional's attempts to design programs. Hence, improved productivity should benefit the organization as well as employees.

Tailoring Tools to the Situation

A wide variety of forecasting techniques are used in employment planning. Some of these are described in Exhibit 6-11, and the interested reader should pursue the references to this chapter.[42] The techniques range from sophisticated quantitative models to the use of qualitative managerial judgements. Researchers have yet to specify the conditions under which specific

EXHIBIT 6-11
Employment Planning Forecasting Techniques

Various authors have reviewed the different forecasting techniques available and have suggested classifications into types of models. Those summarized here serve the purposes of this book. More complex approaches involve programming (linear, nonlinear, dynamic) with future needs defined by constraints, and/or comprehensive integrated simulation models combining a number of techniques.

Unit demand forecasting: A bottom-up approach to forecasting demand. The unit can be a project team, an entire department, or other readily identifiable group. Manager analyzes the unit's current situation of, and anticipated demand for, staff on a person-by-person, job-by-job basis. Estimations of future demand for the unit's products and services are made (using methods similar to trend projection techniques at the organizational level) to determine unit staffing level. Headquarters sums unit forecasts to derive the demand forecast for the organization. When bottom-up and top-down approaches are used together and yield different results, differences are reconciled by averaging and examining major variances in detail.

Expert estimate approach: Frequently used, but is the least sophisticated method. Individual "expert" forecasts employment needs based on experience, intuition, and guesswork. Can be improved by the *Delphi* technique, a procedure for obtaining the most reliable consensus of a panel of experts (who do not meet or communicate directly with each other). Inputs solicited through a series of questionnaires are compiled by an intermediary at each stage and revealed to the panel for further refinement. Responses tend to converge after several rounds. The final round's average is used as the consensus judgement for the forecast. Can also be used to help resolve differences between forecasts in organizations using both bottom-up and top-down approaches.

Trend projection: Based on determining and relating the relevant factor(s) used in business planning to employment needs in terms of work force size and composition. Analyzes past trends in the forecasting factor(s) in relation to staffing level and projects to determine what the future trend is expected to be. Specific steps are: (1) identifying the appropriate business factor(s); (2) plotting the historical record of the factor in relation to work force; (3) computing labour productivity (i.e., average output per employee per year); (4) determining the trend in labour productivity; (5) making adjustments to the trend; and (6) projecting to the target year.

Regression analysis: Uses quantitative procedures that allow quantification of the relationship between future staffing requirements (the dependent variable) and predictors such as unit costs, production, sales, and labour productivity (independent variables). It may be necessary to generate separate equations to predict demand for different job categories (e.g., factory, office, professional, managerial employees). In some cases, overall forecast of total employees can be allocated according to current proportions (as in Exhibit 6-9).

EXHIBIT 6–11 *(concluded)*

Succession analysis: Projects retirements, transfers, and promotions to develop plans for key positions and levels for the future. Lists position incumbents along with targetted mobility; identifies prospective successor candidates and projected time of readiness. Data generated in the form of replacement/succession charts.

Markov analysis: Projects future flows to obtain availability estimates through a straightforward application of historical transition rates. Historical transition rates are derived from analyses of personnel data concerning losses, promotions, transfers, demotions, and, perhaps, recruitment.

Simulation (based on Markov analysis): Alternative (rather than historical) flows are examined for effects of future human resource availabilities. Alternative flows reflect the anticipated results of policy or program changes concerning voluntary and involuntary turnover, retirement, promotion, etc.

Renewal analysis: Estimates future flows and availabilities by calculating: (1) vacancies as created by organizational growth, personnel losses, and internal movements out of states; and (2) the results of decision rules governing the filling of vacancies. Alternative models may assess the effects of changes in growth estimates, turnover, promotions, or decision rules.

Goal programming: Optimizes goals—in this case a desired staffing pattern—given a set of constraints concerning such things as the upper limits on flows, the percentage of new recruits permitted, and total salary budgets.

---

techniques work better than others. Elaborate quantitative devices require both advanced databases to support them and professionals trained to apply and understand the results. Models such as regression and time series often require several years of historical data to estimate parameters and their relationship to employment needs.

Some evidence suggests that the particular proclivities of the manager influence the techniques used. It is sort of like children with a hammer—once they learn to use the tool, they apply it to everything. Buller and Maki report the historical evolution from design to implementation, evaluation, and ultimate disuse of a forecasting model of Weyerhaeuser.[43] They present the model's life cycle, shown in Exhibit 6–12, and offer the following reasons for the decline in the model's use:

- Weyerhaeuser's human resources requirements stabilized.
- The personnel department shifted its orientation from an organizational to an individual/developmental approach.
- The leadership changed; the designer of the model was promoted.

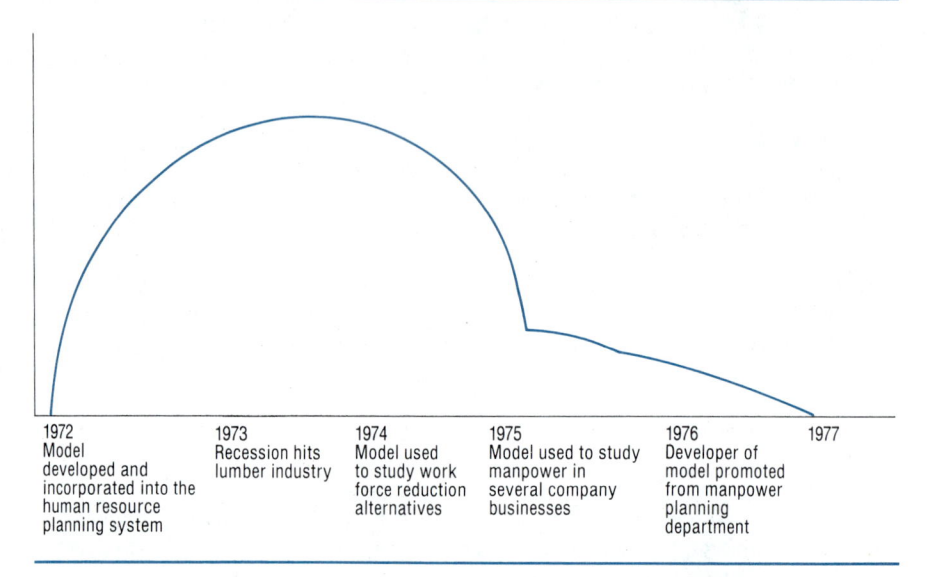

EXHIBIT 6–12
Weyerhaeuser Experience: History of Utilization of the Employment Planning Model*

1972	1973	1974	1975	1976	1977
Model developed and incorporated into the human resource planning system	Recession hits lumber industry	Model used to study work force reduction alternatives	Model used to study manpower in several company businesses	Developer of model promoted from manpower planning department	

*This graph was constructed from subjective assessment of the authors. At its peak the model was used on a weekly, sometimes daily, basis. In 1976 the model was used on a quarterly, then semiannual basis.

Source: P. F. Buller and W. R. Maki, "A Case History of a Manpower Planning Model," *Human Resource Planning* 4, no. 3 (1981), p. 132.

Buller and Maki observed, "A given model may outlive its usefulness. The personnel professional shouldn't foster the use of a model if a particular problem no longer warrants it."[44]

What is intriguing about the Weyerhaeuser experience is the questions it raises. What effects do changing economic and organizational circumstances have on the employment planning techniques used? And what difference does changing the techniques make on the results obtained?

The best advice for an employment planner is: be familiar with several techniques and don't be afraid to try different ones to see which best fit the circumstances.

Prediction Accuracy versus Objectives Achieved

But how do we judge a forecasting model? Some research into employment forecasting focuses on the accuracy of the results.[45] That is, the results of a forecast are compared to the actual employment behaviour of the organization. Results of such studies have been very disappointing, suggesting that relying on historical relationships to predict future employment needs is not a fruitful endeavour.

However, the emphasis on accuracy of forecasts may be misplaced. The models may have a greater payoff in helping managers achieve productivity goals. For example, if productivity is treated as a human resource objective, then the required human resources are simply derived from it. Under this view, the productivity goal and the resulting employment forecasts become a control device or goal rather than a prediction. For example, a company may set its productivity figures at $120,000 sales revenues per person, and no employee can be added to the work force unless anticipated sales revenue permits. The emphasis is on goals and control rather than predictive accuracy. No one claims such a goal is optimal—all that is claimed is that the productivity goal is achieved. And employment levels are controlled to guarantee that result.

Keep Employment Forecasts in Perspective

We have emphasized that employment planning procedures need to be designed to fit the circumstances. Too often, employment planning is limited in scope. There are several reasons for this. In many cases, the business plans are not sufficiently developed. Even in cases where they are, the human resource variables may be difficult to define and quantify. Think about the nature of employment planning. It is to translate one set of estimates (future sales or production) into another set of estimates (future numbers and skills of employees required). It often seems like constructing a structure on shifting sand.

Another problem faced in demand forecasting is that its output is expressed in terms of the right number and right types of employees in the right place at the right time. But human resource objectives are broader than simply the right numbers. They include labour costs, achievement of safe working conditions, employee satisfaction, and more.[46]

Nevertheless, the process of determining employment needs still has value beyond the numbers obtained. In many organizations, it alerts top management to the human resources implication of financial, manufacturing, and marketing plans and directs attention toward the management of those resources. Witness Dahl and Morgan's suggestions to managers of Upjohn's 17 profit centres.[47] Before adding employees to the work force, they are asked to address the following questions:

1. What purposes does the new position serve?
2. What alternatives were considered to accomplish the same purposes?

3. If the position is filled, what are the projected five-year costs?
4. What impact will this position have on:
   a. Maintenance or improvement of sales?
   b. Maintenance or improvement of earnings?
   c. Improved utilization of people?

A survey of human resource/employment planning practices in 154 Canadian companies (from 15 industrial sectors and located in Alberta, Ontario, Quebec, and Nova Scotia) helps illuminate several of the points made in our discussion of forecasting demand. The following conclusions were reached:[48]

- The median number of years planned increases with company size. A critical point seems to be 1,000 employees, at which the incidence of five-year forecasts increases markedly.
- Longer-term planning is highest in the energy/petrochemical sector, followed by mining/smelting, forest products, trade, and manufacturing/automotive sectors. Requirements for high capital outlays and considerable lead times appear to explain this trend.
- Employment planning tends to be done for the categories of employees that are most important to the particular industry or region. Most industries plan their human resources in a rank order, with a descending order of time frames: managerial (most important/longest time frame); professional/technical; skilled trades; clerical; semi- and unskilled (shortest time frame). Some exceptions are manufacturing/machine equipment (with greater emphasis on the last two categories) and mining/smelting (which plan for skilled trades longer than for all other categories).
- Industry material, company surveys, and extrapolated historical data were used most often as data sources. These self-generated data were followed by reliance on industry or management association data and consultant reports. Little use was made of government data (seldom used, considered out of date, or unknown to some of the planners interviewed).

We have now examined the first phase of employment planning: demand forecasting. Next we turn to the second phase: the analysis of the supply of human resources.

FORECASTING HUMAN RESOURCE SUPPLY

Analysis of the available human resource supply focuses on such issues as: How many people, with what qualifications and interests, do we currently employ? How many of these do we estimate will be available during the planning period?

Supply analysis considers two sources of human resources, external (available in labour markets) and internal (available in the organization). Both these sources are analyzed not only for the numbers of people available but also for other factors, including their abilities, interests, and work experience. Supply analysis begins with an internal inventory of human resources. This is a count of the numbers of people and skills currently employed.

The next step is to project current supply into the future. This is done to estimate what human resources will be available internally during the plan year. As Exhibit 6–4 showed, in the box labelled turnover patterns, the current internal supply changes. Some workers will be promoted, retire, transfer, and so on. Forecasting future supplies involves estimating this movement in the work force and adjusting the projected supply accordingly.[49]

Turnover Rates as an Objective

Many employment planners establish specific rates of turnover (or patterns of mobility) as an objective. Subsequently, P/HRM programs are designed to achieve the objective, perhaps through the use of early retirement programs such as at Alcan, Air Canada, and Kodak (parent of Kodak Canada, Inc.).[50] Kodak designed early retirement programs to encourage older, experienced, and more expensive employees to leave. It also designed layoffs and instituted a recruiting freeze. Other firms may attempt to reduce the losses of employees, particularly those who are highly skilled and high performers. Specific turnover rates can be established as human resource objectives, just as productivity improvement rates are. Whether to seek increased or decreased turnover rates depends on the circumstances the organization faces.[51]

The experience of a large aluminum smelter in Western Canada illustrates a situation that required the employer to seek lower turnover rates.[52] Due to a combination of factors (e.g., underrepresentation of P/HRM in senior management levels, more militant worker attitudes, plenty of jobs elsewhere) during a two-year period in the 1970s, employees quit in higher numbers than ever in the company's history. The P/HRM department was unable to meet the staffing demands of plant supervisors. Selection standards were lowered, but many of the increasing number of young, single, and mobile workers hired quit after only a few months. The situation so deteriorated that P/HRM was scrambling to find replacements for employees recently hired as replacements. An outside consultant was engaged to develop a model to forecast plantwide terminations. The turnover forecast model and actual experience proved remarkably close and gained the confidence of plant managers. With better planning, the company introduced a "stability bonus" program that combined an increase in the labour costs of production with lower turnover.

Human Resource Supply Estimates

As Exhibit 6–6 showed, once expected turnover rates are established, they are combined with the current supply of employees to determine the expected future supply of human resources. For a small employer, it is relatively easy to know how many employees there are, what they do, and what they can potentially do. A grocery store may be operated by the owners, who have two part-time helpers to "plan" for. When they expect turnover (one part-time employee is going to graduate from college and take a new job in June), they know they need a replacement. Sources of supply could include their own children, converting their other part-time helper into a full-time employee, or calling the school's employment office for possible applicants.

It is quite different with an organization employing hundreds at numerous locations.[53] To analyze their supply of human resources, these organizations must know how many full-time and peripheral workers they have and where. They must also know what types of skills and experience the employees who leave take with them.

Supply Analysis Techniques

A range of tools for analysis of internal supplies are available. We will examine three: skills inventories, replacement/succession charts, and Markov models.

Skills Inventories

Recall from Chapter Three that a skills inventory is an important component of a comprehensive human resource information system. In its simplest form, a skills inventory contains a list of employees' names, certain characteristics, and skills of the people working for the organization.[54]

Many organizations introduced skills inventories when computers became available for this purpose. Most organizations do have the information in one form or another, but frequently it is buried in personnel folders, and time and effort are needed to get at it. Good skills inventories enable organizations to determine quickly and expeditiously what kinds of people with specific skills are available. This information is useful whenever an employer decides to expand and accept new contracts or to change strategies. It is also useful in planning for training, management development, employment equity, promotion, transfer, and related P/HRM activities.

Designing Skills Inventory Systems

Once the decision is made to have a skills inventory system, the challenge is what data the system should contain. An organization can retrieve only what is designed into the system.

The list of data coded into skills inventories is almost endless and must be tailored to the needs of each organization.[55] Some of the more common items include: name, employee number, present location, date of birth, date of employment, job classification or code, prior experience, history of work experience in the organization, specific skills and knowledge, education, field of education (formal education and courses taken since leaving school), knowledge of the two official languages and others, health, professional qualifications, publications, licences, patents, hobbies, a supervisory evaluation of the employee's capabilities, and salary/salary range. Items often omitted, but becoming increasingly important, are the employee's own stated career goals and objectives, including geographical preferences, and intended retirement date.

Skills inventory data identify employees for specific assignments which will fulfill not only organizational objectives but individual ones as well.

Examples of Skills Inventory Systems

One of the main problems in designing such a system is developing a standard data format, with records stored in an easily accessible form for all units. Sophisticated computerized skills inventories have many P/HRM and nonpersonnel uses.[56] IBM's system contains information on such data as career plans and educational goals for more than 100,000 of its employees. This system allows IBM to project five-year engineering and other P/HRM needs for various rates of corporate growth, and a monthly personnel transaction report is developed for all divisions that can be used to pinpoint possible imbalances within the total organizational system.[57]

Other computerized systems are available in a variety of configurations. Office Data Systems of Toronto provides a software package called "Recruiter," an automated skills inventory filing system.[58] TDM Software Systems' HRbase allows the P/HRM manager instant desktop access to all relevant details of any number of employees and applicants. "Microprospect," developed by Swiftsure Data Systems of Vancouver, can be used for identifying human resource shortfalls or surpluses before they occur.[59]

Smith points out several uses of skills inventory systems:

> A carefully prepared skills inventory can be used as a basis for long-range personnel planning and development by providing precise definitions of the aptitudes and abilities available and needed by the organization. It can be used to assist in the evaluation of growth potential of the present executive work force and help to

identify group strengths and weaknesses for future recruiting strategies. It may uncover interdivisional imbalances (e.g., understaffing) which could lead to future overall corporate personnel problems. Most importantly, it will serve as a motivating device by demonstrating through written feedback that the organization has a systematic approach to personal data utilization and that it is eager to develop each employee to full potential.[60]

Maintaining Inventory Systems

While designing the system is the most difficult part of developing a skills inventory, planning for the gathering, maintaining, handling, and updating of data is also important.[61] The two principal methods for gathering data are the interview and the questionnaire. Each method has unique costs and benefits. The questionnaire is faster and less expensive when many employees are involved, but inaccuracies are usually greater; people often do not spend enough time on a questionnaire. There are those who contend, therefore, that the trained interviewer can complete the reports more quickly and accurately, and this in the long run more than offsets the costs of the interviewer. A procedure for keeping the files updated also must be planned.

Computerized systems have the advantage of providing faster data and more detailed information.[62] They also are useful in wider applications. Employee turnover can be projected to determine the work force required to maximize the capital investment. Comparative analysis of employment on a time series basis can also be generated on the computer; observing the changes in promotable personnel over time may provide insights into the effectiveness of recruitment and development activities. Computerized systems can analyze all the sequential events necessary in a production process. With an estimation of their associated time and cost factors, these systems can enhance planning accuracy by defining all the necessary work activities, suggesting the latest allowable starting date for each activity, and identifying the potential costs of various courses of action.[63]

Replacement and Succession Charts

Replacement or succession charts are widely used to analyze and project the supply of managerial talent available.

Replacement planning is typically implemented by the use of charts like those shown in Exhibit 6–13. These charts, based on organization charts, provide a "snapshot" of key positions in the organization and the availability of replacements in the current work force. Replacement charts allow judgements about employees' knowledge, skills, and abilities to be documented. This aids decision making when informal knowledge is less complete.

Replacement planning usually is designed to help identify the top 10 to 20 percent of managers who are above standard and who can be promoted at a faster-than-average rate; the middle 60 to 80 percent who should be developed through normal position growth and the bottom 10 to 20 percent who may not be qualified for present jobs and require some other P/HRM action.[64]

Walker highlights several of the inherent shortcomings in replacement planning.[65]

- Little consideration is given to the actual requirements of the positions or the prospective changes that will occur in a job when a new person moves into it.
- Identification of backups or replacement candidates is largely subjective, based on personal knowledge of the nominating managers. There are rarely objective indicators of performance, individual capabilities, or past achievements.
- A high-potential candidate may be qualified for more than one management position, but may be "boxed in" by the vertical line-oriented replacement planning or, alternatively, may be named as a backup for several positions, giving a false impression of management depth.

**EXHIBIT 6–13
Replacement Chart**

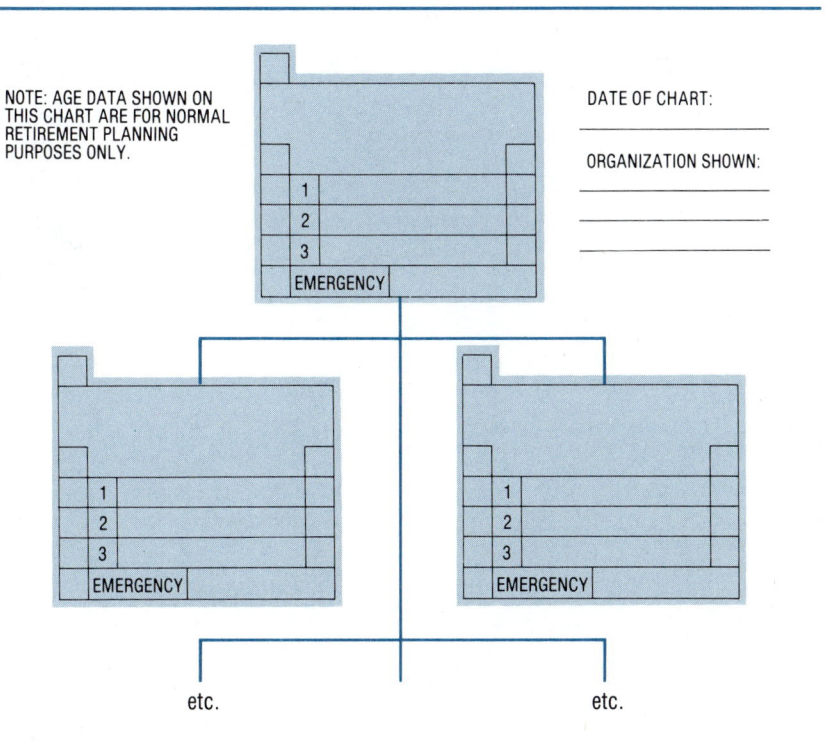

EXHIBIT 6–13 (continued)

	Title	Promotability of Incumbent
Age of incumbent	Incumbent	Performance of incumbent
Replacement candidates in order of preference	1	Readiness of replacements to assume position
	2	
	3	
	EMERGENCY	

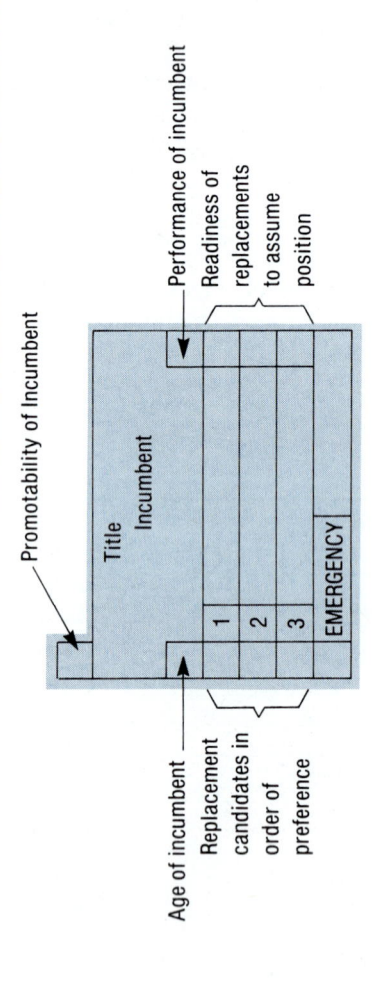

PROMOTABILITY OR READINESS

R	Should be replaced (RED)	PS	Promotable or ready short-term (1-3 years) (YELLOW)
HL	Highest Level (WHITE)	PL	Promotable or ready long-term (3-5 years) (ORANGE)
PN	Promotable or ready now (GREEN)		

EXHIBIT 6-13 *(concluded)*

Performance Rating

1. **Unacceptable**

   Performance is well below the expected standard for the position to such an extent that it cannot be accepted. Performance at this level is probationary and employment will be terminated unless performance reaches a satisfactory level within a stated period of time. Employee should be on a formal improvement program (not more than three months).

2. **Needs improvement**
   or
   Progressing (if applicable for recently hired employee)

   Certain areas of work require improvement before the incumbent can be judged to be fully competent. For a longer service employee, performance at this level for more than six months requires a formal improvement program. Acceptable from a *recently* hired employee or an employee in a new position if normal progress is being made in acquiring full job knowledge and skills.

3. **Expected**

   Performance at this level is fully adequate and is satisfactory in most major aspects of the job. To achieve this rating, an employee must be doing nearly everything that full performance of the job requires. Experienced employees are expected to perform at this level.

4. **Exceeds expectations**

   Performance in most important areas of the job exceeds normal expectations to such a marked and obvious degree that it deserves special recognition. An employee who earns this rating is achieving greater results than were anticipated and is making a contribution to the Company which goes beyond the basic expectations of the job.

5. **Exceptional**

   This category is reserved to properly single out, recognize and compensate those employees who through truly outstanding performance genuinely excel in their jobs in a particular year. This rating reflects significantly greater than expected results with respect to most job responsibilities. It would be rare for an individual to achieve this rating on a continuing basis.

Note: +/− ratings may be used for even greater preciseness.

- Planning is fragmented and vertically oriented; rarely is there provision for lateral or diagonal moves across organizational units.
- There is rarely any input from the individuals themselves regarding their own self-assessments and career interests.
- Most significantly, the charts rarely result in the moves planned or in other developmental activities; the process is often a static, annual paperwork exercise.

To overcome these shortcomings, some employment planners have introduced succession charting.[66] According to Walker, the principal differences are that succession charting is longer range, more developmental, and offers greater flexibility.[67]

An Example of Management Succession Planning

Ontario's Ministry of Transportation and Communications (MTC) is one of the leading transportation authorities in North America. Its responsibilities include managing about 20,800 km (13,000 miles) of provincial roads, managing subsidy allocations for an additional 100,000 km (62,500 miles) of municipal roads, and being involved in the planning for provincial commuter rail and air services. The full-time work force consists of 7,700 bargaining-unit employees and approximately 2,600 management personnel.

MTC's management succession system encompasses middle and senior management (about 1,300 positions) and can prepare separate analyses for each of five primary and eight secondary operational functions. Data used by the forecasting model (for each level of operational function) are:[68]

- Current strength, determined from the personnel inventory.
- Losses, comprised of resignations, dismissals, transfers, and retirements. The first four items are assessed from historical data and then modified according to current and future trends.
- Backup, which is determined from two sources: (1) as part of the formal annual appraisal process, managers identify employees considered promotable within the next one-year planning cycle, and (2) as part of a separate annual process, management identifies high potential employees whose ability suggests progress—in more than one function—to two responsibility levels higher during a five-year forecast period.
- Future demand, forecast on the basis of current as well as future business plans, as determined by MTC's strategic policy committee.

These data are then processed by a computerized forecasting model (see Exhibit 6-14). The numbers in each box are explained in the enlarged portion. At job level 17/18 in 1987, for example, staff strength is shown as 120 persons, of whom 24 had been identified as promotable; 4 persons were promoted "out" (up to level 19), 8 were promoted "in" (from level 15/16), 1 was

EXHIBIT 6–14
MTC Succession Planning Model

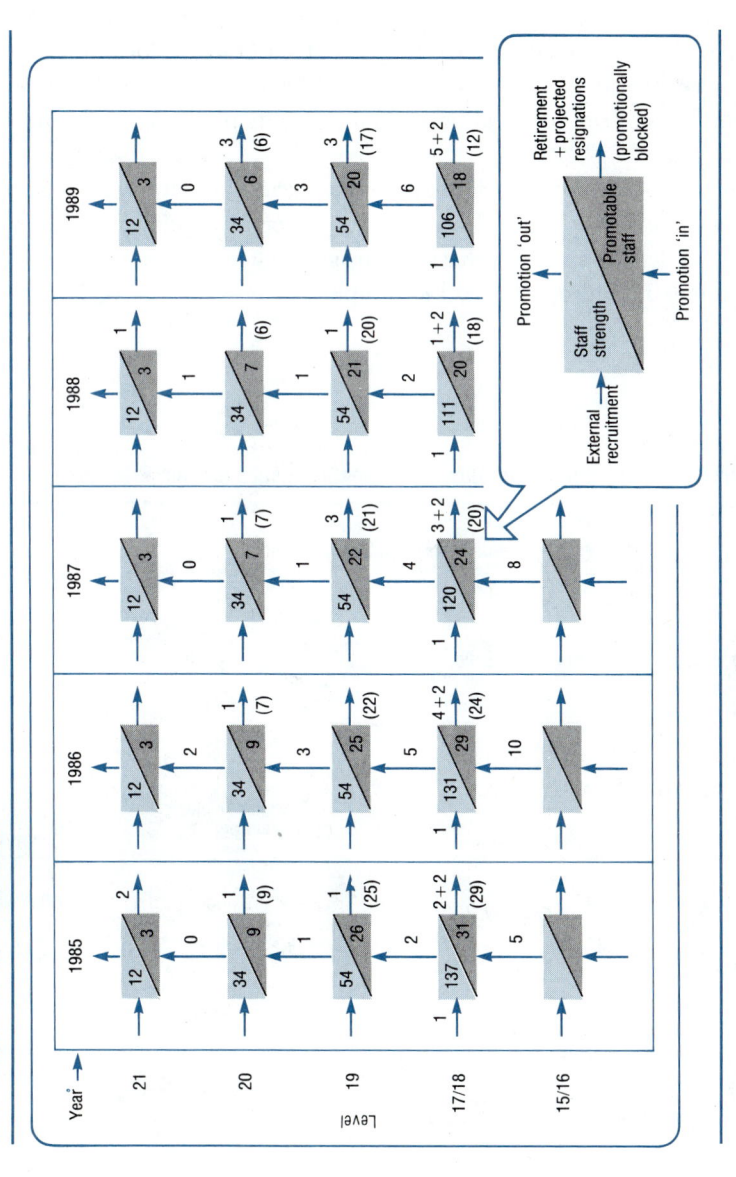

Source: Adapted from L. J. Reypert, "Succession Planning in the Ministry of Transportation and Communications, Province of Ontario," *Human Resource Planning* 4 (1981), pp. 151–56. Reprinted by permission of the publisher from *Human Resource Planning* 4, no. 3 (1981). Copyright 1981 by the Human Resource Planning Society.

recruited externally, 3 retired, 2 were projected to resign, and 20 were promotionally blocked.

Surveys of employment planning practices show that replacement planning and succession planning are widely practiced. Yet little is known about the payoffs from such practices. In one case, a firm's succession plans from 10 years back did not include either the current CEO or the president. Several current vice presidents had received rather lukewarm evaluations. None of these employees had been earmarked on previous plans as part of the future executive team.

Exhibit 6–15 shows the framework Carnazza derived from an analysis of the succession/replacement planning practices of 79 employers.[69] He reports current practices tend to emphasize managers while often neglecting the nature of the work and the demand for employees.

EXHIBIT 6–15
Schematic Representation of the Succession/Replacement Planning Process

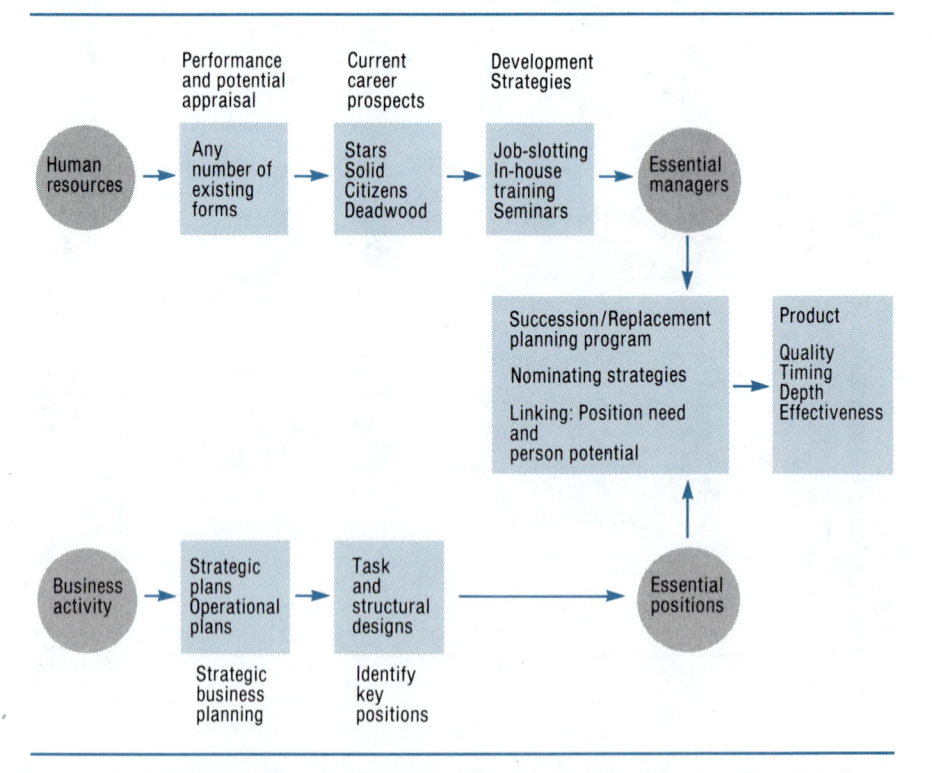

Source: J. Carnazza, *Succession/Replacement Planning: Programs & Practices* (New York: Center for Career Development, Columbia School of Business, 1982), p. 5.

Transitional Matrixes

A third, somewhat more advanced, tool used for the analysis and projection of human resource supplies is transitional probability matrixes.[70] Basically such tables show the movement (promotion, demotions, transfers, hires, and turnover) of employees into, through, and out of the organization.

The usefulness of this technique can be seen with the aid of Exhibits 6–16 and 6–17. There are three basic features of a transitional matrix to keep in mind.

1. *"State" definitions:* States may be salary grades, performance levels, or other characteristics to be analyzed. They represent the way the planner has divided the organization. For example, in Exhibits 6–16 and 6–17, the letters A to J represent positions in the organization's job hierarchy, with A at the *top* of the organization and J at the *bottom*.
2. *Time interval:* The matrix represents the movement of employees in a time period. The vertical axis (Time I) shows the job structure (A through I) at Time I, the beginning of the time period. The horizontal axis (Time II) shows the structure at the end of the time period. The time period analyzed may be one day, one month, one year, or one decade; it is established at the discretion of the planner.
3. *Cell entries:* The entries in the cells of the matrix indicate the proportion of individuals moving from one position at Time I to another position at Time II. For example, cell AA (1.00) tells us that all the people who were in position A at Time I were still there at time II. Cell BA indicates that 15 percent of the individuals in position B in Time I have moved up to position A at Time II.

All the cells in the diagonal represent the probability of remaining in the same job, and off-diagonals represent promotions and demotions. These proportions were calculated by placing the number of employees in a job at the beginning of the time period in the denominator and the number who move from the job to another job at the end of the period in the numerator. For example, consider position B. Suppose that at the beginning of the period (Time I, vertical axis) 100 people were employed as Bs. At Time II (horizontal axis), we find that of these original 100 people employed in B, 15 went up to A (Cell BA), 80 remained in B (Cell BB), and 5 have left the organization. By calculating the proportion, we see that 15 percent (15/100) of those who started in B moved up to A, 80 percent (80/100) remained in B, and 5 percent (5/100) left.

Through the transitional probability matrix we can analyze the movement, the staffing patterns, that occurred during the period. For example, we can identify career patterns in the organization. In our example, there is a

EXHIBIT 6–16
Descriptive Use of Transitional Probability Matrix (internal human resources movement)*

Time II

Job States†	A	B	C	D	E	F	G	H	I	J	Exit	Total
A	1.00										—	1.00
B	.15	.80									.05	1.00
C		.16	.76	.04		◀ Organizational career I					.04	1.00
D		.01	.23	.73							.03	1.00
E					.85	.05					.10	1.00
F					.25	.65	.05				.05	1.00
G			Organizational career II ▲			.40	.50	.03			.07	1.00
H						.02	.15	.75			.08	1.00
I								.20	.50		.30	1.00
J					Organizational career III ▲			.20	.30	.40	.50	1.00
Recruit level				.10							—	1.00

*Cell entries are proportions.
†A to J are different jobs arranged hierarchically.

EXHIBIT 6–17
Interpreting the Transitional Probability Matrix

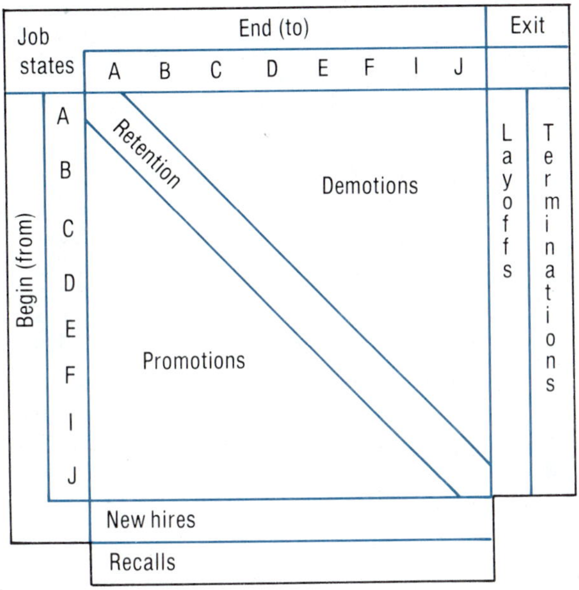

career pattern DCBA. A is its top job and D is the entry-level job. Another career pattern has E at the top and I as the entry job. But for job J, people just come into position J and stay (50 percent during this period) or leave (50 percent left). It appears that there is no possibility of promotion if you are in job J. Through these analyses we can identify "dead-end" positions (J, E, and A) and entry-level positions (people come into the organization at D, H, I, J), perform turnover analysis, and study the rate of employee movement through the organization.

To see how a matrix works, assume we wanted to eventually be in job A. Where would we have to enter this organization? Options are to enter at D, H, I, or J. Based on data from this period, the only way to get to A is to start at job D; the other careers are "dead-ended" before getting to A.

Forecasts and Simulations

So far we have illustrated the uses of the matrix to describe the employer's current behaviour.[71] But matrixes can also be used to simulate the expected future supply of personnel by projecting the employer's current behaviour into the future. Simulating the future tells us what the employer can expect if it continues to hire, move, and lose people in the future at the same rate

EXHIBIT 6-18
Forecasting and Simulation Use of Transitional Probability Matrixes (Markov Analysis)

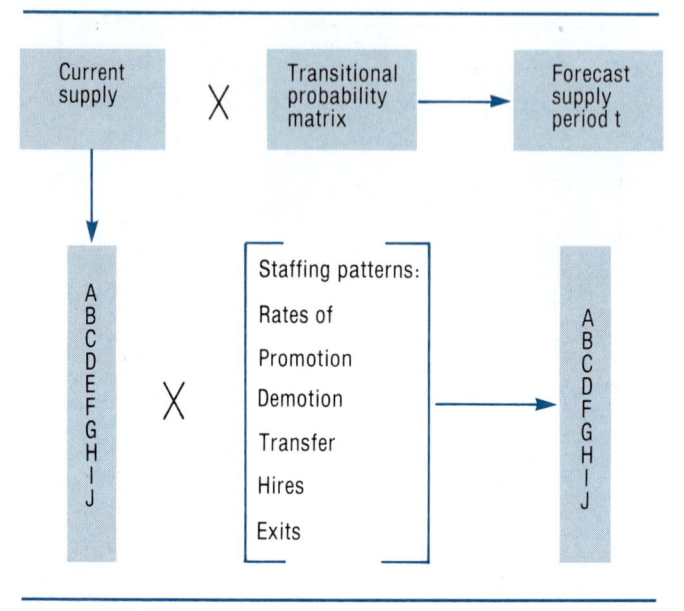

Current supply × Transitional probability matrix → Forecast supply period t

A B C D E F G H I J × [Staffing patterns: Rates of Promotion, Demotion, Transfer, Hires, Exits] → A B C D E F G H I J

Note: t represents the number of periods into the future that the current supply is being forecast.

that it currently hires, moves, and loses people. The forecasting and simulation uses are illustrated in Exhibit 6-18. The calculations can all be performed by a microcomputer.[72]

Conceptually, all we need are three basic pieces of data:

1. The numbers of employees in each position at the beginning of the period (Time I).
2. A matrix that reflects the expected movement (staffing patterns) of employees. This matrix can be based on past history such as described in Exhibit 6-16, or it can represent hypothetical staffing rates that we plan to apply in the future. In other words, the matrix can calculate "what would happen *if?*"
3. How many periods into the future we wish to project the current supply.

By causing the current supply of human resources to move according to the staffing patterns reflected in the matrix, we can forecast the supply in a future period. In other words, this tool will help answer the question: given our current supply of personnel and our staffing plans (promotions, demotions, transfers) what will our expected supply of personnel be in our planning period?

Turning back to the employment planning process in Exhibit 6-4, we see that the forecast supply of personnel available is an important component of an employment plan. If the forecast supply of human resources available differs from the human resources required, then corrective action to reconcile this difference is necessary (Phase III).

The use of matrixes is widely discussed and illustrated, and several actual applications (e.g., at AT&T, Merck, and Weyerhaeuser) have been reported.[73] Heneman and Sandver argue that the uses of matrixes may have been oversold, especially in terms of the accuracy of the forecasts.[74] However, their greatest potential lies not in forecasting but in description and simulation. They have been applied to testing the cumulative effects of differing recruiting and training programs, and to staffing and budgeting problems in the several organizations. One of the greatest uses can be in employment equity analysis. In this case, an employer could calculate what percentage of workers in each job or job category are members of designated groups, and how staffing patterns might be adjusted to change the percentages in a future time period.

We have now examined the first two phases of the employment planning process, analysis of demand and supply; next we turn to Phase III, programming strategies to reconcile differences.

DESIGNING PROGRAMS

There are several managerial decisions to be made once demand and supply of people have been forecast and compared. Exhibit 6-19 presents a more detailed scheme of the personnel programming considerations. Employment equity (EE) leads the list, whether we are over- or understaffed. Since the next chapter is devoted to EE issues, we will examine other possibilities in this chapter. But bear in mind that EE is a priority item in employment planning.

Actions with No Difference in Supply and Demand

Sometimes the demand for employees and the projected supply match, but this is rare. More frequently, if the total supply is correct, there are variances in subgroups. Thus, while the total employment level required and the total available match, the distribution of employees among different positions, with various skills, or in various plant locations may not match. The balancing process may involve transfers, promotions, demotions, and even retraining employees.

EXHIBIT 6-19
Employment Planning Action Plans

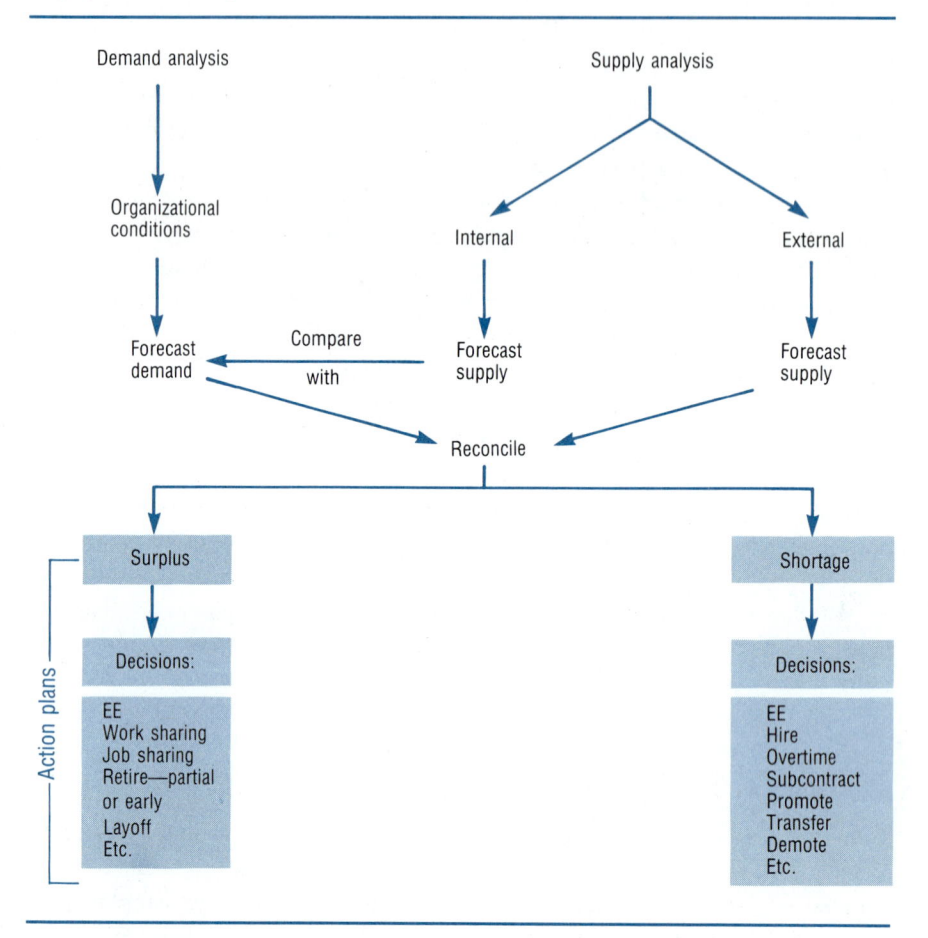

```
Demand analysis                          Supply analysis
     │                                    ╱         ╲
     ▼                                   ▼           ▼
Organizational                      Internal      External
conditions                             │             │
     │                                 ▼             ▼
     ▼          Compare            Forecast      Forecast
  Forecast  ◄───────────           supply         supply
  demand       with                    │             │
     │                                 │             │
     └──────────────► Reconcile ◄──────┘─────────────┘
                          │
             ┌────────────┴────────────┐
             ▼                         ▼
          Surplus                   Shortage
             │                         │
             ▼                         ▼
        Decisions:                Decisions:
        EE                        EE
        Work sharing              Hire
        Job sharing               Overtime
        Retire—partial            Subcontract
        or early                  Promote
        Layoff                    Transfer
        Etc.                      Demote
                                  Etc.
  ◄── Action plans ───
```

Actions with a Shortage of Employees

When employment specialists compare demand to supply and find the supply of workers is less than the demand, several actions are possible. If the shortage is small and employees are willing to work overtime, it can be filled with present employees. If the shortage is of higher-skilled employees, training and promotions of present employees, together with recruitment of lower-skilled workers, is a possibility. Previous employees who may have been laid off can be recalled. Additional employees can be hired, or some of the work can be subcontracted. The upcoming chapters focus principally on strategies to add people to the organization, so we will consider surplus conditions here.

Actions under Surplus Conditions

Reducing labour costs with minimal disruption is one of the greatest challenges to P/HRM specialists. Although we often hear about staff layoffs to reduce costs, other forms of organizational retrenchment exist.[75] Some organizations go to great lengths to avoid laying off surplus staff.[76] A hiring freeze is one of the least painful options, reducing employment costs through attrition alone. Unfortunately, turnover tends to decline so dramatically during times of restraint that this action is usually insufficient. Two other retrenchment strategies used frequently in Canada are reducing work hours and providing early retirement.

Reducing Work Hours. Part-time work is the fastest-growing type of employment in Canada. More than 15 percent of employment time in Canada is worked by part-time employees. By the year 2000, this is expected to rise to 20 percent. Part-time work increases flexibility so employers can match the work force with peak demand.[77] In sudden economic downturns, it keeps everyone on the payroll so recruitment and selection costs are minimized when product demand increases again. Two special forms of part-time work are work sharing and job sharing.

Work sharing refers to an arrangement between the employer and the Canadian government whereby employees work for part of the week and receive unemployment insurance on the other days that would normally have been worked.[78] This scheme, which was introduced in 1977, is essentially a layoff avoidance strategy whereby all employees in a group "share" part of the layoff. The main benefit is that all employees stay on the company payroll and receive some work during the week. Work-sharing arrangements are implemented only on a temporary basis to avoid layoffs due to reduced demand or technological change. Through a work-sharing program at Pratt and Whitney Aircraft of Canada, more than 300 jobs were saved. Motorola was able to save 20 jobs by asking 100 employees to work four days a week instead of five.[79]

Job sharing involves dividing responsibilities of a single position between two or more people.[80] Many job-sharing plans are started by employees who want to work fewer hours. For example, London Life Insurance Company introduced job sharing in 1982 when several employees asked for more flexible work hours. Job sharing can also be used to reduce the organization's labour costs, although the reduced work time is not covered by unemployment insurance.

Providing Early Retirement. Encouraging older employees to take early retirement is a frequently used retrenchment strategy.[81] Typically, the organization provides a time-limited "window of opportunity" whereby individuals who would reach normal retirement age within 5 or 10 years can retire immediately with nearly full pensions. In many cases, the early retirement package also includes employee benefits up to normal retirement age. Early retirement can effectively reduce labour costs. However, this practice may also demoralize remaining staff and cause the organization to lose the most valued staff. In some cases, the costs of early retirement exceed labour savings.[82]

An innovative alternative to early retirement is partial retirement.[83] Partial retirement allows employees to retire early (but typically without a pension top-up) and to continue work on a part-time basis. Woodwards Ltd. introduced a partial retirement plan that allows its older employees across Canada to retire and yet work up to 16 hours per week. Partial retirement plans reduce employment costs because the partially retired individual is hired only when needed. This scheme also encourages retirement among employees who would not take advantage of an early retirement offer. At the same time, this plan enables employers to retain key staff.

To avoid staff layoffs, companies facing organizational retrenchment must rely on several strategies. Control Data Corporation attempts to avoid layoffs through its "rings of defence" strategies shown in Exhibits 6–20 and 6–21.[84]

The first defence is to cut overtime, then call back work subcontracted to outside vendors. Next, supplemental and part-time employees are dismissed. Finally, if the surplus still remains, Control Data turns to retrenchment programs affecting full-time employees—its "inner rings of defence." These programs include hiring freezes, voluntary layoffs, and dismissing poor performers. Job-sharing arrangements are also considered before any full-time employees are laid off.

Many organizations have employment stabilization programs, although they may not be as elaborate as Control Data's. These firms are committed to providing continuous employment to employees wherever possible. However, with increasing competition and technological change, employment flexibility has become the dominant strategy for many companies. We look at this employment planning strategy next.

The Flexible Firm

Perhaps one of the most dramatic changes in the 1980s in Canada is the emerging flexible firm. With increasing turbulence in the organization's environment, P/HRM professionals must find ways to quickly adjust employment costs. In one sense, flexible-firm practices are used when employment planning fails to forecast an imbalance between the supply of and demand for employees. A recent survey of flexible-firm practices highlights four broad approaches used in Canada to increase the flexibility of the organization's work force.[85]

Numerical Flexibility. As noted earlier, employment costs can be adjusted by changing either the number of people employed or the number of hours each employee works. The retail industry moved toward numerical flexibility by dramatically increasing the percentage of part-time employees and

EXHIBIT 6–20
Rings of Defence Strategies

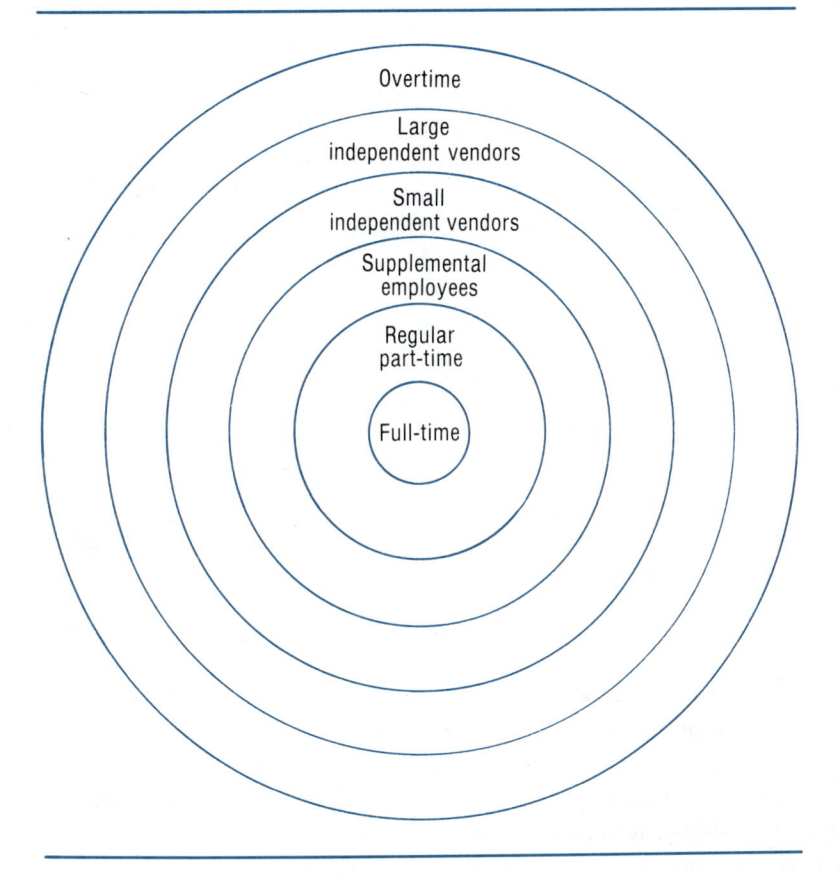

[Concentric rings diagram, from outer to inner: Overtime; Large independent vendors; Small independent vendors; Supplemental employees; Regular part-time; Full-time]

Source: Control Data Corporation.

carefully matching their work hours with peak customer demand. School boards rely on numerical flexibility by using a "float" of fixed-term, or "contract" teachers. When student enrollments declined during the past few years, many of these contracts were not renewed.[86]

Functional Flexibility. Organizations also create a more flexible work force by breaking down traditional skill boundaries (multiskilling) and redesigning traditional job categories. Major technological changes have blurred traditional skill boundaries in some organizations. This has led to new jobs that more closely fit organizational needs. Other firms have introduced skill-based pay systems that reward employees who acquire a broader range of skills.

Subcontracting. Many organizations turn to subcontracting as a means of reducing employment costs and increasing labour force flexibility. Work that

EXHIBIT 6–21
Inner Rings of Defence

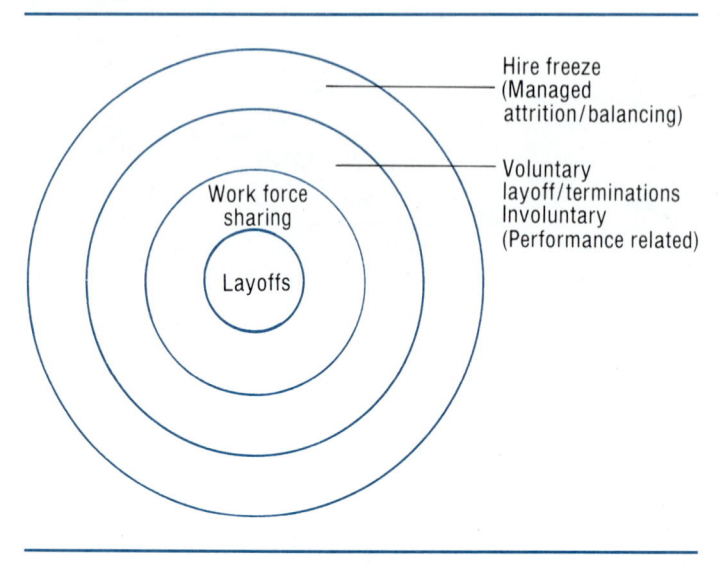

- Hire freeze (Managed attrition/balancing)
- Voluntary layoff/terminations Involuntary (Performance related)
- Work force sharing
- Layoffs

Source: Control Data Corporation.

is peripheral to the central business function is assigned to an outside organization. For example, Canada Post released its janitorial staff and subcontracted this work to independent janitorial firms. The forest products industry relies heavily on small contractors for its logging operations. Many trucking firms have shifted to subcontracting by requiring their employees to purchase rigs and become independent contractors.

Pay Flexibility. Employment flexibility also includes changes to the way employees are paid. This may include stronger emphasis on performance-based pay, task-based (rather than time-based) fee schedules for subcontractors, and restrictions on the payment of overtime. Some organizations have been able to negotiate seven-day work schedules so employees normally scheduled to work weekends do not receive overtime pay. Some trucking firms have negotiated with independent contractors (former employees) to pay for the distance hauled rather than the time required to haul.

SUMMARY

The basic premise of this chapter is that employment planning is positively related to an organization's chances of achieving its goals. But is it? Does employment planning pay? The truth is that those organizations that undertake it believe it does. Those that don't are skeptical.

Believers and skeptics are found in the research literature too. Some point to successful firms in which little or no employment planning is performed. Rowland and Summers concluded from a study of 20 organizations that "it is a fantasy to believe that it (employment planning) ever was a systematic (rational) process in business decision making."[87] And they imply it never will be. Perhaps they interviewed the wrong managers? Often employment planning is done in finance, manufacturing, or other areas of a company because human resource managers have abrogated their function. Instead, they function solely as recruiters of the number and types of personnel that finance or manufacturing recommends. Other researchers have documented the extensive use of employment planning in numerous organizations.[88]

We believe employment planning is a useful means of preparing for future risks and uncertainty. It permits systematic judgement about the number and types of employees needed to staff the organization. The precise techniques and procedures used must be tailored to fit the context. To adopt a completely ad hoc and reactive stance seems foolhardy. The real danger with planning is to avoid becoming so ossified and bureaucratic that managers fail to take advantage of unforeseen opportunities.

DISCUSSION AND REVIEW QUESTIONS

1. What factors in the external environment will influence the extent of employment planning an organization does? What factors in the organization influence it?
2. Compare strategic human resource planning and employment planning? How are they related? What questions does each address?
3. What is the employment process? What is its primary purpose?
4. Why should an organization bother with employment planning?
5. What are the three major phases of analysis conducted in employment planning? How are they interrelated?
6. Compare and contrast alternative demand forecasting techniques. Under what conditions would you consider using each?
7. What are the two major sources of supply?
8. Compare and contrast skills inventories, replacement and succession charts. Under what conditions and for what purposes would you consider using each?
9. What programming options are available when an employer is overstaffed? Understaffed?
10. Which programming options developed in Question 9 are best? Under what conditions?
11. Interview a resource person in the CEIC and prepare a 10-minute class presen-

tation to describe the uses of COPS in human resource planning/employment planning.
12. Interview an employment planner in a local company about the forecasting approaches used and prepare a short class presentation. Better yet, invite a guest speaker.

NOTES AND REFERENCES

1. J. Murphy, "The Corporate Kings," *The Financial Post*, May 10, 1986, pp. 1–2.
2. General Electric annual report, 1983.
3. Eva Innes, Robert L. Percy, and Jim Lyon, *100 Best Companies to Work for in Canada* (Don Mills: Collins, 1986).
4. J. R. Galbraith and D. A. Nathanson, *Strategy Implementation: The Role of Structure and Process* (St. Paul, Minn.: West Publishing, 1978); Robert M. James, "Effective Planning Strategies," *Human Resource Planning* 2, no 1 (1980), pp. 1–10; James Brian Quinn, "Strategic Change: Logical Incrementalism," *Sloan Management Review*, Fall 1978; Richard F. Vancil, "Strategy Formulation in the Complex Organizations," *Sloan Management Review*, Winter 1976; James W. Walker, *Human Resources Planning* (New York: McGraw-Hill, 1980); Mary A. Devanna, C. Fombrun, and N. Tichy, "Human Resource Management: A Strategic Approach," *Organizational Dynamics*, Spring 1981; J. A. Craft, "A Critical Perspective on Human Resource Planning," *Human Resource Planning* 3, no. 2 (1980), pp. 39–52.
5. George Milkovich and Thomas Mahoney, "Human Resources Planning and PAIR Policy," in *ASPA Handbook of Personnel and Industrial Relations*, ed. D. Yoder and H. Heneman, Jr. (Washington, D.C.: Bureau of National Affairs, 1979); Lee Dyer, "Human Resource Planning," in *The Management of Personnel/Human Resources: New Perspectives*, ed. K. Rowland and G. Ferris (Boston: Allyn & Bacon, 1982).
6. George Milkovich, Lee Dyer, and Tom Mahoney, "HRM Planning," chap. 2 in *Human Resource Management in the 1980s*, ed. Stephen J. Carroll and Randall S. Schuler (Washington, D.C.: Bureau of National Affairs, 1983); *Manpower Planning*, ed. John Edwards, Chris Leek, Ray Loveridge, Roger Lumley, John Mangan, and Mick Silver (New York: John Wiley & Sons, 1983); G. G. Alpander, *Human Resources Management Planning* (New York, AMACOM, 1982); James F. Bolt, Management Resources Planning: Keys to Success, *Human Resource Planning* 5, no. 4 (1982), pp. 185–97; D. M. Atwater, E. S. Bres III, R. J. Niehaus, and J. A. Sheridan, "An Application of Integrated Human Resources Planning Supply-Demand Models," *Human Resources Planning* 5, no. 1 (1982), pp. 1–15; Eric Vetter, *Manpower Planning for High Talent Personnel* (Ann Arbor: University of Michigan, Bureau of Industrial Relations, 1967).
7. "Notions and Numbers—The Canadian Occupational Projection System" (Ottawa: Employment and Immigration Canada, WH-3-418, undated).
8. This description of the Candide model draws on material from several sources: "The Candide Model," *Manpower Review* 10 (1977), pp. 31–33; Pierre Paul Proulx, Luce Bourgault, and Jean-Francois Manegre, "Candide-Cofor and Forecasting Manpower Needs by Occupation and Industry in Canada," in *Manpower Planning for Canadians*, 2nd ed., ed. Larry F. Moore and Larry Charach (Van-

couver, B.C.: Institute of Industrial Relations, University of British Columbia, 1979).
9. Ibid.
10. Proulx, Bourgault, and Manegre, "Candide-Cofor and Forecasting Manpower Needs."
11. A general introduction to COPS is available in "Notions and Numbers"; more detailed discussions of COPS are presented in the following: "The Canadian Occupational Projection System-Supply Issues and Approaches" (Employment and Immigration Canada, WH-3-335E, January 1983); and "Demand Methodology" (Employment and Immigration Canada, WH-3-341, January 1983); Innovation and Jobs in Canada, A Research Report Prepared for the Economic Council of Canada (Ottawa: Minister of Supply and Services Canada, 1987; Cat. No. EC22-141/1987E).
12. "Demand Methodology."
13. Innovation and Jobs in Canada, chap. 4.
14. *Human Resource Planning: A Challenge for the 1980s* (Ottawa: Minister of Supply and Services, 1983; Cat. No. MP 43-125/83).
15. Ibid., p. 7.
16. Ibid., p. 5.
17. Ibid., p. 8.
18. For more advanced treatment, the reader is encouraged to examine John Anderson and Morley Gunderson, *Union-Management Relations in Canada* (Don Mills: Addison-Wesley Publishing, 1982); and Morley Gunderson, *Labour Market Economics* (Toronto: McGraw-Hill Ryerson Ltd., 1980).
19. See, for example, *Labour Market Bulletin–B.C./Yukon Region* (Labour Market Outlook), August 1985; and *Career News* (the B.C. Labour Market/Changes and Prospects), September 1985, both published by the Economic Services Branch, Employment and Immigration Canada.
20. Lee Dyer and N. O. Heyer, "Human Resource Planning at IBM: A Field Study" (working paper, Ithaca, N.Y.: Cornell University, 1984); James C. Rush and Laurie C. Borne, "Human Resources Planning at Ontario Hydro," *Human Resources Planning* 6, no. 4 (1983), pp. 193–207; Donald F. Parker, John A. Fossum, Jan H. Blakslee, and Anthony J. Rucci, "Human Resources Planning at American Hospital Supply," *Human Resources Planning* 6, no. 4 (1983), pp. 207–19.
21. Ray Sata, "Human Resources—The Limitation to High-Technology Growth," in *Strategic Human Resources Management: A Guide for Effective Practice*, ed. Fred F. Foulkes (Englewood Cliffs, N.J.: Prentice-Hall, 1986).
22. See, for example, Exhibit 6–3, and *Human Resource Planning: A Challenge for the 1980s*.
23. Vetter, *Manpower Planning*.
24. K. M. Rowland and S. L. Summers, "Human Resources Planning: A Second Look," *Personnel Administrator*, December 1981, pp. 73–80; Thomas G. Gutteridge and Elmer H. Burack, "Industrial Manpower Planning: Rhetoric versus Reality," *California Management Review* 10, no. 3 (1978), pp. 13–22.
25. Walker, *Human Resources Planning*; also see R. B. Frantzreb, "Confessions of a Manpower Modeler," in *Manpower Planning for Canadians*, 2nd ed., ed. L. F. Moore and L. Charach (Vancouver: Institute of Industrial Relations, University of British Columbia, 1979).
26. R. V. Dawis, L. H. Lofquist, and D. J. Weiss, "A Theory of Work Adjustment:

A Revision," in *Minnesota Studies in Vocational Rehabilitation* (Minneapolis, Minn.: IRC, University of Minnesota, 1968) p. 23.
27. Jeffrey Pfeffer, "Organizational Demography," in *Research in Organizational Behaviour*, Vol. 5, ed. Barry M. Staw and Larry L. Cummings (Greenwich, Conn.: JAI Press, 1983), pp. 299–357; Ralph Katz, "Project Communication and Performance: An Investigation into the Effects of Group Longevity," *Administrative Science Quarterly* 27 (1982), pp. 81–104; B. E. McCain, C. O'Reilly, and J. Pfeffer, "The Effects of Departmental Demography on Turnover: The Case of a University," *Academy of Management Journal* 28 (1983), pp. 626–41; K. McNeil and J. D. Thompson, "The Regeneration of Social Organizations," *American Sociological Review* 36 (1971), pp. 624–37.
28. Milkovich and Mahoney, "HRP and PAIR Policy."
29. G. Milkovich and T. Mahoney, "Human Resource Planning Models: A Perspective," *Human Resources Planning* 1, no. 1 (1978); J. Wadel and R. Bush, "Probalistic Forecasting of Manpower Requirements," *IEEE Transactions on Engineering Management*, August 1962, pp. 136–38; N. Kwak, Walter Garrett, and S. Barone, "A Stochastic Model of Demand Forecasting for Technical Manpower Planning," *Management Science* 23, no. 10 (1977), pp. 1089–98; G. Milkovich, A. Annoni, and T. Mahoney, "The Use of Delphi Procedures in Manpower Forecasting," *Management Science*, December 1972, pp. 381–88; and A. Delbecq, A. Van de Ven, and D. Gustafson, *Group Techniques for Program Planning* (Dallas, Tex.: Scott, 1975); A. Drui, "The Use of Regression Equations to Predict Manpower Requirements," *Management Science* 9, no. 4 (1963), pp. 667–77; I. M. Gascoigne, "Manpower Planning at the Enterprise Level," *British Journal of Industrial Relations*, March 1968, pp. 94–106; Wendell W. Burton, "Manpower Planning in an Inflationary Period," *Personnel Administrator*, August 1979, pp. 33–38.
30. W. S. Wickstrom, *Manpower Planning: Evolving Systems* (New York: Conference Board, Report No. 521, 1971); Wayne F. Cascio, *Applied Psychology in Personnel Management*, 2nd ed. (Reston, Va.: Reston Publishing Company, 1982).
31. Cascio, *Applied Psychology in Personnel Management*, 2nd ed.
32. Ibid.
33. Ibid.
34. Burton, *Manpower Planning*.
35. Henry Dahl and K. S. Morgan, *Return on Investment in Human Resources* (Kalamazoo, Mich.: Upjohn Company Report, 1982).
36. F. A. Muckler, "Evaluating Productivity," chap. 2 in *Human Performance and Productivity*, ed. M. D. Dunnette (Hillsdale, N.J.: Lawrence Erlbaum Associates, 1982); Committee for Economic Development, *Productivity Policy: Key to the Nation's Economic Future* (Washington, D.C.: U.S. Government Printing Office), April 1983; T. K. Connellan, *How to Improve Human Performance* (New York: Harper & Row, 1981); Work in American Institute, *Productivity through Work Innovations*, 1982; D. L. Rowe, "How Westinghouse Measures White Collar Productivity," *Management Review*, November 1981, pp. 42–47; Jon English and Anthony R. Marchione, "Productivity: A New Perspective," *California Management Review* 25, no. 2 (1983), pp. 57–66; Peter F. Drucker, "Managing Productivity," (working paper, 1983).
37. *People & Productivity* (Minneapolis, Minn.: Honeywell Corporate Human Resources, 1982).

38. See S. Makridukis and S. C. Wheelwright, *Forecasting Studies in the Management Services*, vol. 12 (New York: North Holland Publishing, 1979); Edwards et al., *Manpower Planning*.
39. Vetter, *Manpower Planning*; W. Rudelius, "Lagged Manpower Relationships in Development Projects," *IEEE Transactions on Engineering Management*, December 1976, pp. 188–95.
40. Ibid.
41. *People & Productivity*, Honeywell.
42. See references No. 6, 29, and 38. The Markov analysis through goal programming section of Exhibit 6–11 was adapted from Lee Dyer, "Human Resource Planning," in *Personnel Management*, ed. K. Rowland and G. Ferris (Boston: Allyn & Bacon, 1982).
43. P. F. Buller and W. R. Maki, "A Case History of a Manpower Planning Model," *Human Resource Planning* 4, no. 3 (1981), pp. 129–38.
44. Ibid.
45. Rowland and Summers, *HRP: A Second Look*; Gutteridge and Burack, *Industrial Manpower Planning*; Gascoigne, *Manpower Planning*.
46. George Milkovich and D. Phillips, "Human Resources Planning at Merck: A Field Study" (working paper, Ithaca, N.Y.: Cornell University, 1984).
47. Dahl and Morgan, *Return on Investment*.
48. R. J. Clifford and Associates, *Survey of Manpower Practices in Canada*, Technical Study No. 7, prepared for the Task Force on Labour Market Development (Ottawa: Minister of Supply and Services, July 1981, Cat. No. MP15-4/7-1981E).
49. Dyer, "Human Resource Planning."
50. Berg, "The Kodak Way."
51. W. H. Mobley, R. W. Griffith, H. H. Hard, B. M. Maglino, "Review and Conceptual Analysis of Employee Turnover Process," *Psychological Bulletin* 16, no. 3 (1979), pp. 493–522; Charles E. Michaels and Paul E. Specter, "Cause of Employee Turnover," *Journal of Applied Psychology* 67, no. 1 (1982), pp. 53–59; James E. Rosenbaum, "Organizational Career Mobility: Promotion Choices in a Corporation during Periods of Growth and Contraction," *American Journal of Sociology* 85, no. 1 (1979), pp. 21–48.
52. L. T. Pinfield, "A Case Study of the Application of a Termination Forecast Model," *Human Resource Planning* 4 (1982), pp. 18–32.
53. R. C. Grinold and K. T. Marshall, *Manpower Planning Models* (New York: North-Holland Publishing, 1977); W. L. Price, A. Martel, and K. A. Lewis, "A Review of Mathematics Models in Human Resource Planning," *Omega* 8, no. 6 (1980), pp. 639–45; D. J. Bartholomew and A. F. Forbes, *Statistical Techniques for Manpower Planning* (New York: John Wiley & Sons, 1979); R. J. Niehaus, *Computer-Assisted Human Resources Planning* (New York: John Wiley & Sons, 1979).
54. R. G. Murdick and F. Schuster, "Computerized Information Support for the Human Resource Function," *Human Resource Planning* 6, no. 1 (1983), pp. 25–35.
55. Ibid.
56. B. H. Johnson, G. Moorhead, and W. Griffin, "Human Resource Information Systems & Job Design," *Human Resources Planning* 6, no. 1 (1983), pp. 35–41.
57. William F. Glueck, *Personnel: A Diagnostic Approach* (Plano, Tex.: Business Publications, 1982).
58. Robert M. Cohen and Jennifer Garland, "Computerizing the Personnel Department," *The Human Resource*, February–March 1986, pp. 13–14.

59. Günter Ott, "A Variety of Personnel Software Solutions," *The Human Resource*, February–March 1986, pp. 12–13.
60. Robert Smith, "Information Systems for More Effective Use of Executive Resources," *Personnel Journal*, June 1969, pp. 452–65.
61. Robert Martin, "Skills Inventories," *Personnel Journal*, January 1967, pp. 28–30.
62. S. Simon, "The HRIS: What Capabilities Must It Have?" *Personnel*, September–October 1983, pp. 36–49; see also SKOPOS, *Personnel Data Base Systems for MICRO'S* (Los Altos, Calif., 1984) and *1st Advanced HR Systems* (Flemington, N.J.: Integral Systems); *Executrak: A Microcomputer Succession Planning System* (Fairfield, Iowa: Corporate Education Resources, 1984).
63. Walker, *Human Resources Planning*.
64. Merck and Company, Inc., Rahway, N.J.: *HR Planning Portfolio*, 1984.
65. Walker, *Human Resources Planning*.
66. E. S. Brewer and W. H. Hoffman, "Multiple Career Paths: An Organization Concept," *Human Resource Planning* 5, no. 4 (1982), pp. 209–17; *Succession Planning & Management Development for the 1980's*, 21st Annual IRC Symposium in Advanced Research in Industrial Relations (New York: IR Counselors, 1983).
67. Walker, *Human Resources Planning*.
68. L. J. Reypert, "Succession Planning in the Ministry of Transportation and Communications, Province of Ontario," *Human Resource Planning* 4 (1981), pp. 151–56.
69. J. Carnazza, *Succession/Replacement Planning: Programs & Practices*, (New York: Center for Career Development, Columbia Business School, 1982), p. 5.
70. Several references exist on this subject: the advanced reader is directed to R. C. Grinold and K. T. Marshall, *Manpower Planning Models* (New York: North-Holland Publishing, 1977); D. J. Bartholomew, *Stochastic Models for Social Processes*, 2nd ed. (New York: John Wiley & Sons, 1973); and Harrison White, *Chains of Opportunity: System Models of Mobility in Organizations* (Cambridge, Mass.: Harvard University Press, 1970). Students new to this topic are directed to Thomas A. Mahoney, George T. Milkovich, and Nan Weiner, "A Stock and Flow Model for Improved Human Resources Measurement," *Personnel*, May–June 1977, pp. 57–66; and Victor H. Vroom and K. R. MacCrimmon, "Towards a Stochastic Model of Management Careers," *Administrative Science Quarterly*, June 1968, pp. 26–46; K. M. Rowland and M. G. Sovereign, "Markov-Chain Analysis of Internal Manpower Supply," *Industrial Relations* 9, no. 1 (1969), pp. 88–89; T. Mahoney and G. Milkovich, "Markov Chains and Manpower Forecasts," Office of Naval Research Technical Report NR 151-323-7002, 1970; and D. J. Bartholomew and A. R. Smith, eds., *Manpower and Management Science* (London: English University Press, 1970).
71. Some examples of Markov simulation applications include: S. H. Zanakis and M. W. Maret, "A Markov Application to Manpower Supply Planning," *Journal of the Operational Research Society* 31, no. 4 (1980), pp. 1095–1102; L. B. Bleau, "The Academic Flow Model: A Markov Chain Model for Faculty Planning," *Decision Sciences*, April 1981, pp. 294–309; H. L. Clark and D. R. Thurston, *Planning Your Staffing Needs* (Washington, D.C.: Bureau of Policies and Standards, U.S. Civil Service Commission, 1977); C. C. Pegels, "A Markov Application to an Engineering Manpower Policy Problem," *IEE Transactions on Engineering Management*, May 1981, pp. 39–42; J. A. Hooper and J. Catalavello, "Markov Analysis Applied to Forecasting Technical Personnel," *Human Resource Planning*

4, no. 2 (1981), pp. 41–54; Bartholomew and Forbes, *Statistical Techniques for Manpower Planning*; W. G. Piskor and R. C. Dudding, "A Computer-Assisted Manpower Planning Model," in *Manpower Planning and Organization Design*, ed. D. T. Bryant and R. J. Niehaus (New York: Plenum Press, 1978), pp. 145–54; Grinold and Marshall, *Manpower Planning Models*; E. S. Bres III, D. Burns, A. Charnes, and W. W. Cooper, "A Goal Programming Model for Planning Officer Accessions," *Management Science* 26, no. 8 (1980), pp. 773–82; S. H. Zanakis and M. W. Maret, "A Markovian Goal Progamming Approach to Aggregate Manpower Planning," *Journal of Operational Research* 32, no. 2 (1981), pp. 55–63.
72. See, for example, Milkovich and Phillips, "HRP at Merck," 1984; N. Mathys and H. LaVan, "A Survey of Human Resource Information Systems (HRIS) of Major Companies," *Human Resources Planning* 5, no. 2 (1982), pp. 57–69.
73. Several examples of application have been reported in the literature. See reference 70.
74. H. G. Heneman III and M. G. Sandver, "Markov Analysis in Human Resource Administration," *Academy of Management Review* 2, no. 3 (1977), pp. 535–42.
75. Sally Luce, *Retrenchment and Beyond* (Ottawa: Conference Board of Canada, 1983); Sally Luce, "Human Resource Policy under Pressure: Learning from Restraint," *Canadian Business Review* 10, no. 1 (1983), pp. 24–27; Steven L. McShane and Lawrence T. Pinfield, "Teacher Expectations Regarding the Impact of Two Staff Reduction Policies," *Alberta Journal of Educational Research* 32, no. 4 (December 1986), pp. 286–96.
76. Lee Dyer, F. Foltman, and G. Milkovich, "Employment Stabilization" (working paper, Ithaca, N.Y.: Cornell University, 1984); Mark Thompson, "The Permanent Employment System: Japan and Mexico," Sixth World Congress of Industrial Relations, Kyōto, Japan, March 28–31, 1983; R. Fuller, C. Jordan, and R. Anderson, "Retrenchment: Layoff Procedures in a Nonprofit Organization," *Personnel*, November–December 1982, pp. 19–24; R. H. Ketchum, "Retrenchment: The Uses and Misuses of Life in Downsizing and Organization," *Personnel*, November–December 1982, pp. 25–30; Linda Wintner, *Employee Buyouts: An Alternative to Plant Closings* (New York: The Conference Board, 1983); F. Foltman, "Managing a Plant Closing: An Overview" (working paper, ILR School, Ithaca, N.Y.: Cornell University, 1981); T. Bailey and T. Jackson, "Industrial Outplacement at Goodyear," *Personnel Administrator*, March 1980, pp. 42–48; D. L. Ward, "The $34,000 Layoff," *Human Resources Planning* 5, no. 1 (1982), pp. 35–43; Dick Schaaff, "Are You Training Yet for Outplacement and Retirement?" *Training*, May 1981, pp. 70–84; E. B. Silverman and S. D. Sass, "Outplacement," *Training and Development Journal*, February 1982, pp. 71–84; R. S. Barkhaus and Carol L. Mak, "A Practical View of Outplacement," *Personnel Administrator*, March 1982, pp. 77–85; C. H. Driessnank, "Outplacement—The New Personnel Practice," *Personnel Administrator*, October 1980, pp. 81–93; P. D. Johnston, "Personnel Planning for a Plant Shutdown," *Personnel Administrator*, August 1981, pp. 53–60.
77. T. D. Little, "Part-time Work: Crisis or Opportunity," *Canadian Business Review*, Spring 1986, pp. 18–20.
78. Noah M. Meltz, Frank Reid, and G. Swartz, *Sharing the Work* (Toronto: University of Toronto Press, 1981); Frank Reid, "Combatting Unemployment through Work Time Reductions," *Canadian Public Policy* 12, no. 2 (1986), pp. 275–85; J. M. Mesa, "Short Time Working or Layoffs? Experience from Canada and

California," *International Labour Review* 123 (February 1984), pp. 99–114.
79. Heywood Klem, "Interest Grows in Worksharing, which Lets Concerns Cut Workweeks to Avoid Layoffs," *The Wall Street Journal*, April 7, 1983, p. 4.
80. "Job Sharing: Good Outweighs Bad," *Globe and Mail*, July 26, 1985; David A. Bratton, "Moving Away from Nine to Five," *Canadian Business Review*, Spring 1986, pp. 15–17; Lesley Krueger, "When Half a Job Is Better than None," *Maclean's*, November 15, 1982, p. 614; Julianne LaBreche, "Two Can Work as Cheaply as One," *Financial Post Magazine*, October 31, 1981, p. 226.
81. Monsanto, "Incentives for Early Retirement Are Offered to 1900," *The Wall Street Journal*, September 22, 1982, p. 4.
82. J. Perham, "The 'Open Window' to Early Retirement," *Dun's Business Monthly* 120 (October 1982), pp. 61–62; Virginia Galt, "Staff Held Demoralized by Early Retirement Plan," *The Globe and Mail*, April 13, 1983; McShane and Pinfield, "Teacher Expectations," p. 288; D. H. Gravitz and F. W. Rumack, "Opening the Early Retirement 'Window'," *Personnel*, February 1983, pp. 53–57.
83. B. Constantineau, "600 at Woodward's Get Retirement Offer," *Vancouver Sun*, September 12, 1986; M. Honig and G. Hanoch, "Partial Retirement as a Separate Mode of Retirement Behaviour," *Journal of Human Resources* 20, no. 1 (Winter 1985), pp. 21–46.
84. Adapted from Dyer, Foltman, and Milkovich, "Employment Stabilization."
85. Lawrence T. Pinfield and John S. Atkinson, "The Flexible Firm in British Columbia" (working paper, Burnaby, B.C.: Simon Fraser University, November 1986).
86. Lawrence T. Pinfield and Steven L. McShane, "Applications of Manpower Planning in Two School Districts," *Human Resource Planning* 10 (1987), pp. 103–13.
87. Rowland and Summers, "HRP: A Second Look."
88. Some of the surveys of HRP practices include: G. E. Miller and E. H. Burack, "A Status Report on Human Resource Planning from the Perspective of Human Resource Planners," *Human Resource Planning* 4, no. 2 (1981), pp. 33–41; G. G. Alpander, "Human Resource Planning in U.S. Corporations," *California Management Review* 22, no. 2 (Spring 1980), pp. 24–32; C. R. Greer and D. Armstrong, "Human Resources Forecasting and Planning: A State of Art Investigation," *Human Resource Planning* 4, no. 2 (1980), pp. 67–78; and H. Kahalas, H. L. Pazer, J. S. Hoagland, and A. Levitt, "Human Resource Planning Activities in U.S. Firms," *Human Resource Planning* 3, no. 2 (1980), pp. 53–66; T. Hercus, "Human Resource Planning in Government and Business: Potential and Reality," *Human Resource Planning* 2, no. 3 (1979), pp. 147–55; Clifford and Associates, *Survey of Manpower Practices in Canada*.

CHAPTER SEVEN
EMPLOYMENT EQUITY

CHAPTER OUTLINE

I. A Diagnostic Approach to Employment Equity
II. What Is Employment Equity?
    A. The Need for Employment Equity in Canada
III. Legal Foundations of Employment Equity
    A. Canadian Charter of Rights and Freedoms
    B. Human Rights Legislation
IV. Emerging Concepts in Employment Equity
    A. From Intent to Effect
    B. Bona Fide Occupational Qualification
    C. Reasonable Accommodation
    D. Sexual and Other Harassment
    E. Mandatory Retirement
V. Employment Equity Programs in Canada
    A. Mandatory Employment Equity Programs
VI. Implementing Employment Equity Programs
    A. Step One: EEP Planning
    B. Step Two: Utilization Analysis
    C. Step Three: Employment Systems Review
    D. Step Four: Plan Design and Implementation
VII. Summary
    Appendix / Prohibited Grounds for Screening and Selection in Employment

Canadian National Railway hired K. S. Bhinder in 1974 as a maintenance electrician in its Toronto coach yard. For the next four years, Bhinder worked in that capacity servicing the turbo train between 11 P.M. and 7 A.M. But in November 1978, the company announced that all employees in the Toronto coach yard would be required to wear hard hats to comply with safety regulations in the Canada Labour Code.

This job requirement presented a dilemma for Bhinder. As a member of the Sikh faith, he was forbidden from wearing anything on his head except a turban. Bhinder presented his concerns to the company, but CN said there would be no exceptions to the hard-hat rule, and Bhinder would not be permitted to work if he did not wear a hard hat on the job. Bhinder was not prepared to work in any capacity other than that of an electrician. Unfortunately, the company had no positions open for electricians in which a hard hat was not required. In December 1978, Bhinder's employment with CN was terminated. Two days after his dismissal, Bhinder filed a complaint with the Canadian Human Rights Commission. The case eventually went to the Supreme Court of Canada.[1]

The case of *Bhinder* v. *CN Rail* raises many issues with far-reaching implications for P/HRM professionals. Is the hard-hat rule discriminatory even though CN did not intend to discriminate against members of the Sikh faith? Is the hard-hat rule a "bona fide occupational requirement"? That is, can the hard-hat rule be continued even though it effectively excludes all members of the Sikh faith from holding a job? Should CN have made an exception or taken other steps to "reasonably accommodate" Bhinder in this situation? These are some of the issues we will address in this chapter on employment equity.

Employment equity touches on every aspect of P/HRM from recruitment and selection to retirement and labour relations. Due to its statutory foundations, employment equity is also concerned with legal concepts and principles. This chapter introduces the applicable legal principles as well as the P/HRM practices used to implement employment equity programs.

A DIAGNOSTIC APPROACH TO EMPLOYMENT EQUITY

Government regulations and societal values are part of the environment in which an employer operates. A diagnostic approach examines the impact of these factors on the organization. Society's concerns for egalitarian treatment have resulted in human rights laws that regulate P/HRM decisions.

If you read a P/HRM text written more than a decade ago, you have difficulty finding any mention of employment equity (or human rights) in Canada. Canadian human rights laws first appeared during World War II. Yet organizations tended to give employment equity a relatively low priority. The profile of this controversial subject was raised during the 1970s as various groups voiced their concerns about inequity in our society. Legislative changes in the United States during the 1960s and 1970s also raised our awareness of the problems.

But these events pale against the impact of recent legislative changes throughout Canada. With the entrenchment of certain concepts pertaining to discrimination (e.g., systematic discrimination, reasonable accommodation) and the recent introduction of mandatory employment equity programs in some jurisdictions, employment equity is certain to become an important P/HRM issue in Canada for the next decade.

In addition to societal values and legislative reforms, employment equity is affected by economic conditions. Improved sales and earnings create job opportunities. Job opportunities in turn affect the ability of employers to hire and promote more people who have been underrepresented in the past. It is difficult to make the composition of the work force more representative when an organization is laying off staff.

Employment equity practices are also influenced by the composition of the organization's work force. The present demographic structure of the work force affects the speed of change toward a more equitable structure. Existing practices and attitudes also must be recognized for their influence on employment discrimination and the amount of resistance P/HRM managers may expect when they introduce employment equity changes.

WHAT IS EMPLOYMENT EQUITY?

> **Definition**
> *Employment equity* refers to employment practices designed to eliminate discriminatory barriers and to provide in a meaningful way equitable opportunities in employment.[2]

On the face of it, employment equity—and its opposite, employment discrimination—seems so simple and intuitive that its definition would be obvious. Yet recent human rights tribunal and court decisions suggest this concept is anything but simple.

According to the definition stated here, employment equity refers to a comparison of the occupational attainment of people in designated groups (gender, disability status, visible minority, aboriginal status). Specifically, employment equity occurs when members of a designated group *have the same probability of obtaining a particular job for which they are qualified as other individuals with the same qualifications.* Employment discrimination, on the other hand, exists when the occupational attainment of people with similar qualifications depends on their demographic or disability characteristics.

Equal Pay and Pay Equity

Employment equity should be distinguished from the concepts of *equal pay* and *pay equity*. Discussion of equal pay and pay equity requires some understanding of the compensation system. Therefore, we leave the details of this subject until Chapter Fifteen. At this point, however, it is useful to introduce these concepts.

Equal pay refers to the idea that individuals doing the same or similar work should receive the same level of remuneration. For example, pay discrimination exists in an organization that pays seamstresses (mostly women) less than tailors (mostly men) even though people in both jobs perform similar tasks.

Pay equity, often called "equal pay for work of equal value," is more comprehensive than equal pay. It refers to the extent that employees receive the same level of pay for performing work of similar value. Under this principle, discrimination occurs if truck drivers (mostly men) working for a hospital receive higher pay than nurses (mostly women) in the same organization even though both jobs have the same value to the organization.

In summary, equal pay compares the pay of jobs with similar content, whereas pay equity compares the pay of jobs of similar value to the organization. The equal pay concept is more widely applied in Canadian laws, although the pay equity concept has recently been adopted in an increasing number of jurisdictions.

Who Is Responsible for Employment Equity?

Everyone in the organization has a role to play in employment equity. The board of directors and CEO have an obligation to develop policies pertaining to employment equity. They must also reinforce the importance of these policies by delegating sufficient resources to those in charge of employment equity operations.

P/HRM professionals actively review their operating policies and practices to ensure they do not have an adverse effect on certain groups of employees and members of the labour force. The P/HRM department is also responsible for educating operating managers and employees about employment equity practices and for ensuring that the organization satisfactorily completes all government reporting requirements.

The supervisor may play the most important role in employment equity. It is the supervisor who translates much policy into action, and it is on the basis of the supervisor's actions that employees decide whether or not they have been treated fairly. The supervisor must also counsel employees to give members of designated groups—indeed, all other employees—an opportunity to perform the work without discriminatory actions or statements.

The Need for Employment Equity in Canada

Employment discrimination exists in Canada. Some forms of discrimination explicitly and malevolently limit employment opportunities of certain people based on their visible demographic or disability status. Other forms of discrimination are more subtle. They can eventually be identified through the employer's apparently neutral policies and practices. But they are most evident through differences in occupational attainment between two identifiable groups of people with similar qualifications.

Occupational Attainment of Women

Consider the occupational attainment of women compared with men. Women constitute 41 percent of the Canadian labour force. Yet their occupational distribution is quite polarized compared with the occupational distribution of men. As Exhibit 7-1 indicates, nearly three fourths of working women in 1981 were employed in just five occupational groups: clerical, service, sales, medicine and health, and teaching. These tend to be the lowest-paying jobs in the organization and offer the least opportunity for advancement. People in these positions are less likely to receive training support for career development or participate in recognized activities such as policy development.[3] In contrast, the occupational distribution of men in Canada is more broadly based. Slightly less than half of the male labour force in 1981 was employed in construction, product fabricating and related jobs, service and sales, and managerial types of occupations.

The occupational segregation (or *ghettoization*) of women is further illustrated in Exhibit 7-2. This table shows the number of women and men as well as their average full-time income in the top-paying jobs in 1980. Two facts are quite clear from Exhibit 7-2. First, women earn substantially less than men within every occupational category. While some of this salary gap is probably due to variations in specific job duties and seniority, the rest of the difference is undoubtedly caused by pay discrimination. The issue of pay equity is covered in Chapter Fifteen.

The exhibit also shows that women are consistently underrepresented in all of Canada's highest-paying jobs. Although many explanations for this phenomenon exist, the increasingly apparent conclusion is that we live in a sex-

EXHIBIT 7-1
Occupational Distribution of Men and Women in 1981

	Women				Men			
	Number		Percent Distribution of Females in Labour Force		Number		Percent Distribution of Males in Labour Force	
	1971	1981	1971	1981	1971	1981	1971	1981
1. Managerial, administrative, and related occupations	58,310	202,295	2.0%	4.2%	313,935	611,740	5.5%	8.7%
2. Occupations in natural sciences, engineering, and mathematics	17,105	56,880	0.6	1.2	217,025	346,085	3.8	4.8
3. Occupations in social sciences and related fields	29,525	99,050	1.0	2.0	49,525	89,565	0.9	1.3
4. Occupations in religion	3,710	8,545	0.1	0.2	19,880	23,730	0.4	0.3
5. Teaching and related occupations	211,125	290,940	7.1	6.0	138,175	198,235	2.4	2.8
6. Occupations in medicine and health	242,685	403,055	8.2	8.3	83,865	116,125	1.5	1.6
7. Artistic, literary, recreational, and related occupations	21,895	65,815	0.7	1.4	58,585	99,645	1.0	1.4
8. Clerical and related occupations	940,180	1,702,515	31.8	35.1	433,385	488,075	7.6	6.8
9. Sales occupations	247,765	467,395	8.4	9.6	567,985	678,860	10.0	9.5
10. Service occupations	447,985	748,260	15.2	15.4	521,935	682,785	9.2	9.5
11. Farming, horticultural, and animal husbandry occupations	106,845	107,565	3.6	2.2	405,305	401,130	7.1	5.6
12. Fishing, hunting, trapping, and related occupations	520	2,235	—	—	25,655	37,590	0.5	0.5

13.	Forestry and logging occupations	1,410	5,105	—	0.1	65,850	76,430	1.2	1.1
14.	Mining and quarrying occupations	375	1,625	—	—	58,780	73,640	1.0	1.0
15.	Processing occupations	59,560	104,610	2.0	2.2	275,175	367,385	4.9	5.1
16.	Machining and related occupations	13,675	20,900	0.5	0.4	227,260	286,165	4.0	4.0
17.	Product fabricating, assembling, repairing occupations	150,205	226,720	5.1	4.7	484,140	703,590	8.5	9.8
18.	Construction trade occupations	5,125	15,350	0.2	0.3	563,435	754,280	9.9	10.5
19.	Transport equipment operating occupations	8,190	29,650	0.3	0.6	330,245	427,685	5.8	6.0
20.	Materials handling and related occupations	40,455	55,040	1.4	1.1	165,385	188,100	2.9	2.6
21.	Other crafts and equipment operating occupations	13,545	30,240	0.5	0.6	95,300	113,240	1.7	1.6
22.	Occupations not elsewhere classified	21,730	31,050	0.7	0.6	145,905	147,710	2.5	2.1
23.	Occupations not stated	319,270	178,275	10.8	3.7	417,995	240,415	7.4	3.4
	Total*	2,961,210	4,853,120	100.0%	100.0%	5,665,720	7,152,205	100.0%	100.0%

Dash indicates less than one tenth of 1 percent.

*Totals are independently rounded and do not necessarily equal the sum of individually rounded figures in distributions.

Source: *Equality in Employment*, a Royal Commission Report (Abella, Commissioner), Cat. No. MP43-157/1-1984E (Ottawa: Minister of Supply and Services Canada, pp. 64–65. Reproduced with permission of the Minister of Supply and Services Canada.

stereotyped society that creates psychological and institutional barriers against women entering high-paying, career-oriented occupations. Stereotyping strongly influences employer perceptions regarding the ability of women to perform nontraditional work. It also causes women to restrict their own occupational goals, particularly in jobs with few female role models.[4] As noted in Chapter Two, women are entering the professions in larger numbers. Nevertheless, employment discrimination continues to impede these changes.

EXHIBIT 7–2
Number and Income of Men and Women in Occupations with Highest Male Average Income in 1980

		Males Number	Males Average Income	Females Number	Females Average Income
1.	Physicians and surgeons	18,995	$59,834	3,065	$36,115
2.	Dentists	3,875	58,128	295	40,510
3.	Judges and magistrates	1,335	51,795	—	—
4.	Salespeople and traders, securities	6,385	46,718	1,575	18,375
5.	General managers and other senior officials	68,120	46,160	5,205	24,915
6.	Optometrists	920	42,256	—	—
7.	Lawyers and notaries	21,970	40,978	2,835	23,935
8.	Other managers (mines and oil wells)	2,280	40,506	555	19,303
9.	Managerial occupations in natural sciences and engineering	10,085	38,948	595	23,322
10.	Osteopaths and chiropractors	1,385	38,869	—	—
11.	Pilots, navigators, and flight engineers	5,325	37,125	—	—
12.	Petroleum engineers	3,035	36,882	—	—
13.	University teachers	22,340	35,944	4,905	26,585
14.	Administrators in teaching and related fields	16,345	35,434	4,450	25,772
15.	Administrators in medicine and health	4,620	34,339	4,310	23,832
16.	Mining engineers	2,240	33,980	—	—
17.	Geologists	4,325	33,728	315	21,207
18.	Chemical engineers	3,945	32,388	—	—
19.	Architects and engineers	5,050	32,188	—	—
20.	Veterinarians	2,210	32,173	—	—
21.	Members of legislative bodies	1,380	32,120	—	—
22.	Nuclear engineers	600	32,027	—	—
23.	Government administrators	17,030	31,655	3,600	21,846
24.	Civil engineers	23,775	31,311	440	24,201

EXHIBIT 7–2 *(concluded)*

		Males		Females	
		Number	Average Income	Number	Average Income
25.	Metallurgical engineers	1,325	31,306	—	—
26.	Health diagnostic and treating occupations	860	31,269	910	16,339
27.	Economists	7,635	31,034	1,430	22,222
28.	Organization and methods analysts	6,190	31,032	1,565	21,109
29.	Personnel—industrial relations managers	15,945	30,844	5,115	20,746
30.	Supervisors—sales occupations, services	11,180	30,692	3,080	17,756
31.	Physicists	930	30,680	—	—
32.	Managers—construction operations	19,700	30,320	395	20,840
33.	Managers—transportation and communication	12,555	30,312	1,685	23,155
34.	Financial management occupations	40,240	30,039	10,765	18,635

— indicates that either no women were in this category or that the estimated number of women was less than 250. Statistics Canada does not release data on earnings where the numbers in the occupations are less than 250.

Source: *Equality in Employment*, a Royal Commission Report (Abella, Commissioner), Cat. No. MP43-157/1-1984E (Ottawa: Minister of Supply and Services Canada, 1984), pp. 64–65. Reproduced with permission of the Minister of Supply and Services Canada.

Native People and Visible Minorities

Stereotyping and the adverse effect of various employment policies restrict employment opportunities of aboriginal people and visible minorities. Native people experience twice the level of unemployment and only 60 percent of the income of nonnative people. Their training opportunities are limited, resulting in employment in low-skilled occupations. Visible minorities also experience labour market barriers, although this varies by group and region. Some minorities face racial prejudice. Many also encounter occupational barriers built into employment policies and practices.[5]

A recent Ontario study dramatically reveals the extent to which visible minorities experience intentional employment discrimination.[6] One phase of the research matched pairs of white and black subjects who were instructed to appear as applicants in job interviews around Toronto. Even though the subject-pairs applied for the same jobs and had very similar qualifications, the white applicants were offered three times as many jobs as the black applicants. Moreover, black applicants were treated discourteously or rudely in nearly 20 percent of the job postings, whereas white applicants were treated well. A few particularly blatant examples of racial prejudice occurred when the white applicant was offered a position even though the black applicant had been told earlier the same day that the job was filled. Similar results were found in the second phase of the study involving telephone inquiries by people with foreign accents.

Accommodating the Disabled

Employment discrimination against disabled people has only recently gained public attention.[7] Canadians mistakenly categorize disabled people as a single group when, in reality, there are many types of disability. These distinctions are important because a person with one type of disability may be unable to perform a particular job, whereas someone with another disability would not have any "handicap" with respect to that job. Discrimination may occur when employers fail to make these distinctions. In some cases, a disabled person is qualified to do the job but has special needs that the employer can reasonably accommodate. Unfortunately, even though the cost may be small, companies are often reluctant to meet these special needs. This is a form of employment discrimination against disabled people.[8]

Native people, women, visible minorities, and disabled people represent only four of the groups designated in human rights legislation. Labour market participants also experience discrimination due to their age, religion, marital status, and other factors. In the next section, we look more closely at employment equity legislation in Canada.

LEGAL FOUNDATIONS OF EMPLOYMENT EQUITY

The principles of employment equity and discrimination are entrenched in the human rights legislation of every Canadian jurisdiction. Individual rights are also protected in the Charter of Rights and Freedoms, although its application to employment equity has not yet crystallized. This section begins with an overview of these statutes and the Charter, the prohibited grounds of discrimination, and the human rights complaint process. A careful examination follows of the legal concepts and principles that affect management of human resources.

Canadian Charter of Rights and Freedoms

Section 15 of the Canadian Charter of Rights and Freedoms protects every individual's right to equality.[9] This section prevents discrimination on the basis of race, national or ethnic origin, colour, religion, sex, age, or mental or physical ability. At first glance, this appears to form a powerful legal foundation for employment equity. Section 15 only came into force in 1985, so it is too early to say exactly what its implications are for P/HRM. However, the Charter's scope is generally limited to the relationship between individual citizens and the federal and provincial governments. This means the Charter probably applies directly only to employment policies in the public sector. Private sector (and possibly even quasi-public sector) organizations would not be directly affected except through the Charter's influence on employment legislation.[10]

The Charter also states that individual equality rights are not absolute. They must be balanced against the rights of Canadian society. Specifically, Section 1 places "reasonable limits" on individual rights to the extent that these limits "can be demonstrably justified in a free and democratic society." As we shall later see, this has implications for the legality of mandatory retirement policies.

Human Rights Legislation

The first Canadian human rights legislation was introduced in Ontario in 1944. Although fairly restrictive by today's standards, the Racial Documentation Act marked the first time a Canadian legislature had declared that racial and religious discrimination was against public policy and that human rights could not be subordinate to commerce, contract, or property.[11] In 1951, Ontario also became the first jurisdiction to introduce equal pay legislation. Canada ratified the equal remuneration convention (No. 100) of the International Labour Organization (ILO) in 1972. This convention advances the principle of equal pay for work of equal value (i.e., pay equity).[12] The federal government introduced pay equity legislation in 1977, 20 years after it had passed an equal pay statute.

Canada has also ratified the ILO convention on employment and occupation discrimination (No. 111). The 1958 convention embodies the principle of equal opportunity and treatment in employment (i.e., employment equity). By 1962, Ontario had enacted the first full-fledged human rights statute. Other jurisdictions subsequently enacted legislation, with most adopting the Ontario model.

Every province and territory as well as the federal government now has its own human rights code or act to prohibit discrimination in employment and the delivery of services to the public. In each of these 13 jurisdictions, the appropriate human rights statute is administered by a human rights commission or council. With respect to employment, human rights legislation prohibits various types of discrimination in recruitment, selection, training, compensation, promotion, and working conditions. These standards apply to employers as well as employer associations, labour unions, and professional associations.

The provincial and territorial statutes generally apply to people living in those geographic areas. However, as outlined in Chapter Two, approximately 12 percent of the labour force is protected by human rights legislation enacted by the Parliament of Canada. The federal statute covers federal government departments, Crown corporations, and federally regulated industries, which include banking (but not trust companies or credit unions), interprovincial transportation, broadcasting and telecommunications, and firms regulated by legislation pertaining to radioactive materials.

Prohibited Grounds of Employment Discrimination

Each human rights statute specifies the grounds on which individuals should not be distinguished. Exhibit 7-3 lists these factors (as of March 1987) for each of the 13 Canadian jurisdictions. Every statute prohibits discrimination on the basis of race, colour, marital status, and sex. Except for the Yukon, every jurisdiction also includes age and disability status as prohibited grounds. Notice that many statutes restrict the upper and lower bounds of the protected age group. This has implications for mandatory retirement, as we will later see. Other factors in Exhibit 7-3, such as ancestry and place of origin, have similar meaning but are stated slightly differently from one statute to the next.

Although human rights legislation was written to protect members of traditionally disadvantaged groups (e.g., visible minorities, disabled people, aboriginal people, women), it applies to all employees. For example, the Canadian Human Rights Commission resolved a complaint involving a man who was allegedly refused an interview for a job in a candy factory because the employer wanted to hire only women.[13]

The proportion of complaints filed for each of the prohibited grounds varies with each jurisdiction. In British Columbia, approximately 30 percent of recent complaints were based on sex; 25 percent were related to race, colour, or place of origin; 20 percent dealt with sexual harassment; 10 percent were related to disabilities; the other 15 percent covered the remaining grounds of discrimination in that province.[14] As Exhibit 7-4 indicates, the distribution of discrimination complaints (including those not related to employment) filed in the federal jurisdiction is quite different. The most frequent complaints filed with the Canadian Human Rights Commission relate to disabilities, sex, race/colour, and age, respectively.

Prohibited Employment Inquiries

A distinction is sometimes made between the preemployment and postemployment actions of employers. Employers are prohibited (or discouraged) from asking certain questions of job applicants. The Appendix illustrates some guidelines for preemployment interviewing. While some restricted informa-

EXHIBIT 7–3
Prohibited Grounds of Discrimination in Employment*

Jurisdiction	Federal	British Columbia	Alberta	Saskatchewan	Manitoba	Ontario	Quebec	New Brunswick	Prince Edward Island	Nova Scotia	Newfoundland	Northwest Territories	Yukon
Race	●	●	●	●	●	●	●	●	●	●	●	●	●
National or ethnic origin₁	●				●	●	●	●	●	●	●		●
Ancestry		●	●	●		●			●			●	●
Nationality or citizenship			●	●	●							●	
Place or origin		●	●	●		●		●				●	
Colour	●	●	●	●	●	●	●	●	●	●	●	●	●
Religion	●	●		●	●		●	●	●	●	●	●	●
Creed₂			●	●		●			●	●	●	●	●
Age	●	● (45-65)	● (18+)	● (18-65)	●	● (18-65)	●	● (19+)	●	● (40-65)	● (19-65)	●	●
Sex	●	●	●	●	●	●	●	●	●	●	●	●	●
Pregnancy or childbirth	●		●	●			●						
Marital status₃	●	●	●	●	●	●	●	●	●	●	●	●	●
Family status₃	●					●	●	●			●		
Pardoned offence	●						●				●		
Record of criminal conviction		●				●	●						
Physical handicap or disability	●	●	●	●	●	●	●	●	●	●	●		
Mental handicap or disability	●	●			●	●	●	●	●	●	●		
Dependence on alcohol or drug	●												
Place of residence												●	
Political belief		●			●		●	●		●			
Assignment, attachment or seizure of pay₄							●						
Source of income													
Social condition₄							●						
Language							●						
Social origin₄											●		
Sexual orientation₅						●	●						
Harassment₅	●					●	●			●			

This chart is for quick reference only. For interpretation or further details, call the appropriate commission.

*Any limitation, exclusion, denial or preference may be permitted if a bona fide occupational requirement can be demonstrated.

[1] New Brunswick includes only "national origin."
[2] Creed usually means religious beliefs.
[3] Quebec uses the term *civil status*.
[4] In Quebec's charter, "social condition" includes assignment, attachment, or seizure of pay and social origin.
[5] The federal, Ontario, and Quebec statutes ban harassment on all proscribed grounds. Ontario, Nova Scotia, and Newfoundland also ban sexual solicitation.

Source: Canadian Human Rights Commission, *Dossier 87–3*, March 1987. Reproduced with permission.

EXHIBIT 7-4
Distribution of Complaints Received in 1986 by the Canadian Human Rights Commission by Grounds for Discrimination

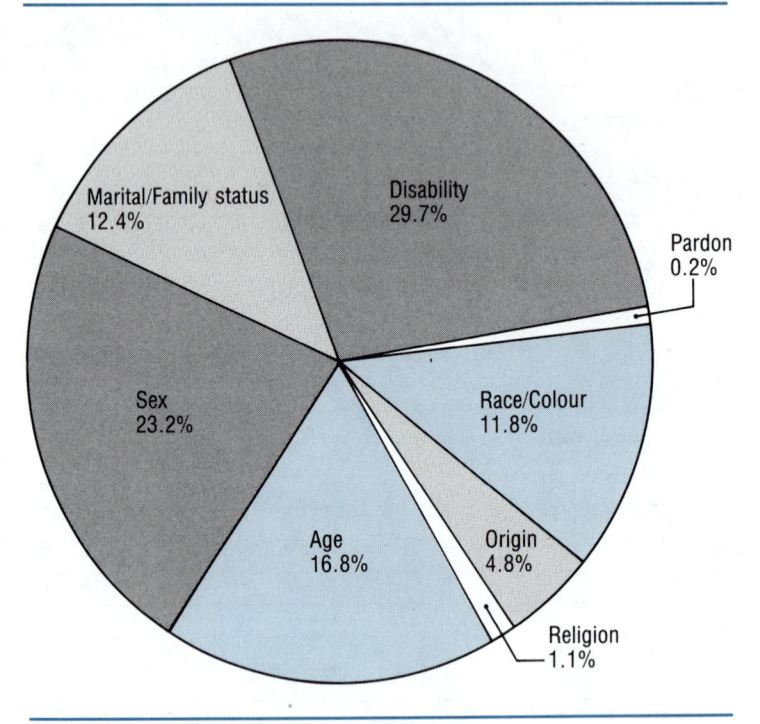

- Disability 29.7%
- Pardon 0.2%
- Race/Colour 11.8%
- Origin 4.8%
- Religion 1.1%
- Age 16.8%
- Sex 23.2%
- Marital/Family status 12.4%

Source: Canadian Human Rights Commission, *1986 Annual Report* (Ottawa: Minister of Supply and Services Canada, 1987), p. 24. Reproduced with permission.

tion may be requested under an employment equity program (in some jurisdictions), these guidelines are applicable to most situations. It is also good policy to consider these recommendations when making promotion decisions.

Employers can sometimes request information on current employees that is prohibited during preemployment. For example, employers may require the names and relations of people to contact in case of emergency. This may reveal the person's family status and, consequently, should be asked only after the decision to hire has been made. The Appendix suggests which information can be requested after job applicants are hired.

Processing Human Rights Complaints

The human rights complaint process varies from one jurisdiction to the next. Generally, the human rights commission/council must investigate a complaint if it appears to fall within the jurisdiction and is not trivial or made in bad faith. An impartial investigator from the commission/council gathers relevant information from all parties. A report is then usually filed and is disclosed to both the complainant and the person toward whom the allegation of discrimination is directed (called the respondent). The report may conclude that the complaint is based on insufficient evidence or it may include a recommendation for settlement of the dispute. Most human rights complaints are settled at this point.

If a settlement is proposed by the investigator but is rejected by either the complainant or respondent, the minister in charge (or the commission/council in some jurisdictions) appoints a tribunal or board of inquiry. The tribunal hears evidence from both sides of the complaint using quasi-legal protocol and makes a binding decision. In its decision, the tribunal may either dismiss the complaint or order the respondent to cease the discriminatory practice and pay damages for lost wages and hurt feelings. The decision may also order the employer to rehire the employee. Some statutes additionally give the tribunal the power to order the employer to introduce a formal employment equity program.

Role of the Courts

The object of human rights legislation in Canada is remedial rather than punitive. Consequently, unlike the United States where allegations of discrimination are challenged directly in the courts, the Canadian human rights complaint process goes through the appropriate human rights commission/council and, if necessary, a tribunal. However, either the complainant or respondent may appeal the tribunal's decision to the appropriate court of law if it is believed the tribunal has erred. Similarly, these lower (or appeal) court decisions may be appealed to the Supreme Court of Canada.

EMERGING CONCEPTS IN EMPLOYMENT EQUITY

In addition to changing human rights legislation, the legal concepts and principles embodied in the decisions of Canadian courts and human rights tribunals have evolved. In this section, we review the concepts of greatest relevance to P/HRM professionals.

From Intent to Effect

The concept of employment equity has evolved over the years. The earliest cases relied on the *adverse intent* principle to reach the conclusion that the employer had discriminated.[15] From this perspective, a discriminatory practice must be based on hostility or an otherwise biased attitude toward the person because of the identifiable designated group to which he or she belongs. For example, adverse intent discrimination would be found where an organization refused to promote women into management because the employer believed women are unable to manage. Unfortunately, adverse intent discrimination is very difficult to prove because the malevolence or attitude toward the identifiable group could be concealed or denied. In the above example, the company could probably win a discrimination complaint by simply denying the employer doubted the managerial abilities of women.

The Shift to Adverse Effect

Eventually it became apparent to human rights tribunals that many of the barriers facing various groups do not result from an overt intent on the part of employers to discriminate. Rather, they are based on the *adverse effect* that certain employment systems (i.e., policies, procedures in P/HRM) have on specific groups.

Employment systems are often neutral in their intent toward these social groups. Indeed, employers may not even be aware of the adverse effect the practices have on the employment opportunities of certain groups of people. For example, a company might decide against installing elevators in a multi-story building to save money. Yet this apparently neutral decision may exclude individuals confined to wheelchairs from being gainfully employed in that organization.[16] Because the discrimination is due to the employment system rather than the intent of the employer, adverse effect is often called *systemic discrimination*.

The shift from adverse intent to adverse effect did not occur overnight. The change began in the United States with the 1971 case of *Griggs* v. *Duke Power Co.*[17] The Supreme Court decided Griggs, a black employee, had been discriminated against because the company used employment tests and educational requirements that screened out a greater proportion of blacks than whites. The tests and qualifications were set too high for satisfactory performance in the janitorial job to which Griggs had applied. These employment practices were not established to discriminate against blacks or any other designated group. Yet they had the effect of restricting black applicants from holding certain jobs even though they could perform them satisfactorily.

Although the *Griggs* case had a dramatic impact on the definition of discrimination in the United States, the shift to adverse effect was much slower in Canada. This is due not only to the fact that *Griggs* was an American case, but also to different language in the Canadian human rights statutes. Some support for the adverse effect principle in Canada appeared in Canadian tribunals deciding equal pay complaints during the mid-1970s.[18] However, the first major endorsement of the adverse effect definition in the area of employment equity came in the 1977 Ontario Board of Inquiry decision of *Singh* v. *Security and Investigation Services Ltd.*[19]

Ishar Singh was refused a job as a security guard because company policy stated that all employees must be clean-shaven, wear a company cap as part of the uniform, and have properly cut hair. As a Sikh, Singh could not abide by these rules on religious grounds. The board of inquiry found that although the company did not intend to discriminate against Sikhs, it nevertheless discriminated against the applicant through the effect of its employment policies.

The adverse effect principle gained further support in subsequent decisions of human rights tribunals and courts throughout most Canadian jurisdictions.[20] Today, adverse effect is an entrenched principle in the definition of employment equity and discrimination. It is used to establish a prima facie case of discrimination. In other words, adverse effect demonstrates that an employer appears (on the surface) to be discriminating. It does not necessarily mean the employer is *actually* discriminating, however, because the employment policy may specify a bona fide occupational qualification.

Bona Fide Occupational Qualification

When prima facie evidence of discrimination is established, the employer's major defense is that the apparently discriminatory practice is, in fact, based on a bona fide occupational qualification (BFOQ).[21] A BFOQ has both objective and subjective components.[22] Subjectively, a BFOQ is an employment practice imposed honestly and in good faith. In other words, the rule was not established to deliberately discriminate against designated groups. Objectively, the employment practice requires individuals to perform or have the capacity to perform the essential functions of the job safely, efficiently, and reliably. This practice must apply to the job or occupational requirements, not to the characteristics of a certain group of individuals.[23] At the same time, the employer must assess the ability of each individual to perform the job rather than basing the decision on that person's membership in a particular group.

An example might clarify these important points. Michael Nowell was employed as a trainman at Canadian National Railway in Winnipeg until 1971, when he was diagnosed as a diabetic. He worked in other positions at CN until 1979, when he requested a transfer back to his trainman job. His request was refused because CN had a policy prohibiting insulin-dependent diabetics from working as trainmen. The company believed that people with this disability pose a safety risk because of the potential side effects of insulin.

The human rights tribunal decided CN discriminated against Nowell because its policy of excluding insulin-dependent diabetics from trainmen positions was not based on a bona fide occupational qualification. The policy referred to a designated group (i.e., insulin-dependent diabetics) rather than to the essential job functions. Furthermore, the company excluded Nowell based on his disability status rather than on an individual assessment of his ability to perform essential tasks. CN lost this case because its policy applied to employee characteristics rather than occupational requirements. Nowell's medical exam only confirmed his diabetic condition. It did not test whether he was physically able to perform the job of trainman.[24]

In the *Bhinder* v. *CN* case described at the beginning of this chapter, the Supreme Court of Canada decided the company had *not* discriminated against Bhinder because the hard-hat rule was based on a bona fide occupational qualification. The rule did not refer to the employee's status in a designated group. CN did not say Sikhs are forbidden from working in the Toronto coach yard. The policy, which was introduced in good faith, stated that people working in this area must wear hard hats for reasons of job safety.

Implications of BFOQ

The challenge to P/HRM managers is to establish policies that apply to essential job requirements rather than the characteristics of applicants in designated groups. Tests that realistically examine each applicant's ability to perform the essential aspects of the job should also be used rather than relying on the person's demographic or disability status. These tests must be applied consistently and universally. Job standards for which applicants cannot easily be tested may be determined through more subjective means, including the expert opinion of medical professionals.[25] Finally, tribunals and courts have been more lenient on the company's claim that an employment practice is based on a BFOQ where public safety is involved.[26]

Reasonable Accommodation

Canadian human rights laws require some flexibility on the part of both the employer and individual. The concept of "reasonable accommodation," or "duty to accommodate," refers to the employer's obligation to provide or permit alternatives to qualified individuals who cannot perform a job in the standard way. In other words, the company must show some degree of flexibility, short of undue hardship, by altering the conditions of work to meet the special needs of otherwise qualified people.

The relationship between reasonable accommodation and BFOQ is still somewhat fuzzy.[27] Generally, it appears that reasonable accommodation deals with the conditions of employment (e.g., hours of work, physical layout), whereas BFOQ relates to job requirements. The employer has a duty to accommodate where the conditions of the workplace have an adverse effect on the employment of target group members. But if the employment policy is based on a BFOQ, there is no duty to accommodate because the employee could not fulfill the job requirements even with accommodating working conditions. We should also note that the employee or applicant also has some obligation to reasonably accommodate the situation.[28]

The implications of this principle are best illustrated in an important case involving Simpsons-Sears Ltd. Mrs. O'Malley was employed full-time as a salesperson at the Simpsons-Sears store in Kingston, Ontario. In 1978, she became a member of the Seventh-Day Adventist Church, which proscribes members from working on the Sabbath (from sundown Friday to sundown Saturday). Unfortunately this conflicted with Mrs. O'Malley's work schedule. When she explained the dilemma to the store's P/HRM manager, he indicated that regular salespeople were required to work Saturdays because of the large volume of business. If Mrs. O'Malley could not work Saturdays, Simpsons-Sears would have to dismiss her. The next week, the P/HRM manager offered Mrs. O'Malley a part-time job that would not conflict with her religious beliefs and indicated she would be considered for any full-time jobs that might be suitable.

The full-time jobs that became available either required Saturday work or could not be filled by a person with the complainant's qualifications. Mrs. O'Malley eventually filed a complaint to the Ontario Human Rights Commission. The case was heard by a tribunal and was twice appealed. It was heard by the Supreme Court of Canada, which determined that Simpsons-Sears had discriminated against Mrs. O'Malley.[29] In the court's opinion, Simpsons-Sears could have given Mrs. O'Malley full-time employment that did not require working Saturdays. In other words, the company failed to prove that further steps to accommodate Mrs. O'Malley—rearranging her schedule so she did not have to work on the Sabbath—would have caused the company undue hardship.

Types of Reasonable Accommodation

Many examples of reasonable accommodation for disabled employees are found in the literature.[30] These include provision of special safety devices or fixtures to either protect the employee or alert others of the disability. A major form of accommodation involves altering the work area. For example, people in wheelchairs require ramps, wider hallways, and taller desks. In some cases, accommodation may also involve creating more flexible job assignments. In this regard, one recent tribunal concluded that the Liquor Control Board of Ontario should assign cashier work to a store clerk with a bad back and pass on tasks requiring heavy lifting to other clerks. The tribunal discovered that the other employees would welcome this alteration because they generally disliked cashier work.[31]

Reasonable accommodation also applies to employees in other designated groups, as the O'Malley case illustrates. Gunderson observes that the employment of women in various occupations may be facilitated by arranging more flexible hours of work, permitting job sharing, and introducing fair parental leave policies. There is also some suggestion that child care facilities provide reasonable accommodation for women.[32]

The employer's duty to accommodate employees having special needs is actually one aspect of an employment equity program. We will discuss employment equity programs later. Next, we turn to two emerging issues in employment equity: sexual and other harassment at work and mandatory retirement.

Sexual and Other Harassment

Harassment is a significant employment problem that has only recently gained the attention of employers and human rights officials.[33] More than 100 cases of harassment are filed annually with the Ontario Human Rights Commission. At least one fifth of discrimination cases filed in many other jurisdictions relate to this issue.[34] Virtually all harassment cases in Canada have been sexually motivated. However, in some jurisdictions, harassment may be related to other discriminatory grounds such as the victim's race, religion, age, or disability.[35]

Harassment in the workplace is broadly defined and may include either explicit or subtle behaviour. For example, human rights legislation in Newfoundland defines harassment as engaging "in a course of vexatious comment or conduct that is known or ought reasonably to be known to be unwelcome."[36] According to the Canadian Human Rights Commission, harassment may include: verbal abuse or threats; unwelcome statements about the individual's body, attire, age, race, and the like; displaying pornographic, racist, or other offensive material; unwelcome invitations or requests; leering or related gestures; condescending actions that undermine the person's self-respect; unnecessary physical contact; and physical assault.[37]

In their recent analysis of published Canadian cases, Jain and Andiappan report that the creation of an intimidating, offensive, or "poisoned" work environment also constitutes sexual harassment, even if no concrete employment consequences are apparent.[38] They also note that seriously offensive conduct may constitute sexual harassment even though it is not persistent.

Some human rights statutes make no direct reference to sexual or other harassment. In these jurisdictions, harassment has been included by inference as a form of sexual or other discrimination. However, more explicit statutory language may be required. A 1987 Manitoba court case rejected the idea that sexual harassment is a form of sex discrimination. Since harassment is not explicitly prohibited in that province, the court overturned the tribunal's award to the employees even though it was evident they had been sexually harassed.[39]

Sexual harassment is a particularly difficult problem to address because it must be distinguished from workplace romance or flirtation. Harassment involves the *power and coercion* of one person over another. For example, an employee may tolerate unwanted advances from her supervisor because she fears reprisals or adverse economic consequences. Workplace flirtation, on the other hand, is based on mutual consent between the parties.[40] The victims of sexual harassment are almost always women, although a male deckhand was sexually harassed in one case by the skipper of the tug on which he worked.[41]

In awarding damages for sexual harassment, human rights tribunals have considered any lost wages, loss of self-respect, and health problems resulting from the experience.[42] A 1982 Ontario decision outlines the factors that increase the amount of compensation payable for injury to feelings and self-respect. These include the nature of the harassment (i.e., whether it was verbal or also physical), the persistence and frequency of harassment, the age and vulnerability of the victim, the degree of aggressiveness and physical contact in the harassment, and the psychological impact of the harassment on the victim.[43]

Organizational Actions

Harassment, particularly sexual harassment, may be difficult to eliminate from the workplace, but P/HRM professionals have an obligation to minimize its prevalence. The first step is to prepare a formal written policy against workplace harassment and communicate this message to all employees. Exhibit 7-5 presents an example of such a policy at B.C. Telephone.

Special seminars can inform managers about the seriousness of the problem and its implications for the company. Appointing a manager to fight harassment is also helpful to symbolize the importance of this issue. An internal redress system should be established that fairly, impartially, and in confidence investigates complaints of harassment. Disciplinary actions against harassers should be established and made known.[44] Many of these actions are already required by law for some employers. All companies in the federal jurisdiction, for example, are required to develop and issue a policy against sexual harassment and to provide a redress mechanism for the victims of sexual harassment.

Mandatory Retirement

Mandatory retirement has been a standard policy in many Canadian businesses most of this century. Typically, it has been introduced in conjunction with the company's pension plan. For example, the Royal Bank's formal retirement policy was established when it introduced its pension plan in 1909.[45] Even

EXHIBIT 7–5
B.C. Telephone Company Personal Harassment Policy

PERSONAL HARASSMENT POLICY

B.C. Telephone has implemented the following Personal Harassment Policy:

Employees of B.C. Telephone and the public with whom we do business are entitled to be treated with dignity, free from personal harassment. In exercising its responsibility as an employer, the Company endeavours at all times to provide a work environment which is supportive of the productivity, personal goals and self-esteem of every employee.

The mutual respect, co-operation and understanding of all employees is necessary to reach this objective.

B.C. Telephone cannot and will not, and employees must not, condone behaviour in the workplace that is unacceptable and likely to undermine work relationships or productivity.

Personal harassment based on race, national or ethnic origin, colour, religion, age, sex, marital or family status, and disability are all prohibited under the Canadian Human Rights Act.

Harassment means any conduct, comment, gesture or contact based on any of the prohibited grounds of discrimination that is likely to cause offence or humiliation to any person, or that might, on reasonable grounds, be perceived as placing a condition on employment or any opportunity for training or promotion.

Harassment by an employee in the workplace is a serious offence, subject to disciplinary action up to and including discharge, and will be treated accordingly.

Individuals who believe they are being subjected to personal harassment as defined above from any person in the workplace should bring their complaint to the attention of their immediate supervisor, or if that is inappropriate, to higher levels of management.

The Human Rights Coordinator should be contacted in the event no satisfactory resolution of the matter is achieved. The name of a complainant or the circumstances of the complaint will not be disclosed to any person except where disclosure is necessary for the purpose of investigating the complaint or taking any related disciplinary measures.

Employees should also be aware that provisions of the Canadian Human Rights Act pertain to the above and an entitlement exists to seek redress through the Canadian Human Rights Commission.

B.C.TEL
BRITISH COLUMBIA
TELEPHONE COMPANY

GENERAL INFORMATION

- In all circumstances, an individual who is accused of harassment must be provided the opportunity to fully explain themselves and to have those explanations properly considered.
- To intentionally accuse someone of harassment, knowing it to be false, is a serious matter. The rights of a person accused of harassment must also be protected.
- No documentation on the harassment is to be placed in the complainant's personal file at any time.

COMPLAINT GUIDELINES

Employees who believe they are being harassed on one of the proscribed grounds should take the following steps to stop the harassment and prevent reoccurrences.

- Make your disapproval and/or unease known to harasser immediately.
- If there is more than one incident, keep a written record of dates, times, the nature of the behaviour and witnesses, if any.
- If the unfair treatment of harassment does not stop after you have spoken to the harasser, speak to your supervisor or departmental manager and then confirm your conversation in a letter. If your supervisor is the harasser, speak immediately to your departmental manager.
- Send copies of this letter to the B.C. Telephone Human Rights Coordinator at 6-3777 Kingsway, Burnaby, B.C. V5H 3Z7 or to the Telecommunications Workers' Union, if appropriate, at 5261 Lane Street, Burnaby, B.C. V5H 4A6.
- Ensure that the harasser is advised that you have taken the above steps.

NOTE:

Clearly, because each case is unique, there may be a time when you feel it is more appropriate to bypass the complaint guidelines listed above. You may speak directly with:

- Your Supervisor,
- The B.C. Telephone Human Rights Coordinator at 432-2250 (toll free).

If appropriate you may also contact:

- The Union Representative in your area,
- The T.W.U. Human Rights Coordinator at 437-8601 (Collect).

FOR FURTHER INFORMATION CONTACT:
B.C. TELEPHONE
HUMAN RIGHTS COORDINATOR

Source: British Columbia Telephone Company Ltd.

government policies on "normal retirement age" are historically based on public pension plan systems. Mandatory retirement policies are traced to government pension systems a century ago in Germany and England.[46]

Mandatory retirement is a controversial issue. Some applaud it as a graceful way for aging employees to leave the organization. It also facilitates human resources planning and opens positions to hire and promote younger people. Others see mandatory retirement as a waste of valuable talent because it arbitrarily terminates employees based on their age rather than ability.[47] It also infringes on the employee's human rights by restricting the opportunity to be gainfully employed after age 65. At least two government commissions have recommended abolishing mandatory retirement.[48]

Mandatory retirement has recently been abolished as a legal business practice in Quebec, Manitoba, and the federal sector. The Ontario government, which currently permits mandatory retirement as a BFOQ, is reviewing this policy. Several Canadian firms, including Noma Industries and Mohawk Oil, have never had mandatory retirement policies, while others have ended theirs.

Challenges to Mandatory Retirement

Mandatory retirement has been challenged from two directions as a form of age discrimination. Where mandatory retirement is not explicitly permitted in the human rights act, tribunals and courts have had to determine whether the policy is a BFOQ. Manitoba courts, which have had many of these cases, have repeatedly indicated that mandatory retirement is fundamentally a political rather than a legal issue. They argue the issue should be resolved through legislation rather than the court's interpretation of human rights statutes, particularly since these statutes make no mention of mandatory retirement.[49] Mandatory retirement has been accepted as a BFOQ under some circumstances, but not others.[50]

In addition to human rights legislation, mandatory retirement has been challenged under Section 15 of Canada's Charter of Rights and Freedoms. In two recent cases involving universities in Ontario and British Columbia,[51] lower courts decided the policy of mandatory retirement at age 65 is not discriminatory for two reasons. First, universities are separate from government and therefore are outside the domain of the Charter. Second, both courts stated that mandatory retirement is a "reasonable limit" on individual rights (from Section 1 of the Charter). The Ontario Court of Appeal upheld this position but the B.C. Court of Appeal came to the opposite conclusion. Consequently, the effect of the Charter on mandatory retirement will eventually be decided by the Supreme Court of Canada. The judges concluded that the benefits to society of mandatory retirement outweighed the cost to individual rights.

EMPLOYMENT EQUITY PROGRAMS IN CANADA

Growing public awareness of employment discrimination, especially the adverse effect of some employment practices, has caused employers to look more closely at their employment systems. Some changed their recruitment and selection practices so more people in designated groups are considered for employment. Others introduced educational programs to increase management and employee awareness of employment equity. A few voluntarily compared the proportion of target group members employed by the company with the proportion of qualified members in the labour force. These actions represent part of a comprehensive system known as an employment equity program (EEP).

> **Definition**
> *Employment equity programs* are comprehensive planning processes for eliminating systemically induced inequities and redressing the historic patterns of employment disadvantage suffered by members of target groups.[52]

As this definition indicates, EEPs are results-oriented strategies aimed at reducing the adverse effect of employment policies and practices. They include several steps we will describe later. First, a brief background on EEPs in Canada is in order.

EEPs are not new to Canada. After World War II, the Canadian government introduced a preferential hiring program for war veterans. This provision is still in place. In the late 1960s, the federal government introduced a program to create greater French-Canadian and bilingual representation in the federal civil service. In 1975, the federal government established an EEP aimed at improving the representation of women in the civil service, particularly at the management level. Other federal programs were subsequently introduced for other target groups.[53]

Several private sector companies have started voluntary EEPs over the past decade. Air Canada's program, which began in 1973, is aimed at increasing the number of women in nontraditional occupations such as pilots and technicians. A decade later, the program has increased the percentage of women in these jobs only slightly.[54] In 1975, Warner-Lambert also launched an EEP directed toward the employment of women at all levels in the organization. Recruitment practices and compensation systems were reviewed, and the company monitored the percentage of women in each occupational category. The proportion of women represented in management at Warner-Lambert has jumped substantially, although most are at the lower management level.[55]

Most human rights commissions have established special services to encourage introduction of EEPs and assist employers in their development. In 1975, the Ontario government launched one of the first services of this kind. Later it also provided funds to subsidize the cost of EEPs in municipalities. In 1984, the government announced that more than 200 firms had introduced EEPs. One source suggests, however, that most of these voluntary programs only marginally qualify as EEPs.[56]

Mandatory Employment Equity Programs

EEPs are controversial, particularly when they are legislated. Part of this controversy stems from the U.S. experience requiring many organizations to set strict quotas on the number of women and minorities hired.[57] In Canada, governments are quick to point out that mandatory programs in this country rely on targets and timetables. The difference is that targets and timetables are long-term objectives that may be altered to reflect conditions beyond the organization's control, such as layoffs. Quotas, on the other hand, impose a relatively fixed distribution of job vacancies over a short period of time to job applicants based on their gender or minority status.

Quebec was the first province to introduce mandatory employment equity programs in any significant way. In 1978, the province legislated an EEP that required employers to file plans with the government showing how they will improve access to the disabled.

The federal government, Saskatchewan, and Quebec empower human rights tribunals to impose EEPs as a remedy to a finding of discrimination. A federal tribunal applied this provision in the 1984 case *Action Travail des Femmes* v. *Canadian National*.[58] In its lengthy decision, the tribunal concluded CN had discriminated against women with respect to nontraditional positions. CN was required to set up a special hiring program in which one out of every four nontraditional positions would be filled by a woman until women represented 13 percent of this occupational group. This figure was based on the percentage of blue-collar jobs in the region held by women. Although the tribunal's decision included quotas (i.e., one in four hires must be a woman), the case was unanimously upheld in 1987 by the Supreme Court of Canada. The Court concluded that imposing quotas was within the scope of the Canadian Human Rights Act because tribunals are permitted to remedy past instances of discrimination. It is unclear whether this decision will lead tribunals and courts to impose quotas in place of a more flexible procedure using targets and timetables.

Federal Government Legislation

The major thrust for mandatory EEPs came from the Commission on Equality in Employment, headed by Judge Rosalie Abella.[59] The final report, which was delivered in October 1984, concluded that the federal government's reliance on voluntary programs was largely ineffective. Instead, all federally regulated employers should be required by legislation to implement EEPs and annually report on changes in the organization's demography. The report also urges provincial and territorial governments to introduce mandatory EEPs consistent with the federal program.

In 1985, the federal government introduced legislation requiring EEPs for federally regulated employers with more than 100 employees. In 1986, a similar program was introduced for companies bidding on contracts to supply goods and services to the federal government. The federal contract compliance program has already affected industry. In early 1987, two bids in a $5 million contract for high-quality paper were rejected because the tendering companies failed to submit the required employment equity documentation.[60] Both statutes require the implementation of EEPs by 1988 in the businesses affected. In the next section, we describe the process of implementing employment equity programs.

IMPLEMENTING EMPLOYMENT EQUITY PROGRAMS

As with so many P/HRM systems and programs, designing and implementing an employment equity program involves managing significant organizational change. It requires careful planning, participation, and monitoring.[61] Exhibit 7–6 outlines the process of EEP development.

Step One: EEP Planning

As an objectives-based system, an EEP requires careful planning and execution. This process is easier in smaller organizations where fewer people need to be consulted. However, the features of an effective EEP are the same no matter how large or small the firm.

Top Management Commitment and Support

A successful EEP needs the continued support of the chief executive officer and other senior staff in the organization. A major study of large corporations in the United States discovered top management commitment is considered the second most important contributor to a successful program.[62] (The most important factor was existence of employment equity laws and regulations.) This support is manifested through executive actions as well as formal statements.

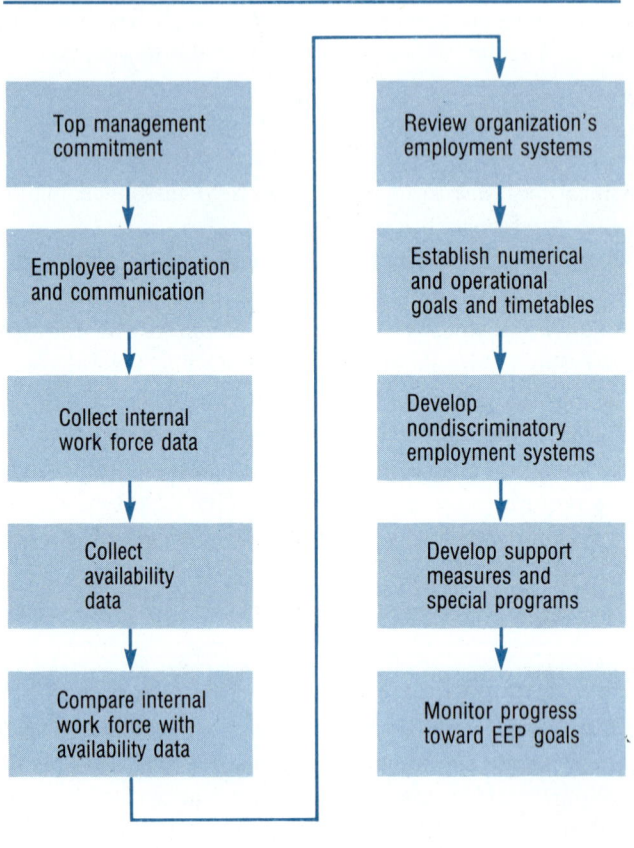

EXHIBIT 7-6
The Employment Equity Program Design Process

```
Top management              Review organization's
commitment          ──┐     employment systems
    │                 │           │
    ▼                 │           ▼
Employee participation│     Establish numerical
and communication     │     and operational
    │                 │     goals and timetables
    ▼                 │           │
Collect internal      │           ▼
work force data       │     Develop
    │                 │     nondiscriminatory
    ▼                 │     employment systems
Collect               │           │
availability          │           ▼
data                  │     Develop support
    │                 │     measures and
    ▼                 │     special programs
Compare internal      │           │
work force with       │           ▼
availability data     │     Monitor progress
    │                 │     toward EEP goals
    └─────────────────┘
```

A formal corporate policy on employment equity is the first step in the planning process. This policy should be clearly communicated to all employees and the general public. This informs employees that employment equity is an important organizational objective. It also provides authorization for the employment equity structure. In a unionized environment, a joint statement with the union executive is recommended.

Corporate commitment to employment equity is also manifested by the appointment of a senior person to oversee the EEP. Phillips suggests two alternative models.[63] The more common approach is to assign responsibility for designing and implementing the EEP to a senior P/HRM manager at the outset. With sufficient resources, this action is effective. However, Phillips argues that this model fails to symbolize the unique importance of employment equity.

The other approach is to temporarily appoint a senior executive advisor on employment equity who reports directly to the CEO. The authority of the special advisor is derived from the direct relationship with the top corporate official, thereby providing a sufficient basis from which to apply the EEP at all levels within the corporation. When the EEP is fully implemented after a couple of years, the program is transferred to the P/HRM department. This model was recently adopted by the City of Scarborough. In 1985, the city hired a senior official from the Canadian Human Rights Commission on a two-year contract to administer its fledgling EEP.[64]

Whether the EEP is developed through the P/HRM department or through a special executive advisor, employment equity managers must be knowledgeable about the problems and concerns of the target groups. They must have the status and authority needed to gain the cooperation of employees, managers, and unions. This usually means they should report directly to the CEO or to a senior vice president. The federal government's contract compliance program requires that these duties be assigned to a person with senior-level authority.

Corporate commitment is also demonstrated through the actions of the CEO and the focus of the management reward system. NOVA, An Alberta Corporation president Robert Blair talked extensively with native leaders in their communities when the company expanded its operations in Northern Canada. His commitment to the employment of aboriginal people was instrumental in introducing the company's native job training program. Native and disabled persons are also given attention in the management reward system. NOVA's performance evaluation of managers includes examining how well they handle the employment of native people and the disabled.[65]

Participation and Communication

Participation is another critical feature of a successful EEP. Most legislated programs in Canada require employers to consult with designated bargaining agents. They must supply sufficient information and opportunity for these groups to ask questions and submit advice on EEP implementation.

Most sources recommend establishing a joint union-management committee or similar mechanism to facilitate participation.[66] Phillips points out that union involvement is important despite the potential difficulty in establishing a cooperative approach. In particular, the EEP may affect several aspects of the collective agreement. Also, union involvement can help to communicate the program on a regular basis to bargaining unit members. In nonunion firms, employee representatives may be appointed to sit on an employment equity advisory committee. Supervisory and management staff also participate in developing and implementing the EEP either through appointment to the advisory committee or separate meetings with the employment equity manager.

The announcement of an employment equity policy and establishment of an EEP can raise many questions and concerns among employees. Some are concerned about how these changes will affect their progress within the company. For example, Westinghouse Canada Ltd. faced a backlash among Anglo-Saxon men and some professional women who were concerned that employment equity would limit their promotional opportunities.[67] At the same time, targetted employees are often concerned about revealing their minority or disabled status.

These apprehensions call for a major campaign communicating to all employees the implications of employment equity within the organization. At Westinghouse, a two-day workshop for all 5,800 employees across Canada explained the program and addressed employee concerns. Some firms use company newsletters to describe the implications of the EEP. Others educate supervisors so they can address many of these concerns directly with employees.

Step Two: Utilization Analysis

Utilization involves comparing the representation and distribution of target group members within the organization with their availability in the relevant labour market. This requires collecting data on the demography of the organization's work force as well as on the proportion of target group members within the geographic and occupational parameters from which the employer would reasonably recruit.

Collecting Internal Work Force Data

Two approaches are used to identify employment discrimination through demographic analysis. One approach examines the *stock* of employees in various occupations by target group variables (i.e., gender, race, disability). Stock data indicate where members of the targetted groups are employed within the organization, including their relative occupational and salary levels. The other approach gathers data on the demographic characteristics of individuals who are hired, promoted, and terminated within the year. These *flow* data provide information on the movement of individuals into, through, and out of the organization.

When compared with availability data (described below), stock data help P/HRM specialists identify the extent to which past employment practices have had an adverse effect on designated groups. Flow data, on the other hand, indicate the extent to which current employment practices have an adverse effect. Organizations regulated by the Canadian government's employment equity legislation must submit both stock and flow data annually for each geographic area on the 12 occupational groups established in the regulations.

Employers regulated by the federal government are required to provide information on the gender, salary, occupational group, geographic location, seniority, employment status (e.g., full-time, part-time), minority status, and disability status of the internal work force. Collecting information on the employee's minority and disability status typically occurs after the individual has been hired. In many jurisdictions, these data may also be collected at the point of application for a job if the information is provided voluntarily by applicants and is separated from the interview and hiring process.[68] The self-identification of target group members is more successful when the company creates a climate of trust and the purpose of the data is clearly communicated. Gathering internal work force data is aided by the development of human resource information systems (Chapter Three) and skills inventories (Chapter Six).

Collecting Availability Data

Availability data provide a profile of the labour force (numbers of qualified persons available to work) in a defined geographical recruitment area appropriate for each occupation from which the employer may reasonably be expected to draw. In other words, an availability analysis indicates the number of target group members available to work in the labour market relevant to each occupation. For senior management and highly specialized occupations, availability data would be collected on the national labour market. Clerical jobs, on the other hand, would typically have an availability profile based on local labour market data.

The type of data collected to estimate target group availability depends on the statistics available, the company's assumptions about those statistics, and the legislative requirements. Many organizations will probably collect availability data only on the external labour market using documentation from Statistics Canada. However, the relevant labour market also includes graduates from educational institutions as well as current employees eligible for promotion, transfer, or training. For example, the City of Vancouver uses the percentage of women in engineering programs as one source of availability analysis information.[69] Occupations at different levels in the organization will rely on these three sources to varying degrees. For example, senior-level positions may draw candidates from lower jobs within the organization and the labour market, whereas entry-level positions may rely more on recent graduates.

Phillips proposes a method of determining target group availability that considers the sources of recruiting.[70] Specifically, the company collects information on the percentage of target group members from each source available for work in a particular occupation. These percentages are then combined by weighting the extent to which each source is used.

EXHIBIT 7–7
Hypothetical Availability Analyis of Women in Skilled Crafts Occupations

Occupation Group	Data Source	Target Group Availability	×	Source Weight	=	Availability Weight
Skilled crafts and trades	Community college grads	27.0%		65%		17.55%
	Provincial labour market	14.6		20		2.92
	Transferable employees*	38.2		15		5.73
	Composite availability estimate					26.20%
	Add: Pull factor†					5.30
	Adjusted availability estimate					31.50%

Note: Women currently represent 12 percent of the skilled crafts and trades positions in this organization.
*This is based on the percentage of women currently working in clerical, service, and semiskilled occupations who would be able to train for skilled crafts jobs.
†This is 10 percent of working age women in the province (the relevant labour market).

An example of the availability of qualified women to work in skilled crafts is shown in Exhibit 7–7. Skilled crafts employees at this company (and in this area of the country) are selected from all three sources to varying degrees. In the past, most were hired from local educational institutions. Another 20 percent were hired as experienced workers from the labour market, and approximately 15 percent were promoted and trained from the company's own supply of unskilled employees.

The target group availability information was collected from various sources. The percentage of qualified women from educational institutions is based on estimates from those institutions. The labour market availability percentage is based on Statistics Canada information for the province (if the relevant labour market is regional). The percentage of women available from other occupations within the company is based on the internal work force analysis described earlier. These percentages are weighted and summed to arrive at the composite availability estimate.

An additional "pull factor" is added to the composite availability estimate to compensate for underutilization of target group members due to past recruitment practices. The size of the pull factor is somewhat arbitrary, but typically represents up to 10 percent of the target group in the relevant population census area (e.g., the province in this example). In Exhibit 7–7, women represent 53 percent of the population in the relevant labour market. Consequently, the pull factor is 5.3 percent. Adding this pull factor results in an adjusted availability estimate of 31.5 percent. This figure indicates the percentage of the relevant labour market for skilled craftspeople represented by women. Similar calculations should be made for visible minorities, aboriginal people, and persons with disabilities.

Comparing Internal Work Force and Availability Data

The underutilization or concentration of target group members is determined by comparing the internal work force data with the adjusted availability estimates. Underutilization occurs where the percentage of employees in a designated group is lower than the percentage an organization would expect to have employed in each occupational category. Concentration refers to a higher percentage of target group employees in a particular occupation within the organization than is found in the relevant labour market.

In the example in Exhibit 7–7, the company would be underutilizing women in its skilled crafts work force because only 12 percent of its skilled crafts work force is represented by women, whereas 31.5 percent of the relevant labour market consists of people in this designated group (based on the adjusted availability estimate above).

Two methods are frequently used to decide whether this gap is large enough to suggest adverse effect. U.S. firms usually rely on the "four-fifths rule." Adverse effect exists if the proportion of target group members in the company's work force is less than four fifths of the proportion of target group members in the external work force. This rule is also used to examine selection rates. The other approach is to use a standard deviation test. This procedure determines whether the number of target group members employed by the company is less than two standard deviations from the number estimated in the availability analysis. The four-fifths rule and the standard deviation test are described in more detail in Exhibit 7–8. Mandatory EEP legislation in Canada has not referred to any statistical estimate of adverse effect. However, Cronshaw believes these procedures may be required in the future as tests of adverse effect become more refined.[71]

Step Three: Employment Systems Review

Through utilization analysis, employment equity programs focus mainly on results. However, Canadian programs also consider the process of discrimination. Specifically, EEPs typically include an employment systems review. The basic purpose of the employment systems review is to measure and analyze the impact of employment systems, policies, practices, and procedures on the participation of designated groups and to identify barriers to their equitable employment.[72] Where the utilization analysis reveals serious problems, this review is nothing short of a comprehensive P/HRM evaluation and audit (see Chapter Seventeen).

EXHIBIT 7–8
Determining Adverse Effect with the Four-Fifths Rule and Standard Deviation Test

The standard deviation test and four-fifths rule are used to statistically compare the percentage of people in one group with the percentage in another group. These tests may be used to compare current employees with people in the relevant labour market. Alternatively, these tests may compare the group of people recently selected for employment with the group of applicants for those jobs.

Here we use the example from Exhibit 7–7. The percentage of women in the organization's internal work force in skilled crafts and trades occupations is compared with the percentage of women in the relevant labour market.

Standard Deviation

Standard deviation (SD) is a statistical measure of variability of data. It indicates the extent to which there are variations around an expected value. The standard deviation test indicates acceptable variability (i.e., variability due to chance) around the ideal percentage of target group members. If the employment of target group members is random, their percentage in the organization would be within *two standard deviations* of the percentage available in the relevant labour market. A percentage below or above two standard deviations would be a chance occurrence less than 5 percent of the time. This would be significant evidence of underutilization or concentration.

One standard deviation is calculated by the following formula:

$$SD = \sqrt{npq}$$

where:

n = Total number of employees in that occupational group
p = Proportion of the occupational group represented by target group members (e.g., women in our example)
q = Proportion of the occupational group not represented by target group members (i.e., $1 - p$)

In our example, women represent 12 percent of skilled crafts employees in the organization and approximately 31.5 percent of the qualified labour market. The company employs 200 skilled craftspeople. This means 24 of them (200 × .12) are women. Ideally, the company should employ 63 women (200 × .315) in these positions. Thus, the standard deviation in this case would be:

$SD = \sqrt{npq}$
$n = 200$
$p = .12$
$q = 1 - .12 = .88$
$SD = \sqrt{200 \times .12 \times .88} \approx 4.6$
$2 \text{ SDs} \approx 9$

Using the standard deviation test, 54 is the minimum number of women the company should have employed in skilled crafts positions (63 − 9). The number

EXHIBIT 7–8 *(concluded)*

of women actually employed by the company in this occupational group is 24. Consequently, the company's employment practices have a significant adverse effect on the percentage of women in this occupational group.

Four-Fifths Rule

The four-fifths rule also corrects for chance in comparing the actual and ideal number of target group members employed in a specific occupational group. Instead of two standard deviations, however, the four-fifths rule allows 20 percent fewer target group members employed than in the available labour market.

Referring to our example, the company should ideally employ 63 women in skilled crafts positions. Correcting for random factors, the company's employment practices would have a significant adverse effect if it employs less than four fifths the ideal number (i.e., 63 × ⅘ = 50.4). Since four fifths of the ideal number is still larger than the actual number, significant adverse effect is found.

The employment systems review begins by fully outlining the organizational actions that constitute the employment system. This should include actual practices and not just the organization's formal policies and procedures. Next, each practice is scrutinized to determine whether it may be a source of systemic discrimination. If so, the P/HRM manager must determine whether the employment practice is job-related, a business necessity, consistently applied, and in compliance with the applicable human rights legislation. Even if the employment practice has an adverse effect on target group members, it may be acceptable on the grounds that it is based on a bona fide occupational qualification.

The number of employment system activities may be large even in small firms. The employment system review should examine job analysis methods, recruitment processes, training and development practices, performance evaluation systems, promotion criteria, compensation decision processes, discipline procedures, work schedules and rules, physical design and layout of the organization and its facilities, termination/layoff processes, and access to employee benefits.

Some aspects of the employment systems review may involve joint labour-management efforts. For example, as part of its review of the job classification system, the Saskatchewan Government Insurance Corporation worked with the union to determine the realistic minimum requirements for each classification and the positions within each classification. The joint committee was particularly concerned with the minimum levels of formal education stated in the existing job classification schedule. The committee also sought to identify equivalances to established knowledge and skill requirements in each classification.[73]

Step Four: Plan Design and Implementation

When the utilization analysis and employment systems review are completed, the organization can begin to develop an employment equity plan that will correct the previously identified problems. In most jurisdictions, the EEP must include specific goals and timetables, support measures and special programs, and a system for monitoring the change.

Numerical Goals and Timetables

According to several sources, specific numerical goals and corresponding timetables represent the hallmark of effective EEPs.[74] Numerical goals refer to the number or percentage of qualified target group members selected, trained, or promoted into each occupational group over a specific period. In Canada, government officials repeatedly emphasize that numerical goals are *not quotas*.[75] Instead, they are targets the organization believes it can achieve by eliminating discriminatory practices and implementing special programs. Numerical targets should be viewed as management tools that are flexible enough to respond to the changing conditions of the organization and the designated groups. In the long term, numerical goals usually represent the percentage of target group members calculated in the availability analysis.

The 20-year employment equity plan at the Saskatchewan Government Insurance Corporation (SGI) is shown in Exhibit 7–9. Based on its utilization analysis, SGI specified the number of women it hopes to employ in the five underrepresented occupational groups. Eventually, it expects the percentage of women in each group to approximate the percentage of women in the relevant labour market (currently 39 percent). Notice that SGI's availability analysis is less specific than we have presented above. SGI has taken the percentage of target group members in the general labour force as the relevant figure for all occupational groups rather than the percentage of qualified members within each occupational group.

The numerical goals for native and disabled employees are less specific. SGI expects that 25 percent of all new hires during the next 20 years will be people of native ancestry and 10 percent will be individuals with physical disabilities. By that time, 11.5 and 7.1 percent of SGI's work force (in any occupation) should consist of native and disabled people, respectively.

Operational Goals

Operational goals refer to changes in specific employment practices believed to have an adverse effect on one or more of the designated groups. In other

EXHIBIT 7-9
Targets and Timetables at Saskatchewan Government Insurance Corporation

Target Group	Current 1983	Short Term	Mid Term	Long Term	Number	(Percent)
Total employees	1,342	1,342	1,342	1,342		
Total female employees (underrepresented categories)	652	652	652	652		
Executive	0	1	1	0	2	(39.0)
Management (excluding secretaries)	33	5	10	20	68	(39.0)
Technical	89	9	18	33	149	(39.0)
Trades	1	3	6	10	20	(39.0)
Labour	1	6	11	20	38	(39.0)
Native employees	14	25% of all new hires			154	(11.5)
Disabled employees	32	10% of all new hires			95	(7.1)

Note: This chart will be revised whenever changes occur in SGI's work force (1,342) and in the target group working age population figures: 39%, 11.5%, and 7.1%.
Source: Saskatchewan Government Corporation et al. (1984), 5 CHHR D/2059.

words, they represent changes from a discriminatory to neutral employment system. Since many employment system practices require time to change, specific timetables should be established. Where complex alterations are required, the relevant operational goals should include interim objectives.

The operational goals selected depend on the sources of systemic discrimination. Below we itemize a few of the more prevalent sources of systemic discrimination and the operational goals that companies have established.

Traditional Recruitment Practices. Many firms rely exclusively on word-of-mouth hiring and promotion from within to fill job vacancies. These policies tend to exclude qualified people in designated groups because they are not currently employed with the company and are not usually within the circle of friends of current employees. Thus, underrepresented group members don't apply for job vacancies because they do not know about them. The employer can neutralize the adverse effect by contacting community organizations representing designated groups when job vacancies occur. For example, in an effort to correct its underrepresentation of native people, the City of Winnipeg sends native organizations bulletins of job openings along with instructions on how to apply.[76] The Saskatchewan Government Insurance Corporation has initiated a variety of outreach activities, including participation in career days and advertising in newspapers directed toward target groups.[77]

Work Schedules. Work schedules that have been established by tradition rather than job requirements may restrict employment of some designated groups. As we saw in the O'Malley case, religious beliefs sometimes conflict with established work schedules. Certain hours of work may also have an adverse effect on women, particularly single parents, because of conflicts with child care responsibilities. Other schedules may compete with cultural activities such as traditional hunting and fishing seasons for native people.[78] Employers should review all work schedule systems to determine whether they can be made more flexible.

Physical Layout of the Workplace. The design of the workplace may be a source of systemic discrimination against physically disabled people. In particular, narrow passageways, heavy doors, and stairs with no corresponding ramps or elevators restrict the movement of these people. As explained earlier, employers can introduce a variety of changes to facilitate the special needs of the disabled. Some human rights commissions have prepared accessibility standards that describe the physical barriers to employment. Several organizations have conducted accessibility studies or audits to determine whether their buildings comply with these standards.

Selection Criteria. Overstated qualification levels and culturally biased tests may limit employment opportunities of designated group members. The *Griggs* case described earlier illustrates how tests can unfairly discriminate against minorities when the cutoff levels are set higher than the job requires. Few people in disadvantaged groups with little education will find employment if employers require a high school diploma for unskilled positions. P/HRM managers must reexamine the minimum job qualifications and identify alternative qualifications where possible (e.g., experience in place of formal education).

Culturally biased tests are selection criteria that have different degrees of validity for various groups of people. For example, a linguistic reasoning test might be strongly correlated with job performance for white applicants but be unrelated to performance for native people or some visible minorities. Cronshaw suggests that the cultural bias of tests in Canada may be less prevalent than many people believe.[79] Nevertheless, employers should examine the validity of their selection criteria for each designated group. Manulife did just that with its 11 selection tests. Together with several U.S. life insurance firms, the Toronto-based company found the tests were job-related for entry-level positions and this validity did not vary by race, sex, or ethnicity.[80]

Career Paths. Earlier we observed that women are typically employed in sex-segregated occupations that offer little opportunity for advancement. This has a dramatic effect on the underutilization of women in higher-paying occupations. Several companies have begun to combat this problem by redesigning the career advancement process. For example, the North York Board of Education created special bridging positions so women stuck in traditional secretarial and clerical jobs can master managerial and supervisory duties. A voluntary job exchange program was also introduced to enable women to broaden their experience and knowledge base in the organization.[81]

Corporate Culture. The organization's dominant values are translated into managerial actions and entrenched in the reward system. When these values diminish the worth of women and minorities, the result can be underutilization of qualified people. In 1976, the chairman of the Royal Bank of Canada angered many people when he said there weren't any women qualified to run a bank. Partly as a result of this public reaction, the bank introduced a voluntary EEP in 1977. However, the senior vice president of P/HRM at the Royal Bank of Canada recognized that employment equity would become reality in his organization only when the traditional attitudes toward women and minorities changed. The company brought about this change by educating management and employees through a series of seminars and meetings about the need for employment equity. Today, women represent about 20 percent of middle and senior management at the Royal Bank.[82]

Support Measures and Special Programs

Support measures are designed to alleviate problems specific to target group members, but they are available to all employees. Rather than changing discriminatory aspects of the employment system, support measures provide additional opportunities for employment equity. For example, a career counselling program may be introduced because target group employees have had little opportunity to learn about career path planning. This support measure would accelerate achievement of EEP goals even though it is available to all employees in the company.[83]

Special programs are developed to redress extreme imbalances in employment of target group members. They attempt to hasten the rate of change toward EEP goals by providing remedial support only to target group members. Although the Canadian Charter of Rights and Freedoms (as well as most human rights legislation) exempts these programs from charges of reverse discrimination, they are treated cautiously by government officials.

To avoid potential controversy, special programs must have a limited duration and be acceptable to the appropriate human rights commission.[84] It must be evident from the utilization analysis that a special program is required. The employment system review must demonstrate that a particular program addresses the underutilization or concentration of target group members. The organization must also consider the effect of the special program on nontarget groups and select measures that minimize any problems in this regard. Finally, the program must be evaluated periodically to ensure it is achieving the expected goals with minimal effect on other employees.

Monitoring Progress toward EEP Goals

A system of monitoring and control must be set up to evaluate the organization's progress toward EEP goals and make necessary adjustments. The monitoring system should also be able to identify which programs and practices are working. Monitoring includes statistical analysis similar to the utilization analysis described earlier. It particularly includes a careful examination of flow data on job applications, interviews, hirings, promotions and transfers, training and apprenticeships, and terminations to determine whether target group members continue to be adversely affected by employment practices. The achievement of operational goals are also monitored.

SUMMARY

Employment equity affects all P/HRM decisions. In one sense, human rights legislation simply requires employers to adopt sound P/HRM practices. The treatment employees receive must be based on work- and business-related factors rather than on the individual's demographic or disability status. This makes good business sense and ensures compliance with the law.

Dispute continues over whether any progress at eliminating employment discrimination has been made. Differences in occupational attainment and earnings for designated groups remain. There are no magical cures for these problems. However, one approach that seems to go a long way is *participation* in the employment equity process. Too often, employment equity is treated as the exclusive province of P/HRM professionals and corporate legal counsel. Involving line management in planning and implementing employment equity programs will increase their commitment to this important process.

The employment equity programs recently mandated by federal government legislation will likely be the centre of controversy for several years. They will be loudly resisted by managers who see these programs as an infringement on their "right to manage." Others already are viewing EEPs as good business practice. As the P/HRM manager at the Royal Bank of Canada observed, employment equity "is an extension of the social responsibility that society has come to expect from the corporation."[85] Human rights legislation in Canada is continuing to evolve. P/HRM professionals will continue to play an important role in this evolution toward a more equitable workplace.

APPENDIX / Prohibited Grounds for Screening and Selection in Employment

Subject	Avoid Asking	Preferred	Comment
Name	About name change whether it was changed by court order, marriage, or other reason Maiden name Christian name		If needed for a reference, to check on previously held jobs or on educational credentials, ask after selection
Address	For addresses outside Canada	Ask place and duration of current or recent addresses	
Age	For birth certificates, baptismal records, or about age in general Age or birthdate	Ask applicants if they have reached age (minimum or maximum) for work as defined by law	If precise age required for benefits plans or other legitimate purposes it can be determined after selection

(CONTINUED)

Subject	Avoid Asking	Preferred	Comment
Sex	Mr./Mrs./Miss/Ms. Males or females to fill in different or coded applications. If male or female on applications		Any applicants can be addressed during interviews or in correspondence without using courtesy titles such as Mr./Mrs./Miss
	About pregnancy, childbirth, or child care arrangements, includes asking if birth control is used or child-bearing plans	Can ask applicant if the attendance requirements or minimum service commitment can be met	
Marital status	Whether applicant is single, married, divorced, engaged, separated, widowed, or living common-law		If transfer or travel is part of the job, the applicant can be asked if this would cause a problem
	Whether an applicant's spouse is subject to transfer. About spouse's employment	Ask whether there are any known circumstances that might prevent completion of a minimum service commitment, for example	Information on dependents for benefits can be determined after selection
Family status	Number of children or dependents. About arrangements for child care	If the applicant would be able to work the hours required and, where applicable, if the applicant would be able to work overtime	Contacts for emergencies and/or details on dependents can be determined after selection

(CONTINUED)

Subject	Avoid Asking	Preferred	Comment
National or ethnic origin	About birthplace, nationality of ancestors, spouse, or other relatives. Whether born in Canada. If naturalized or landed immigrants. For proof of citizenship	Since those who are entitled to work in Canada must be citizens, landed immigrants, or holders of valid work permits, applicants can be asked if they are legally entitled to work in Canada	Documentation of eligibility to work (i.e., papers, visas, etc.) can be requested after selection
Military service	About military service in other countries	Inquiry about Canadian military service where employment preference is given to veterans, by law	
Language	Mother tongue. Where language skills obtained	Ask if applicant understands, reads, writes, or speaks languages which are required for job	Testing or scoring applicants for language proficiency is not permitted unless fluency is job related
Race or colour	Any inquiry which indicates race or colour, including colour of eyes, skin, or hair		Information required for security clearances or similar purposes can be obtained after selection
Photographs	For photo to be attached to applications or sent to interviewer before interview		Photos for security passes or company files can be taken after selection
Religion	About religious affiliation, church membership, frequency of church attendance		Employers are to reasonably accommodate religious needs of workers

(CONTINUED)

Subject	Avoid Asking	Preferred	Comment
	If applicant will work a specific religious holiday For references from clergy or religious leader	Explain the required work shifts, asking if such a schedule poses problems for applicant	
Height and weight			No inquiry unless there is evidence that they are bona fide occupational requirements
Disability	For listing for all disabilities, limitations, or health problems Whether applicant drinks or uses drugs Whether applicant has ever received psychiatric care or been hospitalized for emotional problems	Ask if applicant has any condition that could affect ability to do the job Ask if the applicant has any condition which should be considered in selection	A disability is only relevant to job ability if it: Threatens the safety or property of others Prevents the applicant from safe and adequate job performance even if reasonable efforts were made to accommodate the disability
Medical information	If currently under physician's care Name of family doctor If receiving counselling or therapy		Medical exams should be preferably conducted after selection and only if an employee's condition is related to the job duties. Offers of employment can be made conditional on successful completion of a medical

(CONCLUDED)

Subject	Avoid Asking	Preferred	Comment
Affiliations	For list of club or organizational memberships	Membership in professional associations or occupational groups can be asked if a job requirement	Applicants can decline to list any affiliation that might indicate a prohibited ground
Pardoned conviction	Whether an applicant has ever been convicted. If an applicant has ever been arrested. Does applicant have a criminal record	If bonding is a job requirement ask if applicant is eligible	Inquiries about criminal record/convictions—even those which have been pardoned are discouraged unless related to job duties
References			The same restrictions that apply to questions asked of applicants apply when asking for employment references

Source: Canadian Human Rights Commission, *A Guide to Screening and Selection in Employment* (Ottawa: Minister of Supply and Services Canada, 1985). Reproduced with permission.

DISCUSSION AND REVIEW QUESTIONS

1. Describe the different forms of employment discrimination.
2. What role does the Canadian Charter of Rights and Freedoms play in protecting human rights in the workplace?
3. Which employees are protected by human rights legislation?
4. Why are employers prevented from asking certain questions during preemployment that they may ask after the employee is hired?
5. How are human rights complaints processed in most Canadian jurisdictions?
6. What role do the courts play in human rights complaints?
7. What is systemic discrimination? Describe three sources of systemic discrimination.
8. When is a company policy or practice a "bona fide occupational qualification (or requirement)"?

9. When does an employer have a "duty to accommodate" an employee or job applicant?
10. What actions should be taken to minimize sexual harassment in the workplace?
11. What are the basic steps in employment equity programs?
12. How do utilization analysis results differ when company flow data are used rather than stock data?
13. When should "special programs" be introduced as part of the company's employment equity program?

NOTES AND REFERENCES

1. *Re Bhinder et al. and Canadian National Railway Co.* (1986) 23 DLR (4th) 481.
2. Royal Commission on Equality in Employment (Abella Commission), *Equality in Employment* (Ottawa: Minister of Supply and Services Canada, 1984), p. 7.
3. Abella, *Equality in Employment*, pp. 24–32; Pat Armstrong and Hugh Armstrong, *The Double Ghetto: Canadian Women and Their Segregated Work* (Toronto: McClelland and Stewart, 1979); Pat Armstrong and Hugh Armstrong, *A Working Majority: What Women Must Do for Pay* (Ottawa: Information Canada, 1983).
4. Harish Jain and Peter Sloane, *Equal Employment Issues* (New York: Praeger Publishers, 1981).
5. Special Committee on Visible Minorities in Canadian Society (Daudlin Committee), *Equality Now* (Ottawa: Minister of Supply and Services Canada, 1984); Abella, *Equality in Employment*, pp. 33–38, 46–51.
6. Frances Henry and Effie Ginzberg, *Who Gets the Work? A Test of Racial Discrimination in Employment* (Toronto: Social Planning Council of Metropolitan Toronto and Urban Alliance on Race Relations, 1985). Another Canadian study of white and visible minority MBA graduates also illustrates differences in occupational attainment. See Elia Zureik, *The Experience of Visible Minorities in the Work World: The Case of MBA Graduates* (Toronto: Ontario Human Rights Commission, 1983).
7. Special Committee on the Disabled and the Handicapped, *Obstacles* (Ottawa: Minister of Supply and Services Canada, 1981).
8. Marcia H. Rioux, "Labelled Disabled and Wanting to Work," in *Research Studies of the Royal Commission on Equality in Employment* (Ottawa: Minister of Supply and Services Canada, 1985), pp. 613–39.
9. *The Constitution Act 1982* C. 11 (U.K.). Section 15 came into effect after April 17, 1985.
10. For a discussion of the Charter and its impact on P/HRM, see Abella, *Equality in Employment*, pp. 11–16; Marc Gold, "The Constitutional Dimensions of Promoting Equality in Employment," in *Research Studies of the Royal Commission on Equality in Employment* (Ottawa: Minister of Supply and Services Canada, 1985), pp. 249–73; Katherine Swinton, "Restraints on Government Efforts to Promote Equality in Employment: Labour Relations and Constitutional Considerations," in *Research Studies of the Royal Commission on Equality in Employment* (Ottawa: Minister of Supply and Services Canada, 1985), pp. 275–96.

11. I. A. Hunter, "Human Rights Legislation in Canada: Its Origin, Development, and Interpretation," *University of Western Ontario Law Review* 21 (1976), p. 25.
12. Abella, *Equality in Employment*, p. 239.
13. Canadian Human Rights Commission, *1985 Annual Report* (Ottawa: Minister of Supply and Services, 1986).
14. British Columbia Council of Human Rights, *1984–1985 Annual Report* (Victoria: Queen's Printer, 1986).
15. For example, see *Britnell v. Brent Personnel Services*, Ontario Board of Inquiry, unreported, June 7, 1962; cited in William Black, "From Intent to Effect: New Standards in Human Rights," *Canadian Human Rights Reporter* (CHRR), 1 (February 1980), pp. C1–C5.
16. Black, "From Intent to Effect," pp. C2–C3.
17. *Griggs v. Duke Power Co.*, 401 U.S. 424, 1971.
18. For example, see *Attorney-General for Alberta v. Gares*, (1976) 67 DLR (3rd) 635.
19. *Singh v. Security and Investigation Services Ltd.*, Ontario Board of Inquiry, unreported, May 31, 1977.
20. Many of these cases are listed in Aidan Vining, David McPhillips, and Anthony Boardman, "Use of Statistical Evidence in Employment Discrimination Litigation in Canada," *Canadian Bar Review* 64 (December 1986), pp. 660–702. A lower court in the O'Malley case discarded the adverse effect principle in 1982 based on the language of the Ontario statute. However, this was overturned by the Supreme Court of Canada. See *Re Ontario Human Rights Commission et al. and Simpsons-Sears Ltd.* (O'Malley case), (1986) 23 DLR (4th) 321.
21. In several Canadian jurisdictions, the term used is *bona fide occupational requirement* (BFOR) rather than BFOQ. Tribunals and courts appear to give these terms the same meaning. See *City of Winnipeg et al. v. Ogelski et al.* (1986) 6 WWR 289; Patricia Hughes, "Discrimination and Related Concepts," in *Research Studies of the Royal Commission on Equality in Employment* (Ottawa: Minister of Supply and Services Canada, 1985), p. 229.
22. *Ontario Human Rights Commission v. Borough of Etobicoke* (1982), 132 DLR (3d) 14, pp. 19–29.
23. *Re Bhinder et al. and Canadian National Railway Co.*, p. 500.
24. *Michael Nowell v. Canadian National Railway Ltd.*, Canadian Human Rights Tribunal Decision, unreported, November 27, 1986. CN has appealed this decision to a review tribunal.
25. *Brideau v. Air Canada* (1983) 4 CHRR 267.
26. Patricia Hughes, "Discrimination and Related Concepts," pp. 233–34.
27. Some authorities claim the duty to accommodate arises when a BFOQ has not been established (e.g., *Central Alberta Dairy Pool v. Alberta Human Rights Commission* [1986] 5 WWR 35). Others suggest reasonable accommodation is considered after a BFOQ has been established (e.g., Patricia Hughes, "Discrimination and Related Concepts," p. 238). The Supreme Court addressed the reasonable accommodation issue in the *Bhinder* case, but the opinion of the minority and the majority differed on its relationship with BFOQ.
28. *Central Alberta Dairy Pool v. Alberta Human Rights Commission* (1986) 5 WWR 35.
29. *Re Ontario Human Rights Commission et al. and Simpsons-Sears Ltd.* (O'Malley case), (1986) 23 DLR (4th) 321.

30. R. Menchel and A. Ritter, "Keep Deaf Workers Safe," *Personnel Journal* 63 (1984), pp. 49–51; M. Jailer, "Accommodating the Handicapped in the Office," *Administrative Management* 39 (1978), pp. 81–83; S. Jarvis, "For Employers of Handicapped Workers: Obligations and Ideas," *Personnel* 62, no. 7 (1985), pp. 42–44; M. Nester, "Employment Testing for Handicapped Persons," *Public Personnel Management* 60 (1985), pp. 417–54.
31. *White v. Liquor Control Board of Ontario* (1985) 7 CHHR.
32. Morley Gunderson, "Labour Market Aspects of Inequality in Employment and Their Application to Crown Corporations," in *Research Studies of the Royal Commission on Equality in Employment* (Ottawa: Minister of Supply and Services Canada, 1985), pp. 17–18. Regarding child care, also see: Abella, *Equality in Employment*, chap. 5.
33. One Canadian study suggests that half of the women surveyed experienced unwanted sexual attention. Canadian Human Rights Commission, *Unwanted Sexual Attention and Sexual Harassment: Results of a Survey of Canadians* (Ottawa: CHRC, 1983).
34. Harish C. Jain and P. Andiappan, "Sexual Harassment in Employment in Canada," *Relations Industrielles* 41, no. 4 (1986), pp. 758–76.
35. Canadian Human Rights Commission, *What Is Harassment?* (Ottawa: CHRC, 1984).
36. Labour Canada, Women's Bureau, *1984 Canadian Women and Job Related Laws* (Ottawa: Minister of Supply and Services Canada, 1985), p. 21. One of the earliest cases to identify sexual harassment as a form of sex discrimination is *Cherie Bell and Ann Korczak v. Ernest Ladas and the Flaming Steak House Tavern* (1980) 1 CHRR 1383.
37. Canadian Human Rights Commission, *Harassment: Commission Policy* (Ottawa: CHRC, 1985). Also see Constance Backhouse and Leah Cohen, *The Secret Oppression: Sexual Harassment of Working Women* (Toronto: Macmillan of Canada, 1979).
38. Jain and Andiappan, "Sexual Harassment in Employment in Canada."
39. *Janzen and Govereau v. Platy et al.* (1987) 1 WWR 385.
40. "Sexual Harassment in the Workplace—A Social Problem," *Women's Bureau Newsletter* (Ontario Ministry of Labour) 6, no. 2 (August 1981); *Jane Kotyk and Barbara Allary v. Canadian Employment and Immigration Commission and Jack Chuba* (1983) 4 CHRR 12156.
41. *Rodney Romman v. Sea-West Holdings Ltd.* (1984) 5 CHRR 19489.
42. For a summary of several representative cases in the federal jurisdiction see Canadian Human Rights Commission, *Sexual Harassment Casebook, 1978–1984* (Ottawa: CHRC, 1984).
43. *Rosanne Torres v. Royalty Kitchenware Ltd. and Francesco Guercio* (1982) 3 CHRR 176.
44. "Sexual Harassment in the Workplace," p. 3; Jain and Andiappan, p. 774; G. E. Biles, "A Program Guide for Preventing Sexual Harassment in the Workplace," *Personnel Administrator* 26 (1981), pp. 49–56.
45. Special Senate Committee on Retirement Age Policies (Croll Committee), *Submission from the Royal Bank of Canada to the Senate Committee on Retirement Age Policies*, December 7, 1978.
46. Canada Pension Plan Advisory Committee, *Retirement Ages: A Report to the Minister of National Health and Welfare* (Ottawa: CPPAC, 1980).

47. Margaret Polanyi, "Mandatory Retirement: Graceful Exit or Painful Deprivation?" *The Globe and Mail*, March 12, 1986, p. A3; Virginia Galt, "65 Arouses Concern," *The Globe and Mail*, September 30, 1985, pp. B1, B11; Ray Whitney, "Mandatory Retirement: Can Companies Cope if It's Abolished?" *Executive*, April 1983, pp. 40–44.
48. Special Senate Committee on Retirement Age Policies (Croll Committee), *Retirement without Tears* (Ottawa: Minister of Supply and Services, 1979); Parliamentary Committee on Equality (Boyer Committee), *Equality for All* (Ottawa: Minister of Supply and Services, 1985).
49. *City of Winnipeg et al.* v. *Ogelski et al.* (1986) 6 WWR 289; *McIntire* v. *University of Manitoba* (1981) 1 WWR 696.
50. *Craig and Saskatchewan Human Rights Commission* v. *City of Saskatoon et al.* (1985) CLLR 17004.
51. *Harrison* v. *University of B.C.* (1986) 6 WWR 7; Thomas Claridge, "Universities' Retirement Policies Not Bound by Charter, Court Says," *The Globe and Mail*, October 17, 1986, pp. A1, A2.
52. Abella, *Equality in Employment*, p. 193.
53. Lance W. Roberts, "Understanding Affirmative Action," in *Discrimination, Affirmative Action, and Equal Opportunity* (Vancouver: Fraser Institute, 1982); Joan Wallace, "Affirmative Action Isn't Anything New," *Vancouver Sun*, July 13, 1985, p. A6; Susan Semenak, "In Pursuit of Equality," *Montreal Gazette*, March 22, 1985, pp. D1, D3.
54. "What Some Firms Are Doing," *Financial Post*, September 8, 1984, p. 18.
55. Nancy Handisyde, *Affirmative Action—One Company's Way*, Warner-Lambert unpublished mimeo, March 1984.
56. Jackie Smith, "Affirmative Action Facts Misleading?" *Toronto Star*, November 19, 1984, p. B1.
57. For a discussion of mandatory programs, quotas, and related issues, see Lance W. Roberts, "Understanding Affirmative Action,"; Conrad Winn, "Affirmative Action and Visible Minorities: Eight Premises in Quest of Evidence," *Canadian Public Policy* 11, no. 4 (1985), pp. 684–700; Conrad Winn, "Affirmative Action for Women: More Than a Case of Simple Justice," *Canadian Public Administration*, Spring 1985, pp. 24–46; Arthur Schafer, "Racial Quotas in Job World May Be Remedy for Canada," *The Globe and Mail*, June 4, 1984, p. 7; P. K. Kuruvilla, "A Fair Chance," *Policy Options*, March 1985, pp. 35–36.
58. *Actions Travail des Femmes* v. *Canadian National* (1984) 5 CHRR D/2327; Ann Rauhala, "Court Backs Order Imposing Job Quota," *The Globe and Mail*, June 27, 1987, pp. A1, A2.
59. Abella, *Equality in Employment*. Although the report's recommendations extend to all businesses in the federal sector as well as federal contractors, the original mandate of the commission was limited to inquiring into the employment opportunities of designated groups in Crown corporations of the federal government.
60. Ann Rauhala, "Toe Line on Job Equity, Ottawa Says," *The Globe and Mail*, February 17, 1987, pp. 1–2.
61. The material in this section is drawn from D. Rhys Phillips, "Equity in the Labour Market: The Potential of Affirmative Action," in *Research Studies of the Commission on Equality in Employment* (Ottawa: Minister of Supply and Services Canada, 1985), pp. 51–111; Employment and Immigration Canada, Consultative Services, Employment Equity Branch, "Employment Equity: A Guide for

Employers," in *Employment Equity Act and Reporting Requirements* (Ottawa: Minister of Supply and Services Canada, 1986); Treasury Board of Canada Secretariat, Human Resources Division, Personnel Policy Branch, *Employment Equity for Crown Corporations: Policy and Reference Guide* (Ottawa: Minister of Supply and Services Canada, 1986).
62. Ruth Gilbert Shaeffer and Edith F. Lynton, *Corporate Experience in Improving Women's Job Opportunities* (Toronto: Conference Board of Canada, 1979).
63. Phillips, "Equity in the Labour Market," p. 69.
64. Royson James, "Scarborough Staff Mainly White Male, 1-Year Study Says," *Toronto Star*, March 24, 1986, p. A6.
65. Peter Silverman, "Hire Handicapped for Ability, Not Disability," *Financial Post*, June 20, 1981, p. 24; "Minority Groups Are Made to Feel Right at Home," *Calgary Herald*, February 17, 1985, p. A8.
66. Phillips, "Equity in the Labour Market," p. 70; Employment and Immigration Canada, "Employment Equity: A Guide for Employers," pp. 16–17.
67. Joan Wallace, "Affirmative Action Falls off the Shelf," *Executive*, October 1985, p. 34.
68. Employment and Immigration Canada, "Employment Equity: A Guide for Employers," pp. 19–20.
69. City of Vancouver, *Equal Employment Opportunity Program* (progress report prepared by Reva Dexter), August 1982.
70. Phillips, "Equity in the Labour Market," pp. 73–76. Although Phillips describes this weighting system as part of utilization analysis, it is specifically relevant to estimating work force availability. For additional suggestions on availability analysis see Edward B. Harvey and John H. Blakely, "Strategies for Establishing Affirmative Action Goals and Timetables," in *Research Studies of the Commission on Equality in Employment* (Ottawa: Minister of Supply and Services Canada, 1985), pp. 115–29.
71. Steven F. Cronshaw, "The Status of Employment Testing in Canada: A Review and Evaluation of Theory and Professional Practice," *Canadian Psychology* 27, no. 2 (1986), pp. 183–95.
72. Treasury Board of Canada Secretariat, Human Resources Division, Personnel Policy Branch, *Employment Equity for Crown Corporations*, p. 11.
73. *Saskatchewan Government Insurance Corporation et al.* (1984) 5 CHHR D/2059.
74. Carol Agocs, "Affirmative Action, Canadian Style: A Reconnaissance," *Canadian Public Policy* 12, no. 1 (1986), pp. 148–62; Jackie Smith, "Affirmative Action Facts Misleading?"
75. Treasury Board of Canada Secretariat, Human Resources Division, Personnel Policy Branch, *Employment Equity for Crown Corporations*, p. 5; Employment and Immigration Canada, "Glossary," in *Employment Equity Act and Reporting Requirements*, p. 5.
76. Val Werier, "Affirmative Action Needed for Minorities," *Winnipeg Free Press*, October 13, 1984, p. 6.
77. *Saskatchewan Government Insurance Corporation et al.* (1984) 5 CHHR D/2059.
78. Employment and Immigration Canada, "Employment Equity: A Guide for Employers," p. 12.
79. Cronshaw, "The Status of Employment Testing in Canada," pp. 187–89.
80. "Tests Used for Hiring," *Financial Post*, November 21, 1981.
81. Jackie Smith, "Affirmative Action that Works," *Toronto Star*, November 20, 1984,

pp. B1, B2. Also see Judy Erola, "Affirmative Action: Prescription for Equality," *Business Quarterly*, Spring 1984, pp. 101–5.
82. "What Some Firms Are Doing," *Financial Post*, September 8, 1984, p. 18. The powerful effect of corporate culture is also apparent in the case *Actions Travail des Femmes* v. *Canadian National* (1984) 5 CHRR D/2327. Numerous discriminatory actions were reported in that case, most perpetrated by line managers, even though CN had introduced an employment equity program a few years earlier.
83. Phillips, "Equity in the Labour Market," pp. 78–79.
84. Canadian Human Rights Commission, *Criteria for Compliance with Section 15 of the Canadian Human Rights Act as Applied to Employment Systems*, mimeo, undated; Employment and Immigration Canada, "Employment Equity: A Guide for Employers," p. 12; Phillips, "Equity in the Labour Market," pp. 78–79.
85. "Tests Used for Hiring," *Financial Post*, November 21, 1981.

CHAPTER EIGHT
RECRUITING AND JOB SEARCH

CHAPTER OUTLINE

I. Introduction
    A. Recruitment Process—Components
    B. Dual Responsibility for Recruiting
    C. The Recruiter
II. A Diagnostic Approach to Recruiting
    A. Recruitment Planning
    B. External Influences
    C. Organization Influences
    D. Individual Candidate's Preferences
    E. Employer–Applicant Matching
III. Sources and Methods
    A. Internal Recruiting
    B. External Recruiting
    C. Locating Other External Candidates
IV. Evaluating Recruiting Programs
    A. Recruiting Costs and Benefits
V. Realism or Flypaper?
    A. Realistic Job Previews
VI. The Potential Employee's View of Recruiting
    A. Occupational Choice
    B. Organizational Choice
VII. Summary
    Appendix / How to Get a Job

INTRODUCTION

Early every spring, placement offices at colleges and universities become the campus busy spots. Students and recruiters come and go. Student résumés and company annual reports are studied, and interviews are scheduled. *Dress for Success* and *The Woman's Dress for Success Book*[1] become the order of the day. Gone are running shoes, blue jeans, unpressed shirts, and casual blouses. Some students even take to carrying a copy of *The Financial Post* or *Canadian Business* around campus. Others find that all copies of *The 100 Best Companies to Work for in Canada* have been checked out of the library.

The campus employment centre and placement office illustrates a labour market. Exchanges occur between buyers (employers) and sellers (students), and elaborate mechanisms have been developed to facilitate and regulate the exchange. Students may be required to bid for interviews with an allocated number of interview points assigned by the placement centre. Various bidding strategies soon become evident. Some students may bid all their allotted points to ensure an interview with a highly desired firm. Other students, trying to bypass the process, call the employer directly in an attempt to save points and schedule an off-campus interview.

Both employers and prospective employees (students) face several important issues. For the organization, recruiting decisions involve where to find candidates (sources), how to recruit them (methods), and how to judge the results (evaluation). Students must decide which firms to interview with, how to market themselves, and so on. The job the student accepts will define earnings and social status and become a major source of self-identity and satisfaction or dissatisfaction in his or her life. For the employer, recruiting represents a stream of new blood, new ideas, and new talent. Imperfect as the system is, it is very important to all participants.

Definition

Recruitment is the process through which the organization informs, searches for, and attracts a sufficient flow or pool of applicants with the necessary abilities, attitudes, and motivation to offset shortages identified in human resource planning.

Subsequent human resource activities will be less effective if qualified employees have not been recruited. P/HRM managers rate recruiting as one of their most important functions. "When we remember that individuals brought into a company today may still be working there in 30 years or more and that among today's new recruits is probably at least one future company president, we can get some idea of the importance of the whole process."[2]

One approach to recruiting employees, the prospecting theory, views the employer as a prospector searching for potentially qualified applicants. However, this view of recruitment as a one-way process is limited. In practice, job searchers seek organizations they have identified as good employers, just as organizations search for qualified applicants. This mating approach is more realistic.

Recruitment Process—Components

Recruiting means attracting and screening candidates; it also serves as an important public relations function on behalf of the organization. The recruitment process involves a series of key contact points between the organization and its environment. As shown in Exhibit 8–1, recruitment activities are comprised of a number of components. Basically, employment planning identifies the employee shortage by providing a clear specification of human resource needs (e.g., numbers, experience and skill mix, levels, race/gender composition) and the time frame by which the various requirements should be met. In summary, these are the "how many, of what type, where in the organization, by when" specifications. Recruitment planning follows, along with a diagnostic approach to assessing relevant external and internal conditions. Next, the design of the recruitment program requires three basic decisions: where to search (sources), how to attract qualified people to apply (methods), and how to judge the results (evaluation).

Recruiters influence the size and quality of the applicant pool by making people aware of job openings and enticing them to apply. After establishing the applicant pool, recruiters sift out those applicants who are clearly unqualified or who are not a good match with the organization. In rejection letters, organizations typically tell recipients how wonderful the applicant pool was and wish them success in their future endeavours.

With the pool of potentially qualified applicants established, the selection process determines the subgroup to which job offers are extended. Recruiters try to persuade successful applicants to accept the offers extended. Before reporting for work, the recruit may be contacted by the prospective supervisor. This postacceptance contact is intended to maintain a link with the recruit and serves a useful pre-employment socialization function (Chapter Ten). Judgement of the recruiting effort is initiated when data on the number of job offers and acceptances are available.

Along with applicants, important participants in the recruitment process are operating managers, P/HRM managers, and the recruiter.

EXHIBIT 8–1
Components of the Recruitment Process

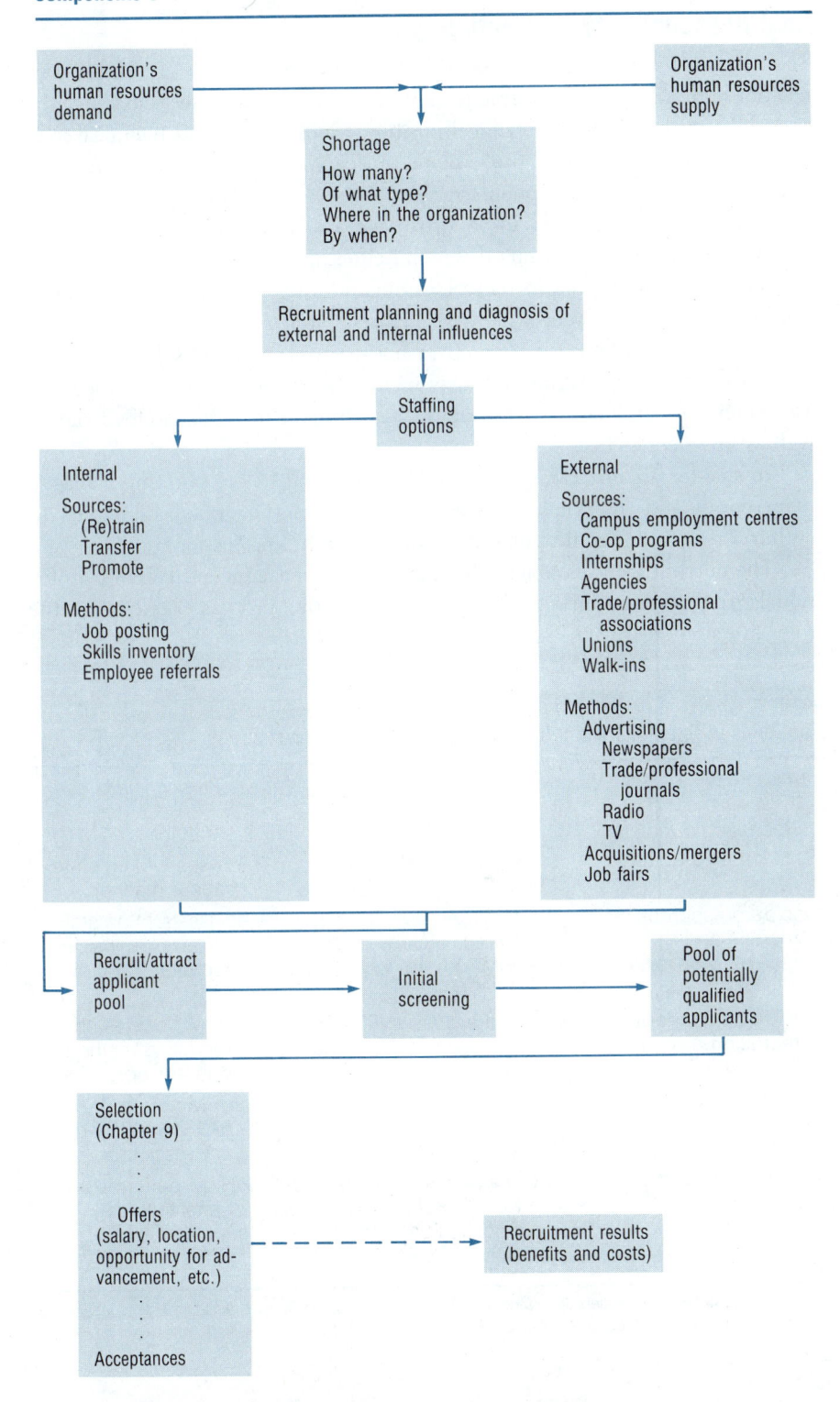

```
Organization's                                          Organization's
human resources ──────────►   ◄────────── human resources
demand                                                  supply
                            │
                            ▼
                    Shortage
                    How many?
                    Of what type?
                    Where in the organization?
                    By when?
                            │
                            ▼
                Recruitment planning and diagnosis of
                external and internal influences
                            │
                            ▼
                    Staffing
                    options
                  ┌─────┴─────┐
                  ▼           ▼
```

Internal

Sources:
   (Re)train
   Transfer
   Promote

Methods:
   Job posting
   Skills inventory
   Employee referrals

External

Sources:
   Campus employment centres
   Co-op programs
   Internships
   Agencies
   Trade/professional
      associations
   Unions
   Walk-ins

Methods:
   Advertising
      Newspapers
      Trade/professional
         journals
      Radio
      TV
   Acquisitions/mergers
   Job fairs

```
Recruit/attract      Initial          Pool of
applicant    ─────►  screening ─────► potentially
pool                                  qualified
                                      applicants
    │
    ▼
```

Selection
(Chapter 9)
 .
 .
 .
Offers
(salary, location,
opportunity for ad-   ─ ─ ─ ─ ─► Recruitment results
vancement, etc.)   (benefits and costs)
 .
 .
 .
Acceptances

Dual Responsibility for Recruiting

The responsibility to recruit does not rest with one position. In larger organizations, the P/HRM department may be staffed by specialists in recruiting and interviewing. But for technical positions, most firms send technical managers as well as personnel professionals to campuses or locations where recruitment interviews have been arranged. For example, an employer in Montreal may find it necessary to advertise nationally, identify several pools of potentially qualified applicants in several cities, prescreen résumés, and then conduct initial interviews in these locations on a two-on-one basis. Organizations can also engage recruitment specialists, often referred to as "headhunters." These consultants' services cover both recruitment and selection testing activities in various locations and may include videotaping interviews for later assessment of candidates by the employer's human resource professionals as well as line managers.

In smaller organizations, either P/HRM generalists or operating managers may recruit and interview applicants. Sometimes the organization puts together a recruiting team of operating and personnel professionals.

The current trend is to have both operating managers and P/HRM professionals participate in various phases of the recruiting process. Their respective roles are summarized in Exhibit 8–2.

EXHIBIT 8–2
The Roles of Operating and P/HRM Managers in Recruitment

Recruiting Function	Operating Manager (OM)	Personnel/Human Resource Manager (P/HRM)
Set recruiting goals	Set by OM with advice of P/HRM	Advises OM on state of labour market
Decide on sources of recruits and recruiting policies	Policy decision, outside versus inside, set by OM with advice of P/HRM	Advises OM on status of possible inside recruits
Decide on methods of recruiting	OM advises P/HRM on methods of recruiting	P/HRM decides on recruiting methods with advice of OM
College/university recruiting	OM occasionally recruits at colleges/universities	P/HRM normally recruits at colleges/universities
Cost/benefit studies of recruiting	OM evaluates results of cost/benefit studies and decides accuracy	P/HRM performs cost/benefit studies

Source: Adapted from John M. Ivancevich and William F. Glueck, *Foundations of Personnel/Human Resource Management*, 3rd ed. (Plano, Tex.: Business Publications, 1986).

The Recruiter

The recruiter is usually the first person from the organization applicants meet, and applicants' impressions of the entire organization are based in large part on their encounter with the recruiter.[3] Therefore, the recruiter should be thoroughly familiar with the entire organization, the relationship between various departments, and the specifications of the jobs to be filled in order to convey an accurate impression to applicants.

From the perspective of college and university students, successful recruiters are enthusiastic, convey an interest in the applicant, avoid too-personal questions and deliberate creation of stress, and use interview time well; that is, they allow ample time to answer questions or explore applicants' interests. They are familiar with the potential job and with the information on the candidate's résumé. From an organization's perspective, a successful recruiter accurately represents the organization, kindles applicant enthusiasm, and is sensitive to the possibility of unconscious bias in evaluating recruits.[4]

A DIAGNOSTIC APPROACH TO RECRUITING

In the diagnostic approach, the design of an effective recruiting process depends on a number of factors. Of primary concern are recruitment planning, effects of external and organizational influences, consideration of candidates' preferences, and employer-applicant matching.

Recruitment Planning

During employment planning (Chapter Six), the number and mix of qualifications of employees required to achieve organization objectives are determined. To project a realistic timetable for reaching the desired staffing level, both external and internal work force composition and readiness (for promotion or transfer) need to be considered. Also of relevance are the setting of employment equity goals and timetables.

Primed with a comprehensive human resource plan for the various segments of its work force, the employer's recruitment planning can utilize three key parameters: the time, the money, and the recruiting staff necessary to achieve a given hiring rate.[5] The main statistic needed to estimate these parameters is the number of leads required "to generate a given number of hires in a given time."[6] This can be derived on the basis of prior recruitment experience if accurate records have been maintained. If current labour market conditions are comparable, yield ratios and time-lapse data (illustrated below) may be determined. Even if no experience data exist, some "best guesses" or hypotheses can be established and progress monitored as the operational recruitment program unfolds.[7]

326 Human Resource Activities: Staffing

Suppose CanEng Consultants is planning to open two new offices and needs 50 additional engineers in the next six months. Based on past expansions involving engineering recruitments, the company is able to collate the following data: the offer-to-acceptance ratio is 2:1 (two offers must be extended to gain one acceptance); the interviews-to-offer ratio is 3:2 (of three candidates interviewed, two are made offers); the invites-to-interview ratio is 4:3 (of four invited for job interviews, three candidates present themselves); leads required to find suitable candidates to invite for interviews are in a 5:1 proportion. These data can be arranged to form a recruiting yield pyramid (shown in Exhibit 8-3).[8] *Yield ratios* are the ratios of leads (résumés) to invites, invites to interviews, interviews (and other selection instruments) to job offers, and offers to hires over some specified period. The total number of leads required is 1,000 (i.e., 50 times the product of the yield ratios).

Additional information required can be derived from time-lapse data, which indicate the average intervals between events. For CanEng Consultants, past data show the interval from receipt of a résumé to invitation (for a job interview) averages five days. If still interested, the candidate will be interviewed five days later. Records also show job offers, on average, are extended three days after interviews, the candidate accepts or rejects the offer within seven days, and, if he or she accepts, reports to work three weeks from the date of acceptance. These time-lapse data make for a "recruitment pipeline" of 41 days. If CanEng receives the first résumé today, the best estimate is it will take 41 days before the first new engineer is added to the payroll. The "length" of the pipeline also suggests the 1,000th résumé should be received not later than 41 days *before* the target date of six months.

This type of information can then be integrated into staffing graphs or weekly activity charts, showing at each point in time the production of leads,

EXHIBIT 8-3
Recruiting Yield Pyramid—Engineering Personnel, CanEng Consultants

			Yield ratio
Hires	50		
Offers	100	Offers/Hires	2:1
Interviews	150	Interviews/Offers	3:2
Invites	200	Invites/Interviews	4:3
Leads	1,000	Leads/Invites	5:1

EXHIBIT 8–4
Staffing Graph—CanEng Engineering Personnel Recruitment

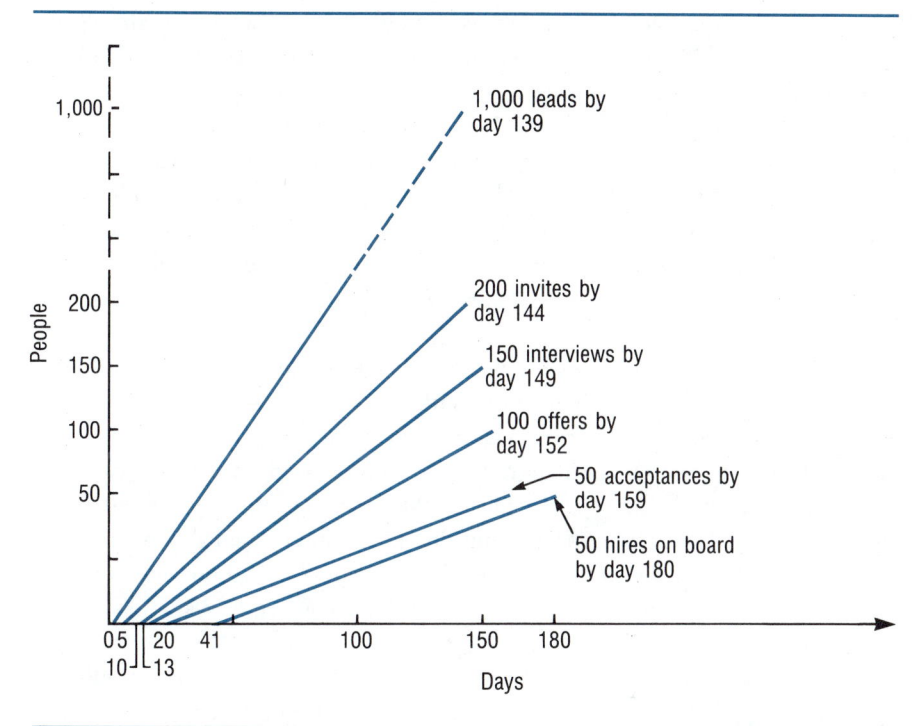

invitations, interviews, offers, and acceptances. The six-month staffing graph for the CanEng data is presented in Exhibit 8–4. Complementary data would include the relative yield of internal versus external sources of applicants at each stage of the process.

Obviously, yield ratios and time-lapse data are a function of the job group being recruited and of the extent to which labour market conditions during recruiting are comparable to those prevailing at the time of data collection.

External Influences

External factors include not only the supply and demand for labour in the external market, but also government and union restrictions.

Labour Market Conditions. Conditions in the labour market are a major factor in the design of the recruiting process.[9] If there is an abundant supply of the skills being sought, informal recruiting will probably attract plenty of applicants. But during periods of full employment, more elaborate and prolonged recruiting may be necessary to attract promising applicants.

Classical economic theory views wage differences as the principal mechanism for the allocation of labour. Jobs for which there is an abundant supply of skilled labour attract many applicants, holding down wages for those jobs. Jobs requiring skills that are less common or that require long periods to gain the necessary training and experience need to pay relatively higher wages to attract sufficient people.[10]

In addition to wages, other factors, such as job security, location, the challenge of the job, time required for training, and skill transferability influence labour force behaviour. Economists combine all these factors into one concept, the "net advantage" of one job over another. People tend to choose the employer and job with the greatest "net advantage" for their own circumstances.[11]

In addition to differences in "net advantage" among jobs and employers, there are also differences in labour markets. As discussed in Chapter Two, some markets are national, regional, or local; some vary by occupation (engineers, teachers, crafts).[12] Further, labour market conditions vary over time. They fluctuate with the overall state of the economy (unemployment rates), societal expectations (women entering the labour force), and demographics.[13]

The point of all this is that the demand and supply of labour are extremely dynamic and are significant factors that influence recruiting in the external labour market.

Government and Union Measures. Laws and regulations, specifically employment equity laws, are another environmental factor that must be considered when designing recruiting programs.[14] Government agencies may review the recruitment sources, advertising, and applicant data to determine an organization's compliance. Recruiting plays a key role in employment equity programs. *Qualified* minorities and women not well represented in the present work force may need to be sought and encouraged to apply, perhaps through special outreach programs that advertise openings more widely and create awareness that the employer has made a commitment to employment equity. For example, CN Rail's management hires about 150 university graduates every year. Part of the company's employment equity target is that 50 percent of the graduates hired be women.[15] A somewhat different approach is followed by an employer in Western Canada. Its recruitment plan envisions hiring female engineers in proportion to their representation in the graduating engineering classes of the applied science programs this organization has traditionally recruited from.[16]

Another federal government measure is the JOBSCAN project, introduced in Chapter Two.[17] The objective of JOBSCAN is to provide an effective computer-assisted job-worker matching system. Its task includes determining the factors that are significant for placement in any given industry or groups of jobs and determining a method to profile all a worker is able and willing to do. The associated database consists of significant placement variables (SPVs), which are defined in terms of specific information an employer can use in making placement decisions. JOBSCAN's configuration allows for appropriate consideration of different tiers of the labour market.

As pointed out in Chapter Seven, human rights regulations also affect the behaviour of recruiters in interviews. The wise recruiter is careful not to probe into "prohibited grounds of discrimination" items (see the Appendix in Chapter Seven).

Obviously, government measures can affect who is recruited, how, and even where. In addition, some union contracts, particularly those in the construction and maritime industries, restrict recruiting to union hiring halls, turning the recruiting function for unionized employees over to the union.

Organization Influences

The decision to recruit springs from the objectives of the organization and the nature of the work. Employment planning translates these objectives into human resource requirements. Management must decide whether to fill these requirements by recruiting or use other options such as subcontracting, offering overtime to current employees, or redesigning the work.[18]

Once a decision to recruit is made, the human resource requirements drive the system. The qualifications desired help define who is to be recruited and where. Information regarding the specific qualifications is obtained from job analysis information, including job descriptions and job specifications (Chapter Four). Job information serves a very basic function in recruiting by defining the tasks, responsibilities, and job activities the successful applicant must do when hired. This information also serves as the guide for selecting an applicant, so it must be accurate, complete, and up-to-date. The designer of an effective recruiting program must make certain the qualifications sought are necessary. For example, if specifications for a custodian's job call for a Grade 12 diploma, it must be shown that this level of education is necessary to perform the work. If it is not demonstrably work-related, not only is the requirement not legal, but it also may affect the sources used for job applicants.

Organization Strategy and Recruiting

Organizations that wish to maximize their recruiting effectiveness often look beyond their immediate job requirements. Hiring standards and requirements may also reflect the organization's long-term goals. Using Miles and Snow's three categories of organization strategies, discussed in Chapter

Three, Olian and Rynes postulate that organizations with different business strategies need to recruit different types of people for their executives and managers.[19] Thus, a *defender* organization operating in a narrow, relatively stable market will seek people with backgrounds in finance or production. *Prospectors* exploiting new products or markets will look for people with basic engineering research or marketing skills. And *analyzers* operating in mixed markets will look for individuals with abilities in applied research, marketing, and production. Further, for employees outside these main functional areas, Olian and Rynes hypothesize that these characteristics will still be favoured. In other words, a defender organization hiring a human resource manager prefers one with some knowledge of finance or production. All else being equal, a prospector organization may favour P/HRM specialists with knowledge or experience in marketing. According to prospectors, recruiting employees with these backgrounds creates a body of common knowledge in the organization that encourages communication and cooperation among functions.

Not only will organization strategy affect the skills an organization seeks, but it may also affect the attitudes and personality traits deemed likeliest to match the organization culture.[20] For example, individuals with high needs for security and structure or low tolerance for change and ambiguity seem well suited to defender organizations. Independent, creative thinkers who are risk takers will be better matched to prospector organizations. Thus, employers' preferences may extend beyond the basic skills required to do a job. At the same time, however, the company must be sure its selection requirements are job-related and consistent with the strategies and culture of the organization. Specifying such requirements is often difficult, leaving much to the judgement of recruiters and managers who make the hiring decisions. Olian and Rynes caution that their propositions are speculative. They rest on the assumptions that staffing decisions are consistent with one another and consistent with the strategic direction of the firm.

Specifying Criteria and Employment Equity Issues

Specifying the criteria to be used for considering candidates presents a dilemma for managers. If criteria are too high, the number of applicants may be insufficient. Potential applicants may complain to human rights agencies that the standards are unnecessarily stringent and not job-related. But if criteria are too low, processing costs for a flood of applicants will be high, and there may be no increase in applicant quality. Further, the race and sex characteristics of the applicant pool in a given area may become the availability standard for employment equity performance, even though the pool is too encompassing. Unfortunately, there is little research to help resolve this dilemma.

Individual Candidate's Preferences

Accurate communication of job specifications and organization's strategies and objectives helps applicants.[21] If a candidate has a clear idea of the requirements of the job, the rewards the job offers, as well as where the organization is headed, then a more accurate assessment can be made as to whether the job offers a good match with personal needs and abilities.[22] Determination of interest on the part of the candidate is called self-selection.[23]

Employer–Applicant Matching

Exhibit 8–5 diagrams some details of effective recruiting (omitted in Exhibit 8–1 for the sake of clarity): an organization with unique characteristics seeks a job applicant possessing certain qualifications and offers certain rewards. The recruit has abilities and interests to offer and is looking for a kind of job that meets some expectations. The expectations on both sides are tempered by the external environment. A match is made when sufficient overlap exists between the expectations of the employer and the recruit.[24] The recruiting process usually requires some modifications and compromises on both sides in response to interactions between job seekers and organizations.

Recruitment planning and diagnosing external and internal influences are followed by decisions on the sources and methods to be utilized.

SOURCES AND METHODS

Two basic sources of applicants exist: internal (current employees) and external (those not affiliated with the organization). Whether an employer elects to look inside or outside for applicants depends on many factors, including what qualified people are available in both sources, the economic conditions and plans of the organization (growth, steady state, or decline), how quickly the vacancy needs to be filled, its employment equity condition, and relative costs. All firms must recruit externally for some of their human resources. Typical entry-level jobs include clerks/typists, management trainees, operatives, or sales or service personnel. Larger organizations are more likely to use internal sources to fill higher-level positions, since training and career development programs are designed to create a pool of qualified resources.[25] Recruiting primarily from internal sources is believed to enhance employee motivation and work behaviours.[26]

Often the organization's needs dictate the source of the recruit. If an experienced engineer or product manager is needed in a younger organization, the organization may have to turn to the external market. Organizations

EXHIBIT 8–5
Employer–Applicant Matching Process

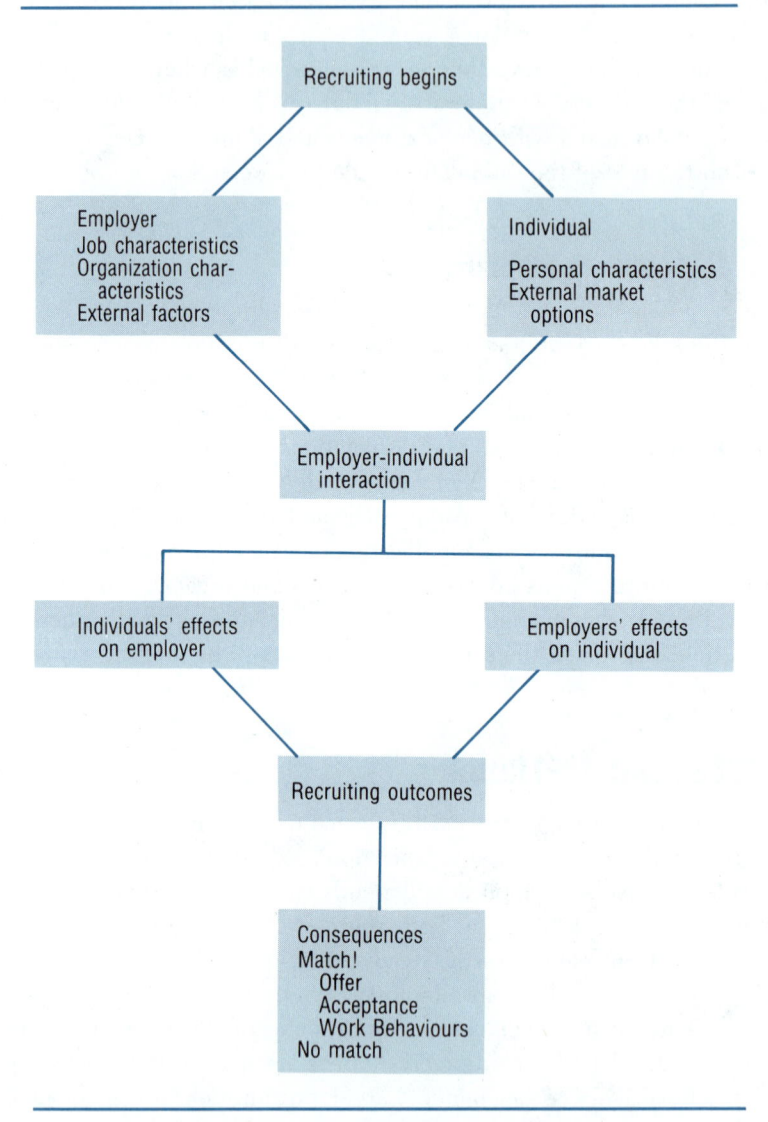

```
                    Recruiting begins
                    /              \
        Employer                      Individual
        Job characteristics           Personal characteristics
        Organization char-            External market
          acteristics                   options
        External factors
                    \              /
                    Employer-individual
                       interaction
                    /              \
        Individuals' effects        Employers' effects
          on employer                 on individual
                    \              /
                    Recruiting outcomes
                            |
                    Consequences
                    Match!
                       Offer
                       Acceptance
                       Work Behaviours
                    No match
```

Source: Adapted from Judy Olian and Sara Rynes, "On the Evolution of the Job Match: Integration and Future Research Directions," working paper (College Park: University of Maryland, 1983).

changing rapidly may find that training programs can't retrain the work force fast enough to keep pace. Conversely, managers may opt for people who already know the organization's systems and are familiar with the way the organization operates. There are good reasons to choose either an internal or an external candidate, depending on the circumstances and the candidates available. A conscious decision to go outside or inside must be made on sound organization and job reasons.

Other human resource policies influence the decision to recruit externally or internally. If managers regard human resources as an asset to be developed and maintained, they may utilize internal recruiting when possible. Training, job experiences, and the like are considered investments in human resources. If employees are viewed primarily as an expense to be controlled and minimized, management is more likely to recruit externally, thereby trying to capitalize on the investments made in employees by other employers.

An employer that prefers to recruit internally also tends to spend relatively more on training and development programs to develop employees and on programs (e.g., services and benefits) to retain them. An external recruitment strategy leads to relatively larger expenditures for recruiting, selection, and initial compensation. Recruiting and selection costs may be relatively larger for external recruiting organizations because such firms are likely to be recruiting and selecting more employees in a given time period than the organization that emphasizes internal sources. Firms that emphasize external sources may also have to offer higher initial pay rates to attract experienced employees from other firms. These comparisons are oversimplified, since most organizations periodically recruit both internally and externally. But they do represent basic considerations in deciding where to seek employees and whether to train and promote from within or recruit employees from external sources.

Internal Recruiting

The three main recruiting methods are: job posting, skills inventories, and referrals. Employers often combine several methods. Referrals are the least formalized of these; human rights concerns and improved computer applications have led to greater use of job posting and skills inventories. Some employers stress their almost exclusive reliance on internal sources, which reflects a promote-from-within policy.

Job Posting

In job posting, the organization notifies its present employees of openings, using bulletin boards and company publications. Employees who respond to these announcements are considered for the position. In some cases, the requirement for and duration of job posting for certain positions are part of the collective agreement.

Many organizations find job posting useful. Some, for example, publish a job opportunities bulletin each week. These bulletins list various job openings and publish brief descriptions of the work involved and the qualifications required. Additionally, they give salaries, grades, and the departments, subsidiaries, or branches offering the jobs. Copies are placed in staff lounges, hallways, and other places frequented by employees. On the back of the bulletin is an application form. Interested employees fill out forms, mail them to a coordinator, and are then considered.

Such systems have been widely adopted. The preponderance of most job posting usage is for office, clerical, administrative, and technical positions. One reason for their popularity is the implicit openness of the system, enabling all employees, including members of designated groups, to nominate themselves for positions. Posting may be a valuable tool when incorporated in employment equity programs. Job posting permits self-selection and expressions of interest by employees. CP Hotels' job posting program helps fill 50 to 60 percent of supervisory and higher vacancies internally; Procter & Gamble recruits only at the entry level and promotes from within.[27]

Dahl and Pinto provide a useful set of guidelines for effective job posting:

- Post all permanent promotion and transfer opportunities.
- Post the jobs for at least one week before recruiting outside the organization.
- Clarify eligibility rules. For example, minimum service in the present position might be specified; decision rules used to choose between several equally qualified applicants, if such rules will be used, should be stated.
- List job specifications. Application forms should be available.
- Later, inform all applicants how the job was filled.[28]

Skills Inventories

Another approach to internal recruiting is using skills inventories (discussed in Chapter Six). The organization searches its files for potentially qualified candidates for vacancies. Identified candidates are contacted and asked whether they wish to apply. Skills inventory information can also be used in conjunction with posting and bidding to ensure openings are known to all qualified applicants and that none is overlooked.

Referrals

A final internal source consists of referrals from present employees. Research has found referrals to be a good source of recruitment. Using one-year survival rates as the criterion of success, Schwab reviewed a number of studies comparing recruiting methods. In all reported samples, new hires that resulted from employee referrals showed the highest survival rate.[29] Vancouver City Savings Credit Union usually promotes from within, and its word-of-mouth approach is sufficient to yield more than enough referrals.[30]

What accounts for the success? Employees giving the referral may also give a realistic preview of jobs and thus ease adjustment once on the job. Or perhaps the referrer exerts pressure on the person referred to meet performance standards. This source of applicants, while successful, may be questioned by human rights officials on the grounds that it tends to perpetuate the race and sex composition of the present work force. Another problem may arise if the referred person is a relative and the "sponsor" is her or his potential supervisor. Many organizations avoid such a potential conflict of interest by not assigning relatives to the same department.

The referral form of recruiting might also have adverse consequences for social relations on the job if informal groups develop that hinder communication and cooperation. If an organization uses this form of recruiting, it must treat all applicants equitably and should provide employees with feedback regarding the status of persons they recommend to the company.

Whatever internal recruiting methods are used, records must be kept so the methods' effectiveness may be evaluated, including adherence to employment equity guidelines.

External Recruiting

No organization can meet all its human resource needs from internal sources. Even if possible, it would not be desirable. Even mature industries that need to reduce employment rolls can benefit from the fresh approaches that often come with new people. Thus, almost every organization does some recruitment in the external labour market. The next section discusses various methods of recruiting externally. We begin with college/university recruiting. The methods chosen are contingent upon many factors, including the source, the qualifications sought, how many new hires are needed, and the costs.

College/University Recruiting

Recruiting at colleges and universities serves as a major source of managerial, professional, and technical talent, but also serves other functions.[31] Many companies recruit on campuses even when they have few positions to fill. Recruiting primarily at prestigious universities may be part of a company's image, or the employer may wish to be a familiar name to potential future employees or customers. Information exchanged by recruiters and college/

university placement officials keeps a company informed as to labour market conditions, pay rates among competitors, and job vacancies. Interviewing on campus usually must be arranged well in advance, so many organizations continue with past arrangements to keep their options open, regardless of their short-term hiring plans.

Some employers stay ahead of the competition by forming cooperative work-study programs with universities. After students' first year of satisfactory full-time studies, the university and employers arrange for students to alternate terms of on-campus study and meaningful, career-related employment with firms across Canada. This allows both employers and students to assess each other, provides work experience for the student, and produces a more mature graduate. Such work assignments can also lead to formal recruiting for permanent employment. Some examples are the business school at Memorial University of Newfoundland and the engineering program at the University of Waterloo.

Campus Recruitment Ethics

The University and College Placement Association (UCPA) is Canada's national association dedicated to improving the process of matching students with jobs, providing services to employers, students, and career counsellors. UCPA has also adopted a set of guidelines addressing the principles and practices of campus recruitment at postsecondary educational institutions. These guidelines provide safeguards for employers as well as students.[32]

Canada Employment Centre (CEC)—Campus

To assist employers in meeting their staffing needs, Employment and Immigration Canada maintain placement offices on campuses. For employers, this year-round service offers two types of recruiting methods, as well as a direct listing facility.[33] Under the prescreening service, students submit their applications to the Canada Employment Centre, which sends them to the employer by a specific date. The employer's responsibilities are to select applicants for interviewing, notify applicants directly in time to schedule interviews through the Campus CEC, and supply a list of students selected for interviews. The other service, direct sign-up, means students from faculties specified by the employer are invited to the CEC to sign up for interviews and submit applications at that time.

The Campus CEC encourages employers to provide job descriptions, brochures, annual reports, and other information before the campus visit. This procedure assures the employer of interviewing a well-informed applicant. In addition, briefing sessions may be arranged through student and faculty employment representatives, and audiovisual equipment can be leased on campus.

Specifying Schools

The first decision in designing a college/university recruiting program is choosing schools at which to recruit. Smaller organizations are more likely to recruit only at regional or local schools. The positions to be filled make a difference in selecting schools. For example, professionals (engineers, accountants) are usually recruited nationally and most intensively at the specialized and prestigious schools, while sales personnel may be recruited nationally or regionally, depending on the resources and needs of the organizations. Some organizations designate key schools and focus on them.

Attracting Students to Initial Interview

The second stage of college/university recruiting is attracting students to sign up for and participate in interviews with the organization's recruiter. The nature of the organization's work is an important factor in students' decisions to sign up for an interview. The company's image also makes a difference. A lot of pre-interview activity needs to occur before the recruiter appears on campus. Preliminary contacts with selected students are frequent. Employers often sponsor wine and cheese parties, come to classes as resource people, or attend job fairs. Some companies also work through option clubs in a given faculty and have a recent graduate from that faculty as part of the campus team. Faculty members who know the students' work and interests are also helpful in giving information to both students and recruiters.

Site Visits

The third stage consists of inviting candidates who survived the campus interview to the organization site, to be evaluated by the department in which the vacancy exists and to receive further job information. This visit is followed by the decision to extend job offers.

Locating Other External Candidates

While college and university recruiting is a major source of an employer's professional human resources, an employer has broader needs. The director of compensation is not recruited right out of school, nor is the assembler. Yet the employer may need to acquire these skills in the external market.

Other Educational Institutions

High schools and vocational-technical schools and institutes are another major source of job applicants. High schools are a major source of clerical and sales personnel as well as trainees and apprentices for many semiskilled jobs. Recruiting in high schools is usually done through contacts with school officials and teachers, bulletin boards, part-time jobs and summer intern programs, or participation in "career day" programs.

Vocational and technical schools supply semiskilled and skilled labour in mechanics, refrigeration, electronics, data processing, and other fields. As the number of these schools increased, recruiting became more formalized and intensive, especially at those schools identified by employers as responding quickly by tailoring their courses to meet industry needs.

Walk-Ins

Walk-ins are simply people who come to an organization seeking employment, often in response to "help wanted" signs at work sites. This is a very inexpensive source of job applicants, especially for lower-skilled labour. It is likely to yield the greatest number of applicants when local unemployment is high, but the quality of applicants may be mixed.

Employment Agencies: Public and Private

More than 800 Canada Employment Centres, operated by the federal government, are located throughout Canada. The purpose of the centres is to match workers and employers and to offer advice on labour market conditions and trends. While this public agency is a virtually no-cost recruiting source offering a number of services to employers, its use has been limited. Those centres not designed to service a specific campus seem to be limited to the placement of unskilled labourers, technicians, clerical, sales and service workers, and applicants for generally lower-level supervisory positions. Relatively few placements are effected in primary, managerial, and professional occupations.[34] This may be partly the fault of employers, who have not been interested in providing job requisitions for a broader range of job vacancies or who have been unaware of the development of JOBSCAN.

Further sources for personnel are private placement agencies. Most of these agencies specialize in certain types of applicants, ranging from computer specialists to accountants to executives. Some companies even limit themselves to placing women executives. These firms have usually received good acceptance by industry, as they are often able to meet specific organization needs in a timelier manner than the organization could through its own recruiting efforts. Additionally, by prescreening candidates, a good agency may save an employer both time and money for high-level jobs filled infrequently.

Professional associations are major sources of both experienced and new graduates in many professions. Recruiting highly educated professionals is similar to college/university recruiting, but is usually more informal. Such recruiting is often done by professionals themselves rather than by a recruiter, and often occurs in conjunction with professional meetings.

Some unions require employers to submit their job requisitions to union hiring halls. The unions send job applicants to the employers, who then select those fitting their needs. This means unions become primary recruiters of labour.

Media Advertising

Advertising is the most commonly used recruiting method. Recruiting ads should influence a variety of market segments.[35] The first and major market segment is qualified applicants (that is, applicants who have the abilities and interest required to do the job). This means writing the ad in forms the reader can understand and placing it in the appropriate source. A review of the literature on newspaper advertising found the majority of published work in this area to be nonempirically based "advice" pieces by experts.[36] A frequently repeated piece of advice is that specific information in ads leads to more self-selection, especially when the ad lists specific job functions that need to be performed as well as quantified standards of performance.[37] A recent study that manipulated the specificity of job descriptions and applicant qualifications in recruitment ads found that qualified individuals responded more favourably than unqualified ones to all ads containing specific information, but the most preferred ad for the qualified group was the one combining a specific job description with a vague job specification statement.[38]

Companies also usually have a good understanding of what the motivated, potentially qualified applicant reads (i.e., the local newspaper, the *Financial Post*, the *Financial Times*, a trade or professional journal).

A second important market segment consists of readers who are already employed. Ads help build an organization's image, which may determine where people seek jobs in the future. The third segment is the organization's own employees; the fourth includes potential customers, investors, government officials, and others. Thus, recruitment advertising can influence both the applicant pool and the organization's image to the entire public. Exhibit 8–6 shows two recruiting ads that cover all the bases.

Other recruiting methods include radio and television advertising, participation in job fairs, mergers/acquisitions, and summer internships. Job fairs and radio and television advertising may attract a great number of unqualified candidates, but it may be useful in specialized situations. Mergers/acquisitions allow an employer to obtain an entire pool of trained talent all at once, However, this approach can have unintended consequences (Chapter Two). A recent innovation is recruiting by computer.[39] Engineers, designers, and programmers can have their computer terminals dial a telephone number, and their terminal will display pertinent data on jobs available at competing employers.

Summer internships can be advantageous to both students and organizations if expectations on both sides are clear. Students get experience, and

EXHIBIT 8–6A

Safety Coordinator

Reporting to the Manager, Administration and Employee Services, your primary challenge will be to encourage and promote all aspects of on-the-job safety. To meet this objective, you will collect and maintain pertinent statistical data, conduct physical inspections and provide remedial recommendations and follow-ups. You will also coordinate safety training courses, provide on-the-job instruction, and offer guidance to site management on matters of legislation, safety standards and environmental measurements. Maintaining good working relationships with relevant government agencies and conducting safety meetings and awareness campaigns will also rank highly among your priorities. You will be on shift rotation at the mine site with an alternate assistant.

To qualify, your minimum of 6 years' related experience must be complemented by a technical school or community college diploma, preferably in a mining-related discipline. A standard Instructor's First Aid Certificate and knowledge of Neil George's "Principals of Safety" are also required, as are excellent organizational, communication and interpersonal abilities.

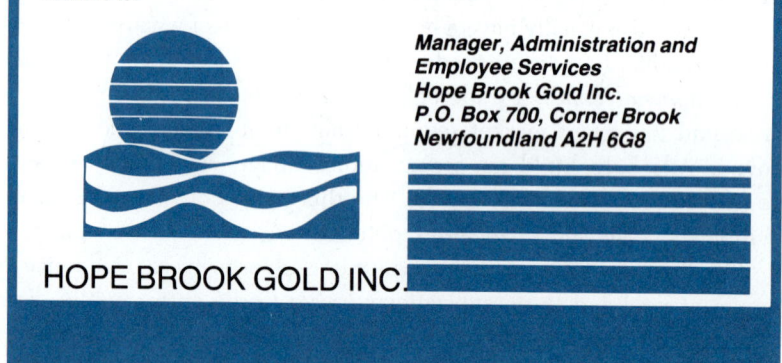

If you're the experienced specialist we seek, please forward your confidential résumé to:

Manager, Administration and Employee Services
Hope Brook Gold Inc.
P.O. Box 700, Corner Brook
Newfoundland A2H 6G8

HOPE BROOK GOLD INC.

Reproduced with permission of Hope Brook Gold Inc.

employers can get special projects done that the regular staff may not have time for, as well as a chance to appraise a potential future employee on the job. But corporate life can disillusion students, and organizations must expend time and energy organizing and supervising projects to ensure meaningful results.

EVALUATING RECRUITING PROGRAMS

So what difference do recruiting programs make? Boudreau and Rynes state that differences in recruiting programs have different costs and benefits to the

EXHIBIT 8–6B

SENIOR HUMAN RESOURCES CHALLENGE

Our client, a major international manufacturer, is seeking an experienced human resources/labour relations professional. The challenge is exciting and unique, an opportunity to create a dynamic, innovative human resources group in a unique, start-up manufacturing organization.

This senior executive will create and manage a department with overall responsibility for organization planning, recruitment, training, compensation, employee benefits, labour relations, employee relations policy, health and safety, and a variety of related functions. This individual will play a key operating role as a member of the senior management team, strategizing and implementing policy, programs and directions for this sophisticated manufacturing operation.

Candidates should be well educated with a minimum of 10 years combined hands-on and management expertise in the aforementioned functional areas, preferabaly in large, diverse manufacturing environments.

Self motivation and excellent interpersonal skills are critical, coupled with an ability to juggle multiple activities, meet tight schedules and achieve results through individuals and committees.

If you can demonstate a track record of innovation and achievement and are interested in a unique opportunity, please send your resume, in confidence, referring to File No. 3790.

Price Waterhouse
Management Consuitants
Box 51, 53rd Floor
Toronto-Dominion Centre
Toronto, Ontario M5K 1G1

Member Canadian Association
of Management Consultants

Price Waterhouse

INTERNATIONAL EXECUTIVE SEARCH SERVICES WITH OFFICES WORLDWIDE

Reproduced with permission of *The Globe and Mail*.

**EXHIBIT 8–7
Recruitment Programs**

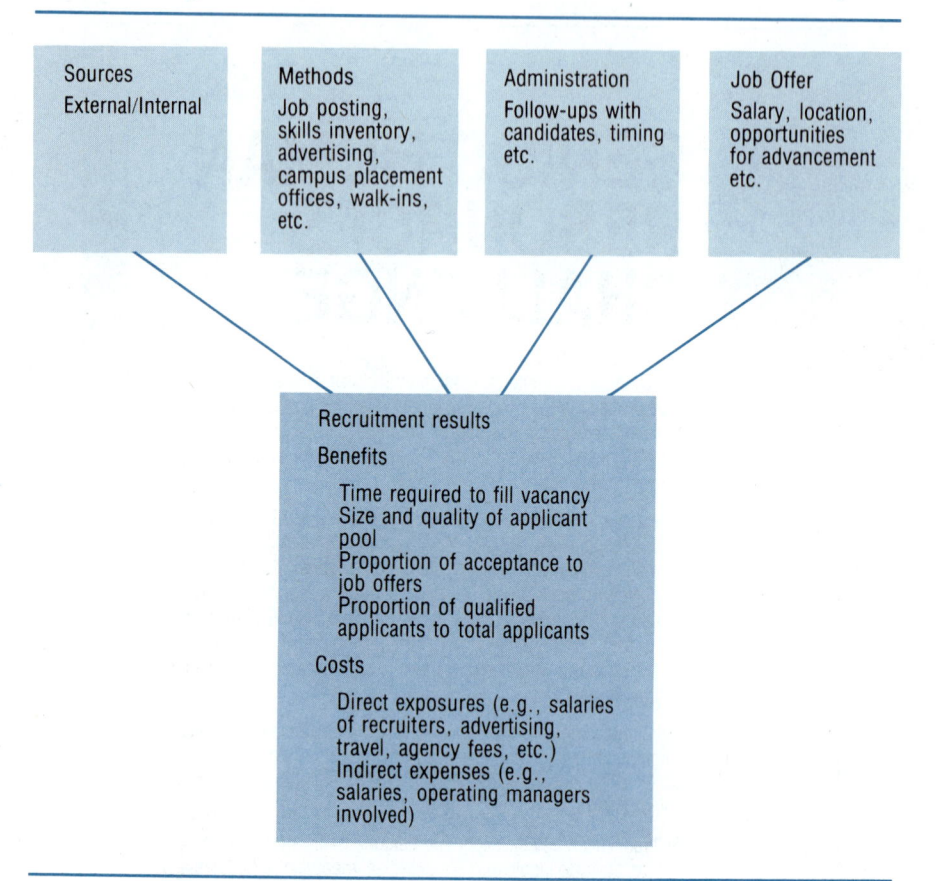

Sources	Methods	Administration	Job Offer
External/Internal	Job posting, skills inventory, advertising, campus placement offices, walk-ins, etc.	Follow-ups with candidates, timing etc.	Salary, location, opportunities for advancement etc.

Recruitment results

Benefits

  Time required to fill vacancy
  Size and quality of applicant pool
  Proportion of acceptance to job offers
  Proportion of qualified applicants to total applicants

Costs

  Direct exposures (e.g., salaries of recruiters, advertising, travel, agency fees, etc.)
  Indirect expenses (e.g., salaries, operating managers involved)

Source: Adapted from J. W. Boudreau and S. Rynes, "The Role of Recruitment in Staffing Utility Analysis" (working paper, Ithaca, N.Y.: Cornell University, 1983).

organization.[40] Exhibit 8–7 shows that using different sources and methods as well as differences in job offers and administrative procedures all may affect results. The results of various recruiting programs are shown as benefits, which include the time to fill a vacancy and the size and quality of the applicant pool. Quality of the pool can be estimated by the proportion of applicants judged to be qualified and the proportion of those who are made job offers and accept them.

Another method of evaluating the quality of hire (QH) incorporates job performance ratings.[41] This measure is calculated as follows:

$$QH = (PR + HP + HR)/N$$

where

QH = Quality of recruits hired
PR = Average job performance ratings (20 items on scale) of new hires (e.g., 4 on a 5-point scale or 20 items × 4)
HP = Percent of new hires promoted within one year (such as 30 percent)
HR = Percent of hires retained after one year (e.g., 80 percent)
N = Number of indicators used

Therefore,

$$QH = (80 + 30 + 80)/3$$
$$= 190/3$$
$$= 63.33\%$$

The 63 percent quality of hire rate is a relative value. Management must decide whether this represents an excellent, good, fair, or poor level.

Caution must be exercised with the quality of hire measure when evaluating the recruitment strategy. Performance ratings and promotion rates are beyond the control of a recruiter. A good new employee can be driven away by few promotion opportunities, inequitable performance ratings, or job market conditions that have nothing to do with the effectiveness of the recruiter. Nevertheless, the quality of hire measure can provide some insight into the recruiter's ability to attract good employees.

A survey asking P/HRM executives to judge the most effective recruiting method found that newspaper advertising was considered most effective for every occupation group.[42] Employee referrals received relatively few endorsements. This questionnaire sampled executives' impressions; it did not require data nor did it define "effective." The survey's results are in sharp contrast with Schwab's findings that employees hired through referrals had the greatest likelihood of still being on the job one year later.[43] Schwab's data show that people who use employment agencies had the lowest job retention. He speculated that this might be because people who used agencies were more aware of employment alternatives. Additional research is needed to clarify the effectiveness of various recruiting methods.

Another study related recruiting method to subsequent work performance, absenteeism, and work attitudes.[44] Degreed scientists recruited through newspapers and college placements were judged to be less dependable than hires resulting from self-initiated contacts and convention/professional journal ads. Those recruited through newspaper ads missed almost twice as many workdays as did those recruited from any other source.

Comparisons of various research results are confounded by variability in research methods. Not all studies compared the same recruiting methods.[45] Additionally, when individual characteristics are held constant, differential effects of recruiting method tend to disappear.[46] The findings highlight the need for directly identifying the individual characteristics related to job success and tuning recruiting methods to enhance the likelihood of attracting those individuals.

Recruiting Costs and Benefits

Recruiting is costly.[47] Recruiting costs have been estimated to run as high as 50 to 60 percent of the first-year salary for professionals and managers. Cost includes not only the direct costs associated with recruiter salaries and various methods used, but also the time of operating personnel.

The best sources of cost-benefit information are the data collected from previous recruiting activities.[48] Too often, these data are not collected or readily accessible. Even with accurate records, subsequent changes in external conditions (e.g., labour markets) may make accurate cost-benefit estimation difficult.

While an organization might obtain some information from local employers' associations regarding recruiting costs, each organization should design its own system to collect recruiting costs and effectiveness data. Computer programs to organize such data are commercially available. Exhibit 8–8 presents samples of possible measures to evaluate different stages of the recruiting process. When recruiters and/or interviewers are used, they may be individually evaluated, as well as sources and methods. The organization can calculate the cost of each method (e.g., advertising) and compare it to the benefits it yields (e.g., acceptances of offers). Some methods may produce a high percentage of qualified applicants (for example, referrals) but may not be able to produce sufficient numbers of applicants to meet the needs of the organization. It is unusual for an organization to meet all its needs through one recruiting method, no matter how cost-effective that method.

The cost-effectiveness of various recruiting methods may vary with external conditions, the time required to fill openings, the nature of the work, and the individual characteristics of applicant and recruiter. Therefore, evaluation should consider these factors. The professionalism with which the whole recruitment procedure is administered also makes a difference. Long delays between contacts with a prospective employee or an overly demanding process may cause applicants to turn elsewhere. Additionally, good candidates who have more options may be lost faster than poorer candidates with few prospects.

We have now examined recruitment planning, diagnosing conditions, sources, methods, and evaluation—basic issues faced in the design of a re-

EXHIBIT 8–8
Possible Measures to Evaluate Each Recruiting Method

Attracting	Screening
Number of applicants	Total visits offered
Cost per applicant	Visits offered
Time required to locate applicants	Applicants
	Qualified minorities and females
Qualified applicants / Total applicants	Qualified applicants
Minority and female applicants / Total applicants	Visits offered to minorities and females / Visits offered
Offers and Hires	*Results*
Offers extended / Visits accepted	Performance rating of hires
	Tenure of hires
Offers extended / Qualified applicants	Costs per level of performance
	Absenteeism per hire
Offers accepted / Offers extended	
Costs per hire	
Time lapsed per hire	
Same ratios for minorities and females	

cruiting program. Next we turn to some recent research and then examine recruiting from the perspective of the individual searching for a job.

REALISM OR FLYPAPER?

Earlier we stated that one of the primary purposes of recruiting is to attract potential employees—to sell the organization as a great place to work. Too often the seeds of dissatisfaction and eventual turnover are sown during recruitment. A candidate may develop inflated expectations of the nature and rewards of the work. The recruiter, in his or her zeal to sell the firm, may foster those expectations in what has been called the "flypaper" approach—telling candidates the organization is attractive on all dimensions.[49] When expectations are unmet, dissatisfaction and lack of commitment to the organization may result, with an eventual decision to leave the organization.

Graver consequences of the flypaper approach are possible. For example, an employee may sue the employer if the job characteristics do not generally reflect what was promised at the time of hiring.[50]

Many researchers believe there is a better approach to recruiting. By giving recruits a more accurate picture of the job and the organization, including their negative aspects, potential dissatisfaction may be avoided. Bringing expectations of newly hired employees closer to reality through "realistic job previews" may reduce turnover, absenteeism, or other negative work behaviours caused by unmet expectations.[51]

Realistic Job Previews

In the realistic job preview (RJP), job applicants are presented with a balanced view of the positive and negative features of work in a particular organization.[52] The major premise behind the use of RJPs is that providing accurate and complete information to job applicants lessens subsequent disillusionment; consequently, this should lead to increased job satisfaction, lower turnover, and possibly higher job performance.[53]

The RJP may be viewed as akin to a medical vaccination, for it exposes the person to a small dose of organizational reality, thereby inoculating the individual against a larger, more extensive exposure.[54] It has also been argued that RJPs are useful in helping newcomers cope better with unpleasant job characteristics—the advance warning allows them time to discover methods of dealing with difficult aspects of the job.[55] Another suggestion is that the RJP enhances attitudes toward the employer because it fosters perceptions of high credibility, honesty, and openness.[56]

While there is a lot of research on realistic job previews, the results are mixed. For example, in one firm, a film for potential telephone operators made it clear the work was closely supervised, repetitive, and sometimes required dealing with rude or unpleasant customers. Use of the RJP was related to decreased turnover rates.[57] It had no effect on job performance, nor did its use hamper the organization's ability to recruit. However, other researchers found evidence of an adverse effect of realistic previews in that more candidates refused to accept job offers.[58] Some have been unable to find any reduction in turnover that could be related to RJPs.[59] A more recent summary indicates recruits who receive RJPs are less likely to leave an organization, the general reduction in turnover is offset by a tendency for the job offer acceptance rate to decline in the face of unfavourable information, and there is generally no significant impact on job performance.[60] Premack and Wanous state that reviews conducted before their study may be misleading because the methods used to draw conclusions have potentially serious flaws.[61] Using a quantitative meta-analytic approach to examine 21 RJP studies, they conclude RJPs tend to lower initial job expectations "while increasing self-selection, organizational commitment, job satisfaction, performance, and job survival."[62] The unanimous conclusion of studies is that the major effect of the RJP is to lower inflated expectations.

Part of the problem may be poorly designed research on a concept too widely applied.[63] For example, some common jobs such as supermarket checkers are so familiar that few people may have unrealistic expectations when applying for those jobs.[64] Furthermore, if an applicant has no other job possibilities, any effect from an RJP may be overwhelmed by economic reality. More careful investigation may be required.

Two possible explanations have been advanced for how the RJP might work to reduce turnover and increase satisfaction:[65]

1. It may facilitate more effective matching between applicant and job by giving better information. The better the information the job candidates possess, the more effective their own organizational choice can be. But self-selection must be preceded by realistic expectations.
2. It may increase commitment to a choice that is made without external pressure or coercion. For commitment to be enhanced, however, multiple job offers must be under consideration at the same time.

For any of these explanations to operate, the potential applicant must have (1) unrealistic expectations to begin with, (2) multiple options, (3) an RJP of each option, and (4) difficulty in coping with job demands without the RJP.

A final issue is whether RJPs are too limited. It may be that intrinsic, rather than extrinsic, job factors seem most in need of a realistic job preview.[66] Others argue that job applicants need more than task-related information and propose the use of realistic organizational previews (ROPs).[67]

THE POTENTIAL EMPLOYEE'S VIEW OF RECRUITING

Thus far, we have focused on recruiting from the organization's perspective. But the process involves matching and interaction, "individuals and organizations attracting and selecting each other."[68] From the recruit's perspective, we should consider how he or she develops preferences for an occupation/profession (e.g., science versus business) and a job (e.g., research chemist versus accountant), searches for a job, and makes an organizational choice (i.e., evaluates job offers to choose a specific organization to work for).

Just as organizations have ideal specifications for recruits, recruits have a set of preferences for a job. A student leaving university may want a job in Vancouver, preferably near the beach, that pays $30,000 a year and requires little or no responsibility or supervision. This recruit is unlikely to get all expectations fulfilled. Recruits anticipate compromises just as organizations do.

From the individual's point of view, choosing which organization to work for is based on a multistage process (see Exhibit 8–9). The individual makes an occupational choice probably in secondary school or just after. Then the type of job and an organization to work for within the occupation must be selected.[69]

Occupational Choice

The subject of occupational choice or entry is quite broad. It includes, for example, how vocational/occupational choices are made, how individuals adjust to vocations, the meaning of occupational success, and satisfaction with one's vocation.[70] Occupational choice has been analyzed from a number of perspectives. The three most notable are psychological, economic, and sociological.

Occupational choice is influenced by the person's preferences (psychological), the realities of the labour market, the person's calculation of net advantage (economic), and the structural limitations of organizations and the individual's socialization to them (sociological).

Psychologists analyze occupational choice as part of the person's emotional and intellectual growth. Occupational choice is influenced by the person's needs, desires, hopes, and aspirations. Economists see the process as the way people seek to maximize the future flow of income and minimize their time and effort to obtain it. Sociologists emphasize how the family, educational system, peer group, and guidance agencies influence occupational choice.

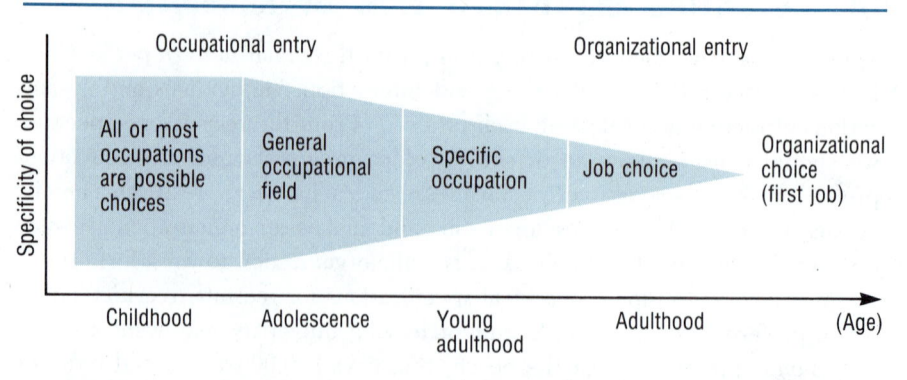

EXHIBIT 8–9
The Narrowing Down from Occupational Entry to Organizational Entry

Source: Adapted from J. O. Crites, 1969, *Vocational Psychology*, p. 162. Reprinted by permission of the McGraw-Hill Book Company.

All three approaches to understanding occupational choice are interrelated. To understand an individual's aspirations without reference to the economic and organizational limitations on them, or to study the idea of maximizing net advantages without including a person's motivations, makes little sense.[71] To this list, reflecting on our own occupational choice, we also add chance or luck.

A convenient framework for representing the entire process of occupational choice was composed by Blau et al. in terms of a developmental sequence of long-term factors and immediate determinants.[72] Long-term factors include the native endowment of the person, aspects of social structure (e.g., cultural values and norms, social stratification system) and those comprising personality development (e.g., educational development, available financial resources, differential family influences). These influence the more immediate determinant of sociopsychological attributes, consisting of abilities and educational level, social position and relations, and orientation to occupational life (its importance, identification with occupational role models, aspirations, and so on).

The next stage of the sequence encompasses social role characteristics, technical qualifications, occupational information, and the person's reward value hierarchy. These, in turn, lead to a preference hierarchy of occupations (as well as an expectancy hierarchy), which eventually yields the individual's choice. The final essence of the sequence is best expressed through Blau's own words: "The process of occupational choice involves a descent in a hierarchy of preferences (or the acquisition of new qualifications), which comes to an end, at least temporarily, by being selected for an occupation."[73]

As shown in Exhibit 8-9, the flow of events described leads to a job choice (e.g., research chemist rather than other work in the field of chemistry), followed by the choice of selecting a specific organization in which to implement this job choice.

Organizational Choice

Most of the research on how people evaluate competing offers concentrates on college and university students. The postgraduate organization choice is unique for several reasons. First, it may be the only time an individual has more than one job offer to consider at a time. Usually a person has only one alternative to compare to the present job. For example, a loan officer in a bank may be offered a job in the trust department for the same employer or for a different employer, but rarely is there more than one option to consider at a time. Second, because of the number of students and recruiters exchanging information at the same time, most students probably have more accurate information on labour market conditions than they will ever possess again.

People who are currently employed but seeking to change jobs or those who are unemployed will not have the information network to provide them such data, nor may they have the option of searching until the perfect job is found. Instead, they may take the first offer above some minimum level.

The minimum level of pay required to make a job offer acceptable is called the reservation wage.[74] In contrast to this approach is the compensatory model, in which trade-offs between job attributes are made. For example, little job responsibility can be offset by a promise of rapid promotion, or an unattractive geographical location can be compensated for by high pay, or a job for a spouse, or an effective management training program. While the compensatory model may seem logical when multiple offers are under consideration, there is more research support for noncompensatory-reservation wage strategies (i.e., take the first offer that meets minimum requirements).[75]

Research on attributes of the job itself (i.e., pay, location) generally concludes that different people respond to different attributes. In one study, Jurgenson asked applicants to rank their preferences among job attributes and then asked them to rank what they felt were other people's preferences.[76] He found some interesting differences (see Exhibit 8–10), especially in the importance of pay. People agree that pay is very important to others, but are less willing to indicate it is important to them. This may be because it is socially unacceptable for an individual to indicate an unseemly interest in money.[77]

EXHIBIT 8–10
Median Ranks of 10 Job Attributes Obtained from Applicants

	Sex and Preference Source			
	Men		Women	
Attribute	Self	Others	Self	Others
Advancement	3.3	3.8	5.3	4.3
Benefits	6.8	5.2	8.0	5.9
Company	4.5	6.8	4.6	7.1
Co-workers	6.0	7.7	5.2	7.3
Hours	7.6	5.4	6.9	5.0
Pay	5.6	2.1	6.0	2.1
Security	2.5	3.6	4.9	5.4
Supervisor	6.3	7.4	5.3	7.0
Type of work	3.3	4.9	1.5	3.5
Working conditions	7.9	6.9	6.5	6.8
Number of respondents	(39,788)	(32,810)	(16,833)	(15,138)

Source: C. E. Jurgensen, "Job Preferences (What Makes a Job Good or Bad?)," *Journal of Applied Psychology*, 1978, pp. 267–76. Copyright 1978 by the American Psychological Association. Adapted by permission of the publisher and author.

How People Seek a Job

Research on job search focusses on two variables: method and intensity of search. Generally, methods vary somewhat by occupation, level of education, and employment status (employed versus unemployed). Managerial and clerical job seekers are more likely to use a private employment service than are blue-collar job seekers.[78] However, differences in search behaviour may disappear in times of economic downturn. For example, during the 1982 recession the most frequent method of job search—by unemployed persons—regardless of gender, occupation, and education was to contact employers directly.[79]

The second variable, search intensity, measures the effort searchers expend. Much research has found that search intensity is inversely related to financial security.[80] If a person has nonwage income or unemployment benefits, fewer hours will be spent each week looking for a job.[81] A study of MBAs found that those who conducted more intensive searches were more satisfied than their less informed counterparts both one and three years after the job choice.[82] However, initial postchoice dissatisfaction may occur if attractive alternatives have to be rejected. The same study also found high search intensity related to higher salary increases over the three-year period.

Glueck categorized business and engineering students according to which of three approaches they used to search for jobs.[83]

1. *Maximizers* took as many interviews as possible, got as many offers as possible, and then rationally chose the best one, based on self-specified criteria.
2. *Satisfiers* took the first offer they got. They tended to believe one company was about the same as another.
3. *Validators* were in between maximizers and satisfiers. They would get an offer (their favourite), get one more just to see if their favourite was a good one, and then take the favourite one.

Little is known about the relationship of intensity of search and efficiency of methods used or about the relationship between methods used and duration of unemployment. Some research suggests there may be differences. For example, one study found that male users of public employment services tended to remain unemployed longer than users of alternative methods.[84] It also found that those who get help from friends and relatives in obtaining a job were more likely to experience a reduction in wage level from a previous job than were those who used alternative methods. So friends and relatives who provide job information may also apply pressure to accept a job offer, even at a lower wage, and to meet performance standards once on the job.

Using a variety of search methods seems to be the best advice for both organizations and individuals.

From a more immediate practical perspective, the book *The 100 Best Companies to Work for in Canada* makes it easier for both the novice and more experienced job searcher to evaluate and select employers.[85] An example is included in the Appendix.

The perceived likelihood of receiving job offers appears to affect search behaviour, especially if the costs of job pursuit are borne by the applicants. But Rynes and Lawler tried to apply expectancy theory to search behaviour and found their subjects evaluated expectancies in ways not directly predictable from expectancy theory.[86] Some subjects chose job interviews based solely on job attractiveness (valences) and appeared to ignore likelihood of getting a job (expectancies). Others chose on the expectancy of securing a job in a geographical location and ignored the job attractiveness. For others, personal characteristics (lack of confidence, risk aversion) seemed to be the source of differences in search and job choice behaviour.

SUMMARY

This chapter examines the recruiting process. Properly designed recruitment programs influence the quality of the flow of new talent into an organization. Consequently, some see recruitment (and selection) as a key human resource program.

In conjunction with recruitment planning and the analysis of external and internal conditions, three major issues—sources, methods, and evaluation—need to be considered in the design of effective recruitment programs. No single best approach to each of these issues exists. Rather, recruitment design is contingent on several factors, including effective planning, economic conditions, the time allotted to fill the opportunities, the number and qualifications required, and the relative costs of various options.

Recruitment is a two-sided process, a market exchange in which prospective employees and employers interact. Recruiters attempt to induce people to apply, help perform preliminary screening, induce people to accept job offers, and leave all applicants with a favourable impression. Applicants tend to choose occupations and, subsequently, employers and jobs. Some evidence based on the behaviour of college and university students suggests applicants, rather than selecting the option to maximize returns (compensatory models), tend to satisfice (select the option that satisfies some standard). The recruitment process plays a major role in ensuring a match between the employer's needs for qualified employees and the individual's needs for challenging and rewarding work.

APPENDIX / How to Get a Job

You: Career Planning and Job Preferences

Before you can be effective as a job seeker and jobholder, you must know what you are looking for. This helps you seek a job effectively and answer recruiting questions honestly.

The process of looking for a job is modelled in Exhibit 8–11. Your first job choice is part of your career objectives. Do you see this job as the first of a chain of jobs with this company? Or is this just a job to get experience before you start your own business?

There are also questions to answer about potential employers (Step 3 in Exhibit 8–11):

1. Do I have a size preference: small, medium, or large, or no size preference?
2. Do I have a sector preference (private, not for profit, public sector)?
3. What kinds of industries interest me? (This is usually based on interests in company products or services.)
4. Have I checked to make sure the sector or product or service has a good future and will lead to growth in opportunity?

At this point, you may have determined, for example, what you really want is a job near home in a small firm you can buy some day.

EXHIBIT 8–11
Career Decision Strategy

STEP 1. Realize that you're looking for a career objective and the sequence of jobs you'll use to achieve it

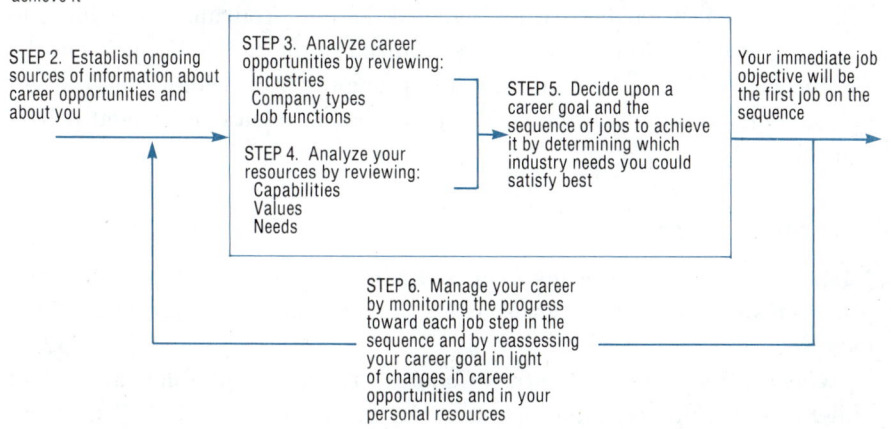

STEP 2. Establish ongoing sources of information about career opportunities and about you

STEP 3. Analyze career opportunities by reviewing:
Industries
Company types
Job functions

STEP 4. Analyze your resources by reviewing:
Capabilities
Values
Needs

STEP 5. Decide upon a career goal and the sequence of jobs to achieve it by determining which industry needs you could satisfy best

STEP 6. Manage your career by monitoring the progress toward each job step in the sequence and by reassessing your career goal in light of changes in career opportunities and in your personal resources

Your immediate job objective will be the first job on the sequence

Source: B. Greco, *How to Get a Job That's Right for You* (Homewood, Ill.: Dow Jones-Irwin, 1975).

For Step 4 in the exhibit, you need to answer:

1. How hard do I like to work?
2. Do I like to be my own boss, or would I rather work for someone else?
3. Do I like to work alone, with a few others, or with large groups?
4. Do I like to work at an even pace or in bursts of energy?
5. Does location matter? Do I want to work near home? In warmer climates? In ski country? Am I willing to be mobile?
6. How much money do I want? Am I willing to work for less money but in a more interesting job?
7. Do I like to work in one place or many? Indoors or outdoors?
8. How much variety do I want in work?

Questions of this type are almost unlimited. You should rank them by importance so you know the trade-offs between them. You will not find a job with all the characteristics you choose.

Step 4 also involves preparing a list of your comparative advantages to help sell yourself to employers you have chosen. A sample list of your advantages might be:

- Education: grades, kind of courses, skills developed.
- Experience: variety, relevance to company, amount, skills developed.
- Personal characteristics: interpersonal skills, leadership skill.
- Contacts with company: businesspeople, bankers, professors.

Recognizing the Factors in the Environment

As discussed in Chapter Two, several factors in the environment affect your job-seeking behaviour. The first is the labour market. If jobs are scarce, you will have to start looking earlier and look harder. You must be willing to compromise if you do not want to find yourself in the unemployment line.

Realize that in an organization that promotes from within, you can get only an entry-level job. If the firm or group has an open employment policy, you can apply at any level.

Your Job Sources

Next, you want to use as many sources of jobs and job information as possible. And you want to use the right sources. Sources you should use include the following:

Canada Employment Centre—Campus. The CEC publishes a series of bulletins covering recruiting activity. The bulletins are published at about two-week intervals during the recruitment season and are available through student employment representatives, faculty advisors, and campus bulletin boards. The student's direct involvement entails registering with the CEC, determining which employers interest you, signing up for the free résumé writing and interviewing skills workshops most campuses offer, completing the UCPA application for employment form, and, finally, interviewing. Observe the deadlines scrupulously and follow the procedure outlined for contacting prescreening and direct sign-up employers.

Newspapers and Professional Publications. Read the local and national media ads for the type of job you want, and professional publications and newspapers for the area you have selected. *The Financial Post, Financial Times,* and *The Globe and Mail* are examples of where to look. Respond to ads that sound interesting.

Professional Associations. Many professional associations provide job placement services. Get your name in the placement application file. Job ads are run in their publications too. You may also discover the hidden job market. Monthly dinner meetings, for example, are an excellent opportunity for finding out who is hiring and for establishing an initial contact point. The contacts you make (yes, even as a student member) can lead to an internal referral, which usually obligates the employer's representative to go forward with an interview.

Private Employment Agencies and Executive Search Firms. Another source of jobs is private employment agencies. Generally, you should visit with them and bring a résumé. They charge a fee, often payable by the employer, but sometimes payable by you. The fee can be as much as 15 percent of the first year's salary. Executive search firms tend to recruit middle managers and up (salaries in the $50,000 range).

Some firms also offer résumé preparation and testing services and career counselling. They often charge up to $1,500, whether you get a job or not. Though this fee is usually paid by employers, you should be aware of any costs you must bear.

Personal Contacts. One of the best sources of jobs is people working for the organization or who have worked there in the past. Develop your contacts from as many sources as possible: parents, relatives, friends, fraternity brothers or sorority sisters, and so on. Some experts estimate that 80 percent of jobs are never advertised. Contacts get these jobs.

Direct Mail. When mailing unsolicited résumés to employers, use a personal approach. Write a personalized letter to the P/HRM manager of the organization, explaining why you are applying. Find out the manager's name. Specify your preferences and advantages in the letter and tell the manager you will call in 10 days to two weeks for a job interview. Waiting for an organization to come to you is not fruitful.

Your Job Search

Preparing a Résumé and Application Form

One of the first things you should do in initiating your job campaign is prepare a résumé and/or complete the UCPA application form at your CEC. The four-page form meets all federal and provincial human rights legislation and is used at institutions all across Canada.[87] Although some prefer résumés, most employers recruiting on campus accept UCPA forms as applications. The form is comprehensive enough for you to include all relevant details, and its standardization helps the employer compare information about a number of job applicants with a minimum of confusion. You will probably be able to use the first three pages (general information, work experience, extracurricular activities) for most of the positions you apply for. The fourth page (additional information) may need to be rewritten each time. See it as an opportunity to link key information from the first three pages with the specific job available and/or the company itself (without being repetitive).[88]

To apply for positions not posted at the Campus CEC you will have to prepare a résumé and a cover letter. Both should create a favourable impression with a potential employer; you want to create a certain image in the employer's mind.

The vast number of self-help books and résumé writing guides makes it difficult to collate all the approaches suggested. For the graduating student, the best strategy is to attend the résumé clinic offered on campus, to consult practical how-to articles (in the most recent issue of *Career Planning*)[89] and the UCPA's Guide to Résumé Writing[90] (see your CEC representative for a copy). The sample format shown in Exhibit 8–12 will help you prepare an effective résumé.

When constructing your résumé, also observe the following guidelines:

- A résumé must state more than just your past. It should also incorporate your goals and give the potential employer some insight into your aspirations.
- A résumé should provide a clear picture of your skills, so use descriptive verbs that will describe your skills (see Exhibit 8–12). In addition to noting job-specific skills, consider transferable skills you may have used in personal activities or community activities. Transferable skills such as analyzing, organizing, leading, and public speaking should always be mentioned.
- Concentrate on emphasizing problem-solving skills and specific accomplishments rather than just a listing of duties. You should aim to differentiate your résumé from others.
- Remember to place the most important information first. An employer may not have time to read the entire résumé, and you do not want him

EXHIBIT 8–12
Sample Résumé Format

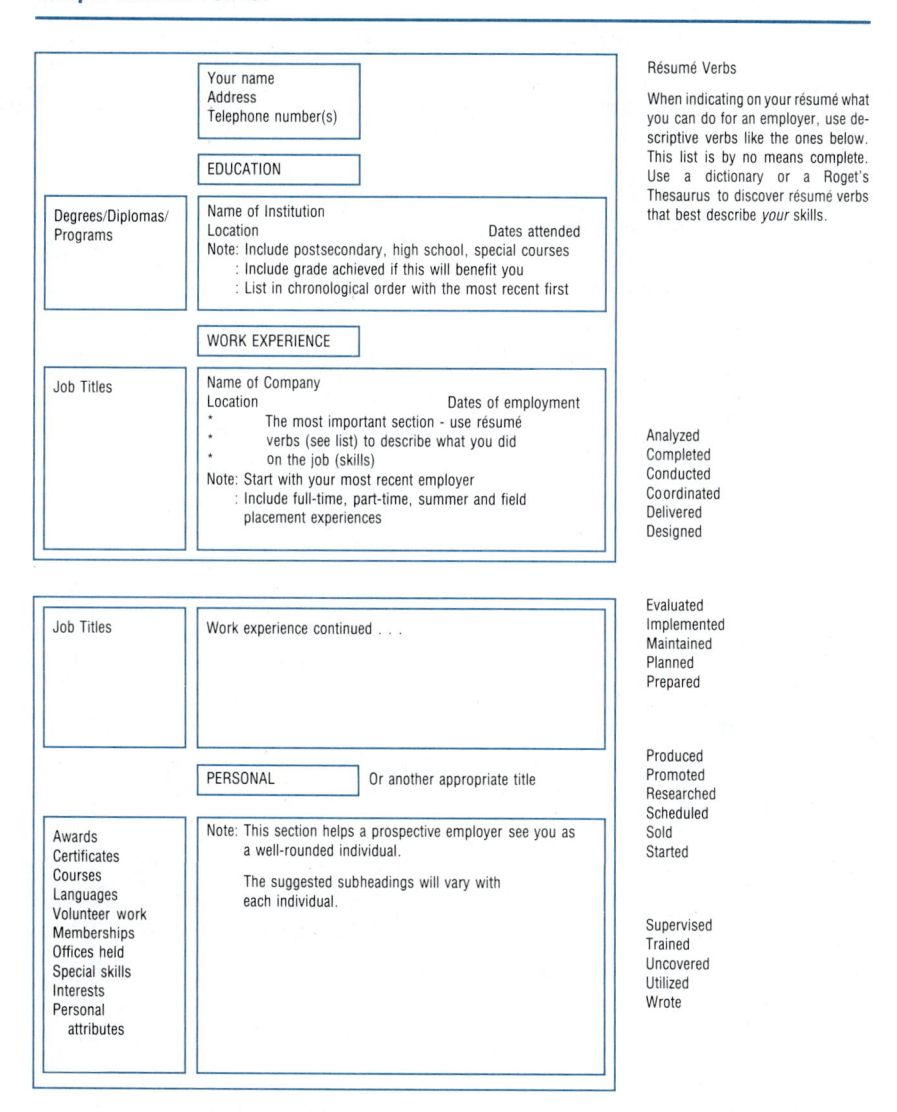

```
┌─────────────────────────────────────────────────┐      Résumé Verbs
│                 Your name                       │
│                 Address                         │      When indicating on your résumé what
│                 Telephone number(s)             │      you can do for an employer, use de-
│                                                 │      scriptive verbs like the ones below.
│                 ┌─────────────┐                 │      This list is by no means complete.
│                 │ EDUCATION   │                 │      Use a dictionary or a Roget's
│                 └─────────────┘                 │      Thesaurus to discover résumé verbs
│ Degrees/Diplomas/  Name of Institution          │      that best describe *your* skills.
│ Programs           Location      Dates attended │
│                    Note: Include postsecondary, high school, special courses
│                        : Include grade achieved if this will benefit you
│                        : List in chronological order with the most recent first
│
│                 ┌──────────────────┐
│                 │ WORK EXPERIENCE  │
│                 └──────────────────┘
│ Job Titles         Name of Company              │
│                    Location     Dates of employment
│                    *   The most important section - use résumé
│                        verbs (see list) to describe what you did    Analyzed
│                        on the job (skills)                          Completed
│                    Note: Start with your most recent employer       Conducted
│                        : Include full-time, part-time, summer and field   Coordinated
│                          placement experiences                      Delivered
│                                                                     Designed
```

```
┌─────────────────────────────────────────────────┐
│ Job Titles         Work experience continued... │      Evaluated
│                                                 │      Implemented
│                                                 │      Maintained
│                                                 │      Planned
│                                                 │      Prepared
│
│                 ┌─────────────┐
│                 │ PERSONAL    │   Or another appropriate title
│                 └─────────────┘                        Produced
│ Awards            Note: This section helps a prospective employer see you as   Promoted
│ Certificates           a well-rounded individual.                              Researched
│ Courses                                                                        Scheduled
│ Languages              The suggested subheadings will vary with                Sold
│ Volunteer work         each individual.                                        Started
│ Memberships
│ Offices held                                                                   Supervised
│ Special skills                                                                 Trained
│ Interests                                                                      Uncovered
│ Personal                                                                       Utilized
│   attributes                                                                   Wrote
```

Source: "Résumés—Market Yourself," *Career Planning: 1985–86,* vol. 16, (Toronto: University and College Placement Association, 1985), p. 38.

or her to lose interest. Tailor your résumé to fit the requirements of the job for which you are applying. Stress the skills and qualities that have the most direct relationship to the job. Résumés must be positive and demonstrate potential for effectiveness. Minimize less relevant experience.

- Do not focus heavily on dates at the expense of other relevant information. Employers are more concerned with a thorough description of *what* you did rather than when you did it.
- A résumé must always be factual. Avoid statements of opinions about yourself and statements you cannot substantiate. Résumés are no place for gimmicks. This turns employers off.[91]

Once you have decided what to include, you have to decide between the two major types of résumés, chronological and functional.[92] The chronological résumé format is more widely used. Education and work history are listed in reverse chronological order, with the present activity heading the list. From the employer's point of view, this format permits an easy check of the progress and promotional path of the applicant. In the functional résumé format, experience and education are arranged in order of their importance, with the most significant appearing first. Either the job title or the basic functions of the job are featured. This approach is suited to experienced individuals who have impressive job titles and duties to highlight.

Company Research

The CEC requests that employers submit job descriptions and a variety of other information (e.g., annual reports and other company literature). The CEC also has copies of employer directories.

Company-specific data about an employer's history, operations, personnel, type of corporate culture, newsworthy events, and so on can also be obtained from the business sections of newspapers, the local Chamber of Commerce, libraries, the firm's public relations department, and personal contacts (friends and alumni association members who work there). Other sources include the *Canadian Business Index*, *Canadian Periodicals Index*, annually updated microfiche collections such as *The Financial Post Corporation Service*, and databases such as *Infoglobe* (which contains most of the material published in the Toronto *Globe and Mail*). Another useful source is the *Financial Post*'s book which identifies Canadian firms that are great to work for.[93]

Thorough research on companies does two things for you: it helps pin down the employers you're really interested in, and it provides you information you can use to your advantage during the interview. Identifying several specific items indicates to the recruiter that your knowledge about the company is current. For example, has the company recently made an acquisition, is it expanding, has it been mentioned in the newspaper or other media as a leader in its industry, as a firm known for having progressive management and employee relations systems, and so on. Also know the names of several of the organization's corporate officers and the North American and overseas (if any) locations of major plants.

Interview Preparation

Work with a friend to practice and hone your interviewing skills. Take turns as recruiter and applicant. Videotape the result, examine your responses (verbal and body language), and work toward improvement. Make these practice interviews as realistic as possible by also observing interviewee guidelines pertaining to "interviewing uniform," accessories, the "Magic Four Hello," avoiding a subordinate role, aligning with the interviewer (through the use of job-related and company buzzwords, "action" vocabulary, and certain success phrases), admiring achievements of the employer, projecting an image with staying power, and the "Magic Four Goodbye."[94]

While each employer's protocol is somewhat different from others, the following dimensions encompass the kind of items that make up the interview evaluation form:

1. Personal characteristics—assertiveness, confidence, appearance, manners, poise, friendliness.
2. Maturity—realistic self-assessment and goals, judgement indicated in evaluating and answering questions.
3. Desire/ambition—self-responsibility, goal-oriented efforts and activities, need to achieve.
4. Communication skills (written and oral)—command of language, voice, sincerity.
5. Interest (in job/career applied for)—long-range development/career goals, enthusiasm, attitude.
6. Work experience—relevance, diversity, degree of responsibility/supervision exercised, work attitude.
7. Extracurricular activities—sports, hobbies, student government, volunteer activities.
8. Academic record—class standing (available from the résumé or copies of academic records).

Each of the items in the first seven dimensions usually has a scale attached to it, ranging from "unsatisfactory" to "outstanding." Based on the 20- to 30-minute interview, the recruiter rates the applicant on each item and generates two additional pieces of information: an overall global assessment rating, which is not necessarily the average of the item ratings, and a yes or no answer to the important question of whether the applicant should be considered further.

While the recruiter's evaluation of your suitability is influenced by a number of factors (see Chapter Nine), you can increase your chances of a successful interview by also preparing and practicing answers to a variety of interviewer questions. There is no one standard list, and the number of questions varies. Get a copy of whatever version is available through the CEC, consultants, or published sources, and use it.[95]

Interview Follow-Up

Be sure to keep a record of your contacts. Immediately after leaving the interview make the following notations:

- The name of the interviewer.
- The type of opportunity for which you were considered.
- The location of work.
- Your reaction and possible interest.
- Your next action.

Answers to Invitations for Visits

If you receive an invitation for a plant visit, acknowledge it in one of three ways:

1. Accept and set the date when you will be there.
2. Indicate your desire to accept at a later date if you need more time to consider.
3. Decline for whatever honest reason you have.

Follow-Up to Site Visit

As soon as you return from a site visit send a letter of thanks to the individual who issued the invitation, as well as to any others you believe should receive a special note of appreciation.

Evaluating Job Offers

Offers of employment may be made verbally, by telegram, or by letter, the last two being the most usual means. When dealing with an offer, remember that both you and the employer are expected to observe the UCPA's principles of good recruitment practice.[96] Employers are required to verify job offers and terms of employment in writing, are prohibited from pressuring candidates to accept offers before the agreed on acceptance date, and are not to rescind offers or renege on acceptances of employment. The student's responsibilities include responding to every offer (even if rejecting it), notifying employers of acceptance (or rejection) as soon as a decision is made, and not accepting more than one offer or reneging on acceptances of employment.

Earlier in this chapter we discussed some of the research on how individuals generally evaluate job offers. We found that a satisfier takes the first offer received. Maximizers and validators make choices among competing offers in a vigilant manner. We also know vigilant decision making is employed by those who realize there are risks involved in all choices, believe there is a best choice, and feel there is enough time to make a thoroughly systematic decision.[97] Further, discussion of the career decision strategy model listed specific questions to ask to sort out what you really want.

From a "how to" perspective, a useful approach in making your choice is the balance sheet procedure. Although several versions are available, it is basically a grid in which you lay out the pros and cons of each job offer.[98] Based on your career and job preferences (see Steps 3 and 4 of Exhibit 8–11), you may find it useful to compare offers by organizing the data in terms of a balance work sheet as illustrated in Exhibit 8–13. The job offer dimensions are factors you believe are relevant to your decision making. Weigh each factor according to its importance to you at this time in your career, rate each in light of the opportunity it represents, multiply, and calculate the total of the products to get a score for the job offer. Although this approach is not objective, it allows for a systematic comparison of job offers based on your preferences and interests.

Replying to an Offer

There are innumerable ways of handling an offer. The quickest is to accept. However, for every acceptance, there are many rejections. Most companies

EXHIBIT 8–13
Evaluating Job Offers

Job Offer Dimensions	Weight	Rating	Weight × Rating
Company culture			
Promotion potential			
Salary			
Job security			
Profit sharing			
Career development			
etc. . . .			
		Total: _____	

do not expect an immediate acceptance or rejection, but they do expect an acknowledgement. *Be sure to reply within three days* after receiving the offer, thanking the sender and stating a date when you will send definite word, provided a deadline has not already been specified. If it has, your letter should indicate that your final answer will be forthcoming by the deadline specified.

Delaying a Final Answer
If you need more time to answer than previously agreed to, send another letter to the employer, stating your reasons and requesting indulgence. Always remember the employer's position as well as your own.

Accepting an Offer
In accepting an offer, send an enthusiastic note of appreciation indicating when you will report for work. This latter point will be developed by mutual agreement.

Rejecting an Offer
Letters of rejection should be sent as soon as you realize you are not interested in the job. It is not necessary to state your exact reasons for turning down an offer or to say where you expect to go, but it is courteous to express your sincere thanks for having been favourably considered. It is helpful for the organization to know what your true feelings are regarding the company, such as preference for a different location, another type of product, or different initial training.

DISCUSSION AND REVIEW QUESTIONS

1. How are recruiting and job search related?
2. How do external conditions affect recruiting?
3. How do organizations formulate a recruiting strategy?
4. What are the positive and negative aspects of a "promotion from within" recruiting policy?
5. What is a realistic job preview? When is it a good idea?
6. Compare the advantages and disadvantages of various recruiting methods, such as advertising, employment agencies, personal referrals, and others.
7. How do employers recruit college and university students for jobs? What are effective and ineffective recruiters like?
8. Discuss the relationship between organizational and occupational choice decisions. How are they similar? How are they different?
9. Outline an approach to specifying the job characteristics you want before your job search.
10. Describe how you plan to get your job when you leave college or university.

11. Collect a list of questions most commonly asked by recruiters, and prepare a set of well-thought-out answers.
12. Team with a fellow student and act out a good (and bad) interview in front of the class (use videotape facilities, if available).
13. Interview the recruiter of a local company about the process and procedures used to recruit managerial personnel, professional technical personnel, and skilled trades. Are different procedures used? Prepare a 20-minute class presentation to report your findings.
14. Interview the coordinator of your campus CEIC employment centre to update your class on the services available.

NOTES AND REFERENCES

1. John T. Malloy, *Dress for Success* (New York: Warner Books, 1975); John T. Malloy, *The Woman's Dress for Success Book* (New York: Warner Books, 1978); see also Letitia Baldrige, *Letitia Baldrige's Complete Guide to Executive Manners* (New York: Rawson Associates, 1985).
2. Paul F. Wernimont, "Recruitment Policies and Practices," in *ASPA Handbook of Personnel and Industrial Relations*, ed. Dale Yoder and Herbert C. Heneman, Jr. (Washington, D.C.: Bureau of National Affairs, 1979).
3. S. L. Rynes and H. E. Miller, "Recruiter and Job Influences on Candidates for Employment," *Journal of Applied Psychology* 68, no. 1 (1983), pp. 147–54.
4. Kenneth N. Wexley and W. F. Nemeroff, "Effects of Racial Prejudice, Race of Applicant, and Biographical Similarity on Interviewer Evaluations of Job Applicants," *Journal of Social and Behavioral Sciences* 20, no. 1 (1974), pp. 66–78.
5. Wayne F. Cascio, *Applied Psychology in Personnel Management*, 2nd ed. (Reston, Va.: Reston Publishing, 1982); our discussion also draws on the excellent treatment presented in Roger E. Hawk, *The Recruitment Function* (New York: American Management Associations, 1967).
6. Cascio, *Applied Psychology in Personnel Management*.
7. Ibid.
8. Ibid., p. 181; see also Hawk, *The Recruitment Function*.
9. J. Ullman and T. G. Gutteridge, "Job Search in the Labor Market for College Graduates: A Case Study of MBA's," *Academy of Management Journal* 17, no. 2 (1974), pp. 381–86.
10. Sara Rynes, Donald Schwab, and Herbert G. Heneman III, "The Role of Pay and Market Pay Variability in Job Application Decisions," *Organizational Behavior and Human Performance* 31, no. 2 (1983), pp. 353–64.
11. Kenneth G. Wheeler, "Perceptions of Labor Market Variables by College Students in Business, Education and Psychology," *Journal of Vocational Behavior* 22, no. 1 (1983), pp. 1–11.
12. R. E. Azevedo, "Scientists, Engineers, and the Job Search Process," *California Management Review* 17, no. 1 (1974), pp. 40–49.
13. L. C. Thurow, *Generating Inequality: Mechanisms of Distribution in the United States Economy* (New York: Basic Books, 1975).
14. Richard R. Reilly and Georgia T. Chao, "Validity and Fairness of Some Alternative Employee Selection Procedures," *Personnel Psychology* 35, no. 1 (1982), pp. 1–62; R. D. Arvey, *Fairness in Selecting Employees* (Reading, Mass.: Addison-

Wesley Publishing, 1979); see also Chapter Seven of this book.
15. Louise Piché, "Employment Equity: On Track at CN," *The Canadian Business Review*, Summer 1985, pp. 19–22.
16. Private communication to authors.
17. Based on Section D - JOBSCAN Concept (pp. 43–47) supplied by Employment and Immigration Canada, April 29, 1986.
18. Judy D. Olian and Sara L. Rynes, "Organizational Staffing: Integrating Practice with Strategy," *Industrial Relations*, Spring 1984, pp. 170–83; Noel M. Tichy, Charles Fombrun, and Mary Anne Devanna, "Strategic Human Resource Management," *Sloan Management Review*, Winter 1982, pp. 47–61.
19. Raymond E. Miles and Charles C. Snow, *Organization Strategy, Structure and Process* (New York: McGraw-Hill, 1978); C. Snow and R. E. Miles, "Organizational Strategy, Design and Human Resources Management," presented at 43rd Meeting of Academy of Management, Dallas, Texas, August 1983; Olian and Rynes, "Organizational Staffing."
20. Sara L. Rynes, Herbert G. Heneman III, and Donald P. Schwab, "Individual Reactions to Organizational Recruiting: A Review," *Personnel Psychology*, Autumn 1980, pp. 529–42.
21. Herbert E. Gerson and Louis P. Britt III, "Hiring—the Dangers of Promising Too Much," *Personnel Administrator*, March 1984, pp. 5–8, 112.
22. John P. Wanous, Thomas L. Keon, and Janina Latack, "Expectancy Theory and Occupational/Organizational Choices: A Review and Test," *Organizational Behavior and Human Performances* 32, no. 1 (1983), pp. 66–86.
23. J. L. Farr, B. S. O'Leary, and C. J. Bartlett, "Effect of Work Sample Test upon Self-Selection and Turnover of Job Applicants," *Journal of Applied Psychology* 58, no. 2 (1973), pp. 283–85; D. P. Schwab, "Organizational Recruiting and the Decision to Participate," in *Personnel Management: New Perspectives*, ed. K. Rowland and G. Ferris (Boston: Allyn & Bacon, 1982).
24. J. P. Wanous, *Organizational Entry: Recruitment, Selection, and Socialization of Newcomers* (Reading, Mass.: Addison-Wesley Publishing, 1980).
25. Sanford M. Jacoby, "The Development of Internal Labor Markets in American Manufacturing Firms," in *Internal Labor Markets*, ed. Paul Osterman (Cambridge, Mass.: MIT Press, 1984); Rosabeth Moss Kanter, "Variations in Managerial Career Structures in High-Technology Firms: The Impact of Organizational Characteristics on Internal Labor Market Patterns," in *Internal Labor Markets*, ed. Paul Osterman (Cambridge, Mass.: MIT Press, 1984).
26. Robert E. Hall, "The Importance of Lifetime Jobs in the U.S. Economy," *American Economic Review*, September 1982, pp. 716–24; Paul Ryan, "Job Training, Employment Practices, and the Large Enterprise: The Case of Costly Transferable Skills," in *Internal Labor Markets*, ed. Paul Osterman (Cambridge, Mass.: MIT Press, 1984); Terry Beehr, Thomas Taber, and Jeffrey Walsh, "Perceived Mobility Channels: Criteria for Intraorganizational Job Mobility," *Organizational Behavior and Human Performance* 26, no. 2 (1980), pp. 250–64.
27. J. R. Garcia, "Job Posting for Professional Staff," *Personnel Journal*, March 1984, pp. 189–92; G. A. Wallropp, "Job Posting for Nonexempt Employees: A Sample Program," *Personnel Journal*, October 1981, pp. 796–98; Eva Innes, Robert L. Perry, and Jim Lyon, *The Financial Post Selects the 100 Best Companies to Work for in Canada* (Don Mills, Ont.: Collins, 1986).

28. Dave Dahl and Patrick Pinto, "Job Posting: An Industry Survey," *Personnel Journal*, January 1977, pp. 40–42.
29. J. C. Ullman, "Employee Referrals: Prime Tool for Recruiting Workers," *Personnel* 43, no. 1 (1966), pp. 30–35; D. P. Schwab, "Recruiting and Organizational Participation," in *Personnel Management*, ed. K. Rowland and G. Ferris (Boston: Allyn & Bacon, 1982); P. J. Decker and E. T. Cornelius, "A Note on Recruiting Sources and Job Survival Rates," *Journal of Applied Psychology* 64, no. 3 (1979), pp. 463–64; M. J. Gannon, "Source of Referral and Employee Turnover," *Journal of Applied Psychology* 55, no. 1 (1971), pp. 226–28.
30. Innes, Perry, and Lyon, *The Financial Post Selects the 100 Best Companies to Work for in Canada*.
31. A. E. Marshall, "Recruiting Alumni on College Campuses," *Personnel Journal*, April 1982, pp. 264–66.
32. "Principles and Practices of Recruitment," *Career Planning: 1985–86*, vol. 16 (Toronto: University and College Placement Association), p. 88.
33. Canada Employment Centre on Campus—University of British Columbia, Summary and Description of Services, 1985.
34. Sunder Magnum, "The Placement Activity of the Canadian Employment Agency," *Relations Industrielles* 38, no. 1, (1983), pp. 72–94.
35. V. M. Evans, "Recruitment Advertising in the '80s," *Personnel Administrator* March 1978, pp. 21–25, 30.
36. Nancy A. Mason and John A. Belt, "Effectiveness of Specificity in Recruitment Advertising" (paper presented at the Academy of Management National Meeting, August 1985, San Diego).
37. Ibid.; R. M. Hochheiser, "Recruitment: A Prescription for Hiring Headaches," *Personnel Journal*, 1982, pp. 578, 580–82.
38. Mason and Belt, "Effectiveness of Specificity in Recruitment Advertising," pp. 7–8.
39. William M. Bulkeley, "Some Firms Are Recruiting by Computer," *The Wall Street Journal*, February 11, 1984, pp. 35, 40.
40. John W. Boudreau and Sara Rynes, "The Role of Recruitment in Staffing Utility Analysis" (working paper, Ithaca, N.Y., Cornell University, August 1983).
41. Jac Fitz-enz, *How to Measure Human Resources Management* (New York: McGraw-Hill, 1984), pp. 86–87.
42. *Personnel Policies Forum* (Washington, D.C.: Bureau of National Affairs, 1979).
43. Schwab, "Recruiting and Organizational Participation."
44. J. A. Breaugh, "Relationships between Recruiting Sources and Employee Performance, Absenteeism and Work Attitudes," *Academy of Management Journal* 24, no. 3 (1981), pp. 142–47.
45. G. L. Reid, "Job Search and the Effectiveness of Job-Finding Methods," *Industrial and Labor Relations Review* 25, no. 3 (1972), pp. 479–95; M. S. Taylor and D. W. Schmidt, "A Process-Oriented Investigation of Recruitment Source Effectiveness," *Personnel Psychology* 36, no. 3 (1983), pp. 343–54.
46. Rebecca Ellis and M. Susan Taylor, "The Role of Self-Esteem within the Job Search Process" (Working paper No. 34, Madison, Wis., August 1982); S. L. Rynes and J. Lawler, "A Policy-Capturing Investigation of the Role of Expectancies in Decisions to Pursue Job Alternatives," *Journal of Applied Psychology* 68, no. 4 (1983), pp. 620–31.

47. Robert Sibson, "The High Cost of Hiring," *Nation's Business*, February 14, 1975, pp. 85–88.
48. R. Stoops, "Recruitment Strategy," *Personnel Journal*, February 1982, p. 102.
49. Wanous, *Organizational Entry*.
50. Gerson and Britt, "Hiring"; Howard A. Levitt, *The Law of Dismissal in Canada* (Aurora, Ont.: Canada Law Book, 1985).
51. J. P. Wanous, "Effects of a Realistic Job Preview on Job Acceptance, Job Attitudes, and Job Survival," *Journal of Applied Psychology* 58, no. 3 (1973), pp. 327–32; D. R. Ilgen and W. Seely, "Realistic Expectations as an Aid in Reducing Voluntary Resignations," *Journal of Applied Psychology* 59, no. 4 (1974), pp. 452–55; Roger A. Dean and J. P. Wanous, "Reality Shock: When a New Employee's Expectations Don't Match Reality" (paper presented at the Academy of Management National Meeting, August 15, 1982, New York City).
52. Wanous, *Organizational Entry*.
53. Richard E. Kopelman, *Managing Productivity in Organizations* (New York: McGraw-Hill, 1986).
54. Ibid.; Paula Popovich and John P. Wanous, "The Realistic Job Preview as a Persuasive Communication," *Academy of Management Review* 7 (1982), p. 571.
55. Kopelman, *Managing Productivity*.
56. Ibid.; Bernard L. Dugoni and Daniel R. Ilgen, "Realistic Job Previews and the Adjustment of New Employees," *Academy of Management Journal* 24, no. 3 (1981), p. 580.
57. Wanous, *Organizational Entry*.
58. R. R. Reilly, S. M. Sperling, and M. L. Tenopyr, "The Effects of Job Previews on Job Acceptance and Survival of Telephone Operator Candidates," *Journal of Applied Psychology* 64 (1979), pp. 218–20.
59. R. R. Reilly, B. Brown, M. R. Blood, and C. Z. Malatesta, "The Effects of Realistic Previews: A Study and Discussion of the Literature," *Personnel Psychology* 34 (1981), pp. 823–34; Bernard L. Dugoni and Daniel R. Ilgen, "Realistic Job Previews and the Adjustment of New Employees," pp. 579–91.
60. Todd D. Jick and Leonard Greenhalgh, "Realistic Job Previews: A Reconceptualization" (paper presented at the Academy of Management National Meeting, August 1980, Detroit).
61. Steven L. Premack and John P. Wanous, "A Meta-Analysis of Realistic Job Preview Experiments," *Journal of Applied Psychology* 70 (1985), pp. 706–19.
62. Ibid., p. 706.
63. James A. Breaugh, "Realistic Job Previews: A Critical Appraisal and Future Research Directions," *Academy of Management Review* 8, no. 4 (1983), pp. 612–19.
64. Roger A. Dean and John P. Wanous, "Effects of Realistic Job Previews on Hiring Bank Tellers," *Journal of Applied Psychology* 69, no. 1 (1984), pp. 61–68; Paula Popovich and John P. Wanous, "The Realistic Job Preview as a Persuasive Communication," *Academy of Management Journal* 7, no.4 (1982), pp. 570–78; S. O. Horner, W. H. Mobley, and B. M. Meglino, "An Experimental Evaluation of the Effects of a Realistic Job Preview on Marine Recruit Affect, Intentions and Behavior," (working paper, Center for Management and Organizational Research, University of South Carolina, 1979); J. P. Wanous, "Realistic Job Previews: Can a Procedure to Reduce Turnover Also Influence the Relationship between Abilities and Performance?" *Personnel Psychology*, Spring 1978, pp. 249–458.
65. Wanous, *Organizational Entry*.
66. Cascio, *Applied Psychology in Personnel Management*.

67. Jick and Greenhalgh, "Realistic Job Previews."
68. L. W. Porter, E. E. Lawler III, and J. R. Hackman, *Behavior in Organizations* (New York: McGraw-Hill, 1975).
69. J. H. Greenhaus and O. C. Brenner, "How Do Job Candidates Size Up Prospective Employers," *Personnel Administrator*, March 1982, pp. 21–25; L. W. Porter and R. M. Steers, "Organizational, Work, and Personal Factors in Employee Turnover and Absenteeism," *Psychological Bulletin* 80, no. 3 (1973), pp. 151–76; S. Rottenberg, "On Choice in the Labor Markets," *Industrial and Labor Relations Review* 9, no. 2 (1965).
70. Wanous, *Organizational Entry*; J. O. Crites, *Vocational Psychology* (New York: McGraw-Hill, 1969).
71. J. F. Dillard, "An Update on the Applicability of an Occupational Goal-Expectancy Model in Professional Accounting Organizations," *Decision Sciences* 12, no. 1 (1981), pp. 32–38; N. Schmitt and L. Son, "An Evaluation of Valence Models of Motivation to Pursue Various Post–High School Alternatives," *Organizational Behavior and Human Performance* 27, no. 2 (1981), pp. 135–50; V. L. Holmstrom and L. R. Beach, "Subjective Expected Utility and Career Preferences," *Organizational Behavior and Human Performance* 10, no. 3 (1973), pp. 201–7; T. R. Mitchell, "Expectancy Models of Job Satisfaction, Occupational Preference and Effort: A Theoretical, Methodological, and Empirical Appraisal," *Psychological Bulletin* 81, no. 4 (1974), pp. 1053–77; K. G. Wheeler and T. M. Mahoney, "The Expectancy Model in the Analysis of Occupational Preference and Occupational Choice," *Journal of Vocational Behavior* 19, no. 2 (1981), pp. 113–22.
72. P. M. Blau, J. W. Gustad, R. Jesson, H. S. Parnes, and R. C. Wilcox, "Occupational Choices: A Conceptual Framework," *Industrial and Labor Relations Review* 9 (1956), p. 534.
73. Ibid., p. 336.
74. George T. Milkovich and Jerry Newman, *Compensation*, 2nd ed. (Plano, Tex.: Business Publications, 1987).
75. Rynes and Lawler, "Policy-Capturing Investigation"; Wanous, Keon, and Latack, "Expectancy Theory."
76. C. E. Jurgensen, "Job Preferences (What Makes a Job Good or Bad?)," *Journal of Applied Psychology*, May 1978, pp. 267–76.
77. R. L. Opsahl and M. D. Dunnette, "The Role of Financial Compensation in Industrial Motivation," *Psychological Bulletin*, October 1966, pp. 94–118.
78. Royal Commission on the Economic Union and Development Prospects for Canada (McDonald Commission), *Report* (Ottawa: Minister of Supply and Services, 1985).
79. A. Hasan and S. Gera, "Aspects of Job Search in Canada" (Discussion Paper No. 156; Ottawa: Economic Council of Canada, 1980); and Statistics Canada, *Labour Force Surveys*.
80. L. D. Dyer, "Job Search Success of Middle-Aged Managers and Engineers," *Industrial and Labor Relations Review*, January 1973, pp. 969–79; J. Barron and D. W. Gilley, "The Effect of Unemployment Insurance on the Search Process," *Industrial and Labor Relations Review*, March 1979, pp. 363–66.
81. Martin Feldstein, "The Economics of the New Unemployment," *Public Interest*, Fall 1973, pp. 3–42; Ronald G. Ehrenberg and Ronald L. Oaxaca, "Unemployment Insurance, Duration of Unemployment and Subsequent Wage Gain," *American Economic Review*, December 1976, pp. 754–66; Finis Welch, "What Have

We Learned from Empirical Studies of Unemployment Insurance," *Industrial and Labor Relations Review*, July 1977, pp. 451–61.
82. Thomas Gutteridge and Joseph Ullman, "On the Return to Job Search," in *Proceedings of Academy of Management*, Boston, August 1973, pp. 366–72; and J. C. Ullman and T. G. Gutteridge, "The Job Search," *Journal of College Placement* 33, no. 2 (1973), pp. 67–72.
83. William Glueck, "Decision Making: Organization Choice," *Personnel Psychology*, Spring 1974, pp. 66–93; and "How Recruiters Influence Job Choices on Campus," *Personnel*, March–April 1971, pp. 46–52.
84. *Empirical Analysis of the Search Behavior of Low-Income Workers* (Menlo Park, Calif.: Stanford Research Institute, 1975); G. L. Reid, "Job Search and the Effectiveness of Job-Finding Methods," *Industrial and Labor Relations Review*, June 1972, pp. 479–95.
85. Innes, Perry, and Lyon, *The 100 Best Companies to Work for in Canada*.
86. Rynes and Lawler, "Policy-Capturing Investigation"; J. H. Greenhaus, C. Seidel, and M. Marinis, "The Impact of Expectations and Values on Job Attitudes," *Organizational Behavior and Human Performance* 23, no. 1 (1983), pp. 3–17.
87. Jim Duncan, "On-Campus Interview," *Career Planning: 1985–86* (Toronto: University and College Placement Association, 1985), pp. 95–96; Rosemary Gaymer, "Coping with Application Forms . . . and the UCPA Form in Particular," *Career Planning: 1985–86*, pp. 42–44.
88. Gaymer, "Coping with Application Forms"; "The Five Steps to Finding a Job," sponsored by Placement Services and Affiliates Program, Faculty of Commerce and Business Administration, University of British Columbia, Vancouver, B.C., 11 pp., undated.
89. *Career Planning* (Toronto: University and College Placement Association, 1987).
90. *Guide to Résumé Writing* (Toronto: University and College Placement Association, 1978).
91. "The Five Steps to Finding a Job."
92. Ibid., p. 5.
93. Innes, Perry, and Lyon, *The 100 Best Companies to Work for in Canada*.
94. Jeffrey G. Allen, *How to Turn an Interview into a Job* (New York: Simon & Schuster, 1983).
95. See, for example, Allen, *How to Turn an Interview into a Job*, chap. V; Suzanne Landau and Geoffrey Bailey, "What Every Woman Should Know," in *Organizational Reality: Reports from the Firing Line*, 3rd ed., ed. Peter J. Frost, Vance F. Mitchell, and Walter R. Nord (Glenview, Ill.: Scott, Foresman, 1986); Stephen K. Merman and John E. McLaughlin, *Out-Interviewing the Interviewer* (Englewood Cliffs, N.J.: Prentice-Hall, 1983); "The 70 Most Asked Questions," supplementary readings for Commerce-220 (Vancouver: Faculty of Commerce and Business Administration, University of British Columbia, 1986); Joseph P. Zima, *Interviewing: Key to Effective Management* (Chicago: Science Research Associates, 1983), especially pp. 155–57.
96. *Career Planning: 1985–86*, p. 88.
97. I. L. Janis and L. Mann, *Decision Making: A Psychological Analysis of Conflict, Choice, and Commitment* (New York: Free Press, 1977).
98. For several applications, see I. L. Janis and D. Wheeler, "Thinking Clearly about Career Choices," *Psychology Today*, May 1978, p. 75; John E. McLaughlin and Stephen K. Merman, *Sound Advice for Job and Career Strategists* (Denver, Colo.: Portland Management Group, 1977).

CHAPTER NINE
SELECTION

CHAPTER OUTLINE

I. A Diagnostic Approach to Selection
II. Employment Testing
III. Reliability
    A. Reliability Methods
        1. Test-Retest Reliability
        2. Alternate (or Equivalent) Forms Reliability
        3. Internal Consistency
        4. Conspect Reliability
IV. Validation
    A. Empirical (Criterion-Related) Validation Methods
        1. Predictive Validation
        2. Concurrent Validation
    B. Rational Methods
        1. Content Validity
        2. Construct Validity
        3. Synthetic Validity—A Combination
V. Usefulness of a Selection Procedure
VI. Validity Generalization
VII. Selection Process
VIII. Selection Procedures
    A. Application Blanks/Biographical Data
    B. Employment Interview
    C. Employment Tests

      D. Medical Testing/Screening
      E. Formal Education
      F. Experience
      G. Reference Checks and Recommendation Letters
      H. Comparison of Job Performance Predictors
IX. International Dimensions
X. Summary
    Appendix A / Technical Note—Selection Study
    Appendix B / Valid Selection Means Higher Work Force Productivity

This chapter is about designing and managing selection programs that contribute to employee effectiveness and organization performance.

Selection is an integral part of the staffing process. When employment planning leads managers to expect that additional staff will be required, recruiting takes place. Recruiting generates the pool of potential employees. Selection involves deciding who from the pool of applicants would be the best job performers and should get job offers. High-level managers, and even chief executives, pour over volumes of dossiers on candidates for top management jobs. Every spring companies cull through the qualifications of graduating students to select the most promising.

Selection decisions are critical to the success of any organization, and particularly to the P/HRM function. Why? Because selection is an area of P/HRM that (along with training/development) provides the greatest opportunity to save (or waste) organizational financial resources. Selection should be viewed as a P/HRM activity that is part of the organization's *feedforward* control system. Feedforward control focusses on the resources (financial, physical, information, and human) taken into the organization, and is designed to assess their quantity and quality *before* they are accepted by the organization.[1] Although effective selection requires great expertise, carefully designed selection programs incoporating valid selection devices *do pay off.*[2]

Who actually makes the selection decision varies. In some organizations, selection is centralized in one office; in others, the selection function is decentralized. In medium-sized and larger organizations, personnel specialists screen the applicants and make a recommendation, while the operating manager makes the final selection. In smaller organizations with no P/HRM unit, the operating manager does both screening and selecting. When unions act as the selection agent, they control the supply of talent available to the employer. Exhibit 9–1 outlines the involvement of both operating and P/HRM managers in selection decisions.

EXHIBIT 9-1
The Role of Operating and P/HRM Managers in Selection

Selection Function	Operating Manager (OM)	Personnel/Human Resource Manager (P/HRM)
Choice of selection criteria	Selected by OM	Recommends and implements the selection criteria based on job specifications
Validation of criteria		Performed by P/HRM
Screening interview		Normally performed by P/HRM
Supervision of application/biodata form		Normally by P/HRM
Employment interview	OM and P/HRM	OM and P/HRM
Testing		Performed by P/HRM
Background/reference check		Normally performed by P/HRM
Physical exam		Normally performed by P/HRM
Selection/decision	OM decides after considering P/HRM recommendation	Recommendation by P/HRM to OM

Source: Adapted from John M. Ivancevich and William F. Glueck, *Foundations of Personnel/Human Resource Management,* 3rd ed. (Plano, Tex.: Business Publications, 1986).

Some employers also give co-workers a voice in the selection decision by allowing them to interview applicants. This procedure is used at universities where the faculty and students express preferences about applicants. At the Canadian General Electric plant in Bromont, Québec, self-regulating work teams participate in hiring, and in some cases firing, team members.

Given the importance of selection, and in light of the professionalization trend of P/HRM (see Chapter One), it is disappointing that selection as practiced by some is still not drawing fully on state-of-the-art techniques. To illustrate, a recent survey of almost 600 Canadian organizations (small, medium, large) revealed that over two thirds of the P/HRM respondents had never heard of, or were not familiar with how to determine, the validity of selection instruments.[3] From a somewhat different perspective, noted author and management consultant Peter F. Drucker reports that most managers make good hiring decisions in only about one third of all selection situations; he claims, however, that well-designed selection procedures can help managers improve on this "0.333 batting average."[4] Understanding and applying the material covered in this chapter are steps in the right direction.

> **Definition**
> *Selection* is the process by which managers choose from a pool of applicants the person or persons who are most likely to meet the requirements of the job opening, given the external and organizational conditions.

A DIAGNOSTIC APPROACH TO SELECTION

Designing a selection system depends on the context in which selection decisions are to be made. Accordingly, P/HRM professionals need to diagnose conditions in the external environment and the organization when designing selection systems.

Strategies and Objectives

The strategies and objectives of an organization influence the selection process.[5] For example, organizations with emerging or new products may require experienced people who possess marketing and technical skills to focus on product design and establishing sales in a new market. Units with more established product lines face mature markets and may select people with finance and manufacturing skills to control product quality and costs.

In addition to affecting the qualifications selected, strategies determine the source of people. Emerging, or prospector, units tend to select from outside; mature units, or defenders, tend to be more willing to promote from within. Consequently, selection systems are designed with the source in mind.

Research may not have advanced enough to prescribe the employee qualities that best match different strategies. Some executives even question the soundness of matching strategies with different selection systems. For example, some seem to believe a well-trained manager is a jack-of-all-trades who can run any unit, no matter its strategy or condition. However, given the renewed emphasis on corporate culture and its relationship to strategy (Chapter Three), a matching of individual values with core and operational values of the employer may become as important as matching KSAOs with job requirements.[6]

Snow and Miles also point out that dominant coalitions within an organization influence the selection process.[7] Powerful managers will try to influence the selection process to make certain their strategies and policies are continued. A study of hospitals found the major source of financing influenced the selection process.[8] When a major portion of the hospital's budget came from private insurance, administrators with accounting backgrounds were selected. When the largest portion of the budget was derived from private donations, managers were selected on the basis of their business or professional contacts.

Labour Markets

Labour market conditions also must be considered in designing and implementing selection systems. For example, hospital dieticians trying to hire dishwashers or food preparation helpers do not have much of a selection decision to worry about. The job can be unpleasant and is performed at unpopular hours (the breakfast crew might have to arrive at 5:30 A.M.). The workday can be long, the pay is not good, and frequently there are no chances for promotion. For such jobs, an applicant who can walk in the door and is free of communicable diseases will usually be hired. Rarely are there enough applicants. On the other hand, a civil service specialist who must choose from hundreds of applicants for foreign service postings to certain overseas embassies has a much more difficult selection system to design.

Labour market conditions show up in the size and quality of the applicant pool. Those who work in P/HRM analyze this factor by use of the selection ratio. Conceptually, the selection ratio (SR) can be defined as the proportion of people in the job applicant population who would score above some threshold score on an employment selection test.[9] In practice, the selection ratio is defined as:

$$\text{Selection ratio} = \frac{\text{Number of applicants selected}}{\text{Number of applicants available for selection}}$$

If every applicant is hired, the selection ratio is 1.00. If only one out of every four applicants is hired, the selection ratio is 0.25. A value of SR=0 means none of the applicants is deemed sufficiently qualified. An SR larger than 1.00 means there are more job openings than applicants.

Government Regulations

The accelerating emphasis in Canada on human rights legislation pertaining to employment is the most significant influence on the design of selection systems. Under the human rights legislation, discussed in Chapter Seven, the principle of employment equity means fair access to employment opportunities and fair treatment in the workplace. It requires that selection procedures be job-related and selection decisions be based on individual assessment. For example, if a selection procedure has adverse impact (e.g., a smaller proportion of female or minority applicants than white male applicants meet hiring standards), the P/HRM professional needs to demonstrate that the procedure is job-related and legally defensible.

In Canada, acceptable methods for demonstrating that hiring decisions are job-related have not been as definitively specified as in the United States. In the United States, lack of compliance has meant considerable financial consequences for employers (e.g., Burlington Northern agreed to a $40 million settlement, due to its inability to show that its selection standards for locomotive engineer training programs were job-related).[10] While Canadians pride themselves on not being as litigious as Americans, the possibility of lengthy human rights actions and unfavourable publicity may cause more Canadian employers to take a proactive stance to ensure their selection procedures are soundly designed and implemented.

The debate about how stringent, complex, and unreasonable human rights guidelines are is far from over. Proponents of the guidelines, while admitting there is some truth in such complaints, may argue that the guidelines were intended to call for little more than adequate development of selection procedures—procedures advocated by industrial psychologists for decades.[11] However, guidelines based on "false theories" about selection research, a "getting-even" attitude, and incorporating inflationary regulations are doomed to failure.

Our thinking on the topic is best concluded with the "fairness principle": fairness exists when applicants (for a job/training program/promotion) with equal probabilities of success (on the job/in the training program/in the higher position) have equal probability of being selected (for the job/training program/promotion). Individuals are of primary importance to our free society, in which each has a fundamental right to the work for which he or she is *qualified*—given that the KSAOs are there to fulfill the job's demands.

Union Requirements

If the organization is wholly or partly unionized, union membership before or soon after hiring is a factor in the selection decision. Some union contracts require that seniority (experience at the job with the company) be the only criterion, or a major one, in selection. If the union has a hiring hall, the union makes the selection decision for the organization. Thus, openly and subtly, a union affects an organization's selection process.

Composition of Client/Customer Base

Organizations sometimes attempt to hire a labour force that reflects the makeup of their clients or customers. For example, in cities to which large numbers of immigrants are attracted, the police department and social welfare agencies attempt to hire personnel fluent in the prevailing languages of the ethnic-immigrant groups. The Royal Canadian Mounted Police engage native persons as special constables with due consideration afforded their native origin in light of the special location of their duty assignment.

Location of the Organization

The location of an organization also affects the selection process. Many high-technology firms are in "Silicon Valley North," located in Kanata, near Ottawa. However, "pockets" of high-technology activity also exist, for example, in Alberta, British Columbia, and Saskatchewan. These regions attract skilled individuals trained to work for high-technology firms. Also, high unemployment in one region may cause the unemployed to move to more promising locations.

EMPLOYMENT TESTING

Employment tests comprise the core of selection procedures. A central issue in designing selection systems is to develop ways to show that the selection procedures are significantly related to successful performance on the job. There is always a risk of making one of two types of errors in selection decisions: selecting someone who should have been rejected (erroneous acceptance), and rejecting someone who should have been accepted (erroneous rejection). These errors can be minimized by selection procedures based on employment tests that are reliable and valid. We will give a brief definition of "test," identify some sources of tests, comment on the status of employment testing, and then focus on available reliability and validation approaches.

According to Cronbach, a test is a systematic procedure for observing an individual's behaviour and describing it with the aid of a numerical scale or a category system; Blum says a test is a sample of an aspect of a person's behaviour, performance, or attitude.[12] Thus, a test may be defined as *a systematic procedure for sampling human behaviour*.[13] The procedure should be systematic with respect to test content, method of administration, and scoring protocol. This definition covers any selection procedure, including interviews, application blanks, aptitude tests, assessment centres, and the like.

Determining which test or tests to use can pose a difficult problem. Catalogues of test developers list several thousand available tests. Sources containing the most extensive bibliographies of commercially available tests are *The Mental Measurements Yearbook, Tests in Print—Volume 2, Vocational Tests and Reviews*,[14] and *Tests*.[15] The latter is a quick-search reference book that describes, but does not critique, more than 3,000 tests for assessment in business, psychology, and education. The first three, by Buros, review and also evaluate the applicability of each test.

A 1986 review of the status of employment testing in Canada drew two important conclusions and presented some tentative recommendations. First, employment testing in Canada is at a formative stage of development compared to that in the United States. Second, although general standards for the use of selection tests are being developed, further guidance is required to produce principles for the validation and use of personnel selection procedures.[16] Guidelines for Canadian testing principles include the following: (1) the importance of reliability and its role within employment testing, (2) the crucial role of job analysis in test validation, (3) appropriate validation strategies, (4) potential applications of validity generalization, (5) identifying types of utility or value-added analyses, (6) methods to detect test bias, and (7) the use of cut-off strategies versus ranking procedures.[17] Understanding these techniques and applying them correctly to selection practices is a must for the P/HRM practitioner who claims to be a professional. Failure to do so will fail to provide sufficient support to clarify the nature and function of employment testing to operating managers and executives. There is also the danger that society at large may force us to settle for "a suboptimal, or even hostile, testing climate imposed by politicians and judicial authorities who have limited technical expertise and may hold uncorrected misconceptions of the nature and purpose of testing in employment."[18]

Current concern with the less than desirable level of sophistication in employment testing practices is justified. Along with relatively little understanding of the seven items already delineated, it appears that: (1) in-house validation studies are often not conducted (instead, validity information accompanying the test booklet is accepted at face value); (2) there is still a strong belief that the interview is one of the most effective selection devices; (3) about half the P/HRM participants surveyed did not know what a weighted application blank is; (4) almost one fifth of medium-size organizations were not familiar with assessment centres; and (5) 25 percent did not know about work sample tests.[19]

RELIABILITY

How good is this test or test procedure? Does it work? These questions often result in confusion when it is not clear whether the questioner is concerned with how well a test measures what it was designed to measure (a question of validity) or with the extent of its consistency of measurement (a question of reliability). Reliability refers to consistency of measurement or repeatability. Since reliable measurement implies stability from one situation to another, a reliable selection instrument should produce either similar scores or at least similar rankings of a set of individuals each time they take the test. An ability test, for example, is considered reliable if the same person's scores do not vary greatly when the test is administered at different times.

Reliability is an important characteristic of selection tests because it is a necessary, but not sufficient, condition for high validity; it serves as a limit or ceiling for validity.[20] Unreliable information cannot be used to predict job performance.

Reliability Methods

The methods and definitions of reliability are (*a*) test-retest reliability, (*b*) alternate forms reliability, (*c*) internal consistency reliability (split-halves, KR-20, Cronbach's alpha), and (*d*) conspect (interscorer) reliability.

Test-Retest Reliability

One obvious method of evaluating the reliability of a selection instrument consists of administering it twice to the same sample of individuals and then determining the similarity of scores. When the correlation coefficient is used to measure the similarity of these scores, it is called a test-retest reliability coefficient or, in this case, a coefficient of stability.[21]

The time interval between testing should be short enough so testees' learning or maturation does not influence scores; also, enough time should pass so testees do not remember the responses made at the first sitting. The appropriate time interval is a function of the type of instrument being examined. A one-week interval is probably sufficient for assessing the reliability of application blanks, interviews, and some personnel tests; a two- or three-month interval may be required for determining reliability of a mental ability test.[22]

Alternate (or Equivalent) Forms Reliability

This method uses two comparable forms of the same test. The two forms differ in that they are developed by drawing two separate random samples of equivalent test items from a larger set of questions (which were constructed to measure the same thing). Each of the forms is composed of the same number and difficulty of items. One of the forms is administered immediately after the other (*immediate* alternate form procedure) or after a certain time interval (*delayed* alternate form). The relationship between the scores obtained on the two forms represents the reliability. For the immediate approach, the reliability estimate is known as the coefficient of equivalence; the delayed approach yields a coefficient of equivalence and stability. The alternate forms approach may be more useful than the basic test-retest because the test items on each form are not the same.

Internal Consistency

The split-halves method is often referred to as a measure of internal consistency. Its mechanics are simple. The test is administered at one sitting. When scoring, it is split into two halves with items as equivalent as possible. Often the test is simply subdivided by putting all the odd-numbered items into one half and forming the other half from even-numbered items. This is called the odd-even version. After each half-test is scored, the relationship between the two halves is determined in terms of the correlation coefficient $r_{(1/2)(1/2)}$. This correlation between halves is an underestimate of the reliability of the total test. To obtain an estimate of the reliability of the entire test, the Spearman-Brown Prophecy formula is applied.[23]

Related to the internal consistency method are techniques which involve the analysis of item variances. Widely used (and requiring only a single test administration) are the "Kuder-Richardson formula 20" (KR-20) and Cronbach's Alpha. Both approaches treat *each item* of the test as a "minitest." The KR-20 formula is used when test items are scored as "right" or "wrong"; the KR-20 coefficient is the mean of all possible split-half coefficients. Cronbach's Alpha is based on a more generalized formula and accommodates tests that have multiple-scored items.[24]

Conspect Reliability

The degree of agreement between the scores or ratings assigned by two (or more) scorers or raters is referred to as conspect reliability. Although not a problem with purely objective scoring procedures, in many instances assessment involves the judgement of raters. For selection procedures such as interviews, conspect reliability can be determined in terms of inter-rater reliability. Decisions about the same applicants are made independently by two or more evaluators, and the results are compared. Low inter-rater reliability means decision makers evaluating the same applicants reach different decisions. Inter-rater reliability is also important in performance evaluation and in scoring certain types of tests (e.g., tests of creativity, projective tests of personality). Unfortunately, inter-rater reliabilities of selection interviews and performance reviews are generally quite low. This may be due to the use of *un*trained raters as well as the particular protocol employed.

VALIDATION

Validation essentially answers two questions: (1) *What* does a selection procedure measure? (2) *How well* does it measure it? It answers these questions by providing evidence that a selection procedure is related to, or predictive of, subsequent work behaviours (e.g., performance, safety, absenteeism, and turnover).

Making certain a selection procedure is work-related is important for at least two reasons. First, increasing work-relatedness of selection decisions has a significant effect on an employee's performance and on the organization's revenues and expenses. Even a slight improvement in job relatedness of a hiring decision translates into significant improvements in productivity. Schmidt, Hunter, McKenzie, and Muldrow showed that using a valid test (versus no test or a less valid test) to select computer programmers saved a company $6,500 per year per selectee over an average job tenure of 10 years. This corresponded to a productivity increase of 20 percent.[25]

The second reason for ensuring that selection procedures are work-related is the wisdom to develop employment equity based on KSAOs.

There are two general approaches to the validation of selection procedures: empirical and rational. The empirical approach employs the criterion-related methods of predictive and concurrent validation; the rational approach focusses on content and construct validity methods. A fifth method, synthetic validity, is a combination of criterion-related and content validities.

Empirical (Criterion-Related) Validation Methods

The empirical approach compares the results of a selection procedure (e.g., interview, work history, test) with one or more independent criteria taken from production or performance evaluation records of on-the-job performance. The relationship between scores on a predictor (selection procedure) and criteria (work behaviours) reflects the job-relatedness of the selection procedure. For example, if a job in the research laboratory at Medtronics, a manufacturer of pacemakers and other implant mechanisms, involves implanting artificial valves into animal hearts, the speed and accuracy of fitting and sewing might be two important performance criteria. A test of hand-eye coordination might be used to select people. Scores on the test might be validated against actual accuracy (a performance quality dimension) and speed shown (quantity dimension) in carrying out the job.

The methods of conducting criterion-related validation studies are predictive and concurrent validation. Exhibit 9–2 compares the two.

Predictive Validation

Under predictive validation (sometimes called the follow-up method), a potential selection technique (e.g., a hand-eye coordination test) is administered to all job applicants but is not used in the decision to hire them. After the applicants have become employees and been on the job for some period, their job performance (criterion) is assessed and correlated with the technique being validated. If a high degree of correlation exists between the scores obtained at the time of application and the later job performance, the test predicts future job performance. Therefore, it may be useful for selecting future employees.

EXHIBIT 9–2

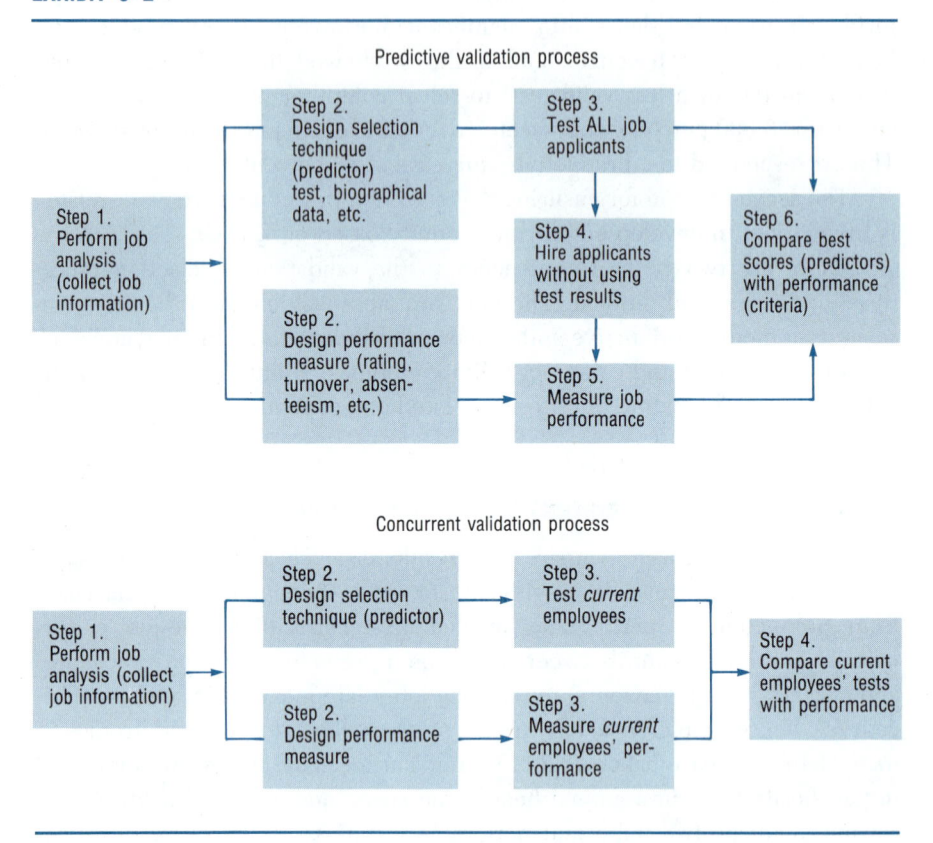

Predictive validation process

- Step 1. Perform job analysis (collect job information)
- Step 2. Design selection technique (predictor) test, biographical data, etc.
- Step 2. Design performance measure (rating, turnover, absenteeism, etc.)
- Step 3. Test ALL job applicants
- Step 4. Hire applicants without using test results
- Step 5. Measure job performance
- Step 6. Compare best scores (predictors) with performance (criteria)

Concurrent validation process

- Step 1. Perform job analysis (collect job information)
- Step 2. Design selection technique (predictor)
- Step 2. Design performance measure
- Step 3. Test *current* employees
- Step 3. Measure *current* employees' performance
- Step 4. Compare current employees' tests with performance

Concurrent Validation

Under concurrent validation (sometimes called present-employee method), current jobholders—instead of applicants—are tested, and their test results correlated with their current job performance. If the predictors are highly related to the job performance criteria, it may be assumed the test results correlated with their performance.

Considerable controversy surrounds use of the concurrent method.[26] If current employees and applicants differ on key factors related to job performance, the concurrent method picks up only those factors possessed by current employees. The applicants could have the potential to do even better on the job than current employees, but if that potential was related to factors not possessed by the current work force, this validation method would miss it. On the other hand, current employee performance may be the result of experience. Very few applicants would have had the opportunity to acquire that experience; yet the test might falsely indicate they will not do well on the job.

A limited, homogeneous sample of current employees usually means a restricted range of available scores on the selection test and criterion scores. A narrowing of the range of either will lower the size of the correlation.[27] As a result, a concurrent validity study provides a conservative (i.e., lower) estimate of what would be obtained through a predictive validation study. Recent studies indicate well-conducted concurrent studies can provide useful estimates of predictive validity. Given the expense of obtaining predictive validity, many researchers believe this useful estimate is close enough.[28]

Exhibit 9–2 also highlights again the importance of conducting a job analysis that is accurate, nondeficient, and not contaminated by aspects not part of the actual job domain. An error in job analysis will have a domino effect on subsequent stages of the validation process and may lead to inconclusive results. Similarly, the use of performance evaluation methods that do not provide valid job performance measures will limit the validation study.

The two criterion-related validity methods should be used by employers when responding to, or anticipating, legislative guidelines calling for empirical data to demonstrate whether a selection procedure is predictive of, or significantly correlated with, important and relevant elements of job performance. The predictive approach is the more elegant method scientifically, but it is not always used in its purest form because some employers may view it as too costly and too slow.[29]

Rational Methods

The second major validation strategy is based on rational methods. These should be utilized with small sample sizes when empirical validation is not feasible.

Content Validity

This method is concerned with the extent to which a selection procedure actually measures some aspect of the job itself (i.e., has content similar to job content). The focus is on analyzing the tasks and behaviours on the job and the knowledge and abilities required to perform them and then testing applicants for such knowledge and abilities. The selection techniques are designed to include the key aspects of the job. Examples are a typing test for an applicant seeking employment as a typist, a shorthand test for use in hiring stenographers, or an assembly test for selecting electronic component assemblers. The more completely one can tap the entire domain of the job, the more content-valid the selection process is. Because it measures current knowledge and abilities, the content approach is less appropriate for entry-level jobs where many skills are to be taught on the job. The assessment of the degree of content validity is primarily a matter of expert judgement; statistical procedures are seldom used.

The choice is not between criterion-related and content-oriented validation approaches. Many employers are including content-oriented data in their criterion-related studies. Dunnette used such an approach for selecting nuclear power plant operators.[30] The validation study collected detailed data on the tasks and behaviours required of the operators, plus experts' judgements of the skills and abilities required to perform the job. Selection tests were designed and used to collect data on the applicants' abilities and skills to successfully perform the required tasks. In this way Dunnette was able to combine criterion- and content-related validation.

Construct Validity

Construct validity of a test is the extent to which it measures a "theoretical construct" or trait.[31] Examples of such constructs are verbal ability, perceptual speed, spatial ability, and empathy. For example, if careful job analysis shows employees must be able to read blueprints, a test of space visualization may be valid as part of the selection process. The effort involved in establishing construct validity involves much research, including criterion-related, and possibly also content, validity studies.

Synthetic Validity—A Combination

This type of validity (sometimes erroneously called artificial validity), attempts to overcome the dilemma of other approaches that depend on relatively large sample sizes. Designed for small organizations, it is sometimes referred to as "validation by parts."[32] It is partly a combination of criterion-related and content validities and is included here because future human rights legislation may specify that even very small organizations will be subject to employment equity considerations.

Consider an organization that has a relatively small number of people in each of several jobs. Synthetic validity analysis would proceed by first analyzing each job into its job behaviour elements, identifying the elements common across the jobs under consideration, and determining their relative importance for these jobs. This part of the process can use the Position Analysis Questionnaire (see Chapter Four), a job analysis instrument that permits the rating of jobs in terms of common behavioural requirements. The organization may find that several jobs involve similar requirements (e.g., creative business judgement, organizational skills, and supervisory ability). One chooses potentially relevant tests (perhaps from existing test batteries developed for similar jobs in larger organizations) and determines the extent to which each actually measures, or predicts proficiency in performing, each of the job elements. The resulting individual test element validities are now combined (synthesized) to obtain a valid test battery for each job. Thus, the output of the analysis identifies which predictors are valid in predicting which job element and specifies the combination of predictors to use for a given job. The statistical procedure developed for computing this type of validity is essentially an adaptation of multiple regression equations.[33]

USEFULNESS OF A SELECTION PROCEDURE

Upon completion of the appropriate validation study, a determination must be made whether to use the predictor in the selection process. This decision involves assessing how much usefulness the prospective predictor would have to the organization. The assessment of usefulness should incorporate a utility analysis perspective. This means that costs and expected benefits must be taken into account. The utility of a selection device is defined as "the degree to which its use improves the quality of the individuals selected beyond what would have occurred had that device not been used."[34] Quality of individuals selected, in turn, can be defined in terms of the proportion of those selected who are considered successful performers, the effect of improved employee effectiveness on productivity, and the dollar payoff to the organization.

Exhibit 9–3 shows the factors used to judge the usefulness of a selection technique. Reliability is included to recall that it is a necessary, but not sufficient, condition for validity; it serves as a limit or ceiling for validity.

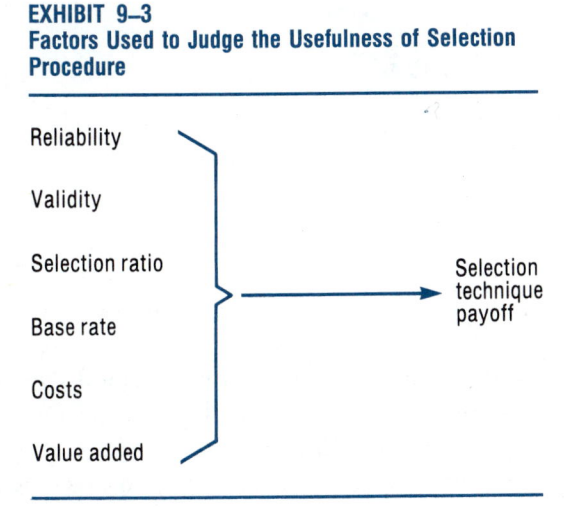

EXHIBIT 9–3
Factors Used to Judge the Usefulness of Selection Procedure

Reliability
Validity
Selection ratio
Base rate
Costs
Value added

→ Selection technique payoff

EXHIBIT 9–4
Scatter Plots Depicting Relationship between Selection Procedure and Job Behaviour

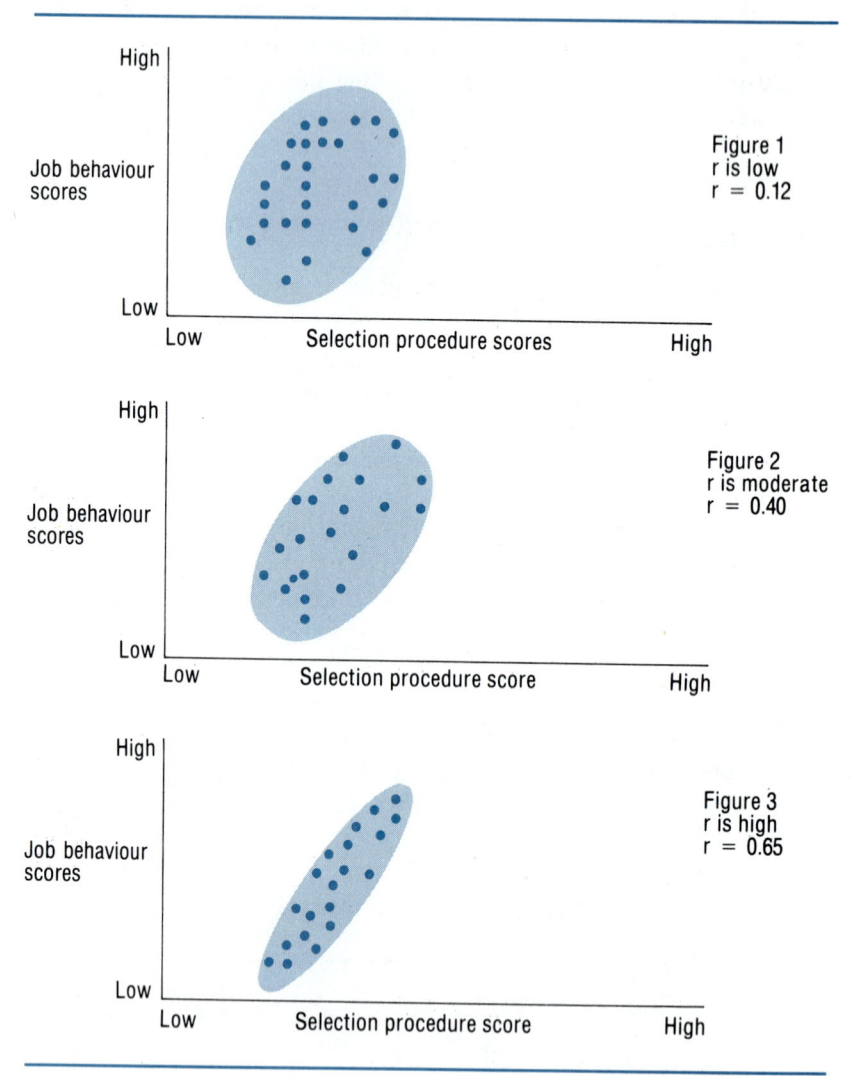

Figure 1
r is low
r = 0.12

Figure 2
r is moderate
r = 0.40

Figure 3
r is high
r = 0.65

Validity. One of the first factors is the relationship between the selection procedure (predictor) and the job behaviour (criterion). Two aspects of the relationship are considered: its strength and its statistical significance.

Exhibit 9–4 presents scatterplots that show the relationship of a hypothetical selection procedure and the job behaviour for each person studied. Figure 1 shows very little relationship between the two. Figure 2 shows a small relationship; there is a tendency for people who do well on the selection technique to also perform well. Figure 3 shows a strong relationship between the selection procedure and subsequent job behaviour. The stronger the relationship, the more "valid" the selection procedure.

All the data shown in a scatterplot can be summarized into a single index called a correlation coefficient (*validity coefficient* in selection design). Numerically, it is identified by the symbol r; the values of r range from -1.0 to $+1.0$. In the figures in Exhibit 9-4, Figure 3 has a higher r (0.65) than Figure 2 (0.40) and Figure 1 (0.12). Coefficients close to zero indicate no significant relationship exists between the predictor and the criterion. The validity coefficient approaches 1.0 as the shape of the scatterplot becomes longer and narrower; if all the points in Figure 3 were arrayed in a straight line we would have perfect validity.

A validity coefficient is said to be statistically significant if the relationship between the selection procedure and the job behaviour is not due to chance.[35] The use of statistical significance is important. If the procedure is to be used to select successful performers, we need to be confident the decision is not due to chance. In practice, validity coefficients seldom exceed $+0.50$.

Each of the three cases shown in Exhibit 9-4 employs a single predictor (independent variable). As most jobs require several abilities, many selection situations utilize a combination of predictors (e.g., various tests, application blanks) in terms of a test battery. One of the methods employed for combining predictive information is multiple regression. It involves assigning different weights to the predictors. The weights are derived through a fairly complicated statistical procedure, which need not concern us here.[36] The output of the procedure includes a predicted criterion score and the multiple correlation coefficient (R), which can be called a *multiple* validity coefficient. (See the Appendix for a simple illustration.)

Note the definition of usefulness so far is how well a selection tool predicts (is related to) a job behaviour. It focusses on the relationship. But in doing so, it treats all errors equally. Underpredictions (predicting lower levels of performance than will actually occur) are the same as overpredictions (predicting better performance than will occur).

Think about selecting insurance agents from an applicant pool. An aspiring applicant goes through the selection procedure, which predicts this person will produce an estimated $70,000 yearly sales. The person is hired and produces $100,000, an error of $30,000. For another applicant, $70,000 is predicted again. But this time the person sells policies worth only $40,000, which is also a $30,000 error. Both errors would be treated the same using only validity coefficients, but the two different performance levels ($40,000 sales and $100,000 sales) are not the same for the employer. Selecting the poor performer is more serious than the underestimation made of the first applicant. So by focussing only on the strength of the relationship between the predictor and the criteria, validity coefficients do not reflect all the facts needed to judge the usefulness of a selection procedure.

A convenient way to consider the influence of base rate and selection ratio on the usefulness of a predictor is illustrated in Exhibit 9–5. The arrangement shown is basically derived from a predictor-criterion scatterplot with the data points deleted (for clarity of illustration).

Selection Ratio. The selection ratio (SR) was defined as the proportion of applicants hired. A very low selection ratio allows the employer to be more "choosy" in terms of who is hired, as there are many more applicants than

EXHIBIT 9–5
Base Rates

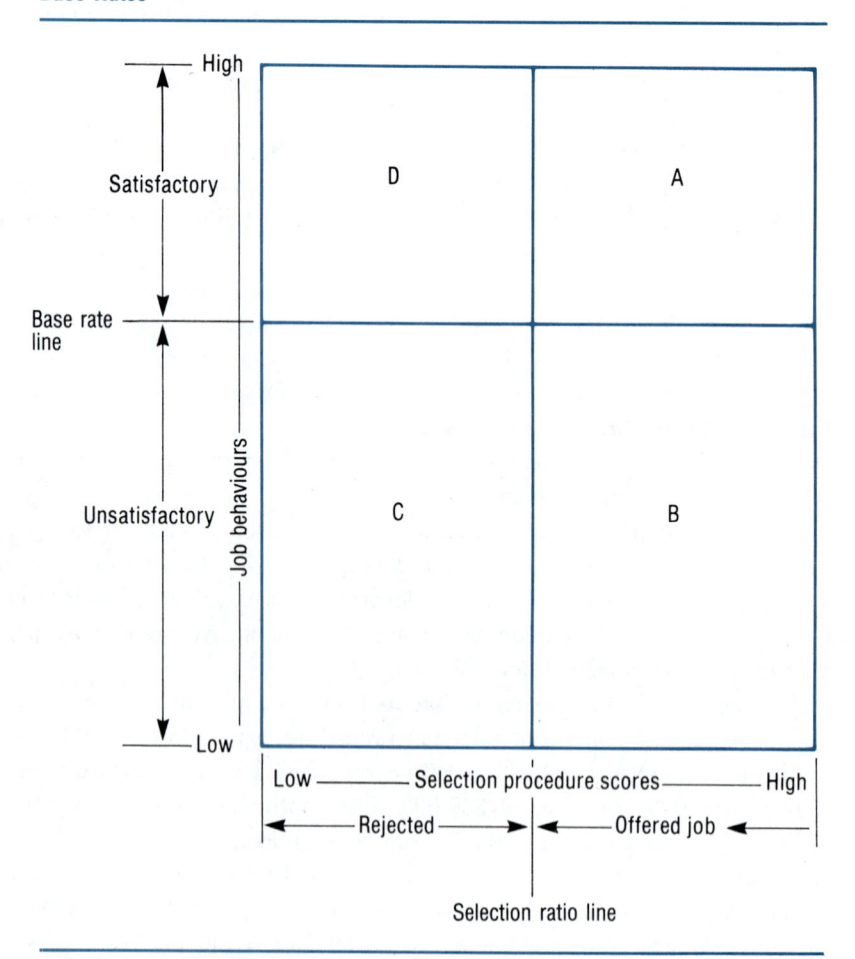

openings. The lower the selection ratio, the more useful a new predictor will be. In Exhibit 9–5, the selection ratio is (A + B) / (A + B + C + D).

Base Rate. The base rate (BR) is defined as the percentage of current employees that would be considered effective performers (using current selection techniques). The placement of the base rate line shown in Exhibit 9–5 is determined by the employer according to prevailing acceptable performance standards. The base rate is calculated by (A + D) / (A + B + C + D) and can vary from zero to 100 percent.

The base rate makes a great deal of difference. A high base rate for a given job indicates existing selection procedures may be more than adequate; using a new predictor may yield little, if any, improvement. However, lower base rates suggest there is room for improvement, and the new predictor takes on greater potential usefulness.

Relationships among Validity Coefficient, Selection Ratio, and Base Rate. Now we combine validity coefficient (strength of the predictor-criterion relationship), selection ratio, and base rate. Lower selection ratios and lower base rates permit valid selection techniques to make a contribution to usefulness.

Note how the focus has shifted. Usefulness of a selection device is judged by the extent to which it may increase the proportion of successful selections and by the extent to which it makes a difference in the process.

A series of tables is available to allow the P/HRM professional to consider the effects of the three factors simultaneously (for they act in combination) when judging the improvement in the percentage of successful employees. Exhibit 9–6 shows three examples from these tables (called Taylor-Russell tables), which were developed to specify the percentage of successful employees resulting from various combinations of validity, base rate, and selection ratio.[37]

Consider Example A in Exhibit 9–6. The current base rate is assumed to be 30 percent. Three different validity correlations and three different selection ratios are shown. The percentages in each line represent the proportion of successful employees a new selection procedure would yield for the various combinations of validity and selection ratio. Example A shows that with a validity of 0.40 and a selection ratio of 0.10, 58 percent of the applicants hired would be successful performers on the job. This represents a 28 percentage point improvement over the current base rate of 30 percent. For the same validity of 0.40, but a selection ratio of 0.70, the base rate of successful performance would rise from the current 30 percent to only 37 percent.

The other two factors to consider when judging usefulness are costs and value added.

EXHIBIT 9–6
Improvement in the Percentage of Successful Employees for Different Combinations of Validity Coefficients, Selection Ratios, and Base Rates

Example A. Base Rate = 30%

Validity (r)	Selection Ratio .10	.40	.70
.20	43%	37%	33%
.40	58	44	37
.60	74	52	40

Example B. Base Rate = 50%

Validity (r)	Selection Ratio .10	.40	.70
.20	64%	58%	54%
.40	78	66	58
.60	90	75	62

Example C. Base Rate = 80%

Validity (r)	Selection Ratio .10	.40	.70
.20	89%	85%	83%
.40	95	90	86
.60	99	95	90

Source: Adapted from H. C. Taylor and J. T. Russell, "The Relationship of Validity Coefficients to the Practical Effectiveness of Tests in Selection: Discussion and Tables," *Journal of Applied Psychology* 23 (1939), pp. 565–78.

Costs. Costs of a selection technique involve the actual costs of design, implementation, use, and the potential costs of any errors made. The actual costs of design can be considerable, since outside experts are often required.

The idea of potential costs of errors has already been introduced. Some errors are more costly than others. Recall the two aspiring insurance agents. Both predictions were in error by $30,000, but the "over" prediction (of the poor performer) was an expensive error, one to try to avoid. Exhibit 9–7 shows a scatterplot of selection procedure and job performance results. Two objectives of the selection procedure are to increase the proportion of correct decisions (C and A; rejecting poor performers and selecting good ones, respectively) and to minimize the chances of making the two types of errors, D and B. The false negatives result in rejection of persons who would have been

EXHIBIT 9–7
Correct Selection Decisions and Errors

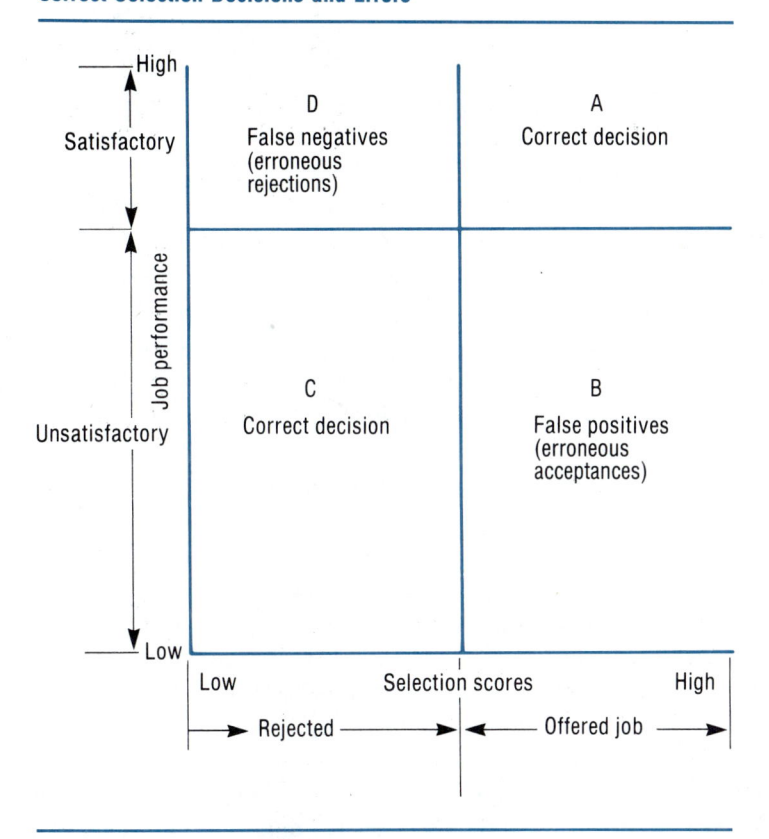

	Low Selection scores	High Selection scores
Satisfactory (High Job performance)	**D** False negatives (erroneous rejections)	**A** Correct decision
Unsatisfactory (Low Job performance)	**C** Correct decision	**B** False positives (erroneous acceptances)
	← Rejected →	← Offered job →

successful (erroneous rejections); the false positives in selection of persons who turn out to be unsuccessful (erroneous acceptances).

Additionally, willingness to risk error varies with the job being filled. The cost of hiring a poor performer for president or key manager would have enormous consequences to the organization. So the designers of the selection procedure will attempt to minimize the risk of selecting false positives (accepting a poor performer). It might be worth running the risk of rejecting a few good performers to avoid a false positive. But in other situations the costs of hiring people who turn out to be poor performers are more tolerable. Lower-level, less expensive jobs can be staffed this way; poor performers can either be trained, transferred, or easily replaced.

Value Added. The final factor used to judge a selection procedure is the value it adds to the organization's effectiveness.

Although the general utility formula has been available for almost 40 years and its derivation is relatively straightforward,[38] it was not until the mid-1970s that researchers began to focus on the relationship of validity, SR, and BR to employee behaviour, and on its impact on the organization in dollar terms. In recent years, a number of studies have examined this relationship, perhaps both in response to the hard economic times and to highlight the significant benefits available through improved selection.[39] An overview of the basic equation used is presented in Appendix B.

In their approach to develop methods for estimating a procedure's contribution, Schmidt and Hunter and others[40] ask managers to estimate the dollar value of different levels of performance on a particular job. By showing the improvement in performance attributed to a selection procedure, they can estimate the value it adds. In a study already mentioned, they estimated the value added in selecting computer programmers. By using a computer programming test, they increased the proportion of successful programmers selected for employment. Managers estimated the dollar value of differences in performance levels of programmers. By translating the improved performance of the new programmers into these dollar values Schmidt and Hunter were able to show that the test is worth $64,725 per hire per year. For the organization in which the study was conducted, which hires hundreds of programmers each year, the potential payoff is enormous.

Cascio and Ramos estimated value added by using the average salary paid for a job as the measure of the value of satisfactory performance.[41] For example, say that the average salary of accountants is $35,000. One set of tasks performed, handling billing problems for suppliers, makes up 15.7 percent of the accountants' jobs. Therefore, these tasks are worth 15.7 percent × $35,000, or $5,495. If accountants could be selected who performed above the average on this set of tasks, let's say 1.5 times better, then the increased performance level would be worth 1.5 × $5,495, or $8,242.50. This could be done across all the accountants' activities to determine the potential value added of selecting better-performing accountants.

Fear and Ross describe the usefulness of a new selection system, which included the use of aptitude tests, whose results were compared to the effectiveness of an earlier one.[42] The benefits of the new system included declines in absenteeism (by 42 percent), turnover (by 28 percent), social insurance program claims (by 51 percent), frequency of lateness (by 33 percent), grievances (by 82 percent), and reported accidents (by 25 percent). For the first three of these items, the estimated dollar savings was $1 million, or roughly $3,000 per employee hired. The overall improvement in productivity approximated 5.7 percent.

A recent utility analysis of the clerical/administrative job group in the Canadian military revealed that use of the existing ability test composite yields long-term productivity gains of more than $50 million for a single year of testing.[43]

These studies and a recent review of others by Kopelman indicate the use of selection procedures based on ability and aptitude tests can be consistently effective in increasing productivity.[44]

A recent novel approach by Cronshaw and colleagues[45] applies methods from the capital-budgeting literature to examine utility in terms of the net present value (NPV) of an organization's selection investment. This may lead to more realistic and useful decision models for P/HRM managers engaged in utility analyses.

VALIDITY GENERALIZATION

For many years, the conventional wisdom was that demonstrated validity in one setting implied nothing about validity in another setting, even with similar jobs. For example, a test for police officers in one city would require a new validation study before being used in another city. But Hunter, Schmidt, and associates claim this is not necessarily so. In a series of studies, they demonstrated validity generalization for various job families. They contend observed differences in test validities across similar situations and jobs are primarily a result of statistical errors attributable to small sample size. The small samples are more susceptible to sampling error (drawing an unrepresentative sample from the population) and greater fluctuations in test validities. They conclude the relationship between predictors and job success is much more stable than the statistics imply, and therefore test validity is far more generalizable than previously thought. An examination of IBM's Programmer Aptitude Test, for example, showed that 65 percent of the variance from one study to the next could be attributed to statistical "artifacts" that were correctable.[46]

Mattinson and Cronshaw addressed the issue of transnational validity generalization, on the grounds that Canadian practitioners have often assumed selection tests developed and validated in the United States can be used in Canada without loss of validity.[47] Using Armed Forces occupational data from both countries and ensuring maximum comparability of predictors between the two data sets, the researchers subjected validity data in six job groups to validity generalization analysis. They found that validities generalize for five of the military job groups—clerical, combat, electronics repair, general maintenance, and skilled technical—but not for mechanical maintenance. However, these results must be tempered, pending further validity generalization research between the two countries. They point out that we do not know whether validities of other tests used in the public and private sectors of the two countries generalize transnationally. Also, the distributions of validity coefficients examined were based on relatively small numbers of studies and may not have been particularly stable. In addition, the cross-national validity generalization was demonstrated only for same-language groups; further research is required to determine whether validities generalize across English-French language groups.[48]

The notion of validity generalization will undoubtedly be receiving more attention from test users and researchers.

We turn now to examining the selection process.

SELECTION PROCESS

The typical selection process includes multiple procedures to collect information about applicants. Exhibit 9–8 illustrates a typical process. Its purpose is to gather information to be used in deciding whom to hire from the applicant pool. Multiple procedures allow the process to be adjusted to fit a particular situation.

Multiple-Hurdles Process

In a multiple-hurdles process, each selection procedure serves as a screen. Each applicant must get through a screen to proceed to the next. Failure to qualify at any hurdle means rejection. A multiple-hurdles process assumes an applicant's strengths and weaknesses do not balance each other. The lack, or a low level, of one quality cannot be overcome by an abundance of others. This makes sense for jobs in which a certain minimum level of each KSAO is required. An accountant needs a certain aptitude with numbers, and a commercial pilot needs a high degree of hand-eye coordination. P/HRM practitioners are advised to make sure that, in the use of multiple-hurdles, every single stage is job-related and free from discrimination.

Compensatory Process

Compensatory selection processes are designed to recognize that applicants' limitations on some qualifications can be counterbalanced, or compensated

EXHIBIT 9–8
Typical Selection Process

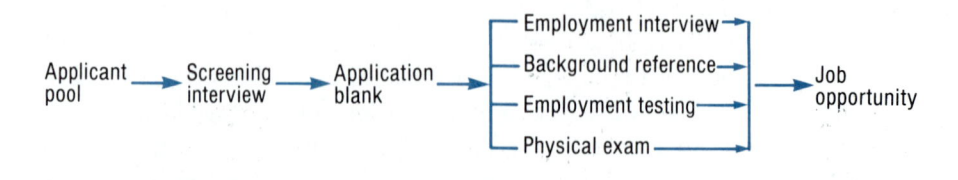

Applicant pool → Screening interview → Application blank → {Employment interview, Background reference, Employment testing, Physical exam} → Job opportunity

for, by strengths in others. Further, an applicant is not rejected or hired until after the entire process is completed. In that way, data obtained from all the selection procedures are combined to assist managers in making the decision.

Hybrid Process

In a hybrid process, multiple hurdles and compensatory logic are both used. For most jobs, certain minimum qualifications are required for successful performance. Examples include university degrees, typing speed, "two years of experience." These qualifications are essential for successful performance, so they become part of the hurdles. Applicants without them are rejected. Beyond these minimums, a blend of other qualifications may lead to success. Some talents compensate for others, so the compensatory process is used. Usually the hybrid process begins with hurdles to screen out those not minimally qualified. Again, however, employers must be sure these hurdles comply with human rights regulations.

SELECTION PROCEDURES

Application Blanks/Biographical Data

One of the oldest procedures in personnel selection is use of the application blank. Surveys show that practically all employers use them.[49] Most forms ask for personal data (address, phone number, and the like), previous training, experience, and work references.

Using these data for selection assumes behavioural consistency, that past behaviour is the best indicator of future behaviour. Thus, a person's personal data and experience need to be gathered in a form that lends itself to validation and interpretation.

Two types of application blanks are the biographical information blank (BIB) and the weighted application blank (WAB). The BIB usually uses a multiple-choice answer system. It also asks opinion questions, such as:

How do you feel about being transferred from this city by this company?
1. Would thoroughly enjoy a transfer.
2. Would like to experience a transfer.
3. Would accept a transfer.
4. Would reject a transfer.

To use the BIB as a selection tool, each item on the form must correlate with measures of job success. Those items that predict the best outcome for a position are used to select applicants.

The WAB procedure uses an application blank developed to be scored, capitalizing on the three hallmarks of progress in selection: standardization, quantification, and understanding.[50] Once developed by an organization, it can serve both as a rapid screening device and in combination with other devices to improve selection decisions. The technique is especially applicable in organizations having a relatively large number of employees doing similar kinds of work and for whom both application blank and work performance data are available. Its rapid screening ability makes it particulary valuable in employment situations where the selection ratio is relatively low (many applicants for very few positions).

Exhibit 9–9 illustrates an application of the results of the WAB approach in terms of an expectancy chart developed (and continuously updated) for the British Columbia Real Estate Association.[51] The performance criterion in this case is "surviving one year or longer in real estate sales." Weights were developed for specific application blank items from data obtained on more than 1,400 real estate salespeople. Results indicate an applicant with a WAB score of 24 or higher has a 100 percent chance of surviving the first year; a score of 18 to 20 reduces the chance of success to 60 percent, and so on. The WAB cut-off score to use depends on the selection ratio and the desired rate of entry to the profession.

EXHIBIT 9–9
Chances of Being Successful* Given WAB Test Score

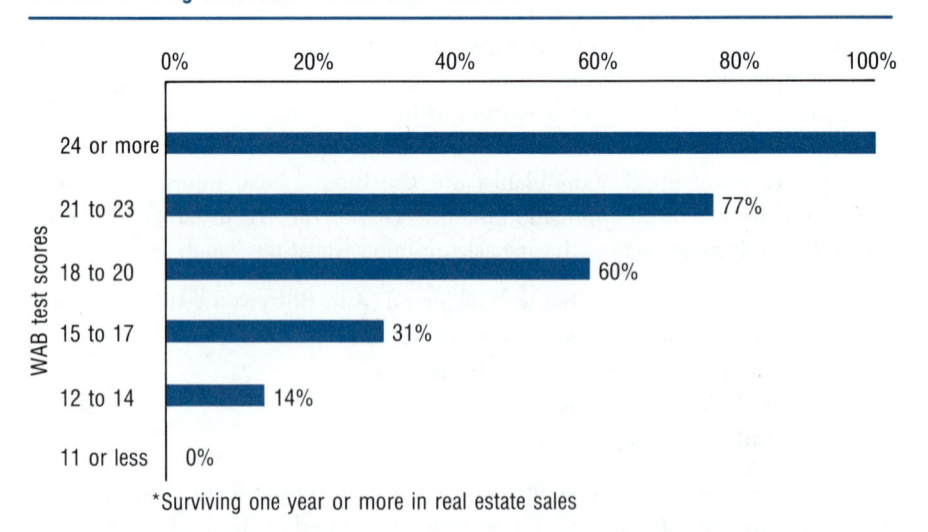

WAB test scores	Chance of Success
24 or more	100%
21 to 23	77%
18 to 20	60%
15 to 17	31%
12 to 14	14%
11 or less	0%

*Surviving one year or more in real estate sales

Source: Merle Ace, "A Good Match = Dollars and Sense," B.C. Real Estate Association, Vancouver, B.C.

Research on Biographical Data

Research shows that biographical data are useful.[52] Relative to other selection procedures, biodata comprise one of the most valid. Two independent reviews (Asher; Reilly and Chao) concluded that biographical data are useful for selection decisions but require constant updating and analysis to ensure their validity.[53] However, surveys indicate that although most organizations use application blanks for selection, fewer than a third of the larger employers had validated them.

The Accomplishment Record. Recently, Hough devised a new approach to biographical data.[54] She found that many applicants felt "my record speaks for itself"; why bother with all the other selection procedures? This feeling was especially strong among professionals, particularly lawyers at a government regulatory agency. They argued that the best selector was their record—their prior accomplishments and achievements—and refused to take employment tests. To solve the problem of validating a selection procedure, Hough designed the Accomplishment Record, a form the lawyers filled out. It does not measure typical biographical data such as college or university grades, quality of schools attended, interests, and so on. Instead, the focus is on actual legal accomplishments and critical dimensions of the regulatory jobs. Exhibit 9–10 shows one dimension of the job: "using knowledge" and an applicant's response to it. Exhibit 9–11 shows a scale used to score the applicant's accomplishment. Hough found the accomplishment record validly predicts job success. Further, it provides applicants with a way to show their accomplishments throughout their careers. It is likely to be seen by applicants as a fairer selection tool than other biographical data.[55] The accomplishment record has "face validity." That is, people using it believe the data make sense and are relevant on the face of it.

Employment Interview

The employment interview is one of the most widely used selection techniques. One survey reports 56 percent of participating companies stated that interviews are the most important aspect of the selection process.[56] Ninety percent reported that of all selection procedures, they had the most confidence in the employment interview. Yet reviewers of more than 150 research studies conducted over 20 years conclude the interview is rarely a valid predictor of job success.[57]

Underscoring this view is Tenopyr's recent review in which she reports the history of validity of the interview to be dismal, believes it represents a poor alternative to testing, and claims that during the three years from 1978 to 1980 only one published interview validation study appears to have been conducted.[58] However, while the accumulated evidence documents the poor

EXHIBIT 9–10
Accomplishment Record Method

> Using Knowledge
> Interpreting and synthesizing information to form legal strategies, approaches, lines of argument, etc.; developing new configurations of knowledge, innovative approaches, solutions, strategies, etc.; selecting the proper legal theory; using appropriate lines of argument, weighing alternatives and drawing sound conclusions.
>
> Time Period: *1974–75*
>
> General statement of what you accomplished:
>
> *I was given the task of transferring our antitrust investigation of. . . . into a coherent set of pleadings presentable to. . . . and the Commission for review and approval within the context of the Commission's involvement in shopping centres nationwide.*
>
> Description of exactly what you did:
>
> *I drafted the complaint and proposed order and wrote the underlying legal memo justifying all charges and proposed remedies. I wrote the memo to the Commission recommending approval of the consent agreement. For the first time, we applied antitrust principles to this novel factual situation.*
>
> Awards or formal recognition:
>
> > *none*
>
> The information verified by: *John B. Goode, Compliance*

Source: L. Hough, "Development of the Accomplishment Record Method of Selecting and Promoting Professionals," *Journal of Applied Psychology* 69, no. 1 (1984), pp. 135–46. Copyright 1984 by the American Psychological Association. Reprinted by permission of the author.

accuracy of the traditional unstructured interview in predicting job performance, more recent research by Janz and his associates in a number of Canadian organizations holds promise for improving the interview's validity.[59] In this section, we will look at the interview, the research on it, and some guidelines for its use. Regardless of the approach taken, the interviewer should observe relevant human rights legislation (see Appendix in Chapter Seven).

Types of Interviews

The three general types of employment interview are structured, semistructured, and unstructured. The main differences in the three lie in the approaches the interviewer takes.

Structured. In the structured type, the interviewer prepares a list of questions in advance and does not deviate from it. A standard form is used

EXHIBIT 9–11
Accomplishment Record Method Rating Scale for "Using Knowledge"

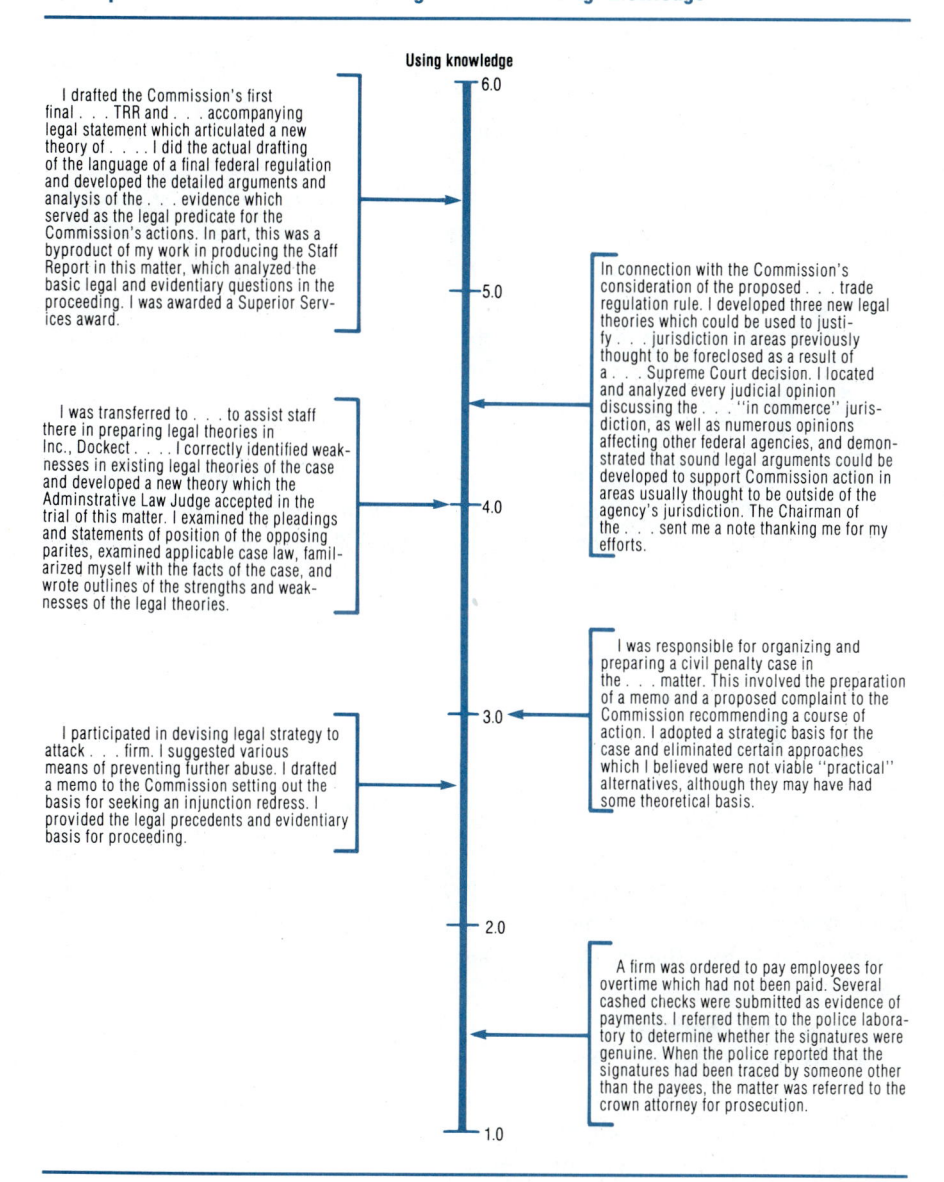

Using knowledge

— 6.0

I drafted the Commission's first final . . . TRR and . . . accompanying legal statement which articulated a new theory of . . . . I did the actual drafting of the language of a final federal regulation and developed the detailed arguments and analysis of the . . . evidence which served as the legal predicate for the Commission's actions. In part, this was a byproduct of my work in producing the Staff Report in this matter, which analyzed the basic legal and evidentiary questions in the proceeding. I was awarded a Superior Services award.

— 5.0

In connection with the Commission's consideration of the proposed . . . trade regulation rule. I developed three new legal theories which could be used to justify . . . jurisdiction in areas previously thought to be foreclosed as a result of a . . . Supreme Court decision. I located and analyzed every judicial opinion discussing the . . . "in commerce" jurisdiction, as well as numerous opinions affecting other federal agencies, and demonstrated that sound legal arguments could be developed to support Commission action in areas usually thought to be outside of the agency's jurisdiction. The Chairman of the . . . sent me a note thanking me for my efforts.

I was transferred to . . . to assist staff there in preparing legal theories in Inc., Dockect . . . . I correctly identified weaknesses in existing legal theories of the case and developed a new theory which the Adminstrative Law Judge accepted in the trial of this matter. I examined the pleadings and statements of position of the opposing parites, examined applicable case law, familarized myself with the facts of the case, and wrote outlines of the strengths and weaknesses of the legal theories.

— 4.0

— 3.0

I was responsible for organizing and preparing a civil penalty case in the . . . matter. This involved the preparation of a memo and a proposed complaint to the Commission recommending a course of action. I adopted a strategic basis for the case and eliminated certain approaches which I believed were not viable "practical" alternatives, although they may have had some theoretical basis.

I participated in devising legal strategy to attack . . . firm. I suggested various means of preventing further abuse. I drafted a memo to the Commission setting out the basis for seeking an injunction redress. I provided the legal precedents and evidentiary basis for proceeding.

— 2.0

A firm was ordered to pay employees for overtime which had not been paid. Several cashed checks were submitted as evidence of payments. I referred them to the police laboratory to determine whether the signatures were genuine. When the police reported that the signatures had been traced by someone other than the payees, the matter was referred to the crown attorney for prosecution.

— 1.0

Source: Adapted from L. Hough, "Development of the Accomplishment Record Method of Selecting and Promoting Professionals," *Journal of Applied Psychology* 69, no. 1 (1984), pp. 135–46. Copyright 1984 by the American Psychological Association. Reprinted by permission of the author.

on which the interviewer notes the applicant's responses to the predetermined questions. The interviewer may also follow a prearranged sequence of questions. The structured interview is very restrictive, however. The information elicited is narrow, and there is little opportunity to adapt to the individual applicant. This approach is equally constraining to applicants, who are unable to qualify or elaborate their answers.

Semistructured. In the semistructured interview, only the major questions to be asked are prepared in advance, though the interviewer may also prepare some potential follow-up questions in areas of interest. While this approach calls for greater interviewer preparation, it also allows for more flexibility than the structured approach. The interviewer is free to probe into those areas that merit it. Since these interviews have less structure, however, they are more difficult to replicate. This approach combines enough structure to facilitate the exchange of factual information with adequate freedom to develop insights.

Unstructured. The unstructured interview involves little preparation. The interviewer prepares a list of possible topics to be covered and sometimes does not even do that. The overriding advantage of the nondirective approach is the freedom it allows the interviewer to adapt to the situation and to the changing stream of applicants. Spontaneity characterizes this approach, but in the hands of an untrained interviewer, digressions, discontinuity, and eventual frustration for both parties may result. Students frequently encounter personnel recruiters whose sole contribution, other than the opening and closing pleasantries, is, "Tell me about yourself, your career plans, the contribution you can make to the organization, etc." The unstructured approach can be a powerful tool, but *only* when used by a highly trained interviewer.

The conventional wisdom that "the more structure the better" is based on the assumption that the questions asked are highly job-related. If they are not, structure alone will contribute primarily to reliability, not validity. To achieve the latter, the pattern of questions must probe specific job behaviours.

Behaviour Description (BD) Interviewing. Based on research by Janz, Hellervik, and Gilmore,[60] the behaviour description interview uses a structured pattern of questions designed to probe the applicant's past behaviour in specific situations, selected for their relevance to critical job events. The questions asked are derived from behaviours that differentiate effective and ineffective performers. Once the questions are asked and the applicant's responses noted, BD interviewing requires that each applicant be assessed against specific behavioural job dimensions. In this way, the rating process cements the direct relationship between job behaviour and interview content. BD interviewing accuracy exceeds traditional interviewing accuracy by three to seven times; the improved accuracy also makes this process cost-effective.[61]

The typical interview is usually a one-on-one situation. However, interviews can also be categorized according to the number of interviewers involved and the use of videotape.

Panel (Board) Interview. This type of interview is often used by government agencies, the military, police and fire departments, and school boards, especially when a candidate's final selection must be approved by a selection committee. Private-sector employers utilize panel interviews primarily when selecting for high-level positions.[62] The panel gets involved after applicants have been prescreened and found eligible. Each candidate is questioned and observed by a panel of interviewers. At the outset, the interviewee may be told which interviewer will ask questions first, who the next one will be, and so on. In some cases, an easy question may be followed immediately by one requiring a lengthy answer. To inject realism, the panel may also pose a realistic work situation and ask the candidate how he or she would deal with it.

Videotape Approach. An innovative approach to improving the accuracy of the selection interview was proposed by Moore.[63] First, the usual one-on-one interview is videotaped (with the permission of the interviewee), and the interviewer rates the candidate immediately following the live interview. The videotape is taken to the company for viewing by one or more operating managers, and perhaps even other interviewers. Before and during each viewing, raters also have access to the candidate's completed application form. The independent ratings by managers are then supplemented by raters pooling their judgements after postreplay discussion.

Using this approach, Moore videotaped a series of 34 initial screening employment interviews at the western headquarters of a large Canadian bank.[64] The normal interview procedure of the bank was utilized, including a standardized semistructured interview format and a multitrait (e.g., self-expression, leadership, appearance) descriptive rating form. It was concluded that, in general, closer agreement exists between the combined judgements of groups of managers and the actual interviewers than between the interviewers and individual managers. Moore also reports that the split-screen staging technique was preferred, as it offers a close-up, simultaneous presentation of both interviewer and interviewee.

The method allows for closer involvement of operating managers in the selection process; another advantage is the use of taped interviews for training interviewers.

An "electronic matchmaking" service of the type described here is being offered by selection consultants. Using questions supplied by employers, videotape interviews can be arranged at regional offices. Within several days after interviewing the last candidate, the company sends the employer a videotape of the applicants.

Stress Interview. Anyone who has been through an interview would probably agree that stress was involved, if simply because of the interview's evaluative nature. A panel interview is often perceived as more stressful than the one-on-one type. Sometimes, however, interviewers intentionally create additional stress through certain questions and behaviours. They justify doing so by claiming the purpose is to find out how the applicant responds under pressure and deals with a stress level presumably similar to that found on the job. Sometimes the approach utilizes verbal attacks on the responses of the applicant, or even derogatory comments about overall suitability for the position. Even if applicants are debriefed at the conclusion of the interview, the use of non–job-related stress questions is unethical.

Research on Interviews

Schmitt summarizes the voluminous research on the interview with the following conclusions:[65]

1. *Overemphasis on negative information.* The interview has been called a search for negative information, and often the finding of even a small amount of negative information can lead to rejection of an interviewee.
2. *Interviewer stereotypes.* Often, interviewers develop a stereotype of the ideal job candidate; successful interviewees are thus not necessarily the ones best qualified, but the ones who conform to the stereotype. If different interviewers have different stereotypes, an interviewee could be evaluated positively by one and negatively by another.
3. *Job information.* Lack of relevant job information can increase the use of irrelevant attributes of interviewees in decision making.
4. *Different use of cues by interviewers.* Some interviewers may place more weight on certain attributes than on others, or they may combine attributes differently as they make their overall decisions.
5. *Visual cues.* Interviewees' appearance and nonverbal behaviour (e.g., whether they "look" interested) can influence their evaluation in an interview, yet perhaps be unrelated to job success.
6. *Similarity to interviewer.* Sex, race, and/or attitude similarity to interviewers may lead to favourable evaluations.
7. *Contrast effects.* The order of interviewees influences ratings; for example, strong candidates who follow weak ones look even stronger by contrast.

These findings suggest that what seems like a simple process, the interview, is actually a complex interaction between applicants and interviewers. This interaction is affected by conditions in the environment and the organization.

Arvey and Campion use a model, shown in Exhibit 9–12, to highlight all the variables and processes that affect the interview and its result.[66]

EXHIBIT 9–12
Variables Affecting the Employment Interview

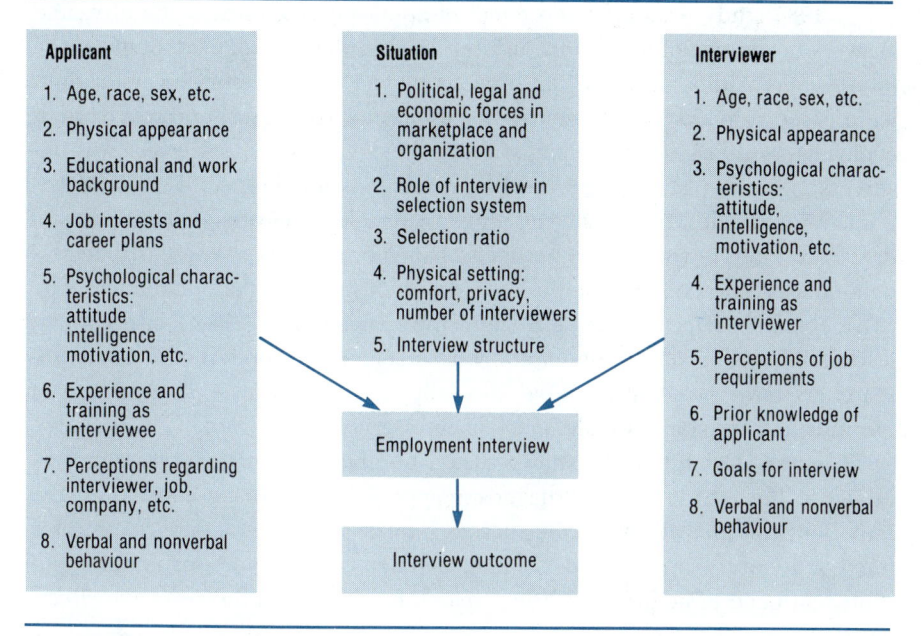

Applicant
1. Age, race, sex, etc.
2. Physical appearance
3. Educational and work background
4. Job interests and career plans
5. Psychological characteristics: attitude intelligence motivation, etc.
6. Experience and training as interviewee
7. Perceptions regarding interviewer, job, company, etc.
8. Verbal and nonverbal behaviour

Situation
1. Political, legal and economic forces in marketplace and organization
2. Role of interview in selection system
3. Selection ratio
4. Physical setting: comfort, privacy, number of interviewers
5. Interview structure

Interviewer
1. Age, race, sex, etc.
2. Physical appearance
3. Psychological characteristics: attitude, intelligence, motivation, etc.
4. Experience and training as interviewer
5. Perceptions of job requirements
6. Prior knowledge of applicant
7. Goals for interview
8. Verbal and nonverbal behaviour

Employment interview

Interview outcome

Source: Richard D. Arvey and James E. Campion, "The Employment Interview: A Summary and Review of Recent Research," *Personnel Psychology* 35, no. 3 (1982), pp. 281–322.

Applicant Characteristics. The applicant's characteristics should influence the selection decision. Research shows that qualifications and experience do.[67] However, what about other characteristics? Does the sex or ethnicity of the applicant have any effect on the decision? What about the topics covered, the types of questions asked, or the interviewer's interpretation of applicant responses?

More than 50 studies have examined effects of the applicant's sex, race, physical attractiveness, age, and marital status on the selection decision.[68] The results are mixed. A thorough review in 1979 concluded that stereotyping in the interview does exist.[69] Evidence showed that female applicants were generally evaluated less favourably than males, especially for jobs traditionally held by men. Yet in 1982, another study found that differences in assessing males and females were not of sufficient magnitude to be significant. The later study did find that stereotyping seems most evident when the interviewer has little data or time to collect it. Consider the typical campus interview, which runs about 30 minutes. Some of that time is devoted to giving data on the job and employer. If stereotyping occurs in the college interview, it has serious consequences, since it acts as a hurdle that must be crossed. Campus interviewers are powerful gatekeepers to job opportunities, yet the validity of their decisions has not been well studied.[70]

A 1985 study examined the effect of applicant race, sex, suitability, and answers on ratings of applicants and the questioning strategy adopted by the interviewer. Although initial impressions played a part, interviewers' ratings were based primarily on the content of applicants' responses, and no clear-cut confirmatory information-seeking strategy on the part of interviewers was observed.[71] Another study used the hiring recommendations of 77 P/HRM administrators to determine the influence of female applicants' "masculinity of dress" on interviewers' selection decisions. The most masculine costume was defined as a navy, tailored suit and a white blouse with an angular collar. The researchers reported a positive relationship between masculinity of dress and favourability of hiring recommendations received by applicants.[72] Some researchers have even investigated the influence of female applicants' use of perfume and cologne on male and female interviewers.[73]

Context. Exhibit 9–12 shows that a number of situational factors may influence the interview. The diagnostic approach has already considered the important role played by factors such as human rights regulations, base rates (the quality of the applicant pool), and selection ratio (the proportion of applicants that need to be hired). Little research has examined their specific effects on the interview.

Interviewer. The characteristics of the interviewer, such as race, sex, beliefs, and experience, influence the selection decision. Arvey suggests that some interviewers are better predictors of job success than others.[74] According to this view, we should focus our efforts on selecting interviewers who are good at making correct selection decisions. Perhaps some interviewers are more valid than others.

Research on the interview shows it has relatively low validity and reliability, and it is susceptible to bias and distortion. Then why is it so widely used? Arvey suggests some answers.[75] First, perhaps the interview assesses the interpersonal qualities important in work. Most other selection devices do not focus on interpersonal competence, sociability, or verbal fluency. Perhaps the interview is really valid, but validity research has failed to be sufficiently sophisticated to include such qualities and relate them to job performance.

Other reasons offered are more practical. The interview has "face validity." Would any manager be willing to hire someone without an interview? Or would you be willing to take a job without one? Probably not. As the discussion on recruiting noted, interviews are used for public relations and information giving as well as selection and data gathering. So the interview serves multiple purposes.

Guidelines. Drawing upon all this research, Hakel offers some guidance (Exhibits 9–13 and 9–14) to the interviewer and interviewee.[76] Other re-

EXHIBIT 9-13
Basic Interviewing Skills for the Interviewer

I. *Planning the interview.* Examination of the application blank, the job requirements, and also mapping out areas to be covered in the interview. Planning and organizing questions pertinent to these areas. Ensuring that the interview will be held in an optimal environment, free from interruption.

II. *Getting information.* Use of appropriate questioning techniques to elicit relevant information in the same sequence over all interviewees. Probing incomplete answers and problem areas while maintaining an atmosphere of trust. Structuring the interview. Comprehensive questions and follow-up comments.

III. *Giving information.* Effectiveness in communicating appropriate and accurate information about the organization and available jobs for which the applicant would qualify, and in answering the applicant's questions. Closing the interview.

IV. *Personal impact.* The total effect the interviewer has on the applicant, both as an individual and as a representative of the organization. This includes the applicant's first impression of the interviewer, given to the applicant through the interviewer's tone of voice, eye contact, personal appearance and grooming, postures and gestures, as well as the interviewer's impact throughout the interview.

V. *Responding to the applicant.* Concern for the applicant's feelings while maintaining control over the interview. Reacting appropriately to the applicant's comments, questions, and nonverbal behaviours. Convey a feeling of interest in the applicant, encourage an atmosphere of warmth and trust, and make use of encouragement and praise.

VI. *Information processing.* Gathering, integrating, and analyzing interview information, culminating in a final placement decision. Identifying personal characteristics and judging them in the context of the job requirements. Skill in assimilating, remembering, and integrating all information relevant to the final evaluation.

Contributed by Milton D. Hakel, Department of Psychology, Ohio State University.
Source: Richard W. Beatty and Craig Eric Schneier, *Personnel Administration: An Experiential Skill-Building Approach*, 2nd ed. (Reading, Mass.: Addison-Wesley Publishing, 1981).

cruiter/interviewer guidelines are available, with differing emphasis on the "how to" versus the interviewing skills needed.[77] Gilmore and Ferris, for example, suggest the recruiter should develop a "game plan" for the interview, do so on the basis of job-relevant information, read the applicant's résumé before the interview, attempt to make the applicant feel at ease, conduct the interview so the applicant does most of the talking, have active listening skills, provide a clear description of the job and the organization to the prospective employee, have skills for both observing and providing appropriate nonverbal communication, record observations during the interview, be aware of current legal and ethical issues surrounding the interview process, and, finally, not allow too much time to pass between contacts with applicants.[78]

EXHIBIT 9-14
Effective Interviewing: Guidelines for Interviewees

Dress appropriately.

Be punctual.

Know the interviewer's name and correct pronunciation.

Make sure your "body language" communicates your interest and attentiveness.

Do some research regarding the organization and the interviewer to ask pertinent questions.

Pause briefly and pensively before answering complex questions.

Try not to discuss salary in preliminary interviews.

Be responsive to each part of each question.

Ask how any personal or potentially illegal questions are related to job performance before responding.

Bring pencil and paper in case some information (for example, a telephone number) must be recorded.

Make some notes regarding high (and low) points of interview shortly after it ends in order to follow up in subsequent interviews.

Thank the interviewer for his/her time.

Be certain that any responses on applicant blanks or résumés are consonant with those provided in the interview.

Contributed by Milton D. Hakel, Department of Psychology, Ohio State University.

Source: Richard W. Beatty and Craig Eric Schneier, *Personnel Administration: An Experiential Skill-Building Approach*, 2nd ed. (Reading, Mass.: Addison-Wesley Publishing, 1981). © 1981 by Addison-Wesley.

Research in connection with the behaviour description approach emphasizes the importance of structure, knowledge, and the use of behaviour-based questions; provides evidence on the side of taking notes before assessing applicants; and suggests methods in which the interviewers gather information during the interview and make assessments on specific items following a review of interview notes.[79]

It should be clear to employers that the interview is to be treated the same as any other selection technique, such as employment tests. The low validity of the interview makes it highly vulnerable to legal attack. In the United States, the number of court cases concerning interviewing practices has been growing,[80] a trend that has somewhat replaced the earlier focus on questioning the validity of psychological and aptitude tests. A similar trend may emerge in Canadian human rights cases after concern with employment tests has been resolved.

Employment Tests

In this section, we will consider only tests of ability, personality and interest, and work or performance samples.

Ability Tests

Ability tests assess an individual's aptitudes and achievements.[81] Achievement covers the effects of training and experience, such as the learning that occurred in apprenticeship training or an accounting course. Aptitude refers to the individual's potential to acquire a skill. An aptitude is a characteristic of a person. Examples of aptitudes include intellectual abilities; perceptual accuracy; spatial, mechanical, and motor abilities; and personality. Thus, the results of an aptitude test indicate what a person might be able to do, given training or experience. For example, a test that requires the individual to follow a complex path with a pencil, graded on speed and accuracy, would be an aptitude test of motor ability. Aptitude tests also serve to estimate the extent to which an individual may profit from training.

Ability and aptitude tests often are combined into a test battery to predict performance on different jobs within organizations. One of the most researched and extensively used test batteries is the General Aptitude Test Battery (GATB). It was adapted for Canadian use by Canada Employment and Immigration through a validation program that utilized Canadian occupational data and developed Canadian norms.[82] A full administration of the GATB requires 2½ hours. As shown in Exhibit 9–15, nine aptitudes are measured through testing on 12 subtests. The aptitudes covered include cognitive, perceptual, and manipulative ones. For example, the job of all-around mechanical repairing would mean testing for G, N, S, and F; an applicant for the

EXHIBIT 9–15
Aptitudes Measured by the GATB

The nine aptitudes measured by the GATB are listed below. The letter used as symbol to identify each aptitude and the part or parts of the GATB measuring each aptitude are also shown.

Aptitude	Tests
G—Intelligence	Part 3—Three-dimensional space
	Part 4—Vocabulary
	Part 6—Arithmetic reason
V—Verbal aptitude	Part 4—Vocabulary
N—Numerical aptitude	Part 2—Computation
	Part 6—Arithmetic reason
S—Spatial aptitude	Part 3—Three-dimensional space
P—Form perception	Part 5—Tool matching
	Part 7—Form matching
Q—Clerical perception	Part 1—Name comparison
K—Motor Coordination	Part 8—Mark making
F—Finger dexterity	Part 11—Assemble
	Part 12—Disassemble
M—Manual dexterity	Part 9—Place
	Part 10—Turn

EXHIBIT 9-15 *(concluded)*

The following are the definitions of the nine aptitudes measured by the GATB:

G—Intelligence—General learning ability. The ability to "catch on" or understand instructions and underlying principles; the ability to reason and make judgements. Closely related to doing well in school. Measured by Parts 3, 4, and 6.

V—Verbal aptitude—The ability to understand meaning of words and to use them effectively. The ability to comprehend language, to understand relationships between words and to understand meanings of whole sentences and paragraphs. Measured by Part 4.

N—Numerical aptitude—Ability to perform arithmetic operations quickly and accurately. Measured by Parts 2 and 6.

S—Spatial aptitude—Ability to think visually of geometric forms and to comprehend the two-dimensional objects. The ability to recognize the relationships resulting from the movement of objects in space. Measured by Part 3.

P—Form perception—Ability to perceive pertinent detail in objects or in pictorial or graphic material. Ability to make visual comparisons and discriminations and see slight differences in shapes and shadings of figures and widths and lengths of lines. Measured by Parts 5 and 7.

Q—Clerical perception—Ability to perceive pertinent detail in verbal or tabular material. Ability to observe differences in copy, to proofread words and numbers, and to avoid perceptual errors in arithmetic computation. A measure of speed of perception that is required in many industrial jobs even when the job does not have verbal or numerical content. Measured by Part 1.

K—Motor coordination—Ability to coordinate eyes and hands or fingers rapidly and accurately in making precise movements with speed. Ability to make a movement response accurately and swiftly. Measured by Part 8.

F—Finger dexterity—Ability to move the fingers, and manipulate small objects with the fingers, rapidly or accurately. Measured by Parts 11 and 12.

M—Manual dexterity—Ability to move the hands easily and skillfully. Ability to work with the hands in placing and turning motions. Measured by Parts 9 and 10.

Reprinted by permission (Nelson Canada).

position of typist would require V, Q, K, and F. Some examples of typical GATB test items are shown in Exhibit 9-16.

In contrast to ability tests, achievement tests get at what the individual already knows. Hough's accomplishment record measures achievement. The Standardized Achievement Test, the Graduate Management Admission Test used by business schools, and other university admissions tests are achievement tests. They focus on measuring the knowledge presumed necessary for successful work behaviours. Other examples include knowledge of mechanics, plumbing, electrical principles, and recognition of various tools and their

EXHIBIT 9–16
Examples of GATB Test Items

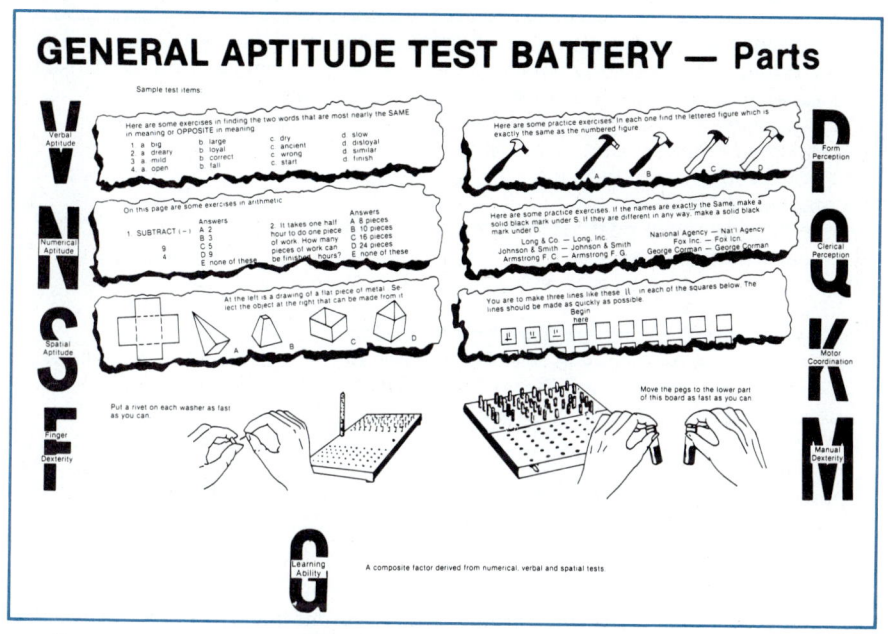

[Figure: General Aptitude Test Battery — Parts, showing sample test items for Verbal Aptitude (V), Numerical Aptitude (N), Spatial Aptitude (S), Form Perception (P), Clerical Perception (Q), Motor Coordination (K), Finger Dexterity (F), Manual Dexterity (M), and Learning Ability (G) — a composite factor derived from numerical, verbal and spatial tests.]

Reproduced by permission (Nelson Canada).

uses. Most achievement tests used for selection have been developed for semiskilled and craft jobs.

Personality and Interest Tests

Personality tests were not originally designed for use in employment selection.[83] Conceptually, the notion that an employee's personality affects job performance makes sense, at least for managerial jobs. But there are few published examples where personality tests are valid predictors of successful performance. The Guilford-Zimmerman Temperament Survey (Exhibit 9–17) is an example of a test that presumably measures personality traits, including general activity, restraint, aggressiveness, sociability, emotional stability, objectiveness, friendliness, and more.[84] Some studies have found that the sociability and emotional stability factors were valid predictors of managerial performance.[85]

Interest inventories assess an applicant's preferences. For example, the Strong Vocational Interest Test asks individuals to state whether they like, are indifferent to, or dislike certain activities, school subjects, behaviours of people, and jobs.[86] By comparing their responses to those of successful people in

EXHIBIT 9–17
Sample Items from the Guilford-Zimmerman Temperament Survey

You start to work on a new project with a great deal of enthusiasm.
In being thrown by chance with a stranger, you wait for him to introduce himself.
You avoid arguing over a price with a clerk or salesman.
You find yourself hurrying to get places even when there is plenty of time.
The thought of making a speech frightens you.
You would rather apply for a job by writing a letter than by going through with a personal interview.
You seldom give your past mistakes a second thought.
You nearly always receive all the credit that is coming to you for things you do.
Most people are paid as well as they should be for what they contribute to society.
You hesitate to tell people to mind their own business.
Most people use politeness to cover up what is really "cut-throat" competition.
If anyone steps ahead of you in line, he is likely to hear from you about it.
You would rather be a miner than a florist.

Source: J. P. Guilford and Wayne S. Zimmerman. Copyright 1949, 1976, Sheridan Psychological Services, Orange, Calif. Reprinted by permission. All rights reserved. No reproduction or use is permitted by any means without the express written consent of Sheridan Psychological Services.

a field, it is possible to find similar and different patterns of interest. The primary use of an interests test is vocational counselling, not selection.

Work or Performance Samples

Work samples are replicas of on-the-job behaviours. Work sample tests involve collecting data on applicants performing in simulated but realistic work conditions. Examples include shorthand or word-processing tests, hydraulic repairs, blueprint reading, managerial in-baskets, or police officer judgement tests.

The design of work sample procedures is based on the previously discussed notion of behavioural consistency.[87]

Assessment Centres. The assessment centre (AC) approach is a widely used standardized off-the-job procedure employed to identify managerial potential for purposes of selection, placement, promotion, and/or development.[88] Some of the Canadian employers using assessment centres are Alcan, B.C. Forest Products, Steinbergs Ltd., The Justice Institute of B.C., Northern Telecom, as well as a number of municipal, provincial, and federal government units. T.S. Turner Consulting reports that the assessment centre method is being used increasingly in connection with employment equity programs, and more attention is being given to integrating the method with other human resource programs.[89]

The assessment centre approach relies on multiple methods of assessment, based on the observations by trained assessors of candidates' behaviour in performing in situations that simulate (or are actual examples of) required job activities. The assessment process can vary in length from a few hours to several days, depending on the complexity of behaviour patterns to be evaluated. Typically, a centre for first-level supervisors will last one to two full days. The content of each centre is tailored around the problems and situations faced in specific jobs.

Some employers have begun to use an assessment centre approach with nonsupervisory and trades personnel as well. General Motors, for example, refined the selection process of applicants for production-related jobs at its Autoplex by introducing an 18-hour assessment centre. The process was extended a year later to skilled tradespeople (e.g., electricians, tool and diemakers).[90]

Steps of the assessment centre process include the following, given that job descriptions and specifications are current: Identification of key factors or dimensions for successful job performance (see Exhibit 9–18 for some of the dimensions usually included in centres designed for managerial jobs); design of job simulation exercises; training of assessors (managers and/or outside consultants); administration of the exercises and observation of participants (up to 12); evaluation of participants on each dimension as well as in terms of a global rating; and feedback to participants, including developmental counselling to those rated "unsuccessful." Final assessments are based on combined judgements of several assessors.

Research on Employment Tests

The accumulated research shows that properly designed ability, achievement, and work sample tests can be valid and useful predictors of performance on the job. Tests based on behavioural consistency, such as actual work samples, are most valid.[91]

The usefulness of several tests, together in a test battery, is usually greater than such tests individually. Test batteries are designed to collect data on several factors. Personality and interest inventories may be useful in selection if part of a test battery, but by themselves the validation results are poor.

After an extensive review of the research on employment testing, Schmidt and Hunter conclude:[92]

1. Professionally designed abilities tests are valid predictors of performance in all settings.
2. They are equally valid for minorities and majority applicants in that they do not underestimate the job performance of minority groups.
3. Abilities tests used in selection can produce large labour-cost savings, ranging from $18 million per year for smaller employers (5,000 employees) to several billion per year for very large employers.

EXHIBIT 9-18
Common Dimensions Used in Managerial Assessment Centres

Oral communication skill	Effective expression in individual or group situations (includes gestures and nonverbal communications).
Oral presentation skill	Effective expression when presenting ideas or tasks to an individual or to a group when given time for preparation (includes gestures and nonverbal communication).
Written communication skill	Clear expression of ideas in writing and in good grammatical form.
Job motivation	The extent to which activities and responsibilities available in the job overlap with activities and responsibilities that result in personal satisfaction.
Initiative	Active attempts to influence events to achieve goals; self-starting rather than passive acceptance. Taking action to achieve goals beyond those called for; originating action.
Leadership	Utilization of appropriate interpersonal styles and methods in guiding individuals (subordinates, peers, superiors) or groups toward task accomplishment.
Planning and organization	Establishing a course of action for self and/or others to accomplish a specific goal; planning proper assignments of personnel and appropriate allocation of resources.
Analysis	Relating and comparing data from different sources, identifying issues, securing relevant information, and identifying relationships.
Judgement	Developing alternative courses of action and making decisions that are based on logical assumptions and reflect factual information.
Management control	Establishing procedures to monitor and/or regulate processes, tasks, or the job activities and responsibilities of subordinates. Taking action to monitor the results of delegated assignments or projects.

Source: W. C. Byham, "Starting an Assessment Center the Correct Way," *Personnel Administrator*, February 1980, pp. 27–32. Copyright 1980 by the American Society for Personnel Administration, 606 North Washington Street, Alexandria, VA 22314.

Generally, research on assessment centres reveals that, if properly designed and conducted, they can be valid predictors of promotion or advancement; they appear to be less valid for predicting job success.[93] However, Cascio, Ramos, and others have found that even moderately valid results translated into significant performance-cost results.[94] ACs also show validity generalization.[95] Moreover, Moses and Boehm's large-scale study provided evidence that the assessment centre is equally valid for predicting the management progress of male *and female* candidates.[96]

Companies show increasing interest in administering tests by computer. AT&T gives about 100,000 tests a year.[97] It is already administering tests for word processors and computer operators by computer and anticipates expanding the use of computers. Even researchers at the Education Testing Service are looking to offer computerized college admission tests.

The Polygraph

Although originally developed for police work, polygraph tests today are also used to check data during personnel selection.[98] Its use appears to be more widespread among employers concerned about employee theft and the protection of proprietary information and processes. Both supportive and negative views have been expressed.[99]

There are many objections to the use of the polygraph in personnel selection. It is an invasion of the applicant's privacy and insults the dignity of the applicant. As severe as these objections are, the most serious question is whether the polygraph is reliable. The polygraph records physiological changes in response to stress. It does not record lying, or even the conditions necessarily accompanying lying. Most of us have heard of cases in which persons who lie easily have beaten the polygraph, and it has been shown that the polygraph brands as liars some people who respond emotionally to questions. There is significant evidence that polygraphs are neither reliable nor valid.

Such criticisms have led to the banning of the polygraph for employee selection in some jurisdictions. Arbitrators often hold against forcing employees to take such tests, and polygraph evidence is not admissible in court unless both sides agree. Despite strong criticisms, use of the polygraph in employee selection persists.

Graphology

Handwriting analysis, called graphology, is used to study an individual's personality and is viewed as legitimate in most European countries (particularly in Germany, France, and Holland). European graphologists generally adopt a holistic approach in their interpretation of handwriting. North Americans usually regard graphology as skeptically as fortune-telling and astrology. However, some Canadian firms do use it.[100]

Cherrington recently summarized two major reviews of this technique and reports (a) changes in personality are accompanied by changes in handwriting; (b) a person's handwriting is fairly stable over long periods of time; (c) intelligence can be inferred from handwriting; and (d) specific personality characteristics are associated with specific handwriting characteristics. He also reports that, although handwriting analysis is surprisingly reliable, its validity is questionable.[101] Reilly and Chao also found that handwriting analysis is not a valid predictor of job performance.[102]

Medical Testing/Screening

Some employers have begun to screen applicants (and, we anticipate, employees) for drug abuse. Others would welcome a reliable test to screen for acquired immune deficiency syndrome (AIDS).[103]

Relatively common in the United States, drug testing (via urine samples) crossed the border in 1986 when CN Railways began using it as a pre-employment screen with applicants for blue-collar positions.[104] While other employers have followed (e.g., Air Canada, Weyerhaeuser Canada Ltd.), some are reviewing their drug-testing stance (e.g., General Motors) or anticipate raising the issue at the bargaining table (e.g., Chrysler Canada). Recent discussions of drug testing suggest the "battle lines" between employers and unions, civil libertarians, and the human rights commissions will become more sharply defined with adoption or report of errors in analysis.[105] In what appears to be a trade-off between safety and productivity and the rights and dignity of employees, the final decision makers may have to be the courts.

Another emerging practice, genetic screening, extends considerably beyond testing for drug abuse. Its introduction to the selection process is a response to the high cost of work-related injuries and disease.[106]

A growing body of genetic research suggests individuals with various genetic conditions are hypersusceptible to toxins in the work environment, thereby increasing their likelihood of contracting occupational diseases. As discussed by Olian, genetic testing in the employment context involves identification of such hypersusceptible individuals to allow selective placement of new hires or incumbents on the basis of genetic information.[107]

Evidence of individual differences in susceptibility to toxic exposure suggests that people are endowed with certain genetic features that result in vulnerability, in unequal degrees, to substances in the work environment. There is strong evidence that many genetic syndromes are distributed unequally across different ethnic groups. For example, genetic conditions distributed unequally across ethnic groups are alpha thalassemia (a potentially fatal form of anemia), the sickle cell trait (which may lead to fatal anemia if both parents are trait carriers), and the Z or S genes (which reduce the body's defences against chronic pulmonary disease). Accordingly, there may be instances in which genetic testing information will reveal adverse effect, by ethnicity.[108] A related issue concerns possible differences of susceptibility across gender lines.

While the judicious and ethical use of genetic tests may result in improved worker health, their high degree of intrusiveness may be repugnant to employees. Their use may lead to contentious issues regarding employee privacy and adverse effect in job selection and placement.

Formal Education

Most employers attempt to screen for abilities by specifying educational and experiential criteria.

Employers tend to specify as a selection requirement the completion of certain levels of formal education and types of education. For the job of accountant, the employer may list a bachelor's degree in accounting as a minimum qualification. The employer may prefer that the degree be from one of certain institutions and that the grade point average is above some minimum. To be legal, such requirements must relate to performance of successful accountants at the firm.

Formal education can indicate ability or skills, and level of accomplishment may indicate the degree of work motivation and intelligence of the applicant. Employers are most likely to have educational requirements upheld when they can assert validity, can demonstrate a strong employment equity program, or have conducted a criterion-related validity study. They are least likely to make a case when their only defence is intent to upgrade the quality of their work force. Requiring a secondary school diploma may be discriminatory if it bars minorities from applying for jobs they would be able to perform; the employer should also specify "or equivalent experience."

Thus, educational factors must be validated against job performance. The employer must examine the amount and type of education that correlates with effectiveness on a particular job. This is more effective than relying on preferences, and it is the legal and professionally sound way to set an educational requirement. In society's rush for more and more education, we may have reached a point where credential requirements are simultaneously too restrictive and too lax (i.e., too lax in their "sloppy" relation to the skills that truly make for competence).[109]

Experience

Another criterion for selection is experience.[110] Employers usually prefer more experience to less, and relevant experience to less relevant, and significant to insignificant. They equate experience with ability as well as with attitude, reasoning that a prospect who has performed the job before and is applying for a similar job likes the work and will do it well.

Reference Checks and Recommendation Letters

For years, as part of the selection process, applicants have been required to submit references or recommendation letters. These are supposed to indicate past behaviour and how well the applicant did at the last job. The letter of recommendation has been called "much used but little researched." A recent study concluded that giving specific behavioural examples produced the most positive perceptions of the recommendee.[111]

For a letter of recommendation to be useful, it must meet certain conditions:

- The writer must have known the applicant's performance level and be competent to assess it.
- The writer must communicate the evaluation effectively to the potential employer.
- The writer must be truthful.

Many people are reluctant to put in writing what they really think of the applicant, since the applicant may see this information. As a result, the person writing the reference either glosses over shortcomings or overemphasizes the applicant's good points. Many prior employers will verify in writing only the last job title, salary, and dates of employment; inquiries asking, "Would you rehire this person?" are often ignored. Because of these and other shortcomings, studies of the validity of written references have not been comforting to those using them in selection.[112]

Although little data for reliability exist, it would be useful to find out how the applicant performed on previous jobs. This can be the most relevant information predicting future work behaviour. Reference checks are in order for the most crucial jobs at any time. Cost of these checks varies from a few cents for a few quick telephone calls to several hundred dollars for a thorough field investigation.

Comparison of Job Performance Predictors

A recent meta-analysis (a study of studies) by Hunter and Hunter analyzed the cumulative research on alternative predictors of job performance.[113] Results from thousands of validity studies were examined and integrated, including the findings of meta-analytic studies conducted by others.

Exhibit 9-19 presents a comparison of the predictors reported by Hunter and Hunter. To allow a direct comparison, the job performance criterion had to be the same for all predictors. Accordingly, these results are based on studies that used supervisory ratings as the criterion.

The figures in Exhibit 9-19 show the comparisons separately for two sets of selection procedures—those useful for predicting job performance in entry-level jobs for which training occurs after hiring and those used for promotion or certification. Both figures reveal the relative advantage of ability tests. For

EXHIBIT 9-19
Mean Validities of Predictors

Figure 1: For Entry-Level Jobs for Which Training Will Occur after Hiring

Predictor	Mean Validity
Ability composite	.53
Job tryout	.44
Biographical inventory	.37
Reference check	.36
Experience	.18
Interview	.14
Training and experience ratings	.13
Academic achievement	.11
Education	.10
Interest	.10
Age	−.01

Figure 2: To Be Used for Promotion or Certification, Where Current Performance on the Job Is the Basis for Selection

Predictor	Mean Validity
Work sample test	.54
Ability composite	.53
Peer ratings	.49
Behavioural consistency experience ratings	.49
Job knowledge test	.48
Assessment centre	.43

Compiled from John E. Hunter and Ronda F. Hunter, "Validity and Utility of Alternative Predictors of Job Performance," *Psychological Bulletin* 96 (1984), pp. 72–98.

entry-level jobs, its validity is higher than validities of 10 other predictors. Figure 1 also highlights the drop in validity once we go beyond "job tryout" and biographical inventories. Note the low validities for some of the other predictors discussed in the preceding section. A somewhat different picture applies to promotion; the validity of the six predictors in Figure 2 is relatively close in magnitude. By a small margin, the work sample is a better predictor than ability. The average validity of the assessment centre is still respectable.

INTERNATIONAL DIMENSIONS

Broadly speaking, multinational companies follow three basic models in the recruitment and selection of executives. They may (1) select only from the national group of the parent company, (2) recruit and select only from within their own country and the country where the international branch is located, or (3) adopt an international perspective and emphasize the unrestricted use of qualified candidates of all nationalities. Each of these strategies has some advantages and disadvantages.

The first strategy (parent country executives only) may be appropriate during the early phases of international expansion. However, this policy of ethnocentrism implies blocked promotional paths for local executives. The second strategy is often used after acquisition of a local company in the host country. Its use helps ease language barriers and cross-cultural adjustment problems. It also allows MNCs the benefit of lower local salary levels while still paying a premium to attract high-quality employees. A possible disadvantage is that local managers experience difficulty in bridging the gap between the foreign subsidiary and the parent company. Although the third strategy ("geocentrism") may appear optimal, it has several potential problems: it can be very expensive, takes a long time to implement, requires a great deal of centralized control over managers and their career patterns, and must be rooted in a deep commitment that cross-national service is important to the firm. Relatively few MNCs have developed a truly international executive cadre.[114]

SUMMARY

You should now know the role the selection process plays in P/HRM plus the basic issues involved in its design and administration. The basic premise underlying selection is that the nature of individuals (abilities, experience, motivation, interests) and jobs (requirements) differs. Selecting individuals who are more likely to match the job requirements should lead to both employee and organization effectiveness. In selection, differences in individuals are used to fit the nature of the work. In job design, the work may be redesigned to better fit the nature of individuals. Ideally, selection and job design are considered together, rather than as alternatives. You should now begin to be aware of how human resource activities operate as a system, as interlinking components.

Selection is the final chapter in Part Three, which deals with staffing. The objective is to staff the organization with people who will be effective. We examined four major components of the employment process: employment planning (how many and which types of human resources are required), recruitment (where and how to attract them to apply), selection (deciding which ones to choose), and employment equity (making certain that human rights are observed throughout the process). In the next part, we turn to training, developing, and utilizing employees.

APPENDIX A / Technical Note—Selection Study

The performance of logging-machine operators is a major factor determining logging productivity, cost, and the success or failure of new technology. Data were obtained for 757 shifts of tree-felling activity carried out by operators of tractor-mounted hydraulic tree shears used in industrial timber felling.[115] The study attempted to relate a number of predictors to observed job performance (measured in terms of trees cut per productive machine hour). The following eight predictors were used as independent variables:

- Motivation.
- Coordination (K), from the GATB.
- Spatial aptitude (S), from the GATB.
- Form perception (P), from the GATB.
- Manual dexterity (M), from the GATB.
- Visual depth perception.
- Physical fitness.
- Forest stand information, to also allow for the quality of operator performance.

Regression models examined resulted in the following equation relating observed productivity (with an adjustment for environmental conditions) to the predictors:

Trees cut per PMH = 22.92 + 0.21 (number of merchantable trees/acre, T)
+ 0.65 (months experience, EXP)
+ 0.65 (manual dexterity score, M)
− 33.85 (if depth perception poorer than normal, D)
+ 6.37 (motivation expectancy score, E)

This approach yielded a multiple validity coefficient of $R = 0.77$, and all regression coefficients (the weights determined for the predictors) were significant beyond the $p < 0.01$ level. Note that only five of the eight predictors were included in the final model. The other three were not significantly associated with performance.

After conducting cross-validation, it appears that experience, manual dexterity, depth perception, and motivation expectancy are four KSAOs each applicant should be tested for.

APPENDIX B / Valid Selection Means Higher Work Force Productivity[116]

The net payoff (utility) in *dollars*, per selectee, expected to result from the use of an improved selection procedure can be determined as:

Dollar gain in productivity per selectee = Difference in validity coefficients × Variability in job performance (in dollars per year) × Average score of selectees on the selection procedure

$$- \left(\frac{\text{Difference in selection costs to fill one vacancy}}{\text{Selection ratio of new method}} \right)$$

In symbolic notation, the formula is (subscript 2 refers to the new procedure):

$$\Delta U/\text{Selectee} = (r_2 - r_1)(SD_y)(\overline{Z}_x) - (C_2 - C_1)/SR$$

The sources referenced address how each term of the utility equation can be measured. Coefficients r_2 and r_1 are the respective validity coefficients. The state of the art of behavioural estimation indicates that SD_y is approximately 40 percent of average annual salary (Hunter and Schmidt's "40 percent rule"). $\overline{Z}_x$ is the average predictor score of those hired. If applicants' predictor scores have a bell-shaped distribution (normal curve), $\overline{Z}_x$ is the ordinate (height) of the distribution corresponding to the selection procedure's cutoff point, which defines the proportion of applicants selected. The lower the selection ratio (i.e., the smaller the A + B shown in Exhibit 9–7), the higher will be $\overline{Z}_x$. The cost term is based on differences in startup costs of the new versus current procedure and the increased costs of operating the new procedure. SR is the selection ratio.

Let's apply the formula to illustrate how an increase in validity affects the dollar value of a new test procedure. A provincial government agency hires a number of claims examiners annually to replace normal retirements and turnover, and perhaps even expands agency staff. A new selection test has been validated ($r_2 = 0.40$) to improve the current procedure ($r_1 = 0.15$). The average annual salary of examiners is $25,000. Estimating in a generally conservative direction, we use 30 (rather than 40) percent as the standard deviation; $SD_y = (0.30) \times (\$25,000) = \$7,500$. Taking SR as 0.20, $\overline{Z}_x = 1.40$. Assume $C_1 - C_2 = \$12$.

Substituting these values into the equation, we determine that the yearly dollar value, per selectee, in improved performance productivity is $2,625 − $60 = $2,565. If we assume that 20 examiners are hired, the annual productivity gain is (20)($2,565) = $51,300. This gain continues to accrue to the agency over the employment period of the new selectees.

The total payoff of applying the new selection procedure can be estimated by multiplying the benefit component of the equation (the part of the formula before the minus sign) by t, the average job tenure (in years). Assuming $t = 25$ years (not an unreasonable assumption for government employment), the total dollar value of the productivity improvement for *each group* of 20 hired is (25)($51,300) = $1.2825 million.

This illustration, and the utility studies cited in the chapter, show that methods are available for an organization of any size to demonstrate the effectiveness of valid selection procedures. As we noted at the outset to this chapter, they do pay off.

DISCUSSION AND REVIEW QUESTIONS

1. Describe the external and organization conditions that influence personnel selection? How?
2. Which government regulations affect personnel selection?
3. What are selection ratios and base rates? How do they apply to personnel selection? What happens if either changes?
4. Compare and contrast the empirical and rational validation methods.
5. What is reliability? Validity?
6. How does the validity of a selection device differ from its usefulness or utility?
7. Describe a typical selection process for a manual labourer, a top executive, a typist.
8. How are biographical data forms used in selection? How effective are they? Are they reliable and valid?
9. How does the accomplishment record compare to biographical data?
10. What does research say about employment interviews?
11. What is an abilities test? A work sample? An interest test? An assessment centre? Discuss the usefulness of each.

NOTES AND REFERENCES

1. For a summary of the classification of types of control, see John H. Jackson, Cyril P. Morgan, and Joseph P. Paolillo, *Organization Theory: A Macro Perspective for Management* 3rd ed. (Englewood Cliffs, N.J.: Prentice-Hall, 1986), pp. 299–302; successful feedforward control requires a good measure of inputs (i.e., a valid selection system) and an understanding of the effects of resource variations (i.e., variations in the labour market, etc.).
2. Wayne F. Cascio, *Costing Human Resources: The Financial Impact of Behavior in Organizations* (Boston: Kent Publishing, 1982).
3. James W. Thacker and R. Julian Cattaneo, "The Canadian Personnel Function: Status and Practices," in *ASAC 1987 Conference Proceedings, Supplement 2* (Personnel and Human Resources, pp. 56–66), ed. Thomas H. Stone and Jean Le Louarn, June 1–3, 1987, Toronto, Ontario.
4. "Improve Hiring Decisions," *Small Business Report,* April 1987, p. 18.
5. Charles C. Snow and Raymond E. Miles, "Organizational Strategy, Design and Human Resources Management" (paper presented at Academy of Management Meetings, Dallas, 1983); also see Marc Gerstein and H. Reisman, "Strategic

Selection: Matching Executives to Business Conditions," *Sloan Management Review*, Winter 1983, pp. 33–34; A. D. Szilagy, Jr., and D. M. Schweiger, "Matching Managers to Strategies: A Review and Suggested Framework" (working paper, University of Houston, Houston, Texas, 1984).

6. Ibid.; see also "Wanted: A Manager to Fit Each Strategy," *Business Week*, February 25, 1980; Theodore T. Herbert and Helen Deresky, "Should General Managers Match Their Business Strategies?" *Organizational Dynamics*, Winter 1987, pp. 40–51; Anil K. Gupta, "Matching Managers to Strategies," *Human Resource Management*, 25, no. 2 (1986), pp. 215–34. For the importance of matching values, see, for example, Richard T. Barth, "Value Noncomplementarity and Organizational Commitment of Engineers," *R&D Management* 4 (1973), pp. 13–24; Richard T. Barth and Ilan Vertinsky, "The Effect of Goal Orientation and Information Environment on Research Performance: A Field Study," *Organizational Behavior and Human Performance*, 13 (1975), pp. 110–32; and Warren Gross and Shula Shichman, "How to Grow an Organizational Culture," *Personnel* 64, no. 9 (1987), pp. 52–57.
7. Snow and Miles, "Organizational Strategy."
8. G. R. Salancik and J. Pfeffer, "Who Gets the Power—and How They Hold on to It," *Organizational Dynamics*, Winter 1977, pp. 3–21.
9. R. A. Alexander, G. V. Barrett, and D. Doverspike, "An Explication of the Selection Ratio and Its Relationship to Hiring Rate," *Journal of Applied Psychology* 68 (1983), pp. 342–44.
10. Personal interview with Fran Coyne, vice president, personnel, at Burlington Northern.
11. Mary L. Tenopyr and Paul D. Oeltjen, "Personnel Selection and Classification," *Annual Review of Psychology* 33 (1982), pp. 581–618; Sheldon Zedeck and Wayne F. Cascio, "Psychological Issues in Personnel Decisions," *Annual Review of Psychology* 35 (1984), pp. 461–518.
12. Lee J. Cronbach, *Essentials of Psychological Testing*, 3rd ed. (New York: Harper & Row, 1970), p. 26; Milton L. Blum, *Industrial Psychology and Its Social Foundations*, new ed. (New York: Harper & Row, 1956), p. 267.
13. Dale S. Beach, *Personnel: The Management of People at Work*, 5th ed. (New York: Macmillan, 1985).
14. Oscar K. Buros, ed., *Tests in Print—Vol. 2* (Highland Park, N.J.: Gryphon Press, 1974); O. K. Buros, ed., *The Eighth Mental Measurements Yearbook, Vols. 1 and 2* (Highland Park, N.J.: Gryphon Press, 1978); O. K. Buros, ed., *Vocational Tests and Reviews* (Highland Park, N.J.: Gryphon Press, 1975).
15. R. C. Sweetland and D. J. Keyser, eds., *Tests* (Test Corporation of America, 1983, distributed by Gale Research Company, Detroit, Michigan).
16. Steven F. Cronshaw, "The State of Employment Testing in Canada: A Review and Evaluation of Theory and Professional Practice," *Canadian Psychology* 27 no. 2 (1986), pp. 183–95.
17. Ibid.; see also "Guidelines for Educational and Psychological Testing" (Ottawa: Canadian Psychological Association, 1986).
18. Cronshaw, "The Status of Employment Testing in Canada," p. 193.
19. Thacker and Cattaneo, "The Canadian Personnel Function: Status and Practices."
20. E. E. Ghiselli, J. P. Campbell, and S. Zedeck, *Measurement Theory for the Behavioral Sciences* (San Francisco: W. H. Freeman, 1981); who show that $r_{xy} \leq$

$\sqrt{r_{xx}}$, where r_{xy} is the validity coefficient and r_{xx} the reliability coefficient.
21. Robert M. Guion, *Personnel Testing* (New York: McGraw-Hill, 1965), chap. 2.
22. David J. Cherrington, *Personnel Management* (Dubuque, Iowa: Wm. C. Brown, 1983).
23. Guion, *Personnel Testing*, p. 43; the Spearman-Brown Prophecy Formula may be applied as follows:

$$r_{tt} = \frac{2r_{1/2\ 1/2}}{1 + r_{1/2\ 1/2}}$$

where

r_{tt} = Reliability of the total test (estimated)

$r_{1/2\ 1/2}$ = Observed correlation between the two halves of the test

For example, if the observed correlation between halves were 0.45, then the Prophecy Formula would estimate the reliability of the complete test as:

$$r_{tt} = \frac{2(0.45)}{1 + 0.45} = \frac{0.90}{1.45} = 0.62$$

24. Ibid., p. 44; see also L. J. Cronbach, "Coefficient Alpha and the Internal Structure of Tests," *Psychometrika* 16 (1951), pp. 297–334; Anne Anastasi, *Psychological Testing*, 5th ed. (New York: Macmillan, 1982); computational routines are presented in Chapter 13 of *Users Guide-SPSS^x* (New York: McGraw-Hill, 1983).
25. F. L. Schmidt, J. E. Hunter, R. McKenzie, and T. W. Muldrow, "The Impact of Valid Selection Procedures on Workforce Productivity," *Journal of Applied Psychology* 64, no. 3 (1979), pp. 609–26; Frank F. Schmidt and John E. Hunter, "Individual Differences in Productivity: An Empirical Test of Estimates Derived from Studies of Selection Procedure Utility," *Journal of Applied Psychology* 68, no. 3 (1983), pp. 407–14.
26. D. D. Baker and D. E. Terpstra, "Employee Selection: Must Every Job Tested Be Validated?" *Personnel Journal* 61, no. 8 (1982), pp. 602–5; Robert M. Guion and C. J. Cranny, "A Note on Concurrent and Predictive Validity Designs: A Critical Reanalysis," *Journal of Applied Psychology* 67, no. 2 (1982), pp. 234–44; F. L. Schmidt and J. E. Hunter, "The Future of Criterion-Related Validity," *Personnel Psychology* 33, no. 1 (1980), pp. 41–60.
27. Wayne F. Cascio, *Applied Psychology in Personnel Management* (Reston, Va.: Reston Publishing, 1982), chap. 8.
28. Dreher and Sackett, *Perspectives on Employee Staffing*.
29. Floyd L. Ruch, "The Impact on Employment Procedures of the Supreme Court Decision in the Duke Power Case," in *Contemporary Problems in Personnel: Readings for the Seventies*, ed., W. C. Hamner and F. L. Schmidt, (Chicago: St. Clair Press, 1974).
30. M. D. Dunnette, *Predicting Job Performance of Electrical Power Plant Operators* (Minneapolis, Minn.: Personnel Decision Research Institute, 1983).
31. Anne Anastasi, *Psychological Testing*, 5th ed. (New York: Macmillan, 1982), chap. 6.
32. Guion, *Personnel Testing*, pp. 169–74.
33. Anastasi, *Psychological Testing*, pp. 436–37.
34. M. L. Blum and J. C. Naylor, *Industrial Psychology: Its Theoretical and Social Foundations*, rev. ed. (New York: Harper & Row, 1968).

35. See Dreher and Sackett, *Perspectives on Employee Staffing*; Richard R. Reily and Georgia T. Chao, "Validity and Fairness of Some Alternative Employee Selection Procedures," *Personnel Psychology* 35, no. 1 (1982), pp. 1–62.
36. Fred N. Kerlinger and E. J. Pedhazur, *Multiple Regression in Behavioral Research* (New York: Holt, Rinehart & Winston, 1973); Roger C. Pfaffenberger and James H. Patterson, *Statistical Methods for Business and Economics* (Homewood, Ill.: Richard D. Irwin, 1987), chap. 15; an introduction to available computer programs and relevant statistics is provided in the following: $SPSS^x$—*User's Guide*, (Chicago: SPSS Inc., 1983); and Marija J. Norusis, *Introductory Statistics Guide to SPSS*, (New York: McGraw-Hill, 1983).
37. H. C. Taylor and J. T. Russell, "The Relationship of Validity Coefficients to the Practical Effectiveness of Tests in Selection: Discussion and Tables," *Journal of Applied Psychology* 23 (1939), pp. 565–78.
38. Wayne F. Cascio, *Costing Human Resources*; H. E. Brogden, "When Testing Pays Off," *Personnel Psychology* 2 (1949), pp. 171–83.
39. Much of the initial development and application of such methods is due to the work of Schmidt and Hunter and their colleagues, and Cascio; see F. L. Schmidt, J. E. Hunter, R. C. McKenzie, and T. W. Muldrow, "Impact of Valid Selection Procedures on Work Force Productivity," *Journal of Applied Psychology* 64 (1979), pp. 609–26; J. E. Hunter and F. L. Schmidt, "Fitting People to Jobs: The Impact of Personnel Selection on National Productivity," in *Human Performance and Productivity: Human Capability Assessment*, M. D. Dunnette and E. A. Fleishman, eds. (Hillsdale, N.J.: Lawrence Erlbaum Associates, 1982); Wayne F. Cascio, "Responding to the Demand for Accountability: A Critical Analysis of Three Utility Models," *Organizational Behavior and Human Performance* 25 (1980), pp. 32–45; J. W. Boudreau, "Economic Considerations in Estimating the Utility of Human Resource Productivity Improvement Programs," *Journal of Applied Psychology* 68 (1983), pp. 551–76; T. J. Janz and L. E. Etherington, "Using Forecasted Net Benefits in Designing Improved Recruitment and Selection Systems," *International Journal of Forecasting* 1 (1985), pp. 287–96; Ralph B. Alexander and Murray R. Barrick, "Estimating the Standard Error of Projected Dollar Gains in Utility Analysis," *Journal of Applied Psychology* 72 (1987), pp. 463–74.
40. Virginia R. Boehm, "Are We Validating More but Publishing Less? The Impact of Governmental Regulations on Published Validation Research," *Personnel Psychology* 5, no. 2 (1982), pp. 175–80; J. E. Hunter and F. L. Schmidt, "Noncompensatory Aspects of Personnel Selection" (working paper, East Lansing: Michigan State University, Department of Psychology 1980); M. J. Mack, F. L. Schmidt, and J. E. Hunter, *Estimating the Productivity Costs in Dollars of Minimum Selection Test Cutoff Scores* (Washington, D.C.: Office of Personnel Research and Development, U.S. Office of Personnel Management, 1981); J. Rauschenberger, "The Utility of Valid Selection Procedures: Dollars and Sense" (paper presented at the conference on "Recent Directions in Testing and Fair Employment Practices," Washington, D.C., sponsored by the Personnel Testing Council of Metropolitan Washington and BNA Systems, April 23, 1981); Schmidt, Hunter, McKenzie, and Muldrow, "The Impact of Valid Selection Procedures on Workforce Productivity"; F. L. Schmidt, J. E. Hunter, A. Outerbridge, and M. Trattner, *The Economic Impact of Job Selection Methods on the Size, Productivity, and Payroll Costs of the Federal Workforce: An Empirical Demonstration*

(Washington, D.C.: Office of Personnel Research and Development, U.S. Office of Personnel Management, 1981); F. L. Schmidt, *An Empirical Analysis of the Economic Impact of the Luevano Consent Decree on the Size, Productivity and Payroll Costs of the GS S-7 Federal Workforce* (Office of Personnel Research and Development, U.S. Office of Personnel Management, 1981); F. L. Schmidt, "The Impact of the Maintenance-Helper Selection Test Batteries of the Philadelphia Electric Company on Workforce Productivity and Payroll Costs" (unpublished paper, 1981); F. L. Schmidt, "The Impact of the Clerical Employees Selection Test Battery of the Philadelphia Electric Company on Clerical Productivity and Payroll Costs" (unpublished paper, 1981); J. E. Hunter and F. L. Schmidt, "Fitting People to Jobs: Implications of Personnel Selection for National Productivity," in *Human Performance and Productivity*, vol. 1, ed. E. A. Fleishman and M. D. Dunnette (Hillsdale, N.J.: Lawrence Earlbaum Associates, 1982), pp. 233–84; J. E. Hunter, *Fairness of the General Aptitude Test Battery (GATB): Ability Differences and Their Impact on Minority Hiring Rates* (Washington, D.C.: U.S. Employment Service, U.S. Department of Labor, 1980); J. E. Hunter, *The Economic Benefits of Personnel Selection Using Ability Tests: A State of the Art Review Including a Detailed Analysis of the Dollar Benefit of U.S. Employment Service Placements and a Critique of the Low Cutoff Method of Test Use* (Washington, D.C.: U.S. Employment Service, U.S. Department of Labor, January 15, 1981); F. L. Schmidt, J. E. Hunter, and K. Pearlman, "Assessing the Economic Impact of Personnel Programs on Workforce Productivity," *Personnel Psychology* 35, no. 3 (1982), pp. 333–43.

41. Wayne F. Cascio, *Costing Human Resources: The Financial Impact of Behavior in Organizations*, p. 163.
42. Richard A. Fear and James F. Ross, *Jobs, Dollars, and EEO: How to Hire More Productive Entry-Level Workers* (New York: McGraw-Hill, 1983), pp. 11–14.
43. Steven F. Cronshaw, "The Utility of Employment Testing for Clerical/Administrative Trades in the Canadian Military," *Canadian Journal of Administrative Sciences* 3, no. 2 (1986), pp. 376–85.
44. Richard E. Kopelman, *Managing Productivity in Organizations: A Practical, People-Oriented Perspective* (New York: McGraw-Hill, 1986), chap. 5.
45. Steven F. Cronshaw, Ralph A. Alexander, Willi H. Wiesner, and Murray R. Barrick, "Incorporating Risk into Selection Utility: Two Models for Sensitivity Analysis and Risk Simulation," *Organizational Behavior and Decision Processes* 40 (1987), pp. 270–86.
46. F. L. Schmidt and J. E. Hunter, "Development of a General Solution to the Problem of Validity Generalization," *Journal of Applied Psychology* 62 (1977), pp. 529–40; F. L. Schmidt, J. E. Hunter, and J. R. Caplan, "Validity Generalization Results for Two Job Groups in the Petroleum Industry," *Journal of Applied Psychology* 66 (1981), pp. 261–73; Michael J. Burke, "Validity Generalization: A Review and Critique of the Correlation Model," *Personnel Psychology* 37, no. 1 (1984), pp. 93–117; M. H. Trattner, "Synthetic Validity and Its Application to the Uniform Guidelines Validation Requirements," *Personnel Psychology* 35, no. 3 (1982), pp. 383–97.
47. Glenda Mattinson and Steven F. Cronshaw, "A Transnational Validity Generalization Study: Transportability of Employment Tests between the United States and Canada," *Canadian Journal of Administrative Sciences* 3, no. 1 (June 1986), pp. 15–28.

48. Ibid.
49. William Owens, "Background Data," in *Handbook of Industrial and Organizational Psychology*, ed. M. Dunnette (Chicago: Rand McNally, 1976); Allen Schuh, "Application Blank and Intelligence as Predictors of Turnover," *Personnel Psychology*, Spring 1967, pp. 59–63; Allen Schuh, "The Predictability of Employee Tenure: A Review of the Literature," *Personnel Psychology*, Spring 1967, pp. 133–52.
50. G. W. England, *Development and Use of Weighted Application Blanks*, rev. ed. (Minneapolis: University of Minnesota, Industrial Relations Center, 1971). Although a number of techniques are available for statistically weighting items, the horizontal percent method is probably the simplest. See W. A. Owens, "Background Data," in *Handbook of Industrial and Organizational Psychology*, ed. M. D. Dunnette (Chicago: Rand McNally, 1976).
51. M. E. Ace, *A Good Match = Dollars and Sense* (Vancouver: B.C. Real Estate Association).
52. Terry W. Mitchell and R. J. Klomoski, "Is It Rational to Be Empirical? A Test of Methods for Scoring Biographical Data," *Journal of Applied Psychology* 67, no. 4 (1982), pp. 411–18.
53. Reilly and Chao, "Validity and Fairness"; James J. Asher, "The Biographical Item: Can It Be Improved?" *Personnel Psychology* 25, no. 2 (1972), pp. 251–69.
54. Leaetta Hough, "Development and Evaluation of Accomplishment Record Method of Selecting and Promoting Professionals," *Journal of Applied Psychology* 69, no. 1 (1984), pp. 135–46.
55. Ibid.
56. Milton D. Hakel, "Employment Interview," in *Personnel Management: New Perspectives*, ed. K. Rowland and G. Ferris (Boston: Allyn & Bacon, 1982).
57. G. P. Latham, L. M. Saari, E. D. Pursell, and M. A. Campion, "The Situational Interview," *Journal of Applied Psychology* 65, no. 4 (1980), pp. 422–27; Eugene Mayfield, "The Selection Interview—A Re-Evaluation of Published Research," *Personnel Psychology*, Autumn 1964, pp. 239–60; Lynn Ulrich and Don Trumbo, "The Selection Interview since 1949," *Psychological Bulletin*, February 1965, pp. 110–16; S. Zedeck, A. Tziner, and S. E. Middlestadt, "Interviewer Validity and Reliability: An Individual Analysis Approach," *Personnel Psychology* 36, no. 2 (1983), pp. 355–74; R. D. Arvey, "Unfair Discrimination in the Employment Interview: Legal and Psychological Aspects," *Psychological Bulletin* 86, no. 4 (1979), pp. 736–65.
58. Mary Tenopyr, "The Realities of Employment Testing," *American Psychologist* 36 (1981).
59. Tom Janz, Lowell Hellervik, and David C. Gilmore, *Behavior Description Interviewing: New, Accurate, Cost Effective* (Toronto: Allyn & Bacon, 1986).
60. Janz, Hellervik, and Gilmore, *Behavior Description Interviewing*.
61. Ibid.
62. Herman Smith, "When a Board Hires . . . Making Committee Hiring Work," *Business Quarterly*, Summer 1987, pp. 28–31.
63. Larry F. Moore, "Using the Videotape in Selection Interviewing: A Report of Three Studies" (Academy of Management Proceedings, 1973).
64. Larry F. Moore and Alec J. Lee, "Comparability of Interviewer, Group, and Individual Interview Ratings," *Journal of Applied Psychology* 59 (1974), pp. 163–67.

65. N. Schmitt, "Social and Situational Determinants of Interview Decisions: Implications for the Employment Interview," *Personnel Psychology* 29, no. 1 (1976), pp. 79–101.
66. Richard D. Arvey and James E. Campion, "The Employment Interview: A Summary and Review of Recent Research," *Personnel Psychology* 35 (1982), pp. 281–322.
67. Ibid.; also see Hakel, "Employment Interview."
68. R. C. Carlson et al., "Improvements in the Selection Interview," *Personnel Journal* 50 (1971), pp. 268–74; S. McIntyre, D. Moberg, and B. Pesner, "Preferential Treatment in Pre-Selections according to Sex and Race," *Academy of Management Journal* 23, no. 4 (1980), pp. 738–49; William F. Giles and H. S. Field, "Accuracy of Interviewers' Perceptions of the Importance of Intrinsic and Extrinsic Job Characteristics to Male and Female Applicants," *Academy of Management Journal* 25, no. 1 (1982), pp. 148–52; D. N. Jackson, Andrew Peacock, and R. R. Holden, "Professional Interviewers' Trait Inferential Structures for Diverse Occupational Groups," *Organizational Behaviour and Human Performance* 29 (1982), pp. 1–20.
69. For a thorough review of the research in this area, see Zedeck and Cascio, *Psychological Issues in Personnel Decisions*.
70. Ibid.
71. Tracy McDonald and Milton D. Hakel, "Effects of Applicant Race, Sex, Suitability, and Answers on Interviewer's Questioning Strategy and Ratings," *Personnel Psychology* 38 (1985), pp. 321–34.
72. Sandra Forsythe, M. F. Drake, and C. E. Cox, "Influence of Applicant's Dress on Interviewer's Selection Decisions," *Journal of Applied Psychology* 70 (1985), pp. 374–78.
73. Robert A. Baron, "Sweet Smell of Success? The Impact of Pleasant Artificial Scents on Evaluations of Applicants," *Journal of Applied Psychology* 68, no. 4 (1983), pp. 709–13..
74. Arvey and Campion, "The Employment Interview."
75. Ibid.
76. Hakel, "Employment Interview."
77. See also, for example, J. G. Allen, *How to Turn an Interview into a Job* (New York: Simon & Schuster, 1983).
78. D. C. Gilmore and G. R. Ferris, "The Recruitment Interview," in *Current Issues in Personnel Management*, ed. K. M. Rowland, G. R. Ferris, and J. L. Sherman (Boston: Allyn & Bacon, 1983).
79. Janz, Hellervik, and Gilmore, *Behavior Description Interviewing*; G. P. Latham, L. M. Saari, E. D. Purall, and M. A. Campion, "The Situational Interview," *Journal of Applied Psychology* 65 (1980), pp. 422–27; T. J. Janz, "Initial Comparisons and Patterned Behavior Description Interviews vs. Unstructured Interviews," *Journal of Applied Psychology* 67 (1982), pp. 577–80; G. P. Latham and L. M. Saari, "The Situational Interview: Examining What People Say versus What They Do versus What They Have Done" (unpublished manuscript, University of Washington, Seattle, 1983).
80. George T. Milkovich and William F. Glueck, *Personnel Human Resource Management: A Diagnostic Approach*, 4th ed. (Plano, Tex.: Business Publications, 1985), p. 307.
81. Judy D. Olian and Tom C. Snyder, "The Implications of Genetic Testing," *Per-

sonnel Administrator, January 1984, pp. 19–23; Edwin Ghiselli, *The Validity of Occupational Aptitude Tests* (New York: John Wiley & Sons, 1966); J. E. Hunter and F. Schmidt, "Ability Tests: Economic Benefits versus the Issue of Fairness," *Industrial Relations* 21 (1982), pp. 293–308.

82. The Canadian version of the General Aptitude Test Battery includes changes to reflect the procedures and forms used by the Canada Department of Employment and Immigration, Ottawa, Ontario. The Canadian editions are: Section I—*Administration and Scoring* (Cat. No. 016); Section II—*Norms, Occupational Aptitude Pattern Structure*; Section III—*Development* (Cat. No. 021); Section IV—*Norms, Specific Occupations* (Cat. No. 022, October 1972).

83. Lee J. Cronbach and G. A. Schaeffer, *Extensions of Personnel Selection Theory to Aspects of Minority Hiring* (Stanford University, Institute for Research on Educational Finance and Governance, 1981).

84. J. P. Guilford and W. S. Zimmerman, *The Guilford Zimmerman Temperament Survey* (Orange, Calif.: Sheridan Psychological Services, 1949, 1976).

85. See Tenopyr and Oeltjen, *Personnel Selection*; and Zedeck and Cascio, *Personnel Decisions*.

86. John L. Holland, "Vocational Preferences," in *Handbook of Industrial and Organizational Psychology*.

87. J. J. Asher and J. A. Sciarrino, "Realistic Work Sample Tests: A Review," *Personnel Psychology* 27 (1974), pp. 519–33; Michael A. Campion, "Personnel Selection for Physically Demanding Jobs: Review and Recommendations," *Personnel Psychology* 36, no. 3 (1983).

88. L. W. Slivinksi, R. P. Bourgeois, L. D. Pederson, J. L. McCloskey, V. S. McDonald, and L. A. Crooks, *Identification of Senior Executive Potential, Development and Implementation of an Assessment Centre* (Personnel Psychology Centre, Public Service Commission of Canada, 1981); A. Wolfson, *Assessment Centres Ten Years Later* (paper presented at the American Psychological Association Ninety-Third Annual Convention, Los Angeles, August 1985); D. W. MacKinnon, "An Overview of Assessment Centers" (Greensboro, N.C.: Center for Creative Leadership, Technical Report No. 1, May 1975; G. C. Thornton and W. C. Byham, *Assessment Centers and Managerial Performance* (New York: Academic Press, 1982); W. C. Byham, "Starting an Assessment Center the Correct Way," *Personnel Administrator*, February 1980, pp. 27–32; P. R. Sackett, "A Critical Look at Some Common Beliefs about Assessment Centers," *Public Personnel Management* 11, no. 1 (1982), pp. 140–47; Frederick D. Frank and James R. Preston, "The Validity of the Assessment Center Approach and Related Issues," *Personnel Administrator*, June 1982, p. 94; Milan Marovee, "A Cost-Effective Career Planning Program Requires Strategy," *Personnel Administrator*, January 1982, p. 30; Anthony J. Plento, *A Review of Assessment Center Research* (Washington, D.C.: U.S. Office of Personnel Management, May 1980), p. 8; Stephen L. Cohen, "The Bottom Line on Assessment Center Technology: Results of a Cost-Benefit Analysis Survey," *Personnel Administrator*, February 1980, p. S7; Task Force on Assessment Center Standards, "Standards and Ethical Considerations for Assessment Center Operations," *Personnel Administrator*, February 1980, p. 18; James C. Quick, William A. Fisher, Lawrence L. Schkade, and George W. Ayers, "Developing Administrative Personnel through the Assessment Center Technique," *Personnel Administrator*, February 1980, p. 46; Donald H. Bush and Lyle F. Schoenfeldt, "Identifying Managerial Potential: An Alternative to Assessment

Centers," *Personnel* (AMACOM), May–June 1980, p. 69; Stephen L. Cohen, "Pre-Packages vs. Tailor-Made: The Assessment Center Debate," *Personnel Journal*, December 1980, p. 989; Barry A. Friedman and Robert W. Mann, "Employee Assessment Methods Assessed," *Personnel* (AMACOM), November–December 1981, p. 70; G. L. Hart and P. H. Thompson, "Assessment Centers: For Selection or Development IBM Workshop Experience," *Organization Dynamics*, Spring 1979, p. 63; J. T. Turnage and P. M. Muchinsky, "Transitional Variability in Human Performance within Assessment Centers," *Organizational Behavior and Human Performance* 30 (1982), pp. 174–200; D. W. Bray and D. L. Grant, "The Assessment Center in the Measurement of Potential for Business Management," *Psychological Monographs* 80, no. 625 (1966).
89. Private communication, T. S. Turner Consulting, Richmond, B.C., January 7, 1987.
90. "The Best People for the Best Technology," *Financial Times* (advertising feature), March 30, 1987, p. A11.
91. P. R. Sackett and M. A. Wilson, "Factors Affecting the Consensus Judgment Process in Managerial Assessment Centers," *Journal of Applied Psychology* 67, no. 1 (1982), pp. 10–17.
92. Schmidt and Hunter, *Employment Testing: Old Theories and New Research.*
93. Barbara B. Gaugler, Douglas B. Rosenthal, George C. Thornton III, and Cynthia Bentson, "Meta-Analysis of Assessment Center Validity," *Journal of Applied Psychology* 72, no. 3 (1987), pp. 493–511; Paul R. Sackett and George F. Dreher, "Constructs and Assessment Center Dimensions: Some Troubling Empirical Findings," *Journal of Applied Psychology* 67, no. 4 (1982), pp. 401–10; V. R. Boehm, "Assessment Centers and Management Development," in *Personnel Management*, ed. K. Rowland and G. R. Ferris (Boston: Allyn & Bacon, 1982); Peter Bycio, Kenneth M. Alvares, and June Hahn, "Situational Specificity in Assessment Center Ratings; A Confirmatory Factor Analysis," *Journal of Applied Psychology* 72, no. 3 (1987), pp. 463–74.
94. W. F. Cascio and V. Silbey, "Utility of the Assessment Center as a Selection Device," *Journal of Applied Psychology* 64 (1979), pp. 107–18.
95. Gaugler, Rosenthal, Thornton III, and Bentson, "Meta-Analysis of Assessment Center Validity."
96. J. L. Moses and V. R. Boehm, "Relationship of Assessment Center Performance to Management Progress of Women," *Journal of Applied Psychology* 60 (1975), pp. 527–29.
97. R. Koenig, "Interest Rising in Testing by Computer," *The Wall Street Journal*, April 18, 1983, p. 29.
98. Robert J. Ferguson, Jr., *The Polygraph in Private Industry* (Springfield, Ill.: Charles C Thomas, 1966); Mary Ann Coghill, *The Lie Detector in Employment* (Ithaca, N.Y.: Industrial and Labor Relations Library, Key Issues Series no. 2, 1970); Bruce Gunn, "The Polygraph and Personnel," *Personnel Administrator*, May 1970, pp. 32–37; M. Smith Burke, "The Polygraph," *Scientific American*, January 1967, pp. 25–31.
99. See, for example, Gordon H. Barland, "The Case *for* the Polygraph in Employment Screening," *Personnel Administrator*, September 1985, pp. 58, 61–62, 64–65; and David T. Lykken, "The Case *against* the Polygraph in Employment Screening," *Personnel Administrator*, September 1985, pp. 59, 61–62, 64–65.

100. Mia Stainsby, "Would You Hire a Person Who Writes Like This?" *The Sun*, February 22, 1986, p. 6.
101. Cherrington, *Personnel Management*.
102. R. R. Reilly and G. T. Chao, "Validity and Fairness of Some Alternative Employee Selection Procedures," *Personnel Psychology* 35 (1982), pp. 1–62.
103. F. S. Chapman, "The Ruckus over Medical Testing," *Fortune*, August 1985, pp. 57–58, 60–63; Carsten Stroud, "Do What's Fair," *Canadian Business*, April 1987, pp. 68–70, 101–2, 104; Mark A. Rothstein, *Medical Screening of Workers* (Washington, D.C.: Bureau of National Affairs, 1984); "How to Deal with AIDS in the Workplace," *Venture*, May 1987, p. 110; Dale A. Masi, "AIDS in the Workplace: What Can Be Done?" *Personnel*, July 1987, pp. 57–60.
104. Colin Languedoc, "Battle Lines Forming over Worker Drug Tests," *The Financial Post*, April 13, 1987, pp. 1, 4.
105. Ibid.; Stroud, "Do What's Fair"; "Rights May Be Violated by Random Drug Testing," *COSHL Monthly Report*, June 1987, p. 5.
106. Chapman, "The Ruckus over Medical Testing"; Alan L. Often, "Genetic Examination of Workers Is an Issue of Growing Urgency," *The Wall Street Journal*, February 24, 1986, pp. 1, 41.
107. Judy D. Olian, "Genetic Screening for Employment Purposes," *Personnel Psychology* 37 (1984), pp. 423–37.
108. Ibid.; see also Z. Harsanyi and R. Hutton, *Genetic Prophecy: Beyond the Double Helix* (New York: Bantam Books, 1981).
109. James Fallows, "The Case against Credentialism," *The Atlantic Monthly*, December 1985, pp. 49–67.
110. Michael E. Gordon and William J. Fitzgibbons, "Empirical Test of the Validity of Seniority as a Factor in Staffing Decision," *Journal of Applied Psychology* 67, no. 3 (1982), pp. 311–19; Michael E. Gordon and William A. Johnson, "Seniority: A Review of Its Legal and Scientific Standing," *Personnel Psychology* 35 (1982), pp. 255–75.
111. Bruce D. Wonder and Kenneth S. Keleman, "Increasing the Value of Reference Information," *Personnel Administrator*, March 1984, pp. 98–103; Martin J. Gannon, "Sources of Referred and Employee Turnover," *Journal of Applied Psychology* 55, no. 3 (1971), pp. 226–28.
112. Zedeck and Cascio, "Psychological Issues in Personnel Decisions."
113. John E. Hunter and Ronda F. Hunter, "Validity and Utility of Alternative Predictors of Job Performance," *Psychological Bulletin* 96 (1984), pp. 72–98.
114. This discussion was adapted (with permission) from Wayne F. Cascio, *Managing Human Resources* (New York: McGraw-Hill, 1986); see also Rosalie L. Tung, "Expatriate Assignments: Enhancing Success and Minimizing Failure," *Academy of Management Executive*, May 1987, pp. 117–25; Nancy J. Adler, *International Dimensions of Organizational Behavior* (Boston: Kent Publishing, 1986); H. W. Lane and J. J. DiStefano, *International Management Behavior* (Toronto: Methuen, 1987); Samuel D. Johnson Jr., "Knowing *That* Versus Knowing *How*: Toward Achieving Expertise through Multicultural Training for Counseling," *The Consulting Psychologist* 15, no. 2 (1987), pp. 320–31; Mark E. Mendenhall, Edward Dunbar, and Gary R. Oddou, "Expatriate Selection, Training, and Career-Pathing: A Review and Critique," *Human Resource Management*, Fall 1987, pp. 331–46.

115. R. T. Barth and P. L. Cottell, "Factors Related to Performance Variation," *Relations Industrielles* 32 (1977), pp. 565–85.
116. Readers interested in more detail and applications should consult the sources included in notes 39 through 46 of this chapter.

Exhibit IV
THE DIAGNOSTIC MODEL

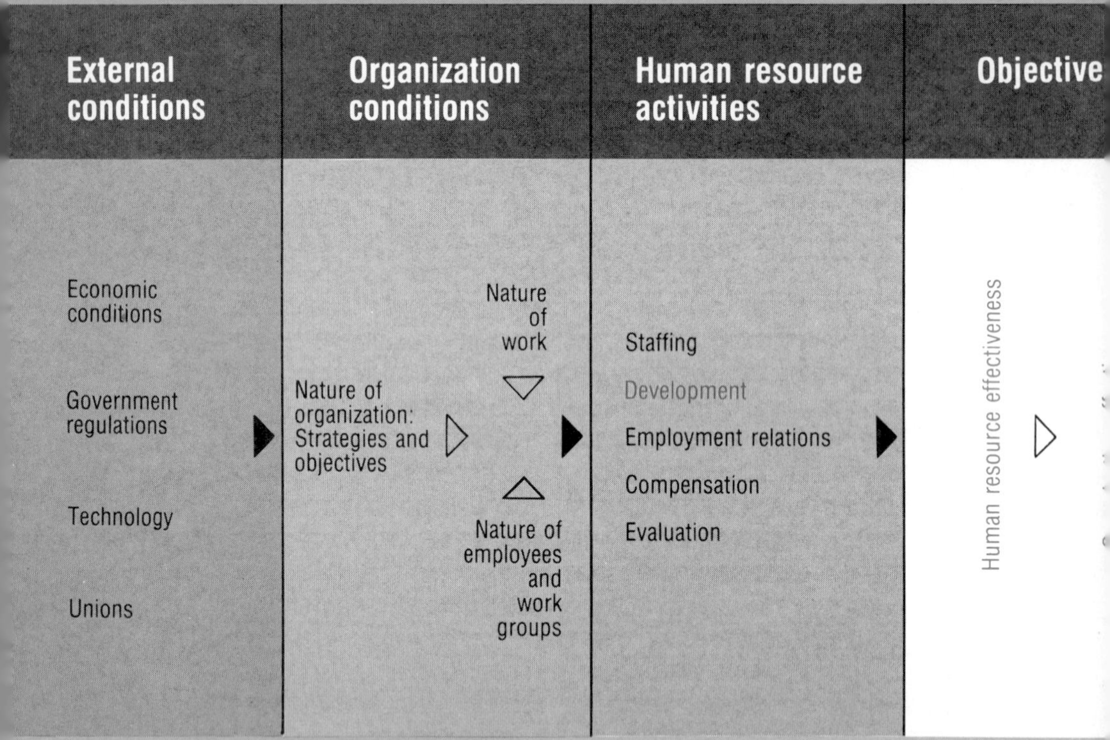

External conditions	Organization conditions	Human resource activities	Objective
Economic conditions Government regulations Technology Unions	Nature of organization: Strategies and objectives	Nature of work Nature of employees and work groups	Staffing Development Employment relations Compensation Evaluation	Human resource effectiveness

PART FOUR
HUMAN RESOURCE ACTIVITIES:
DEVELOPMENT

This part of the book explores the management and development of employees. The object of development activities is to provide the necessary conditions to allow individuals to perform at levels that increase their personal effectiveness as well as the organization's. As the diagnostic model shows (Exhibit IV), the process is affected by external conditions, especially labour, technological, and product market conditions, and also by governmental regulation. Within the organization, a variety of conditions affect the amount of resources the organization devotes to developing employees. Some organizations view human resources as an asset to be conserved, developed, and utilized. Other organizations view human resources more like interchangeable commodities, to be used or abandoned at the employer's discretion.

Staffing, the topic of Part Three, assists managers to employ effective people in the right jobs. New employees usually require orientation, socialization, and additional training, and mature or experienced employees may need retraining, as requirements change in a dynamic organization. Orientation, socialization, and training (Chapter Ten) comprise one of the major activities of P/HRM. Once people are trained, the organization must determine how they are performing. Performance evaluation is discussed in Chapter Eleven. Both training and performance evaluation enhance the effectiveness of employees, and, therefore, organization effectiveness.

CHAPTER TEN
ORIENTATION, SOCIALIZATION, AND TRAINING

CHAPTER OUTLINE

I. The Orientation Process
II. The Socialization Process
III. The Training Process
   A. Introduction
IV. A Diagnostic Approach to Training
   A. External Influences
   B. Internal Influences
   C. Who Is Involved in Training
   D. Major Decisions
V. Determining Training Needs and Objectives
   A. Organizational Analysis
   B. Operational Analysis
   C. Individual Performance Analysis
   D. Training Needs as a Function of Organizational Level
   E. Stating Objectives
VI. Translating Needs into Programs
   A. Learning Principles
   B. Individual Differences
VII. Instructional Techniques
   A. On-the-Job Training
   B. Off-the-Job Training
   C. Combinations

VIII. Evaluating Results
  A. Four Evaluation Questions
  B. Criteria for Evaluation
  C. Experimental Designs
  D. Costs and Benefits
  E. Costs, Benefits, and Productivity
IX. Summary
  Appendix / Orientation—International Assignments

When the diagnostic model was introduced in Chapter One, we distinguished between a reactive, or problem-solving approach to human resource management, and a proactive, or forward-looking approach. While orientation and training are used by both types of organizations, a proactive stance puts more emphasis on ensuring that the design of the two processes is current, and that they do contribute to both individual and organizational effectiveness.

The newcomer's formal orientation usually leads to some degree of training. Orientation can be considered a form of training. Concomitantly, the new employee also enters a period of organizational socialization. For example, entry into an organization is part of a definite phase of socialization. All three processes—orientation, socialization, and training—are important in preventing the employee's derailment and in contributing to effective alignment (i.e., aligning personal values, interests, and skills with task requirements of the job).[1]

THE ORIENTATION PROCESS

> ### Definition
> *Orientation* is the P/HRM activity that introduces new employees to the organization and to the employees' new tasks, superiors, and work groups.[2]

The employee orientation process has not been studied a great deal, and relatively little research has been done on whether orientation programs are adequate.[3] A recent Canadian study of orientation practices concluded there are few sources on this subject. Virtually nothing has been published in Canada, and the U.S. literature is also surprisingly sparse.[4]

Purposes of Orientation

Orienting new employees has two main objectives. One is learning job procedures. The other objective involves establishing relationships with coworkers, subordinates, and superiors, and fitting the new employee into the employer's way of doing things.[5] Within these objectives are several specific purposes:

To Reduce Start-Up Costs. The new employee does not know the job, how the organization works, or whom to see to get the job done. This means that for a while he or she is less productive than the experienced employee, and additional costs are involved in getting the new employee started. Effective orientation reduces start-up costs and enables the new employee to reach performance standards sooner.

To Reduce the Amount of Anxiety and Hazing. Anxiety in this case means normal fear of failure on the job. This anxiety can be compounded by initiation rites, or hazing. Hazing serves several purposes. It lets the recruit know he or she has a lot to learn and thus is dependent on the others for his or her job, it is fun for the old-timers, and it tests the newcomer's potential for group membership. But it can cause great anxiety for the recruit. Effective orientation alerts the new person to hazing and reduces anxiety.

Anxieties existing early in the new job can reduce competence and lead to dissatisfaction and turnover.[6] This was clearly demonstrated in a study of electronic component assemblers. Their anxiety resulted from awareness that they were expected to reach the competence level observed in experienced employees. Often they did not understand their supervisor's instructions but were afraid to ask further questions and appear stupid.

A comparison of two different orientation approaches revealed anxiety to be a very important factor. One group of newly recruited assemblers was given the traditional orientation training: a typical two-hour briefing on the first day by the personnel department. This included the topics normally covered in orientation—description of the organization and its products/services; safety regulations; personnel and pay policies; daily routine—and the usual description of the minimum level of performance desired. Then they were introduced to the supervisor, who gave them a short job introduction, and they were off.

Another group was given the same two-hour orientation training and then six hours of training in social orientation. Four factors were stressed.

1. They were told their opportunity to succeed was good. They were given facts showing that more than 99 percent of the employees achieved company standards. Learning curves of how long it took to achieve various levels of competence were discussed. Five or six times during the day it was stressed that all in the group would be successful.

2. New employees were tipped off about typical hazing. It was suggested that they take it in good humour.
3. They were told to take the initiative in communication. Supervisors would be glad to help, but the worker must ask for it and would not appear stupid for doing so.
4. Their supervisor was described in important details—brief work history, approach to supervision, and hobbies.

This social orientation training had dramatic results. The employees receiving it had 50 percent less tardiness and absenteeism, waste was reduced by 80 percent, product costs were cut 15 to 30 percent, training time was cut 50 percent, and training costs cut by two thirds.

To Reduce Employee Turnover. If employees perceive themselves to be ineffective, unwanted, or unneeded they may react to these feelings by quitting. Turnover is high during the break-in period, and effective orientation can reduce this costly reaction.

To Save Time for Supervisor and Co-Workers. Improperly oriented employees must still get the job done, and to do so they need help. The most likely sources of help are co-workers and supervisors, who will have to spend time breaking in new employees. Good orientation programs save everyone time.

To Develop Realistic Job Expectations, Positive Attitudes, and Job Satisfaction. In what sociologists call the older professions (law, medicine) or total institutions (the church, prison, the army), job expectations are clear because they develop over years of training and education. Society builds up a set of attitudes and behaviours considered proper for these jobs. For most of the world of work, however, this is not true. New employees must learn what the organization expects of them, and their own expectations of the job must be neither too low nor too high.[7] Each worker must incorporate the job and its work values into his or her self-image. Orientation helps this process.

Who Orients New Employees?

Exhibit 10–1 describes how operating and P/HRM managers conduct orientation programs in medium and large organizations. In smaller organizations, the operating manager does all the orienting. In some unionized organizations, union officials are involved. Besides direct involvement, P/HRM also helps train the operating manager for more effective orientation behaviour.

Available Canadian data indicate the relative allocation of orientation roles.[8] Overall, the P/HRM department is most involved in conducting formal employee orientation, followed by the newcomer's supervisor. In most cases, human resource managers coordinate the orientation process and present organizationwide information; the supervisor manages the employee's introduc-

EXHIBIT 10-1
Relationship of Operating and P/HRM Managers in Orientation

Orientation Function	Operating Manager (OM)	P/HRM Manager (P/HRM)
Design the orientation program		P/HRM is consultant with OM
Introduce the new employee to the organization and its history, personnel policies, working conditions, and rules. Complete paperwork		P/HRM performs this
Explain the task and job expectations to employee	OM performs this	
Introduce employee to work group and new surroundings Encourage employees to help new employee	OM performs this	

Source: Adapted from John M. Ivancevich and William F. Glueck, *Foundations of Personnel/Human Resource Management,* 3rd ed. (Plano, Tex.: Business Publications, 1986).

tion to the department and job. Senior executives are involved in a minor capacity in about 75 percent of the organizations studied, consultants in about 5 percent. Other participants in orienting employees included heads of various departments, fire and safety officials, representatives from public relations/corporate communications, and union officials.

A new and progressive idea uses experienced retired employees to orient recent hires. Newcomers may believe the firm must be a good place to work if retirees come back.[9]

Orientation Program Content

Orientation programs can vary from informal, primarily verbal efforts to formal schedules that supplement verbal presentations with written handouts. Slides, charts, pictures, and videotapes are often used. A good orientation program also includes a tour of the facilities. The latter helps the new employee get the feel of the place. A variety of approaches is required to cover the extensive array of information that needs to be transmitted. Exhibit 10-2 presents areas covered in comprehensive orientation programs.

After an employee receives a general orientation of the organization, a more job-specific orientation should be given. Exhibit 10-3 presents the areas that can be covered in a job-specific orientation program.

Some Canadian employers' orientation emphasizes communicating corporate culture, the importance of teamwork (including "the *company* is a team"), and a pioneering spirit as well as customer-oriented attitudes (in keeping with the external focus of "excellent" companies).[10]

EXHIBIT 10-2
Areas Covered in a Comprehensive Orientation Program

1. **Overview of the company**
   - Welcoming speech
   - Founding, growth, trends, goals, priorities, and problems
   - Traditions, customs, norms, and standards
   - Current specific functions of the organization
   - Products/services and customers served
   - Steps in getting product/service to customers
   - Scope of diversity of activities
   - Organization, structure and relationship of company and its branches
   - Facts on key managerial staff
   - Community relations, expectations, and activities

2. **Key policies and procedures review**

3. **Compensation**
   - Pay rates and ranges
   - Overtime
   - Holiday pay
   - Shift differential
   - How pay is received
   - Deductions; required and optional, with specific amounts
   - Option to buy damaged products and costs thereof
   - Discounts
   - Advances on pay
   - Loans from credit union
   - Reimbursement for job expenses
   - Tax shelter options

4. **Fringe benefits**
   - Insurance
   - Medical-dental
   - Life
   - Disability
   - Workers' compensation
   - Holidays and vacations (patriotic, religious, birthday)
   - Leave: personal illness, family illness, bereavement, maternity, military, jury duty, emergency, extended absence
   - Retirement plans and options
   - On-the-job training opportunities
   - Counselling services
   - Cafeteria
   - Recreation and social activities
   - Other company services to employees

5. **Safety and accident prevention**
   - Completion of emergency data card (if not done as part of employment process)
   - Health and first aid clinics
   - Exercise and recreation centres
   - Safety precautions
   - Reporting of hazards
   - Fire prevention and control
   - Accident procedures and reporting
   - WCB requirements (review of key sections)
   - Physical exam requirements
   - Use of alcohol and drugs on the job

6. **Employee and union relations**
   - Terms and conditions of employment review
   - Assignment, reassignment, and promotion
   - Probationary period and expected on-the-job conduct
   - Reporting of sickness and lateness to work
   - Employee rights and responsibilities
   - Manager and supervisor rights
   - Relations with supervisors and shop stewards

EXHIBIT 10–2 (concluded)

- Employee organizations and options
- Union contract provisions and/or company policy
- Supervision and evaluation of performance
- Discipline and reprimands
- Grievance procedures
- Termination of employment (resignation, layoff, discharge, retirement)
- Content and examination of personnel record
- Communications: channels of communication—upward and downward—suggestion system, posting materials on bulletin board, sharing new ideas
- Sanitation and cleanliness
- Wearing of safety equipment, badges, and uniforms
- Bringing things on and removing things from company grounds
- On-site political activity
- Gambling
- Handling of rumours

7. **Physical facilities**
   - Tour of facilities
   - Food services and cafeteria
   - Restricted areas for eating
   - Employee entrances
   - Restricted areas (e.g., cars)
   - Parking
   - First aid
   - Washrooms
   - Supplies and equipment

8. **Economic factors**
   - Costs of damage by select items with required sales to balance
   - Costs of theft with required sales to compensate
   - Profit margins
   - Labour costs
   - Cost of equipment
   - Costs of absenteeism, lateness, and accidents

Source: W. D. St. John, "The Complete Employee Orientation Program," *Personnel Journal*, May 1980, pp. 376–77. Reprinted with the permission of *Personnel Journal*. Costa Mesa, California; all rights reserved.

Guidelines for Conducting Orientation

Some guidelines for conducting employee orientation have been proposed by Thorp:[11]

- Begin the orientation with the most relevant and immediate kinds of information and company policies. (Conducted off the job.)
- Emphasize the human side, one of the most significant parts of orientation. Give new employees knowledge of what supervisors and co-workers are like. Tell them how long it should take to reach standards of effective work, and encourage them to seek help and advice when needed. (Off the job.)
- Have new employees be sponsored, or directed, by an experienced worker or supervisor who can respond to questions and keep in close touch. (On the job.)
- Introduce new employees gradually to the people with whom they will work, rather than give a superficial introduction to all of them on the first day. (On the job.)

EXHIBIT 10–3
Areas Covered in a Job-Specific Orientation Program

1. **Department functions**
   - Goals and current priorities
   - Organization and structure
   - Operational activities
   - Relationship of functions to other departments
   - Relationships of jobs within the department
2. **Job duties and responsibilities**
   - Detailed explanation of job based on current job description and expected results
   - Explanation of why the job is important, how the specific job relates to others in the department and company
   - Discussion of common problems and how to avoid and overcome them
   - Performance standards and basis of performance evaluation
   - Number of daily work hours and times
   - Overtime needs and requirements
   - Extra duty assignments (such as changing duties to cover for an absent worker)
   - Required records and reports
   - Checkout on equipment to be used
   - Explanation of where and how to get tools, have equipment maintained and repaired
   - Types of assistance available; when and how to ask for help
   - Relations with provincial and federal inspectors
3. **Policies, procedures, rules, and regulations**
   - Rules unique to the job and/or department
   - Handling emergencies
   - Safety precautions and accident prevention
   - Reporting of hazards and accidents
   - Cleanliness standards and sanitation (such as cleanup)
   - Security, theft problems and costs
   - Relations with outside people (e.g., drivers)
   - Eating, smoking, and chewing gum, etc., in department area
   - Removal of things from department
   - Damage control (e.g., smoking restrictions)
   - Time clock and time sheets
   - Breaks/rest periods
   - Lunch duration and time
   - Making and receiving personal telephone calls
   - Requisitioning supplies and equipment
   - Monitoring and evaluating of employee performance
   - Job bidding and requesting reassignment
   - Going to cars during work hours
4. **Tour of department**
   - Washrooms and showers
   - Fire-alarm box and fire extinguisher stations
   - Time clocks
   - Lockers
   - Approved entrances and exits
   - Water fountains and eye-wash systems
   - Supervisors' quarters
   - Supply room and maintenance department
   - Sanitation and security offices
   - Smoking areas
   - Locations of services to employees related to department
   - First aid kit
5. **Introduction to department employees**

Source: W. D. St. John, "The Complete Employee Orientation Program," *Personnel Journal*, May 1980, p. 377. Reprinted with permission of *Personnel Journal*, Costa Mesa, California; all rights reserved.

- Allow sufficient time for new employees to get their feet on the ground *before* demands on them are increased. (On the job.)

Feldman reports that orientation does not occur at one point. It is achieved over time and usually starts before a person enters an organization with such activities as job choice, attraction to organizations, and selection.[12]

McShane found that some of the Canadian firms surveyed made efforts at pre-employment orientation.[13] These occurred during recruitment and selection and before the first day on the job. This formal "early start" orientation demonstrates that the new employee is appreciated, maintains a nurturing link once the job offer has been accepted, and helps smooth the information load. In addition to written material, a phone call from the prospective supervisor provides an additional gesture of appreciation.

About two thirds of the firms begin formal orientation as soon as the person reports for work. Others do it within the first two weeks, although some delay orientation between two weeks and six months. Once initiated, about one half of orientation programs are conducted in less than half a day. Only about one in five organizations spread their programs over more than one week (not including follow-up).

Follow-Up. Once the employee is assigned to the new job, the supervisor is expected to continue the orientation process. However, busy supervisors easily overlook some facts needed by the new employee. There may also be gaps in program content.

One way to check that orientation is adequate is to design a feedback system to monitor the program, or use the management by objectives technique. In its simplest form, a follow-up procedure should employ a checklist through which the employee can evaluate the program, especially with respect to its best and least useful aspects. At the same time, the employee should be given an opportunity to meet with the supervisor, and perhaps with the orientation group, ask additional questions, and review how well he or she is adjusting. The procedure is not intended to test knowledge or to appraise performance.

The time interval between orientation and follow-up sessions depends on the nature of the job. About one third of the Canadian sample utilizes such sessions within one month; another third administers follow-up between one to three months.[14]

International Assignments

Comprehensive orientation is also important when preparing employees for overseas assignments, both before departure and after arrival. Key components of a three-phase program (initial/predeparture/arrival orientation) are summarized in the Appendix at the end of this chapter.

THE SOCIALIZATION PROCESS

Orientation is usually followed by training. However, before, during, and after the formal and informal components of orientation and training, the newly recruited employee is also exposed to a process of socialization.

> **Definition**
>
> *Organizational socialization* of new employees is the process concerned with the acquisition of a set of appropriate role behaviours, the development of work skills and abilities, and the adjustment to both the organizational culture and the work group's norms and values.

This definition is based on Feldman's model, which includes a three-phase socialization process.[15] The first is anticipatory socialization, which encompasses all the learning that occurs before a new member joins an organization. During the encounter phase, the new recruit sees what the organization is really like. Some initial shifting of values, skills, and attitudes occurs, along with role definition and initiation to task and work group. Progressively sharper perceptions increase awareness of the importance of interpersonal factors and organizational politics. If the newcomer survives to the third stage, change and acquisition, relatively long-lasting changes take place: new recruits master the skills required for their jobs, successfully perform their new roles, and make adjustments to their work group's values and norms and the organizational culture. Although viewed as a sequential process, the three stages overlap. Progress in socialization can be measured in terms of three attitudinal variables (general satisfaction, internal work motivation, job development) and three behavioural outcomes (dependably carrying out role assignments, remaining with the organization, innovation/spontaneous cooperation to achieve objectives that go beyond role specifications).[16]

Other views of the socialization process focus on relinquishing preexisting attitudes, values, and behaviours,[17] or emphasize acquiring new self-images and involvements.[18] A model proposed by Schein consists of three stages encompassing entry, socialization, and mutual acceptance.[19] The first step of the entry stage of his model is occupational choice, followed by occupational image, anticipatory socialization to the chosen occupation or profession, and entry into the labour market. Formal organizational socialization begins when the new employee reports for work and leads to locating one's place in the organization and developing an identity. Schein's final stage, mutual acceptance, culminates in bonding the new employee and the organization through a psychological contract indicating their mutual acceptance and trust of one another.

The formality and intensity of the socialization process are influenced by the history, image, and philosophy of an organization. The integrated models outlined here capture the variety of experience faced by a newcomer, regardless of the type or size of organization. For example, most would agree that the process provides for "a rite of passage, a paying of dues, an initiation (into a very exclusive club) . . . it also breeds an attitude, an enduring sense of fellowship, and esprit de corps that comes with membership in an organization (steeped in tradition and legend)."[20] These process and outcome variables are part of the socialization and initial training undergone by recruits at the RCMP's training depot, but also apply to any socialization scheme.

THE TRAINING PROCESS

Introduction

Managers at IBM Canada Ltd. must attend a five-day management training and development course within three months of their appointment; they follow up with a five-day refresher six months later. *All* managers take an annual, five-day development course. Overall, the company averages 11 training days annually for each employee.[21]

At General Motors of Canada Ltd., supervisors and managers receive regular management training as they are promoted.[22] McDonnell Douglas Canada Ltd. credits the training given to all of its 3,000 employees for a major improvement in productivity.[23]

Training and development is big business. It is a major expense and an important method for improving employee productivity. Canadian organizations spend about $200 million a year on training and development.[24] The outlay of private and public organizations is about $16 per person in the work force, which amounts to approximately one tenth of 1 percent of Canadian corporate profit.[25] The Canada Employment and Immigration Commission alone offers about $140 million each year to employers willing to train workers in important skills; the federal government's Canadian Jobs Strategy effort involves an allocation of $1.65 billion.[26]

Some companies develop training/development material themselves. Others use a mix of in-house and outside training. The packaged material of outside programs can cost between $5,000 and $15,000, plus an average $100 to $150 for material for each participant. For example, Toronto's Achieve Enterprises Ltd. has a five-day packaged program called "Toward Excellence," which costs $15,000 plus $145 per participant for materials.[27]

Properly designed, training and development can help employees maintain or develop their skills. It also may be the best way for employees to improve their own wealth-producing capacity, that is, their skill, knowledge, and internal/external marketability.[28]

Despite sizable budgets, good intentions, and real needs, many training/development programs fail to achieve lasting results. Too often, it is because the purported goals of the training are vague. If we don't know where we're going, we can't tell if we got there. Nor can we tell if it's where we wanted to be. Also, in-house trainers historically have been judged by how many course hours they deliver, rather than by the quality of that training. This leads some managers to remain cynical about the value of training and has shifted more attention to training evaluation.[29] More trainers and researchers are developing appropriate evaluation methodologies, according to Goldstein.[30]

The remainder of this chapter emphasizes (1) specifying training needs, (2) designing programs that meet those needs, and (3) evaluating whether the training results in what was intended.

A DIAGNOSTIC APPROACH TO TRAINING

A reactive type of organization conducts training only in response to direct deficiencies. The proactive employer's approach reflects an anticipatory stance to training. For example, a program of high scrap rates or low quality on an assembly line may be attributed to employees unfamiliar with a new part. Training may be offered to solve this problem. Or a group of workers may be selected for a supervisory skills class, and their potential for promotion determined in part on their performance in that class. The organization may not need additional supervisors at present, but through employment planning, it knows it will need them in the future. A proactive organization will use training both to encourage employees to invest in their own human capital and to solve current problems.

> **Definition**
> *Training* is a planned, systematic effort by the organization to facilitate the acquisition of job-related behaviour, knowledge, skills, motivation, and attitudes by employees in order to improve their performance and help increase organizational goal achievement.[31]

External Influences

Government
The government influences training in several ways:

1. Employment Equity. The government exerts pressure to upgrade the skills of women and other designated groups; this increases the demand for training or retraining. The government also seeks to ensure that access of qualified candidates to training is free of discriminatory practices. Every aspect of training—needs analysis, program design, trainee selection, and evaluation—may become subject to scrutiny for adverse effect. For example, subsequent to the Abella report, the federal government passed Bill C-62.[32] According to its contract compliance provisions, the required reporting encompasses an employer's progress toward providing *equal access to training*.[33]

Chapter Seven discussed the need to ensure that personnel decisions are demonstrably work-related. The fairness principle of Chapter Nine suggests that eligibility for training and evaluation of trainees' performance are included in P/HRM decisions designed to yield employment equity.

2. Occupational Health and Safety. As part of their efforts to ensure safe and healthful working conditions, the federal government and the various provincial workers' compensation boards set certain standards. Employers subject to safety and health standards (see Chapter Twelve) are required to provide training based on identification of actual tasks performed by employees, actual and potential hazards encountered, and the equipment and practices that can minimize these hazards. Initial exposure to training in this area occurs as part of the orientation program.

3. The Canadian Jobs Strategy Policy. A third way government influences training is by supporting training programs or strategies that have public policy purposes. The Canadian Jobs Strategy approach includes several programs,[34] each directed at specific target groups. The objective of the Job Development program, for example, is to develop the long-term labour market potential of Canadians who have been out of work for 24 of the last 30 weeks. The program focusses on individual needs and improved long-term employment prospects in the context of local economic growth and potential. It is not a make-work project; the short-term, stop-gap job creation measures of the past have not worked.

In some industries, appropriately skilled workers may be in short supply and in high demand. For the employer, this shortage may represent a fundamental obstacle to maintaining a competitive position. The Skill Shortages program provides financial assistance (for up to three years) to employers who want to train workers. An employer can train current employees or ask the Canada Employment Centre to refer qualified candidates, who can be hired and trained. One example of the program would be support in the following situation: to remain competitive, a large manufacturer of knitwear introduces state-of-the-art, computer-aided design terminals and microprocessor-controlled looms to replace traditional design and weaving techniques.

Two other programs are more future-oriented. Skill Investment is the first program to help employed workers plan for change in advance and to train before their skills become obsolete. For employers, the program provides a practical way to avoid laying off adaptable, capable employees during times of change. It also allows management and labour to set their own agenda for training. Several options are available.

One option, designed to foster individual initiatives to cope with change, is full-time training leave at two thirds of regular wages (the employer pays one third, the federal government another third). A second option is targetted at women, managers and owners in small business as well as self-employed individuals. This option generally involves a combination of on- and off-the-job training. Training trust funds are the third option. These are set up by employee associations, or unions and employers, to pay for their members' future training and skill development. A good example of how the Skill Investment program benefits workers who are employed in jobs sensitive to technology (or changing market conditions) is the worker who has operated a machine lathe for 20 years and is informed that numerically controlled machines will be installed. To adapt to the new technology, the employee and her employer agree she should take leave from her regular job to be trained by a neighbouring firm that has the expertise necessary for training.

Innovations, a fourth program of the Canadian Jobs Strategy, is designed to act as a catalyst to tap the creative resources of Canadians. Innovations provides financial assistance for pilot and demonstration projects that test new solutions to labour market problems. Proposals from all sectors are encouraged and may address regional concerns or labour market problems that are national in scope. Priority areas include:

- New training technologies, including computer-assisted learning.
- Innovative bridging programs to help workers entering or reentering the work force.
- Alternative work arrangements related to labour market adjustment.
- More effective links between training and job creation.
- Economic shifts.

A current nationwide survey of Training in Industry is being conducted by Statistics Canada with a sample of about 20,000 employers from various industries.[35] The survey, sponsored by Employment and Immigration Canada, is designed to determine how much training Canadian firms do, who receives training, how much in-house training occurs in individual industrial sectors, and what role the Canadian Jobs Strategy plays. This snapshot of industrial training activity will be used for planning future governmental activities.

The scope of the Canadian labour market is divided jurisdictionally between the federal and provincial governments. Training is viewed as shared or solely under federal jurisdiction because of Ottawa's overall responsibility for economic matters.[36] These divisions have occasionally led to conflicts over the administration of programs relating to the labour market.[37]

Economic and Technological Shifts

Economic conditions also influence the design and administration of training programs. If necessary skills are in short supply in the external labour market, an organization may find that developing these skills among its internal labour supply is cost-effective. Similarly, under surplus conditions, organizations may find they can readily purchase the skills and experience they need in the external market. Under these conditions, investing in developing their own human capital may be less attractive.

External shifts in technology were delineated in Chapter Two. It was stated that continuing technological change has been the hallmark of the Canadian economy. The range of emerging or fast-growing technologies is broad, diverse, and advancing with increasing rapidity. Triggered by the chip, microelectronics drives a whole cluster of technologies, such as computer-aided design (CAD), computer-assisted manufacturing (CAM), robotics, digital signal processing, speech processing, and expert systems.[38]

Unions

Unions also play a varying role in training. In the construction industry, where unions are often larger than the employer, unions provide all or most of the training through apprenticeship programs.

As part of their wider boundary-spanning role of linking members to both employers and societal concerns, unions encourage training in areas other than technological and safety or health. For example, as part of a 1987 contract settlement with the Canadian Auto Workers, General Motors of Canada Ltd. agreed to finance a voluntary three-hour course (of on-the-job seminars) on human rights issues for its 38,000 unionized employees.

Internal Influences

Some firms, such as General Motors, allocate a large share of their human resource budget to training. An organization's business strategies, sense of social responsibility, policies toward human resources, culture, as well as the trainability of its employees all influence the emphasis placed on training. For many of these factors, the reasons for training are the flip side of the reasons for recruiting.

Make or Buy Strategies

Organizations in new or emerging product markets tend to hire experienced personnel (buying talent), while business units in more mature, stable markets tend to develop their own human resources internally (developing talent).[39] Depending on the strategic direction taken by top management, an employer's buy approach may be in terms of acquisitioning another firm in order to "capture" an entire cadre of trained talent already possessing the specific expertise required. However, little is known about why some firms expend more per employee on training than others. More importantly, very little is known about the payoffs from make-or-buy options.

Nevertheless, even in units that recruit experienced workers, some training must occur. Orientation is needed for new employees. Company policies and procedures must be learned, the specific tasks to be performed must be reviewed, and many jobs are unique to the organization and require special training.

Technological Change

The impact of technological change on an organization may be discontinuous and drastic. Much of the existing "organizational technology" used to convert inputs into outputs may need to be modified (see Chapter Three). A virtual "skill twist" can occur: current KSAOs of part of the work force are suddenly insufficient. While the overall economy gains from new technologies, workers whose jobs are substantially changed may experience hardship and some degree of "technology shock." Similarly, professionals who fail to keep up with new technological developments may find their expertise has become obsolete. Training and reskilling can help lessen some of these negative effects of change.

Obsolescence can be defined as a reduction in competence resulting from lack of knowledge of new techniques or technologies developed since completion of one's professional or job training.[40] As the rate of change accelerates, it becomes harder for professionals to keep abreast of developments without employer assistance. Organizations that employ large numbers of scientists or engineers cannot afford to let these expensive resources become obsolete. So organizations and individuals have a common interest in avoiding obsolescence.

In addition to threatening professionals who don't maintain their knowledge and skills, technological change can threaten workers whose jobs are substantially changed by new technologies. Robots frequently change the job from a manual one, where the workers perform the tasks, to a job requiring judgement and decision making, in which the workers control the robots. Workers may believe they should have more say in deciding where the robots should be placed and who should run them. Robots are an example of the kind of technological change that dictates a need for training.[41] This sentiment is echoed by both workers and employers.[42] For example, the British Columbia Telephone Company's submission to the Labour Canada Task Force on Microelectronics and Employment stated, "Training is the key to adapting to technological change and increased investment must be made in order to meet the growing skill and technical manpower requirements of the new technology."[43] Another illustration is the recent "retuning" of the auto industry.[44]

The ability to learn "may emerge as the premium skill of the future."[45] We hope that, once acquired, the employee's ability to learn is applied to anticipatory learning. There are also indications that technological change will alter drastically the educational attributes sought by employers and the emphasis on in-house training will increase.[46] The latter response is based on the realization that robotics programs offered by schools are not specific enough to meet employers' training needs.[47]

Need for Training and Development

In Chapter Five, we stated that employees' performance is a function of their ability and motivation to perform. Training, as Exhibit 10–4 shows, can be designed to affect both.[48] Programs can be designed to improve specific skills or to make supervisors more proficient at working with and motivating employees.[49] Much of IBM's required annual training, for example, is devoted to learning how to work with or manage employees. Some programs are designed to improve abilities and to serve as a reward as well.

Training can further socialize or orient new employees into the organization's culture, policies, and procedures. It can also help satisfy special needs, such as Burlington Northern's training program This Way Up, designed to assist women in clerical positions to become locomotive engineers. The

**EXHIBIT 10–4
Effects of Training**

Abilities - - -> Motivation ———> Performance

Training programs

women benefit by becoming qualified for higher-paying positions, and BN benefits by improving its employment equity efforts.

Who Is Involved in Training?

For training to be effective, top management must support it in an open manner. Employees must be convinced that top management supports training personally and financially. Exhibit 10–5 summarizes how both operating and P/HRM managers contribute to the training function. Occasionally, more than these two groups are involved. For example, outside consultants may also participate, especially if they helped develop the training package or the company lacks in-house expertise in a specific area. Or, for example, the training and labour relations departments may combine forces with theatre actors to prepare a videotape training program to train managers to handle grievances and arbitration.

Based on a survey of almost 3,000 practitioners, the scope of activities performed by training and development professionals can be summarized as follows:[50]

- Needs analysis and diagnosis.
- Determine appropriate training approach.
- Program design and development.
- Develop material resources (make).
- Manage internal resources (borrow).
- Manage external resources.
- Individual development planning and counselling.
- Job/performance-related training.
- Conduct classroom training.
- Group and organizational development.
- Training research.
- Manage working relationships with managers and clients.
- Manage the training and development function.
- Professional self-development.

Another survey (in progress) will provide further insights by identifying the types of training/development done by Canadian practitioners (e.g., train the trainer, safety training, team building, decision making).[51]

Major Decisions

Exhibit 10–6 provides a broad overview of the interrelated phases of the training process. The assessment phase provides the foundation of the entire training effort. As shown, both the training and development phase and the evaluation phase are determined by inputs from the assessment of training needs. If the assessment phase is deficient or contaminated (with irrelevant

EXHIBIT 10–5
The Role of Operating and P/HRM Managers in Training

Training Activities	Operating Manager (OM)	P/HRM Manager (P/HRM)
Determining training needs and objectives	Approved by OM	Done by P/HRM
Developing training criteria	Approved by OM	Done by P/HRM
Choosing trainer	Jointly chosen: nominated by OM	Jointly chosen: approved by P/HRM
Developing training materials	Approved by OM	Done by P/HRM
Planning and implementing the program		Done by P/HRM
Doing the training	Occasionally done by OM	Normally done by P/HRM
Evaluating the training	OM reviews the results	Done by P/HRM

Source: Adapted from John M. Ivancevich and William F. Glueck, *Foundations of Personnel/Human Resource Management,* 3rd ed. (Plano, Tex.: Business Publications, 1986).

needs), the training program will have little chance of accomplishing its purpose. With needs clarified, it is possible to specify training objectives.

The next phase involves translating training needs and objectives into a training program that will meet the needs of the organization through the trainees selected. Consideration is normally given to program content, the delivery system (i.e., training methods), desired outcomes, learning principles, and trainee characteristics. In a well-designed program, trainees are pretested before actual training occurs.

Finally, there is evaluation, a twofold process that involves (1) establishing indicators of trainees' success during and at completion of the training as well as on the job, and (2) determining which job-related changes have occurred due to the training.[52] The results of the evaluation phase provide a continuous stream of feedback to those who will reassess needs and plan, develop, and deliver future programs.

The rest of this chapter is organized around the three phases shown in Exhibit 10–6.

DETERMINING TRAINING NEEDS AND OBJECTIVES

Methods of determining the needs that training can fulfill may be subsumed under three levels of analysis (Exhibit 10–7): organizational analysis, operational analysis, and individual performance analysis.[53] Once conducted, the diagnosis of needs can proceed to the following questions: (1) Does an actual or potential performance discrepancy exist? (2) Is it important to the organization? (3) Is it correctable through training? Given our proactive view of P/HRM, we view training needs as consisting of actual as well as potential performance discrepancies.

**EXHIBIT 10–6
Training Model**

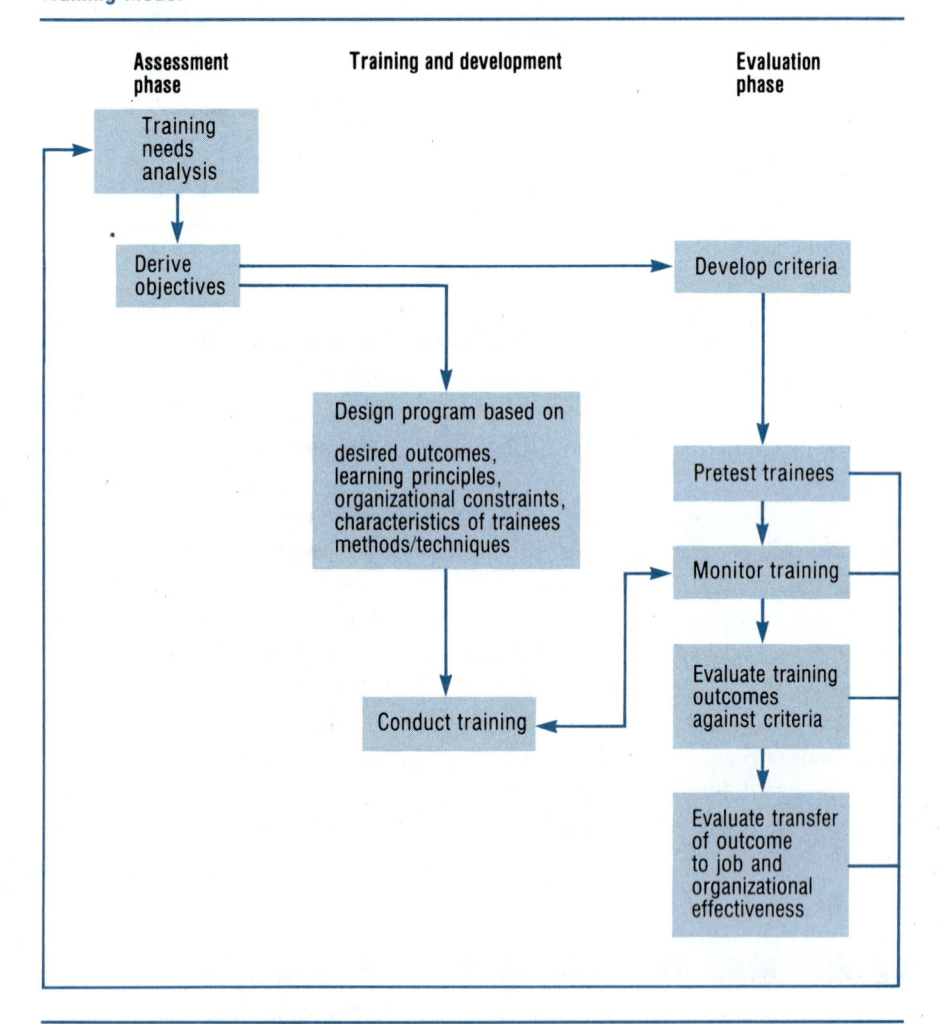

```
Assessment          Training and development        Evaluation
phase                                                phase

Training needs analysis
    ↓
Derive objectives ──────────────────────→ Develop criteria
         │                                           ↓
         ↓                                    Pretest trainees
Design program based on                              ↓
desired outcomes,                            Monitor training
learning principles,                                 ↓
organizational constraints,                  Evaluate training outcomes
characteristics of trainees                  against criteria
methods/techniques                                   ↓
         ↓                                    Evaluate transfer
Conduct training ←─────                       of outcome to job and
                                              organizational effectiveness
```

Source: Adapted and modified from *Training: Program Development and Evaluation* by I. L. Goldstein, Copyright © 1974 by Wadsworth Publishing Company, Inc. Reprinted by permission of the publisher, Brooks/Cole Publishing Company, Monterey, California.

EXHIBIT 10–7
Training Needs Analysis

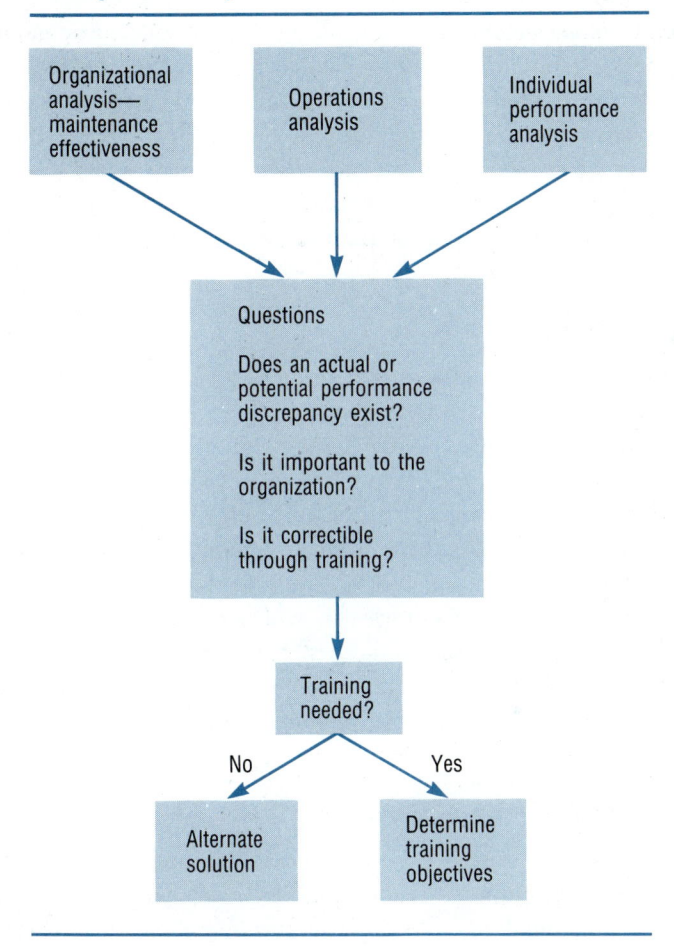

```
┌──────────────┐   ┌──────────────┐   ┌──────────────┐
│Organizational│   │              │   │              │
│analysis—     │   │ Operations   │   │ Individual   │
│maintenance   │   │ analysis     │   │ performance  │
│effectiveness │   │              │   │ analysis     │
└──────┬───────┘   └──────┬───────┘   └──────┬───────┘
       │                  │                  │
       └──────────────────▼──────────────────┘
                 ┌─────────────────────┐
                 │ Questions           │
                 │                     │
                 │ Does an actual or   │
                 │ potential performance│
                 │ discrepancy exist?  │
                 │                     │
                 │ Is it important to  │
                 │ the organization?   │
                 │                     │
                 │ Is it correctible   │
                 │ through training?   │
                 └──────────┬──────────┘
                            ▼
                     ┌────────────┐
                     │ Training   │
                     │ needed?    │
                     └──┬──────┬──┘
                   No   │      │   Yes
              ┌─────────▼─┐  ┌─▼──────────┐
              │ Alternate │  │ Determine  │
              │ solution  │  │ training   │
              │           │  │ objectives │
              └───────────┘  └────────────┘
```

Organizational Analysis

Organizational analysis is the process of focussing on where in the organization training is needed. This involves a broad look at companywide needs: the purpose is to link the assessment of training needs to strategic planning considerations and the attainment of organizational objectives. A thorough analysis might look at organizational maintenance and effectiveness.

Organizational maintenance aims at ensuring a steady supply of critical skills. If succession plans point out the need to develop managerial talent, training may include transferring high potential employees through a variety of positions and locations in order to ensure broad exposure to a variety of responsibilities.[54]

Organizational effectiveness, a major goal in the diagnostic model, might include checking on productivity, labour costs, output quality, or various other efficiency measures. Managers examine the organization's strategies, the results of employment planning, and the major variances between the units' successes and failures to determine what role training could play.

Finally, *specific requests for training* from operating managers and the union provide additional inputs to training needs analysis.

Operational Analysis

Operations analysis involves a careful study of job requirements. This entails (1) a systematic collection of data about a job in order to delineate, (2) the behaviour (KSAOs) required of the incumbent, (3) the standards of performance that must be met, and (4) how the tasks constituting the job are to be performed. An operational analysis not only helps specify training objectives, but also attempts to identify the content of training and the criteria for judging its effectiveness.[55] Job and task analysis, work sampling, critical incident analysis, the use of task inventories in which employees indicate how frequently they carry out a particular activity and the importance of each activity to the job, and analyses of operating problems (e.g., downtime, quality control) are all methods to help analyze training needs.

Individual Performance Analysis

At this level, the focus is on how well individual employees are performing their jobs. The training need is identified by a gap between desired performance (based on standards identified in the operations analysis phase) and actual performance. Information on actual performance is obtained through formal performance appraisal methods and can include the recording and analysis of critical incidents, or work sample, situational, and job knowledge tests.

In sum, there are three levels of analysis to identify training needs: organizational, operational, and individual. A wide range of alternative methods to assess training needs is evaluated in Exhibit 10–8.

While alternatives abound, in reality it appears that systematic analysis is only rarely used.[56] Many companies identify training needs by reacting only to problems that crop up.[57] Fewer organizations even claim to have regular ongoing processes for defining training needs. Training needs analysis must flow as part of the ongoing process of managing human resources, must be linked through the organization's human resource plans to the numbers and

EXHIBIT 10–8 Needs Assessment Methods

Technique \ Criteria	Potential participant involvement	Management involvement	Time required	Cost	Relevant quantifiable data
Advisory committees	Low	Moderate	Moderate	Low	Low
Assessment centres	High	Low	Low	High	High
Attitude (opinion) surveys	Moderate	Low	Moderate	Moderate	Low
Group discussions	High	Moderate	Moderate	Moderate	Moderate
Interviews with potential participants	High	Low	High	High	Moderate
Management requests	Low	High	Low	Low	Low
Observations of behaviour (on the job performance)	Moderate	Low	High	High	Moderate
Performance appraisals	Moderate	High	Moderate	Low	High
Performance documents	Low	Moderate	Low	Low	Moderate
Critical incident method	High	Low	Moderate	Low	High
Questionnaire surveys and inventories (needs assessment)	High	High	Moderate	Moderate	High
Skills test	High	Low	High	High	High
Evaluations of past programs	Moderate	Low	Moderate	Low	High

Source: John Newstrom and John Lilyquist, "Selecting Needs Analysis Methods," *Training and Development Journal*, October 1979, p. 56. ©1979, *Training and Development Journal*, American Society for Training & Development. Reprinted with permission. All rights reserved.

skills required (employment planning), to the jobs performed (job analysis), and to the individual employees (career planning and performance evaluation).

Training Needs as a Function of Organizational Level

Different levels of management may have different training and development needs. While key managerial skills are commonly categorized into the dimensions of technical, interpersonal, and conceptual skills, diagnostic and analytic skills are also prerequisites to managerial success. Exhibit 10–9 summarizes the extent to which managerial work at different levels draws on these five skills. In general, as a manager advances in the organization, fewer technical skills are required: top managers are more concerned with the broader strategy, and mission, aspects of the organization. Conceptual and diagnostic skills become more important at higher levels, supported by analytic skills.

EXHIBIT 10–9
Managerial Skills at Different Organizational Levels

First-line management	Middle management	Top management	Description
Conceptual skills	Conceptual skills	Conceptual skills	Ability to think in the abstract, to understand cause-and-effect relationships in the organization and how its parts fit together, to view it in a holistic manner
Interpersonal skills	Interpersonal skills	Interpersonal skills	Ability to communicate with, understand, and motivate both individuals and groups
Diagnostic skills	Diagnostic skills	Diagnostic skills	Ability to diagnose a number of symptoms and determine their probable cause
Analytic skills	Analytic skills	Analytic skills	Ability to identify the key variables in a situation, their interaction, and decide which should receive most attention; similar to conceptual skills and complementary to diagnostic skills
Technical skills	Technical skills	Technical skills	Needed to perform specialized activities such as operating equipment, preparing a budget, writing a computer program

Source: Adapted (with permission) and summarized from Ricky W. Griffin, *Management,* 2nd ed. (Boston: Houghton Mifflin, 1987); see also Robert L. Katz, "The Skills of an Effective Administrator," *Harvard Business Review,* September–October 1974, pp. 90–102.

Stating Objectives

From the analysis of training needs, specific objectives must be derived. Objectives guide selection of program content, and to some extent selection of methods and techniques. The idea is to state objectives in such a way that the degree of success or failure of the training program can be ascertained.[58]

Well-defined training objectives contain three elements: (1) a statement of desired performance, (2) a description of any important conditions under which the desired performance is to occur, and (3) a statement of the success criteria to be used to evaluate the trainee's behaviour and performance after training. They can take one or more of the following forms:[59]

1. Knowledge objectives refer to the material participants are expected to know when the program ends.
2. Attitudinal objectives state the beliefs and convictions participants are expected to hold as a result of the program.
3. Skill objectives describe the kinds of behaviours participants should be able to demonstrate under learning conditions.
4. Job behaviour objectives indicate the desired responses of participants once they are back on the job.
5. Organizational results objectives state changes in profitability, sales, service, efficiency, costs, employee turnover, and the like that should result from the program.

Exhibit 10–10 shows how each type of objective might be stated for a training program on performance appraisal. This illustration shows that a training program may have multiple instructional objectives that encompass several levels. Generally, short-run objectives are stated in terms of knowledge, attitudes, or skills and often serve as requisites for the new job behaviours.

Stating measurable objectives is particularly difficult for programs designed to increase self-awareness, such as sensitivity training or assertiveness training. Nevertheless, clear behavioural standards of expected results are necessary and should contain verifiable statements that provide a basis for later evaluation. Decisions on content, potential trainees, and training method flow logically from behavioural objectives.

TRANSLATING NEEDS INTO PROGRAMS

With objectives specified, the next issue involves designing the program.

The purpose of a formal program is to manage the learning process by controlling the *what* and *how* of the learning, linking this with employee and

EXHIBIT 10–10
Examples of Objectives—Performance Evaluation Training

Type of Objective	Examples
Knowledge	All trainees will understand and be able to attain a grade of 80 or better on a test designed to measure the principles of performance appraisal, including types, uses, assessment procedures, errors and their avoidance, providing feedback, and employment equity issues.
Attitudes	All trainees will believe that performance appraisal is important to effective management and that every employee has a right to receive an accurate appraisal annually. To be judged by their statements in class and their behaviour back on the job.
Skills	All trainees will be able to appraise accurately three videotaped examples of employee performance. All trainees will be able to provide high-quality feedback to these "subordinates" in role playing.
Job behaviour	All trainees will provide all of their subordinates with high-quality appraisals (including feedback) within six months after completion of training.
Organizational results	All trainees' work groups will improve their performance levels by 5 percent during the first year following training.

Source: Adapted from Herbert G. Heneman III, Donald P. Schwab, John A. Fossum, and Lee D. Dyer, *Personnel/Human Resource Management,* 3rd ed. (Homewood, Ill.: Richard D. Irwin, 1986).

organization needs, and increasing the efficiency of the process. This requires first consideration of the following: (1) incorporation of learning principles and (2) individual differences among trainees. The design process then considers (3) the methods to be used (i.e., specific approaches selected from off-the-job versus on-the-job techniques), and (4) cost in relation to various factors.[60]

Let us now focus on the first two of these in greater detail.

Learning Principles

Learning can be defined as a relatively permanent change in behaviour that occurs as a result of practice. Through countless experiments, certain variables affecting learning have been identified.[61] Those relevant to training include:

Conditions of Practice. For maximum learning, active practice of the skill to be acquired is necessary. Practice should continue beyond the point where the task can be performed successfully several times (overlearning). Distributed practice sessions (divided into spaced segments) have been found to be more effective than massed practice, a fact often ignored in training programs for the sake of expediency. The size of the unit to be learned at each practice session affects the learning rate.

Whether a task should be divided into subparts depends on the difficulty of the task and the degree of interrelationship between the subtasks. For example, a parts clerk would probably learn to correctly identify the stock before learning the computerized system for maintaining a parts inventory. On the other hand, a tool and die maker's tasks of feeding, aligning, and stamping is more difficult to subgroup into simpler elements without those elements becoming meaningless, so should probably be taught as a single unit.

Knowledge of Results. Errors will be eliminated faster if trainees are given feedback on how they are doing. Guidance and/or role modelling can provide this feedback, reinforce appropriate learning, and prevent inadequate behaviour patterns from developing.[62]

Meaningfulness of Material. Material that is rich in associations for trainees is more easily understood. Meaningfulness can be enhanced by providing an overview of how the training fits with the job, how the training sequences fit together, and the anticipated consequences of applying the key behaviours on the jobs.

Transfer to the Job. The issue of what learning is transferred to the job is a perplexing one for every training program. The traditional approach to boost transfer has been to maximize the number of identical elements between the training situation and the actual job. Besides this practical reason, matching program content with job content as much as possible is advised for employment equity reasons. It is also generally agreed that the transfer of learning problem is lessened if training material is presented in the same sequence it is to be used on the job.[63] While this is feasible for skills training, such as operating a cash register, it is less so for teaching leadership or conceptual skills. Often what is learned in a training session faces resistance on the job. Techniques for overcoming this resistance include creating positive expectations on the part of the trainee's supervisor, creating opportunities to implement the new behaviour on the job, and ensuring that the behaviour is reinforced when it occurs.[64] Commitment from top management to the training program will also help in overcoming resistance to change.

Individual Differences

A key criterion for selecting/designing training programs is recognition of individual differences among employees. Substantial differences exist in individuals' abilities and motivations. Both factors affect training.

EXHIBIT 10–11

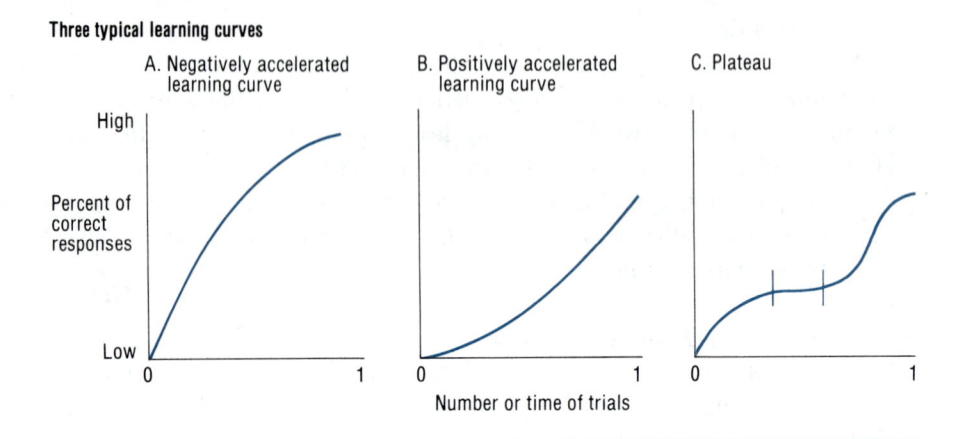

Three typical learning curves

A. Negatively accelerated learning curve

B. Positively accelerated learning curve

C. Plateau

Percent of correct responses (Low to High)

Number or time of trials

Ability

Individuals differ in the amount of learning that has occurred before training, their ability to learn, and the ways they learn.

Exhibit 10–11 shows some typical learning curves. For many individuals, rapid gains from initial practice are followed by a plateau where improvement levels off. A plateau may occur because material to be learned may become more difficult, fatigue or boredom may inhibit performance, or individuals may have reached the upper limits of their capacity. Not every individual's learning rate plateaus at the same time, nor do all individuals learn at the same rate, as the three curves indicate. It is difficult to accurately predict where an individual is on the learning curve. But a good trainer will use knowledge of this common learning pattern to design training programs that can be adjusted to the observed needs of the individual trainees. Changes in instructional method, additional examples, breaks to allow fatigue to dissipate, or pacing changes may be needed to reenergize learning.

Motivation

Motivation cannot be measured. It can only be inferred from behavioural observation. In Chapter Five, we discussed theories of motivation and work performance. Theories of motivation have implications for training as well.

Goal Setting. Goal-setting models postulate that individuals' conscious goals or intentions regulate their behaviour. The trainer's job is to get the trainees to adopt or internalize the training goals of the program.[65] Wexley and Latham identify three key points in motivating trainees:

- Learning objectives of the program should be conveyed at the outset and at various strategic points throughout the program.
- Goals should be difficult enough to adequately challenge the trainees and, thus, allow them to derive satisfaction from achievement, but not so difficult as to be unattainable.
- The final goal of program completion should be supplemented with subgoals (periodic quizzes, work samples) to maintain feelings of accomplishment and encourage anticipation of the next hurdle.[66]

Reinforcement. Reinforcement theory says the frequency of a behaviour is influenced by its consequences. Behaviour can be shaped by reinforcing progressively closer approximations to the goal behaviour. Reinforcement needs to be administered as soon after the desired behaviour occurs as possible. However, the same reinforcers are not effective for all people. The more familiar a trainer is with a group of trainees, the more likely that reinforcers can be tailored to the trainees.[67]

Expectancy. Expectancy theory holds that individuals will be motivated to choose a behaviour alternative that is most likely to have desired consequences. There are two aspects to expectancy. First, the trainee must believe improved skills or knowledge will lead to valued outcomes, for example, increased pay, promotions, or self-esteem. Second, the trainee must believe effort (level of participation in the training program) will lead to improved skills and knowledge, and therefore the program will have positive payoffs for the trainee. People who have been unemployed for a long time often do not expect these effort/behaviour/reward contingencies.[68] They may have little expectation that effort expended to learn new behaviours in a training program will lead to meaningful employment. Wexley and Latham caution that trainers should not assume trainees have accurate perceptions of reward contingencies.[69] Trainees must be told exactly which outcomes can be expected if the training program is successfully completed. These outcomes must occur.

Another issue in designing training programs is which format to use. This requires deciding whether the training should be done on the job, off the job, or utilize a combination of these, and what particular training techniques to employ.

INSTRUCTIONAL TECHNIQUES

Deciding on the best training technique and approach is more art than science.[70] The decision is often constrained by the number of trainees, budgetary considerations, the availability of facilities and technologies (e.g., audiovisual aids, computers, and so on), and the experience and flexibility of the trainer.

A recent raw list of loosely defined methods, techniques, devices, and assorted other ways to conduct training shows 92 ways to train.[71] Given the training techniques available, program designers must decide whether training should occur off the job or on the job. Within these two broad categories, choices must be made as to specific approaches.

On-the-Job Training

Exhibit 10–12 shows the major types of training techniques that occur on the job.

A typical on-the-job training program places the trainee in the real work situation, where an experienced worker or the supervisor demonstrates the job. On-the-job training avoids the major difficulties with off-the-job training: lack of relevance and reinforcement in the actual job situation.[72] For example, the literature offers many examples of managers who did well in formal classrooms but made no changes in their behaviours at work. The importance of a job or task, how it fits in with other tasks and other jobs, and the conse-

EXHIBIT 10–12
On-the-Job Employee Development Methods and Techniques

Methods and Techniques	Description
Coaching	This method has been described as the process of assuring that employee development occurs in the day-to-day supervisor-subordinate relationship. Basically, in coaching, the supervisor acts much as a tutor in an academic setting. His or her function is to serve as a favourable role model and to facilitate the learning process by providing guidance, assistance, feedback, and reinforcement.
Special assignments	A common method of employee development. Involves putting trainees on special committees, projects, or jobs, usually on a temporary basis. Often the purpose is to give the trainees an opportunity to work on special problems to which they otherwise would not become exposed. This approach often is combined with coaching.
Job rotation	Involves the systematic movement of trainees through a predetermined set of jobs, usually with the objective of providing exposure to many parts of an organization and to a variety of functional areas. It may be combined with coaching at each stop. Often newly hired graduates are involved in job rotation before receiving permanent assignments. Another common usage: to provide broad exposure to fast-track managers whose career plans suggest they will reach general management positions.

Source: Adapted from Herbert G. Heneman III, Donald P. Schwab, John A. Fossum, and Lee D. Dyer, *Personnel/Human Resource Management,* 3rd ed. (Homewood, Ill.: Richard D. Irwin, 1986).

EXHIBIT 10–13
Job Instruction Training (JIT) Methods

First here's what you *must do* to *get ready* to teach a job:
1. Decide what the learner must be taught in order to do the job efficiently, safely, economically, and intelligently.
2. Have the right tools, equipment, supplies, and material ready.
3. Have the workplace properly arranged, just as the worker will be expected to keep it.

Then, you should *instruct* the learner by the following *four basic steps:*

Step I—*Preparation* (of the learner)
1. Put the learner at *ease.*
2. Find out what is already known about the job.
3. Get the learner interested and desirous of learning the job.

Step II—*Presentation* (of the operations and knowledge)
1. *Tell, show, illustrate,* and *question* in order to put over the new knowledge and operations.
2. Instruct slowly, clearly, completely, and patiently, one point at a time.
3. Check, question, and repeat.
4. Make sure the learner really knows.

Step III—*Performance tryout*
1. Test by having the learner perform the job.
2. Ask questions beginning with *why, how, when* or *where.*
3. Observe performance, correct errors, and repeat instructions if necessary.
4. Continue until you *know* the learner knows.

Step IV—*Follow-up.*
1. Check frequently to be sure instructions are being followed.
2. Taper off extra supervision and close follow-up until the learner is qualified to work with normal supervision.

Remember—If the learner hasn't learned, the teacher hasn't taught.

---

quences of improper performance are usually far easier to demonstrate to the trainee on the job.

However, on-the-job training also entails some risks. Damaged machinery, low quality, unsatisfied customers, misfiled forms, or less than optimal performance are examples. On-the-job trainers must be well trained. They should be good performers on the job and have experience with training techniques. The Job Instruction Training approach (see Exhibit 10–13) is one way to systematize the training and ensure follow-up.[73]

Apprenticeships

The apprenticeship approach dates to the Guild system of the Middle Ages.[74] It combines on-the-job training with some institutional training and involves the cooperation of the employer, schools, government agencies (which frequently subsidize apprenticeships and establish standards), and unions.

Most apprenticeships require commitment to a three- to five-year period of training and learning. The apprentice spends most of the training time on the job with a certified skilled worker. The rest of the time is spent receiving classroom instruction in subjects related to the job training. During this period, the apprentice is paid wages, which increase as he or she becomes more skilled. In unionized plants, the training schedules and rates of pay for apprentices are negotiated in collective agreements.[75]

The type and amount of instruction required vary across the country and are regulated by provincial departments of labour. The apprenticeship program normally concludes with a set of provincial examinations that lead to the relevant licences or certifications. A nationwide comparison of apprenticeships is available through the well-known Ellis Chart.[76]

While there are a number of valid criticisms of Canadian apprenticeship programs, especially when compared to those in West Germany, there is renewed interest in standardizing qualifications for trades and training to the greatest extent possible.[77]

On-the-Job Management Training

Training managers on the job can take several approaches. The main ones are role modelling and job transfers (employing the techniques shown in Exhibit 10–12).

Role Models. One of the best methods of developing new managers is for effective managers to teach them. The role model sets a good example of how to be a manager, answers questions, and explains why things are done the way they are. It is the manager's obligation to help the manager-trainee make the proper contacts so the job can be learned easily and performed well.[78]

Research on role modelling stresses that if the trainees are to develop, the superior must delegate enough authority to let them make decisions and even mistakes.[79] A climate for learning not only provides opportunities to learn, but also encourages a feeling of mutual confidence.

Appropriately chosen task-force and special assignments are often used as a form of coaching and counselling in the role model approach. Although most organizations use coaching and counselling by a role model, it is not without its problems. Argyris points out that coaching reinforces or perpetuates current executive styles, which may not be desirable.[80] He also says that too often superiors are not rewarded for providing an effective role model, or the system will not allow the subordinate to make mistakes.

Despite these difficulties, coaching and counselling by a role model are probably the most widely used management development techniques and may yield good results. However, there has been little systematic study or evaluation of these techniques, so it is difficult to demonstrate their effectiveness.

If one good role model can be useful, perhaps two or more are even better. This is part of the notion behind the second on-the-job management training approach: job transfers.

Transfers. In this on-the-job approach, trainees are rotated through a series of jobs to broaden their managerial experience. The jobs typically involve exposure to a variety of functions, product lines, and geographic areas.[81]

Advocates of rotation and transfer contend this approach broadens the manager's background, accelerates the promotion of highly competent individuals, introduces new ideas across the organization, and increases organization effectiveness.[82] However, some research questions the wisdom of rotation. The organization may be moving employees before they have experienced the consequences of their decisions.

There may also be negative reactions to transfers. Some employees maintain that IBM really means "I've Been Moved." Changing social values, the increase in dual-career couples, and economic uncertainty have combined with skyrocketing relocation costs to make organizations consider transfers more thoroughly than they used to.[83] Brett and Werbel investigated why some employees and their families are willing to move and others are not, what conditions make moving difficult, and the effects of a mobile lifestyle.[84] They concluded that employees are most willing to move when the new job promises to be a challenge and a contribution to their career development.

Based on this research, they recommend that companies:

1. Give the first-choice employee the job transfer opportunity, even if management thinks it will be turned down. It may not be.
2. Discuss with the employee how each transfer furthers career development.
3. Make the new job challenging.
4. Do not "dead end" an employee who turns down a transfer.
5. Assist spouses to find challenging jobs at the new location.
6. Be sure benefits are sufficient with respect to current economic conditions.

How fast do transferees adjust to their new positions? Do transfers help employees in their professional development? Pinder obtained data from a sample of Canadian managers to address these questions.[85] The study found it took transferees about three to four months to become effective at the new job assignment and to decipher the new informal networks. The best predictors of adjustment time were the levels of support the transferee received from the new supervisor and co-workers and the degree of increase in job difficulty. A somewhat surprising finding was that employees who had been transferred more frequently than others did not report shorter adjustment times. This result supported similar findings from two earlier Canadian transfer studies in the mid-1970s.[86]

In examining the second question, Pinder took the view that the learning which follows a transfer might be a function of the type of transfer. Three types of transfer were considered: transfers including job changes accompanied by promotion (but no change in type of department); transfers involving changes in job function; and transfers encompassing a disproportionate number of moves initiated by the transferees. The first type of transfer also featured high levels of increases in the verbal, cognitive (thinking), planning, and interpersonal skills required of the transferee. The following results linking type of learning to type of transfer emerged:[87]

1. The best predictor of the amount of feedback the transferee perceived about where he or she stood in the organization was the degree of increase in the level of cognitive skill required on the posttransfer job.
2. The amount of political insight gained due to the transfer was best predicted by the amount of verbal and cognitive skill increase accompanying the transfer and by whether the organization had initiated the transfer.
3. Learning about the organization's structure, goals, and problems seemed to be highest when the transfer entailed a promotion and large increases in the cognitive skill levels required of the transferee.
4. The degree of learning of new ways of conceptualizing problems and processing information was best predicted by changing function (departments).
5. The degree of learning of new behavioural styles was highest when supervisory support after the transfer was high, cognitive skill requirements increased, the employee had not previously experienced many transfers, and the organization (rather than the employee) initiated the transfer.

Overall, it appears that different types of transfer experiences do promote different types of on-the-job learning.

Off-the-Job Training

Off-the-job training is more common for management and professional development than for skills training.

Exhibit 10–14 shows the major types of off-the-job training techniques.[88] They are divided into three types: (1) information presentation, (2) information processing, and (3) simulation.

Information Presentation Techniques. These are preferred when instructional objectives focus on knowledge, the content is not too complex, participants are relatively capable and self-motivated, large numbers are to be trained, and the budget is limited (except in the case of programmed or computer-based instruction, where developmental costs may be quite high).

These techniques provide a relatively efficient way to organize and present a large volume of material to a great many people in a limited period of time. The problem is that they are very much trainer (or technology) centred, and thus may not appeal to adult learners who are used to taking a more active role in their own development.[89] Furthermore, most of them (programmed or computer-based instruction aside) provide few opportunities for pacing the material to allow for individual differences in learning rates. Still, it is rare not to have at least some lecture time, perhaps augmented by films or panel discussions, to introduce concepts and organize or summarize material that has been dealt with using other instructional techniques.

Among the information presentation techniques, computer-based instruction is clearly in the ascendency. This parallels the sharp increase in the use of computers in P/HRM more generally. It also reflects the value of this approach, particularly in the development of technical skills. Research has shown significant reductions in learning time and instructional costs over more conventional training techniques, with no significant differences in learning or subsequent job performance.[90]

Information Processing Techniques. Such techniques, particularly conference or discussion groups, are particularly well suited as adjuncts when the objective is to enhance knowledge—especially when the material is complex,

EXHIBIT 10–14
Off-the-Job Training/Development Methods and Techniques

1. *Information presentation techniques*—designed primarily to impart information with a minimum amount of activity by the learner.
   a. Reading list.
   b. Correspondence course.
   c. Film.
   d. Lecture.
   e. Panel discussion.
   f. Programmed or computer-based instruction—material to be learned is presented in a series of carefully planned steps either in a booklet or on a screen. Learners move at their own pace, answering preprogrammed questions when ready. Answers are immediately "graded." Correct responses are reinforced, and the learner moves to new material. Incorrect responses require that the material be repeated.
2. *Information processing techniques*—designed to involve groups of learners in the generation and discussion of material to be learned.
   a. Conference or discussion group—a problem is presented to a group of learners who are expected to discuss the issues and reach a conclusion. Usually a leader provides guidance and feedback.
   b. T (training) Group—similar to the conference or discussion group technique, except that attention is focussed on the behaviour of the group and the learners' behaviour as part of the group rather than on a substantive problem. Emphasis is on open and honest communications, especially concerning personal feelings.

EXHIBIT 10–14 *(concluded)*

3. *Simulation* techniques—designed to represent the work environment to a greater or lesser degree and to actually involve the learner (experiential learning).
    a. Case method—trainees study a written description of real decision-making situations, analyze and choose solutions. (Effectiveness: Best if there is interaction between trainer and trainee and among trainees. Can be effective with good cases and trainees, but little research exists to evaluate this technique.)
    b. Role-playing—each participant is assigned a role and reacts to other players' role-playing. Background information on other players and the situation is given, but there is no script. Can be videotaped for reanalysis. (Effectiveness: Success depends on ability of participants to play the roles believably. Evidence on effectiveness is mixed.)
    c. In-basket—trainee is given material that includes items from a manager's mail and telephone messages. Important and pressing matters are mixed in with routine items. Different subordinates' or supervisors' versions of a situation make solutions less clear cut. Trainee is critiqued on the number of decisions made in the allotted time period, quality of decisions, and priorities used in making them. (Effectiveness: Some evidence that method is useful in predicting managerial success.)
    d. Vestibule—a duplicate work operation is set up independent of the usual work site. Trainees learn under realistic situations but apart from production pressures.
    e. Mock-up—the essential aspects of a work environment are duplicated, usually in a manner that allows specific problems to be introduced. Classic example is the link trainer used to train airline pilots.
    f. Business management game—attempts to simulate the economic functioning of an entire organization either manually or on a computer. Trainees make decisions concerning market strategies, pricing, staffing levels, and so forth and observe the results on sales, profits, and so on. (Effectiveness: Advantages include integration of interacting decision makers, provision of feedback, and the requirement that decisions be made with inadequate data, which simulates reality. Disadvantages include development and administration costs and the sometimes unrealistic or limited models underlying the equations.)

Source: Adapted and modified from George T. Milkovich and William F. Glueck, *Personnel/Human Resource Management: A Diagnostic Approach,* 4th ed. (Plano, Tex.: Business Publications, 1985); and Herbert G. Heneman III, Donald P. Schwab, John A. Fossum, and Lee D. Dyer, *Personnel/Human Resource Management,* 3rd ed. (Homewood, Ill.: Richard D. Irwin, 1986).

the participants are experienced or lacking in self-motivation, and the number of trainees is (or can be made) manageable. This approach is applied in many introductory employee training courses where lectures are supplemented by weekly discussion sessions allowing for in-depth exploration of the material.

Information processing techniques may also be effective in changing attitudes. Research has shown that simply presenting information has relatively little effect on attitudes, but group discussions can be more effective in this respect because trainees feel peer pressure to change, and the new attitudes can be reinforced by the group. A relatively beneficial use of this approach can be to eliminate sexist or racist attitudes on the part of white male supervisors soon to be assigned work teams that include women and other employees drawn from a more culturally diverse work force. New skills, particularly communication and interpersonal skills, may also be learned through information processing techniques, either directly or as a by-product; this is the main purpose of T-groups, for example.

Simulation Techniques. When it comes to developing skills, simulation techniques are generally most effective. The reason for this may be summed up in one word: *practice*. Manual or motor skills are sharpened through vestibule training and the use of mock-ups; leadership and supervisory skills can be honed through the use of role playing; and problem-solving and decision-making skills are developed through cases, in-basket exercises, and business games.

The more elaborate simulations of corporate life are viewed as real enough to bring out the manager in any trainee, and their use is gradually reshaping the way managers are trained.[91]

One simulation technique—role-playing—may be as effective in changing attitudes as in developing skills. Role-playing requires that one project oneself into the cognitive, emotional, and perceptual "roadmap" of the role's usual incumbent, and see "reality" from that person's perspective and job responsibilities. Role reversals involve the exchange of roles (e.g., assigning white males to assume the roles of female employees or of members of designated groups, and vice versa). This approach has been found particularly effective when the new attitudes are reinforced on the job.

Of the major simulations on the market, Looking Glass is the oldest and most widely used. Adding certain features and debriefing sessions transformed the simulation, originally intended as a research tool, into a training device whose air of reality grips even veteran managers.[92]

Looking Glass re-creates a day in the lives of the 20 managers of a midsize manufacturing corporation.[93] Each of the corporation's three divisions faces a unique external environment; more than 100 problems are built into the simulation. The issues involved cover a variety of areas and require participants to deal with items such as the opportunity to acquire a new plant, supply shortages, pollution and discrimination concerns, and competition with foreign manufacturers. Because of its realism, the trainee learns about the activity pattern, pace, pressure, and variety of problems of managerial work. They experience issues covered in lecture or case study exposure. The simulation also teaches trainees about themselves and their behaviour in a management context.

The relatively widespread use of Looking Glass may also be due to its ability to serve different corporate objectives in different training programs.

For example, after an acquisition it can be used to show employees they can work together. It can help managers from different segments of a company to put more emphasis on organizational integration; it can also be part of a management course aimed at dispelling stereotypes in order to encourage company scientists and engineers to consider executive jobs.[94]

Within the past few years, several other management simulations have come into use. One of these, Simmons Simulator Inc., represents a high-technology multinational company. Its development was commissioned by IBM, which went to great pains to tailor this simulation to its needs. Simmons was developed because IBM needed a way to initiate fast-track managers into the company's top-level planning process. Alcoa and Shell recently also became users of this simulation.[95]

Some simulations focus on a specific functional area. MarkStrat, for example, requires participants to operate the marketing department of a simulated company as part of a microcomputer-based approach.[96] Participants receive information about the competitive position of the simulated company and make a set of marketing decisions with a view to improving their position. MarkStrat takes the input and simulates the market response to determine the new position for the next cycle of decisions. The program is cosponsored by Air Canada Express and IBM Canada and is viewed as sufficiently realistic to allow Canadian executives to "test their ability to compete in an arena where mistakes will not cost their company millions of dollars."[97]

Combinations

Many training and development programs combine on-the-job and off-the-job efforts.[98] In fact, successful programs probably must be designed to incorporate real work situations with more formal off-the-job analysis and development. Very often the three major types of off-the-job training techniques—information presentation, information processing, and simulation—are used in various combinations during a single training program. To cite one example, the objectives of the training described in Exhibit 10–10 were to improve managers' understanding of the performance appraisal process and to improve the quality of their performance appraisal ratings and feedback sessions. One program involved only an information presentation technique—computer-aided instruction (CAI). The other added to CAI a 12-hour workshop that combined information presentation (lectures, videotapes), information processing (group discussions), and simulation (role-playing) techniques. The CAI alone was as effective as the CAI plus the workshop (CAIW) in improving trainees' knowledge and rating skills, but the latter was more effective in improving quality of their on-the-job appraisal feedback.

Behaviour modelling is an increasingly popular training approach.[99] One of its attractions is the use of all three types of off-the-job training techniques in a single, integrated package. Program content is usually based on careful job analysis and is presented in logical modules, each with its own "learning points." In each module, trainees observe desired behaviours in films and videotapes and reinforce and practice these behaviours in group discussions and role-playing exercises. Constant feedback is provided by trainers and fellow trainees during group discussions and role-playing. At the end of each module, trainees are provided copies of key "learning points," given instructions on how to use them on the job, and instructed to do so soon and often. At the beginning of the next module, they are asked to report on their successes and failures. (Sometimes supervisors are also trained on how to reinforce trainees who exhibit desired behaviours on the job.)

Not surprisingly, given the strong theoretical base and comprehensiveness of behaviour modelling, the available research suggests it is often successful, especially in increasing knowledge and skills and in changing attitudes. Mixed findings with respect to job behaviours and results, however, have led some to suggest the need to ensure that considerable post-training reinforcement is provided to increase the motivation to apply newly attained abilities once trainees return to their jobs.[100]

Regardless of technique or place of training, evaluation of its effectiveness is required. We will now examine the training evaluation process.

EVALUATING RESULTS

Evaluation is the final phase of training. As Exhibit 10–6 suggested, methods of evaluation must be designed into the training program from the very beginning, at the time the objectives are specified. Training evaluation is based on comparing training results with the program objectives, which were set in the assessment phase. In practice, unfortunately, it is like brushing your teeth after every meal; everyone advocates it, but few actually do it.

A student recently put the question to a leading training consultant who was visiting our class. "Why don't you evaluate your programs?" The response was, "Because our client firms refuse to do it. Even when we offer to cover the expenses involved, our clients begin to question whether we have confidence in the programs we designed. They ask, 'If your programs are tailored to our needs, why evaluate them?'"

Attempts to measure the effectiveness of training should include several elements: (*a*) asking the right questions, (*b*) utilizing multiple criteria, with some attempt to study the criteria themselves, (*c*) having sufficient experimental control to enable the causal arrow to originate in the training program (i.e., training → effect), and (d) comparing costs and benefits to provide information about the practical and theoretical significance of training outcomes.[101]

Four Evaluation Questions

From a practical perspective, the training analyst is concerned with answering four crucial questions when evaluating training.[102]

1. Are the trainees happy?
2. Do the materials used in the training session teach the concepts specified?
3. Are the concepts applied on the job after training?
4. Does the application of the concepts contribute to organizational effectiveness?

Questions 2, 3, and 4 reflect concern with whether change has occurred, at what level, and the extent to which change can be attributed to the training program. The effect on the organization remains the bottom line in training. The evaluation matrix presented in Exhibit 10–15 suggests approaches to answering the four questions and provides a useful parallel to the following sections.

The training literature suggests training evaluators should also consider questions beyond the basic ones listed here. For example, Goldstein shows a concern with whether it is likely that similar changes will occur with new participants in the same training program.[103] Cascio points to the importance of comparing a training program with other possible ways to developing work force capability, such as improved selection procedures or job redesign.[104]

Criteria for Evaluation

Evaluation criteria are set before training when instructional objectives are specified and can be considered according to time, type, and level.

Timing

This aspect of evaluation is concerned with the question of when, relative to the actual conduct of the training, criterion data should be obtained. Since evaluation is concerned with the change in criteria due to training, it follows that appropriate measures should be obtained both before (see "pretest trainees," Exhibit 10–6) and after the program takes place. How much before and after depends on the criteria used and the employer's interest in comparisons of short- versus long-term training effects.

Types and Levels of Criteria

It is useful to classify criteria into two types: internal and external.[105] These, in turn, are composed of criteria that refer either to organizational levels from which criterion data are drawn or to the relative level of rigour adopted in measuring training outcomes.[106]

Internal Criteria. Criteria of the internal type are associated with the content of the training program, are linked directly to the training situation, and are used to assess trainees' reactions and learning (but not the transfer of these to the on-the-job situation). Reaction and learning comprise the internal criteria and represent two levels of rigour. Their use helps address the first two of our evaluation questions (see Exhibit 10–15).

Reaction criteria represent the lowest level of rigour and are defined in terms of trainees' impressions, opinions, or feelings about various aspects of the training. Training departments generally use questionnaires (and sometimes group interviews) to collect reactions to the relevance, quality, and comprehensiveness of training content, to the method of training and quality of training aids (e.g., handouts, videotaped presentations), and effectiveness of the trainer. These data are usually collected immediately after training; sometimes a follow-up administration of the same questionnaire some time later can add useful information. Glowing comments and accolades do not guarantee that learning has occurred. Alternatively, continuance of a training program should not hinge on the comments of only a few disgruntled participants. The ease of gauging participant reaction probably explains why this is, unfortunately, often the only information collected.

Learning criteria are based on more rigorous measurements and attempt to provide objective and quantifiable indicators of the learning absorbed by trainees. The training analyst is concerned with assessing the (pretraining to post-training) change in knowledge of the principles, facts, techniques, and attitudes that were specified as part of the training objectives. Objective achievement tests (true-false and/or multiple choice questions), essay exams, and "demonstration" tests are illustrative of internal criteria. For example, an employer may conduct a two-day training program on employment equity issues and their implications for P/HRM. A written exam at the conclusion of training can be used to assess mastery of the training material. A more meaningful procedure would also administer the same test just before training to allow measurement of the change in knowledge imparted by the program. A program to train typists in the use of word processors could be judged on how fast and accurately the trainees operate the machine at the conclusion of the training, before reporting to the new position.

External Criteria. These are used to provide measures that are successively closer to the ultimate purpose of training, in parallel with the third and

EXHIBIT 10–15
Evaluation Matrix*

What We Want to Know	What Might Be Measured	Measurement Dimensions	What to Look At (sources of data)	Alternative Data Gathering Method	Evaluation Criteria
I. Are the trainees happy? If not, why not? a. Concepts not relevant b. Workshop design c. Trainees not properly positioned	Trainee reaction during workshop	Relevance Threat Ease of learning	Comments between trainees Comments to instructor Questions about exercises "Approach behaviour" to exercises	Observation Interview Questionnaire	
	Trainee reaction after workshop	Perceived "worth" V—Relevance; or C—Learning energy	"Approach behaviour" to project Questions about project concepts	Observation Interview Questionnaire	

II. Do the materials teach the concepts? If not, why not?
a. Workshop structure
b. Lessons
  (1) Presentation
  (2) Examples
  (3) Exercises
	Trainee performance during workshop	Understanding
		Application
			Learning time
			Performance on exercises
			Presentations
				Observation
				Document review	

	Trainee performance at end of workshop	Understanding Application Facility Articulation	Action plan for project Use of tools on exercises Presentations	Observation Document review Interview Questionnaire	

III. Are the concepts used? If not, why not? a. Concepts 　(1) Not relevant 　(2) Too complex 　(3) Too sophisticated b. Inadequate tools c. Environment not supportive	Performance improvement projects	Analysis Action plan Results	Discussions Documentation Results	Observation Interview Document review Questionnaire (critical incident)
	Problem solving technique	Questions asked Action proposed Action taken	Discussions Documentation Results	Observation Interview Document review Questionnaire (critical incident)
	Ongoing management approach	Dissemination effort Language People management process	Discussions Meetings Documentation	Observation Interview Document review Questionnaire (critical incident)
IV. Does application of concepts positively affect the organization? If not, why not?	Problem solving	Problem identification Analysis Action Results	Discussions Documentation Results	Interview Document review Questionnaire (critical incident)
	Problem prediction and prevention	Potential problem identification Analysis Action	Discussions Documentation Results	Interview Document review Questionnaire (critical incident)
	Performance measures Specific to a particular workshop	Output measures Interim or diagnostic measures	Performance data	Document review

*Copyright 1976, Praxis Corporation. Used by permission.
Source: K. Brethower and G. Rummler, "Evaluating Training," *Training and Development Journal*, May 1979, pp. 14–22.

fourth of the evaluation questions (Exhibit 10–15). Their use is intended to demonstrate essentially two things: (*a*) what, and how much, of the learning is transferred to the post-training job situation; and, as a consequence, (*b*) what is the program's eventual contribution to organizational effectiveness and goal achievement. The two levels of external criteria are behaviour and results.

Behavioural criteria are concerned with changes in job behaviour and performance on the job. Measures employed include well-designed performance appraisal scales (preferably of the behaviourally anchored kind; see Chapter Eleven); self-reports; certain critical incidents observed by subordinates, peers, and supervisors; and other qualitative and objective assessments of individual performance. In the case of the word-processing operators, the degree of positive transfer reflected in job behaviour can be assessed by tracking speed and accuracy on a periodic or relatively continuous basis. A relevant behavioural criterion for the trainees exposed to the employment equity program would be ratings of their on-the-job application of employment-related human rights principles.

In assessing behavioural changes, sufficient time should be allowed for the newly trained employee to demonstrate the required set of relevant behaviours. Time is needed to overcome anxiety and uncertainty that exist even after the training. The appropriate time interval for the word-processing operations would be shorter (about two weeks) than for a development program designed to improve problem-solving and decision-making skills, interpersonal competence, and leadership styles. Several months are probably required before changes in these are fully manifested in behavioural changes.

Results criteria, when possible to apply, represent the highest level of rigour. They provide measures of the training program's utility in terms of its impact on organizational performance and goals. In practice, their use is generally delayed until after behavioural criteria have been employed. Typical results criteria include changes in sales volume and operating costs, absenteeism rate, grievances, turnover rate, production quality and quantity, profitability, work unit morale, and frequency or severity of accidents (and the attendant assessment by the provincial workers' compensation board). A specific results criterion for the employment equity program would measure, for example, the dollars (and time) saved and goodwill (company image) created due to a reduction of sexual harassment and valid complaints of discrimination in hiring and promotion.

Experimental Designs

Exhibit 10–16 summarizes four of the numerous experimental designs suggested for determining the effects of training on learning, behaviour, and re-

EXHIBIT 10–16
Training Evaluation Designs

Training Evaluation Design	Measure before Training	Exposure to Training	Measure after Training
A. Training group	No	Yes	Yes, X2
B. Training group	Yes, X1	Yes	Yes, X2
C. Training group	Yes, X1	Yes	Yes, X2
Control group	Yes, Y1	No	Yes, Y2
D. Training group	Yes, X1	Yes	Yes, X2
Control group 1	Yes, Y1	No	Yes, Y2
Control group 2	No	Yes	Yes, Y'2

sults.[107] These designs differ a great deal in terms of scientific rigour and, consequently, their value and degree of confidence with which the organization can identify the cause → effect linkage of the training. While use of an experimental approach will not solve all problems of accountability, utilization of even a simple design will dramatically improve the validity of the obtained information.[108]

In the designs, X1 and X2 represent the before and after measures of the training group; Y1 and Y2 refer to the control group. Design A, which obtains measures only after training, makes it impossible to determine whether knowledge or job skills were developed as a result of training or existed before training. A slight improvement over this method is Design B, which uses a before and after measurement approach with the training group. However, the trainer still has no idea whether the X2 − X1 differences are due to training and/or extraneous factors to which trainees were exposed in addition to the training. Design C is a further improvement by meeting a third guideline: changes in the training group are compared with changes in the same measures(s) for an equivalent control group that did not receive the training. Introduction of a control group attempts to account for the effects of both the initial measurement and contemporaneous factors. Pretraining equivalency can be achieved by randomly assigning individuals to each of the groups or checking that they are at about the same level of performance, skill level, and so on before the training. Differences between the control group and training group after training measure the effectiveness of the training alone. Either the final scores, (X2 and Y2), or their respective change scores [i.e., (X2 − X1) and (Y2 − Y1)] may be compared. If the two groups were truly equivalent before training (i.e., X1 = Y1), the training effect is measured by X2 − Y2. Although Design C is not perfect, it controls for most extraneous factors and is feasible in most organizations. The use of two (or even more)

EXHIBIT 10–17
Cost Breakdown for an Off-Site Management Meeting

Cost Elements		Total Costs	Cost per Participant per Day
A. Development of programs (figured on an annual basis)			
1. Training department overhead			
2. Training staff salaries			
3. Use of outside consultants			
4. Equipment and materials for meeting (films, supplies, workbooks)		$100,000	$100*
B. Participant cost (figured on an annual basis)			
1. Salaries and benefits of participants (figured for average participant)	$20,000		
2. Capital investment in participants (based on an average of various industries from *Fortune* magazine)	25,000	45,000	190.68†
C. Delivery of one meeting for 20 persons			
1. Facility costs			
a. Sleeping rooms	1,000		
b. Three meals daily	800		
c. Coffee breaks	60		
d. Miscellaneous (tips, telephone)	200		
e. Reception	200	2,260	56.50‡
2. Meeting charges			
a. Room rental			
b. A/V rental			
c. Secretarial services			
3. Transportation to the meeting		2,500	62.50§

Summary: Total per day per person cost
A. Development of programs $ 100
B. Participant cost   190
C. Delivery of one meeting (hotel and transportation)   119
                               Total $ 409

Note: Meeting duration: two full days. Number of attendees: 20 people. These costs do not reflect a figure for the productive time lost of the people in the program. If that cost were added—and it would be realistic to do so—the above cost would increase dramatically.
    *To determine per day cost, divide $100,000 by number of meeting days held per year (10). Then divide answer ($10,000) by total number of management people (100) attending all programs = $100 per day of a meeting.
    †To determine per day cost, divide total of $45,000 by 236 (average number of working days in a year) = $190.68 per day of work year.
    ‡To determine per day, per person cost, divide group total ($2,260) by number of participants (20) and then divide resulting figure ($113) by number of meeting days (2) = $56.50 per day.
    §To determine per day, per person cost, divide group total ($2,500) by number of people and then divide resulting figure ($125) by number of meeting days (2) = $62.50 per day.
    Source: Adapted from W. J. McKeon, "How to Determine Off-Site Meeting Costs," *Training and Development Journal*, May 1981, p. 117.

control groups, as in Design D, permits more sophistication and allows for better isolation of nontraining effects from those of the training. However, the realities and constraints of most organizational settings usually preclude Design D.

Costs and Benefits

In addition to analyzing training results, McKeon and others emphasize cost comparisons to account for the cost involved.[109] Exhibit 10–17 shows one approach to determining cost of an off-site program. Costs associated with alternative programs could be calculated and then compared.[110]

Another approach is to compare costs to the benefits associated with the training.[111] When using this approach, a distinction should be made between cost benefit (CB) and cost effectiveness (CE) analysis.[112] Cost benefit analysis is based on the examination of "training costs in monetary units as compared to benefits derived from training in nonmonetary terms."[113] Cost effectiveness involves consideration of monetary terms on the benefit side as well; training costs are compared to monetary benefits. This means translating benefits into dollar values. Benefits might include estimating the dollar value of improved performance ratings, production improvements, quality improvements, diminished downtime, and the like.[114] Cullen et al. developed a model, shown in Exhibit 10–18, to assess the cost effectiveness of two approaches to training.[115] In the model, a structured training program is compared to an unstructured program.

Cost, Benefits, and Productivity

Another approach examines the productivity of a training program by comparing the different levels of training expenditure with possible outcomes.[116] Kearsley's training productivity model, shown in Exhibit 10–19, shows these trade-offs. The straight line A represents an equal increment in training outcomes for every increment in training costs. Curves B, C, and D represent different training approaches. B depicts a situation in which each improvement in results is obtained at a considerable increase in training costs. Curve D, where gains in training effectiveness are initially greater than costs but then become less, is most realistic, Kearsley says. Many programs get significant improvements for relatively small effort. But to achieve greater improvement requires more and more resources. The trick is to know when to switch from one training program to another, or even from training to another human resource activity (e.g., compensation) to enhance behavioural outcomes. Clearly, training cannot achieve maximum contribution independent of other P/HRM functions.

EXHIBIT 10–18
Industrial Training Cost-Effectiveness Model

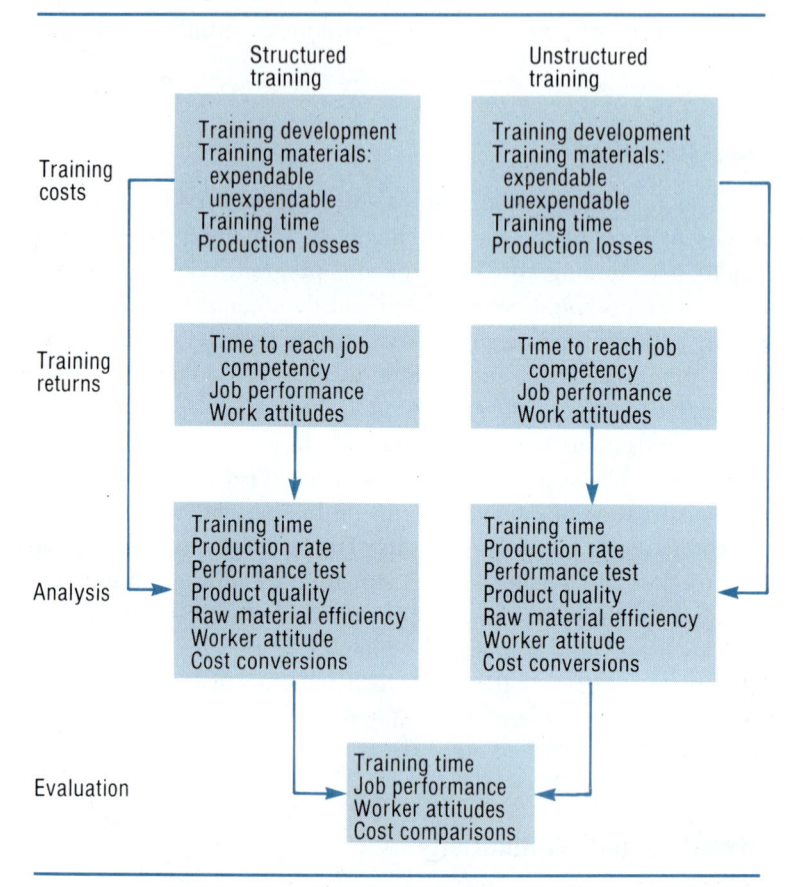

	Structured training	Unstructured training

Training costs	Training development
	Training materials:
	  expendable
	  unexpendable
	Training time
	Production losses
		Training development
		Training materials:
		  expendable
		  unexpendable
		Training time
		Production losses

Training returns	Time to reach job competency Job performance Work attitudes	Time to reach job competency Job performance Work attitudes
Analysis	Training time Production rate Performance test Product quality Raw material efficiency Worker attitude Cost conversions	Training time Production rate Performance test Product quality Raw material efficiency Worker attitude Cost conversions
Evaluation	Training time Job performance Worker attitudes Cost comparisons	

Source: J. G. Cullen, S. A. Sawzin, G. R. Sisson, and R. A. Swanson, "Cost-Effectiveness: A Model for Assessing the Training Investment," *Training and Development Journal* 32 (1978), p. 27.

**EXHIBIT 10–19
Productivity Functions**

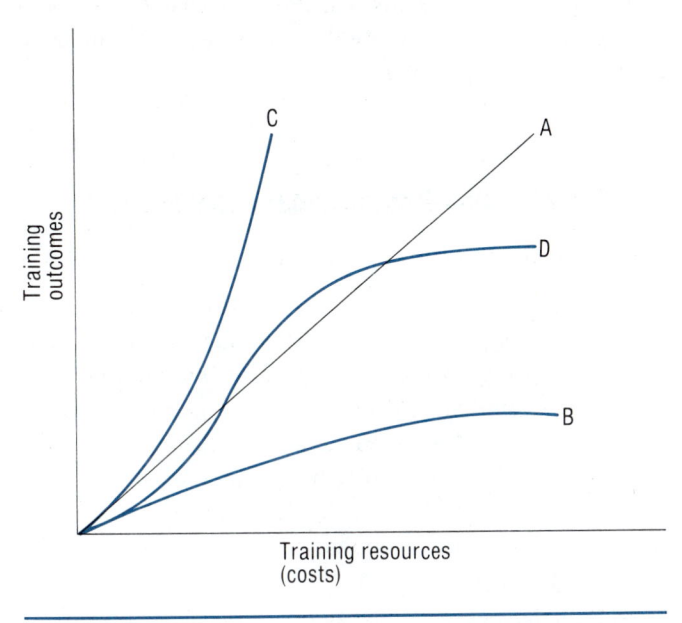

Source: Greg Kearsley, *Costs, Benefits, and Productivity in Training Systems* (Reading, Mass.: Addison-Wesley Publishing, 1982), p. 18.

SUMMARY

Given the dollars and time spent on training and development, it is astonishing that we know so little about effectively managing this investment. Unfortunately, training, of all the activities in P/HRM, seems most subject to passing fads and fashions.

Managers need to approach training decisions more systematically. Assessment of needs and objectives is required, program alternatives designed to meet these needs and to achieve the objectives must be planned, and cost-benefit evaluation conducted. Until these issues are dealt with, managers will remain unguided in their expenditure of the millions of dollars in training. As it now stands, research in the management of training offers little comparative evidence by which to evaluate the impact or generalizability of various approaches to training the work force.

Finally, it is important to call out a basic premise underlying this chapter. In training today, we tend to shape the individual to fit the job requirements. Perhaps training and development in the future must include managing the job design process as well. We need to study ways to design jobs differently—

to build in *future-needed* skills in the present job so employees can begin to prepare for future jobs. Human resource professionals need to create expectations in all employees that skills learning and change will be an ongoing process throughout their careers. Both employees and employers have responsibility to adapt to this change.

APPENDIX / Orientation—International Assignments*

Initial orientation (may last as long as two full days).

- *Cultural briefing.* Traditions, history, government, economy, living conditions, clothing and housing requirements, health requirements, and visa applications. Attention is given to the differences among drug laws in foreign countries. Alcohol use gets special attention when candidates are going to Moslem countries, such as Saudi Arabia.
- *Assignment briefing.* Length of assignment, vacations, salary and allowances, tax consequences, and repatriation policy.
- *Relocation requirements.* Shipping, packing, or storage and home sale, rental, or acquisition.

Predeparture orientation (may last another two or three days).

- Introduction to the language. (The amount of language instruction provided depends on how long a company allows for training.)
- Further reinforcement of important values, especially open-mindedness.
- Enroute, emergency, and arrival information.

Arrival orientation (usually takes place on three levels).

- *Orientation toward the environment.* Language, transportation, shopping, and other subjects that—depending on the country—may be understandable only through actual experience.
- *Orientation toward the work unit and fellow employees.* Often a supervisor or a delegate from the work unit will introduce the new person to his or her fellow workers, discuss expectations of the job, and share his or her own initial experiences as an expatriate. The ultimate objective, of course, is to relieve the feelings of strangeness or tension the new expatriate feels.
- *Orientation to the actual job.* This may be an extended process that focusses on cultural differences in the way a job is done. Only when this process is complete, however, can we begin to assess the accuracy and wisdom of the original selection decision.

*Source: Adapted from Wayne F. Cascio, *Managing Human Resources* (New York: McGraw-Hill, 1986); used with permission.

DISCUSSION AND REVIEW QUESTIONS

1. What factors in the diagnostic model help explain why there is such a wide range among employers in what they spend on training?
2. Distinguish between training and development.
3. What organization measures indicate a need for training?
4. What job analysis method would be most useful for training purposes for a production job? A managerial job?
5. What performance evaluation method would be most useful for training purposes for a production job? A managerial job?
6. What is obsolescence, how can it be reduced, and whose responsibility is it?
7. What learning principles affect training? How?
8. Why is it difficult to evaluate training?
9. What are possible criteria for evaluating training? What are the pros and cons of each?
10. What is socialization? Should an organization try to control it? Why? How?
11. Why should both operating managers and P/HRM personnel be involved in orientation and training?
12. Interview a training professional of a local company to find out how training/development is being done, why it's being done a certain way, and how outcomes are evaluated by the company. Give a short report to your class.

NOTES AND REFERENCES

1. Samuel A. Culbert and John J. McDonough, "The Invisible War: Pursuing Self-Interest at Work," in *Organizational Reality: Reports from the Firing Line*, 3rd ed., ed. Peter J. Frost, Vance F. Mitchell, and Walter R. Nord (Glenview, Ill.: Scott, Foresman, 1986).
2. John M. Ivancevich and William F. Glueck, *Foundations of Personnel/Human Resource Management*, 3rd ed. (Plano, Tex.: Business Publications, 1986).
3. David F. Jones, "Developing a New Employee Orientation Program," *Personnel Journal*, March 1984, pp. 86–87.
4. Steven L. McShane and Trudy Baal, "Employee Socialization Practices on Canada's West Coast: A Management Report," Faculty of Business Administration, Simon Fraser University, Burnaby, B.C., December 1984. This study collected data from 85 companies with headquarters or regional offices in the lower mainland of British Columbia. The surveyed companies together employ approximately 200,000 people in British Columbia and at least 600,000 across Canada.
5. Daniel C. Feldman, "A Socialization Process that Helps New Recruits Succeed," in *Current Issues in Personnel Management*, ed. K. Rowland, G. Ferris, and J. Sherman (Boston: Allyn & Bacon, 1985); David F. Jones, "Developing a New Employee Orientation Program," *Personnel Journal*, March 1984, pp. 86–87.
6. John Van Maanen, "Breaking In: Socialization to Work," in *Handbook of Work, Organization, and Society*, ed. Robert Dubin (Chicago: Rand McNally, 1976).
7. Walter D. St. John, "The Complete Employee Orientation Program," *Personnel Journal*, May 1980, pp. 377–78.
8. McShane and Baal, "Employee Socialization Practices on Canada's West Coast."

9. "Companies Calling Retirees Back to the Workplace," *Management Review*, February 1982, p. 29.
10. McShane and Baal, "Employee Socialization Practices on Canada's West Coast."
11. This list is heavily dependent on a list compiled by Dr. Cary Thorp, Jr., University of Nebraska.
12. Daniel C. Feldman, "A Contingency Theory of Socialization," *Administrative Science Quarterly*, 2nd quarter, 1976, pp. 433–52; Daniel C. Feldman, "The Role of Initiation Activities in Socialization," *Human Relations* 30, no. 4 (1977), pp. 977–90.
13. McShane and Baal, "Employee Socialization Practices on Canada's West Coast."
14. Ibid.
15. Daniel C. Feldman, "The Multiple Socialization of Organization Members," *Academy of Management Review* 6 (1981), pp. 309–18.
16. Ibid.
17. Van Maanen, "Breaking In: A Consideration of Organizational Socialization"; J. Van Maanen, "People Processing: Strategies of Organizational Socialization," *Organizational Dynamics* 7 (1978), pp. 18–36.
18. T. Caplow, *Principles of Organization* (New York: Harcourt, Brace, Jovanovich, 1964).
19. E. H. Schein, *Career Dynamics: Matching Individual and Organizational Needs* (Reading, Mass.: Addison-Wesley Publishing, 1978).
20. Tony Leighton, "Red Serge and High Spirits," *Equinox*, July–August 1985, p. 42.
21. Michael Salter, "Makeovers, Executive-Style, Back in Business," *The Financial Post*, September 1, 1984, p. 19.
22. Ibid.
23. Andrew Campbell, "Training Helps Keep Employees on Toes," *The Globe and Mail*, March 10, 1986, p. B2.
24. Michael Salter, "Makeovers, Executive-Style, Back in Business," p. 19.
25. Ibid. (based on a statement by F. Gump, president of Menergy Co., a Toronto-based educational firm).
26. *Human Resource Planning: A Guide for Employers* (Ottawa: Minister of Supply and Services Canada, 1983, Cat. No. MP43-146/1983), p. 8; and "$16 Million in Job Fund Goes to Youth," *The Vancouver Sun*, May 31, 1986, p. A6.
27. Salter, "Makeover, Executive-Style, Back in Business," p. 19.
28. Peter F. Drucker, "A Corporation Should Be Inflation-Proofed," *The Wall Street Journal*, May 28, 1981, p. 35.
29. Salter, "Makeover, Executive-Style, Back in Business," p. 19.
30. Irwin L. Goldstein, *Training in Organizations: Needs Assessment, Development, and Evaluation*, 2nd ed. (Monterey, Calif.: Brooks/Cole Publishing, 1986).
31. This definition draws on John Hinrich's given in "Personnel Training," in *Handbook of Industrial and Organizational Psychology*, ed. M. Dunnette (Chicago: Rand McNally, 1976); and on Irwin L. Goldstein, *Training in Organizations*, p. 3.
32. Judge Rosalie Silberman Abella, *Equality in Employment: A Royal Commission Report* (Ottawa: Government of Canada, 1984).
33. *Employment Equity: Discussion Paper*, proposed contents for regulations, Bill C-62, Employment Equity (Ottawa: Government of Canada, 1985), p. i.
34. *The Canadian Jobs Strategy: Working Opportunities for People* (Ottawa: Employment and Immigration Canada, 1985). The description of the four programs is based,

with permission of the Minister of Supply and Services Canada, on WH-3-500 (Job Development), WH-3-501 (Skill Shortages), WH-3-498 (Skill Investment), and WH-3-502 (Innovations), all dated September 1985.
35. "Survey of Training in Industry," *Business News*, October 1986.
36. John C. Anderson and Morly Gunderson, *Union Management Relations in Canada* (Reading, Mass.: Addison-Wesley Publishers, 1982).
37. J. Stefan Dupré, David M. Cameron, Graeme H. McKechnie, and Theodore B. Rotenberg, *Federalism and Policy Development: The Care of Adult Occupational Training* (Toronto: University of Toronto Press, 1973).
38. *In the Chips: Opportunities, People, Partnerships*, report of the Labour Canada Task Force on Micro-Electronics and Employment (Ottawa: Minister of Supply and Services Canada, 1982; Cat. No. L35-1982/1E).
39. Charles Snow and Raymond Miles, "Organizational Strategy, Design and Human Resources Management" (paper presented at 43rd meeting of the Academy of Management, Dallas, August 1983).
40. Robert McCarthy and Joseph Yeager, "Training and Change: The Automated Office," *Training and Development Journal*, December 1982, pp. 46–48; A. N. Jones and G. L. Cooper, *Combating Managerial Obsolescence* (Westport, Conn.: Greenwood, 1980).
41. H. Allan Hunt and Timothy L. Hunt, *Human Resources Implications of Robotics* (Kalamazoo, Mich.: W. E. Upjohn Institute for Employment Research, 1982).
42. Linda Argote, Paul S. Goodman, and David Schkade, "The Human Side of Robotics: How Workers React to a Robot," *Sloan Management Review*, Spring 1983, pp. 31–41.
43. *In the Chips*, p. 22.
44. Chris Lee, "Retuning the Auto Industry," *Training*, April 1986, pp. 55–60.
45. Samuel Ehrenholt, "No Golden Age for College Graduates," *Challenge*, July–August 1983, pp. 42–50.
46. Keith Newton, "Impact of New Technology on Employment," *Canadian Business Review*, Winter 1985, pp. 27–30.
47. Carol Fey, "Working with Robots: The Real Story," *Training*, March 1986, pp. 49–51, 56.
48. Kenneth L. Wexley and Gary P. Latham, *Developing and Training Human Resources in Organizations* (Glenview, Ill.: Scott, Foresman, 1981), p. 112.
49. A. P. Goldstein and M. Sorcher, *Changing Supervisory Behavior* (New York: Pergamon Press, 1974).
50. P. R. Pinto and J. W. Walker, "What Do Training and Development Professionals Really Do?" *Training and Development Journal*, July 1978, pp. 58–64.
51. "Take Part in Our HRD Survey," *The Human Resource*, February–March 1986, p. 2.
52. Wayne F. Cascio, *Managing Human Resources* (New York: McGraw Hill, 1986).
53. The three levels of analysis are detailed in W. McGehee and P. W. Thayer, *Training in Business and Industry* (New York: John Wiley & Sons, 1961); see also M. Moore and P. Dutton, "Training Needs Analysis: Review and Critique," *Academy of Management Review* 3 (1978), pp. 532–54; the three specific questions posed are discussed in R. F. Mager and P. Pipe, *Analyzing Performance Problems* (Belmont, Calif.: Pitman Learning, 1984), pp. 7–57.
54. James Walker, *Human Resource Planning* (New York: McGraw-Hill, 1980); James

Walker, "Training and Development," in *Human Resources Management in the 1980s*, ed. Stephen J. Carroll and Randall Schuler (Washington, D.C.: Bureau of National Affairs, 1983).
55. Cascio, *Managing Human Resources*; Bernard Bass and James A. Vaughan, *Training in Industry: The Management of Learning* (Belmont, Calif.: Wadsworth Publishing, 1966).
56. S. Newstrom and J. Lilyquist, "Selecting Needs Analysis Methods," *Training and Development Journal*, October 1979, pp. 52–56.
57. L. A. Digman, "Determining Management Development Needs," *Human Resource Management*, Winter 1980, pp. 12–17.
58. R. F. Mager, *Preparing Instructional Objectives* (Belmont, Calif.: Pitman Learning, 1984), pp. 19–88.
59. Herbert Heneman III, Donald P. Schwab, John A. Fossum, and Lee D. Dyer, *Personnel/Human Resource Management*, 3rd ed. (Homewood, Ill.: Richard D. Irwin, 1986); several sections of this chapter draw heavily on their Chapter 12.
60. W. McGehee and P. Thayer, *Training in Business and Industry* (New York: John Wiley & Sons, 1961).
61. K. W. Wexley and G. P. Latham, *Developing and Training Human Resources in Organizations*, pp. 59–61.
62. D. R. Ilgen, C. D. Fisher, and M. S. Taylor, "Consequences of Individual Feedback on Behavior in Organizations," *Journal of Applied Psychology* 64, no. 4 (1979), pp. 349–71.
63. Wexley and Latham, *Developing and Training*.
64. Melissa Leifer and J. W. Newstrom, "Solving the Transfer of Training Problem," *Training and Development Journal*, August 1980, pp. 42–46.
65. Dov Eden and Gad Ravid, "Pygmalion versus Self-Expectancy: Effects of Instructor and Self-Expectancy on Trainee Performance," *Organizational Behavior and Human Performance* 30 (1982), pp. 351–64.
66. Wexley and Latham, *Developing and Training*.
67. David A. Kolb, "Experiential Learning Theory and the Learning Style Inventory: A Reply to Freedman and Stumpf," *Academy of Management Review* 6, no. 2 (1981), pp. 289–96.
68. Eli Ginzburg, ed., *Employing the Unemployed* (New York: Basic Books, 1980).
69. Wexley and Latham, *Developing and Training*.
70. Heneman, Schwab, et al., *Personnel/Human Resource Management*, 3rd ed.
71. Ora A. Spaid, *The Consummate Trainer: A Practitioner's Perspective* (Englewood Cliffs, N.J.: Reston/Prentice Hall, 1986).
72. Paul Ryan, "Job Training Employment Practices, and the Large Enterprise: The Case of Costly Transferable Skills," in *Internal Labor Markets*, ed. Paul Osterman (Cambridge, Mass.: MIT Press, 1984).
73. Fred Wickert, "The Famous JIT Card: A Basic Way to Improve It," *Training and Development Journal*, February 1974, pp. 6–9.
74. Ronald L. Crawford, "Employee Development," in *Human Resource Management: Contemporary Perspectives in Canada*, ed. K. M. Srinivas (Toronto: McGraw-Hill Ryerson, 1984).
75. *Work for Tomorrow: Employment Opportunities for the '80s* (Ottawa: Published under authority of the Speaker of the House of Commons, (Cat. No. XC2-321/4-01E, undated), pp. 75–76.

76. *Ellis Chart—The Ellis Company Chart of Apprenticeship Training Programmes* (Ottawa: Employment and Immigration Canada, 1985).
77. *Work for Tomorrow*; "Training for Work," *The Economist*, December 20, 1986, pp. 93–101.
78. Jerry I. Porras and Brad Anderson, "Improving Managerial Effectiveness through Modeling-Based Training," *Organizational Dynamics*, Spring 1981, pp. 60–77.
79. P. J. Decker, "The Enhancement of Behavior Modeling Training and Supervisory Skills by the Inclusion of Retension Processes," *Personnel Psychology* 35 (1982), pp. 323–32.
80. C. Argyris, "Some Limitations of the Case Method: Experiences in a Management Development Program," *Academy of Management Review* 5, no. 2 (1980), pp. 291–98.
81. Jeanne M. Brett and James Werbel, *The Effect of Job Transfer on Employees and Their Families* (Washington, D.C.: Employer Relocation Council, 1980); Jeanne M. Brett, "Job Transfer and Well-Being," *Journal of Applied Psychology* 67, no. 4 (1982), pp. 450–63.
82. Karen E. Debats, "The Current State of Corporate Relocation," *Personnel Journal*, September 1982, pp. 664–70.
83. Ceil Blomquist, "Study Shows Relocation Resistance Reversing," *Personnel Administrator*, December 1982, pp. 55–56.
84. Brett and Werbel, *Effect of Job Transfer*.
85. Craig C. Pinder, "Employee Transfer Studies—Summary," Faculty of Commerce and Business Administration, University of British Columbia, Vancouver, B.C., November 8, 1985.
86. Craig C. Pinder, "A Study of Personnel Transfers and Organizational Transfer Policies," *U.B.C. Business Review*, 1979, pp. 25–31.
87. Pinder, "Employee Transfer Studies—Summary," p. 4; John Newstrom, "Evaluating the Effectiveness of Training Methods," *Personnel Administrator*, January 1980, pp. 55–60.
88. Based on material drawn from Heneman et al., *Personnel/Human Resource Management*, 3rd ed.; George T. Milkovich and William F. Glueck, *Personnel/Human Resource Management: A Diagnostic Approach*, 4th ed. (Plano, Tex.: Business Publications, 1985).
89. D. W. Lacey, R. J. Lee, and L. J. Wallace, "Training and Development," in *Personnel Management*, ed. K. Rowland and G. Ferris (Boston: Allyn & Bacon, 1982).
90. Wexley, "Personnel Training," pp. 534–36.
91. Peter Petre, "Games that Teach You to Manage," *Fortune*, October 29, 1984, pp. 67–70.
92. Ibid.
93. Michael M. Lombardo, Morgan W. McCall, Jr., and David L. DeVries, *Looking Glass: Administrator's Guide* (Glenview, Ill.: Scott, Foresman, 1983).
94. Petre, "Games that Teach You to Manage."
95. Ibid.
96. "The FP-UBC Strategic Marketing Challenge: 30 Corporate Teams Test Their Marketing Skills," *Viewpoints*, Spring 1986, p. 4.
97. Ibid., p. 4.
98. William McGehee, "Training and Development."

99. First popularized by G. P. Goldstein and M. Sorcher, *Changing Supervisory Behavior* (New York: Pergamon Press, 1974); see also Wexley and Latham, *Developing and Training*, pp. 176–79.
100. J. S. Russel, K. N. Wexley, and J. E. Hunter, "Questioning the Effectiveness of Behavior Modeling Training in an Industrial Setting," *Personnel Psychology* 37 (1984), pp. 465–82.
101. John Campbell, Marvin D. Dunnette, Edward E. Lawler III, and Karl E. Weick, Jr., *Managerial Behavior, Performance, and Effectiveness* (Toronto: McGraw-Hill Book Company, 1970).
102. Karen Brethower and Geary Rummler, "Evaluating Training," *Training and Development Journal*, May 1979, pp. 14–22.
103. Goldstein, *Training in Organizations*.
104. Cascio, *Applied Psychology in Personnel Management*.
105. H. O. Martin, "The Assessment of Training," *Personnel Management* 39 (1957), pp. 88–93.
106. D. L. Kirkpatrick, "Techniques for Evaluating Training Programs," *Journal of American Society of Training Directors* 13 (1959), pp. 3–9; D. L. Kirkpatrick, "Evaluating Training and Development Programs: Evidence vs. Proof," *Training and Development Journal*, November 1977, pp. 9–12; Cascio, *Applied Psychology in Personnel Management*.
107. The designs reviewed here are based on Claire Sellitz, Marie Jahoda, Morton Deutsch, and Stuart W. Cook, *Research Methods in Social Relations*, rev. one-volume ed. (Toronto: Holt, Rinehart & Winston, 1959), chap. 4.
108. Goldstein, *Training in Organizations*, p. 113; W. J. McKeon, "How to Determine Off-Site Meeting Costs," *Training and Development Journal*, May 1981, pp. 108–20; P. Ryan, "The Costs of Job Training for a Transferable Skill," *The British Journal of Industrial Relations*, November 1983, pp. 334–51.
109. W. J. McKeon, "How to Determine Off-Site Meeting Costs."
110. P. Ryan, "The Costs of Job Training for a Transferable Skill."
111. G. E. Head and G. C. Buchanan, "Cost/Benefit Analysis of Training," *Performance and Instruction*, November 1981, pp. 25–27.
112. Wayne F. Cascio, *Costing Human Resources: The Financial Impact of Behavior in Organizations* (Boston: Kent Publishing Company, 1982).
113. Ibid., p. 208.
114. Ibid.
115. J. G. Cullen, S. A. Swazin, G. R. Sisson, and R. A. Swanson, "Cost Effectiveness: A Model for Assessing the Training Investment," *Training and Development Journal* 32 (1978), pp. 20–29.
116. Greg Kearsley, *Costs, Benefits, and Productivity in Training Systems* (Reading, Mass.: Addison-Wesley Publishing, 1982).

CHAPTER ELEVEN
PERFORMANCE EVALUATION

CHAPTER OUTLINE

I. A Diagnostic Approach to Performance Evaluation
    A. Environmental Conditions
    B. Organizational Conditions
II. Performance Evaluation Effectiveness
    A. Purpose of Performance Evaluation
    B. Reliability and Validity
    C. Sensitivity
    D. Acceptability
    E. Practicality
III. Evaluation Criteria and Standards
    A. Multiple, Global, or Composite Criteria
    B. Measuring Performance Criteria
    C. Standard of Evaluation
IV. Performance Evaluation Methods
    A. Subjective Criteria, Absolute Standard
    B. Objective Criteria, Absolute Standard
    C. Relative Evaluation Methods
    D. Assessment Centres
    E. Using Multiple Techniques
V. The Evaluation Process
    A. Who Should Evaluate?
    B. Processing Performance Information

    C. Performance Evaluation Training
    D. Observing Performance
VI. The Evaluation Interview
VII. Summary
    Appendix A / Performance Evaluation at First City Trust
    Appendix B / Performance Evaluation at Chevron Canada Limited

The 1982 recession forced Imperial Oil Ltd. to take a close look at itself. In the words of Donald McIvor, chief executive officer from 1982 to 1985: "I realized that this organization was as bureaucratic as the post office. There was a horrible stultifying atmosphere." The company rewarded seniority and seemed to stifle individual achievement. Tumbling profits and increasing turbulence in the energy industry caused top management to change this culture. Imperial Oil began to emphasize individual effort and performance.

To accomplish this dramatic transformation, Imperial Oil needed a good performance evaluation system. The company wanted to know which employees were achieving results so they could be properly rewarded. It wanted to identify those who were ready for higher responsibilities in the organization so they could be promoted. Imperial Oil also could no longer afford to retain poor performers. It turned to its performance appraisal system to identify job performance problems so these people could be properly trained or transferred to more suitable jobs.

In 1983, Imperial Oil made performance evaluation a top priority. Its P/HRM department spent 18 months making the system more accurate and acceptable. Employee participation in the process was increased, performance ratings were scrutinized, criteria were more carefully developed, and information about each individual's performance was collected more diligently. The company is more confident that the best people are identified for promotion and reward and that performance problems are more quickly identified and corrected.[1]

Definition

Performance evaluation is a systematic process designed to assess the extent to which employees are performing jobs effectively.

As this definition states, performance evaluation is a formal process. It is designed to regularly and systematically evaluate employee performance on specified criteria. (Criteria are standards of excellence against which the employee is compared.) This should be contrasted with the informal discussions supervisors have with their employees on a daily or weekly basis. Informal counselling and coaching are important activities in the development of employees. However, spontaneous evaluations of employee performance are subject to political and interpersonal biases and must not replace the formal process. Formal performance evaluation is the focus of this chapter.

Performance evaluation is another P/HRM activity that involves both operating managers and P/HRM specialists. Generally, P/HRM specialists design the performance evaluation system, train the operating managers in the use of these systems, and maintain the records. Operating managers conduct the evaluation and discuss the results with their employees. Without top management commitment, however, performance evaluation can become a paperwork exercise.[2] Says the former CEO of Imperial Oil: "We all take performance appraisals seriously. I hope that my managers view it not just as a chore, but as one of the most important duties of being a supervisor."[3]

A DIAGNOSTIC APPROACH TO PERFORMANCE EVALUATION

Environmental Conditions

As with most P/HRM activities, government regulations are a significant external factor influencing the design and operation of a performance evaluation system. Human rights legislation requires employers to demonstrate that they do not discriminate against designated groups in deciding promotions, pay raises, or training opportunities. Common law and labour union rights also affect the performance evaluation system.

Human Rights Cases

A growing number of human rights tribunals in Canada have discussed the quality of performance evaluation data. One of the main concerns raised in these cases is the validity and objectivity of the system. For example, Ontario Hydro was found to have discriminated when it used a ranking procedure with no clear set of performance criteria to lay off employees.[4] The ranking had an adverse effect on the employment of black employees.

Another Ontario Human Rights Commission tribunal harshly criticized the poor quality of an employer's performance evaluation system. In addition to rejecting the evaluation results, the tribunal saw the poorly designed system as further evidence of the employer's tendency to use discriminatory practices.[5] Other human rights cases have emphasized the need to properly communicate performance information to employees.[6]

Some human rights tribunals refer to U.S. cases with respect to the quality of performance evaluation systems. Canadian P/HRM managers are advised to look closely at these decisions and their implications in this country.[7]

Wrongful Dismissal Cases

Employees have certain common law rights (civil law rights in Quebec) protected by the courts. These employee rights will be discussed in more detail in Chapter Twelve. However, we should mention that several court decisions have considered the quality of the performance evaluation system in deciding the weight of performance results presented. In particular, judges will determine whether the performance criteria are reasonable, whether performance problems could be attributed to the employee, and whether the employer's concerns about poor performance were clearly communicated to the employee.[8] Some judges have even awarded compensation for mental distress in cases where the employee was subjected to an ill-conceived performance evaluation.[9]

Labour Unions

Unions can have a profound effect on performance evaluation. With a strong interest in seniority-based decisions, unions often oppose implementation of performance-based systems or try to limit application of performance ratings. They are also concerned about inequities resulting from poorly designed systems. This does not mean performance evaluations are absent from unionized firms. Rather, employers must work harder to gain employee acceptance of the performance evaluation process and outcomes.

Union influence on the performance evaluation system is evident in labour arbitration decisions. Some arbitration hearings will not allow performance evaluation information because the collective agreement prevents this information from being used for disciplinary purposes.[10] Where performance ratings can be introduced as evidence, arbitrators may look carefully at the conditions under which the evaluation is conducted, including the degree of mutual trust and employee participation in the process.[11]

Organizational Conditions

As Exhibit 11–1 indicates, performance evaluations are linked with other P/HRM activities. Through job analysis and interpretation of organizational objectives, performance standards are established.[12] Next, evaluation systems are designed to assist managers and employees in developing a common set of performance expectations. Performance is evaluated over a predetermined period of time, and the manager's observations are fed back to employees. These performance results are also used to make other P/HRM decisions.

EXHIBIT 11–1
Performance Evaluation Process

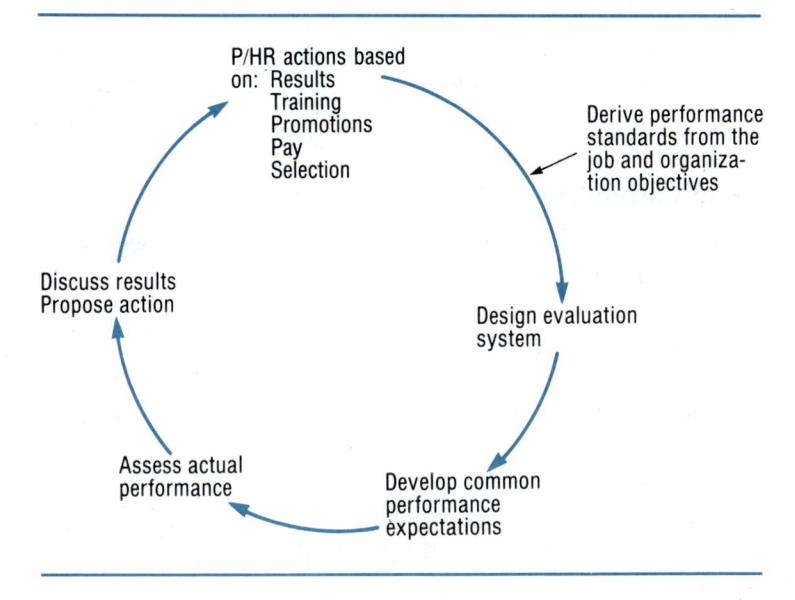

```
        P/HR actions based
        on: Results
            Training              Derive performance
            Promotions            standards from the
            Pay                   job and organiza-
            Selection             tion objectives


Discuss results
Propose action
                                  Design evaluation
                                  system


Assess actual
performance         Develop common
                    performance
                    expectations
```

The particular evaluation system used may be affected by the nature of the work, the employee characteristics, and the abilities of supervisors using the process. For example, employees in professional and managerial jobs are more likely than some blue-collar jobs to receive formal performance evaluation. Performance in professional and managerial jobs is not as easily measured in the short term by quantifiable units of output. Instead, performance includes the quality of interpersonal activities, dependability under deadlines, problem-solving initiative, and other intangibles.[13] Performance evaluation systems try to capture these complex and often subjective dimensions, whereas blue-collar performance is fairly accurately captured by objective criteria alone.

Generally, employees want to be recognized for their good performance. To high achievers, the performance evaluation process is particularly important. If this process is badly handled, morale may decline, unwanted turnover may increase, and productivity may drop. If employees think the evaluation process is unfair, the performance→outcome (reward) link described in expectancy theory weakens, resulting in lower motivation (see Chapter Five). So the degree of trust among employees and supervisors also influences the design and ultimate effectiveness of performance evaluation systems.

PERFORMANCE EVALUATION EFFECTIVENESS

A variety of performance evaluation systems are used throughout Canada. P/HRM professionals must consider several factors before deciding which performance evaluation system will be most effective for their organization.

Purpose of Performance Evaluation

In the opening story, Imperial Oil rediscovered the important role performance evaluation plays in organizational effectiveness. In that organization as well as others, the performance evaluation system serves two fairly distinct purposes: evaluative and developmental.

Evaluative. As its name implies, performance evaluation is used to rate the performance of individual employees. This information becomes the basis for strategic reward decisions. In particular, performance ratings are used to determine salary increases, decide layoffs and dismissals, and award promotions. Many Canadian organizations—such as Imperial Oil, NOVA, and General Motors of Canada—have placed greater emphasis on performance evaluation results to decide salary increases.[14] A major Canadian study on organizational retrenchment also discovered that performance ratings are used extensively in dismissing employees with marginal performance records.[15]

Developmental. Performance evaluation results are also used to develop employees. This is accomplished by using performance results to communicate performance improvement and feedback as well as to decide which employees require further training. Used for developmental purposes, performance evaluation systems provide a variety of benefits. They give managers the opportunity to demonstrate their interest in employee development. This interest can help retain ambitious, capable employees instead of losing them to competitors. They provide encouragement to the employee who has been trying to perform well. They also provide a formalized means of communicating and documenting dissatisfaction with unacceptable employee performance and efforts to improve it.[16]

Organizations typically use their performance evaluation system for both evaluative and developmental purposes. Unfortunately, systems introduced for developmental purposes may not be suited for evaluative purposes.[17] It is therefore important that the organization understands why it requires a performance evaluation system and selects the system that best meets those requirements.

It is also important that the performance evaluation results are actually used. For example, a work force audit at the Secretary of State in 1981 discovered that, contrary to policy, its administrators usually ignored performance evaluation ratings when making promotion decisions. As a result, women in the department were significantly underrepresented in managerial ranks even though they tended to have high performance ratings.[18]

Reliability and Validity

The effectiveness of a performance evaluation system also depends on whether the results are both reliable and valid. Recall from Chapter Nine that reliability refers to the consistency of measurement. In the context of performance evaluation, reliability means different raters arrived at the same performance ratings for a particular employee during the same performance period (conspect or inter-rater reliability). It also means the performance ratings provided by one rater do not change within a very short period of time, such as a few hours or days (test-retest reliability).[19]

Validity refers to the idea that performance ratings accurately estimate the employee's true performance level during the performance period. This is called construct validity (see Chapter Nine) because we are interested in knowing how accurately the performance evaluation instrument measures th theoretical construct (in this case, employee performance).[20]

To accurately measure employee performance, the evaluation criteria must be tied to the critical elements of the employee's job. Consequently, job analysis is the foundation on which valid performance evaluation systems are built. All of the relevant performance dimensions should be included in the evaluation instrument. These job elements must be linked with organizational objectives. At the same time, the evaluation system should ignore information that is either irrelevant to job performance or beyond the control of job incumbents.

The construct validity of a particular evaluation system depends on its use. Performance criteria used for making merit increase decisions might not provide valid information for making promotion decisions. This is because some of the performance dimensions relevant to the current job may not be relevant in the job to which the employee is promoted. In this respect, the anticipated use of the performance evaluation results determine the appropriate evaluation criteria.

Sensitivity

The performance evaluation system should be sufficiently sensitive to differentiate among employees and performance dimensions.[21] Systems designed for evaluative purposes need to differentiate employees so the higher performers receive higher rewards. For developmental purposes, performance systems need to differentiate the various performance dimensions within each employee so the job performance aspects needing improvement are clearly identified.

Sensitivity may seem like a rather obvious characteristic of an effective evaluation system, but some systems do not distinguish among employees or dimensions very well. One problem is that there are too few (or too many) levels on the rating scale. Some performance evaluation instruments give the evaluator only three performance levels (satisfactory, unsatisfactory, unable to evaluate) on which to rate the employee when six or seven levels could actually be distinguished.

Another problem is that evaluators fail to distinguish among employees or performance dimensions because of rater bias and cognitive distortions. As we will later discuss, some supervisors tend to rate all employees near the middle or top of the scale. In other cases, an employee is given the same rating for all performance dimensions even though he or she actually performs well on some dimensions and poorly on others.

Acceptability

Employee attitude toward the performance evaluation system is one of the most important and, until recently, most overlooked characteristics of an effective performance evaluation system.[22] *Perceived fairness* of the evaluation system is the watchword here. The extent to which employees believe the evaluation process is fair has a strong influence on the credibility and meaningfulness of the performance results. This may influence employee motivation as well as organizational commitment and turnover.[23]

The perceived fairness of the evaluation system is affected by the favourableness of the employee's performance ratings. Those with better ratings are more likely to believe the system is fair. Controlling for favourable outcomes, several characteristics of the performance evaluation process also seem to affect perceived fairness. A recent study of performance evaluation in two large Canadian organizations discovered the characteristics affecting employee fairness perceptions may vary with organizational and job characteristics.[24] In general, however, employees are more likely to believe the system is fair when:[25]

- Employees are given the opportunity to participate in the evaluation process.
- Performance outcomes are based on established and agreed on goals, and these objectives are discussed in the performance interview.
- Employees believe the rater is knowledgeable of the job and has had sufficient opportunity to observe the employee perform the job.
- The performance dimensions on which employees are evaluated are perceived to be relevant.
- The performance evaluation is conducted at least once a year.

Supervisors must also accept the performance evaluation system. Evaluators who believe in the legitimacy of the system may be more motivated to avoid rating errors and thereby rate employees accurately. According to Bernardin and Beatty, rater motivation could explain much of the difference between accurate and inaccurate performance evaluation results.[26]

Practicality

One of the realities of managing organizations is that the goal of collecting accurate information often conflicts with the goal of minimizing costs. A system requiring supervisors to daily record critical performance incidents on each employee may be effective in terms of accurate ratings and employee perceptions of fairness. But the system would be costly and probably soundly rejected by most supervisors. Many well-intentioned performance evaluation systems have failed because their developers did not consider the administrative realities of time and cost.[27] In other situations, the performance evaluation system may be relatively easy to use but is prohibitively costly to develop.

Jones conducted a systematic assessment of evaluation costs in one situation.[28] Costs from development stages through maintenance are shown in Exhibit 11-2. Notice that the earliest costs are for job analysis. Cost per rating is approximately $34. Is this cost reasonable? The answer depends on the quality of information resulting from the evaluation and the appropriateness of the uses to which this information is applied. Further cost-benefit studies are required to judge the practicality of the entire performance evaluation system.[29]

Individualization versus Standardization

Practicality also becomes an issue in the conflicting goals of individualizing and standardizing the performance evaluation system.[30] Recall that performance evaluation criteria must be tied to the critical elements of the employee's job in order to accurately measure performance. To accomplish this, the system should be individualized to the point where each job uses a different evaluation instrument. Some methods we will later describe, such as management by objectives, tailor performance criteria to individual jobs.

Unfortunately, highly individualized systems are often expensive to develop because each job group requires its own evaluation instrument. Individualized systems may also be impractical for evaluative purposes such as salary decision making because these P/HRM decisions require standardized information on employees in different jobs. In effect, individualized systems make it more difficult to compare employees in different jobs.[31] For these reasons, many organizations rely on only one or two standardized instruments for

EXHIBIT 11-2
Cost Estimates of the Elements in a Performance Appraisal System

Cost Element	1975–1977	1977–1978
Operating costs		
DP production	$ 11,406.00	$ 3,483.00
DP develop and enhancement	41,688.00	14,643.00
Keypunch (hardware)	0.00	385.00
Paper (OPM)	1,691.00	179.00
Paper (agency)	N/D	637.00
Mailing and distribution (postage and messenger)	500.00	6,583.00
Training workshops (5 hrs.)	0.00	23,492.00
Total operations cost	$ 55,285.00	$ 49,402.00
Operations cost per rating	$ 0.00	$ 9.31
Staffing costs		
Job knowledge experts (time)	$ 15,072.00	$ 0.00
Job analyst (time)	21,887.00	0.00
Clerical support (OPM)	10,179.00	6,786.00
Professional coordinator (1)	0.00	7,223.00
Rater time	0.00	80,696.00
Ratee time	0.00	29,783.00
Clerical processing (Agency)	1,000.00	4,353.00
Consultant	25,480.00	1,500.00
Staffing totals	$ 73,618.00	$130,341.00
Staffing cost per rating	$ 0.00	$ 24.55
Grand totals	$128,903.00	$179,743.00
Cost per rating		$ 33.86

Source: M. A. Jones, "Estimating Costs in the Development and Implementation of a Performance Appraisal System" (paper presented at the first annual Scientist-Practitioner Conference in Industrial-Organizational Psychology, Old Dominion University, Norfolk, Va., 1980).

employees in most job groups (e.g., one for management and another for nonmanagement staff). Standardized systems may result in less accurate performance results because employees in some jobs are evaluated on irrelevant criteria. Yet they allow the organization to compare results across employees in a wide spectrum of jobs at a reasonable cost. P/HRM specialists must decide the optimal balance between the cost and utility of individualized systems and the imperfection of standardized systems.

EVALUATION CRITERIA AND STANDARDS

Properly developed performance evaluation systems must carefully consider the relevant dimensions of the job and the corresponding criteria on which the job incumbent will be rated. Two questions must be answered in this regard: (1) Should the system use multiple, global, or composite criteria? and (2) How should these criteria be measured? Once the criteria have been established, the P/HRM manager must make a third decision: the standard against which employee performance is compared. We address each of these issues in this section.

Multiple, Global, or Composite Criteria

Job performance is multidimensional. A foreign exchange trader at the Bank of Montreal, for example, must be able to identify profitable trades when they arise, work cooperatively (in a stressful environment) with account representatives and customers, assist in training new staff, and work on special telecommunications equipment without error. Properly developed performance evaluation systems should include all relevant dimensions pertaining to the employee's job.[32] By considering all dimensions, evaluators provide more accurate estimates of each employee's total performance.

Multiple Criteria. A logical way to assess employee performance on all dimensions is to use multiple criteria in the performance evaluation instrument. By rating each dimension, supervisors are more likely to have a common understanding of job performance. The information available from the multiple criteria approach is also beneficial for developmental purposes. Supervisors are able to document the areas where employees have performed well and the areas where improvement is required. Exhibit 11–3 lists some multiple criteria used in standard rating scales. Exhibit 11–4 shows some multiple criteria in a management-by-objectives system used to evaluate sales representatives.

While multiple criteria improve the quality of performance feedback, organizations also need a single overall rating of employee performance to make decisions such as salary increases.[33] This is accomplished either by having evaluators provide a global rating of performance or by creating a composite performance score.

EXHIBIT 11–3
Some Multiple Criteria Used in Standard Ratings Scales

Work attitude	Work under pressure
Dependability	Interaction with others
Adaptability	Reliability/responsibility
Punctuality	Resourcefulness
Communication skills	Job knowledge
Judgement	Quality of work
Initiative	Supervisory skills
Leadership skills	Quantity of work

EXHIBIT 11-4
Multiple Criteria Used in an MBO Evaluation Report for Salespersons

Objectives Set	Period Objective	Accomplishments	Variance
1. Number of sales calls	100	104	+4%
2. Number of new customers contacted	20	18	−10
3. Number of wholesalers stocking new product 117	30	30	0
4. Sales of product 12	10,000	9,750	−2.5
5. Sales of product 17	17,000	18,700	+10
6. Customer complaints/service calls	35	11	−68.6
7. Number of sales correspondence courses successfully completed	4	2	−50
8. Number of sales reports in home office within 1 day of end of month	12	10	−17

Global Criterion. According to one survey, many Canadian organizations use global ratings for evaluative purposes and are apparently satisfied with this system.[34] Global ratings are usually the supervisor's overall impression of employee performance, although specific results or behaviours are sometimes used. At First City Trust, for example, supervisors are asked to assign an overall performance rating to each employee ranging from "unsatisfactory" to "excellent." This is in addition to their ratings of employee performance on specific performance dimensions (see Appendix A).

When arriving at an overall rating, the supervisor should consider how well the employee has performed in each aspect of the job. But global ratings can lead to inconsistent weighting of performance dimensions from one employee to the next. Supervisors may emphasize the quality of work when deciding the overall performance of one individual and practically ignore that dimension for another employee in the same job.[35]

Composite Criterion. Rather than relying on global impressions, some performance evaluation systems use the composite criterion approach to arrive at a single performance score for each employee. A composite criterion is simply a statistical combination of multiple criteria. Supervisors rate employees on each performance dimension. Each employee's ratings are then combined to create a single overall score. Composite scores are superior to global ratings because they ensure the relevant dimensions are not overweighted or excluded from the single score.

Your instructor probably uses the composite approach to determine the performance of students in this course. Exams, cases, and other assignments are weighted and summed to arrive at a single final grade. Contrast this with the global criterion method. Using the global approach, the instructor looks at assignment grades and then assigns a final grade based on his or her overall impression of your performance in the course. You can see why students and employees alike feel more comfortable with the composite criterion approach.

Weighting Criteria

Using the composite criterion approach raises another question: How do we weight performance criteria? Generally, criteria are weighted according to their importance. The relative importance of each performance dimension may be a topic of negotiation between the employer and employee. At both Cominco and the Bank of Montreal, performance criteria weights are based on an importance index in the job description.

Carroll and Schneier provide some alternate weighting methods in Exhibit 11–5.[36] Some of these methods can become very statistical and may not be understood or accepted by employees. This jeopardizes the perceived fairness of the evaluation system. Some may require an unreasonable amount of time and effort to calculate. Consequently, the validity, acceptability, and practicality of these methods must be carefully compared with a simple method of equally weighting the ratings assigned to each performance dimension.

EXHIBIT 11–5
Methods for Weighting Subcriteria

1. Judgement	Experts judge the relative importance of each subcriterion to overall job performance or success on the job.
2. Reliability	Subcriteria on which multiple judges agree most regarding their ratings are weighted highest.
3. Predictability	Subcriteria that are most closely related or highly correlated with overall performance are weighted highest.
4. Factor analysis	A statistical technique reduces the number of subcriteria into a more meaningful, somewhat mutually exclusive set, with weights determined by statistical properties.
5. Correlation	Weights are determined by the degree to which subcriteria are correlated with, and hence in a sense redundant with, other subcriteria.
6. Dollar value	Weights are assigned relative to the dollar value of each subcriterion to job success or to the organization's effectiveness.
7. Equality	All subcriteria are weighted equally.

Source: Stephen J. Carroll and Craig E. Schneier, *Performance Appraisal and Review Systems* (Glenview, Ill.: Scott, Foresman, 1982), p. 34. Copyright © 1982 by Scott, Foresman and Company. Reprinted by permission.

Measuring Performance Criteria

Performance criteria vary in the extent to which they are results-oriented and objectively based. Exhibit 11–6 provides examples of these two perspectives of performance criteria.

Results versus Process Criteria

Results-oriented criteria focus on the outcomes of the employee's work, whereas process-oriented criteria examine employee performance on the work process. Results-oriented methods have the advantage of linking criteria directly with organizational objectives. It is fairly easy to see that sales volume and product quality measures are associated with organizational effectiveness. It is less clear that process criteria, such as the number of clients contacted each month, are linked to organizational effectiveness.

Results-oriented criteria have their problems, however. The results of an employee's effort may not be easily measured or may become apparent only after several years. Measuring performance with short-term results may omit important performance dimensions or may lead to "the end justifies the means" philosophy. Results-oriented criteria may also be inadequate for de-

EXHIBIT 11–6
Types of Performance Criteria

	Subjective Criteria	Objective Criteria
Process Oriented	Initiative Dependability Enthusiasm	Checks equipment at the end of shift Follows safety procedures
Results Oriented	Customer satisfaction Quality of work	Percent wastage Sales volume

veloping employees because they don't indicate *why* the employee has poor results. Consequently, many evaluation systems also include process-oriented performance criteria.[37]

Objective versus Subjective Criteria

Performance evaluation criteria also vary in the degree to which they are objectively based. Objectively based criteria focus on observable information such as quantifiable results or employee behaviours. For the "quality of work" dimension of a professional engineer's job performance, for example, the supervisor might record the percentage of assignments in which significant errors were detected. Subjective criteria, on the other hand, are the evaluator's personal impressions of employee performance. Using a subjective evaluation system to record the "quality of work" dimension, the project engineer's supervisor recalls errors made over the past year and indicates whether this performance is "unsatisfactory," "commendable," or some other performance level.

Objectively based criteria are usually considered superior to subjective criteria because the rater simply records the presence of employee behaviours or results. This supposedly minimizes the rater's personal biases because no subjective judgements are made. However, Carroll and Schneier argue that objective measures are also vulnerable to rating errors. Moreover, subjective criteria are better able to capture performance dimensions that are difficult to observe and quantify.[38]

Standard of Evaluation

All performance evaluations are based on either a relative or absolute standard against which employee performance is compared. Relative standard systems compare employee performance with that of other employees. Actual performance is rated as "outstanding" only if it exceeds the performance of most other employees in the department or organization. Thus, the employee's performance results depend on how well other employees have performed.

In absolute standard methods, the supervisor compares actual performance with a carefully constructed definition of the various levels of proficiency. For example, an absolute evaluation method may have a clear definition of the quality of work required and the level of accomplishment deserving an "outstanding" performance rating. As we shall see in the following section, most performance evaluation methods use an absolute standard. However, employee ranking and other relative standards are still used, particularly for evaluative purposes.

PERFORMANCE EVALUATION METHODS

So far, we have distinguished performance evaluation systems based on whether the criteria used: (1) are multiple, global, or composite; (2) are results- or process-oriented; (3) are objectively or subjectively based; and (4) use a relative or absolute standard of comparison. This produces a wide variety of procedures with which to evaluate employee performance. Some methods, such as standard rating scales and management by objectives, are commonly found in Canadian industry. Other methods have gained the respect of academic researchers but have received limited application in business.

To help organize this section, we categorize the performance evaluation techniques based on whether they use objective or subjective criteria and an absolute or relative standard of comparison. Most performance evaluation methods fall into one of the four categories shown in Exhibit 11–7. However, any of these methods may use multiple or global criteria and may include a combination of results-oriented and process-oriented criteria.

Subjective Criteria, Absolute Standard

Several performance evaluation systems require the evaluator to provide subjective impressions of employee performance against an absolute standard.

EXHIBIT 11–7
Taxonomy of Performance Evaluation Methods

	Subjective Criteria	Objective Criteria
Absolute Standard	Standard rating scales Behaviourally anchored rated scales	Behavioural observation scales Management by objectives Weighted checklists Mixed standard scales
Relative Standard	Alternation ranking Paired comparison Forced distribution	Alternation ranking Paired comparison Forced distribution

Standard Rating Scales

One of the oldest and most widely used performance evaluation techniques is the standard (or graphic) rating scale.[39] In this technique, the evaluator is presented with a list of subjective performance dimensions (such as "quality of work") on which each employee is rated. In some cases, the evaluator has the option of using only dimensions that clearly apply to the individual's job. More often, all employees are evaluated on all dimensions. Standard rating scales are popular because they provide standardized results and require relatively little time to complete. They are also more acceptable and easier to use for those doing the evaluation.[40]

Exhibit 11–8 shows an example of a standard rating scale used by Air Canada. This instrument includes seven performance dimensions and is used for administrative and technical support personnel. The evaluator rates each dimension of the employee's performance on a six-point scale—from "unsatisfactory" to "outstanding"—and provides written comments on each dimension. Each of the four performance levels is defined. The evaluator also provides a global rating of the employee's performance.

Despite their popularity, standard rating scales have received much criticism. Since most dimensions are broadly defined, this method may provide inadequate information for developmental purposes such as employee feedback and training needs assessment.[41] Standard ratings are subject to a number of rating errors (which we will discuss later) because evaluators make subjective value judgements. Other studies, however, suggest this procedure can be quite reliable and valid, particularly when the evaluators are properly trained.[42]

Standard rating scales can also be improved by clearly defining each performance dimension and anchoring each level on the rating scale.[43] For example, the first scale format (a) in Exhibit 11–9 may lead to inaccurate results because the performance dimension is ambiguous and the performance levels are undefined. The second format (b) is better, but the meaning of the performance levels may still be ambiguous. If evaluators have different interpretations of "average," then employees may be rated inconsistently from one department to the next. The final format (c) should provide the most reliable and valid results because the performance dimension is defined and the performance levels are clearly anchored.

Behaviourally Anchored Rating Scales

Behaviourally anchored rating scales (BARS) are standard rating scales with the performance levels anchored by job-related behaviours. The last rating format (c) in Exhibit 11–9 would become a BARS if the performance levels were defined behaviourally. By anchoring scales with concrete behaviours, the BARS format makes the standard rating scale even less subjective.

EXHIBIT 11–8
Example of a Standard Performance Rating Scale

PERFORMANCE REVIEW - ADMINISTRATIVE & TECHNICAL SUPPORT PERSONNEL
ÉVALUATION DU RENDEMENT - PERSONNEL DE SOUTIEN ADMINISTRATIF ET TECHNIQUE

PLEASE REFER TO GUIDELINES ON REVERSE FOR COMPLETION *POUR REMPLIR LA FICHE, VOIR DIRECTIVES AU VERSO*

Emp. No. *Matricule*	Name *Nom*	Title *Fonction*	Location *Lieu*

Group *Groupe*	Service Date *Date d'entrée en service*	Entry date present job *Date d'affectation au poste actuel*	Review date *Date de l'évaluation*	Last review date *Date de la dernière évaluation*	Next review date *Date de la prochaine évaluation*

Probation - First 6 months *Fin période d'essai*	Six months Review *Évaluation semestrielle*	Annual Review *Évaluation annuelle*
☐	☐	☐

CHECK APPROPRIATE BOX
COCHER LA CASE APPROPRIÉE

		OUTSTANDING *EXCEPTIONNEL*	SUPERIOR *SUPÉRIEUR*	FULLY COMPETENT *PLEINEMENT SATISFAISANT*	SOME IMPROVEMENT/DEVELOPMENT REQUIRED *À AMÉLIORER/PERFECTIONNER LÉGÈREMENT*	SUBSTANTIAL IMPROVEMENT REQUIRED *À AMÉLIORER NETTEMENT*	UNSATISFACTORY *INSATISFAISANT*	**COMMENTS** (including development recommendations) ***OBSERVATIONS*** *(y compris les recommandations de perfectionnement)*
RESULTS *RÉSULTATS*	WORK ACCOMPLISHMENTS — QUALITY OF WORK *RÉALISATIONS PROFESSIONNELES — QUALITÉ DU TRAVAIL*							
	WORK ACCOMPLISHMENTS — QUANTITY OF WORK *RÉALISATIONS PROFESSIONNELLES — QUANTITÉ DE TRAVAIL*							
SKILLS *APTITUDES*	ATTITUDE & INTERPERSONAL SKILLS COMPORTEMENT ET RELATIONS AVEC AUTRUI							
	INITIATIVE *INITIATIVE*							
	ABILITY TO LEARN, INCLUDING SELF DEVELOPMENT ACTIVITIES *FACILITÉ D'ADAPTATION, EFFORTS DE PERFECTIONNEMENT*							
	TECHNICAL SKILLS *QUALITÉS TECHNIQUES*							
	ATTENDANCE, PUNCTUALITY *ASSIDUITÉ, PONCTUALITÉ*							
OVERALL PERFORMANCE *NOTATION GÉNÉRALE*								

	Name *Nom*	Title *Fonction*	Date
Prepared by *Établi par*			
Approved By *Visa*			

Employee's comments, interests & aspirations
Observations de l'employé, intérêts & aspirations

Employee's Signature
Signature de l'employé

ACF683A(9-87)

EXHIBIT 11–8 *(concluded)*

PERFORMANCE REVIEW
ADMINISTRATIVE & TECHNICAL SUPPORT PERSONNEL

It is Air Canada's objective to have its managers/supervisors conduct performance reviews with all their subordinates in the Administrative and Technical Support/Technical category.

For individuals who are progressing through the salary scale this review must occur immediately before the granting of the progression increases, which takes place every 26 weeks. For employees who have attained the maximum of the scale this review must take place each year between mid-December and mid-March prior to the salary schedule change and the general increase.

THE REVIEW PROCESS

PREPARATION

The manager should review the individual's performance for the period covered against the factors outlined on the reverse side. The Manager should assess the level of performance on each factor and provide supporting comments. The manager should obtain information from any other party who had any dealings with the individual.

DISCUSSION AND DOCUMENTATION

In a meeting with the subordinate the manager should review and discuss the subordinate's performance in terms of strengths and weaknesses. The manager should also recommend corrective action to improve performance, as required. For individuals whose performance is exceptional or below standards: the manager should recommend a specific salary adjustment as per Publication 706. Pay Administration, Chapter 5.

In the "Overall evaluation & comments" section the manager can summarize, as required, the subordinate's interests and aspirations, as well as development recommendations.

EMPLOYEE'S COMMENTS

Self explanatory.

CONCLUSION

The original of the form is forwarded to the local Personnel Services office for action and filing in the individual's personal file.

LEVELS OF PERFORMANCE

OUTSTANDING

Usually high level of accomplishment **in all major** areas. Performance and results are consistently and significantly above expected level.

SUPERIOR

Performance in **some major areas** of responsibility exceeds the fully competent level, and in all other areas can be rated as fully competent.

FULLY COMPETENT

All areas of responsibility are performed at a competent level, job requirements and expected results are met.

SOME IMPROVEMENT/DEVELOPMENT REQUIRED

Most major areas of responsibility are performed at the competent level. However to achieve proficiency in all areas, some improvement is required.

SUBSTANTIAL IMPROVEMENT REQUIRED

Performance is **inconsistent** and is frequently below minimum job requirements. Substantial improvement is required before performance can be regarded as satisfactory.

UNSATISFACTORY

Performance is **consistently** below minimum job requirements. For newer incumbent, there is little or no evidence of progress toward the fully competent level.

ÉVALUATION DU RENDEMENT
PERSONNEL DE SOUTIEN ADMINISTRATIF ET TECHNIQUE

Air Canada s'est proposée de demander aux chefs de service et responsables de faire une évaluation du rendement de tout leur personnel de soutien administratif et technique.

Pour les employés dont l'avancement suit l'échelle des salaires, cette évaluation se fera juste avant l'augmentation de salaire qui a lieu toutes les 26 semaines. Pour les employés qui ont atteint le haut de l'échelle, l'évaluation se fera entre la mi-décembre et la mi-mars, avant l'augmentation de salaire habituelle.

LA MÉTHODE D'ÉVALUATION

PRÉPARATION

Le supérieur doit évaluer le rendement de l'employé pendant la période couverte en se référant aux éléments considérés dans la fiche. Pour chacun de ces éléments, il doit évaluer le niveau de l'employé et apporter des commentaires à l'appui. Pour cela, il se renseigne auprès de toute personne ayant eu affaire à l'employé.

DISCUSSION ET UTILISATION DE LA FICHE

Au cours d'une entrevue avec le subalterne, le supérieur évalue les points forts et les points faibles de l'employé et en discute avec l'intéressé. Au besoin il précise quelles sont les mesures à prendre pour améliorer son rendement. Conformément au chapitre 5 de la publication 706 (Gestion des salaires), le supérieur, dans le cas d'un employé dont le rendement est supérieur ou inférieur au niveau demandé, indique comment cela doit se traduire sur le salaire.

Dans la section "Évaluation globale et observations" le supérieur peut résumer, au besoin, les souhaits et aspirations du subalterne, y compris les recommandations de perfectionnement.

OBSERVATIONS DE L'EMPLOYÉ

explicite

CONCLUSION

L'original doit être envoyé au bureau local des Services du Personnel qui prend les mesures nécessaires et classe la fiche dans le dossier de l'employé.

NIVEAUX DE RENDEMENT

EXCEPTIONNEL

Le niveau des réalisations est exceptionnellement élevé. Le rendement dépasse largement et constamment les critères normaux dans **tous les domaines** de responsabilités.

SUPÉRIEUR

Le rendement est plus que satisfaisant dans **certains des principaux domaines** de responsabilités et est pleinement satisfaisant dans tous les autres.

PLEINEMENT SATISFAISANT

Le rendement est d'un bon niveau dans **tous les domaines** de responsabilités et les résultats sont jugés pleinement satisfaisants.

À AMÉLIORER/PERFECTIONNER LÉGÈREMENT

Le rendement est satisfaisant dans **la plupart des principaux domaines** de responsabilités. Certaines améliorations sont toutefois indiquées pour atteindre un niveau satisfaisant dans tous les domaines.

À AMÉLIORER NETTEMENT

Le rendement est **irrégulier** et souvent inférieur aux exigences du poste. Des améliorations substantielles sont indiquées pour atteindre un niveau jugé satisfaisant.

INSATISFAISANT

Le rendement est constamment **inférieur** aux exigences du poste. Peu ou aucun progrès n'a été démontré en vue d'atteindre un niveau pleinement satisfaisant.

Reproduced with permission of Air Canada

EXHIBIT 11-9
Anchoring Standard Rating Scales

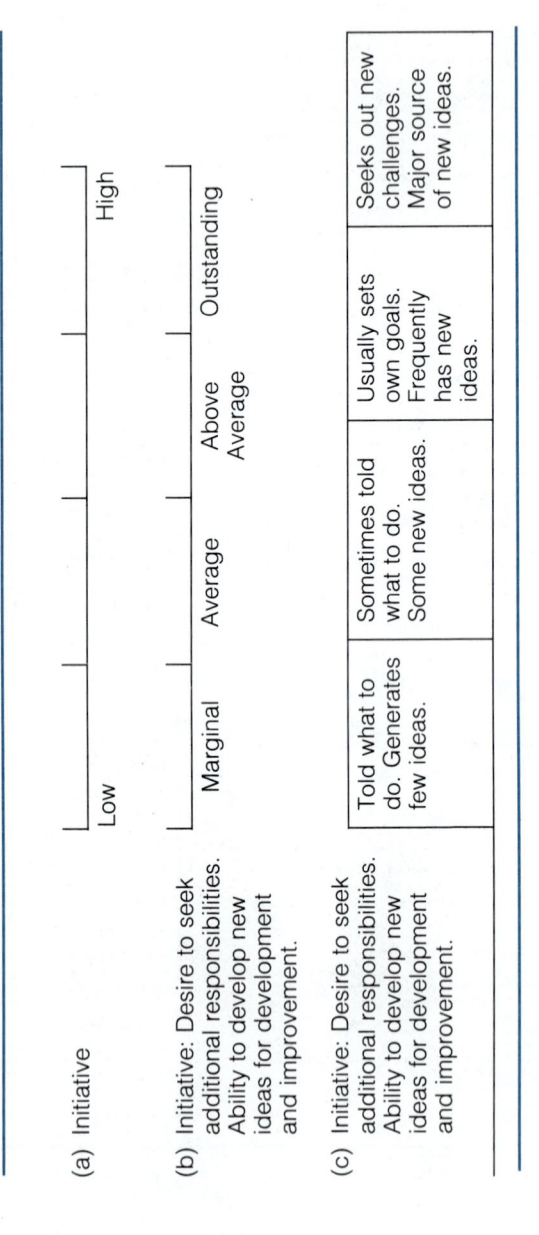

(a) Initiative

|———|———|———|———|———|
Low   High

(b) Initiative: Desire to seek additional responsibilities. Ability to develop new ideas for development and improvement.

|———|———|———|———|———|
Marginal   Average   Above Average   Outstanding

(c) Initiative: Desire to seek additional responsibilities. Ability to develop new ideas for development and improvement.

Told what to do. Generates few ideas.	Sometimes told what to do. Some new ideas.	Usually sets own goals. Frequently has new ideas.	Seeks out new challenges. Major source of new ideas.

The development of BARS, which can be time-consuming, usually includes the following steps.[44] First, supervisors or other "experts" describe specific examples of both effective and ineffective behaviour in a particular job. These *critical incidents* are clustered into a smaller set of performance dimensions, usually by P/HRM specialists. A second group of people familiar with the job then assigns each incident to the performance dimensions developed in the previous step. Incidents that are not consistently placed into the same dimension are discarded. This group of participants also rates each incident in terms of its effectiveness or ineffectiveness on the assigned dimension. The average effectiveness rating is used to place each incident on the scale range. Incidents with wide-ranging effectiveness ratings are discarded.

Exhibit 11–10 illustrates a BARS scale used to evaluate the performance of logging crew supervisors with respect to crew training in a Canadian forest

**EXHIBIT 11–10
Behaviourally Anchored Rating Scale for One Dimension of Logging Crew Supervisor Performance**

	Job Dimension: Ensures Effective Crew Training
Totally unacceptable (incompetent)	Ignores agreed on training procedures. Doesn't have sufficiently trained back-up on key jobs. When crew member calls in sick or is pulled off job, supervisor has no immediate replacement—has to train someone to fill in. Doesn't check knowledge level of trainee before starting the training. New people assigned to crew stand around waiting for instructions. Has no written plans or schedule for crew training and upgrading. Doesn't follow up on newly trained operations and check job knowledge. Supervisor tells someone on crew "Here is new man, show him the ropes," does not set training guidelines to follow up.
Needs improvement	Tells person how to do job, shows them when done wrong, but doesn't explain why or check whether person understands what he is doing and reason for method. Replacements filling in for vacations/sickness cause drop in production/quality. Expects understanding by "telling." No follow-up on training—does it once. Does not have all jobs covered with back-up people. Spends little time with crew in operating area—"expects but doesn't inspect" correct control. Does some training but no skills inventory taken for department upgrading. Has key position covered but not others.

EXHIBIT 11–10 *(concluded)*

	Job Dimension: Ensures Effective Crew Training
Satisfactory or adequate	Has crew fully trained for normal job functions and adequate back-up for all jobs. Uses slack periods for training if people are spare. When crew member calls in sick or is pulled off job, supervisor is able to cover job with trained person in crew. Supervisor delegates training of new person to crew member who is a good coach, knows job well, and rechecks new or reassigned crews. Supervisor uses job instruction training (JIT) approach to structure skills training. Instructor who is crew member uses JIT approach in training new operator.
Commendable	Supervisor encourages crew members to take outside courses related to industry. Has clear objectives for crew training and keeps abreast of changes in the operation that will require operator retraining. Cross-trains crew where feasible to increase overall effectiveness of crews.
Outstanding	Supervisor promotes and organizes upgrading program for crew (e.g., grading course). Supervisor determines training needs for each person on crew and sets up plan and schedule to complete this training by specified date. Understands various training techniques (e.g., learning curves) and uses them. Looks for more efficient training methods and upgrading programs. Influences others in achieving a high level of crew training and assists with training in other departments.

Source: Douglas H. Lawson. Lawson and Associates.

products company. As with most BARS, this example applies to a specific job (logging crew supervisors). Goodale and Burke have developed an evaluation scale that follows the BARS approach, but is applicable to several jobs.[45] The performance dimension checklist used by Chevron Canada Ltd. (shown in Appendix B) also uses the BARS format to evaluate employees in several jobs.

One major advantage of BARS is that evaluators participate in its development. This increases the chance that they will accept the procedure and will have a common understanding of the performance dimensions. BARS has received much fanfare and support from some writers.[46] Others conclude, however, that BARS is not superior to alternative performance evaluation methods.[47] Evaluators tend to make rating errors even with behavioural anchors because some inference and judgement are still required. As a result, performance ratings are only slightly more reliable and valid. Finally, BARS doesn't provide precise information for developmental purposes.

Objective Criteria, Absolute Standard

An increasingly popular alternative to subjective evaluation methods is procedures in which evaluators indicate whether and to what extent the employee fits a set of descriptions. These descriptions are typically job behaviours or results. The supervisor makes no direct judgement about whether the employee is "marginal" or "outstanding." Rather, these performance levels are systematically determined by the P/HRM department from the descriptive information provided by the supervisor.

Behavioural Observation Scales

Behavioural observation scales (BOS) were introduced by Latham and Wexley only a decade ago. Yet this method has quickly gained the attention of researchers and practitioners alike.[48] BOS instruments consist of a list of performance-related behaviours for a specific job. These behaviours are identified using the *critical incident method* described above to develop BARS scales.[49] Evaluators are asked to indicate on a five-point scale the frequency with which the employee engages in each behaviour. Total scores for each performance dimension are calculated by summing the scores for behaviours pertaining to each dimension.

Toronto-based Delta Hotels uses the BOS method for some of its nonmanagement jobs. A BOS for the coffee emporium waiter/waitress performance evaluation consists of 73 behaviours grouped into eight performance dimensions. A sample of items from this instrument is presented in Exhibit 11–11. At no time is the supervisor asked to judge the employee's performance level (e.g., "unsatisfactory," "outstanding"). Instead, this is derived from the frequency each behaviour is observed.

The BOS method purportedly overcomes some of the problems with subjective evaluation methods because evaluators merely report how often they have observed each behaviour. Moreover, separate ratings for each behaviour provide a wealth of specific feedback for developmental purposes. This detail may also help evaluators recall employee performance.[50] According to one survey, BOS is also preferred to BARS and, in most cases, standard rating scales.[51]

But the BOS method may not be a panacea for performance evaluation problems. One study found that the behaviour frequency ratings degenerated into general impressions as the time between the observation and the evaluation increased.[52] Another problem is that behaviour frequencies have different levels of satisfactoriness across behaviours. A frequency of 85 to 94

EXHIBIT 11–11
Sample of Items from a Behaviour Observation Scale for a Waiter/Waitress

◿ DELTA HOTELS
Performance Appraisal
Coffee Emporium Waiter/ess

Employee Information:
Name: _____ Position: _____
Department: _____ Period from: _____ to _____
Occasion of appraisal (please circle)

| Probationary | Annual | Change of supervisor | Promotion or transfer | Special or termination |

In completing this form circle a 1 if the employee has engaged in a behaviour 0–64 percent of the time, a 2 if the employee has engaged in a behaviour 65–74 percent of the time, a 3 if the employee has engaged in a behaviour 75–84 percent of the time, a 4 for 85–94 percent of the time, a 5 for 95–100 percent of the time.

1. Customer awareness   Almost never   Almost always
   a. Greets the customer with a smile   1   2   3   4   5
   b. Introduces themselves and lets customer know they will be their waiter/ess for evening or day   1   2   3   4   5
2. Initiative
   a. Keeps sugar, creamers, salt, and pepper refilled without constant reminding   1   2   3   4   5
   b. Cleans and refills ketchup bottles—when quiet   1   2   3   4   5
3. Service
   a. Knows menu—and can inform customers what each item is, how it is served, and how it is prepared   1   2   3   4   5
   b. Asks customers how they would like their meat or eggs done. Brings rolls to the table promptly   1   2   3   4   5
4. Selling technique
   a. Asks customers if they would like wine or a cocktail before meal   1   2   3   4   5
   b. Suggests wine with meal   1   2   3   4   5

EXHIBIT 11–11 *(concluded)*

	Almost never			Almost always	
5. Wine, liquor service					
a. Knows house wines and is able to inform customers about them	1	2	3	4	5
b. Presents wine bottle to table before opening	1	2	3	4	5
6. Bills					
a. Ensures everything is rung in appropriately; example: wine under wine	1	2	3	4	5
b. Writes out orders clearly and neatly and in proper order; i.e., hot items at top of bill, cold and hot sandwiches in middle, soup, dessert, and beverages in lower part of bill	1	2	3	4	5
7. Appearance and attendance					
a. Uniform always clean and pressed	1	2	3	4	5
8. Team work					
a. Offers to help others	1	2	3	4	5
b. Brings out others' orders	1	2	3	4	5

Source: Delta Hotels Ltd., Toronto. Reproduced with permission.

percent may be exemplary for some behaviours but dismal for others.[53] BOS ignores these differences. Finally, BOS requires much effort to develop and results in rather lengthy evaluation instruments. In organizations with many jobs, this cost may be prohibitive.

Management by Objectives

Management by objectives (MBO) is possibly the most popular technique using objective criteria. MBO developed out of a disenchantment with more subjective evaluation methods and an increasing recognition of goal setting as a powerful motivational tool.[54] It is widely used in Canada for evaluating managerial performance in both the private and public sectors.[55] To a lesser extent, the MBO approach has been used to evaluate the performance of technical and support staff. In some firms, such as Black and Decker Canada Inc., MBO is more than just a performance evaluation tool. It is a management philosophy. The performance evaluation systems at First City Trust Company Ltd. and Chevron Canada Ltd.—both in the appendixes to this chapter— include an MBO section. Notice that both organizations use the MBO jointly with at least one other method to evaluate employee performance.

While numerous variations exist, MBO typically includes four basic steps: (1) establish individual objectives, (2) develop action plans, (3) periodically review performance, and (4) evaluate goal accomplishment.

Establish Individual Goals. The first step in the MBO process is to identify specific, measurable goals for the employee to accomplish over a specific time period. Some organizations, such as IBM Canada and several departments of the Canadian government, base individual goals on tasks listed in the job description. Elsewhere, these goals are based on organizational and departmental objectives through a *cascading* goal-setting procedure. Organizational objectives are cascaded down to establish departmental goals. Departmental goals are then cascaded down to become the foundation on which individual goals are established.[56] Although based on departmental objectives, individual goals should be mutually agreed on by the supervisor and employee. Many MBO systems also include agreement on the priority of individual goals and their weighting in an overall assessment of performance.[57]

Develop Action Plans. As part of the goal-setting process, the supervisor and employee identify the means by which each of the individual goals should be achieved. In effect, the process of goal accomplishment is outlined and intermediate goals are often specified. These action plans also clarify the resources required and indicate other employees with whom the individual will work to fulfill performance objectives.

Periodically Review Performance. Periodically throughout the performance period, the supervisor and employee review progress toward each performance goal. This provides feedback to the employee and keeps the supervisor vigilant of the employee's progress. These interim reviews also provide the opportunity for goals to be altered if circumstances have changed.

Evaluate Goal Accomplishment. At the end of the performance period the supervisor works with the employee to identify the extent to which goals have been met or exceeded. Goal accomplishment is often stated in terms of a percentage. An example is shown in Exhibit 11–4. A predetermined formula may be applied to calculate a composite score for the employee's overall performance.

MBO has been advocated on the grounds that it focusses on objective criteria clearly associated with organizational objectives. In most cases, the employee participates in the process, thereby potentially enhancing goal commitment and perceived fairness. The periodic reviews provide the employee with plenty of constructive feedback. Most important, MBO is goal-oriented. It directs the employee toward specific targets of future performance rather than reflecting on ambiguous definitions of past accomplishments or failures.[58]

MBO also has its limitations.[59] The system is very time-consuming and can degenerate into a paperwork jungle. While the evaluation stage is relatively objective, establishing performance goals is open to a number of human errors and inconsistencies. In particular, it is difficult to determine whether the assigned goals have comparable difficulty between employees and performance periods. When used to decide organizational rewards, MBO may lead employees to direct their energy only toward the measurable goals that have been identified in the performance review. More subtle forms of performance with long-term consequences may be overlooked.

Other Objective Criteria, Absolute Standard Methods

Other methods using objective criteria and absolute standards include the weighted checklist and the mixed standard scale.

Weighted Checklist. In its simplest form, the weighted checklist is a set of adjectives or behavioural statements. When the checklist is developed, each item is weighted in terms of its level of performance effectiveness. These weights are not usually known to the people doing the evaluation. Behaviours indicating average performance are assigned lower weights than items representing outstanding performance. To assess employee performance, the evaluator checks those behaviours that the job incumbent engages in. The other items are left blank. A rating score from the checklist equals the sum of the weights of the items checked.

Mixed Standard Scale. The mixed standard scale uses three statements to represent the range of each performance dimension. Typically, one statement represents poor performance on that dimension, another average, and the third good. Statements from all performance dimensions in mixed standard scales are mixed randomly to form a single list of items. Similar to weighted checklists, these statements have been weighted in terms of the item's level on that dimension, although the weights are unknown to those using the instrument. But instead of checking the presence of a behaviour, mixed standard scales ask the evaluator to indicate whether the employee's performance is better than (+), equal to (0), or worse than (−) each statement listed. A total score for each performance dimension is derived from the number of +, 0, and − symbols assigned to the three statements. For example, three + symbols might translate into a score of 7; two + and a 0 would score 6, and so on.[60]

Relative Evaluation Methods

Evaluation procedures using a relative standard rely on other employees as the standard. Most are variations of ranking employees either on overall performance or a specific performance dimension. Relative evaluation methods are typically based on the supervisor's subjective impression of each employee's performance level; however, objective criteria could also be used. Ranking is the simplest, fastest, easiest to understand, and least expensive performance evaluation technique. Ranking simply involves ordering employees from highest to lowest in performance.

Different ranking procedures exist.[61] Alternation ranking orders employees alternatively at each extreme. The best employee is identified, followed by the worst, the second best, the second worst, and so on until all employees in the group have been ranked.

The paired comparison ranking technique compares all possible pairs of employees being evaluated. The number of pairs compared is calculated: $[n \times (n - 1)]/2$, where n is the number of employees. Five employees result in 10 paired comparisons $[(5 \times 4)/2]$. The paired comparison method assigns scores based on the percentage of comparison pairs in which the employee was rated more favourably. In a department of 11 people, an individual would score 70 if he or she was superior in 7 out of 10 comparisons $[7/10 \times 100 = 70]$.

The forced distribution technique requires the evaluator to place all employees on a performance distribution with a fixed percentage in each level. For example, only 10 percent of employees may be assigned an "outstanding" rating; 20 percent, "good"; 40 percent, "satisfactory"; 20 percent, "fair"; and 10 percent, "unsatisfactory." This procedure is most appropriate where many employees are compared and the range of performance is quite wide.

Unlike absolute standard methods that potentially allow supervisors to give high or low ratings to all staff, relative evaluation procedures force evaluators to distinguish employees. This is useful for salary administration purposes. Nevertheless, relative evaluations are subject to a variety of rating errors. They may also result in incomparable results from one group to the next. A top-ranked employee in one group may be placed much lower in another group. Finally, relative evaluations force the supervisor to differentiate employees even where no differences exist. This is particularly true when ranking employees near the middle of the range.

Relative evaluation methods are rarely used alone, but they are occasionally found in conjunction with other performance evaluation procedures. Supervisors may complete a standard rating scale as well as a forced distribution of employees within the department. For example, employees at Chevron Canada are ranked by their supervisors in terms of overall performance based on the performance evaluation results (standard rating scale and management by objectives). These rankings are used to decide salary increases. Separate rankings are also conducted to distinguish employees within each area of the organization for promotion, retention, and development decisions. The Imperial Oil evaluation system described at the beginning of this chapter also uses ranking to determine salary increases.[62]

Assessment Centres

Assessment centres were introduced in Chapter Nine as a method of selecting people for managerial and technical jobs. Job candidates are evaluated by trained observers on several simulations and other tests. The simulations and tests can last for several days after which the evaluators pool their results to make the final selection decision.

Assessment centres can also be used as a form of performance evaluation.[63] This procedure is frequently used to identify current employees for promotion as well as to assess each employee's need for further development. The majority of assessment centres in Canada appear to exist for these purposes. Considering their high cost, it is not surprising that assessment centres are used more for current employees than for external job applicants.

As a performance evaluation method, assessment centres are generally restricted to more complex jobs. Both the Government of Manitoba and the City of Edmonton have used this method to identify the management potential of employees currently in nonmanagement positions. In particular, this procedure has benefited both organizations by identifying minorities and women for employment equity purposes. Several departments of the Government of Canada have also used assessment centres to identify management talent among employees in designated groups as well as other staff.

One of the best-known examples of assessment centres as a performance evaluation technique is at Alcan's Kitimat Works in British Columbia.[64] Alcan's centre, which has been ongoing since the mid-1970s, is used to identify production staff who are ready to assume the job of foreman/woman. The one-day assessment includes four main tasks: two leaderless group discussions (one with an assigned and the other an unassigned role), a performance interview exercise, and a personal background interview. The assessors include operating managers throughout the Kitimat Works as well as a program administrator from the P/HRM department. It takes almost three days for the assessors to complete their work.

Using Multiple Techniques

Earlier we warned that no single evaluation technique will be entirely appropriate across all jobs for all purposes in an organization. Keeley suggests that the method used is largely dependent on the nature of the work. He argues that tasks can be ordered along a continuum from observable and routine behaviours to unspecified and complex behaviours. Exhibit 11–12 illustrates this continuum. Behaviourally based evaluation procedures that define specific performance criteria are only appropriate or feasible for jobs with highly routine tasks.[65] BARS and BOS methods fall into this category. The behavioural

EXHIBIT 11–12
Interaction between the Nature of the Work and Evaluation Technique

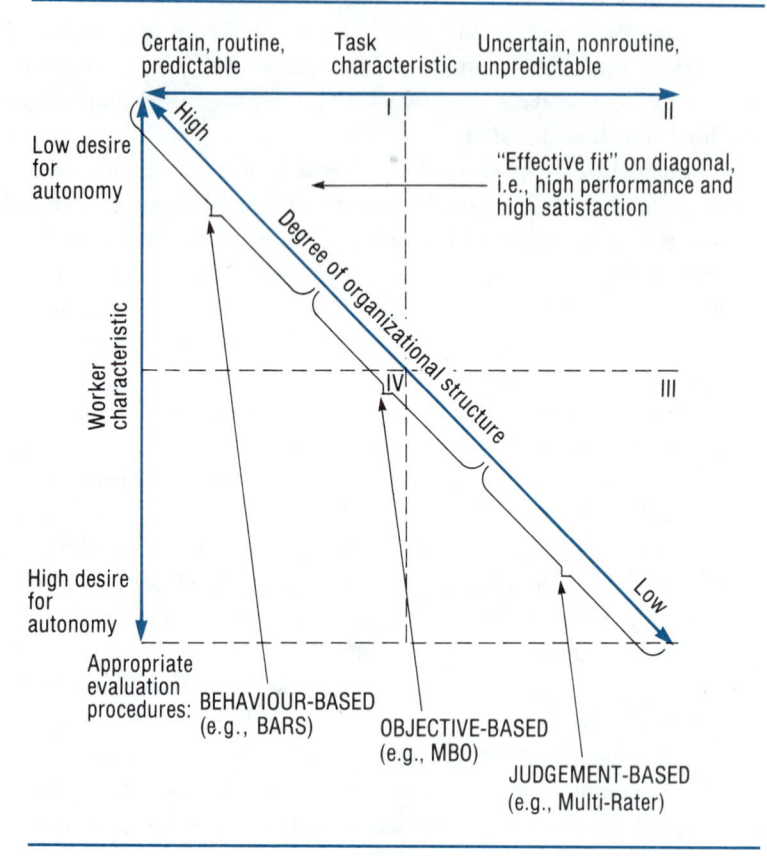

Source: Michael Keeley, "A Contingency Framework for Performance Evaluation," *Academy of Management Review*, July 1978, pp. 428–38.

anchors and statements define specific performance expectations and specify different levels of performance possible by an employee.

In jobs with less routine tasks, however, it is more difficult to specify the behaviour required to accomplish a goal. Rather, different actions are both feasible and appropriate. Under these circumstances, Keeley argues the technique should evaluate the extent to which the final goal is accomplished—the results rather than the process of goal attainment. For such jobs, MBO would be appropriate. As long as job output can be specified, performance can be evaluated without examining the behaviours required to produce those results. The focus is exclusively on the results, not the process.

At the other extreme are jobs for which neither behaviour nor results can be specified. In these situations, subjective evaluation procedures are most appropriate. The evaluator's impressions of employee performance are specified for each performance dimension. As noted earlier, subjective evaluation procedures are the most vulnerable to personal biases and cognitive errors. Consequently, this approach should be implemented only when other procedures are not feasible.

In the next section, we look more closely at the evaluation process, including potential rating errors and training solutions.

THE EVALUATION PROCESS

So far we have mainly discussed characteristics of various performance evaluation techniques. At one time, researchers and practitioners paid almost total attention to this perspective of the system. More recently, however, attention has shifted from techniques to process in performance evaluation.[66] This perspective looks more closely at who conducts the evaluation and what problems need to be resolved when evaluators observe and rate employees. These process-oriented issues are addressed in this section.

Who Should Evaluate?

Throughout this chapter, the immediate supervisor has been identified as the main person who evaluates employee performance. This is the case in most Canadian organizations. However, other people may participate in the evaluation process.

Canadian Pacific Hotels and MacMillan Bloedel are two of the many firms that begin the performance evaluation process by having the job incumbent complete a self-appraisal form. Self-appraisals usually give inflated results, but at least they indicate the employee's own perspective of his or her performance. Self-appraisals may also increase the perceived fairness of the system because employees are more actively participating in the process.[67]

Peer evaluations are occasionally found in professional organizations. In most Canadian universities, for instance, faculty- and universitywide committees comprised of professors assess the performance of other professors. Imperial Oil encourages co-workers and supervisors to provide one-page "mini-appraisals" of other employees.[68] These forms are given to the immediate supervisor who, together with a management committee, evaluates the employee's performance. A few studies have found problems with the validity of peer ratings and their effect on group cohesiveness in some situations.[69] However, peer appraisals are useful where the work is complex and the supervisor is unable to regularly observe performance.

Subordinate evaluation also exists in a few organizations, such as Gulf Oil and IBM in the United States.[70] Subordinates are asked to evaluate their supervisor in a variety of ways. We are aware of one Canadian insurance company that administers organizational surveys as a form of subordinate evaluation. The results are used only for developmental purposes. A federal government employee association has recommended introducing subordinate evaluations in the public sector. It points to Sun Life, Sears Canada, and several banks where this source is used.[71] Most colleges and universities also use subordinate evaluations by having students rate the performance of their instructors.

Senior management reviews are a frequent component of the performance evaluation process. Occasionally the senior manager directly evaluates the performance of employees two levels below. More often, the senior manager or management committee reviews the evaluations supervisors have conducted on their employees. These reviews act as a control mechanism against distorted ratings and may provide some consistency among supervisors. For example, the Treasury Board of Canada has set up a process whereby the senior manager or management committee reviews the supervisor's evaluation of his or her employees.[72] At Mohawk Oil, a human resources committee reviews all evaluations for an employee group (for example, all station managers) at one time to ensure they are properly done and the results are acceptable to everyone on the committee.

Other sources of employee evaluation include clients, P/HRM professionals, and independently trained observers (as in assessment centres).[73] Whenever possible, multiple sources should be used because no single source is usually able to gain an accurate view of all performance dimensions. But where only one source conducts the evaluation, that source should:

- Be in a position to observe the employee's behaviour and performance.
- Be knowledgeable about the dimensions or features of performance.
- Have an understanding of the scale format and the instrument itself.
- Be motivated to do a conscientious job evaluating.[74]

Processing Performance Information

The objective of the performance evaluation process is to accurately estimate the employee's true level of performance on each dimension. However, a variety of information processing problems exist that can lead to incorrect conclusions about employee performance.[75] Three general types of errors or biases may occur in information processing.[76]

Observation. Raters may improperly observe employee behaviour or the outcomes of that behaviour. For a variety of reasons, some information is ignored while other information about the employee's performance is given undue attention.

Memory Storage. Raters bias information when it is stored in memory. Rather than memorizing factual information, they tend to combine facts to form global impressions of the employee in a particular context. For example, by subconsciously tallying the number of times a particular employee argues with co-workers, supervisors develop a sense of how well that employee works with others. This impression is remembered, whereas the specific events that led to this impression are forgotten.

Memory Retrieval. Raters cognitively distort the previously formed impressions when these impressions are retrieved from memory. They may ignore minor impressions in favour of more general impressions of the employee.

These information processing problems may lead to a variety of specific rating errors, which can undermine the accuracy of performance evaluation results. Several specific rating errors are discussed below.

The Halo Effect

The halo effect is the tendency to rate an employee similarly across all performance dimensions based on an overall or global impression of that employee.[77] The overall evaluation is usually based on one or two of the performance dimensions or even irrelevant characteristics of the employee that the evaluator favours.

Say that a supervisor is a fanatic about punctuality. If two employees actually have the same quality and quantity of work output but one tends to be late for work, the supervisor is likely to rate that employee lower on all performance dimensions. The punctual employee will tend to receive higher ratings on the quality and quantity of work dimensions even though his or her performance level is actually the same as that of the tardy employee. This could result in highly distorted performance ratings, particularly where punctuality is an unimportant aspect of job performance.

Not all halo is due to the supervisor's cognitive distortion of reality. In many jobs, employees who perform well on one dimension of the job tend also to do well on other dimensions. Nevertheless, halo bias is prevalent in the performance evaluation process. It is more likely to occur when the supervisor lacks concrete information about the employee on which to base sound judgements about each performance dimension. When the supervisor lacks evidence of the employee's performance on a specific performance dimension, the global impression of that employee is used to infer a rating. Halo bias also occurs when supervisors either are not motivated to carefully observe and rate subordinates or are unaware that halo bias can occur. As we will discuss later, various types of training may reduce halo bias.

Standards of Evaluation

Supervisors may vary their ratings of employees because of different standards of excellence or different interpretations of the rating anchors. It may be easier to receive a "satisfactory" rating from one supervisor than from another. Leniency error occurs when the supervisor inflates the ratings of employees above their true performance. Severity error has the opposite effect. Employees are assigned lower performance ratings than their actual performance level. Central tendency error occurs when performance ratings are artificially bunched together near the centre of the rating scale. Exhibit 11–13 illustrates these three evaluation standard problems.

The presence of inaccurate evaluation standards depends on the actual distribution of performance among the group of employees. In Exhibit 11–13, "true" performance is fairly normally distributed. In other situations, however, most employees may actually be outstanding or marginal. In one study, Cascio and Valenzi discovered a "lenient" distribution of police officer performance would be accurate rather than biased because the selection process effectively weeded out people at the lower end of the scale.[78] Thus, iden-

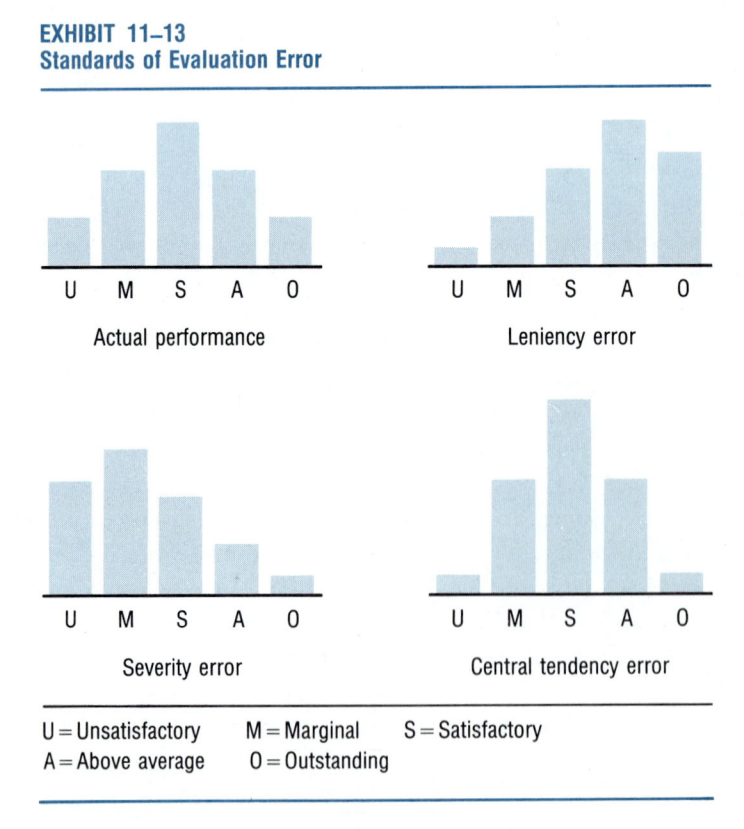

EXHIBIT 11–13
Standards of Evaluation Error

Actual performance

Leniency error

Severity error

Central tendency error

U = Unsatisfactory   M = Marginal   S = Satisfactory
A = Above average   O = Outstanding

tification of leniency, severity, or central tendency cannot be easily interpreted from a review of the supervisor's ratings at one time. These biases become apparent over time or when the supervisor's ratings are compared with the evaluation of the same employees by other raters.

Recent-Behaviour Bias

Another common problem in the evaluation process is that evaluators remember recent behaviour better than past behaviour.[79] Employees are often evaluated more on the results of the past few weeks than on a representative sample of behaviour over the entire performance period. Some employees are well aware of this difficulty. They know the dates of the evaluation, and the name of the game is to get some good projects on the manager's desk just before evaluation time. Later we will describe the critical incident technique as one solution to recent-behaviour bias.

Contrast Effects

Recall that most performance evaluation systems rely on absolute comparisons between employee performance and predetermined performance standards. For example, MBO systems evaluate individuals based on how well they have accomplished the performance objectives set out at the beginning of the performance period. In reality, however, supervisors tend to make relative comparisons of performance among employees even when the system calls for an absolute standard. Consequently, the performance ratings of one employee may be influenced somewhat by the performance ratings of other employees. This is known as the contrast effect. An individual will receive higher performance ratings when other employees in the department perform poorly than when others perform the job well.[80] One solution to this problem is to provide performance standards training (also called frame-of-reference training) so supervisors have the same "ideal" performance benchmark.

Attribution Errors

Supervisors want to know why employees perform the job well or poorly. In particular, they try to determine whether performance is caused mainly by the employee's own motivation and ability (internal attribution) or by factors beyond the employee's control (external attribution). These causal attributions are inferred from information about the employee's previous performance as well as the performance of others in that job. Internal attributions about an employee's behaviour are typically made when: (1) the employee has performed that particular task consistently well (or poorly) in the past (high consistency), (2) some people don't perform the task as well as the employee (low consensus), and (3) the employee performs well on other tasks (low distinctiveness). External attributions are usually made under conditions of low consensus, high consistency, and high distinctiveness.[81]

Assigning internal or external attributions to employee behaviour affects the supervisor's performance ratings of that person, the corrective actions taken, and the type of feedback provided to the employee.[82] For example, say an individual completes an excellent project, but the supervisor believes this performance is due mainly to the assistance of co-workers rather than the individual's own skill and motivation. This external attribution results in a lower performance rating because the supervisor believes credit should go to the co-workers, not to the employee.

Causal attribution is a rational process of assigning credit and blame to either the person or the situation. Unfortunately, supervisors make attribution errors that reduce the validity of performance ratings.[83] Fundamental attribution error (also called actor-observer error) is a tendency for observers to underestimate the importance of situational contingencies and overestimate the importance of personal factors in the behaviour of others. Basically, it is easier to see an employee perform the job poorly than to notice the situational influences on that ineffective behaviour. But this means an employee's performance may be rated too low because the supervisor does not recognize that the poor performance is partly due to factors beyond the employee's control.

A second attribution error, known as self-serving bias, is a tendency for people to internally attribute their own favourable outcomes and externally attribute unfavourable outcomes. Simply put, we take credit for our successes and blame the situation for our mistakes. Self-serving bias can cause supervisors to discount the good performance of subordinates and inflate their responsibility for poor performance. When a subordinate performs the job well, the supervisor may take more credit than deserved for this success, leaving the employee with less credit. When the subordinate performs poorly, self-serving bias may cause the supervisor to attribute most of the folly to the subordinate.

Attribution errors are difficult to remove from the performance evaluation process. However, some training programs aimed at increasing supervisors' awareness of attribution errors may help. Some research also suggests supervisors are less likely to make fundamental attribution errors when they have good knowledge of the subordinate's job.[84]

Performance Evaluation Training

To some extent, information processing problems can be minimized by developing performance evaluation instruments with clearly defined and measurable criteria. However, researchers and practitioners are learning that rater training is also an effective way to improve the performance evaluation process. While some problems may develop,[85] most research supports rater training as a means of reducing rating errors and improving the accuracy of the evaluation results.[86] (See Exhibit 10-10 in the previous chapter for an example of rater training.)

Rater training varies in terms of its content and method used. Training programs may include three types of content: rater error training, performance dimension training, and performance standards training.[87] Rater error training attempts to reduce leniency, severity, central tendency, halo, and contrast errors by raising awareness of these problems and encouraging raters to avoid them. Performance dimension training attempts to familiarize raters with the meaning of the performance dimensions on the rating instrument. This is accomplished by reviewing the job qualifications and the rating scale used. In some performance dimension training, raters actually participate in the development of the rating scale. Performance standards training is sometimes called *frame-of-reference* training because it tries to establish a common frame of reference among the raters. This is achieved by presenting samples of job performance along with some indication of the level at which that performance should be rated on the performance evaluation instrument.

Research on these three types of rater training content points to performance standard and performance dimension training as the most effective at increasing rating accuracy and reducing many of the errors discussed above. While rater error training is popular, it may lead to inaccurate results because supervisors are taught to avoid performance rating distributions that may, in some cases, reflect the true distribution of employees.

In addition to content, the success of rater training depends on the method used. Three different methods exist. Lecture presentations are often given where supervisors learn from an instructor about the different types of rating error and how they can be overcome. Another approach is to have group discussions so those in attendance fully understand the training content. The discussions often require supervisors to generate solutions to specific rating problems and to reach consensus on the definition of each performance dimension. Finally, some training involves practice and feedback, where the rater evaluates the performance of a fictitious employee (usually on video) and then compares his or her ratings with those of "experts" or other raters in attendance. The rater receives feedback indicating the type of rating errors made.

From the available research, the lecture method of rater training appears to be the least effective in reducing most types of rating error. Participation in the learning process through small group discussions produces better results, particularly in reducing leniency, severity, and halo errors. Rater training programs are most effective, however, when the discussion method is combined with practice and feedback.

Observing Performance

Even with rater training, evaluators may draw inaccurate conclusions about employee performance because they lack either the skills or motivation to observe or recall performance-relevant information.

The critical incident technique is one way to improve observation and reduce recent behaviour bias. Throughout the performance period, the supervisor documents observations of effective and ineffective behaviour considered critical to the job. These critical incidents are filed away until the formal evaluation, when they are carefully reviewed. This procedure forces evaluators to record important events when they occur rather than relying on memory. It also provides specific feedback during the evaluation interview.[88] As noted earlier, critical incidents also provide a useful foundation for several performance evaluation techniques. However, this process is time-consuming and has been resisted by supervisors.[89]

Possibly a more acceptable alternative to the critical incident method is to train supervisors in the use of memory aids.[90] Although little research has been conducted in the performance evaluation context, techniques that help supervisors remember job-relevant behaviours should reduce recent behaviour bias.

As well as possessing observation and memory skills, supervisors must be motivated to accurately observe and rate employee behaviour. Many systems actually motivate evaluators to be inaccurate. For example, leniency error is a persistent problem because supervisors don't like to give poor ratings. Central tendency is frequently found in evaluation systems requiring additional documentation for extreme ratings because supervisors try to avoid the extra work involved.

There is no easy answer to the problem of rater motivation. P/HRM managers can introduce control systems such as the management committee process described earlier. Ultimately, however, the willingness to accurately observe and evaluate employee performance must be based on deeply embedded management beliefs in the value of the performance evaluation system.

THE EVALUATION INTERVIEW

Probably no other area of management is so fraught with anxiety on the part of both supervisors and subordinates and has so much potential for either positive or negative consequences in terms of motivation, development, and satisfaction as the evaluation interview.[91]

The purpose of the interview is to let employees know the results of the performance evaluation process, explain how these results were determined, discuss future performance goals, and identify the means by which performance shortcomings may be improved. Unfortunately, some writers have found the typical evaluation interview does more harm than good. The supervisor is often defensive, authoritarian, and ambiguous.[92] Employees frequently feel more uncertainty about their performance and express less favourable opinions about their supervisor *after* the interview!

Despite existing problems, the evaluation interview is a potentially valuable source of feedback and motivation for employees. It is therefore important that both managers and P/HRM staff try to improve this process. This may be accomplished by considering the frequency and timing of the meeting, the preparation required, and the purpose and style of the interview.

Interview Frequency and Timing

Earlier in this chapter we distinguished the formal evaluation process from informal counselling and coaching. The informal process is beneficial because it includes frequent discussions with the employee throughout the performance period.[93] At the same time, it is difficult to ensure that informal discussions occur. As Landy warns, performance feedback must be part of the formal process to ensure that the employee receives any feedback at all.[94]

The frequency and timing of formal evaluation interviews typically coincide with the formal performance evaluation. In many organizations, this means formal reviews are often held only once a year with all employees within the work unit receiving their reviews at the same time. But this procedure is at odds with the literature, which suggests performance feedback should be received soon after a goal has been accomplished.[95] Consequently, developmental meetings should be more frequent and timely.

Some organizations have taken steps in this direction. IBM Canada and A&W Food Services of Canada require supervisors to arrange quarterly reviews to ensure that employees receive ongoing feedback. A&W calls its quarterly review process a "No Surprises System" because it ensures that employees are regularly informed of their progress.[96] Some companies have annual reviews but recognize the need for more frequent meetings under special circumstances. For example, First City Trust encourages special performance evaluations and interviews for employees who have completed a temporary assignment or major project. This enables the performance evaluation process to be more closely aligned with natural work cycles.

Interview Preparation

The most important preparation for the evaluation interview is supervisor training in interview and interpersonal skills. Few Canadian firms spend any time developing these supervisory skills. Supervisors must learn how to give useful feedback, how to handle the difficult task of communicating negative feedback, how to minimize employee (and supervisor) defensiveness, and how to keep the interview discussion on a positive and future-oriented track. To prepare for the evaluation interview, the supervisor must also carefully review the evaluation results, particularly the facts and criteria on which the employee was evaluated.[97]

Interview Purpose and Style

Most performance evaluation systems are used for both evaluative and developmental purposes. Since these applications carry over to the evaluation interview, supervisors must play two roles. They must take the role of helper by providing feedback to the employee and assisting with an action plan to improve performance shortcomings. At the same time, they must take the role of judge by communicating the results of the performance evaluation and the consequences for the employee's salary increase and future promotion opportunities.

Some time ago, Meyer and his colleagues concluded that the roles of helper and judge were incompatible and were having an adverse effect on the evaluation process.[98] In particular, salary discussion overshadows the developmental objectives of the interview. As the P/HRM vice president at Toronto-based Honeywell Ltd. explains: "Sometimes an employee won't hear a word you're saying about his performance and development because he's waiting for the raise."[99] This problem is aggravated by the fact that employees tend to rate themselves higher than the supervisor's evaluation. To resolve this dilemma, Meyer and others recommend that salary and other evaluative issues be discussed at a separate meeting from the developmental issues. Employee development issues should be discussed several times throughout the year, preferably on a flexible basis.

The style of the interview should reflect the need to communicate performance information without the employee becoming defensive. Here are some of the main points to remember in conducting the evaluation interview:[100]

- Allow adequate time to conduct the interview and remove any interruptions.
- Encourage employees to participate in the interview by asking open-ended questions about their behaviour and feelings about the evaluation results.
- Discuss job-related behaviour, not personalities or ambiguous criteria.
- Give the interview a future-oriented perspective by focussing on goals and performance improvement.
- Think and act supportively and constructively throughout the interview.

SUMMARY

Performance evaluation is potentially one of the most important aspects of P/HRM because of its impact on employee productivity. Yet in practice, the evaluation process is typically far from perfect. Employees may try to perform well, but managers often fail to identify and reward these contributions. The consequences of a poorly developed and implemented system can be disheartening to all.

Performance evaluation provides a format for rating employee performance and giving formal feedback. The evaluative function provides the basic information required to distribute organizational rewards. The developmental function assists employees in their quest for better performance and organizational rewards. Thus, designing a performance evaluation system deserves a substantial amount of consideration from P/HRM managers.

An effective evaluation system must consider the purpose to which the results are used. Since different techniques serve different purposes, this may mean more than one technique should be implemented. The evaluation system must produce reliable and valid results that distinguish good and poor performers. It must also be acceptable to both employees and management and must be practical to all concerned. Evaluation criteria should consider all relevant job dimensions and, where possible, should be objectively defined and measured. These criteria are based on current job analysis and should be clearly communicated to employees before the performance period begins.

Many people other than the employee's immediate supervisor can (and often should) contribute to the evaluation process. Input from other supervisors and higher-level managers, peers, subordinates of the person being evaluated and even the employee's own self-appraisal may be part of the final evaluation.

An effective performance evaluation system depends as much on the rating process as on the rating format. Specifically, evaluators should be trained to avoid information processing errors. They should be both motivated and able to observe employee behaviour throughout the performance period.

Although supervisors should informally counsel and coach employees throughout the year, the formal performance evaluation interview is the primary means of communicating evaluation results. Evaluators must be properly trained in interview and counselling skills and should carefully review the evaluation results before these meetings. Whenever possible, developmental reviews should be frequent and timely—certainly more often than once a year for most jobs—and possibly be separated from the salary discussion.

Ultimately, the success of the performance evaluation system depends on top management's symbolic and actual commitment to its use. Everyone must believe the system is more than pieces of paper placed in P/HRM files once or twice a year. These records must actually be used as part of the employer's developmental, reward, and employment planning decisions.

APPENDIX A / Performance Evaluation at First City Trust

FirstCity Trust COMPANY Confidential

EMPLOYEE PERFORMANCE APPRAISAL

Form A: To be completed for positions at C5 and above

Instructions to Appraiser

1. Employee performance appraisal is a part of the process of management.
2. The Employee Appraisal Form is to be completed by the Immediate Supervisor of the employee.
3. The appraisal is to be as objective as possible. Errors the appraiser must watch out for are:
    a. **The halo effect.** Be sure to describe the individual's performance on each dimension independently. Do not allow the description assigned to one dimension to influence the assessment assigned to another.
    b. **Bias or prejudice.** The appraiser's personal likes or dislikes should not have a bearing in determining the value of an individual's contribution to the company.
    c. **Central tendency.** Few individuals are totally "average" with respect to all performance dimensions; be sure to assign either high or low descriptions where appropriate.
    d. **Leniency and severity.** Ensure that the assigned description accurately reflects the individual's performance on the job and that it is not used to justify other considerations.
    e. **Hearsay.** Descriptions must be assigned on the basis of the appraiser's personal experience with and observations of the individual's performance and not on the basis of rumour.
4. The appraiser should take the following steps to prepare for the appraisal:
    a. Advise the employee of the appraisal; distribute a blank appraisal form so the employee can complete a self appraisal; set a date for the appraisal interview.
    b. Review the employee's file to ensure complete familiarity with the employee's background, training, previous appraisals, development program, etc.
    c. Review the relevant sections of the Human Resource Department Manual.
    d. Review the major duties from the job description, the objectives established at the time of the last review and their assigned weightings.
    e. Assemble all necessary information to assess the employee's achievements.
5. The appraiser is measuring the employee's performance according to established objectives. If factors beyond the control of the employee make it difficult for him/her to achieve these, the appraiser will take this into consideration.
6. The Employee Appraisal Form is to be reviewed with the employee. This interview is one of the most important steps in the appraisal process. It is an opportunity for honest, frank discussion and if conducted properly, it will —
    Clarify objectives;
    Give the employee satisfaction about the areas where he/she is effective and an understanding of how performance can be improved in other areas;
    Give the employee an opportunity to discuss the job and career interests;
    Identify necessary training and development activities.
7. When the appraiser has completed the Employee Appraisal Form, including the development section, the Form is to be signed by the employee and the appraiser and forwarded to the appropriate executive for review and authorization of the salary recommendation.
8. **Employee Appraisal Form distribution:**
    a. Original to Executive for authorization of salary recommendation, then to Human Resources Division.
    b. Copy for appraiser for future reference and action.
    c. Copy for employee for future reference and action.

CG 043 (11/82)

Performance Evaluation at First City Trust *(continued)*

General Information

Review Type	Date of Review
☐ Scheduled ☐ Other	

Employee Name	Employee No.	Position Title	Position No.	Job Grade

Branch/Dept. and Location	Time in current position	Time with current supervisor	Supervisor's name

Current Salary	Date of last review	Salary Range min. $	mid. $	max. $

Objectives Recap

Attach copy of Performance Appraisal Worksheet

Major Duties	Objectives	Wgt. %	Achievements	Pts.

Performance Evaluation at First City Trust *(continued)*

Behaviour/Skills

Appraisal Codes
1. Particularly strong skills at this level.
2. Has normal skills expected of this position.
3. Would require improvement before skill level would be considered satisfactory.
4. N/R Not rated/not applicable.

1	2	3	4.

Planning & Organizing
  Selects realistic, yet challenging objectives
  Develops programs and activities to achieve objectives
  Establishes priorities

Communication Skills — Written
  Logic, clarity, conciseness
  Empathy, tact, style
  Persuasiveness

Communication Skills — Verbal
  Listens, comprehends and identifies needs
  Speaks clearly, concisely, and confidently
  Tactful, persuasive and inspirational

Supervisory Skills
  Selection of people for tasks
  Control of task execution
  Production of results through subordinates
  Employees treated fairly, firmly and with understanding
  Group operates as a "Team"

Personnel
  Writing and dealing with performance appraisals
  Training, improving and developing subordinates
  Administration of personnel policies, e.g. Compensation, Benefits, Hours of work, etc.
  Recruitment

Analytical Skills
  Identification and organization of Data
  Analysis of Data
  Quality of conclusions and recommendations

Administration
  Accuracy of forecasts
  Preparation of budgets
  Control of expenses
  Up-keep of premises and equipment
  Systems and Methods

Credit Skills
  Financial Statement Analysis
  Negotiation
  Collection and follow-up
  Realistic loan pricing
  Interpretation of policy
  Appropriate security

Marketing
  Service to the Public
  Public Relations
  Selling services
    — Retail
    — Commercial
    — Investments & Securities

Performance Evaluation at First City Trust *(concluded)*

Development

1. The supervisor and the employee will undertake the following steps to develop the employee in areas requiring improvement and/or to prepare the employee to undertake additional responsibility.

   a. _____

   b. _____

   c. _____

2. For what other positions in First City might the employee be considered and what training is required to prepare the employee for these positions?

Position	Time Frame	Additional Training
a.		
b.		

3. Recommendation for attendance at First City Trust training programs:

   Managing for Effectiveness ☐   This Year ☐   Next year ☐

   Supervisory Skill Building ☐

   Other ☐

Performance Rating

Excellent ☐ — Consistently achieves or surpasses objectives. This employee contributes substantially more than expected and demonstrates a high level of commitment. Applies a high degree of imagination and energy and strives to improve.

Superior Competent ☐ — Job performance consistently exceeds that expected in most of the major job responsibilities. Unusual problems and situations are properly considered and handled well.

Competent ☐ — Employee demonstrates a consistently satisfactory level of work performance. Individuals receiving this rating regularly handle major responsibilities in a completely competent manner.

Low Competent ☐ — Some important objectives are not met. Improvement is required before an individual is considered to be delivering a consistently satisfactory level of work. (Refer to HR 0402)

Unsatisfactory ☐ — Key objectives are not achieved. Substantial improvement required before it can be said that the job is being covered adequately. (Refer to HR 0402).

Recommended Increase

_____ % (Refer to HR 0305)

Head Office Approval

_____

Acknowledgement

Employee's Signature _____ Date _____

Appraiser's Signature _____ Date _____

Rec'd. by HRD _____ Date _____

APPENDIX B / Performance Evaluation at Chevron Canada Limited

Chevron Canada Limited

Performance Dimension Checklist
GO-1035-2

Before filling out this form, you should be thoroughly familiar with the procedures described in "A Supervisor's Guide for Performance Planning Evaluation and Documentation".

Employee's Name		Date	
Department	Position Title	Salary Group	

Comment on the dimensions below which are significant to this employees performance, either as strengths or as areas to improve or develop. The statements along each scale describe general kinds of performance at various levels. Try to write your own brief statements that illustrate specific examples of your employee's work. You may place a check mark on the scale at the point which best represents employee's performance on the dimension.

Ability to Work Independently — Degree of assistance and supervision required to complete assignments.

| Rarely completes an assignment without lots of prodding. | Works efficiently once general direction is established but needs help in getting started. | Works with minimal supervision. Supervisor does not have to constantly check work. | Initiates and carries out complex projects with little or no supervision. |

Examples/Comments

Problem-Solving — Ability to think through a problem, identify possible causes, and develop workable solutions.

| Analysis is superficial. Does not critically review available data. Conclusions are not supported by facts. | Jumps to conclusions. Overlooks alternatives that may lead to more practical solutions to problems. | Reviews all aspects of a situation before coming to conclusions or recommending action to be taken. | Very persistent in attacking problems. Quickly sorts out relevant information and comes up with workable solutions. |

Examples/Comments

Working with Others — Effectiveness in relating to people; cooperativeness; keeping others informed and considering their opinions.

| Is an impatient listener and does not consider people's opinions. Loses their interest and support. | Sometimes fails to share ideas in order to gain support of other people. | Establishes and maintains workable relationships with others. | Initiates and cultivates key contacts; tact and diplomacy allow accomplishment of even unpopular tasks. |

Examples/Comments

Job Knowledge — Knowledge of methods, techniques, skills, policies, etc., required to do the job.

| Does not have good mastery of job fundamentals. Must frequently consult peers for information. | Knowledge of job is adequate to handle most assignments without consulting others. | Keeps informed of trends affecting work— new developments, regulations, etc. | Thoroughly understands own and related work. Sought out by peers for information. Considered an expert. |

Examples/Comments

Performance Evaluation at Chevron Canada Limited *(continued)*

Planning and Organizing — Skill in establishing goals, priorities, and courses of action; using resources, personnel and time efficiently.

| Does not establish priorities. Spends more time than necessary on less essential tasks. | | Organizes work to keep productively occupied under normal circumstances. | | Carefully plans work so that support services can be obtained when needed. | | Always has a long-range plan with enough flexibility to handle contingencies. |

Examples/Comments

Effectiveness under Stress — Ability to work under pressure, e.g., in handling multiple assignments, rapidly changing conditions, meeting tight deadlines, etc.

| Easily flustered when given more than one assignment to do at the same time. | Keeps work flowing smoothly in normal situations but loses effectiveness when pressures mount. | | | Stays calm during hectic periods and maintains steady work output. | | When a crisis occurs, can drop everything to meet new demands and produces high quality work. |

Examples/Comments

Supporting Management Objectives — Understanding and working in concert with goals of the organization.

| Quick to disagree with management. Criticizes policies and resists their implementation. | | | | Frequently discusses work with supervisor to assure compatibility between personal and organization objectives. | Understands overall objectives of organization and works to achieve those objectives. |

Examples/Comments

Cost/Profit Awareness — Skill at working within budget constraints; making use of cost reduction and profit opportunities.

| Shows disregard for cost consciousness. Fails to monitor budget and cannot support expenditures. | | Keeps within budget on most items but overspends in a few areas. | | Monitors expenditures to keep costs within budget. | Regularly checks expenditures to control operating costs. Minimizes overtime and supply purchases. | Thoroughly understands the economics of operation. Recognizes and capitalizes on profit opportunities. |

Examples/Comments

Commitment to Job — Diligence, involvement, and interest in one's work.

| Frequently tardy or absent for reasons others would consider frivolous. | | Works dependably on regular assignments but avoids extra work that requires overtime. | | | Very attentive to responsibilities. Discourages casual conversation when there is work to be done. | Eagerly seeks new assignments and challenges. Pursues development activities on own time. |

Examples/Comments

Originating and Adapting to New Ideas — Ability to generate innovative ideas that will benefit the organization; developing and adapting to more efficient ways of doing work.

| Has difficulty shifting to new work procedures. Requires considerable time to change old patterns. | Very comfortable in following established procedures. Seldom suggests changes. | Does not initiate change but easily adapts and follows through when a new plan has been established. | | | | Continually experiments with new concepts. Very imaginative in coming up with profitable ideas. |

Examples/Comments

Performance Evaluation at Chevron Canada Limited *(continued)*

Decisiveness/Self-Assurance — Willingness to make decisions, commit oneself to a course of action, and accept accountability.

| Easily influenced by others and likely to change mind depending on most recent contact. | Reluctant to make decisions when the outcome will have a major effect on operations. | | Takes a firm stand in supporting opinions and does not shrink from a challenge. | Accepts accountability even in difficult situations. Does not ignore responsibility or pass the buck. |

Examples/Comments

Written Communication — Effectiveness in expressing thoughts in writing.

| Written communications are incomplete and poorly organized. | Written communications are rambling with too much detail. | | Written communications anticipate knowledge and position of reader. | Has a command of English that makes writing clear, concise, and accurate. |

Examples/Comments

Oral Communication — Effectiveness in expressing thoughts orally.

| Oral presentations are disorganized and cover too much detail. | Uncomfortable in oral communication with others at different educational/professional levels. | | Uses visual aids effectively to support ideas in oral presentations. | Tailors presentation to audience. Not upset by complex questions or challenges to positions taken. |

Examples/Comments

Developing Subordinates — Helping subordinates grow in their capacity to handle increasing responsibility.

| Is unaware of subordinates' performance unless problems arise. Makes no effort to train them. | Does not make use of subordinates' talents. Delegates only routine assignments. | | Conducts regular performance review sessions to inform subordinates how they're doing. | Makes specific plans to build on subordinates' strengths. Spots their development needs and creates training assignments. |

Examples/Comments

Handling Personnel Problems — Willingness to face sensitive employee relations issues and take action.

| Lets emotions get in way of acting on personnel problems. Cannot reach sound conclusions. | | Resolves and documents routine personnel problems. Seeks guidance on situations having greater impact. | Handles personnel problems with fairness. Bases decisions on facts. Does not back away from unpleasant personnel tasks. |

Examples/Comments

Comments: _____

Performance Evaluation at Chevron Canada Limited *(continued)*

Review/Discussion —
Supervisor should review this evaluation with the employee. Upon employee request, supervisor must show this evaluation to the employee.

Date discussed with employee _____ if not discussed, explain: _____
Comments on discussion, if appropriate: _____

Endorsement/Review

Comments, if desired: _____

Endorsed by _____ Title _____ Date _____

Performance Evaluation at Chevron Canada Limited *(continued)*

Chevron Canada Limited

**Performance Evaluation —
Unclassified Employees GO-1035-1**

Confidential

Name _____ Soc. Ins. No. _____ Date _____

Company _____ Department _____ Location _____

Position _____ Salary Group _____ Service Date _____

Time in Present Position _____ Period Covered _____ To _____

Section I — Goals/Assignments/Results
Describe employee's performance planning goals and/or major assignments and the degree to which these were met. Cite specific examples.

GO-1035-1 1/82

Performance Evaluation at Chevron Canada Limited *(continued)*

Section II — Summary Evaluation — On the scale, place a check at the point which best represents employee's overall performance.

Unsatisfactory Performance
Performance does not meet minimum standards and improvement is necessary to maintain this job assignment.

Lowest Acceptable Performance
Performance is below what is typically expected on this job. Often fails to meet desired standards of quality, quantity or timeliness.

Performance meets all normal requirements. Exceeds what is typically expected in a few aspects of job, but improvement in some areas is desirable.

Exceptional Performance
Performance far exceeds what is typically seen in this job. Consistently achieves outstanding results and/or makes unique contributions.

Comments to support above: (e.g., indicate strengths; assignments employee has done particularly well; any areas where growth or improvement is needed.)

Evaluation prepared by _____ Title _____ Date _____
How long have you supervised this employee? _____ years _____ months
In consultation with _____ Title _____ Date _____

Section III — Endorsement/Review — Comments, if desired:

I concur that this evaluation reflects the employee's performance.

Endorsed by _____ Title _____ Date _____

Section IV — Review/Discussion — Supervisor should review this performance evaluation with the employee.

Date discussed with employee _____ if not discussed, explain: _____
Comments on discussion, if appropriate:

Human Resource Activities: Development

Performance Evaluation at Chevron Canada Limited *(continued)*

Placement Recommendation GO-311-1

CONFIDENTIAL

Name _____ Soc. Ins. No. _____ Date _____

Company _____ Department _____ Location _____

Position Title _____ Salary Group (e.g., 3B, 1C, 1AA, etc.) _____ Service Date _____

Time in Present Position _____ Period Covering _____ To _____ Date of Last GO-311-1 _____

Is the employee presently in the Management Planning Inventory? Yes ☐ No ☐

Instructions:
Note: For employees in the Management Planning and Development Inventory, promptly forward **typed** copies of up-to-date GO-311-1 and GO-1035 forms (stapled together) to Management Planning and Development.

A GO-311-1 must be completed for all unclassified employees at the frequency described in the Supervisors Guide for Performance Planning, Performance Evaluation and Career Planning. The GO-311-1 serves as a record of the employee's estimated potential, development needs, and considerations relating to job changes. After management review, it should be discussed with the employee and any pertinent comments or observations recorded at the end of the form. A copy of the completed form should be placed in the employee's personnel file.

I — Assessment of Employee Promotability

Is employee promotable? ☐ Now   ☐ With Experience   ☐ Not at Present

Please explain _____

_____

_____

_____

_____

If promotable now, or with experience, what positions might be suitable as a next step? Please list several.

Within Present Organization   Outside Present Organization

_____   _____
_____   _____
_____   _____
_____   _____
_____   _____

II — Assessment of Employee Potential

1. Based on your observations what do you think the employee's potential might be in relationship to his current group level?

   ☐ Can advance at least one level
   ☐ Can advance 2 or more levels
   ☐ Satisfactorily placed at current level

2. List any higher-level jobs for which you think the employee might eventually be a realistic candidate. Please give your rationale for this projection.

_____

_____

_____

_____

GO-311-1 1/82

Performance Evaluation at Chevron Canada Limited *(concluded)*

III — Career Planning (Fill this section out for all unclassified employees, whether or not they are in the MP&D Inventory.)

1. List the kinds of work or functional areas in which this employee would like experience. Be as specific as possible.

2. From your knowledge of this employee's performance and expectations, would such experience be a realistic career step? Please explain.

3. What development do you propose for this employee? (Be specific, e.g., lateral assignment or promotion giving duration of the assignment and the organization, course work, seminars, new job responsibilities, etc.)

   A. Over the next year

   B. Beyond the next year

IV — Special Considerations for Career Planning

A. **Job Related:** Please comment on important characteristics and special skills which should be considered during career planning. Comment on both strengths and weaknesses — e.g., in interpersonal relationships, analytical ability, communications, managerial skills, etc.

B. **Other:** Are there any factors (e.g., health, schooling, family needs or problems, etc.) that will affect changes in assignment or work location?

V — Is employee interested in a foreign assignment? (Comment and indicate areas of particular interest.)

☐ Yes ☐ No

Comments on Discussion

Prepared By	Title	Date
Endorsed by Management — Name		Date
Discussed with Employee By		Date

Reprinted with permission of Chevron Canada Limited. These forms are to be revised in 1988.

DISCUSSION AND REVIEW QUESTIONS

1. How can performance evaluation influence organizational effectiveness?
2. How can organizations increase the validity of performance evaluation results?
3. Under what conditions are performance evaluation results more likely to be accepted by employees?
4. Describe the potential conflict between individualization and standardization in performance evaluation systems.
5. Describe the different performance evaluation criteria and standards. What are the advantages and disadvantages of each?
6. Describe the stages of management by objectives. What problems may develop with this method of performance evaluation?
7. How can performance evaluations using standard rating scales be made more effective?
8. Compare and contrast the strengths and weaknesses of behaviourally anchored rating scales versus management by objectives.
9. Who should conduct performance evaluations?
10. Describe the three general information processing errors that occur in performance evaluation. How may each of these errors be minimized?
11. How do attribution errors affect performance evaluation results?
12. Describe the characteristics of an effective performance evaluation interview.

NOTES AND REFERENCES

1. John Terry, "In Praise of Appraisals," *Canadian Business*, December 1984, pp. 81–85; Eva Innes, Robert L. Perry, and Jim Lyon, *The 100 Best Companies to Work for in Canada* (Don Mills, Ont.: Collins, 1986).
2. Michael Beer, R. Ruh, J. A. Dawson, B. B. McCaa, and M. J. Kavanagh, "A Performance Management System: Research Design, Introduction, and Evaluation," *Personnel Psychology* 31 (1978), pp. 505–35.
3. Terry, "In Praise of Appraisals," p. 81.
4. *B. L. Mears et al. v. Ontario Hydro et al.* (1984) 5 C.H.R.R. D/343.
5. *Ingram v. Natural Footwear* (1980) 1 C.H.R.R. D/59.
6. *Reid v. Russelsteel Ltd.* (1981) 2 C.H.R.R. D/402.
7. For two excellent analyses of U.S. cases between 1976 an 1981, see H. S. Feild and W. H. Holley, "The Relationship of Performance Appraisal System Characteristics to Verdicts in Selected Employment Discrimination Cases," *Academy of Management Journal* 25, no. 2 (1982), pp. 392–406; W. F. Cascio and H. J. Bernardin, "Implications of Performance Litigation for Personnel Decisions," *Personnel Psychology* 34, no. 2 (1981), pp. 211–26.
8. A few of the better-known cases include: *Robson v. General Motors of Canada Ltd.* (1982) 37 O.R. (2d) 229; *Wallace v. Toronto Dominion Bank* (1981) 39 O.R. (2d) 350; *Ibrahim v. Association of Professional Engineers etc. of Alberta* (1985) 41 A.L.R. (2d) 126; and *MacDonald v. Seaboard G.M. Diesel Ltd. and Cullen Canadian Inc.* (1984) 61 N.S.R. (2d) 229.

9. See, for example, *Young* v. *Huntsville District Memorial Hospital et al.* (1984) 5 C.C.E.L. 113.
10. *Georgian College of Applied Arts and Technology* (1983) 10 L.A.C. (3rd) 359.
11. *B.C. Tel and Telecommunication Workers Union* (1980) W.L.A.C. (Vol. 2) 457.
12. Richard Henderson, *Performance Appraisal: Theory to Practice*, 2nd ed. (Reston, Va.: Reston Publishing, 1984); H. John Bernardin and Richard W. Beatty, *Performance Appraisal: Assessing Human Behavior at Work* (Boston: Kent, 1984).
13. George T. Milkovich and Jerry M. Newman, *Compensation*, 2nd ed. (Plano, Tex.: Business Publications, 1987), p. 334.
14. Bruce Gates, "Managers Look to Merit Pay to Boost Productivity," *Financial Post*, November 23, 1985, p. 18; Michael Salter, "Pay Now Tagged More to Results," *Financial Post*, October 25, 1983, p. 24; Virginia Galt, "Employers Tying Pay to Performance," *The Globe and Mail*, November 4, 1985, p. B1; Michael Ryval, "The Corporate Report Card," *Financial Post Magazine*, March 1981, pp. 44–46.
15. Sally Luce, *Retrenchment and Beyond: The Acid Test of Human Resource Management* (Ottawa: Conference Board of Canada, 1983), pp. 43–45.
16. L. L. Cummings and D. P. Schwab, "Designing Appraisal Systems for Information Yield," *California Management Review*, Summer 1978, pp. 18–25; Michael Beer, "Performance Appraisal: Dilemmas and Possibilities," *Organizational Dynamics*, Spring 1981, pp. 24–36.
17. D. L. DeVries, A. M. Morrison, S. L. Shullman, and M. L. Gerlach, *Performance Appraisal on the Line* (Greensboro, N.C.: Centre for Creative Leadership, 1981); Stephen J. Carroll and Craig E. Schneier, *Performance Appraisal and Review Systems* (Glenview, Ill.: Scott, Foresman, 1982); Bernardin and Beatty, *Performance Appraisal*.
18. Honourable Judy Erola, "Affirmative Action: Prescription for Equality," *Business Quarterly*, Spring 1984, p. 103.
19. For detailed reviews of reliability in performance appraisal, see Jeffrey S. Kane and Edward E. Lawler III, "Performance Appraisal Effectiveness: Its Assessment and Determinants," in *Research in Organizational Behavior, Vol. 1*, ed. Barry M. Staw (Greenwich, Conn.: JAI Press, 1979), pp. 425–78; Bernardin and Beatty, *Performance Appraisal*.
20. Ibid.
21. Wayne F. Cascio, "Scientific, Legal, and Operational Imperatives of Workable Performance Appraisal Systems," *Public Personnel Management* 11 (1982), pp. 367–75.
22. R. Folger and J. Greenberg, "Procedural Justice: An Interpretive Analysis of Personnel Systems," in *Research in Personnel and Human Resources Management, Vol. 3*, ed. Kendrith M. Rowland and Gerald R. Ferris (Greenwich, Conn.: JAI Press, 1985), pp. 141–85; R. J. Burke and D. S. Wilcox, "Characteristics of Effective Employee Performance Reviews and Development Interviews," *Personnel Psychology* 22 (1980), pp. 291–305; J. Greenberg, "Determinants of Perceived Fairness of Performance Evaluations," *Journal of Applied Psychology* 71 (1986), pp. 340–42.
23. J. J. DeMarco and J. G. Nigro, "Using Employee Attitudes and Perceptions to Maintain Supervisory Implementation of CSRA Performance Appraisal Systems," *Public Personnel Management Journal* 12, no. 1 (1983), pp. 43–51.

24. Elaine M. Evans and Steven L. McShane, "Employee Perceptions of Performance Appraisal Fairness in Two Organizations," *Canadian Journal of Behavioural Science* (in press).
25. Ibid.; R. J. Burke, W. Weitzel, and T. Weir, "Characteristics of Effective Employee Performance Review and Development Interviews: Replication and Extension," *Personnel Psychology* 31 (1978), pp. 903–19; R. L. Dipboye and R. de Pontbriand, "Correlates of Employee Reactions to Performance Appraisals and Appraisal Systems," *Journal of Applied Psychology* 66 (1981), pp. 248–51; M. M. Greller, "Subordinate Participation and Reactions to the Appraisal Interview," *Journal of Applied Psychology* 60 (1975), pp. 544–49; F. J. Landy et al., "Correlates of Perceived Fairness and Accuracy of Performance Evaluation," *Journal of Applied Psychology* 63 (1978), pp. 751–54.
26. Bernardin and Beatty, *Performance Appraisal*, pp. 267–77.
27. For example, see Wayne F. Cascio, "Scientific, Legal, and Operational Imperatives of Workable Performance Appraisal Systems." For a detailed discussion of the practicality of various methods, see Bernardin and Beatty, *Performance Appraisal*, pp. 208–15.
28. M. A. Jones, "Estimating Costs in the Development and Implementation of a Performance Evaluation System" (paper presented at the first annual Scientist-Practitioner Conference in Industrial-Organizational Psychology, Norfolk, Va., Old Dominion University, 1980).
29. H. J. Bernardin, B. B. Morgan, and P. S. Winne, "The Design of a Personnel Evaluation System for Police Officers," *JSAS Catalog of Selected Documents in Psychology* 10 (1980), pp. 1–280.
30. Bernardin and Beatty, *Performance Appraisal*, pp. 30–34.
31. R. I. Lazer and W. S. Wikstrom, *Appraising Managerial Performance: Current Practices and Future Directions* (New York: The Conference Board, 1977), p. 5.
32. F. J. Landy, J. L. Farr, and R. R. Jacobs, "Utility Concepts in Performance Measurement," *Organizational Behaviour and Human Performance* 30 (1982), pp. 15–40; Carroll and Schneier, *Performance Appraisal*, pp. 32–35.
33. Frank J. Landy, *Psychology of Work Behavior*, 3rd ed. (Chicago, Ill.: Dorsey Press, 1985); F. L. Schmidt and L. B. Kaplan, "Composite vs. Multiple Criteria: A Review and Resolution of the Controversy," *Personnel Psychology* 24 (1971), pp. 419–34.
34. L. W. Mealiea and J. F. Duffy, "Contemporary Training and Development Practices in Canadian Firms" (working paper, Halifax, Dalhousie University, 1986).
35. Charles J. Holson and Frederick W. Gibson, "Capturing Supervisor Rating Policies: A Way to Improve Performance Appraisal Effectiveness," *Personnel Administrator*, March 1984, pp. 59–68.
36. Carroll and Schneier, *Performance Appraisal*, pp. 32–35; also see Bernardin and Beatty, *Performance Appraisal*, pp. 34–38.
37. Latham and Wexley, *Increasing Productivity through Performance Appraisal*, pp. 41–47.
38. Carroll and Schneier, *Performance Appraisal and Review Systems*, pp. 36–83.
39. Lazer and Wikstrom, *Appraising Managerial Performance*.
40. T. A. DeCotiis, "An Analysis of the External Validity and Applied Relevance of Three Rating Formats," *Organizational Behaviour and Human Performance* 19 (1977), pp. 247–66; T. L. Dickinson and P. M. Zellinger, "A Comparison of the Behaviorally Anchored Rating and Mixed Standard Scale Formats," *Journal of*

Applied Psychology 65 (1980), pp. 147–54; Uco Wiersma and Gary P. Latham, "The Practicality of Behavioral Observation Scales, Behavioral Expectation Scales, and Trait Scales," *Personnel Psychology* 39 (1986), pp. 619–28.

41. DeVries et al., *Performance Appraisal on the Line*, p. 45; Wiersma and Latham, "The Practicality of Behavior Observation Scales."
42. L. M. King, J. E. Hunter, and F. L. Schmidt, "Halo in a Multi-Dimensional Forced Choice Performance Evaluation Scale," *Journal of Applied Psychology* 65 (1980), pp. 507–16.
43. R. M. Guion, *Personnel Testing* (New York: McGraw-Hill, 1965); Edwin E. Ghiselli and Clarence W. Brown, *Personnel and Industrial Psychology*, 2nd ed. (New York: McGraw-Hill, 1955), pp. 103–10.
44. Donald P. Schwab, H. G. Heneman III, and T. A. DeCotiis, "Behaviorally Anchored Rating Scales: A Review of the Literature," *Personnel Psychology* 28 (1975), pp. 549–62. Variations of BARS development are described in: Carroll and Schneier, *Performance Appraisal and Review Systems*, pp. 109–12; and Bernardin and Beatty, *Performance Appraisal*, pp. 83–85.
45. James Goodale and Ronald Burke, "BARS Need Not Be Job Specific," *Journal of Applied Psychology* 60, no. 3 (1975), pp. 389–91.
46. In particular, see Bernardin and Beatty, *Performance Appraisal*, chap. 6.
47. Schwab et al., "Behaviorally Anchored Rating Scales"; Wiersma and Latham, "The Practicality of Behavioral Observation Scales"; W. C. Borman, "Format and Training Effects on Rating Accuracy and Rater Errors," *Journal of Applied Psychology* 64 (1979), pp. 410–21; Frank J. Landy and James L. Farr, *The Measurement of Work Performance: Methods, Theory, and Application* (New York: Academic Press, 1983); P. O. Kingstrom and A. R. Bass, "A Critical Analysis of Studies Comparing Behaviorally Anchored Rating Scales (BARS) and Other Rating Formats," *Personnel Psychology* 34 (1981), pp. 263–89.
48. Gary P. Latham and Kenneth N. Wexley, "Behavioral Observation Scales for Performance Appraisal Purposes," *Personnel Psychology* 30 (1977), pp. 255–68.
49. For a detailed description on developing a BOS instrument, see Latham and Wexley, *Increasing Productivity through Performance Appraisal*, pp. 55–61.
50. Ibid., pp. 61–64.
51. Wiersma and Latham, "The Practicality of Behavioral Observation Scales."
52. K. R. Murphy, C. Martin, and M. Garcia, "Do Behavioral Observation Scales Measure Observation?" *Journal of Applied Psychology* 67 (1982), pp. 562–67.
53. Sheldon Zedeck and Wayne F. Cascio, "Psychological Issues in Personnel Decisions," *Annual Review of Psychology* 35 (1984), pp. 461–518; Jeffrey S. Kane and H. John Bernardin, "Behavioral Observation Scales and the Evaluation of Performance Appraisal Effectiveness," *Personnel Psychology* 35 (1982), pp. 635–42.
54. MBO was first brought to public attention in Peter Drucker, *The Practice of Management* (New York: Harper & Row, 1954), chap. 11. In that book, Drucker described an early form of MBO at General Electric. The case for MBO was also strengthened in works by McGregor and Odiorne. See Douglas McGregor, *The Human Side of Enterprise* (New York: McGraw-Hill, 1960); and George Odiorne, *Management by Objectives* (New York: Pitman, 1964).
55. J. S. Hodgson, "Management by Objectives: The Experiences of a Federal Government Department," *Canadian Public Administration* 16, no. 4 (1973), pp. 422–31.
56. Carroll and Schneier, *Performance Appraisal and Review Systems*, pp. 142–43;

Heinz Weihrich, *Management Excellence: Productivity through MBO* (New York: McGraw-Hill, 1985), chaps. 4 and 5.

57. Edwin A. Locke and Gary P. Latham, *Goal Setting: A Motivational Technique that Works* (Englewood Cliffs, N.J.: Prentice-Hall, 1984).
58. J. Carroll, Jr., and H. L. Tosi, Jr., *Management by Objectives* (New York: Macmillan, 1973); J. N. Kondrasuk, "Studies in MBO Effectiveness," *Academy of Management Review* 6 (1981), pp. 419–30; Edwin A. Locke, "The Ubiquity of the Technique of Goal Setting in Theories of and Approaches to Employee Motivation," *Academy of Management Review* 3 (1978), pp. 594–601.
59. For a review of these limitations, see Carroll and Schneier, *Performance Appraisal and Review Systems*, pp. 149–52; Bernardin and Beatty, *Performance Appraisal*, pp. 116–24.
60. For a thorough description of developing and implementing mixed standard scales, see Frank J. Landy, *Psychology of Work Behavior*, pp. 182–84; Bernardin and Beatty, *Performance Appraisal*, pp. 88–96.
61. For details of these and other ranking procedures, see Richard I. Henderson, *Performance Appraisal*, 2nd ed., pp. 160–67. More advanced statistical procedures on ranking are found in J. P. Guilford, *Psychometric Methods* (New York: McGraw-Hill, 1954), chaps. 7 and 8.
62. John Terry, "In Praise of Appraisals," p. 81.
63. For a detailed discussion of assessment centres in performance evaluation, see Latham and Wexley, *Increasing Productivity through Performance Appraisal*, pp. 92–94; DeVries et al., *Performance Appraisal on the Line*, pp. 18–19; George C. Thornton III and William C. Byham, *Assessment Centres and Managerial Performance* (New York: Academic Press, 1982).
64. Tom S. Turner and Jim A. Utley, "Foreman Selection: One Company's Approach," *Personnel*, May–June 1979, pp. 47–55.
65. Michael Keeley, "A Contingency Framework for Performance Evaluation," *Academy of Management Review*, July 1978, pp. 428–38.
66. Jack M. Feldman, "Instrumentation and Training for Performance Appraisal: A Perceptual-Cognitive Viewpoint," in *Research in Personnel and Human Resources Management, Vol. 4*, ed. Kendrith M. Rowland and Gerald R. Ferris (Greenwich, Conn.: JAI Press, 1986), pp. 45–99.
67. Herbert H. Meyer, "Self-Appraisal of Job Performance," *Personnel Psychology* 33 (1980), pp,. 291–95.
68. John Terry, "In Praise of Appraisals."
69. John S. Kane and Edward E. Lawler III, "Methods of Peer Assessment," *Psychological Bulletin* 85 (1978), pp. 555–86; Angelo S. DeNisi, W. Alan Randolph, and Allyn G. Blencoe, "Potential Problems with Peer Ratings," *Academy of Management Review* 26, no. 3 (1983), pp. 457–64.
70. G. W. Bush and J. W. Stinson, "A Different Use of Performance Appraisal: Evaluating the Boss," *Management Review*, November 1980, pp. 14–17.
71. "Union Urges Workers Get Right to Evaluate Bosses," *Winnipeg Free Press*, August 25, 1985, p. 1.
72. Treasury Board of Canada Secretariat, Personnel Policy Branch, *Personnel: A Manager's Handbook* (Ottawa: Minister of Supply and Services Canada, 1982), pp. 49–50.
73. Latham and Wexley, *Increasing Productivity through Performance Appraisal*, chap. 4; Kane and Lawler, "Performance Appraisal Effectiveness," p. 445.

74. Kenneth N. Wexley and Richard Klimoski, "Performance Appraisal: An Update," in *Research in Personnel and Human Resources Management, Vol. 2*, ed. Kendrith M. Rowland and Gerald R. Ferris (Greenwich, Conn.: JAI Press, 1984), pp. 35–79.
75. Some authors question the practicality of some information processing research, but suggest a number of ways supervisors' information processing may be improved. See Cristina G. Banks and Kevin R. Murphy, "Toward Narrowing the Research-Practice Gap in Performance Appraisal," *Personnel Psychology* 38 (1985), pp. 335–45.
76. Stephan J. Motowidlo, "Information Processing in Personnel Decisions," in *Research in Personnel and Human Resources Management, Vol. 4*, ed. Kendrith M. Rowland and Gerald R. Ferris (Greenwich, Conn.: JAI Press, 1986), pp. 1–44.
77. Ibid. For a detailed analysis of the halo effect, see William H. Cooper, "Ubiquitous Halo," *Psychological Bulletin* 90, no. 2 (1981), pp. 218–44.
78. Wayne F. Cascio and E. R. Valenzi, "Relations among Criteria of Police Performance," *Journal of Applied Psychology* 63, no. 1 (1978), pp. 22–28.
79. Robert L. Heneman and Kenneth N. Wexley, "The Effects of Time Delay in Rating and Amount of Information Observed in Performance Rating Accuracy," *Academy of Management Journal* 26 (1983), pp. 677–86; H. John Bernardin and R. L. Cardy, "Appraisal Accuracy: The Ability and Motivation to Remember the Past," *Public Personnel Management* 11 (1982), pp. 352–57.
80. John M. Ivancevich, "Contrast Effects in Performance Evaluation and Reward Practices," *Academy of Management Journal* 26, no. 3 (1983), pp. 465–76.
81. H. H. Kelley, "The Processes of Causal Attribution," *American Psychologist* 28 (1973), pp. 107–28; J. M. Feldman, "Beyond Attribution Theory: Cognitive Processes in Performance Appraisal," *Journal of Applied Psychology* 66 (1981), pp. 127–48; Dean Tjosvold, "The Effects of Attribution and Social Context on Superiors' Influence and Interaction with Low Performing Subordinates," *Personnel Psychology*, Summer 1985, pp. 361–76.
82. Terence R. Mitchell and R. E. Wood, "Supervisor's Responses to Subordinate Poor Performance: A Test of an Attribution Model," *Organizational Behaviour and Human Performance* 25 (1980), pp. 123–38; Andre de Carufel and Jak Jabes, "Intuitive Prediction and Judgement on a Personnel Task by Naive and Experienced Judges," *Canadian Journal of Administrative Sciences*, June 1984, pp. 78–94.
83. Daniel R. Ilgen and Jack M. Feldman, "Performance Appraisal: A Process Focus," in *Research in Organizational Behavior*, ed. Barry Staw and Larry Cummings (Greenwich, Conn.: JAI Press, 1983), pp. 141–97.
84. Terence R. Mitchell and L. S. Kalb, "Effects of Outcome Knowledge and Outcome Valence on Supervisors' Evaluations," *Journal of Applied Psychology* 66 (1981), pp. 604–12.
85. H. J. Bernardin and E. C. Pence, "Effects of Rater Training: Creating New Response Sets and Decreasing Accuracy," *Journal of Applied Psychology* 65 (1980), pp. 60–66.
86. Bernardin and Beatty, pp. 254–67; David E. Smith, "Training Programs for Performance Appraisal: A Review," *Academy of Management Review* 11, no. 1 (1986), pp. 22–40.
87. David E. Smith, "Training Programs for Performance Appraisal"; H. John Bernardin and M. R. Buckley, "Strategies in Rater Training," *Academy of Management Review* 6, no. 2 (1981), pp. 205–12.

88. John C. Flanagan, "The Critical Incident Technique," *Psychological Bulletin* 51 (1954), pp. 327–58; John C. Flanagan and Robert K. Burns, "The Employee Performance Record: A New Appraisal and Development Tool," *Harvard Business Review*, September–October 1955, pp. 95–102.
89. Bernardin and Beatty, *Performance Appraisal*, p. 82.
90. Banks and Murphy, "Toward Narrowing the Research-Practice Gap," p. 341.
91. Berkeley Rice, "Performance Review: The Job Nobody Likes," *Psychology Today*, September 1985, pp. 30–36; Carroll and Schneier, *Performance Appraisal and Review Systems*, pp. 161–62.
92. D. R. Ilgen, R. B. Peterson, B. A. Martin, and D. A. Boescher, "Supervisor and Subordinate Reactions to Performance Appraisal Sessions," *Organizational Behaviour and Human Performance* 28 (1981), pp. 311–36; Bernardin and Beatty, *Performance Appraisal*, p. 277.
93. DeVries et al., *Performance Appraisal on the Line*, pp. 72–73; Latham and Wexley, *Increasing Productivity through Performance Appraisal*, pp. 154–55.
94. Landy, *Psychology of Work Behavior*, p. 203.
95. Douglas Cederblom, "The Performance Appraisal Interview: A Review, Implications, and Suggestions," *Academy of Management Review* 7, no. 3 (1982), pp. 219–27; D. R. Ilgen, C. D. Fisher, and M. S. Taylor, "Consequences of Individual Feedback on Behavior in Organizations," *Journal of Applied Psychology* 64 (1979), pp. 349–71; Carroll and Schneier, *Performance Appraisal and Review Systems*, chap. 7.
96. Terry, "In Praise of Appraisals."
97. Bernardin and Beatty, *Performance Appraisal*, pp. 278–80.
98. Herbert H. Meyer, Emanuel Kay, and John R. P. French, Jr., "Split Roles in Performance Appraisal," *Harvard Business Review*, January–February 1965, pp. 123–29. However, one study reports the opposite effect: salary discussion has a positive impact on the interview session. See Bruce Prince and Edward E. Lawler III, "Does Salary Discussion Hurt the Developmental Performance Appraisal?" *Organizational Behaviour and Human Decision Process* 37 (1986), pp. 357–75.
99. Terry, "In Praise of Appraisals," p. 85.
100. R. S. Burke and D. S. Wilcox, "Characteristics of Effective Employee Performance and Development Interviews," *Personnel Psychology* 22 (1969), pp. 291–305; Cederblom, "The Performance Appraisal Interview"; Bernardin and Beatty, *Performance Appraisal*; DeVries et al., *Performance Appraisal on the Line*.

Exhibit V
THE DIAGNOSTIC MODEL

External conditions	Organization conditions	Human resource activities	Objective
Economic conditions Government regulations Technology Unions	Nature of organization: Strategies and objectives Nature of work Nature of employees and work groups	Staffing Development Employment relations Compensation Evaluation	Human resource effectiveness

PART FIVE
HUMAN RESOURCE ACTIVITIES:
EMPLOYMENT RELATIONS

In the preceding part of the book, we discussed the necessary conditions to encourage maximum development of employees. Another aspect of human resource management involves the daily relationship between employees and the organization. Employees may have problems, either job-related or personal, that inhibit their performance. Or managers, through their supervisory styles, may inhibit employee creativity and contributions. Chapter Twelve describes ways organizations might assist employees.

Often, employees faced with unsatisfactory conditions join together in unions to collectively bargain to improve these conditions. In Chapter Thirteen, Labour Relations, the impact of unions on human resource management is considered. Although unions receive the most attention in the popular press, the influence of unions extends beyond their membership. It also affects nonunionized organizations, notably in conflict resolution and wage setting. Unions are part of the social and political fabric of Canada.

The quality of employment relations, as the diagnostic model shows (Exhibit V), is affected by external conditions. Collective bargaining agreements are legal contracts subject to regulation. The whole unionizing and negotiating process is regulated too in order to provide some semblance of a balance of power among participants. Economic conditions affect employment relations by limiting what options each side can afford to utilize. Within the organization, the culture and values set the tone about how the employee/employer relationship is viewed. Both employees and employers have rights and responsibilities. Employers differ in initiating systems to protect the rights of

PART FIVE   continued

employees. Some employers still try to avoid any formal systems that recognize employee rights. The issue is one of governance and justice in the workplace.

These chapters can be viewed as continuing the discussion of the employee development process, since they are also concerned with the conditions that allow individuals to develop their abilities and to contribute to the organization. Obviously the quality of employment relations has an impact on the objective of organization effectiveness.

CHAPTER TWELVE
EMPLOYEE RELATIONS AND RIGHTS

CHAPTER OUTLINE

I. A Diagnostic Approach to Employee Relations and Rights
   A. External Factors
   B. Internal Factors
II. Quality of Work Life
   A. QWL Approaches
   B. QWL Outcomes
III. Employee Counselling and Conflict Resolution
   A. Career Development
   B. Employee Assistance
   C. Conflict Resolution
IV. Occupational Health and Safety
   A. Costs and Causes of Occupational Injuries and Diseases
   B. Occupational Health and Safety Legislation
V. Termination of Employment
   A. Statutory Rights
   B. Common Law Wrongful Dismissal
VI. Summary

The low point in Budd Canada's rocky history of labour-management relations was 1979. The company's Kitchener, Ontario, plant was shut down 68 times that year by illegal work stoppages. More than 300 grievances had been filed (an average of 16 per 100 unionized employees), and absenteeism had reached 7.4 percent. By September, the company was in court trying to put the leaders of the union in jail for violating a cease-and-desist ruling from the Ontario Labour Relations Board. Budd Canada's West German parent company was thinking about closing the operation and moving the work to an older plant in the United States where labour-management relations were better.

Now, under a quality of work life program between Budd Canada and Local 1451 of the Canadian Auto Workers, labour-management tensions have eased, and employee participation in product quality improvement has increased through weekly problem-solving sessions. The number of wildcat strikes has fallen to zero, the grievance rate is only 3 per 100 employees, absenteeism is much lower, and the company reports record profits. One study of the Budd Canada experience notes that product quality has improved demonstrably. Another investigation, which conducted surveys before and after the intervention, reports that employees now feel a greater sense of pride in their performance and more optimism toward union-management relations.[1] The official logo of Budd Canada's Employee Involvement Program, shown in Exhibit 12–1, illustrates this dramatic change in philosophy between management and employees.

> **Definition**
> *Employee relations* activities are those that seek greater organizational effectiveness through the enhancement of human dignity and growth, with manager and employees learning to approach work in a cooperative rather than adversarial manner.

The previous two chapters in this book dealt with enhancing employee and organization effectiveness through training and performance evaluation. This chapter discusses enhancing effectiveness through employee relations. Here we include programs that encourage employee participation in decision making, such as quality of work life (QWL) programs, to foster employee growth such as career development, employee assistance programs that aid troubled employees, and employment security programs.

This chapter also extends our discussion of employee rights. We have already examined employment equity (Chapter Seven), but other employee rights also exist, such as the rights to a healthful and safe work environment

EXHIBIT 12-1
Official Logo of Budd Canada's Employee Involvement Program

Budd Kitchener ✦ C.A.W. Local 1451
PEOPLE
OUR STRONGEST LINK
EMPLOYEE INVOLVEMENT

Source: Budd Canada (Design by Steve Deacon, maintenance tradesperson at Budd Canada).

and to reasonable notice in dismissal. First, employee relations and employee rights are placed into the context of the environment and organization.

A DIAGNOSTIC APPROACH TO EMPLOYEE RELATIONS AND RIGHTS

The quality of employee relations and rights in an organization is a function of many things. While corporate culture is perhaps the most important, external factors play a role too.

External Factors

Economic
There is no doubt that a company making a profit and experiencing growth will find it easier to commit to an open, supportive employee relations policy. Job security is enhanced, promotions become possible, and careers can be

developed. But during an economic crunch, avoiding layoffs and the rumours of layoffs becomes more difficult. Dofasco Inc. is an example.[2] Since the Great Depression of the 1930s, the Hamilton, Ontario, steelmaker has been seen as a "rock of Gibraltar" regarding job security. With a deeply embedded philosophy of taking care of its employees, Dofasco avoided layoffs by carefully managing inventories and customer orders. But the severe recession of 1982 forced the company to lay off more than 2,000 of its 11,500 employees until the economy improved a year later.

A fundamental tenet underlying sound employee relations is that employees and management must have confidence in each other's intention to be fair and equitable. Fairness and trust are harder to maintain when markets are shrinking and cutbacks are required. Dofasco's carefully nurtured relationship with its employees weathered this unprecedented event. The company went out of its way to assist those who were laid off and communicated to all employees why other options were not feasible. Fortunately, Dofasco was able to offer jobs to all of the laid-off employees one year later. The economy plays a significant role in setting the context for employee relations.

Government

Government also plays a role in employee relations and rights. Federal, provincial, and territorial legislation requires employers to monitor and improve health and safety in the workplace. Employment Standards Acts, Labour Codes, and other laws also regulate the actions of employers and employees. Government also facilitates employee relations and rights through a variety of programs and services. Several jurisdictions have introduced quality of work life centres to study and publicize innovative workplace arrangements.

To more effectively disseminate information on occupational health and safety matters, the federal government created the Canadian Centre for Occupational Health and Safety in 1978. Located in Hamilton, Ontario, the centre responds to public inquiries about health and safety matters and has set up a computerized information facility (called CCINFO) with terminals in nearly 300 organizations across Canada. CCINFO consists of two parts: (1) a detailed listing of chemical information and (2) a bibliography of published research and materials on occupational health and safety.

Unions

Unions play a substantial role in shaping employee relations and rights. Through their support and participation, unions can ensure the success of quality of work life programs. They are often the strongest advocates of occupational health and safety programs. Many employee rights are negotiated into collective agreements, as we shall see in Chapter Thirteen.

Internal Factors

Corporate Culture
The employee relations atmosphere reflects the culture of the organization. In many organizations, employee relations programs emphasize safeguarding employee rights, employee input into work and job decisions, and a communication system that makes employees aware of problems and objectives of the organization and makes managers aware of problems and objectives of the employees.[3]

Some organizations committed to employee relations programs evaluate managers on whether discipline procedures or conflict resolution systems are fairly administered; or whether women and minorities are given equal access to training, promotions, or other job rewards; and on the results of surveys of employees' attitudes about the organization and its management practices.

Nature of Employees
The rising educational level of the work force is often cited as a fundamental change. These employees, some assert, want a greater say in work decisions and are more willing to challenge management.[4] The rising number of employees suing employers supports such assertions. But such assertions contrast with the fact that formalized worker participation programs exist mainly in manufacturing firms, where the bulk of jobs do not require high levels of education.[5] So while we cannot say for certain what differences the educational level of employees makes, it is safe to say some workers want to be involved in decision making, others do not; the desires of both groups should be accommodated.

To see how all these factors influence the design of employee relations programs, let us begin by examining some quality of work life projects.

QUALITY OF WORK LIFE

If any concept in P/HRM has an elusive definition, it is quality of work life (QWL). In its most general form, QWL refers to creation of a work environment that helps employees to fulfill their social, psychological, and emotional needs. This typically includes a higher degree of participative decision making and/or a restructuring of the work process. Profit and equity sharing, improved health and safety, and alternative work schedules have also been included under the QWL heading.[6] The QWL concept has been expanded so broadly, it is in danger of becoming a victim of its own success. Therefore, let us describe some of the more specific approaches to QWL.

QWL Approaches

Sociotechnical Systems

The sociotechnical concept emerged out of the work of Eric Trist and his colleagues at Britain's Tavistock Institute in the 1950s.[7] The basic principle of this approach is that organizational objectives are best met by the joint optimization of the social and technical aspects of the work environment. Essentially, this suggests that for a workplace to attain its potential productivity, those implementing the technology must pay equal attention to the human element through the design of work around that technology. The employee and work group are complementary to the technology, not merely extensions of it. Moreover, this theory proposes that the work group, not management, should regulate the work system. In other words, autonomous work groups represent a major feature of sociotechnical systems.

There are several examples of sociotechnically designed operations in the Canadian petroleum industry. The best known is the Shell Canada chemical plant in Sarnia, Ontario.[8] Rather than build a new plant around traditional departmental divisions, the company set up a task force in 1975 to identify solutions to problems in other operations. The task force's recommendation was to dramatically redesign the work relationships. In particular, the new operation would be run by six multiskilled work teams, each with 18 members and a coordinator, and one special craft team. An important prerequisite for the success of this new system is that each group would be fully capable of operating all sections of the plant. Therefore, an intensive training program was developed to enable each member of the work team to eventually become proficient in all aspects of the process. A skill-based compensation system was introduced to encourage employees to expand their knowledge through the training program. Along with a redesign of the social system, the technical system was adapted to facilitate the work team's operational control of the process. Part of the philosophy behind these and other changes at Shell Canada's chemical plant is shown in Exhibit 12-2.

Problem-Solving Groups

Many types of problem-solving groups exist. Union-management committees can become constructive forums for problem solving when both sides are able to identify areas of mutual concern and work toward integrative solutions. The General Motors of Canada plant in Ste.-Therese, Quebec, experienced a dramatic turnaround in 1986, in part due to joint union-management problem-solving groups. Rather than being permanently closed, the operation has significantly improved productivity and worker morale.[9] The Ontario Ministry of Labour and the Ontario Education Relations Commission introduced a type of preventative mediation, called Relationships by Objectives, which is also

EXHIBIT 12–2
Philosophy of Shell Canada Chemical Plant QWL Project

The primary objective of Shell Canada Limited at the Sarnia Refinery and Chemical Plant is to obtain an optimum return on investment in capital and human resources, operating in a safe environment as a responsible member of the community, while being responsive to its employees' needs. It is believed that this objective can best be achieved by establishing and sustaining an organization and management system consistent with the following philosophy.

The Company recognizes that, in order to achieve its primary objective, it is necessary to give appropriate consideration to the design and management of both the social and technical aspects associated with its operation. The former is related to employees and encompasses such areas as organizational structure, levels of responsibility and authority, supervisory roles, communication networks, interpersonal relationships, reward systems, etc., while the latter deals with the physical equipment—its capacity, layout, degree of automation, etc. Although our operations involve a high degree of sophisticated technology which can be exploited to improve efficiencies, it is only through the committed actions of our people that the full benefits can be realized. The social and technical systems are interrelated and must be jointly taken into account to achieve overall optimization.

Source: Normal Halpern, "Sociotechnical Systems Design: The Shell Sarnia Experience," in *Quality of Working Life: Contemporary Cases*, ed. J. B. Cunningham and T. H. White (Ottawa: Labour Canada, 1984).

---

based on the joint problem-solving approach. This program helped improve relations between Budd Canada's management and union local.

The *quality circle* is quickly becoming the most popular type of problem-solving arrangement. The quality circle is based on the efforts of American quality control experts sent by the Allied Forces after second World War II to rebuild the Japanese economy. These ideas were incorporated into a series of quality control lectures presented first by William Deming. Although Deming emphasized the participation of middle and top management in quality control systems, the Japanese extended involvement to rank-and-file employees.[10] The innovation to include blue-collar participation was based on the belief that properly trained workers are in the best position to see unrecognized quality problems. Thus, quality circles emerged as small groups of production employees who meet on a regular basis to identify, analyze, and solve quality and related problems in their area of responsibility.

Although Canada lags behind Japan and the United States, several hundred firms in this country have implemented the quality control concept. It is interesting to note, however, that few Japanese subsidiaries operating in Canada have quality circles. According to one study,[11] this is due to union resistance and the fact that many Japanese subsidiaries are service firms where quality circles are more difficult to introduce. In contrast, quality circles are found in a variety of manufacturing and processing firms, such as

Garrett Manufacturing Ltd., Canadian Gypsum Co., McCain Foods Ltd., and Ford Motor Company of Canada Ltd.

TRW Canada Limited introduced quality circles to its Thompson Products Division in St. Catherines, Ontario, in 1981.[12] A steering committee established the policies to be followed by the quality circle groups. It was decided membership in the circle would be voluntary. The groups would not exceed 15 members, would meet weekly for one hour before the end of the work shift, and would confine their problem-solving activities to their own areas. A quality circle facilitator was appointed from company staff to train group leaders, meet with the steering committee, and act as a resource person. Other members of the quality circles also received training on problem-solving methods and an orientation on the quality circle concept. A pilot quality circle was initiated in 1982, and several other circles were later formed as the success of the project became apparent. According to the personnel manager at TRW Canada Ltd., part of this success has been due to the awareness of the quality circle program created through the extensive use of bulletin boards, in-house newspapers, and media advertisements.

The organization of the quality circle program at TRW Canada is very similar to the structure shown in Exhibit 12–3. The steering committee, which consists of employee and management representatives, establishes policy and oversees the operation of the program. Each circle is comprised of 5 to 10 employees, one of which is the circle leader. A facilitator is appointed to act as a liaison between the steering committee and the circle leaders and to provide training to the group. In larger organizations, several facilitators may be needed. At the Toronto-Dominion Bank, for example, a full-time facilitator is assigned to each major branch or district. In these larger operations, a coordinator's position is created to supervise the facilitators and provide administrative support. In smaller programs, such as at TRW Canada, only one facilitator is needed. Consequently, the facilitator works with the P/HRM department and steering committee to provide administrative support.[13]

Employee Equity Investment and Ownership

Potentially the highest degree of employee involvement in organizational decisions occurs when employees are shareholders or complete owners of the company. In some firms, employee ownership has led to a substantial improvement in commitment, productivity, and morale. This appears to be the case at Britex Ltd. of Bridgetown, Nova Scotia.[14] The original owner, J. P. Stevens and Co., was about to permanently close the elastic fabric manufacturing plant in 1980 due to its low productivity and outdated equipment. Rather than face unemployment, several managers bought the operation with financial assistance from both federal and provincial governments. In addition

EXHIBIT 12–3
Structure of a Quality Circle System

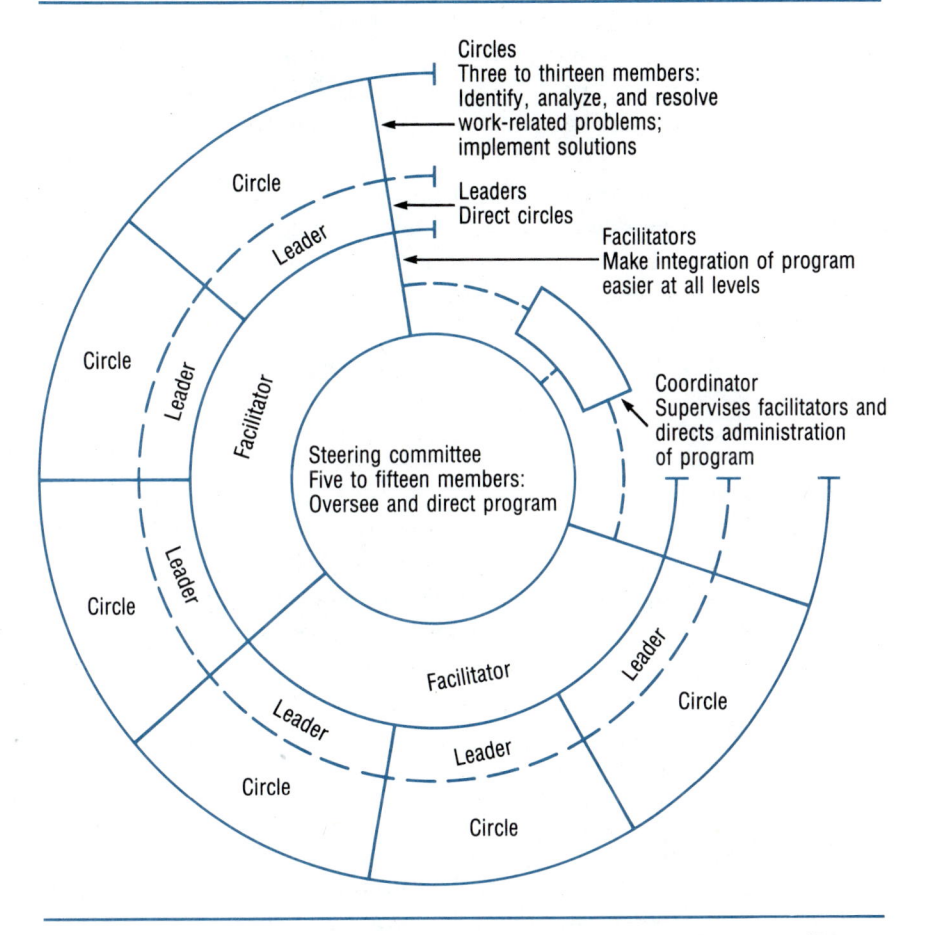

Circles
Three to thirteen members: Identify, analyze, and resolve work-related problems; implement solutions

Leaders
Direct circles

Facilitators
Make integration of program easier at all levels

Coordinator
Supervises facilitators and directs administration of program

Steering committee
Five to fifteen members: Oversee and direct program

Source: Joseph Hanley, "Our Experience with Quality Circles," *Quality Progress* 13 (February 1980), p. 24. © 1980 American Society for Quality Control. Reprinted by permission.

to profit sharing and a formalized system of participative decision making, the new owners set aside 20 percent of the company's shares for employee ownership. Approximately half the eligible employees own shares in Britex. The company's productive efficiency has since tripled, and there is a distinct sense that employees and management share common objectives. The extent to which the company's turnaround is attributable to employee ownership rather than other factors is unknown. But similar improvements have also been reported at Lamford Forest Products in British Columbia, Tembec Inc. in Quebec, and Byers Transport in Alberta (before the employees sold the company in 1979).

Employee-owned companies are not always successful (e.g., failure of Societe Populaire Tricofil in St. Jerome, Quebec). Even where these initiatives are financially successful, research has found that most employee-owners view their ownership only as a financial investment. Employees tend to exercise their full decision-making rights infrequently. Typically, the managerial and collective bargaining arrangements under the previous ownership are retained.[15]

In Europe, employee participation in organizational decisions, either directly or through representatives, is frequently required by law. Nightingale notes that these reforms were based on political doctrine but are unlikely to receive wide appeal in North America. Rather than attempting to impose workplace democracy through omnibus legislation, federal and provincial governments would be more successful by encouraging joint employee-management committees in targetted areas such as health and safety.[16] Through these experiences, the philosophy of participation would spread.

Employment Security

Evidence exists to suggest layoffs and dismissals hurt the productivity of the remaining employees and weaken their psychological attachment to the company.[17] Consequently, a few companies have introduced employment security policies in order to increase organizational effectiveness. Generally, guaranteed employment meets the following conditions:

> Top management is committed—or required by labour contract—to make every effort to provide continuous employment or income for at least some segment of its work force, and has put in place at least some activities or programs to support this commitment.[18]

Hewlett-Packard and IBM have guaranteed employment policies in both Canada and the United States.[19] In neither organization, however, is employment security an unwavering policy. For instance, Hewlett-Packard's Statement of Corporate Objectives indicates it is the company's intent to "provide job security based on (employee) performance." But the document also declares this policy "does not mean we are committed to an absolute tenure status." In 1987, when profits dipped, Hewlett-Packard's president reminded employees that employment security may mean changing jobs and locations within the company.[20] Even if a guarantee of lifetime employment becomes part of the written or implied employment contract, it is unlikely to be binding in a Canadian court.[21]

Rather than total job security for all staff, some firms maintain a no-layoff policy for permanent employees by implementing buffers. S. C. Johnson and Son Ltd., makers of Johnson's Wax, has avoided layoffs among its full-time staff in Canada and abroad by hiring temporary employees for peak production. Overtime and delivery schedule flexibility also act as buffers.

While still maintaining employment security, work force adjustments can be made by reducing the number of hours of work. During the last recession, several organizations avoided layoffs by having all employees work fewer hours per week at proportionately reduced pay. Alternatively, some surplus staff has been lent to other organizations temporarily. A third option, introduced in the late 1970s in Canada, is a work-sharing arrangement through the unemployment insurance system. Rather than laying off some people, all employees in that job group work for part of the week and receive UI benefits for the remainder.[22]

QWL Outcomes

Quality of work life interventions have received considerable interest, but few have been systematically evaluated. One such evaluation was conducted by Ondrack and Evans.[23] The authors measured employee attitudes and job perceptions in five Canadian petrochemical plants with QWL programs. These attitudes and perceptions were also collected on employees in non-QWL plants in that industry. A comparison revealed few significant differences.

Another study of QWL programs at 18 General Motors plants found mixed support for the impact of these programs on economic performance and labour-management relations in the company.[24] The authors speculate, however, that QWL efforts may enable union and management to break out of a cycle of high conflict and low trust in the collective bargaining relationship. The key test of QWL success, they say, is whether effective collaboration can be maintained at the workplace during periods of difficult negotiations at the bargaining table.

QWL is an important approach to employee relations. It focusses on individuals as part of work groups and the larger organization. Participation, cooperation, and fair treatment are key ingredients. Another approach to employee relations is employee counselling. It focusses more on individuals and their ability to cope with work and other events that may influence work effectiveness.

EMPLOYEE COUNSELLING AND CONFLICT RESOLUTION

Human resource managers are increasingly responsible for helping employees resolve their personal and work-related problems. Career counselling, employee assistance, and conflict resolution assist employees in their quest for a better quality of life. These forms of employee relations may also increase organizational effectiveness by enabling employees to work more effectively.

Career Development

While the responsibility for planning a career lies with the individual, a specific career is not solely determined by actions of the individual. Rather, the organization has a large role to play by creating job opportunities for employees.[25] Career planning is therefore more effective if done jointly by the individual and the organization. The organization has a stake in successful career planning, as it needs a steady supply of adequately trained people to do jobs at every level of the organization.[26] This mutual participation, shown in Exhibit 12-4, makes career planning a valuable component of employee relations.

> **Definition**
> *Career development* is the formal, structured activity offered by an organization for its members for the purpose of increasing their awareness, knowledge, or capabilities affecting the direction and progression of their careers.

Career development implies more than the organization offering a set pattern of advancement, which an employee is free to accept or reject, or an employee setting career goals without regard to the organization. Career development implies the employee is heavily involved in designing a career with input from the organization as to what it expects and anticipates for the employee.[27]

The organization's role includes assisting the development of insight into abilities and career needs; assisting the formulation of a possible career plan; and providing training and development opportunities to meet the requirements for movement along the career path.

Career Development Activities

Bowen and Hall delineate four categories of career development activities to increase awareness, knowledge, and skills of employees.[28]

1. Individual activities.
2. Counsellor/client activities.
3. Supervisor as counsellor or coach.
4. Group activities.

Exhibit 12-5 lists the advantages and disadvantages of each of these activities.

EXHIBIT 12–4
A Working Model of Organizational Career Development

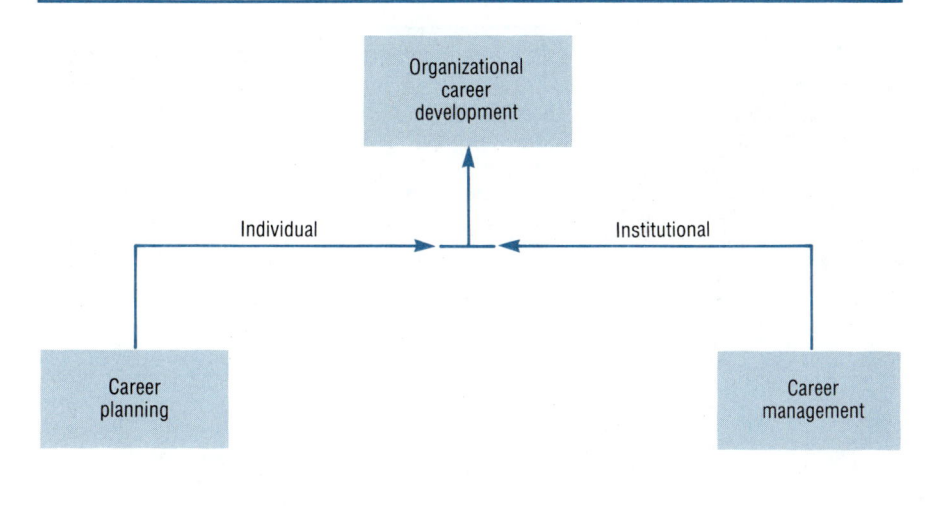

```
                    Organizational
                        career
                     development
                           ▲
                           │
        Individual ───────┴─────── Institutional
           │                              │
           ▼                              ▼
        Career                         Career
       planning                       management
```

Sub Processes
—Occupational Choice
—Organizational Choice
—Choice of Job Assignment
—Career Self-Development

Sub Processes
—Recruitment and Selection
—Human Resource Allocation
—Appraisal and Evaluation
—Training and Development

A. Career: The sequence of a person's work-related activities and behaviours and associated attitudes, values, and aspirations over the span of one's life.
B. Organizational Career Development: The outcomes emanating from the interaction of individual career planning and institutional career management processes.
C. Career Planning: A deliberate process for: becoming aware of self, opportunities, constraints, choices, and consequences; identifying career-related goals; and programming work, education, and related developmental experiences to provide the direction, timing, and sequence of steps to attain a specific career goal.
D. Career Manangement: An ongoing process of preparing, implementing, and monitoring career plans undertaken by the individual alone or in concert with the organization's career systems.

Source: Thomas G. Gutteridge and Fred L. Otte, "Organizational Career Development: What's Going On out There?" *Training and Development Journal*, February 1983, pp. 22–26.

The type of program used will be based, in part, on the nature of the users. With programs that are open to all employees, economics dictate there will be more emphasis on self-directed activity. Counselling and coaching will play a larger role in career development for managerial and professional people whose leadership or potential contribution is critical for the organization.

Individual activities can be done with or without organizational assistance. In larger Canadian businesses, the individual's career decisions are assisted

EXHIBIT 12–5
Characteristics of Various Career Planning Activities and Probable Contribution to Career Success

Individual Activities	Potential Advantages	Potential Shortcomings
1. Personal planning with possible aid of self-help materials.	a. For persons with strong motivation and adequate sources of information, may be adequate for goal setting. b. Cost is minimal.	a. Most people need interpersonal feedback to develop a complete and accurate self-evaluation. b. No built-in mechanism for checking completeness of information on occupational opportunities or for correcting distorted views of self. c. No opportunity to explore new occupational possibilities.
2. Testing approach: Guidance counsellor administers vocational interest and aptitude tests and feeds data back to client; may also provide information on occupations, job market, and job hunting techniques.	Test results and information supplied may be of considerable value for client.	a. Usually expensive. b. Client has no way of testing validity of counsellor's views or test results. c. Interpersonal feedback likely to be minimal.

Boss as Counsellor or Coach

3. Superior regularly or periodically assesses subordinate's performance and provides feedback and suggestions for improving performance and/or career opportunities.	a. Superior may have an excellent opportunity to observe subordinate's behaviour in a number of work activities. b. Superior knows career opportunities within the organization. c. Superior can provide assignments to expand subordinate's capabilities.	a. The superior's power can be highly threatening, causing subordinate to be defensive, cautious, and closed to feedback. b. Superior's first loyalty is likely to be seen as to the interests of the organization, not subordinate. c. Not likely to integrate nonwork aspects of subordinate's life with career issues.

EXHIBIT 12–5 *(concluded)*

Group Activities	Potential Advantages	Potential Shortcomings

4. Assessment centre: usually conducted by or sponsored by employer. Employee is tested by a number of pencil and paper tests and is presented with situational tests and interviews where performance is observed and evaluated. Evaluators are often other managers trained in the technique. Psychologists design centre and interpret test results.	a. Substantial amounts of data can be developed quickly.
	b. Multiple judges on panel and results of several tests provide variety of perspectives for candidate.
	c. Moderate cost, usually borne by employer.
		a. High threat situation
		  1. Employee likely to feel "on the spot" and anxious about results—not an optimal situation for feedback.
		  2. Centre serves interests of employer first, which may be incompatible with interests of employee.
		b. Data generated primarily applicable to career with employing organization only.

Life Planning Workshop: Conducted within Organization

5. A set of semistructural experiences are presented which encourage participants to assess their values, situation, etc. to set goals, and to develop greater self-awareness through interpersonal interaction with other participants.	a. No cost to participant. b. Wide exploration of self and needs encouraged. Copious interpersonal feedback generated. c. Other participants are frequently valuable sources of information on career alternatives. d. Goals developed and development needs can be integrated into parallel organizational programs.	a. Normally do not provide occupational information, especially for careers outside of the organization. b. Employers leery of processes that may encourage employees to leave organization. c. Provision for periodic follow-up probably necessary to maximize value to most participants. d. Participants may not be encouraged to explore changing jobs or careers.

Source: Adapted from D. Bowen and D. T. Hall, "Career Planning for Employee Development: A Primer for Managers," *California Management Review*, Winter 1977, pp. 33–35.

by formalized programs and in-house career counselling specialists. At Great-West Life Assurance Co. of Winnipeg, employees are provided with a career development program to help them identify their career goals and explore effective ways to achieve them. They are also strongly encouraged to visit one of the company's career information counsellors to discuss which training

EXHIBIT 12-6
Employer-Assisted Career Planning

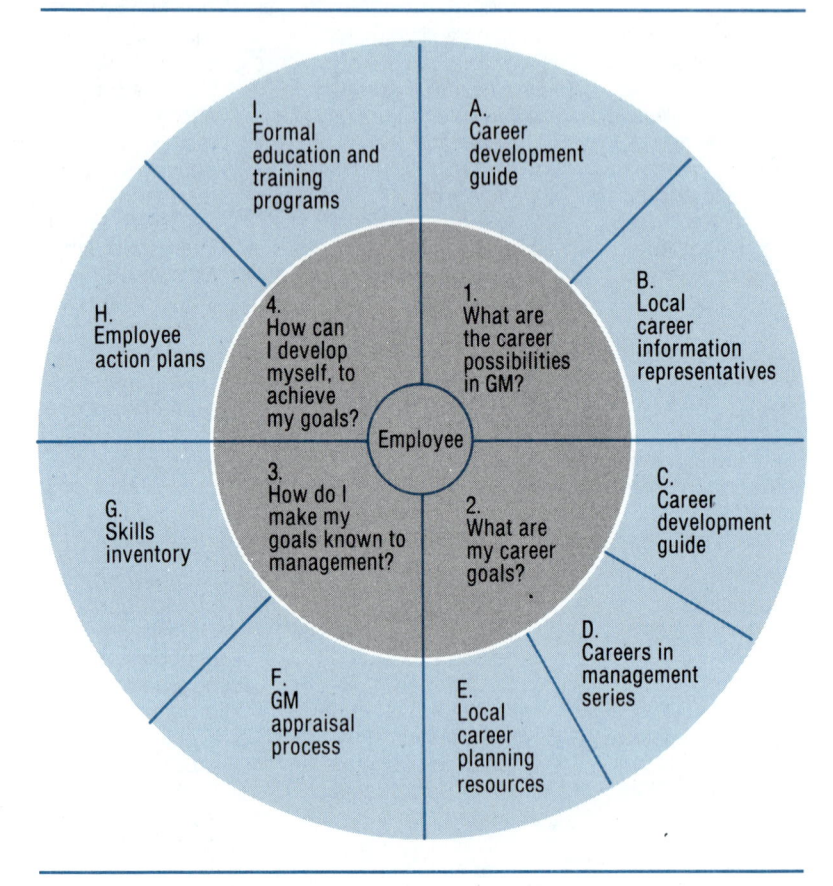

Inner ring (four basic career development questions, surrounding Employee):
1. What are the career possibilities in GM?
2. What are my career goals?
3. How do I make my goals known to management?
4. How can I develop myself, to achieve my goals?

Outer ring (elements of the system):
- A. Career development guide
- B. Local career information representatives
- C. Career development guide
- D. Careers in management series
- E. Local career planning resources
- F. GM appraisal process
- G. Skills inventory
- H. Employee action plans
- I. Formal education and training programs

Note: As you look at the diagram, you'll see that the employee is in the centre surrounded by the four basic career development questions. The elements of the system are in the outer ring and relate to each question.

Source: *Career Development Guide*, General Motors, 1977.

courses to take and in which areas of the company they should get their work experience.

Supervisors can also play an important role in assisting the individual, particularly in smaller companies where it is not feasible to employ career specialists. In particular, supervisors can assist or redirect employees and ensure that they assume their proper responsibilities for the career planning and development process. Exhibit 12–6 gives an example of employer-assisted career planning at General Motors.

Group activities offer the advantage of peer support for the assessment process. In addition, other participants can provide a reality check to ensure career goals are reasonable.

Counselling may be effectively combined with the interview that provides performance evaluation feedback. Discussing past performance can logically be extended to include where that behaviour might lead in the organization.[29] Employee interest in promotion or transfer can be explored easily in this same interview. Counselling and development remain essential aspects of the supervisor's job, in order to assist both subordinates and employers to reach their goals.

Results of Career Development

What constitutes successful career development programs? Few measures to evaluate programs exist. Many rely on asking participants for their reactions to a program, but this provides little useful information for judging long-term results.[30] One reason for the lack of measures is the great variety in programs as well as the variety in definitions of careers. Another reason is programs are designed to meet organization needs, rather than to test theories; thus, controlled experiments are not performed to assess impact. Nevertheless, London and Stumpf list some guidelines for evaluating a career development system.[31] An organization's career development system should:

- *Establish career paths.* Their existence communicates to employees specific step-by-step objectives and identifies possible role models in the organization.
- *Provide feedback on performance and potential.* Feedback enhances learning and helps clarify which behaviours will be rewarded.
- *Foster realistic expectations.* Unrealistic expectations lead to dissatisfaction, whereas realistic expectations can provide motivation. The likely rewards and the levels of performance required to attain them should be jointly understood by the worker and the person who will evaluate performance. The ability of employees to set realistic career goals is a key outcome of career development activities.
- *Manage information.* Career planning programs must be grounded in objective information. The organization's responsibility is to provide this information. Job requirements, career paths, and development programs are all examples of this information.
- *Match jobs and people.*
- *Maintain program continuity and flexibility.* No matter how good a program is, it must be revised as more information becomes available and situations change.
- *Integrate career planning with other human resource functions.* This is especially so in training and development and staffing decisions.

Career development ensures that qualified people are available and interested in jobs at all levels of the organization. Other counselling activities, such as employee assistance programs, are sponsored by employers to deal with more troubling employee problems.

Employee Assistance

Employee assistance programs (EAPs) have a long and interesting history. The earliest programs emerged in the United States during the time known as Welfare Capitalism (i.e., 1910–1929). This was the era when thousands of "welfare workers" were hired by industry to assist employees in their personal problems. More often than not, these early welfare staff only monitored employee behaviour and reported any problems to management.[32] In a few organizations, genuine employee assistance was provided. At Ford Motor Company, for example, employees could receive counselling on legal matters as early as 1917. The company's medical department maintained an operating room and six-bed ward. Ford also introduced an English school that taught thousands of employees rudimentary language skills.[33]

In Canada, employee assistance programs emerged in the 1950s out of alcoholism rehabilitation efforts conducted by various social service agencies. Provincial and federal ministries of health and welfare also encouraged development of occupational alcoholism programs. According to one estimate by Health and Welfare Canada, problem drinking costs Canadian industry more than $2 million a day in lost productivity. Between 3.5 and 7 percent of the work force in this country has severe alcoholism problems and another 15 to 17 percent has moderate problems. One of the longest-running occupational alcoholism programs was introduced in 1953 by Cominco in British Columbia. Today, more than 1,000 Canadian firms have addiction-related assistance programs.[34]

Broad Brush Programs

Broad brush employee assistance programs, which assist employees with a variety of work-related and personal problems, are also gaining in popularity, although at a slower pace. Ontario Hydro pioneered this approach when it appointed a staff psychologist to its health services department in 1955. However, a formal program was not introduced until the late 1970s. Warner-Lambert Canada began its broad brush employee assistance program in 1974 when the company's medical and personnel departments realized many employees suffered from stress, alcoholism, family conflicts, and other personal and work-related problems. Warner-Lambert approached the Canadian Mental Health Association to provide training and orientation to the company's employees, management, and health services staff. It then contracted with the

Family Services Association of Metropolitan Toronto to provide counselling services.

While alcoholism remains a major concern, family problems often represent the largest percentage of referrals in broad brush programs.[35] The type of problems counselled also depends on the occupation and industry. The Bank of Montreal began working with a professional social worker at the McGill University School of Social Work in 1973 to help employees in Montreal through the trauma following bank robberies. The program has since been expanded to deal with most other employee problems.[36]

The EAP function is contracted out in smaller organizations because hiring a full-time health service professional is not cost-effective. There is also evidence that employees prefer to receive counselling away from the workplace because of the greater sense of confidentiality. However, a few large organizations, including Ontario Hydro, Alcan, CBC, and Imperial Oil Limited, have developed their own programs. These internal EAPs have the advantage of greater control by the employer over the selection of qualified health care professionals. They also ensure that the counsellor has a solid understanding of the organization.[37]

Based on the data available, EAPs appear to be cost-effective. Canadian National Rail estimates its alcoholism and drug abuse rehabilitation program cost $600,000 in 1982 and saved the company at least $5 million that year in higher productivity and lower absenteeism. And for every dollar invested in Warner-Lambert's broad brush EAP, the company saves $10 to $11 in reduced absenteeism, workers' compensation, and group insurance claims and premiums.

Developing an Employee Assistance Program

Many of the early alcoholism-related assistance programs were developed by management alone. The newer EAPs are usually introduced through joint union-management committees. Even in nonunion settings, many of the social service agencies and private practitioners who provide counselling insist on having a planning committee that includes employee representation. A senior P/HRM specialist also sits on the committee along with managers from other areas.[38]

The committee assists the agency in setting up the program and later in monitoring its effectiveness. It is usually also responsible for establishing the objectives of the EAP. Exhibit 12–7 displays the objectives of the employee assistance program at the Toronto Transit Commission.

Orienting all employees to the new EAP is an important step in the program's success. From its work with several major employers, the Family Service Association of Metropolitan Toronto has learned that the penetration rate (i.e., the percentage of employees using the service) increases more rapidly

EXHIBIT 12–7
Objectives of the TTC Employee Assistance Program

1. To provide a confidential counselling service to assist employees and their families with problems that could affect their personal and on-the-job functioning.
2. To offer a training and orientation program to Toronto Transit Commission employees which will assist them to use the program appropriately.
3. To create and distribute to all members of the organization publicity material designed to motivate employees who have problems to accept the program and cooperate with its procedures and policies.
4. To motivate supervisory personnel and union officials to carry out the actions and policies described in the project design.
5. To continuously strive to design and promote the program in such a way as to motivate employees to seek help early, before their job performance is affected.
6. In addition to counselling troubled employees, to continue to acquaint members of the organization and clients of the service as to other helping resources available to them in the community.
7. To effect regular program evaluations, through the office of the Joint Committee.

Source: "Employee Assistance Programs—The TTC Design," *Contract Clauses*, December 1983, pp. 1–4.

and to a higher level when every employee attends an educational session in small groups at the time the program begins. At these sessions, the presenters describe the program, the employee problems served, and the counsellor's independence from the company. The confidentiality of the referral sessions is particularly stressed. A few weeks later, when the brochures are sent out, employees have a better understanding of the program and are more willing to voluntarily seek assistance. Each year thereafter, letters are sent to employees reminding them of the EAP.

In addition to orientation, the effectiveness of the EAP depends on training supervisors and union stewards to recognize the symptoms of a troubled employee and how to deal with these situations. This may involve discussions, role plays, and case analyses. Films on the progression of alcoholism are also available for presentation. Special emphasis should be placed on the supervisor's (or union steward's) skills in confronting employees about their problems and convincing them to receive counselling.

Once the EAP has been in place for a year or more, the joint committee is able to meet less frequently (usually quarterly) to monitor its progress and make recommendations on its improvement or continuation. Monitoring is done through statistical feedback on information such as the penetration rate, the number of counselling interviews given, and the total number of hours spent by the agency on the company's program.

Constructive Coercion

One of the more important decisions regarding the design of the EAP is the degree of "constructive coercion" in the referral process. In some organizations, such as Air Canada, the program is mainly voluntary. Although the EAP does not limit management's right to discipline employees, the written policy states the "decision to request/accept assistance and treatment is the personal responsibility of the individual employee."[39] In effect, the program relies on self-referral. The supervisor and union steward can only recommend that the employee seek help.

In contrast, the Toronto Transit Commission (TTC) and many other organizations implemented a system that includes mandatory as well as voluntary and suggested referral. EAPs that include mandatory referral typically are more closely aligned with the company's disciplinary process. At the TTC, the voluntary referral is confidential and no entry is made in the employee's personnel record. In the early stages of the disciplinary process, the supervisor may suggest that the employee seek assistance if there is reason to believe a personal problem is contributing to the poor performance. This suggested referral will be noted in the written record of discipline. In the latter stages of the disciplinary procedure, management may offer the employee referral to an EAP counsellor as a condition of continued employment. This procedure applies to both union and nonunion staff at the TTC.[40]

Conflict Resolution

Even in the best managed firms, conflicts may arise over promotions, pay, admission to training programs, sexual harassment, and a host of other sources of disagreement. Organizations may have procedures for handling these conflicts. These procedures provide a mechanism for employees and managers to voice their disagreements and receive a fair hearing. Exhibit 12–8 reproduces one employer's discipline policy.[41]

Employees who belong to a union collectively bargain some of these disputes and take others through a formal grievance procedure.[42] Union-management relations are discussed in Chapter Thirteen. Here we examine some of the conflict resolution or "voice" procedures designed for managerial, professional, and other nonunionized employees.

Types of Systems

The type of system an organization uses may depend on the types of problems it deals with and its compatibility with other organizational structures.

EXHIBIT 12–8
Progressive Discipline Policy

In order to provide a fair method of disciplining employees, the employer has established a formal progressive discipline procedure.

A. Discipline—general guidelines
   1. Discipline may be initiated for various reasons, including but not limited to, violations of the employer's work rules, insubordination or poor job performance. The severity of the action generally depends on the nature of the offence and an employee's record, and may range from verbal counselling to immediate dismissal.
   [A portion of the sample policy is omitted here.]
B. Progressive discipline
   1. With the exception of offences requiring more stringent action, employees will normally be counselled once verbally before receiving a written warning.
   2. In the event of another performance problem or a violation of any employer policy or rule, a written warning should ordinarily be issued.
      a. The warning should be signed and dated by the employee. If the employee refuses to sign the warning, another supervisor should be immediately brought in and asked to sign and witness that the employee has seen, but refused to sign, the warning.
      b. The warning should inform the employee of the possible consequences, including final written warning, suspension and/or discharge, should additional violations or performance problems occur.
      c. A written warning need not pertain to the same or similar offence for which the verbal counselling was given.
   3. If a third offence occurs within 12 months of the previous written warning, a final warning should be issued.
      a. The warning should be signed and dated by the employee. If the employee refuses to sign the warning, another supervisor should be immediately brought in and asked to sign and witness that the employee has seen, but refused to sign, the warning.
      b. The warning should inform the employee that termination may result if further violations or performance problems occur.
      c. A final written warning need not pertain to the same or similar offence for which any prior verbal or written warning was issued.
      d. In addition to the final written warning, the supervisor may also suspend the employee without pay or take other disciplinary action deemed appropriate.
   4. If the employee violates any policy of the employer or fails to improve his or her level of performance, termination may result.
C. The employer must, of course, reserve the right to deviate from this policy when it feels that circumstances warrant such a deviation.

Reproduced with permission from *Employee Handbook and Personnel Policies Manual* by Richard J. Simmons © 1983 Richard J. Simmons, Castle Publications, Ltd., P.O. Box 580, Van Nuys, California 91408.

Procedures can vary on two dimensions:

1. Degree of formality. High formality means explicit statements concerning appealable issues, steps to follow, and roles and responsibilities of parties.
2. Degree of independence from management. Are workers forced to complain to their immediate superiors, or does the system use people further removed?[43]

The most independent system uses an outside arbitrator and may even provide independent legal counsel to employees.[44] Many writers imply that the more formal and independent a process, the more likely it will be accepted. Unfortunately, no research has addressed this issue.[45]

Most organizations have an informal conflict resolution process whereby employees are encouraged to discuss their concerns with the immediate manager or, in some cases, a manager one level beyond. If this procedure does not resolve the issue to the mutual satisfaction of the parties, a number of firms have introduced more formal mechanisms. In addition to finalizing the dispute, these formal systems may protect the employee from fear of supervisory reprisal.

Peer Systems

Some conflict resolution procedures rely on the employee's peers to assess the situation and recommend action. At Queen's University in Kingston, Ontario, nonunion support staff have access to this procedure.[46] If a frank discussion with the supervisor or department head does not resolve an issue, the staff member can request an appeal board hearing and the assistance of a grievance officer. The grievance officer may be a senior member of the P/HRM department or one of the employee's peers who has been trained in this conflict resolution process. The appeal board is a panel of three members of Queen's support staff and is formed to hear the complaint of any support staff member. One member of the board is selected by the employee, the second by the head of the department to whom the complaint is directed, and the third by the first two appointees. The appeal board convenes the meeting within one week of its formation and listens to the presentations from both sides of the dispute. A report is prepared by the board and submitted to the principal of Queen's University within one month. Soon after, the staff member, the department head, and the director of personnel services are informed of the principal's decision as well as the appeal board's recommendations.

Ombudsperson

Another form of conflict resolution is the use of an ombudsperson. An ombudsperson may be a specially trained employee or an independent mediator who will investigate complaints, hear all sides, and try to help the parties arrive at a solution they all can live with.[47] This form of conflict resolution is widely used by governments to resolve disputes with the public, but it is still uncommon in Canadian organizations.

Judging a System

The effectiveness of a conflict resolution system lies in its outcomes for employees and employers. A way to examine those outcomes is to consider employees' options without a resolution system. Valued, disgruntled employees can leave an organization fairly easily and go on to other opportunities. Less valued employees have fewer options to leave, but they can reduce their commitment and motivation, or even sabotage other employees' work efforts.[48]

A second option for disgruntled employees is to unionize to pool their efforts to change the workplace.[49] A third option is to sue the employer or, in the case of alleged discrimination, take the case to a human rights commission. More employees are taking this option, and it can be costly to the company. As we will see later in this chapter, Canadian courts will compensate employees whose jobs have been substantially altered without their consent. The costs of one lawsuit can be several hundred thousand dollars.

To be effective, the conflict resolution system must appear more attractive than quitting or suing. Aram and Salipante conclude this implies four criteria for evaluating such systems.[50]

1. *Fairness of settlement.* Employees must perceive that an organization is both capable and willing to change a situation leading to the problem.
2. *Timeliness of settlement.* Reducing the period of uncertainty and the loss of benefits stemming from continuance of the dispute is one of the main advantages of resolution over litigation.
3. *Ease of utilization.* Time and effort required to file and follow through with an appeal must be minimal.
4. *Protection from recrimination.* Future raises and promotions must not be perceived to be threatened by filing a grievance or complaint.

OCCUPATIONAL HEALTH AND SAFETY

Dan Hanuse, president of Cheslakee Logging Co. Ltd., can't afford another 20 percent increase in workers' compensation premiums. The Vancouver Island logging firm paid nearly $250,000 in premiums to the Workers' Compensation Board of British Columbia to cover the 80 people employed in 1984. With the proposed increase, premiums would rise to an average of $4,000 for each employee. Hanuse doesn't know where he's going to find the extra money.[51]

Lloyd Godsall had suspected for several years that his hearing was deteriorating. In 1982, the 59-year-old forklift operator at Stelco's fence manufacturing plant submitted a claim to the Ontario Workers' Compensation Board. This was rejected, however, on the grounds that the noise levels in the workplace were not excessively high, according to documents submitted by the company. In 1985, with the assistance of the Hamilton Workers' Occupational Health and Safety Centre, Godsall learned that Stelco actually had documented his hearing deterioration since 1973. After a lengthy internal investigation, Stelco's director of industrial relations revealed that the company's recordkeeping system had erred. Godsall's noise exposure had been much higher than earlier reported. Based on the new evidence, the WCB ruled that Godsall's cumulative hearing loss in both ears was indeed caused by excessive work-related noise over his 27 years of employment. In 1986, Godsall received $11,375 as compensation for his hearing loss.[52]

These two stories illustrate a few of the many issues facing P/HRM specialists in the area of occupational health and safety. What rights do employees have to a safe workplace? At what point do the costs of health and safety overcome the benefits? When are industrial accidents and diseases primarily caused by the work environment or the employee? Some of these questions are clarified in legislation. Others remain unresolved.

Costs and Causes of Occupational Injuries and Diseases

Despite tougher regulations and a greater awareness of the issue by management and employees, about 1.2 million workplace injuries are reported annually in Canada. This results in 15 million lost workdays—more lost productivity than is attributed to strikes or lockouts. Between two to three workers are killed on the job every day. Many more fatalities due to occupational illnesses are not counted in these figures. For example, according to the conservative estimates of a report by Paul Weiler, Ontario workplaces produce 700 cancer fatalities annually. Yet only about 50 of these are reported in workers' compensation statistics.[53] Very few occupational diseases are compensated. This is largely due to the difficulty of proving the illness was work-related.

Exhibit 12–9 shows the types of claims reported in Manitoba. These statistics are comparable to claims in other Canadian jurisdictions. Most reported industrial accidents involve the hand or back. Industrial diseases represent only 1 out of every 100 claims.

Industrial injuries and diseases are very costly. More than $3 billion in compensation claims are paid annually by Canada's 12 workers' compensation boards (10 provinces and 2 territories). The Alberta board estimates it costs $7 million to support just one totally disabled young worker with dependents until the age of 72. But these are only direct economic costs. The loss of

EXHIBIT 12–9
Workers' Compensation Claims in Manitoba by Region of Injury

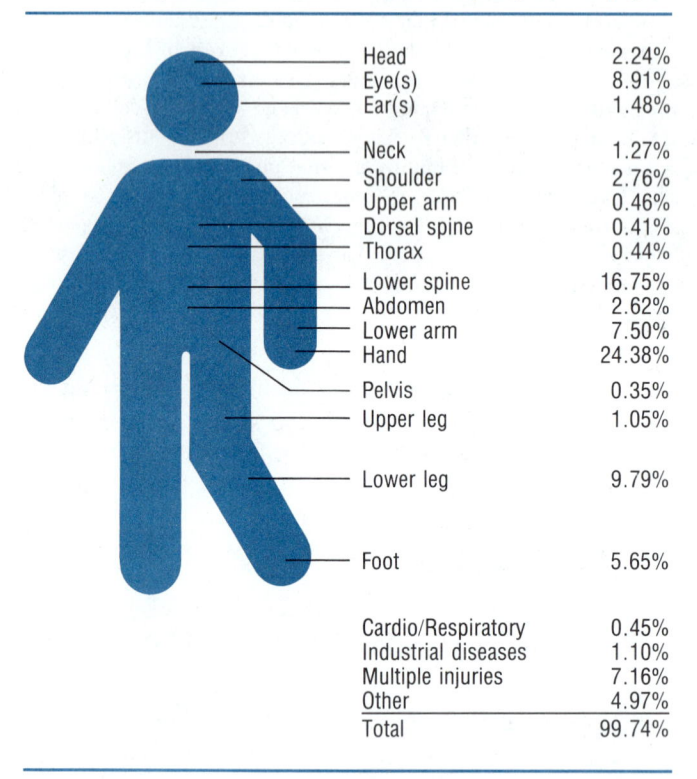

Region	Percent
Head	2.24%
Eye(s)	8.91%
Ear(s)	1.48%
Neck	1.27%
Shoulder	2.76%
Upper arm	0.46%
Dorsal spine	0.41%
Thorax	0.44%
Lower spine	16.75%
Abdomen	2.62%
Lower arm	7.50%
Hand	24.38%
Pelvis	0.35%
Upper leg	1.05%
Lower leg	9.79%
Foot	5.65%
Cardio/Respiratory	0.45%
Industrial diseases	1.10%
Multiple injuries	7.16%
Other	4.97%
Total	99.74%

Source: Workers' Compensation Board of Manitoba, *1984 Annual Report* (Winnipeg: Queen's Printer, 1985).

productivity due to absenteeism, recruiting and training replacements, downtime, and lower morale could push the financial losses well beyond $10 billion annually. There are also the immeasurable costs of pain and suffering by the victims and their families.

Causes of Work-Related Accidents and Illnesses

Occupational health and safety problems are caused to varying degrees by employees and the work environment. In the early years of industrial accident prevention, it was generally believed unsafe worker behaviour was the primary cause. Several studies focussed on unsafe acts and even tried to document the characteristics of employees who were "accident prone."[54] Today, industrial health and safety still emphasizes the employee. Most funds are spent on safety awareness and training programs for employees. Pre-employment medical tests are given to screen out job applicants who would be more susceptible to illness resulting from certain substances in the workplace.[55] Some firms even look at the job applicant's previous accident record to screen out the accident prone employee.

Critics of this approach suggest that attributing the cause of industrial accidents to unsafe acts perpetuates an image of the "dumb worker" and draws attention away from the work environment as the source of the trouble. They point to recent studies indicating the causes of occupational injuries are split about equally between unsafe work conditions and unsafe work behaviours.[56]

Increasingly, attention is shifting to the work environment. In the past decade, dangerous substances have been listed in occupational health and safety statutes for the purpose of greater legislative control over the workplace. The legislation of health and safety committees and workplace inspections has also helped to place more emphasis on safe working conditions. Hazardous conditions include poorly designed or inadequately repaired machinery, inadequate ventilation, poorly designed work space, lack of protective equipment, and the presence or inadequate storage of dangerous substances. Other working conditions of concern include excessive noise and psychological stressors, improper lighting, and excessive hours of work leading to worker fatigue.

The Ergonomic Perspective

Many firms are beginning to look more closely at the long-term effects of workplace design on employee health and safety. Engineering and medical specialists plan and adapt equipment, furniture, and work processes to promote comfort and efficiency. This perspective is referred to as *ergonomics*. By carefully designing the location of equipment, the structure of furniture, and the process of repetitive tasks, ergonomists can reduce fatigue, physical strain, and a variety of injuries.

To prevent back injuries and fatigue among supermarket cashiers, the Retail Clerks Union initiated a project with financial assistance from Labour Canada to construct and test on site an ergonomically designed laser/scanner checkout stand. This was the first use of ergonomic principles on supermarket workstations in North America. With minimal costs, the site test resulted in a 15 percent reduction in back muscle strain. The project also found an increase in performance and job satisfaction resulting from the ergonomically redesigned checkout stand. Ergonomic projects elsewhere in Canada have focussed on designing visual display terminals and standardizing tools with workplace materials.[57]

Overall, P/HRM managers should be aware of both worker behaviour and the work environment as potential sources of health and safety problems. Government regulations play an important role in directing employers and workers in their control of both causes. Two sets of worker protection legislation exist in Canada: occupational health and safety statutes and workers' compensation statutes. The 10 provinces, the 2 territories, and the federal government each have their own legislation. Many of these jurisdictions still have separate statutes for each major industry, although there is a move to more omnibus legislation. This creates a complex set of statutes, especially for companies with employees in several areas of the country. Nevertheless, several common themes emerge across jurisdictions.

Occupational Health and Safety Legislation

The main objective of occupational health and safety legislation is to control industrial hazards. The earliest Canadian regulations, which appeared soon after Confederation, merely required owners and operators of machines to take certain precautions so people working on or near them would not be injured. There were no inspectors until a decade later to ensure that these safety regulations were enforced.[58] Today, the regulations have dramatically expanded to cover procedures of workplace inspection, the labelling and containment of toxic substances, and a variety of employee rights. In most jurisdictions, these statutes are managed by the Ministry of Labour. In others, such as British Columbia, they are managed by the Workers' Compensation Board.

The Internal Responsibility System

For the past 15 years, responsibility for industrial hazards and the identification of regulatory violations has been placed on both employees and employers. The primary vehicle for this internal responsibility system is the joint health and safety committee.[59] In some areas, such as Saskatchewan, Ontario, and the federal jurisdiction, every establishment must have a committee unless otherwise exempted. In other jurisdictions, committees must be formed by statute in certain businesses or in accordance with a specific request by the minister responsible. Quebec and a few other provinces rely on a health and safety representative appointed by employees in addition to, or instead of, committees, particularly on construction sites or other places with few workers.

Joint health and safety committees are required by law to perform a variety of duties. Exhibit 12–10 lists the powers and functions of committees in the federal government jurisdiction (e.g., transportation, communication, banking). In Quebec, committees have the authority to choose individual protective devices, select the physician responsible for the company's health services, and approve the physician's health program. For the most part, how-

EXHIBIT 12–10
Powers and Functions of Federally Regulated Health and Safety Committee

- To deal with health and safety complaints by employees.
- To identify hazards and to regularly monitor workplaces for hazards.
- To monitor records of injuries and illnesses.
- To participate in investigations of health and safety–related injuries.
- To develop, establish, and promote health and safety programs and procedures.
- To obtain information from the employer and government agencies concerning existing or potential hazards in the workplace.

Source: Labour Canada, *A Guide to the Revised Canada Labour Code Part IV* (Ottawa: Minister of Supply and Services Canada, 1985), p. 7.

ever, committees in all jurisdictions have only an advisory role in decisions affecting the workplace.

Researchers are beginning to understand the conditions under which joint health and safety committees are more likely to improve workplace health and safety. A major study of committees in more than 3,000 Ontario workplaces revealed that committees are more effective when:[60]

- Management has a strong commitment to health and safety in the workplace.
- Employees throughout the company have a good knowledge of health and safety matters.
- Committee members receive sufficient health and safety information in the workplace.
- Committee processes, such as regular meetings, recorded minutes, and frequent workplace inspections, are institutionalized.
- Labour-management relations are good.
- The committee is given some decision-making power (rather than having only an advisory role).

Other studies confirm many of these observations. They also find that joint health and safety committees are less effective when committee members are unable to discuss health and safety matters integratively and when employee representatives fail to communicate with the employees they represent.[61]

In addition to joint health and safety committees, the internal responsibility system is supported by statutory provisions giving employees the right to know about the hazards of work and other health and safety information. In most places, employers are obliged to identify and inform employees of all dangerous substances in the workplace. They are also responsible for adequately training employees in health and safety matters. Generally, employees must also be told about their legal rights and responsibilities. In British

Columbia, employers must meet monthly with employees to answer their questions about workplace safety.[62]

The third dimension of the internal responsibility system is the employee's right to refuse unsafe work.[63] Whether the employee's right to refuse to work can be based on subjective perceptions rather than objective evidence of the hazard depends on the jurisdiction. Whether the danger must be "imminent" rather than long term also depends on the statute. In a few regions, an individual may stop work if another employee's health or safety is at risk. Generally, someone who refuses to work on the grounds of health and safety must be paid for the time off or be placed in another job without loss of pay. Employees cannot refuse to work where the danger is a normal part of the job (e.g., a firefighter working near burning buildings).

Dangerous Substances

A rapidly expanding area of occupational health and safety legislation in Canada addresses the control of toxic substances. Several jurisdictions have enacted restrictions on the introduction and use of dangerous chemicals and gases. For gases, this usually includes a limit on the levels of concentration. Certain employers must also test for the presence of substances listed in the regulations.

New workplace hazards are added to the designated lists every year. Noise has recently become another contaminant that must be limited and monitored in some provinces.[64] Several workers' compensation boards have also compensated employees affected by substances not mentioned in the legislation. For example, at least one board has compensated workers suffering from job burnout. Robert Sass argues that government inspectors and workers' compensation boards should also scrutinize the nature of the work and other dimensions of the quality of work life in their determination of a hazardous work environment.[65] The primary function of workers' compensation boards, however, is to *compensate* the victims of occupational hazards, not to regulate or control those hazards. In the next section, we look more closely at the foundations of workers' compensation in Canada.

Workers' Compensation

In Canada's early years, employees could seek compensation for industrial accidents only by suing the employer for negligence. This process was risky and costly and contributed to an unfortunate antagonism between workers and management. To resolve this conflict, the Quebec government enacted no-fault legislation in 1909. A year later, the Ontario government established a Commission of Inquiry headed by Sir William Meredith. His report recommended that employers should contribute to a fund out of which all employees could be compensated for their work-related injuries and illnesses without consideration of fault. In return, employees should forfeit their right to sue employers for health and safety negligence. This model of no fault/no litigation was adopted by the province in 1915 and today is embodied in workers' compensation legislation throughout Canada.[66]

Collective Liability

One of the principles of workers' compensation in Canada is that employers bear the burden of occupational injuries collectively by paying premiums into a central fund. Within most jurisdictions, employers are classified on the basis of their specific industrial undertaking and the types of accidents likely to occur. All firms in each industry group are assessed an annual premium at the same percentage of payroll. The funds collected are pooled to compensate employees injured in that group of businesses. This premium ranges from a fraction of a dollar per $100 of payroll in accounting firms to more than $20 in high-risk industries. The exceptions to this procedure are large companies such as governments, Canadian National Rail, and the Cape Breton Development Corporation, which are self-insured.

During the past decade, several provinces have moved from this purely collective liability model to an experience rating system whereby premiums vary with the accident record of each firm. For example, in 1980, Quebec started rating companies' accident records individually and assessing their premiums accordingly. If a particular organization has a better safety record than in the past, its assessment is lowered. It may even be eligible for a merit rebate from the previous year's assessment. The experience rating model has the potential for motivating employers to improve health and safety records. One concern, however, is that this system will put undue pressure on injured employees to return to work before they are well enough in order to save the employer money. For various reasons, the Workers' Compensation Board of Manitoba has recommended that its pilot program on experience ratings not be implemented more widely in the province.[67]

Methods of Compensation

The methods of compensating disabled employees vary from province to province. Many still apply Meredith's recommendation that disabilities can be assigned a percentage of wages that accounts for the person's lost ability to function in the labour force. Employees with temporary disabilities are awarded a lump sum benefit based on this percentage loss. Those with permanent disabilities—that is, those who will never recover their full ability to work—receive a pension. For example, an individual who loses the use of one hand on the job will be awarded a permanent partial disability pension that represents a small percentage of preinjury earnings. The calculation of percentage loss is based on a formula (sometimes called a *meat chart*) that establishes the loss for each bodily part.

In 1979, the Saskatchewan government implemented an alternative system of compensation that awards damages to disabled workers based on their actual wage loss. This creates a more accurate assessment of economic loss by the employee. However, it also requires additional controls to ensure the disabled person actually returns to work in his or her fullest capacity. In this respect, many boards adopting the Saskatchewan model have expanded their vocational and physical rehabilitation to minimize the amount of wage loss. This system also awards lump sum payments to employees who have been permanently disabled even if they suffer no loss of earnings.[68] New Brunswick, Newfoundland, the Yukon, and Quebec have also switched to the Saskatchewan model.

This brief excursion through Canada's occupational health and safety system shows this is one of the more complex areas of P/HRM. Most of the larger companies have a health and safety manager or department that reports to the senior P/HRM executive. This department coordinates workplace monitoring, health and safety training, accident analysis, and a host of other functions in conjunction with the joint health and safety committee, government representatives, and other P/HRM professionals. However, the greatest responsibility for occupational health and safety lies with employees and the operating supervisors. They are at the job site and are closest to potentially dangerous work behaviours and working conditions.

Occupational health and safety covers a variety of employee rights, as we have described above. Another employee rights area of increasing relevance to P/HRM professionals is the termination of employment.

TERMINATION OF EMPLOYMENT

With a changing economy, many P/HRM managers have had to face the difficult task of laying off employees. Effective management of poor performers has become critical in a competitive environment. At the same time, more dismissed employees are challenging the actions of employers. Hundreds of wrongful dismissal lawsuits are heard annually in the Canadian courts. Other claims are raised through government statutory bodies. Each of these courts or tribunal decisions has considerable relevance to P/HRM managers in areas ranging from recruitment to salary administration.

Statutory Rights

Except in the Northwest Territories, every area of Canada has legislation requiring an employer to give notice or an equivalent severance payment to employees who have been dismissed without just cause.[69] The length of notice varies with the length of service and can range from one to eight weeks. Most jurisdictions also require longer notice when many people are laid off. The period of notice for group terminations depends on the number of employees affected. In Newfoundland, for example, employers laying off 50 to 199 people must give 8 weeks' notice; this rises to 16 weeks when 500 or more are laid off. These statutes provide some protection for dismissed employees, but they represent only the minimum requirements for compensation.

In 1978, the federal government established a system of arbitration for nonunion employees in federally regulated industries. When a complaint of wrongful dismissal occurs, an inspector is dispatched from Labour Canada to mediate the conflict. If the dismissal appears to be wrongful but the officer is unable to reach a settlement, the Minister of Labour usually assigns an adjudicator to decide the case. The adjudicator has the power to reinstate or award damages if wrongful dismissal is found. Several hundred cases have been heard using this process.[70] Similar procedures exist in Quebec and Nova Scotia. The Nova Scotia procedure is rarely used, however, because the employee must have at least 10 years of service.

Common Law Wrongful Dismissal

Most employees in Canada also have certain rights pertaining to dismissal that are based on common law. These rights are adjudicated by the courts and have evolved from previous court decisions in Canada and Great Britain. Modern Canadian common law principles on wrongful dismissal can be traced back to 16th-century British statutes that have long since been repealed.[71]

Contract of Employment

At common law, every employee has a contract with his or her employer. Sometimes the conditions of this contract are written. If there is a dispute in these circumstances, the courts will ensure that the parties have complied with the written contract if it is valid. For most employees, however, there is no written contract of employment. In these cases, the courts will search for any conditions of employment that could reasonably be implied at the time of hiring. Some of these implied conditions are found in verbal agreements, written memos, industry customs, previous practices by the employer, and actions condoned by the employee.

In the absence of a written contract to the contrary, some conditions of employment are implied by the courts from basic common law principles. One of these conditions is that the employment is for an indefinite period. This means either the employer or employee can terminate the employment relationship for any reason simply by giving reasonable notice. Alternatively, the employee can be dismissed immediately if the employer pays a severance equivalent to what would have been earned during the notice period.

Wrongful dismissal is determined when the courts decide the length of notice or amount of severance is insufficient.

If the employer has just cause to dismiss the employee, then no notice or severance payment is necessary. For example, employees who have stolen expensive company property can be fired immediately without severance. However, as we will describe later, employers are frequently unsuccessful at proving just cause to the courts.

Constructive Dismissal

Wrongful dismissal also occurs when the employer unilaterally changes a fundamental condition of the employment contract. If the new arrangement is unacceptable, the employee is constructively dismissed and may sue the employer for damages. These damages amount to the earnings that would have been received during a period of reasonable notice.

Constructive dismissal might result from an unjustifiable demotion of the employee, a unilateral reduction in salary, a job transfer that was not contemplated at the time of hiring, a unilateral downward change in job responsibilities, a major change in the form or method of compensation, abusive treatment by the employer, a forced resignation, or a forced early retirement. Whether the employer's action constitutes constructive dismissal depends on the written or implied terms of the contract and the extent to which the action repudiates a fundamental aspect of the employment relationship.

Several constructive dismissal decisions have implications for wage and salary administration. In *Allison* v. *Amoco Production Co.*, the employee was transferred to Alberta from the United States in 1952.[72] In 1964, Amoco decided to supplement Allison's salary with an expatriate allowance. This continued until 1974, when the employee became a Canadian citizen. Allison sued for wrongful dismissal on the grounds that Amoco had unilaterally changed a fundamental aspect of the employment contract by ending the expatriate payments. At trial, the court agreed that a fundamental breach of contract had occurred and awarded Allison one year of severance plus costs. In other decisions, constructive dismissal has been found where the company ended an automobile allowance as an employee benefit, changed an employee's remuneration from fixed salary to straight commission, and altered the formula for calculating commissions and salary adjustments. One Ontario court even awarded damages to an employee whose job was going to be red-circled for a significant length of time.[73]

Who Has Access to Common Law

The common law of dismissal does not apply to everyone. The individual must be an employee and not an independent agent or contractor. Unionized employees do not have access to wrongful dismissal at common law because the contract of employment is between the company and the trade union rather than the employees. Many public sector employees are governed by statutes that restrict their access to common law. Even where no statute exists, the courts have historically recognized that public servants are hired and fired "at the pleasure of the Crown." Individuals employed in Quebec are protected from wrongful dismissal by the civil code in that province, which replaces the common law remedy found elsewhere in Canada.

Just Cause for Dismissal

What constitutes just cause for dismissal? In general, an employee may be fired when he or she violates a fundamental aspect of the implied or written contract of employment.

Unfaithful Service. One of the essential conditions of the employment relationship is that the employee serves the employer faithfully. Just cause, therefore, exists when there is sufficient evidence of dishonesty, theft, or conflict of interest. This fiduciary responsibility increases with the employee's position in the organizational hierarchy. For example, in *Jewitt* v. *Prism Resources Ltd.*, the president of a mining company forged the signature of the chairman of the board to the company's financial figures.[74] The intentions behind this forgery were honest because the president didn't want to inconvenience the chairman who was on vacation. Also, the chairman had already approved the preliminary figures. Yet the British Columbia Supreme Court upheld the discharge on the grounds that the forgery made it impossible for the board of directors to trust the president in the future.

Willful Misconduct. Another essential condition of the employment relationship is that the employee must obey the employer's instructions. Consequently, willful disobedience is another justification for summary dismissal under certain conditions. These conditions are described in Exhibit 12-11. In one case, a dental technician working in a Halifax laboratory was discharged for refusing to remove containers of garbage and waste from time to time. This task was part of the normal duties expected of all male dental technicians. Nevertheless, the employee adamantly refused to carry out those duties even though he was warned by the employer that such a refusal could lead to his dismissal. The court found the dismissal was justified.[75]

Incompetence. One of the more difficult grounds to justify dismissal without notice is employee incompetence. Except for situations where the individual is a probationary employee, the employer must be able to prove the employee's behaviour was grossly incompetent rather than merely unsatisfactory. To establish just cause for dismissal due to incompetence, employers must be able to establish to the satisfaction of the courts the factors listed in Exhibit 12–12. Notice that many of these conditions reflect the characteristics of an effective performance appraisal system discussed in Chapter Eleven.

EXHIBIT 12-11
Just Cause for Dismissal Due to Willful Disobedience

In order for willful disobedience to constitute just cause for dismissal, the following conditions must exist:

1. The order must be either clear and specific or must be a breach of policies and procedures well known by the employee.
2. The order must be within the scope of the employee's job duties.
3. The order must be reasonable and lawful.
4. The disobedience must be both deliberate and intentional.
5. The order must involve some matter of importance to the employer.
6. Unless the act of disobedience is particularly serious, it has to be repeated rather than be an isolated act in order to constitute cause.
7. It must be shown that the employment relationship was so damaged by the act of disobedience that it cannot continue.
8. Willful disobedience will not be cause for dismissal if there is a reasonable explanation for the employee's actions.

Source: Adapted from Howard A. Levitt, *The Law of Dismissal in Canada* (Aurora, Ontario: Canada Law Book, 1985).

The importance of the conditions stated in Exhibit 12–12 is evident in *Robson v. General Motors of Canada Ltd.*[76] Robson was hired by General Motors in October 1979 to work as a plant engineer at the Trim Plant in Windsor, Ontario. His supervisor conducted a performance appraisal after three months (in January 1980) as required by company policy. However, the appraisal was never discussed with Robson and was not shown to him until June 1980. Another appraisal was conducted at the end of the fifth month (in March 1980) but was not shown to Robson until mid-June. The supervisor did meet informally with the employee in early May, at which time he discussed several serious problems with Robson's performance and provided advice for improvement. In June, a third appraisal was conducted, this time with the employee in attendance. A rating of "required slight improvement" was given and, consistent with General Motors' policy for below standard ratings, the supervisor established an action plan and a one-month deadline for improvement. One month later, the employee met again with the supervisor for another appraisal. The supervisor noted Robson had made some improvement, but advised him this progress was insufficient. Robson's employment was terminated, and the employee sued General Motors for wrongful dismissal. The court found there was insufficient evidence of incompetence because of the way the issue was handled. General Motors was ordered to pay Robson damages.

Many P/HRM managers are surprised to learn the company's economic difficulties do not justify dismissing employees without notice. Unless otherwise specified in a written contract of employment, employees cannot be permanently laid off without sufficient notice. Even if the business is sold and the new owner doesn't want certain employees, the original owner must pay adequate severance to those who are dismissed as a result of the sale.

Reasonable Notice

At common law, Canadian courts can neither reinstate wrongfully dismissed employees nor alter the conditions of work in cases of constructive dismissal. Instead, they decide the length of notice that should have been given and award the employee an equivalent severance payment (along with other costs). Reasonable notice has ranged from 1 month to 30 months.

To avoid litigation, many P/HRM specialists calculate a severance payment for laid off employees based on length of service or some other formula.

EXHIBIT 12–12
Just Cause for Dismissal Due to Incompetence

In order for incompetence to constitute just cause for dismissal, the following conditions must exist:

1. The employee's job duties and the standards of performance established by the organization must be clearly communicated.
2. The employee who is performing poorly must be made aware there is a discrepancy between his or her performance and the standards for the job. Recent positive feedback or evaluations will seriously weaken the evidence of incompetence.
3. Incompetence will not be acceptable as a grounds for dismissal if other employees with similar job duties are also performing below standard but are not recognized by the organization as poor performers.
4. The employee must be provided with adequate training or, if already trained, must be informed of what to do to improve the unsatisfactory job performance.
5. The employee must be given a reasonable amount of time to improve performance after he or she has been warned. Similarly, if new to the job, the employee must be given a reasonable opportunity to learn the job.
6. If the performance continues to be below standard, the employee must be informed his or her job is in jeopardy.
7. The standards of performance expected of a new employee should not be increased above the level of competence on which the individual was hired.
8. In order to establish incompetence, the employee's poor performance must not have been partly due to actions of the company (such as failing to provide the necessary support) or, in some cases, factors beyond the employee's control.
9. If employees are routinely dismissed for failing to attain a specific standard of performance, this must be made clear to the employee at the time of hire.
10. The organization cannot use incompetence as a justification for dismissal where the employee's performance is improving or where there is a reasonable belief that the poor performance is temporary.

Source: Adapted from Howard A. Levitt, *The Law of Dismissal in Canada* (Aurora, Ontario: Canada Law Book, 1985).

Unfortunately, many companies have wound up in court anyway. B.C. Hydro is an example. In 1984, the utility laid off 660 nonunion professional engineers because the demand for new hydro construction disappeared. These employees were paid severances based on their years of service with the company. Some had been employed by B.C. Hydro for 20 years and were paid the equivalent of 10 months of salary. Believing their severances were inadequate, many professional engineers sued the utility for wrongful dismissal. In the first of four cases, the courts agreed with the employees' assessment and awarded roughly twice the notice that B.C. Hydro had calculated. Three other cases followed with similar results. In these latter decisions, the chief justice of British Columbia outlined the criteria used to determine reasonable notice. These include the employee's length of service, job status and responsibility, age, and availability of alternate employment.[77]

Even with these factors clarified, the calculation of reasonable notice remains a guessing game unless these criteria can be weighted. McShane and McPhillips recently estimated these weights using a statistical analysis of all British Columbia wrongful dismissal cases over a six-year period.[78]

Earlier in this chapter, we mentioned that many firms try to avoid laying off qualified employees because of their direct and indirect costs. Litigation is one obvious economic cost to the company. But the noneconomic costs, such as the company's image in the community and the morale of remaining staff, are much greater. This is not to suggest employees should never be dismissed. Rather, through careful human resource planning, effective recruitment, valid selection procedures, and a number of other management practices, the need for termination of employment can be minimized.

Where terminations are necessary, whether due to poor performance or economic recession, good employee relations calls for outplacement counselling. These outplacement services help terminated employees cope with this event and prepare them for job search. Usually the counselling begins as soon as the dismissal notice has been issued. Outplacement consultants also prefer to work with employers before the decision to terminate is made.[79]

SUMMARY

A wide variety of activities in an organization are aimed at enhancing the quality of the employment relationship. Some of the programs are formal, such as conflict resolution procedures or quality circles. Other activities are more casual, such as organizing and funding an employee picnic. Encouraging a cooperative rather than adversarial relationship is the goal. The underlying assumption is that such an atmosphere will better allow employees to perform their jobs and contribute a creative spark to the organization.

The effects of employee relations programs are difficult to assess. Most of their benefits take the form of cost-avoidance—lawsuits that were not filed, turnover or absenteeism that did not occur, productivity that did not decline. Additionally, many of the programs contribute to a better atmosphere. They demonstrate that the employer is committed to cooperative relationships, respects the employees, views them as a source of profitable suggestions, and will make efforts to accommodate their preferences.

Because of the difficulty in justifying these programs on a cost basis, top management commitment to employee relations is essential. If this commitment falters, often through a change in management, it seems an easy choice to cut these programs to improve the bottom line. So the P/HRM manager must be in touch with employees—to be sure programs are working effectively—and with top managers—to maintain their commitment.

DISCUSSION AND REVIEW QUESTIONS

1. How would sociotechnical systems improve the quality of work life for employees?
2. Describe the structure of a typical quality circle program.
3. What actions can employers take to provide employment security?
4. Whose responsibility is career development? How can others assist?
5. What actions can make employee assistance programs more effective?
6. What are the characteristics of an effective conflict resolution system in organizations?
7. Should P/HRM professionals deal with employees or the work environment when attempting to improve health and safety in the workplace?
8. What is the internal responsibility system in occupational health and safety?
9. The dominant principle of workers' compensation in Canada is "collective liability." What does this mean?
10. Based on common law principles, when does an employer have just cause to dismiss an employee without notice?
11. What is "constructive dismissal"?

NOTES AND REFERENCES

1. Wayne Lilly, "Over the Volcano," *Canadian Business*, September 1984, pp. 91–100; Ron Eade, "Dignity in Workplace Led to Turnaround of Budd's Labour Strife," *Financial Post*, May 12, 1984, p. 6; Bernard Simon, "Budd's Challenge: Maintain Its Footing on Growth Path," *Financial Post*, December 28, 1985, p. 36.
2. Virginia Galt, " 'Our Strength Is People,' but Dofasco to Lay Off 2,100," *The Globe and Mail*, July 16, 1982, p. B5; Robert English, "Dofasco Comes Back in a Profitable Way," *Financial Post*, November 19, 1983, pp. 1, 2.

3. Daniel Spencer, "Employee Voice and Employee Retention" (paper presented at 1982 Academy of Management meetings, New York); Stanley E. Seashore, Edward E. Lawler III, Philip H. Mirvis, and Cortlandt Cammann, eds., *Assessing Organizational Change: A Guide to Methods, Measures, and Practices* (New York: John Wiley & Sons, 1983); John Van Maanen and Edgar Schein, "Career Development," in *Improving Life at Work*, ed. J. Richard Hackman and J. Lloyd Suttle (Santa Monica, Calif.: Goodyear Publishing, 1977).
4. Clark Kerr and Jerome Rosow, *Work in America* (New York: Van Nostrand Reinhold, 1979).
5. D. Nadler and E. E. Lawler III, "Quality of Work Life: Perspectives and Directions," *Organizational Dynamics*, Winter 1983, pp. 20–30; E. Rendall, "Quality Circles—A 'Third Wave Intervention,'" *Training and Development Journal*, March 1981, pp. 28–31; W. Thompson, "Is the Organization Ready for Quality Circles?" *Training and Development Journal*, December 1982, pp. 115–18.
6. R. Keidel, "QWL Development: Three Trajectories," *Human Relations* 35, no. 1 (1982), pp. 743–61; A. V. Subbarao, "Worker Participation in Management of Human Resources: Lessons from Abroad and Experience at Home" (paper presented at the ASAC 1983 Conference, Vancouver); J. B. Cunningham and T. H White, eds., *Quality of Working Life: Contemporary Cases* (Ottawa: Labour Canada, 1984); A. W. Azim and Kirby Wright, "A Discussion of Quality of Work Life," *Proceedings of the ASAC 1984 Conference* (Guelph, Ontario: University of Guelph), pp. 26–34.
7. E. L. Trist, G. W. Higgin, H. Murray, and A. B. Pollock, *Organizational Choice* (London: Tavistock, 1963); F. E. Emery, "Characteristics of Socio-Technical Systems," in *Design of Jobs*, ed. L. E. Davis and J. C. Taylor (Harmondsworth, England: Penguin, 1972), pp. 177–98; Malcolm Chadwick and Fred Clark, *Design of a New Plant at CSP Foods* (Ottawa: Labour Canada, 1984).
8. Norman Halpern, "Sociotechnical Systems Design: The Shell Sarnia Experience," in *Quality of Working Life: Contemporary Cases*.
9. Brian Brinks, "Turnaround at Ste.-Therese," *Financial Times*, February 16, 1987, pp. 1, 14.
10. W. Ouchi, "Theory Z Organizations: Straddling U.S. and Japanese Molds," *Industry Week*, May 4, 1981, pp. 49–52.
11. Hem J. Jain, "Industrial Relations Practices of Japanese Multinationals and Their Subsidiaries in Canada: Are They Transferable to Canadian Firms?" *Canadian Journal of Administrative Science*, June 1985, pp. 77–94.
12. L. J. Knight, "Quality Circles in Action: A Canadian Experience," *CTM: The Human Element*, February 1983, pp. 20–21; Brent King, "Quality Circles Have Achieved Acceptance," *Financial Post*, January 18, 1986, p. 15; Bernard Portis, Paul Ingram, and David Fullerton, "Effective Use of Quality Circles," *Business Quarterly*, Fall 1985, pp. 44–47.
13. Olga L. Crocker, J. S. L. Chiu, and C. Charney, *Quality Circles: A Guide to Participation and Productivity* (Toronto: Methuen, 1984); Joseph Hanley, "Our Experience with Quality Circles," *Quality Progress*, February 1980, pp. 22–24; B. G. Dale and J. Lees, "Quality Circles: From Introduction to Integration," *Long-Range Planning*, February 1987, pp. 78–83.
14. Kathy Fiske, "Back to Shape," *Executive*, September 1984, p. 12; Daniel Staffman, "Great Workplaces and How They Got That Way," *Canadian Business*, September 1984, pp. 30–38; Deborah Jones, "Britex Success Attributed to Employee

Participation," *The Globe and Mail*, April 29, 1985, p. B10; Brent King, "Employee Participation a Key to Steady Expansion of Britex," *Financial Post*, October 26, 1985, p. 27; James Bagnall, "Most Employees Come Out Winners in Ownership Gamble," *Financial Post*, April 12, 1980, p. 2; Judy Steed, "The Rewards of Running Your Own Show," *The Globe and Mail Report on Business Magazine*, March 1985, pp. 22–28; Donald Nightingale and Richard Long, *Gain and Equity Sharing* (Ottawa: Labour Canada, 1984).

15. Richard J. Long, "Job Attitudes and Organizational Performance under Employee Ownership," *Academy of Management Journal* 23, no. 4 (1980), pp. 726–37; Susan Rhodes and Richard Steers, "Conventional vs. Worker-Owned Organizations," *Human Relations* 34, no. 12 (1981), pp. 1013–35; Jeanne M. Brett and Tove Helland Hammer, "Organizational Behavior and Industrial Relations," in *Industrial Research in the 1970s: Review and Appraisal*, ed. T. A. Kochan, D. J. B. Mitchell, and L. Dyer (Madison, Wis.: Industrial Relations Research Association, 1982).

16. Donald Nightingale, *Workplace Democracy: An Inquiry into Employee Participation in Canadian Work Organizations* (Toronto: University of Toronto Press, 1982); John Crispo, *Industrial Democracy in Western Europe: A North American Perspective* (Toronto: McGraw-Hill Ryerson, 1978).

17. Sally R. Luce, *Retrenchment and Beyond: The Acid Test of Human Resource Management* (Ottawa: Conference Board of Canada, 1983); "Employment Security Strategies," *Worklife/IR Research Reports* 4, no. 3 (1985), pp. 8–9; Jocelyn F. Gutchess, *Employment Security in Action: Strategies That Work* (New York: Pergamon Press, 1985); Leonard Greenhalgh and Robert B. McKersie, "Cost Effectiveness of Alternative Strategies for Cutback Management," *Public Administration Review* 40, no. 6 (1980), pp. 575–84; Michael Fein, "Motivation to Work," in *Handbook of Work, Organization, and Society*, ed. Robert Dubin (Chicago: Rand McNally, 1976).

18. Stan Luxenburg, "Lifetime Employment, U.S. Style," *New York Times*, April 17, 1983, p. 12F; Lee Dyer, Felician Foltman, and George Milkovich, "Contemporary Employment Stabilization Practices," in *Industrial Relations and Human Resource Management: Text, Readings, and Cases*, ed. T. A. Kochan and T. A. Barocci (Boston: Little, Brown, 1984); Mark Thompson, "The Permanent Employment System: Japan and Mexico" (paper presented at the Sixth World Congress of Industrial Relations, Kyoto, Japan, March 28–31, 1983).

19. Eva Innes, Robert L. Perry, and Jim Lyon, *The 100 Best Companies to Work For in Canada* (Don Mills, Ont.: Collins, 1986); William G. Ouchi, *Theory Z: How American Business Can Meet the Japanese Challenge* (Reading, Mass.: Addison-Wesley Publishing, 1981), app. 1.

20. Peter Cook, "Giving the Death Sentence to Lifetime Jobs," *The Globe and Mail*, March 18, 1987, p. B3.

21. Howard A. Levitt, *The Law of Dismissal in Canada* (Aurora, Ont.: Canada Law Book, 1985).

22. Frank Reid, "Combatting Unemployment through Work Time Reductions," *Canadian Public Policy* 12, no. 2 (1986), pp. 275–85; Frank Reid, "UI-Assisted Worksharing as an Alternative to Layoffs: The Canadian Experience," *Industrial and Labour Relations Review* 35 (1982), pp. 319–29; "Employment Security Strategies," *Worklife/IR Research Reports*; Jocelyn F. Gutchess, *Employment Security in Action*; Wilfred List, "Pay Cuts, 4-Day Week: Work-Sharing Helps Avoid Layoffs," *The Globe and Mail*, May 27, 1982.

23. Daniel A. Ondrack and Martin G. Evans, "Job Enrichment and Job Satisfaction in Quality of Working Life and Nonquality of Working Life Work Sites," *Human Relations* 39, no. 9 (1986), pp. 871–89.
24. Harry C. Katz, Thomas A. Kochan, and Kenneth R. Gobeille, "Industrial Relations Performance, Economic Performance, and QWL Programs: An Interplant Analysis," *Industrial and Labor Relations Review*, October 1983, pp. 3–17.
25. Andrew F. Sikula and John F. McKenna, "Individuals Must Take Charge of Career Development," *Personnel Administrator*, October 1983, pp. 89–97; William L. Mihal, Patricia A. Sorce, and Thomas E. Comte, "A Process Model of Individual Career Decision Making," *Academy of Management Review* 9, no. 1 (1984), pp. 95–103; Mary Ann VonGlinow, Michael J. Driver, Kenneth Brousseau, and J. Bruce Prince, "The Design of a Career-Oriented Human Resource System," *Academy of Management Review* 8, no. 1 (1983), pp. 23–32; Richard W. Scholl, "Career Lines and Employment Stability," *Academy of Management Journal* 26, no. 1 (1983), pp. 86–103; John F. Veiga, "Mobility Influences during Managerial Career Stages," *Academy of Management Journal* 26, no. 1 (1983), pp. 64–85; Susan R. Rhodes and Mildred Doering, "An Integrated Model of Career Change" (working paper, Syracuse, School of Management, Syracuse University, December 1981); Thomas G. Gutteridge and Fred L. Otte, "Organizational Career Development: What's Going On out There?" *Training and Development Journal*, February 1983, pp. 22–26; Zandy Leibowitz, Caela Farren, and Beverly Kaye, "Will Your Organization Be Doing Career Development in the Year 2000?" *Training and Development Journal*, February 1983, pp. 14–21.
26. E. G. Schein, *Career Dynamics: Matching Individual and Organizational Needs* (Reading, Mass.: Addison-Wesley Publishing, 1978).
27. M. C. Hanson, "Career Counseling in Organizations," in *Career Development in the 80's*, ed. D. H. Montross and C. J. Shinkman (Springfield, Ill.: Charles C Thomas, 1981); J. Walker, *Human Resource Planning* (New York: McGraw-Hill, 1980); M. A. Morgan, D. T. Hall and A. Martier, "Career Development Strategies in Industry—Where Are We and Where Should We Be?" *Personnel*, March–April 1979, pp. 13–30.
28. D. Bowen and D. T. Hall, "Career Planning for Employee Development: A Primer for Managers," *California Management Review*, Winter 1977, pp. 33–35.
29. D. Super and D. T. Hall, "Career Development: Exploration and Planning," in *Annual Review of Psychology*, ed. M. R. Rosenzweig and L. W. Porter (Palo Alto, Calif.: Annual Reviews, 1978).
30. George T. Milkovich and John C. Anderson, "Careers and Career Systems," in *Personnel Management: New Perspectives*, ed. K. Rowland and G. Ferris (Boston, Mass.: Allyn & Bacon, 1982); Linda Kapurch, "Following Up on the Effects of a Goals Workshop," *Training and Development Journal*, February 1983, pp. 27–33.
31. Manuel London and Stephen A. Stumph, *Managing Careers* (Reading, Mass.: Addison-Wesley Publishing, 1981).
32. Ray Thomlison, "Industrial Social Work: Perspectives and Issues," in *Perspectives on Industrial Social Work Practice*, ed. Ray Thomlison (Ottawa: Family Service Canada, 1983).
33. *Essays on American Industrialism: Selected Papers of Samuel M. Levin* (Detroit, Mich.: Wayne State University, 1973).
34. Joan Lynch, "Labour-Management Issues: The Interlock Experience," in *Perspec-*

tives on Industrial Social Work Practice; Glenn Thede, "Employee Assistance Programs: How They Began and Where They Stand," *CTM: The Human Element*, August–September 1983, p. 14.
35. "How One Company Helps Its Staff," *Financial Times of Canada*, April 20, 1981, p. H4; "Social Workers Get Nod in Care, Nurturing of Employee Psyches," *The Globe and Mail*, April 21, 1979, p. B1; Alan Morantz, "Helping Employees Cope with Personal Problems," *Worklife* 3, no. 1 (1983), pp. 10–12.
36. Marie Roy-Brisebois, "Victim Assistance: An Example of Meeting the Work-Related Needs of Employees," in *Perspectives on Industrial Social Work Practice*.
37. Michael Salter, "Employee Assistance Comes of Age," *Financial Post*, May 28, 1983, p. 11; "Employee Assistance Programs: The Inside View from Imperial Oil," *CTM: The Human Element*, October–November 1983, p. 21.
38. David Wright, "Marketing, Planning and Implementation of Industrial Social Work Programs," in *Perspectives on Industrial Social Work Practice*; Sally MacEwen, "Training and Orientation in the Workplace," in *Perspectives on Industrial Social Work Practice*.
39. "Employee Assistance Programs—The Air Canada Model," *Contract Clauses*, November 1983, pp. 1–4. For a more detailed analysis of constructive coercion, see Donald G. Finlay, *Constructive Coercion and the Alcoholic Employee: Problems and Prospects* (Vancouver: Education Department of the B.C. Alcohol and Drug Commission, 1975).
40. "Employee Assistance Programs—The TTC Design," *Contract Clauses*, December 1983, pp. 1–4.
41. Richard J. Simmons, *Employee Handbook and Personnel Policies Manual* (Van Nuys, Calif.: Castle Publications, 1983).
42. Robert T. Boisseau and Harvey Caras, "A Radical Experiment Cuts Deep into the Attractiveness of Unions," *Personnel Administrator*, October 1983, pp. 76–79.
43. John D. Aram and Paul F. Salipante, Jr., "An Evaluation of Organizational Due Process in the Resolution of Employee/Employer Conflict," *Academy of Management Review* 6, no. 2 (1981), pp. 197–204.
44. Alan F. Westin, "Individual Rights and Fair Procedure Systems," *ILR Report*, Fall 1982, pp. 5–8.
45. A. Thomson, *The Grievance Procedure* (Lexington, Mass.: Lexington Books, 1976); J. Gandz, *Grievance Arbitration* (working paper series no. 206, School of Business Administration, University of Western Ontario, 1978); W. Scott, *The Management of Conflict* (Homewood, Ill.: Richard D. Irwin, 1965).
46. *Queen's University Personnel Policy and Procedure Manual for Support Staff* (Kingston, Ont.: Queen's University).
47. Ronald E. Berenbeim, *Nonunion Complaint Systems: A Corporate Appraisal* (New York: The Conference Board, 1980); "Listening and Responding to Employees' Concerns: An Interview with A. W. Clausen," *Harvard Business Review*, January–February 1980, pp. 101–14.
48. Albert O. Hirschman, *Exit, Voice and Loyalty* (Cambridge, Mass.: Harvard University Press, 1971).
49. Chris Berger, Craig A. Olson, and John Boudreau, "Effects of Unions on Job Satisfaction" (working paper, Krannert Graduate School of Management, Purdue University, Lafayette, Ind.); Chester A. Schriescheim, "Job Satisfaction," *Journal of Applied Psychology*, October 1978, pp. 548–52; Richard Freeman and James

Medoff, *What Do Unions Do?* (New York: Basic Books, 1984); Thomas Kochan, "How American Workers View Labor Unions," *Monthly Labor Review*, April 1979, pp. 22–31.
50. Aram and Salipante, "Organizational Due Process."
51. Margaret Wente, "The Coming Crisis in Workers' Compensation," *Canadian Business*, February 1984, pp. 46–50.
52. Bertrand Marotte, "Provincial Officials Probing Stelco Workers' Allegations," *The Globe and Mail*, August 24, 1985, p. 17; John Deverell, "Health Data Faulty Stelco Admits," *Toronto Star*, July 5, 1986, pp. A1, A18.
53. Labour Canada, *Employment Injuries and Occupational Illnesses: 1972–1981* (Ottawa: Minister of Supply and Services Canada, 1984); Wente, "The Coming Crisis in Workers' Compensation"; Paul Weiler, *Protecting the Worker from Disability: Challenges for the Eighties* (Toronto: Report submitted to the Ontario Minister of Labour, 1983); Ian Robinson, "Health and Safety in Ontario's Uranium Mines," *Alternatives*, Summer–Fall 1983, pp. 44–52; Charles E. Reasons, Lois L. Ross, and Craig Paterson, *Assault on the Worker: Occupational Health and Safety in Canada* (Toronto: Butterworths, 1981); Bernard Brody et al., "Les Accidents Industriels au Canada: Le Portrait d'une D'ecennie," *Relations Industrielles* 40, no. 3 (1985), pp. 545–66.
54. R. M. Harano et al., "The Prediction of Accident Liability through Biographical Data and Psychometric Tests," *Journal of Safety Research*, March 1975, pp. 16–52; G. V. Barrett and C. L. Thornton, "Relationship between Perceptual Style and Driver Reaction to an Emergency Situation," *Journal of Applied Psychology* 52, no. 2 (1968), pp. 169–76; C. A. Drake, "Accident-Proneness: A Hypothesis," *Character and Personality* 8 (1940), pp. 335–41; J. T. Kunce, "Vocational Interests and Accident Proneness," *Journal of Applied Psychology* 51 (1967), pp. 223–25.
55. Wilfred List, "Safety Groups Come under Fire over High Accident Rates, Costs," *The Globe and Mail*, August 11, 1986, pp. B1, B3; James Bagnall, "Work Safety Everyone's Goal, but Achieving It Is the Problem," *Financial Post*, October 3, 1981, p. 21; Gordon R. C. Atherley et al., "Medical Monitoring: Occupational Health and Human Rights," *Alternatives*, Summer-Fall 1983, pp. 19–27.
56. J. F. Follman, Jr., *The Economics of Industrial Health* (New York: AMACOM, 1978); N. A. Ashford, *Crisis in the Workplace: Occupational Disease and Injury* (Cambridge, Mass.: MIT Press, 1976).
57. Canadian Council on Working Life, "Ergonomic Design of Supermarket Checkout," *Inventory of Worklife Improvements in B.C.: Pilot Project* (Vancouver: CCWL, October 1986), pp. 25–26; Rhonda Birenbaum, "Designer Screens," *Occupational Health and Safety Canada*, March–April 1986, pp. 56–57.
58. Eric Tucker, "The Determination of Occupational Health and Safety Standards in Ontario, 1860–1982: From Market to Politics to . . .?" *McGill Law Journal*, March 1984, pp. 260–311.
59. Michael Izumi Nash, *Canadian Occupational Health and Safety Law Handbook* (Don Mills, Ont.: CCH Canadian Ltd., 1983); Richard M. Brown, "Canadian Occupational Health and Safety Legislation," *Osgoode Hall Law Journal*, March 1982, pp. 90–118; R. D. Clarke, "Worker Participation in Health and Safety in Canada," *International Labour Review*, March–April 1982, pp. 199–206; L. Gauthier, "Ontario's Occupational Health and Safety Act and the Internal Responsibility System: Is the Act Working?" *Canadian Community Law Journal* 7 (1984),

pp. 174–83; Katherine E. Swinton, "Enforcement of Occupational Health and Safety Legislation: The Role of the Internal Responsibility System," in *Studies in Labour Law*, ed. K. P. Swan and K. E. Swinton (Toronto: Butterworths, 1983), pp. 143–75; Labour Canada, *Establishment and Operation of Safety and Health Committees* (Ottawa: Ministry of Supply and Services Canada, 1986).

60. SPR Associates, "An Evaluation of Joint Health and Safety Committees in Ontario" (report prepared by Ted Adam Harvey, Michael Krashinksy, and Steven L. McShane), in *Eighth Annual Report of the Ontario Advisory Council on Occupational Health and Occupational Safety*, Vol. 2 (Toronto: Queen's Printer, 1986).

61. George K. Bryce and Pran Manga, "The Effectiveness of Health and Safety Committees," *Relations Industrielles* 40, no. 2 (1985), pp. 257–83; Kenneth George, "Les Comités de Santé et de Sécurité du Travail: Tables de Concertations on de Négociation?" *Relations Industrielles* 40, no. 3 (1985), pp. 512–28.

62. Michael Grossman, "A Worker's Right-to-Know about Workplace Chemicals," *At the Centre*, September 1986, pp. 8–11; E. G. Fisher and I. F. Ivankovich, "Alberta's Occupational Health and Safety Amendment Act, 1983," *Relations Industrielles* 40, no. 1 (1985), pp. 115–38; Brown, "Canadian Occupational Health and Safety Legislation."

63. Nash, *Canadian Occupational Health and Safety Law Handbook*; Brown, "Canadian Occupational Health and Safety Legislation"; G. Leslie, "The Statutory Right to Refuse Unsafe Work: A Comparison of Saskatchewan, Ontario, and the Federal Jurisdiction," *Saskatchewan Law Review* 46 (1982), pp. 235–70.

64. Brian Cole, "Province Establishes Guidelines to Limit Workplace Noise," *Winnipeg Free Press*, May 31, 1985, p. 2; Caitlin Kelly, "Government's Silence on Noise in Workplace Deafening, Groups Say," *The Globe and Mail*, March 14, 1986, p. A18.

65. Robert Sass, "The Need to Broaden the Legal Concept of Risk in Workplace Health and Safety," *Canadian Public Policy* 12, no. 2 (1986), pp. 286–93; Bagnall, "Safety Reforms Are in Danger."

66. Nash, *Canadian Occupational Health and Safety Law Handbook*; Dianne Pother, "Workers' Compensation: The Historical Compromise Revisited," *Dalhousie Law Journal*, April 1983, pp. 309–46.

67. Weiler, *Protecting the Worker from Disability*; Bagnall, "Safety Reforms Are in Danger"; Wente, "The Coming Crisis in Workers' Compensation"; Workers' Compensation Board of Manitoba, *1984 Annual Report* (Winnipeg: Queen's Printer, 1985).

68. Ibid.; Nash, *Canadian Occupational Health and Safety Law Handbook*.

69. Labour Canada, *Labour Standards in Canada*, 1986 ed. (Ottawa: Minister of Supply and Services Canada, 1986).

70. G. England, "Unjust Dismissal in the Federal Jurisdiction: The First Three Years," *Manitoba Law Journal* 12, no. 1 (1982), pp. 9–30; Levitt, *The Law of Dismissal in Canada*, pp. 22–28.

71. Levitt, *The Law of Dismissal in Canada*; David Harris, *Wrongful Dismissal*, 2nd ed. (Toronto: Richard De Boo, 1980); Brian A. Grosman, *The Executive Firing Line* (Toronto: Methuen, 1982); G. England, "Recent Developments in Wrongful Dismissal Laws and Some Pointers for Reform," *Alberta Law Review* 16 (1978), pp. 470–520; R. J. Harrison, "Termination of Employment," *Alberta Law Review* 10 (1972), pp. 250–87; Lessey Sooklal, "An Analysis of Wrongful Dismissal Lawsuits in Canada" (paper presented at the ASAC 1986 Conference, Whistler, B.C.);

R. J. Adams and Maureen E. Donnelly, "Wrongful Dismissal: Employee Challenge and Corporate Response" (McMaster University working paper, December 1986).
72. *Allison* v. *Amoco Production Company* (1975) 5 WWR 501.
73. Howard Levitt, *The Law of Dismissal in Canada*, pp. 54–56; Harris, *Wrongful Dismissal*, 2nd ed., p. 31.
74. *Jewitt* v. *Prism Resources Ltd.* (1980) 110 DLR (3d) 713; 127 DLR (3d) 190.
75. *Lewis* v. *Associated Laboratories Ltd.* (1981) 44 NSR (2d) 567.
76. *Robson* v. *General Motors of Canada Ltd.* (1982) 37 OR (2d) 229.
77. *Ansari et al.* v. *B.C. Hydro* [1986] 4 WWR 123.
78. Steven L. McShane and David C. McPhillips, "Predicting Reasonable Notice in Canadian Wrongful Dismissal Cases," *Industrial and Labor Relations Review* 41, no. 1 (1987), pp. 108–17; David C. McPhillips and Steven L. McShane, "Notice in Wrongful Dismissal: A Proposal for Reform" (University of British Columbia, Working Paper No. 1155, September 1986); Steven L. McShane, "Reasonable Notice Criteria in Common Law Wrongful Dismissal Cases," *Relations Industrielles* 38 (1983), pp. 618–33.
79. Murray Axmith, "The Art of Firing," *Business Quarterly*, Spring 1981, pp. 36–45; Carl H. Driessnack, "Outplacement: A Benefit for Both Employee and Company," *Personnel Administrator*, January 1978, pp. 24–29.

CHAPTER THIRTEEN
LABOUR RELATIONS*

CHAPTER OUTLINE

I. A Diagnostic Approach to Labour Relations
    A. External Conditions
    B. Organizational Conditions
II. Canadian Unionism: A Historical Perspective
III. Why Employees Join Unions
IV. The Organizing Campaign
V. Union Structure
VI. Negotiating a Contract
    A. Preparation for Contract Negotiations
    B. Negotiation Issues
    C. Formalizing the Contract
VII. Impasses in Collective Bargaining
    A. Mediation and Conciliation
    B. Interest Arbitration
    C. Strikes and Lockouts
    D. Labour Disputes in Canada
VIII. Collective Agreement Administration
    A. Grievance Process
    B. Grievance Arbitration

*This chapter was prepared by Brian Bemmels, University of Alberta, in collaboration with R. T. Barth and Steve McShane. Copyright © 1988 Business Publications, Inc.

IX. The Public Sector
X. Labour Union Effects
   A. Union Impact on Wages
   B. Union Impact on Productivity
   C. Union Impact on Employee "Voice"
XI. Summary

The introduction of the diagnostic model (see Chapter One) identified unions as an important element of the external conditions component. In Chapter Two, we provided a glimpse of union membership and discussed a number of emerging union expectations and concerns. In contrast, this chapter focusses on the union-management relationship and how this affects human resource management.

The economic recession of the early 1980s hit unions as hard as industry. Unions reacted in much the same way organizations reacted. Services were cut and staff were laid off. This recession hit especially hard at heavily unionized economic sectors—auto, steel, rubber, forestry, construction, and eventually, the public sector too. As a result, unions have stepped up their efforts to penetrate the service sectors and to organize workers outside their traditional areas of strength. Some unions have merged to provide greater service to members at less cost. Others have split from international unions based in the United States to form independent Canadian unions (such as the Canadian Auto Workers that split from the United Auto Workers), in order to better represent Canadian workers' interests without restrictions from the internationals.

Why do people join unions? What advantages do unions provide their members? What impact does a union have on human resource management? This chapter will consider the union-management relationship: the historical development of unionism in Canada, how unions organize, the structure of union organizations, negotiating a contract, and jointly administering that contract. As will be seen throughout this chapter, unions have a profound impact on human resource management, especially in such areas as promotions, layoffs, compensation, and benefits. At nonunion organizations, employers have individual contracts (implicit, if not explicit) with their employees, and most P/HRM decisions are made essentially unilaterally by management. However, at a unionized organization, many P/HRM decisions are subject to negotiation with the union or specific contractual restrictions from the collective agreement.

A DIAGNOSTIC APPROACH TO LABOUR RELATIONS

Labour relations is frequently an emotionally charged P/HRM activity; few employers or employees get as emotionally involved over recruiting methods or career development plans, for example, as they do over this aspect of the personnel function. Collective bargaining goes to the heart of employee relations problems—power. Whoever has the power to fire an employee has power over that employee's economic and psychological well-being. Whoever has the power to evaluate an employee's performance has the power to affect significant human needs. Thus, labour relations is one of the most significant areas of human resource management.

> ### Definition
> *Labour relations* is a continuous relationship between a defined group of employees (represented by a union or association) and an employer. The relationship includes the initial recognition of the rights and responsibilities of union and management, the negotiation of a written collective agreement concerning wages, hours, and other conditions of employment, and the interpretation and administration of this contract over its period of coverage.

In a nonunionized organization, management has flexibility in hiring and promoting people, establishing the nature of the work and work rules, administering pay and benefits, and in other P/HRM matters. Much of this changes when employees elect to join a union. Then, the union and the employer negotiate a collective agreement that spells out details of the union-management relationship.

Human resource management professionals are of necessity technical experts in labour relations. They train and advise operating managers on the contract provisions. They also bargain with the union on the collective agreement and serve in the grievance process. But operating managers are the people who make the contract work on a daily basis. They identify problem areas in the contract to be improved during the next negotiations, and they are the first to face grievances.

External Conditions

Economic and Technological

Perhaps more than any other human resource activity, labour relations is affected by economic conditions on a global scale. Foreign competition in the product market had a devastating impact on union membership, employment, and wage scales in the early 1980s in the auto and steel industries. Wage freezes and cuts were the order of the day, and even those concessions couldn't stave off layoffs.

Product market conditions affect unions and employers in the same direction. Hard times for an employer constitute hard times for the union. In contrast, labour market conditions can affect unions and employers differently. If the labour market is tight, the union's power may be enhanced. If the labour market has a surplus, management may have an advantage: It can sustain a strike, and perhaps even benefit economically from it by replacing workers with new hires at lower pay rates.

Technological change (see Chapter Two) has an important impact on labour relations. Historically unions have been concerned about technological advances that affect employment. They argue that workers will generally be laid off and replaced by machines and their skills may become obsolete, thus adding to unemployment problems. Management generally counters by pointing out that the improved efficiency will create more jobs, although the skills required may change and retraining may be necessary. As high-tech developments continue and robots, CAD/CAM, and CIM become more common in modern industry, this centuries-old debate between unions and management continues, and contractual provisions regulating the introduction of new technology are not uncommon. Research has shown that Canadian unions are not generally opposed to the principle of technological change, but are more concerned with how it is implemented. In 1985, 38 percent of major collective agreements included clauses requiring advance notice or consultation before technological changes are introduced, 31 percent provided for training or retraining of workers, and 23 percent included other technology-related employment security provisions.[1] Unions are also concerned about the health and safety effects of new technology.

Government

The federal and provincial governments create the legal environment within which labour relations occur. Approximately 10 percent of the work force comes under the federal sector jurisdiction, which includes, for example, the banking, airline, and railroad industries, federal crown corporations, and, of course, the federal government. All others come under provincial jurisdiction (see Chapter Two). The federal jurisdiction and each of the provinces have two statutes that regulate labour relations: one for private-sector employers and another for public-sector employers. Consequently, the legal framework for labour relations is very fragmented since there are more than 20 different statutes across the jurisdictions and public and private sectors. The statutes are very similar in their basic provisions, but there are minor variations labour

EXHIBIT 13–1
Framework of Labour Relations Statutes

	Provincial	Federal
Private Sector	Provincial labour relations acts	Canada Labour Code, Part V
Public Sector	Provincial public sector labour relations acts	Public Service Staff Relations Act

relations specialists must be aware of. This legal framework is summarized in Exhibit 13–1.

These statutes stipulate certain rights of employees, including the right to organize a trade union of their choice and to participate in its legal activities. Legal activities include the right to bargain collectively with the employer over wages, benefits, and other terms and conditions of employment, the right to strike (except for many public-sector employees as discussed below), and the right to picket during a legal strike. Employers are also guaranteed certain rights, including the right to form an employer's organization, to bargain collectively through an employer's organization, and to lock out employees in the event of a labour dispute (with the exceptions noted below).

Each of the statutes established a Labour Relations Board (as well as a Labour Court in Quebec) responsible for administering and enforcing the provisions of the statutes. The boards' duties fall into two main categories: overseeing certification procedures and handling unfair labour practice complaints.

Certification procedures are based on the principle of majoritarianism. When a union applies to the board to be certified as the representative for a group of employees, the board first determines the appropriate bargaining unit, that is, the group of employees to be covered by the collective agreements negotiated between the union and the employer. The board is then responsible for determining the wishes of the majority of the employees in the bargaining unit, which may necessitate a certification vote supervised by the board. If the majority wants the union to be certified as the bargaining representative, the board will generally do so. If the majority wishes to remain unorganized, then the union will not be certified. Once certified, the union becomes the exclusive bargaining agent for those employees, and the employer is compelled by law to bargain in "good faith" with the union.[2]

Unfair labour practices are violations of the labour relations statutes, such as, an employer interfering with an employee's right to join a union. If a union or employer files an unfair labour practice complaint against the other party, the labour relations boards will conduct an inquiry, possibly hold hearings, determine the validity of the complaint, and issue an order to remedy the situation if the complaint is valid. Labour relations board orders generally have the same force and effect as a court order. Board orders can be appealed to the courts, but only on limited grounds.

Except for the extension of bargaining rights to public-sector employees in the late 1960s and early 1970s, the basic provisions of the labour relations statutes have remained unchanged since World War II. However, due to several very long and costly strikes, Alberta and British Columbia are reviewing their labour relations statutes. Labour law review committees in each province have been holding public hearings and have received hundreds of suggestions from labour, management, and other organizations. Alberta has already passed legislation, effective June 5, 1987, that established a new integrated/coordinated bargaining stucture for the construction industry.[3] The Quebec labour laws have also received much criticism recently, and a special government task force has recommended several changes in the Quebec statutes.[4]

Organizational Conditions

Employers can adopt a variety of strategies for dealing with organized employees. The specific strategy adopted will depend on organization goals, competitors' strategies, the organization culture, and even the personal values of top management.

Union-Free Strategy

In the previous chapter, we discussed employee relations programs that may be motivated in part by an employer's desire to maintain a union-free environment. Such programs demonstrate concern and respect for employees and give them substantial control for their work lives.

The employee relations program comprises ways in which an organization can change its internal environment to reduce the attractiveness of unions.

Cooperation Strategy

While labour relations disputes—strikes, violence, allegations of illegal behaviour—capture the attention of the public, the vast majority of contract negotiations and day-to-day administration is done in an atmosphere of mutual respect. The interests of all parties are served if an agreement acceptable to all can be reached without resorting to work stoppages. If not harmonious, most relationships are at least cooperative.[5] Issues and programs involved in cooperative union management relations are examined in the remainder of the chapter.

An employer's labour relations strategy—union-free, anti-union, or co-operation—is a major decision made by top management. The strategic choice serves to guide the programs and activities adopted in human resource management.

CANADIAN UNIONISM: A HISTORICAL PERSPECTIVE

The first record of unionism in Canada is an organization of skilled tradesmen in Saint John, New Brunswick, during the War of 1812.[6] By 1850, trade unions had developed in every major city in eastern Canada, most of them organizations of skilled tradesmen. Labour unions had a difficult time during these early days, but they survived and laid the foundation for the developing Canadian labour movement.

Early Organization Issues

Many of the issues that prompted workers to form labour unions in the 1800s are the same issues that attract workers to unions today. One major issue in the workplace at that time was working conditions, especially safety. Many employees worked with high-speed machines that could, and did, remove a limb in a moment's notice. The bone-numbing fatigue caused by the 12- to 14-hour workday, seven days a week, contributed to high accident rates. Consequently, safety, shorter hours, and improving other dismal work conditions were the rallying points for many early trade unions.

Wages were also a major point of contention between workers and employers. No minimum wage laws existed at the time, and many workers toiled at wages below subsistence levels. Furthermore, many unions were organized in an attempt to prevent further wage cuts rather than to increase wages. At these low wage levels, it was often necessary for entire families to work in the factories and mines to supply enough money for the family to survive. This exasperated labour problems since many employers would hire children at lower rates before they would hire adults, leading to unemployment among adults.

Job security was a key issue also. In 1852, the Journeymen Tailors of Toronto formed in an attempt to prevent introduction of the new Singer sewing machine in Toronto tailor shops. As is common today, many skilled tradesmen who saw new technology and machinery threatening their occupations (and consequently their livelihood) tried to stop, or at least slow, its adoption by employers. Many of the trades early unions attempted to protect have disappeared, such as sailmakers and coopers (barrel makers).

Although industrialization then was very different from modern industry, the rallying points of early labour unions are not foreign to modern unions.

The incredible progress in industry over the past 150 years has had little impact on the basic reasons for workers to organize unions.

Legality of Unions

Before 1872, unions were considered illegal organizations. This was based on Common Law doctrines, especially the Criminal Conspiracy Doctrine, and the courts' interpretation that trade unions were criminal conspiracies whose objective was restraint of free trade. The courts would routinely issue injunctions against unions, union organizers, strikers, and picketers, and violators could be fined or imprisoned. Nevertheless, some unions developed even in this hostile legal environment.

In 1872, the Trade Unions Act and the Criminal Law Amendment Act freed labour unions from charges of criminal conspiracy. This legislation followed a strike by the printers in Toronto. The printers were campaigning for a shorter workweek (54 hours a week rather than 60). The Toronto publishers resisted with the usual tactics, and 13 strike leaders were arrested. Eventually, a mass protest developed as 10,000 people gathered at the legislative buildings in Queen's Park, Toronto.

After 1872, unions had a new legal standing. However, although workers could now legally form unions, employers were not legally required to recognize and bargain with the unions. After World War I, neither governments nor the general public were tolerant of unions. A major event in unions' battle to gain recognition was the Winnipeg General Strike on May 15, 1919. Organized by the metalworkers, between 25,000 and 30,000 employees walked out in support of the Winnipeg unions battling for recognition from their employers. Eventually, the North-West Mounted Police drove the strikers from the streets. In elections following this general strike, labour made major victories all across Canada, especially in the West.

Employers adopted new tactics to counter unions, the yellow dog contract and blacklisting. Yellow dog contracts are agreements between the employer and individual employees stating that, as a condition of employment, the employee must not join a labour union. Employers required that applicants sign these contracts before being hired. If employees did join a union, they were dismissed. Blacklists were lists of workers known to be union supporters. These lists were circulated among employers who refused to hire any individual on the lists. These tactics were outlawed in a 1939 amendment to the Criminal Code, establishing the principle that employers could not take away employees' right to unionize.

Canadian labour policy in the early 1900s was heavily influenced by William Lyon Mackenzie King. The Department of Labour was established in 1900, and King was the first deputy minister of labour. One of King's major achievements was instituting compulsory conciliation as a precondition to the right to strike or lock out, as embodied in the Industrial Disputes Investigation Act of 1907. These provisions remain in the statutes of several Canadian jurisdictions today.

In 1944, the Wartime Labour Relations Regulations established certification procedures for unions and required that employers recognize and bargain in good faith with certified trade unions. After World War II, each of the provinces passed labour relations legislation. For a time, the provinces experimented with different models of labour relations. The provinces eventually adopted legislative frameworks similar to the Wartime Labour Relations Regulations, which are patterned after the Wagner Act of 1935 in the United States, and the basic legal framework in Canada has changed little since.

International Unions

Many of the tradesmen who formed the early unions in Canada had immigrated from Britain. Consequently, they brought with them the traditions of the British labour movement, and many of the first unions were affiliated with British unions. Several British unions had branches in Canada. However, over time, Canadian workers developed closer ties with workers in the United States, and ties with British unions were replaced with those to American unions. From 1860 until 1960, the Canadian and American labour movements maintained very close ties.

That close association with the U.S. labour movement began to break down about 1960. In the early 1960s, approximately 70 percent of Canadian union members belonged to international unions based in the United States. Currently, the figure is approximately 36 percent. Much of this decline is due to the belief by many, both inside and outside the labour movement, that Canadian members of international unions pay much more into international union funds than they receive in benefits and services.[7]

Others argue that Canadian unions will be able to better represent Canadian workers' interests without interference and restrictions from international headquarters. This was a key issue in the 1984 contract negotiations between General Motors of Canada and the United Auto Workers and eventually led to the split of the Canadian Auto Workers (a new independent Canadian union) from the international UAW. Others argue that the larger financial base and greater clout of the huge international unions help Canadian workers. Clear conclusions cannot be drawn at this time since the issue has not been adequately studied, but if recent trends continue, the Canadian labour movement will continue to break its ties with the American labour movement.

Labour Federations

Most of the central labour federations in Canada emerged and developed between 1860 and 1960; consequently, their history parallels that of the federations in the United States. The Knights of Labour, which originated in Philadelphia, established its first Canadian assembly in Hamilton, Ontario, in 1875. The Knights of Labour had an open organizational structure and allowed all unions to join its ranks. It remained fairly strong in Canada into the 20th century, but it eventually died because of lack of membership. Most union members found its idealism and support of political action over bargaining action inconsistent with their more immediate concerns.

In 1886, the Trades and Labour Congress of Canada (TLC) emerged. This federation was closely associated with the American Federation of Labor (AFL) in the United States, restricted its membership to craft unions, and adopted the "business unionism" philosophy. Business unionism is characterized by pragmatic action at the bargaining table to obtain immediate benefits for labour rather than pursuing ideological goals through the political process. As did the AFL, the TLC promoted "exclusive jurisdiction" and chartered unions in an attempt to avoid interunion rivalry for membership.

The Canadian Congress of Labour (CCL) emerged as a federation of industrial unions in 1940. This also paralleled the emergence of the industrial-based Congress of Industrial Organizations in the United States in 1938. The TLC and CCL coexisted until 1956, often engaging in bitter rivalry for membership. In 1956, the two federations put this rivalry aside and merged to form the Canadian Labour Congress (CLC). This again paralleled the merger of the AFL and CIO in the United States. Although there are several other labour federations in Canada, the CLC remains by far the largest Canadian labour federation. In 1985, 75.4 percent of Canadian union members belonged to unions affiliated with a labour federation, 57.8 percent of union members being affiliated with the CLC.[8]

Union Membership

The growth of unionization in Canada from 1921 to 1960, as measured by the percentage of nonagricultural workers, is shown in Exhibit 13–2. No reliable data are available for the time before 1920. Several patterns in the growth of unionization can be noted. From 1920 until 1940, union penetration fluctuated between 12 and 18 percent with no clear trend upward or downward. However, unionization almost doubled from 16.3 percent in 1940 to 30.3 percent in 1947. This dramatic increase can be attributed to the more favourable legal environment created by the 1939 amendment to the Criminal Code and the 1944 Wartime Labour Relations Regulations. During this seven-year period, the labour movement gained a very strong foundation in Canadian industry.

EXHIBIT 13–2
The Growth of Unionization in Canada, 1921–1986 (union members as a percentage of nonagricultural workers)

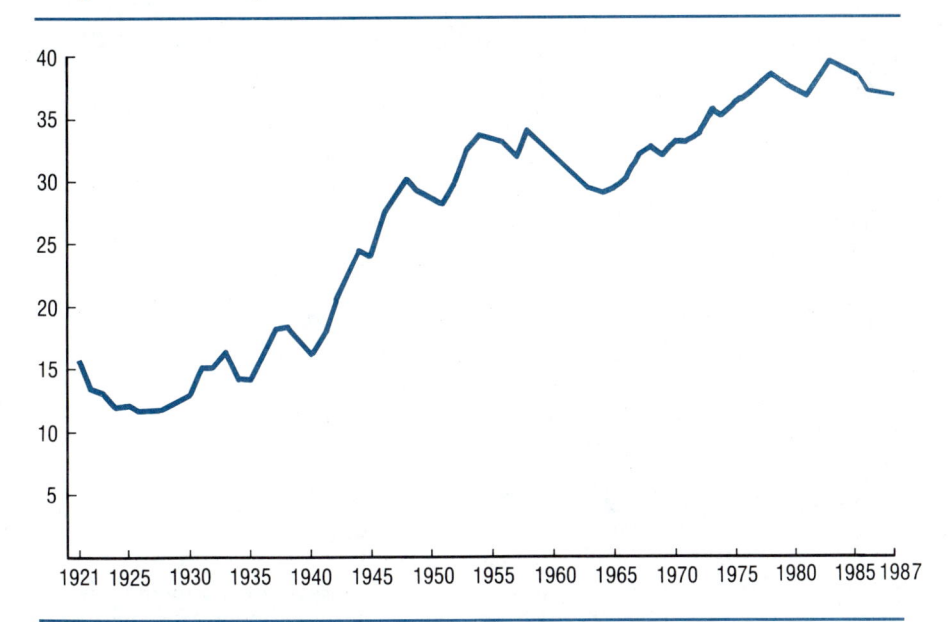

Note: 1987 data are for January.
Source: See Economics and Research Branch, Canada Department of Labour, *Labour Organizations in Canada* (Ottawa: Queen's Printer, 1972), for data from 1921 to 1972; Labour Data Branch, Labour Canada, *Directory of Labour Organizations in Canada 1986* (Ottawa: Supply and Services Canada, 1986), for data from 1973 to 1986; Pradeep Kumar et al., *The Current Industrial Relations Scene in Canada* (Kingston, Ont.: Industrial Relations Centre, Queen's University, 1986 and 1987 editions).

Unionization continued to rise to about 33 percent in the mid-1950s, but declined to less than 30 percent by the mid-1960s. During the late 1960s, bargaining rights were extended to most public-sector employees, and the organization of the public sector over the next 15 years resulted in another long period of growth for the labour movement. Since 1978, unionization has been fluctuating between 37 and 40 percent of the work force.

The industrial structure of unionization shows that unions are much stronger in some industries than others, as shown in Exhibit 13–3. Unions have their highest penetration in the transportation, communication, and utilities industries, and public administration and are weakest in wholesale and retail trade and finance, insurance, and real estate. Unions are also well established in manufacturing industries, but the 45 percent figure for manufacturing masks considerable variation, ranging from 67 percent in the tobacco and paper industries to only 17 percent in petroleum and coal products.[9]

EXHIBIT 13–3
Canadian Unionization by Industry, 1984 (union members as a percentage of workers)

Industry Group	Percent Unionized
Forestry	36.6
Mines, quarries, and oil wells	32.8
Manufacturing	45.0
Construction	38.9
Transportation, communication, and other utilities	60.0
Trade	12.5
Finance, insurance, and real estate	9.2
Community, business, and personal services	38.1
Public administration	66.6

Source: Statistics Canada, Survey of Union Membership (conducted as a supplement to December 1984 labour survey).

WHY EMPLOYEES JOIN UNIONS

To understand labor-management relations we must first understand the *people* involved. Why do people join unions? Kochan developed a model, shown in Exhibit 13–4, which summarizes the research. An individual's decision to join or avoid a union, according to the model, is influenced by three critical determinants:

1. *Perceptions of the work environment.* Dissatisfaction with bread-and-butter aspects of the job, such as wages and benefits, dissatisfaction with supervision, or with the treatment of one group of employees versus another, all can translate into a greater interest in unionism.
2. *Desire to participate or influence* the job and the employment conditions surrounding the job. According to Kochan, a key here is that the lack of other effective alternatives for influence turns employees to unions.
3. *Employee beliefs about unions.* Employees who are dissatisfied have certain expectations about what a union can do for them. If they are predisposed or convinced through organizing efforts that a union will improve their situation, employees are more likely to join.

Sometimes employees join because the representing union and management have negotiated a clause in their contract that makes joining the union a condition of continued employment (a union shop clause).

Based on her research, Brett identifies some factors that boost the likelihood of success of an organizing campaign.[10] First, employees will be more likely to unionize if an employer is perceived to have demanded different

EXHIBIT 13-4
Psychological Determinants of Propensity to Unionize

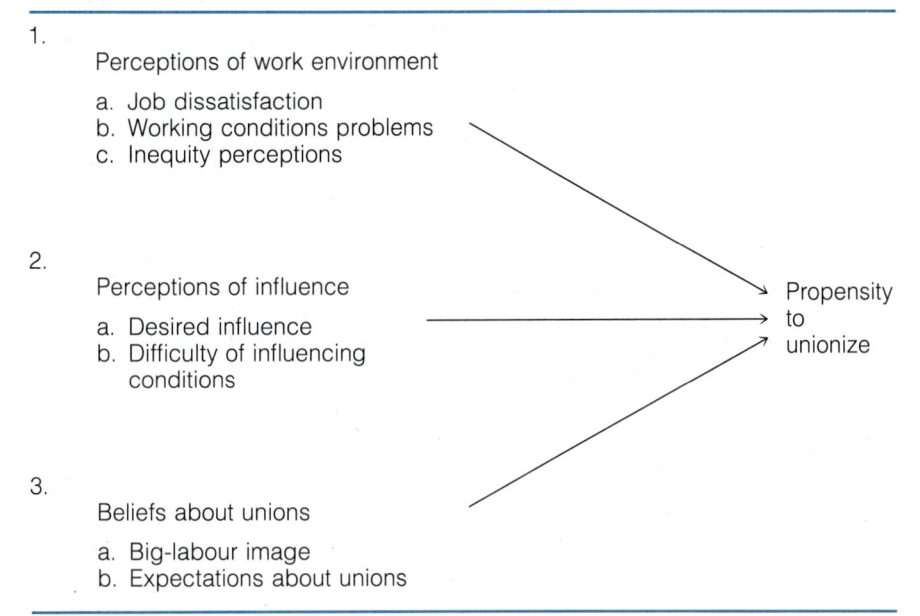

1. Perceptions of work environment
   a. Job dissatisfaction
   b. Working conditions problems
   c. Inequity perceptions

2. Perceptions of influence
   a. Desired influence
   b. Difficulty of influencing conditions

3. Beliefs about unions
   a. Big-labour image
   b. Expectations about unions

→ Propensity to unionize

Source: Thomas Kochan, *Collective Bargaining and Industrial Relations* (Homewood, Ill.: Richard D. Irwin, 1980), p. 144.

behaviour than was expected or failed to provide rewards expected. Second, an individual must believe there is little likelihood of changing conditions except through collective action. Third, some critical mass of like-minded activists is necessary to begin the unionizing attempt. Fourth, unionization by this activist coalition depends on employees' understanding of how collective bargaining works and their belief that the likely benefits of organizing outweigh the losses.

THE ORGANIZING CAMPAIGN

When employees are not represented by a union, either the employees themselves or a union can initiate unionization. When employees are quite dissatisfied, they can take the initiative and invite a union in to begin organizing an employer. There is little empirical evidence on the frequency of employee intiative.

Whether the employees or the union take the initiative, the time of high drama is the organizing campaign itself. Union organizers try to get the minimum employee support required by the relevant statutes to apply for certification. This varies from 25 percent in Saskatchewan to 50 percent in Alberta, Newfoundland, and Prince Edward Island.[11] Union organizers must demonstrate employee support for the union by having the required percentage either join the union or sign a "certification card" that states the employee wishes to have the union certified as the bargaining agent.

In general, the union tries to keep initial stages of the certification campaign secret so it can gather momentum before management can mount a counteroffensive. During the campaign, unions and management try to influence attitudes toward unionization. The union typically stresses how it can improve the workers' lot in terms of compensation, benefits, working conditions, and increased control over decisions related to their jobs (see Exhibit 13–5). Management mounts a countercampaign stressing how well off the employees are already and the costs of union membership in dollars and "loss of freedom." It is illegal for either side to threaten or coerce employees in an attempt to get their support or to commit other unfair labour practices during the organizing period.

Once a union gathers the required support and applies for certification, the labour relations board must decide on the appropriate bargaining unit. An

EXHIBIT 13–5
Prevalent Union Campaign Issues

Issue	Percent of Campaigns
Union will prevent unfairness, set up grievance procedure/seniority system	81
Union will improve unsatisfactory wages	79
Union strength will provide employees with voice in wages, working conditions	79
Union, not outsider, bargains for what employees want	73
Union has obtained gains elsewhere	70
Union will improve unsatisfactory sick leave/insurance	64
Dues/initiation fees are reasonable	64
Union will improve unsatisfactory vacations/holidays	61
Union will improve unsatisfactory pensions	61
Employer promises/good treatment may not continue without union	61
Employees choose union leaders	55
Employer will seek to persuade/frighten employees to vote against union	55
No strike without vote	55
Union will improve unsatisfactory working conditions	52
Employees have legal right to engage in union activity	52

Source: Adapted from Table 4–3 in *Union Representation Elections: Law and Reality*, by Julius G. Getman, Stephen B. Goldberg, and Jeanne B. Herman, © 1976 by Russell Sage Foundation, New York. Reprinted by permission of Basic Books, Inc., Publishers.

important consideration in this decision is the community or mutuality of interest among the workers in the bargaining unit with respect to wages, hours, working conditions, and other issues. The board may also consider the bargaining pattern in the industry, the prior bargaining history of the unit, the structure of the employer, and other factors.[12]

After the appropriate unit of employees is established, the board must determine if there is majority support for the union. In several provinces, the board is required by law to certify the union if a certain percentage of employees in the unit indicate support for the union. If there is doubt, however, the board may hold a certification election. These are supervised by the board to ensure they are unbiased, and each employee in the unit may vote to express his or her preference. Three provinces (New Brunswick, Newfoundland, and Quebec) require 50 percent of the employees in the bargaining unit to vote for the union for it to be certified, while the other provinces require only 50 percent of the employees that actually vote supporting the union. If certified, the union becomes the exclusive bargaining agent for all the employees in the bargaining unit.

Over the two-year period 1984–85, there were 4,142 certification applications in Canada. Of these, 2,803 (67.7 percent) certifications were granted. Over the same period, 469 previously certified unions were decertified.[13]

UNION STRUCTURE

The structure of the Canadian labour movement is shown in Exhibit 13–6. The keystone of the union movement is the 16,000 local unions, each representing all the workers in one bargaining unit. Most local unions are branches of national or international unions, and most have little legal autonomy. Union dues are collected by the local, which in turn distributes the money according to the constitution of the national or international. A substantial portion of the funds generally goes to the national or international union.

A philosophy of "bigger is better" seems to be emerging in the Canadian labour movement. In some cases, this has resulted in internal mergers, such as the United Food and Commercial Workers, which combined four locals in Ontario into one new local that now has 35,000 members. There are also discussions of consolidating diverse unions within some trades and industries to form a smaller number of larger national unions.[14]

Many unions are also affiliated with labour federations. Labour federations generally act as the "spokesperson" for labour. They are generally involved in lobbying and promoting labour's interests in the political process, in addition to research, education, and public relations functions. Some locals are affiliated with local labour councils, such as the Labour Council of

EXHIBIT 13–6
Structure of the Labour Movement in Canada

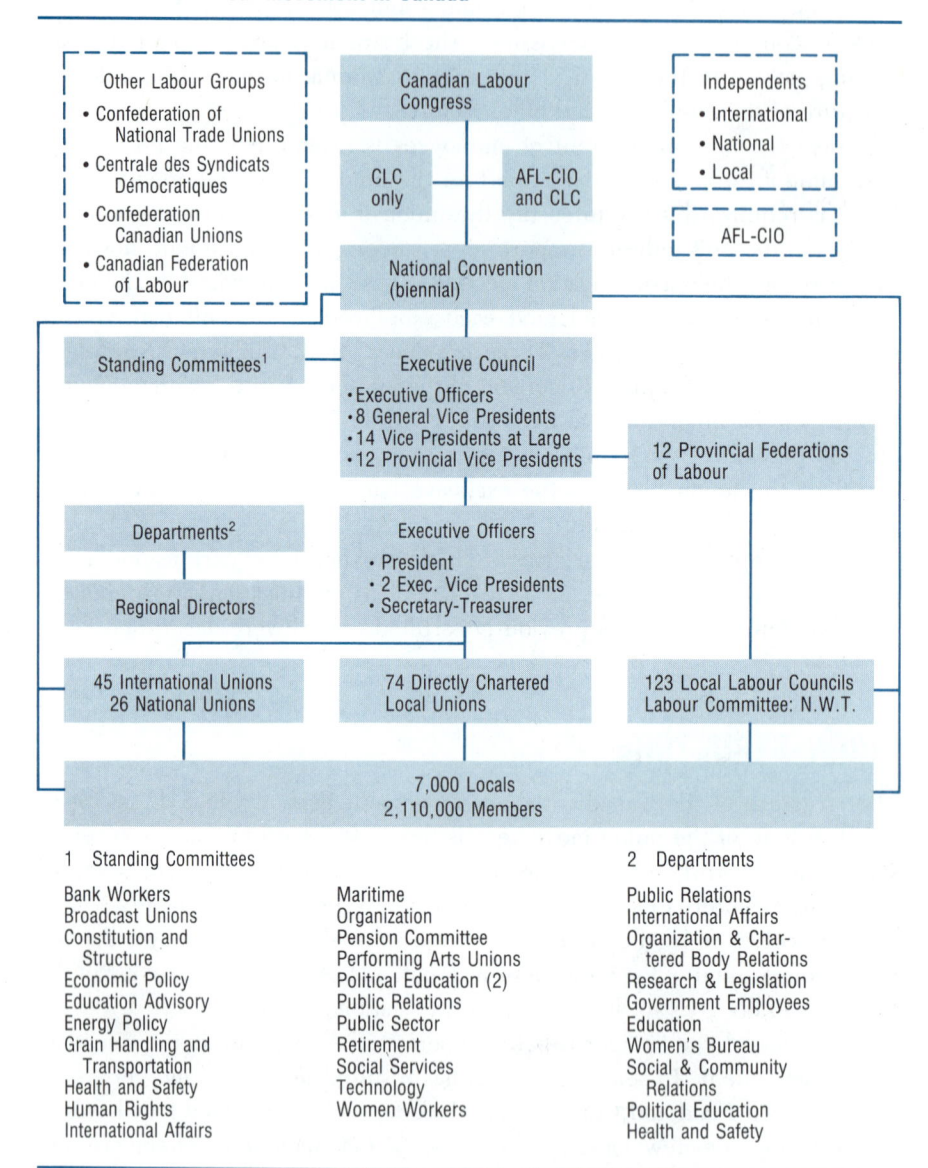

```
┌─────────────────────────┐    ┌──────────────────────┐    ┌──────────────────┐
│ Other Labour Groups     │    │ Canadian Labour      │    │ Independents     │
│ • Confederation of      │    │ Congress             │    │ • International │
│   National Trade Unions │    │                      │    │ • National       │
│ • Centrale des Syndicats│    │  CLC      AFL-CIO    │    │ • Local          │
│   Démocratiques         │    │  only     and CLC    │    └──────────────────┘
│ • Confederation         │    │                      │    ┌──────────────────┐
│   Canadian Unions       │    │ National Convention  │    │ AFL-CIO          │
│ • Canadian Federation   │    │ (biennial)           │    └──────────────────┘
│   of Labour             │    └──────────────────────┘
└─────────────────────────┘
```

Standing Committees[1] — Executive Council
- Executive Officers
- 8 General Vice Presidents
- 14 Vice Presidents at Large
- 12 Provincial Vice Presidents

12 Provincial Federations of Labour

Departments[2] — Regional Directors

Executive Officers
- President
- 2 Exec. Vice Presidents
- Secretary-Treasurer

45 International Unions / 26 National Unions | 74 Directly Chartered Local Unions | 123 Local Labour Councils Labour Committee: N.W.T.

7,000 Locals
2,110,000 Members

1 Standing Committees

Bank Workers
Broadcast Unions
Constitution and
  Structure
Economic Policy
Education Advisory
Energy Policy
Grain Handling and
  Transportation
Health and Safety
Human Rights
International Affairs

Maritime
Organization
Pension Committee
Performing Arts Unions
Political Education (2)
Public Relations
Public Sector
Retirement
Social Services
Technology
Women Workers

2 Departments

Public Relations
International Affairs
Organization & Char-
  tered Body Relations
Research & Legislation
Government Employees
Education
Women's Bureau
Social & Community
  Relations
Political Education
Health and Safety

Source: Pradeep Kumar, Mary Lou Coates, and David Arrowsmith, *The Current Industrial Relations Scene in Canada, 1986* (Kingston, Ont.: Queen's University, Industrial Relations Centre, 1986), p. 351.

Metropolitan Toronto. These represent labour's interests at the local level. Most provinces also have provincial labour federations, such as the Alberta Federation of Labour. Many national unions and the Canadian branches of international unions are affiliated with the Canadian Labour Congress or other Canadian federations, and many of the Canadian branches of international unions are also affiliated with the American AFL–CIO through their international parent organizations.

Most contract negotiations occur at the level of the local union. However, it is also common for several locals within one organization to negotiate a common contract. This is especially so for employers with multiple plants, each plant organized as a separate local of the same national union (such as in the auto industry).

NEGOTIATING A CONTRACT

Once a union is recognized as the bargaining representative for a group of employees, its officials are authorized to negotiate an employment contract. There are usually three phases to this: preparation for negotiations, negotiation, and settlement.

Preparation for Contract Negotiations

Preparation for contracts is an area in which little research has been done, mainly because the parties of the negotiation prefer secrecy. The more complex the bargaining, the further ahead preparations begin.

The beginning part of the preparation concerns problems in contract administration and changes in contract language. Both offensive and defensive strategies regarding contract changes are prepared. If management or the union wishes to make changes in a contract, it must notify the other party and generally the labour relations board in writing of desire to terminate or modify the contract at least 60 days before the contract expires. This notification also should include an offer to meet the other side to discuss the issue.

Probably since the signing of the last contract, both sides have been compiling a list of issues to be brought up the next time. Management has asked its supervisors how they would like the contract modified to avoid problem areas. The personnel department has been studying patterns in grievances to see where problems lie. The contract has been examined to identify undesirable sections, especially those that management believes restrict its rights.

Based on these data, statistical information is gathered and bargaining positions are prepared. For example, management seeks information on economic conditions affecting the job (e.g., wage rates, productivity) from its staff, industry data, and published sources.

An attempt is made to determine the cost of each likely union demand. Computer simulation can help here. Preliminary trade-offs are considered. The union tends to ask for more than it knows it can get, so management tries to calculate the best strategy. If the organizing effort is industrywide, as it is in the auto, steel, rubber, and trucking industries, intercompany preparations begin.

Often there are differences within management groups over bargaining objectives.[15] A common complaint is: "I'm having more trouble with my company than I am with the union." If these management differences are worked out before the negotiations start, the bargaining process will be more effective. An employer who negotiates with more than one union must prepare carefully, for what it negotiates with one union will be brought up by the other.[16] Typically, a careful balance of wage, benefit, and status differentials must be maintained among unions. Careful preparations will help maintain that balance.

The union also prepares for negotiations by preparing lists of problems with the contract. It too gathers statistical information, studies the opponent closely, and coordinates with other unions involved. Unions may also have internal differences, usually over what the bargaining objectives are; for example, younger workers may want job security and re-skilling, older workers better pensions. Increasingly, unions poll their members on their preferred objectives for negotiation.

Very few studies have been done of how unions set their priorities. It is probable that members' expectations are formalized by the union leadership, which may compare past trends and extrapolate them to the present situation.

Negotiation Issues

Any labour contract can have a large number of clauses; studies show that the number of items an employer must bargain over is increasing. They can be categorized into the six groups named below.

1. Compensation and Working Conditions. All contracts stipulate compensation and working conditions, such as direct compensation rates, benefits, and hours of work. Issues concern whether overtime should be voluntary and the size of cost-of-living adjustments. Unions may bargain about not only payments for pensions but also the details of early retirement provisions, for example.

2. Job Security. Seniority is a special concern in this bargaining category. Seniority is continuous service in a work unit, plant, or organization. Unions believe seniority should be the determining factor in promotions, layoffs, and recalls. Management contends it is its right to make these decisions on the basis of job performance, or efficiency will suffer. Many contracts stipulate that in cases of promotion and layoff, when efficiency and ability are substantially equal, the most senior employee shall be favoured. As mentioned earlier, unions are also concerned about employees being replaced by new technology and often try to ensure that jobs are not lost by the introduction of new technology into the workplace. Job security is also the main reason why unions have opposed the Canada–U.S. free-trade deal, since they believe this will result in jobs being "exported" to the United States.

3. *Union Security.* To have as much influence over members as possible, the union tries to write a requirement for a union shop into the contract. If the union shop clause cannot be won, an agency shop may be acceptable to the union. In this, those who do not join the union must pay the equivalent of union dues to the union.

4. *Management Rights.* This issue usually presents an especially difficult set of problems. Management lists certain areas or decisions as management rights or prerogatives, which are thus excluded from bargaining. Management tries to make these lists long, and unions try to chip away at them. In many cases, the wage concessions unions made in the early 1980s were in exchange for reduction in the items of management's sole discretion.[17]

5. *Contract Duration.* This issue is of special concern to the organization. Companies tend to prefer longer contracts to avoid the turmoil of frequent negotiation.

6. *Grievance Procedure.* Legislation in most jurisdictions requires that collective agreements include a grievance procedure with binding arbitration as the final step of the procedure and outlaw "wildcat" strikes throughout the duration of the contract. Some statutes include model clauses deemed to be a part of the collective agreement if the parties have not negotiated their own specific grievance procedure. Most contracts do include a grievance procedure that the parties find most workable for their circumstances.

Formalizing the Contract

An agreement occurs when both sides believe they have produced the best contract they can. Their perceptions are influenced by the negotiations, their relative power at the time, and other factors. Power factors such as a weak union or a strong employer are very important in settlement of the contract. If the economy is slack, the union may be under more pressure to settle than in times of full employment. If the employer's business has certain crucial times (e.g., during the summer for construction, harvest time for food, Christmastime for the post office), the union may choose that time for negotiation to give it an advantage. If the government is committed to few strikes, it may intervene.[18] All these external factors, and more, enter the bargaining process.

After the two sides have tentatively agreed, the union leadership must receive the membership's support. The members must ratify the contract. Ratification is not automatic, and union negotiators must keep an eye toward membership ratifications or the negotiation process will have to be repeated.

The agreement or contract sets out the rules of the job for the contract period. It restricts some behaviour and requires other behaviour. Proper wording of the agreement can prevent future difficulties in interpretation. Both sides should thoroughly discuss the meaning of each clause to prevent misunderstanding, if possible.

Even if the contract is accepted at one level, it may require adjustments at other levels. For example, when General Motors of Canada signs a contract with the Canadian Auto Workers at the national level, local plants must then settle disputes on work rules and other issues at each plant. Only when these are settled is a comprehensive agreement reached.

In 1986, wage increases in major settlements averaged 3.4 percent, which was the lowest average annual increase in two decades. Furthermore, over the period 1982–86, the average wage settlements have been below the rate of price inflation. That means the average unionized worker in Canada has been losing in terms of "real" wages after adjusting for inflation. Two-tier wage systems are becoming more common as well. These systems maintain those employed at the time the contract is settled on a higher wage scale, but all new employees hired after that date are on a separate, lower wage scale.[19]

IMPASSES IN COLLECTIVE BARGAINING

The description of contract negotiation above suggests a smooth flow, from presentation of demands to settlement. But this flow is not always smooth, and impasses may develop at which one or both sides cannot keep the process moving. Four things can happen when an impasse develops: mediation, conciliation, a strike or lockout, or arbitration.

Mediation and Conciliation

> ### Definition
> *Mediation or conciliation* is the process by which a professional, neutral third party gets involved to help remove an impasse to the negotiations.

All experts agree it is better for the two parties to negotiate alone. However, when it appears this process has broken down, a mediator may be invited in to help the two sides find common grounds for further bilateral negotiations. Mediators have no legal authority to force the parties to make concessions or agree to specific contract terms. In general, mediation appears to work best when the negotiators are inexperienced and to be least effective when major differences exist between the expectations of each party to the dispute.

Conciliation is similar to mediation, especially in its initial stages. The key difference is that conciliators (or conciliation boards) are required to file a report that indicates how they believe the dispute should be settled. These reports may be made public and released to the press, and public pressure on the parties to settle the dispute on the terms recommended may get negotiations going again. However, as with mediation, the parties are free to accept or reject the recommendations. They are not legally binding.

Interest Arbitration

Definition
Interest arbitration is the process by which the union and management submit negotiation issues under dispute to an independent arbitrator or arbitration board. Arbitration decisions are final and binding on both parties.

No other topic in labour relations has more confusing jargon and labels than interest arbitration. Interest arbitration refers to a process that ends in a decision, not a recommendation. Kochan's clarification of the different forms of arbitration is shown as Exhibit 13–7.[20] He starts with differentiating voluntary and compulsory arbitration. Under voluntary arbitration, the parties agree to submit their differences to arbitration, whereas under compulsory arbitration the law requires the parties' impasses be submitted to arbitration. Under conventional arbitration, the arbitrator is free to generate any resolution that seems appropriate. Final-offer arbitration is a process during which the arbitrator must choose either the employer's or the union's last proposal. Arbitrators may deal with a single issue or the total contract. Arbitration may be done by a single individual or by a panel of arbitrators.[21]

Once the arbitrator has heard all the evidence, the arbitration award, which is binding on both parties, is written. Arbitration, no matter the form, assumes a high priority is placed on avoiding strikes. Some experts argue that the threat of arbitration (especially compulsory) stifles innovative solutions and the ability of the parties to make major breakthroughs.[22] The parties simply wait for the arbitrator to make a decision rather than collectively bargain.

EXHIBIT 13-7
The Terminology of Alternative Forms of Interest Arbitration

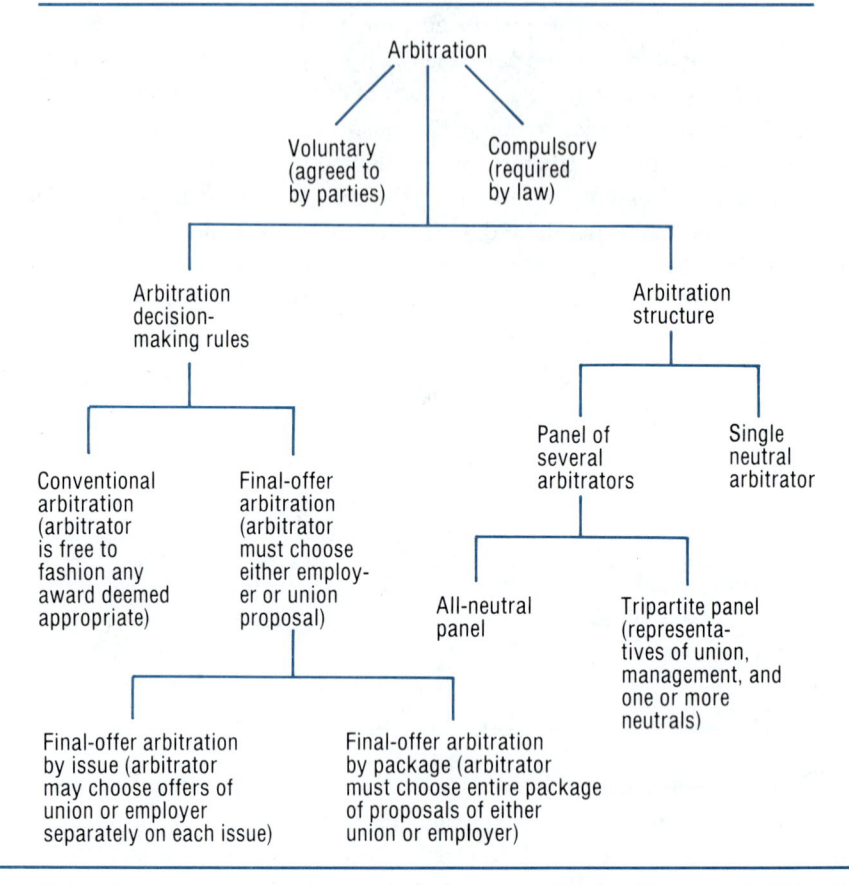

```
                            Arbitration
                           /          \
              Voluntary              Compulsory
              (agreed to             (required
              by parties)            by law)
                  |                      |
            Arbitration             Arbitration
            decision-               structure
            making rules                |
                 |                 ┌─────┴─────┐
          ┌──────┴──────┐      Panel of      Single
    Conventional   Final-offer  several      neutral
    arbitration    arbitration  arbitrators  arbitrator
    (arbitrator    (arbitrator       |
    is free to     must choose  ┌────┴────┐
    fashion any    either employ- All-neutral  Tripartite panel
    award deemed   er or union   panel        (representa-
    appropriate)   proposal)                  tives of union,
         |                                    management, and
         |                                    one or more
         |                                    neutrals)
   ┌─────┴─────┐
  Final-offer arbitration   Final-offer arbitration
  by issue (arbitrator      by package (arbitrator
  may choose offers of      must choose entire package
  union or employer         of proposals of either
  separately on each issue) union or employer)
```

Source: Thomas Kochan, *Collective Bargaining and Industrial Relations* (Homewood, Ill.: Richard D. Irwin, 1980), p. 290.

Others argue that the high costs associated with strikes in certain basic industries (e.g., steel) and public-sector jobs (e.g., police and fire protection) require some form of arbitration.[23]

Strikes and Lockouts

If an impasse in negotiations is serious, a strike or lockout can take place. A strike is a refusal by employees to work, and a lockout is a refusal by management to allow employees to work.

Strikes in Canada are generally of two types. A *contract* strike occurs when management and the union cannot agree on terms of a new contract. This is the only type of strike that is legal in Canada; consequently, most strikes in Canada are contract strikes. A *grievance*, or *wildcat*, strike occurs when the union disagrees on how management is interpreting the contract or handling day-to-day problems such as discipline. Grievance strikes are prohibited by law in all provinces and the federal sector, but they still occur.

Strikes differ too in the percentage of employees who refuse to work. A *total* strike occurs when all unionized employees walk out; if only a percentage of the workers does so, the result may be a partial strike, semistrike, or slowdown. In a *slowdown*, all employees come to work, but they do little work; the union insists on all work rules being followed to the letter, with the result that output slows. In a *partial strike*, many employees strike, but others come to work. This type is especially prevalent in the public sector where employees cannot legally strike.

Anatomy of a Strike. For a strike to take place, both sides must make decisions. Management must decide it can afford to "take a strike"; that is, it has built up its inventories, has sufficient financial resources, believes it will not lose too many customers during a strike, and believes it can win. The union must believe it will win more than it loses, that the employer will not go out of business, and that management will not replace union employees with strikebreakers. Union members must be willing to live with hardships and worries about no paychecks and be willing to give the union a strike vote. When members give the union the authority to strike, its bargaining hand is strengthened, and it can time the strike to occur when it will most hurt management.

During the strike, the union sets up the legally allowed number of pickets at the plants and tries to mobilize support among allies in other unions and the public.

What does management do if there is a strike? Lockouts are rarely used. In general, it tries to encourage workers to return to work by advertising circulars, phone calls, and so on. The longer the strike, the harder it is on the strikers. If the union has only limited strike funds and workers' savings run out, a back-to-work movement can cause the strike to collapse. In recent years, management has tended to play a defensive "wait them out" game and to keep operating during a strike. Nonunionized employees such as white-collar workers and managers may try to keep things going, and if management goes on the offensive, it may hire strikebreakers (except in Quebec, where this practice is illegal). Hiring strikebreakers is a very sensitive issue with unions and often results in violence on the picket lines. This was a key issue in the long and violent strike at the Gainers meat-packing plant in Edmonton in 1986. In this case, management attempted to retain the strikebreakers as permanent employees and lay off a substantial number of striking workers.

A number of theories have been advanced to explain why some employers and industries have more strikes than others.[24] It has been contended that strikes occur when there is uncertainty about the other side's position, and thus poor chances for advantageous collective bargaining; when management's expectations are too low and union members' are too high—in this case, a strike may take place to adjust expectations; when the bargaining power of one side is substantially greater than the other's.

Strikes or the threat of strikes put added pressures on both sides to settle their differences. Most strikes do not seriously affect the public welfare, but if it appears this is the case, the government often intervenes and may order the strikers back to work. This has become common over the last decade.[25]

Labour Disputes in Canada

Exhibit 13–8 provides data on the number of labour disputes and the percentage of work time lost due to labour disputes. The number of disputes increased as the Canadian economy grew. However, the percentage of work time lost due to labour disputes has not followed the same pattern. This figure tends to fluctuate with general economic conditions. When business is good, such as during the 1970s and early 1980s, unions are more demanding and labour disputes are more common. When business conditions are poor, such as during the Great Depression of the 1930s and, in more recent years, during the 1982–83 recession, the number generally declines.

EXHIBIT 13–8
Strikes and Lockouts in Canada, 1920–1985

Years	Average Number of Disputes	Percentage of Work Time Lost
1920–29	118	.14
1930–39	141	.06
1940–49	230	.15
1950–59	209	.17
1960–69	436	.20
1970–79	877	.37
1980	1,028	.38
1981	1,048	.37
1982	677	.25
1983	645	.19
1984	718	.16
1985	825	.13

Source: A. W. J. Craig, *The System of Industrial Relations in Canada*, 2nd ed. (Scarborough, Ontario: Prentice-Hall Canada, 1986), pp. 308–9; P. Kumar, Mary Lou Coates, and David Arrowsmith, *The Current Industrial Relations Scene in Canada 1987* (Kingston, Ont.: Industrial Relations Centre, Queen's University, 1987).

The percentage of work time lost due to labour disputes is a more appropriate statistic for gauging the impact of labour disputes on the economy since this reflects not only the number of labour disputes, but also the number of workers involved and the length of the disputes. Furthermore, this statistic is relative to the total amount of work time available to account for the changing size of the economy. This indicates the impact of strikes on the economy in 1984 was proportionately almost identical to the average impact during the decade of the 1920s.

The impact of labour disputes on the Canadian economy can be further investigated by comparing the percentage of work time lost due to labour disputes in Canada to other countries. A comparison of strike activity for 17 industrialized countries from 1970 through 1985 reveals Canada had the second highest level of the 17 countries.[26] Only Italy had a higher average percentage of work time lost due to labour disputes. The average percentage of work time lost in Britain was more than one third less than in Canada, and the percentage lost in the United States was approximately two thirds less than in Canada. For several countries (Switzerland, West Germany, Austria, Holland, and Norway), the average percentage of work time lost due to labour disputes was less than one tenth that of Canada.

Thus, on an international basis, labour disputes appear to be a serious problem in Canada. Several reasons can be offered for the high percentage of work time lost in Canada relative to other countries. First, the extent of unionization varies across countries. Almost 40 percent of the Canadian labour force is unionized, compared to less than 20 percent in the United States. This alone explains why the percentage of work time lost due to industrial disputes in the United States is much lower than in Canada even though the industrial relations systems in the two countries are very similar.

Second, the labour relations laws in Canada are more supportive of unions and strikes than the laws in some countries. For example, before a strike can legally occur in West Germany, 75 percent of the workers must vote to support the strike compared to the 50 percent support required in most provinces in Canada.

A third reason is the importance of natural resource industries in the Canadian economy. Natural resource industries tend to have much more volatile business cycles that manufacturing or service industries. That is, the "boom and bust" cycles are more pronounced. These extreme cycles tend to have a detrimental effect on labour relations. During boom periods, unions become very demanding in negotiations as they see employers reaping the benefits. During the bust, unions are also very demanding as workers become concerned about job security. For these and other reasons, natural resource industries (for example, forestry and mining) tend to be relatively strike prone. Compared to most other industrialized countries, natural resources account for a larger portion of total gross national product in Canada, making Canada more strike prone.

It has been well documented that a disproportionate share of industrial disputes occurs in a small number of strike-prone industries. One study found that from 1966 through 1975, six industries accounted for more than half the work time lost due to strikes, even though these six industries employ less than 15 percent of the labour force.[27] These six strike-prone industries are construction, mining, transportation, primary metals, pulp and paper products, and wood products. In most years, construction is the most strike-prone industry. The same study also found that three quarters of all work time lost due to industrial disputes was concentrated in three provinces: Ontario, Quebec, and British Columbia.

Industrial disputes are not the only source of work time lost, and some have argued that in comparison to other sources, the percentage of work time lost due to industrial disputes is insignificant. As indicated in Exhibit 13–8, the average percentage of work time lost due to strikes and lockouts from 1970 through 1985 was 0.34 percent. Another major source of lost time is unemployment. In recent years, the unemployment rate in Canada has been near 10 percent. Unemployed individuals are losing all of their work time; therefore, 10 percent is a reasonable estimate of the percentage of work time lost due to unemployment. If all these unemployed people had full-time jobs, the total work time (and presumably output) of Canada would be approximately 10 percent higher. Compared to this 10 percent figure, the one third of 1 percent of time lost due to labour disputes looks minuscule. In fact, according to these simple estimates, the percentage of work time lost due to unemployment is more than 30 times greater than that due to industrial disputes.

Other sources of lost time are accidents, illness, and other absenteeism. Together, these sources of absenteeism result in an average of five to seven days of absenteeism per employee. Thus, on average, about 2.3 percent of total work time per employee is lost due to absenteeism each year (some estimates have been as high as 4.0 percent). Again, this figure makes the 0.34 percent of work time lost due to industrial disputes look very small. Based on these estimates, the percentage of time lost due to absenteeism is more than seven times higher than that due to industrial disputes.

Thus, the statistics paint a confusing picture. In an international comparison, Canada's record of industrial disputes is among the worst. This would suggest industrial disputes may have a very serious detrimental impact on the Canadian economy. However, when compared to other sources of work time lost, the impact of industrial disputes is seen to be very small.

COLLECTIVE AGREEMENT ADMINISTRATION

Although contract negotiations and labour disputes make sensational headlines, most of the labour relations activities are concerned with the day-to-day administration of the collective agreement. The grievance process is an integral part of collective agreement administration.

Grievance Process

> **Definition**
> A *grievance* is a formal dispute between an employee (or the union) and management involving the interpretation, application, or an alleged violation of the collective agreement.

A grievance may be an *individual grievance*, relating to one individual employee; a *group grievance*, relating to a group of employees all of whom are similarly affected by the employer's action that is being grieved; or a *policy grievance*, which involves a matter of general policy or the general application of the collective agreement.

Grievances arise because of (1) differing interpretations of the contract by employees, stewards, and management; (2) a violation of a contract provision; (3) a violation of work procedures or other precedents; or (4) perceived unfair treatment of an employee by management. The rate of grievances may increase when employees are dissatisfied or frustrated on their jobs or they resent the supervisory style, or because the union is using grievances as a tactic against management. Grievances may also be due to unclear contractual language or employees with personal problems or who are otherwise "difficult."

The grievance process has at least three purposes and consequences. First, by settling smaller problems early, it may prevent larger problems (such as strikes) from occurring. Second, properly analyzed, grievances serve as a source of data to focus the attention of the two parties on ambiguities in the contract for negotiation at a future date. Finally, the grievance process is an effective communication channel from employees to management.[28]

Steps in the Grievance Process

The employee grievance process involves a systematic set of steps for handling an employee complaint. Most union contracts provide the channels and mechanisms for processing these grievances, though the process will vary with the contract.

1. Initiation of the Formal Grievance. When an employee feels mistreated or that some action or application of policy violates rights in the contract, a grievance is filed with the supervisor. It can be done in writing or (at least initially) orally. The grievance can be formulated with the help and support of the union steward.

A shop steward's position is somewhat like that of a first-line supervisor. They represent the union on the job site and are charged with handling grievances and disciplinary matters. Normally the steward is elected by members in the unit for a one-year term. By far, most grievances are settled at this level among the steward, the employee, and the supervisor.

The supervisor must attempt to determine accurately the reason for the grievance. The effective approach is to try to solve the problem, rather than assess blame or find excuses. The supervisor should consider what the contract says as modified by the employer's policies and past precedents in such cases. If the supervisor has a good working relationship with the steward, they can work together to settle the problem at that level.

2. Department Head or Unit Manager. If the steward, supervisor, and employee together cannot solve the grievance, it goes to the next level in the hierarchy. At this point, the grievance must be presented in writing, and both sides must document their cases.

3. Arbitration. If the grievance cannot be settled at this intervening step (or steps), an independent arbitrator must be called in to settle the issue.

Most grievances are settled at the first or second step. Only a few go to arbitration. Relatively few studies have been done on grievances.[29] Studies of the personal characteristics of those who have filed grievances as contrasted with those who have not revealed some differences; in general, those who filed grievances were younger, had more formal education, and got more wage increases.[30]

Grievance Arbitration

Definition

Grievance arbitration is the process by which the union and management submit an unresolved grievance to an independent arbitrator or arbitration board. The decisions are final and binding on both parties.

Grievance arbitration is required by law to be the last step of the grievance procedure in every collective agreement. This corresponds to the prohibition of strikes or lockouts during the term of the collective agreement discussed above. Consequently, grievance arbitration is very common in Canadian labour relations, and most labour arbitration in Canada is grievance arbitration rather than interest arbitration.

Most collective agreements specify the procedure by which the union and management will choose the arbitrator(s). Once this selection is made, a hearing date is established and each party presents its case in a quasi-courtroom procedure. Grievance arbitration is generally described as being "informal but orderly." Witnesses may give testimony and be cross-examined by the other party. The arbitrator(s) may also ask for clarification or additional evidence if it is necessary to make a decision.

The arbitration award normally reviews the facts in the case before stating the decision and usually is presented within 30 days of the hearing. The arbitrator writes the award in language understandable to all parties concerned, including the employee(s) involved in a grievance. It should attempt to clarify the problem situation so as to prevent future problems. The arbitrator will usually look over previous arbitration awards in similar cases but need not be bound by them.

THE PUBLIC SECTOR

Public-sector unions in Canada are relatively recent, although some other countries have had long experience with them.[31] Bargaining rights were not conferred to public-sector employees until the late 1960s, but once they had the right to organize, public-sector unions spread rapidly. The basic provisions of public-sector labour relations statutes are similar to private-sector statutes. Labour relations boards are set up to administer the laws, unions are certified as exclusive bargaining agents, and the unions and employers are required to bargain in good faith.

A key difference for many public-sector employees is they do not have the right to strike. This severely limits the unions' bargaining power during negotiations. Other fundamental differences in collective bargaining between the public and private sectors result from the structural difference between the two sectors.[32] For example, decision making is much more diffuse within the bureaucracy of the public sector, political constraints are predominant rather than economic constraints, many government services are considered essential, and economic sanctions may have little economic impact on employers in the public sector. Public-sector collective bargaining is still fairly new, and the federal and provincial governments continue to grapple with the unique problems that arise in this sector.

LABOUR UNION EFFECTS

Economic theory depicts unions as a constraint on the organization.[33] In a competitive market, unions attempt to obtain monopolistic control over the supply of labour in order to raise wages above the market-determined rate. Moreover, as unions are likely to attempt to establish restrictive work rules to protect their members, productivity is likely to fall. Consequently, unions are frequently viewed as promoting inefficiency and inequality in society. Is that view accurate? Let us examine the research on the impact of unions.

Union Impact on Wages

Does the presence of a union in an organization raise the level of wages for workers above what it would be if the company was not unionized? The commonly held belief among workers is that unions do have a wage impact. Efforts to determine if this perception is accurate have been a focus of research for many years.

Part of the reason for the continuing interest in this area is that the question of union impact on wages has not been totally resolved. Efforts to determine union impact on wages run into several measurement problems. The ideal situation would compare numerous organizations that were identical except for the presence or absence of a union.[34] Any wage differences among these organizations could then be attributed to the unionization. Unfortunately, few such situations exist. One alternative strategy adopted has been to identify organizations within the same industry that differ in level of unionization. For example, consider company A, which is unionized, and company B, which is not. It is difficult to argue with assurance that wage differences between the two firms are attributable to the presence or absence of a union. First, the fact that the union has not organized the entire industry weakens its power. Strike efforts to shut down the entire industry could be thwarted by nonunion firms. A second problem in measuring union impact arises if company B grants concessions to employees. These concessions, indirectly attributable to the presence of a union at company A, would lead to underestimation of union impact on wages.

A second strategy in estimating union impact on wages is to compare two different industries that differ dramatically in the level of unionization.[35] This strategy suffers because nonunionized industries (e.g., agriculture, service) are markedly different from unionized industries in the types of labour employed and the general availability of that labour. Such differences have a major impact on wages, independent of the level of unionization, and make any statements about union impact difficult to substantiate.

Such problems make estimating the union impact on wages difficult. Nevertheless, several studies have been done of the union impact on wages in Canada. Most of these studies found a union impact on wages in the range of 10 to 20 percent, although some have been higher.[36] The studies also found the union wage effect is higher for internationally based unions (31 percent) than for Canadian unions (15 percent),[37] and the impact varies considerably across occupations.[38]

What Determines Union Wage Levels?

The next part of this book will discuss how employers decide what to pay employees. Our discussion here will touch solely on the level of wages in unionized firms in comparison to the level of wages in nonunionized firms.

Among the most important factors affecting wage levels in unionized organizations are the ability of an employer to pay, productivity, and changes in the cost of living.

Changes in Employer's Ability to Pay

In profitable years, unions reason that part of the profits should accrue to the work force responsible for much of the organization's success. And in extremely unprofitable years, unions will even offer wage concessions.[39] Unions suffered dramatic slowdown in wage increases in 1982 and 1983, attributable to declines in cost-of-living adjustments and substantially reduced profitability among employers. However, economists frequently describe wages as "sticky"; that is, they do not rise and fall readily in response to changes in economic conditions.[40] Because of the time lag built into labour contracts, wages don't rise as fast as profits do, nor fall as fast. So changes in wages typically lag changes in an employer's ability to pay.

Changes in the Cost of Living

A second factor affecting wage levels in unionized organizations is the linkage of wages to the change in cost of living. Intent upon maintaining and improving the buying power of its membership, unions made a strong drive for wage escalator clauses during the 1970s. Cost-of-living adjustments (COLA) are designed to automatically increase wages during the life of the contract as a function of changes in the consumer price index. By 1976, 49 percent of the workers covered by major bargaining agreements had COLAs in their contracts. Since then, the percentage has declined (35 percent in 1984), partly because employment has been shrinking in some of the major unionized industries that have COLA clauses, but also because some unions have agreed to remove such clauses, in light of moderating increases in living costs.

Union Impact on Productivity

Although Canada has high labour productivity by international standards, yearly increases in productivity have lagged far behind most other industrial countries over the past decade. Our productivity advantage is rapidly eroding. Many industries, most notably the steel industry, have already experienced huge losses in market share that can be traced in large part to poor improvements, or actual declines, in productivity. This has led to an increasing effort to tie wage increases to productivity increases.[41] Incentive systems, profit-sharing plans, merit-based pay plans are all examples of efforts to make this productivity-wage link stronger. Even productivity bargaining and quality control circles show an increasing emphasis on the level of productivity in unionized and nonunionized organizations alike.

The model in Exhibit 13–9 indicates unions can have a positive or negative effect on productivity. Which it will be depends on how management responds.[42] The model suggests some of the specific ways union and employer behavior can affect productivity. Based on their analysis of the research, Freeman and Medoff conclude, "With management and unions working together to produce a bigger 'pie' as well as fighting over the size of their slices, productivity is likely to be higher under unionism. If industrial relations are poor, with management and labor ignoring common goals to battle one another, productivity is likely to be lower under unionism."[43]

EXHIBIT 13–9
Unionism and Productivity

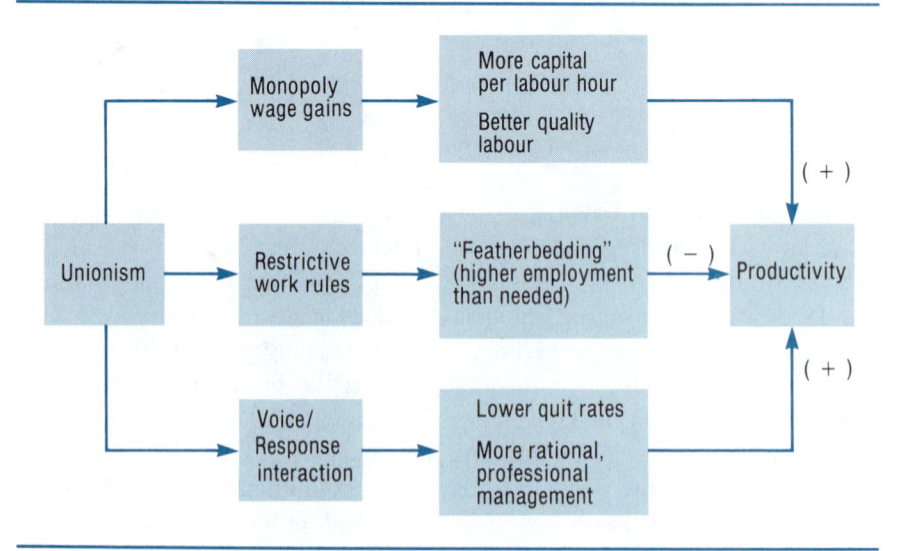

Source: Richard Freeman and James Medoff. *What Do Unions Do?* (New York: Basic Books, 1984). © 1984 by Basic Books, Inc., Publishers. Reprinted by permission of the publisher.

Union Impact on Employee "Voice"

In addition to its effect on members' wages, the other positive effect claimed for unionism is that it provides workers a collective voice on subjects affecting their work.[44] By providing workers with a voice in work-related decisions, unions are likely to have a number of positive effects for both employees and organization. First, unions act as *information collectors* for the organization, obtaining a clearer picture of the preferences of all employees rather than just new entrants to or those leaving the organization. As a result, employers are able to develop better personnel practices that reflect the needs of the existing work force. Second, unions are likely *to increase worker satisfaction by reducing inequality* among workers and guaranteeing some degree of due process in organizational decision making. Berger, Olson, and Boudreau, for example, discovered that unions have a significant positive effect on employee satisfaction with pay.[45] However, job dissatisfaction appears to be higher among union members than nonunion members.[46] Allen found substantially higher absenteeism rates among union members too.[47] Since absenteeism can be interpreted as an expression of job dissatisfaction, it may be that any "voice" the union provides has only limited effect on job satisfaction. Various writers have suggested that by providing the worker with a voice to change organizational conditions, the probability of turnover is likely to be reduced. Freeman and Medoff found consistent evidence that union membership increased tenure and decreased turnover.[48] Becker discovered a 50 percent reduction in turnover among hospital employees due to unionism.[49] Similarly, Pencavel found a 63 percent reduction in turnover.[50]

SUMMARY

Labour unions are an integral part of the external environment. In Canada, unions have concentrated on economic issues, whereas in Latin America and some Western European countries, unions are much more involved in politics and government. Unions affect the work environment through the wage gains, worker protection provisions, and shared decision making they have been able to negotiate. These gains have spilled over to benefit nonunionized employees too. So unions both affect and reflect the external environment.

Organizations differ in their approach to labour relations. Few employers invite a union to organize its workers, because they believe a union inhibits flexibility. Some employers display open hostility. But most labour/management relationships evolve to a position of mutual respect.

An effective union can provide employees with a "voice" to change organization conditions. Giving employees this voice can reduce turnover and enhance employee effectiveness. Many unions are formed as a result of ill-considered human resource management. By correcting poor management practices, unions can also contribute to organization effectiveness. So a constructive labour relations philosophy should be part of sound human resource management activities.

DISCUSSION AND REVIEW QUESTIONS

1. What are the significant diagnostic factors affecting labour relations?
2. Why do people join unions?
3. What role does the government play in labour relations?
4. Describe the various organization strategies for dealing with unions.
5. What factors have contributed to the past success of unions in Canada?
6. Contrast the different methods of dispute settlement.
7. When are mediators helpful to negotiations?
8. Do you believe Canada has a serious problem with labour disputes? If so, what should be done about it?
9. Is the practice of hiring replacement workers for strikers a good idea? Is it fair to the striking employees? Should this practice be allowed?
10. How do unions and collective bargaining differ in the public sector?
11. Discuss the possible impact of unions on employee and organizational effectiveness.

NOTES AND REFERENCES

1. Economic Council of Canada, *Innovation and Jobs in Canada* (Ottawa: Minister of Supply and Services Canada, 1987, (at. No. EC22-141/1978E), p. 114 (Table 8–4).
2. For further discussion on "good faith" bargaining, see Brian Bemmels, E. G. Fisher, and Barbara Nyland, "Canadian-American Jurisprudence on 'Good Faith' Bargaining," *Relations Industrielles/Industrial Relations* 41, no. 3 (1986), pp. 596–621. For general discussion on Canadian labour law, see George W. Adams, *Canadian Labour Law* (Toronto: Canada Law Book Inc., 1985); and H. D. Arthurs, D. D. Carter, and H. J. Glasbeek, *Labour Law and Industrial Relations in Canada*, 2nd ed. (Toronto: Butterworths, 1984).
3. "Seeking the Elusive Better Way," *Alberta Report*, January 12, 1987; *Canadian Labour Law Reports*, no. 857, p. 2.
4. "Quebec Labour Laws Are Blamed for Huge Loss of Jobs to Ontario," *Evening Telegram*, October 8, 1986, p. B–3.
5. Brian Bemmels, "Increasing Productivity at Unionized Organizations," in *Improving Productivity through Labour Management Cooperation* (proceedings of a Conference at the University of New Brunswick, November 14–16, 1985), pp. 41–51.
6. For further reading on the history of the Canadian labour movement, see Canadian Labour Congress, "History of Canadian Labour," *Notes on Unions*; John Crispo, *International Unionism: A Study in Canadian-American Relations* (Toronto: McGraw-Hill Company of Canada, 1967); Eugene Forsey, "The Movement

towards Labour Unity in Canada: History and Implication," in *Readings in Canadian Labour Economics*, ed. A. E. Kovacs (Toronto: McGraw-Hill Company of Canada, 1961); A. E. Kovacs, "Philosophy of the Canadian Labour Movement," in *Canadian Labour in Transition*, ed. Richard U. Miller and Fraser Isbester (Scarborough: Prentice-Hall of Canada, 1971); and C. Brian Williams, *Canadian Trade Union Philosophy: The Philosophy of the English-Speaking Trade Union Movement in Canada, 1936–1967* (Ottawa: Privy Council Office, 1970).

7. "Canadian Unions Hit by Ripoff," *The Globe and Mail*, July 19, 1986, p. A–7.
8. Labour Canada, *Directory of Labour Organizations in Canada 1985* (Ottawa: Supply and Services Canada, 1985), table 2, p. xxvi.
9. Statistics Canada, *Corporations and Labour Unions Returns Act, Report for 1981, Part II—Labour Unions* (Ottawa: Ministry of Supply and Services, 1983), p. 60.
10. Jeanne M. Brett, "Why Employees Want Unions," *Organizational Dynamics*, Spring 1980.
11. See Alton W. J. Craig, *The System of Industrial Relations in Canada*, 2nd ed. (Scarborough, Ontario: Prentice-Hall Canada, 1986), pp. 126–35.
12. Edward E. Herman, *Determination of the Appropriate Bargaining Unit by Labour Relations Boards in Canada* (Ottawa: Canada Department of Labour, 1966).
13. Pradeep Kumar, Mary Lou Coates, and David Arrowsmith, *The Current Industrial Relations Scene in Canada 1987* (Kingston, Ont.: Industrial Relations Centre, Queens University, 1987), p. 380.
14. Kumar et al., *The Current Industrial Relations Scene in Canada 1987*, p. 37.
15. Thomas Kochan et al., "Determinants of Intraorganizational Conflict in Collective Bargaining in the Public Sector," *Administrative Science Quarterly*, March 1975, pp. 10–22.
16. Daniel J. B. Mitchell, *Unions, Wages, and Inflation* (Washington, D.C.: Brookings Institution, 1980); Audrey Freedman and William E. Fullmer, "Last Rights for Pattern Bargaining," *Harvard Business Review*, March–April 1982, pp. 30–48.
17. Prem Benimadhu, "Industrial Relations 1986: Coping with Change," *Canadian Business Review*, Summer 1986, pp. 26–31.
18. For further discussion on government intervention in strikes, see Leo Panitch and Donald Swartz, "Towards Permanent Exceptionalism: Coercion and Consent in Canadian Industrial Relations," *Labour/Le Travail*, Spring 1984, pp. 133–57.
19. Kumar et al., *The Current Industrial Relations Scene in Canada 1987*, pp. 45–46.
20. Thomas A. Kochan, *Collective Bargaining and Industrial Relations* (Homewood, Ill.: Richard D. Irwin, 1980).
21. John C. Anderson, "The Impact of Arbitration: A Methodological Assessment," *Industrial Relations*, Spring 1981, pp. 129–48; Charles Feigenbaum, "Final Offer Arbitration: Better Theory than Practice," *Industrial Relations*, October 1975, pp. 311–17; Peter Feuille, "Final Offer Arbitration and the Chilling Effect," *Industrial Relations*, October 1975, pp. 302–11; Christopher J. Bruce, "The Compatibility of Arbitration and Bargaining: Comment," *Industrial Relations*, Fall 1982, pp. 398–401; David E. Bloom, "The Compatibility of Arbitration and Bargaining: Reply," *Industrial Relations*, Fall 1982, pp. 402–4.
22. Thomas Kochan, "Dynamics of Dispute Resolution in the Public Sector," in *Public-Sector Bargaining*, ed. B. Aaron, J. R. Grodin, and J. L. Stern (Washington, D.C.: Bureau of National Affairs, 1979), pp. 150–90; John Fossum, *Labor*

Relations: Development, Structure, Process, 2nd ed. (Dallas, Tex.: Business Publications, 1982); Kochan, *Collective Bargaining and Industrial Relations*; Robert J. Flanagan, Robert S. Smith, and Ronad C. Ehrenberg, *Labor Economics and Labor Relations* (Glenview, Ill.: Scott, Foresman, 1984).

23. Richard J. Butler and Ronald G. Ehrenberg, "Estimating the Narcotic Effect of Public Sector Impasse Procedures," *Industrial and Labor Relations Review*, October 1981, pp. 3–20; Thomas A. Kochan and Jean Baderschneider, "Estimating the Narcotic Effect: Choosing Techniques that Fit the Problem," *Industrial and Labor Relations Review*, October 1981, pp. 21–28.

24. E. G. Fisher and M. B. Percy, "The Impact of Unanticipated Output and Consumer Prices on Wildcat Strikes," *Relations Industrielles/Industrial Relations* 38, no. 2 (1983), pp. 254–74; Bruce E. Kaufman, "Interindustry Trends in Strike Activity," *Industrial Relations*, Winter 1983, pp. 45–57; Sean Flaherty, "Contract Status and the Economic Determinants of Strike Activity," *Industrial Relations*, Winter 1983, pp. 20–33; J. Paul Leigh, "Risk Preference and the Interindustry Propensity to Strike," *Industrial and Labor Relations Review*, January 1983, pp. 271–85.

25. Panitch and Swartz, "Towards Permanent Exceptionalism."

26. *The Economist*, August 2, 1986, p. 81.

27. Stuart M. Jamieson, *Industrial Conflict in Canada, 1966–75* (Discussion Paper No. 142, Centre for the Study of Inflation and Productivity, Economic Council of Canada, 1979).

28. "Avoiding the Arbitrator: Some New Alternatives to the Grievance Procedure," *Proceedings, 30th annual meeting Washington, D.C.: National Academy of Arbitrators*, 1977; Steven Briggs, "Beyond the Grievance Procedure: Factfinding in Employee Complaint Resolution," *Proceedings of the Industrial Relations Research Association Spring Meeting*, April 1982, pp. 454–58; Mollie H. Bowers, Ronald L. Seeber, and Lamont E. Stallworth, "Grievance Mediation: A Route to Resolution for the Cost-Conscious 1980s, *"Proceedings of the Industrial Relations Research Association, Spring Meeting*, April 1982, pp. 459–63.

29. Briggs, "Beyond the Grievance Procedure"; Bowers et al., "Grievance Mediation"; Joseph P. Cain and Michael J. Stahl, "Modeling the Policies of Several Labor Arbitrators," *Academy of Management Journal* 26, no. 1 (1983), pp. 140–47; Dan R. Dalton and William D. Todor, "Antecedents of Grievance Filing Behavior: Attitude/Behavioral Consistency and the Union Steward," *Academy of Management Journal* 25, no. 1 (1982), pp. 158–60.

30. Arnold M. Zack, "Suggested New Approaches to Grievance Arbitration," *Proceedings of the 30th Annual Meeting National Academy of Arbitrators* (Washington, D.C.: Bureau of National Affairs, 1978), pp. 105–20; Mollie H. Bowers, "Grievance Mediation: Settle Now, Don't Pay Later," *Federal Service Labor Relations Review*, Spring 1981, pp. 25–35; Marcus Sandver, Harry Blaine, and Mark Woyar, "Time and Cost Savings through Expedited Arbitration Procedures: Evidence from Five Industrial Settings," *Arbitration Journal*, December 1981, pp. 11–20.

31. Fossum, *Labor Relations*.

32. C. Brian Williams, "Collective Bargaining in the Public Sector: A Re-Examination," *Relations Industrielles/Industrial Relations* 28, no. 1 (1973), pp. 17–33.

33. Flanagan et al., *Labor Economics*; Milton Friedman and Rose Friedman, *Free to*

Choose (New York: Harcourt Brace Jovanovich, 1980); Edward P. Lazear, "A Competitive Theory of Monopoly Unionism," *The American Economic Review*, September 1983, pp. 631–41.
34. Fossum, *Labor Relations*; James E. Long and Albert N. Link, "The Impact of Market Structure on Wages, Fringe Benefits, and Turnover," *Industrial and Labor Relations Review*, January 1983, pp. 239–50.
35. F. Ray Marshall, Vernon M. Briggs, Jr., and Allan G. King, *Labor Economics*, 5th ed. (Homewood, Ill.: Richard D. Irwin, 1984).
36. Morely Gunderson, "Union Impact on Wages, Fringe Benefits, and Productivity," in *Union-Management Relations in Canada*, ed. John Anderson and Morely Gunderson (Don Mills, Ontario: Addison-Wesley Publishers, 1982), pp. 247–68; G. Starr, *Union-Nonunion Wage Differentials* (Toronto: Ontario Ministry of Labour, 1973); P. Kumar, "Differentials in Wage Rates of Unskilled Labor in Canadian Manufacturing Industries," *Industrial and Labor Relations Review* 26 (1972), pp. 631–45; G. MacDonald and J. Evans, "The Size and Structure of Union-Nonunion Wage Differentials in Canadian Industry," *Canadian Journal of Economics*, May 1981, pp. 216–31.
37. S. Christensen and D. Maki, "The Union Wage Effect in Canadian Manufacturing Industries," *Journal of Labor Research* 2, no. 2, Fall, 1981, pp. 355–67.
38. MacDonald and Evans, "The Size and Structure of Union-Nonunion Wage Differentials."
39. Benimadhu, "Industrial Relations 1986"; Clayton Sinclair, "Real Wages Will Keep on Shrinking," *Financial Times of Canada*, November 3, 1986.
40. Richard B. Freeman and James L. Medoff, "The Impact of Collective Bargaining: Illusion or Reality," in *U.S. Industrial Relations 1950–1980: A Critical Assessment*, ed. J. Steiber, R. B. McKersie, and D. Q. Mills (Madison, Wis.: Industrial Relations Research Association Series, 1981), pp. 47–98.
41. Benimadhu, "Industrial Relations 1986."
42. Brian Bemmels, "How Unions Affect Productivity in Manufacturing Plants," *Industrial and Labor Relations Review* 40, no. 2 (January 1987) pp. 241–53; A. C. Brown and J. Medoff, "Trade Unions in the Production Process," *Journal of Political Economy*, June 1978, pp. 355–78; J. Frantz, *The Impact of Trade Unions on Productivity in the Wood Household Furniture Industry* (undergraduate thesis, Cambridge, Mass.: Harvard University, 1976); S. Allen, "Unionized Construction Workers Are More Productive" (mimeographed, Greensboro: North Carolina State University, 1981); K. Clark, "The Impact of Unionization on Productivity: A Case Study," *Industrial and Labor Relations Review*, July 1980; M. Connerton, R. B. Freeman, and J. L. Medoff, "Industrial Relations and Productivity: A Study of the U.S. Bituminous Coal Industry" (mimeographed, Cambridge, Mass.: Harvard University, 1983 revision); Freeman and Medoff, *Trade Unions and Productivity*.
43. Richard B. Freeman and James L. Medoff, *What Do Unions Do?* (New York: Basic Books, 1984), p. 165.
44. Albert O. Hirschman, *Exit, Voice, and Loyalty* (Cambridge, Mass.: Harvard University Press, 1971); Richard B. Freeman and James L. Medoff, "The Two Faces of Unionism," *The Public Interest*, Fall 1979, pp. 69–93; R. B. Freeman, "The Exit–Voice Trade-Off in the Labor Market: Unionism, Job Tenure, Quits, and Separations," *Quarterly Journal of Economics* 94 (1980), pp. 6433–74; Francine

Blau and Lawrence Kahn, "The Exit-Voice Model of Unionism: Some Further Evidence on Layoffs" (unpublished paper, Champaign: University of Illinois, 1980).
45. Chris J. Berger, Craig A. Olson, and John W. Boudreau, "Effects of Unions on Job Satisfaction: The Role of Work-Related Values and Perceived Rewards" (working paper, Krannert Graduate School of Management, Lafayette, Ind.: Purdue University, 1983).
46. Michael E. Gordon, Laura L. Beauvais, and Robert T. Ladd, "The Job Satisfaction and Union Commitment of Unionized Engineers," *Industrial and Labor Relations Review*, April 1984, pp. 359–71; Michael E. Gordon and Sandra J. Miller, "Grievances: A Review of Research and Practice," *Personnel Psychology*, Spring 1984, pp. 117–46.
47. Steven G. Allen, "Trade Unions, Absenteeism, and Exit-Voice," *Industrial and Labor Relations Review*, April 1984, pp. 331–45.
48. Freeman and Medoff, *Trade Unions and Productivity*.
49. Brian Becker, "Hospital Unionism and Employment Stability," *Industrial Relations* 17 (1978), pp. 96–101; Francine D. Blau and Lawrence M. Kahn, "Unionism, Seniority, and Turnover," *Industrial Relations*, Fall 1983, pp. 362–73.
50. J. Pencavel, *An Analysis of the Quit Rate in American Manufacturing Industry* (Princeton, N.J.: Industrial Relations Section, Princeton University, 1970).

Exhibit VI
THE DIAGNOSTIC MODEL

External conditions	Organization conditions	Human resource activities	Objective
Economic conditionsGovernment regulationsTechnologyUnions	Nature of organization: Strategies and objectivesNature of workNature of employees and work groups	StaffingDevelopmentEmployment relationsCompensationEvaluation	Human resource effectiveness

PART SIX
HUMAN RESOURCE ACTIVITIES:
COMPENSATION

Compensation has a dual nature. On the one hand compensation is a major reason for people to join, stay, and work for an organization. On the other, it is a major cost of operating an organization: something to be carefully managed.

To an increased extent, the approaches for determining compensation are being challenged. These challenges are from managers who are under increased economic pressure, and who are questioning their unit labour costs and whether the pay system aids them in achieving their objectives. And when employees observe differences in earnings between men and women, they are challenging the equity of the entire system of pay determination.

As the diagnostic model shows (Exhibit VI), external conditions play an important role in pay determination. They set the limits on pay. Government laws mandate minimum wages, and economic conditions affect maximum and minimum wages. Chapter Fourteen discusses how organizations design their pay systems to incorporate product and labour market conditions, as well as the conditions in the organization that affect pay. Market surveys are designed to assess market conditions; job evaluation takes account of the nature of jobs in compensation decisions.

In Chapter Fifteen, pay is linked to the nature of employees. Various pay techniques are discussed for recognizing the individual's contribution to the organization's objectives. Budgeting and other administrative issues are also covered.

Chapter Sixteen examines an area of compensation that is receiving a

PART SIX continued

greater share of attention: benefits. For years, benefits were routinely expanded by major employers, in large part in response to collective bargaining agreements. But now, rapidly escalating costs have required sounder management.

A recurring theme in these chapters on compensation is the need to constantly understand why systems are designed as they are, in addition to understanding the mechanics.

CHAPTER FOURTEEN
PAY LEVEL AND STRUCTURE

CHAPTER OUTLINE

I. Introduction
    1. Forms of Pay
    2. Compensation Decision Makers

II. A Diagnostic Approach to Pay Administration
    A. External Influences on Pay
    B. Organizational Influences on Pay

III. A Pay Model
    A. Compensation Objectives
    B. Equity: The Conceptual Foundation

IV. Pay Decisions and Techniques
    A. External Equity
    B. Internal Equity
    C. Job Evaluation and the Pay Model

V. Summary
    Appendix / The Hay Guide Chart–Profile Method

Canadian Pacific, Ltd., one of Canada's largest corporations, employs a variety of people. These include a chief executive officer, engineers and technicians, plant managers, market analysts, financial planners, mechanics, accountants, security guards, word-processing operators, clerical personnel, and so on. How does the organization determine the pay scale for these different jobs? Is a financial planner worth more than an accountant, or a mechanic more than the word-processing operator? What procedures are used to set pay rates? Who is responsible for setting the rates? How important are the characteristics of the employee—knowledge, skills, abilities, or experience? How important are the characteristics of the work, the conditions under which it is done, or the value of what is produced? Do the procedures differ according to an employer's business strategies and its financial condition? What role do unions play?

The next two chapters address these questions. In this chapter, the external and organizational influences on pay decisions and the basic decisions and techniques used to set pay levels and structures are discussed. In the next chapter, the various approaches for paying individual employees, based on their performance and the performance of the organization, are examined.

INTRODUCTION

Compensation is one of the most important P/HRM functions for the employer and employee. An employee may think of compensation as a return for the efforts expended or a reward for satisfactory or outstanding work. The level of compensation may indicate the value the employer attaches to each employee's skills and abilities—the return on investment in education and training.[1] For most, the pay received for the work performed is the major source of personal wealth; hence, it is an important determinant of economic and social well-being.

Managers have two views of compensation. First and foremost, pay is seen as a major operating expense. Labour costs in many organizations account for more than 50 percent of operational expenses. For this reason alone, pay requires sound administration. In addition, pay can influence employees' work behaviours and attitudes. It may affect their decision to apply for a job, remain with an employer, work more productively, or undertake more training to be eligible for a higher-paying job.[2] If managed inequitably, pay may cause employees to diminish their efforts, to search for alternative employment, and/or to form a union.[3] Thus, the potential to influence employees' work attitudes and behaviours is another compelling reason for ensuring that pay systems are designed and administered fairly and equitably.

Compensation is also significant to the economy. Over the past 30 years, salaries and wages have equaled approximately 60 percent of the gross national products of Canada and the United States.

Forms of Pay

> **Definition**
> *Compensation* refers to all forms of financial returns and tangible services and benefits employees receive as part of an employment relationship.

Exhibit 14–1 shows the variety of forms compensation can take. It may be received directly in the form of cash (e.g., wages, merit increases, bonuses, incentives) or indirectly through services and benefits (e.g., pensions, health insurance, vacations.) This definition excludes other forms of rewards and returns, such as promotions, recognition for outstanding work, feelings of accomplishment, choice office locations, and the like. Such rewards may be thought of as part of an organization's "total reward system," and their administration should be coordinated with compensation whenever possible.[4]

Compensation Decision Makers

How much for whom? Who decides? As shown in Exhibit 14–2, both the operating manager and P/HRM manager have a role in making pay decisions.

EXHIBIT 14–1
Forms of Compensation

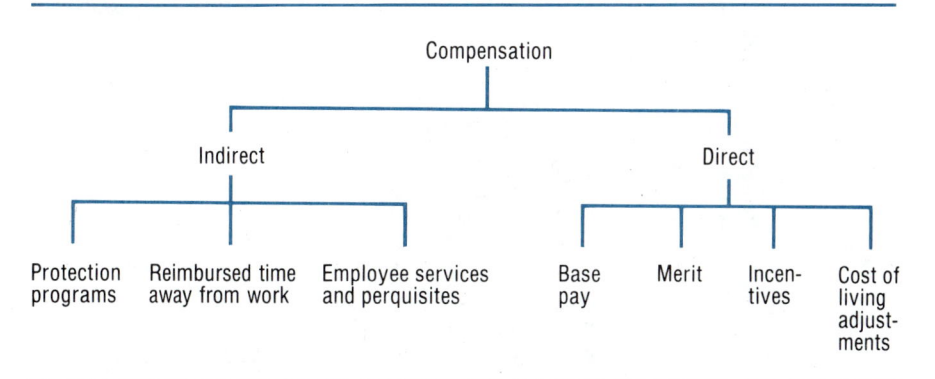

```
                          Compensation
                  ┌────────────┴────────────┐
               Indirect                   Direct
         ┌────────┼────────┐      ┌───────┼───────┬───────┐
    Protection  Reimbursed  Employee  Base  Merit  Incen-  Cost of
    programs    time away   services  pay          tives   living
                from work   and                            adjust-
                            perquisites                    ments
```

Source: George T. Milkovich and Jerry M. Newman, *Compensation*, 2nd ed. (Plano, Tex.: Business Publications, 1987).

EXHIBIT 14–2
The Roles of Operating and P/HRM Managers in Making Pay Decisions

Pay Decision Factor	Operating Manager (OM)	P/HRM Manager (P/HRM)
Compensation budgets	OM approves or adjusts P/HRM preliminary budget	P/HRM prepares preliminary budget
Pay-level decisions: Pay survey design and interpretation		P/HRM designs, implements, and makes decisions
Pay-structure decisions: Job evaluation design and interpretation		P/HRM designs, implements, and makes decisions
Pay classes, rate ranges, and classification design and interpretation		P/HRM designs, implements, and makes decisions
Individual pay determination	Joint decision with P/HRM	Joint decision with OM
Pay policy decisions: method of payment	OM decides after advice of P/HRM	P/HRM advises OM
Pay secrecy	OM decides after advice of P/HRM	P/HRM advises OM
Pay security	OM decides after advice of P/HRM	P/HRM advises OM

Source: John M. Ivancevich and William F. Glueck, *Foundations of Personnel/Human Resource Management* 3rd ed. (Plano, Tex.: Business Publications, 1986).

Generally, top management (including the vice president, P/HRM) make the decisions that determine the total amount of the budget allocated for pay, the pay form to be used (e.g., time pay versus incentive pay), and pay policies. Top management also sets the pay strategy. The P/HRM department provides advice on these issues. As shown, operating managers at the supervisory and middle-management level also have an impact on P/HRM decisions, including pay.

A DIAGNOSTIC APPROACH TO PAY ADMINISTRATION

Exhibit 14–3 shows some of the possible determinants that influence pay decisions. As indicated, pay decisions are affected by both external and organizational influences.

EXHIBIT 14–3
Possible Determinants of Pay Decisions

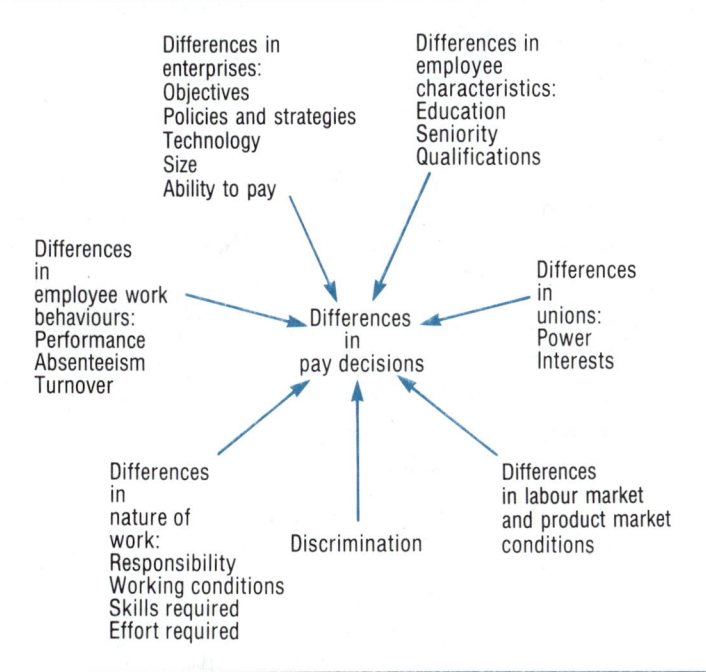

Differences in pay decisions are influenced by:

- Differences in enterprises: Objectives, Policies and strategies, Technology, Size, Ability to pay
- Differences in employee characteristics: Education, Seniority, Qualifications
- Differences in employee work behaviours: Performance, Absenteeism, Turnover
- Differences in unions: Power, Interests
- Differences in nature of work: Responsibility, Working conditions, Skills required, Effort required
- Discrimination
- Differences in labour market and product market conditions

Source: Adapted and modified from George T. Milkovich, "The Emerging Debate," in *Comparable Worth: Issues and Alternatives*, ed. E. Robert Livernash (Washington, D.C.: Equal Employment Advisory Council, 1980).

External Influences on Pay

Important external influences that must be considered when administering pay include the economy, government regulations (embodied in labour standards legislation), and unions' interest and power.

Economy: Product and Labour Markets

Although some believe people should not be subject to forces of supply and demand, they are.[5] During times of expanding demand for products and services, job opportunities expand and employers are more willing and able to increase pay to attract and retain employees with the needed skills and experience. Often, increased wages may be translated into increased costs of production. Organizations that face greater costs as a result of pay increases may try to pass the costs on to consumers in the form of higher prices. Passing costs on is easier during periods of strong demand for products or services. Even public-sector employers such as provinces or universities attempt to pass on their increased labour costs in the form of increased taxes or tuition.

Increased competition also affects pay decisions. Managers faced with increased competition from foreign producers, surplus inventories, and the like seek to control costs. A major line item in the budget is labour costs. Compensation in large part determines labour costs. So it is not too surprising that increased competition in product markets causes managers to think twice about the amount of pay to offer.[6]

Labour market conditions directly affect pay decisions. During periods of shortages of qualified employees, pay increases at a faster rate to help attract and retain needed workers. In recessions, or when surpluses of qualified employees are available, rates of pay increases slow; pay may even decrease.[7]

Government Regulations

The government influences pay both directly through laws, regulations, and controls and indirectly through socioeconomic policies. For example, governments' fiscal and monetary policies directly affect demand for goods and services and, subsequently, the employer's demand for employees. These actions create economic forces that affect pay.

The government more directly affects compensation through wage controls and guidelines, which limit increases in compensation for certain workers at certain times, and laws that establish minimum wage rates, wage and hour regulations, as well as prevent pay discrimination.[8]

As indicated earlier (see Chapter Two), both the Parliament of Canada and the provincial legislatures have the power to enact employment laws. Judicial interpretation gives provincial legislatures major jurisdiction. However, Parliament has exclusive jurisdiction in the federal sector.

Wage Controls and Guidelines. Sometimes the federal government establishes wage freezes or guidelines, as was done in the early 1970s. In addition, provincial governments may enact legislation to form compensation stabilization boards or programs. Usually headed by a commissioner, such boards have the authority to review, modify, or reject pay increases that have been through arbitration.

Wage freezes are government orders that permit no wage increases; wage controls limit the size of wage increases. Wage guidelines are similar to wage controls but are voluntary rather than legally required restrictions.[9] Economists differ on the usefulness of wage and price freezes. Critics argue that controls are an administrative nightmare, seriously disrupt the effective resource allocation by market forces, and lead to frustration and strikes.[10] Even critics admit, however, that during times of national emergencies, and for relatively brief periods, the controls might help slow (but not indefinitely postpone) inflation.[11] The important point is that managers must adjust their compensation decisions to fit any governmental wage guidelines or controls.

Wage Regulations. Minimum wage legislation is in force in the federal jurisdiction, all Canadian provinces and the two territories.

The Canada Labour Code, Part III, Division II, sets a minimum rate for employees 17 years of age and older in the federal industries. Employees who are paid on other than a time basis, such as pieceworkers and persons paid a mileage rate, are required to be paid the equivalent of the minimum wage. In most provinces, minimum wage boards or other labour boards are authorized by law to recommend minimum rates of wages or to establish such rates with the approval of the lieutenant-governor-in-council. Minimum wage orders apply to both men and women. The rates are imposed by minimum wage orders or, in British Columbia, Alberta, Manitoba, Ontario, Quebec, Nova Scotia, and Newfoundland, by regulations under the provincial employment standards act. Coverage usually excludes farm labour and certain other classes of workers (e.g., supervisory and managerial employees, certain categories of employed students, registered apprentices, certain salespersons, and members and students of professions).

Hours of Work Regulations and Overtime Provisions. Hours of work of employees in undertakings within the federal jurisdiction are regulated by the Canada Labour Code, Part III, Division I. The code sets a standard workday (8 hours) and workweek (40 hours) and requires payment of an overtime rate for work done beyond the hours specified. It also specifies a maximum workweek, overtime hours being restricted to eight in a week, except in special circumstances defined by the Minister of Labour. Maximum weekly hours may also be exceeded to make up for time lost due to an accident, breakdown in machinery, or other emergency. Overtime compensation is at one and one-half times the regular rate.

At the provincial level, differences exist among the various employment standards or labour standards acts. For example, under the Labour Standards Act in Saskatchewan, standard hours are set at 8 in a day and 40 in a week. Ontario's Employment Standards Act specifies 8 and 48 hours. In Newfoundland, the Labour Standards Regulations provide for standard hours of 8 in a day and 40 in a week for assistants (shop employees) and 44 in a week for other employees.

Overtime provisions generally specify one and one-half times the regular pay rate for hours in excess of the standard hours prescribed (Alberta, British Columbia, Saskatchewan, Manitoba, Quebec, New Brunswick, Northwest Territories, Yukon Territory). In Ontario the overtime rate applies after 44 hours; in Nova Scotia, after the maximum of 48 hours. Newfoundland and Prince Edward Island define overtime compensation in terms of a minimum rate per hour.

Equal Pay and Pay Equity. Provisions for equal pay and pay equity are delineated in Chapter Fifteen (and summarized in Exhibit 15–14).[12] Most provisions allow for "reasonable factors" to justify a difference in pay. These are specified by some jurisdictions merely as "any factor other than gender"; most specify seniority, merit, and a performance evaluation system that measures quantity and/or quality of production. Almost uniformly, the criteria specified for determining job content and job worth include skills, effort, responsibility, and working conditions.[13] This makes it essential that these be part of the *job evaluation* methods used (discussed later in this chapter).

Weekly Rest Day. The Canada Labour Code, Section 31, provides that employees must be given at least one full day of rest in the week, on Sunday if possible. With the exception of Prince Edward Island, the provinces and territories provide for a weekly rest day, but the provisions vary in scope.

Union Influences

Unions are another important external influence on employers' compensation decisions. Frequently, the real or perceived fear of becoming unionized encourages managers to improve wages and other conditions of employment.[14] This is called *spillover effect*, named after the fact that improvements obtained in unionized firms often spill over to nonunion firms seeking ways to lessen workers' incentives to form unions.

The vast majority of collective bargaining contracts specify seniority as a basis for pay increases.[15] We discussed the effects of unions on all human resource programs, including pay, in Chapter Thirteen.

Organizational Influences on Pay

Several organizational factors affect pay decisions. Among these are the firm's objectives and strategies, its policies and culture, the type of work performed, and the types of skills and preferences of employees.

Tailoring the Pay System to the Organization Strategies

All pay systems have a purpose. Answer the question—for what do we want to pay?—and you will begin to specify the objectives of the pay system. Some are clearly identified; others are implied. But the pay system objectives should be tailored to the organization's operating objectives and strategies.[16]

Strategy refers to the fundamental direction of the organization (Chapter Three). It guides the development of all resources, including compensation. An example might be Sears Canada signing a contract to market an exclusive designer line. Historically, Sears Canada had established a reputation for providing good value for the price of its merchandise. But a new strategy seeks to adjust the firm's image and also attract a more upscale, affluent shopper. This reflects a fundamental change in directions. Organization resources—financial, capital, and human—need to be deployed in a manner consistent with these new directions. As part of such an effort, Sears Canada has to design pay incentives tied to sales targets to try to ensure a maximum return on its investment in the new product line.

Strategic Stages and Pay. Pay decisions can be guided by an organization's strategic stage. Exhibit 14–4 shows six strategic stages ranging from start-up through decline and renewal. Hypothetical examples of the pay

EXHIBIT 14–4
An Example of Pay Tailored to Strategic Stages of a Product or Unit

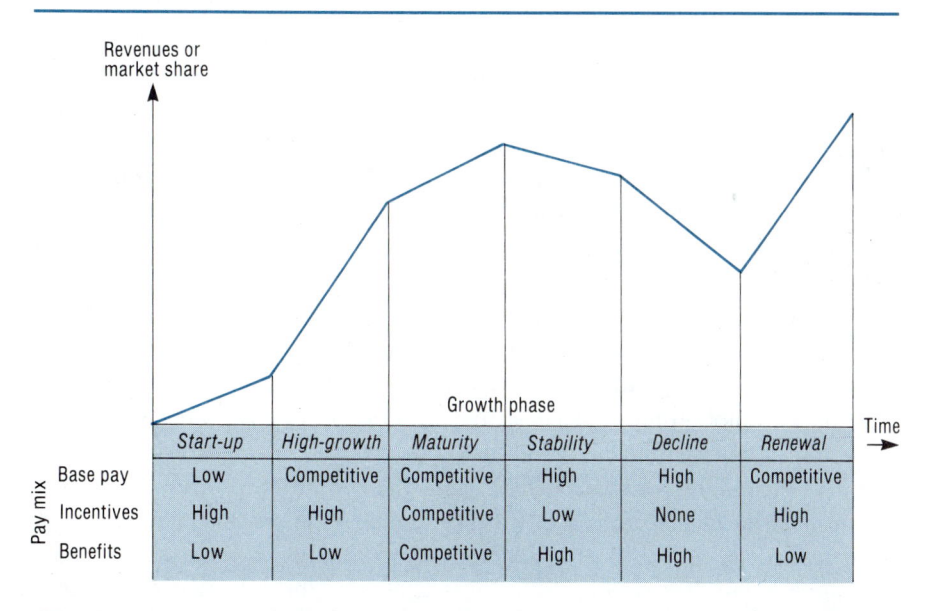

Pay mix	Start-up	High-growth	Maturity	Stability	Decline	Renewal
Base pay	Low	Competitive	Competitive	High	High	Competitive
Incentives	High	High	Competitive	Low	None	High
Benefits	Low	Low	Competitive	High	High	Low

Source: George T. Milkovich and Jerry M. Newman, *Compensation*, 2nd ed. (Plano, Tex.: Business Publications, 1987).

tailored to each state are also shown. Business units just starting usually have a limited, closely related set of products and are exploring their markets. Cash-flow problems are common at this stage, but employees are confident of the future success of the business. The pay in the example includes relatively low base pay (to conserve cash) and strong emphasis on incentive pay (to emphasize unit and individual performance and to share the results of growth). Benefits may be kept low to control costs, unless the organization is competing for scarce labour; then benefits may have to be set to meet those offered by competitors. Declining business units or products may have high fixed costs, including base pay and benefits. Incentives may be restricted to encourage phase-out or reintroduced to encourage renewal.

The exhibit oversimplifies the real world: not all business units go through all stages. Units may be divested; others acquired. Labour market competition may preclude offering low benefits or base salaries. A variety of reasons make it difficult to characterize any single organization as being in any one stage.

The important point is that pay systems can be tailored to the organizations' overall strategies. In highly decentralized organizations, this means different business units may even adopt different pay systems.

Tailoring the Pay Systems to Organization Culture and Values

Not only can pay programs be tailored to organization strategies and objectives, but they can also be congruent with the organization's culture and values. Lawler points out that because pay is just one of many systems that make up an organization, its design must be partially influenced by how it fits with the other structures and systems in the organization.[17] A highly centralized and confidential pay system, controlled by a few people in a corporate unit, will not, according to this view, operate effectively in a highly decentralized and open organization. Unfortunately, the influence of such factors as the degree of centralization, the decision-making style of management, or the maturity of the union-management relationship, is not well understood.

The importance of the congruency of pay programs with other management processes is clearest in the case of other human resource management programs, such as recruiting, hiring, and promoting. The pay tied to a job offer or a promotion must be consistent with other systems. Some employers do not maintain significant pay differences between manufacturing workers (such as assemblers or inspectors) and their first-line supervisors. This diminishes the incentive to acquire the training required to be a supervisor or to accept the promotion to supervisor. The situation is reversed for many engineering and research jobs, where the pay for managerial positions induces people to leave engineering and research positions. Pay coexists with other structures in the organization. An effective pay system cannot be designed without considering the nature of the organization and its culture and values.

Tailoring Pay to Employee Needs

Within some legally imposed limits, compensation can be delivered to employees in the forms identified in Exhibit 14–1. The allocation of compensation among these pay forms to emphasize performance, seniority, entitlements, or the long versus short term should be tailored to the pay objectives of the organization. It should also be tailored to the needs of individual employees.

The simple fact that employees differ is too easily and too often overlooked in designing pay systems. Individual employees join the organization, make investment decisions, design new products, assemble components, and judge the quality of results. Individual employees receive the pay. Opsahl and Dunnette were among the first to observe that a major limitation of contemporary pay systems is the degree to which individual attitudes and preferences are ignored.[18] Others agree.[19] For example, older, highly paid workers may wish to defer taxes by putting pay into retirement funds, while younger employees may have high cash needs to buy a house, support a family, or finance an education. Dual-career couples who are overinsured medically may prefer to use more of their combined pay for child care, automobile insurance, financial counselling, or other benefits.

Thus, a wide variety of external and organizational factors influence pay. To understand how they all interact in the design and management of pay systems, let us examine a model of the pay process.

A PAY MODEL

The pay model shown in Exhibit 14–5 contains three basic components: (1) the *concepts* that form the foundations of the pay system, (2) the *techniques* that make up much of the mechanics of compensation management, and (3) the *compensation objectives*, or desired results. Each of these components and their interrelationships are discussed.

Compensation Objectives

Pay systems are designed to achieve certain objectives, shown at the right side of the model. Typical objectives might be to facilitate organization performance, control labour costs, influence employee attitudes and behaviours, and comply with laws and regulations. This set includes examples of the most common objectives employers use to guide compensation decisions. An example of one employer's pay objectives is shown in Exhibit 14–6.

**EXHIBIT 14–5
A Pay Model**

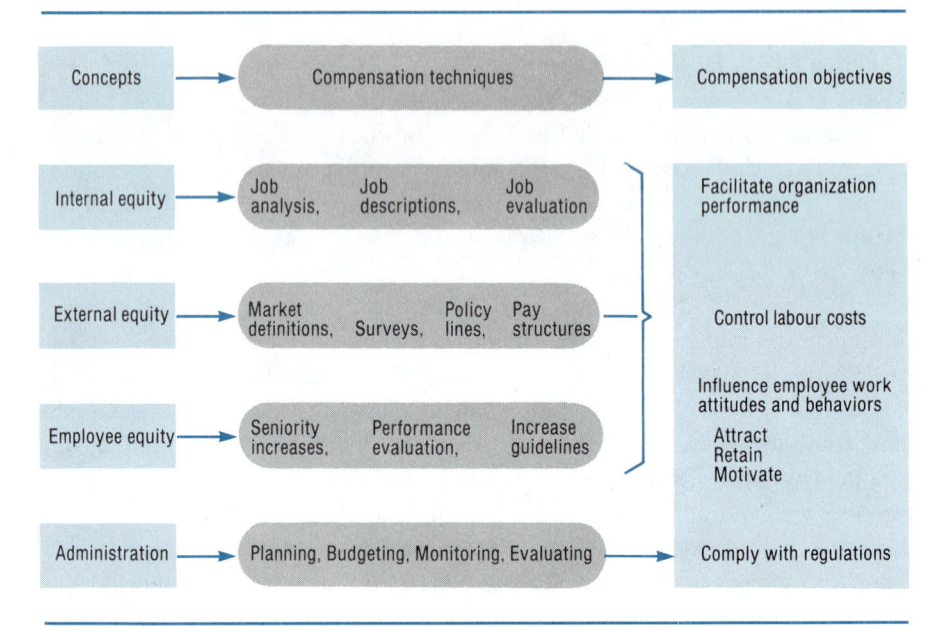

Concepts	Compensation techniques	Compensation objectives
Internal equity	Job analysis, Job descriptions, Job evaluation	Facilitate organization performance
External equity	Market definitions, Surveys, Policy lines, Pay structures	Control labour costs
Employee equity	Seniority increases, Performance evaluation, Increase guidelines	Influence employee work attitudes and behaviors — Attract, Retain, Motivate
Administration	Planning, Budgeting, Monitoring, Evaluating	Comply with regulations

Source: Adapted from George T. Milkovich and Jerry M. Newman, *Compensation*, 2nd ed. (Plano, Tex.: Business Publications, 1987).

Patten suggests that an organization's compensation policy and objectives meet several standards.[20] The compensation should be:

Adequate—Minimum governmental, union, and managerial levels should be met.

Equitable—Each person should be paid fairly, in line with his or her effort, abilities, and training.

**EXHIBIT 14–6
Illustration of Compensation Objectives**

Salary Program Objectives:

1. Competitiveness — Attract and retain competent employees.
2. Pay for performance — Reward individual contribution and performance.
3. Consistency — Maintain consistency by paying employees with similar responsibilities similar pay.
4. Cost control — Plan and control salary expenditures within goals established by the company and division.
5. Legal requirements — Conform to various provincial and federal wage and salary laws and guidelines.

Balanced—Pay, benefits, and other rewards should provide a reasonable total reward package.

Cost effective—Pay is not excessive, considering what the organization can afford to pay.

Secure—Pay should be enough to help an employee feel secure and aid him or her in satisfying basic needs.

Incentive-providing—Pay should motivate effective and productive work.

Acceptable to the employee—The employee should understand the pay system and believe it is a reasonable system for both the enterprise and himself or herself.

Establishing objectives is important because they serve several purposes. Some organizations' objectives emphasize pay for performance. These organizations use incentives or merit plans. Other organizations focus on maintaining a stable and experienced work force and may have seniority-based pay. So the objectives influence the pay forms and underlying pay procedures. Recent trends indicate greater concern with measuring white-collar productivity, and more Canadian employers are shifting compensation emphasis toward pay for performance—away from the former across-the-board increases for everyone.[21]

Besides affecting the mechanics of pay systems, objectives serve as the standards against which the success of the pay system is evaluated. If the pay objective is to attract and retain a highly competent staff, yet skilled employees are leaving to take higher-paying jobs at other employers, the pay system may not be performing effectively. While there may be many reasons for undesired turnover, pay objectives do serve as a standard for evaluating the pay system.

Equity: The Conceptual Foundation

The basic concept underlying the pay model in Exhibit 14–5 is equity.[22] Three types of equity are identified: external, internal, and employee. Equity forms the foundation on which pay systems are designed. These systems must also be equitably administered.

External equity refers to comparisons outside an organization. It examines how competitive an employer's pay is in the external market. External equity has a twofold concern: (1) to ensure pay rates are competitive enough to attract and retain employees, and (2) to control the cost of human resources so the organization's prices of products or services remain competitive.

Internal equity refers to the internal consistency of the relationships among *jobs* (in terms of each job's worth) inside an organization. How, for example, does the work of a word processing operator compare to the work of the computer operator, the programmer, or the systems analyst? Does one job require more (or less) skill or experience than another? The focus is on the relative similarities and differences in the work content of jobs and their relative contribution to the organization's objectives.

Employee (individual) equity refers to comparisons among *individuals* doing the same job for the same organization. Should all such employees receive the same pay? Or should one programmer be paid more than another for better performance and/or greater seniority? Employee equity is an important concept in the design and administration of pay systems since it may directly affect employees' attitudes and work behaviours.

Administration of the Pay System. The administration of the pay system is the fourth building block of the conceptual segment of the pay model. A system that incorporates internal, external, and employee equity will not achieve its objectives unless it is administered properly. Does the pay system help attract skilled workers? Does it help keep them? Do employees believe the system is equitable? Do they understand what factors are considered in setting their pay? Do they agree that these factors are important? How does labour cost per unit produced compare with costs for other employers? Administration includes monitoring and evaluating how the pay system is operating and judging whether it is achieving its objectives.

Balancing Internal, External, and Employee Equity

The balance, or relative emphasis, among internal, external, and/or employee equity is a key decision in any employer's compensation strategy. Does it ever make sense to emphasize one type of equity over another? For example, many high-technology firms grant sizable salary increases to match outside offers from competing employers (an external equity issue). Sometimes it makes sense to emphasize external equity because the relationship of an employer's pay level to a competitor's pay level directly affects the ability to attract a competent work force, to control labour costs, and to compete with products or services. Yet ignoring internal and employee equity may increase an employer's vulnerability to litigation, as well as increase employee dissatisfaction. If the person next to me is doing the same job but is paid more, there had better be a good reason for this differential. Internal pay differences can affect employees' willingness to accept promotions, pay satisfaction, absenteeism, turnover, and unionization activity.

Thus, all three—internal, external, and employee equity—are critical in the design and administration of pay systems. Achieving the desired balance among them is part of the art involved in making pay decisions.

PAY DECISIONS AND TECHNIQUES

The remaining portion of the model in Exhibit 14–5 lists various pay techniques. The techniques link equity to the compensation objectives. The combination of external equity and internal equity helps define the dimensions of the pay strucure.

External Equity

External equity focusses attention on how the employer's pay rates compare to the rates paid by competitors. In practice, external equity gets translated into decisions about the pay level and pay policy lines.

Pay level refers to an average of the rates paid by an employer. There are three "pure" alternatives in setting a pay level—to set average pay to (1) lead competition, (2) match competition, or (3) be lower than what others are paying. Evidence suggests the most common policy is to match what is paid by competitors.

Pay Level Effects

What difference does pay level make? Exhibit 14–7 shows the potential effects on compensation objectives.

Match Competition. By setting the pay level to match competition, organizations try to ensure their labour costs are approximately equal to the labour costs of competitors. Equal labour costs help place competing employers on an equal footing in their ability to attract and maintain a qualified work force.[23]

EXHIBIT 14–7
Probable Relationships between Pay Level Policies and Objectives

Policy	Ability to Attract	Ability to Retain	Contain Labour Costs	Reduce Pay Dissatisfaction	Increase Productivity
Pay above market (lead)	+	+	?	+	?
Pay with market (match)	=	=	=	=	?
Pay below market (lag)	−	?	+	−	?

Source: George T. Milkovich and Jerry M. Newman, *Compensation*, 2nd ed. (Plano, Texas: Business Publications, 1987).

Lead. Employers who offer higher pay rates than competitors seek to maximize their ability to attract and retain quality employees and to minimize employee dissatisfaction with pay.[24] The idea is that higher pay increases the number of applicants. A larger applicant pool permits the properly designed selection process to skim the cream of the applicants. These higher-quality employees should exhibit greater productivity, thereby offsetting the higher wages. However, little research has been reported to support (or refute) these contentions. Some industries (e.g., petroleum and pharmaceuticals) do pay higher rates for similar skills (e.g., MBA or accountants) than other industries, but this may be because they can pass these rates on to consumers and because labour costs are not a significant portion of total operating costs in these industries.

Lag. Setting pay rates below competitors' rates may hinder an employer's ability to attract or retain employees. However, the opportunity to work overtime, to secure promotions and avoid layoffs, or to work in a secure, friendly environment may offset lower pay rates for many potential employees.[25]

No matter which pay level option is selected, it needs to be translated into practice. As shown in the pay model, this is usually done by surveying relevant external labour markets and establishing the pay policy line.

Compensation Surveys

What's the going wage? Who are the wage leaders—locally, regionally, nationally, or even internationally? Can we compete with them? A compensation survey seeks to answer these and related questions (e.g., regarding benefits) by systematically collecting information on what other employers are paying for similar jobs and skills.

Pay surveys are conducted by employers either individually or through associations, by consulting firms, and by government agencies. A do-it-yourself survey can be costly and requires expertise in survey design, statistical sampling, data collection, and data analysis. This may be why use of "canned" pay surveys of varying degrees of specificity appears to be increasing.

One primary source of Canadian data is the *Compensation Data Sourcebook*.[26] Published by The Conference Board of Canada, the *Sourcebook* is a reference guide to major Canadian surveys of wages, salaries, benefits, perquisites, and working conditions. The surveys include employers from the public, private, and not-for-profit sectors. Details of each survey are fully documented in terms of frequency and coverage (geographical, industrial, occupational), method (sample, job matching, data gathering and processing), format and availability of the findings, and include a description of the surveying organizations. The list in Exhibit 14–8 shows some of the more than 70 different surveys contributing to the *Sourcebook*.

EXHIBIT 14–8
Sample of Salary Survey Participants

Associations
"Report on Engineers' Salaries—Survey of Employers"
  Association of Professional Engineers of Ontario
"Canadian Directorship Practices: Compensation"
  The Conference Board of Canada
"Hourly Wage Survey—Maintenance, Service and Production Occupations"
  Quebec Industrial Relations Institute/L'institut de relations industrielles du Quebec
"Office Salaries Directory"
  Administrative Management Society
"Salaries and Working Conditions of Office and Other Selected Salaried Employees"
  The Canadian Manufacturers' Association

Government bodies
"Survey of Wage Rates"
  Greater Vancouver Regional District
"Wage Rates, Salaries and Hours of Labour"
  Labour Canada
"Wages, Salaries and Hours of Labour"
  New Brunswick Department of Labour and Manpower

Consulting firms
"Data Processing Salary Survey"
  Peat Marwick
"Salary Survey of Canadian Personnel and Industrial Relations Positions"
  Hansen Consultants Limited
"Salary Survey: Administration, Finance and Data Processing Report"
  Stevenson, Kellogg, Ernst & Whinney
"Professional, Scientific and Technical Remuneration—Canada"
  Executive Compensation Service, Inc.

Source: *Compensation Data Sourcebook* (Ottawa: The Conference Board of Canada, annual).

A good survey includes a brief description of job duties. This aids survey users in matching their jobs to those covered in the survey. Surveys usually collect the minimum, mid (50th percentile or median), maximum, and average rates from each participating firm. This provides a sense of the distribution of rates paid for the job within each employer. However, survey data can be collected in considerably greater detail. Exhibit 14–9 shows the results of a pay survey of computer programmers in terms of 90th through 10th percentiles.

Survey users may find it is not always easy to identify the "going rate"; a range of rates may be paid for the same job in a given city. Such differences may be attributable to the effects of seniority or experience but may also reflect different pay level decisions (lead, lag, match) by employers.

EXHIBIT 14–9
Maturity Curves Based on Scatterplot for Computer Programmers (90th through 10th percentiles)

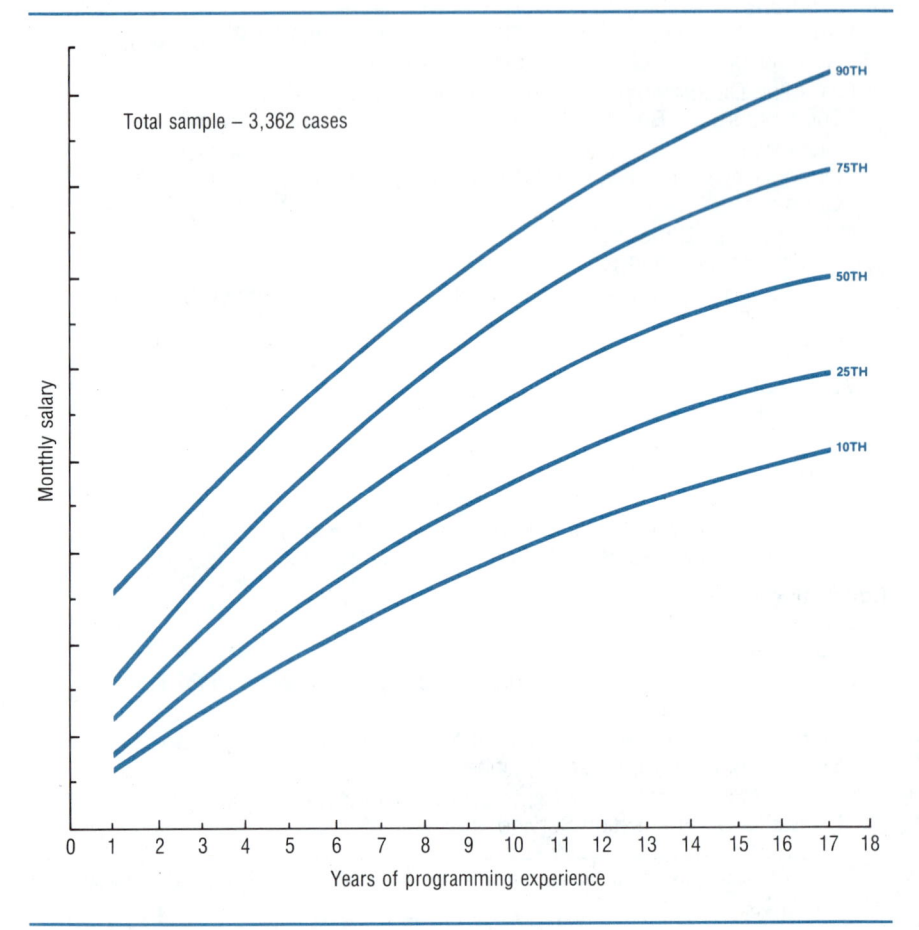

[Graph: Monthly salary vs. Years of programming experience (0–18), showing curves for 90TH, 75TH, 50TH, 25TH, and 10TH percentiles. Total sample – 3,362 cases.]

Source: Organization Resources Counselors, Inc.

Survey Decisions

There are two basic methods to collect pay data—interviews (in person or by phone) and mailed questionnaires. The method used is usually determined by the purpose of the survey and the extensiveness of the data required. Field interviews conducted by trained interviewers are the most effective but also the most costly and time-consuming. Mailed questionnaires are the most frequently used method because of lower costs. Jobs being surveyed by mail must be clearly defined. Telephone inquiries can be used to follow up the questionnaires or to gather additional data.

A number of critical features of surveys can be used to evaluate their usefulness: the employers included, the jobs covered, the method used in gathering the data, the age of the data, and its accuracy are examples.

Key Jobs

In practice, employers do not seek market data for all jobs. Rather, only selected jobs, called *key*, or *benchmark*, jobs, are included in the survey. Benchmark jobs are defined as reference points having the following characteristics:

- The contents are well known, relatively stable, and agreed on by the employees involved.
- The supply and demand for these jobs are relatively stable and not subject to recent shifts.
- They represent the entire job structure under study.
- A sizable proportion of the work force is employed in these jobs.
- Some employers use the percentage of incumbents who are women and men to try to ensure that the benchmarks are free of possible employment discrimination.[27]

Survey Results and Pay Policy Line

The results gained from a pay survey are distilled into a distribution of rates paid by competitors. Exhibit 14–10 illustrates a set of hypothetical pay distributions for five key jobs (A, D, G, M, and N). In the illustration, the pay level policy line has been set to equal the average paid by the competition for each of the key jobs: a matching-competition policy. The employer could establish a lead or lag policy by simply shifting the pay level policy line up or down. Thus, market survey data help translate the concept of external equity into pay-setting practice (vertical axis of Exhibit 14–10).

Once pay level has been determined, we turn to internal equity.

Internal Equity

Internal equity refers to the pay relationships among jobs within a single organization. Job evaluation helps translate internal equity into practice through job structure, the horizontal dimension of pay structure.

Pay Structure Decisions

Pay structures are combinations of external and internal equity, and depict pay rates for different jobs within a single organization. Another way to think about pay structures is in terms of the differences in compensation paid for jobs within a firm.

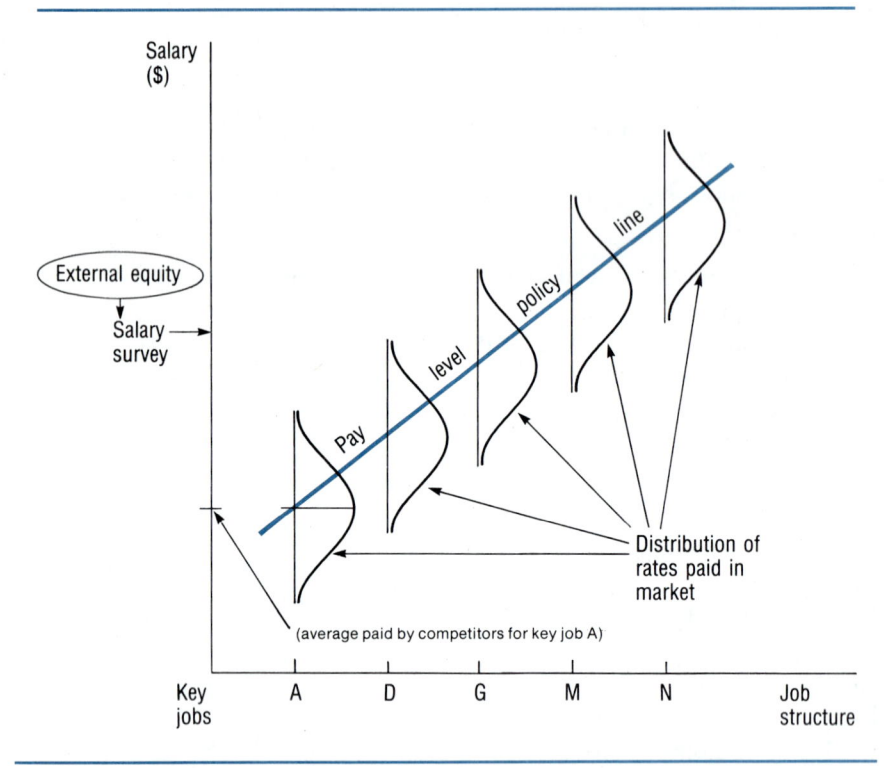

EXHIBIT 14–10
Survey Rates: Rates Paid by Competitors; Pay Policy Line: Match Competition

Source: George T. Milkovich and Jerry M. Newman, *Compensation* (Plano, Tex.: Business Publications, 1984).

Pay structures are designed to provide internal equity by paying more for jobs that require greater qualifications to perform, or must be performed under less desirable conditions, and/or whose output is more valued.

Exhibit 14–11 shows an example of pay structures found within a single organization. Each career path, or grouping of jobs, is arranged in a hierarchy reflecting pay differentials between jobs within it. In the managerial group, for example, the pay for the job of division manager exceeds that for the job of project leader.

Considering the importance of pay structures, it is surprising that relatively little is known about employee perception of what constitutes fair or equitable pay differences among jobs. Mahoney concluded from his study of business school students and compensation administrators that "a compensation differential of approximately 30 percent is considered appropriate for the higher of two (adjacent) managerial levels."[28] Belcher poses the question, "Equity for whom?"[29] For example, little is known about whether different

EXHIBIT 14–11
Hypothetical Job Structure with Four Occupational/Skill Groups

MANAGERIAL GROUP	TECHNICAL GROUP	MANUFACTURING GROUP	ADMINISTRATIVE GROUP
Vice Presidents		Assembler I / Inspector I	Administrative Assistant
Division General Managers		Packer	Principal Admin. Secretary
Managers	Head/Chief Scientist	Materials Handler / Inspector II	Administrative Secretary
	Senior Associate Scientist	Assembler II	Word Processor
Project Leaders	Associate Scientist	Drill Press Operator / Grinder, Rough	
Supervisors	Scientist	Machinist I / Coremaker	
	Technician		Clerk/Messenger

Note: Exhibit is not intended to depict pay differences between the four groups.
Source: George T. Milkovich and Jerry M. Newman, *Compensation*, 2nd ed. (Piano Tex.: Business Publications, 1987).

employee groups (older versus younger, women versus men, office versus production workers, engineers versus accountants, and so on) hold different ideas about what constitutes fair pay differences among jobs. Litigation over equal pay and pay discrimination may reveal that substantial disagreement exists over what constitutes equitable pay differences among different jobs.

Pay Structure Effects

Why should managers concern themselves with differences in pay among jobs? How do internally equitable structures help managers achieve their objectives?

Pay structures focus attention on the link between employee perceptions and their work behaviours. Many compensation experts argue that equitable pay structures are related to everything from employee performance to strikes.[30] Exhibit 14–12 shows some of the potential effects of fair pay structures, including employee decisions to join, stay, or leave the organization and to invest in the additional training required for promotions or new jobs. Pay differences among jobs influence these decisions. Consequently, equitable pay structures can be a very important management tool.

EXHIBIT 14–12
Some Consequences of Equitable Pay Structures

Equitability of pay structure →
- Undertake training
- Increase experience
- Reduce turnover
- Facilitate career/job progression
- Facilitate performance
- Reduce pay-related grievances
- Reduce pay-related work stoppages

Source: George T. Milkovich and Jerry M. Newman, *Compensation*, 2nd ed. (Plano, Tex.: Business Publications, 1987).

Let us now turn to the techniques employed to define the job structure dimension of the pay structure.

Job Evaluation and the Pay Model

Recall from the pay model (Exhibit 14–5) that job analysis and job evaluation are typically used to achieve internal equity. A more detailed perspective is shown in Exhibit 14–13. Job analysis, a systematic process for collecting information about jobs, was examined in Chapter Four. The information collected is summarized into job descriptions. These descriptions serve as input into the job evaluation process. Appendix B in Chapter Four contains examples of job descriptions that could be used in the compensation system.

Job evaluation involves the systematic evaluation of job descriptions. It helps develop and maintain pay structures by comparing jobs within an organization in terms of relative similarities and differences in their content and value.[31] When properly administered, job evaluation can help ensure that pay structures are internally equitable and acceptable to the employer and employee.

Job evaluation is an area for which definitions are as diverse as the proverbial blind men's elephant. To highlight the intent of determining the relative worth of a job, the following definition is adopted:

> **Definition**
> *Job evaluation* is the formal systematic process by which the relative worth of various jobs in the organization is determined for pay purposes. Essentially, it attempts to relate the amount of the employee's pay to the extent that her or his job contributes to organizational effectiveness. (It is *not* an evaluation of the jobholder's work performance.)

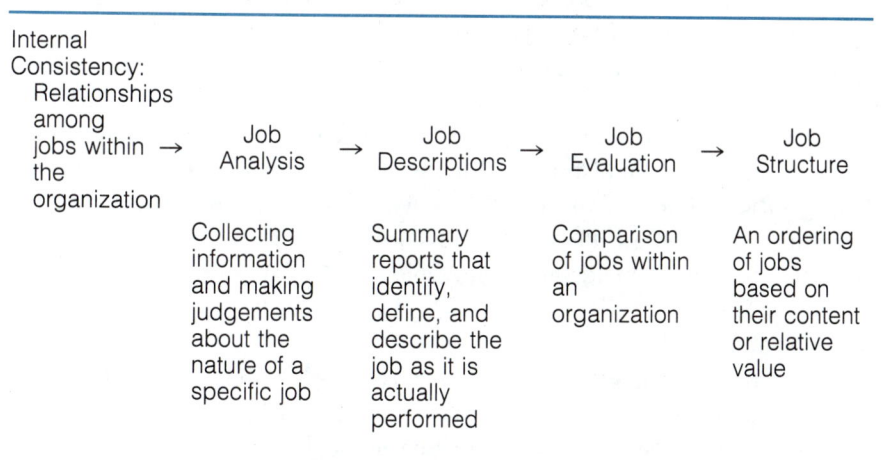

Major Decisions in Job Evaluation

Exhibit 14–13 also calls out the major decisions involved in the design and administration of job evaluation. They include (1) determining its purpose(s), (2) deciding whether to use single/multiple plans and choosing among alternative approaches, (3) obtaining the involvement of relevant parties, and (4) evaluating the plan's usefulness.

Purposes

Job evaluation emphasizes a systematic, rational assessment of jobs as a basis for deciding pay. The resulting pay structure should be internally equitable

EXHIBIT 14–13
Determining an Internally Consistent Job Structure

Internal Consistency: Relationships among jobs within the organization →	Job Analysis	→	Job Descriptions	→	Job Evaluation	→	Job Structure
	Collecting information and making judgements about the nature of a specific job		Summary reports that identify, define, and describe the job as it is actually performed		Comparison of jobs within an organization		An ordering of jobs based on their content or relative value

Some Major Decisions in Job Evaluation
- Establish purpose of evaluation
- Decide whether to use single or multiple plans
- Choose among alternative approaches
- Obtain involvement of relevant parties
- Assess plan's usefulness

Source: Adapted from George T. Milkovich and Jerry M. Newman, *Compensation*, 2nd ed. (Plano: Tex.: Business Publications, 1987).

and consistent with the goals of the organization.[32] Job evaluation results must be relevant to managers whose responsibility includes making pay decisions as well as to employees whose pay rates are affected. In some cases, varying perspectives on job evaluation have led to controversy over its role in setting pay differentials among jobs. So the purpose of the evaluation should be clearly specified.

Relevant Parties—Whom to Involve?
If job evaluation is an aid to managers and if gaining employees' understanding and acceptance of the pay structure is an important objective, then these groups need to be included in its design and administration. A common approach to gaining acceptance, understanding, and valuable ideas from managers and employees is through the use of compensation committees. Through these committees, key managers and nonmanagerial employees advise compensation professionals about job evaluation results and broader pay issues.

Several case studies of employee participation in the design and administration of pay systems have been reported. Lawler and Jenkins, for example, report on a plan designed with the assistance of a committee of employees and managers.[33] Within six months after the system went into effect, significant improvements in turnover and satisfaction with pay were observed. Employee participation in both the design and decisions involved in compensation is a key feature of what Lawler calls the "new pay."[34] He asserts that participation leads to increased trust, commitment, and perceptions of pay equity on the part of employees.

Management probably will find it advantageous to include union officials in the design and administration of job evaluation as a source of ideas and to help gain acceptance of the results. However, some union leaders may believe that philosophical differences prevent their active participation and that collective bargaining yields more equitable results than job evaluation.

Job Evaluation Methods
A recent report claims that there remains an astounding lack of Canadian evidence as to the prevalence of various types of formal job evaluation plans.[35] Basically, four fundamental job evaluation methods are in use: ranking, classification, factor comparison, and point method. They can be distinguished by determining (1) whether the evaluation is based on the whole job or only specific factors, (2) whether jobs are evaluated against some standard or against each other, and (3) whether the process is qualitative or quantitative. Of these, the key distinguishing feature is the degree of specificity of the standard with which the jobs are compared. Imagine a continuum of specificity from ranking to classification to factor comparison to point methods. In

ranking, a whole job is compared against other whole jobs on some general concept of value or job content. In classification, the job content and value are divided into categories or classes, and jobs are slotted into them. In factor comparison and point methods, content *and* value are broken into factors, and jobs are evaluated by the degree of each factor the job possesses. While these are the four basic methods, uncounted variations exist (including several single-factor, unidimensional systems).[36]

The following sections offer some specifics on each of the four methods.

Ranking. Ranking the jobs according to relative value is the simplest, fastest, easiest to understand, and least expensive job evaluation method. Exhibit 14–14 lists the typical steps involved. However, ranking is seldom the recommended approach. There are several reasons for this. The criteria on which jobs are ranked are usually so crudely defined the results are subjective opinions and are difficult to explain or justify. Furthermore, ranking requires that users be knowledgeable about every single job under study. In larger, changing organizations this becomes a formidable task. Finally, even though ranking is simple, fast, and inexpensive, in the long term it may be more costly. Since the results are difficult to explain and defend, costly solutions are often required to overcome problems the ranking method creates.

Classification. This method involves slotting job descriptions into a series of classes or grades covering the range of jobs in the organization. Exhibit 14–15 lists the typical steps in this method. Exhibit 14–16 illustrates class definitions with examples of typical jobs in each class. This method is widely used in the public sector. For example, provincial and federal government departments identify occupational groups and subgroups. Grades are differentiated according to the degree to which a set of compensable factors applies to each job. In the personnel administration group, the factors of knowledge, decision making, and managerial responsibility would be relevant when evaluating the job of a "classification officer" (job analyst).[37] The method is also commonly used for managerial and engineering/scientific jobs in the private sector.[38]

EXHIBIT 14–14
Typical Steps in Ranking

1. Determine jobs and units to be included.
2. Obtain job descriptions.
3. Select evaluators.
4. Define contribution or value.
5. Rank: Alternation ranking.
      Paired comparison.
6. Merge unit rankings.

Source: George T. Milkovich and Jerry M. Newman, *Compensation* (Plano, Texas: Business Publications, 1984).

EXHIBIT 14–15
Typical Steps in Classification System

1. Determine jobs/units to be included in study.
2. Conduct job analysis/prepare job descriptions.
3. Select evaluators.
4. Define classes.
5. Identify and slot benchmarks.
6. Prepare classification manual.
7. Apply system to nonbenchmark jobs.

Source: George T. Milkovich and Jerry M. Newman, *Compensation* (Plano, Texas: Business Publications, 1984).

In practice, the most troublesome feature of the classification method is the need to describe each class properly. The description must be general enough to cause little difficulty in slotting jobs, yet it must capture sufficient detail of the work to have meaning. Questions about how many classes, who defines them, and the like must also be answered.

Typically, sufficient vagueness exists in the way classes are described to permit what Patten calls "aggrandizing language" in the job description.[39] In these cases, the classification method may generate into a "title" game. Managers may try to pick the class they want the job assigned to before any analysis. Then they try to influence the results by assigning the job an inflated title. Managers who view evaluation as a bureaucratic hindrance may define this manipulation as "flexibility." But lack of a work-related logic to the pay structure is a serious shortcoming when trying to reassure disgruntled employees who believe their job is undervalued compared to their co-workers' jobs.

Factor Comparison. Factor comparison permits the job evaluation process to be done on a factor-by-factor basis. Essentially, jobs are evaluated or compared against a benchmark of key jobs on the basis of several predetermined compensable factors. The five universal factors used to compare jobs encompass mental demands, skill, working conditions, responsibility, and physical demands.

The job evaluation committee follows several formal steps in examining jobs:

1. Select and define the comparison factors to be used.
2. Choose the key jobs to be evaluated. These benchmark jobs (10 to 20 may be necessary) are well known in the organization and, in the opinion of the evaluators, are properly paid at present.
3. Rank the key jobs on important factors. Mental requirements, skills requirements, physical requirements, responsibility, and working conditions are some factors commonly used.

EXHIBIT 14-16
Illustration: Class Definitions and Benchmarks

Class II

Ability to perform unskilled routine jobs that are almost entirely manual, requiring the use of simple tools or equipment. Jobs usually do not require a knowledge of company methods or the exercise of judgement and decision.
Versatility may be the prime characteristic and assignments will coincide with ability to assume tasks dependent on training and skill. Work performed under direct or limited supervision.

Benchmarks

Casual plant and field labour
Car and truck loaders
Apprentice factory mechanic
Guard
Janitor
Apprentice machine operator

Class IV

Ability to perform work of a skilled or specialized nature. Mechanically must have the ability to set up repair, overhaul, and maintain machinery and mechanical equipment without being subject to further check. Must have ability to read blueprints, material specifications and the use of basic shop mathematics or comparable experience with the company layout to offset these requirements.
Work may be specialized or a nonmechanical nature requiring the ability to plan and perform work where only general operations methods are available and requires the making of decisions involving the use of considerable ingenuity, initiative, and judgement. Work under limited supervision.

Benchmarks

Skilled machinist
Skilled electrician
Skilled mechanic
Packaging supervisor
Shipping supervisor

Class III

Ability to perform tasks of a semiskilled nature, either manual or nonmanual. Mechanically must have ability to operate or to examine machines for defects, dismantle, reassemble, and adjust for efficient operation without direct or constant supervision.
May have ability to perform work of nonmechanical status, but work that requires the making of some general decisions as to quality, quantity, operations, and the exercising of independent judgement.

Benchmarks

Stockroom clerk
Semiskilled mechanic
Semiskilled machine operator
General truck operator
Research technician

Class V

Ability to perform work of the highest level in a trade or craft. This skill may be recognized with a licence or other certification after formal apprenticeship training; or after a considerable period of formal on-the-job training by demonstrated competence to perform equivalent level of skill. Other employees to be considered for classification into grade V must regularly supervise others in the technical and other aspects of the work, perform other supervisory functions and may, in addition, perform work of a nonsupervisory nature.

Benchmarks

Master electrician
Master (chief) mechanic
Power plant—chief engineer
Factory supervisor
Maintenance planner

4. Divide the current pay among the factors. If the job pays $15.75 per hour, how much of the $15.75 is for mental requirements? How much for skill requirements?
5. Reconcile the differences in ranking found in steps 2 and 3.
6. Place the key jobs on a scale for each factor. This becomes the basis for evaluating nonkey jobs in the structure. Exhibit 14–17 gives an example.

According to Nash and Carroll, only about 10 percent of employers that do a formal job evaluation use the factor comparison method.[40] The complexity of the above explanation demonstrates why. There is also the issue of subjectivity. Despite its systematic nature, the method still relies on a committee or group of evaluators' judgement. It does have the advantage of demonstrating how differences in factor rankings translate into dollars and cents.

Point Method. The point method system is a frequently used job evaluation method.[41] It is more sophisticated than ranking and classification systems and, once designed, relatively simple to understand and administer.

Point methods have three common features: (1) compensable factors, (2) factor degrees numerically scaled, and (3) weights reflecting the relative importance of each factor. Exhibit 14–18 illustrates the steps in the design of a point plan. Let us consider each of these elements.[42]

Choose Compensable Factors. Taking job analysis/job description data as the input, there are two ways to select and define compensable factors: (1) adapting from an existing plan or (2) custom designing. In practice, most applications fall between those two.

The factors included usually pertain to skills required, physical and mental effort needed, the degree of hazardous or unpleasant working conditions, and the amount of responsibility. Some point system plans use as many as 10 factors.

Due to their pivotal role in the point method, the factors chosen should pos-

EXHIBIT 14–17
Factor Comparison Method Ranking Benchmark Jobs by Compensable Factors

Benchmark Jobs	Mental Requirements	Experience/ Skills	Physical Factors	Supervision	Other Responsibilities
A. Punch press operator	6	5	2	4	4
B. Parts attendant	5	3	3	6	1
C. Riveter	4	6	1	1	3
D. Truck operator	3	1	6	5	6
E. Machine operator	2	2	4	2	5
F. Parts inspector	1	3	5	3	2

Note: Rank of 1 is high.
Source: George T. Milkovich and Jerry M. Newman, *Compensation*, 2nd ed. (Plano, Tex.: Business Publications, 1987).

EXHIBIT 14–18
Steps in Design of Point Job Evaluation

1. Conduct job analysis.
2. Choose compensable factors.
3. Establish factor scales.
4. Derive factor weights.
5. Prepare evaluation manual.
6. Apply to nonbenchmark jobs.

Source: George T. Milkovich and Jerry M. Newman, *Compensation*, 2nd ed. (Plano, Tex.: Business Publications, 1987).

sess the following characteristics. They should be work-related, which means demonstrably derived from the actual work performed. Appropriate documentation (i.e., job description, job analysis, employee and/or supervisory interviews) must support the factors. The factors must also be acceptable to (and understood by) managers and employees. Third, the compensable factors need to be business-related in terms of being consistent with the organization's culture and values, its business directions, and the nature of work. Changes in the organization or its directions may necessitate a different mix of factors.

Establish Factor Scales. This involves establishing gradations within each factor in terms of "degrees." Each degree is anchored by the typical skills, tasks, and behaviours taken from benchmark jobs that illustrate each factor degree. Exhibit 14–19 shows a typical scaling for the factor of knowledge. The different factors used in a point plan do not necessarily contain the same number of degrees. Some plans employ two-dimensional grids to define degrees (e.g., Hay Plan—see Appendix).

Derive Factor Weights. Factor weights are assigned in order to indicate differences in importance attached to each factor by the employer. They are established by committee judgement and statistical analysis. In the first method, the compensation committee allocates 100 percent of value among the factors. This may involve a structured process such as Delphi or some other nominal group technique to facilitate consensus.[43] In the statistical approach, weights are empirically derived so as to correlate as closely as possible to a set of pay rates agreed on by the parties involved.[44]

Prepare Evaluation Manual. A written evaluation manual is an important output of the design phase of job evaluation: It becomes the yardstick for the plan and should contain sufficiently detailed information to permit the accurate evaluation of the bulk of jobs. The manual also needs to contain a description of review and appeal procedures.

EXHIBIT 14-19
Illustration of a Compensable Factor

1. Knowledge

This factor measures the knowledge or equivalent training required to perform the position duties.

1st Degree
Use of reading and writing, adding and subtracting of whole numbers; following of instructions; use of fixed gauges, direct reading instruments and similar devices; where interpretation is not required.

2nd Degree
Use of addition, subtraction, multiplication and division of numbers including decimals and fractions; simple use of formulas, charts, tables, drawings, specifications, schedules, wiring diagrams; use of adjustable measuring instruments; checking of reports, forms, records, and comparable data; where interpretation is required.

3rd Degree
Use of mathematics together with the use of complicated drawings, specifications, charts, tables; various types of precision measuring instruments. Equivalent to 1 to 3 years applied trades training in a particular or specialized occupation.

4th Degree
Use of advanced trades mathematics, together with the use of complicated drawings, specifications, charts, tables, handbook formulas; all varieties of precision measuring instruments. Equivalent to complete accredited apprenticeship in a recognized trade, craft or occupation; or equivalent to a 2-year technical college education.

5th Degree
Use of higher mathematics involved in the application of engineering principles and the performance of related practical operations, together with a comprehensive knowledge of the theories and practices of mechanical, electrical, chemical, civil or like engineering field. Equivalent to completion of 4 years of technical college or university education.

Source: George T. Milkovich and Jerry M. Newman, *Compensation*, 2nd ed. (Plano, Tex.: Business Publications, 1987).

Evaluating Nonbenchmark Jobs. The evaluation of nonbenchmark jobs may again involve committees. Typically, each member independently evaluates each job description.[45] These evaluations are then compared. If no consensus emerges, employees with firsthand knowledge of the jobs may become part of the evaluation discussions.

The following illustrations demonstrate how to determine total points and how to place nonbenchmark jobs.

An Illustration

Each job's relative value, and hence its location on the pay structure, is determined by the total points assigned to it. The point plan shown in Exhibit 14–20 is based on four compensable factors: skills required, effort required, responsibility, and working conditions; the weights add to 100 percent. Each factor has a possible five degrees. According to the weights (expressed in percent), the total points of a job requiring two degrees of skills (2 × 40 = 80), three degrees of effort (3 × 30 = 90) and responsibility (3 × 20 = 60), and two degrees of working conditions (2 × 10 = 20) is 250 points (80 + 90 + 60 + 20 = 250). Once the total points for all jobs are computed and a hierarchy established, the jobs are compared to make certain their *relative* place in the hierarchy makes sense.

Our second illustration is based on setting pay rates for key jobs based on what other employers are paying and determining pay rates for all other jobs by slotting them, via job evaluation, around the key job rates. For example, Exhibit 14–21 reproduces the pay level decision made earlier (shown in Exhibit 14–10). This decision was based on market data and the organization's policy decision to lead, lag, or meet competition. This permits us to set pay rates for the five key jobs, A, D, G, M, and N. Assume a point job evaluation method is in use. By evaluating all jobs (A through N), a job structure (horizontal axis) is established. Each job is assigned job evaluation points. The job structure represents the similarities and differences among jobs based on job content (compensable factors) and other variables (factor weights). Based on this job structure, it is now possible to place each nonkey job into the appropriate place on the pay level line. In the example, key jobs A (100 points), D (150), G (200), M (250), and N (300), and nonkey jobs B (130 points), C (140), E (165), F (170), H (210), I (215), J (220), K (230), and L (240) are the total point results. Based on these point totals, the nonkey jobs are placed into the structure. Their place is based on market rates (reflected in the pay level line

EXHIBIT 14–20
Characteristics of the Point Job Evaluation Method: Factors, Scaled Degrees, and Weights

Weights	Factors	Degrees				
40%	Skills required	1	2	3	4	5
30	Effort required	1	2	3	4	5
20	Responsibility	1	2	3	4	5
10	Working conditions	1	2	3	4	5

Source: George T. Milkovich and Jerry M. Newman, *Compensation*, 2nd ed. (Plano, Tex.: Business Publications, 1987).

and rates for key jobs) plus content of the work and compensable factors (reflected in the job evaluation process). Hence, job evaluation links internal and external market factors. Through job evaluation, pay rates for nonkey jobs can be determined.

Obviously, a point method of job evaluation is not required. Any of the job evaluation methods could be substituted to achieve a pay structure. The key is to ensure that whatever method is used is demonstrably work-related, as well as understood and acceptable to managers and employees.

EXHIBIT 14–21
Establishing a Pay Structure via Job Evaluation

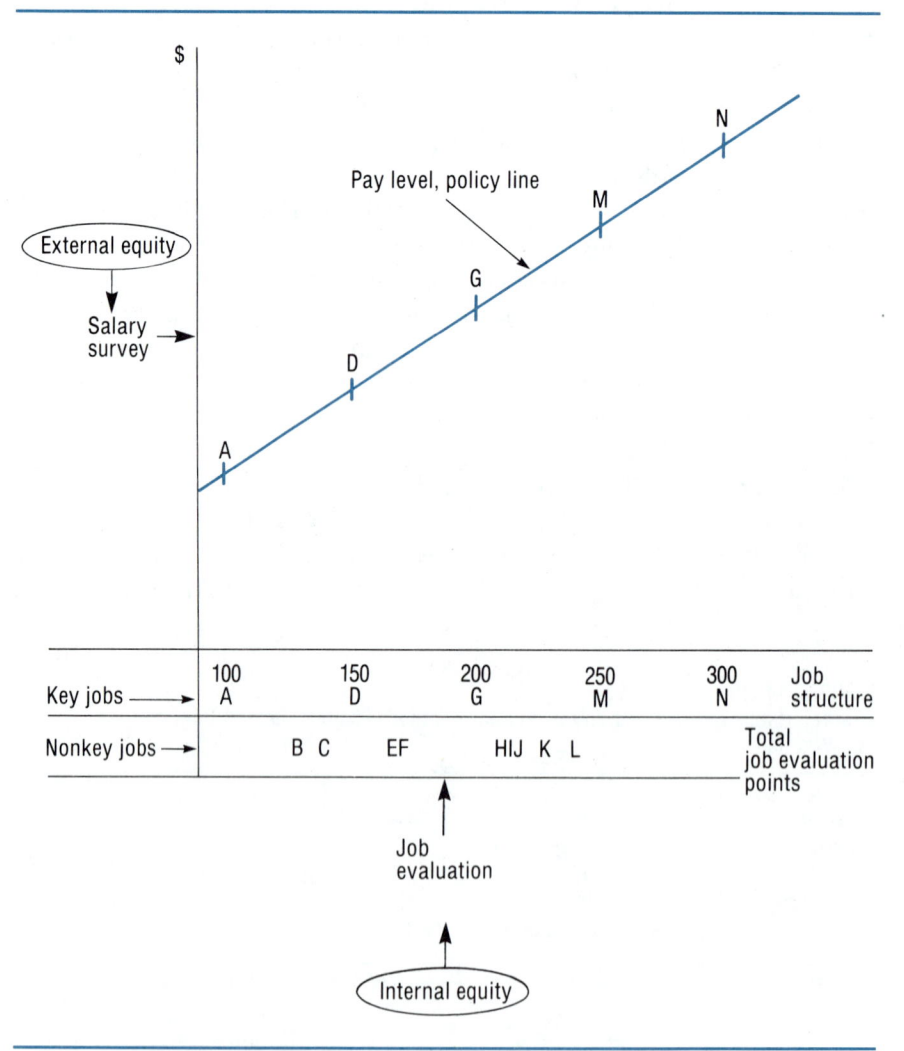

EXHIBIT 14–22
Job Evaluation Approval Process

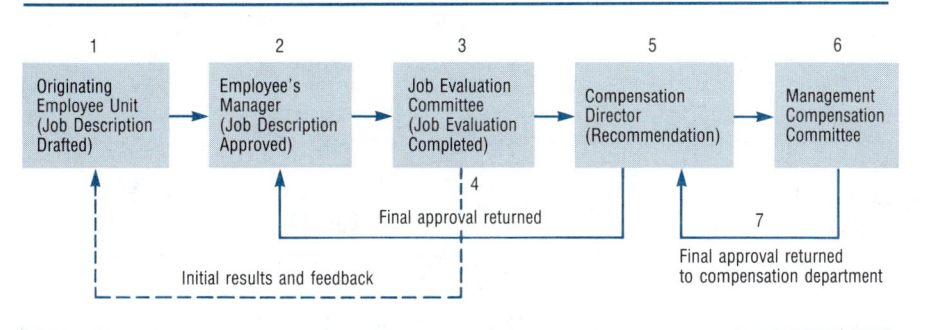

1	2	3	5	6
Originating Employee Unit (Job Description Drafted)	Employee's Manager (Job Description Approved)	Job Evaluation Committee (Job Evaluation Completed)	Compensation Director (Recommendation)	Management Compensation Committee

4 — Final approval returned

7 — Final approval returned to compensation department

Initial results and feedback

Source: George T. Milkovich and Jerry M. Newman, *Compensation*, 2nd ed. (Plano, Tex.: Business Publications, 1987).

Evaluating the Plan's Usefulness

The final major decision (Exhibit 14–13) calls for assessment of the job evaluation plan. Job evaluation procedures have been subjected to extensive evaluation.[46] In general, evaluation efforts focus on job evaluation as a measurement device: its reliability, its validity, the costs included in design and implementation, its compliance with laws and regulations (e.g., the absence of gender effects), and the procedural equity of the process.

When all evaluations are completed, approval by higher levels in the organization (e.g., vice president of human resources) is usually required. The approval process serves as a control and helps ensure that any changes resulting from job evaluation are consistent with the organization's operations and directions. Exhibit 14–22 is one example of the approval process.

SUMMARY

No single best pay program exists. Rather, the design and administration of pay programs are contingent on the organizational and environmental context in which they must operate.

Within this context, there are several basic concepts and issues of concern. This chapter examined two of them. One is to establish external equity by setting the pay level. This was accomplished through market surveys and determining the pay policy line. The other is to establish internal equity in the pay structure. The structure, usually designed with the aid of job analysis and job evaluation, focusses on pay differentials among jobs.

We have begun to develop the pay system. In the next chapter, we will develop it further to pay employees. Employee equity and individual pay are examined along with several alternative methods of paying employees. Merit pay, gainsharing, and lump sums are discussed. Some major concerns in pay administration and pay discrimination are also considered.

APPENDIX / The Hay Guide Chart–Profile Method

The *Hay Guide Chart–Profile Method* is perhaps the most widely used job evaluation plan. It has been installed in approximately 5,000 profit and nonprofit organizations in more than 30 countries. Its Canadian users include a number of firms listed in the *Financial Post*'s 500. The chances are high that many readers of this book will eventually work for a company that uses the Hay plan.

The four Hay factors—know-how, problem solving, accountability, and working conditions—employ a total of 12 dimensions (see Exhibits A–1 through A–4 for definitions). The use of working conditions has become more prevalent as a result of pay equity initiatives and is now a standard part of the evaluation process. Job evaluation experts point out (with some disagreement) that the Hay plan combines features of the point method and factor comparison. The materials shown are proprietary to Hay Associates Canada.[47]

Upon engagement, a set of guide charts is prepared specifically for each client organization. Installation of the Hay procedure involves a number of steps, including use of wage surveys to keep the point-dollar relationship up-to-date. The charts provided here are subject to continuing refinements by Hay Associates.

A simple example helps illustrate how points are assigned. Consider the three jobs shown across the bottom of the know-how (KH), problem solving (PS), and accountability (AC) charts.

Know-how (KH): A key punch supervisor's job may require an "advanced vocational" level of knowledge (the fourth of eight levels), only a "minimal" level of managerial know-how, but human face-to-face relation skills that are "critical." The job would be evaluated as 152 points for know-how. The actuary's job requires a similar level of managerial know-how, only basic human relations skills, but knowledge of much more depth (specialized mastery), and merits 304 points. The requirements for the job of area manager are seen as being 700 points. Compared to the actuary's job, the area manager's work has the same depth, but much more scope (i.e., managerial know-how).

Problem solving (PS) is treated as a percentage utilization of know-how. For example, the level of novelty and complexity of the thinking required combined with the degree to which the thinking environment is defined yield 66 percent for the actuarial specialist. This translates into 200 points (i.e., 66 percent of the 304 points allocated to KH).

EXHIBIT A-1

XYZ COMPANY OF CANADA LIMITED

GUIDE CHART FOR EVALUATING KNOW-HOW

DEFINITION: Know-How is the sum total of every kind of knowledge and skill, however acquired, needed for acceptable job performance. Know-How has 3 dimensions—the requirements for:
- Practical procedures, specialized techniques, or scientific disciplines.
- Planning, organizing, coordinating, integrating, staffing, directing and/or controlling the activities and resources associated with an organizational unit or function, in order to produce the results expected of that unit or function. This skill may be exercised consultatively ("Thinking like a manager") as well as directly.
- Active, face-to-face skills needed for various relationships with other people. Defined as:
  1. **BASIC:** Ordinary courtesy and effectiveness in dealing with others.
  2. **IMPORTANT:** Understanding and influencing people are important requirements in the job.
  3. **CRITICAL:** Alternative or combined skills in understanding and motivating people are important in the highest degree.

*** HUMAN RELATIONS SKILLS

MEASURING PRACTICAL, TECHNICAL KNOW-HOW: This type of know-ledge and skill may be characterized by breadth (variety) or depth (complexity) of both. Jobs require, in varying combinations, some knowledge about many things or a good deal of knowledge about a few things. Thus, the measuring of Practical, Technical Know-How requires an understanding of "HOW MUCH KNOWLEDGE IS NEEDED ABOUT HOW MANY THINGS AND HOW COMPLEX ARE THEY?"

** MANAGERIAL KNOW-HOW

		IN NONSUPERVISORY Performance of an activity as an individual (not as a supervisor or professional)			I. MINIMAL Performance or direction of activities which are similar as to content and objectives with appropriate awareness of other company activities			II. RELATED Direction of a unit with varied activities and objectives OR guidance of a subfunction(s) or several important elements across several organizational units			III. DIVERSE Direction of a large unit with functional variety OR guidance of a function(s) which affects all or most of the company			IV. BROAD Direction of a major unit with substantial functional diversity OR guidance of a strategic function(s) which significantly affects company planning and operations.		
		1	2	3	1	2	3	1	2	3	1	2	3	1	2	3
A	**PRIMARY:** Familiarization with simple work routines.	38 43 50	43 50 57	50 57 66	50 57 66	57 66 76	66 76 87	66 76 87	76 87 100	87 100 115	87 100 115	100 115 132	115 132 152	115 132 152	132 152 175	152 175 200
B	**ELEMENTARY VOCATIONAL:** Experienced in uninvolved, standard procedures and/or use of simple equipment or machines.	50 57 66	57 66 76	66 76 87	66 76 87	76 87 100	87 100 115	87 100 115	100 115 132	115 132 152	115 132 152	132 152 175	152 175 200	152 175 200	175 200 230	200 230 264
C	**VOCATIONAL:** Procedural or systematic proficiency which may involve a facility in the use of specialized equipment.	66 76 87	76 87 100	87 100 115	87 100 115	100 115 132	115 132 152	115 132 152	132 152 175	152 175 200	152 175 200	175 200 230	200 230 264	200 230 264	230 264 304	264 304 350
D	**ADVANCED VOCATIONAL:** Knowledge of practical procedures or systems which are moderately complex, and/or specialized skills which require some technical (usually non-theoretical) knowledge to apply.	87 100 115	100 115 132	115 132 152	115 132 152	132 152 175	152 175 200	152 175 200	175 200 230	200 230 264	200 230 264	230 264 304	264 304 350	264 304 350	304 350 400	350 400 460
E	**BASIC SPECIALIZED OR VARIED:** Basic understanding of theory and principles in a scientific or similar discipline OR a combination of a sound understanding and skill in several activities which involve a variety of practices and precedents.	115 132 152	132 152 175	152 175 200	152 175 200	175 200 230	200 230 264	200 230 264	230 264 304	264 304 350	264 304 350	304 350 400	350 400 460	350 400 460	400 460 528	460 528 608
F	**SEASONED SPECIALIZED OR DIVERSE:** Extensive knowledge and skill gained through broad or deep experiences in a field (or fields) which requires a command of either scientific, theory and principles OR involved, diverse practices and precedents OR both.	152 175 200	175 200 230	200 230 264	200 230 264	230 264 304	264 304 350	264 304 350	304 350 400	350 400 460	350 400 460	400 460 528	460 528 608	460 528 608	528 608 700	608 700 800
G	**BROAD OR SPECIALIZED MASTERY:** Determinative mastery of principles and complex techniques OR the diverse cumulative equivalent gained through broad seasoning and/or special development.	200 230 264	230 264 304	264 304 350	264 304 350	304 350 400	350 400 460	350 400 460	400 460 528	460 528 608	460 528 608	528 608 700	608 700 800	608 700 800	700 800 920	800 920 1056
H	**PROFESSIONAL EMINENCE:** Authoritative expertise in a complex scientific field or other learned discipline.	264 304 350	304 350 400	350 400 460	350 400 460	400 460 528	460 528 608	460 528 608	528 608 700	608 700 800	608 700 800	700 800 920	800 920 1056	800 920 1056	920 1056 1216	1056 1216 1400

PRACTICAL PROCEDURES — SPECIALIZED TECHNIQUES — SCIENTIFIC DISCIPLINES

KH	PS	AC	Total
152			

Supervisor key punch

KH	PS	AC	Total
304			

Actuarial specialist
Research associate

KH	PS	AC	Total
700			

Area manager

EXHIBIT A–2

XYZ COMPANY OF CANADA LIMITED

GUIDE CHART FOR EVALUATING
PROBLEM SOLVING

DEFINITION: Problem Solving is the amount and nature of the thinking required in the job in the form of analyzing, reasoning, evaluating, creating, using judgment, forming hypotheses, drawing inferences, arriving at conclusions, and the like.

Problem Solving has two dimensions:
- The environment in which the thinking takes place — the extent to which assistance or guidance is available from others or from practice and precedents.
- The challenge of the thinking to be done — the novelty and complexity of the thinking required.

N.B. The evaluation of Problem Solving should be made without reference to the job's authority to make decisions or take action; this is measured on the Accountability Chart.

MEASURING PROBLEM SOLVING: All thinking requires the presence of knowledge in the form of facts, principles, procedures, standards, concepts, etc. This is the raw material to which the thinking processes are applied.

Problem Solving measures the degree to which thinking processes must be applied to the required knowledge in order to obtain the results expected of the job.

To the extent that thinking is limited or reduced by job demands or structure, covered by precedent, simplified by definition, or assisted by others, Problem Solving is diminished and results are obtained by the automatic application of skills rather than by the application of the thinking processes to knowledge.

		THINKING CHALLENGE			
THINKING ENVIRONMENT	**1. REPETITIVE** Identical situations requiring resolution by simple choice of learned things	**2. PATTERNED** Similar situations requiring resolution by discriminating choice of learned things.	**3. INTERPOLATIVE** Differing situations requiring search for resolutions within area of learned things.	**4. ADAPTIVE** Variable situations requiring analytical, interpretive, evaluative and/or constructive thinking.	**5. UNCHARTED** Novel or nonrecurring path-finding situations requiring the development of new concepts and imaginative approaches.
A RIGIDLY STRUCTURED: Thinking within very detailed and precisely defined rules and instructions and/or with continually present assistance.	10% / 12%	14% / 16%	19% / 22%	25% / 29%	33% / 38%
B ROUTINE: Thinking within detailed standard practices and instructions and/or with immediately available assistance or examples.	12% / 14%	16% / 19%	22% / 25%	29% / 33%	38% / 43%
C SEMI-ROUTINE: Thinking within well-defined somewhat diversified procedures; many precedents covering most situations and/or readily available assistance.	14% / 16%	19% / 22%	25% / 29%	33% / 38%	43% / 50%
D STANDARDIZED: Thinking within clear but substantially diversified procedures; precedents covering many situations and/or access to assistance.	16% / 19%	22% / 25%	29% / **33%**	38% / 43%	50% / 57%
E CLEARLY DEFINED: Thinking within a well-defined frame of reference and toward specific objectives, in situations characterized by functional practices and precedents.	19% / 22%	25% / 29%	33% / 38%	43% / 50%	57% / 66%
F GENERALLY DEFINED: Thinking within a general frame of reference toward functional objectives, in situations with some nebulous, intangible or unstructured aspects.	22% / 25%	29% / 33%	38% / 43%	50% / 57%	**66%** / 76%
G BROADLY DEFINED: Thinking within concepts, principles, and broad guidelines towards the organization's objectives or pervasive functional goals; many nebulous, intangible or unstructured aspects to the environment.	25% / 29%	33% / 38%	43% / 50%	**57%** / 66%	76% / 87%
H ABSTRACT: Thinking within business philosophy and/or natural laws and/or principles governing human affairs.	29% / 33%	38% / 43%	50% / 57%	66% / 76%	87%

KH	PS	AC	Total
152	50		

Supervisor key punch

KH	PS	AC	Total
304	200		

Actuarial specialist
Research associate

KH	PS	AC	Total
700	400		

Area manager

Accountability (AC) is the answerability for action and for the consequences thereof. The allocation of 115 points for the actuarial job reflects the combination of its impact on a unit of medium magnitude and the "generally regulated" level of freedom to act.

Exhibit A–5 shows the total evaluation points and profiles for each of the three jobs. Given the final, agreed on evaluations, their most common application is to serve as a basis for setting pay structures.

EXHIBIT A-3

XYZ COMPANY OF CANADA LIMITED

GUIDE CHART FOR EVALUATING ACCOUNTABILITY

GENERAL: Accountability is the answerability for action and for the consequences thereof. It is the measured effect of the job on end results. It has three dimensions in the following order of importance:

* **Freedom to Act** — the degree to which personal or procedural controls exist, as defined in the left-hand column below.
* **Job Impact on End Results** — as defined at upper right.
* **Magnitude** — the size of the unit or function (as indicated by the dynamic, annual dollars) most clearly affected by the job.

IMPACT — the degree to which the job affects or brings about the results expected of the unit or function being considered.

- **P — PRIMARY:** Controlling impact — the position has effective control over the significant activities and resources which produce the results, and is the sole position (with level of freedom to Act) which must answer for the results.
- **S — SHARED:** Equal and joint control, with one other position, of the activities and resources which produce the results. OR control of what are clearly most (but not all) of the significant variables in determining results.
- **C — CONTRIBUTORY:** Interpretive, advisory, or other supporting services for use by others in achieving results.
- **R — REMOTE:** Informational, recording or other facilitating services for use by others in achieving results.

FREEDOM TO ACT

MAGNITUDE (annual basis) → IMPACT →	(M) MINIMAL Up to $10M				(1) VERY SMALL $10M–$100M				(2) SMALL $100M–$1MM				(3) MEDIUM $1MM–$10MM				(4) LARGE $10MM–$100MM			
	R	C	S	P	R	C	S	P	R	C	S	P	R	C	S	P	R	C	S	P
A PRESCRIBED: These jobs are subject to direct and detailed instructions and/or very close supervision.	8	10	14	19	10	14	19	25	14	19	25	33	19	25	33	43	25	33	43	57	A
	9	12	16	22	12	16	22	29	16	22	29	38	22	29	38	50	29	38	50	66
	10	14	19	25	14	19	25	33	19	25	33	43	25	33	43	57	33	43	57	76
B CONTROLLED: These jobs are subject to instructions and established work routines and/or close supervision.	12	16	22	29	16	22	29	38	22	29	38	50	29	38	50	66	38	50	66	87	B
	14	19	25	33	19	25	33	43	25	33	43	57	33	43	57	76	43	57	76	100
	16	22	29	38	22	29	38	50	29	38	50	66	38	50	66	87	50	66	87	115
C STANDARDIZED: These jobs are subject, wholly or in part, to standardized practices and procedures. General work instructions. Supervision of progress and results.	19	25	33	43	25	33	43	57	33	43	57	76	43	57	76	100	57	76	100	132	C
	22	29	38	50	29	38	50	66	38	50	66	87	50	66	87	115	66	87	115	152
	25	33	43	57	33	43	57	76	43	57	76	100	57	76	100	132	76	100	132	175
D GENERALLY REGULATED: These jobs are subject, wholly or in part, to practices and procedures covered by precedents or well-defined policies. Supervisory review.	29	38	50	66	38	50	66	87	50	66	87	115	66	87	115	152	87	115	152	200	D
	33	43	57	76	43	57	76	100	57	76	100	132	76	100	132	175	100	132	175	230
	38	50	66	87	50	66	87	115	66	87	115	152	87	115	152	200	115	152	200	264
E DIRECTED: These jobs, by their nature or size, are subject to broad practice and procedures covered by functional precedents and policies. Achievement of a circumscribed operational activity. Managerial direction.	43	57	76	100	57	76	100	132	76	100	132	175	100	132	175	230	132	175	230	304	E
	50	66	87	115	66	87	115	152	87	115	152	200	115	152	200	264	152	200	264	350
	57	76	100	132	76	100	132	175	100	132	175	230	132	175	230	304	175	230	304	400
F GENERAL DIRECTION: These jobs, by their nature or size, are broadly subject to functional policies and goals. Management direction of a general nature.	66	87	115	152	87	115	152	200	115	152	200	264	152	200	264	350	200	264	350	460	F
	76	100	132	175	100	132	175	230	132	175	230	304	175	230	304	400	230	304	400	528
	87	115	152	200	115	152	200	264	152	200	264	350	200	264	350	460	264	350	460	608
G BROAD GUIDANCE: These jobs are subject to the guidance of general policies and directives from top management.	100	132	175	230	132	175	230	304	175	230	304	400	230	304	400	528	304	400	528	700	G
	115	152	200	264	152	200	264	350	200	264	350	460	264	350	460	608	350	460	608	800
	132	175	230	304	175	230	304	400	230	304	400	528	304	400	528	700	400	528	700	920
H STRATEGIC GUIDANCE	152	200	264	350	200	264	350	460	264	350	460	608	350	460	608	800	460	608	800	1056	H
	175	230	304	400	230	304	400	528	304	400	528	700	400	528	700	920	528	700	920	1216
	200	264	350	460	264	350	460	608	350	460	608	800	460	608	800	1056	608	800	1056	1400

KH	PS	AC	Total
152	50	66	268

Supervisor key punch

KH	PS	AC	Total
304	200	115	619

Actuarial specialist
Research associate

KH	PS	AC	Total
700	400	608	1708

Area manager

EXHIBIT A-4

XYZ COMPANY OF CANADA LIMITED
GUIDE CHART FOR MEASURING WORKING CONDITIONS

GENERAL: Working Conditions includes two dimensions, Physical and Mental, each consisting of two elements as defined below.

- • **Physical Effort:** Jobs require levels of physical activity that vary in intensity, duration and frequency, or any combination of these factors, to produce physical stress and fatigue. Some examples of these activities include lifting, handling of materials or objects, stretching, pulling, pushing, climbing, walking, carrying, sitting, standing, and/or working in awkward positions, or other unusual circumstances.

- • **Physical Environment:** Jobs may include progressive degrees of exposure of varying intensities to unavoidable physical and environmental factors which result in discomfort or increase the risk of accident or ill-health. Some examples of these include: fumes, temperature, noise, vibration, dirt, dust, and unavoidable exposure to hazardous substances, equipment, and/or situations.

- • • **Sensory Attention:** Jobs may require levels of sensory attention (i.e. seeing, hearing, smelling, tasting, touching) during the work process that vary in intensity, duration and frequency. Some examples include: auditing, inspecting, operating mechanical equipment, tabulating data, monitoring video display terminals, proofreading, or technical troubleshooting.

- • • • **Mental Stress:** Mental stress refers to progressive degrees of exposure of varying intensities to factors inherent in the work process or environment which increase the risk of tension or anxiety. (These are different from the factors considered in the "Physical Environment" element. See definition at left.) Some examples of such factors include: disruptions in lifestyle caused by travel requirements, work repetition, lack of control over work pace because it is irregular or machine controlled, emotional deprivation resulting from isolation or lack of privacy, exposure to emotionally disturbing experiences.

	• • • MENTAL STRESS → • • SENSORY ATTENTION ↓ The job demands:	1 Minimal mental stress.	2 Moderate mental stress.	3 Considerable mental stress.	4 Severe mental stress.
• PHYSICAL ENVIRONMENT → • PHYSICAL EFFORT ↓	The combination of intensity, duration, and frequency of exposure to factors in the environment is such that it results in:	I Limited sensory attention.	II Moderate sensory attention.	III Considerable sensory attention.	IV Intense sensory attention with little or no interruption.
The combination of intensity, duration, and frequency of physical activity is such that it results in:	a. Minimal discomfort or risk of accident or ill-health.	b. Considerable discomfort or moderate risk of accident or ill-health.	c. Great discomfort or substantial risk of accident or ill-health.	d. Extreme risk of accident or ill-health.	
A. Mild fatigue or physical stress.					
B. Moderate fatigue or physical stress.					
C. Considerable fatigue or physical stress.					
D. Severe fatigue or physical stress.					

EXHIBIT A–5

	Points					Percentages		
KH	PS	AC	Total			KH	PS	AC
152	50	66	268		PS 19% / KH 56% / 25%	56	19	25
Supervisor key punch						= 100%		

KH	PS	AC	Total
304	200	115	619
Actuarial specialist Research associate			

PS 32% / KH 49% / AC 19%

49 32 19
= 100%

KH	PS	AC	Total
700	400	608	1708
Area manager			

PS 23% / KH 41% / AC 36%

41 23 36
= 100%

DISCUSSION AND REVIEW QUESTIONS

1. How do product market conditions affect compensation?
2. How do labour market conditions affect compensation?
3. How will the business directions of the organization affect forms of pay?
4. How will strategic stages of an organization affect pay?
5. Distinguish among the three concepts of equity contained in the pay model presented in this chapter. Give an example where an organization would emphasize one type of equity over the others.
6. What are some potential problems in emphasizing one type of equity over the others?
7. What are the three alternatives in setting a pay level? Under what circumstances would you recommend each alternative?
8. What is a key benchmark job?
9. What is a pay structure? How do you construct one?
10. What are the four main job evaluation methods? What is the major advantage and disadvantage of each?

11. What is the relationship between job analysis and job evaluation?
12. What is the relationship between key jobs and job evaluation?

NOTES AND REFERENCES

1. See Edward E. Lawler III, *Pay and Organization Development* (Reading, Mass.: Addison-Wesley Publishing, 1981); and Gary S. Becker, *Human Capital* (New York: National Bureau for Economic Research, 1964).
2. R. L. Opsahl and M. D. Dunnette, "The Role of Financial Compensation in Industrial Motivation," *Psychological Bulletin* 66 (1966), pp. 94–118.
3. Chester A. Schriesheim, "Job Satisfaction," *Journal of Applied Psychology*, October 1978, pp. 548–52; Tover Helland Hammer and Michael Berman, "The Role of Noneconomic Factors in Faculty Union Voting," *Journal of Applied Psychology*, August 1981, pp. 415–21; Thomas A. DeCotiis and Jean-Yves LeLourn, "A Predictive Study of Voting Behavior in a Representation Election Using Instrumentality and Work Perceptions," *Organizational Behavior and Human Performance*, February 1981, pp. 103–18.
4. We thank Chris Berger and Bill Whitely for this comment. Readers interested in a broader perspective of reward systems in organization can turn to M. A. Von Glinow, "Reward Strategies for Attracting, Evaluating and Retaining Professionals," *Human Resource Management*, Summer 1985, pp. 191–206; or L. L. Cummings, "Compensation, Culture, and Motivation: A Systems Perspective," *Organizational Dynamics*, Winter 1984, pp. 33–44.
5. Arne L. Kalleberg and Aage B. Sorensen, "The Sociology of Labor Markets," *Annual Review of Sociology*, 1979, pp. 351–79.
6. R. Ehrenberg and R. S. Smith, *Modern Labor Economics* (Glenview, Ill.: Scott, Foresman, 1982).
7. Ibid.
8. The "sketch" of labour standards legislation in this section draws heavily on *Labour Standards in Canada—1984 edition* (Ottawa: Labour Canada, 1984); *Labour Standards—Summary* (Ottawa: Minister of Supply and Services Canada, 1983; Cat. No. L40-2/1-1983E); and reference tables detailed in Pradeep Kumar, with Mary Lou Coates and David Arrowsmith, *The Current Industrial Relations Scene in Canada: 1987* (Kingston, Ont.: Queen's University, Industrial Relations Centre, 1987), pp. 273–320.
9. Daniel J. B. Mitchell and Ross E. Azevedo, *Wage-Price Controls and Labor Market Distortions* (Los Angeles: Institute of Industrial Relations, University of California, 1976).
10. George P. Schultz and Kenneth W. Dam, "Reflections of Wage and Price Controls," *Industrial and Labor Relations Review*, January 1977, pp. 139–51.
11. Arnold R. Weber and Daniel J. B. Mitchell, "Further Reflections on Wage Controls: Comment," *Industrial and Labor Relations Review*, January 1978, pp. 149–58.
12. *Labour Standards in Canada*, p. 38; Kumar et al., *The Current Industrial Relations Scene in Canada: 1987*, pp. 316–20.
13. Ibid.

14. Fred F. Foulkes, *Personnel Policies in Large Nonunion Companies* (Englewood Cliffs, N.J.: Prentice-Hall, 1980).
15. See, for example, Kumar et al., *The Industrial Relations Scene in Canada: 1987;* and *Collective Bargaining Review,* a monthly publication of Labour Canada.
16. Bruce Ellig, *Executive Compensation—A Total Pay Perspective* (New York: McGraw-Hill, 1982); Jude T. Rich, "Strategic Incentives," in *1980 National Conference Proceedings* (Scottsdale, Ariz.: American Compensation Association, 1981).
17. Lawler, *Pay and Organization Development.*
18. Opsahl and Dunnette, "Financial Compensation."
19. George T. Milkovich and Michael Delaney, "A Note on Cafeteria Pay Plans," *Industrial Relations,* February 1975, pp. 112–16; Edgar Schein, *Career Dynamics: Matching Individual and Organizational Needs* (Reading, Mass.: Addison-Wesley Publishing, 1978).
20. Thomas H. Patten, Jr., *Pay: Employee Compensation and Incentive Plans* (New York: Free Press, 1977).
21. Virginia Galt, "Employers Tying Pay to Performance," *The Globe and Mail,* November 4, 1985, p. B1; Michael Salter, "Pay Now Tagged More to Results," *Financial Post,* October 25, 1983, p. 24.
22. David Belcher, *Wage and Salary Administration* (Englewood Cliffs, N.J.: Prentice-Hall, 1974).
23. Lester C. Thurow, *Generating Inequality: Mechanisms of Distribution in the U.S. Economy* (New York: Basic Books, 1975).
24. Daniel J. B. Mitchell, "How to Find Wage Spillovers (Where None Exist)," *Industrial Relations,* Fall 1982, pp. 392–98; H. Gregg Lewis, "Union Relative Wage Effects: A Survey of Macro Estimates," *Journal of Labor Economics,* January 1983, pp. 1–27.
25. Thomas A. Mahoney, *Compensation and Reward Perspectives* (Homewood, Ill.: Richard D. Irwin, 1979).
26. *Compensation Data Sourcebook* (Ottawa: The Conference Board of Canada, 1983).
27. George T. Milkovich and Jerry M. Newman, *Compensation,* 2nd ed. (Plano, Tex.: Business Publications, 1987), p. 231.
28. Thomas A. Mahoney, "Organizational Hierarchy and Position Worth," *Academy of Management Journal,* December 1979, pp. 726–37.
29. David W. Belcher, "Pay Equity or Pay Fairness?" *Compensation Review,* Second Quarter 1979, pp. 31–37.
30. E. Robert Livernash, "The Internal Wage Structure," in New Concepts in *Wage Determination,* ed. G. W. Taylor and Frank C. Pierson (New York: McGraw-Hill, 1957).
31. George Milkovich and Jerry Newman, *Compensation,* 2nd ed.
32. Ibid., p. 106.
33. E. E. Lawler III and G. D. Jenkins, "Employee Participation in Pay Plan Development" (unpublished technical report to Department of Labor, Ann Arbor, Mich., 1976).
34. E. E. Lawler III, "The New Pay," in *Current Issues in Human Resource Management,* ed. S. L. Rynes and G. T. Milkovich (Plano, Tex.: Business Publications, 1986).

35. Lorna L. Kaufman, *Job Evaluation Systems: Concepts and Issues* (Kingston: Industrial Relations Centre, Queen's University, 1986). Other surveys of job evaluation systems in Canada include Public Service Staff Relations Board, Pay Research Bureau, *Salary Administration in Canadian Industry—1980* (Ottawa: Minister of Supply and Services Canada, 1981); and Labour Canada, Equal Pay Division, *Job Evaluation Survey—1984* (Ottawa: Minister of Supply and Services Canada, 1985).
36. Milkovich and Newman, *Compensation*, 2nd ed., p. 109; see also their pp. 136–40 for a review of single-factor systems. These appear to focus on assessing the amount of discretion an employee has in a job. The two most widely known are Jacques' Time Span of Discretion (TSD) and Arthur Young's Decision Banding. Many employees are not convinced that only one factor can adequately capture the entire domain of their jobs.
37. See, for example, *Report on Job Evaluation Systems in the Ontario Public Sector* (Kingston: Queen's University, Industrial Relations Centre, 1986).
38. Robert B. Pursell, "R&D Job Evaluation and Compensation," *Compensation Review*, Second Quarter 1972, pp. 21–31; T. Atchinson and W. French, "Pay Systems for Scientists and Engineers," *Industrial Relations*, 1967, pp. 44–56.
39. Thomas H. Patten, Jr., *Pay, Employee Compensation and Incentive Plans*, (New York: Free Press, 1977).
40. Allan N. Nash and Stephen J. Carroll, Jr., *The Management of Compensation* (Belmont, Calif.: Wadsworth, 1975).
41. Milkovich and Newman, *Compensation*, 2nd ed.; *Report on Job Evaluation Systems in the Ontario Public Sector*.
42. A more detailed discussion is available in Milkovich and Newman, *Compensation*, 2nd ed., pp. 125–36.
43. Dov Elizur, *Job Evaluation: A Systematic Approach* (London: Gower Press, 1980); Dov Elizur, "The Scaling Method of Job Evaluation," *Compensation Review*, Third Quarter 1978, pp. 34–46; Dov Elizur and Louis Guttman, "The Structure of Attitudes toward Work and Technological Change within an Organization," *Administrative Science Quarterly*, December 1976, pp. 611–21.
44. Andre L. Delbecq, Andrew H. Van de Ven, and David H. Gustafson, *Group Techniques for Program Planning: A Guide to Nominal Group and Delphi Processes* (Glenview, Ill.: Scott, Foresman, 1975); and D. D. Robinson, O. W. Wahlstrom, and R. C. Mecham, "Comparison of Job Evaluation Methods: A Policy-Capturing Approach Using the PAQ," *Journal of Applied Psychology* 59, no. 5 (1974), pp. 633–37.
45. Harry Walter Daniels, "Winning Acceptance for the Job Evaluation Plan," *Personnel* 30, no. 1 (July 1953), pp. 30–33; Vincent S. Wilkins, "Seven Traps in Job Evaluation," *Management Review*, February 1961, pp. 120–29; G. K. Warner, "Using Salary Administration Committees Effectively," *Personnel Journal*, July–August 1961, pp. 116–18; Arthur H. Dick, "Job Evaluation's Role in Employee Relations," *Personnel Journal* 53, no. 3 (March 1974), pp. 176–79.
46. Milkovich and Newman, *Compensation*, 2nd ed.
47. The charts shown in Exhibits A–1 through A–4 are copyrighted by HAY Associates Canada. We appreciate HAY Associates' permission to use this material for educational purposes as part of this book. The illustrative examples for the three jobs were inserted by the authors.

CHAPTER FIFTEEN
INDIVIDUAL PAY AND ADMINISTRATION

CHAPTER OUTLINE

I. Individual Pay Policies
II. Individual Pay Techniques
    A. Pay Ranges
    B. Pay Increase Guidelines
    C. External, Internal, and Employee Equity
III. Pay-for-Performance
    A. Is Money Important?
    B. Should Pay Increases Be Based on Performance?
    C. Is Pay Based on Performance?
    D. Negative Evidence
IV. Pay and Satisfaction
V. Incentives
    A. Individual Incentives
    B. Group Incentives
VI. Pay Administration
    A. Cost Controls
    B. Communication
    C. Participation
    D. Special Groups
VII. Executive Pay
    A. Compensation Decisions
    B. Is Executive Pay Effective?

VIII. Pay Equity
   A. Equal Pay versus Pay Equity: An Example
   B. Features of Pay Equity Legislation
   C. The Continuing Controversy
IX. Summary

The most important pay question for most of us is: How much of it do we get? The topics discussed in the previous chapter—external and internal equity, pay levels, and pay structures—seem abstract in comparison. This chapter examines various approaches to paying individual employees. It also considers a variety of issues associated with administering the entire pay system. These include budgeting, communication, and paying special groups of employees.

How much should one employee be paid relative to another when both hold the same job in the same organization? For example, should all first-line supervisors working at the Alberta Wheat Pool's facilities in Vancouver receive the same pay? Or should they receive different pay levels based on individual performance and/or longevity in the job?

Employee equity, the third element of the conceptual foundation in the pay model presented in the last chapter (Exhibit 14–5), helps answer these questions. Employee equity refers to the pay relationships between people in the same job within a single organization. Employee equity is translated into practice through policies and techniques that include pay ranges, pay increase guidelines, individual incentives, and group gainsharing programs.

INDIVIDUAL PAY POLICIES

At the individual level, pay policies need to address two issues. Should a pay system permit employees doing the same work to receive different levels of pay? If so, what criteria should be used to determine these differences? Performance? Seniority? Some combination of the two?

Many employers pay different rates to employees in the same job. These differences reflect external labour market pressures and organizational strategies.[1] Two external influences are:

1. Variations in the quality (skills, abilities, experience) among applicants in the external market.
2. Recognition that employers place differing values on these variations in quality.

Differences in rates paid to employees on the same job also occur in response to the following organizational factors:

1. Policies to recognize individual differences in experience, skill, and performance with pay.
2. Employees' expectations that longer seniority and/or higher performance deserve greater pay.

So pay differences permit managers to recognize differences among employees.

Flat Rates

In some jobs, all employees receive a single flat rate of pay. For example, all cafeteria assistants at the North Vancouver School Board receive an hourly rate of $9.16; all sheet metal mechanics at Versatile Pacific Shipyards earn $17.40 per hour. Paying the same rate within a job does not mean all job incumbents have the same performance or experience. Rather, the parties have chosen to ignore individual differences. Unions argue for flat rates on the grounds that performance measures are biased. In other circumstances, a flat rate of pay may be assigned where individuals earn separate bonuses or incentives. Many sales jobs are paid in this manner. Employees receive a flat hourly rate plus a percentage of sales.

Policy Effects

Choosing between paying a flat rate or different rates depends on the objectives established for the pay system. Recognizing individual differences in performance and/or experience assumes that workers are not interchangeable and equally productive. By using pay to recognize experience and/or performance differences, managers are trying to encourage an experienced, efficient work force. All managers may desire such a work force; the difference is that some use differences in pay to help achieve it.

A variety of techniques provide managers with the option to pay different amounts to employees in the same job. The most common technique is pay ranges.

INDIVIDUAL PAY TECHNIQUES

Ranges set limits on the rates an employer will pay for a particular job. Exhibit 15–1 shows pay ranges constructed for the pay level and structure designed in the last chapter. Five pay ranges (I–V), one for each key job (A, D, G, M, and N), have been established.

Pay Ranges

Designing ranges is relatively simple.[2] There is no "best" approach, but two basic steps are typically involved.

1. Develop Classes or Grades. In Exhibit 15–1, the horizontal axis is the job structure generated through job evaluation. A grade or class is a grouping of different jobs; thus, each grade may be made up of a number of jobs. There are five grades (I–V) in Exhibit 15–1; grade I has one job (A) in it; Grade II has jobs B, C, D, E, and F; and so on. The jobs in each grade are considered substantially similar for pay purposes. They may have approximately the same job evaluation points (e.g., within 30 or 50 points in a 700-point job evaluation plan).

Each grade has its own pay range and all the jobs within the grade also

EXHIBIT 15–1
Establishing Ranges

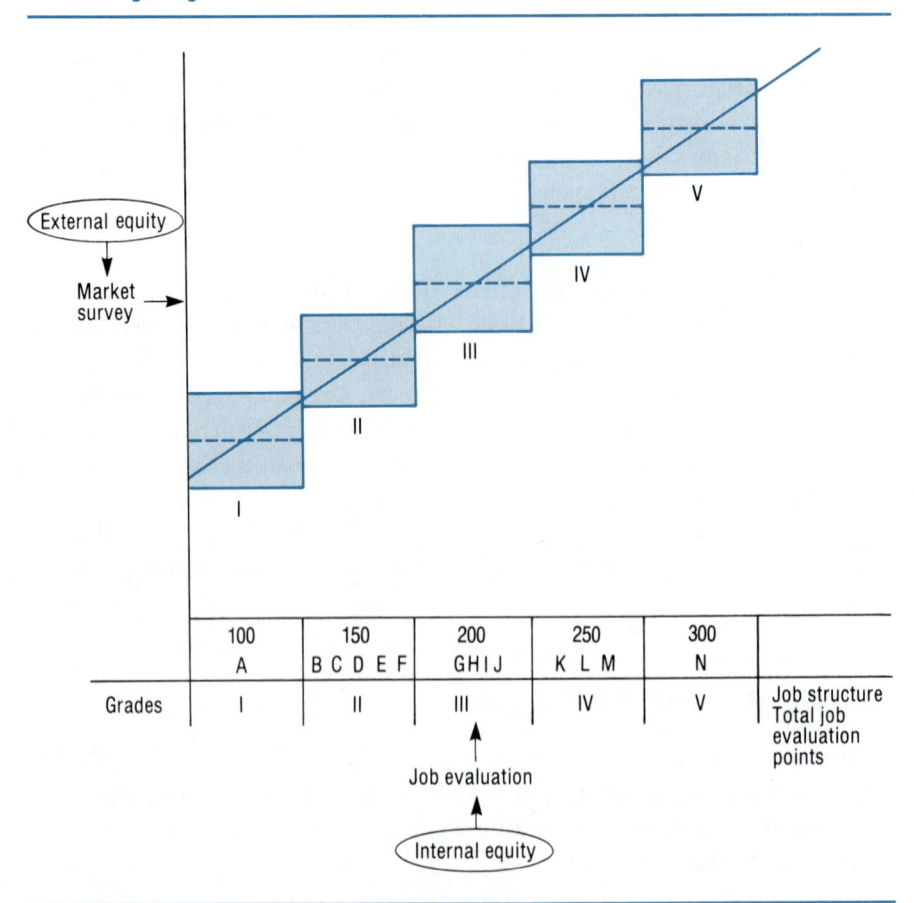

EXHIBIT 15-2
Typical Pay Grade Range

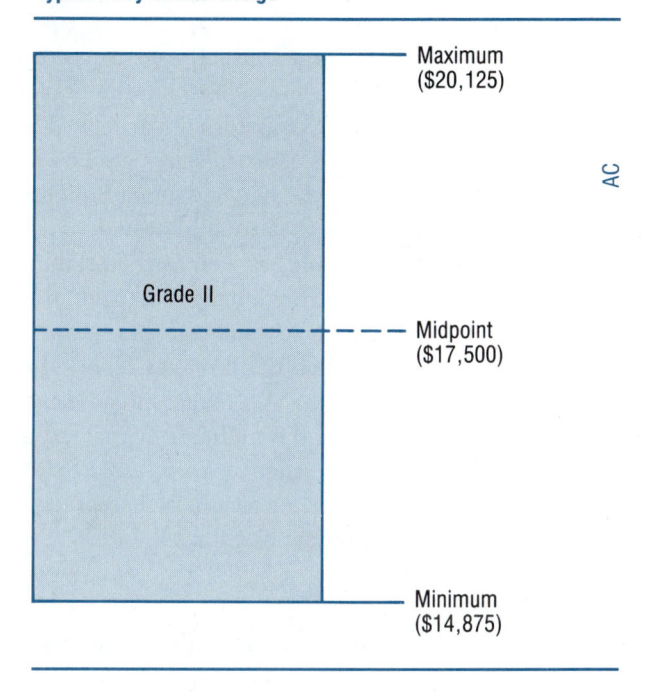

Grade II

Maximum ($20,125)

AC

Midpoint ($17,500)

Minimum ($14,875)

have that same range. Jobs within a grade (e.g., jobs K, L, and M in Grade IV) should be dissimilar from jobs in other grades (e.g., jobs G, H, I, and J) and will have a different pay range.

The correct number of job grades depends on the circumstances. Designing the grade structure that fits each organization involves trial and error. The use of grades recognizes the imprecision in job evaluation. Some consulting firms, professing a high degree of confidence in their job evaluation system's ability to generate precise measurements, argue that grades are meaningless.[3] They state that each job evaluation point has a dollar value, and each job with its own point total should have its own range. Thus, they would say the number of ranges should equal the number of jobs.

2. *Set Midpoints, Maximums, and Minimums.* Exhibit 15–2 shows a typical pay range with a maximum, midpoint, and minimum. Ranges permit managers to pay on the basis of employee experience or performance. The pay range for any job should approximate the range of differences in performance and/or experience that managers wish to recognize. For example, a job of plant manager accommodates a wide variation in performance level and experience, so the pay range for this job may be quite large. But there is less latitude in the job of insurance claims processor, and consequently a smaller

pay range for processors. Ranges also act as control devices. A range maximum sets the lid on what the employer is willing to pay for the job; the range minimum sets the floor.

The midpoint rates for each range are usually set to correspond to the employer's pay policy line. The policy line represents the organization's pay level policy relative to what competitors pay for similar jobs. The maximums and minimums (the range width or spread) are usually based on a combination of what other employers are doing and some judgement about what makes sense for a particular organization. Surveys usually provide data on both the actual maximum and minimum rates paid, as well as the established ranges.[4] Some compensation professionals use the actual rates paid, particularly the 75th and 25th percentiles (if available), to establish the maximum and minimum; others use the average of the established ranges reported in the survey as a starting point to design the ranges. The range spread can vary from 10 percent to 50 percent on either side of the midpoint with ±20 to 30 percent of the midpoint most common. Wider range spreads, ±30 to 50 percent are common for managerial/professional/technical jobs, whereas ±10 to 20 percent are common in office/clerical/production jobs.[5]

Progression through Ranges

Once ranges are established, the next issue is to decide how employees will move through the range. Two criteria are commonly used, seniority and merit.

Seniority pay increases are based on experience or seniority on the job. Seniority-based pay increases recognize the value of an experienced, stable work force. However, as the work force grows older, it also grows more expensive. So without turnover or productivity increases, unit labour costs will increase under seniority-based systems.

Merit pay increases link pay to employee job performance. Merit pay—pay for performance—will be discussed in more detail later. If pay is tied to productivity increases, then unit labour costs are less likely to increase than they will in seniority-based systems.

The choice of which criteria to use—merit, seniority, or some combination of the two—depends on the objectives of the pay system. If managers want to try to reinforce performance improvements with pay, then some part of pay must be linked to performance. If they also wish to ensure a stable, experienced work force, then seniority needs to be included, too.

Pay Increase Guidelines

Most employees have come to expect annual pay increases. A variety of pay increase guidelines exist.[6] One, the *general increase*, typically is found in unionized firms. A contract is negotiated that specifies an across-the-board (equal for all employees) percentage increase for each year the contract is in effect. Another method of general increase is the *cost-of-living adjustment* (COLA). With COLA, increases are triggered by changes in the consumer price index (CPI).[7] Some contracts have wage adjustments corresponding to the full increase in the CPI. More recently, a number of contracts have included limited CPI-based increases. Under these formulas, wage increases are triggered only when the CPI rises beyond a specified percent. Exhibit 15–3 shows an example of this type of COLA.

Another increase guideline, the seniority or automatic increase, was discussed above. For example, a pay range might be divided into 10 equal steps and employees moved to higher steps based on their seniority on the job.

With increasing competition, many firms have shifted to pay increases based on performance. These are most commonly applied to managerial and professional staff. But pay increases based on merit are also replacing seniority and general increases for production and clerical employees. One survey reports that at least half of Canada's major employers are using performance-based pay increases compared with only one quarter of those surveyed in the early 1980s.[8]

Most performance-based pay increase guidelines use performance evaluations as the indicator of performance. The largest salary increase is awarded to employees in the highest performance category, the second highest increase is awarded to those in the second highest category, and so on.

Some firms also vary the amount of increase with the employee's position in the pay grade range using a *merit guide chart matrix*. An example of this matrix used by Royal Trust appears in Exhibit 15–4. Xerox Canada, Scott Paper, the Bank of British Columbia, and a growing number of other major firms in this country have similar merit guide charts. Merit guide charts attach higher pay increases to higher performance evaluation ratings. But within each pay grade, merit guide charts also assign relatively lower increases to employees in the upper region of the pay range. For example, "competent" employees in the lower part of the pay grade range receive a larger increase (D percent) than those in the upper part of the range (E percent). The idea behind this practice is that employees in the upper portion of a pay range are expected to be superior performers.

Re-Earnable Bonuses

With merit guide charts, average employees are less likely to receive above-average pay within the range. Nevertheless, those who performed well a few years ago might still receive salaries above the midpoint in the pay grade even if their recent performance has been marginal.

To ensure the highest salaries within a pay grade go only to employees with the best performance within the past year, some companies have established a system of re-earnable bonuses.[9] Re-earnable bonus systems typically include a combination of salary increase and cash award. At CNCP Telecommunications, for instance, employees with good performance ratings receive a salary increase plus a cash award calculated as a percentage of annual

EXHIBIT 15–3
Cost-of-Living Adjustments Clause

Cost of Living Allowance

1. Effective 29 June 1987 and terminating 23 July 1988, a Cost of Living Allowance (COLA) formula will apply for each employee covered by this Collective Agreement.
2. Payments generated by the COLA formula shall only be paid for hours actually worked and shall not be used in the calculation of overtime rates, vacation and Statutory Holiday pay, or in the calculation of any pay allowance or benefit provided for in this Collective Agreement.
3. The COLA calculation shall be based on the Consumer Price Index for Canada, All Items, 1971 = 100, published by Statistics Canada (hereinafter referred to as CPI).
4. The COLA payment shall be equal to one cent (1¢) for each 0.30 point rise in the CPI as hereinafter determined, adjusted downward to the nearest tenth of a cent.
5. The calculation of the COLA and timing of payment shall be as follows:
    a. The COLA payable from 29 June 1987 to 4 October 1987 shall be calculated on the difference between the CPI for May 1987 and one hundred and six percent (106%) of the CPI for February 1987 provided that the CPI for May is the greater of the two values.
    b. The COLA payable from 5 October 1987 to 27 December 1987 shall be calculated on the difference between the CPI for August 1987 and one hundred and six percent (106%) of the CPI for February 1987 provided that the CPI for August 1987 is the greater of the two values.
    c. The COLA payable from 28 December 1987 to 3 April 1988 shall be calculated on the difference between the CPI for November 1987 and one hundred and six percent (106%) of the CPI for February 1987 provided that the CPI for November 1987 is the greater of the two values.
    d. The COLA payable from 4 April 1988 to 23 July 1988 shall be calculated on the difference between the CPI for February 1988 and one hundred and six percent (106%) of the CPI for February 1987 provided that the CPI for February 1988 is the greater of the two values.
    e. There shall be no reduction of the COLA due to a decline of the CPI during a measuring period.
6. In the event that Statistics Canada does not issue the CPI on or before the beginning of periods referred to in clause 5, any pay adjustments required shall be made at the beginning of the first pay period after publication of the CPI, and shall be retroactive to the commencement of the appropriate period. In the event that a retroactive adjustment is made by Statistics Canada to the CPI, it is agreed that the COLA already paid to employees will not be adjusted retroactively.

Source: Collective agreement between Alcan Smelters and Chemicals Ltd. and Local 1, Canadian Association of Smelter and Allied Workers; effective July 24, 1985, to July 23, 1988.

EXHIBIT 15-4
Merit Pay Guide Chart Matrix

	\multicolumn{6}{c}{Position within Grade Range}
Performance Level	80–87.9%	88–95.9%	96–103.9%	104–111.9%	112–120%	Above Range Maximum
Distinguished	A%	A%	A%	A%	A%	0 to A%
Commendable	B	B	B	C	C	0 to C
Competent	D	D	D	E	E	0 to E
Adequate	F	F	F	0	0	0
Marginal	G	0	0	0	0	0

Note: Percentages A through G represent merit increases based on budget constraints. Employees who receive a "distinguished" performance rating will receive a larger percent increase (A%) than someone who performs at an "adequate" level. Within most performance levels, those in the lower part of the grade range will receive a larger increase than those in the higher part of the range.

Source: Royal Trust Salary Guide, 1986.

salary. Satisfactory performance is awarded the salary increase without the cash award. Employees with a marginal performance rating receive less than the full salary increase.

Lump Sum Payments

Another individual reward practice is to give employees the option of receiving their pay increase in a lump sum rather than an increment in the regular pay cheque.[10] To correct for the higher present value of the reward, the lump sum is usually less than the total value of the increase for the year. In the following year, employees can fold the previous year's increase into the base salary. Alternatively, they can receive the two years of increases as a lump sum.

The effectiveness of the lump sum and re-earnable bonus payment methods have not yet been systematically researched. However, Lawler claims large cash awards can enhance motivation by increasing the salience of the reward. The re-earnable bonus has the added advantage of providing employers with greater control over who receives the highest salary within each pay grade.

External, Internal, and Employee Equity

At this point, we have covered three major elements of the pay model introduced in the previous chapter. External equity is translated through market surveys into the pay policy line. It establishes the firm's pay position relative to its competitors for human resources in the labour market. Next, internal equity is translated through job analysis and evaluation into the pay structure. Internal equity addresses the differences in pay among dissimilar jobs and the equality of pay among substantially equal jobs. In this chapter, employee equity has been included. Individual employee pay is determined through use of flat rates or pay ranges for those working on the same job. Ranges permit pay to be used to recognize differences in seniority and/or performance.

Before going on to discuss the pay techniques, let's step back a moment. Recall that in addition to being a major expense, pay is presumed to affect employee attitudes and behaviours. A basic premise underlying much of pay administration is that if it is properly designed and managed, pay can affect employee performance and work satisfaction. Let's examine the concepts and research related to this assumption.

PAY-FOR-PERFORMANCE

Can employee performance be affected by properly designed and managed pay programs?[11] One way to examine this question is to consider three subquestions: (1) Is pay important to employees? (2) Should pay increases be based on performance? and (3) Are pay increases based on performance?

Is Money Important?

From the motivational theories discussed in Chapter Five, it is apparent there is no instinctive or basic need for money. Money becomes important insofar as it can satisfy recognized needs. Lawler infers from research that money is capable of satisfying physiological, security, and esteem needs.[12] If these needs are satisfied by other means, or if they are not currently prepotent (e.g., other needs are greater), then money is seen as having lower instrumental value and is not particularly useful in motivating performance or any other behaviour.[13]

If different needs are, in fact, of varying importance across individuals, this information could be used to design a pay-for-performance system. Lawler argues for a two-step sequential process: (1) identify groups for which differential need strength is evident, and (2) devise selection programs that will identify those individuals who have needs that can be satisfied through a pay system tied to performance.[14] Such a program, if successful, would permit organizations that subscribe to a pay-for-performance philosophy to implement a pay system designed to use pay for improved performance.

There is some evidence that organizations may be experiencing problems by assuming that employees place a high value on monetary rewards. One study suggests that managers overestimate the importance of pay to subordinates.[15] Given a belief that pay can motivate performance, supervisors become disillusioned when improved performance does not result from pay increases. This failure results in a general condemnation of pay as a motivator.

In reality, however, it may be more advantageous not to view money as the supreme motivator, but rather as one of the numerous factors in the work environment that affects employee motivation.

Should Pay Increases Be Based on Performance?

Given that money can satisfy at least a subset of basic needs, the question now becomes *should* salary increases be based on level of performance? Substantial evidence exists that management and workers alike believe pay *should* be tied to performance.

Dyer, Schwab, and Theriault asked 180 managers from 72 companies to rate 9 possible factors in terms of the importance they should receive in determining the size of salary increases.[16] As Exhibit 15–5 indicates, workers believed the most important factor for salary increases should be job performance. Following close behind is a factor that presumably would be picked up in job evaluation (nature of job) and a motivational variable (amount of effort expended).

In a second study of managers, similar results were obtained.[17] Quality of job performance and productivity were ranked first and third (of seven alternatives), respectively, as criteria that should be used for determining salaries of managers in the private sector.

The role that performance levels should assume in determining pay increases is less clear-cut for blue-collar workers. Unions frequently oppose merit and pay-for-performance plans. Much of the discontent with performance-based plans may be a reaction to the specific type of plan and the way it is administered. Lawler notes, "In many situations opposition to (merit) pay comes about because the employees feel they cannot trust the company to administer the schemes properly."[18]

EXHIBIT 15–5
Mean Range of Criteria that *Should Be* Used to Determine Size of Salary Increases

Criteria	Mean Rating
1. Level of job performance	6.23
2. Nature of job	5.91
3. Amount of effort expenditure	5.56
4. Cost of living	5.21
5. Training and experience	5.15
6. Increase outside organization	4.64
7. Budgetary considerations	4.53
8. Increases inside organization	3.69
9. Length of service	3.31

Source: L. Dyer, D. P. Schwab, and R. D. Theriault, "Managerial Perceptions regarding Salary Increase Criteria," *Personnel Psychology* 29 (1976), pp. 233–42.

Is Pay Based on Performance?

Many of the studies that attempt to determine if pay is tied to performance support the conclusions of the classic study by Georgopoulos, Mahoney, and Jones.[19] In this study, 621 production employees on an incentive system were asked to complete a questionnaire to determine how important high and low performance were for a series of outcomes, one of which was long-run pay increases. The findings indicated that employees who saw high performance as important to obtaining salary increases tended to be higher producers. Since this study, numerous other research projects have resulted in similar conclusions.[20]

Based on this evidence, the pay-for-performance concept appears to have considerable support. It reflects the notion from expectancy theory that motivation increases under conditions where valued rewards are linked to performance (Chapter Five). A few writers are skeptical, however. They argue the disadvantages of developing a merit-based system outweigh the advantages.[21]

Negative Evidence

Most of the evidence arguing against a pay-for-performance system is based on problems encountered in implementing the system. Hamner offers the best summary of these problems. He lists four problems that make it difficult to implement a performance-contingent pay system.

1. Pay is not perceived as contingent on performance. Many employers adopt a policy of secrecy in their pay administration practices.[22]

Hamner argues that the secrecy surrounding pay increases may lead employees to believe there is no direct relationship between pay and performance. It may lead to beliefs that administrators are trying to hide bad pay practices under a cloak of secrecy.

2. Performance evaluations are viewed as biased. If performance evaluations are based on subjective judgements by supervisors, and not on objective criteria (e.g., units produced) many employees believe ratings have the potential to be biased. Substantial evidence exists to support this position. At least one study suggests this problem can be overcome, however, if performance criteria are carefully defined so raters understand fully the different work behaviours being tapped.[23]

If performance evaluations are viewed as biased, then the pay-performance link is particularly difficult to establish. If employees view the evaluations they receive as arbitrary, little incentive exists to improve performance. Chapter Eleven discussed additional issues in evaluating performance.

3. Rewards are not viewed as reward. Assume, for the moment, that pay is supposed to be based on performance in Company A. It would be expected that A's employees compare the pay increase they receive with that of other employees in Company A. What happens if employees have an inflated view of their own performance relative to others in the company? They conclude that pay is not tied to performance; otherwise their pay would be higher.

This is the problem Meyer uncovered in a study of several occupational groups in a number of companies.[24] People were asked to rate themselves on job performance relative to other employees doing similar work. Across all occupational groups, in excess of 95 percent of the employees rated themselves above average. For each of the groups, at least 68 percent of the employees thought they were in the top 25 percent of all similarly situated employees in performance. This is statistically impossible. But the important point is that these employees expect a pay increase commensurate with their perceived performance and do not receive it, even though the employer thinks it was given.

4. *Organizations fail to recognize sources of motivation other than money.* One of the difficulties faced in compensation is the belief that money is a general panacea, capable of compensating for all other organizational problems. If one thing has been learned from the problems with poor productivity, absenteeism, and sabotage in the automobile industry, it is that money may attract workers to unsatisfying jobs; it may also help to retain workers, at least in the short run. But the ability of money to motivate under conditions where numerous other factors work in opposition is limited at best. Money can be a motivator, but not to the exclusion of other factors, including the job itself. A pay system must complement a well-designed job, rather than compensate for one that is poorly designed.

PAY AND SATISFACTION

Besides performance, pay is presumed to affect employee attitudes toward work. Particularly important is satisfaction and dissatisfaction, since certain employee behaviours may be related to these attitudes. Lawler derived a model, shown in Exhibit 15-6, based on his review of pay satisfaction and dissatisfaction research.[25] He makes the following general findings:

1. Satisfaction with pay is a function of how much is received, how much others are perceived to receive, and perceptions of what should have been received.
2. Satisfaction with pay can influence overall job satisfaction as well as absenteeism, recruitment, and turnover.
3. The evidence generally supports the view that pay dissatisfaction is related to turnover. It clearly indicates, however, the two are not always

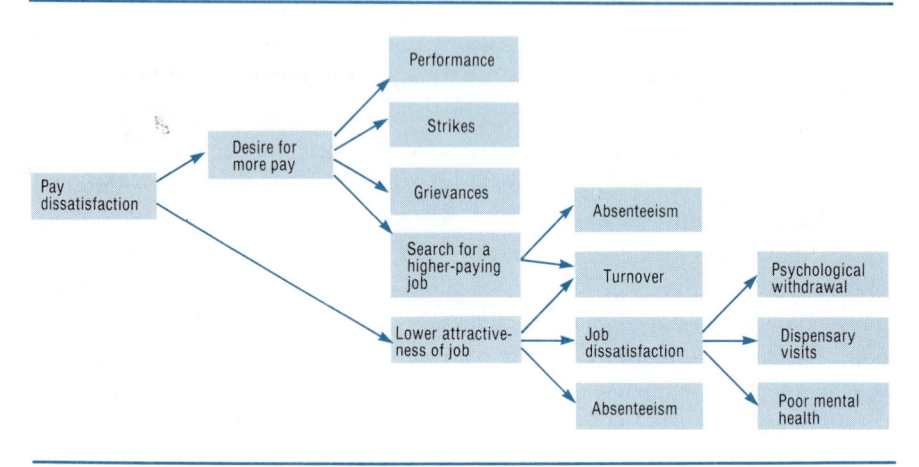

EXHIBIT 15–6
Consequences of Pay Dissatisfaction

Source: E. Lawler, *Pay and Organizational Effectiveness* (New York: McGraw-Hill, 1971), p. 233.

highly related. The relationship seems to be strongly affected by the importance the employee attaches to pay.

4. The stronger causal tendency is *that performance causes pay satisfaction rather than pay satisfaction causing performance.* Interestingly, pay satisfaction appears to be related to performance only when pay is based on employee performance.

5. The evidence quite clearly shows that pay dissatisfaction can lead employees to join unions, go on strike, and file grievances.

Lawler concludes that pay dissatisfaction can be quite costly to organizations. It erodes commitment to work and may lead to absenteeism, turnover, and even lower productivity.

But what does the pay satisfaction/dissatisfaction research reveal about designing fair and equitable pay systems? Not much. Most of the studies fail to distinguish among internal pay comparisons, external market comparisons, individual pay, the mix of different pay forms, or how pay is administered.[26] For example, Dyer and Theriault found that the perceived adequacy of management of the pay system and the adequacy of the performance evaluation plan also affected pay satisfaction.[27]

In sum, there is evidence to support the premise that pay is linked to employee performance and satisfaction. However, in the case of the pay and performance relationship, certain potential problems often make it difficult to design a pay-for-performance system. The relationship between certain aspects of pay (level, structure, amount, and form) and satisfaction needs further research.[28]

The remainder of this chapter examines three topics: incentive pay plans, administering the pay system, and executive pay. First we will discuss incentive plans; they are another method, in addition to ranges, used to recognize differences in employee performance.

INCENTIVES

The idea of basing pay increases upon improvement in performance is an old and well-established practice.[29] Hundreds of formulas exist for calculating payments to employees based on performance.[30] Incentives can be based on an individual's performance or on the operating results of a work team, plant, or even the entire corporation.

Individual Incentives

Perhaps the oldest form of compensation is the individual incentive plan, in which the employee is paid for units produced. Today, individual incentives take several forms: piecework, production bonus, standard hour plans, commissions, and suggestion plans.

Piecework and Production Bonus

In piecework, an employee is guaranteed a rate of pay for performing an expected minimum output. This minimum output is usually called a *standard*.[31] For production over the standard, the employee is paid so much per piece produced. The standard is established through work measurement studies and collective bargaining. The base rate and piece rates may be developed by surveys of compensation practices as well as financial analysis of revenues and expenses.

A variation of the straight piece rate is the differential piece rate. In this plan, the employer pays a smaller piece rate up to the standard and then a higher piece rate above the standard.

Standard Hour Plans

Rather than assigning a reward directly to each unit produced, standard hour plans assign a unit of time the task should take to complete. These standard hour time units are calculated from industrial engineering studies of the job or are estimated from past experience.

Standard hour plans are commonly used to pay automobile mechanics. Each task, such as an engine tune-up or brake repair, is assigned a standard hour time unit. These units are found in a "blue book" established by the industry. At the end of each pay period, pay cheques are calculated by multiplying the hourly rate of pay times the total number of standard hour time units (rather than by the actual number of hours worked).

Many companies in the Canadian mining industry use another type of standard hour plan to reward productive miners. Miners receive a regular salary based on the number of hours worked plus a bonus based on the ratio of standard hour time units to hours actually worked. For example, a productive miner might complete enough tasks during 160 actual hours of work to accumulate 240 standard hour time units. This means the miner will earn a 50 percent bonus in addition to his or her regular salary.

Commissions

Another type of individual incentive, commonly used in sales jobs, is the commission. Straight commission is the equivalent of straight piecework and is typically calculated as a percentage of sales. Salespeople in realty and brokerage firms, auto dealerships, and insurance companies are often paid straight commission.

More often, employees receive a combination of straight salary and commission.[32] Typically, sales staff in Canadian manufacturing and wholesale firms receive between 20 and 40 percent of their annual income from commissions. Many employees in retail sales, particularly clothing and consumer goods, also receive a combination of salary and commission. Higher commissions can be earned by selling certain products or services. These extra incentives are known as "spiffs" and are used by firms to move overstocked or more profitable inventory faster.

Suggestion Systems

One incentive found in a variety of Canadian firms is the employee suggestion system.[33] This incentive tries to encourage employees to think creatively about how to make the organization more effective. Typically, a suggestion is submitted in writing and is screened by a committee to determine its value. If the idea is implemented, the employee receives a financial reward based on a percentage of the first year's savings. For example, suggestions at British Columbia Railway are awarded 15 percent of the first year's estimated savings up to a maximum of $10,000. If the savings are difficult to calculate, the employee receives a lump sum payment based on the suggestion committee's estimate of its value. The maximum award at B.C. Railway for immeasurable savings is $500. Some firms use a point rating system to award suggestions with immeasurable savings. As Exhibit 15-7 shows, Sears Canada uses a point rating system to evaluate suggestions with immeasurable savings and

EXHIBIT 15-7

AWARD WORKSHEET
(To be completed by Evaluator)

INTANGIBLE AWARD	OR	TANGIBLE AWARD

COMPLETENESS OF IDEA (Check one)

- [2] A general idea; caused action to be taken
- [3] Idea requires further development
- [5] Suggestion used as presented

Points _____

Most suggestion awards will be determined by using the Intangible Award schedule. The Tangible Award schedule is to be used only in those instances where there is an actual measurable dollar savings of $500.00 or more after costs. Labour is defined as actual payroll eliminated and not as time freed up to do other tasks. An increase in sales would not be considered Tangible since there are too many variables such as advertising, payroll, rent, etc.

INGENUITY (Check one)

- [2] Normally used in this department
- [3] Commonly used in this unit
- [4] Commonly used by other merchants/businesses
- [5] Original idea

Points _____

TANGIBLE FACTORS	FIRST YEAR $ SAVINGS	IMPLEMENTATION $ COSTS*
LABOUR (Actual payroll saved):		
MATERIAL (Forms, postage, printing expense, etc.)		
OTHER: (Explain)		
TOTAL of first year savings		

USE (Check one, whichever applies the most.)

Degree of Use

Great*	Moderate	Small	
40	25	12	Personal Convenience/Time Savings/Accuracy
45	27	14	Product Appearance/Presentation
50	30	17	Safety/Security
60	33	20	Customer Satisfaction
75	36	23	Product/Equipment Reliability
90	40	27	New or Increased Product Sales

*Great to be used only when significant changes are made.

Points _____

*If there are no implementation costs, indicate "None" in appropriate area.

APPLICATION (Check one)

- [1] One Activity/Department/Division
- [2] Several Departments/Divisions
- [3] Entire Unit
- [4] Several Units (Group/Headquarters approval only)
- [5] National (Headquarters approval only)

Application Factor _____

FOR SUGGESTION COMMITTEE USE ONLY

Total Points _____ X Application _____   Total savings _____ Less costs _____

_____ Award   Net savings _____ X 10% = _____ Award

AMOUNT OF AWARD $ _____ APPROVED BY _____ DATE _____

Suggestion Program Administrator
(Suggestion Chairperson)

Source: Sears Canada.

offers 10 percent of first-year savings for suggestions with measurable savings. Individual suggestions may receive as much as $10,000.

The literature contains many examples of successful systems. In 1985, Northern Telecom reported savings of $2.7 million from the 3,900 suggestions implemented during the previous year. In return, the firm paid more than $500,000 in rewards. The Canadian Government's suggestion plan, which has been administered by the Treasury Board since 1952, yielded savings of $12 million in 1984. At Canadian Pacific Ltd., which has been rewarding employee suggestions since 1934, an estimated $2.3 million was saved in 1984.

Effective management is essential to the success of a suggestion system. The process must be clearly explained to all employees. Winning suggestions should be communicated and publicly celebrated to facilitate role modelling. For example, the success of Northern Telecom's suggestion plan is partially attributed to its annual suggestion system awards dinner. Most of all, the system must be fair. The reasons for rejecting an idea must be carefully explained. The organization must also be careful that everyone who proposes a valuable suggestion gets rewarded for it.

Problems with Individual Incentives

There is little doubt that many individual incentive schemes do motivate employees. Nevertheless, they can also create problems.[34] The quantity of sales or output may increase, but other aspects of performance may be ignored. Piecework may increase the number of units produced per day, but the quality of the product may decrease. Sales commissions may increase the amount of goods sold, but reduce the employee's motivation to service accounts or stock inventory. Consistent with expectancy theory (Chapter Five), incentives tend to draw effort toward those things that get rewarded and away from other job duties.

The standard hour plan seems to have this effect on the safety of employees in the Canadian mining industry.[35] The plan is credited with improving productivity, but it has also been linked with the number and severity of occupational accidents among miners. By motivating miners to complete more jobs in less time, the standard hour plan encourages miners to ignore safety procedures. For example, as one of the few sites *without* special incentives, the Kidd Creek mine near Timmins, Ontario, has one of the *lowest* accident records in metal mining. Based on the evidence, a 1981 commission on mining safety recommended the standard hour plan be terminated in the mining industry.

Group Incentives

Incentives are often more effectively paid to work groups than to individual employees.[36] Exhibit 15–8 summarizes some factors influencing whether to

EXHIBIT 15–8
Factors Influencing Aggregation Level

Characteristic	Individual Level of Incentives Appropriate	Group Level of Incentives (Unit, Department, Organization) Appropriate
Performance measurement	Good measures of individual performance exist. Task accomplishment not dependent on performance of others.	Output is group collaborative effort. Individual contributions to output cannot be assessed.
Organizational adaptability	Individual performance standards are stable. Production methods and labour mix relatively constant.	Performance standards for individuals change to meet environmental pressures on relatively constant organization objectives. Production methods and labour mix must adapt to meet changing pressures.
Organizational commitment	Commitment strongest to individual's profession or superior. Supervisor viewed as unbiased and performance standards readily apparent.	High commitment to organization built upon sound communication of organizational objectives and performance standards.
Union status	Nonunion. Unions promote equal treatment. Competition between individuals inhibits "fraternal" spirit.	Union or nonunion. Unions less opposed to plans that foster cohesiveness of bargaining unit and distribute rewards evenly across group.

Source: George T. Milkovich and Jerry Newman, *Compensation*, 2nd ed. (Plano, Tex.: Business Publications, 1987).

use individual or group incentives. Group incentives are preferred where individual output is difficult to measure. For example, chemical plants and other process technologies are better suited to group incentives because employee tasks are highly interdependent. Rather than focussing on each employee's output, the entire plant's operating results are used to calculate financial rewards.

Group incentives come in many forms. Some focus on cost savings, others on company profits, and still others emphasize quantity of production. However, the basic premise underlying each of these plans is to share the gains with employees.[37] To many, gainsharing is part of a total management approach or philosophy, not just a group incentive scheme. In addition to the factors listed in Exhibit 15–8, gainsharing tends to be more effective where the level of trust is high, production is relatively stable, and employees have both the technical skills and opportunity to control production and costs.[38]

Productivity-Sharing Plans

Some gainsharing plans, such as the Scanlon, Rucker, and Improshare plans, focus on cost savings and productivity improvement. Each plan has its own formula for calculating group productivity. Scanlon plans typically divide payroll costs by the value of production. Rucker plans determine productivity gains by subtracting raw material costs from net sales to arrive at a value-added figure. Improshare compares the standard hours required to produce the output with the actual hours (similar to standard hour plans described earlier). According to one estimate, only a few dozen productivity-sharing plans exist in Canada.[39]

For each of these productivity-sharing plans, the employees and company share financial gains based on a predetermined formula. Bonuses are distributed monthly or quarterly using a moving average to smooth out dramatic changes in payouts. Some of the gains are held in escrow for a year as a buffer in case productivity falls.[40]

A Closer Look at the Scanlon Plan

The Scanlon plan is perhaps the best-known productivity-based gainsharing system. Developed in the 1930s by Joseph Scanlon, a union leader in the steel industry, the plan is both a group suggestion plan and an employee participation scheme.

Each unit in the plant has a production committee composed of the supervisor and employee representatives. The committee screens suggestions presented by employees and management. The savings attributed to each suggestion are paid to the work group, not just to the person who made the suggestion. The distribution of bonuses varies from one plan to the next. Some divide the gains equally among employees, while others distribute bonus amounts in proportion to hourly rates or position in the organization.

Advocates of the Scanlon plan contend there are positive results for everyone. These include increased participation by employees, less resistance to change, increased organizational effectiveness, and improved union-management relations. In general, the research is supportive, but hardly conclusive.[41]

Profit Sharing

Profit sharing is a form of gainsharing and group incentive.[42] It is defined as any arrangement where the employer shares a portion of corporate profits with a designated group of employees. The underlying philosophy is that employees who participate in profit-sharing plans identify more closely with the company and its goal of profitability. This will motivate them to reduce waste and improve productivity. As a substitute for higher salaries, profit sharing also acts as a buffer by adjusting payroll costs to the prosperity of the business. This increases the employee's burden of sharing the costs of economic recession, but it also reduces the need to lay off staff.

An estimated 30,000 profit-sharing plans exist in Canada. The majority of these limit participation to senior executives (called "top hat" plans), although the number of broad-based plans (plans that allow nonmanagement staff to participate) has increased considerably during the past decade. Profit-sharing plans differ in the way profits are distributed. In *current distribution* schemes, a percentage of profits is paid out quarterly or annually in the form of a cash bonus. Lincoln Electric Co. of Canada Ltd., which has had an all-cash plan since 1940, claims this form of distribution provides a clear incentive to employees.

Deferred profit-sharing plans (DPSPs) represent another form of distribution. DPSPs place the employee's share of profits in a trust fund for distribution at retirement or termination of employment. Basically, they are a form of money purchase pension plan (see Chapter Sixteen) and therefore must be registered with Revenue Canada. Some DPSPs also permit or require employees to add their own contributions to the pool of deferred funds.

A variation of the current distribution and DPSP approaches is the *employees' profit-sharing plan* (EPSP). As with DPSPs, EPSP contributions are placed in an investment trust rather than distributed to employees as cash income. However, unlike DPSPs, which are taxable in the year funds are withdrawn from the investment trust, EPSP contributions are taxable in the year of allocation (as are current distribution plans).

Many employers use both cash awards and deferred payments to distribute profits. These *combination plans* offer the advantages of immediate reward and income protection for the employee. Many also let employees decide the proportion of the distribution to defer. Comcheq Services Limited of Winnipeg has a broad-based profit-sharing plan that combines current and deferred distribution methods. The company allocates 10 percent of pretax profits to its employees, who have the option of withdrawing up to 50 percent of their share in cash. The remainder is registered as a DPSP and invested by trustees of the plan.[43]

The popularity of broad-based profit sharing is increasing in Canada. But is it an effective incentive system? While research on this issue is sparse, profit sharing does appear to increase employee identification with corporate goals. However, this type of gainsharing system is less likely to have incentive value to most employees in the long term, particularly in larger firms.[44] This is because the efforts of individual employees have a very indirect effect on corporate profits. For instance, even if employees cut costs and work hard, profits may still slump badly due to an economic recession or expensive but ineffective marketing program.

PAY ADMINISTRATION

As with any P/HRM area, compensation tries to improve organizational effectiveness and employee well-being. Unfortunately, pay systems often degenerate into bureaucratic burdens. Rather than focussing on the diagnostic objectives, the techniques become ends in themselves. So any discussion of compensation management must also consider administration of pay systems. Three important administrative issues will be discussed here: cost controls, communication, and participation.

Cost Controls

One of the key reasons for being systematic about pay decisions is to control costs. Pay systems have two basic approaches that serve to control costs: (1) those inherent in the design of the techniques, and (2) the formal budgeting process.

Inherent Controls

Think back to the several techniques already discussed: job analysis and evaluation, pay policy lines, ranges, pay increase guidelines, and more. In addition to their primary purposes, they also regulate managers' pay decisions. Controls are embedded in the design of these techniques.

Range maximums and minimums set the limits on the rates to be paid for each job. The maximum is an important cost control. It represents the top value the organization places on the output of the job. The skills and abilities a particular employee possesses may have greater potential value than the range maximum but in a particular job for a particular employer it is the work output that is valued and paid. Presumably, some employees in this job may be qualified for other, higher-paying jobs. However, their extraneous qualifications do not affect the value of their present job. In other words, balancing a ledger has a certain value for an employer, whether it is done by a high school graduate or a certified public accountant. Range maximums and minimums are tied to the value of the work and the skills used to perform that work.

Budgeting

Budgeting, as part of the pay system, helps to ensure that future expenditures are coordinated and controlled. Exhibit 15–9 shows an example of a budgeting process.

**EXHIBIT 15–9
An Example of Compensation Forecasting and Cycle**

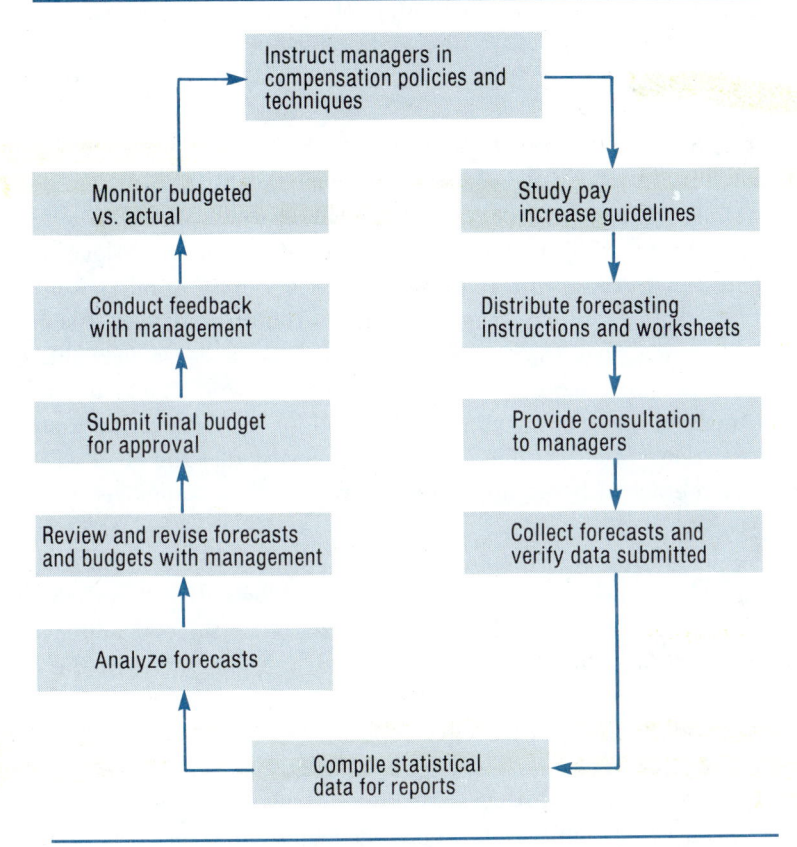

```
                    ┌─────────────────────────┐
              ┌────▶│ Instruct managers in    │────┐
              │     │ compensation policies   │    │
              │     │ and techniques          │    │
              │     └─────────────────────────┘    ▼
    ┌─────────────────┐                  ┌─────────────────┐
    │ Monitor budgeted│                  │ Study pay       │
    │ vs. actual      │                  │ increase        │
    │                 │                  │ guidelines      │
    └─────────────────┘                  └─────────────────┘
             ▲                                    │
    ┌─────────────────┐                  ┌─────────────────┐
    │ Conduct feedback│                  │ Distribute      │
    │ with management │                  │ forecasting     │
    │                 │                  │ instructions    │
    │                 │                  │ and worksheets  │
    └─────────────────┘                  └─────────────────┘
             ▲                                    │
    ┌─────────────────┐                  ┌─────────────────┐
    │ Submit final    │                  │ Provide         │
    │ budget for      │                  │ consultation    │
    │ approval        │                  │ to managers     │
    └─────────────────┘                  └─────────────────┘
             ▲                                    │
    ┌─────────────────┐                  ┌─────────────────┐
    │ Review and      │                  │ Collect         │
    │ revise forecasts│                  │ forecasts and   │
    │ and budgets     │                  │ verify data     │
    │ with management │                  │ submitted       │
    └─────────────────┘                  └─────────────────┘
             ▲                                    │
    ┌─────────────────┐                  ┌─────────────────┐
    │ Analyze         │                  │                 │
    │ forecasts       │                  │                 │
    └─────────────────┘                  │                 │
             ▲                           │                 │
             │     ┌─────────────────────┴──┐              │
             └─────│ Compile statistical    │◀─────────────┘
                   │ data for reports       │
                   └────────────────────────┘
```

Source: George T. Milkovich and Jerry Newman, *Compensation*, 2nd ed. (Plano, Tex.: Business Publications, 1987).

The cycle involves instructing managers in the use of compensation policies and techniques. The pay increase guidelines are used by the managers to forecast their employees' anticipated pay rates for the next year. Then forecasts are reviewed and summarized; eventually the pay budget for next year emerges.

Another approach to pay budgeting is to calculate the percentage increase in labour costs the employer is willing (and able) to pay. This percentage increase may be influenced by factors such as changes in the economy, the cost of living, and the firm's ability to attract and retain its employees. Once this percentage increase is determined, it is allocated to the various units in the organization.

Budgeting enables managers to foresee the financial impact of pay expenditures on the organization's performance. This encourages them to better manage the expenditure and distribution of compensation dollars.

Communication

The literature on pay administration usually exhorts employers to communicate pay information.[45] Two reasons are usually given. One is that according to some research, employees seem to misperceive the pay system.[46] For example, they tend to overestimate the pay of those with lower-level jobs and to underestimate the pay of those in higher-level jobs. In other words, they tend to think that the pay structure is more compressed than it actually is. What difference does that make? It is important because pay differentials were designed to encourage employees to seek promotions, to undertake added training, and gain experience required for higher-level positions. Furthermore, there is even some evidence to suggest that the good will engendered by the act of being open about pay also affects employee satisfaction with pay.[47]

The danger in pay communications should be obvious. If the pay system is not based on work-related or business-related logic, the wisest course may be to avoid formal, detailed communication. Nevertheless, employees are constantly getting intended and unintended messages through the pay increase they receive and the gossip floating among co-workers.

Some managers take a proactive approach. They reason that a pay system, properly designed, is intended to influence employee attitudes and behaviours. To help accomplish these objectives, employee perceptions of the pay system need to be influenced. Hence, actively telling employees about the system, its techniques, and rationale is in order.

Participation

Lawler argues persuasively that employee participation can make a difference in the success of a pay system.[48] He cites two work groups doing the same kinds of jobs and operating under similar pay plans. One group had high productivity that continued to increase; the other had low and stable productivity. The first had a long history of participation in decision making; the second had the pay plan imposed by management.[49]

According to Lawler, a design process that includes employees can be successful in overcoming resistance to change.[50] Employees are more likely to be committed to the system if they have some control over what happens.

All-Salaried Work Force

As the name implies, the all-salaried work force involves paying all employees in the organization a regular salary rather than an hourly wage. This includes removing time clocks and equalizing benefits for all staff. The objective is to improve employee commitment to the organization and promote greater unity between management and nonmanagement by adopting more egalitarian pay practices.[51]

The effects of the all-salaried approach have not been systematically researched. Several case studies indicate employee loyalty increases if this practice is part of a broader management philosophy of treating employees maturely. Lawler notes that high-technology and knowledge-based companies are more likely to put all employees on salary. For instance, IBM and Digital Equipment have adopted this practice in Canada for several years. Yet several manufacturing and processing firms in this country also pay their employees on salary. Examples include Kidd Creek Mines, Hayes-Dana, and Supreme Aluminum.[52]

Special Groups

A few groups of employees require unique pay systems because of the nature of the work performed. Engineers and scientists represent one group with special compensation needs. Since their career paths are usually distinct from most other job groups, scientific and professional jobs are often placed in a separate compensation structure. Employees on international assignment also require special compensation programs to deal with exchange rate and cost-of-living inequities. Typically, the financial well-being of these people is maintained by supplementing base pay with various premiums and allowances.[53]

A separate compensation system is also established for executives. Executive pay will be discussed as an illustration of how pay systems are tailored for special groups of employees. The point is that firms typically have several pay systems, not just one.

EXECUTIVE PAY

For purposes of compensation management, an executive is usually defined as any individual in the highest levels of management. The executive group usually includes the chief executive officer (the president or chairman of the board), chief operating officer, and vice presidents. Since executives are responsible for the direction of the organization, their compensation program must link executive actions with corporate performance.[54]

Compensation Decisions

At which competitive level should pay be set (external equity)? What should the pay structure look like (internal equity)? How much should each executive be paid (employee equity)? What forms should the compensation take (cash, benefits, and so on)? Designers of executive pay packages must address these four questions. The answers may vary with external and organizational conditions.

Pay Level

Surveys on executive compensation are regularly conducted in Canada. Most compare the base and total compensation by executive officer title, industry subgroup, and some indicator of organization size (usually sales volume). Exhibits 15–10 and 15–11 summarize the results of one executive compensation survey. Notice in both exhibits that executive compensation varies considerably by the industry and size (i.e., sales volume) of the organization.

Several studies have tried to identify the determinants of executive pay level.[55] Agarwal analyzed executive compensation as a function of three basic factors: job complexity (measured as firm size), ability to pay, and the executive's human capital (education, work experience, and so forth). These factors accounted for almost 80 percent of the variance in executive compensation with most of the variance explained by job complexity. In other words, how much executives earn depends less on their qualifications than the size of the company for which they work. The results of a more recent study, however, indicate that executive compensation levels reflect corporate performance more than size of operation when the organization is controlled by a dominant outside shareholder. In firms without dominant shareholders—that is, in firms where executives hold power—company size is the strongest predictor of executive pay.[56]

No matter which criteria are applied, a policy decision must be made regarding the level of executive pay. Once the decision is made to lead, lag, or meet the competition, other pay issues are addressed.

Pay Structure

The executive pay structure is usually based on the organizational hierarchy as an indicator of job worth. Except in very large corporations with many executives, the concept of pay grades and ranges may have little meaning in the executive pay structure.

Individual Pay and Pay Form

In executive compensation, the issues of how much each individual should receive and what form the compensation should take become intertwined. The financial performance of the firm usually plays a significant role in deter-

EXHIBIT 15-10
Executive Compensation in Canada by Position and Industry

Industry	CEO	No. 2 Executive	Top Sales/ Marketing	Top Finance	Top Industrial Relations
Food	$129,642	$105,756	$ 66,334	$ 78,260	$69,931
Rubber	135,816	115,884	73,474	71,201	47,802
Textiles	98,630	85,420	77,148	66,692	56,656
Wood	80,662	67,677	48,825	55,745	50,130
Paper	101,972	81,780	—	68,295	47,950
Printing	130,560	136,800	81,217	65,091	—
Primary metal	107,851	—	—	80,018	59,058
Fabricated metal	110,510	80,127	62,077	59,709	47,997
Machinery	100,449	53,880	75,241	66,526	56,580
Transportation	129,559	94,125	72,400	73,246	65,443
Consumer electrical	103,125	—	73,450	63,210	49,088
Industrial electrical	120,989	92,547	68,670	70,089	61,390
Mining and petroleum	203,105	111,940	—	102,682	56,300
Chemical	105,853	—	78,795	64,972	—
Pharmaceutical	108,863	85,795	75,529	76,081	45,102
Cosmetics	90,742	—	57,300	56,681	—
Construction	62,779	58,000	—	—	—
Wholesale	153,533	75,033	61,990	65,214	56,066
Retail	154,396	—	96,760	78,450	—
Utility	198,900	132,230	101,300	108,627	77,450
Service	101,718	75,044	65,333	65,107	55,420
General insurance	101,362	70,056	69,177	66,897	—
Life insurance	165,400	139,983	91,117	83,801	—
Other financial insurance	145,140	143,360	—	84,549	—
Miscellaneous	123,117	83,687	72,397	72,999	57,625

Note: Figures refer to the base salaries (excluding bonuses) of five top executive positions as of January 1, 1987. Varying sample sizes may affect the statistics.

Source: Sobeco Group Inc., *Management Compensation in Canada, 1987* (Toronto: Sobeco Group Inc., 1987); Sobeco Group Inc., *Remuneration of Chief Executives in Canada, 1987* (Toronto: Sobeco Group Inc., 1987). Reproduced with permission of Sobeco Group Inc.

mining the amount paid. But the form of compensation also reflects the overall strategy of the firm and often the personal circumstances of the executive. A few typical forms of executive pay are described here.

Bonuses

Executive bonuses are short-term incentives designed to reward the achievement of specific objectives over one or two years. Bonuses supplement salary and can either be paid at the end of the performance period or deferred for several years. They are typically associated with measures of corporate financial performance such as profit level, sales volume, or market share. This

EXHIBIT 15–11
Executive Compensation in Canada by Position and Sales

Company Sales Volume ($ millions)	CEO	No. 2 Executive	Top Sales/ Marketing	Top Finance	Top Industrial Relations
Under 18	$ 93,171	$ 67,859	$58,054	$53,917	$42,172
18–32	103,182	81,248	69,384	62,865	51,305
32–64	118,217	86,542	66,554	68,775	49,394
64–96	141,446	104,940	84,175	76,989	56,750
96–125	150,783	98,742	83,991	77,908	60,698
125–300	138,496	105,321	80,572	85,233	66,985
Over 300	163,610	110,014	87,896	92,835	75,628

Note: Figures refer to the base salaries (excluding bonuses) of five top executive positions as of January 1, 1987. Varying samples sizes may affect the statistics.

Source: Sobeco Group Inc., *Management Compensation in Canada, 1987* (Toronto: Sobeco Group Inc., 1987); Sobeco Group Inc., *Remuneration of Chief Executives in Canada, 1987* (Toronto: Sobeco Group Inc., 1987). Reproduced with permission of Sobeco Group Inc.

contrasts with bonuses in lower levels of management, which are often based on subjective performance evaluations (see discussion of re-earnable bonuses earlier in this chapter).

Bonuses comprise an increasing proportion of executive compensation in Canada. According to recent surveys, these short-term incentives represent approximately 25 percent of total compensation compared with 17 percent a decade ago. However, these figures pale against the extensive use of executive bonuses in the United States.[57]

Capital Accumulation

Long-term incentives have objectives similar to short-term bonuses except their value depends on corporate performance over several years. Capital accumulation is typically used as an incentive device to tie executive rewards to long-term corporate performance. The most common forms of capital accumulation are stock options and performance share plans.

Stock options give the executive the right to purchase a fixed number of the company's shares at a fixed price (called the exercise price) by a certain date. The executive gains if the stock's value rises above the exercise price. If the price does not rise sufficiently, the executive can let the stock option expire.

For example, the chief executive officer of Abitibi-Price was granted the right in 1985 to purchase 30,000 shares of the company's stock at an exercise price of $18. He can exercise this stock option at any time after one year (probably up to a five-year time limit).[58] In November 1986, Abitibi-Price shares were trading on the Toronto Stock Exchange at $26. If the option was exercised at that time, the CEO would have realized a net gain of $240,000 [($26 − $18) × 30,000].

Many types of stock options exist. Options are attractive to both executives and shareholders for the following reasons:

1. Executives must put up some of their own money as do the shareholders.
2. The value of the option, the same as that of the shareholders' stock, varies with the price of the company stock.
3. Options are a form of profit sharing, which links the executive's financial success to that of the shareholders.

Performance share units are another major long-term incentive plan. A performance share plan provides stock awards in return for meeting specific long-term financial performance targets.[59] Contingent share units are granted at the start of each performance period, which is usually between three and five years. At the end of the period, the units are converted into stock to the extent the financial targets are met. Usually, a minimum performance level must be met before any award is made.

Benefits and Perquisites

Benefits represent a substantial proportion of employee compensation and, consequently, are a major expense to the employer. The next chapter examines them in detail. Here we will examine some unique perquisites (perks) available to Canadian executives.[60] Each perk is designed to encourage executives to remain with the firm in a "tax effective" way.

No-Interest Loans. A tax effective way to get cash in the hands of executives is to grant them the right to an interest-free loan from the corporate treasury. Revenue Canada assesses income tax based on a reasonable rate of interest for the borrowed money. If the money is used for investment purposes, however, the gains to the executive could be substantial. While most loans are limited to the executive's annual salary, others have been much higher. For example, a 32-year-old vice president at Mitel borrowed nearly $1 million interest-free from the corporate treasury.

Financial Counselling. Executives who borrow a lot of interest-free money from the corporation could use professional advice on how to invest it. Some firms purchase in-house financial counselling seminars for their senior executives. More frequently, corporations cover the cost of individual counselling with a private financial consultant. According to one survey, nearly half of Canadian firms with at least $500 million sales include financial counselling as an executive perk. This compares with less than 10 percent of the firms in 1971.[61]

Vacations and Resorts. One of the better-known (and probably most widely used) perquisites is the company-paid vacation. As long as executives are involved directly in a business-related activity, the company can cover airfare and accommodation to exotic destinations as a business expense. A few corporations even lease residences in vacation spots, presumably for business purposes. Fully paid vacations are also used with increasing frequency to reward top corporate performers.

Golden Parachutes. The golden parachute is an employment contract that stipulates, among other things, the executive will receive a large severance payment in the event of a change in corporate control. These agreements address the tenuous job security of top management at the time of corporate takeovers. Concerns over the size of golden parachutes led to statutory restrictions on their use in the United States. They have not received nearly as much attention in Canada, possibly because information on executive salaries is not made public here. (Unlike the United States, Canadian securities commissions do not require the disclosure of executive compensation. Our information is largely restricted to executives of Canadian firms trading on U.S. stock exchanges.) One known Canadian example of a golden parachute is the $2 million in severance pay awarded to each of Genstar's two top executives when the firm was taken over by Imasco Ltd. of Montreal in 1985.[62]

Is Executive Pay Effective?

In 1986, Frank Stronach, founder and chief executive officer of Magna International, earned $200,000 in base salary and more than $2 million in a profit-based bonus. Edgar Bronfman, chief executive officer at Seagram Co. Ltd., took home $1,887,000 in salary and bonuses. These are two of the highest-paid executives in Canada. Does the size of their compensation correlate with the company's performance?

A simple test of this question is to compare total compensation of the chief executive officer with return on capital. Exhibit 15–12 makes this comparison for the largest Canadian firms with shares traded in the United States. (As noted above, these firms must disclose executive compensation to the U.S. Securities and Exchange Commission.) It appears that executive compensation is unrelated to this measure of corporate performance. But it is just as likely the relationship is far more complex than this simple correlation. The effectiveness of executive performance might show up in corporate performance many years down the road. Executive pay also varies by industry, as we discovered earlier. This factor should first be considered along with other possible moderating variables. Recall, for example, that firms controlled by an external shareholder are more likely to have performance-based executive pay.

EXHIBIT 15-12
Executive Pay and Corporate Financial Performance

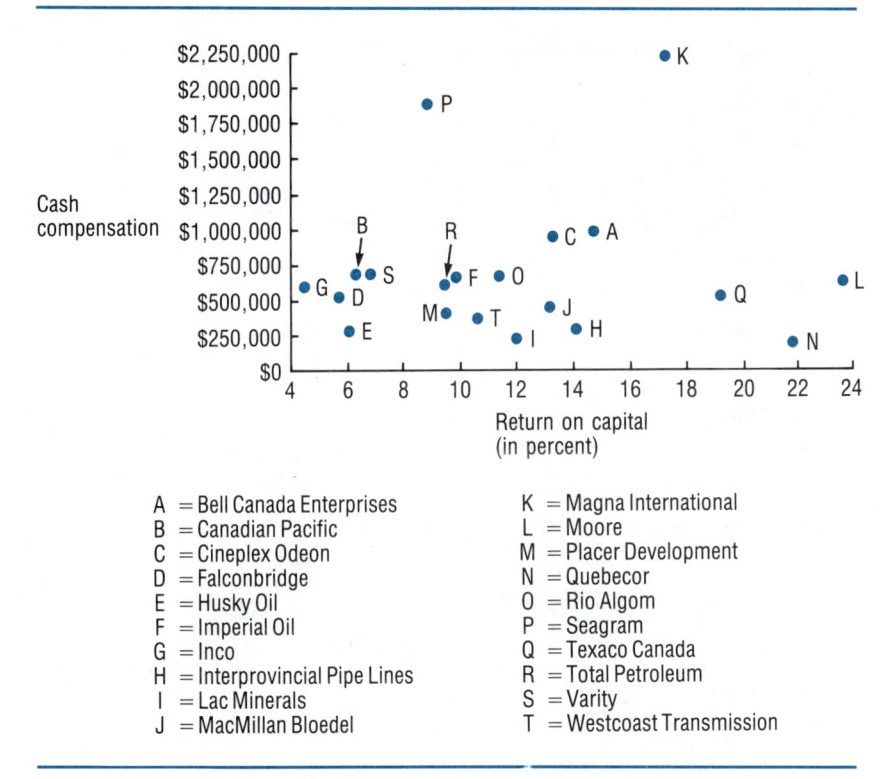

A = Bell Canada Enterprises
B = Canadian Pacific
C = Cineplex Odeon
D = Falconbridge
E = Husky Oil
F = Imperial Oil
G = Inco
H = Interprovincial Pipe Lines
I = Lac Minerals
J = MacMillan Bloedel
K = Magna International
L = Moore
M = Placer Development
N = Quebecor
O = Rio Algom
P = Seagram
Q = Texaco Canada
R = Total Petroleum
S = Varity
T = Westcoast Transmission

Note: Salaries are those of the highest paid executive in the organization.
Source: Salary data are from Caroline Meinbardis, "Options Swell Super Salaries," *Financial Times*, April 13, 1987, pp. 1, 11–13; Sheila Arnott, "What Our Top Executives Are Earning," *Financial Post*, April 13, 1987, p. 16. Return on capital data are from Financial Post, *The Financial Post 500*, Summer 1987.

A related issue is whether executives are overpaid. Again, the student must look carefully at the details of each case. The total compensation of Frank Stronach and Edgar Bronfman may look excessive, but an examination of their unique contributions to these firms may give a different perspective.

Another way to look at executive pay levels is to compare the total compensation of a chief executive officer in Canada with people in a similar position in other countries. As Exhibit 15–13 reveals, corporate heads in the United States earn the highest total compensation, about 67 percent higher than Canadian CEOs. Top executives in Switzerland receive, on average, the second highest earnings. In contrast, Australian CEOs take home (before taxes) only one half the level of pay earned by their Canadian counterparts.

EXHIBIT 15–13
Compensation of Chief Executive Officers in Selected Countries

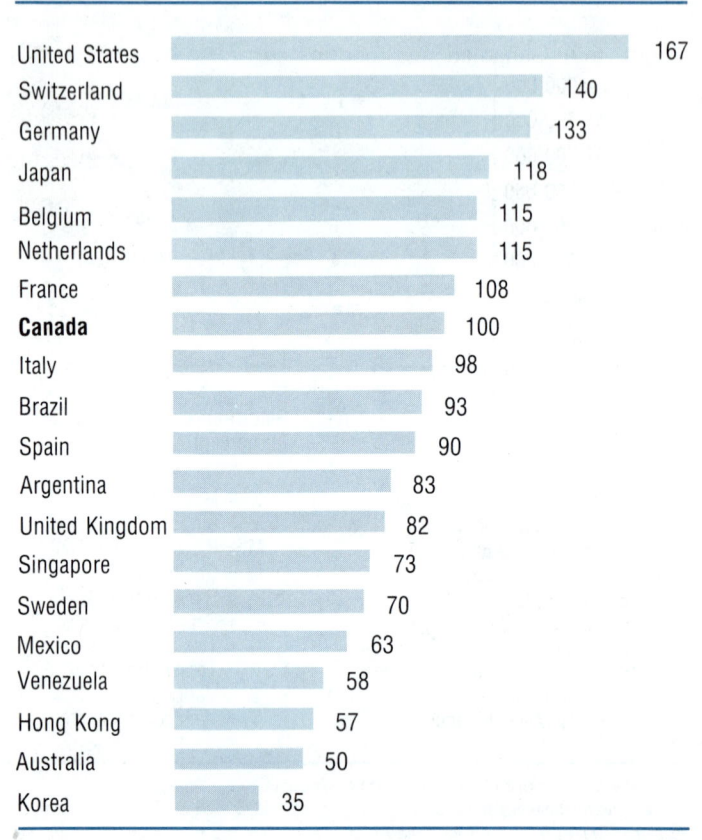

United States	167
Switzerland	140
Germany	133
Japan	118
Belgium	115
Netherlands	115
France	108
Canada	100
Italy	98
Brazil	93
Spain	90
Argentina	83
United Kingdom	82
Singapore	73
Sweden	70
Mexico	63
Venezuela	58
Hong Kong	57
Australia	50
Korea	35

Note: This exhibit compares the total cash remuneration of a Canadian CEO with a similar executive—head of a locally based company—in other countries. For all countries, company size is averaged around U.S. $100 million in sales. Cash compensation includes base salary plus bonuses and other cash payments.

Source: Adapted with permission from Towers, Perrin, Forster, & Crosby, *Paying the Chief Executive: A TPF & C Update,* June 1987 (New York: Towers, Perrin, Forster, & Crosby).

PAY EQUITY

Recall from Chapter Seven that employment equity is different from equal pay and pay equity. Employment equity refers to fairness in the occupational attainment of people. Equal pay and pay equity, on the other hand, refer to fairness in the pay-setting process. Equal pay (also called "equal pay for equal work") occurs where men and women in jobs with the same or similar duties receive similar levels of pay. Pay equity (also called "equal pay for work of equal value") occurs where men and women in jobs with the same or similar value (as determined by job evaluation) receive similar levels of pay.

Equal pay legislation was introduced in Ontario in 1951.[63] Subsequently, other jurisdictions introduced similar protection against pay discrimination either in their human rights or employment standards legislation. As Exhibit 15–14 shows, four Canadian jurisdictions currently have pay equity legislation. Quebec was first to adopt the pay equity concept in Canada when it introduced its Charter of Human Rights and Freedoms in 1975. The federal government's pay equity legislation, covering the public-service and private-sector employers in the federal jurisdiction, followed in 1978. In 1985, Manitoba introduced pay equity legislation covering public-sector organizations only. Ontario introduced two pay equity statutes in 1986 and 1987 covering

EXHIBIT 15–14
Equal Pay and Pay Equity Legislation in Canada

Jurisdiction	Legislation	Equal Pay/Pay Equity
Federal	Canadian Human Rights Act, Canada Labour Code, and Equal Wages Guidelines	Pay equity—skill, effort, responsibility, working conditions
Alberta	Individual's Rights Protection Act	Equal pay—similar or substantially similar work
British Columbia	Human Rights Act	Equal pay—similar or substantially similar work, determined by skill, effort, and responsibility
Manitoba	Pay Equity Act (public sector only)	Pay equity—composite of skill, effort, and responsibility normally required in work performance and conditions of work
	Employment Standards Act	Equal pay—same or substantially the same job, duties, or services
New Brunswick	Employment Standards Act	Equal pay—substantially the same work requiring substantially the same skill, effort, responsibility, performed under similar working conditions
Newfoundland	Human Rights Code	Equal pay—Same or similar work under same or similar working conditions, similar skill, effort, responsibility
Nova Scotia	Labour Standards Code	Equal pay—substantially the same work, requiring substantially equal skill, effort, responsibility

EXHIBIT 15–14 *(concluded)*

Jurisdiction	Legislation	Equal Pay/Pay Equity
Ontario	Public Service Pay Equity Act	Pay equity—composite of skill, effort, and responsibility normally required in work performance and conditions of work
	Bill 154 (Pay Equity Act)*	Pay equity—composite of skill, effort, and responsibility normally required in work performance and conditions of work
	Employment Standards Act*	Equal pay—substantially the same work requiring substantially the same skill, effort, responsibility, performed under similar working conditions
Prince Edward Island†	Human Rights Act	Equal pay—substantially the same work, requiring equal education, skill, experience, effort, responsibility, performed under similar working conditions
Quebec	Charter of Human Rights & Freedoms	Pay equity—performance of equivalent work (interpreted as work of equal value)
Saskatchewan	Labour Standards Act	Equal pay—similar work requiring similar skill, effort, responsibility under similar working conditions
Northwest Territories	Fair Practices Act	Equal pay—similar or substantially similar job, duties, or services
Yukon	Employment Standards Act	Equal pay—similar work requiring similar skill, effort, responsibility under similar working conditions

*Ontario's Bill 154 had not been passed at the time of writing. The name of the legislation is therefore uncertain. The equal pay provisions in Ontario's Employment Standards Act are in effect until Bill 154 is passed.

†At the time of writing, PEI had introduced Bill 75, pay equity legislation for the public sector.

public- and private-sector employers, respectively. All other Canadian jurisdictions (and the private sector in Manitoba) use the equal pay concept (although the Yukon may soon introduce pay equity legislation for the public sector).[64]

Notice in Exhibit 15–14 that skill, effort, responsibility, and working conditions factors are used to determine both job content *and* job worth. Under equal work legislation, government investigators (human rights officers) use these factors to identify the relevant job duties for comparison. Under pay equity legislation, these factors represent the critical components of the job evaluation system used to compare the worth of different jobs.

Equal Pay versus Pay Equity: An Example

The distinction between equal pay and pay equity is illustrated in the 1975 case *Re Harris et al. and Bell Canada*.[65] For many years before 1968, Bell Canada had two pay structures for people in management and supervisory positions. One pay structure consisted of predominantly male-dominated jobs and was described as "the male hierarchy." The other pay structure included mainly female-dominated jobs and was known as "the female hierarchy." Salary grades in the female structure were designated by numbers in the 50s (e.g., salary grade 51); salary grades in the male structure were designated by numbers in the teens (e.g., salary grade 15).

In 1968, Bell Canada carried out an extensive job evaluation that integrated the two groups into one pay structure for management and supervisory staff. Results indicated jobs in the "female hierarchy" were assigned lower pay rates than jobs of equal value in the "male hierarchy." For example, jobs in salary grade 54 of the female hierarchy had similar job evaluation points as jobs in salary grade 14 of the male hierarchy. Yet the maximum pay rate in the male salary grade 14 was $880 per month compared with $770 per month in the female salary grade 54. Bell Canada indicated it might increase salaries in the underpaid jobs more quickly over five years until salaries reached parity with those of male-dominated jobs of equal value.

Soon after the job evaluation was completed, three female labour relations assistants filed a pay discrimination complaint with the federal government against Bell Canada. Their job was originally in salary grade 54 of the female pay structure and, consequently, was assigned a maximum pay level $110 less per month than jobs of equal value in the male hierarchy (i.e., salary grade 14). The company had earlier indicated to the complainants that the discrepancy would be eliminated after five years, depending on Bell Canada's reconsideration of its pay structure philosophy. The women claimed they were being discriminated against as long as the discrepancy existed.

Under pay equity legislation, the facts suggest Bell Canada probably did discriminate against the complainants. Based on Bell Canada's own job evaluation, the complainants' job was in a lower salary range than male-dominated jobs of equal or comparable value. However, this case was heard at a time when equal pay legislation was in place, not pay equity. The equal pay concept only allows salary comparisons between jobs with the same or similar tasks. The jobs in salary grade 14 of the male hierarchy had similar value to the company as the labour relations assistant job, but all had quite different duties from those performed by a labour relations assistant. Consequently, no evidence of pay discrimination was found and the case was dismissed.

Features of Pay Equity Legislation

Several issues pertaining to pay equity legislation affect compensation management. The more important issues are briefly described below.

Proactive versus Reactive. Pay equity legislation may be proactive or reactive. Reactive legislation uses a complaint-oriented procedure. It relies on individuals to identify pay discrimination and lodge a complaint. Pay equity legislation in Quebec and the federal jurisdiction is mainly reactive. All equal pay statutes in Canada are also reactive. Proactive legislation requires compliance with government guidelines and includes a government agency (such as a pay equity commission) that actively monitors guideline compliance. Proactive legislation often requires the employer to file a report with the pay equity commission regarding its pay equity practices. Pay equity laws in Manitoba and Ontario are based on the proactive approach.[66]

Determining Job Worth. At the heart of pay equity legislation is the notion that two jobs with different duties can be compared in terms of their value to the organization. This is accomplished through job evaluation, as learned in Chapter Fourteen. But whose job evaluation system should be used when a complaint arises? Rather than imposing an externally designed system, the human rights commissions in Quebec and the federal jurisdiction rely on the employer's job evaluation system if that system is gender-neutral and includes factors resembling skill, effort, responsibility, and working conditions. The human rights commission may introduce its own job evaluation system to investigate the complaint if the company's system is unacceptable or nonexistent.[67] Gender-neutral job evaluation systems must be implemented in companies covered by pay equity legislation in Manitoba and Ontario. Consequently, these pay equity commissions primarily respond to complaints about the systems themselves.

Assessing Gender Dominance. Under pay equity, discrimination occurs when someone in a job category dominated by one gender earns significantly less than someone in another job category of equal value that is dominated by the other gender. This requires the government investigator to determine whether the job groups have predominantly female and male incumbents. For example, if nurses earn less than truck drivers in a particular hospital but their value is allegedly similar, the investigator must first determine that nurses are predominantly female and truck drivers are predominantly male (or vice versa). If at least one group is not gender-dominated, then the complaint is dismissed because the difference in pay could not be due to sex discrimination. All pay equity legislation in Canada defines the minimum percentage of women or men required for the job group to be labelled female or male dominated (e.g., in Manitoba, the minimum is 70 percent).

Reasonable Factors. In all pay equity legislation, pay differences between male and female employees performing work of equal value is justifiable under certain circumstances. For instance, the Canadian Human Rights Commission includes the following "reasonable factors": performance ratings, seniority, red circling, rehabilitation assignments, a demotion procedure, a temporary training position, an internal labour shortage, a position reclassification, and wage rate variations between regions.

Making Pay Equity Adjustments. Where pay discrimination is found, the discrepancy must be corrected by increasing the salaries of the underpaid employees. No pay levels may be reduced. In Manitoba and Ontario, where pay equity legislation may lead to major pay structure adjustments, limits have been established on the amount of adjustment the employer is required to make in a single year. The Manitoba law, for instance, limits wage adjustments to a maximum of 1 percent of total payroll in a 12-month period. No adjustments are required after four consecutive years of adjustments.

The Continuing Controversy

The introduction of proactive pay equity legislation in Manitoba and Ontario rekindled the controversy over equal pay for work of equal value. While few people would dispute the moral value of pay equity, there is still much disagreement over the need for legislation and the ability to control pay discrimination.[68]

Economic studies indicate women earn, on average, less than two thirds of the average earnings of men.[69] Pay equity legislation is based on the premise that a significant proportion of this wage gap is due to pay discrimination. But some sources suggest pay discrimination accounts for only five percentage points in the gap.[70]

Another concern is the subjectivity of job evaluation and related compensation management processes. Several writers describe the many ways in which gender bias may enter the pay-setting process.[71] Job analysts may distort the information documented in job descriptions based on the incumbent's gender. The selection, weighting, and anchoring of factors in the job evaluation system may further undervalue the worth of female-dominated jobs. Job evaluation committee members may also undervalue the worth of female-dominated jobs by cognitively distorting information from the job descriptions or the meaning of job evaluation factors.

Debate also surrounds the relationship between pay equity and labour market forces. Some economists argue the labour market is more or less efficient and job evaluation interferes with the natural forces of supply and demand.[72] They further suggest the labour market will eventually rid society of most pay discrimination because other employers will quickly bid up the salaries of those in undervalued jobs.

Finally, many employers worry about the cost of implementing pay equity. One pay equity case in the federal jurisdiction resulted in a settlement totalling more than $2 million. Another settlement was estimated at $19 million.[73] Gunderson estimates the cost of implementing pay equity in Ontario would cost employers between $1 billion and $3 billion.[74] Others point to the potentially burdensome task of implementing job evaluation systems, negotiating new pay structures with labour unions, and resolving grievances during implementation.[75]

Valid arguments may be found on both sides of these issues. As P/HRM managers, the important concern is that the organization is prepared for pay equity legislation when it is introduced. Many firms covered by Quebec and federal pay equity legislation for the past decade say meeting pay equity law requirements simply involves application of good P/HRM practices.[76] While the Ontario and Manitoba statutes differ from those in Quebec and the federal sector, the future is unlikely to be quite as gloomy as some have predicted.

SUMMARY

The last two chapters examined the basic pay issues and illustrated alternative techniques designed to aid managers facing these issues. It is important to place compensation in perspective. It is only one, albeit an important one, of the human resource management activities. However, it does represent a major portion of the expense budget for most managers. Consequently, the systems used to determine and administer pay must be well designed. Unfortunately, much of contemporary compensation administration is bureaucratic and technique-oriented. The concepts and objectives are often replaced with forms and paperwork. But change is in the wind. Challenged by increased economic competition, managers are beginning to manage pay. Similarly, challenges from employees and pay equity advocates are also causing some current practices to be reexamined.

The next chapter examines a major form of compensation that has long been ignored: benefits. Rising costs, concerns about their tax-free status, and questions about their value have caused P/HRM professionals to reexamine management of employee benefits.

DISCUSSION AND REVIEW QUESTIONS

1. In what circumstances may an employer wish to pay different wages to individuals in the same job? In what circumstances may an employer wish to pay the same wages to individuals in the same job?
2. What employee and organizational factors are usually considered in paying different rates to employees in the same job?
3. What are the advantages and disadvantages of using pay ranges?
4. Why would an organization want to use each of the following pay increase methods: (*a*) merit guide chart matrix, (*b*) re-earnable bonus, (*c*) lump sum payment.
5. What are some difficulties in a merit pay system?
6. What conditions may lead to more effective suggestion systems?
7. When would you use group rather than individual pay incentives?
8. What are "inherent controls"? Give an example.
9. What employee groups might need a separate pay system? Why?
10. How does the concept of "equal pay" differ from "pay equity" in pay discrimination matters?
11. What job evaluation factors must be included in a job evaluation system to make it acceptable to pay equity legislation?

NOTES AND REFERENCES

1. Walter A. Fogel, "Job Rate Ranges: A Theoretical and Empirical Analysis," *Industrial and Labor Relations Review*, July 1964, pp. 584–97; W. A. Fogel, "Wage Administration and Job Rate Ranges," *California Management Review*, Spring 1965, pp. 77–84; George T. Milkovich and Jerry M. Newman, *Compensation*, 2nd ed. (Plano, Tex.: Business Publications, 1987).
2. Compensation texts that the reader may find useful include David W. Belcher and Thomas J. Atchison, *Compensation Administration*, 2nd ed. (Englewood Cliffs, N.J.: Prentice-Hall, 1987); Leonard R. Burgess, *Wage and Salary Administration* (Columbus, Ohio: Charles E. Merrill, 1984); Richard I. Henderson, *Compensation Management* (Reston, Va.: Reston Publishing, 1984); Milton L. Rock, ed., *Handbook of Wage and Salary Administration* (New York: McGraw-Hill, 1984); Thomas Patton, *Pay, Employee Compensation, and Incentive Plans* (New York: Free Press, 1977).
3. Hay Associates argues that each job has its own evaluation point total and its own range. That is, each job evaluation point has a dollar value.
4. Milkovich and Newman, *Compensation*, part 2; Belcher and Atchison, *Compensation Administration*.
5. Burgess, *Wage and Salary Administration*.
6. Belcher and Atchison, *Compensation Administration*, part IV; Milkovich and Newman, *Compensation*, part 3.
7. For example, see the discussion of COLAs in Milkovich and Newman, *Compensation*, chaps. 15 and 17; also see Janet L. Norwood, "Two Consumer Price Index Issues," *Monthly Labor Review*, March 1981, pp. 58–61.
8. Kimberley Noble, "Study Shows Firms to Link Pay with Performance," *The

Globe and Mail, October 3, 1984, p. B19; David Tyson, "Pay-for-Performance Makes Sense for More Major Companies," *Financial Post*, November 12, 1983, p. 14; Michael Salter, "Pay Now Tagged More to Results," *Financial Post*, October 15, 1983, p. 24.

9. Bruce Gates, "Managers Look to Merit Pay to Boost Productivity," *Financial Post*, November 23, 1985, p. 18; Virginia Galt, "Employers Tying Pay to Performance," *The Globe and Mail*, November 4, 1985, p. B1.
10. C. A. Smith, "Lump Sum Increases—A Creditable Change Strategy," *Personnel* 56 (1979), pp. 59–63; Edward E. Lawler III, *Pay and Organization Development* (Reading, Mass.: Addison-Wesley Publishing, 1981).
11. Much of this section is based on Milkovich and Newman, *Compensation*, chap. 8.
12. E. E. Lawler III, and L. Porter, "Perceptions Regarding Managerial Compensation," *Industrial Relations* 3, no. 1 (1969), pp. 41–49; A. Maslow, *Motivation and Personality* (New York: Harper & Row, 1954).
13. Maslow, *Motivation*.
14. E. E. Lawler III, *Pay and Organization Effectiveness* (New York: McGraw-Hill, 1971).
15. F. A. Heller and L. W. Porter, "Perceptions of Managerial Needs and Skills in Two National Samples," *Occupational Psychology* 40, no. 1 (1966), pp. 1–13.
16. L. Dyer, D. P. Schwab, and R. D. Theriault, "Managerial Perceptions Regarding Salary Increase Criteria," *Personnel Psychology* 29, no. 2 (1976), pp. 233–42.
17. E. E. Lawler III, "Managers' Attitudes toward How Their Pay Is and Should Be Determined," *Journal of Applied Psychology* 50 (1966), pp. 273–79.
18. E. E. Lawler III and E. Levin, "Union Officer's Perceptions of Members Pay Preferences," *Industrial and Labor Relations Review* 21, no. 4 (1968), pp. 509–17.
19. B. S. Georgopolous, G. M. Mahoney, and N. W. Jones, "A Path Goal Approach to Productivity," *Journal of Applied Psychology* 41, no. 3 (1957), pp. 345–53.
20. George Green, "Instrumentality Theory of Work Motivations," *Journal of Applied Psychology* 53, no. 2 (1965), pp. 1–25; Lawler, "Managers' Attitudes"; D. P. Schwab and L. Dyer, "The Motivational Impact of a Compensation System on Employee Performance," *Organization Behavior and Human Performance* 9 (1973), pp. 215–25.
21. Clay W. Hamner, "How to Ruin Motivation with Pay," *Compensation Review*, Third Quarter 1975, pp. 88–98; Herbert H. Meyer, "Pay for Performance Dilemma," *Organizational Dynamics*, Winter 1975, pp. 71–78.
22. E. E. Lawler III, "Manager's Perceptions of Their Subordinate's Pay and of Their Supervisor's Pay," *Personnel Psychology* 18, no. 3 (1965), pp. 413–22; T. Mahoney and W. Weitzel, "Secrecy and Managerial Compensation" *Industrial Relations* 17, no. 2 (1978), pp. 245–51.
23. Hamner, "How to Ruin Motivation with Pay."
24. Meyer, "Pay for Performance Dilemma."
25. Lawler, *Pay and Organization Development*; also see Stephan J. Motowidlo, "Relationship between Self-Rated Performance and Pay Satisfaction among Sales Representatives," *Journal of Applied Psychology* 67, no. 2 (1982), pp. 209–13.
26. H. G. Heneman III, "Multi-Dimensionality of Pay Satisfaction" (working paper, Madison, Wis., Graduate School of Business, University of Wisconsin 1983).
27. L. Dyer and R. Theriault, "The Determinants of Pay Satisfaction," *Journal of Applied Psychology* 61, no. 4 (1976), pp. 596–604.

28. Chris Berger, "The Effects of Pay Levels, Pay Values and Employee Benefits on Pay Satisfaction" (working paper, Lafayette, Ind., Purdue University Graduate School of Business, 1984); Carla O'Dell, *Gainsharing Involvement, Incentives, and Productivity* (New York: American Management Associations, 1981); also see Belcher and Atchison, *Compensation Administration*, chap. 13; Rock, *Handbook of Wage and Salary Administration*, chaps. 27–31.
29. James Lincoln, *Incentive Management* (Cleveland: Lincoln Electric Co., 1969).
30. Ibid.
31. Ibid.; E. E. Lawler III, "Managers' Attitudes towards How Their Pay Is and Should Be Determined," *Journal of Applied Psychology* 50, no. 3 (1966), pp. 273–79.
32. John K. Moynahan, *Designing an Effective Sales Compensation Program* (New York: AMACOM, 1980); David Toole, "In Pay, the Trend Is to Salary," *Financial Times*, January 26, 1981, pp. 27–28.
33. Bruce Gates, "Employees' Ideas Can Pay Dividends if Taken Seriously," *Financial Post*, March 16, 1985, p. 20; John Hein, "Employee Suggestion Systems Pay," *Personnel Journal*, March 1973, pp. 218–21; "Northern Telecom Canada Limited's Employee Suggestions Program Record," *Canadian Industrial Relations and Personnel Developments*, June 12, 1985, p. 685.
34. Milkovich and Newman, *Compensation*, 2nd ed.
35. Ontario Ministry of Labour, *Towards Safe Production: Report of the Joint Federal-Provincial Inquiry Commission into Safety in Mines and Mining Plants in Ontario (Burkett Commission)*, (Toronto: Queen's Printer, 1981); Terry Pender, "Miner's Bonus Wage System Comes under Ontario Scrutiny," *The Globe and Mail*, August 22, 1986, p. A10; Linda McQuaig, "Between a Rock and a Soft Bonus," *Maclean's*, November 24, 1980, pp. 54, 56; Mick Lowe, "End Bonus Pay System, Miner Tells Safety Probe," *The Globe and Mail*, November 28, 1980, p. 9; T. F. Cawsey and P. R. Richardson, "Employee Relations at the Kidd Creek Operations of Texasgulf Limited," in *Employee Relations Initiatives in Canadian Mining, Proceedings No. 5* (Kingston, Ont.: Centre for Resource Studies, Queen's University, 1979), pp. 45–59.
36. Belcher and Atchison, *Compensation Administration*; O'Dell, *Gainsharing*; Lawler, *Pay and Organizational Development*.
37. *Gainsharing: A Collection of Papers* (Norcross, Georgia: Institute of Industrial Engineers, 1983).
38. Lawler, *Pay and Organization Development*, p. 144.
39. Royal Commission on the Economic Union and Development Prospects for Canada (MacDonald Commission), *Report* (Ottawa: Minister of Supply and Services Canada, 1985), volume 2, pp. 714–15.
40. Donald Nightingale and Richard Long, *Gain and Equity Sharing* (Ottawa: Labour Canada, 1984); Timothy L. Ross and J. James Keyser, "Gainsharing: Is It a Human Resource Strategy or a Group Incentive System?" *Business Quarterly*, Winter 1984, pp. 92–95; Bruce Gates, "Gainsharing Seen as Productivity Aid," *Financial Post*, September 27, 1986; Catherine Motherwell, "Managers Take Second Look at Gainsharing," *The Globe and Mail*, December 10, 1984, p. B8.
41. Fred Lesieur and Elbridge Puckett, "The Scanlon Plan Has Proved Itself," *Harvard Business Review*, September–October 1969, pp. 109–18; A. J. Geare, "Productivity from Scanlon-Type Plans," *Academy of Management Review*, July 1976, pp. 99–108; George Schultz and Robert McKersie, "Participation-Achievement-

Reward Systems," *Journal of Management Studies*, May 1973, pp. 141–61; Brian Moore, "The Scanlon Plant-Wide Incentive Plan," *Training and Development Journal*, February 1976, pp. 50–53; George Sherman, "The Scanlon Plan: Its Capabilities for Productivity Improvement," *Personnel Administrator*, July 1976, pp. 17–20; T. Gilson and M. Lefcowitz, "A Plant-Wide Productivity Bonus in a Small Factory," *Industrial Labor Relations Review* 10, no. 3 (1957), pp. 284–96.

42. Nightingale and Long, *Gain and Equity Sharing*; Donald V. Nightingale, *The Profit Sharing Handbook* (Toronto: Profit Sharing Council of Canada, 1982); Ronald Knowles, "Firms Turn to Profit Sharing to Enhance Productivity," *Financial Post*, February 9, 1985, p. 37; Ann Auman, "Profit Sharing Gains More Converts," *Toronto Star*, April 17, 1984, pp. D1, D7; Tracy LeMay, "Not Only Bosses Get a Piece of the Profits," *Financial Post Moneywise Magazine*, November 1986, pp. 18, 20; L. Till and A. Waite, "Sharing the Wealth," *Office Management & Automation*, October 1987, pp. 32–35.
43. Jack Francis, "Profit Sharing Gaining Ground," *Winnipeg Free Press*, June 8, 1984, p. 46.
44. Lawler, *Pay and Organization Development*, p. 152.
45. Mahoney and Weitzel, "Secrecy and Managerial Compensation"; George W. Hettenhouse, Wilbur G. Lewellen, H. Lanser, and H. James, "Communicating the Pay Package," *Personnel*, November–December 1975, pp. 19–30.
46. E. E. Lawler III, "Secrecy and the Need to Know," in *Managerial Motivation and Compensation*, ed. Henry Tosi, Robert House, and M. Dunnette (East Lansing: Michigan State University Press, 1972). .
47. Ibid.; also see Mahoney and Weitzel, "Secrecy and Managerial Compensation."
48. Lawler, *Pay and Organization Development*; G. Douglas Jenkins, Jr., and E. E. Lawler III, "Impact of Employee Participation in Pay Plan Development," *Organization Behavior and Human Performance* 28, no. 2 (1981), pp. 111–28.
49. Jenkins and Lawler, "Impact."
50. Ibid.
51. David Peach, "Salaries for Production Workers—What Happens?" *Business Quarterly*, Spring 1974, pp. 67–69; Lawler, *Pay and Organization Development*, pp. 62–65; Robert D. Hulme and Richard V. Bevan, "The Blue-Collar Worker Goes on Salary," *Harvard Business Review*, March–April 1975, p. 110.
52. Edward E. Lawler III, "The Strategic Design of Reward Systems," in *Strategic Human Resource Management*, ed. Charles Fomburn, Noel M. Tichy, and Mary Anne Devanna (New York: John Wiley & Sons, 1984) pp. 140–41; Sheldon Lush, "A New Class of Capitalists—How One Company Develops Them," *Business Quarterly* 41, no. 1 (1976), pp. 51–54; Eva Innes, Robert L. Perry, and Jim Lyon, *The 100 Best Companies to Work for in Canada* (Don Mills: Collins, 1986).
53. Milkovich and Newman, *Compensation*, chap. 16; Belcher and Atchison, *Compensation Management*, chap. 18; Rock, *Handbook*, Part I.
54. Bruce Ellig, *Executive Compensation: A Total Pay Perspective* (New York: McGraw-Hill, 1982); James E. Cheeks, *How to Compensate Executives* (Homewood, Ill.: Dow Jones-Irwin, 1982).
55. Naresh Agarwal, "Determinants of Executive Compensation," *Industrial Relations* 20, no. 1 (1981), pp. 36–46; Marc Wallace, "Type of Control, Industrial Concentration and Executive Pay," *Academy of Management Proceedings*, 1976, pp. 284–88; Harland Fox, *Top Executive Compensation: 1978* (New York: The Conference Board, 1980).

56. Luis R. Gomez-Mejia, Henry Tosi, and Timothy Hinkin, "Managerial Control, Performance, and Executive Compensation," *Academy of Management Journal* 30, no. 1 (1987), pp. 51–70.
57. Wayne Lilley, "More Money," *Canadian Business*, April 1985, pp. 48–56; Helen Kohl, "Surprise Packages," *Canadian Business*, August 1982, pp. 83–92; Cecil Foster, "Canadian Executives Go for Cash Up Front," *The Globe and Mail*, December 3, 1985, p. B2; Noble, "Study Shows Firms to Link Pay with Performance."
58. Edward Greenspon, "Executives' Pay Cheques Jump 22.5%," *The Globe and Mail*, May 3, 1986, pp. B1, B4.
59. Ellig, *Executive Compensation*.
60. Brent King, "Sweets from the Suite," *Financial Post Moneywise Magazine*, October 1986, pp. 34–37; Helen Kohl, "Executive Sweets," *Financial Post Magazine*, May 1981, pp. 14–18.
61. Colin Mills, "The Perk that Pays—and Pays . . . ," *Benefits Canada*, October 1984, pp. 27–30.
62. Sheila Arnott, "What Our Top Executives Are Earning," *Financial Post*, April 13, 1987, p. 16; Caroline Meinbardis, "Options Swell Super Salaries," *Financial Times*, April 13, 1987, pp. 1, 11–13.
63. For a history of pay equity legislation in Canada, see Lindsay Niemann, *Wage Discrimination and Women Workers: The Move towards Equal Pay for Work of Equal Value in Canada* (Ottawa: Minister of Supply and Services Canada, 1984).
64. John G. Campbell, "Equal Pay for Work of Equal Value in the Federal Public Service of Canada," *Compensation Review*, 3rd Quarter 1983, pp. 42–51; Labour Canada, *Labour Standards in Canada, 1986 Edition* (Ottawa: Minister of Supply and Services Canada, 1986); Cynthia Goodwin, *Equal Pay Legislation and Implementation: Selected Countries* (Ottawa: Labour Canada, 1984); Labour Canada, *Equal Pay for Work of Equal Value* (Ottawa: Minister of Supply and Services Canada, 1986).
65. *Re Harris et al. and Bell Canada* (1975) 58 D.L.R. (3d) 58.
66. Carole Geller, "Manitoba's Pay Equity Act," in *Equal Pay for Work of Equal Value* (Ottawa: Minister of Supply and Services Canada, 1986), pp. 14–17; Sandy Fife, "Learning to Live with Pay Equity," *Financial Times*, March 9, 1987, pp. 1, 7; Business Council of British Columbia, *Equal Pay for Work of Equal Value: A Background Paper* (Vancouver: Business Council of British Columbia, 1987).
67. Muriel Garon, "Pay Equity: An Element in a System," in *Equal Pay for Work of Equal Value* (Ottawa: Minister of Supply and Services Canada, 1986), pp. 18–22; Canadian Human Rights Commission, *Methodology and Principles for Applying Section 11 of the Canadian Human Rights Act* (Ottawa: Canadian Human Rights Commission, 1983); "Equal Wages Guidelines, 1986," *Canada Gazette, Part II*, December 10, 1986, pp. 4794–98.
68. Joan Breckenridge, "Equal Pay's Unequal Effect," *Report on Business*, December 1985; "Reason Is Loser as Pay Equity Rolls On," *Financial Post*, September 13, 1986, p. 8.
69. Roberta Robb, "Conceptual and Operational Issues Confronting the Equal Value Approach to Equal Pay," in *Proceedings of the 21st Annual Meeting of the Canadian Industrial Relations Association*, ed. Bryan Downie, University of Guelph, May 1984, pp. 314–30; Morley Gunderson, "Spline Function Estimates of the Impact of Equal Pay Legislation: The Ontario Experience," *Relations Industrielles*

40, no. 4 (1985), pp. 775–91; Business Council of B.C., *Equal Pay for Work of Equal Value: A Background Paper*.
70. MacDonald Commission, *Report, Vol. 2*.
71. Richard D. Arvey, "Sex Bias in Job Evaluation Procedures," *Personnel Psychology* 39 (1986), pp. 315–35; D. J. Trieman and H. Hartmann, *Women, Work, and Wages* (Washington, D.C.: National Academy of Sciences, 1981).
72. William Watson, "Pay Equity: Idea Whose Time Has Passed," *Financial Post*, April 2, 1986; MacDonald Commission, *Report, Vol. 2*.
73. Campbell, "Equal Pay"; Canadian Human Rights Commission, *Equal Pay Casebook 1978–84* (Ottawa: Canadian Human Rights Commission, 1984).
74. Morley Gunderson, *Costing Equal Value Legislation in Ontario: A Report to the Ontario Ministry of Labour* (Toronto: Ontario Ministry of Labour, 1985).
75. Business Council of B.C., *Equal Pay for Work of Equal Value: A Background Paper*, p. 13.
76. Ann Rauhala, "Implementing Pay Equity No Big Deal for Some Firms," *The Globe and Mail*, December 27, 1986; Frances Russell, "Apples vs. Oranges," *Winnipeg Free Press*, July 14, 1986, p. 7; Walter McLean, "Pay Equity Can and Should Be Made to Work," *Montreal Gazette*, March 24, 1986, p. B3.

CHAPTER SIXTEEN
BENEFITS

CHAPTER OUTLINE

I. A Diagnostic Approach to Benefits
   A. External Influences
   B. Internal Influences
II. Types of Employee Benefits
   A. Compensation for Time Not Worked
   B. Insurance-Based Benefits
   C. Employee Services
III. Canada's Retirement Income System
   A. Government Income Security Programs
   B. Canada/Quebec Pension Plan
   C. Employer-Sponsored Pensions and Individual Savings
IV. Managing Benefits
   A. Benefit Objectives
   B. Benefits Communication
   C. Containing Benefit Costs
   D. Flexible Benefits
V. Summary

Human Resource Activities: Compensation

The story is told about a gunman who suddenly appeared at the paymaster's window in a large plant and demanded: "Never mind the payroll! Just hand over the welfare and pension funds, the group insurance premiums, and the withholding taxes." With the cost of employee benefits rising much faster than direct pay, the gunman would have made off with a good haul.

Once called "fringe benefits," employee benefits are no longer on the fringe of total compensation. They represent a large percentage of labour costs in most organizations. Before the Great Depression, benefits cost employers only 2 or 3 percent of gross annual payroll. Today, benefit costs have escalated to one third of gross payroll.

Exhibit 16–1 depicts this growth based on biennial surveys conducted by the management consulting firm Stevenson Kellogg Ernst & Whinney. In 1953 (the first survey year), employee benefits accounted for 15.1 percent of gross annual payroll. This figure jumped in the late 1950s and again in the late 1960s. As a percentage of gross payroll, benefit costs decreased slightly in 1982 and 1984, but continued their upward climb again in 1986. Benefits currently average 36.3 percent of gross annual payroll in the surveyed firms.

EXHIBIT 16–1
The Rising Cost of Employee Benefits

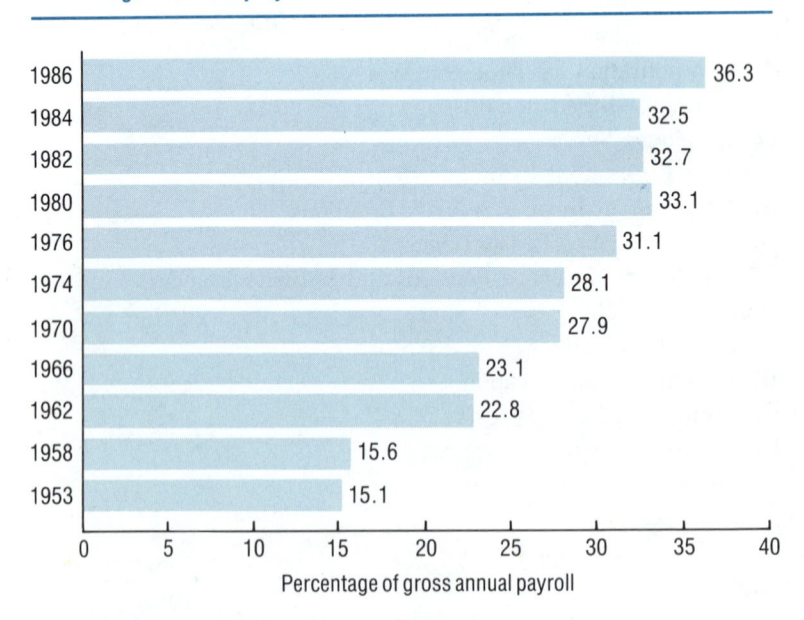

Year	Percentage of gross annual payroll
1986	36.3
1984	32.5
1982	32.7
1980	33.1
1976	31.1
1974	28.1
1970	27.9
1966	23.1
1962	22.8
1958	15.6
1953	15.1

Source: Stevenson Kellogg Ernst & Whinney, *Employee Benefit Costs in Canada, 1986* (and previous survey years), (Toronto: Stevenson Kellogg Ernst & Whinney, 1986). Reproduced with permission.

Much of the decline during the early 1980s was due to relatively lower group benefit costs resulting from more competition in the insurance industry. The economic recession also had an influence, particularly through lower pension plan premiums as employees were laid off. However, pension reform and premium increases for mandatory benefits will likely lead to benefit cost increases during the next decade.[1]

The cost of employee benefits varies considerably by industry. In the primary metals and metal fabrication industries, benefits average 45 percent of payroll. In some firms, benefits actually account for more than 50 percent of total compensation. In contrast, benefit costs in textile, footwear, and publishing represent only 26 percent of gross payroll.

> **Definition**
> *Employee benefits* are the indirect part of total compensation. Major benefits include pay for time not worked, insurance, pensions, and other services.

Benefits are part of the total compensation system. The previous chapters examined three basic compensation decisions: pay level (external equity), pay structure (internal equity), and individual pay relationships (employee equity). This chapter addresses the fourth basic decision: the form of pay. Specifically, employee benefits are indirect forms of compensation. Within benefits, various forms of compensation are possible. Exhibit 16–2 lists the variety of employee benefits provided by B.C. Tel to its management and exempt staff.

A DIAGNOSTIC APPROACH TO BENEFITS

External Influences

External factors play a major role in influencing both the amount and type of employee benefits offered by employers.

Government Regulations

Government requirements have affected the benefits area significantly.[2] Legislation requires employers to partially or fully pay the premiums for unemployment insurance, Canada/Quebec Pension Plans (C/QPP), and workers' compensation. Other statutes influence voluntary benefits. For example, employer-sponsored pension plans have been regulated by the Income Tax

EXHIBIT 16–2
Benefits for Management and Exempt Staff at B.C. Tel

Health care benefits	Death benefits after retirement
Medical Services Plan of B.C.	Employee-paid life insurance
B.C. Hospitals Program	Survivor benefit
Extended health care benefits	Company pension spouse's benefit
Dental plan	Canada pension plan death benefit
	Dependent's life insurance
Disability benefits	Retirement benefits
Short-term benefits	Company pension plan
Disability benefit program	Pension investment plan
Occupational accident disability plan	Canada pension plan
Long-term disability benefits	
Canada pension plan disability benefits	
Workers' compensation disability benefits	
Survivor benefits	Other benefits
Company-paid life insurance	Vacation
Employee-paid life insurance	Paid personal leave
Voluntary life insurance	Concession telephone service
Company pension plan death benefit	Personal lines insurance
Pension investment plan death benefit	Management relocation expense
Business travel accident insurance	Education assistance plan
Canada pension plan death benefits	Autoplan
Workers' compensation death benefits	

Note: The benefits listed may include some fully paid by the employee. Other benefits not on the list may include the company fitness centre, in-house training, or subsidized cafeteria.

Source: B.C. Tel, *Summary of Management and Exempt Benefit Programs.*

Act since 1919. Provincial governments have passed legislation in this area since 1963.[3] As we will discuss later, recent changes in this legislation will have a profound effect on future pension plans in Canada.

Governments have also indirectly encouraged growth of employee benefits. For example, during World War II, when wages (but not benefits) were controlled by the National War Labour Board, employers competed for the short supply of labour by offering more generous benefits. Canadian income tax policies allowing employers to deduct the costs of many benefits have also indirectly encouraged their growth. In other words, employee benefits are more tax effective than similar services and programs purchased outside the company. The significance of taxation on benefits is evident from public reaction when the federal government has attempted to tax more of these benefits.

Unions

If governments provided the initial impetus, unions have continued to push for improved benefits. Since the 1940s, the union movement has given a high priority to both the variety of benefits provided and the proportion of costs borne by the employer. As an example, the Canadian Auto Workers union is credited with introducing dental plans to Canada many years ago. More recently, it negotiated with General Motors, Ford, and International Harvester to provide the first prepaid legal aid for its members in this country.[4] Unions have also actively lobbied government for improvements in legally required benefits such as unemployment insurance and C/QPP.

Internal Influences

Corporate strategies, objectives, and culture can affect the benefits package. P/HRM managers may aim at employee satisfaction or may try to avoid unionization by offering a highly competitive package. Many organizations claim their benefit plan attracts better job applicants. Others, such as Shell Canada, try to maintain a stable, loyal work force through the benefits program.[5] Later in this chapter, we will examine the strategic development of benefit packages.

Another significant organizational influence on employee benefits is the firm's ability to pay. Smaller companies usually have less generous benefit packages for this reason. With tighter budgets, businesses of all sizes are looking for ways to rationalize benefit costs.[6]

Employee Preferences

Preferences for a particular form of compensation vary from one employee to the next. According to two Canadian studies conducted more than a decade ago, the pay increase is the most preferred form of compensation overall.[7] However, its importance decreases among employees who are older or have longer service with the company. In contrast, the importance of pensions increases from third place among young employees to the most preferred form of compensation among employees older than 55. The importance of pensions also increases with the employee's length of service. Vacations become increasingly important to those in the middle of their working lives. Medical and life insurance benefits generally rank lowest on the employee preference scale.

Research on employee benefit preferences in the United States gives a different picture.[8] Americans tend to place hospital and medical insurance at or near the top of the list. This possibly reflects the lack of a publicly funded universal health system and substantially higher medical insurance rates in that country. The pay raise is rated much lower than in Canada, usually below vacations, which have the second-highest preference. Life insurance is usually rated at the bottom of the list of benefits.

Employee preference is only one factor to consider in managing employee benefits. Before discussing the management of benefits, let us describe the variety of benefits that might be included in the compensation system.

TYPES OF EMPLOYEE BENEFITS

There are many types of employee benefits. Some are required by federal, provincial, or territorial law. Others have been introduced voluntarily by the employer or through negotiations. Exhibit 16–3 lists the various types of employee benefits and their average cost as a percentage of gross annual payroll. In this section, we describe compensation for time not worked (paid time off), insurance-based benefits, and employee services. Due to the complexity and importance of retirement income, pensions will be discussed separately later in the chapter.

Compensation for Time Not Worked

At one time, people worked 12 hours a day, 6 days a week, 52 weeks a year. They received no vacations or holidays. Some were able to take lunch and rest breaks, but at their own expense. Today, Canadian laws require most employees to receive a minimum number of employer-paid days of vacation and holiday. Legislation also limits the number of hours worked in a day (and week) and requires employers to provide paid time for rest breaks.[9] Most companies have added other benefits beyond the legal requirements that amount to paid time off. As Exhibit 16–3 indicates, compensation for time

EXHIBIT 16–3
Average Employee Benefits Costs in Canada in 1986

Employee Benefit	Cost as a Percentage of Gross Annual Payroll
Vacations	6.5%
Holidays	3.7
Coffee breaks, rest periods	3.9
Other paid time off	1.1
Subtotal: Paid time off	15.2
Disability plans	1.6
Provincial medical insurance	1.4
Unemployment insurance	2.3
Workers' compensation	2.0
Other insurance-based benefits	2.4
Subtotal: Insurance-based benefits	9.7
Employer pension plans	4.1
Canada/Quebec pension plan	1.3
Subtotal: Pension plans	5.4
Subtotal: Employee services	1.4
Subtotal: Cash benefits	4.6
Total benefits cost	36.3%

Source: Stevenson Kellogg Ernst & Whinney, *Employee Benefit Costs in Canada, 1986* (Toronto: Stevenson Kellogg Ernst & Whinney, 1986).

EXHIBIT 16–4
Vacation Entitlements in Major Collective Agreements

	Weeks of Vacation			
Seniority Requirement	*Three*	*Four*	*Five*	*Six*
Not stated/no provision	19.7%	15.6%	22.6%	56.7%
1 year	31.3	8.2	N/A	N/A
2–4 years	26.9	3.3	N/A	N/A
5 years	19.2	2.8	N/A	N/A
6–9 years	2.5	27.5	N/A	N/A
10 years/or less	0.5	27.3	3.1	N/A
11–14 years	N/A	10.1	4.4	N/A
15 years/or more/or less	N/A	5.1	6.6	1.9
16–19 years	N/A	N/A	21.8	2.1
20 years	N/A	N/A	26.9	4.1
21–24 years	N/A	N/A	7.0	5.7
25 years/or more	N/A	N/A	7.7	11.9
26–29 years	N/A	N/A	N/A	8.4
30 years or more	N/A	N/A	N/A	9.3
Total	100.0%	100.0%	100.0%	100.0%

Note: "No provision" means the collective agreement does not make reference to that particular benefit. This does not necessarily mean the benefit is not provided by the employer.

Source: Labour Canada, *Provisions in Major Collective Agreements in Canada Covering 500 and More Employees, July 1985* (Ottawa: Minister of Supply and Services Canada, 1985), tables 49–53.

not worked is the most costly type of employee benefit in the average Canadian firm.

Vacations are the most common and expensive employee benefit. Every Canadian jurisdiction requires individuals employed for more than one year to receive a minimum of two weeks of paid time off. In Saskatchewan, the minimum is three weeks. Many statutes also provide three weeks of vacation (four in Saskatchewan) for those with longer seniority. In many cases, employees are required to take their vacations in unbroken periods of at least one week.

Most companies voluntarily provide vacation entitlements beyond the legal requirements. As Exhibit 16–4 indicates, the majority of workers covered by a major collective agreement receive four weeks of vacation annually after six to nine years of service. Most receive five weeks after 15 to 20 years of service. In some collective agreements, long service employees may receive six or more weeks of vacation.

Legislation throughout Canada (except P.E.I.) requires employers to provide staff a certain number of paid holidays. These holidays are specifically stated and usually include New Year's Day, Good Friday, Victoria Day, Canada Day, Labour Day, and Christmas. Some companies also pay for holidays not listed in the statutes. A few firms provide floating paid personal holidays.

As an example, Canadian Tire's benefit package includes five days of paid "noncontrolled absenteeism." At Maritime Life Assurance in Halifax, employees can arrange days off as "recovery time" before or after stressful times of the year.

Coffee breaks and rest periods represent a significant amount of paid non-productive time in most organizations. Other paid time off may include leave for bereavement, jury duty, and parental responsibilities. Paid educational leave is also provided by several companies, but research suggests it is restricted mainly to managerial and executive staff. Moreover, educational leave is usually paid only for company-specific training.[10]

Parental Leave

Parental (or child care) leave—which includes maternity, paternity, and adoption leave—is quickly gaining interest in Canada. Legislation currently provides women with the right to unpaid leave during and immediately after pregnancy. In five provinces and the federal jurisdiction, employers are also required to provide unpaid paternity and adoption leave.[11]

Women on maternity leave are eligible for unemployment insurance benefits up to 60 percent of their normal wage. There is a two-week waiting period during which no income is received. Consequently, a growing number of employers—including Canada Post, Gaz Metropolitan, and Bell Canada—supplement unemployment insurance benefits for women on maternity leave.[12] Through formal agreements with the Unemployment Insurance Commission, employers may add to maternity benefits to a maximum of 95 percent of the employee's normal salary.

Paid paternity leave is also gaining popularity. Approximately half of Canadians covered by major collective agreements are given one or more days of paid paternity leave at the time of their child's birth. Paid adoption leave is also provided by several major employers.

Insurance-Based Benefits

The many risks encountered throughout life—illness, accident, and early death, among others—can be made less costly by buying insurance. Insurance is well suited as an employee benefit because group rates are usually much less expensive than individual premiums. These premiums are paid by the employer, employee, or both parties. Insurance-based benefits include health insurance, unemployment insurance, workers' compensation, short-term sickness and long-term disability, and group life insurance.

Health Insurance

All Canadian residents are covered by basic provincial health and medical insurance plans. The federal government began sharing the cost of provincial hospital insurance plans in 1958. In 1966, coverage was extended to medical care services.[13] Government health insurance covers basic hospital expenses; the medical plan pays for physicians' and medical specialists' fees and medical laboratory expenses. Some provinces have increased coverage to include dental care for children and prescription drugs for the elderly.

The cost of maintaining Canada's national health care system is borne primarily by general tax revenues. Quebec also levies a special payroll tax on employers. A few provinces have health insurance premiums and require employers to deduct these premiums from the employee's pay cheque. A survey by the Pay Research Bureau indicates most large employers in Ontario pay the provincial health premiums rather than deducting the cost from the employee's earnings.[14]

Beyond basic health care, most major employers in Canada include supplemental medical coverage in the benefit package. These plans typically insure individuals for the cost of a semiprivate or private hospital room, ambulance and paramedical services, and private nursing. Coverage may also include the costs of prescription drugs and often extends to costs of health care outside of the country. Vision and hearing care insurance is provided by one third of large Canadian companies.

Basic and extended health insurance may be important, but dental insurance takes top prize for the most dramatic growth. More than 10 million people (employees and their families) are covered by dental insurance plans. The benefit is offered in 90 percent of Canadian firms and most employers pay the full cost. Compare this with 1970 when only 100,000 people had dental insurance. One explanation for such dramatic growth is that dental insurance is tax deductible. But some writers note that many unions made this one of their top negotiating items in the past decade. It is also a highly visible benefit because it is used frequently. Employers tend to like the benefit because it provides for the employee's welfare.[15]

Unemployment Insurance and Workers' Compensation

Canada's unemployment insurance program (UI) was introduced in 1940 and has since undergone several changes.[16] The main objective is to provide income support during temporary interruptions in employment. By reducing the financial burden during a job search, it is also intended to facilitate the match between individual abilities and job requirements and thereby improve the operation of the labour market. Except for a few special groups, participation in UI is compulsory for individuals younger than 65 in wage earning positions (called insurable employment). Self-employed members of the work force are generally excluded from the program.

With annual disbursements of $12 billion, UI is now the most expensive social program in Canada. It is funded by both employer and employee premiums as well as tax revenues. Employee premiums are fixed at 2.35 percent of earnings (in 1987) up to the maximum insurable earnings, while employer premiums are 1.4 times this amount. The premiums are tax deductible.

There are two types of UI payments, both of which are considered taxable income. Regular benefits are paid to eligible claimants who are unemployed for seven days or longer and are actively looking for work. This excludes those on strike or lockout. Payments are 60 percent of the person's average insurable earnings over the last 20 weeks of work. Benefits are received for up to 50 weeks. Special benefits are provided to eligible claimants who are injured, sick, on maternity leave, or in quarantine. Maternity and sickness benefits are payable for up to 15 weeks. Some employers offer their laid-off employees supplementary unemployment insurance benefits (SUB) which restore the unemployed person's income to a maximum of 95 percent of previous salary.

From its beginning, unemployment insurance in Canada has been a major source of debate. Who should be eligible for UI? How generous should the benefits be? Is UI just an insurance plan, or should it be the foundation of universal income support? Who should bear the costs of the program? These and other questions have been addressed in several parliamentary committees and task forces, including the MacDonald Commission in 1985 and the Forget Commission in late 1986.[17] The main issues have been the cost of UI and the effect of benefit levels on unemployment. On the latter point, research indicates increasing benefit levels lengthens the average job search duration and, consequently, increases the level of unemployment.[18] Whatever changes have been enacted in the past or are proposed for the future, unemployment insurance will remain a significant part of the employee benefit package.

Workers' compensation, discussed in Chapter Twelve, is another insurance-based benefit. It is also a mandatory benefit, with all premiums paid by the employer. Premiums are calculated as a percentage of payroll and vary with the accident/illness rate of the industry and, in some provinces, the experience rating of each company.

Disability and Life Insurance

Workers' compensation and other government programs provide modest income protection for individuals who suffer wage loss due to illness or accident. As a consequence, most employers offer short-term sick leave and long-term disability insurance to cover any gaps in these public income security programs.

Sick Leave. This benefit often provides partial or fully paid leave for up to six months to cover the waiting period of long-term disability. Other companies restrict paid sick leave to only a few days each year. Many sick leave plans assign credits for each unit of time worked. For example, one day of sick leave may be awarded for each month of service. These credits may be cumulative, with the unused credits paid to the employee at either the end of the year or retirement, or the unused credits may be forfeited at year's end. Sick leave costs are usually absorbed directly by the employer, although policies may be purchased from insurance companies.

Long-Term Disability. This insurance protects against wage loss for prolonged injury or illness. Disbursements from long-term disability plans usually begin several (typically six) months after the employee has ceased work. Payments are a percentage of salary at the time of the disability and usually continue until the employee returns to work, retires, or is declared fit and qualified for other work. In some cases, the percentage of salary paid increases with the employee's length of service before the disability. Given the potentially long benefit period, many long-term disability plans increase disbursements with inflation.

Group Life. Life insurance is found in almost every employee benefit package in Canada. More than half these plans are contributory (i.e., the employee pays some portion or all of the premiums). Typically, group life insurance pays the beneficiary one or two times the employee's annual salary at the time of death. Many plans also permit the individual to voluntarily purchase supplemental life insurance for higher multiples of annual salary. Some firms offer separate travel insurance, which pays a lump sum benefit to survivors of employees killed while travelling on business.

Accidental Death and Dismemberment (AD&D). AD&D insurance provides a lump sum payment to employees or their survivors in the event of an accident or death. The value of the lump sum payment varies according to the bodily part dismembered and is typically listed as a fraction of the highest amount.

Employee Services

This catch-all category of employee benefits includes a variety of perquisites such as subsidized cafeterias, free parking lots, employee assistance programs (described in Chapter Twelve), in-house fitness centres, discounts on company products, counselling programs—even the Christmas turkey many employers still distribute to their employees!

Training and development is big business in Canada (see Chapter Ten). Employers spend millions of dollars annually to educate and train their employees. This varies from teaching basic skills—such as second language training at Honda Canada Inc.—to tuition refunds. Some major employers send a select number of their best managers back to university on salary with all expenses paid to earn an MBA. Others, including Syncrude Canada Ltd., offer scholarships to the dependents of employees.[19] Canterra Energy Ltd. of Calgary pays $750 a year for the postsecondary education of any employee dependent who maintains at least a C average.

A large number of firms have introduced recreational facilities. Several, such as Manufacturers Life Insurance Co. (Manulife), pay the capital costs but let participating employees cover operating costs. Dofasco's facilities must be among the most lavish. Within a 100-acre park, the company provides two NHL-size hockey rinks, baseball diamonds, an all-weather track, tennis courts, soccer and football fields, and a golf driving range. Smaller companies are more likely to subsidize membership fees at local health clubs.

Child Care

Child care (or day care) is the emerging employee benefit of the late 1980s and 1990s. With record numbers of women entering the labour force, the demand for quality child care centres has increased dramatically.[20] Working mothers list adequate child care as the most important problem they face. An Ontario Hydro survey in 1979 reported 72 percent of female employees viewed day care as a social right and more than two thirds were in favour of it as a bargaining issue. However, a higher percentage of men in the sample were opposed to child care on the bargaining agenda.[21] (A day care facility has since been established in the Ontario Hydro building.) Several labour union organizations have already made workplace child care a major policy issue.

For P/HRM managers, the issues are whether child care is a worthwhile benefit and, if so, what form it should take. With respect to the value of employer-sponsored child care, research indicates the introduction of this benefit reduces absenteeism and turnover, improves the company's ability to recruit employees, and increases morale.[22] One firm in British Columbia estimates its on-site facility reduced average absenteeism for all staff from 12 to 5 days per year. Montreal-based Lavelin Inc. also experienced a lower rate of absenteeism. Riverdale Hospital in Toronto, which has one of the longest-running employer-sponsored child care centres, introduced a day care facility in 1964 in response to its inability to recruit enough staff to operate at full capacity. The number of qualified applicants jumped by 40 percent within six months after the day care centre opened.[23]

Whether child care is a cost-effective benefit also depends on the form of employer support. Much attention has been centred around the on-site facility. More than 100 hospitals, municipalities, and other public-sector organizations in Canada have set aside space for day care centres, many of which are independent nonprofit organizations. In contrast, only a handful of private-sector employers have child care facilities. Child care has become a relatively important public policy issue, however, and government response may include tax incentives for employers to expand this benefit.[24] Some municipal and provincial governments are already active in this regard. With zoning incentives from the City of Toronto, one building developer redesigned its office tower to accommodate a nonprofit centre operated by George Brown College.[25]

Exhibit 16–5 lists some workplace child care arrangements in the private sector. Most of these facilities are employer-subsidized nonprofit organizations with day care licences located at or near the work site. Smaller businesses might try a less formal arrangement by renovating and loaning space to employees who are responsible for sharing the wages of a child care worker or nanny. Another approach, used by ManuLife in Toronto, is to secure places by contributing funds to an existing facility near the workplace. Finally, the benefit arrangement might take the form of a voucher or reimbursement provided to employees with day care expenses.

CANADA'S RETIREMENT INCOME SYSTEM

Pensions are more than another employee benefit in Canada. They are an important part of national policy and are the dominant business of many consulting firms. In the past decade, Canada's retirement income system has been studied more than any other social program.[26] Substantial changes will occur over the next decade in public, employer-sponsored, and individual retirement programs resulting from these commissions and inquiries.

To understand pensions within the employee benefit package, we need to examine the components of the retirement income smorgasbord. These income sources are roughly divided into three tiers: (1) government retirement income security programs, (2) Canada/Quebec Pension Plan (C/QPP), (3) employer-sponsored pension plans and individual savings initiatives. As Exhibit 16–6 illustrates, employer-sponsored pension plans (EPPs) represent a sizable proportion of retirement income in Canada.

Government Income Security Program

Retirement income policy in Canada is directed toward minimizing the number of elderly living below the poverty line. To accomplish this, the Canadian government established three income security programs: Old Age Security (OAS), the Guaranteed Income Supplement (GIS), and Spouse's Allowance (SA). Several provinces have supplementary programs.[27]

Old Age Security was introduced in 1952 as Canada's first universal pension program, replacing a means-tested program, which had been operating since 1927.[28] As with all of the government retirement income security

EXHIBIT 16-5
Some Workplace Child Care Arrangements in the Private Sector

Name of Centre	Employer Contribution	Weekly Parent Fees (per child)	Number of Spaces	Number of Staff
Garderie Pomme de Reinette Montreal, Quebec Banque Nationale du Canada	Phone, maintenance, rent, computer services, postage	$65 for infants, $55 for toddlers and preschoolers	40	6 staff, 1 supervisor, 1 cook
Garderie sur une Patte Drummondville, Quebec Celanese Canada	Space, food, maintenance, and accounting	$50	60	9 staff, 1 supervisor, 1 cook, 7 full-time, and 2 part-time instructors
Down's Child Centre Winnipeg, Manitoba Horsemen's Association	Rent and utilities, loans as needed	$39	26	
Garderie L'Enfanfreluche Montreal, Quebec Lavalin Inc.	Accounting, payroll, subsidy 1 hot meal and 2 snacks	$50 and $37 for 2 children	60	8 staff full-time, 1 supervisor, 1 secretary, part-time 2 cooks, 2 p/t staff, 4 on call

Mutual Life Assurance Co. of Canada Day Care Centre Waterloo, Ontario Mutual Life of Canada Limited	All capital costs, some administrative services, (renovations and equipment to be paid back out of any profits)	$65 (to increase January 1985)	40	5 staff with E.C.E., 1 supervisor
7/11 Daycare Centre Burnaby, B.C. Southland Canada	Rent, utilities, repairs and maintenance, administrative support, and food	$46 toddlers $35 preschoolers	25	
Garderie de la Place Ville Marie Montreal, Quebec Trizec	Space, services	$85	30	1 director 1 staff
Nanisivik Daycare Centre Nanisivik, NWT Strathcona, Mineral Services	Employer covers all costs	No charge to users		

Source: Susan Deller, "The Daycare Dilemma," *Benefits Canada*, April 1986, pp. 15–20. Reproduced with permission from *Benefits Canada*, a Maclean-Hunter publication.

EXHIBIT 16–6
Distribution of Total Retirement Income among Employer-Sponsored Pension Plan Recipients 65 Years and Older

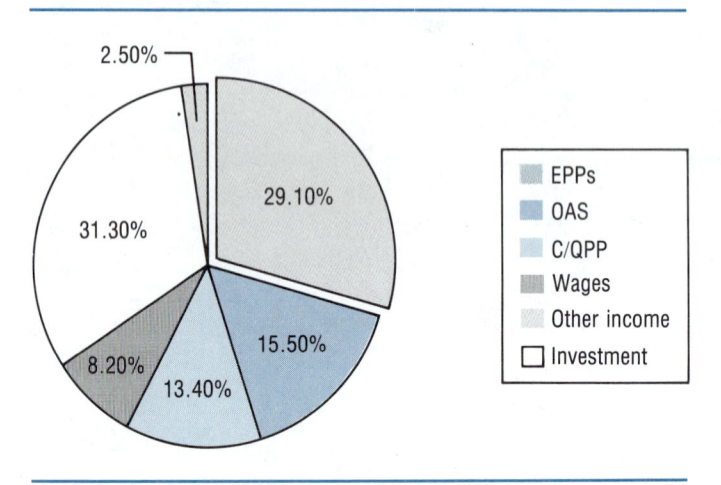

- 2.50%
- 29.10%
- 31.30%
- 8.20%
- 13.40%
- 15.50%

Legend:
- EPPs
- OAS
- C/QPP
- Wages
- Other income
- Investment

Note: These data only include members of employer-sponsored pension plans. Among all retirees (including those without pension plans), the percentage attributed to EPPs would presumably be much lower.
Source: Statistics Canada, *Pension Plans in Canada* (Ottawa: Minister of Supply and Services Canada, 1986). Reproduced with permission.

programs described in this section, OAS is funded through general tax revenues. All persons older than 65 who meet the residency qualifications of the OAS program are entitled to a taxable monthly income that is raised quarterly with inflation.

For retirees with few alternate sources of income, the OAS is usually insufficient to cover living expenses. Consequently, the Guaranteed Income Supplement was introduced by the federal government in 1967 as an income-tested addition to retirement income.[29] GIS benefits are paid monthly with the OAS cheque and are adjusted quarterly for inflation. In 1975, the federal government introduced the Spouse's Allowance to assist low-income couples where one person receives GIS and the other is between 60 and 64. The program essentially gives the younger spouse monthly benefits equivalent to OAS and GIS. The Spouse's Allowance is also income-tested.

The final piece in the government retirement income security system is various supplements provided by six provinces and the two territories. These are similar to the GIS program because they are directed toward assisting low-income persons older than 65. Some provincial retirement supplements are income-tested; others are means-tested.

Canada/Quebec Pension Plan

The second tier of the retirement income system, the Canada/Quebec pension plan, was established in 1965. The program was developed with the belief that employer-sponsored plans and personal savings alone could not fully meet retirement income needs. As a publicly administered pension system funded jointly by the employer and employee, C/QPP would minimize dependence on OAS and GIS. Almost all employed Canadians between the ages of 18 and 70 and earning above a basic exemption level must participate in C/QPP.

Before 1987, the tax-deductible contributions to C/QPP were 3.6 percent of employment earnings up to a yearly maximum pensionable earnings (YMPE), which is approximately the average industrial wage. Contributions are shared equally (i.e., 1.8 percent) between the company and employees. Self-employed persons pay the full contribution.

With concerns about the long-term viability of the C/QPP reserves, the funding formula has been revised, as shown in Exhibit 16–7. Total C/QPP contributions increased to 3.8 percent in 1987 and will further increase by 0.2 percentage points annually until 1991. Then, CPP premiums will increase by 0.15 percentage points for each of the 20 following years. By 2011, combined employer/employee contributions will be 7.6 percent of the YMPE.[30] The Quebec government is not yet committed to the CPP contribution adjustments after 1991.

EXHIBIT 16–7
Revised Total Annual Contribution Rate to Canada's Pension Plan

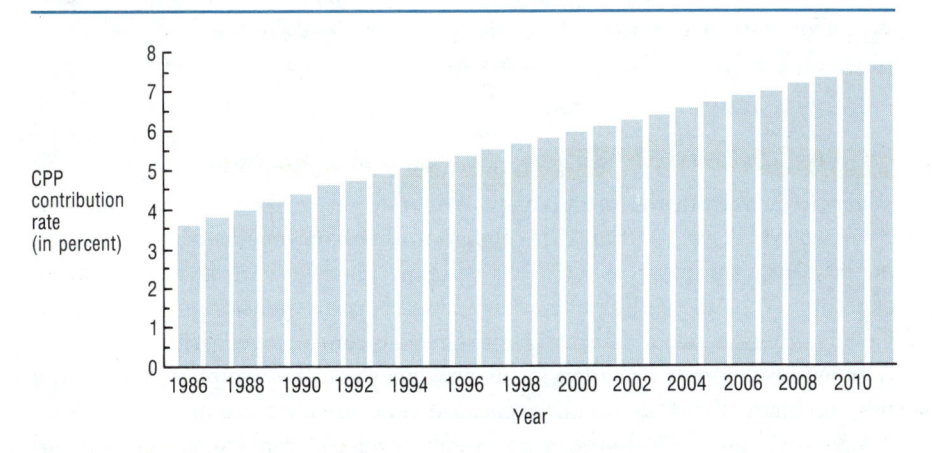

Note: Quebec Pension Plan contributions will follow the CPP schedule only until 1991.

The amount of C/QPP pension received depends on two factors. First, the pension increases with the employee's average pensionable earnings over the entire working life (adjusted for inflation). For example, an employee who earned an average of $22,000 over the years (in 1987 dollars) would receive a higher pension than someone earning a lifetime average of $18,000. Employees earning different average incomes above the YMPE would receive the same pension. We should also point out that lifetime average earnings are calculated as income in every year the person *could* have been in the labour force, even years when there was no labour force participation. Fortunately for those who have long illnesses, are unemployed, or enjoy year-long vacations, the calculation disregards up to 15 percent of the working years when income was low.

The second factor determining the C/QPP pension is the age of the employee when the pension commences. Until recently, C/QPP pensions were automatically received when the individual turned 65. At that age, the pension amounts to 25 percent of the person's average pensionable earnings. However, since 1987 (1984 in Quebec), C/QPP participants have been allowed to receive their pension anytime between the ages of 60 and 70. For those retiring early, the pension decreases by 0.5 percent for each month between the time of commencement and the person's 65th birthday. The pension increases by the same percent for those retiring after age 65. In Quebec, where this option was first introduced, approximately 20 percent of those aged 60 to 64 who are eligible for QPP pension benefits have taken early retirement.[31]

The C/QPP program also provides benefits to surviving spouses and children, a death benefit, and a pension to the severely disabled. Other provisions deal with pension sharing and splitting pension credits upon divorce. Although the idea of C/QPP pensions for homemakers has received much discussion, it has not yet been incorporated into the program.[32]

Employer-Sponsored Pensions and Individual Savings

When C/QPP was introduced, it was generally believed that retirement income would be sufficient only if the government intervened with a mandatory public pension program. C/QPP has certainly improved the financial security of retirement, but public policy now views company pension plans and individual savings as major sources of retirement income as well. This philosophy is reflected in recent changes to legislation governing employer-sponsored pension plans (EPPs) as well as registered retirement saving plans (RRSPs).[33]

As of January 1984 (the latest data available), there were 17,711 employer-sponsored pension plans covering more than 4.5 million employees.

This represents 47 percent of all paid employed (not self-employed) workers in Canada.[34]

Pensions are probably the oldest cash-based employee benefit. Several organizations, including the Hudson's Bay Company and some provincial legislatures, paid retirement gratuities on an ad hoc basis before Confederation. The first known pension plan was developed in 1870 for employees of the Canadian federal government. Grand Trunk Railroad (now part of Canadian National Railway) began its pension plan four years later. By the end of the 1880s, a few financial institutions had also introduced plans for their staff.[35]

Despite the long history of EPPs, these benefits had almost no statutory regulation until 1965 when the Ontario government introduced legislation. Pension legislation is still absent in several provinces. Where legislation does exist, fairly dramatic reforms are under way. The major changes are discussed later. First, we will outline the various types of EPPs found in this country.

Types of EPPs

Employer-sponsored pension plans basically vary by the type of contribution required or pension provided. As Exhibit 16–8 indicates, two major groups exist: defined contribution and defined benefit plans.

In defined contribution (also called money-purchase) plans, the amount of money contributed to the pension fund is known or determined while the amount of pension upon retirement depends on the quality of the investment strategy. For example, a company pension plan might require the employer and employee to each contribute an amount equivalent to 5 percent of the

EXHIBIT 16–8
Membership in Different Employer-Sponsored Pension Plans

	Pension Plans		Membership	
Type of Pension Plan	Number	Percent	Number	Percent
Defined contribution plans				
General defined contribution	8,613	48.6%	252,498	5.5%
Profit sharing	417	2.4	16,125	0.4
Subtotal: Defined contribution	9,030	51.0	268,623	5.9
Defined benefit plans				
Final earnings	3,472	19.6	2,720,709	59.6
Career average earnings	3,562	20.1	592,030	13.0
Flat benefit	1,352	7.6	930,509	20.4
Subtotal: Defined benefit	8,386	47.3	4,243,248	93.0
Combination and other plans	295	1.7	52,752	1.2
Grand total	17,711	100.0%	4,564,623	100.0%

Source: Statistics Canada, *Pension Plans in Canada* (Ottawa: Minister of Supply and Services Canada, 1986), text table M.

employee's salary in regular installments. Upon retirement, the accumulated contributions and return from investments are used to purchase either an annuity or registered retirement income fund (RRIF). The amount of money entering the pension fund is known, but the size of the employee's annuity varies. A variation of defined contribution plan is a profit-sharing plan (see Chapter Fifteen) where the amount of employer contribution depends on profits.

In contrast to defined contribution plans, defined benefit plans define the amount of pension received at retirement, but vary the total contributions required to meet the benefit objective. If the plan is contributory—that is, employees are required to make contributions along with the employer—the amount of employee contribution is fixed and the employer must make up any shortfall. Whether or not the defined benefit plan is underfunded or overfunded is determined by regular actuarial inspections.

Defined benefit plans also vary with the type of benefit provided. Some are flat benefit plans that provide a fixed dollar pension for each year of service. The most common defined benefit plans use a unit benefit formula. Employees receive a unit of pension that is expressed as a percentage of earnings for each year of service. For instance, most of these plans award 2 percent of earnings for each year of service, usually to a maximum of 35 years. A participant in this type of plan who retires after 25 years would receive a pension equivalent to 50 percent (25 × 2%) of his or her earnings base. But what is the earnings base? As Exhibit 16–8 reveals, some plans use career average earnings, others use some variation of final or best earnings as the base.

The variety of employer-sponsored pension plans is limited only to the imagination of pension specialists. New types of plans are developing each year.[36] All EPPs must fit within the applicable regulatory guidelines, however, where they exist. These guidelines address important public policies and have been subject to much debate and reform within the past few years. In particular, EPPs must comply with changes in vesting, portability, coverage, retirement flexibility, fund disclosure, and survivor benefits.

Vesting

Nearly 70 percent of all pension plan members in 1984 belonged to contributory plans. That is, both the employee and employer pay into the pension fund. For the remainder, contributions are made only by the company. Employees who quit or otherwise leave the plan before retirement age have access to the money they have contributed. However, the employer's contributions do not automatically belong to the employee.

In the earliest pension plans, employer contributions were received only by those who stayed in the plan until retirement. The reason behind this policy was that pensions were initially viewed as long-service rewards, and company contributions were gratuities to those who stayed until retirement. But as time passed, particularly as labour unions negotiated for higher pension benefits, employer contributions became more of a deferred wage.[37] In 1965, the Ontario government's pension legislation gave employees the right to the employer's contributions when they were at least 45 years old and had 10 years or more of service (the 45-and-10 rule). Other provinces followed with similar legislation. This right to the employer's contributions is known as vesting.

Although statutory vesting requirements helped to ensure that more employees received a pension, employee turnover is still high enough that many company contributions are forfeited. Consequently, the federal government and a few provinces have changed (or will soon change) their legislation to require vesting after two years of membership in the plan regardless of age. This means both higher pensions for employees in the future as well as higher pension costs for employers (because fewer contributions will be forfeited).

Portability

What happens to pension contributions when employees leave before retirement? If the funds are not vested, the employee's contributions are typically paid out in cash or deposited into an RRSP. However, if the funds are vested, they are typically locked in, that is, held by the employer until retirement. This is less than ideal because it fragments pension benefits and can result in a lower total pension at retirement. A better solution for the employee is to arrange for the accrued pension benefits to be transferred to the new employer. This is the concept of pension portability.

Multiemployer pension plans provide one form of portability. If the employee moves to another company participating in the plan, the pension fund contributions are continuous. Currently 14 percent of pension plan members belong to multiemployer plans. One of the largest is the Ontario Municipal Employees Retirement System (OMERS). C/QPP is also fully portable because Canadians stay in the plan when changing jobs without losing the employer's contributions.

The recent legislative changes have addressed the portability issue by giving employees the option of transferring the lump sum value of the vested benefit to a new employer's pension plan or locking it into an RRSP or deferred annuity. This promises to be one of the more challenging technicalities of pension plan management in the future.

Other Pension Legislation Changes

Although it is not possible to detail all the recent changes and proposals to pension legislation, several are briefly listed below:

Part-Time Employees. Pensions laws in several jurisdictions now require part-time employees above a stated income level to be eligible to participate in the employer's pension plan after two years of service. Previously, these people were excluded from most plans.

Spouses' Rights. Pension credits may be split between spouses where a plan member has a marriage breakdown. Previously, the spouse's right to part of the pension was not clear.

Employee Participation. In most plans, employers must establish a pension committee with representation from both current employees and retirees. Before this change, employee influence in pension plan activities was limited except where permitted by the employer or negotiated by the union.

Nondiscriminatory Benefits. The amount of annual pension income from defined contribution plans is determined from life expectancy tables, the person's pension assets at retirement, the person's age, and special features of the annuity or retirement income fund (e.g., inflation protection). In the past, women have received lower pension income than men of the same age with the same pension assets because women are expected to live longer. Now pension income must be based on unisex life expectancy tables. These tables do not differentiate the life expectancy of men and women, so all employees retiring at the same age with the same pension assets will receive the same annuity income.

All these changes will significantly affect employer-sponsored pensions and the duties of P/HRM professionals in this area of employee benefits.

Individual Retirement Savings

In 1957, the Canadian government introduced the Registered Retirement Savings Plan (RRSP). With tax deferral as an incentive, it was hoped that RRSPs would encourage individuals to save for retirement. For various reasons, the plans got off to a slow start, although the number of people with RRSPs recently increased dramatically. In the 1983 taxation year, about one fifth of the labour force had an RRSP. Most participants are middle- and high-income earners. Changes to RRSPs throughout the late 1980s will permit higher annual contributions, but are unlikely to increase the participation rate of low-income workers.

This completes discussion of the types of employee benefits. It is evident that P/HRM professionals have no shortage of options to include in the benefit package. With divergent employee preferences and such a wide variety of benefits, employers must carefully manage the benefits package to meet the objectives for which it was designed.

MANAGING BENEFITS

The benefits offered by an employer should reflect the organization's objectives, strategies, and culture.[38] Some perquisites, such as recreational facilities and holidays, emphasize the short term. These may help a growth-oriented company attract new employees. Longer-term benefits, which may be used in more mature organizations, emphasize security. For instance, pension plans reward employees for their years of service. Vesting arrangements in employee pension plans motivate individuals to stay with the employer long enough to receive the full pension benefit.

With increasing emphasis on pay-for-performance, some benefits are directed toward employee motivation and productivity.[39] For example, one imaginative Canadian firm gives the best parking spot in the company lot to the "employee of the month." Rather than providing guaranteed pension contributions, Mitel and numerous other firms base pension plan contributions on company profits through a deferred profit-sharing plan (see Chapter Fifteen). To increase employee productivity and reduce absenteeism, many firms added fitness-related benefits to the package. These include programs to stop smoking or lose weight and either in-house fitness centres or subsidized memberships to health clubs. Vancouver City Savings Credit Union even provides incentives for employees to jog 150 kilometres because it believes a healthy employee is a productive employee.

Benefit Objectives

In addition to achieving organizational goals, benefits should satisfy the objectives of competitiveness, matching individual needs, adequacy, and cost-effectiveness. Employers must adopt a benefits policy regarding their competition just as they do for direct compensation. Do they wish to lead or lag competitors' benefit levels? The competitiveness of a benefits package is often assessed through pay surveys. Many organizations purchase special benefits surveys that provide detailed information on each industry.

Adequacy of benefits can be assessed by determining the percentage of present income an employee and survivors would require in the event of retirement, death, or disability, and comparing this to the comparable value of the benefits provided by the organization. A company pension plan that provides 35 percent of final pay, with C/QPP and Old Age Security adding 20 percent, results in a combined replacement ratio of 55 percent. Various ratios can be targetted for different employees according to income and/or length of service.

As the work force diversifies, awareness is increasing that benefits must meet individual needs of employees. Some employers survey employees to

EXHIBIT 16–9
Cost Analysis of Employee Benefits

Step 1. Examine the internal cost to the company of all benefits and services, by payroll classification, by profit centre.
Step 2. Compare the company's costs for benefits to external norms. For example, compare its costs to average costs, averages by industry, and so on, as reported in surveys such as those conducted by the Chamber of Commerce, for the package as a whole and for each benefit.
Step 3. Prepare a report for the decision maker, contrasting Steps 1 and 2 and highlighting major variances.
Step 4. Analyze the costs of the program to employees. Determine what each employee is paying for benefits, totally and by benefit.
Step 5. Compare the data in Step 4 with external data such as the Chamber of Commerce data.
Step 6. Analyze how satisfied the individual is with the employer's program, and as compared to competitors' programs.

Source: Bruce Ellig, "Determining the Competitiveness of Employee Benefit System," *Compensation Review*, First Quarter 1974, pp. 8–34.

---

determine which benefits are valued. Later we will discuss a more direct way to tailor benefits to individual needs through flexible benefit systems.

Adequacy is often traded off against another benefit objective: cost-effectiveness. Every organization with substantial benefits costs should conduct a cost analysis. Costs can be compared on four bases:

1. Total annual cost of benefits for all employees.
2. Cost per employee per year [item (1) divided by the number of employees].
3. Percentage of payroll [item (1) divided by annual payroll].
4. Cost per employee per hour [item (2) divided by employee hours worked].

Ellig proposes a mechanism of cost analysis that examines the total benefits picture.[40] The steps he recommends are outlined in Exhibit 16–9. This approach provides the kind of information needed to make executive decisions about employee benefits that will be cost-oriented as well as strategic.

Two other aspects of managing employee benefits that deserve further discussion are benefits communication and containment of benefit costs.

Benefits Communication

An often overlooked method of improving the effectiveness of the benefits package is to regularly communicate its content to employees. Benefits cannot satisfy or motivate if employees do not know about them or understand their value. Yet most studies indicate employees at all levels in the organization are either unaware of the benefits provided or significantly undervalue their actual cost and usefulness.[41]

Increasingly, employers are designing a variety of benefits communication programs. Brochures are probably the most common medium to explain the benefits package, particularly to new employees. A potentially more effective medium is the annual employee benefit report, which briefly describes each benefit and indicates its cost and value. An example is reproduced in Exhibit 16-10. Other benefit reports also calculate how much each benefit would cost if employees purchased it on their own.

Another way to communicate the benefits package is through an annual videotaped message. At Sears Canada, employees are shown a video program each year informing them of the benefits offered, the advantages of these over those provided by other organizations, and the benefit costs borne by the company. Other innovative benefits communications practices include listing both the employer and employee costs of benefits on each pay cheque. Some firms have individual benefit counselling sessions, usually held once every two or three years with an in-house benefits specialist. B.C. Tel has a benefits hot line that employees can use at any time to get answers to questions about their compensation package. At Canadian Tire, a committee of employees invented "Dollars and Sense," a trivia-type board game that asks employees 500 questions about the company's benefits and other information. The game is accompanied by a slide and tape show.[42]

One study has found that employees satisfied with their benefits are also satisfied with their jobs.[43] The cost of benefits is not related to employee satisfaction. But the study reports satisfaction improves with the frequency of benefits communication. When employees know more about their benefits, they are more satisfied.

In sum, employers are spending a large proportion of total compensation on benefits and almost nothing on benefit communications. To make the benefit dollars more cost-effective, they need to increase the quantity and quality of their communications about these benefits.

Containing Benefit Costs

As benefit expenses increase, cost containment becomes a higher priority. Rarely are benefits withdrawn to reduce labour costs. Rather, a variety of cost control strategies are available to manage benefits more cost effectively.

Contributory benefit plans require employees to pay a share of the costs. For example, they may be required to cover some or all of the premiums for the dental plan. The contributory approach may make employees more aware of benefit costs and be more selective in using these services. (Higher usage

EXHIBIT 16–10
Annual Individualized Benefit Report

Simon Fraser University Personal Benefits' Statement

Name _____
Social Insurance Number _____
Birthdate _____
Employment Class _____

All information provided in your Personal Benefit Statement is based on your earnings as of the statement date indicated equal to _____.

Statement Date _____

Health and Dental Care

Basic Health Care benefits are provided through your B.C. Medical Services Plan As of the Statement Date

You have couple benefits at a cost of $32.00/month.

Extended Health Care benefits As of the Statement Date

You have couple MSA benefits at a cost of $5.25/month – 100% paid.

Health and Dental Care

Dental Care benefits as of the Statement Date

CU&C

Your dental benefits include

You have couple dental at a cost of $26.68/mo.-100% pd. 80% of Plan A services 50% of Plan B services

Income Protection

Short-Term Disability benefits (based on your length of service with _____ are provided as follows: _____ 100% of salary for 26 weeks.

Survivor Benefits

Basic Life Insurance—In the event of your death your beneficiary would receive _____

Optional Life Insurance—In addition to your basic life benefit your beneficiary would receive _____

Beneficiary for life insurance is _____

Income Protection

Long-Term Disability benefits provide for continued income on expiry of your short-term benefits

Your Long-Term Disability benefits will provide _____

The cost of your Long-Term Disability benefits _____

Survivor Benefits

Business Travel Protection In the event of accidental death while on business your beneficiary would receive an additional sum of _____ $150,000

Your pension plan death benefit is equal to the value of your money purchase pension account with interest.

EXHIBIT 16–10 *(concluded)*

Retirement Benefits

Your Pension Plan credited service date is ___01 September, 1983___

As of the Statement Date, your rights to deferred pension benefits on termination of employment ___not eligible___

Your normal retirement date is ___01 September, 2020___

Beneficiary for retirement benefits is:
Basic Account ___
Voluntary Contribution Account ___not elected___

Retirement Benefits

Your Pension Plan benefit payable at normal retirement is ___ is determined by the value of your account at retirement.

Government Benefits

Income Protection
Canada Pension Plan provides ___ Total disability benefits up to a maximum of $455.64 per month.

Workers' Compensation provides benefits for absence due to occupational injury ___ Benefits vary with extent of injury.

Unemployment Insurance provides maternity leave benefits for up to 15 weeks

Government Benefits

Survivor Protection
Canada Pension provides ___ a lump sum death benefit up to $2,580 for 1986, plus a spouse's pension (if applicable). Up to a maximum of $486.11 per month for 1986.

Retirement Benefits
Canada Pension Plan provides a pension payable from age 65 ___ Payable at age 65 up to $891.00 for 1986.

Unemployment Insurance provides a lump sum retirement benefit ___

Note: Long-Term Disability and Retirement Plan benefits are integrated with benefits payable from Workers' Compensation and the Canada Pension Plan.

General Information

The cost of each component of your benefits program is shared by you and the University on the following basis:

	Your share	University share
Basic Health		100%
Extended Health	100%	
Dental Care		100%
Short Term Disability		100%
Long Term Disability	100%	
Basic Life Insurance		100%
Optional Life Insurance	100%	
Retirement Benefits		100%

HOMEOWNER/TENANTS INSURANCE PROTECTION

Optional Insurance start date _____
Optional Insurance end date _____
The cost of your insurance is _____ You have no coverage.

Important

All information provided on your Personal Benefit Statement is based on our record of your benefits status as of the Statement Date. To assist in updating our files, should any information provided on your Personal Benefit Statement appear incorrect or you require further clarification, please contact the Personnel Department *in writing* noting your Social Insurance number and indicating the information which is in question.

The Personal Benefit Statement has been prepared to help you gain a better understanding of your total benefits program. Please retain for easy reference. The benefits card can be detached and inserted into your wallet. All terms and conditions are governed by the provisions of applicable policies, contracts, and collective agreements. E&OE.

Health Care Benefits

Basic Health Care Benefits are provided through the B.C. Medical Services Plan.
You are enrolled for _____ couple

Extended Health Care Benefits are provided through _____ MSA

You are enrolled for _____ couple benefits

Dental Care Benefits

Dental Care Benefits are provided through _____ CU&C

You are enrolled for _____ couple

Eligible dental expenses include

Plan A @ 80%
Plan B @ 50%

Claims Procedures

Submit Extended Health Claims directly to MSA
Policy No. _____

Submit Dental Care Claims directly to CU&C
Policy No. _____

Benefits Card

Name _____

Certificate Number _____

Date _____

Signature _____

of some benefits may lead to higher premiums.) Because of the visibility of employee contributions, however, employers are often under pressure to reduce and eventually eliminate the employee's payments. A common bargaining strategy by labour unions is to begin an employee benefit on a contributory basis and later negotiate a noncontributory arrangement (where the employer pays the full cost).

Another method of reducing benefit costs is to increase the amount of the deductible.[44] In an extended health care plan, for example, the premiums are higher if the insurer refunds 100 percent of the medical or prescription bill than if the employee pays a percentage or a fixed amount (say, the first $25).

Self-insurance is another option, although it is usually too risky for small businesses. Rather than purchasing a benefit from an insurer who absorbs the risk, self-insured employers set up an internal fund (known as a reserve) to pay covered expenses. The advantages of self-insurance are that the employer avoids both the federal tax levied on insurance premiums and the extra administrative costs of the insurer. The main disadvantage, of course, is the costs of the benefit are unknown beforehand. For some benefit plans, the self-insured company may be at considerable risk.

The trend toward self-insurance is particularly evident in dental plans because the disbursements are small and regular. One survey estimates that more than half of Canadian firms with 500 or more employees have self-insured their dental plans.[45] Many of these are actually administrative service plans (ASPs), where the employer pays an annual fee to the insurance firm to administer the benefit. At the end of the year, the employer reimburses the insurer for all paid-out claims. Other employers undertake the administration as well as the risk.

Increasing employee awareness and containing costs are two valuable ongoing strategies to meet the objectives of a well-managed benefits program. Next, we look at a new development in benefits management that promises to further enhance the effective use of benefit dollars: flexible benefits.

Flexible Benefits

One of the most significant developments in the management of employee benefits is the introduction of flexible benefit systems.[46] This approach allows employees to participate in the composition of their individual benefit package.

Most organizations already offer employees some degree of flexibility in their benefits package. However, this flexibility is usually restricted to voluntary employee-paid options. All employees receive the same basic plan, but they can supplement this by purchasing additional options with their own money through payroll deductions. For instance, when the Bank of Nova Scotia learned its employees wanted more comprehensive personal injury coverage, it added this option for those who were willing to pay the premium.[47] In many companies, a benefits package that includes one times earnings of life insurance might permit employees to purchase up to two additional earnings multiples with the same carrier through payroll deductions.

The Flexible Dollar System

A growing number of Canadian firms have introduced a flexible benefits system that offers employees more control over employer contributions. These plans include a set of core benefits plus a flexible dollar allowance that employees use to purchase optional benefits. The amount of flexible dollars allotted by the employer typically increases with the employee's base salary. The core benefits, which are required for all employees, are paid by both the employer and employee.

Cominco Ltd. of Vancouver was one of the first companies to introduce the flexible dollar system. Similar plans are found at IMC in Saskatchewan as well as Reichhold Ltd., 3M Ltd., BP Canada, and Pepsi-Cola Canada Ltd. in Ontario.[48]

Exhibit 16–11 illustrates the election form for Cominco's Flex-Com benefits system. It has been completed by a young married woman without dependents, and earning $25,000. In addition to the core benefits (not shown on the form), this employee is given a $483 flexible dollar allowance by Cominco. Notice she increased this allowance by selling her basic medical insurance because this benefit is also covered by her husband's plan.

With the flexible dollars allowance, the employee has purchased full extended health coverage, intermediate dental insurance, two units (two times earnings) of life insurance, and nine additional units of accidental death and dismemberment insurance (AD&D). She has also opted to pay for the long-term disability premiums with after-tax dollars through payroll deduction so in the event of disability the insurance company's payments to her would not be taxed. (With flexible dollars, the premiums are tax free but disability payments are taxable.) The remaining flexible dollars are deposited to the employee's retirement income savings plan (RISP). She could have taken this as cash, but it would have been taxed as income.

Evaluation of Flexible Benefit Plans

Although flexible benefit systems have received a lot of favourable media attention, are they really effective? How do they fare against the objectives of meeting individual needs, adequacy, competitiveness, and cost-effectiveness?

Meeting Individual Needs. The most obvious advantage of flexible benefits is that they are most likely to meet the needs of individual employees.[49] Traditional benefit plans were designed around the typical employee in the 1950s—a male wage earner with a homemaker wife and three children. Yet

EXHIBIT 16-11
Flexible Benefits at Cominco

1987 Flex-Com Election Form

PERSONAL & CONFIDENTIAL

Refer to the guidebook items noted to complete your elections. **It is most important** that you complete and return this form — otherwise **your benefits will be reduced to core** coverage. All values given are annual.

Your 1986 elections (guidebook item 1)

Name: JANE DOE

Options	Option Costs/Values	Election	Flex Dollars	or	Payroll Deduction
Flexible Dollar Allowance (g.b. item 2) **Family Status** COUPLE	N/A	N/A	$ 483 (Allowance)		N/A
Basic Medical & Hospital (g.b. item 3) A. Keep government medical B. Sell government medical	$ 192 (selling value)	Option: B (1) Coverage: N (2)	N/A		N/A
Extended Health Benefits (g.b. item 4) A. Core B. Full	Single $16 Couple $32 Family $48	Option: B (3) Coverage: C (4)	32 (5)		N/A
Dental (guidebook item 5) A. Core B. Basic C. Intermediate D. Full	Single — $120 $168 $252 Couple — $204 $324 $456 Family — $300 $492 $816	Option: C (6) Coverage: C (7)	324 (8)		N/A
Life Insurance (guidebook item 6) Employee A. Core ($ 25,000) B. Core + optional in units of $ ___ (smoker rates) C. Core + optional in units of $ ___ (non-smoker rates)	$ — /unit (guar.) $ — /unit (smoker) $ 9.36 /unit (non-smoker)	Option: C (9) No. of units Age rel.: 2 (10) Guar. rate: N (11)	N/A		18.72 (12)
Spouse-optional Spouse age ___ A. No coverage B. Units of $10,000 at smoker rates C. Units of $10,000 at non-smoker rates	1-15 units at smoker rates 1-15 units at non-smoker rates	Option: A (13) No. of units: N (14)	N/A		N (15)
AD&D (guidebook item 7) Employee A. Core $ 75,000 B. Core + employee-optional AD&D in units of $10,000	1-15 units at $4.80/unit	Option: B (16) Units: 9 (17)	$43.20 (18)	or	N (19)
Spouse-optional A. No coverage B. Units of $10,000	1-15 units at $4.80/unit	Option: A (20) Units: N (21)	N (22)	or	N (23)
Long-term disability (g.b. item 8) A. Pay with flexible dollars B. Pay by payroll deduction C. No coverage in first year	$	Option: B (24)	N/A	N (25)	or	99 (26)
Sale of Flexible Holidays (guidebook item 9) You may sell up to ___ days of your current flexible holidays for $ ___ per day. All sales final.	Days sold: N (27)	N/A		N/A

Retirement Savings plans (guidebook item 10)

Flexible Dollar Accounting (guidebook item 11)

Flex $ Allowance	Basic Medical if sold	Holiday credits	New SSPP credits	Total Flex Dollars	Flex Dollars spent	Cash Account balance
483 (28)	− 192 (29)	+ N (30)	+ — (31)	= 675 (32)	− 399.20 (33)	= 275.80 (34)

EXHIBIT 16–11 *(concluded)*

Cash Account Balance (guidebook item 12)
Distribution of unused balance: % to RISP/SSPP
(subject to specified maximum)

June 30   35 **50**

December 31   36 **50**

Maximum 1986 RISP/SSPP contribution: $3,500 or   37 [ ]

Authorized Payroll Deductions (guidebook item 13)
Total Boxes 12, 15, 19, 23, 26
Authorized Payroll Deductions

38 **$117.72**   Box 38 total **117.72** ÷ 12 = **9.81** deduction   Monthly Flex-Com
Other payroll deductions include RISP/SSPP, CPP, UIC, income tax, etc.

I hereby authorize Cominco Ltd. to arrange my benefit coverage as I have elected above and where designated to make appropriate payroll deductions. I understand that the values shown in this form may change during the year if my family status or salary changes and I declare and confirm as follows (check boxes for parts that apply):

[✓] I am cancelling my provincial medical coverage: I hereby confirm that I am covered under my spouse's medical plan (identity number **1234567** dependent number **2**).

[✓] I am electing optional life insurance at non-smoker rates: I affirm that I have not smoked for at least one year. **JD** (initials)

[ ] I am electing spouse-optional life insurance at non-smoker rates: I affirm that my spouse has not smoked for at least one year. _____ (initials)

[ ] I am electing **new** units of employee or spouse-optional life insurance: I understand that the election must be accompanied by an application, that the additional coverage commences only upon confirmation by the insurer and that any misrepresentation on the application form may result in that insurance becoming void.

[ ] I am cancelling previously held units of optional life insurance: I acknowledge that this is my intention. _____ (initials)

[ ] I am cancelling units of optional life insurance previously held at the guaranteed rate. I understand that I may not buy units at that rate again. _____ (initials)

I understand that the Flex-Com program permits me to select benefit options that suit my current needs. As those needs change, I shall have the opportunity to adapt my benefits as the program permits. I accept full responsibility for the elections I have made on this form, and I take responsibility for ensuring that my coverage remains suitable to my changing needs. I hereby declare that the representations I have made in this form are true and accurately reflect my current personal status. I understand that misrepresentation of non-smoker status may cause my optional group life insurance to become void.

Signature: *Jane Doe*   Date: *January 29/87*

FOR LOCAL PERSONNEL OFFICE USE ONLY

Enclosures
Group Life app. [ ]   Checked   Comments:
  card   [ ]
AD&D card   [ ]
SSPP-RISP
  transfer forms [ ]   _____
  card   [ ]   (Init.)

Source: Updated from Susan Deller, "Cominco's Flex-Com: A Canadian Prototype," *Benefits Canada*, April 1984, pp. 22–26. Reproduced with permission of *Benefits Canada*, a Maclean-Hunter publication.

most households today are two-income families, as women now make up approximately 40 percent of the work force. The traditional family of yesteryear represents less than 25 percent of Canadian households today. Moreover, employee benefit preferences vary with other demographic characteristics such as age and length of service.

Flexible benefit systems challenge the traditional notions by viewing the work force as a group of individuals with different benefit needs and preferences. This individuality is reflected in the fact that most employees alter their benefits package when the flexible system is introduced. Exhibit 16–12 lists the changes made by nonunion employees at Reichhold's operations in North Bay and Thunder Bay when flexible benefits were introduced in early 1986.

Adequacy. Greater flexibility can potentially increase the risk of inadequate coverage because employees might make poor decisions. However, flexible benefit systems developed in Canada have safeguards to ensure adequacy. Every plan has a set of core benefits, so all employees receive the most essential coverage (such as basic protection in the event of long-term disability). Moreover, some P/HRM managers involved with these plans discovered Canadian employees are more likely to overinsure themselves. This reflects similar observations in the United States.[50]

Competitiveness. Lawler argues that flexible benefit schemes can make the compensation system more competitive without increasing the cost of the benefits.[51] Matching benefits to individual needs increases their perceived

EXHIBIT 16–12
Changes to Flexible Benefits at Reichhold Ltd.

- 98 percent of participants made at least one change to their benefits when the flexible dollar plan was introduced in 1986.
- 62 percent opted for a different life insurance plan: 40 percent increased their core coverage of two times earnings; 22 percent reduced the coverage.
- 54 percent changed their dental coverage with most shifting to a more comprehensive plan.
- 23 percent reduced their major medical coverage; virtually all of these were able to integrate with plans provided by their spouse's employer.
- 75 percent opted for one of the 12 accidental death options; the other 25 percent dropped the coverage.
- 88 percent elected to retain the higher of two long-term disability options.
- 46 percent purchased dependent life insurance with their flexible dollars.
- 11 percent were able to waive provincial medical premiums because they were covered by their spouse's plan.
- 11 percent elected to sell some vacation days.

Source: Susan Deller, "Flexing Your Benefits," *Benefits Canada*, March 1986, pp. 31–35. Reproduced with permission from *Benefits Canada*, a Maclean-Hunter publication.

value. Detailed research has not been conducted, but plenty of anecdotal evidence exists. For example, P/HRM managers at Cominco observe that their Flex-Com system has helped the firm's ability to attract and retain employees. In one situation where an employee was asked to transfer to a subsidiary of Cominco, the absence of a flexible benefits system in the subsidiary company became a major issue.

Flexible benefits may also increase the firm's competitive position by presenting a more desirable image. Through surveys conducted at Cominco and Reichhold, several employees have commented that the introduction of flexible benefits is a sign the company treats its employees as responsible adults. Finally, with greater participation in the benefits planning process, employees are more likely to be aware of the cost of their benefits. Recall that the value of most benefit packages is lost by employees' inaccurate perception of their actual cost.

Cost-Effectiveness. One of the major concerns about flexible benefits is that the system is very costly to install. The program requires participant education and communication. Individual accounts must be established for each employee. Annual costs must also be figured in as employees change their plans. Xerox Canada decided against introducing a flexible benefits system when a feasibility study concluded the start-up costs would exceed $200,000. Pepsi's flexible dollar plan cost $80,000 to implement for its 600 salaried staff. At Cominco, a similar scheme cost approximately $190,000 for 1,800 salaried staff.

On the positive side of the cost-effectiveness equation, flexible benefit systems permit employers to add new benefit options without incurring additional costs. To illustrate, a company might have a group insurance plan with liberal life insurance and hospital/medical benefits. The company has no dental plan. By adopting the flexible dollar system, the company includes a dental plan without increasing its benefits cost. Employees who want the dental option shift the employer's cost out of some other benefits to select the dental option. The flexible approach can also have greater control over benefits costs by regulating the amount of flexible dollars allotted to each employee. Finally, software is available for both mainframe and microcomputers to manage the individual accounts with little difficulty.[52]

Flexible benefit systems are developing slowly in Canada. Whether they will become the norm or remain the exception is anyone's guess. The union movement is one potential source of resistance, although some unions are shedding their initial skepticism.[53] The need for actuarial stability in most insurance plans also restricts the installation of flexible benefits to large organizations. However, the insurance industry is currently examining ways to enable small businesses to introduce flexible plans.

SUMMARY

Employee benefits contribute substantially to the firm's labour costs. Yet these benefits are too often underutilized and unappreciated. Some of the pitfalls in the management of benefits include granting or increasing benefits without much regard to what they cost, what the preferences of employees are, or for what organizational objectives and goals they have been provided. With the costs of employee benefits rising faster than direct compensation, it is in the best interests of employees and the firm to manage the benefits package more effectively.

Some benefits are required by law: unemployment insurance, public pensions, and workers' compensation. Most employers offer additional benefits, such as compensation for time off (vacations, holidays, rest and lunch breaks), group insurance (health, life, and disability), private pensions, and other services such as prepaid legal services, health club memberships, or child care centres.

Little is known about the contribution employee benefits make to improving organizational effectiveness. Most researchers believe their impact is minimal. They might have a marginal effect on attracting and retaining employees. Few benefits are designed for motivation or productivity.

The benefit package has typically been poorly communicated to employees. Studies usually find that people are unaware of the type or level of benefits provided them. One solution is to review the benefit package regularly with employees either through a benefits report or personal counselling session. Alternatively, a flexible benefits system, whereby employees select the benefits they want using flexible dollars, increases their awareness. Flexible benefits may also enhance the effective use of benefit dollars by customizing benefits to individual preferences.

This chapter completes the Compensation section of the book. We have now discussed the major human resource activities of staffing, development, employment relations and rights, and compensation. Our remaining activity is Evaluation, the systematic review of P/HRM practices. This topic is discussed in Chapter Seventeen.

DISCUSSION AND REVIEW QUESTIONS

1. What are an employee's main sources of retirement income? What role does an employer play in influencing them?
2. What effect does communication have on various benefit objectives?
3. Describe three employee benefits required by law.
4. Describe three ways employers can introduce child care as an employee benefit.
5. Distinguish "defined contribution" and "defined benefit" pension plans.

6. What are "vesting" and "portability" in employer-sponsored pension plans? What effect do they have on employees?
7. How can employers contain benefit costs?
8. How can employers better match employee benefits with individual employee needs?
9. Describe two potential problems with flexible benefit plans.
10. Which employee benefits have different degrees of importance to employees of different ages?

NOTES AND REFERENCES

1. Virginia Galt, "Rise in Benefit Costs Seen Slowing," *The Globe and Mail*, September 2, 1982, p. B4; John Milne, "Picking Up the Tab," *Benefits Canada*, October 1984, pp. 21–26; Randall J. Dutka, "Reform Will Make Plans Costlier," *The Globe and Mail*, August 21, 1986, p. B18.
2. For a thorough discussion of the role of government in employee benefits, see Laurence E. Coward, *Mercer Handbook of Canadian Pension and Welfare Plans*, 8th ed. (Don Mills, Ont.: CCH Canadian, 1984).
3. Robert M. Clark, *Economic Security for the Aged in the United States and Canada: A Report Prepared for the Government of Canada* (Ottawa: Queen's Printer, 1960); Hart D. Clark, "The Development of the Retirement Income System in Canada," in *The Retirement Income System in Canada: Problems and Alternative Policies for Reform*, Vol. 2 (Ottawa: Minister of Supply and Services Canada, 1980), app. 1.
4. Virginia Galt, "Workers Are Winners on Prepaid Legal Aid," *The Globe and Mail*, July 15, 1985, p. B3; "Prepaid Legal Services—The Newest Benefit," *Contract Clauses* 9, no. 5 (December 1985), pp. 1–2.
5. Ellen Moorhouse, "Three Formulas for Benefits," *Financial Times*, April 20, 1981, pp. H11–13.
6. Randall Dutka, "Firms Struggle to Balance Coverage, Cost," *The Globe and Mail*, August 16, 1985, p. B18.
7. Harish C. Jain and Edward P. Janzen, "Employee Pay and Benefit Preferences," *Relations Industrielles* 29, no. 1 (1974), pp. 99–109; Harish C. Jain, "Employee Pay and Benefit Preferences at Canadian National: New Evidence," *Relations Industrielles* 32, no. 3 (1977), pp. 449–52.
8. For a summary of employee benefit preferences research in the United States, see Allan N. Nash and Stephen J. Carroll, *The Management of Compensation* (Monterey, Calif.: Brooks/Cole Publishing, 1975).
9. For an excellent summary of legally required benefits and working conditions, see Labour Canada, *Labour Standards in Canada, 1986 Edition* (Ottawa: Minister of Supply and Services Canada, 1986).
10. Inquiry Commission on Educational Leave and Productivity (Roy Adams, chairperson). *Statistics from Survey of Educational Leave and Training and Development* (Ottawa: Labour Canada, 1981); Wilfred List, "Growing Number of Unions Seek Paid Educational Leave in Contract," *The Globe and Mail*, March 5, 1979, p. B4; Hem C. Jain, "Paid Educational Leave in Europe," *Relations Industrielles* 33, no. 3 (1978), pp. 485–500; Paul Belanger, "Paid Educational Leave," in

Manpower Training at the Crossroads, ed. Ian Morrison and Paul Belanger (Montreal: ICEA/CAAE, 1976), pp. 49–54.
11. Labour Canada, *Maternity and Child Care Leave in Canada* (Ottawa: Minister of Supply and Services Canada, 1983).
12. Wilfred List, "Paid Maternity Leave Becoming More Important in Negotiations," *The Globe and Mail,* December 14, 1981, p. B6; "Paternity Leave," *Contract Clauses* 7, no. 10 (October 1983), pp. 1–2; Nancy Norman and James Tedeschi, "Paternity Leave: The Unpopular Benefit Option," *Personnel Administrator,* February 1984, pp. 39–43; "Maternity Leave at Bell," *Worklife* 2, no. 4 (1982), p. 19.
13. Coward, *Mercer Handbook.*
14. Susan Deller, "Health Plans Expected Part of Working Life," *Financial Post,* February 9, 1985, p. 33; Virginia Galt, "Employee Fitness Programs Are among Innovative Health Benefits," *The Globe and Mail,* August 16, 1985, p. B15.
15. Darryl Leach and Peter Hirst, "A Dental Discourse," *Benefits Canada,* April 1986, pp. 51–54; Joan Breckenridge, "Dental Plan Changes Tactics," *The Globe and Mail,* August 16, 1985, p. B20.
16. The first unemployment insurance legislation was enacted by the federal government in 1935. However, with employment issues in the provincial jurisdiction, the law was overturned by the Supreme Court of Canada the following year. The Canadian constitution (then the BNA Act) was amended to bring unemployment matters under federal jurisdiction before the Unemployment Insurance Act of 1940 could be passed by Parliament. The history of Canada's unemployment insurance system is described in Statistics Canada, *Unemployment Insurance Statistics* (Ottawa: Minister of Supply and Services Canada, cat. no. 73-202S, 1985).
17. Royal Commission on the Economic Union and Development Prospects for Canada (MacDonald Commission), *Report* (Ottawa: Minister of Supply and Services Canada, 1985), especially Volume Two; Commission of Inquiry into Unemployment Insurance (Forget Commission), *Report* (Ottawa: Minister of Supply and Services Canada, 1986).
18. Ibid.
19. Eva Innes, Robert L. Perry, and Jim Lyon, *The 100 Best Companies to Work For in Canada* (Don Mills, Ont.: Collins, 1986); Megan Perks, "Extras Pay Off for Employers in Many Ways," *Financial Post,* February 9, 1985, pp. 33, 36.
20. Justice Rosalie Silberman Abella, *Report of the Commission on Equality in Employment* (Ottawa: Minister of Supply and Services Canada, 1984), chap. 5.
21. Bureau of Municipal Research, *Work-Related Day Care—Helping to Close the Gap* (Toronto: BMR, 1981); "Day Care Clauses," *Contract Clauses* 8, no. 2 (1984), pp. 1–4; Oscar Ornato and Carol Buckham, "Day Care: Still Waiting Its Turn as a Standard Benefit," *Management Review,* May 1983, pp. 57–62; Jacquelyn McCroskey, "Work and Families: What Is the Employer's Responsibility?" *Personnel Journal,* January 1982, pp. 30–38.
22. George Milkovich and Luis Gomez, "Day Care and Selected Employee Work Behaviours," *Academy of Management Journal,* March 1976, pp. 111–15. For a summary of other U.S. research, see Kathleen Mahoney, "Day Care and Equality in Canada," *Manitoba Law Journal* 14, no. 3 (1985), pp. 305–34.
23. Bureau of Municipal Research, *Work-Related Day Care,* p. 30; Jay Paull, "How to Boost Productivity—Put a Nanny on Your Payroll," *Canadian Business,* March 1986, pp. 122–23; "Day Care Becoming Management Issue," *Financial Post,* October 18, 1986, p. 43. Day care facilities are not new to Canadian business. They

were implemented in several firms during World War II so women could work for the war effort. After the war ended, the day care facilities were closed as many women left the work force.
24. Judith Martin, "High Quality Child Care: A Precondition to Equality of Employment," *Canadian Women Studies* 6, no. 4 (1985), pp. 91–93; Link Byfield, "Feminism's $11 Billion Baby," *Alberta Report*, April 7, 1986, pp. 10–15.
25. Judy Steed, "When Babies Cry, Developers Listen," *The Globe and Mail*, October 10, 1986, pp. B1–B2; Susan Deller, "The Daycare Dilemma," *Benefits Canada*, April 1986, pp. 15–20.
26. Some of the more prominent government inquiries include, Comite d'etude sur le financement du Regime de rentes du Quebec et sur les regimes supplementaires de rentes, *La securite financiere des personnes agees au Quebec* (COFIRENTES + Report), (Quebec: Editeur Officiel du Quebec, 1977); Special Senate Committee on Retirement Age Policies (Croll Committee), *Retirement without Tears* (Ottawa: Minister of Supply and Services Canada, 1979); Government of Canada Interdepartmental Task Force on Retirement Income Policy (Lazar Report), *The Retirement Income System in Canada: Problems and Alternative Policies for Reform* (Ottawa: Minister of Supply and Services Canada, 1979); Government of Canada Parliamentary Task Force on Pension Reform (Frith Report), *Better Pensions for Canadians* (Ottawa: Minister of Supply and Services Canada, 1983); Ontario Royal Commission on the Status of Pensions in Ontario (Haley Report), *Design for Retirement* (Ontario: Queen's Printer, 1980).
27. These government programs are described more fully in the Haley Report, *Design for Retirement*, Vol. 3; National Council on Welfare, *A Pension Primer* (Ottawa: Minister of Supply and Services Canada, 1984); Hart D. Clark, "Development of a Retirement Income System."
28. A "means test" is a method by which a person's assets as well as income are taken into account in determining eligibility for or amount of payment under a government program.
29. An "income test" is a method by which the income (but not the assets) of a person or family is taken into account in determining eligibility for or amount of payment under a government program. In GIS, the amount of benefit is reduced with the amount of alternate income earned (other than OAS).
30. Jacques Pelletier, "CPP Funding: A 25-Year Compromise," *Benefits Canada*, April 1986, pp. 9–12; Laurence Coward, "Pension Plans Will Soon Need Amendment," *The Globe and Mail*, August 16, 1985, p. B17.
31. "Flexible Retirement under the Quebec Pension Plan," *The Mercer Bulletin* 35, no. 9 (September 1985), p. 2.
32. Canada Pension Plan Advisory Committee, *More Effective Participation of Homemakers in the Canada Pension Plan* (Ottawa: CPPAC, 1983); National Council of Welfare, *Better Pensions for Homemakers* (Ottawa: Minister of Supply and Services Canada, 1984); Ailey Bailen, "Debate Rages over Homemaker Pensions," *Financial Post*, February 8, 1986, p. 45.
33. Coward, "Pension Plans Will Soon Need Amendment."
34. Statistics Canada, *Pension Plans in Canada, 1984* (Ottawa: Minister of Supply and Services Canada, 1986). This biennial survey is an excellent source of information about most aspects of employer-sponsored pension plans in Canada.
35. Hart D. Clark, "The Development of the Retirement Income System in Canada." Employees at the Bank of Montreal had established a formal pension society before 1870, but this was operated independently of the bank.

36. Randall J. Dutka, "Reform Will Make Plans Costlier."
37. For a discussion of EPPs as a gratuity or right, see Ontario Committee on Portable Pensions, *Second Report* (Toronto: Queen's Printer, 1961); Haley Report, *Design for Retirement*; James E. Pesando and S. A. Rea, *Public and Private Pensions in Canada: An Economic Analysis* (Toronto: Ontario Economic Council, 1977).
38. George T. Milkovich and Jerry M. Newman, *Compensation*, 2nd ed. (Plano, Tex.: Business Publications, 1987); Michael F. Carter and Kenneth P. Shapiro, "Develop a Proactive Approach to Employee Benefits Planning," *Personnel Journal*, July 1983, pp. 562–66; Bruce Ellig, "What's Ahead in Compensation and Benefits," *Management Review*, August 1983, pp. 56–61.
39. Ibid.; Joanne Blain, "Giving Staff a Lift: More Companies Finding It Pays to Offer Perks," *Vancouver Sun*, February 24, 1986, p. C1.
40. Bruce Ellig, "Determining the Competitiveness of Employee Benefits Systems," *Compensation Review*, First Quarter 1974, pp. 8–34.
41. Richard Huseman, John Hatfield, and Richard Robinson, "The MBA and Fringe Benefits," *Personnel Administration* 23, no. 7 (1978), pp. 57–60; Brent King, "Many Employees Don't Know What Their Firm's Benefits Are Worth," *Financial Post*, December 3, 1983, p. 26.
42. Andrew Webster, "Spreading the Word about Spreading It Around," *Benefits Canada*, October 1985, pp. 33–36.
43. Jerry Geisler and William Glueck, "Benefit Communication and Employee Satisfaction" (mimeographed, University of Georgia, Athens, 1977).
44. Colin Languedoc, "Cost of Benefits Growing Concern to Managers," *Financial Post*, April 13, 1987, p. 17.
45. Leach and Hirst, "A Dental Discourse"; Breckenridge, "Dental Plan Changes Tactics"; Robin Noxon, "Benefits Change to Mate Personal, Company Needs," *The Globe and Mail*, April 12, 1985, p. R8.
46. Jack Hanna, "The Move to Flexible Benefits," *Financial Times*, January 30, 1984, pp. 1, 20; Barbara Aarsteinsen, "Workers Can Choose Own Benefits," *The Globe and Mail*, August 21, 1986, p. B16; Susan Deller, "Flexing Your Benefits," *Benefits Canada*, March 1986, pp. 31–35.
47. Bruce Gates, "New Contents in Benefit Packages," *Financial Post*, February 8, 1986, p. 44.
48. Susan Deller, "Cominco's Flex-Com: A Canadian Prototype," *Benefits Canada*, April 1984, pp. 22–26; Frank Livsey and Robert J. McKay, "Flexible Compensation Schemes Catching On Slowly," *Financial Post*, February 8, 1986, p. 44; George Brett, "Some Companies Overwhelm Their Workers with Benefits," *Toronto Star*, March 29, 1986, pp. G1–G2.
49. Edward E. Lawler III, *Pay and Organization Development* (Reading, Mass.: Addison-Wesley Publishing, 1981); William B. Werther, "Flexible Compensation Evaluated," *California Management Review*, Fall 1976, p. 42; Howard Risher and Colin Mill, "Cafeteria Compensation: Present Status and Future Potential," *Canadian Personnel and Industrial Relations Journal*, March 1974, pp. 35–39.
50. A. S. Schlachtmeyer and R. B. Bogart, "Employee-Choice Benefits—Can Employees Handle It?" *Compensation Review* 11, no. 3 (1979), pp. 12–19; Livsey and McKay, "Flexible Compensation Schemes."
51. Lawler, *Pay and Organization Development*, pp. 72–76.
52. Deller, "Flexing Your Benefits"; W. David Thompson, "Benefits Administration: Changing Direction," *TPF&C Focus*, Spring 1987, pp. 1–2.
53. "Cafeteria Benefits: Long-Term Scam?" *Canadian Labour*, March 1984, p. 12.

Exhibit VII
THE DIAGNOSTIC MODEL

External conditions	Organization conditions	Human resource activities	Objectives
Economic conditions Government regulations Technology Unions	Nature of organization: Strategies and objectives — Nature of work / Nature of employees and work groups	Staffing Development Employment relations Compensation Evaluation	Human resource effectiveness

PART SEVEN
HUMAN RESOURCE ACTIVITIES:
EVALUATION

The last part of the book may contain the most important chapter, Evaluation. While discussing the other human resource activities in the model (Exhibit VII), we have emphasized the need to evaluate the effects of the activities and to weigh these effects against objectives. Evaluating activities should ultimately lead to improved employee and organization performance.

The basic approaches to evaluation are discussed in Chapter Seventeen. Evaluation can be applied to the separate human resource activities and programs as well as the entire personnel function. The P/HRM function should be something more than a collection of activities. Evaluation helps determine and direct its contribution to employee and organization effectiveness.

CHAPTER SEVENTEEN
EVALUATION

CHAPTER OUTLINE

I. A Diagnostic Approach to Evaluation
    A. P/HRM as a Collection of Activities: Maintenance and Control
    B. P/HRM as an Integrated System: Achieving Effectiveness

II. Approaches to Evaluation
    A. Process-Oriented Audits
    B. Reputational Approach
    C. Quantitative Approaches

III. Summary

The setting is an executive conference room. The top officers of a large bank are participating in the annual planning meeting. Each functional vice president presents the department's budget for next year after a review of the past year's accomplishments.

Martha Renstrom, vice president for marketing, has just completed her budget request and had her advertising budget cut for the next year. Last year, return on assets and profits were down at the bank.

Andrew Major, vice president for P/HRM, speaks next.

Andrew: Well, folks, I'm not going to take much of your time. It's been a long day. You know what we do for the bank. We hire, train, and pay the employees, provide benefits, career planning, employment equity, and so on. P/HRM is not asking for any major increases. My budget is simply last year's budget adjusted upward 4 percent for inflation. Any questions?

Martha: Wait a minute, Andy. My budget just got cut and here you come asking for 4 percent more than last year. I suppose we need a P/HRM department. But why shouldn't my advertising budget be increased and your budget cut? After all, advertising brings customers into the bank and helps us make money. What *specifically* does P/HRM do for this bank's profit and loss statement? How *specifically* does P/HRM help us reach our goals of growth and profitability?

Martha's questions are to the point—if Andy's P/HRM department had been systematically evaluating activities, he would have some answers.

This last chapter discusses the evaluation of P/HRM activities. In practice, a variety of approaches to evaluation are used, and this chapter examines and illustrates these alternatives. Let's start with what is meant by evaluation and the purposes it may serve.

Definition
Evaluation of the P/HRM function is a systematic, formal process designed to assess the policies and procedures used, the reactions of users or clients, and the costs to, and benefits obtained by, the organization.

Evaluation serves many purposes. It can:

Improve the operation of activities by providing data on the activities' costs and results.

Assist P/HRM and operating managers to decide which P/HRM activities to continue, modify, or drop.

Help ensure that P/HRM activities are related to achieving the organization's strategies and objectives.

Help ensure that employees, managers, and others are aware and satisfied with P/HRM services provided.

Help justify the existence of P/HRM activities and help formulate the budget for the plan year.

The notion of evaluating the P/HRM function and its activities is not new. Writers and professionals have long advocated it and many companies attempt it.[1] One U.S. survey on the extent of evaluation and the general methods used found that more than 80 percent of the companies answering the survey formally evaluated the P/HRM function.[2] Yet, as you will discover in this chapter, the types of evaluation performed in both Canada and the United States are often very basic and their usefulness quite limited. However, significant recent advances in evaluation techniques offer promise for improvement.

A DIAGNOSTIC APPROACH TO EVALUATION

Throughout this book, the diagnostic model has been used to provide a framework for understanding the role of P/HRM in an organization. In Chapter One, when the diagnostic model was introduced, we suggested thinking of the analogy of physicians. Broadly stated, their objectives are to maintain or improve your health. They do this by evaluating the effects of a variety of treatment and prevention programs. Data on your system's behaviour, such as blood pressure, white blood cell counts, temperature, discussions with you about your health, and the like, all serve in the diagnosis. Evaluation of these data serves three purposes:

To evaluate how healthy the system is and to identify any problem areas.

To evaluate the effectiveness of treatments and activities.

To anticipate future problems and direct future treatments and actions.

Evaluation of personnel/human resource management activities serves similar purposes. Evaluation helps P/HRM professionals maintain and control specific P/HRM activities. Properly designed and administered, evaluation also helps ensure that P/HRM activities aid in achieving effective employees and organizations.

P/HRM as a Collection of Activities: Maintenance and Control

Without evaluation, P/HRM runs the risk of becoming simply a "collection of activities," like those described in each separate chapter of this book. P/HRM without evaluation consists of rather discrete efforts, such as recruiting, monitoring employment equity performance, and designing labour relations, compensation, and training programs. Each of these activities focusses on a specific set of goals (attracting applicants, meeting employment equity goals, controlling labour costs) and draws upon a subset of theories and research related to specific problems. Under such a view, personnel/human resource management tends to be primarily a maintenance and control function. It is less likely to focus on the objectives of employee and organization effectiveness.

P/HRM as an Integrated System: Achieving Effectiveness

A task of the P/HRM professional using the diagnostic approach is to make certain the P/HRM activities are *integrated into a system that is greater than the sum of the parts* and to assist the organization to effectively utilize its human resources. Thus, recruiting, labour relations, and all P/HRM activities are evaluated to assess how well they help organizations and employees achieve their objectives. Evaluation also helps the P/HRM function become more than a loose collection of separate activities. It ensures that activities are integrated with each other and with the overall organization objectives.

APPROACHES TO EVALUATION

According to the diagnostic model, the criteria or measures of effectiveness fall into two basic sets: organizational effectiveness and employee effectiveness. Examples of each include:

1. Organizational effectiveness: Human resource components.
    a. Unit productivity measures, such as earnings-to-compensation ratio, product quality indexes.
    b. P/HRM-related costs such as total labour costs, labour costs per unit of output, benefit costs as a percentage of total labour costs.
    c. Attitudes of employees and managers and others regarding personnel services provided.
    d. Compliance with public regulations, such as rates at which job opportunities are shared with minorities and women, or equitable pay for minorities and women.
2. Employee effectiveness: Assessing employee work behaviours and attitudes.
    a. Employee turnover (voluntary and involuntary) rates.
    b. Employee absenteeism rates.
    c. Production above/below standard.

d. Quality above/below standard.
   e. Accident/health indexes.
   f. Grievance rates.
   g. Employees' job satisfaction and attitudes toward various aspects of their work.
   h. Employees' suggestions for innovation.

Many organizations use these and other indexes to reflect the health or effectiveness of the P/HRM departments' efforts. More than 25 years ago, General Electric developed a series of these measures into an Employee Relations Index.[3] The items are shown in Exhibit 17–1. The results, obtained on a quarterly basis, were used to diagnose how units changed over time as well as how various GE units compared to each other.

There are various other approaches to the evaluation of P/HRM activities. We will examine three: audits, reputation with clients, and quantitative analysis.

Process-Oriented Audits

In its pure form, an audit is simply a review to determine if key P/HRM policies and procedures are in place and followed.[4] The audit approach is usually implemented by developing a checklist of the required policies and procedures. An illustration is shown in Exhibit 17–2. The items are usually grouped by human resource activities, such as staffing, compensation, and labour relations.

Although a checklist audit is better than a totally informal approach, it still is a simplistic approach to evaluation. And even though checklists provide a format that is relatively easy to record and prepare, interpretation of results may be difficult.[5] For example, a negative comment on one group of items may be more or less important than a negative comment on another item. Some policies are more important than others. Ignoring employment equity

EXHIBIT 17–1
Factors Included in General Electric's Employee Relations Index for Production and Assembly Plants

Periods of absence	Grievances filed
Separations	Work stoppages
Visits to dispensary	Participation in health
Suggestions submitted	insurance plans
Disciplinary actions	

EXHIBIT 17–2
An Illustration of a P/HRM Audit (an interview with the operating manager)

1. What would you say are the objectives of your plant?
2. As you see it, what are the major responsibilities of managers?
3. Have there been any important changes in these over the last few years in the plant?
4. Are there any personnel responsibilities on which you think many managers need to do a better job?
5. What are some of the good things about employee relations in this plant?
6. Do you feel there are any important problems or difficulties in the plant? Causes? How widespread? Corrective measures?
7. Do you have any personnel goals for the year?
8. Overall, how well do you feel the personnel department does its job? Changes the department should make?

Community relations

9. What are managers expected to do about community relations? Is there plant pressure? Reaction to pressures?
10. What have you done about community relations? Do you encourage subordinates to participate in them? What are your personal activities?

Safety and medical

11. Who is responsible for safety in your area? Role of group leaders and lead men?
12. What things do you do about safety? Regular actions? Results achieved?
13. Do you have any important safety problems in your operation? Causes? Cures? How widespread?
14. What does the safety specialist do? How helpful are those activities? Other things could be done?
15. Are there any other comments or suggestions about safety you would like to make?
16. Have you any comments about the dispensary? Employee time involved? Types of service offered? Courtesy?

Communication

17. How do you keep your people informed? What are your regular communication activities? Particular problems?
18. How do you go about finding out information from employees? Channels and methods? How regularly are such channels used? How much information is passed on to employee superiors? How much interest do supervisors show? Does personnel provide information?
19. Has the personnel department helped improve communication in the plant? What assistance is needed? Nature of assistance provided?
20. Has the personnel department helped you with your own communication activities?

Communication channels available

21. What improvement is needed in these?
22. Are there any other comments about communication you'd like to make? Any changes or improvements you'd especially like to see?

Manpower planning

23. What kind of plans do you have for meeting the future manpower needs of your own component? Indicate plans for hourly, nonexempt. How far do plans extend into the future?
24. What does your manager do about planning for future manpower needs? How is this planning related to your own planning?
25. What part does the personnel department play in planning for the future manpower needs of your component? Of the plant as a whole?

Personnel development

26. How is the training of employees handled in your group? (on-the-job training) Who does it? Procedures followed?
27. What changes or improvements do you think should be made in the training of employees? (on-the-job training) Why?
28. What changes or improvements do you feel are needed in the amount or kind of classroom training given here? Why?
29. Have you worked with your subordinates on improving their current job performance? Inside or outside regular appraisal? Procedure? Employee reaction? Results? Improvements needed?
30. Have you worked with subordinates on plans for preparing for future job responsibilities? Inside or outside regular appraisal? Procedure? Employee reaction? Improvements needed?
31. What does personnel do to help you with your training and development problems?
32. Do you have any other comments on personnel development or training?

Personnel practices

33. How are employees added to your work group? New employees, for example. (*Probe*: Specify exempt, nonexempt, hourly. Procedure followed? How are decisions made? Contribution of personnel? Changes needed and reasons? Transfers?)
34. How is bumping or downgrading handled? (*Probe*: Specify nonexempt or hourly. Procedure followed? How are decisions made? Contribution of personnel? Changes needed and reasons?)
35. How are promotions into or out of your group handled? (*Probe*: Specify exempt, nonexempt, hourly. Procedure followed? How are decisions made? Contribution of personnel? Changes needed and reasons?)
36. Do you have any problems with layoffs? (*Probe*: Nature of problems? Possible solutions? Contribution of personnel?)
37. How do you handle "probationary" periods? (*Probe*: Specify hourly, nonexempt, exempt. Length of period? Union attitude? How handled?)
38. How are inefficient people handled? (*Probe*: Specify hourly, nonexempt, exempt. How do you handle? How do other supervisors handle? Frequency?)

Salary administration—exempt

39. What is your responsibility for exempt salary administration? (*Probe*: Position evaluation? Determining increases? Degree of authority?)
40. How do you go about deciding on salary increases? (*Probe*: Procedure? Weight given to merit? Informing employees? Timing?)
41. What are your major problems in salary administration? (*Probe*: Employee-centred? Self-centred? Plan-centred?)
42. Has the personnel department assisted you with your salary administration problems? How? (*Probe*: Administrator's role? Nature of assistance? Additional assistance needed and reasons?)

Salary administration—nonexempt

43. What is your responsibility for nonexempt salary administration? (*Probe*: Nature of plan? Position evaluation? Changes needed and reasons?)
44. How has the personnel department helped in nonexempt salary administration? (*Probe*: Specify personnel or other salary administrators. Nature of assistance? Additional assistance needed and reasons?)

Source: Reprinted by permission from "Auditing PAIR," by Walter R. Mahler, in *ASPA Handbook of Personnel and Industrial Relations*, ed. D. Yoder and H. Heneman, pp. 2–103. Copyright © 1979 by The Bureau of National Affairs, Inc., Washington, D.C. 20037.

EXHIBIT 17–3
Personnel Compliance Audit Process at Citibank

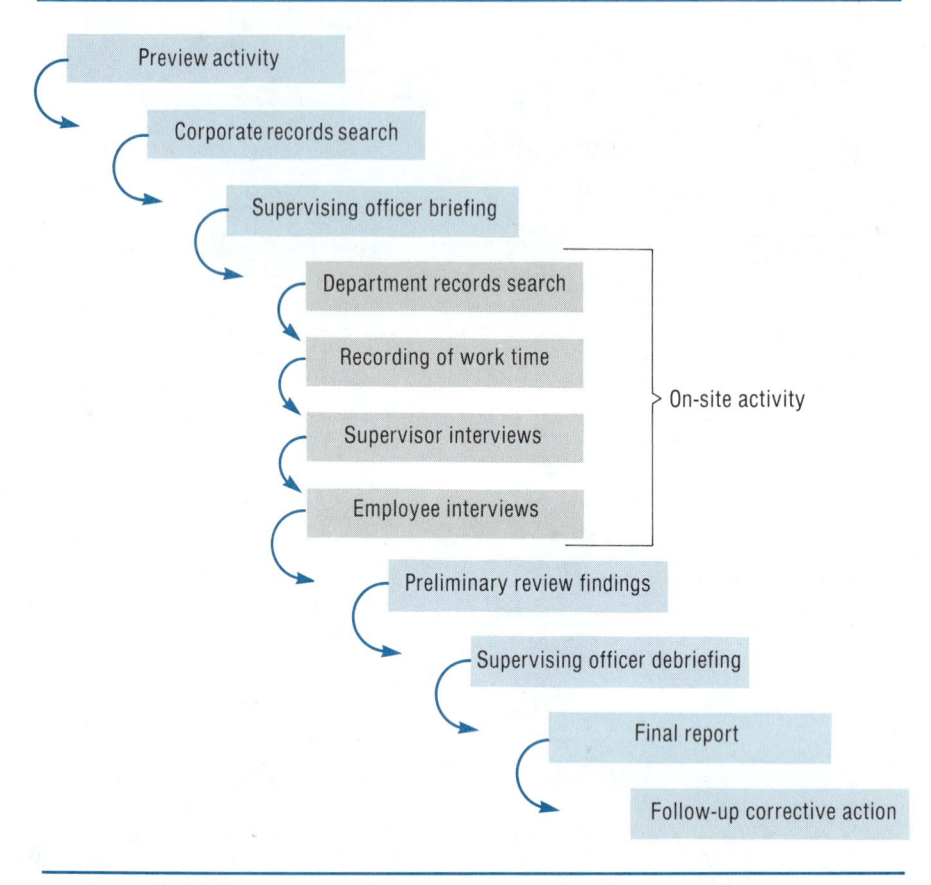

- Preview activity
- Corporate records search
- Supervising officer briefing
- Department records search ⎫
- Recording of work time   ⎬ On-site activity
- Supervisor interviews   ⎪
- Employee interviews   ⎭
- Preliminary review findings
- Supervising officer debriefing
- Final report
- Follow-up corrective action

Source: Paul Sheibar, "Personnel Practices Review: A Personnel Audit Activity," *Personnel Journal*, March 1974, p. 213.

policies and practice may have greater and more costly consequences than the absence of a company picnic, for example.

Often audits are conducted by a team comprising P/HRM professionals and managers. Citibank's approach is shown in Exhibit 17–3.[6] The first step is to identify crucial P/HRM activities that need to be included. Then the bank randomly chooses branches and affiliates to be studied. The review is performed by a Personnel Practices Review Team (six P/HRM professionals, an operations manager, and staff support). Every major organization unit is reviewed on a two-year cycle.

Reputational Approach

The premise of the reputational approach is that the effectiveness of P/HRM units and their activities is determined by its reputation with its constituents or clients.[7] Tsui, in her research on P/HRM effectiveness, observes that a P/HRM department has multiple constituencies.[8] As shown in Exhibit 17-4, these may include functional executives (the top P/HRM position), operating executives (top positions in the business operations), operating managers (middle level and supervisors), all nonmanagerial employees and external clients (unions, human rights officers, etc.).

According to Tsui, the value of P/HRM units, and by implication their policies and actions, is defined in terms of "reputation effectiveness," by which she means the judgements of the users of P/HRM services.[9] She suggests that P/HRM units judged most effective by the users will exhibit patterns of decisions and activities different from those of less effective units. For example, more effective units may concentrate on employment equity and employee relations activities, while the less effective may concentrate on designing staffing models and strategic plans. Whatever patterns emerge, effective units are most likely to satisfy the critical demands of its most important constituents and in turn contribute the most to organization effectiveness.

The reputational approach involves assessing the attitudes of various users of P/HRM activities. Several firms do assess one or more of their constituents.

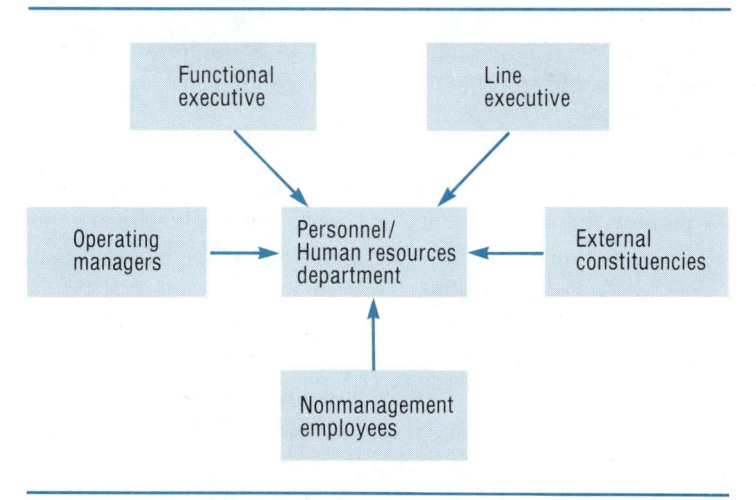

EXHIBIT 17-4
Multiple Constituencies in a Reputational Approach to Evaluating Personnel/Human Resources Department Effectiveness

Source: A. Tsui, "Research on Personnel Department Effectiveness" (paper presented at Cornell University, Ithaca, N.Y., 1983).

EXHIBIT 17–5
Operating Managers' Impressions of Personnel Services at Exxon

How Well Informed Are You about Specific Personnel Services?	Not At All	Little Informed	Somewhat Informed	Quite Informed	Very Well Informed
Benefits, policies, and employee services	1	2	3	4	5
Compensation	1	2	3	4	5
Employment	1	2	3	4	5
Labour relations	1	2	3	4	5
Education and development	1	2	3	4	5
Planning	1	2	3	4	5
Affirmative action	1	2	3	4	5

Source: Exxon Research and Engineering Employee Relations Report 1980.

Exhibit 17–5 lists some of the questions in a survey of operating managers conducted by Exxon Research and Engineering. Other employers (IBM and Merck are examples) also survey employees' attitudes toward the services and activities offered by the P/HRM unit. However, no organization systematically assesses all constituents.[10]

The approach is controversial. Some readers may take issue with the basic premise. Why are constituent's impressions, particularly those of union officials and regulatory agents, relevant to the assessment of the P/HRM effectiveness? Which users' impressions are the most important? For example, policies and actions judged effective by management may be seen as less so by unions and others.

The diagnostic model would suggest that selecting the most important constituents depends on external and organizational conditions. Challenges from government regulatory agents or unions will make them important at one time, whereas shifting business strategies and objectives will make operating or plant managers more salient at another time. Some P/HRM vice presidents argue that the impressions of operating executives and managers are all that count. Whatever the research reveals about this approach, the idea that P/HRM effectiveness depends on its reputation with consumers of its activities has considerable appeal to operating managers.[11]

Both the audit and the reputation-among-users approaches rely heavily on impressions. The third approach is based on cost and the results obtained.

Quantitative Approaches

Quantitative approaches to evaluation may be grouped into three types: personnel indexes, cost–benefit analysis, and work activity-budgeting. In practice, the application of these types tends to overlap, but we have separated them as a convenience for discussion.

Personnel Indexes

Perhaps the most frequently used formal evaluation approaches are based on the measurement of human resource behaviour and unit performance.[12] Most employers analyze these data by using indexes and ratios such as those shown in Exhibit 17–6. The indexes in this exhibit are grouped to correspond to the

EXHIBIT 17–6
Examples of Personnel Evaluation Indexes

Staffing
  Employment distribution by skill types, salary grade, unit, product line.
  Employment distribution by chronological age.
  Employment distribution by length of service with organization.
  Employment distribution by sex, race, national origin, religion.
  Managerial staff distribution by chronological age, sex, race, national origin, religion.
  Average age of work force.
  Average age of managerial work force.

Development
  Proportion of eligible work force that received skills training in last year.
  Proportion of new supervisors who received supervisory training.
  Proportion of employees fully qualified for their jobs.

Employee relations
  Number of grievances and complaints filed.
  Subjects of complaints and grievances.
  Suggestions offered per 100 employees.

Effectiveness ratios
  Sales in dollars per employee for the whole company or by organizational unit (business).
  Output in units per employee hour worked for the entire enterprise or organizational unit.
  Scrap loss per unit of the enterprise.
  Payroll costs by unit per employee grade.

Turnover and absenteeism ratios
  Attendance, tardiness, and overtime comparisons by organizational unit.
  Employee turnover by unit and for the organization.

Accident ratios
  Frequency of accident rates.
  Number of lost-time accidents.
  Compensation paid for accidents per 1,000 hours worked.
  Accidents by type.
  Accidents classified by type of injury to each part of the body.

major human resource activities, such as staffing, development, and employee relations. They may also be grouped by major issues, such as turnover, absenteeism, productivity, and accident rates.

To some, the raw data provided by these indexes may be interesting, but they really serve only as input to the evaluation process. Most organizations compare these indexes to the unit's own past data or to some desired objective or perhaps even to some overall industry average. Such comparisons provide information on the direction of the index (increase or decrease over last period or greater or less than another unit or a goal).

Examples of some indexes reported by W. R. Grace Company are shown in Exhibits 17–7A and 17–7B.[13] Productivity trends in three districts, A, B, and C, measured as sales over total employee compensation are reported in Exhibit 17–7B. It appears that none of the districts produces consistent quarterly results and in some cases significant changes in the ratios are evident. Also note that districts A and C improved in 1981 compared to 1980, while B reported a decline. These data should raise more questions than they answer—for example, what are the possible underlying reasons for the decline in B's performance? What in the external and organization conditions may have contributed to that decline?

The results on university recruiting in Exhibit 17–7A show that employees recruited in 1979 from University B receive greater percentage salary increases than those recruited from A and C. Why? These data are simplistic because they may mask other important information. What, for example, are the minority/gender characteristics of these recruits? Perhaps the firm is discriminating. What were the initial salary offers? Perhaps recruits at B received lower initial offers. What are the jobs and locations? Perhaps geographic and product line differences are important.

The W. R. Grace data are very basic. The General Electric's Employee Relations Index discussed earlier is an example of a series of personnel

EXHIBIT 17–7A
MBA University Recruiting (June 1979–June 1983)

School	Number of Recruits	Average Percentage of Compensation Increase		
		Year 1	Year 2	Year 3
University A/79	16	6.3	7.5	8.6
University B/79	10	10.7	12.5	15.6
University C/79	7	8.7	12.5	13.1

Source: J. R. LaPointe, "Human Resource Performance Indexes," *Personnel Journal*, July 1983, pp. 545–50.

EXHIBIT 17–7B
Compensation/Output Ratios 1980, 1981, by Quarter

Compensation/Output Ratios

Organizational Unit	1980 1st	2nd	3rd	4th	Yr.	1981 1st	2nd	3rd	4th	Yr.
District A	1.36	1.13	2.72	3.63	2.22	1.66	2.91	2.50	3.75	2.70
District B	1.05	3.16	4.74	2.10	2.76	1.22	3.26	1.63	2.45	2.14
District C	1.45	1.82	2.91	2.54	2.18	1.82	1.45	3.64	3.27	2.54
Region 1	1.28	2.04	3.46	2.76	2.39	1.57	2.54	2.59	3.16	2.46

Ratios result from the following calculation:

$$\frac{\text{Sales dollars from a particular unit}}{\text{Total compensation of the employees in that unit (plus any overhead distribution if included)}}$$

Source: J.R. LaPointe, "Human Resource Performance Indexes," *Personnel Journal*, July 1983, pp. 545–50.

indexes in combination.[14] Macy and Mirvis report more detailed indexes from one organization over three time periods.[15] Their results are shown in Exhibit 17–8. They take the analysis a step further by estimating costs associated with behaviour. Estimated costs associated with each of their measures are shown in Exhibit 17–9.

The point is that personnel indexes do provide insights into directions and differences in P/HRM activities and unit performance. As such, they often serve as signs of more important results or trends. But they do not always tell us much about the impact—the results of the activities.

Cost–Benefit Approaches

Cost–benefit approaches to P/HRM evaluation attempt to attach dollar values to both the expenses associated with human resource activities and their results.[16]

Estimating dollar values associated with expenditures on such activities as training and staffing is common.[17] Usually some method of cost accounting is applied. The earlier data reported by Macy and Mirvis in Exhibit 17–9 represent an extension of cost accounting to personnel indexes.[18]

Estimating dollar values associated with the outcomes—the benefits of P/HRM activities—has been more problematic. In the chapters on Selection (9) and Training (10), we examined some recent attempts to estimate P/HRM payoffs. Here we will consider these attempts applied to human resource activities in general.

Two basic approaches to estimating costs and benefits have been suggested: human resource accounting and utility analysis.

Human resource accounting involves the application of basic accounting rules to human resources.[19] It attempts to treat human resources as assets rather than simply as expenses. Under this approach, the accounting conventions applied to capital assets are also applied to the work force. Thus, the asset value of human resources may be estimated by its replacement costs and/or acquisition costs; it would also be depreciated and so on.[20] After an initial flurry of activity in the late 1960s, few recent applications of human asset accounting have been reported.

Utility analysis includes estimating both costs and benefits.[21] Personnel costs are measured through conventional accounting methods. The unique and promising aspect of utility analysis lies in the simple methods used to attach dollar values to the results expected from P/HRM activities.[22] The method is to ask managers to estimate the dollar value of hypothetical performance levels and then to determine the performance level expected to be achieved by the personnel activity.[23]

The classic study conducted by Schmidt, Hunter, McKenzie, and Muldrow

EXHIBIT 17–8
Incidents and Rates of Behaviors at XYZ Corporation

Behaviours and Performance	Period 1 Number of Incidents	Period 1 Rate (percent)	Period 2 Number of Incidents	Period 2 Rate (percent)	Period 3 Number of Incidents	Period 3 Rate (percent)
Absenteeism						
Absences	4,420	3.3	9,604	5.19	6,905	3.76
Leave days*	—	—	12,486	6.75	13,332	7.25
Accidents						
Hourly work force	251	38.35	316	35.34	208	23.76
Salaried work force	16	17.56	12	10.90	9	7.90
Minor†	3,181	421.80	6,713	706.08	5,559	635.26
Revisits†	1,806	216.99	2,455	258.22	2,028	231.74
Turnover						
Voluntary						
Hourly work force	132	24.10	229	29.59	116	14.57
Salaried work force	18	17.00	29	24.17	4	3.25
Involuntary						
Hourly work force	118	21.40	161	20.80	120	16.08
Salaried work force	—	—	5	4.17	4	3.25
Tardiness‡	48	8.68	—	—	—	—
Grievances§	57	10.40	40	5.17	41	5.15

*Hourly work force; leave days were instituted in periods 2 and 3 and are measured and computed as absences.
†Hourly and salary employees combined.
‡This is a daily rate; available only in period 1.
§Hourly work force.

Source: Reprinted from B. A. Macy and P. H. Mirvis, "A Methodology for Assessment of Quality of Work Life and Organizational Effectiveness in Behavioral-Economic Terms," *Administrative Science Quarterly*, June 1976, pp. 212–26. © *The Administrative Science Quarterly*.

EXHIBIT 17-9 Estimated Costs of Behaviour at XYZ Corporation (1972–1975)

Behaviours and Performance	Period 1 (1972–1973) Estimated Cost per Incident	Period 1 (1972–1973) Estimated Total Cost	Period 2 (1973–1974) Estimated Cost per Incident	Period 2 (1973–1974) Estimated Total Cost	Period 3 (1974–1975) Estimated Cost per Incident	Period 3 (1974–1975) Estimated Total Cost
Absenteeism*						
Absences	55.36	$ 286,360	53.15	$ 510,453	62.49	$ 431,494
Leave days	—	—	55.04	687,229	61.64	821,795
Accidents*						
OSHA reported	727.39	194,213	698.31	229,046	1,106.52	240,115
Minor	6.64	21,112	5.71	38,331	6.45	35,856
Revisits	6.64	11,992	5.71	14,018	6.45	13,081
Tardiness*†‡	4.86	56,920	—	—	—	—
Turnover*						
Voluntary	120.59	18,089	131.68	33,973	150.69	18,083
Involuntary	120.59	14,230	131.68	21,859	150.69	18,686
Grievances	32.48	1,851	34.44	1,378	56.10	2,300
Quality below standard‡‡	19,517	663,589	19,517	573,800	19,517	409,857
Production below standard§	22,236	266,838	22,236	335,764	22,236	255,714
Total costs§§#		$1,535,204		$2,445,851		$2,246,971

*Costs associated with absenteeism, leave days, accidents, turnover, and grievances during the last four months of this period are projections. Product quality and production below standard are actual figures.

†Rates and costs for salaried personnel are assumed to be the same as those for hourly employees (period 1: salaried absence costs—$41,669; salaried accident costs—$11,638; salaried tardiness costs—$9,641; salaried turnover costs—$1,829).

‡Average tardiness time was 27 minutes.

‡‡The costs of rejects and scrap was 3.4 percent of total sales for period 1. Each .1 reduction is valued at $19,517 per incident. Period 2 costs were 2.94 percent of total sales: period 3 costs were 2.1 percent of total sales. A constant dollar equivalency of $19,517 was used in periods 2 and 3 to discount inflation. Nondiscounted cost of quality below standard in period 2 was $677,015 ($23,028 per incident); in period 3, nondiscounted cost was $613,970 ($29,237 per incident).

§Plant productivity for period 1 was 88 percent of standard. The production below standard rate is 12 percent, thus, a reduction of 1 percent is valued at $22,236 per incident. Plant productivity in periods 2 and 3 was 84.9 percent and 88.5 percent of standard respectively. A constant dollar equivalency of $22,236 was used in periods 2 and 3 to discount inflation. Nondiscounted cost of production below standard in period 2 was $400,567 ($26,528 per incident); in period 3 nondiscounted cost was $405,938 ($25,299 per incident).

§§The total cost in period 1 is $1,470,427 for hourly personnel; $64,777 for salaried personnel.

#The total cost is reflected in standard labour dollars. The estimated cost in real dollar equivalents in period 1: $1,688,724 or 10.4 percent of sales; in period 2: $2,690,436 or 8.45 percent of sales; in period 3: $2,471,668 or 10.61 percent of sales.

Source: Reprinted from B. A. Macy and P. H. Mirvis, "A Methodology for Assessment of Quality of Work Life and Organizational Effectiveness in Behavioral-Economic Terms," *Administrative Science Quarterly*, June 1976, pp. 212–16. © The *Administrative Science Quarterly*.

was examined in Chapter Nine.[24] Briefly, they asked managers to estimate the dollar value of different performance levels of computer programmers. Then, by showing the improvement in performance that was attributed to a new selection program, they were able to estimate the dollar value of its results.

Others have applied a similar approach to assessment centres and training programs.[25] Landy et al. suggest that the utility approach may be applied to any P/HRM activity.[26] Hence, the potential utility of day care centres, employee assistance programs, gainsharing programs, and other programs can be evaluated using a utility approach.

Work Analysis and Budgeting

Work analysis and budgeting involve quantitative evaluation of what the P/HRM department does (similar to an audit) and how it budgets or allocates its resources (time, staff, and budgets).

Work analysis is typically performed by using work sampling techniques. Carroll describes the technique as "observations made at random intervals of what the personnel professional is doing with the purpose of providing a basis for inferences about the various elements that comprise his(her) total work activity."[27] Exhibit 17-10 reports some of Carroll's findings. It shows that if the strategy of the department included emphasis on benefits and staffing, then their activities were consistent with that strategy, since 50 percent of the time was spent on them. However, if a strategy emphasized training activities, then the department's actual activities are not consistent with the training emphasis, and reexamination is in order.

Budgeting is usually thought of as, at best, a cost-control device rather than an evaluation approach. Yet, back in the 1950s, Yoder pointed out that the basic concern in budgeting includes benefits as well as costs.[28] Accordingly, human resource activities can be evaluated in terms of the percentage of department budget allocated to each and the dollars per employee expended through each activity. The percentage allocated to each activity reflects the strategic directions of the P/HRM department, and the dollars expended per employee within each activity reflects the magnitude of effort. These two indexes along with total expenditures can be used to describe the human resource activity strategy. Changes in the directions and magnitude can be assessed over time as well as compared with other P/HRM activities.

The Bureau of National Affairs periodically surveys employers' P/HRM budgets.[29] Exhibit 17-11 shows the wide variation in the strategic directions and the magnitude of effort expended. For example, in 1982, the lowest

EXHIBIT 17–10
Percentage of Total Work Time Spent on Various Employee Relations Functions by P/HRM Department Members

Type of Function	Five Clerical Workers — Number of Observations	Five Clerical Workers — Percentage of Total Work Time	Four Personnel Department Managers — Number of Observations	Four Personnel Department Managers — Percentage of Total Work Time	Total Staff in Department — Number of Observations	Total Staff in Department — Percentage of Total Work Time
Administration of the department	60	05%	214	22%	274	13%
Staffing	88	08	196	20	284	14
Training	0	0	5	01	5	0
Labour relations	72	06	122	13	194	09
Wage and salary administration	117	10	46	05	163	08
Benefits and services	490	43	257	27	747	36
Research, audit, and review	76	07	35	04	111	05
Personal activities	43	04	61	06	104	05
Insufficient data*	197	17	22	02	219	10
Total	1,143	100%	958	100%	2,101	100%

*These observations could not be classified because two participants failed to explain adequately the purpose of some of their activities.

Source: Stephen J. Carroll, Jr., "Measuring the Work of a Personnel Department." Reprinted by permission of the publisher from *Personnel*, July–August 1969, p. 55. Copyright © 1960 by the American Management Associations, Inc. All rights reserved.

EXHIBIT 17-11 Personnel Budgets—1982

	\multicolumn{5}{c}{Range of Budgets Reported}
	Low	First Quartile	Median	Third Quartile	High
Total budget—1982					
All companies (290)	$ 35,550	$175,000	$ 370,000	$ 950,000	$42,907,000
By industry					
Manufacturing (129)	35,550	175,000	380,000	775,000	42,907,000
Nonmanufacturing (91)	50,000	188,000	550,000	1,665,000	15,704,200
Finance (46)	68,973	183,995	372,800	1,217,256	15,704,200
Nonbusiness (70)	41,520	142,289	300,000	520,595	17,700,000
Health Care (36)	62,136	107,943	215,000	445,800	11,700,502
By size					
Up to 250 employees (24)	35,550	80,347	100,000	159,500	632,114
250–499 employees (47)	50,000	100,744	177,000	298,300	1,249,931
500–999 employees (76)	41,520	134,000	282,000	495,000	2,863,472
1,000–2,499 employees (80)	57,000	273,303	475,600	1,047,440	3,074,020
2,500 or more employees (63)	229,000	795,000	1,681,000	3,000,000	42,907,000
Cost per employee—1982					
All companies (288)	29	216	390	719	3,951
By industry					
Manufacturing (129)	29	287	520	826	2,778
Nonmanufacturing (91)	30	286	403	750	3,951
Finance (46)	141	286	454	691	3,951
Nonbusiness (68)	59	126	186	297	2,934
Health Care (34)	65	126	168	270	2,934
By size					
Up to 250 employees (24)	145	412	667	1,101	3,951
250–499 employees (46)	135	332	473	715	2,778
500–999 employees (75)	59	202	380	742	2,934
1,000–2,499 employees (79)	55	187	325	662	2,200
2,500 or more employees (64)	29	143	300	541	2,500

Note: Figures in parentheses indicate number of companies responding in each category.
Source: Adapted from *ASPA-BNA Survey no. 35, Personnel Activities, Budgets & Staff 1982, Bulletin to Management,* August 15, 1983 BNA Policy and Practice Series for Employee Relations Executives (Washington, D.C.: Bureau of National Affairs). Copyright by the Bureau of National Affairs. Reprinted by permission.

expenditure on programming was $35,550, compared to a high of more than $42.9 million; some employers spend only $29 per employee on P/HRM activities (for an entire year!), whereas others expend about $4,000 per employee. While the accuracy of the data may be suspect due to the survey techniques, they do reflect the variation present. Little research has been conducted to understand the factors that may explain these differences. The diagnostic model would suggest specific organizational and environmental conditions that affect them, such as the organization's life-cycle stage, technology, and strategic direction. We would expect a firm's business strategy, for example, to significantly affect expenditures on P/HRM activities. A new, emerging firm is more likely to emphasize recruiting experienced personnel over training and development activities, for example.

While both work analysis and budgeting are useful quantitative approaches to evaluation activity, they focus on what the P/HRM department does. A vital point is missing—what difference do these P/HRM activities make upon the effectiveness of employees and the organization? Cost–benefit analysis offers an approach to determine the relationship between personnel activities and effectiveness. It holds considerable promise for the future. Unfortunately, it is also the least developed or applied approach.

A Review

We have now reviewed the basic approaches to evaluation of P/HRM units and activities: the audit, reputational assessment, and quantitative analysis. In addition to these approaches, some combination of these three may be used. A firm may employ an audit to assess the extent to which particular procedures are applied, a survey of managers and employees to evaluate how well P/HRM units aid and serve them, and a quantitative analysis to track key indexes and calculate costs and benefits.

Some firms develop their own unique approaches. Upjohn, for example, evaluates the acquisition of new employees in terms of the firm's return on investment. Dahl reports that a new employee, at a $25,000 starting salary, translates into a 30-year investment in excess of $2 million.[30] This includes salaries and benefits but excludes formal training programs. Each Upjohn manager has to justify the addition of each new employee in terms of a three- to five-year return on the initial investment in salary.[31]

In contrast, some firms do not seem to perform any formal evaluation of their personnel unit or activities. Does it make any difference? This is a tough question to answer without formal evaluation. However, we believe formal evaluation is an important activity that increases human resource management's ability to contribute to employee and organization effectiveness.

SUMMARY

The evaluation activity provides data on the effectiveness of human resource management activities as well as on the entire P/HRM system. It assists managers in making decisions about how to more effectively allocate scarce resources (budgets, time, people) to achieve employee and organization effectiveness. Evaluation, properly designed and managed, permits P/HRM to move beyond a mere collection of activities resulting from fads and fashions. Evaluation aids in the integration of human resource activities.

Currently, evaluation is one of the least developed activities in P/HRM; it is emerging as the tools and techniques advance. Most likely the burden for evaluating the P/HRM function and each of its subfunctions falls to P/HRM professionals. However, operating managers and executives may initiate or share the responsibility. Nonetheless, without evaluation, it is unclear how the function can be justified.

DISCUSSION AND REVIEW QUESTIONS

1. What is evaluation and what role does it play in P/HRM?
2. Why do organizations continue to allocate budgets to the P/HRM function if no formal evaluation occurs?
3. Compare and contrast: audits, reputational assessment, and quantitative approaches to evaluation.
4. How might the approach to evaluation depend on organizational conditions (e.g., strategic type) and on environmental conditions (e.g., unions, regulations, economic)?

NOTES AND REFERENCES

1. Paul Sheibar, "Personnel Practices Review: A Personnel Audit Activity," *Personnel*, March–April 1974, pp. 211–17; Malathi Bolar, "Measuring Effectiveness of Personnel Policy Implementation," *Personnel Psychology*, Winter 1970, pp. 463–80; Michael Gordon, "Three Ways to Effectively Evaluate Personnel Programs," *Personnel Journal*, July 1972, pp. 498–504; J. Fitz-Enz, "Quantifying the Human Resources Function, *Personnel*, March–April 1980, pp. 41–52.
2. Bureau of National Affairs, *Labor Policy and Practice: Personnel Management* (Washington, D.C., 1975).
3. W. Merrihue and R. Katzell, "ERI, Yardstick of Employee Relations," *Harvard Business Review*, November–December 1955, pp. 91–99.
4. Walter R. Mahler, "Auditing PAIR," in *ASPA Handbook of Personnel and Industrial Relations*, ed. D. Yoder and H. Heneman, Jr. (Washington, D.C.: Bureau of National Affairs, 1979), pp. 2–103; Geneva Seybold, *Personnel Audits and Reports to Top Management*, Studies in Personnel Policy 191 (New York: The

Conference Board, 1964); Paul Sheibar, "Personnel Practices Review: A Personnel Audit Activity," *Personnel Journal*, March 1974, pp. 211–17.
5. Paul Sheibar, "Personnel Practices Review."
6. Ibid.
7. Terry Connelly, E. J. Conlon, and S. J. Deutsch, "A Multiple Constituency Approach of Organizational Effectiveness," *Academy of Management Review* 5, no. 1 (1980), pp. 211–18; Michael Keeley, "Impartiality and Participant-Interest Theories of Organizational Effectiveness," *Administration Science Quarterly* 29, no. 1 (1984), pp. 1–26; Michael Hitt, R. D. Ireland, B. W. Keats, and A. Vianna, "Measuring Subunit Effectiveness," *Decision Sciences*, January 1983, pp. 87–102; Michael Keeley, "A Social Justice Approach to Evaluation," *Administrative Science Quarterly*, June 1978, pp. 272–92.
8. Anne S. Tsui, "Personnel Department Effectiveness: A Tri-Partite Approach," *Industrial Relations*, Spring 1984, pp. 184–97.
9. Ibid.
10. Ibid.
11. Evidence of reputational assessment popularity is reflected in the willingness of companies to participate in Tsui's studies. Personal communications with A. S. Tsui.
12. Joel R. LaPointe, "Human Resource Performance Indexes," *Personnel Journal*, July 1983, pp. 545–600.
13. Lapointe, "Human Resource Performance," pp. 545–50.
14. Merrihue and Katzell, "ERI."
15. Barry A. Macy and Phillip H. Mirvis, "A Methodology for Assessing the Quality of Work Life and Organizational Effectiveness in Behavioral and Economic Terms," *Administrative Science Quarterly*, June 1976, pp. 212–26.
16. Tom Janz and Lois Etherington, "Comparing Methods for Assessing the Standard Deviation for Performance in Dollars," in *Proceedings of the Administrative Sciences Association of Canada Annual Conference* Vol. 4, Part 5, ed. Gary Johns (1983), pp. 192–200; Tom Janz, "Personnel Decisions: Costs, Benefits, and Opportunities for the Energy Industry," *Journal of Canadian Petroleum Technology*, September 1982, pp. 80–84; Wayne F. Cascio, *Costing Human Resources: The Financial Impact of Behavior in Organizations* (Boston: Kent Publishing, 1982); John W. Boudreau, "Decision Theory Contributions to HRM Research and Practice," *Industrial Relations*, Spring 1984, pp. 198–217; Edward Gramlich, *Benefit-Cost Analysis* (Englewood Cliffs, N.J.: Prentice-Hall, 1981).
17. See Chapter Ten, "Orientation, Training, and Development."
18. Macy and Mirvis, *A Methodology for Assessing*.
19. E. Flamholtz, "Toward a Theory of Human Resource Value in Formal Organizations," *The Accounting Review*, October 1972, pp. 666–67; E. Flamholtz, "Assessing the Validity of a Theory of Human Resource Value: A Field Study," in *Empirical Research in Accounting: Selected Studies 1972*, ed. Nicholas Dopuch (Chicago: Chicago Institute of Professional Accounting, 1972), pp. 241–66.
20. E. Flamholtz, "Replacement Cost as a Surrogate Measure of Human Resource Value: A Field Study," (AIS Working Paper No. 74–1, July 1973, mimeographed); E. Flamholtz, "Human Resource Accounting: Measuring Positional Replacement Costs," *Human Resource Management*, Spring 1972, pp. 8–16; R. Likert, *The Human Organization: Its Management and Value* (New York, McGraw-Hill, 1967); R. Likert and D. G. Bowers, "Organizational Theory and

Human Resource Accounting," *American Psychologist*, September 1969, pp. 585–92; James A. Craft, "Resource Accounting and Manpower Management: A Review and Assessment of Current Applicability," *Journal of Economics and Business* 1 (1980), pp. 42–50.
21. Wayne F. Cascio, "Responding to the Demand for Accountability: A Critical Analysis of Three Utility Models," *Organizational Behavior and Human Performance* 25, no. 1 (1980), pp. 32–45; also see Stanley E. Seashore, Edward E. Lawler III, Phillip H. Miwis, and Coctlandt Cammann, eds., *Assessing Organizational Change: A Guide to Methods, Measures, and Practices* (New York: John Wiley & Sons, 1983).
22. Frank L. Schmidt, John E. Hunter, and Kenneth Pearlman, "Assessing the Economic Impact of Personnel Programs on Workforce Productivity," *Personnel Psychology* 35, no. 2 (1982), pp. 333–47.
23. John W. Boudreau, "Economic Considerations in Estimating the Utility of Human Resource Productivity Improvement Programs," *Personnel Psychology* 36, no. 4 (1983), pp. 551–76; Philip Bobko and John J. Parkington, "Estimation of Standard Deviations in Utility Analysis: An Empirical Test," *Journal of Applied Psychology* 68, no. 2 (1983), pp. 170–76.
24. J. E. Hunter, F. L. Schmidt, R. C. McKenzie, and T. W. Muldrow, "Impact of Valid Selection Procedures on Work-Force Productivity," *Journal of Applied Psychology* 64 (1979), pp. 609–26.
25. Wayne F. Cascio and Val Silbey, "Utility of the Assessment Center as a Selection Device," *Journal of Applied Psychology* 64, no. 1 (1979), pp. 107–18.
26. Frank J. Landy, James L. Farr, and Rick R. Jacobs, "Utility Concepts in Performance Measurement," *Organizational Behavior and Human Performance* 30, no. 1 (1982), pp. 15–30.
27. Stephen J. Carroll, Jr., "Measuring the Work of a Personnel Department," *Personnel*, July–August 1960, pp. 49–56.
28. Dale Yoder, *How Much Do Personnel Activities Cost: 1954 Budget Study*, Reprint Series No. 15 (Minneapolis: University of Minnesota); H. G. Heneman, Jr., *Personnel Audits and Manpower Assets* (Minneapolis: University of Minnesota Industrial Relations Center, 1967).
29. *ASPA-BNA Survey, Personnel Activities, Budgets, and Staffs, 1982* (Washington, D.C.: Bureau of National Affairs, 1983).
30. Henry Dahl, "Measuring the Human ROI," *Management Review*, January 1979, pp. 44–50; Henry Dahl and K. S. Morgan, *Return on Investment in Human Resources* (Upjohn Company Report, 1982).
31. Ibid.

CASES

▶ BLOCK DRUG COMPANY

Block Drug Company is a large firm located near Montreal. It employs several thousand persons.

One subunit of the firm is the research division. Research employs a number of scientists such as chemists and pharmacological scientists, assisted by laboratory technicians. The latter require training in the same fields but not as much as the scientists themselves.

Although much of the technicians' work is routine—to free the scientists for more creative work—many of the technicians are quite competent. These are given more challenging work. Often, teams of several scientists and a half dozen technicians work on the same research project. Synergy develops: all members of the team come up with new ideas and procedures.

Many of the technicians are helping put spouses through college or graduate school at one of Montreal's many colleges and universities. As a result, frequently a technician leaves a project in the middle, when the spouse finishes or drops out of a program.

Dr. Lawrence Pyrbomba, director of research for Block, has requested that the personnel department make recommendations to improve this situation and help develop a career pattern for lab technicians. Because of budgetary constraints, he is not able to increase their salary much above its current level, but employee benefits such as insurance and pensions are very generous.

Discussion Questions

1. Would it be feasible for the personnel department to develop a career pattern for the lab technicians? What benefits may be derived for the company?
2. How else can the company recognize employee performance other than pay increases?
3. What action might the company take to reduce turnover among the technicians?

▶ CANADA EAST INSURANCE COMPANY LTD.*

Canada East Insurance Company (CEI) is a Halifax-based financial institution specializing in group benefit plans and related insurance products. The company was founded in 1922 and currently employs 654 people. Most employees, except some of the sales force, are located in Halifax. Sales employees are stationed throughout the Atlantic provinces and parts of Quebec.

Jay Epstein, vice president of human resources at CEI, recently heard about a Canadian firm that was found to discriminate against women based on evidence that female employees were almost totally absent from the managerial and professional ranks. Instead, they were concentrated in the clerical and service jobs. The part of the story that particularly caught Epstein's attention was that the company did not intend to discriminate against women. In fact, the discriminating firm had earlier introduced a special training program to make supervisors more aware of discrimination and attitudes toward women in nontraditional jobs. Nevertheless, a human rights tribunal decided against the firm because its employment practices had an adverse effect on the employment opportunities of women.

Epstein was concerned about these events and thought it was time for CEI to examine its own work force and employment practices. Using available information from personnel files, the human resources department tabulated the number of men and women in each occupational group within the company. Four disabled employees were also identified from company files, although the human resources vice president was certain this was much lower than the actual number of disabled staff. Unfortunately, more precise information on disabilities, visible minority status, and aboriginal status was unavailable until CEI had the opportunity to conduct a formal survey of employees. Depending on the results from the information now available, the survey would be conducted within the next six months.

---

*© Copyright 1987 Steven L. McShane. This is a fictitious company. Any resemblance to an existing firm in Canada is purely coincidental.

Canada East Insurance Work Force

The occupational distribution of CEI's work force is presented in Exhibit 1. These occupational groups correspond to those required in federal employment equity programs. CEI's employment practices are regulated by provincial legislation, but these occupational categories permit comparisons with labour market data compiled by the federal government on each province and census metropolitan area (CMA). Only 8 of the 12 occupational groups in the federal list are included because CEI employs only a handful of people in skilled crafts, service, and manual jobs.

Clerical and sales staff are the two largest groups of employees, followed by the professional group. The clerical group includes a variety of jobs, particularly insurance, account-recording, and statistical clerks. Almost all of the sales jobs are insurance sales to corporations and other organizations that purchase group insurance plans. CEI also employs approximately 82 professionals, including accountants, actuaries, lawyers, and computer programmers. The company is known for its strong actuarial analysis and actively hires the best people into these jobs.

In addition to the current stock of employees, the human resources staff has prepared information on the number of hires for each occupational group over the past four years by the source of hire. Exhibit 2 presents this information. According to Jay Epstein, these hiring levels are stable and will probably reflect the trend for at least the next four years.

As a company policy, CEI prefers to promote people into upper- and middle-level positions rather than hiring from outside. In the past four years, the company has promoted two people from middle to upper management. Occasionally, promotions also occur from professional positions to upper management. On the few occasions that CEI hired someone from the external labour market to an upper-management job, the company relied on an exec-

EXHIBIT 1
Canada East Insurance Co. Ltd. Occupational Distribution of Work Force by Gender and Disability Status

Occupational Group	Total	Male	Female	Disabled	Percent Female	Percent Disabled
Upper management	17	15	2	0	11.76%	0.00%
Middle management	55	49	6	1	10.91	1.82
Professionals	82	60	22	2	26.83	2.44
Semiprofessionals	29	15	14	0	48.28	0.00
Supervisors	72	32	40	1	55.56	1.39
Foremen/women	3	3	0	0	0.00	0.00
Clerical	216	29	187	0	86.57	0.00
Sales	180	125	55	0	30.56	0.00
Total	654	328	326	4	49.85%	0.61%

EXHIBIT 2
Numbers of Hires by Occupational Group in Past Four Years

Occupational Group	Source of Hire	Total	Male	Female	Disabled	Percent Female
Upper management	Promotions	2	1	1	0	50.00%
Middle management	Promotions	8	6	2	0	25.00
	Labour market	1	1	0	0	0.00
Professionals	Promotions	3	2	1	0	33.33
	Labour market	4	3	1	0	25.00
	Postsecondary graduates	12	7	5	1	41.67
Semiprofessionals	Promotions	1	0	1	0	100.00
	Labour market	1	1	0	0	0.00
	Postsecondary graduates	5	2	3	0	60.00
Supervisors	Promotions	14	8	6	0	42.86
	Labour market	4	3	1	0	25.00
Foremen/women	All sources	0	0	0	0	N/A
Clerical	Labour market	18	3	15	0	83.33
	Graduates	23	5	18	0	78.26
Sales	Promotions	9	2	7	0	77.78
	Labour market	11	8	3	0	27.27
	Graduates	13	7	6	0	46.15
Total		129	59	70	1	

Note: Promotions to sales and semiprofessions were from clerical jobs. Employees promoted to supervisory positions came mainly from clerical and sales jobs. Promotions to middle management came mainly from professional, semiprofessional, supervisory, and sales occupations. Upper management were promoted entirely from middle management.

utive search firm from Montreal that searches throughout the country for job candidates.

Middle-management promotions come mainly from professional and sales jobs. A few promotions also go to people from semiprofessional and supervisory positions. Although performance evaluations include a section on promotability, this information is not usually considered in promotion decisions. Instead, promotions are usually determined from interviews with employees seeking the job. External hires in the middle-management category usually come from Nova Scotia or, occasionally, from other Atlantic provinces.

Professional jobs are filled from a variety of sources, as Exhibit 2 indicates. Most incumbents are hired from specialized postsecondary programs such as business, mathematics, law, and computer science. Graduates are from educational institutions throughout the Atlantic provinces, although most are hired from schools in Nova Scotia. People hired from the general labour market also originate mainly from various places in Nova Scotia.

Employees in semiprofessional occupations, such as statistical officers and computer technicians, are mainly hired from community colleges and universities in and around Halifax. This also reflects the area from which most external hires are drawn. Clerical employees are occasionally promoted to semiprofessional jobs when they have completed the required training. However, CEI has no formal career path from clerical positions, and people in these jobs complete the educational programs part-time without company assistance.

Sales staff members are usually hired from the labour market in Eastern Canada (from central Ontario to Newfoundland), although some also originate from other parts of the country. University and community college graduates entering CEI's sales force are attracted from the Atlantic provinces, Quebec, and parts of Ontario. Some sales positions are filled by employees in clerical positions who have completed company-sponsored training courses on insurance sales.

Employees in supervisory positions at CEI are usually promoted from sales, clerical, and semiprofessional jobs. When external hiring is required, most job candidates originate from the local Halifax area. Clerical employees are also hired locally, either from the general labour market or directly from high schools and community colleges in the area.

Assignment

Jay Epstein has retained your services as an external consultant to prepare a report on the employment opportunities of women and disabled people in CEI. In addition to the two exhibits on CEI's work force, labour force data are attached for your information (Exhibit 3 through Exhibit 7). Your report should address each of the following:

1. In which occupational groups, if any, are women and disabled persons underutilized? In which groups are they concentrated? What assumptions or facts do you make when applying the labour force data in the utilization analysis? (Note: Data on graduates from educational institutions are not available at this time.)
2. Use the standard deviation test to determine whether the gap between the ideal and actual number of women in each occupational group is significant. (Conduct this test only on the gender data, not the disability data.) Using this test, indicate the ideal minimum number of women that CEI should be employing in each occupational group. When should the standard deviation test be interpreted cautiously?
3. What additional information do the data on hiring (Exhibit 2) provide regarding the effect of CEI's employment policies?

EXHIBIT 3
Canadian Population Aged 15 and Older Who Worked in 1980 or 1981 Showing Representation of Designated Groups by Occupational Groups

Occupational Groups	Total No.	Total %	Males No.	Males %	Females No.	Females %	Aboriginal People No.	Aboriginal People %	Visible Minorities No.	Visible Minorities %
All occupations	13,129,260	100.0	7,595,395	57.9	5,533,870	42.1	175,935	1.3	646,085	4.9
Upper-level managers	116,690	100.0	101,945	87.4	14,740	12.6	1,200	1.0	3,330	2.9
Middle and other managers	813,070	100.0	600,740	73.9	212,330	26.1	5,225	.6	28,355	3.5
Professionals	1,437,505	100.0	708,570	49.3	728,935	50.7	10,110	.7	88,250	6.1
Semiprofessionals and technicians	578,645	100.0	306,905	53.0	271,740	47.0	7,925	1.4	30,505	5.3
Supervisors	352,795	100.0	197,435	56.0	155,365	44.0	2,215	.6	20,760	5.9
Foremen/women	402,550	100.0	375,750	93.3	26,800	6.7	3,885	1.0	10,040	2.5
Clerical workers	2,302,765	100.0	468,515	20.3	1,834,250	79.7	18,800	.8	113,430	4.9
Sales workers	984,515	100.0	522,345	53.1	462,175	46.9	5,980	.6	33,915	3.4
Service workers	1,239,625	100.0	476,865	38.5	762,760	61.5	21,590	1.7	85,825	6.9
Skilled crafts and trades	1,077,105	100.0	1,012,830	94.0	64,270	6.0	12,555	1.2	32,225	3.0
Semiskilled manual workers	1,216,715	100.0	1,072,320	88.1	144,400	11.9	19,825	1.6	44,195	3.6
Other manual workers	2,107,125	100.0	1,473,960	70.0	633,165	30.9	46,340	2.2	127,570	6.1
Occupations not stated	500,150	100.0	277,220	55.4	222,935	44.6	20,285	4.1	27,685	5.5

Totals may not equal the sum of components due to rounding and suppression.
Source: Unpublished data, 1981 Census of Canada. Compiled for Canada Employment and Immigration Commission, 1987.

EXHIBIT 4
Nova Scotia Population Aged 15 and Older Who Worked in 1980 or 1981 Showing Representation of Designated Groups by Occupational Groups

Occupational Groups	Total No.	%	Males No.	%	Females No.	%	Aboriginal People No.	%	Visible Minorities No.	%
All occupations	419,260	100.0	247,955	59.1	171,305	40.9	2,890	0.7	7,165	1.7
Upper-level managers	2,505	100.0	2,095	83.6	405	16.2	—	—	—	—
Middle and other managers	21,415	100.0	15,840	74.0	5,570	26.0	120	.6	405	1.9
Professionals	47,105	100.0	22,530	47.8	24,575	52.2	215	.5	1,310	2.8
Semiprofessionals and technicians	18,750	100.0	9,215	49.1	9,530	50.8	165	.9	340	1.8
Supervisors	10,715	100.0	6,030	56.3	4,690	43.8	30	.3	320	3.0
Foremen/women	11,285	100.0	10,620	94.1	665	5.9	30	.3	135	1.2
Clerical workers	63,610	100.0	12,570	19.8	51,045	80.2	355	.6	1,005	1.6
Sales workers	33,030	100.0	16,530	50.0	16,500	50.0	135	.4	550	1.7
Service workers	47,455	100.0	19,750	41.6	27,710	58.4	390	.8	1,130	2.4
Skilled crafts and trades	31,190	100.0	29,965	96.1	1,225	3.9	225	.7	210	.7
Semiskilled crafts and trades	39,905	100.0	36,790	92.2	3,120	7.8	290	.7	435	1.1
Other manual workers	76,750	100.0	57,655	75.1	19,090	24.9	710	.9	1,040	1.4
Occupations not stated	15,540	100.0	8,370	53.9	7,170	46.1	200	1.3	270	1.7

— Numbers too small to be expressed.
Totals may not equal the sum of components due to rounding and suppression.
Source: Unpublished data, 1981 Census of Canada. Compiled for Canada Employment and Immigration Commission, 1987.

EXHIBIT 5
Halifax Population Aged 15 and Older Who Worked in 1980 or 1981 Showing Representation of Designated Groups by Occupational Groups

Occupational Groups	Total No.	Total %	Males No.	Males %	Females No.	Females %	Aboriginal People No.	Aboriginal People %	Visible Minorities No.	Visible Minorities %
All occupations	156,280	100.0	87,485	56.0	68,800	44.0	660	0.4	4,800	3.1
Upper-level managers	1,450	100.0	1,170	80.7	280	19.3	—	—	—	—
Middle and other managers	9,985	100.0	7,295	73.1	2,690	26.9	35	.4	300	3.0
Professionals	22,710	100.0	11,780	51.9	10,935	48.2	65	.3	905	4.0
Semiprofessionals and technicians	8,700	100.0	4,560	52.4	4,140	47.6	40	.5	245	3.8
Supervisors	4,865	100.0	2,710	55.7	2,160	44.4	—	—	185	2.8
Foremen/women	3,480	100.0	3,205	92.1	275	7.9	—	—	85	2.4
Clerical workers	31,385	100.0	6,065	19.3	25,320	80.7	145	.5	780	2.5
Sales workers	13,515	100.0	7,265	53.8	6,245	46.2	50	.4	330	2.4
Service workers	20,025	100.0	10,590	52.9	9,435	47.1	120	.6	715	3.6
Skilled crafts and trades	9,040	100.0	8,725	96.5	315	3.5	—	—	145	1.6
Semiskilled manual workers	10,680	100.0	9,935	93.0	745	7.0	65	.6	295	2.8
Other manual workers	15,500	100.0	11,640	75.1	3,855	24.9	95	.6	605	3.9
Occupations not stated	4,955	100.0	2,555	51.6	2,405	48.5	—	—	195	3.9

— Numbers too small to be expressed.
Totals may not equal the sum of components due to rounding and suppression.
Source: Unpublished data, 1981 Census of Canada. Compiled for Canada Employment and Immigration Commission, 1987.

EXHIBIT 6
Canadian Experienced Labour Pool* by Selected Occupational Major Groups† Showing Representation of Persons with Disabilities by Sex

Major Group	Total Population Total 000s	%	Male 000s	%	Female 000s	%	Persons with Disabilities Total 000s	%	Male 000s	%	Female 000s	%
All occupations	13,644	100.0	7,757	56.9	5,887	43.1	887	6.5	511	3.7	376	2.8
Managerial, administrative, and related	1,032	100.0	712	69.0	320	31.0	54	5.2	34	3.3	20	1.9
Professional and semiprofessional	2,112	100.0	1,001	47.4	1,111	52.6	97	4.6	40	1.9	57	2.7
Clerical and related	2,306	100.0	472	20.5	1,834	79.5	139	6.0	34	1.6	105	4.6
Sales	1,373	100.0	763	55.6	610	44.4	86	6.3	50	3.6	37	2.7
Service	2,154	100.0	922	42.8	1,232	57.2	170	7.9	75	3.5	94	4.4
Primary	936	100.0	728	77.8	207	22.1	93	9.9	72	7.7	20	2.1
Others	3,731	100.0	3,158	84.6	573	15.4	248	6.6	205	5.5	43	1.2
Processing	480	100.0	364	75.8	116	24.2	33	6.9	24	5.0	9*	1.9*
Machining and related	281	100.0	259	92.2	22	7.8	18	6.4	18	6.4	—	—
Product fabricating, assembling, and repairing	1,111	100.0	840	75.6	270	24.3	73	6.6	53	4.8	20	1.8
Construction trades	838	100.0	817	97.5	21	2.5	50	6.0	50	6.0	—	—
Transport equipment operating	482	100.0	453	94.0	29	6.0	35	7.3	31	6.4	—	—
Material handling and related	377	100.0	298	79.0	78	20.7	28	7.4	22	5.8	—	—
Other crafts and equipment operating	163	100.0	126	77.3	37	22.7	12‡	7.4‡	8‡	4.9‡	—	—

— Indicates amount too small to be expressed, i.e., sampling variability (c.v.) is greater than 25%.

*The experienced labour pool consists of individuals who had worked in the previous 17 months. This time period corresponds to the period used for employment equity data from the 1981 Census (population who worked in 1980 or 1981) conducted on June 3, 1981.

†Data for employment equity occupational groups are not available for persons with disabilities. As a result, data using Standard Occupation Classification Major Groups are provided in this table. Major groups cannot be converted to employment equity occupational groups.

‡High sampling variance (c.v.: 16.5% – 25%)—use with caution.

Source: Unpublished data. Canadian Health and Disability Survey, October 1983–June 1984. Compiled for Canada Employment and Immigration Commission, 1987.

EXHIBIT 7
Atlantic Region Experienced Labour Pool* by Selected Occupational Major Groups† Showing Representation of Persons with Disabilities by Sex

Major Group	Total Population							Persons with Disabilities					
	Total		Male		Female		Total		Male		Female	
	000s	%	000s	%	000s	%	000s	%	000s	%	000s	%
All occupations	1,111	100.0	641	57.7	470	42.3	66	5.9	39	3.5	26	2.3
Managerial, administrative, and related	75	100.0	53	70.7	22	29.3	—	—	—	—	—	—
Professional and semiprofessional	155	100.0	67	43.2	88	56.8	7	4.5	—	—	4	2.6
Clerical and related	163	100.0	31	19.0	132	81.0	9	5.5	—	—	7	4.3
Sales	95	100.0	51	53.7	44	46.3	5	5.3	—	—	—	—
Service	191	100.0	73	38.2	118	61.8	13	6.8	5	2.6	8	4.2
Primary	104	100.0	90	86.5	14	13.4	7	6.7	7	6.7	—	—
Others	328	100.0	276	84.1	52	15.9	20	6.1	17	5.2	—	—
Processing	72	100.0	39	54.2	32	44.4	4	5.6	—	—	—	—
Machining and related	13	100.0	13	100.0	—	—	—	—	—	—	—	—
Product fabricating, assembling, and repairing	58	100.0	50	86.2	8	13.8	4	6.9	—	—	—	—
Construction trades	97	100.0	93	95.9	4	4.1	6	6.2	6	6.2	—	—
Transport equipment operating	48	100.0	45	93.8	—	—	—	—	—	—	—	—
Material handling and related	29	100.0	26	89.7	—	—	—	—	—	—	—	—
Other crafts and equipment operating	11	100.0	9	81.8	—	—	—	—	—	—	—	—

— Amount too small to be expressed, i.e., sampling variability (c.v.) is greater than 25%.
*The experienced labour pool consists of individuals who had worked in the previous 17 months. This time period corresponds to the period used for employment equity data from the 1981 Census (population who worked in 1980 or 1981) conducted on June 3, 1981.
†Data for employment equity occupational groups are not available for persons with disabilities. As a result, data using Standard Occupation Classification Major Groups are provided in this table. Major Groups cannot be converted to employment equity occupational groups.
Source: Unpublished data, Canadian Health and Disability Survey, October 1983–June 1984. Compiled for Canada Employment and Immigration Commission, 1987.

4. Based on the facts available in this case, indicate what recruiting, training and development, career path, and performance evaluation policies and practices CEI should change to increase employment opportunities for women. In which occupational groups where underutilization of women is found do you anticipate the slowest progress toward employment equity? Why?

▶ CANADIAN GLOVE COMPANY LTD.*

Canadian Glove Co. Ltd. is a medium-sized firm that manufactures a variety of sporting goods. All domestic production comes from its plant in Sherbrooke, Quebec.

The market for Canadian Glove Co.'s products is growing at a fairly stable rate, as Exhibit 1 indicates. Based on previous sales and economic projections, the firm estimates sales (in 1987 constant dollars) of $63 million in 1990 and $69 million in 1993.

Production technology improved productivity rapidly during the early 1970s, but no major technological advances are expected for the next decade. Consequently, productivity has been growing at a slow but constant rate since 1981 and will likely continue at that rate for the next decade. The firm uses sales per employee as the major indicator of labour productivity. Productivity levels for 1981, 1984, and 1987 are shown in Exhibit 1.

As the company continues to grow, the vice president of human resources sees a need for better projections of the demand for employees at all occupational levels. The proportion of the work force in each occupational group has not changed since 1981 and is expected to remain the same for the next decade. However, even with productivity improvement, the vice president thinks employment will rise. Exhibit 2 shows the number of employees in each occupational group.

The vice president is particularly concerned about the supervisory group. Canadian Glove Co. has a policy of recruiting internally to fill supervisory positions (i.e., promoting rather than hiring to fill vacancies). Technological changes during the early 1970s led to relatively few promotions at this level. But with several supervisors retiring soon, the need for qualified candidates will likely increase more rapidly than in the other groups.

Based on these concerns, the vice president of human resources has asked you to prepare an employment forecast report on the demand for all employees and demographic changes to the supervisory group.

---

*This case was written by Professor Steven L. McShane, Simon Fraser University. © 1987 Steven L. McShane.

EXHIBIT 1
Sales and Productivity Record of Canadian Glove Co. Ltd.

Year	Sales	Employees	Sales per Employee
1981	$43,200,000	810	$53,333
1984	49,800,000	902	55,211
1987	56,400,000	985	57,259
1990	63,000,000		
1993	69,000,000		

Note: Sales are in 1987 constant dollars. Sales figures for 1990 and 1993 are estimates.

EXHIBIT 2
Distribution of Employees at Canadian Glove Co. Ltd. by Occupational Group

Occupational Group	1981	1984	1987
Management/technical	80	90	99
Supervisory*	162	180	196
Clerical	203	225	246
Production	365	407	444
Total	810	902	985

*Includes supervisors, foremen/women, and lead hands.

Assignment

1. Estimate the demand for employees in 1990 and 1993. Include the total number of employees required as well as the number in each of the four occupational groups listed in Exhibit 2. Be sure to show how you arrived at your figures.
2. Conduct a demographic analysis of the supervisory group based on age. Specifically, estimate the age distribution of the supervisory group in 1990 and 1993. Canadian Glove Co. provided the current age distribution of supervisory staff in Exhibit 3. Based upon the movement of people into,

EXHIBIT 3
Distribution of Supervisory Staff at Canadian Glove Co. Ltd. by Age

Age Group	1981	1984	1987
20–29	8	14	25
30–39	23	27	29
40–49	65	58	52
50–59	54	59	60
60–65	12	22	30
Total	162	180	196

EXHIBIT 4
Age Graded Transitional Probability Matrix for Supervisory Jobs

Status at T2 \ Status at T1	20–29	30–39	40–49	50–59	60–65	Vacancies*	Total
20–29	0.39	0.36				0.25	1.00
30–39		0.60	0.30			0.10	1.00
40–49			0.62	0.33		0.05	1.00
50–59				0.63	0.32	0.05	1.00
60–65					0.50	0.50	1.00
Recruits†	0.60	0.20	0.15	0.05	0.00	—	1.00

*"Vacancies" includes all quits, retirements, and promotions out of supervisory jobs.
†"Recruits" include both promotions and external hires into supervisory jobs.

through, and out of the supervisory group between 1981 and 1987, the vice president of human resources also provided you with a transitional probability matrix for this group in Exhibit 4. (Note: The "Vacancies" category includes quits, promotions, retirements, and any other forms of employment exit.)

3. In the demographic analysis of supervisors, draw upon your knowledge of organizational demography to explain what problems may arise as a result of the changing demographic structure of this group.

▶ CONSOLIDATED DEFENSE MANUFACTURING

Consolidated Defense Manufacturing (CDM) is a large Canadian firm, headquartered in Montreal, that produces devices purchased primarily by Canada, the United States, and a few other NATO countries for defense purposes.

CDM is considering bidding on a new contract to make an improved version of its product for the Canadian Armed Forces. This would be a large contract and would require additional hiring of several hundred skilled workers to produce the devices.

These workers (tool and die workers, machinists, etc.) are thought to be in short supply. Before CDM bids on the contract, top management asked for the advice of its management as to feasibility of the project. Thus, the financial people are working with production people on minimum bid. The production people are projecting their needs for plant and equipment.

Assignment

You have been asked to recommend whether the personnel are available and at what cost. Several production sites are available: Fredericton, New Brunswick; Halifax, Nova Scotia; Winnipeg, Manitoba; and Trois Rivieres, Quebec. Your recommended site and projected personnel availability are expected in 30 days. Where do you begin? What kinds of data would you need for each potential site?

▶ EASTERN SCHOOL DISTRICT

Eastern School District is a medium-sized district in the eastern part of the country. The district has 883 employees distributed as follows:

Administrators	
Principals and district administrators	49
Primary teachers	312
Secondary teachers	316
Clerical	87
Operative	
Custodians, maintenance	119

The district operates 1 special education facility, 1 vocational education high school, 26 primary schools, 6 junior high schools, and 4 high schools.

Eastern is located near a university. Many of the younger teachers stay a relatively short time, since they are primarily supporting their spouses through graduate or professional school. The turnover rate for each category of employment is given in Exhibit 1.

Dr. John Fleming, superintendent of schools, attributes the general decline in turnover for a time to several factors. He was able to get an increase in the wages of clerical and operative employees approved by the school board. He believes the decline in teacher turnover is due to the attractiveness of the district and the steady increase in the number of career teachers.

EXHIBIT 1
Turnover at Eastern Schools

	1974	1975	1976	1977	1978
Administrators	3%	3½%	4%	3½%	3%
Primary school teachers	31	28	27	29	23
Secondary school teachers	19	16	15	15	14
Clerical employees	20	22	21	16	17
Operative employees	33	31	28	27	26

	1979	1980	1981	1982	1983
Administrators	2%	1%	0%	2%	3%
Primary school teachers	20	19	20	22	24
Secondary school teachers	12	13	11	9	7
Clerical employees	15	10	13	14	12
Operative employees	23	21	17	16	18

Although there has been a decline in turnover in many categories, Superintendent Fleming wishes to reduce it further. He believes turnover is expensive in training costs, disrupts the system, and lowers morale. He asked Jane Cutler, professor of educational administration at the nearby university, to develop an orientation program for the district. He is not sure whether or not the same program should be given to teachers as to other employees. To ensure that the schools in the district cooperate, Dr. Fleming would like a control system set up to be monitored by the school district office.

At present, the relevant material that might be covered includes (1) salary scales, (2) summer school teaching, (3) extracurricular activities policies, (4) promotion opportunities, (5) adult education policies, (6) benefits (insurance—health, life, and accident; credit union; pension plan; cafeterias; vacations and rest periods; and workers' compensation), and (7) working conditions (hours of work, punctuality, fire protection, clothing to be worn, proper attitude, and parent-teacher meetings).

There might be other factors that should be covered. Professor Cutler thought she might begin her orientation by outlining a good program and a reasonable follow-up system. Then she might sample teacher and other employee responses to her ideas.

Assignment

You are Professor Cutler. Design an orientation program or programs for the district. Prepare a strategy for follow-up control. Describe how you would test the system for acceptance before introducing it into Eastern School District.

▶ EGLOFF PLASTICS

Egloff Plastics Company (EPC) is a medium-sized manufacturer of industrial plastics. The company's main location is in Richmond Hill, just north of Toronto.

Recently, Richard Hutcheon, head of the bookkeeping department, had a chat with Ernest Au, one of the younger bookkeepers in Hutcheon's department.

About a month ago, an opening for a senior bookkeeper had developed. Au had indicated an interest in the job. Hutcheon had not taken this very seriously, for Au was having a hard time doing his present job well. His supervisor, Mervyn Eastman, told Hutcheon that Au made more errors than anyone in the department.

Eastman: Really, he isn't qualified to do what he's doing now. We only hired him because he's Oriental. We thought we'd give him a chance. He's had twice the training our other bookkeepers received. I spend three times as much time with him as I do with others, training him and correcting his work. He seems to be a slow learner.

Later, Au stopped in to see Hutcheon.

Au: I didn't get that promotion. I know the reason. Eastman is prejudiced against Orientals. I think I'll file a complaint with the Ontario Human Rights Commission. There are no Orientals here in jobs other than the lowest ones, even though Toronto has a large percentage of Orientals.

Hutcheon pointed out that the job required more advanced bookkeeping skills than Au possessed, as well as the ability to supervise a clerical staff.

Samuel Rubinowitz, who had gotten the job, had several years of bookkeeping classes and three more years' experience than Au. This didn't impress Au, who walked out mentioning a visit to the Ontario Human Rights Commission.

Hutcheon is 42 years old, a graduate of York University's accounting program. He's had 15 years' experience with EPC, mostly in accounting. He likes his job, and the company, and feels it has not discriminated against Au.

Au is 24 years old, a high school graduate. He took one course in bookkeeping in his junior year of high school. He had a hard time getting a good job. He believes it was because he is Oriental. He has had two years' bookkeeping experience, one at EPC. Before that, he worked in a restaurant and a gas station.

Discussion Questions

1. What can the personnel department do for Au?
2. What can the personnel department do for Hutcheon?
3. What can the personnel department do for Rubinowitz?

▶ FLINT MEMORIAL HOSPITAL*

Flint Memorial is a large hospital, located in a growing, progressive city. Originally built about 20 years ago, it is now in the midst of a large expansion program. Soon the original 250-bed capacity will have been enlarged to

---

*Note: This case is from Richard P. Calhoun, *Cases in Personnel Management and Supervision*, © 1966, pp. 17–20. Reprinted by permission of Prentice-Hall, Inc., Englewood Cliffs, New Jersey.

accommodate about 800 beds. The hospital has enjoyed increasingly good public relations recently because of good patient service and a fine school of nursing. An organization chart showing hospital administration is shown in Exhibit 1.

Many changes have taken place in the administrative staff during the past two years. A new, well-qualified hospital administrator was employed. About the time he arrived, several members of the staff left. Anne Jones, the director of nursing, was employed to replace the former director. This position involved both nursing service and nursing education. An experienced nursing administrator, Miss Jones held a degree in nursing from a well-known university.

The morale of the nursing staff and faculty had been affected adversely by years of inadequate leadership. Henry Collins, the new administrator, was anxious to do something about this morale problem. When he told Miss Jones that she had been employed to meet the growing needs of the hospital and that he expected changes to be made, Miss Jones replied that she intended to make haste slowly. Each agreed that too much change might be even more detrimental to morale during this adjustment period. Collins delegated responsibility readily. Conditions seemed to improve gradually.

EXHIBIT 1
Organization Chart: Flint Memorial Hospital

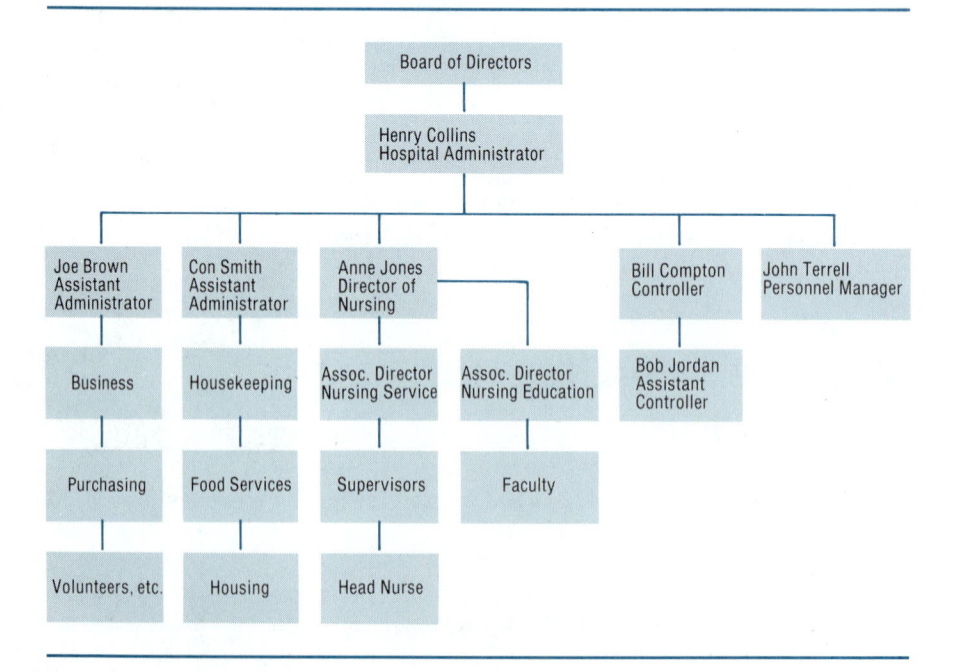

```
                        Board of Directors
                               |
                        Henry Collins
                     Hospital Administrator
   ┌──────────┬──────────────┬──────────────┬──────────────┬──────────────┐
Joe Brown   Con Smith     Anne Jones                    Bill Compton    John Terrell
Assistant   Assistant     Director of                   Controller      Personnel Manager
Administrator Administrator Nursing
   |           |          ┌─────────────┬──────────────┐      |
Business   Housekeeping  Assoc. Director  Assoc. Director   Bob Jordan
                         Nursing Service  Nursing Education Assistant
                                                            Controller
   |           |              |              |
Purchasing  Food Services  Supervisors      Faculty
   |           |              |
Volunteers, etc. Housing   Head Nurse
```

Miss Jones surveyed her staff and concluded that it was above average. The members of the staff with whom she had held discussions seemed friendly and willing to cooperate. The supervisors and faculty members seemed to accept her readily. In reviewing the personnel policies that affected her employees, she realized that no policy changes had been made in years; she was anxious to begin making some necessary revisions. Soon she began holding meetings with the staff to find areas of weakness and of strength.

New problems arose daily, now in nursing service, now in nursing education. Miss Jones and the faculty reviewed the rules and regulations for the student nurses and revised these in the light of present-day democratic principles. Revision was time-consuming and left little time to work on the problems of the staff of nursing service; this was the most pressing need of the moment.

John Terrell, the personnel manager, had been employed about four months after Miss Jones, to head a newly established personnel department. Miss Jones worked cooperatively with the personnel department, transferring records, putting in job requisitions, and exchanging information. The associate director of nursing service and Miss Jones's secretary were less willing to delegate responsibility to the new personnel department, but after some persuasion they began to realize that this would lighten their workload.

Mr. Terrell had previously been employed as an administrative assistant in a small hospital. Because he was apparently insecure at first, Miss Jones tried to cooperate and support him in his efforts. She had several years' experience in hospital personnel management and made available to him the literature and information she had.

Several times Joe Brown, an assistant administrator, remarked about Mr. Terrell's practice of reporting every trivial incident to Mr. Collins; Miss Jones felt Mr. Terrell might just be following directions.

Mr. Terrell and Miss Jones had discussed several times the need to revise and implement the personnel policies. After six months on the job, Mr. Terrell told Miss Jones he was revising the policies and would like her to read them over before he presented them to his committee on personnel policies. She indicated that she was very interested and wished to see them even though reorganization and the daily stress of the many disciplines and personalities in the hospital organization kept her busy.

One Tuesday morning Mr. Terrell called Miss Jones to ask when he could see her to discuss the new personnel policies. Consulting her desk calendar, she suggested Friday morning.

Mr. Terrell: But that's too late! My meeting is Thursday afternoon at 5 P.M.

Miss Jones: In that case bring them down and I'll go over them at home—I certainly want to see them.

Mr. Terrell's secretary brought the suggested policies to Miss Jones's office later that morning. Tuesday evening and Wednesday evening she read the new policy changes; she fumed inwardly. She could see the results of her efforts toward morale and cooperation evaporating. She wrote notes and recommended changes on the margin; she suggested additional policies. On Thursday morning Miss Jones called on Mr. Terrell in his office.

Miss Jones: Terrell, you can't take things away from people and expect a satisfied staff. One of your policies reduces some of the supervisors' vacation period by a week. I have 450 employees in my department. I can see nothing but hostility arising from many of these changes. Here are *my* suggestions—in writing!

Mr. Terrell: I'll look them over before the meeting this afternoon.

Miss Jones: I've been around hospitals too long to be sensitive, and as I've said, most of the employees in this institution are under Nursing. I intend to be at your meeting this afternoon, invited or not.

Miss Jones then angrily left Mr. Terrell's office.

That afternoon she attended the Personnel Policy Committee meeting. Copies of the suggested policies were passed out. Miss Jones asked for the copy on which she had noted her suggestions. Mr. Terrell, looking pained, said he had made her suggested changes. On glancing through her copy, she realized he had. Miss Jones was appeased.

Matters went along smoothly for a while after that; the combination of new-old policies was approved. One of the new personnel policies stated: "Those employees who have been employed over five years and are no longer receiving periodic increment salary raises will have their records reviewed on the anniversary of employment date; merit raises will be given consistent with performance appraisal by the supervisor."

Bob Jordan, one of the assistants to the controller, called Miss Jones about a month after the policy had gone into effect and asked if he could see her for a minute.

Mr. Jordan: This guy Terrell is getting into everyone's hair. I thought you might be interested in these.

Mr. Jordan had two authorization slips for merit raises for two of Miss Jones's supervisors. She had signed these herself, and they had been countersigned by Mr. Brown, the assistant administrator. Mr. Terrell had cancelled the authorization.

Miss Jones took the authorization slips and went to Mr. Brown's office. After he read them, the two of them appeared at Mr. Collin's office and requested a short conference.

Discussion Questions

1. What is happening here?
2. Whose responsibility is it that this situation exists?
3. Could Miss Jones have helped Mr. Terrell?
4. Should this matter of merit raises have been taken up with Mr. Terrell—or had it gone too far?
5. How should Miss Jones approach Mr. Collins?
6. How should Mr. Collins handle the interview with Miss Jones and Mr. Brown?
7. What should Mr. Collins do in his subsequent interview with Mr. Terrell?

▶ GIBSON PETROLEUM, LTD.

Gibson Petroleum (GP) is a moderate-size oil exploration firm. Its headquarters are located in Red Deer, Alberta. The firm explores for oil in Alberta, British Columbia, Northwest Territories, and the Yukon.

Gibson presently employs about 600 persons. This number has gone as high as 800 and as low as 200. The number of employees varies by the amount of business Gibson can sustain.

Gibson's personnel manager, John Sorenson, will retire in nine months. He recommended the firm hire a professionally trained personnel manager with at least 10 years' experience. Instead, J. W. F. Gibson, the firm's president, decided to appoint Harry VonTwistern to this position.

VonTwistern has given 15 years' service to GP. He wants to stay home more instead of going off to the exploration sites as he has for 15 years. VonTwistern is 50 years old. He graduated in petroleum engineering from MIT 25 years ago.

VonTwistern went to see Sorenson.

VonTwistern: John, I'm your replacement, I guess. I am really excited at the prospect of starting out on this new career. But, all I know is oil exploration. I've never spent any time in the office. I know everything there is to know about the field, but I am a complete novice about personnel work. Where do I start?

Exhibit 1 is an organization chart of GP's personnel department. The four-person department also has clerical help, employee consultants, and extra trainers, as needed.

Sandra Sankaran is 27 years old, a graduate of the University of Calgary in personnel several years ago. She has worked at GP for two years. Walter Pollock is 32 years old and has a degree in secondary education. He has worked at GP for six years. Ann Knudson is 37 years old, a graduate of the

EXHIBIT 1

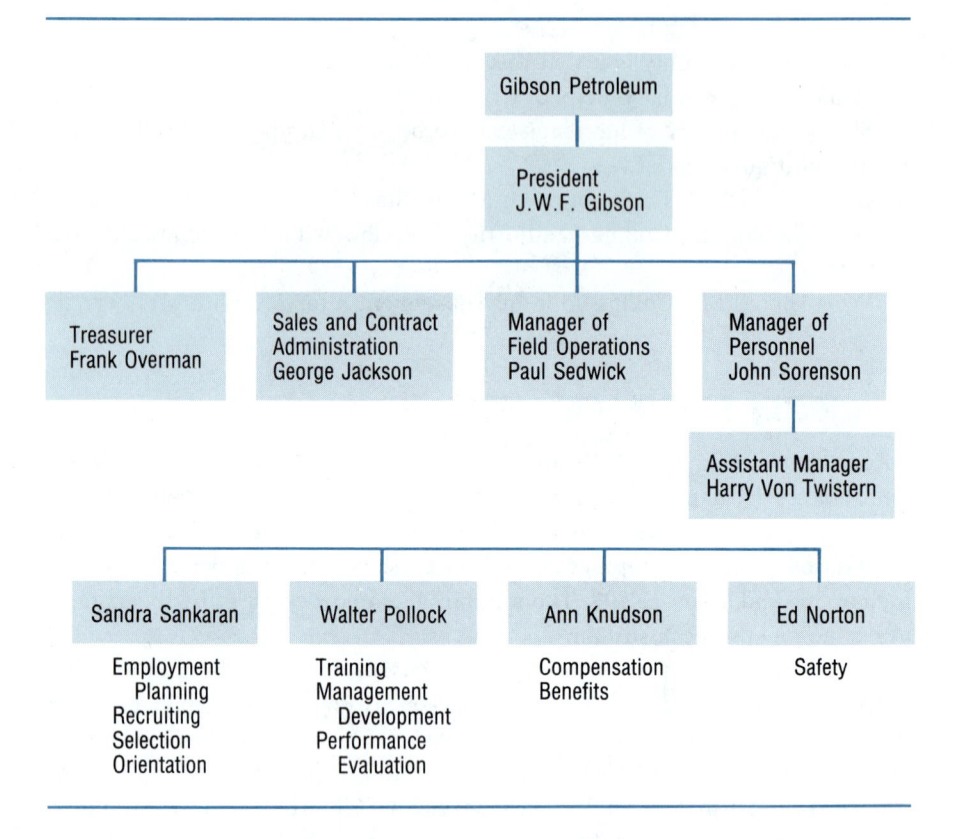

```
                        Gibson Petroleum
                              │
                          President
                         J.W.F. Gibson
   ┌──────────────┬───────────┴──────────┬──────────────┐
Treasurer     Sales and Contract    Manager of        Manager of
Frank Overman Administration        Field Operations  Personnel
              George Jackson        Paul Sedwick      John Sorenson
                                                          │
                                                   Assistant Manager
                                                   Harry Von Twistern
           ┌──────────────┬──────────────┬──────────────┐
      Sandra Sankaran  Walter Pollock  Ann Knudson    Ed Norton

      Employment       Training        Compensation   Safety
      Planning         Management      Benefits
      Recruiting       Development
      Selection        Performance
      Orientation      Evaluation
```

University of British Columbia in economics. She has worked at GP for 15 years. Ed Norton is 42 years old, an engineer and a graduate of the University of Washington. He has worked at GP for 12 years.

Assignment

You are John Sorenson. Design a program to develop VonTwistern into a top-notch personnel executive.

▶ GIGANTIC AIRCRAFT COMPANY

Gigantic Aircraft Company is a large firm with a plant in Winnipeg, Manitoba. The personnel manager called in Joyce Piersol, a management consultant specializing in personnel, for advice on selection policies. Bill Fabris invited Piersol to come in the first thing in the morning. When Piersol arrived, Fabris said: "Joyce, I'm glad you're here. I've been having a lot of trouble in selection recently. My long suit has always been collective bargaining. I'm a lawyer by training, and I think I need help. Briefly, let me outline how we handle selection here now."

> *Blue-collar employees*—Screening interview to separate out the misfits; then a test battery—mostly abilities tests—and then interview the best of the lot. For crucial jobs, either security-wise or if the job involves expensive equipment, get two letters of reference from prior employers.
>
> *White-collar employees*—Clerical and so forth—same as blue-collar procedures except references always are checked out.
>
> *Managerial employees*—Multiple interviews, intelligence test, personality tests, and references.

Fabris added: "I've also been making a list of what's happened in selection in the last six months since I've been in this job."

1. Our best managerial candidate was lost because she refused to take the personality test we use, the Minnesota Multiphasic Personality Inventory. She said it was an invasion of privacy.
2. For employees who handle expensive supplies, we use a polygraph test too. We've had a few refuse to take it. Our thefts are high. We wonder if it's any good! My boss feels the polygraph is essential.
3. One man we hired is doing a good job. We accidentally found out he has a prison record. His supervisor wants to know how we missed that and wants to let him go. We have no policy on this, but I feel he's proved himself in three months on the job.
4. We're having a lot of trouble on the reference letters. When we ask people to rate the applicants on the basis of all factors, including references, we find the supervisors read different things into these letters.
5. Our turnover has been high. My boss thinks it's because we aren't matching the best people to the right jobs. I need your help.

Assignment

You are Joyce Piersol. Make a list of additional information necessary to help Gigantic. How would you acquire the information? Based on what you know now, what are the biggest problems, and what would you do about them?

HALIFAX MANUFACTURING, LTD.

PART A

Halifax Manufacturing is a small manufacturer of heavy equipment. It is located in an older section of Halifax. The plant building was constructed in 1897.

HM employs 278 blue-collar workers. Charles Reinke, president, had always run a tight ship. He tried to keep managerial and staff employment to a minimum. Recently he has been noting more references in his trade magazines to the perils of health and safety legislation. Case studies of reports by these interfering government inspectors worried him.

Reinke believed he ran a safe plant, but at times in the past he had "finessed" safety inspectors on a few minor points of violation. He wondered if the new safety emphasis the politicians were pushing would be different.

Reinke called in his personnel director, Ed Barner, to talk about it. "How likely are we to get hung by these health and safety regulations, Ed? When is the government going to stay out of business? All they want is a big contribution to their election fund anyway."

"Chuck, I really don't know how we'd come out on this one. You know, we've never pushed safety here. Oh, we mention it once in a while and put up those posters the safety group sends out, but other than that. . . . Our accident rate is up, though."

"What should we do to find out, Ed?"

"At a recent meeting of the Halifax and District Personnel Association, Sharon Bentzen, a safety specialist, spoke. She's a consultant, but probably for a couple of hundred bucks we could find out where we stand."

"OK, Ed, hire her and let's get this over with." The consultant was hired. Her report to Reinke was as follows:

To: Charles Reinke
From: Sharon Bentzen
Subject: Accident Prevention Report

I have analyzed your safety records and note that you are running 10 percent higher than your industry on major accidents and 22 percent higher on minor accidents. Some of this can be attributed to the fact that new workers are not given safety orientation. About 20 percent turnover each year means you get 40 new ones yearly. You have no safety program reminders for experienced workers, either.

Because your records are not accurately kept, it was arbitrary to classify accidents as major or minor. No follow-up on accident reports has been made, nor is there even a safety committee at your plant.

Much of your equipment is antiquated. The unsafe areas are not carefully marked or painted. In short, I feel government inspection would cause you real trouble.

I recommend the development of a safety program at once. I could do this for you. I estimate it would involve 10 days of my time at $500 per day.

Sincerely,
Sharon Bentzen

Reinke was discussing the report with Barner. "This is just a snow job to get five big ones for 10 days' 'work.' I think I'm going to file it in the circular file."

"I don't know, Chuck," Barner replied. "I received notice that government health and safety inspectors will make a scheduled inspection in six weeks."

Assignment

You are Ed Barner. How do you induce Reinke to do something, if you feel it should be done?

PART B

Two weeks after Bentzen's report, Harry Conners was severely hurt in a machine accident. His work group, with whom he was popular, was very angry and complained bitterly. Then they walked out in protest. They demanded a meeting of their union, a unit of the Machinists Union. As one of the group, Sam Tender, said to the steward, Chip Flanders, "Chip, when are you going to do your job? Accidents are increasing every day in this place. You know they don't care anything about us. Do we all have to lose an arm before you act? The government is supposed to watch out for things like this, but where have the government inspectors been?"

Another worker, Diane Pendleton, said: "Listen, my husband is really carrying on to me about this. Sally Conners is about to have a nervous breakdown. We want action. There was some kind of safety expert snooping around a couple of weeks ago. You find out what happened on her report. How about us getting the government in here? Or how about a strike? Workers' compensation can never pay you back the pain an accident can cause."

Flanders has rarely seen the employees so mad. The next morning, he went to see Ed Barner. He told Barner what happened at the meeting. Then he said: "Look, Ed, I want to look over the report of that safety consultant to see what she recommended and what you've done about it."

Barner replied, "That report's confidential, Chip."

Flanders yelled. "Don't give me that nonsense about it being confidential! I'm serious. We'll have the government in here or you'll have a wildcat strike on your hands!"

Barner was really worried now. He went to see Charles Reinke and told him all that had happened. Reinke sat and listened impatiently. Then he said, "You are too upset, Barner. This'll all blow over. You wait and see."

Assignment

You are Ed Barner. What do you do now?

▶ HICKLING ASSOCIATES LTD.*

Introduction

For almost seven years prior to June 1983, Tony Azzara had been employed by Pisces Exporters Ltd. The company, located in Vancouver, was a subsidiary of a U.S. food products conglomerate headquartered in Los Angeles. Pisces was one of the largest exporters for fresh and frozen seafood on Canada's west coast and had generated revenues between $40 million and $60 million annually, depending on the quality of the fishing season and market demand. The company's major markets were primarily in Europe as well as several areas of Asia and Japan. Pisces also traded other food products, which, over the years, overtook seafood as the main revenue producer for the firm.

At the age of 27, Tony Azzara began his career with Pisces as a salesperson where he learned the complexities of exporting both fresh and frozen sea products to various countries. Within two and one-half years he was promoted to the position of sales manager responsible for all seafood exports to Europe. This was an exciting job and a respected position. He was given a comfortable office and a very acceptable compensation package. There was an annual bonus based on group sales, which was as high as 100 percent of Tony's base salary in the best years. Even in the poorest years, the bonus was about 20 percent of base salary. He also received a generous car allowance. The work required Tony to develop contacts with other people in the seafood industry in Canada as well as with the major customers in Europe. He was able to take several trips to Europe to expand the market there and develop

---

*© 1985. Steven L. McShane, Faculty of Business Administration, Simon Fraser University. All names and locations have been changed. Any similarity with current names and places is purely coincidental.

better relations with Pisces' existing customers. The job was also a constant challenge because of the increasing international competition in seafood sales and the need to closely coordinate the sales group with the buyers in Pisces. Tony learned early in his career that product quality and delivery time were just as important as price in this market, and only by keeping in touch with the company's seafood buyers could he make those guarantees to his overseas customers.

After about two years as sales manager, it became increasingly clear that Pisces' products were being priced out of the European market. The competition from Asia and Scandinavia was increasing dramatically as they improved their export marketing practices to Europe. Equally important was the appreciation of the Canadian dollar against most European currencies. This dramatically increased the price of Canadian goods in most European countries, whereas the seafood products entering from the Pacific Rim did not experience these fluctuations. By the end of 1982, European seafood sales from Pisces and all other North American exporters had dropped both in volume and market share. Only in the higher end of the market—the expensive seafood products—did the price have only a modest effect on European market share.

Unfortunately, the American parent company of Pisces Exporters Ltd. was also experiencing serious financial problems for several different reasons and, combined with the depressed export market in seafood, the entire fresh and frozen seafood export division of Pisces Exporters Ltd. was discontinued in the second week of June 1983. Consequently, the vice president, 6 sales managers (including Tony Azzara), 10 salespeople, and 5 support staff lost their jobs. The notices of permanent layoff were given in March, and all laid off staff were given reasonable severance payments in June in amounts that corresponded to their position and length of service. For Tony, this was equivalent to about four months' salary.

An Opening at Hickling Associates Ltd.

In the weeks leading up to the final day of work at Pisces Exporters Ltd., Tony Azzara began telephoning around to the people he knew in the Vancouver area in order to let it be known that he was looking for a job in the industry. He had the right experience and had become fairly well known in the city as a good trader in the canned and frozen seafood business. The president of Pisces even approached Tony before he left to say that he would be pleased to write a letter of reference if it would help Tony's search for alternate employment. Tony was flattered by the gesture. In spite of these factors, however, Tony Azzara did not expect to find another job in the seafood exporting business in the near future. With a depressed seafood market and high unemployment throughout British Columbia, securing alternate employment was not going to be easy. In fact, Tony entertained the possibility of changing industries and even began to look through the newspapers for sales positions in other products.

In early June, Mr. James Hickling telephoned Tony Azzara at his office and invited him to lunch the next day. Mr. Hickling owned Hickling Associates Ltd., a medium-sized trading organization in Vancouver that specialized in the import and export of several types of canned and frozen foods. In addition, the company traded a few other commodities such as grains and finishing nails. Tony had met Mr. Hickling in two joint ventures between the two companies a few years earlier. However, Tony worked mainly with Thomas Siu who was the export seafood trader at Hickling Associates.

Following the call from James Hickling, Tony tried to recall what else he knew about Hickling Associates Ltd. and later in the day made several inquiries regarding the firm. He knew that the company was mainly an importer of canned foods such as mushrooms and oriental foods from several Asian countries. Seafood trading was restricted mainly to the export of canned salmon and represented a very small factor in the business. As far as Tony knew, Thomas Siu was the only person responsible for this part of the operation and had been employed by Hickling Associates for about five years. Tony also learned from one of his contacts in the industry that Hickling Associates was financially very strong and well established. It was founded by James Hickling's father in 1934 and grew steadily throughout the years. When the elder Hickling retired in the late 1960s, James Hickling took over the company and is given a lot of credit for the company's current success.

James Hickling was considered by many people in the import-export industry to be something of a maverick and was generally respected for his business sense and solid understanding of the international merchant business. Tony had heard a rumour of a disenchanted trader in canned foods who left Hickling Associates Ltd. a few years ago. The trader joined a rival importer and took with him a few Asian accounts whose contracts with Hickling Associates Ltd. were about to expire. Nevertheless, James Hickling subsequently won back some of those customers and further expanded his business in the import of mushrooms, bamboo shoots, and other canned goods.

The Meeting with James Hickling

Tony Azzara arrived early at the posh restaurant where Mr. Hickling had made reservations and ordered a glass of white wine while he waited. Precisely at 12:15, the time of the scheduled meeting, James Hickling arrived. He was conservatively dressed in a dark blue suit and looked to be in his early 50s. He introduced himself as he arrived at the table and ordered a double scotch on the rocks. After a few initial pleasantries and acknowledgements of the troubles in the European market, Mr. Hickling got right to the point.

"Tony, I'm looking for a man like you to take charge of the seafood export trading in Hickling Associates. It's been a small part of the company for too long, in my opinion. The market is down in a few areas such as Europe and that's knocked the wind out of some of the competition. I believe that you could help me to get a bigger share of the canned salmon market and even get into the export of fresh fish over the next few years as the market rebounds."

Tony took a quick sip of his wine. He was sure that this meeting was about a possible job opening, but he was surprised by the sudden offer. These jobs were rare in Vancouver in 1983, and there were a lot of good traders around.

"This sounds like the sort of challenge that I'd like," Tony replied, trying to sound calm and interested in the position at the same time. "As you know, I've been in this business for a few years now and have developed several contacts in Europe and other markets. I've also worked with Tom Siu on occasion, as you'll recall." Tony was hoping to find out how he and Tom Siu would be working together.

"Yes, indeed," Hickling continued. "Those ventures turned out very well. Siu told me that the two of you worked well together. That's why I think you can do an excellent job in this market."

"What do you have in mind, Mr. Hickling?" It was a risky question but worth asking. Tony had seen situations at Pisces Exporters where two traders clashed because the vice president neglected to clarify their respective duties. He also wanted to avoid stepping on Tom Siu's toes by taking his job away from him.

Hickling took a final bite of his sole florentine and ordered another double scotch. "Siu's done a good job as a trader for me, but his strength is as a buyer, not as a seller," he explained. "He came to us about five years ago from (the Department of) Fisheries in the Canadian government and really knows the quality of seafood. His knowledge of the processing industry on the West Coast has been a real plus. My intention is to bring you in as the export seller and Siu will be primarily responsible as the buyer."

Tony felt satisfied. The job looked challenging and the setup would take advantage of both Tom Siu's and his talents.

Hickling continued. "Tony, there's a lot of opportunity in Hickling Associates if you decide to join our team. I'll start you at $40,000 per year and, depending on your contribution, you'll receive a bonus with no ceiling. That means a virtually unlimited earnings potential if you boost our export seafood business. And I know you will."

The offer was quite satisfactory to Tony, especially considering his employment alternatives. The salary was slightly lower than his current $42,000 salary, but this could be made up in bonus. He was curious about the bonus plan, but felt that this was not diplomatically the right time to go into details on compensation matters. It was not a large company, and written employment contracts were rarely seen in the industry, even at the senior executive level.

"That sounds reasonable." Tony didn't want to sound too enthusiastic. "Of course, I'll have to give this some thought. Could you tell me more about the company's facilities for export trading?"

James Hickling explained the computer system that had recently been introduced to keep track of client accounts as well as purchase inventories. Tony would have complete access to the support staff and would have freedom to develop fresh and frozen seafood sales. In order to develop these sales, Tony would be free to travel as required. In addition, traders at Hickling Associates Ltd. have a company car up to a certain value. This value was about $3,000 lower than Tony's car because Pisces had a higher limit. However, Hickling agreed to raise this limit for as long as Tony had his present automobile. The limit would then be lowered for any subsequent car purchase.

The conversation wandered into the quality of recent salmon catches and the opportunities for international merchants with the rapid growth of fish farms along British Columbia's coast. Tony saw these farms as an excellent source for fresh salmon exports, particularly in competition with the Norwegians, who had been taking an increasing percentage of market share in several areas of the world.

About one and one-half hours after the lunch began, Tony Azzara and James Hickling shook hands and left the restaurant. Tony promised to get back to Hickling within the next couple of days with an answer. That evening, Tony discussed the offer with his wife, and the next day he accepted Mr. Hickling's offer. Tony would start work on July 18, 1983, giving Tony and his wife a few weeks of vacation on Vancouver Island in early July.

The Start of a New Job

Promptly at 8 A.M. on Monday, July 18, Tony Azzara walked into the office of Hickling Associates Ltd. in downtown Vancouver eager to accept his new challenge. Mr. Hickling had not arrived yet, but the receptionist had just sat down at her desk. Tony could hear that other people were already at work behind the partition that separated the receptionist from the rest of the offices.

When Tony introduced himself to the receptionist, she answered in an apologetic way that she knew nothing of his arrival. It was evident from her awkwardness that the receptionist wasn't quite sure how to deal with this situation, so Tony let himself into the general office and wandered through the various areas (see Exhibit 1). There were five secretarial workstations directly behind the reception area and, along the hallway to the left, another larger, open section of the office where several men and a few women were working. As Tony entered this area, an oriental gentleman in his late 30s approached him. It was Thomas Siu. Tom looked genuinely pleased to meet Tony as the two men shook hands. After short introductions, Tom walked Tony over to a far corner of the room and pointed to two of the large desks butted up against each other.

"This is where you'll be working, Tony," Tom said with a smile. "Mr. Hickling likes to have the traders who work together near each other. Since I'm doing the buying and you're doing the selling, I'll be right here." Tom put his hand on the other desk.

The proximity of the work areas was something of a shock to Tony. He was accustomed to his own office and, although aware that Hickling Associates had an open office arrangement, he did not expect to be so physically close to the other traders. Tony looked around the large room. It was an older building with high ceilings and large arched windows. The offices of Hickling Associates took up half of the fourth floor of the 10-story office building. The clerical workstations he had passed earlier were very modern while the trader desks were large oak pieces with wooden swivel rockers. Except for the carpeting and fixtures, the room looked much like it would have 30 years earlier. It was actually rather appealing to Tony except for the physical arrangements. The other traders were at their desks, most of them on the telephone, or just coming in to work.

At that moment James Hickling walked in from the entrance on the far side of the room and walked toward Tony and Tom. "Good morning, Tony. I see that you're getting yourself all settled in." He shook Tony's hand and then sat down at the desk at the head of the room.

Tony's heart sank. Hickling's desk was only 5 feet from his, allowing Hickling to literally look over Tony's shoulder. He sat down and looked around the room again. It then dawned on him that he was the only person wearing a suit. The other traders were dressed casually in slacks and open shirts. Some were even wearing blue jeans. Tony glanced back to Hickling who was on the telephone and looking out the window. He was dressed in corduroy pants and a plaid sport shirt—a sharp contrast from Tony's three piece dark grey pinstripe suit with white shirt and tie.

Not knowing quite what to do, Tony rummaged through his desk to discover what supplies were available. He jotted down the supplies he needed and made a short list of his goals for the next few weeks. Unfortunately, this didn't take very long, and Tony was soon left with the task of finding some-

EXHIBIT 1
Office Layout of Hickling Associates Ltd.

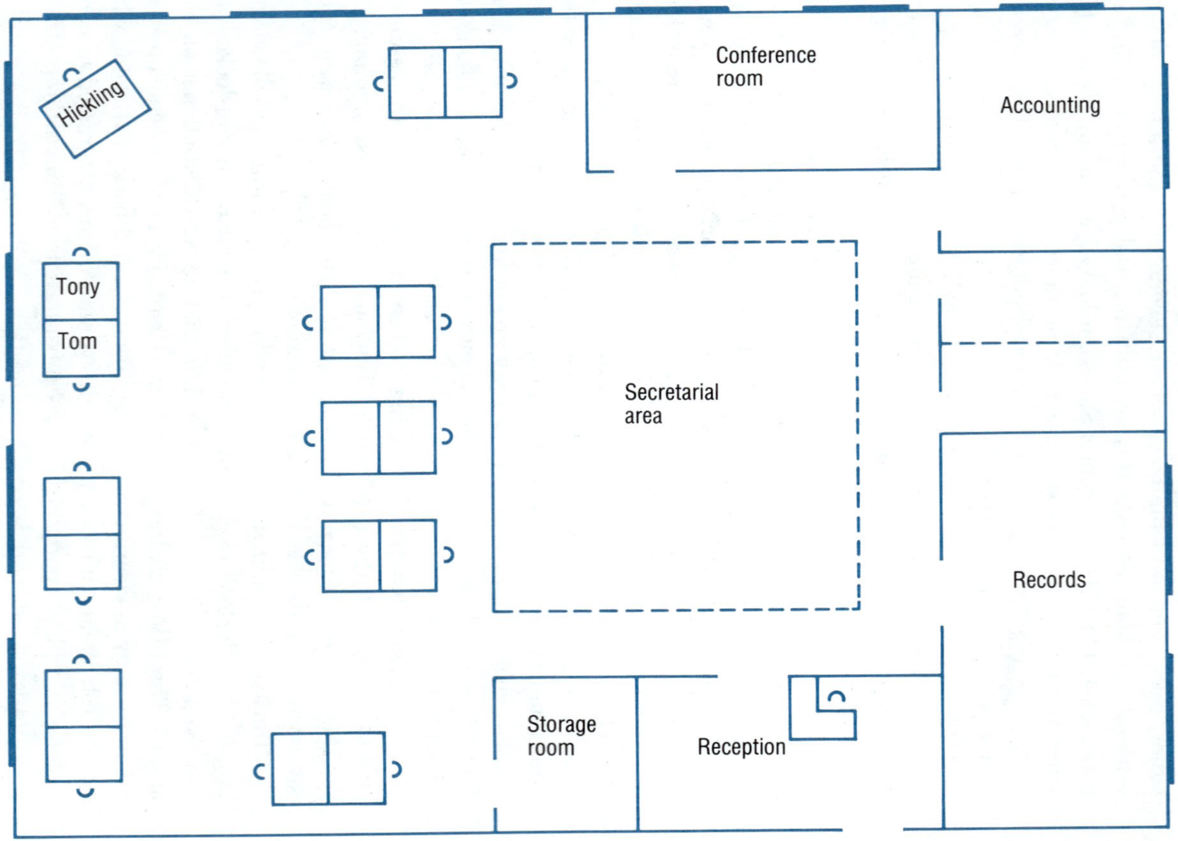

thing else to do. It wasn't a good idea to ask Tom about work procedures yet, with Hickling just a few feet away. That wouldn't leave a good impression. Instead, Tony walked around the office, introducing himself to the other traders and staff in the firm. In a casual manner, he observed some of the forms and procedures the other traders were using while asking them about their product areas. After about half an hour, Tony returned to his desk. His watch said it was only 9:30 A.M. It was going to be an awkward morning. For the next few hours, Tony made telephone calls to some of his contacts to inform them that he was now employed at Hickling Associates Ltd.

James Hickling left the office before lunch and didn't return until late in the afternoon. This gave Tony the opportunity to talk with Tom and learn more about the firm's buy and sell procedures. Tom was very helpful as the two discussed matters over lunch. They also formed a fairly good understanding of how they could coordinate the work. Tom was quite pleased that he was now handling only the purchases of seafood, but Tony felt that Tom wasn't very enthusiastic either about his job or the possibility of expanding the product line to fresh fish exports.

Settling In

During the first month, Tony Azzara made several successful foreign sales of canned salmon and other fish products and was able to use the records and inventory system at Hickling Associates Ltd. with minimal difficulty. Having previous experience in the industry was a definite help. Much of the job could be performed in a similar manner no matter where he worked. However, there was still a lot of uncertainty about some of the more technical procedures and the extent of his authority. Hickling hadn't given Tony any idea about this. The office layout was also difficult to get used to. It was quite clear that Mr. Hickling had tried to overhear some of Tony's telephone conversations. The records people also were putting pressure on Tony to sign all correspondence with the company name rather than his own. This made him feel very uncomfortable because these were contacts and customers that he had established. It was certainly common for traders to sign their own names in other trading firms. For several weeks, these factors took their toll as Tony felt quite worn out by the end of the day.

At the end of the third week, Tony decided to approach Mr. Hickling about a few company policies so that he would have a clearer idea about how to approach certain items on his agenda. For example, Tony was still unsure about the limit of his signing authority for shipments to new customers. There was also the question of the firm's approach to selling odd-sized lots. On both issues, Tony had received conflicting opinions from the other traders. This may have been because they were in such diverse product lines and company policy might vary with the product. So Tony approached James Hickling directly for the answers.

Hickling's reply was hostile. "For God's sake, Tony!" he barked. "Can't you figure these things out for yourself? I haven't time for that trivia!"

Tony's initial feeling was that of embarrassment. Hickling spoke loud enough for all of the traders to hear, and several of them turned to find out what was going on. Embarrassment turned to anger, however, as Tony realized that his questions were not unreasonable. He turned on his heel and, without replying to Hickling, marched out of the room toward the records office. Hopefully, some of the answers might be found there in old invoices and other documents. Later that day, Tom Siu apologized to Tony for not warning him earlier about Hickling. Tom pointed out that most of the traders had received the same dress-down at one time or another and therefore avoided Hickling whenever possible. Hickling may be one of the best traders in the city, but he isn't easy to get along with.

The only exception was when Hickling had been drinking. It became increasingly apparent to Tony that Hickling and several of the traders were heavy drinkers. They almost always drank copious amounts of liquor at lunch. There was also a ritual of sharing a large bottle of rye or scotch whenever a major deal was finalized. Tony figured that at least one bottle was consumed openly in the office each week. Every trader had his or her own glass. Both an ice machine and liquor store were conveniently located around the block from the Hickling Associates offices. It was during these celebrations that Hickling became more personable with the traders, although the traders still watched what they said to him. Tony wasn't much of a drinker, but went along with the ritual and even broke out a bottle of scotch for the group one day in September when he signed up a major European customer. This office behaviour was quite different from Pisces Exporters Ltd. where drinking on the job was strictly forbidden.

The drinking habits of Hickling and the office staff (mainly the traders) paled against a more startling observation that Tony made after about a month on the job. James Hickling was married with three children, but Tony noticed him on several occasions leave for lunch with a female employee in the accounting group and not return until late in the afternoon. He quietly asked Tom Siu about this one day and was told that Hickling was having an affair with the woman. Tony was surprised at how casually Tom said this. Over the next few months, Tony learned about two other relationships in the office between traders and support staff. In both cases, one or both of the employees were married. All three affairs were generally known of and accepted throughout the firm. Apparently, other relationships had formed in the past, and when they dissolved one or both of the employees involved had left the company within a few months. Tony had difficulty accepting the moral standards of the office and couldn't understand how these affairs were condoned so easily by the other members of Hickling Associates Ltd.

After three months, Tony Azzara was beginning to feel a little more comfortable in his position at Hickling Associates Ltd. He hadn't received any feedback from Hickling, but had a fairly good idea that he was doing well by industry standards. The other traders were in diverse product areas and it was difficult to compare performance. Nevertheless, several of them congratulated Tony on the number of new customers he had signed up for the export of canned salmon and other seafood products. Tom Siu's excellent buying skills helped considerably, but in the tough European market, the traders knew that export sales would be the more difficult task.

Tony felt that his earlier contacts had really helped to increase sales. But he was not receiving the industry mail that used to come across his desk at Pisces Exports Ltd. This mail was important because it would inform Tony of upcoming functions in Vancouver and abroad. Instead, the mail was going directly to James Hickling's desk. On several occasions, Hickling attended these functions and Tony would not find out until after the event. In fact, Tony attended only two industry functions during the first year compared with the five or six events he had formerly attended annually.

Another major setback occurred in late November. Hickling had planned a trip to Europe and made arrangements to visit several of Tony's new customers. Tony was angry and frustrated. But when he approached his boss about this, Hickling replied, "It doesn't make sense for both of us to travel." Two more trips were made in February and April 1984. On both of these occasions, Tony was told that he would be able to make these trips in the future. Meanwhile, Tony had to rely on the telephone and other forms of communication to make his important contacts for new business. On none of the trips that Hickling took did any new seafood export sales materialize.

The Bonus and the Final Straw

At the end of six months of work, Tony Azzara had contributed over $425,000 in net profits to Hickling Associates Ltd. Seafood exports had more than doubled, and several new customers had been established in spite of the limitations that were placed on Tony. Hickling still hadn't provided any performance feedback but Tony had high expectations of the bonus, which was paid at the end of the year. In his final pay cheque for 1983, Tony found a bonus in the amount of $10,000. It was a disappointment. He had worked harder than ever before and had personally generated record sales for the company. A few days later, when Hickling had returned from lunch and was in high spirits, Tony confronted Hickling about how the bonus was decided. Hickling looked rather awkward as he explained that it was based on a combination of overall company profitability and individual performance. He then promised Tony that if he sold as well in 1984, the bonus for that year would reflect this performance.

In February, when Hickling was out of town, Tony had the opportunity to talk about the bonus system with a few of the other traders. To his surprise, many of the traders had gone through a similar reaction to their first bonus. Most were still disappointed, but had resigned themselves to the fact that salaries would not be much higher than the base rate. As long as they avoided James Hickling and did their jobs, the traders accepted the situation. It was quite clear that they were doing enough to survive in the job and nothing more.

After a year on the job, Tony was feeling increasingly antagonistic to Hickling and the firm. He still had not been given the opportunity to visit his customers and make new contacts abroad. Tony even began rummaging through Hickling's mail to find out about upcoming industry events. He continued to sign his own name rather than the company's to most telex correspondence, but it was clear that Hickling wanted the customers to identify with him, not the traders. It was fairly easy at first to accept the drinking ritual. However, Tony later separated himself more from Hickling and the other traders when he realized how much alcohol he was drinking. In fact, it was his wife who first noticed this as Tony began to consume more liquor at home.

As the end of 1984 approached, Tony felt somewhat confident that his bonus would be at least as high as last year's. Sales had continued to climb and the seafood export component of Hickling Associates Ltd. represented a larger proportion of the business than ever before. The 1984 bonus was $5,000. Tony Azzara was shocked and upset. Neglecting the possibility of a loud confrontation, Tony again confronted Hickling. Hickling indicated that several other parts of the organization were not producing the expected levels of profit and, as a result, all bonuses were lower. He added that it was important to be part of the team at Hickling Associates Ltd. and share the profits and losses throughout the firm.

A few weeks later, Tony learned from sales records that none of the other trading areas in the company had suffered any serious drop in sales. In February 1985, Tony Azzara submitted his resignation at Hickling Associates Ltd. He accepted a position with a competing international merchant in Vancouver at a lower salary.

Assignment

Hickling Associates has hired you as a human resources management consultant following Tony Azzara's resignation.

1. Identify the problems that you see in this case.
2. Recommend P/HRM activities that would solve the problems at Hickling Associates.

▶ MINISTRY OF TRADE AND COMMERCE*

The Ministry of Trade and Commerce (MOTAC) is a department of a Canadian provincial government. A major role of MOTAC is to work cooperatively with the Canadian federal government in facilitating exports from the province and attracting investment to the province. Based on an increasing emphasis on international trade, MOTAC has been granted a substantial budget increase by the provincial government over the next three years. This will result in a 45 percent increase in the number of field staff and a 15 percent increase in the number of administrative and support staff located at the ministry's headquarters in three years.

Field offices, located throughout the province, are mainly staffed by trade officers and secretarial support. Trade officers explain provincial export programs and assist firms in their region with proposals for government export support. They prepare seminars on exporting for businesses in the region. Additionally, the provincial trade officers assist federal government officials with local arrangements for organizations participating in foreign export fairs sponsored by the federal government. To a lesser extent, trade officers also explain joint venture activities to local firms.

MOTAC is very concerned about recruiting qualified trade officers during the next three years. Ninety-five officers are currently employed in seven field offices throughout the province. With the projected budget increases, this number will grow to 105 officers in 1988, 120 in 1989, and 140 in 1990 (see Exhibit 1). Trade officers are almost always hired externally because of their specialized skills. The typical officer has at least three years of experience in marketing, finance, or management and has participated in export or foreign joint venture activities.

After their initial six-month probationary period, trade officers tend to specialize based on their previous experience. In each region, a few officers are particularly good at assisting with government financial assistance proposals and explaining joint venture arrangements. They are prohibited, however, from providing financial or legal counselling on joint ventures. Other trade officers assist client organizations by providing information on export marketing programs. They also provide firms entering export markets for the first

---

*© 1987 Steven L. McShane. This organization does not actually exist as described and should not be confused with any government department with similar functions.

EXHIBIT 1
Trade Officers at MOTAC

Year	Number Employed	Turnover of Existing Positions	New Positions
1982	75	6	0
1983	75	9	0
1984	80	10	5
1985	85	9	5
1986	95	12	10
1987	95	10	0
1988	105	?	10
1989	120	?	15
1990	140	?	20

time with information about the cultural and political situation in export countries.

Trade officers at MOTAC are recruited from five different sources, as Exhibit 2 indicates. Advertisements for trade officers are placed in three print media each year, including a daily newspaper, a financial newspaper, and a professional trade magazine. All three of these sources have national circulation. The source of each inquiry is easily established because the mailing address in each advertisement is a special mailing number at the newspaper or magazine. As part of the advertising cost, each publication sorts the incoming mail and sends it to the appropriate employer.

MOTAC also receives several unsolicited inquiries and applications. Several inquiries and applications have also resulted from employee referrals. In these cases, employees at MOTAC have either notified the P/HRM department of a potential candidate or the applicant has directly applied and indicated an employee recommended that he or she apply.

The cost of processing inquiries varies with each recruiting source. Advertising space and time are approximately the same for all three print media. However, this currently amounts to an annual expense of $3,700 in the national newspaper, $2,800 in the financial newspaper, and $1,700 in the professional magazine. The cost of advertising in each publication has increased at the same rate over the years. The P/HRM department estimates it costs MOTAC $25 to receive and file each unsolicited application and employee referral. This expense does not apply to print media inquiries because these activities are handled by the publication. Inquiries from all sources have the same cost of reviewing applications, checking references, interviewing, and making the hiring decision.

EXHIBIT 2
Recruiting Statistics at MOTAC by Recruiting Source, 1982–1987

Enquiries Received

Year	National Newspaper	Financial Newspaper	Professional Magazine	Unsolicited Applications	Employee Referrals	Total Inquiries
1982	15	15	45	25	20	120
1983	31	21	52	30	35	169
1984	22	15	50	22	25	134
1985	27	17	61	38	40	183
1986	30	24	57	40	31	182
1987	28	15	58	35	30	166

Number of Applicants

Year	National Newspaper	Financial Newspaper	Professional Magazine	Unsolicited Applications	Employee Referrals	Total Applications
1982	7	6	35	15	16	79
1983	16	8	36	18	27	105
1984	16	5	33	12	20	86
1985	19	7	40	20	29	115
1986	21	10	43	19	22	115
1987	20	8	42	16	23	109

EXHIBIT 2 *(concluded)*

Number of Interviews

Year	National Newspaper	Financial Newspaper	Professional Magazine	Unsolicited Applications	Employee Referrals	Total Interviews
1982	2	1	10	3	9	25
1983	5	2	13	2	11	33
1984	4	0	11	1	12	28
1985	6	2	16	3	13	40
1986	7	4	14	3	13	41
1987	3	1	15	2	10	31

Number Hired

Year	National Newspaper	Financial Newspaper	Professional Magazine	Unsolicited Applications	Employee Referrals	Total Hired
1982	0	0	2	1	3	6
1983	1	1	4	0	3	9
1984	2	0	6	0	7	15
1985	1	0	7	1	5	14
1986	3	2	8	1	8	22
1987	1	0	5	0	4	10

Discussion Questions

1. Assuming that the average recruiting and employment activities of the past six years are representative for the next four years, approximately how many inquiries, applications, and interviews would MOTAC require to employ 105 trade officers in 1988, 120 in 1989, and 140 in 1990?
2. Evaluate the cost-effectiveness of each recruiting source? Which sources have the best and worst hiring yields? Which sources have the highest and lowest cost per hire?
3. What changes would you recommend to improve the effectiveness of trade officer recruitment?

▶ PACIFIC FINANCIAL SERVICES LTD.*

Pacific Financial Services Ltd. is a diversified financial institution that offers insurance, mutual funds, annuities, and other investment vehicles for Canadians. It is headquartered in Vancouver and has offices in major cities throughout the country. Pacific Financial Services began operation in 1937 as an insurance company and diversified into the field of personal investments in the late 1970s. The company employs approximately 1,100 people, 400 of whom are located in the Vancouver headquarters.

Almost all employees at Pacific Financial Services are in white-collar jobs. Approximately 150 people hold management positions, and the same number are employed in technical jobs such as actuarial, statistical, and financial analysis. The largest group of people hold clerical and records jobs. A large number of salespeople, including insurance representatives and account executives, are employed throughout the branch offices. About 60 percent of the employees at Pacific Financial Services are women, most of whom work in the lower-paying clerical and records jobs. Currently, women represent about 20 percent of the employees in technical and sales jobs and 7 percent of those in management jobs.

The vice president of human resources at Pacific Financial Services has been aware for some time that pay equity (i.e., equal pay for work of equal value) is becoming the foundation for human rights legislation in an increasing number of jurisdictions across Canada. The company has not yet faced a charge of pay discrimination, and it wishes to avoid any problems with the human rights commissions.

Pacific Financial Services has two job evaluation systems—one for man-

---

* © 1985 Steven L. McShane. The organization described in this case does not exist.

agement and the other for nonmanagement jobs—that were developed by a consultant (with input from senior management) and formally implemented in 1965. Some changes in factor weights occurred five years later. Both job evaluation systems use the point method. The management system has six compensable factors: problem solving, extent of supervision, education, complexity of duties, accountability, and necessary skills. The nonmanagement system includes supervision required, education, complexity of duties, contact with others, significance of errors, and necessary skills.

Nonmanagement jobs are evaluated by someone in the human resources department in consultation with the vice president of human resources. Job evaluation decision making is based on two-page job descriptions that are usually updated every three or four years. Management job evaluations are conducted by a senior management committee with the vice president of human resources as the chairperson. There is no fixed timetable for reevaluating jobs and some jobs have not been reevaluated since the plan was modified. However, Pacific Financial Services has a request form that any employee may submit in order to have his or her job reevaluated.

In many respects, the vice president is confident Pacific Financial Services has a job evaluation system that will withstand human rights litigation. The company spent a considerable amount of time and money developing the tailor-made plans, particularly in deciding the compensable factors. In fact, it has been due to this initial care that the original system has had only minor changes. The vice president is particularly proud of the fact that the systems were tailor-made so the factor descriptions are more relevant to the organization. Also, having two separate plans has saved time since some of the factors relevant to one group are not relevant to the other.

According to the vice president, another strength of the job evaluation systems at Pacific Financial Services is that every job is reanalyzed every three or four years so job evaluation decisions are usually based on fairly recent job descriptions. On occasion, jobs have been reevaluated due to discrepancies between the original points assigned and the value of the job in the labour market. The vice president recognizes that this conflict between job evaluation and market rates is not unique to Pacific Financial Services. The company believes reassigning point values is the best way to deal with these discrepancies. In fact, the vice president encourages the job evaluation specialist (or senior management committee) to look at the median labour market salary for a job when it is evaluated so this conflict with market rates is less likely to occur.

The main advantage, however, of the job evaluation systems at Pacific Financial Services, according to the vice president, is that the company has not deliberately used them to discriminate against women or members of other designated groups. In fact, the company has a written policy that it will not discriminate against employees because of their race, sex, age, and so on. The vice president believes this policy is one of the strongest protections Pacific Financial Services has against charges of pay or employment discrimination.

Assignment

Despite the vice president's confidence, you have been hired as a consultant to examine the two job evaluation systems at Pacific Financial Services Ltd. Specifically, your task is to:
1. Comment on the strengths and weaknesses of the two job evaluation systems as they have been described to you.
2. Explain what other information, if any, you would examine to determine the defensibility of these job evaluation systems.

▶ PEMBERTON MINING SYSTEMS LTD.*

Susan Lee flipped through the latest salary survey report again. As director of human resources at Vancouver-based Pemberton Mining Systems Ltd., she saw trouble brewing in the salaries of systems analysts. Since 1982, the entry-level salaries of systems analysts in Toronto and Montreal have been increasing faster than those in Western Canada. Much of this discrepancy is due to the economic recovery in Quebec and Ontario. According to the latest survey (see Exhibit 1), which shows the established grade ranges as of September 1987, the market rate for the entry-level systems analyst job was now an average of 15 to 20 percent higher than Pemberton's pay level. The salaries of higher level systems analyst jobs have also lagged in Western Canada but to a lesser extent. The national survey is conducted by a major consulting firm from Toronto that is well known for providing reliable and highly representative surveys.

Susan Lee was convinced the best systems analysts at Pemberton Mining Systems Ltd. would soon be leaving the firm. The exodus would be a serious blow to a firm already hurt by a long economic recession.

Overview of the Company and Its Compensation System

Pemberton Mining Systems Ltd. develops and markets computer software systems for the mining and petroleum industries. While some clients are

---

* © Copyright 1986 Steven L. McShane. This case is based on actual events in another industry. To maintain confidentiality, company names and data have been changed. Therefore, this information should not be compared with actual data in this industry or time period.

EXHIBIT 1 Survey of Established Entry-Level Salary Grade Ranges for Systems Analysts—Mining/Petroleum (effective September 1987)

CANADIAN COMPENSATION CONSULTANTS LTD.

Company Identification	City	Number of Incumbents	Percent Bonus (1)	Number of Job Levels (2)	Established Grade Range (3) Minimum	Midpoint	Maximum	Range Spread (4)
A	Toronto	2	10	2	2,400	3,000	3,600	50
B	Toronto	11	N	2	2,560	3,020	3,500	37
C	Ottawa	1	15	3	2,310	2,890	3,470	50
D	Vancouver	4	N	3	1,950	2,500	3,050	56
E	Edmonton	9	0	3	2,070	2,520	2,970	43
F	Vancouver	3	11	3	1,890	2,330	2,780	47
G	Montreal	3	N	2	2,350	3,050	3,750	60
H	Vancouver	2	12	3	2,050	2,410	2,770	35
I	Toronto	14	9	3	2,510	2,950	3,400	35
J	Calgary	7	0	3	1,900	2,370	2,850	50
K	Toronto	2	N	3	2,420	2,950	3,480	44
L	Toronto	5	10	2	2,390	2,990	3,580	50
M	Montreal	8	N	3	2,500	2,940	3,380	35
N	Halifax	12	11	3	3,030	2,470	2,920	44
O*	Vancouver	5	14	3	2,000	2,440	2,880	44
P	Montreal	8	N	3	2,370	2,820	3,270	38
Q	Toronto	9	0	2	2,530	3,160	3,800	50
R	Ottawa	7	19	2	2,290	2,790	3,300	44
S	Vancouver	4	11	3	1,920	2,400	2,880	50
T	Winnipeg	9	N	3	2,080	2,450	2,810	35
U	Toronto	6	12	2	2,370	3,030	3,700	56
V	Montreal	5	6	3	2,420	2,910	3,400	40
W	Toronto	6	N	2	2,510	3,060	3,610	44
			Low		1,890	2,330	2,770	
			High		2,560	3,160	3,880	
			Weighted average		2,279	2,768	3,262	
			Median		2,350	2,890	3,380	

Number of companies = 23
Number of incumbents = 142

Notes: *Your organization is indicated with an asterisk.
(1) Indicates any bonus paid out between September 1986 and August 1987 expressed as a percentage of base salary. "N" indicates that the company does not have a bonus system for people in these jobs.
(2) Indicates the total number of systems analyst job levels including entry level.
(3) All figures indicate monthly base salaries. None of the companies surveyed pays a market differential.
(4) Indicates the range spread between the minimum and maximum salaries established for this pay grade.

located in Eastern Canada and abroad, most are based in Western Canada, particularly Alberta and British Columbia.

Along with other companies in the mining services industry, Pemberton has suffered through a long recession brought about by depressed mineral and oil prices. As long as prices stay low, most mining and petroleum companies will try to postpone major computer system upgrading, thereby reducing the demand for Pemberton's expertise. This situation is aggravated by an extended economic recession in Western Canada since 1982. A small net loss was reported for the 1987 fiscal year, although a small profit is expected in 1988.

Within the mining service industry, Pemberton Mining Systems Ltd. is well known as a good place to work. It has one of the best benefits packages in the industry with most benefits fully paid by the company. Indeed, there have been no significant complaints regarding salaries or benefits over the past year or more. Unlike some other mining service companies in Western Canada, Pemberton has successfully averted employee layoffs despite large financial losses in 1982 and 1983. Turnover has remained below 5 percent in virtually all professional and management job categories for each of the past four years. This is partly due to the weak demand for managerial and technical skills in Alberta and British Columbia.

Pemberton has a profit-sharing plan that typically pays bonuses between 5 and 25 percent above base salaries for technical, marketing, and management staff. The 1987 profit-sharing bonus (paid out of 1986 profits) represented approximately 14 percent of base salaries in these groups. Due to the financial loss in 1987, however, no bonus will be paid in 1988. While disappointing, this is generally accepted by employees, particularly since most mining service firms in Western Canada suffered financial losses in 1987.

One reason for Pemberton's recognition as a good place to work is that employees are given the opportunity to participate in major decisions. The development of the companywide job evaluation system and the committee process of job evaluation review are two examples of this. In 1978, the company retained a compensation consultant and asked employees to choose four representatives to sit on the task force to develop a new job evaluation system and pay structure. Together with two supervisors and the four top executives, the representatives helped select and weight the factors, identify benchmark jobs, and establish pay structure grades. The resulting job evaluation system is a custom-made point plan.

A job evaluation committee—consisting of two nonmanagement employees, two supervisors, one senior executive, and the director of human resources—meets twice each year to review and update job evaluations. The president of Pemberton Mining Systems Ltd. has the final authority on all committee decisions. Except for the director of human resources, committee

EXHIBIT 2
Pay Structure for Systems Analysts at Pemberton Mining Systems Ltd. (effective January 1, 1987)

			Grade Ranges (monthly salary)		
Job Title	Number of Incumbents	Grade Level	Starting Rate	Job Rate	Maximum Rate
Systems Analyst 1	5	7	$2,000	$2,440	$2,880
Systems Analyst 2	12	9	2,650	3,310	3,970
Systems Analyst 3	4	11	3,260	4,180	5,100

membership changes every three years. Pemberton's employees have frequently expressed their support for this process and the pay structure.

The pay policy line at Pemberton Mining Systems Ltd. is set slightly above the weighted average among western Canadian firms in the annual pay survey. Through hiring and turnover information, it became apparent over the years that most jobs in the company (except senior-management positions) compete in the local and regional labour market. The salary survey data are adjusted upward to reflect the lag between the time the data are collected and the time they are released to Pemberton and other surveyed companies.

The pay structure at Pemberton Mining Systems Ltd. has 14 grade levels with ranges of ±15 percent at the bottom grades and ±25 percent at the highest grades. Employees have knowledge of all pay ranges, but individual salaries are kept confidential. Since systems analysts and other technical jobs are career-oriented, there are three job levels for each job family. For example, new hires would enter the Systems Analyst 1 job. Later, they may be promoted to Systems Analyst 2 and Systems Analyst 3. Each level is two grades above the next. Information about the pay structure for systems analysts at Pemberton Mining Systems Ltd. as of January 1, 1987, is shown in Exhibit 2.

As Exhibit 2 indicates, 21 systems analysts are currently employed at Pemberton Mining Systems Ltd. The five entry-level employees have all been with the firm for at least two years and are above the bottom third of the range. Two employees near the top of the Systems Analyst 1 job have been with Pemberton for more than five years and will likely be promoted later this year. Most systems analysts at all three job levels are married with children. Five of the job incumbents are women, and all have lived in British Columbia for at least five years.

The Approaching Storm

The director of human resources at Pemberton Mining Systems Ltd. sees a storm approaching. Susan Lee's main concern is that the best systems analysts at Pemberton will leave for better-paying jobs in Ontario and Quebec unless they receive a substantial salary increase. For example, she believes the job rate for Systems Analyst 1 should increase from $2,440 to at least $2,750. Smaller adjustments would have to be made for the other two systems analyst job categories.

To add to her problem, the director of human resources has been informed the company may want to hire another systems analyst at the entry level within the next year. Susan Lee has the authority to pay above the minimum rate, although this is rarely done unless the successful job candidate has previous experience. Several dozen unsolicited résumés for such a position are on file, but Susan does not look forward to the problems she anticipates with the existing pay structure.

Assignment

Describe in detail the problem(s) that you see in this case. As an external P/HRM consultant, what recommendations would you make to Pemberton Mining Systems Ltd.?

▶ STRATEGIC HUMAN RESOURCE PLANNING

Background

In Chapter Three we discussed business strategies and presented Miles and Snow's three strategic types: Defenders, Prospectors, and Analyzers. Two points were emphasized: first, that organization units may differ in their financial and marketing directions (i.e., strategies); and second, that different business strategies may require different human resource strategies. We also suggested that there is no single best approach to human resource management. Rather, the "best" depends in part on the organization's strategies and objectives. Hence, we are suggesting the manager of human resources must consider the strategic directions of the organization when designing human resource actions.

Strategic Grids and Screens

The use of analytical techniques to guide strategic decisions has grown rapidly over the past decade. A typical technique is the planning matrix shown as Exhibit 1. The matrix relates an *organization's strengths and weaknesses* to certain environmental characteristics such as *industry attractiveness*, which yield opportunities and risks for the organization. For industry attractiveness, the vertical axis is determined by such factors as the size of the potential

EXHIBIT 1

	STRATEGIC PLANNING MATRIX			
	High	E	I	I
Industry Attractiveness	Medium	D	E	I
	Low	D	D	E
		Low	Medium	High
		Organization Strengths		

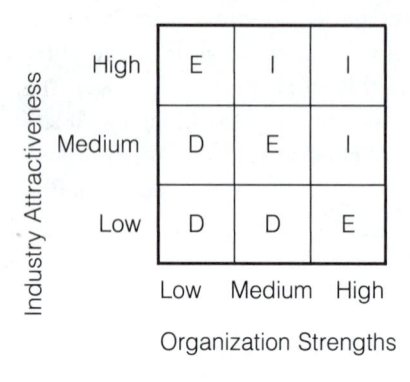

I = Invest (emerging, growth)
  Strong revenue, market share potential
  Cash scarcity
  Individual decision makers
  Entrepreneurial managers
  Long-term orientation
  Invest for future

E = Evaluate (manage selectively)
  Revenue potential unclear
  Control expenses
  Formalizing management systems
  Intermediate to short-term orientation

D = Disinvest (harvest)
  Revenue potential weak
  Control expenses
  Formalized management systems
  Short-term orientation

market, growth rate in consumer demand, or others. Organization strengths (the horizontal axis) may be determined by technology, market share, financial conditions, human resources, or other factors. In the case of nonbusiness establishments, (government units, universities, United Way) the dimensions on a strategic matrix may become "strength of the demand for services provided" and "the organization's strengths and weaknesses."

Several possible states of cells emerge in the matrix. We have identified three strategic stages for illustrative purposes: Invest (grow), Evaluate (manage selectively), Disinvest (harvest). The characteristics of each state are included in the exhibit. For example, a business unit in an invest stage is often characterized in terms of being in a business that is highly attractive (high growth potential, profitability, or high service demand) and has a relatively high business strength (proven management, or good labour relations). According to this conventional strategic analysis, such a business unit should be considered a good risk and may receive increased deployment of resources to take advantage of the opportunity. Conversely, the disinvest stage combines a less attractive business (shrinking market, or highly competitive) with low business strength (obsolete plant). Such a unit may be viewed as a drag on the enterprise, and eliminated.

Such analysis, employed by General Electric and a host of other organizations, should help direct the deployment of resources within the organization and to protect developing business directions. While there is little rig-

EXHIBIT 2
Strategies

Human Resource Activities	Invest (I)	Evaluate (E)	Disinvest (D)
Planning			
Staffing			
Compensation			
Training			
Labour relations			

orous empirical research that supports such models, many industrial and consulting firms subscribe to some variation of the framework.

Discussion Questions

Speculate about the types of P/HRM actions that are most consistent with each type of business strategy.
1. Is planning formalized or not? Is the P/HRM function likely to be centralized in all stragegic types?
2. Which strategy type is most likely to go outside for talent? Which is most likely to "grow on their own"—promote from within and develop employees?
3. Which type would emphasize paying whatever is necessary to hire (competition is key)? Which would emphasize internal pay relationships? Which would focus on incentive plans?
4. Would the types of training (e.g., technical, managerial, specific, general) emphasized differ by strategic type?
5. Is management's approach to unions at all related to the strategy it is following? How would the presence of a union affect the ability of the firm to pursue its strategy?
6. You may wish to return to this project after you have finished this book. Compare your answers now to those you give after reading the text.

▶ SUDBURY SHOES

Ronald Bell has just been employed as a management trainee at Sudbury Shoes, a medium-sized manufacturer of quality shoes and boots, located in Sudbury, Ontario.

Bell came from a small town north of London, Ontario. He attended the University of Western Ontario and took the honours degree in business and commerce. Bell's father is in agribusiness; as a result, Bell worked around the business much of his life. For example, he spent all of his summers working in his father's business. His father naturally expected him to enter his firm. But Bell believed he first should make it on his own. If he didn't, he wasn't sure that he would be respected at home. All he knew was agribusiness; he thought he'd like to try something else for a while.

Bell worked his way through university. He took his summer income and added funds from jobs he had held in London on weekends and on several nights a week. He also had taken out bank loans. He now owed the Toronto Dominion Bank $7,000. He plans to pay this loan off as soon as he can, preferably in the first year. He plans to live modestly. He has taken a flat with two other bachelors, where his cost per month will be $130. He has purchased a small Ford car and his monthly payments will be $80. His beginning salary at Sudbury will be $1,500. The company personnel manager, Richard Mason, who recruited Bell to Sudbury, promises Bell a raise if he does well in the first six months on the job.

Mason said Sudbury has been a family-owned and -run firm. But the last family member in management, H. T. L. Sawyer, had just died of cancer at age 49. Sawyer had been president. His son was a United Church of Canada clergyman and had never shown an interest in Sudbury. Sawyer's daughter was married; her husband was a career officer in the Canadian Forces. Mrs. Sawyer, the Rev. Mr. Sawyer, and Group Captain Higgins were on the Sudbury board of directors. But none of them had the capacity or interest in managing the firm.

Sawyer had begun to develop a professional management team. He was young enough that he wasn't overly concerned. Then he became ill. He appointed as president his long-time associate, James Lawrence, who had been vice president.

Lawrence saw the need for developing a professional management team, too. Exhibit 1 summarizes the characteristics of the current management.

Bell was to be the first of several university graduates brought in to professionalize Sudbury's management.

Because of its size, Sudbury did not really have a formal management training program. For the first several weeks, Mason arranged for Bell to spend several days in each department and area. Mason asked the supervisors to familiarize Bell with the operations of the department.

Then, Bell was assigned to the sales department. It was thought he should spend a year as a salesman, calling on Sudbury's trade. Bell was assigned to John Knotts, a regional sales manager for Sudbury. Knotts has been

EXHIBIT 1
Sudbury's Management Team

	Age Distribution					Educational Background		
Management Level and Number	<25	26–35	36–45	46–55	>56	High School Graduate	Some College	College Degree
Top (6)	0	0	0	2	4	4	1	1
Middle (10)	0	0	3	4	3	2	6	2
First line (44)	1	7	11	13	12	44	0	0

with Sudbury for 15 years. He is a high school graduate who has worked his way up from the job of office boy at Sudbury.

Knotts introduced Bell to the Sudbury line and handed him price sheets and sales records of all the customers in the Toronto area. After a two-day introduction, Knotts drove up in front of Pay-Less Shoes, a store in one of the lower income areas of Toronto.

Knotts said: "Ron, I'm sure this is all simple stuff to you. I'd be in the way. Why don't you make the call on this store. It will be on your list of customers. The owner's name is Azimian."

What Bell didn't know was that Azimian was known in the trade as "the crazy Armenian," because of his unique style of dealing with salesmen. Ron entered the store.

Bell: May I please speak with Mr. Azimian?
Clerk: He's busy.
Bell: I'll wait.
Clerk: What do you want to see him for anyway?
Bell: I'm Ron Bell from Sudbury Shoes. I'd like to talk to him about our new line.
Clerk: You're wasting your time. Azimian doesn't buy Sudbury shoes. They screwed him in the past when he was smaller. Besides, they charge too much.
Bell: Look, I don't want to argue with you. I'll just wait for Mr. Azimian.
Azimian: You *are* talking to him, you little punk!

The man turned. Azimian was tall, burly, about 45 years old. He was wearing work clothes.

Bell: Oh, I'm sorry, I didn't know that.
Azimian: That's obvious. Now go away.
Bell: If I could just have a few minutes of your time, we really do have some outstanding new items for the new season and. . . .

Azimian: Too bad you got physical defects. You must be deaf. I told you to get the hell out of here. I mean it. Conversation ended.

At this, Azimian went into the storeroom. Bell picked up his materials and left. He got in the car.

Knotts: How did you get along with my good buddy, Joe?
Bell: Not so good. No sale.

Later, Knotts was discussing the matter with another regional manager, Ray Kittrell.

Kittrell: Why did you throw Ron at the crazy Armenian. You know he didn't have a chance. Nobody has ever sold him anything from Sudbury; I doubt they ever will. Ron seems like a nice kid.
Knotts: Listen, they sent me the new crown prince, didn't they? With all that college and all, he ought to be able to handle anything. He hasn't cut it as far as I am concerned.

Kittrell repeated the conversation to Mason.

Assignment

1. You are Mason. What, if anything, do you do about the orientation of Bell?
2. Examine the psychology of the orientation from Ron and John's point of view.
3. If you were Ron, how long would you stay at Sudbury?

▶ TIMBER CRAFT LIMITED*

Timber Craft Limited, located in southern British Columbia, is a manufacturer of consumer goods relating to sports and recreation activities. It started as a family-controlled organization nine years ago but has since become a private limited company employing professional managers. Timber Craft is currently considering a major expansion of facilities and product lines to take advantage of the rapidly growing sports goods and recreational market. Selected operating figures for the company during 1975–1984 are given in Exhibit 1.

The company's plant is located in Midsex near Campbell River, British

---

*This case was prepared by Professor Hari Das, St. Mary's University, Halifax, Nova Scotia.

EXHIBIT 1
Operating Figures of Timber Craft, 1975–1984, and Projections 1986–1990 (in thousands of dollars)

	1975	1980	1984	1986	1990
Net sales values	$17,000	$17,850	$21,420	$27,850	$30,630
Cash	49	47	52	56	58
Net receivables	85	223	450	600	674
Other assets (excluding paint and facilities)	212	398	616	1,218	1,399
Net plant and equipment	567	756	1,161	1,625	1,628
Accounts payable	61	112	312	408	439
Stock and retained earnings Other liabilities	192	216	398	476	492
Percent net income on sales (before taxes)	10.4%	11.8%	12.4%	13.6%	14.2%

*Projections based on report of the firm's financial evaluation committee.

Columbia. In 1973, when the company started is operations, it had three sales offices: in Campbell River, Victoria, and Vancouver. However, during 1981–83, Timber Craft opened four more sales offices to cater to the rapidly rising demand for its products. The company currently employs 43 managers (excluding the president).

Over the years, the company has built a reputation for selling quality sports and recreation products. About 70 percent of the company's customers are in the 18–35 age group and tend to look for new products and the avant-garde. The customers tend to treat prices as only one of a number of criteria when buying the firm's products. The company has acquired a solid financial and sales base through a policy of selling *credit*.

In general, Timber Craft has the reputation of offering competitive salaries and good working conditions. Despite this, the company had problems in the past in obtaining personnel for key managerial positions, because of high technical expertise and innovative ability needed on the part of Timber Craft's managers. Basically, the production techniques, the products, and the consumers themselves had grown very sophisticated in the last decade and, to maintain a competitive advantage in the industry, Timber Craft had to be extremely creative in its managerial policies and procedures. By 1980, the company handled two major groups of sports goods; however, this had doubled by 1984. The production process in the company is mainly capital intensive (and not labour intensive). The employee/plant value ratio for managerial personnel in the company is roughly 1:27,000.

Organizational Structure

In 1984, Timber Craft Limited was organized functionally into four major units: marketing, manufacturing, finance and accounting, and administration. Personnel, public relations, and some aspects of customer relations were grouped under the administration. While no formal organization chart existed, Exhibit 2 shows an approximate chain of command in the organization.

The marketing unit performed essentially two types of functions: sales management at the various branches, and market planning (including market research and advertising). Recently, Timber Craft has been considering a possible switchover to a product manager concept, under which a manager would be responsible for the success or failure of one or more products rather than that of a region of a branch. S. P. Johnson indicated the scope of responsibilities of a manager under the proposed system:

> I am sure Timber Craft can significantly benefit from a product-type of organization structure. Most of the large consumer products companies, General Foods, Kellogg, and Procter & Gamble to mention just three, are built on the product

EXHIBIT 2
Organization Chart

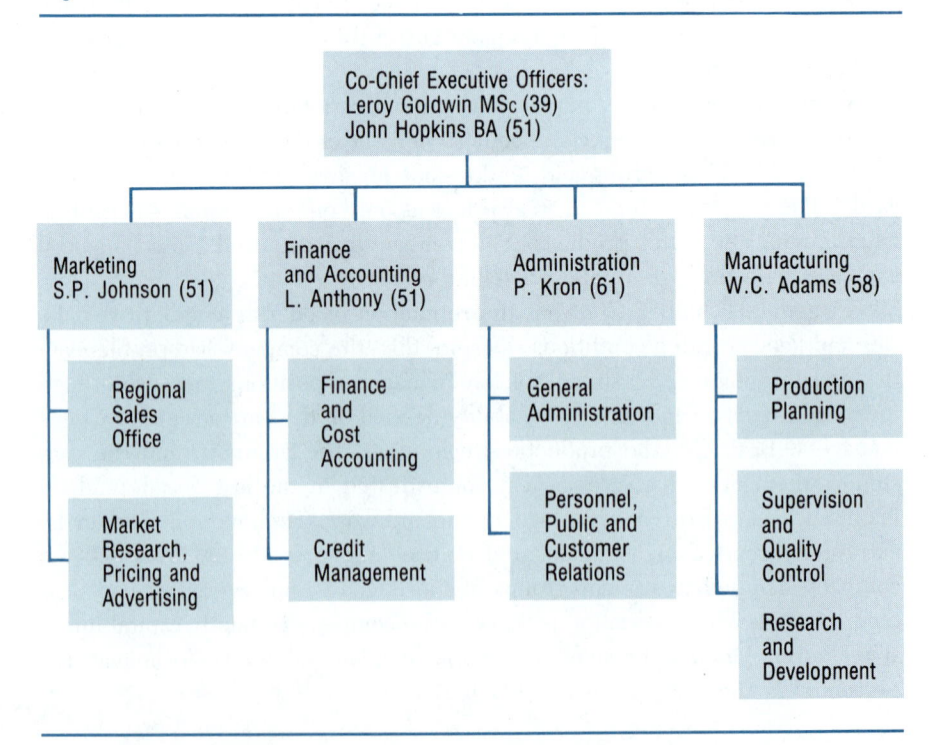

```
                    Co-Chief Executive Officers:
                    Leroy Goldwin MSc (39)
                    John Hopkins BA (51)
        ┌───────────────┬───────────────┬───────────────┐
   Marketing        Finance         Administration   Manufacturing
   S.P. Johnson     and Accounting  P. Kron (61)     W.C. Adams (58)
   (51)             L. Anthony (51)
     │                 │                 │                 │
   Regional          Finance          General           Production
   Sales             and              Administration    Planning
   Office            Cost
                     Accounting
                                      Personnel,        Supervision
   Market                             Public and        and
   Research,         Credit           Customer          Quality
   Pricing and       Management       Relations         Control
   Advertising
                                                        Research
                                                        and
                                                        Development
```

manager idea. The product manager will be held responsible for the product planning and for constant monitoring of the product success. Here in Timber Craft we don't believe in lines and arrows to show relationships among people. If problems at the plant are holding up the sales, we expect the sales manager to go down to the plant or call him to iron out the problems. That is already the way we work here. What we are trying to do is to make it more systematic so that our reward system recognizes responsibility and on-the-job achievement.

W. C. Adams, a 50-year-old BSc, headed the manufacturing division. Reporting to Adams in 1984 were five managers in production planning, eight supervision and quality control officers, and six R&D managers. Most product development activities were centralized in Midsex, British Columbia.

Details of the number of managerial employees in Timber Craft are given in Exhibit 3.

Operations and Future Plans

The company is planning a major expansion of its productive capacity. By 1986, sales are targetted at $27,850,000 (or an increase of 30 percent over 1984 figures). The company hopes to expand its operations to three more centres in British Columbia and Alberta. Also, Timber Craft is planning to enter the field of water sports by introducing three new products in the fall of 1985. Results of market research and financial analyses have shown that the planned expansion is feasible and desirable at this time.

Many of the managers realized the promise of continued rapid growth of

EXHIBIT 3
Details of Managerial Employees in Timber Craft Limited

	1975	1980	1984
Manufacturing	2	3	5
Production supervising and quality control	4	6	8
Research and development	2	3	6
Finance and accounting			
Financial accounting	2	3	3
Cost and management accounting	1	1	1
Credit management	1	2	3
Marketing			
Sales administration	4	5	9
Market research	1	1	2
Administration			
Personnel and staff relations	1	1	2
Labour relations	1	1	1
Office management, customer relations, and public relations	2	2	3
Total	21	28	43

EXHIBIT 4
"Skills Inventory" of Managerial Staff at Timber Craft Limited

Employee	Dept.	Current Performance Level (1–lowest, 5–highest)	Highest Educational Level*	Age	Present Managerial Level (1–lowest, 7–highest)	Assessment Centre Report Rating on Potential Leadership Skill (1–low, 10–high)	Time in Present Job (months)
W. C. Adams	Mfg.	5	BSc	58	6	10	90
S. R. Allen	Acc.	4	CGA	31	5	9	29
P. T. Anderson	Mfg.	5	MSc	63	6	8	92
L. Anthony	Acc.	4	CA	51	6	8	100
R. Arnesen	Acc.	5	BComm	59	6	4	108
L. Belcheff	Mktg.	4	MBA	28	4	8	20
R. Bensoff	Acc.	5	RIA	58	6	8	105
R. K. Bloom	Mfg.	4	BSc	37	5	7	26
M. T. Barberton	Mktg.	4	BSc	49	7	7	39
M. P. Burke	Mktg.	3	BA	24	4	5	24
T. P. Buyer	Mfg.	4	MSc	29	5	9	16
D. Caroon	Mktg.	4	BSc	28	5	6	22
N. T. Cayon	Mfg.	4	HS	28	3	4	17
R. Chapman	Mfg.	3	HS	24	2	6	13
E. S. Conway	Mfg.	3	BSc	29	4	7	36
R. T. Dickoff	Pers.	5	MBA	47	6	8	49
P. Frost	Mktg.	5	BComm	48	6	9	24
W. K. Goodwin	Mktg.	4	MBA	38	5	7	20
K. N. Griggs	Pers.	4	MBA	33	5	7	16
R. Groster	Mktg.	4	MBA	31	5	5	34
P. Hack	Mktg.	5	BComm	44	6	8	62
K. Heneman	Mfg.	4	MSc	44	6	8	43

Name	Dept	Degree				
S. Hickory	Mfg.	BSc	5	64	6	10	108
T. Hitronf	Pers.	BLit	4	29	3	7	32
S. Inckson	Mfg.	BSc	4	37	5	8	79
P. Jackson	Mfg.	HS	3	47	5	5	60
S. P. Johnson	Mktg.	BA	5	51	6	9	64
T. Kennelly	Mfg.	BSc	5	62	5	9	58
S. Kiefel	Mktg.	HS	4	58	5	7	69
P. Q. Kimble	Mfg.	BSc	4	27	4	8	14
S. Kirton	Mktg.	BA	5	51	6	8	39
T. Knoll	Mfg.	MSc	5	29	4	7	19
P. Kron	Adm.	HS	5	61	6	8	31
J. H. Laboy	Mfg.	MSc	4	43	5	6	42
E. F. Pederson	Mfg.	MSc	4	47	5	6	19
N. T. Potler	Mfg.	BTech	5	31	5	7	60
A. Ranallo	Adm.	BA	4	39	5	5	29
H. C. Reeves	Mfg.	BSc	5	60	6	8	63
T. Reitman	Mfg.	BSc	4	28	4	9	20
R. E. Smith	Acc.	BComm	4	29	5	7	19
J. Sorenson	Acc.	HS	5	42	6	7	41
N. F. Trandt	Adm.	BSc	4	28	5	8	17
H. Walden	Acc.	HS	4	49	4	4	69

*Almost everyone in this list has undergone special training programs at some time during their stay at Timber Craft Limited.

the company would mean changes in the structure and processes of the company. As one manager in the manufacturing division pointed out:

> Growth for Timber Craft means something quite different from what it is for most other firms. For a conglomerate, growth may often mean new acquisitions or new diversified units that will be operating independently. For a company like Timber Craft, however, it means entering new and completely different product-market situations and finding new ways of doing things. This may be the end of our present ways of doing things and the loss of informal relationships. Sure, everybody likes growth; but the associated costs are often not apparent.

Growth also meant identifying new methods of rewarding the employees, more formalization of recruiting and training procedures, identifying newer modes of integration of various operations of the company. The need for managers in the areas of planning, research and development, and selling is expected to increase rapidly in the next few years. The need for supporting sources, like finance, personnel, market research, and credit management, is also expected to increase, although not to the same extent as in the case of above functions.

Personnel Policies

Timber Craft has had a policy of promoting qualified personnel from within before seeking outside candidates. The policy further implies consideration of the best-qualified people from all departments within Timber Craft, rather than simply promoting only from within the department in which the opening occurs (unless the skill needed is very specific and cannot be acquired in a relatively short period of time, e.g., design engineer, computer programmer, financial accountant). Typically, the personnel department provides assistance in locating qualified candidates and takes pride in its "skills inventory" of all managerial personnel. The skills inventory consists of names, certain characteristics (e.g., age, education), and skills of the managers working for Timber Craft. Exhibit 4 shows the skill inventory of managerial staff in the company.

The company uses the services of an assessment centre located in Vancouver, British Columbia. Periodically, managers were sent to this centre where, for periods ranging from two to four days, they were given tests and interviews. During their stay, the participants also participated in management games, group discussions, in-basket exercises, and other role-plays. These managers were later rated by the centre for their leadership potential. Exhibit 4 also gives the details of the assessment centre report on leadership abilities of Timber Craft managers.

The salaries offered by Timber Craft are slightly higher than the ruling market rates for similar positions. Despite this, the company had problems in attracting qualified managers. The salaries of the supporting staff are comparable to the market rates. The bonus system for sales staff, however, has been criticized by several employees as being unfair. Several instances of salesmen's territories being taken away after they have cultivated them have been pointed out. Timber Craft has no pension or stock option plans for its employees. Despite these shortcomings, Timber Craft has built up a good name for giving equal and fair opportunities to minority groups.

The mandatory retirement age at Timber Craft is 65. The company is committed to the development of its employees and, in the past, has sent many of its employees for training to the University of British Columbia, Simon Fraser University, British Columbia Institute of Technology, and some of B.C.'s community colleges.

Current and projected employment data for selected job classes in Western Canada for the next decade are shown in Exhibit 5. The reader may assume the company recruits only from Western Canada. (This is more or less true, since currently 91 percent of Timber Craft's managerial personnel come from Western Canada.)

EXHIBIT 5
Current and Projected Employment Data for Selected Job Classes in Western Canada*

Job Class	Latest Employment Data	Predicted Annual Average Job Openings for Next Decade	Predicted Annual Average Supply of Personnel in Job Class in Next Decade
Accountants	94,316	8,390	8,120
Aerospace engineers	11,205	345	410
Agricultural engineers	1,900	120	431
Architects	7,300	1,222	692
Carpenters	8,940	3,860	1,760
Chemists	11,216	4,127	1,673
City managers	512	36	62
Computer programmers	6,382	4,230	3,190
Credit officers	1,700	430	416
Employment counsellors	857	362	118
Lawyers	6,988	636	739
Office managers	12,108	430	378
Other engineers	72,300	16,120	14,002
Personnel managers	6,381	1,785	1,123
Photographers	21,300	9,020	9,108
Physicians and medical personnel	42,130	13,000	9,368
Research and design personnel	9,180	2,127	730
Sales managers	51,320	4,362	2,930
Sales persons	149,346	16,300	17,360
Technicians	231,700	19,216	16,390

*Fictitious data.

Assignment

Assume you are Ron Dickoff, the personnel manager of Timber Craft. You have been asked to prepare an employment forecast for the years 1986 and 1990. Assume the current expansion plans of the company will be implemented by 1985.
1. What are some specific environmental, task, organizational, and human variables that should be considered in making such a forecast?
2. For an organization like Timber Craft, which is poised for a fast growth, what policy related and operational problems do you foresee?
3. What is your evaluation of the personnel policies at Timber Craft Limited?

▶ TYLER MANUFACTURING COMPANY

Tyler Manufacturing Company is a medium-sized firm producing parts for the auto industry. The firm fabricates major metal subassemblies for autos and sells its products on contract to such firms as General Motors, Ford, and Chrysler. Tyler's main plant is located in the Kitchener, Ontario, area, but it has a branch plant in Ste. Jerome, Quebec.

Tyler has always had good employee relations. Its wages and benefits have always exceeded the industry's. Tyler has an independent union. Recently the union leadership asked to see the vice president—Vance Henry. The union leader, Peter Vuychich, said: "Mr. Henry, at our most recent get-together, someone brought up the subject of the four-day week. As you know, the *Kitchener-Waterloo Record* carried an article on this and the TV has played it up some. Some of the workers have boats and others like to hunt. This appeals to them since they could take longer breaks that way. We'd like to give it a try."

Vance said: "Well, Peter, it's a big step. Let me give it some thought." After checking around with other personnel people and reading up on the topic, Vance decided to experiment with it, but in the Kitchener plant only. He asked Peter to come in again. After a brief discussion of the football game the previous weekend, he said: "Look, Peter, about your request on the four-day week. You know we've always gone along with what the employees want. I'm willing to try it and the president, Archibald Seeley, says he is too, if the employees want it. Take a mail poll and let me know how it comes out."

The union polled the workers and 85 percent favoured the move. The new arrangement called for work on Monday through Thursday, 7 A.M. to 6 P.M., with 45 minutes for lunch and a 15-minute break midmorning and midafternoon.

About a month after the experiment started, a rush order came in from

EXHIBIT 1
Productivity Data for Tyler Manufacturing: Four-Day Week and Overtime Week Compared to Previous Five-Day Week Figures

	Monday	Tuesday	Wednesday	Thursday	Friday	Saturday
Week 1						
Morning	Same	Same	−1%	−2%		
Afternoon	Same	Same	−1%	−2%		
Week 2						
Morning	+2%	+1%	Same	Same	−1%	−2%
Afternoon	Same	Same	−1%	−2%	−2%	−3%
Week 3						
Morning	+2%	+1%	Same	−2%		
Afternoon	Same	Same	−1%	−2%		

General Motors. This required some overtime work. There was a lot of grumbling about Friday and Saturday work. A typical comment was found in the suggestion box: "You'll kill us with this pace—six-day 60-hour weeks—leaves us no time for our families."

Vance and Richard Peterson, operations manager at the plant, looked over the productivity figures. They found that quality had dropped (reject rates went up 10 percent) and output rate had dropped 5 percent. This upset them both a great deal. Richard said: "You know, Vance, this is all due to your damn experiment. You never asked me about it before you started, but I knew it would never work. I'll bet those last couple of hours per day are killing us. I'll get some data on productivity per half day and check it out."

Three weeks later, Richard returned with the data. During these weeks, two weeks had had no overtime, one had overtime. The productivity data were worked up to compare an "average" week before the change with these weeks (see Exhibit 1).

Richard said, "Vance, as you can see, this experiment is a disaster. We talked to the employees about the productivity drop, emphasizing that if they wanted to keep the experiment going, they'd have to get production up. As you see, on some of the days, they did. But the later in the week it got, the worse things were. And quality figures parallel these quantity figures. The work is just too heavy for these hours."

Vance agreed something had to be done. He called Peter in, explained the situation, and said: "I'm thinking of dropping the four-day week. My bet is that people have lost some of their enthusiasm too. Let's see."

The poll results came in: 65 percent said they'd like to continue the experiment, 35 percent wanted to revert. Vance is wondering how to handle the situation now.

Discussion Questions

1. You are Vance. How do you handle the situation?
2. What do the statistics prove about the productivity or unproductivity of the employees?
3. What part should the union play in the decision?

NAME INDEX

A

Abella, Rosalie, 295
Adams, J. Stacey, 200, 201
Agarwal, Naresh, 708
Allen, Steven G., 631
Andiappan, P., 288
Aram, John D., 576
Argyris, C., 464
Arvey, Richard D., 400, 402
Asher, James J., 395

B

Beatty, Richard W., 497
Becker, Brian, 631
Bedaux, Charles, 145
Belcher, David W., 660
Berger, Chris J., 631
Bernardin, H. John, 497
Bhinder, K. S., 270
Blair, Robert, 297
Blau, P. M., 349
Blum, Milton L., 375
Boehm, Virginia R., 410
Boudreau, John W., 340, 631
Bowen, D., 564
Brett, Jeanne M., 465, 610
Bronfman, Edgar, 712, 713
Buller, P. F., 237, 238
Burke, Ronald, 510

C

Campion, James E., 400
Carnazza, J., 250
Carroll, Stephen J., Jr., 501, 503, 668, 787
Cascio, Wayne F., 23, 167, 390, 410, 472, 522
Chao, Georgia T., 395, 411
Cherrington, David J., 411
Cronbach, Lee J., 375
Cronshaw, Steven F., 301, 307, 391
Cullen, J. G., 479

D

Dahl, Dave, 334
Dahl, Henry, 239
Decelles, Rene, 148
DeCotiis, Thomas, 156
Deming, William, 559
Dimick, David E., 119
Doeringer, Peter, 113

Drucker, Peter F., 33, 371
Dunnette, Marvin D., 166, 197, 382, 651
Dyer, Lee, 113, 693, 696

E

Ellig, Bruce, 750
Emerson, Harrington, 145
Evans, Martin G., 563

F

Fear, Richard A., 390
Feldman, Daniel C., 441, 442
Ferris, G. R., 403
Fine, J. A., 160
Freeman, Richard B., 630, 631

G

Gantt, Henry L., 145
Georgopoulos, B. S., 694
Gilbreth, Frank, 145
Gilmore, David C., 398, 403
Glueck, William, 351
Godsall, Lloyd, 577
Goldstein, Irwin L., 444, 472
Goodale, James, 510
Gunderson, Morley, 287, 720

H

Hackman, J. Richard, 210
Hakel, Milton D., 402
Hall, D. T., 564
Hamner, Clay W., 694
Hanuse, Dan, 576
Hellervik, Lowell, 398
Heneman, H. G., III, 255
Herzberg, Frederick, 33, 147, 196
Hough, Leaetta, 395, 406
Hull, Clark, 197
Hunter, John E., 379, 390, 391, 409, 414, 784, 787
Hunter, Rhonda F., 414

J

Jacoby, Sanford M., 39
Jain, Harish C., 288
Janger, A. R., 120
Janz, Tom, 395, 398
Jenkins, G. D., 664
Jones, J. J., 156
Jones, M. A., 497

855

Jones, N. W., 694
Jurgenson, C. E., 350

K

Kanter, Rosabeth Moss, 23
Kearsley, Greg, 479
Keeley, Michael, 517, 518
King, William Lyon Mackenzie, 606
Kochan, thomas A., 610, 619
Kopelman, Richard E., 391
Kumar, Pradeep, 22

L

Landy, Frank J., 527, 787
Latham, Gary P., 460, 461, 511
Lawler, Edward E., III, 650, 664, 691, 692, 693, 696, 706, 707, 760
Lawler, J., 352
Levine, Edward L., 165, 166
Levinson, D. J., 203

M

McIvor, Donald, 490
McKenzie, R. C., 379, 784, 787
McKeon, W. J., 479
McPhillips, David C., 590
McShane, Steven L., 441, 590
Macy, Barry A., 784
Mahoney, G. M., 694
Mahoney, Thomas A., 660
Maki, W. R., 237, 238
Maslow, Abraham, 33, 195, 196
Mattinson, Glenda, 391
Mayo, Elton, 146
Medoff, James L., 630, 631
Meredith, Sir William, 582, 583
Meyer, Herbert H., 528, 695
Miles, Raymond E., 104, 329, 372
Mirvis, Phillip H., 784
Moore, Larry F., 399
Morgan, K. S., 239
Moses, J. L., 410
Muldrow, T. W., 379, 784, 787
Murphy, Peter, 65
Murray, Victor V., 119

N–O

Nash, Allan N., 668
Nightingale, Donald, 562
Nowell, Michael, 285–86

Oldham, G. R., 210
Olian, Judy D., 329, 330, 412
Oliver, Robert, 206
Olson, Craig A., 631
Ondrack, Daniel A., 563
Opsahl, R. L., 197, 651
O'Reilly, Charles, 144

P

Patten, Thomas H., Jr., 652, 666
Pencavel, J., 631
Perigoe, J. Rae, 32
Peters, Thomas J., 108
Phillips, D. Rhys, 296, 27, 299
Pinder, Craig C., 465, 466
Pinto, Patrick, 334
Porter, Michael E., 102
Premack, Steven L., 346
Presgrave, Ralph, 145

R

Reilly, Richard R., 395, 411
Reisman, Simon, 65
Ross, James F., 390
Rynes, Sara L., 329, 330, 340, 352

S

Salipante, Paul F., Jr., 576
Sandver, M. G., 255
Sass, Robert, 582
Sathe, Vijay, 108
Scanlon, Joseph, 702
Schein, Edgar H., 107, 202, 442
Schmidt, Frank L., 379, 390, 391, 409, 784, 787
Schmitt, N., 400
Schneier, Craig E., 501, 503
Schwab, D. P., 335, 343, 693
Simon, Sidney H., 125
Singh, Ishar, 285
Smith, Robert, 243
Snow, Charles C., 104, 329, 372
Stronach, Frank, 712, 713

T

Taylor, Frederick W., 145
Tenopyr, Mary, 395
Theriault, R. D., 693, 696
Throp, Cary, Jr., 441
Trist, Eric, 558
Tsui, Anne S., 779

V–Y

Valenzi, E. R., 522

Walker, A. J., 126
Walker, James W., 245, 246
Wanous, John P., 346
Waterman, Robert H., Jr., 108
Watson, Thomas, 144
Weiler, Paul, 577
Werbel, James, 465
Wexley, Kenneth, 460, 461, 511
Woods, J. Douglas, 146

Yoder, Dale, 787

SUBJECT INDEX

A

A&W Food Services of Canada, 527
Ability, 191–93; *see also* Disabilities *and* KSAOs
 and E→P expectancy, 198–99
 and motivation, 193
 tests of; *see* Aptitude tests
 and training, 460
Absenteeism
 and child care benefits, 738
 and fitness, 749
 and recruitment methods, 343
 and unions, 631
 work time lost to, 624
Accents, foreign, 278
Accessibility, 306
Accidental death and dismemberment (AD&D) insurance, 737
Accidents, 577; *see also* Safety, occupational *and* Workers' compensation
 causes of, 578–79
 experience rating for, 583
 under standard hour pay plans, 700
Accomplishment Record, 395
Accountability (AC), 676
Accounting, and P/HRM evaluation, 784
Achievement tests, 406
Action plans, for MBO, 514
Action Travail des Femmes v. *Canadian National*, 294
Actor-observer errors; *see* Attribution errors
Administrative service plans (ASPs), 756
Advertising, recruitment by, 339–40, 355
Age, employment discrimination based on, 280; *see also* Retirement, mandatory
Agency shops, 617
Air Canada, 148, 505, 573
Alberta Federation of Labour, 615
Alcan, 517
Alcoholism, employee assistance programs for, 570
Allison v. *Amoco Production Co.*, 586
Alternate forms reliability, 377
Alternation ranking, 516
American Federation of Labor (AFL), 608, 615
American Society of Personnel Administrators (ASPA), 26
Analyzers, 104
 recruiting for, 330

Annuities, for pension plans, 746
Anxiety, orientation to reduce, 435
Applicants
 criteria for, 330, 359
 preferences of, 347–48; *see also* Self-selection
 quality of, 342
Application blanks, 393–95
Apprenticeship programs, 447, 463–64
Aptitude, 191–92
 tests, of, 405–6
  as performance predictors, 414–15
  value added by, 390
Aquired imune deficiency syndrome (AIDS), 412
Arbitration
 conflict resolution by, 575
 final-offer, 619
 of grievances, 626–27
 interest; *see* Interest arbitration
Assessment centres, 408–9
 performance evaluation at, 517
 validity of, 410
Attitudes
 toward P/HRM department, 779–80
 and role-playing, 469
 and socialization, 442
 and training techniques, 468–69
Attribution errors, 523–24
Audits, process-oriented, 775–78
Authoritarian leadership style, 207
Automation, 72–73; *see also* Technology
 and job engineering, 147
Automobile industry
 product market of, 63–64
 robots in, 71
Automobile mechanics, compensation of, 697–98
Autonomy, 149
 as career anchor, 203

B

Baby boom generation, 46–47
Back injuries, 579
Backward integration, 100
Balance sheet, for job evaluation, 361
Bank of Montreal, 571
Bargaining units, 612–13
Base case economic projection, 59
Base rate, 387

857

858 Subject Index

Behavioural criteria, 476
Behaviourally anchored rating scales (BARS), 505, 509–11
Behavioural observation scales (BOS), 511, 513
Behavioural sciences, 33
Behaviour description (BD) interviewing, 398–99
Behaviour modelling, 471
Bell Canada, 717
Benchmark jobs; see Key jobs
Benefits, see Employee benefits
Bhinder v. *Canadian National Railway*, 270, 286
Biographical data, 395
Biographical information blank (BIB), 393
Birth rates, 46
Blacklists, 606
Blacks, discrimination against, 277–78, 284; see also Discrimination, employment
Blue-collar workers, performance evaluation of, 493
Board interviews; see Panel interviews
Bona fide occupational qualifications (BFOQs), 285–86
  and mandatory retirement, 292
Bonuses
  for executives, 709–10
  for job stability, 241–42
  from profit sharing, 703
  re-earnable, 689–91
Bottom-up forecasting, 230
Bridging positions, 307
Britain
  labour disputes in, 623
  unions imported from, 607
Britex Ltd., 560
British Columbia
  employment discrimination in, 280
  notice of dismissal in, 590
British Columbia Hydro, 590
British Columbia Railway, 698
Broad brush programs; see Employee assistance programs (EAPs)
Brochures, about employee benefits, 751
Budd Canada, 554
Budgeting
  for compensation, 704–5
  for P/HRM evaluation, 787, 790
Bureau of National Affairs, 787
Business factors, and labour demand, 230–31
Business immigrants, 51
Business unionism, 608
Business units, strategy at level of, 103, 111

C

CAE Electronics Ltd., 190
Calgary, 55
Canada
  executive compensation in, 713–714
  high-technology in, 73

Canada—*Cont.*
  human rights laws in, 270–71, 279–80
  national health care system of, 735
  nationalism in, 34
  population growth of, 45–46
  trade with United States, 64–65
Canada/Quebec pension plan, 729, 743–44
Canada Employment Centres (CECs), 338
  Campus, 336, 354–55
Canada Employment and Immigration Commission (CEIC), 52, 55, 221–22
Canadair Ltd., 66
Canada Labour Code, 79
Canada Oil and Gas Act, 224
Canadian Auto Workers, 554, 607, 731
Canadian Centre for Occupational Health and Safety, 556
Canadian Charter of Rights and Freedoms, 79, 278–79
  and mandatory retirement, 292
  unions' attitudes toward, 83
Canadian Classification and Dictionary of Occupations (CCDO), 168, 170
Canadian Congress of Labour (CCL), 608
Canadian Disaggregated Interdepartmental Econometric (CANDIDE) mode, 222
Canadian Jobs Strategy, 443, 445–46
Canadian Labour Congress (CLC), 608, 615
Canadian National Railway, 285–86
  employment discrimination at, 270
Canadian Occupational Forecasting Program (COFOR), 222
Canadian Occupational Projection System (COPS), 59, 222–24
Canadian Pacific Ltd., 642
Cancer, work-related, 577; see also Health, occupational
Capital accumulation, as compensation, 710
Career
  defined, 202
  management of, 206
  orientation toward, 202–3
  planning for, 353–54
  stages of, 203–6
  transitional probability matrixes to chart, 251, 253
  unrest in, 206
Career anchor, 202–3
Career clock, 206
Career development, 564–69
  results of, 569–70
Career paths, 569
  and pay structure, 660
Causal attribution, 523–24
CCH Canada Limited, 29
CCINFO, 556
Centralization, 129–31
Central tendency evaluation error, 522
Certificate in Personnel Management (CPM), 26
Certification cards, 612

Change, and employment planning, 220
Charter of Human Rights and Freedoms, 715
Charter of Rights and Freedoms; see
    Canadian Charter of Rights and
    Freedoms
Checklists
    for P/HRM audits, 775, 778
    weighted, 515
Cheslakee Logging Co., 576
Chevron Canada Limited, 534–41
Chief executive officers (CEOs)
    attitudes toward P/HRM, 33–34
    compensation of, 710–13
    and employment equity programs, 295, 297
    selection of, 101–2
Child care
    as employee benefit, 738
    as reasonable accommodation, 288
Citibank, 778
Clarkson Gordon, 48
Client groups, 18
Collective bargaining, 601; see also Labour
    relations and Unions
    federal regulation of, 79
    impasses in, 618–24
    process of, 615–18
    public-sector, 627–28
    for quality of work life programs, 563
    union concessions in, 629
    over vacations, 733
Collective liability, 583
Colleges, recruiting at, 335–37
Comcheq Services Limited, 703
Cominco Ltd., 757–59, 761
Commission on Equality in Employment, 295
Commissions, 685, 698
Common law
    access to, 586–87
    unions under, 606
    wrongful dismissal in, 584–85
Communication
    of environmental scanning results, 43
    grievances as, 625
    of pay information, 706
Commuting, willingness for, 56
Companies
    research about, 358
    unionized versus nonunionized, 628–29
Compensable factors, 668–69
    examples of, 671
Compensation, 15–16, 642–43; see also
    Reward; Salary; and Wages
    administration of, 704–7
    budgeting for, 704–5
    contract negotiations about, 616
    for dismissal, 585–86
    equity in, 272; see also Pay equity
    of executives, 707–13
    external influences on, 646–48
    flat rates for, 685
    flexibility in, 260

Compensation—Cont.
    forms of, 651, 729
    for executives, 708–12
    importance as job attribute, 350
    increases in, 688–91
    of individuals, 684–85
    internal influences on, 648–51
    and job analysis, 155, 157
    and job search intensity, 351
    levels of, 655–59
    managers' views of, 642
    model of, 651–54
    motivating effect of, 196–97, 695–97
    objectives of, 649–53
    of P/HRM managers, 223
    performance-based, 516, 685, 687, 689,
        692–95; see also Incentive pay and
        Merit pay
    for executives, 707, 709–10
    and performance evaluation, 494, 528
    and product/service market conditions, 63–64
    ranges for, 686–88, 704
    responsibility for setting, 643, 645
    secrecy about, 694, 706
    seniority and, 688
    structure of, 659–62, 671, 691–92
    and pay equity, 719
    surveys of, 656–59, 688, 708
    and benefits, 749
    unions' influence on, 628–29
    workers'; see Workers' compensation
Compensation Data Sourcebook, 656
Compensation stabilization boards, 647
Compensatory model, 350
Compensatory selection processes, 392–93
Compentence, focuses of, 202–3
Competition
    and compensation, 646, 655, 688
    deregulation of, 81
    and employee benefits, 749, 760–61
Competitiveness
    P/HRM's effect on, 102
    and technology, 70
Composite performance criteria, 500–501
Compressed worksheet, 152
Computer-aided design (CAD), 71
Computer-aided instruction (CAI); see
    Computers, training using
Computer-aided manufacturing (CAM), 71–73
Computer-integrated manufacturing (CIM), 72
Computer programmers, selection of,
    390
Computers
    employment tests on, 411
    and flexible benefits administration, 761
    and home work, 153
    for human resource information systems,
        122
    information accessed by, 29–30
    recruitment via, 339

Computers—*Cont.*
  for skills inventories, 242–44
  training using, 467, 470
Concentration, 301
Conciliation, 618–19
  compulsory, 607
Concurrent validation, 380
Conference Board of Canada, The, 29
Conflict resolution, 573–76
Congress of Industrial Organizations, 608, 615
Conspect reliability, 378
Construction industry, strikes in, 624
Constructive coercion, 573
Constructive dismissal, 586
Construct validity, 382
  of performance evaluation results, 495
Consultants
  corporate human resource function as, 129
  for employment equity programs, 297
  for employment planning, 224
  for recruiting, 324
  for selection, 399
Content validity, 381–82
Contingency approach to leadership, 207
Contract strikes, 620–21
Contrast effects, 523
Control Data Corporation, 165, 258
Control groups, in training evaluation, 477
Convenience stores, 98
Core benefits, 757, 760
Core time, 152
Corporate culture, 107–9
  and compensation, 650
  discriminatory, 307
  and employee loyalty, 190
  and mergers, 66–67
  and orientation, 437
  and recruiting, 330
Corporate renewal, 108
Correlation coefficient, 377
  multiple, 385
  for validity; *see* Validity coefficient
Cost benefit (CB) analysis, 479
  of P/HRM department, 784, 787
Cost effectiveness (CE) analysis, 479
Cost-of-living adjustments (COLAs), 64, 629, 689
Costs, orientation to reduce, 435
Cottage industry; *see* Home, work at
Council of Canadian Personnel Associations (CCPA), 26
Counselling, 563, 590; *see also* Employee assistance programs (EAPs)
  on employee benefits, 751
  financial, as employee benefit, 711
Countercultures, corporate, 109
Courts, and employment discrimination, 283
CP Ltd., 103
Cranbach's Alpha, 378

Creativity
  as career anchor, 203
  as job ability, 192
Criminal Conspiracy Doctrine, 606
Criminal Law Amendment Act, 606
Critical incidents
  in BARS, 509
  in BOS, 513
  in evaluation training, 526
Cross-training, and robtos, 76
Culture, corporate; *see* Corporate culture
Current distribution profit sharing, 703

D

Dartmouth College, 32
Day care; *see* Child care
Dead-end positions, 253
Death, work-related, 577; *see also* Health, occupational *and* Safety, occupational
Decentralization, 129–31
Decline career stage, 205–6
Deductibles, 756
Defenders, 104
  P/HRM policies of, 106
  recruiting for, 330
  selection by, 372
Deferred profit-sharing plans (DPSPs), 703
Defined benefit pension plans, 746
Defined contribution pension plans, 703, 745–46; *see also* Pensions
Delta Hotels, 513
Democratic leadership style, 207
Demography, 7; *see also* Population
  and employment equity, 271, 298–99
  organizational, 228
Dental insurance, 735
  self-insurance for, 756
Deregulation, 81
Design, of jobs; *see* Job design
Development, professional, 15; *see also* Career development
  BOS for, 513
  as employee benefit, 737
  and individual ability, 192–93
  and internal recruiting, 333
  performance evluation for, 494, 499, 502–3, 528
  and subordinate evluations, 520
  and transfers, 465
Diabetics, 285–86
Diagnostic approach, 9–11
Diagnostic model, 11–19
  employee benefits in, 729–31
  employee relations in, 555–56
  employment equity in, 270–71
  evaluation in, 773–74
  external conditions in, 40–43
  interaction among components of, 18–19
  labour relations in, 601–5
  pay administration in, 645–51

Subject Index **861**

Diagnostic model—*Cont.*
  performance evaluation in, 491–93
  recruitment in, 325–31
  training in, 444–51
  work in, 142
Direct mail, as job search technique, 355
Disabilities
  compensation for; *see* Workers' compensation
  employment discrimination based on, 278
  insurance against, 737
  numerical goals for employment of people with, 304
  permanent versus temporary, 583–84
  reasonable accommodation of, 286–87
  taxable benefits for, 757
  and workplace design, 306
Discipline, and employee assistance programs, 573
Discrimination, employment, 272; *see also* Employment equity
  age; *see* Age, employment discrimination based on
  and Charter of Rights and Freedoms, 278–79
  complaints of, 282–83
  demographic analysis to identify, 298–99
  against disabled people, 278
  employment systems review to avoid, 303
  intent versus effect of, 283–84
  and native people and visible minorities, 277–78
  in pension income, 748
  in performance evaluation, 491–92
  pre- versus postemployment, 280, 282
  prima facie case of, 285
  prohibited grounds for, 280, 309–13
  in recruiting, 329
  reverse, 308
  sexual harassment as, 288–89
  sources of, 306–7
  in training, 445
  against women, 273–76; *see also* Women
Disease; *see* illness, occupational
Dismissal; *see also* Layoffs
  constructive, 586
  cost of, 590
  and employment security policies, 562
  just cause for, 587–89
  notice required for, 584–85, 589–90
  and performance evaluation results, 492, 494
  wrongful, 585–86
Diversification, 100–101
Dofasco, Inc., 556, 738
"Dollars and Sense," 751
Dress, for employment interviews, 402
Drive theory of motivation, 197
Drug testing, 412

Duties
  description in CCDO, 170
  job descriptions based on, 167

E

Earnings base, 746
Economic conditions, 12
  and compensation, 646
  and employee benefits, 729
  and employee relations, 555–56
  and employment equity, 271
  employment planning for, 225–26
  importance of, 43
  labour disputes as, 623
  in labour market; *see* Labour markets
  and occupational choice, 348–49
  and P/HRM development, 23
  in product/service markets; *see* Product/service markets
  projections of, 59
  and unions, 600–602
  unions as, 628–29
  and wages, 629
Economies of scale, in P/HRM activities, 20
Economy, model of, 222
Education
  as employee benefit, 734, 737–38
  and employee relations, 557
  as investment, 642
  of P/HRM managers, 22
  and participation rate, 45
  and robots, 76
  and selection, 413
Effect, adverse, 284
  and underutilization, 301
Effectiveness
  criteria for, 17
  employment planning for, 227
  organizational versus employee, 774–75
  and P/HRM staffing ratios, 20
  and training, 454
Efficiency, employment planning for, 227
Effort, level of, 197–99
Effort→performance (E→P) expectancy, 197–98
Ellis Chart, 464
Emotional competence, 203
Employee assistance programs (EAPs), 570–73
Employee benefits, 728–29
  communication of, 750–51
  and company strategy, 650
  contributory, 751, 756
  costs of, 750–51, 756, 761
  employee services as, 737–39
  for executives, 711–712
  external influences on, 729–31
  flexible, 756–61
  individuals' needs for, 757, 760
  insurance-based, 734–37

Employee benefits—Cont.
  internal influences on, 731
  objectives of, 749-50
  paid time not worked as, 732-34
  short-term versus long-term, 749
Employee relations, 554-55; see also Quality of work life (QWL)
  external influences on, 555-56
  internal influences on, 557
  to prevent unionization, 604
Employee Relations Index, 775, 782, 784
Employees; see also Individuals and Human resources
  benefit plan contributions of, 751, 756
  career development for, 565
  company ownership by, 560-62
  counselling; see Counselling
  effectiveness of, 774-75
  and employment planning, 228
  focus of attention of, 150-51
  and human resource objectives, 113
  and job evaluation, 664, 670
  and management by objectives, 514-15
  nature of, 14
  and employee relations, 557
  pension plan contributions of, 746
  and performance evaluation, 492, 496, 519
  ranking, 516
  as recruiters, 334-35
  recruitment as seen by, 347-52
  relations with managers, 15
  and relative performance standards, 515
  rights of, 554-55, 603
  satisfaction of, 631, 656; see also Motivation
  and benefits, 751
  and compensation, 695-97
  selection by, 371
  social interaction among, 146-47
  suggestions from, 698-700
  unsafe behavior of, 578-79
  "voice" of, 631
Employees' profit-sharing plans (EPSPs), 703
Employers
  liability for injuries of; see Workers' compensation
  pensions sponsored by, 744-49
Employment
  buffers, 562
  contracts for; see Employment contracts
  forecasts of, 222-23
  government regulation of terms and conditions of, 79-80
  and privatization, 66
  robots' effect on, 75
Employment agencies, 338, 355; see also Canada Employment Centres (CECs)
  and job retention, 343
Employment contracts
  administration of, 625-27
  Common Law, 585-86

Employment contracts—Cont.
  duration of, 617
  negotiating, 615-18
  ratification of, 618
Employment equity
  advisory committees for, 297
  and applicant criteria, 330
  assessment centres to achieve, 517
  communications about, 297-98
  in compensation; see Pay equity
  defined, 271
  employment planning for, 224, 228
  as external condition, 13
  and flexitime, 153
  intent versus effect of, 283-84
  and job analysis, 156
  legal foundations of, 278-83
  versus pay equity, 714
  and performance evluation, 491-92
  policies on, 296
  programs for, 293-95
    design and implementation of, 304-8
    employment systems review for, 301, 303-4
    monitoring, 308
    planning, 295-98
    target groups of, 298-99
    utilization analysis for, 298-301
  and qualifications, 143
  and recruiting, 328-29
  responsibility for, 272-73
  results criteria for, 476
  and selection, 373-74
  support measures for, 307-8
  in training, 445
  transitional probability matrices to forecast, 255
  unions' emphasis on, 83
Employment Equity Act, 79-80
Employment planning, 220
  accuracy of, 238-39, 250
  defined, 227
  for flexible firms, 258-60
  government involvement in, 221-24
  versus human resource planning, 112, 120
  integrating with business plans, 232, 239
  for labour markets, 225-26
  reasons for, 227-28
  and recruitment, 322, 325
  required, 224
  responsibility for, 229
  techniques for, 235-38, 242-55
  technology and, 226
  three phases of, 228
  time frame of, 240
  unions and, 226-27
Employment Requisition, 135
Employment security; see Job security
Employment systems review, 301, 303-4

Employment testing; see Tests
Engineers
  compensation of, 707
  demand for, 11, 234
  recruiting, 326
England; see Britain
Entrepreneurs
  immigration of, 51
  and strategy focus of organization, 106
Entry-level jobs
  ability tests for, 415
  recruitment for, 331
  in transitional probability matrices, 253
Environmental scanning, 40, 42–43
Equality, federal quarantees of, 79
Equal pay, 272, 714–16
  versus pay equity, 717–18; see also Pay equity
Equity
  in compensation; see Pay equity
  in conflict resolution, 576
  and employee relations, 556
  employment; see Employment equity
  and unions, 631
Equity theory of motivation, 200–202
Equivalent forms reliability, 377
Ergonomics, 579–80
Errors, potential cost of, 388–89
Establishment career stage, 205
Ethnicity, and genetic screening, 412; see also Discrimination, employment
Europe, employee participation in, 562
Evaluation
  of performance; see Performance evaluation
  of P/HRM, 16, 112, 772–73
    audits for, 775–78
    and integration of activities, 773–74
    quantitative, 781–87
    reputational, 779–80
Executive search firms, 355
Expatriate payments, 586
Expectancy theory of motivation, 197–200
  and job searches, 352
  and performance-based pay, 694
  of training, 461
Experience, selection and, 413
Exploration career stage, 204
  return to, at maintenance stage, 205
External attribution, 523–24
External conditions, 11–13
  diagnosing, 40
  human resource objectives based on, 113
  and job analysis, 167
  and job design, 151–53
  organizational conditions affected by, 98
  organization's influence on, 19
  and recruitment, 327–29
  and stages of P/HRM development, 23
Extrinsic rewards, 143

F

Facilitators, for quality circles, 560
Factor comparison, 666–68
Factory of the future, 72
Factory system of production, 144
Families
  counselling, 571
  dual career, 47–48
  reasonable accommodation of, 288
Family Services Association of Metropolitan Toronto, 571
Feedback
  in career development, 569
  as characteristic of work, 149
  with critical incidents, 526
  for evaluation training, 525
  in MBO, 514
Feedforward control, 370
File maintenance stage of P/HRM development, 23, 31
Financial conditions, 106–7
Financial counselling, 711
Finger dexterity, 192
First City Trust, 530–33
Five day worker, 39
Flat-rate compensation, 685
Fleet Aerospace Corp., 101
Flex-Com, 757–59, 761
Flexible dollar benefits systems, 757
  cost of, 761
Flexible firm, 258–59
Flexiplace, 153
Flexitime, 152–53
Flexitour, 152
Floater, 39
Flow data, 298–99
Flypaper approach to recruitment, 345
Focus of attention, 150–51
Forced distribution ranking, 516
Ford Motor Company
  employee assistance programs at, 570
  turnover at, 39
Foreign business, environmental scanning, 40
Forgery, 587
Forget Commission, 736
Forms, for HRIs, 134
Forward integration, 100
Four-fifths rule, 301
Frame-of-reference training, 523
Free trade, 64–65
  unions' attitudes toward, 83
Fringe benefits; see Employee benefits
Functional job analysis; see Job analysis, functional
Functional level, strategy at, 103, 111

G

Gainsharing; see Incentive pay, group
Gases, hazardous, 582
Gender dominance, 718–19

General Aptitude Test Battery (GATB),
    405–6, 417
General Electric, 72, 775, 782, 784
    automation at, 72
Generalists, 23
    accreditation as, 26
    in centralized organization structure, 129
    recruiting by, 324
General Motors of Canada, 72, 607
Genetic screening, 412
Geocentrism, 416
Geography
    labour market defined by, 56
    and technology distribution, 73
Gliding time, 152
Global performance criteria, 500
    and rating errors, 521
Golden Horsehoe, 55
Golden parachutes, 712
Government
    and compensation, 646–48
    and employee benefits, 729–30
    and employee relations, 556
    employment equity programs mandated by, 294–95
    and employment planning, 221–24
    as external condition, 13
    information about, 30
    job classification in, 665–66
    jurisdiction of, 79–80
    labour market involvement of, 52
    and labour relations, 602–3
    panel interviews by, 399
    and performance evaluation, 491–92
    P/HRM staffing ratios in, 20
    and privatization; *see* Privatization
    and recruiting, 328–29
    regulation of business by, 39, 78–81
    and selection, 373–74
    and strikes, 622
    and training, 445–47
    and unions, 13, 627–28
    vacation and holiday regulations of, 732
Government accountability stage of P/HRM development, 23
Grace, W. R., Company, 782
Grades, academic, 500–501
Grand Trunk Railroad, 745
Graphology, 411
Great Britain; *see* Britain
Great-West Life Assurance Co., 567
Grievances, 617, 625–26
    arbitration of, 626–27
    group, 625
    officers for, 575
Grievance strikes; *see* Wildcat strikes
Griggs versus Duke Power Co., 284
Groups
    discussions in, 468–69, 525
    for problem-solving, 558–60

Groups—*Cont.*
    T; *see* T-groups
    work; *see* Work groups
Guaranteed employment, 562
Guaranteed Income Supplement (GIS), 742
Guide to Resume Writing, 356
Guilford-Zimmerman Temperament Survey, 407

H

Halo effect, 521
Handwriting analysis; *see* Graphology
Harassment, 288–89
Hard hats, 286
Hawthorne Studies, 146
Hay Guide Chart-Profile Method of job evaluation, 674–76
Hazing, 435
Headhunters, 324
Heath, occupational, 15, 576–80
    employee assistance programs for, 570–71
    and employee relations, 556
    federal regulations about, 79
    information about, 29
    legislation about, 580–84
    and productivity, 749
    and robots, 76
Health insurance, 734–35
Hearing loss, 577
Hewlett-Packard, 562
Hierarchy of needs, 195–96
High schools, recruitment from, 337–38
Hiring; *see also* Staffing
    centralization of, 31
    freeze on, 257
    from outside the organization, 9
    rate of, 325
Holidays, 733–34
Home, work at, 153
Honeywell, 40, 42
Hospitals, selection at, 372–73
Hours of work
    and employment security, 563
    government controls on, 647
HR Canada, 26
Human relations movement, 33, 146–47
Human resource accounting, 784
Human resource activities, 14–15
Human resource information systems (HRISs), 122–23
    example of, 133–35
    input to, 124–25
    output from, 125
    security precautions for, 133
Human resource planning, 110–12
    analysis for, 117
    evaluation step of, 119–20
    and implementation, 117, 119
    responsibility for, 120
Human resource programming, 119

Human resources; *see also* Employees
 effectiveness of, 17–18
 effect on strategy of, 101
 importance of, 6
 management of; *see* Personnel/human resource management
 sources of, 241
 strategic redeployment of, 101
Human rights commissions, 279
 employment equity programs imposed by, 294
Hygiene factors, 196

I

Illness, occupational, 577; *see also* Health, occupational
 causes of, 578–79
Immigrants, 49–50
Imperial Oil Ltd., 109, 490
Implied conditions of employment, 585–86
Improshare plan, 702
Incentive pay, 653, 697; *see also* Commissions
 and company strategy, 650
 for executives, 709–10
 group, 700–703
 individual, 697–700
Inco Ltd., 148
Income Tax Act, 729–30
Incompetence, as cause for dismissal, 587
Individuals
 career anchors of, 202–3
 determinants of performance of, 190–94
 employee benefits for, 749–50, 757–60
 forms of compensation for, 651
 incentive pay for, 697–700
 matching to work, 117
 pay equity among, 684; *see also* Pay equity
 performance evaluation of, 494
 retirement savings of, 748
 training, 454, 456, 459–61
 and work groups, 210
Industrial betterment movement, 30–31
Industrial Disputes Investigation Act, 607
Industrial psychology; *see* Psychology, industrial
Industrial relations
 emergence of, 31
 information about, 29
Industries
 labour market in, 56
 levels of unionization in, 628–29
Inequity, perceived, 201; *see also* Equity
Inflation; *see also* Cost-of-living adjustments (COLAs)
 and development of P/HRM, 34
 and disability insurance, 737
 and government income security, 742
 and labour costs, 64
 and wage levels, 618, 629, 647
Informal groups; *see* Work groups

Informatics, 67
Information; *see also* Human resource information systems (HRISs)
 for career development, 569
 on compensation, 656, 706
 about employee benefits, 750–51
 for employment equity programs, 298–301
 for employment planning, 240
 on forms, 134
 about health and safety, 581
 for human resource programming, 120
 in job ads, 339
 for job analysis, 156–60
 for job candidates, 347
 for job descriptions, 171–72
 on labour market, 226
 for objective setting, 113
 about P/HRM department, 781–82
 presentation techniques in training, 466–67
 processing techniques in training, 467–68
 for recruitment planning, 326
 requirements of, 123
 screening, 42
 for skills inventories, 243
 sources of, 27–30
 for succession planning, 248
 for transitional probability matrixes, 254
 utility of, 126
Innovations program, 446
Inputs, relevant, 201
Insurance
 deductibles for, 756,
 employee benefits based on, 734–37
 employee desire for, 731
Intellectual ability, 192
Intent, adverse, 283–84
Interest arbitration, 619
Interest inventories, 407–8
 validity of, 409
Internal attribution, 523–24
Internal environment; *see* Organization, nature of
Internal responsibility system, 580–82
International Association for Personnel Women (IAPW), 26
International business, 83–84; *see also* Multinational companies
International Business Machines (IBM)
 corporate culture of, 108
 human resources of, 20
 Programmer Aptitude Test of, 391
 training at, 443, 470
International Labour Organization (ILO)
 equal remuneration convention of, 279
 information from, 30
Internships, 339–40; *see also* Work-study programs
Inter-rater reliability, 495

Interviewers
  characteristics of, 402
  skills of, 398, 402–3
Interviews
  for compensation surveys, 658
  employment, and applicant characteristics, 401
    at colleges, 337
    context of, 402
    follow-up of, 360
    preparation for, 359
    types of, 396, 398–400
    validity of, 395–96, 404
    weaknesses of, 400
  guidelines for, 402–4
  for job descriptions, 172
  for performance evaluation, 526–28
  for skills inventories, 244
  versus tests, 376
Intrinsic rewards, 143–44
  and vertical job enrichment, 148
Inventories, for quantitative job analysis, 161
Issues research, 42–43

J

Japan
  management techniques in, 34
  quality circles in, 559
Jewitt v. Prism Resources Ltd., 587
Job analysis, 154–57
  acceptance of results of, 158, 165–66
  and compensation structure, 662–63
  data collection for, 158–60
  error in, 16, 166–67
  functional, 160–61, 166, 170
  and performance evluation, 495
  practicality of, 165–66
  procedures for, 171–73
  quantitative, 161–63
  reliability of, 163, 165
  subjectivity of, 166
  and validation of selection procedures, 381
  validity of, 165
Job burnout, 582
Job descriptions, 167–68
  classification of, 665–66
  and compensation, 657, 662
  for functional job analysis, 160–61
  information for, 171–72
  sample, 173–81
  and unionization, 31
  verifying, 173
Job design, 144–45
  and characteristics of task, 149–50
  and employees' social needs, 146–47
  and job analysis, 156; *see also* Job analysis
  and organizational and external conditions, 151–53
  scientific; *see* Scientific management
  and scope of responsibility, 147–48
  and work groups, 209

Job engineering, 147
Job enlargement, 147
Job enrichment, 145, 147–48
  and employee focus of attention, 151
  Hackman-Oldham model of, 149
Job evaluation, 662–63
  Jay Guide Chart-Profile Method of, 674–76
  illustration of, 671–72
  and labour market, 720
  manual for, 669
  methods for, 664–70
  and pay equity, 717–19
  and pay ranges, 686–87
  purposes of, 663–64
  relevant parties to, 664
  usefulness of, 673
Job Instruction Training, 463
Job opportunities bulletins, 334
Job posting, 333–34
Job rotation, 147–48
Jobs
  attributes of, 350
  choice of, 353–54
  classifications of, 168–70, 665–66, 686–87
  complexity of, 708
  evaluating offers of, 360–61
  evaluation of; *see* Job evaluation
  expectations about, 345–47, 436
  factor comparison of, 666–68
  key; *see* Key jobs
  learning, 458–59; *see also* Training
  net advantage of, 328
  ranking, 665
  rating scales specific to, 510
  replacement planning for, 245
  searches for, 351–52
  sources of information about, 354–55
  unrest in, 206
  worth of, 718
JOBSCAN, 55, 170
  and recruitment, 328–29
Job security, 562–63
  contract negotiations about, 616–17
  and union development, 605
Job sharing, 49, 257
Job simplification, 145
Job specifications, 168
Joint health and safety committees, 580
Journals; *see* Publications
Journeymen Tailors of Toronto, 605

K

Key jobs, 659
  and factor comparison, 666
  pay structure based on, 671
Kidd Creek mine, 700
Knights of Labour, 608
Know-how (KH), 674
Knowledge, training techniques for, 466–69
Kodak, 241

KSAOs, 156–57
Kuder-Richardson formula 20, 378

L

Labatt's, 101
Labour costs, 642
 and competition, 655
 of early retirement, 258
 and product/service market conditions, 63–64
 reducing, 106
 and technology, 78
Labour Council of Metropolitan Toronto, 614–15
Labour demand; see also Labour markets
 equal to supply, 255
 exceeding suply, 256
 forecasting, 222–23, 230–40
 numbers required, 233
 and productivity, 232, 234–35
 and product/service market conditions, 62–64
 and skills mix, 234
 supply exceeding, 257–60
Labour federations; see Unions, federations of
Labour force, 43–45
 and immigration levels, 50–51
 makeup of, 45
 shifts in, 46–52
Labour Force Survey (LFS), 43
Labouring level, 55
Labour markets
 availability data about, for employment equity programs, 299
 campus placement office as, 321
 CEIC influence on, 222
 compensation and, 646
 COPS forecasts of, 223
 defined, 52
 employment planning for, 225–26
 and job searches, 354
 and labour relations, 602
 and pay equity, 720
 prospects for, 59–60
 and recruitment, 327–28
 regional variations in, 55
 relevant, 55–56
 and selection, 373
 and training, 445–47
 trends in, 52, 55
 and unemployment insurance, 735
Labour relations, 601; see also Unions
 disputes, 622–24
 external influences on, 601–4
 internal influences on, 604–5
Labour Relations Boards, 603–4
 in certification campaigns, 612–13
Labour supply; see also Labour markets
 equal to demand, 255
 forecasting, 222–23, 240–55
 shortage in, 256

Labor supply—*Cont.*
 surplus in, 257–60
 turnover and, 241
Laissez-faire leadership style, 207
Language, as selection criterion, 374
Layoffs, 225–26; see also Termination
 alternatives to, 257–58
 counselling after, 590
 and employee relations, 556
 and employment security policies, 562
 notice required for, 584–85, 588–89
 and profit sharing, 703
 unemployment insurance for; see Unemployment insurance
Leadership styles, 207
Learning; see also Training
 individuals', 459–61
 principles of, 458–59
 as training evaluation criterion, 473
 and types of transfers, 466
Learning curves, 460
Lecture
 for evaluation training, 525
 as training technique, 467
Legislation; see also Government
 and development of P/HRM, 23
 on dismissal, 584–90
 for employment equity programs, 294–95
 for health and safety, 580–84
 human rights, 270–71, 279–80
  complaints under, 282–83
 information about, 29
 regulatory, 80
Leniency evaluation error, 522
Life insurance, 737
Line managers; see Operating managers
Linguistic reasoning tests, 307
Literacy, 49
Litigation, cost of, 590
Loans, no-interest, as benefits, 711
Lobbying, 80
Location, and selection, 375
Lockouts, 620–22
 and unemployment insurance, 736
Looking Glass, 469–70
Lump sum pay increases, 691

M

MacDonald Commission, 736
Maintenance
 of HRIS, 125
 organizational, 453
 of robots, 75
Maintenance career stage, 205
Make or buy strategies, 448
Management
 in employee-owned firms, 562
 in joint problem-solving committees, 558
 preparation for contract negotiations by, 616
 relations with unions; see Labour relations
 resistance to unionization by, 612

Management—Cont.
  rights of, 617
  and strikes, 621
Management development, origins of, 33
Management information services, 28–29
Management by objectives (MBO), 513–15
  jobs appropriate for, 518
Managerial competence, 203
Managers
  career development for, 565
  compensation of, 650, 707–13
  and job evaluation, 664
  labour market for, 55
  of multinational companies, 415–16
  operating; see Operating managers
  pay structure for, 660
  performance evaluation of, 493, 513
  relations with employees, 15
  training of, 443, 456
    on-the-job, 464–66
    simulation techniques for, 469–70
  women as, 294
Maniflex, 152
Manitoba, mandatory retirement in, 292
Manpower Consultative Service (MCS), 224
Manufacturing industries, unions in, 609
Manulife, 307
Marketing, and human resource decisions, 11
MarkStrat, 470
Maternity leave, 734
  unemployment insurance during, 736
Maximizers, 351
MBAs, 737
Meat charts, 583
Mechanicl ability, 192
Mediation, 618–19
Medical testing, 412
Memory, in performance evaluation, 521, 526
Merck and Company, Inc., 120
  HRIS at, 133–35
Mergers, 66–67
  severance pay after, 712
  of unions, 613
Merit guide chart matrix, 689
Merit pay, 688
  administration of, 693–94
Microelectronics industry, training in, 447
MicroElectronics SIMulation Model (MESIM), 224
Midcareer crisis, 205
Middle aged people, as employees, 46–47
Middle management, 8
Minimum wage, 24, 647
  and union development, 605
Mining industry, compensation in, 698, 700
Ministry of Transportation and Communications (MTC), Ontario, 248
Minorities
  employment discrimination against, 277–78
  recruiting, 328
Mixed standard scales, 515

Models
  diagnostic; see Diagnostic model
  for employment planning, 237–38
  human resource programming, 119
Molson, 101
Money-purchase pension plans; see Defined contribution pension plans
Montreal Personnel Association, 31
Morale; see Motivation
Motivation, 193
  and compensation, 692–93
  content theories of, 195–96
  and core job characteristics, 148
  and employee benefits, 749
  and internal recruiting, 331
  and lump sum pay increases, 691
  nonmonetary, 695
  and performance-based pay, 694
  and performance evaluation, 493, 526
  process theories of, 197–202
  and productivity, 19
  skills inventories for, 244
  and task design, 209
  and training, 460–61
Motivators, 196
Motor coordination ability, 192
Multinational companies
  compensation in, 707
  orientation in, 441
  selection in, 415–16
Multiple-hurdles selection processes, 392
Multiple performance criteria, 499
Multiple regression, and utility of selection procedures, 385
Multiskilling, 259

N

National occupational classification (NOC) system, 170
  and COPS, 224
Native people
  employment discrimination against, 277–78
  employment equity programs for, 297
  numerical goals for employment of, 304
Natural resource industries, labour relations in, 623
Needs
  hierarchy of; see Hierarchy of needs
  prepotent, 195
  and valence, 199
Network corporation, 77
Newspapers, job ads in, 339–40, 355
Noise, 577, 582
Norms, of work groups, 210
Northern Pipeline Act, 224
NOVA, An Alberta Corporation, 297

O

Objectives, 111–13
  cascading, 514
  of compensation, 649–53

Objectives—*Cont.*
 in decentralized organization structure, 131
 and employment planning, 220, 239
 formulating, 113, 115, 117
 implementing, 117, 119
 numerical, for employment equity programs, 304
 of P/HRM activities, 17–19
 performance evaluation by, 518; *see also* Management by objectives (MBO)
 and selection, 372–73
 of training programs, 457, 460–61, 471
Observation evaluation errors, 520
Obsolescene, 448; *see also* Technology
Occupational groups, prospects for, 59
Occupations
 availability analysis for, 299
 choice of, 348–49
 classifications of, 168–70
 defined, 154
 long-term factors versus immediate determinants of, 349
 women's, 273
Old Age Security (OAS), 739, 742
Older people, as employees, 48–49
Ombudspersons, 575–76
100 Best Companies to Work for in Canada, The, 352
Ontario
 employment discrimination in, 277–78
 employment equity programs in, 294
 equal pay legislation in, 715
 human rights legislation in, 279
 workers' compensation in, 582
Ontario Hydro, 33, 738
Ontario Municipal Employees Retirement System (OMERS), 747
On-the-job training, 462–66
Operating managers; *see also* Supervisors
 compensation set by, 643, 645
 employment planning by, 229
 human resource planning by, 120
 and labour relations, 601
 orientation by, 436
 and P/HRM evaluation, 775–78, 780
 P/HRM managers' relations with, 24–25
 performance evaluation by, 491
 recruiting by, 324
 selection by, 370–71
 as sources of information, 9
 training by, 450
 and videotaped interviews, 399
Operational analysis, for training, 454
Operational goals, for employment equity programs, 304, 306–7
Operational planning, 102
Organization
 changes in, 7–8
 choice of, 349–50
 demography of, 228

Organization—*Cont.*
 effectiveness of, 774
 as P/HRM objective, 17
 influence on external conditions, 19
 and job design, 151–53
 levels of, and strategy, 103
 training needs and, 456
 nature of, 13–14
 and recruitment, 329–30
 size of; *see* Size of organization
Organizational accountability stage of P/HRM development, 23
Organizational analysis, for training, 453–54
Organization charts, and replacement charts, 244
Organization for Economic Cooperation and Development (OECD), 30
Organization structure
 centralized versus decentralized, 129–31
 and robots, 77
Orientation
 defined, 434
 to employee assistance programs, 572
 follow-up to, 441
 guidelines for, 439, 441
 for international assignments, 441
 program content for, 437–39
 purposes of, 435–36
 responsibility for, 436–37
 training for, 449
Outcomes, relevant, 201
Outplacement counselling, 590
Output
 and labour demand, 232
 and leadership style, 207
Overlearning, 458
Overtime, limits on, 260
 by government, 647–48
 and short labour supply, 256

P

Paired comparison ranking, 516
Panel interviews, 399
Parental leave, 734
Partial strikes, 621
Participation rate, 44
 for older workers, 48
 prospects for, 59
 for women, 47–48
Part-time work, 49
 in flexible firms, 258–59
 and labour surpluses, 257
 partial retirement as, 258
 pensions for, 748
Paternity leave, 734
Pay; *see* Compensation
Pay equity, 272, 279, 642, 648, 653–54, 714–17
 continuing controversy over, 719
 cost of, 720
 versus equal pay, 717–18

Pay equity—*Cont.*
  external, 655–59, 672, 691
  among individuals, 684
  internal, 659–62, 671–72, 691–92
  job evaluation for, 662–63
Peer evaluations, 519
Pensions, 739
  defined benefit, 746
  defined contribution, 703, 745–46
  and early retirement, 257–58
  employee desire for, 731
  employer-sponsored, 744–48
  government regulation of, 729–30
  government-sponsored, 739, 742–44
  information about, 29
  legislation about, 745
  and mandatory retirement, 292
  portability of, 747
  and retirement age, 49
  vesting in, 746–47
Performance
  compensation based on, 685, 687, 689, 692–95; *see also* Incentive pay *and* Merit pay
  for executives, 707, 709–10
  criteria for, 498–503
  evaluation of; *see* Performance evaluation
  and individual ability, 192
  and labour demand, 231–32
  long-term, 710
  observing, 526
  and on-the-job training, 463
  and perceived inequity, 201
  predictors of, 414–15
  and quality of hire, 343
  standards for, for work groups, 210
  and training evaluation, 476
  and training needs, 454, 456
Performance evaluation, 490
  with absolute standards, 503–15, 523
  acceptability of results of, 496–97, 514
  biased, 694
  cost of, 497
  criteria for, 498–503
  in diagnostic model, 491–93
  and dismissal, 588
  and employment equity, 297
  errors in, 520–24
  evaluative versus developmental purposes of, 494–95
  fairness of, 496, 514, 519
  formal, 490–91, 527
  to identify training and development needs, 193, 569
  and incompetence, 587
  individualized versus standardized, 497–98
  instruments for, 496, 530–41
  interviews for, 526–28
  and job analysis, 155
  objective criteria for, 511, 513–15

Performance evaluation—*Cont.*
  and pay increases, 689
  and P→O expectancy, 199
  with relative standards, 503, 515–19, 523
  reliability and validity of, 378, 495
  responsibility for, 519–20
  senior management involvement in, 520
  training for, 524–25
  and validation of selection procedures, 381
Performance→outcome (P→O) expectancy, 199–200
Performance share units, 711
Performance standards training, 523, 525
Perquisites, 711–12
Personal holidays, 733–34
Personality
  and heredity versus life experiences, 190
  and leadership style, 207
  tests of, 407
    handwriting in; *see* Graphology
    validity of, 409
Personnel/human resource management
  as collection of activities, 773–74
  constituencies of, 779
  defined, 6
  development of, 22–24
  evaluation of, 772–73
  history of Canadian, 30–34
  integrated, 774
  integrating with organization, 8–9
  objectives of, 17–19
  responsibility for, 7
  support versus functional activities of, 16
Personnel/human resource managers, 19–20
  BARS development by, 509
  compensation set by, 643, 645
  in employment equity program, 296
  employment planning by, 229
  employment systems review by, 303
  functional area knowledge of, 6
  involvement in company strategy, 14
  and labour relations, 601
  and mergers, 67
  numbers of, 21–22
  and operating managers, 24–25
  orientation by, 436
  performance evaluation by, 491
  personal experience of, 10
  professional certification of, 26
  selection by, 370–71
  training by, 450
  women as, 26
Personnel Association of Ontario (PAO), 26
Personnel Association of Toronto (PAT), 32
Personnel evaluation indexes, 781–84
Personnel Management Information System (PMIS), 133–35
Personnel Practices Review Team, 778
Personnel Profile form, 134
Philosophy; *see* Corporate culture

Physical characteristics, 190
Physician analogy, 9–11
Physiological needs, 195
Pickets, 621
Piecework, 697
  quality of, 700
Placement, and individual ability, 192–93
Planning
  employment; see Employment planning
  human resource; see Human resource planning
  operational; see Operational planning
  strategic; see Strategic planning
Point method of job evaluation, 668–71
Polarization, and technology, 71
Policies, formation and evaluation of, 112
Policy grievances, 625
Policy line, 688, 691
Polygraph tests, 411
Population; see also Demography
  growth of, 45–46
  and labour force, 43–45
  shifts in, 46–52
Position
  defined, 154
  promotion possibilities in, 253
Position analysis questionnaire (PAQ), 162–63
  acceptability of, 166
  and selection procedure validation, 382
Position description questionnaire (PDQ), 162–63
Power, 601
Practice
  for evaluation training, 525
  and learning, 458–59
  simulation training as, 469
Predictive validation, 379
Pretesting, for training evaluation, 477
Price(s)
  and compensation levels, 63–64
  deregulation of, 81
  flexibility in, 106
Privatization, 66
Proactive management, 10–11
  orientation in, 434
  of pay equity, 718
  of pay information, 706
  training in, 444, 454
Problem solving (PS), 674
Product/service markets, 62–64
  and compensation, 646
  and labour relations, 602
  and strategy, 104
Production committees, 702
Productivity
  and alcoholism, 570
  and compensation, 233, 656, 685, 688, 702; see also Incentive pay
  and deregulation, 81
  and employee benefits, 749

Productivity—Cont.
  of employee-owned firms, 561
  employment planning for, 239
  human resource objectives to improve, 115, 117
  and labour demand, 232, 234–35
  and morale, 19
  of training programs, 479
  unions and, 630
  and validity of selection procedures, 379, 417–19
  and working conditions, 146
Productivity bargaining, 630
Products, and labour demand, 231
Professional associations, 22
  job placement services of, 355
Professional work
  P/HRM as, 26
  recruitment for, 338
  women in, 48, 276
Profit sharing, 702–4
  pension plans based on, 746
Promotion; see also Transfers
  and assessment centres, 517
  and job posting, 334
  and performance evaluation results, 495
  probability of, 253
  and quality of hire, 343
  from within, 8–9; see also Recruitment, internal
Propensity to be mobile, 56
Prospecting theory of recruitment, 322
Prospectors, 104
  P/HRM policies of, 106
  recruiting for, 330
  selection by, 372
Provinces
  health insurance in, 734–35
  human rights legislation in, 280
  jurisdiction of governments of, 80
  labour laws in, 604, 648
  migration among, 55
  pay equity legislation in, 715–16
  retirement income security supplements in, 742
  strike-prone, 624
  union certification requirements in, 613
Psychology
  industrial, 32
  of occupational choice, 348–49
Publications, 27–28
Public relations, recruitment as, 322
Pull factors, 300
Punctuality, evaluation based on, 521

Q

Qualifications, 143
  bona fide; see Bona fide occupational qualifications (BFOQs)
  and employment equity, 272, 306–7

Qualifications—*Cont.*
  and recruitment, 329
  and selection, 374
Quality
  and employee relations, 554
  of piecework, 700
Quality circles, 559–60, 630
Quality of hire (QH), 342–43
Quality of work life (QWL), 145, 554, 557
  approaches to, 558–60
  and hazardous work environments, 582
  outcomes from, 563
  Quebec; *see also* Canada/Quebec pension plan
  mandatory employment equity programs in, 294
  pay equity in, 715
  workers' compensation in, 582
  wrongful dismissal in, 587
Queen's University, 32, 575
Questionnaires
  for compensation surveys, 658
  for skills inventories, 244
  for training evaluation, 473
Quotas
  for employment equity programs, 294, 304
  production, work-group-decided, 208

R

Racial Documentation Act, 279
Racial prejudice, 277–78; *see also* Discrimination, employment
Rater error training, 525
Rating scales, 505
  anchoring, 505, 509–11
  with forced distribution ranking, 516
  training in use of, 525
Reaction criteria, 473
Real domestic output, 222
Real estate salespeople, selection of, 394
Realistic job previews (RJPs), 346–47
Reasonable accommodation, 286–88
Recent-behaviour evaluation bias, 523
  memory aids to reduce, 526
Recommendation letters, 413–14
Recreational facilities, as employee benefit, 738
Recruiters, 325
Recruitment, 321
  advertising for, 339–40
  applicant's view of, 347–52
  components of, 322
  costs of, 344
  discrimination in, 306
  effectiveness of, 343
  employer-applicant matching in, 331
  evaluating, 340, 342–45
  expectations created during, 345–47
  external, 335–40
    versus internal, 331, 333

Recruitment—*Cont.*
  from target group of employment equity program, 299–300
  government influences on, 328–29
  internal, 333–35
    versus external, 331, 333
  and job analysis, 155
  and labour market conditions, 327–28
  orientation during, 441
  personnel evaluation indexes for, 782
  planning for, 325–27
  principles of good practice in, 360
  responsibility for, 324
  and selection, 370; *see also* Selection
  time requirements of, 326
References, checking, 413–14
Referrals, recruitment by, 334–35, 343
  and compensation level, 351
Refugees, 50
Regional Development Incentives Act, 224
Regions
  employment planning for, 226
  labour market variation between, 55
  technology distribution among, 73
Registered retirement income funds (RRIFs), 746
Registered retirement savings plans (RRSPs), 748
Re Harris et al. and Bell Canada, 717
Reinforcement, in training, 461, 471
Relationships by Objectives, 558
Reliability
  of BARS, 510
  of performance evaluation results, 495
Religion, discrimination based on, 270, 285, 287
Relocation, 48
  willingness for, 56
Replacement planning, 244–45, 248; *see also* Succession planning
Reputational evaluation techniques, 779–80
Research, for policy formulation, 119
Reservation wage, 350
Resources, and nature of organization, 14
Response sets, for job analysis, 166–67
Rest breaks, 732, 734
Rest days, 648
Results, job descriptions based on, 167
Results criteria, 476
  for performance evaluation, 502–3
Resumes, 356–58
Retail Clerks Union, 579
Retirees, orientation by, 437
Retirement, 48
  early, 241, 257–58, 744
  income during; *see* Pensions
  individual savings for, 748
  mandatory, 289, 292
  partial, 258
Retirement income savings plans (RISPs), 757

Retrenchment, employment policies for, 257–60
Rewards
    compensation as, 196, 643; *see also* Compensation
    extrinsic versus intrinsic, 143–44
    inputs compared to, 201
    and P→O expectancy, 199
    valences of, 199
    value of, 694–95
    and work groups, 210
Right to refuse unsafe work, 582
"Rings of defence" strategies, 258–59
Riverdale Hospital, 738
Robots, 71, 73
    and employment, 75
    and training, 449
    union attitudes toward, 82
Robson v. *General Motors of Canada Ltd.*, 588
Role clarity, 194
Role models, for management training, 464
Role perceptions, 194
Role reversals, 469
Rotation; *see* Transfers
Royal Bank of Canada, 307
Royal Canadian Mounted Police, 374
Royal Commission on the Relations of Labour and Capital, 30
Rucker plan, 702

S

Safety, occupational, 15, 576–80
    and BFOQs, 286
    and diabetics, 285–86
    and employee relations, 556
    equipment for, 270
    government regulation of, 79, 580–84
    and illiteracy, 49
    information about, 29
    and job analysis, 156
    and robots, 76
    under standard hour pay plans, 700
    training for, 445
    and union development, 605
Salary; *see also* Compensation
    and value added by selection, 390
    versus wages, 707
Sales jobs, compensation for, 685, 698
Sampling errors, in job analysis, 166
Saskatchewan, workers' compensation in, 584
Saskatchewan Government Insurance Corporation (SGI), 303–4
Satisfiers, 351
Scanlon plan, 702
Scarborough, 297
Scatterplots, 384–85
Schedules, work; *see* Work, schedules for
Scientific management, 145–46
Scientists, compensation of, 707

Sears Canada, 649, 698, 700, 751
Seasons of a Man's Life, The (Levinson), 203
Secondary reinforcers, 197
Secrecy, about compensation, 694, 706
Security
    as career anchor, 203
    needs for, 195
    for personnel records, 133
Selection
    application blanks for, 393–95
    and compensation levels, 656
    cost of, 388–89
    defined, 372
    discriminatory criteria for, 306–7, 309–13
    and education, 413
    employment testing for; *see* Tests
    and experience, 413
    and individual ability, 192–93
    influences on, 372–75
    in multinational companies, 415–16
    multiple-hurdles versus compensatory processes of, 392–93
    net present value of, 391
    orientation during, 441
    and productivity, 417–19
    reliability of, 376–78, 383
    responsibility for, 370–71
    and stereotypes, 400–401
    validation of procedures for, 378–83
    value added by, 389–91
Selection ratio, 373, 386–87
    and weighted application blanks, 394
Self-appraisals, 519
Self-insurance, 756
Self-selection, 330
    and job ad contents, 339
    and job posting, 334
Self-serving bias, 524
Seniority
    and compensation, 648, 653, 688–89
    contract negotiations about, 616–17
    and employment planning, 228
    and vacations, 733
Service industries
    employment prospects in, 59–60
    part-time work in, 49
    unions in, 82
    women working in, 47–48
Severance pay, 585–86
    for executives after mergers, 712
Severity evaluation error, 522
Sexual harassment, 288–89
Shop stewards, 626; *see also* Unions
Sick leave, 736–37
Significant placement variables (SPVs), 329
Sikhs, 270, 285
Simmons Simulator Inc., 470
Simpsons-Sears Ltd., 287
Simulations, with transitional probability matrixes, 253–55

Subject Index

Simulation training techniques, 469–70
Singh v. *Security and Investigation Services Ltd.*, 284
Site visits, 337, 360
Situational contingencies, 194
Size of organization, and labour supply forecasting, 242
Skilled labour, immigration of, 51
Skill Investment program, 446
Skills; *see also* Ability *and* Qualifications
   classifications of, 405–6
   and compensable factors, 668–69
   and employment planning, 226
   for functional flexibility, 259
   interviewing, 398, 402–3
   inventories of, 242–44
      for recruitment, 334
   and labour markets, 56
   mix of, 234, 255
   and organizational level, 456
   rank-ordered importance of, 241
   resume to present, 356
   simulation training for, 469–70
   and technology employed, 75, 106–7
   and training, 445; *see also* Training
   transferable, 356
Skill twist, 448
Slowdowns, 621
Social interaction, in work groups, 208
Socialization, 442–43
   at establishment career stage, 205
   orientation as, 434
   during recruitment, 322
   training for, 449
Sociology, of occupational choice, 348–49
Sociotechnical systems, 558
Software
   for P/HMR systems, 127
   for skills inventories, 243
Source population, 44
Spearman-Brown Prophecy formula, 378
Specialists, P/HRM
   accreditation as, 26
   in decentralized organization structure, 129
   journals for, 28
Specialization
   excessive, 8
   P/HRM management as, 19–20
   and technology, 78
Spiffs, 698
Spillover effect, 13, 648
Split-halves reliability, 377–78
Spouses, pension rights of, 748
Spouse's Allowance (SA), 742
Stability bonuses, 241–42
Staffing, 15
   and career development, 569
   HRIS to assist, 135
   and organization structure, 132
   in P/HRM department, 20

Staffing—*Cont.*
   and product/market conditions, 64
   selection as part of, 370; *see also* Selection
Staffing graphs, 326–27
Standard deviation, for underutilization test, 301
Standard hour pay plans, 697–98
   accidents under, 700
Standards, 697
State definitions, in transitional probability matixes, 251
Steel industry, productivity in, 630
Stereotyping, 276; *see also* Discrimination, employment
   and selection decisions, 400–401
Stock data, 298–99
Stock options, 710–11
Straight commission, 698
Strategic planning, 99
   and career management, 206
   and employment planning, 220, 232
   and training needs, 453
Strategy
   appropriateness of, 99
   and compensation, 649–50
   and corporate culture, 108–9
   and financial condition, 106
   human resources' influence on, 101, 113
   levels of, 103
   make or buy, 448
   and nature of organization, 13
   and nature of work, 142–43
   P/HRM manager's involvement in, 14
   and P/HRM policies, 106
   phases of, 99
   and recruiting, 329–30
   and selection, 372–73
   types of, 104
Stress interview, 400
Strikebreakers, 621
Strikes, 620–22
   arbitration to avoid, 619
   industries prone to, 624
   in natural resource industries, 623–24
   right to, 603, 627
   and unemployment insurance, 736
Strong Vocational Interest Test, 407–8
Structured interviews, 398
Subcontracting, for flexible labour force, 259–60
Subcultures, 108–9
Subjective performance criteria, 503
   evaluation methods using, 504–11
Subordinate evaluation, 519–20
Succession planning, 248, 250; *see also* Replacement planning
   and training, 453–54
Suggestion systems, 698–700, 702
Supervisors; *see also* Operating managers
   assessment centres for, 409

Supervisors—Cont.
  and career development, 568
  compensation of, 650
  and conflict resolution, 575
  and employee assistance programs, 572
  and employment equity, 273
  and grievances, 626
  and job analysis, 163
  and job descriptions, 172
  in MBO, 514
  and motivation, 206–7
  and occupational health and safety, 584
  and orientation, 436
  performance evaluation by, 497, 500, 519, 526, 528
    inconsistent, 522
  performance evaluation of, 519–20
  and relative performance standards, 516
  as role models, 464
  and vertical job enrichment, 148
Supplementary unemployment insurance benefits (SUB), 736
Support staff
  needs estimate for, 234
  P/HRM as, 16
Surpluses, in labour market, 225
Synethetic validity, 382
Systemic discrimination, 284
  sources of, 306–7

T

Takeovers, 66–67
  severance pay after, 712
Task Force on Microelectronics and Employment, 74
Task identity, 149
Task significance, 149
Taxes
  and employee benefits, 729–30
  and RRSPs, 748
  and unemployment insurance, 735–36
Taylor-Russell tables, 387
Technical/functional competence, 202
Technical managers, as recruiters, 324
Technology, 67–74; see also Robots
  and employment planning, 224, 226
  as external factor, 12–13
  implications of, 74–78
  as internal factor, 13
  and quality of work life, 558
  and skill requirements, 106–7
  training for, 445–48
  unions' attitudes toward, 82, 602, 605
Termination, 584–90; see also Layoffs
Territories; see also Provinces
  human rights legislation in, 280
  jurisdiction of governments of, 80
Test-retest reliability, 377
  of performance evaluation results, 495

Tests, 375–76
  for ability; see Aptitude tests
  versus biographical data, 395
  discriminatory, 306–7
  to evaluate training programs, 473, 477
  of health, 578–79
  and job analysis, 155
  reliability of, 376–78
  validity of, 409–11
T-groups, 469
Theft, dismissal for, 586
Theory, for policy formulation, 119
Timetables, for employment equity programs, 304
Top-down forecasting, 230
"Top hat" profit sharing plans, 703
Toronto, day care centers in, 739
Toronto Transit Commission (TTC), 573
Total strikes, 621
Toxic substances, 582
Trades and Labour congress of Canada (TLC), 608
Trade Unions Act, 606
Training, 15, 443–44
  assessing needs for, 451–56, 505
  and career development, 569
  costs and benefits of, 106, 479
  defined, 444
  for employee assistance programs, 572
  as employee benefit, 737
  evaluation of, 471–79
  of experienced workers, 448
  external influences on, 445–47
  for health and safety, 581
  and illiteracy, 49
  and individual ability, 192–93, 454, 456, 460
  internal influences on, 447–50
  and internal recruiting, 333
  and international business, 84
  as investment, 642
  and job analysis, 154
  and labour relations, 602
  materials for, 443, 459
  objectives of, 457
  on-the-job techniques for; see On-the-job training
  and orientation, 434
  and performance evaluation, 494, 523, 524, 525
  phases of, 450–51
  productivity of, 479
  program design for, 457–61
  quality circles for, 559
  responsibility for, 450
  techniques for, 462–71
  and technology, 76, 78, 445–49
  timing of, 472
  transferring to job, 459, 462
Transfers, 465–66; see also Promotion

Transitional probability matrixes, 251, 253–55
Travel insurance, 737
Trust funds, for training, 446
TRW Canada Limited, 560
TRW Corporation of North America, 98
　Employee Information System Project at, 126
Turnover, 39
　and child care benefits, 738
　and labour supply, 241
　with mergers and takeovers, 67
　orientation to reduce, 436
　and pay dissatisfaction, 695–96
　and realistic job previews, 346
　and recruitment, 345
　and unions, 631
Two factor theory of motivation, 196
　and job enrichment, 147–48
Two-tier wage systems, 618

U

Underutilization, 301
Unemployment
　employee ownership to avoid, 560
　and free trade, 65
　and immigration, 51
　and job search methods, 351
　and labour relations, 602
　part-time, 563
　prospects for, 59
　and selection, 375
　technological, 70, 77
　training to reduce, 445, 461
　work time lost to, 624
Unemployment insurance, 735–36
　and maternity leave, 734
　and work sharing, 257
Unfair labour practices, 603–4
Unfaithful service, as cause for dismissal, 587
Unions, 81–83; see also Labour relations
　attitudes toward P/HRM department, 780
　certification of, 603, 611–12
　and compensation, 648
　and conflict resolution, 573; see also Grievances
　and dental insurance, 735
　develpment of, 31, 605–9
　and employee assistance programs, 571
　and employee benefits, 730–31
　and employee participation, 631
　and employee relations, 556
　and employment equity programs, 296, 297
　and employment planning, 226–27
　in employment systems reviews, 303–4
　and equity theory of motivation, 201–2
　as external conditions, 13
　federations of, 608, 614–15
　and flat-rate compensation, 685
　and flexible benefits, 761
　international variation in strength of, 623

Unions—Cont.
　and job analysis, 158
　and job evaluation, 664
　in joint problem-solving committees, 558
　organizing campaigns for, 611–13
　orientation by, 436
　and P/HRM development, 39
　and pay increases, 688–89
　and performance-based pay, 693
　and performance evaluation, 492
　political activism of, 608
　and productivity, 630
　public-sector, 627–28
　reasons for joining, 610–11
　during recessions, 600
　and recruitment, 329, 338–39
　right to participate in, 603, 606
　security of, 617
　and selection, 374
　stewards of; see Shop stewards
　strategies for dealing with, 604–5
　and strikes, 621; see also Strikes
　structure of, 613, 615
　and technology, 602, 605
　and training, 447
　and wages, 628–29
　and wrongful dismissal, 586–87
Union shops, 610, 617
Unit benefit formula, 746
United Auto Workers, 607
United Food and Commercial Workers, 613
United States
　adverse effect principle in, 284
　employee benefits in, 731
　executive compensation in, 713–14
　human rights laws in, 271
　labour disputes in, 623
　P/HRM manager accreditation in, 26
　selection regulation in, 374
　selection tests validated in, 391
　trade with Canada, 64–65
　unions imported from, 607
Universities
　P/HRM degrees from, 22
　recruiting at; see Colleges, recruiting at
University and College Placement Association (UCPA), 336
　application form of, 356
Unskilled labour, employment planning for, 226
Unstructured interviews, 398
Utility analysis, 784

V

Vacations, 733
　employee desire for, 731
　for executives, 712
Valence, 199–200
Validators, 351

Validity
  of BARS, 510
  coefficient of, 385
    example calculation of, 417
    with selection ratio and base rate, 387
  of performance evaluation results, 495
  of selection procedures, 378–79
    biographical data, 395
    empirical, 379–81
    employment tests, 409–11
    face, 395
    interviews, 395–96, 404
    and productivity, 417–19
    rational, 381–82
    scatterplots to indicate, 384–85
    synthetic, 382–83
    transnational generalization of, 391–92
Variable day, 152
Vesting, in pension plans, 746–47
Veterans, hiring program for, 293
Videotapes
  about employee benefits, 751
  interviews on, 399
Vocational schools, recruitment from, 337–38

W

Wages; see also Compensation
  concessions in, 629
  employer pension contributions as, 747
  government controls on, 647–48
  and inflation, 618
  and productivity, 233
  and recruitment, 328
  salary versus, 707
  and technology level, 73
  and union development, 605
  unions' influence on, 628–29
Wagner Act (U.S.), 607
Walk-ins, 338
Warner-Lambert Canada, 570
Wartime Labour Relations Regulations, 607
Weighted application blanks (WABs), 394
Weighted checklists, 515
Weighted performance criteria, 501
Welfare Capitalism, 570
West Germany, strikes in, 623
Wheelchairs, accommodation of, 287
Wildcat strikes, 621
Willful misconduct, 587
Winnipeg General Strike, 606
Women
  career paths of, 307
  and child care, 738–39
  employment discrimination against, 273–76
  employment equity programs for, 293–94
  and flexitime, 153
  income of, 273
  in labour force, 47–48
  masculine dress by, 402
  maternity leave for, 734

Women—Cont.
  numerical goals for employment of, 304
  as P/HRM managers, 26
  pay equity for, 714–15, 717–18
  pension incomes of, 748
  performance evaluation of, 495
  reasonable accommodation of, 288
  recruiting, 328
  selection of, 401–2
  sexual harassment of; see Sexual harassment
  in skilled crafts, 300
  technology's effect on, 75
  training for, 449–50
  in unions, 82
  in work force, 34
Woods Gordon, 146
Word-of-mouth, 306
Work
  at home, 153
  nature of, 7, 14, 143
    and compensation, 707
    and core characteristics, 149
    and hazardous work environments, 582
    and human resource objectives, 113, 117
    and performance evaluation, 493, 517–18
  orientation to, 202; see also Orientation
  schedules for, 151–53
    discrimination in, 306
Work analysis, 787
Workers' compensation, 582–84, 736
Work groups, 208–10
  incentive pay to, 700–703
  nature of, 14
  and peer evaluations, 519
  and quality of work life, 558
  and referral tactics for recruiting, 335
  and transfers, 465
Working conditions
  contract negotiations about, 616
  discriminatory, 306
  and health and safety, 579
  money as, 692–93
  and reasonable accommodation, 286–87
  and union development, 605
Work rules, 81
Work sample tests, 408–9
Work sharing, 257
Work-study programs, 336; see also Internships
Work teams, 7–8
Workweek, compressed, 152
World War II, and personnel function, 32

Y

Yearly maximum pensionable earnings (YMPE), 743
Yellow dog contracts, 606
Yield ratios, in recruiting, 326
York Plan, 146